the christian calendar

OVERLEAF A polyptych by Crivelli
in the Cathedral of St Emidio,
Ascoli Piceno, Italy.

OPVS·KAROLI·CRIVELLI·VENETI · 1473 ·

the christian calendar

A COMPLETE GUIDE TO THE SEASONS
OF THE CHRISTIAN YEAR TELLING
THE STORY OF CHRIST AND THE
SAINTS FROM ADVENT TO PENTECOST

Text by L. W. COWIE *and* JOHN SELWYN GUMMER

G & C Merriam Company, *Publishers*
Springfield, Massachusetts

Edited by JOHN SELWYN GUMMER
Designed by ELWYN BLACKER

ACKNOWLEDGMENTS
All illustrations except those mentioned separately are reproduced from the archives of Photo Fratelli Fabbri Editore, Milan.
The pictures on pages 84, 156, 212 are reproduced by gracious permission of H.M. The Queen; Associated Press 41; Bayerisches Nationalmuseum 155; Bodleian Library 167, 187; British Museum 20, 142, 165, 176; Cooper Bridgeman Library 207; Department of the Environment 162; Glasgow Art Gallery 234; Sonia Halliday 16, 64, 80, 107, 110, 157, 175, 193/1, 210; Robert Harding 60; A. F. Kersting 183, 185, 244; Keystone Press 9; Mary Evans Picture Library 11/2, 174, 180, 189, 191, 201, 208, 237; MAS 164; Museum of Art, University of Michigan 141; Museo Capitolino 91; National Gallery 27, 29, 49, 143, 146, 148, 158, 161, 172, 181, 193/2, 197, 216, 220, 221, 238, 241; National Portrait Gallery 10, 12, 163, 200; Toledo Cathedral 207; Trinity College, Dublin 219; The Dean and Chapter, Winchester, 64.

If we have unwittingly infringed copyright in any picture reproduced in this book, we tender our sincere apologies and will be glad to hear from the copyright owner.

Library of Congress Cataloging in Publication Data

Cowie, Leonard W
  The Christian calendar.
  1. Church year. 2. Christian saints – Calendar.
  I. Gummer, John Selwyn, joint author. II. Title.
BV30.C7 263'.9 74–955
ISBN 0–87779–040–X

Manufactured in Italy

contents

introduction

THE CHRISTIAN CALENDAR is a direct inheritance from the Jewish religion in which the keeping of regular commemorations and observances had long been important. About 250 years before the birth of Christ, an Alexandrian Jew – Jesus the son of Sirach, wrote, 'Why doth one day excel another whereas all the light of every day in the year is of the sun? By the knowledge of the Lord God they were distinguished; and He altered seasons and feasts. Some of them He hath made high days and hallowed them, and some of them hath He made ordinary days.'

The Jewish calendar was a lunar one because, as they were originally nomadic people and travelled by night, they attached great importance to the moon. It is from their calendar that the Christian Church took the concept of great festivals like the Passover and Pentecost being fixed according to the moon's phase. Of course, they gave a new significance to the old feasts. The Passover became Easter and Pentecost commemorated the coming of the Holy Spirit. From very early times, the Church adopted also the Jewish custom of a seven-day week with regularly recurring fasts on Wednesdays and Fridays – Wednesday acquiring a Christian significance as the day of the Passion of Christ, and Friday as the day of the Crucifixion. Only the Jewish Sabbath was changed by the Christians. They chose as their Holy Day, the day of the Resurrection, the Lord's Day, and the change originated with the Apostles. It was, however, only in 321 that the Emperor Constantine forbade unnecessary work on Sundays.

Yet just as vital an influence on the calendar is the fact that the Christian Church grew up in the Roman Empire, which followed a calendar controlled by the sun.

This divided the year into twelve months and therefore, when the Church began to institute festivals which were of unique importance for itself and not originally Jewish, they were observed on dates in the Roman calendar. These included the saints' days, which at first were only commemorations of martyrs, and later Christmas Day.

This is the reason why the Christian calendar is a complicated one. Unlike all others it is a double calendar, governed in some parts by the moon and in others by the sun. The Church distinguishes between 'fixed' and 'movable' feasts, but in reality the movable feasts, such as

Introduction

Easter, are fixed according to the Jewish lunar calendar, while the fixed festivals, such as Christmas, run according to the Roman solar calendar.

For ten months, from Septuagesima to the last of the Sundays after Pentecost (which vary from twenty-two to twenty-eight), the Christian calendar is lunar. The movable festivals during this period depend upon the date of Easter. For instance, Septuagesima is sixty-three days – the ninth Sunday – before Easter, and Pentecost is seven weeks after Easter. Other movable festivals depend upon the position of a Sunday. Such are the Sunday after the Epiphany, 6 January, and Advent, the opening season of the Christian year, which begins on the Sunday nearest to 30 November. On the other hand, the fixed festivals are associated mostly with Christmas and the main events in the life of the Virgin Mary. These and the saints' days occur on definite dates in the Roman calendar.

The history of the development of the individual seasons and festivals which make up the Christian year are described under the appropriate headings in this book and detailed information is shown in the glossarial index. The earliest Christian calendar extant was drawn up in the fourth century, but the earliest for the Church in England belongs to the eighth century and has been attributed to Bede. The first calendars were mainly intended to indicate the days on which the martyrs and confessors of the Church were to be commemorated, and in the course of time the names of others who had been canonized were added.

Canonization, the process by which a name is added to the canon or list of saints, has changed over the centuries. The custom was probably derived from the Roman practice of exalting heroes to the ranks of the gods by decree of the Senate. The Apostles and a few others, such as John the Baptist, seem to have been regarded as saints from very early times, and others were added by popular acclamation. Local bishops began to control the canonization of saints within each diocese, but often the veneration of some saints extended beyond the bounds of their own diocese or even country, though no official recognition had been given. The need to regularize the situation brought about papal intervention. Pope John xv in 993 was the first to authorize the canonization of a saint for the whole Church and in 1170 Alexander iii confined all canonization to the Papacy.

In the Roman Catholic Church, canonization follows the procedure laid down by Urban viii in 1634. An appeal for canonization must be made at Rome to the Congregation of Rites, which consists mainly of cardinals. One of its members, the Promotor Fidei, commonly called the

8

'Devil's Advocate', has the duty of examining critically the alleged virtues and miracles of a candidate for canonization, so as to prevent any rash decision. If the enquiry is satisfactory, and the eminent virtue of the proposed saint can be proved and certified by well-authenticated miracles, then three successive congregations are convened, the last being in public and in the presence of the Pope. When papal consent has been given, a day is fixed for canonization to take place in St Peter's, Rome, at which a Mass is said in honour of the new saint, his statue is un-veiled, a day is fixed as his annual festival, and thanksgiving is offered to God because the Church has now another patron and intercessor.

In 747 the Roman calendar was adopted in England. But at the Reformation it was adapted considerably both because the Reformers wanted to observe only Scriptural commemorations and for the practical reason that Parliament wished to reduce the number of holy days, especially during harvest-time. The Book of Common Prayer, therefore, includes thirty-two days traditionally connected with the life of Christ, or dedicated to saints mentioned in Holy Scripture, for which a Collect, Epistle and Gospel are provided, and these are known as Red Letter

The canonization of the Forty Martyrs on 3 October 1970.

Introduction

Archbishop Cranmer, the most important influence on the creation of the Anglican calendar.

Days because originally they were printed in red ink in the calendar. The remaining days, Black Letter Days, for which no special provision is made, were retained mainly for everyday convenience to indicate the dates of university and law terms or the patronal festivals of churches.

In 1662 a Red Letter Day was added for 30 January, the anniversary of the execution of King Charles the Martyr in 1649, but this was removed in 1859, though several parish churches are still dedicated to him. In addition, a number of recent churches, such as John Keble Church, Mill Hill, and Bishop Hannington Church, Brighton, have been dedicated to figures regarded as saints by a modern form of popular acclamation. The Church of England has not revised its calendar to include such recent commemorations but this has been done in the United States of America, Canada, South Africa and other branches of the Anglican Communion, and some of the new saints honoured by them have been included in this book.

Lutherans, like Anglicans, retained after the Reformation the general framework of the Christian calendar and continued to observe the more important festivals. Calvinists, on the other hand, kept only the Lord's Day and discarded completely all other commemorations. They did, however, recognize the value of fasting as a disciplinary exercise, and their congregations were sometimes called upon to observe specially-appointed days which had no relation to the fast-days of the medieval Church.

Martin Luther (right) saved the major elements of the Christian calendar for the Lutherans, while Calvin (far right) reacted strongly against any continuation of the ancient observances.

Calvin's reasons for abandoning the Christian calendar were two-fold. Firstly, he objected to the medieval doctrine of the invocation of the saints which was defined by the Council of Trent (1545–63) as 'to invoke the saints as suppliants and to resort to their prayers, aid and help for obtaining benefits from God'. Secondly, he disliked as irreligious and superstitious many of the popular practices associated with the observance of many of the festivals of the Christian calendar, the processions and pilgrimages, feasting and games. Calvinism, therefore, considered that the calendar was inconsistent with the purity of religion it wished to establish, and insisted upon its entire rejection.

This attitude had lasting and widespread consequences. Since the English Puritans were Calvinists, they were opposed to the observances of the Christian calendar and forbade them during the period of the Commonwealth when they were in power. Though their political rule did not last, their religious influence remained. The Protestant bodies descended from them attached little importance to the Christian calendar, and there was a decline in its observance by the Church of England.

The early Puritan settlers in America had a similar outlook. Among the Pilgrim Fathers in New Plymouth, 'on the day called Christmas Day' in 1621, Governor William Bradford 'called the people to work as usual', but when those among them who were not Puritans objected, he had to 'spare them until they were better informed', though he stopped

Introduction

them playing stool-ball and other sports on the day. He insisted that 'it was against his conscience that they should play and others work', and he told them that 'if they made the keeping of it a matter of devotion, let them keep to their houses, but there should be no gaming or revelling in the streets'.

In more recent times, however, there has been a growing appreciation of the value of the Christian calendar and a renewal of its observance. All Christians nowadays keep at least the three great festivals of the year – Christmas, Easter and Whitsun – and many recognize other holy days as well. In the Church of England, the lead in this revival was taken by the nineteenth-century Tractarians, especially John Keble, whose poems in *The Christian Year* did much to make people understand the purpose of the Church's annual observances, and the movement has inspired all Christians and strengthened the growth of unity among them.

This renewed interest in the Christian calendar has led in the Roman Catholic Church and the Anglican Communion to the production of new lectionaries and forms of service. Some of these have tables of Epistles and Gospels extending over a two-year cycle. Most include Old Testament lessons as well. Different provinces of the Church have compiled their own experimental series. The Roman Catholic Church has a new calendar in which the 'Sundays of the Year' begin after Epiphany and are numbered consecutively except for the period from the beginning of Lent to Whit Sunday, so that there are thirty-three or thirty-four 'Sundays of the Year' according to the date of Advent, six Sundays of Lent and eight Sundays of Eastertide, the last being Whit Sunday. These developments may well lead to a more unified pattern in the future, but meanwhile in this book, the Christian year has been followed through the traditional lectionary of the Roman Missal and the English Book of Common Prayer.

The Christian calendar is a reminder to all followers of Christ that they share a common faith as members of one family in Him and are not even divided by death. This is the truth expressed by Charles Wesley in his fine hymn:

> *Let saints on earth in concert sing*
> *With those whose work is done;*
> *For all the servants of our King*
> *In heaven and earth are one.*

John Keble's *Christian Year* brought a renewed observance of the calendar to the Church of England.

PART ONE

the
year of
our lord

'The voice of one crying in the wilderness,

Prepare ye the way of the Lord.'

(Matthew 3:3)

advent

This is the great season of looking forward. We prepare for Christ's birth at Christmas; we proclaim His future ministry as did John the Baptist; and we watch expectantly for His second coming. Advent is the beginning, the preparation for the Christian Year.

ADVENT I

Then shall they see the Son of Man coming in a cloud with power and great glory.
LUKE 21:27

In the Roman rite, Advent begins with our eyes firmly set on the Second Coming of Christ. The Gospel is the prophecy of the destruction of Jerusalem which was to occur in AD 70 when the city was razed to the ground by the Romans after the Jewish revolt. It continues with the picture of the signs and portents which will precede the arrival of Christ to judge the world. In the English Prayer Book this passage is pushed forward one week and for Advent I there is the story of Christ's triumphal entry into Jerusalem and his cleansing of the Temple on Palm Sunday. This is to emphasize the purification of the Church when He comes again. Both stories concentrate upon the judgement which is to come, the physical judgement of Jerusalem and the final judgement of the world. It is an essential part of the Christian gospel. As Dr Johnson said 'I cannot forget that my Saviour has said that He will separate the sheep from the goats'. In this way the beginning of the Christian year establishes Christ as the central and eternal figure in the redemption of the world. We prepare, not just for the earthly life of Jesus, but for His continuing role as mediator between God and man.

> *That day, when sent in glory by the Father,*
> *The Prince of Life His blest elect shall gather;*
> *Millions of angels round about Him flying,*
> *While all the kindreds of the earth are crying,*
> *And He, enthroned above the clouds, shall give*
> *His last just sentence, who must die, who live.*
>
> HENRY VAUGHAN

The Last Judgment
portrayed in a
fifteenth-century
stained glass window
by Hans Acker.

Three great strands of meaning are blended on this Sunday. John the Baptist sends his disciples to ask whether Christ is in truth the Messiah and it is in answering that question that the Gospel focuses our attention upon the Advent theme of preparation for the coming ministry of Jesus. He is the Messiah because in His life can be seen the signs which the prophet Isaiah predicted would accompany His coming. The blind can see, the lame walk, the lepers are healed, the deaf hear, the dead are raised up, and the poor have the good news preached to them.

Yet it is not only to prepare for the ministry of Christ that this Gospel is placed here. It is to place that preparation in its historical context in reference to the preaching of John the Baptist. He had proclaimed Jesus as the Messiah and seen himself as His precursor. Now, wearied with Herod's long imprisonment, he was unsure and sent his disciples to ask. We move from the life of Christ and its meaning to all men, to its meaning to one man, suffering because of what he had said about Him. In this John represents much more than himself. He is the priest whose life is spent in preparing the way for Christ in others; the priest who under the pressure of events has his doubts. Advent is the season of ordination and so this third theme is particularly important. When John's disciples have gone away Jesus turns to those round about Him and commends His faithful forerunner as a 'prophet and more than a prophet' because he was the expected messenger, sent to prepare the way of the Messiah. John, as a true minister of God, is therefore exalted by Jesus because, however great his human failings, he has faithfully accomplished that duty of opening the way into the hearts and minds of the people. These are words to comfort all whose vocation it is to prepare the way for Christ. Even their doubts cannot destroy the unique importance of their task.

In all religion, at least in any deeper kind of religion, there must be isolation from the world, that we may be alone with God. The religious teacher or thinker is no longer liable to be persecuted for his opinions; he is not like the older prophets 'wandering about in sheep-skins and goat-skins'; yet any man who thinks or feels deeply is always liable to find himself more or less estranged from his fellow men. They cannot enter into his thoughts, nor can he join always in their trivial and passing interests. Like the prophets he has to go into the wilderness, that he may be alone with God.

BENJAMIN JOWETT

17

ADVENT III

I baptise you with water but He shall baptise you with the Holy Spirit. MARK 1:8

The first word of the introit sung on this Third Sunday in Advent has given it the name 'Gaudete Sunday'. It became the custom to exchange the purple vestments and altar hangings for rose-coloured ones to mark the special rejoicings of the day. This was primarily because it was considered as the last Sunday before Christmas, because Advent IV was so taken up with ordinations that the Pope would spend much of the vigil of this day in prayer and meditation in preparation for the Nativity of Christ.

The Gospel is therefore specifically concerned with the real nature of Christ. Again we see Him through the eyes of John the Baptist who is being cross-questioned by priests and Levites who were sent by the Pharisees in Jerusalem to discover who he was. In replying to them John declines to give himself any position but concentrates upon proclaiming the coming Messiah. He explained that he was not the Christ, nor 'the Prophet' who had been foretold in Deuteronomy 18:15–18, nor was he the returned prophet Elijah whom Malachi expected. Instead he was 'the voice' sent from God to prepare the way for the Messiah.

When this statement brought the riposte that such humility was inconsistent with the fact that John baptized people who accepted his message, the Baptist claimed that he was still merely preparing the way for one immeasurably greater than he. That one was already among them, but as yet unknown, and He would baptize men with the Holy Spirit. This is, therefore, the clearest statement of the coming of the Messiah. It prepares us directly for the ministry of Jesus and sets Him and John the Baptist in the context of Jewish prophecy.

It is not merely that John looked forward to the coming of Our Lord but that the Old Testament itself prepares the way for the Messiah and His new dispensation. We are seeing Christ as the fulfilment of the long story of God's chosen people. This Sunday in Advent is preparing us for the Incarnation which completes the revelation of God to man begun in the Jewish scriptures.

> *Because the world might not pretend*
> *It knew not of the coming day,*
> *Thou didst, O Christ, before Thee send*
> *A cryer, to prepare Thy way.*
> *Thy kingdom was the bliss he brought,*
> *Repentance was the way he taught.*
>
> GEORGE WITHER, *John the Baptist*

Breugel's John the Baptist fascinates a crowd drawn from every section of society – with others clambering up trees and pushing their way in to hear his words.

And he came into all the country about the Jordan, preaching a baptism in token of repentance for the forgiveness of sins. LUKE 3:3

The Wednesday, Friday, and Saturday before the Fourth Sunday in Advent are Ember Days, when there are solemn vigils for those who are to be ordained. In earlier centuries the Saturday vigil was conducted with a Mass in the very early hours of the morning at which the ordinations took place. The people were then not expected to assemble for another Mass that day. In the Roman rite the Gospel again tells a story of John the Baptist. This time it goes right back to the account of his preaching in the wilderness and his fulfilment of Isaiah's prophecy:

> *The voice of one crying in the wilderness*
> *Make ye ready the way of the Lord,*
> *Make his path straight,*
> *Every valley shall be filled*
> *And every mountain and hill shall be brought low.*
> *And the crooked shall become straight,*
> *And the rough ways smooth,*
> *And all flesh shall see the salvation of God!*

This Gospel is not found in the Book of Common Prayer but it does complete the message of the previous Sunday in presenting Christ as indeed the One whom the prophets foretold.

እዘእዘዝኩ፡ስዮሴፍ፡ትኩዛ፡ነ   ስድ፡ጽ፡ሙ፡ስ፡እጋ፡ኝ፡ት፡እ፡ሃ፡በ
ጽ፡ሐ፱ነ፡ያገ፡ዱ፡ይ፡እ፡መ፱ተ፡   ሐ፡ረ፡ል፡በ፡ዩ፡ግ፡ብ፡ጽ፡ወር፡እ
ሂ፡ሮድ፡ስ፡ሕ፡ሁ፡ፉ፡እ፡ግ፡ዚ፡እ፡በ፡ሐ   ስ፡ጣ፡ያ፡ቅ፡ሙ፡ቀ፡ጦ፡ቅ፡ጥ፡በ፡በ፡ት
ር፡ጓ፡ያ፡ል፡በ፡ሠ፡ረ፡ተ፡ቃ፡ል፡ክ፡ሐ፡ዕ፡   ር፡ኩ፡ዕ፡ጽ፡

christmas

And the word was made flesh and dwelt among us. JOHN 1:14

As it was time for the census, Joseph, the village carpenter from Nazareth, had to go with his wife to Bethlehem, the town from which his family came. They reached there late and found no room at the inn, but were allowed to camp out in the stable. It was there that Christ, the creator incarnate, was born, and there that the shepherds became the first to worship Him.

NO TRADITION about the date of the birth of Jesus has survived, and even the year remains doubtful. There is not even a definite date for the beginning of the custom of celebrating Christmas, and it does not seem to have been general until late in the fourth century. Moreover, the early Church had no fixed date for Christmas. It was observed by some Christians in May and by some in January, while in the Eastern Church the date first kept was 6 January, when it was combined with the festival of the Epiphany. It was St John Chrysostom who is said to have persuaded the East to adopt the same date as the Western Church.

The earliest mention of the observance of Christmas on 25 December is in a list of Roman bishops compiled in 354, which describes this date as 'the day Christ was born in Bethlehem of Judea'. The choice of this day was partly influenced by the theory of the Roman ecclesiastical writer, Hippolytus (*c.* 170–*c.* 236), who concluded that the Crucifixion took place in AD 29 on 25 March (which tradition held also to have been the date of the Creation), and that the Annunciation took place on the same day, because he believed that an exact number of days elapsed between the Incarnation and the death of Christ. It followed, therefore, that Christ's birth was on 25 December.

The strongest reason for the choice of this date in the Western Church, however, was doubtless because of the pagan associations of the day and the desire of the Church to persuade the people to replace these by Christian observances. In Rome, 25 December was the feast of the Birth of the Unconquered Sun, which commemorated the winter solstice, when the days begin to get lighter. The Church replaced this by the celebration of the birth of the 'Sun of Righteousness' and the coming of the 'Light of the World'.

The festivities accompanying Christmas are also thought to come from another pagan Roman festival held in mid-December. This was in

This Ethiopian manuscript shows God watching over and blessing the Incarnation of His Son and the flight into Egypt.

honour of Saturn the god of seed-corn, which was celebrated on 17, 18 and 19 December. In late Roman times, these three days, known as the Saturnalia, were an occasion of merriment, feasting and the exchange of presents. Temples were decked with greenery and flowers, while no public business could be transacted, the law courts were closed, the schools had a holiday, no criminal could be punished, and no war could be declared. Under the Roman Empire, the festival was extended to seven days.

As Christianity spread to northern Europe, it met with the observance of another pagan festival held in December in honour of the sun. This time it was the Yule-feast of the Norsemen, which lasted for twelve days. During this time log-fires were burnt to assist the revival of the sun. Shrines and other sacred places were decorated with such greenery as holly, ivy, and bay, and it was an occasion for feasting and drinking. Equally old was the practice of the Druids, the caste of priests among the Celts of ancient France, Britain and Ireland, to decorate their temples with mistletoe, the fruit of the oak-tree which they considered sacred. Among the German tribes the oak-tree was sacred to Odin, their god of war, and they sacrificed to it until St Boniface, in the eighth century, persuaded them to exchange it for the Christmas tree, a young fir-tree adorned in honour of the Christ child. Luther is said to have originated the lighting of the Christmas tree with candles, and Queen Victoria's consort, Prince Albert, to have popularized it in England as part of the Christmas celebrations. It was the German immigrants who took the custom to America.

Such pagan practices were made part of the Christian celebration of Christmas, but at the same time new specifically Christian observances were introduced to recall the birth and early life of Christ. Plays and symbolic ceremonies were performed in church. The crib, said to have been introduced by St Francis of Assisi, became especially popular in Italian homes, where it was set up in a prominent place, and around which candles were lighted on Christmas Eve. The singing from house to house of carols – songs telling of the birth of Christ or describing the festivities of Christmas – also dates back to the Middle Ages. Among old English carols are 'I saw Three Ships Come Sailing By' and 'The Holly and the Ivy', but one of the most popular was originally German and is of comparatively recent date – 'Holy Night', which was written by Franz Gruber and Joseph Mohr in 1818.

During the sixteenth century, the Protestant dislike of keeping feast days extended particularly to Christmas. Calvinist influence in Scotland led to the abolition of Christmas Day as a public holiday and its replacement by New Year's Day. In England, the Puritans of the sixteenth and seventeenth centuries objected to the 'drinking, roaring, healthing, dicing and carding' which accompanied its observance as 'liberty to carnal and sensual delights'. Under their influence, Parliament in 1644 ordered that 25 December was to be kept as a fast-day, in order that all might call to remembrance their own sins and those of their fathers in transforming a day sacred to the memory of Christ into an occasion of revelry. And troops were ordered on the day itself to go round houses in London to see that no Christmas dinners were being cooked in the kitchens. The Pilgrim Fathers and other Puritan settlers in New England brought with them the same attitude towards the observance of Christmas.

The revival of the celebration of Christmas and its development into a family festival owes much to the pen of the nineteenth-century novelist, Charles Dickens, who was very influential in both England and the United States. For him, the joy of Christmas was connected with the memory of childhood – 'it is good to be children sometimes, and never better than at Christmas when the mighty Founder of Christianity was a child himself.' To him Christmas in the home and among the family was the supreme example of human goodwill, and in his books, particularly *Pickwick Papers* and *Christmas Carol*, he successfully communicated this to his readers.

Nowadays, the story of Bethlehem, the singing of carols, the message of goodwill, and other parts of the Christian observance of Christmas mingle with the giving of presents, family reunions and the reversion to the pagan tradition of feasting and carnival. For Christmas, however, the truth of what it commemorates outshines all other truths, as John Betjeman has said:

> *No love that in a family dwells,*
> *No carolling in frosty air,*
> *Nor all the steeple-shaking bells*
> *Can with this single Truth compare –*
> *That God was Man in Palestine*
> *And lives today in Bread and Wine.*

This was the true light which enlighteneth every man that cometh into the world.

JOHN I : 9

Originally Christmas had two Masses, the first of the vigil, which was said in the late afternoon of the preceding day, and the second of the feast. When the observance of Christmas began in Rome, Mass was added to that of the vigil and celebrated in the Church of St Anastasia, whose martyrdom is commemorated on this day, and then a third Mass was celebrated in the Vatican Church. Later, the first two Masses came to be considered Christmas Masses and were celebrated at midnight and dawn. And so all three became Masses of the feast, and yet another was added in celebration of the vigil. In the Roman Catholic Church Christmas still remains unique as being the only day in the year on which priests are allowed to celebrate three Masses.

Albertus Argentinensis says that in the year 800 Charlemagne stood in Rome with drawn sword and read the Gospel, 'A decree went forth from Caesar Augustus', and after the Mass, while he still knelt before St Peter's Shrine, the Pope, Leo III, crowned him and named him the successor of the ancient Roman Emperors. After this it was the custom that whenever a sovereign was present at the Mass on that night in Rome, he would read the Gospel with his sword in his hand, and the Pope would give him some present.

In medieval times, the boar's head was the favourite dish at the Christmas feast, and in great houses it was brought in at the head of a procession with music and much ceremony. Geese, capons, pheasants, bustards, swans, pickled oysters and, above all, peacocks were also eaten. Since the introduction of the turkey from America in the sixteenth century, most European countries have given this the supreme place on the Christmas table. Christmas cakes and Christmas puddings, made of dried fruit, and mince pies are also part of the fare in English-speaking countries. In France the traditional Christmas cake is made in the shape of a log, decorated with icing sugar and thickly covered with a layer of chocolate marked to look like the bark of a tree; and in Poland a favourite dish is *Kutia*, made from wheat soaked in water to which is added honey, raisins and poppy-seeds, and eaten cold and uncooked.

The Nativity in strikingly fifteenth-century terms. All the home comforts of a prosperous household with the merest apology for holes in the stable walls! This miniature is the forerunner of all the Christmas scenes which stylize Christ's birth and avoid the real harshness of the situation.

The modern Father Christmas has a strange story of development. In England, originally he was a shadowy personification of the season. He had nothing especially to do with children and did not bring gifts or fill stockings. This was the role of Santa Claus, who had evolved in New York State from the St Nicholas of the Dutch colonists in the nineteenth century. The linking of the traditional English Father Christmas with the Dutch–American Santa Claus produced a myth which gained world-wide acceptance. Perhaps the clearest reminder of its American origin is

LEFT This fifteenth-century manuscript illustration captures the stark surroundings of Christ's birth and the real concern of the ageing Joseph. The children on their way to see the baby could be children of any age but only a medieval mind could portray God's brooding presence so directly and materially.

Crivelli's sophisticated *Madonna and Child Enthroned* shows an entirely different view of the Incarnation. Fifteenth-century primitive realism is replaced by fifteenth-century high fashion and grandeur. The baby born in the stable is also the Prince of the House of David.

the notion that this new character is the bringer of gifts in a sleigh drawn by reindeer, for St Nicholas was always shown as travelling on horseback.

The Christmas card is an entirely modern development and a British invention. It came when the introduction of penny postage in 1840 had made it possible to send Christmas greetings cheaply to distant friends and relatives. The first Christmas cards are said to have been sent in 1843 and rapidly became popular throughout the world.

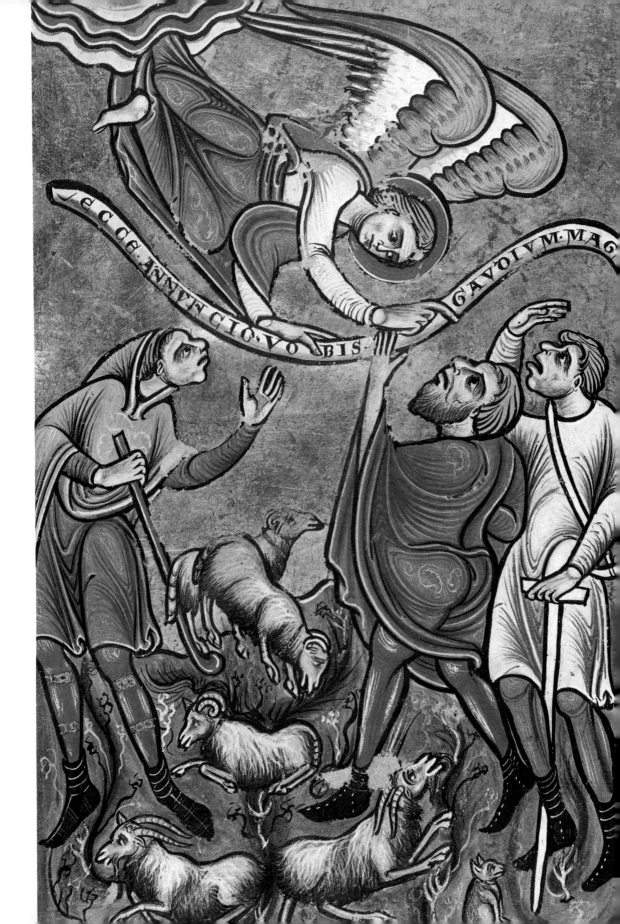

You are therefore no longer a slave but a son, and if a son, then also by God's own act, an heir. GALATIANS 4:7

The message of this Sunday does more than merely repeat the good news proclaimed on Christmas Day. Then the coming of Christ into the world was commemorated; this day now sets forth the meaning of that coming for mankind. This is expressed in the Epistle which in both the Roman Missal and the English Prayer Book is the opening chapter of Galatians beginning, 'So long as the heir is a minor, he is no better than a slave, even though the whole estate is his; he is under guardians and trustees until the date fixed by his father.' Mankind, St Paul said, was like that when it was under the law. It was heir to the fullness of God's grace, but could no more enjoy it than could the son, who was bound by the restrictions laid down in his father's will.

LEFT This twelfth-century miniature seizes upon the fear of the shepherds as they hear of the birth of Christ from an angel. Rough, hard men, they react like their sheep – bewildered and astonished at their visitors.

Parenzo's shepherds come to the stable. They are the first outsiders to worship Christ. Fellow-Jews and fellow labourers, they recognise Him – the Messiah first coming to His own people – even though they were so soon to refuse to receive Him.

THE CIRCUMCISION

There is neither Greek nor Jew, circumcision nor uncircumcision, Barbarian, Scythian,
bond nor free; but Christ is all and in all. COLOSSIANS 3:11

This festival, kept on 1 January, the eighth day after Christmas, commemorates the Circumcision of Christ, said by St Luke to have taken place 'when eight days were accomplished'. At first it was simply the octave day of Christmas, and the Roman Missal hardly mentions the Circumcision on this day. Its observance as the feast of the Circumcision does not seem to go back further than the middle of the sixth century. It then spread, at first particularly in Gaul, but did not become established at Rome until the ninth century.

Its comparatively late introduction into the Christian calendar was probably because the Church did not want to establish a festival on New Year's Day which was a day of riotous pagan celebration. For this reason it seems originally to have been observed as a fast. The Council of Tours in 567 stated, 'In order to tread underfoot the custom of the heathen, our fathers ordained that private litanies should be held at the beginning of January, psalms sung in the churches, and at the eighth hour on the first of the month the Mass of the Circumcision, pleasing to God, should be said.'

Many early missals provided a second Mass for use on that day in honour of the Virgin Mary. A Roman Mass book of the eleventh century explains this custom – 'Lately, when we celebrated our Lord's Nativity, we could not give any special office to His Mother. Therefore not unsuitably do we venerate her more specially on the Octave of our Lord; lest she should seem to have no share in the solemnity of her Son, though we do not doubt that in that same solemnity she deserves the chief honour after our Lord.' There is a relic of this in the repeated references to the Virgin Mary in the Roman Mass for the day; and a reminder of the pagan festivities in the Collect in the English Prayer Book with its mention of 'being mortified from all worldly and carnal lusts'.

The down-to-earth directness of this illustration from a Flemish breviary shows the Holy Family carrying out the requirements of the Jewish Law. It is a public occasion and the interested bystanders look on as the priest prepares to circumcise Christ.

Now, singing, homeward let us carry
The babe unto his mother Mary;
And when we have the child commended
To her warm bosom, then our rites are ended.
ROBERT HERRICK Circumcision's Song

31

epiphany

The nations shall march towards thy light and their kings towards the brightness of thy rising. ISAIAH 60:3

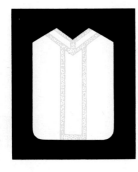

The Wise Men came to Bethlehem, led by a star. They had first called on King Herod expecting to find the new born king. Herod was very disturbed. As a client of Rome, his position was too precarious for any claimants, so when the kings went home avoiding him, he killed all the baby boys in Israel to make sure he killed Jesus.

THE WORD 'EPIPHANY' is the Greek for 'manifestation' and this festival, observed on 6 January, originated in the Eastern Church. It is older than Christmas and is mentioned by Clement of Alexandria as far back as AD 200. In the East it is still celebrated in commemoration of the Baptism of Christ as the manifestation of the Incarnation. By the fourth century it had come to rank with Easter and Pentecost as one of the three great festivals of the Eastern Church, and its vigil was a day commonly chosen for the baptism of converts.

It was first adopted in the Western Church in southern Gaul. There, by the middle of the fourth century, it was kept as a separate festival from Christmas. In Rome it became instead a commemoration of the manifestation of Christ to the Gentiles. The Magi are seen as representative of all the non-Jews to whom Christ came. Their gifts symbolize three aspects of His life – gold for kingship; frankincense for priesthood; myrrh for death. Frankincense is, of course, incense and myrrh is a spice used in embalming the dead.

From the few sentences in St Matthew, a whole legend developed in the Middle Ages. The Magi became three in number, were promoted to be kings and finally acquired the names of Melchior, Caspar and Balthazar. Then in 1158 three bodies were found in the Church of St Eustorgio, just outside a new moat surrounding Milan, which were presumed to be those of the Magi. When the Emperor Frederick Barbarossa captured the city, he took them to Germany, where they were deposited in Cologne Cathedral in 1164. Henceforward the shrine of the Three Kings of Cologne became a famous place of pilgrimage. It was among those visited by the wife of Bath in Chaucer's *Canterbury Tales*.

Also in the Middle Ages it was the custom for the rich and powerful to make offerings in church of gold, frankincense, and myrrh. This is still done by the Queen in England at a service in the Chapel Royal, St

Christ stretches forward to welcome the three wise men in this picture from the *Bedford Breviary*. Joseph is pushed into the background as the Virgin and her child meet these first representatives of the gentile world. This is, in fact, a strip picture telling each incident in the Epiphany story and providing captions for the key statements.

33

The Adoration of the Magi by Botticelli. It is a set piece, one of the tableaux in the story of man's redemption. Fallen man kneels before his Saviour.

James's Palace, where two Gentlemen Ushers make the offering at the altar on her behalf. The gift of twenty-five golden sovereigns is changed into notes and distributed to the aged poor, the frankincense is used in a church, and the myrrh is given to a hospital.

The Epiphany was once popularly known as Twelfth Day, being

twelve days after Christmas Day, and the evening preceding the Epiphany was Twelfth Night – a time of merry-making marking the end of the Christmas holiday. The Twelfth Cake was an ornamental cake, containing a bean or coin, the drawer of which became the 'King' or 'Queen' of the festivities.

EPIPHANY I

Jesus increased in wisdom and stature and in favour with God and man. LUKE 2:52

The Gospel for this Sunday is the account, contained in Luke 2:41–52, of the self-manifestation by Jesus as a boy. It is the only glimpse given of His childhood, when at the age of twelve, the time when a Jewish boy became a 'son of the law', he went up to Jerusalem with His parents for the Passover and stayed on to talk with the teachers in the Temple.

This Sunday used to be known as Plough Sunday because it marked the beginning of the ploughing season. The plough was brought into the village church to be blessed; and on the next day, Plough Monday, boys with blackened faces, decorated with ribbons, wearing masks and cowhides, went from house to house, cracking whips, singing and dancing with swords in their hands and sometimes dragging along a plough with them. These were pagan survivals of ceremonies originally intended to drive away evil spirits from the earth before the new crops.

Inside the capital letter, from an antiphonal produced in Bologna, is Christ, portrayed as priest. God's sacrifice for man blesses the gift of incense and in their rush to kneel before Him the kings trample on their own crowns.

EPIPHANY II

This beginning of miracles did Jesus in Cana of Galilee and manifested forth his glory, and his disciples believed on him. JOHN 2:11

The Gospel for this Sunday continues the record of the self-manifestation of Christ with an account of the 'first miracle that he wrought' as described in the second chapter of St John's Gospel. This is the miracle at Cana of Galilee, the turning of the water into wine at a marriage-feast.

The great nineteenth-century preacher, F. W. Robertson of Brighton, expressed in a sermon on Christ at Cana the meaning of this miracle for the Christian life: 'Here again, then, Christ manifested His peculiar glory. The Temptation of the Wilderness was passed; the Baptism of John, and the life of abstinence to which it introduced, were over; and now the Bridegroom comes before the world in the true glory of the Messiah – not in the life of asceticism, but in the life of godliness – not separating from life, but consecrating it; carrying a Divine spirit into every simplest act – accepting an invitation to a feast – giving to water the virtue of a nobler beverage. For Christianity does not destroy what is natural, but enobles it. To turn water into wine, and what is common into what is Holy, is indeed the glory of Christianity.'

It is a continuous theme of the Gospels that God transforms what is available: the five loaves and the two fishes, the Passover bread and wine, the water at the marriage feast. It is as if He demands from men and from nature all that they can manage and then takes it and changes it to use it for His purposes.

The Gospel, indeed, shows in example what is taught in the exhortation of St Paul in the Epistle for this day. It is the discourse upon the practice of the Christian virtues, the 'gifts differing according to the grace that is given to us'; and the call to 'rejoice with them that do rejoice' is a reminder that Jesus was as ready to join in the festivity of the marriage-feast at Cana as in the mourning of the bereaved sisters at Bethany.

Thou water turn'st to wine, fair friend of life;
Thy foe, to cross the sweet arts of thy reign,
Distils from thence the tears of wrath and strife,
And so turns wine to water back again.

RICHARD CRASHAW

EPIPHANY III

Many shall come from the east and west and shall sit down with Abraham and Isaac and Jacob in the kingdom of heaven. MATTHEW 8:11

The two stories in the Gospel for this Sunday continue the self-manifestation of Jesus by miracle. This time it is the miracle of healing the sick. The stories tell of men who came to Jesus asking for help, one for himself and one for another, and who both shared the common experience of living in some way in estrangement from their fellow-men.

One was suffering from the terrible disease of leprosy, which imposed upon the sufferer, through dread of infection, exclusion from the Temple and the synagogues, from the towns and the homes of the people. To the Jews leprosy was an unclean disease, which required not healing but cleansing, and to touch a leper was to be defiled according to the law.

The other man, a Roman centurion, also experienced the ostracism of those who lived around him. He was an officer in a foreign army which occupied Palestine as a conquered country; he was a Gentile and a pagan among God's people.

To Jesus both these men came. The leper asked to be cleansed from his disease; the centurion asked Him to heal his sick slave. Their faith in Jesus brought them the granting of their request. In both stories Jesus brought hope and comfort to those who came to Him. It is the manifestation expressed in His great invitation, 'Come unto me, all ye who labour and are heavy laden, and I will give you rest.'

Joseph and Mary make the regulation sacrifice at the Temple when they present their boy child to God. Again they carry out all the requirements of the Old Law which Christ has come to fulfil.

38

Candlemas: Botticelli's *Madonna and Child* celebrates the crowning glory of the Mother of God on this her first feast of the year.

CANDLEMAS

In common with all Jewish mothers, the Blessed Virgin Mary took her child to the Temple at about six weeks old to present him at the Temple and would complete the ceremonies of Purification. There the priestess Anna and the aged Simeon recognised that this child was the special one – 'The glory of Thy salvation'.

From about the year 350 this festival was kept locally at Jerusalem on 14 February and later, on the 2 February. In 542 the Emperor Justinian ordered it to be observed at Constantinople as an act of thanksgiving for the ending of a plague in the city, and from there it spread throughout the East. Candlemas was then called the *Hypapante* or 'Meeting' (of Jesus with Simeon and Anna in the Temple as described in the second chapter of St Luke's Gospel). This is the reference in today's alternative, though not commonly used, title of this festival – 'The Presentation of Christ in the Temple'. The story of St Simeon's recognition of the Lord continues the pattern of manifestation. His work is 'the glory of thy people Israel' and Simeon describes it in a psalm full of reference to the prophecies of the Old Testament. It is indeed Christ presented to His own people in the form laid down by the Jewish law.

When the festival was later adopted in the Western Church, the growing cultus of the Virgin Mary led it to be regarded as a day in honour of her rather than of Christ. It was called 'The Purification of the Blessed Virgin Mary' in commemoration of the completion of the 'days of her purification', forty days after Christmas Day, as required by Jewish law (Leviticus 13). The service in the Roman Missal, however, still refers to the Presentation in the Temple and scarcely mentions the Purification.

The English name Candlemas refers to the custom of blessing and distributing candles and carrying them in procession before the Mass of the day, which probably originated in the seventh century. This may have superseded the heathen festival of carrying torches in honour of Ceres, the Roman name for Mother-Earth, the protectress of agriculture and of all the fruits of the earth, which took place in the early part of February. The symbolism of the candles in the Christian festival is direct and clear. They are blessed, distributed to the congregation and lit while the *Nunc Dimittis* is sung and are then carried round the church in procession to commemorate the entry of the 'True Light' into the world and the gradual illumination of the whole world by Him.

Various old superstitions were connected with Candlemas Day. Some people carefully preserved the candles they received in church in the

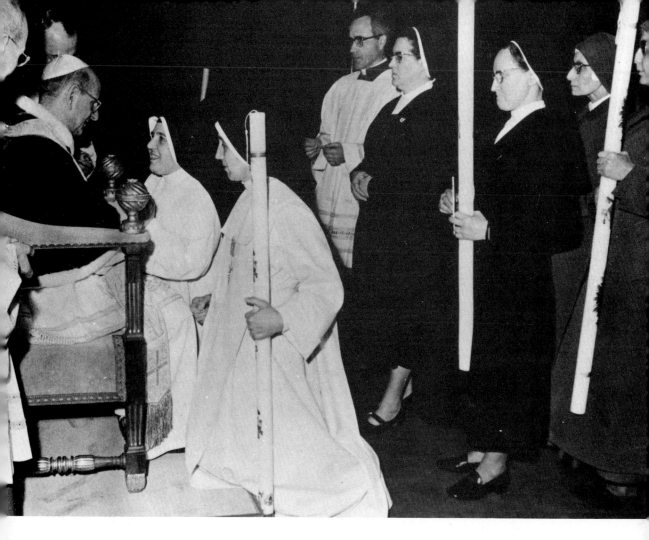

A procession on the feast of Candlemas brings candles to the Pope for blessing.

belief that these would drive away storms and evil spirits. Others believed that 'if the day be clear and sunshiny, it portends a hard weather to come; if cloudy and lowing, a mild and gentle season ensuing.'

Robert Herrick, in his poem *Candlemas Eve*, refers to the country custom in seventeenth-century England of taking down the last greens of the old year on that night:

> *Down with the Rosemary, and so*
> *Down with the Bays and Mistletoe;*
> *Down with the Holly, Ivy, all*
> *Wherewith ye drest the Christmas Hall;*
> *That to the superstitious find*
> *Not one least Branch there left behind:*
> *For look, how many leaves there be*
> *Neglected there, maids, trust to me,*
> *So many goblins you shall see.*

EPIPHANY IV

What manner of man is this that even the winds and sea obey him? MATTHEW 8:27

The record of the self-manifestation of Christ by miracle is further expounded in the Gospel for this Sunday. Here it is a nature miracle in which He is described as controlling the forces of the physical world. It is the story of the stilling of the storm when Jesus and the disciples were crossing the Sea of Galilee in a boat. He said to them all, when the storm suddenly arose, 'Why are ye afraid, O ye of little faith?' and He turned and rebuked the winds and the sea, and there was a sudden calm. Jesus underlines the disciples' cowardice and lack of faith. Their fear was great because their faith was small.

Two illustrations from a thirteenth-century French psalter continue the story of the birth of Christ. The killing of the boy children by Herod's soldiers has a terrifying immediacy. As one mother kisses the head of her decapitated child and another holds the legs of her boy running with blood, Mary and Joseph make their way with Jesus into the safety of Egypt.

The Fifth and Sixth Sundays after the Epiphany only occur when Easter is particularly late, and the Gospels do not carry on the scheme of instruction of the previous Sundays. Here the parable of the wheat and the tares, which appears only in St Matthews Gospel, teaches that the evil in man's make-up is best destroyed not by concentration upon remorse, but by cultivation of goodness.

The 'tares' of the parable are generally thought to be a weed called 'darnel', a plant only distinguishable from wheat by the black poisonous grain formed in its ear. The proposal of the servants to weed the corn-field is not so absurd as might appear because often in Palestine the darnel was carefully weeded out by hand by women and children.

EPIPHANY VI

If ye have faith as a grain of mustard seed ... nothing shall be impossible unto you.
MATTHEW 17:20

In the Roman Missal, the Gospel is the parable of the grain of mustard seed, but since 1662 the Gospel for this Sunday in the English Book of Common Prayer proclaims the last and greatest of the epiphanies of Christ, the epiphany of the future when He will be manifested in power and glory at the end of the age. The words come from Christ's own prophecy to his disciples on the eve of His Passion on Mount Olivet, as told in St Matthew's Gospel. The passage foretells that there will appear in heaven 'the sign of the Son of Man', which old writers believed was the Cross; but it also states, 'This gospel of the kingdom shall be preached in the whole world for a testimony unto all nations, and then shall the end come.'

Joseph is busy asking Mary what is going on as they stand outside the Temple where Christ is teaching the scribes and Pharisees. He is uncomprehending, but she understands; dimly, and inside herself, His mother can accept that Jesus is about His Father's business.

septuagesima

So run that we may obtain. I CORINTHIANS 9:24

The designation of this cycle of three Sundays – Septuagesima, Sexagesima and Quinquagesima – as a preparation for Lent, originated with the great disasters which finally brought the declining Roman Empire to an end.

SEPTUAGESIMA is sixty-four days before Easter and its name may come from the fact that in some parts of the Church, Sundays, Thursdays, and Saturdays were never fast-days and if Lent was to have forty fast-days then it would have to start on this Sunday. An alternative view is that Quinquagesima is fifty days before Easter and Sexagesima and Septuagesima are incorrect titles by analogy from that.

At first sight the parable of the labourers in the vineyard, which is the Gospel for this Sunday, appears to be one of the most difficult to understand. A modern commentator has said that this story contains what deserves to be called a 'bolt from the blue' and has suggested that it might well be called 'Last come, first served'. It seems to involve a complete reversal of accepted values, a strange example of unfairness because all the labourers were paid the same, however long they worked.

It is a story about the harvesting of grapes in Palestine, where perfect weather may threaten to change into a storm that would damage the fruit on the vines. The owner desperately hires more men and more men and yet more men again, and by evening the crop has been safely gathered into his barns. It is natural for him to feel especially grateful to the late-comers, who have saved the situation, and to be generous to them.

The purpose of the parable is to teach about the Kingdom of Heaven. It makes it clear that entry into the Kingdom is not governed by conditions which might seem to us the obvious ones. God does not value human achievements as the world does. Many humble Christian men and women have given themselves to the work of the Kingdom and have not received the recognition accorded in this life to those who have performed more spectacular deeds. Their reward will be from God. This is the meaning of the words of Jesus at the end of the parable, 'So the last shall be first, and the first last: for many be called, but few chosen'.

SEXAGESIMA

The seed is the Word of God. LUKE 8:11

Again the meaning of Sexagesima is obscure. It comes either by analogy from Quinquagesima or because of different fasting rules which, like those referred to on the previous Sunday, meant that Lent had to begin here.

The parable of the sower, which is the Gospel for this Sunday, might more accurately be called the 'parable of the four kinds of soil'. The skill of the sower and the quality of the seed are not questioned, but the results of the sowing depend upon the nature of the soil; and so the results of teaching depend much upon the response of the hearer. Criticism of the pulpit by the pew is common; this is criticism of the pew by the pulpit.

Some seed fell on a hard pathway beside the field and was at once snatched up by birds – the hearers recognize the truth of the Word, but lack the moral strength to obey. Some seed fell on shallow soil, with rock underneath, and it germinated rapidly, but had not enough roots to enable it to survive the dry weather. The hearers fail because of lack of depth of character and do not persist in obeying the message. Some seed falls on rough, unweeded ground, where it is choked by thorns. The hearers cannot concentrate and are distracted by worldly cares which choke the religious life.

Some seed, however, falls on good ground and produces an abundant harvest – 'they on the good ground are they which, in an honest and good heart, having heard the word keep it, and bring forth fruit with patience'. Those profit from the Word who are honest and sincere, who remember and meditate upon what they have heard and who act upon it with perseverance and patience.

Of all parables of the Christian life, this has had the clearest teaching appeal. It is founded on the daily experience of farming in Palestine. The broadcast sower, with his basket secured on one shoulder, cannot choose where the seed shall land. The fields are of uneven fertility. Outcrops of rock, then patches of soil and places where the weeds grow apace, the seed falls on them as well as on the rich productive areas. There is a prodigality about the sower who must scatter widely if he is to ensure a good crop. It is the prodigality of God's grace and the uncertainty of man's response which is here expounded.

> *It is not causeless, Christ did use compare*
> *Man's mind unto the soil that tilled is;*
> *They both full well indeed agree in this,*
> *Untilled, they unfruitful are and bare.*
>
> HENRY LOK

The parable of the sower, interpreted for the fifteenth-century readers of the *Très Riches Heures*. Broadcast sowing was still part of the agricultural scene and the careful details of the harrow, weighed down with a rock, and the figure of a bowman acting as a scarecrow gave this the considerable contemporary realism demanded by the wealthy French magnate who commissioned this work.

QUINQUAGESIMA

Jesus, thou Son of David, have mercy on me. LUKE 18:38

This is the only one of these three Sundays where the meaning of the name is certain: fifty days from Easter. It was a suitable day to begin to prepare for Lent, particularly at the time of its institution when the whole of the civilised world crumbled as the barbarian descended upon the Roman Empire. In the East, this Sunday is Cheese-Fast Sunday. It marks the beginning of the great fast where even cheese and eggs are forbidden.

The Gospels for the previous two Sundays have been parables about entry into the Kingdom of Heaven and receiving the Word of God. For this Sunday, the Gospel tells of two incidents during the last journey of Christ with the disciples to Jerusalem. One is an announcement by Him to the disciples, and the other is an act of healing.

The announcement by Jesus is His prediction of the Passion and Resurrection, when the Son of Man 'shall be delivered up unto the Gentiles, and shall be mocked, and shamefully entreated, and spat upon: and they shall scourge and kill him: and the third day he shall rise again'. The disciples, Luke is at pains to add, failed to understand anything of this.

The act of healing is the opening of the eyes of the blind beggar, whose perception of the mission of Jesus is greater than that of the disciples. He recognized Him as the Messiah and hailed him as the Son of David, which was a Messianic title. The crowd, alarmed by such treasonable talk, urged him to be quiet, but Jesus said, 'Receive thy sight: thy faith hath made thee whole.'

These two parts of the Gospel are about blindness – spiritual blindness and physical blindness. The disciples were spiritually blind because they could not see the true nature of Christ, which the beggar, though physically blind, could. The blind beggar was immediately healed, but the disciples were to be still longer unaware of the truth about Christ. Crucially important is the irony that the blind man whom no-one expected to be able to see, understood more of Christ than the disciples whom everybody knew were close to Jesus and understood His inner-most thoughts and real purposes.

Since to be loved endures,
To love is wise:
Earth hath no good but yours,
Brave, joyful eyes:

Earth hath no sin but thine,
Dull eye of scorn:
O'er thee the sun doth pine
And angels mourn.

ROBERT BRIDGES

48

In Duccio's painting of Christ healing the blind, the fascination of the crowd in the miracle is evident. Jesus heals because it is the demand of love; as such it is an evidence of His divinity. He never let it become mere wonder-working to draw an audience.

Almighty and everlasting God, who hatest nothing
that thou hast made, and dost forgive the sins of all
them that are penitent: Create and make in us new
and contrite hearts, that we worthily lamenting our
sins, and acknowledging our wretchedness, may
obtain of thee, the God of all mercy, perfect remission
and forgiveness; through Jesus Christ our Lord.

Lent

Having nothing and yet possessing all things. II CORINTHIANS 6:10

Jesus' preparation for His ministry begins with forty days of fasting and prayer in the wilderness. He was then tempted to achieve His great work by the expected means – by force and political action. He refused and chose instead the way of the Cross.

ORIGINALLY GOOD FRIDAY and Easter Day were observed as a single festival of the Crucifixion and Resurrection of Our Lord, and from very early times this probably included a fast which was kept before the commemoration of the Resurrection, but it certainly did not last nearly as long as the present forty days of Lent. Irenaeus (*c.* 130–*c.* 200), referring to differences of opinion about the celebration of Easter in his time, wrote, 'For the difference of opinion is not about the day alone, but about the manner of fasting; for some think they are to fast one day; some two, some more; some measure their day as forty hours of the day and night'. The idea of this fast came from the words of Christ, 'The days will come when the bridegroom shall be taken away from them, and then they shall fast in those days'; but the interpretation placed upon them varied. Commonly people kept a strict, unbroken fast either on Good Friday only, or for the time between the death of Christ and His Resurrection, which came to be estimated at forty hours.

The period before Easter was the time when converts from paganism were instructed in the Christian religion and prepared for baptism. The same barbarian invasions and collapse of the Roman Empire in western Europe, which turned the three Sundays of Septuagesima, Sexagesima and Quinquagesima into penitential days, brought about the long Lenten fast. The collects for the Third, Fourth and Fifth Sundays in Lent, written in the sixth century, express the outlook of that time with their recurrent thought of adversity, punishment, relief and defence.

The actual duration of the longer Lenten fast varied in different Churches. Some made it last three weeks, some six, some seven; some omitted Saturdays as well as Sundays from the days they observed. In the Eastern Churches it was observed during seven weeks, but as Saturdays and Sundays – with the exception of Holy Saturday – were excluded, there were only thirty-six days of actual fasting. On the other hand, while the Western Church fasted during six weeks, it also had a total of thirty-six fast-days since it usually left out only the Sundays. The Church of Jerusalem was perhaps the first to observe an actual fast of a total of forty days as early as the fourth century. The Roman Church made up the number to forty days under Pope Gregory the Great, towards the close of the sixth century, by adding the four days from Ash Wednesday to the First Sunday in Lent, and this practice spread from Rome throughout the Western Church. The Eastern Church begins Lent on the Monday after Quinquagesima Sunday.

When the original space of forty hours had been abandoned as too short, it was natural that the length of the Lenten fast should come before long to be forty days. This was identical with the Fasting and Temptation of Christ, the forty days spent by Moses and Elijah in the wilderness and the forty days' grace given in the preaching of Jonah to Nineveh. It also had a connection with baptism, since on the fortieth day before Easter the candidates for baptism were enrolled and thenceforth were called '*competentes*' or 'qualified'. In the Middle Ages, when the custom became general of communicating chiefly, and even only, at Easter, the period of Lent became a time of preparation for the Easter Communion by fasting, prayer and religious exercises.

The degree of fasting also varied widely. St Chrysostom wrote, 'There are those who rival one another in fasting and show a marvellous emulation in it; some, indeed, who spend two whole days without food; and others who, rejecting from their tables not only the use of wine and of oil, and of every dish, and taking only bread and water, persevere in this practice during the whole of Lent'. In the Western Church, the observance of the fast during the first centuries was very strict. Only one meal a day, taken towards the evening, was permitted, and this could not include flesh-meat and fish and, in most places, eggs and milk, butter and cheese; but from the ninth century greater leniency was introduced. The meal was gradually brought forward to three o'clock in the afternoon, and by the fifteenth century it was generally served, even in monasteries, at mid-day. This meant that the evening service of Vespers was said before noon, so as to keep the rule of fasting until after Vespers, and the granting of permission to take an evening 'collation', which consisted at first merely of a drink, but, from the thirteenth century, included also some light food. Fish was allowed throughout the Middle Ages, and from the fifteenth century so also were generally milk, butter and cheese.

Immediately after His baptism, at which it had been revealed to Him that He was called by God to be the Messiah, Jesus sought solitude in

Even though this fifteenth-century Flemish devil has horns, he is a real, and obviously dangerous, adversary. In the background are the other temptations but the main emphasis is on the suggestion to turn the stones into bread. The devil is clearly persuasive and the miniature catches the feeling of a real battle between well-matched participants. This is no pantomime character but Satan out to win.

ortam̅ audint te · in die salutis
uos ne adiuni te · R̅ Emedem?
in uaci udi Hympn̅
um gra renigue condi
tiam dei tor ñris preces
recipia cũ fletibz in h̅c sacro ie
tis. ait unio fusas qdragenario
crum tempore · accepto et Sentator alme cor

the wilderness of the wild, hilly limestone country south of Jerusalem so that He might think about the mission that lay before Him. There He was tempted to establish the Kingdom of God among men by resorting to three ways of asserting His influence over them, and He rejected all of them as not being the ways in which God intended Him to proclaim His message. At the end of the forty days, Jesus knew, not only what His future work was to be, but also on what principles He was to set about it.

The first temptation was doubtless suggested by His own hunger from fasting and the rocky countryside around Him. It was to 'tell these stones to become bread'. This suggested that He should win over the poverty-stricken people of the land by offering them bread and economic security. It would have been a policy like that of the contemporary Roman emperors who set out to gain the loyalty of their people by providing them with 'bread and circuses'. Jesus rejected this temptation because He had not come to bring comfort or material well-being for those who followed Him. His work was spiritual. A sentence from the Book of Deuteronomy emphasized for Him the inadequacy of this notion to inspire His Messiahship – 'Man cannot live on bread alone; he lives on every word that God utters.' Man had to have food for his physical existence, but the Word of God was also essential for his well-being, and that was what Jesus had come to proclaim. His purpose was not to make people content with their materialistic wishes, but to lead them on to the higher things of God.

The second temptation turned from materialism to the miraculous. It was that He should win people to Him by means of magic. Many Jews at this time were looking for a Messiah who would prove His Messiahship to them by 'signs and wonders' – supernatural happenings. The particular way in which Jesus was tempted to do this was by appearing suddenly on the topmost pinnacle of the Temple in Jerusalem and throwing Himself down 430 feet to the Kedron gorge below, secure in the belief that the angels of God would support Him in His descent, so that He came to no harm. No one who saw this happen could doubt that He had really been sent by God, and they would readily hear His message. Another sentence from Deuteronomy came into His mind – 'You are not sent to put the Lord your God to the test.' It would be presumptuous to challenge God to support Him in this way. His duty was to proclaim God's message to men and to bring them to see its truth.

The third and last temptation was political. The popular expectation of the Messiah was that He would be a great king and conqueror, a second David, who would put down the enemies of the Israelites and

A twelfth century Byzantine version of the temptation for Christ to throw Himself off the Temple in order to astonish men into belief. The curious perspective concentrates upon the essentials. Christ and Satan are in the centre of the drama – the Temple is merely a prop. No-one doubts Jesus' ability to jump unharmed – the debate is about something much more important, how He must win men to Him.

make them supreme in the world. So Jesus was tempted to seek to gain control of 'all the kingdoms of the world in their glory'. This would mean that He would make Himself a military leader who would encourage His people to rise in revolt against the Roman conquerors and regain their independence as a nation. This was the ideal which had inspired the Maccabean heroes of the past and still animated the nationalist zealots. If He set Himself at the head of such a movement, there would be many people who would follow Him in the hope of establishing the great messianic kingdom on earth. Jesus expressed His rejection of this temptation in yet a further sentence from Deuteronomy

'You shall do homage to the Lord your God and worship him alone'. To give in to this temptation would mean using the methods of the world and worshipping force and power. He would not attain what He had come to accomplish because men would not be any better morally and spiritually than they had been, and He could only succeed by using means that were entirely inconsistent with His whole nature. To resort to violence and domination would mean, not the coming of the Kingdom of God, but rather submission by the Messiah to the forces of evil. To worship God alone, to do His will and to achieve His righteousness, was the message that He must proclaim to the world.

These temptations, which Jesus resisted at the outset of His ministry, reappeared during the whole period of it. The Hebrew religious leaders tempted Him by saying, 'Show us a sign from heaven', to which He replied, 'It is a wicked generation that asks for a sign, and there shall be no sign given to it'. Again, He was forcefully presented with the same temptation when, after the confession of His Messiahship at Caesarea Philippi by Peter, He told His disciples that Messiahship for Him involved the shame and suffering of the Cross. When Peter told Him that He was mad, He replied, 'Away with you, Satan; you think as men think, not as God thinks.'

Throughout His ministry, Jesus never departed from the resolve He had made in the wilderness. He did not rest His Messiahship upon either the offer of economic benefits or the display of miraculous signs or the resort to political intrigue and military force. On the contrary, His sole aim was to arouse and create the spiritual life of those among whom He worked. He would not do any of the things popularly expected of a Messiah, but bade them fulfil God's will as He himself did, even though it meant for Him the final sacrifice of the Cross.

Sophisticated symbolism is the medium in this fifteenth-century miniature from the *Très Riches Heures*. Christ surveys the kingdoms of the world, accompanied by a shadowy flying Devil. He offers all that is greatest in the world, the most elegant of castles standing for everything that material power can give. Christ still refuses to become the revolutionary leader out to win men's hearts by force.

Lent

The Monday before the beginning of Lent was in some parts of England known as Collop Monday because it was the last day of eating flesh before the fast. People would cut up their fresh meat into collops or steaks for salting or hanging up until Lent was over; and they often had a last meal of eggs and collops or slices of bacon on that day. Daniel Defoe in his *Tour of Great Britain* in 1726 said that the day was 'called, everywhere in the North, Collop Monday from an immemorial custom there of dining that day on eggs and collops'.

The next day, Shrove Day, was so named from the shriving (confession and absolution) of the people in the churches on that day. It was also a holiday in preparation for the Lenten fast-days ahead and the day when housewives used their butter and eggs to conserve the perishable food in their larders before the fast. The 'pancake bell' was rung in the morning to show that the holiday had begun and again towards sunset to show that it was over.

The day was marked in England by cock-fighting and other sports. The pancake race at Olney (Buckingham), probably five hundred years old, is a survival of these sports, and so also is the football played in the streets of Ashbourne (Derbyshire) between the Up'ards and the Down'ards, where the goals are millwheels three miles apart; and the hurling of the silver ball (made of wood covered with silver leaf) at St Columb (Cornwall), in which huge teams of up to a thousand play a wild game between goals a mile apart.

In France the week before the beginning of Lent has traditionally been celebrated by a carnival (which means literally 'to put away flesh'), reaching its climax in Mardi Gras (Fat Tuesday), and this observance was taken by French settlers across the Atlantic to Louisiana, where New Orleans is famous for its pre-Lenten street processions, glittering floats, military bands and flickering flares, which reach their climax in the parades and balls of Mardi Gras, all coming to an end at midnight when Lent begins.

ASH WEDNESDAY

Jesus was led up of the spirit into the Wilderness. MATTHEW 4:1

When this day was made the first day of Lent, the name first given to it in the Roman service books was '*Caput Jejunii*' – 'the Head of the Fast'. Later it was called '*Dies Cinerum*' – the 'Day of Ashes' – and so assumed its present name.

From about the seventh century those who had committed serious sins and were prepared to submit to public penance, presented themselves at the beginning of Lent to the Bishop in his church, clothed in sackcloth and with bare feet, where they joined with him and the rest of the clergy in repeating the seven penitential psalms. Then they were sent into a monastery for their penitential exercises and remained there until shortly before Easter.

This practice was gradually replaced by the whole Church putting itself to penance during Lent, and this was symbolized by the ceremonial use of ashes with a solemn penitential service in the churches. To strew ashes upon the head was in Old Testament times a sign of grief and mourning. It was an early custom for penitents under excommunication to sprinkle ashes upon their heads and stand at the door of a church to beseech the prayers of those who were entering, that they might be absolved and re-admitted to Communion. In the rite for Ash Wednesday ashes, made by burning the palm leaves which had been blessed on the Palm Sunday of the year before, are placed upon the altar, blessed, sprinkled with holy water and censed. The congregation then kneel at the altar rails and the priest touches their forehead with a portion of the ash, saying, 'Remember, O man, thou art dust, and unto dust thou shalt return'.

Jesus goes out into the wilderness, the barren and rough hillside, to be alone with God.

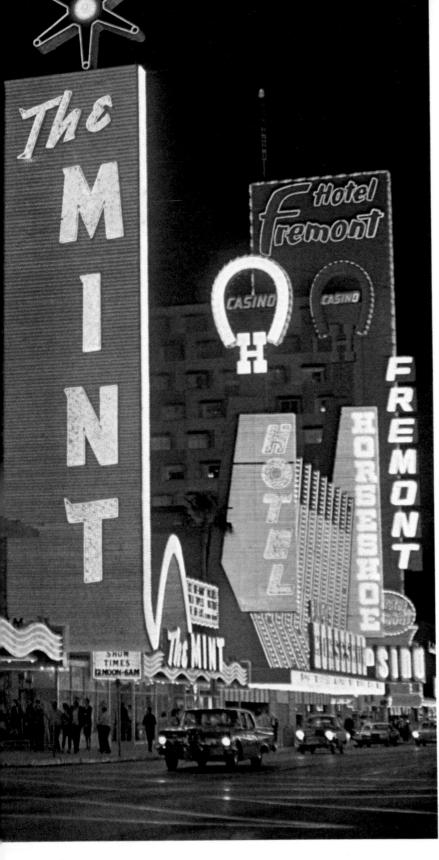

When ye fast, be not as the hypocrites, of a sad countenance: they disfigure their faces, that they may appear unto men to fast. Verily I say unto you, They have their reward. But thou, when thou fastest, anoint thine head, and wash thy face, that thou appear not unto men to fast, but unto thy Father which is in secret; and thy Father, which seeth in secret, shall reward thee openly. Lay not up for yourselves treasures upon earth, where moth and rust doth corrupt, and where thieves break through and steal: but lay up for yourselves treasures in heaven, where neither moth nor rust doth corrupt, and where thieves do not break through nor steal: for where you treasure is, there will your heart be also. ST MATTHEW 6:16

Las Vegas.

Thou shalt worship the Lord Thy God, and Him only thou shalt serve.
MATTHEW 4:10

Since this Sunday was originally the beginning of Lent, the Gospel for the day sets the tone for the whole season. It is the account in St Matthew's Gospel of the Temptation of Jesus in the Wilderness, with which the season has long been associated.

In his novel *The Brothers Kamarazov*, Dostoevsky tells the fable of the Grand Inquisitor, to explain the meaning of the Temptation. It recounts how Jesus, revisiting the world and appearing in medieval Spain, was arrested and condemned by the Grand Inquisitor because He had been offered the three things by which men may be controlled – bread, authority and mystery. Men will follow one who gives them bread, obey one who rewards the obedient and punishes the disobedient, and believe in one who is wrapped in mystery; but He would not use these things. Men were to follow Him, obey Him, and believe in Him, out of love and devotion or not at all. This attitude the Inquisition had had to set aside or there would have been very few to accept Him. And now He had come to repeat His great mistake and spoil their work, and He was to be burnt at the stake the next day. When the Inquisitor had finished speaking, the Prisoner simply crossed the prison-cell and kissed the old man on his bloodless lips. The Inquisitor opened the door and bade Him go. He went out into the night and was never seen again. That kiss burned in the old man's heart, but he did not alter his opinion or practice.

Lent is the time when Christians are called upon to change their opinion and practice in the light of Christ's person and message. His forty days of Temptation in the Wilderness preceded the beginning of His public mission in which He put into practice the principles He had there adopted.

> *Was the trial sore?*
> *Temptation sharp? Thank God a second time!*
> *Why comes temptation but for man to meet*
> *And master and make crouch beneath his foot,*
> *And so be pedestalled in triumph? Pray*
> *'Lead us into no such temptations, Lord!'*
> *Yea, but O Thou whose servants are the bold,*
> *Lead such temptations by the head and hair,*
> *Reluctant dragons, up to who dares fight,*
> *That so he may do battle and have praise!*
>
> ROBERT BROWNING, *The Ring and the Book*

O woman, great is thy faith, may it be unto thee even as thou wilt. MATTHEW 15:28

Like the Fourth Sunday in Advent, this Sunday follows an Ember week and was originally a vacant Sunday without a Mass for the people. Hence the sort of 'patchwork composition' of the Roman Mass for this day which arises because, when a Mass was needed for a day otherwise without one, it was necessary to provide the changing elements – the Collect, Epistle and Gospel from various sources. Accordingly, the Gospel for this day in the Roman Missal, like that provided for the Fourth Sunday in Advent, is a repetition of the one for the Saturday. It is the account in St Matthew's Gospel of the Transfiguration of Jesus.

The English Book of Common Prayer, however, has the story, also from Matthew, of the healing by Jesus of the sick child of the Syro-Phoenician woman. She seems to have been a Greek by language, a Phoenician by descent and a Syrian by residence. She belonged, therefore, to a race which hated and despised the Jews and was hated and despised by them. Yet she came to Jesus and threw herself at His feet, begging Him to heal her daughters, and she persevered, replying to Him with an apt retort. Her faith brought her what she wanted. Like the other Gentile for whom Jesus performed an act of healing, the centurion at Capernaum, she was commended for her 'great faith'. Since both her child and his servant were healed at a distance, St Augustine saw in this the prophetic symbolism that the Gentiles would be saved by faith in Christ's gracious promise even without His bodily presence.

> *Had Christ rebuffed me as He did that mother,*
> *I had been mortified so bitterly,*
> *My smarting pride, all further speech to smother.*
> *Had filled my heart with such black ecstasy*
> *The miracle had ended differently –*
> *The fiend had left my child, but entered me.*
>
> *Yet if I'm human, was she so much better?*
> *Or saw she something which the books omit –*
> *Christ's eyes a-twinkle, as he spoke, that set her*
> *Though whelmed in trouble, catching at her wit?*
> *Did he not laugh, who owned her 'saying' fit?*
> *And if he then blessed humour – cherish it.*

ANON

There is nothing glamorous about this group. Christ and his disciples are portrayed with the primitive realism of fifteenth-century Flanders. The healing of the Syro-Phoenician woman is the reward of her faith and it is the faith of the real world not of some pious existence unconnected with daily life.

LENT III

He that is not with Me is against Me; and he that gathereth not with Me scattereth.
LUKE 11:23

Christ casts out a devil from the twelfth-century *Winchester Bible*.

It was an ancient custom that the Pope celebrated Mass on certain days in one of the churches of Rome. On this Sunday it was in the Basilica of St Lawrence, and this fact explains the choice of both the Epistle and Gospel.

Late in the sixth century, Pope Pelagius II rebuilt the Basilica, adding a new nave and admitting the light from this into the older part of the building. An inscription composed by the Pope himself likens the change to the glare of the flames of St Laurence's martyrdom. This was taken to illustrate this image in the Epistle for this Sunday – 'For ye were sometimes darkness, but now are ye light in the Lord: walk as children of light . . .' Similarly there may be an allusion in the Gospel for the day to the victory of God through his martyr Laurence and also to the dedication of the new nave in honour of the Virgin Mary. St Matthew recounts how Jesus insisted that he cast out devils, not by Beelzebub, the 'prince of devils', but 'with the finger of God', and how a woman exclaimed, 'Blessed is the womb that bare Thee'.

When the people saw the miracle that Jesus did, they said, This is truly that prophet that was to come into the world. JOHN 6:14

This mid-Lent Sunday was kept in the East as a festival of the Holy Cross, and in Rome the Pope celebrated at the Basilica of 'the Holy Cross in Jerusalem', hence the frequent mention of Jerusalem in the Mass. From the opening words of the introit ('Rejoice ye with Jerusalem') it came to be known as Laetare Sunday. In the Western Church it was marked by certain relaxations of the penitential observances of Lent. Rose-pink, instead of purple vestments, were worn, and rich currant simnel cakes were eaten in some countries. This relaxation, together with the Gospel of the feeding of the five thousand, led some to call it 'Refreshment Sunday'.

In England, however, the day was known as Mothering Sunday because it was originally when young servants were allowed by their employers to go home to visit their mothers, taking gifts with them for her and feasting on 'mothering cakes'. School-children also sometimes had the day as a holiday from boarding-school.

Once it was known as Rose Sunday for on this day the Pope blessed a 'Golden Rose' and afterwards sent it as a mark of special favour to some distinguished individual or community. King Henry VIII of England, strange though it may seem, received it from three popes! The Golden Rose sent by Clement V to the city of Basle in 1308 is preserved in the Musée de Cluny at Paris. It is not known when the custom originated, but Pope Leo IX as early as 1049 spoke of it as an ancient practice.

This is Rejoicing Day in Germany. In Augsburg, boys carry plaited bread on long sticks and two men play Summer and Winter. They fight, Summer wins, and establishes the fact that Winter's rule is over.

The five thousand kneel to receive their bread in this picture by Jean Colomb. Christ Himself blesses it and the link is established with the everlasting bread on which we feed in the Eucharist.

This was sometimes called Judica Sunday from the opening words of the introit of the Mass ('Give sentence with me, O God'). More commonly it was named Passion Sunday because of the anticipation of the Passion in the Epistle which comes from that part of Hebrews which compares Christ's sacrifice with those of the Hebrews and sets forth as the object of His Passion, the shedding of His blood that He might obtain eternal redemption for mankind.

In the Roman Catholic Church, since 1956, this day has been officially named the 'First Passion Sunday', while the following Sunday is the 'Second Passion Sunday'. During these last two weeks of Lent, which form the season of Passiontide, all crucifixes, pictures, and images in church are covered with purple drapery. The practice is said to refer to the last words of the gospel for the day, 'Jesus hid himself and went out of the temple'. The practice symbolises the growing pull of events, as Lent's links with the Temptation of Christ give way to the story of His death and Resurrection. With the beginning of Passiontide we start to look towards the Cross.

In the north of England this day was called Carling Sunday, because it was marked by the eating of parched peas or 'carlings'. The custom is said to be the continuation of a pagan springtime bean-feast. An old rhyme refers to the Sundays in Lent and Easter Day as: '*Tid, Tid, Misere, Carling, Palm and paste egg day*'.

I wake and feel the fell of dark, not day.
What hours, O what black hours we have spent
This night! what sights you, heart, saw; ways you went!
And more must, in yet longer light's delay.

With witness I speak this. But where I say
Hours I mean years, mean life. And my lament
Is cries countless, cries like dead letters sent
To dearest him that lives alas! away.

I am gall, I am heartburn. God's most deep decree
Bitter would have me taste: my taste was me;
Bones built in me, flesh filled, blood brimmed the curse.

Selfyeast of spirit a dull dough sours. I see
The lost are like this, and their scourge to be
As I am mine, their sweating selves; but worse.

GERARD MANLEY HOPKINS

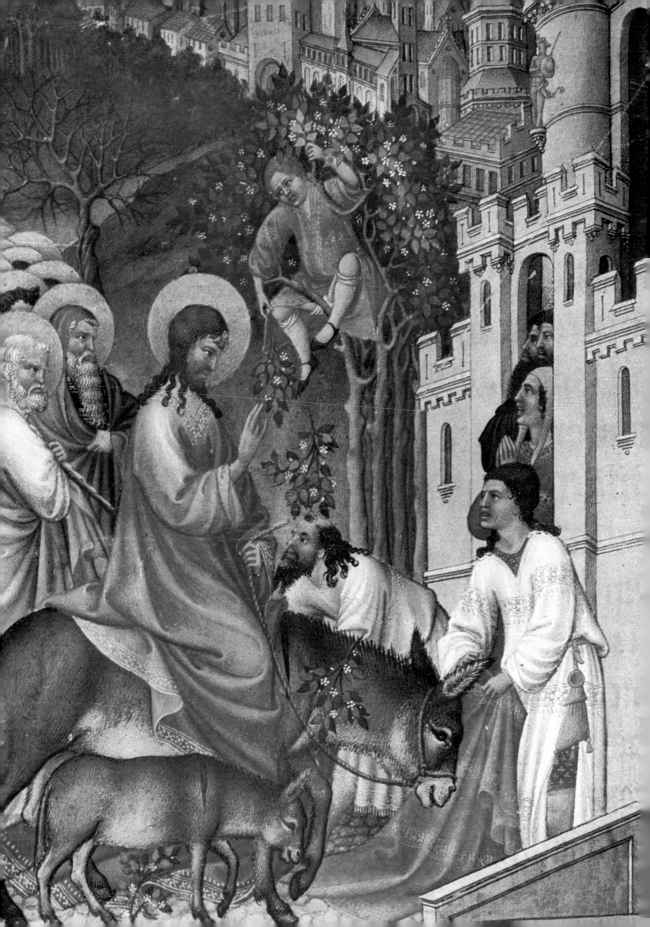

The name of Palm Sunday, for the day celebrating the entry of Christ into Jerusalem, is ancient, but the Mass of the day, including the Gospel, has always been completely concerned with the Passion. The commemoration of the events of the original Palm Sunday was observed in Jerusalem as early as the fourth century. The whole city went in the afternoon to the Mount of Olives and sat on the spot whence Jesus ascended, singing and hearing lessons from Scripture, and then went home in slow procession, all carrying branches of palm or olive and singing, 'Blessed is he that cometh in the name of the Lord', and the people did not return to their houses until late in the day. The earliest mention of the day in the Western Church is in service-books of the seventh century in Gaul, which contain a blessing of palms to be carried as symbols of the victory of Christ and protection against the devil, but no service for the procession is found until the ninth century.

An impulse to the observance of the day in the West was undoubtedly given by the fine Latin hymn by Theodulph, a Spaniard who was Bishop of Orleans in the time of Charlemagne – 'All glory, laud and honour to thee Redeemer, King'. During the Middle Ages the procession of clergy and choirs usually set out from one church and proceeded to another, where the palms or olive-branches were blessed and distributed to the people, and then it returned from the church from which it had started. Often a representation of Christ, such as the Gospel book or a crucifix or a carved figure seated upon a wooden ass, was carried in the procession.

The day before this Sunday was known in England as Palm Saturday, when it was the custom for people to go into the woods and gather willow-branches with which they decorated their houses. In English history, 29 March 1463 was Sad Palm Sunday, the day of the Battle of Towton, near Tadcaster in Yorkshire, the bloodiest of all the fights of the Wars of the Roses.

> *Hark! how the children shrill and high*
> * 'Hosanna' cry;*
> *Their joys provoke the distant sky,*
> *Where thrones and seraphim reply;*
> *And their own angels shine and sing*
> * In a bright ring:*
> * Such young, sweet mirth*
> * Makes heaven and earth*
> *Join in a joyful symphony.*
>
>   HENRY VAUGHAN

Zacchaeus climbs up into a tree to catch a glimpse of Christ entering into Jerusalem with the hosannas of the crowd ringing in His ears. It is the nearest Christ gets to earthly kingship and even then He rides on a donkey and drinks with the outcast tax collector. This miniature from the *Très Riches Heures* captures Jerusalem's symbolic position as the Holy City – the city to be re-established by Christ at His second coming.

HOLY WEEK

The last week in Lent has long been observed in both the Eastern and the Western Church as a commemoration of the death and burial of Christ. It is variously called by early writers the Great Week, the Holy Week, the Week of the Holy Passion and the Week of Forgiveness. In the East, Holy Week was distinguished from the rest of Lent by the extreme strictness of the fast.

Originally Holy Week seems to have begun with the last Sunday in Lent, but when this became Palm Sunday, the week began with the Monday. The various traditional rites, and particularly those on Maundy

El Greco's Christ whips the traders out of the Temple in this superbly physical interpretation. The gentle Jesus meek and mild is shown up for the partial view it is, beside the virile Christ who cleanses the Temple of God.

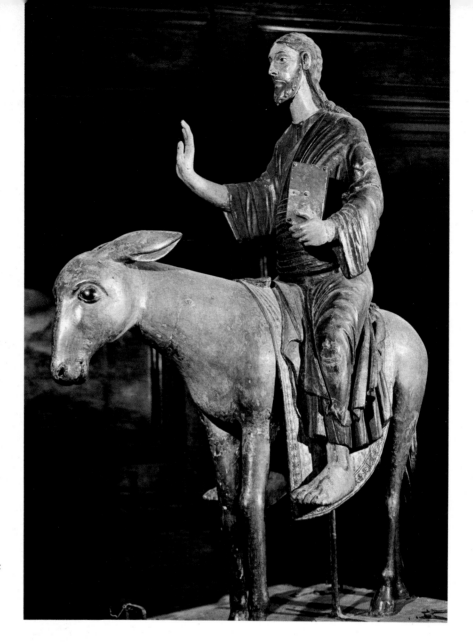

A primitive view of Christ riding upon the donkey, this Lombardic sculpture is restricted to the bare and telling essentials.

Thursday, Good Friday and Holy Saturday, probably evolved at Jerusalem during the fourth century, when access to the city by pilgrims became easier, and Christians were able to express their devotion to the Passion of Christ in ceremonial enactments. As time passed, the old observances throughout the week came to commemorate the historical events some hours before the time they actually took place, probably through a desire to do this in the early morning of each day.

In the Roman Catholic Church the service of Matins and Lauds of the last three days of Holy Week are known as Tenebrae and are sung by anticipation on the preceding evening of Wednesday, Thursday, and Friday. The name means 'darkness' and comes from the very old ceremony of putting out the lights in the church one by one in the course of the service. At the beginning of Tenebrae fifteen lighted candles are placed on a triangular candelabrum. Fourteen of the candles, arranged seven on each side, represent the eleven apostles, the Virgin Mary, and the women that were with her at the Crucifixion, while the single candle at the top represents Christ. At the end of each psalm, a candle is put out (to denote the flight or mourning of the apostles and the women) until only the single candle at the top is left burning. This is then placed behind the altar to symbolize the laying of Christ in the tomb, but it is not extinguished, since death had no dominion over Him.

I was a stricken deer that left the herd
Long since; with many an arrow deep infixt
My panting side was charged when I withdrew
To seek a tranquil death in distant shades.
There was I found by one who had Himself
Been hurt by the archers. In His side He bore
And in His hands and feet the cruel scars.
With gentle force soliciting the darts,
He drew them forth, and heal'd, and bade me live.

WILLIAM COWPER, *The Task*

This medieval portrayal of the Last Supper shows the simplicity of the traditional Jewish meal which marked the coming of the Passover and which was transformed into the Christian Eucharist. On the left Christ is shown washing the feet of the disciples.

ne familiam tua; pro qua
is ur ihs xps non dubita
et manibz tradi nocentui;
ucis subire tormentum
ut. Copleti solito more
q; prostratione dicatur
edictio pplet detur In
ob; uero sequentibz ñ det
edictio Ant de beata uirg
hac die z duob; seqtibz

non dicatur. Ad matutina
Inuitatoriu nõ dicatur Do
mine labia nec ds in adiut
neq; inuitatorium uno. B do
Pater nr z Credo. postq; sig
nauerint se fratres q; etia
fiat ad alias horas. statim
incipiatur. In primo noct
no. Antiphona. z hic in
cipitur.

MAUNDY THURSDAY

As often as you eat this bread and drink the cup, you proclaim the Lord's death until he comes. I CORINTHIANS II: 26

This traditional name for the Thursday before Easter is said to be a corruption of 'Mandati' (*Dies Mandati*, the Day of the Commandment), referring to the commandment given that night by Jesus to His disciples to love one another. The account of this washing of the feet – a task usually assigned to slaves, forms the Gospel of the Roman Mass for this day.

As early as the fourth century, the day had been observed as the commemoration of the Institution of the Eucharist by Jesus at the Last Supper. The Epistle for the day is the earliest written account of the Institution as recorded by Paul in his First Epistle to the Corinthians.

In the early centuries, three Masses were celebrated. The first was connected with the reconciliation of penitents and excommunicated persons, the second with the consecration of the holy oils, and the third, in the evening, commemorated the Last Supper. In the modern Roman Catholic Church, however, one Mass only may be said in the same church during Maundy Thursday, and it must be a public one.

Though white vestments are worn at this Mass as a sign of thanksgiving for the Eucharist, the ceremonies at the service signify the approach of the Crucifixion. All the bells are rung at the *Gloria in Excelsis* and then not rung again until Easter. The Kiss of Peace is omitted in remembrance of the kiss of Judas. A second Host is consecrated, placed in a chalice and taken in procession to an Altar of Repose prepared for it and decked with flowers and lights. Afterwards the altars are stripped and the holy water stoups emptied. In some churches the altars are ceremonially washed with water or wine. 'The whole life of the Church,' a writer has said, 'has dwindled to its lowest pulse before the catastrophe of Good Friday.'

During the Middle Ages, bishops, abbots and noblemen washed the feet of the poor on Maundy Thursday in imitation of the action of Christ, and English sovereigns washed the feet of 'as many old men as the Sovereign is years of Age'. So it was in 1572, when Queen Elizabeth I washed the feet of thirty-nine poor people at Greenwich Palace. James II was the last monarch to do it in person, but in the eighteenth century it was still being performed by the Archbishop of York, as the Sovereign's representative.

Though this part of the ceremony has now been abandoned, another part is still carried out by English monarchs, usually in Westminster Abbey. It is a continuation of the further custom of bestowing gifts of money, food and clothing on the poor on this day, and it has been called Britain's oldest charity, for it began in the reign of Edward III (1327–76).

In washing His disciples' feet, Christ was performing the most menial of tasks which was usually assigned to the humblest servant. That is why they are protesting as He teaches them the lesson in humility.

Maundy Thursday

The Maundy gifts nowadays take the form of silver coins, specially minted, a penny for each year of the Sovereign's age, which the Queen distributes in white leather purses with red thongs. After the Maundy service it is customary for her to walk the length of the choir and make the actual distribution in the nave as an act of humility. She, and the clergy present, each carry a posy of flowers, which was a traditional protection against the plague of which the recipients might be carriers. The clergy have a towel on their shoulders, as a survival of the time when the monarch also washed the feet of the poor.

A former popular name for Maundy Thursday was Shere Thursday, the reason for this being explained by the *Liber Festivalis* of 1483 – 'For in alde faders days men wold make hem that day shere hem and pollen her heedes and clippen her berdes, and so make hem honeste (seemly) ageyn ester day'.

The usual name in Germany, and also occasionally elsewhere, for this day is Green Thursday. This is probably connected with the custom of providing penitents, who had made their confession on Ash Wednesday, with green branches on this day, as a sign that their penance had been completed and that they were therefore received back into full membership of the Church.

> *He was the Word that spake it,*
> *He took the bread and brake it;*
> *And what that Word did make it,*
> *I do believe and take it.*
>
> ANON (sixteenth century)

Judas betrays his Master to the soldiers of the Chief Priest. Each little group in this early German painting tells one part of the story. John Mark is about to lose his robe and run off naked into the darkness, while St Peter chops off one of the soldier's ears. In the centre is the archetype of treason, one of the chosen band using a kiss – the mark of their relationship – to sell His life away.

When Jesus had cried out with a loud voice, he said, Father, into thy hands I commit my spirit; and with these words he died. LUKE 23:46

The name of Good Friday for the day on which the anniversary of the Crucifixion is kept, originated with the English Church. In early Christian writings, the day is called the Paschal Day, and later names for it include the Day of Preparation, the Day of our Lord's Passion and the Day of Absolution. In England, during Anglo-Saxon times, it was known as Long Friday, probably because of the long fasts and services which marked the day. In the Eastern Church it is called Great Friday, and from the very earliest times the day appears to have been observed with strict fasting and humiliation in sorrow for the death of Christ and the sin which brought it about.

'On the Paschal Day,' wrote Tertullian at the end of the second century, 'the strict observance of the fast is general and, as it were, public.' Eusebius, writing early in the fourth century, said that long before his time the day had been kept with watching and fasting; and

among the decrees issued in 321 by the Emperor Constantine, legalizing Christianity in the Roman Empire, was one making Good Friday a general day of rest. At the Fourth Council of Toledo in 633, all those who only fasted up to three o'clock in the afternoon of the day were severely censured and were forbidden to communicate at the Easter Eucharist.

The three parts of the rite of the Roman Catholic Church on this day go back in origin to the early days of Christianity. The ancient service was one of instruction and prayer for the catechumens, who had been ceremonially bathed the day before. It resembled a 'Mass of the Cate-chumens', that is to say, the first part of the Eucharistic service which was the only part the catechumens were allowed to attend. This has survived in the Roman rite as readings from passages of the Old Testament, followed by the story of the Passion according to St John's Gospel and prayers for all mankind.

To this was afterwards added the ceremony of the Veneration of the Cross, sometimes also called Creeping to the Cross. The crucifix on the altar is divested of the black cloth with which it has been covered and is kissed by the clergy and people. The ceremony originated at Jerusalem in the veneration of the relics of the true cross, discovered there by Helena, the mother of Constantine in 326, and then spread to Constantinople and other places which claimed to possess fragments of the original cross. To begin with, naturally enough, observance of this ceremony was not confined to Good Friday.

The second addition to the services on this day is the Mass of the Presanctified. From very ancient times it was considered that the Eucharist, being a feast, was not appropriate for a fast day. The Eastern Church, accordingly, abstained from the celebration of Mass during Lent, except on Saturdays and Sundays, but substituted for it the Mass of the Presanctified at which a Host consecrated at a previous Mass was used for Communion. In the Western Church, however, this practice was restricted to Good Friday. In the present form of the Roman rite, it is preceded by a procession in which the Host is carried back from the Altar of Repose, where it was placed the day before, to the high altar. Until recent times only the celebrant communicated at this service, but now the traditional communion of the people has been restored. Black vestments are worn, and both bells and organ remain silent. The altars stay stripped, and the empty Tabernacle is left open.

As well as these ancient services, several popular devotions have been adopted in the Roman Catholic Church. The best-known of these is the Three Hours' Service, held during the three hours of the Passion from

Memlin's painting of the carrying of the Cross makes of the procession the ritual it was. The condemned man had to bear the sign of his condemnation. It was part of the grim business of a crucifixion which began with the scourging and the mocking soldiers, continued with this public statement of the punishment that was to come, and would end in hours of agony on the cross which the victim himself carried to Golgotha – the place of skulls.

noon until three, which was instituted by the Jesuits after an earthquake at Lima in 1687, and which spread from South America to Spain and then to Rome in 1736. There is also the ceremony of walking the Stations of the Cross, first instituted by the Franciscans in the seventeenth century, which is usually made at three o'clock in the afternoon. The Pope himself does it publicly in Rome, carrying a wooden cross and sometimes there is also an evening service with a sermon called the 'Devotion of Mary'.

At the Reformation, the English reformers abolished the traditional services for Good Friday. The Book of Common Prayer provided for a normal celebration of the Eucharist, which seems to have become a common practice in English churches, but is seldom observed nowadays. In some Protestant churches in Europe and elsewhere, Good Friday is kept as a festival rather than a fast, and often it is a special day for the celebration of the Lord's Supper.

Hot Cross Buns, spiced buns with the figure of a cross impressed upon them, are probably a Christianization of cakes which were eaten at an earlier pagan spring festival. They have long been commonly eaten at breakfast on Good Friday, and used to be sold early in the morning to the street cry of 'One-a-penny, two-a-penny, hot cross buns!' In London for a long time the best hot cross buns came from the Chelsea Bun House, which was closed in 1836. During the Middle Ages there was a belief that any bread or buns baked on Good Friday would last the whole of the coming year, and one loaf or bun was always saved so that a few gratings of it, in water, could be used for curing all complaints during the next twelve months.

The Christian's great conquest over the world is all contained in the mystery of Christ upon the Cross. It was there, and from thence, that He taught all Christians how they were to come out of and conquer the world, and what they were to do in order to be His disciples. And all the doctrines, sacraments and institutions of the gospel are only so many explications of the meaning and applications of the benefit of this great mystery. And the state of Christianity implieth nothing else but an entire, absolute conformity to that spirit which Christ showed in the mysterious sacrifice of Himself upon the Cross.

WILLIAM LAW, *A Serious Call to a Devout and Holy Life*

Christ is crucified. It is complete. His earthly work is done and the world waits for the Resurrection. A sixteenth-century stained glass window from Notre Dame, Chalons sur Marne.

HOLY SATURDAY

The last day of Holy Week, known nowadays as Holy Saturday or Easter Even, was in early times called by both the Eastern and Western Church the 'Great Sabbath'. To this name was attached a threefold interpretation. It was the Sabbath of Christ's rest in the sepulchre; the last Sabbath for His disciples before the Jewish ordinance was superseded by the Lord's Day, the day of the Resurrection; and the anticipation for Christians of the Sabbath rest of the unseen world, into which Christ's human spirit entered on this day, the expectation of the Second Easter of the general Resurrection.

The ancient way of opening this day was to treat it as a solemn fast without public worship until midnight when the Lenten fast abruptly terminated and the Easter vigil began.

In the Eastern Church the original evening vigil has never been altered, but in the West it was put back to Holy Saturday in the middle ages. Since 1956, however, this Mass has been restored to its ancient time at midnight, and now this day and Good Friday are the only days of the year on which there is no celebration of the Mass.

RIGHT St John comforts the Virgin Mary as the body of Christ is laid in the tomb. A fifteenth-century miniature by the Master of Albrecht.

There is a profound emptiness in the faces of those who take the body of Christ from the Cross. The most important part of their own selves is dead because He is crucified. Now they must hurriedly make the arrangements for His burial because the Day of the Passover is upon them and they cannot deal with death on that holy day. For the moment the tomb will be occupied and the disciples will be away at their devotions. Soon the day of the Resurrection will dawn.

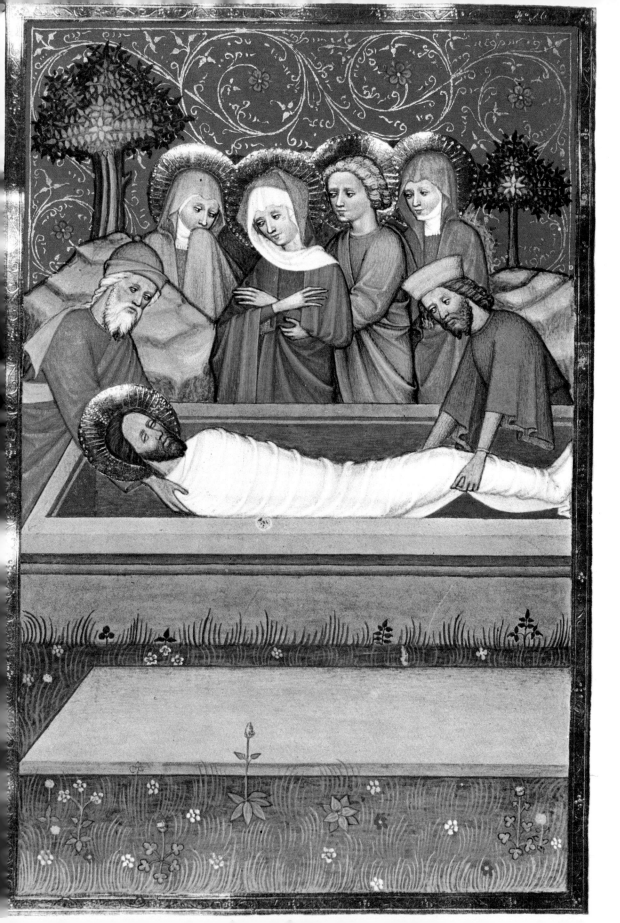

easter

After the disillusion of Good Friday, the followers of Jesus spent the Passover season in dejected withdrawal. Then, early on Easter Morning, Mary Magdalene came to mourn at the tomb only to find it empty and the body gone. She called to a gardener to find where its new resting place was and discovered, as the other disciples were to find later, that her Lord was risen indeed.

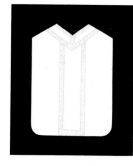

EASTER is the greatest and the oldest of Christian festivals, the 'feast of feasts' as Pope Leo the Great called it early in the fifth century. It has always been regarded as the chief and most joyous of the observances of the Church as the commemoration of the Resurrection of Christ and the restoration of life to the world which sin had ruined. Its importance is indicated in the Christian calendar by the long period of preparation of Lent and Passiontide, by the special observances of Holy Week and by the following Eastertide between Easter and Pentecost.

Yet there was a long and complex dispute in the early Church about the day on which Easter should be kept. There were those who wanted to keep it always on the Lord's Day and those who wished to keep it on the day in the lunar month, the third day after the fourteenth Nisan, whatever the day of the week, which represented its historical connection with the Jewish Passover. The Western Church, and especially the Church of Rome, supported the former view and many Eastern Churches the latter. Finally by a decree of the Council of Nicea in AD 325 the Western outlook prevailed; and since then Easter Day has been the Sunday nearest to the calculated anniversary of the actual Resurrection, this being determined by the Paschal moon, the first full moon that occurs on or after the spring equinox (21 March). The earliest date, therefore, for Easter Day is 21 March and the latest 25 April.

Rembrandt's gardener is Christ, recognized only when He speaks Mary Magdalene's name. He calls her as she looks for Him, just as once before He called her away from sin and to Himself. The risen Christ appeared first to the humble penitent who came to mourn him. She sought and as He promised, she found her Master.

In the early Church, Easter was the great day for baptism since it was believed that the plunging of the believer beneath the baptismal water and his rising again from it re-enacted for him the death and Resurrection of Christ.

Easter became the festival of both the Resurrection of Christ and the sacrament of Christian baptism.

In Rome thousands of people were sometimes baptized at Easter. For months and even for years previously they had been candidates under instruction and on probation. During the last weeks of Lent they had been engaged in repeated 'scrutinies', exorcisms, fastings and prayers. Then, at the Easter midnight vigil, they presented themselves to receive the sacrament of 'illumination' in the baptistry, the magnificent structure that had been built in the Lateran Palace and had in its centre a large circular reservoir or font. There the twelve Old Testament prophecies of baptism were read, psalms and litanies were sung, the paschal candle was lit, and finally the catechumens descended by three steps into the font, where they were baptized by the bishop and immediately confirmed by the laying on of hands.

By now the dawn of Easter Day was approaching and the bishop and deacons led the newly-baptized, barefooted, carrying candles and robed in white chrisoms, into the great church where they joined the whole congregation of the faithful in the celebration of the Easter Mass. As the day was breaking, the congregation greeted each other with the salutation, 'Christ is risen!', in the way observed in the Eastern Church to this day. Meanwhile, churches, houses and even streets had been illuminated to herald the coming day.

In the present Roman rite the Easter Mass at midnight preserves many features of the old vigil. It has no introit, creed or *Agnus Dei* because it goes back to the time before these were introduced into the Mass. The paschal candle is solemnly lit as it was when the 'great light' was illuminated. The twelve prophecies are read, and the font is blessed though there are now no catechumens awaiting presentation to the bishop to be baptized. And the service ends with the Easter Alleluia which brought the vigil to an end and ushered in the day of rejoicing.

During the Middle Ages a dramatic ceremony was performed in church on Easter morning. Two days previously, on Good Friday, the crucifix from the high altar, wrapped in a veil, had been laid upon a curtained tomb set against the north wall of the chancel where it had remained until the clergy removed it on Easter Eve. After the Gospel had been read on Easter Day, a priest, robed in white as an angel, sat by the tomb and, as three other priests approached, representing the three Marys, asked them, 'Whom seek ye in the tomb, O followers of Christ?' When they replied, 'Jesus of Nazareth, O dweller in heaven', he exclaimed triumphantly, 'He is not here; He is risen, as He foretold', and he pulled back the curtain to reveal only the veil which had wrapped the crucifix. Then the three Marys seized the veil and displayed it, singing, 'The Lord is risen!', and the church-bells began to ring.

A common medieval practice was to eat tansies at Easter in remembrance of the bitter herbs eaten by the Jews at the Passover. These were a kind of cake or fritter flavoured with tansy, rue, wormwood or other bitter-tasting herb. An old recipe for tansies said they should be made with 'a pint of cream, twenty yolks of eggs, ten egg-whites, two spoonfuls of rosewater, juice of oranges, six or eight pippins, shredded very small, with added leaves of 'tansy, feaver-few, violets, spinage or primrose, to make it green', before being fried with butter.

The eating of eggs at Easter is a very old custom that has survived into the present, and in the Middle Ages the day was sometimes called Egg Sunday. Pace, paste, pascal, paschal or pasque eggs, hard-boiled and coloured, were taken to church to be blessed by the clergy and were given away as gifts. A record of the thirteenth century relates that King Edward I ordered four hundred painted eggs to be distributed to the royal household.

The connection of eggs with Easter is also derived from the pagan spring festival. They symbolize new life and so the Resurrection as well.

> *Most glorious Lord of life, that on this day*
> *Didst make thy triumph over death and sin;*
> *And having harrowed hell, didst bring away*
> *Captivity thence captive, us to win:*
> *This joyous day, dear Lord, with joy begin,*
> *And grant that we, for whom thou didst die,*
> *Being with thy dear blood clean washed from sin,*
> *May live for ever in felicity.*

EDMUND SPENSER

Jesus came and stood among them and said, Peace be unto you. JOHN 20:26

Traditionally in England this Sunday is called Low Sunday. The derivation of this is uncertain. It may be in contrast with the 'high' feast of Easter Sunday itself, or a corruption of '*Laudes*', the opening word of the sequence or hymn sung before the Gospel on this day. Some suggest that it is a corruption of Close Sunday, another name for this day, signifying the close of the Easter festivities. Whichever it may be, the ancient name for the day was *Dominica in Albis deponendis*, meaning that on this day those baptized at Easter put aside their white robes. The previous Saturday was correspondingly known as *Sabbatum in Albis*. In the Eastern church this day is called New Sunday, an allusion to the new life entered upon by the recently-baptized.

The Easter octave is the oldest of all octaves. In Rome the whole week was kept holy, no one engaged in secular business, and even slaves were not put to work. Originally the octave ended on Saturday, but now this First Sunday after Easter is part of the Easter festival.

The Gospel for the day continues the story of the Resurrection. It passes from the discovery of the empty tomb in the early morning of Easter Day to the appearance of the risen Lord to His disciples in the evening of the same day, as recounted in St John's Gospel. On this, His first self-manifestation to them in His Resurrection glory, 'He showed them His hands and His side', both to assure them that it was He, their crucified Messiah, who was present with them, and to remind them of the meaning of the Cross, for, as William Temple wrote, 'The wounds of Christ are His credentials to the suffering race of men'. Now risen, the work which He had been sent to do was complete and so, as His Father had sent Him, He sent the Apostles. Christ's commission to them is the assurance that the work that He had completed was not for one generation but would be continually shown forth to all men at all times.

> *Though dead, not dead:*
> *Not gone, though fled:*
> *Not lost, though vanished.*
> *In the great gospel and true creed,*
> *He is yet risen indeed:*
> *Christ is yet risen.*

> ARTHUR HUGH CLOUGH,
> *Easter Day at Naples*

The glory of the Resurrection. Christ rises in majesty while the soldiers gaze with amazement at the empty tomb.

EASTER II

I am the good shepherd: the good shepherd layeth down his life for the sheep.
JOHN 10:11

A popular name in the past for this Sunday has been 'Good Shepherd Sunday' because of the reference to Christ as the shepherd in both the Epistle and the Gospel for the day. The Epistle (from the First Epistle of St Peter), says, 'You were as sheep gone astray, but now you have turned towards the Shepherd and Guardian of your souls', which is probably addressed particularly to the newly-baptized; and the Gospel (from St John's Gospel) emphasizes the message by recounting the discourse by Jesus about Himself as the Good Shepherd.

In taking this theme, the Second Sunday after Easter goes back to the meaning of the sacrifice of the Cross for 'the good shepherd layeth down his life for the sheep'. His sole concern is for the flock; there is no limit to His care for them or the sacrifice He will make for them; He will surrender His own life for their welfare.

In contrast with the rather sentimental modern associations that have grown up around the idea, Christian art in the earliest times represented the Good Shepherd in association with a sacrificing death. In the catacombs of Rome, the Christians of the second and third centuries made crude drawings of the Shepherd who gave His life for the sheep. A motif in the Catacomb of Priscilla shows Christ accompanied by sheep but bearing a goat on His shoulder to emphasize that His care and devotion is for both those inside and outside the fold of the church.

Christ is both the Shepherd and the sheep. As Shepherd He protects His flock even giving His life for them. As the sacrificial lamb He takes the place of the sheep who would otherwise suffer and He dies that they might live.

> *The infant Church; of love she felt the tide*
> *Stream on her from her Lord's yet recent grave.*
> *And then she smiled; and in the Catacombs,*
> *With eye suffused, but heart inspired true,*
> *On those walls subterranean, where she hid,*
> *Her head 'mid ignominy, death and tombs,*
> *She her Good Shepherd's hasty image drew;*
> *And on His shoulders, not a lamb, a kid.*
>
> MATTHEW ARNOLD,
> *The Good Shepherd with the Kid*

A third-century
sculptured relief of
Christ as the Good
Shepherd.

EASTER III

Your joy no man taketh from you. JOHN 16:22

The Gospel for this Sunday, like those for the next four Sundays (including Whitsun), is taken from the last discourses of Jesus to His disciples in the upper room on the night of the betrayal. All the passages come from St John's Gospel and refer in some way to the Holy Spirit. Their inclusion in the rite goes back to the time when Eastertide was also considered as Whitsuntide; they prepare the worshipper to consider the meaning of Pentecost.

The theme of the Gospel for this day is joy after sorrow or sorrow turned into joy. Jesus speaks of the sorrow filling the minds of the disciples at His approaching departure from them and assures them that their grief will be replaced by rejoicing. The disciples find it difficult to follow His meaning, and He does not try to resolve their perplexities. He tells them that they must look forward in faith to the supreme joy of a new fellowship with Him in the Spirit.

The record of this conversation expresses the purpose in the mind of the Evangelist when he wrote for the Christians of his time. By then the years were passing, and the hopes of those who looked for the Second Coming of Christ seemed in vain. Had Christ deluded them? No, the Evangelist insisted, they had misunderstood His words. As He explained in this passage, He was now already among them.

After the sorrow of the Cross, the Resurrection, Ascension and Pentecost had brought them great joy, joy to be compared to that of a mother after the birth of her child, because they are able to 'behold' Him clearly with the eye of faith and be assured that He can 'see' them, coming always to them through their spiritual 'asking' and willingness to receive Him. The concept of the Second Coming of Christ as an immediate event was certainly a general belief in the early Church and the Gospel writer needed therefore to press home the real significance of Christ's promise.

> *For thee I wait, for thee I tarry still,*
> *Mine eyes do long to gaze on thee my fill;*
> *For thee I watch, for thee I pry and pore,*
> *My soul for thee attendeth evermore.*
>
> GEORGE GASCOIGNE

Now I go my way to him that sent me. JOHN 16:5

Again the Gospel for this Sunday comes from Christ's farewell discourse to His disciples in the same sixteenth chapter of St John's Gospel, though, strangely enough, from the passage preceding that of the last Sunday. Here also the Evangelist is concerned with the true interpretation of the Second Coming and the promise of judgment. From the first Pentecost God has been judging men according to their attitude towards Christ. As Bishop Westcott says, 'Because after Christ was withdrawn from human eyes He had passed into a new sphere, there was fixed for all time that by which men's estimate of righteousness might be tried'. Men are now declared righteous or sinful by the standard of Christ, which is final and fixed by His departure. The Prince of this World—human plans and aims and ambitions—is found wanting in comparison with it. This passage also contains the promise that there will be further truths which the time has not yet come to reveal, but which will be revealed by the Holy Spirit when the moment is right. The text has been an important one in the discussions of how far the Gospels contain all that is necessary for salvation or whether there is a continuing revelation of the mind of God through His Church. In general the Eastern Churches and the Church of England have seen the General Councils of the Church as being able further to define doctrine, while the Roman Catholic Church has confined the power to the Popes as successors of St Peter.

> *Unchanging God, by that one Light*
>   *Through which we grope to Truth and Thee,*
> *Confound not yet our day with night,*
>   *Break not the measures of Thy sea.*
> *Hear not, though grief for chaos cry*
>   *Or rail at Thine unanswering Throne.*
> *Thy Law, Thy Law, is Liberty*
>   *And in Thy Law we find our own.*
>
> ALFRED NOYES, *The Trumpet of the Law*

In the world ye have tribulation, but be of good cheer, I have overcome the world.

JOHN 16:33

On this Sunday, the Gospel continues the words of Jesus which formed the Gospel for the Third Sunday after Easter and which close His teachings to the disciples on the night of the betrayal. This is His farewell to them.

In this last message, He urges them to pray in future 'in His name', which, as William Temple said, 'means that we pray as His representatives, as He would pray in our place, as He does pray in Heaven.' He also assures them that their faith in Him will be strengthened by their understanding of His divine mission which is to be revealed to them more clearly in His victory over the world, which will be the foundation of their peace and joy.

Christ's promise in the Gospel, that whatsoever we shall ask in His name His Father will give us, is appropriate for this Sunday, which is sometimes called Rogation Sunday. The three days following it are Rogation Days (from the Latin *rogare*, to ask or beseech). These were days set aside by the Church for prayer for the growing crops. Processions were led through the cornfields and litanies sung. All this was a Christianized version of an ancient pagan practice. It was adopted in England in the eighth century and was suppressed in 1547. However, under Elizabeth I, the royal injunctions of 1559 ordered the 'perambulation of parishes' and the use of the Litany in the Book of Common Prayer.

The Homily for Rogation Week, written in 1562, explains the sermon's purpose very clearly:

We be now assembled together, good Christian people, most principally to laud and thank Almighty God for his great benefits, by beholding the fields replenished with all manner of fruit, to the maintenance of our corporal necessities, for our food and sustenance; and partly also to make our humble suits in prayers to his fatherly providence, to conserve the same fruits in sending us seasonable weather, whereby we may gather in the said fruits, to the end for which his merciful goodness hath provided them.

It was when Christ blessed the bread that His two disciples recognized who it was who had shared their journey to Emmaus.

ASCENSION DAY

So then the Lord Jesus, after he had spoken to them, was received up into heaven and sat at the right hand of God. MARK 16:19

Ascension Day, known as Holy Thursday in old English usage, is kept on the fifth Thursday, which is the fortieth day, after Easter. It is one of the great festivals of the Christian year, and there is considerable evidence for its observance from the later years of the fourth century. St Augustine speaks of it as universally observed and thought it was of very early origin – 'For those things which are received and observed over all the world, not as written in Scripture, but as handed down to us by tradition, we conceive to be instituted by the Apostles themselves or some numerous Council whose authority is of very great use in the Church. Such are the anniversary solemnities of our Saviour's passion and resurrection and ascension into heaven, and the coming of the Holy Ghost from heaven.'

The earliest celebration of Ascension Day seems to have originated in Jerusalem, when visiting pilgrims made a procession on this day in memory of the journey made by the Apostles from Jerusalem to Bethany and the Mount of Olives in continuation of the dramatic representations of Holy Week. In the Western Church, the paschal candle, which is lighted during the more important services of Eastertide, is extinguished after the Gospel at the Mass on Ascension Day in commemoration of Christ's departure from the Apostles.

In England from the ninth century the ceremony of 'beating the bounds' was performed on Ascension Day. The bounds were small boundary stones marking the limit of parishes and also of a town's meadows and fields. The children were marched in procession round the bounds, accompanied by the clergy and parish officers, and beaten with peeled willow switches at each stone. This was to teach the children to remember the boundary marks of their parishes when they grew up and so be able to prevent farmers removing them.

> *Salute the last and everlasting day,*
> *Joy at the uprising of this Sunne, and Sonne,*
> *Yee whose just teares, or tribulation*
> *Have purely washt, or burnt your drossie clay;*
> *Behold the Highest, parting hence away,*
> *Lightens the darke clouds, which hee treads upon,*
> *Nor doth hee by ascending show alone,*
> *But first hee, and hee first enters the way.*
>
> JOHN DONNE, *Ascention*

Mantegna's very
stylized view of
Christ's ascension
concentrates on the
wonder of the disciples
at the glory of His going
into Heaven. It
celebrates His
statement that He has
to leave the world in
order that the
Comforter could come,
and that He goes to
prepare a place for us.

ASCENSION I

When the Comforter is come, whom I will send to you from the Father, even the spirit of truth, which proceedeth from the Father, he shall testify of me. JOHN 15:26

This day was originally known as Expectation Sunday, and it looked forward to Pentecost since, during the ten days between the Ascension and Whitsunday, the Apostles were waiting for the promised gift of the Holy Spirit. The expectation of Pentecost was vividly expressed during ancient times in Rome by the custom of showering roses through the opening of the roof of the Pantheon during the sermon at the stational Mass.

The Gospel for this Sunday deals with the Comforter, the Spirit of truth, which will lead the Church into all truth. Christ tells the Apostles that when this comes at Pentecost, they will be taught by the Spirit, testify to Jesus among men and incur the hatred and hostility of the world.

RIGHT With His feet protruding from the cloud, Christ is taken up to Heaven in this illustration from a fifteenth-century Flemish breviary. It may be too literal for our demythologizing age but its statement is still strikingly clear. Christ really and bodily rose from the dead and has gone on before us into Heaven.

'And He ascended into heaven and sitteth on the right hand of God the Father from whence He shall come to judge both the quick and the dead whose kingdom shall have no end.' In this picture of the Coronation of the Virgin Christ is shown in glory at the side of God, amidst the saints in heaven. The Holy Spirit in the form of a dove hovers beside Him.

ugilia ascensionis Ad
trinas In mutatoriuz
meius uts. s̄m iohez

n illo. t̄e
Sublenat
ihus ocul
in celum.
dixit. Pa
te venit ho
auifica filium tuum.

ut filius tuus clarificet
te. Et rel'. Omelia beati:
augustini lectio prima.

oterat dūs ir
quingentus ⁊
cōetenus p̄n
in forma seu: ⁊ ex formi
p̄r̄i si hoc op̄s ēēt orare si
lentio. s̄z ita p̄n se exhibe
re volunt precatorē ut me

The story of the Tower of Babel explained to the Jews why the languages of the nations of the earth were so different. It was man's presumption that had brought it about. He tried to build a tower to Heaven and was confounded when God ensured that no builder could understand another as they began to speak their various tongues.

At Pentecost the barriers between men are broken down and everyone hears and understands the good news, preached by the Apostles, in their own language. On this the birthday of the Church, it is manifestly true there is neither Jew nor Greek, neither male nor female, for we are all one in Christ Jesus. The divisions symbolized by the Tower of Babel, and brought on by man's own presumption, are healed by the redemptive power of Christ.

pentecost

I will pray the father, and he shall give you another Comforter.

JOHN 14:16

The disciples were gathered together on the Jewish feast of Pentecost, no longer the miserable and defeated band which they had been before the Resurrection but ready now to receive the inrush of the Holy Spirit which so filled them that the cosmopolitan crowd thought them drunk and were astonished to find that they could understand these simple Galileans in their own languages.

THE CHRISTIAN SEASON OF PENTECOST or Whitsuntide corresponds to the Jewish festival of Weeks or Pentecost in the same way that the Christian Easter corresponds to the Passover. These two annual Jewish feasts have a story of development from nature-festivals to historical commemorations. The Passover, originally a spring-time, lambing-season festival, coincided with the Feast of Unleavened Bread, marking the beginning of reaping the harvest. The two feasts became fused in biblical times into a single festival commemorating the exodus of the Israelites from slavery in Egypt. Just as the Passover marked the beginning of the reaping season, so the Feast of Weeks marked its end. After forty-nine days, a week of weeks, came the day of the festival, Pentecost being the Greek for the fiftieth day. Later Rabbinical writers treated it as a commemoration of the delivery of the Law to Moses on Mount Sinai.

Just as both these Jewish festivals correspond to Christian ones, so they both actually played a part in the events of Christian history commemorated at Easter and Pentecost. The Last Supper of Jesus and the disciples was the meal shared in every Jewish household on the night of the Passover. Later the outpouring of the Holy Spirit occurred when multitudes had come to Jerusalem for the observance of the Jewish feast of Pentecost, and the disciples were 'all together in one place' (which may have been a private house or part of the Temple) precisely for this reason.

A further comparison may be made between the Jewish and Christian festivals of Pentecost. The giving of the Law of Moses came during the formative period of the Hebrew people and made possible the union of the twelve tribes into a single nation with a common moral standard. In the same way the gift of the Holy Spirit converted the disciples into the Church of God, the New Israel, devoted to the task of proclaiming

Pentecost

Christ's message and performing His mission in the world. So Pentecost has sometimes been called the 'birthday of the Christian Church'.

After Easter, Pentecost ranks as the second festival of the Christian year and has been observed from ancient times. Some early writers use the word 'Pentecost' for the whole period of the 'great fifty days' of Eastertide and others only for the concluding day of the period (Whitsunday), but from the beginning of the fourth century the latter sense began to prevail. The celebrations after the day seem always to have been confined to the octave. The Apostolic Constitutions, a collection of ecclesiastical law dating from the latter half of the fourth century, state, 'After you have kept the festival of Pentecost, keep one week more festival, and, after that, fast'. In the Roman Catholic Church, Monday and Tuesday within the octave rank as Doubles of the First Class and in the English Book of Common Prayer as 'Red Letter Days' while Wednesday, Friday and Saturday are Ember Days.

In likeness of a dove and in semblance of fire was the Spirit of God manifested; for he causes those to be meek in innocence and burning in the will of God, whom he fills with his grace. Meekness is not pleasing to God without wisdom, nor wisdom without meekness; as it is said by the Blessed Job, that he was meek and righteous. What is righteousness without meekness? Or what is meekness without righteousness? But the Holy Ghost, who teaches both righteousness and meekness, should be manifested both as fire and as love, for he causeth the hearts of those men whom he enlightens with his grace to be meek through innocence and kindled by love and wisdom. God is, as Paul said, a consuming fire. He is a fire unspeakable and invisible. Concerning that fire, Jesus said: 'I come because I would send fire upon the earth, and I will that it burn.' He sent the Holy Ghost on earth, and he by his inspiration kindled the hearts of earthly men. Then burns the earth, when the earthly man's heart kindles to love of God, which before was cold through fleshly lusts.

Anglo-Saxon Homily for Whitsuntide

I will not leave you comfortless, I will come to you. JOHN 14:18

The common English name for the festival of Pentecost is thought most likely to have been originally 'White Sunday' from its association with the white robes of baptism. In the Western Church, the vigil of Pentecost soon joined Easter as a great time for baptism and in the colder northern countries most converts may have preferred it as the occasion for undergoing baptism by immersion and would, therefore, have worn their white chrisoms on this day.

Baptism was administered with many of the same ceremonies as those of the Easter vigil, but the lighting of the candle was omitted. The number of the Old Testament lessons in the Roman Missal is six, and it also prescribes a form for the blessing of the font. Among the old customs which prevailed in some churches in Spain and other countries on Whitsunday were the blowing of trumpets at the singing of the *Veni, Sancte Spiritus* (Come, Holy Ghost), the throwing down of burning torches from the roof, the releasing of doves in the church and the scattering of roses.

In England during the Middle Ages, Whitsun was traditionally a time when people were called upon to contribute money towards the upkeep of church buildings. Everyone who lived in a house with a chimney made an offering, called Whitsun-farthings or smoke-farthings, to the cathedral of the diocese in which they lived. Parish churches raised money by Church Ales or Whitsun Ales. Malt was brewed into strong ale, and often sold in the church itself, where the girls of the parish stood at the door to receive the contributions of those who came to drink. In some villages, the inn may have originally been the church house, especially if its sign is derived from the dedication of the church, for instance, the Cross Keys of St Peter or the Lamb and Flag of St John the Baptist.

> *Where is the fire which once descended*
> *On Thy Apostles? Thou didst then*
> *Keep open house, richly attended,*
> *Feasting allcomers by twelve chosen men,*
>
> *Lord, though we change, Thou art the same,*
> *The same sweet God of love and light:*
> *Restore this day, for thy great name,*
> *Unto his ancient and miraculous right.*
>
> GEORGE HERBERT, *Whitsunday*

TRINITY SUNDAY

Go, ye, therefore, and make disciples of all the nations, baptizing them in the name of the Father and of the Son and of the Holy Spirit. MATTHEW 28:19

The festival of Trinity Sunday is of comparatively recent institution and is observed in the Western Church only, the day being kept in the Eastern Church as the festival of all Holy Martyrs. Originally, as with other Sundays following the Ember vigil, this day was left vacant; and from the eighth to the fourteenth century it was treated as the octave of Pentecost. The institution of the festival of the Holy Trinity made the octave end, as the Easter octave originally did, on Saturday.

From quite early times, some of the clergy in various places initiated annual festivals in honour of the Trinity, but Pope Alexander II in the eleventh century discouraged this practice as unnecessary, since the doctrine was recognized in the daily worship of the Church in the *Gloria Patri*. It would seem that at this period some churches chose the Sunday before Advent for their festival of the Trinity, while others celebrated it in this octave of Pentecost. This day became increasingly observed as Trinity Sunday, and in 1334 Pope John XXII ordered its acceptance by the whole Church. It seemed the most appropriate day since it com-

The essential nature of the Three in One is here expressed by Gozzoli with complete simplicity. The Three Persons combine in one action and that the blessing of the cup. In the Eucharist we offer to God the Father, His own Son, through the operation of the Holy Spirit.

Pesellino uses the traditional ways of presenting the Trinity. The majesterial Father both supports the Cross and presents His Son upon it to the world; while the Holy Spirit hovers like a dove above Christ's head. The doctrine of the Trinity is at the centre of the Christian faith and one of the great tests of orthodoxy. Its representation in concrete terms must always be difficult and can only be possible at all through some such mannered construction as this.

pleted the liturgical commemorations of the life of Christ and the coming of the Holy Spirit during the first half of the Church's year by a commemoration of the central Christian doctrine that the One God exists in Three Persons and One Substance.

In England, the feast was especially popular perhaps because of its association with Thomas Becket, who was consecrated Archbishop of Canterbury in the octave of Pentecost in 1162. In English parishes processions were held in which the children wore garlands and the choirs sang special anthems, while in London the judges and great law officers of the crown, together with the lord mayor, aldermen and common council of the city, attended divine service in St Paul's Cathedral and heard a sermon preached by the lord mayor's chaplain. The Book of Common Prayer follows the old Sarum use in reckoning the succeeding Sundays as after Trinity instead of as after Pentecost as in the Eastern and Roman Catholic Churches.

CORPUS CHRISTI

He that eateth my flesh and drinketh my blood abideth in me and I in him. JOHN 6:56

From very early times the Institution of the Eucharist was recalled on Maundy Thursday, but through its association with the Passion this has a largely mournful and penitential character, and by the thirteenth century many thought that another day should be set apart for this commemoration of the Last Supper. The day most favoured was the sixtieth day after Easter, the Thursday after Trinity Sunday, the first free Thursday after the cycle of festivals is over.

The celebration of the festival on this day was due largely to the Blessed Juliana, a nun of Liège, who about 1230 said that while gazing at the full moon she had seen a gap in it and received a special revelation that the moon represented the Christian Church and the gap the want of a festival for the adoration of the Sacrament. In 1246 she was able to persuade the Bishop of Liège to order the day to be kept throughout his diocese.

The festival remained a local one until the pontification of Pope Urban IV (1261–4), who had at one time been Archdeacon of Liège. His doubts about making it universal are said to have been removed by the miracle of Bolsena, where a priest, who disbelieved in the recently declared doctrine of transubstantiation, saw blood issuing from the consecrated Host when he was celebrating Mass. In 1264 Urban ordered the observance of the festival throughout the Church, and at his bidding Thomas Aquinas drew up a service for the day which includes such fine hymns as *Pange Lingua*.

Corpus Christi remained a widely observed festival throughout the Western Church until the Reformation, and in England the name was given to two colleges, one at Cambridge in 1352 and one at Oxford in 1516. The Council of Trent (1545–63) spoke of Corpus Christi as a triumph over heresy and condemned those who censured the feast or the procession of the Blessed Sacrament.

> *Sing, my tongue, the glorious battle,*
> *Sing the last, the dread affray;*
> *O'er the Cross, the Victor's trophy,*
> *Sound the high triumphal lay,*
> *How, the pains of death enduring,*
> *Earth's Redeemer won the day.*
> THOMAS AQUINAS

A fifteenth-century painting by Philip Goul of the communion of the Apostles. Corpus Christi is a separate festival from the events of Maunday Thursday because otherwise the continuing significance of Christ's words 'Do this in remembrance of me' must be submerged in the gathering drama of His death and Resurrection.

PENTECOST II

They all began to make excuses. LUKE 14:18

The second half of the Christian calendar begins with this Sunday. The first half has been devoted to the commemoration of the events of the life of Jesus on earth, the coming of the Holy Spirit and the doctrine of the Trinity. The Sundays after Pentecost are concerned with the practical life of those who believe in Christ and accept His teaching.

Since, in England, the Sarum use numbered this and all the other Sundays to Advent 'after Trinity', this Sunday in the English rite became the First Sunday after Trinity and is the first of twenty-five such Sundays. For the first few Sundays of this season of Pentecost, the Gospel for the day in the Roman Missal is one in advance of the Book of Common Prayer, and, though they generally kept to the old Gospel, the English reformers occasionally changed the length of the passages.

The Gospel for this Sunday is the story of the invited guests who decline to come to the banquet prepared for them and are replaced, on the orders of the host, by 'the poor, the maimed, the halt and the blind' and by those from 'the highways and hedges'. Those who have no need for the Kingdom of Heaven are supplanted by those who want to share in its duties and promises. As Professor A.B.Bruce has said, 'The parable teaches that the kingdom of heaven is not for the full, but for the hungry. In concrete, pictorial form, it declares that God filleth the hungry with good things and sendeth the rich empty away.'

> *Unto Thy princely wedding, Lord, are bid*
> *Of every sort some guests to feast with Thee;*
> *One that a spouse but late before had wed,*
> *One oxen bought, one taken land to fee;*
> *They from the banquet therefore absent be,*
> *Regarding not Thy messengers of grace.*
> *In number of the like, Lord, hold not me,*
> *But let me have, I crave, the offered place.*
> *Yet e'er that I appear before Thy face,*
> *A wedding garment first I must put on,*
> *My own unrighteous clothing is too base,*
> *And merchandise of merits now are gone;*
> *Then since Thou call'st, with faith do Thou me clothe,*
> *A lame blind begger, Lord, do Thou not loathe.*
>
> HENRY LOK, *The Great Supper*

In this *Codex Aureo*, the story of the Great Feast is told as a strip cartoon. The guests who are first invited point to the various pre-occupations that forbid their attendance. Only the man who has married a wife does not point, her very presence on his horse is sufficient for him to say 'And therefore I cannot come'. The halt and the lame, with their various props and crutches, crowd up along the edge of the picture to get into the supper where the Lord presides at His table with an unmistakable air of real authority.

There is joy in the presence of the angels of God over one sinner that repenteth.

LUKE 15:10

Two short parables of the lost form the Gospel for this day. They are the parable of the lost sheep and the parable of the lost coin. The first of these is the better known of the two. This is because most people subconsciously identify the shepherd, who lost and searched for his sheep, as the Good Shepherd in the passage in St John's Gospel which forms the Gospel for the Second Sunday after Easter. There is, however, no reason for this. He is intended to be no more than an ordinary shepherd, just as the woman who looked for her coin in the other parable is an ordinary housewife.

Both the shepherd and the housewife, when they lose something they own, do not remain content with what they still have – the ninety-nine sheep in the flock or the nine coins in her purse – but are determined at once to do all that they can to find it again. They do this because the human instinct of possession leads them to want everything that belongs to them, and they rejoice when they find what they had lost. The point of the parable is that God shares this same feeling. All human souls are His property, and He therefore rejoices whenever those that are lost or strayed return to Him.

There is no idealisation whatever in either parable. They unveil something of the mystery of the Kingdom in facts which are genuinely commonplace, because they show them as illustrating a universal principle of order. The sense of ownership is a very primitive element in man's nature. It develops early in every human child. Yet in every child it is a tiny instance of a law which penetrates also to what is deepest and greatest in the universe. It indicates and reflects a relation which exists between God Himself and His creation. And the joy in property regained has its analogue, its fulfilment, its source, in something which is known in the presence of the angels of God.

The immediate popular appeal of the story is reflected in the famous Sankey hymn, 'The Ninety and Nine':

> *Lord, Thou hast here Thy ninety and nine;*
> *Are they not enough for thee?*
> *But the Shepherd made answer: 'This of mine*
> *Has wandered away from me;*
> *And although the road be rough and steep*
> *I go to the desert to find my sheep.'*

The parable of the lost sheep portrayed in a stained-glass window at Hillesden Church, Buckinghamshire.

PENTECOST IV

They forsook all and followed him. LUKE 5:11

Since the Gospel for the previous Sunday in the Book of Common Prayer (the Fourth Sunday after Trinity) does not appear at all in the Roman rite, the Gospels in the Roman Missal are henceforward two ahead of the Prayer Book, though the Epistles remain only one.

The Gospel for this Fourth Sunday after Pentecost is the story, so dramatically told by Luke, of the miraculous draught of fishes and the calling by Jesus of Peter and the other three fishermen who became His first disciples. This is action by Jesus rather than teaching, but the inclusion of this incident for the Gospel for this day is entirely consistent with the purpose of these Sundays in this part of the Christian calendar. The story emphasizes that when Christ was on earth He called men to follow Him and still does today.

The account brings home the fact that the disciples were indeed taken straight from their very humble jobs. There is an arresting directness in the way which Christ appeals to them through the things which really concerned them. The lesson was taught by the miraculous catch – something dear to every fisherman's heart – and the explanation of their future mission was itself put in the terms of their trade – they were to be fishers of men. It is this direct appeal which has been seen as the prototype of the way in which God calls his people.

In *The Quest for the Historical Jesus* Albert Schweitzer uses this story as just such a prototype: 'He comes to us as one unknown, without a name, as of old by the lake-side He came to those men who knew Him not. He speaks to us the same word: "Follow thou ME", and sets us to the same task which He has to fulfil for our time. He commands. And to those who obey Him, whether they be wise or simple, He will reveal Himself in the toils, the conflicts, the sufferings which they shall pass through in His fellowship, and as an ineffable mystery they shall learn in their own experience who He is.'

> *Thou hast the art on't, Peter, and canst tell*
> *To cast thy nets on all occasions well:*
> *When Christ calls, and thy nets would have thee stay,*
> *To cast them well's to cast them quite away.*
>
> RICHARD CRASHAW

'Launch out into the deep.' This is the ringing call of Christ to St Peter and its immediacy is mirrored in the stark simplicity of this illustration from a thirteenth-century German psalter. The variety of expressions on the faces of the Apostles as they greet the miracle of the draught of fishes are as eloquent as is St Peter's own look of reluctant acceptance of the fact that he has walked on the water. He has obviously removed most of his clothes just in case, and he is reaching to grasp Christ's hands immediately he gets near enough to the shore. Man's faith, even when great enough to start to trust God, is still timid enough to need constant reassurance. In the very act of walking on the sea, Peter fears for the last few steps.

PENTECOST V

Except your righteousness shall exceed the righteousness of the scribes and Pharisees,
ye shall in no wise enter into the kingdom of heaven. MATTHEW 5:20

The Sermon on the Mount, the discourse of Jesus setting out the principles of Christian conduct, provides the Gospel for this Sunday. The passage is from the part of the Sermon in which, after the opening description of the Christian character in the Beatitudes and the duty of Christians to be 'the salt' and 'the light' of the world, He briefly contrasts the provisions of the old Law with the higher righteousness demanded by His teaching. In dealing with the nature of the Law, Jesus contrasts legalistic acceptance of the letter with a real understanding of the spirit. The scribes and the Pharisees become the embodiment of those who religiously keep to the minutiae of the regulations with no real conception of the demands of morality. The scribes were learned Jews who devoted their lives to a study of the Law and made an occupation of its exposition. The Pharisees had grown out of the long conflict between the Jews and the surrounding heathen states. They stood for a strict monotheism and observance of the Sabbath. They demanded an undeviating acceptance of the Old Testament as interpreted by the scribes and they laid great emphasis on the strict observance of the synagogue service.

By contrast Christ took the meaning of the Law to a deeper level. Here He singles out particularly the sixth commandment 'Thou shalt do no murder' but deals with it in the same way as He does with all the commandments. He always insisted that whenever anything is forbidden as contrary to God's will, all else of the same thought, even all thought about it, is also forbidden; and when anything is not to be done, the opposite is always to be required in thought and word and deed.

The Law prohibits murder and punishes the crime, but angry thoughts are as bad; and anyone who insults someone may be prosecuted, but he will also have to answer to God for it. This means that in everyday life, therefore, no one should ever entertain anger towards others. If people do fall out with each other they should make up their quarrels quickly while they still have time.

> *Think, and be careful what thou art within;*
> *For there is sin in the desire of sin.*
> *Think, and be thankful, in a different case;*
> *For there is grace in the desire of grace.*
>
> JOHN BYROM

Is the story of the feeding of the four thousand by Jesus, which forms the Gospel for this Sunday, a second account of the feeding of the five thousand, or does it describe a separate incident? Mark undoubtedly regarded it as a separate occurrence. His account opens with the word 'again', and later he cites Jesus as definitely referring to both miracles of feeding. On the other hand, the language of the two accounts is similar, and the differences in numbers may very likely have occurred in the first years after the death of Jesus when the stories were spread by word of mouth.

Their spiritual meaning is expressed by Thomas Aquinas:

> *O bread to pilgrim given,*
> *O food that angels eat,*
> *O manna sent from heaven,*
> *For heaven-born natures meet,*
> *Give us, for Thee long pining,*
> *To eat till richly filled;*
> *Till, earth's delights resigning,*
> *Our every wish is stilled.*

This is the thought expressed in the best commentary on this miracle, the discourse by Jesus in St John's Gospel beginning 'I am the bread of life'. Jesus Himself will satisfy all who come to Him in hunger with the bread of everlasting life, which is Himself and has sustained, strengthened and inspired Christians in all times and in all circumstances. The image of bread has a continuing importance in the Bible. The Old Testament archetype is the manna which fed the Children of Israel in the desert, but it is carried on through this miracle to the concept of Christ as the Bread of Life and shown supremely in the use of bread in the Last Supper which in the hands of Christ becomes His body.

> *Twas August, and the fierce sun overhead*
> *Smote on the squalid streets of Bethnal Green,*
> *And the pale weaver, through his windows seen*
> *In Spitalfields, looked thrice dispirited.*
>
> *I met a preacher there I knew, and said:*
> *'Ill and o'erworked, how fare you in this scene?'* –
> *'Bravely!' said he; 'for I of late have been*
> *Much cheer'd with thoughts of Christ, the living bread'.*
>
> MATTHEW ARNOLD

The disciples seem really concerned at the left-overs from the feeding of the four thousand in this sixteenth-century illustration from the Master of Boqueteaux. The crowd is fully satisfied with the loaves and fishes, and still baskets full of food remain. God gives so generously that He more than fulfils all our needs.

Wherefore by their fruits ye shall know them. MATTHEW 7:20

The Gospel for this Sunday is again taken from the Sermon on the Mount. It is a part of Christ's final warning against unreality in religious teaching and practice. It begins with a condemnation of 'false prophets', wolves in sheep's clothing. As in the rest of the New Testament, the word 'prophet' means 'one who interprets the will of God' rather than 'a foreteller of the future' as common usage today suggests, and a 'false prophet' here does not mean one who prophecies what is false, but rather a bogus prophet, one who claims to proclaim God's message and does not, and is to be judged by his fruits, the effect he has on the life of others.

From a good man a good example will come for he will do good things. Much-desired fruits like the fig and the grape are not gathered from such weeds as thorns and thistles. As Lord Byron wrote:

The thorns which I have reaped are of the tree
I planted: they have torn me, and I bleed:
I should have known what fruit would spring from such a seed.

Jesus insists that true piety must result in good actions, as a good tree produces good fruit. True disciples are not those who profess allegiance to Him and call Him 'Lord', but 'only those who do the will of my heavenly Father'. Fine words are no substitute for good deeds, which are the ultimate test of Christian sincerity.

There is a practicality about this which is rooted in the simplicity of the image. In the subsistence farming community to which He was speaking, good crops were not just desirable they were vital to life itself. It is therefore difficult for us to recapture the immediacy of an image like 'I am the true vine' yet it is in the transformation of everyday things that Jesus' language still lives even in a world which only knows of cultivation at second hand.

Like as the gentle heart itself bewrays
In doing gentle deeds with frank delight,
Even so the baser mind itself displays
In cankered malice and revengeful spite.
ANON. (R. CARLTON'S *Madrigals 1601*)

PENTECOST VIII

For the sons of this world are wiser in their own generation than the sons of light.
LUKE 16:8

This Sunday, like Septuagesima Sunday, has for its Gospel another of Christ's parables which presents problems to those who would understand it. It is the parable of the unjust steward, described by Dr Inge as 'a very strange parable, on which expositors have broken their teeth in vain'. He himself suggested, 'It may have been a humorous story, suggested by some clever fraud which the disciples reported to Jesus. "Why cannot you be as clever in making the best of your opportunities?"'

Certainly there can be no suggestion that Jesus was expressing approval of the steward's dishonest mismanagement of his employer's estate, but the story does suggest appreciation of the shrewdness and decisiveness displayed by the steward when, being accused of wasting his master's goods and instantly dismissed, he had to provide for his future. He secured the friendship of his master's debtors by allowing them to pay less than they owed him, and when the master heard of it, he had to admire his audacity and ingenuity. And Jesus finished the story by turning to the disciples and saying, 'For the sons of this world are wiser in their own generation than the sons of light'.

Jesus was making the point that religious people rarely devote such whole-hearted energy to the fulfilment of God's purposes as others do to forwarding their own interests. They are often careless, indolent and half-hearted about eternal things, but how great an effect they could have if they emulated the determination of those who concern themselves with worldly matters.

One good man, one man who does not put on his religion once a week with his Sunday coat, but wears it for his working dress, and lets the thought of God grow into him, and through and through him, till everything he says and does becomes religious, that man is worth a thousand sermons – he is a living Gospel – he comes in the spirit and power of Elias – he is the image of God. And men see his good works, and admire them in spite of themselves, and see that they are Godlike, and that God's grace is no dream, but that the Holy Spirit is still among men, and that all nobleness and manliness is His gift, His stamp, His picture: and so they get a glimpse of God again in His saints and heroes, and glorify their Father who is in heaven.

CHARLES KINGSLEY

The traders escape Christ's wrath in this illustration of the Gospels produced by Arabs in the seventeenth century. Most sold animals for sacrifice – the doves and other birds and even a small pig. Others changed Roman coins into the Temple currency which was used for offerings. All existed because of the Jewish faith, but their motives were exclusively secular – they had turned His Father's house into a den of thieves.

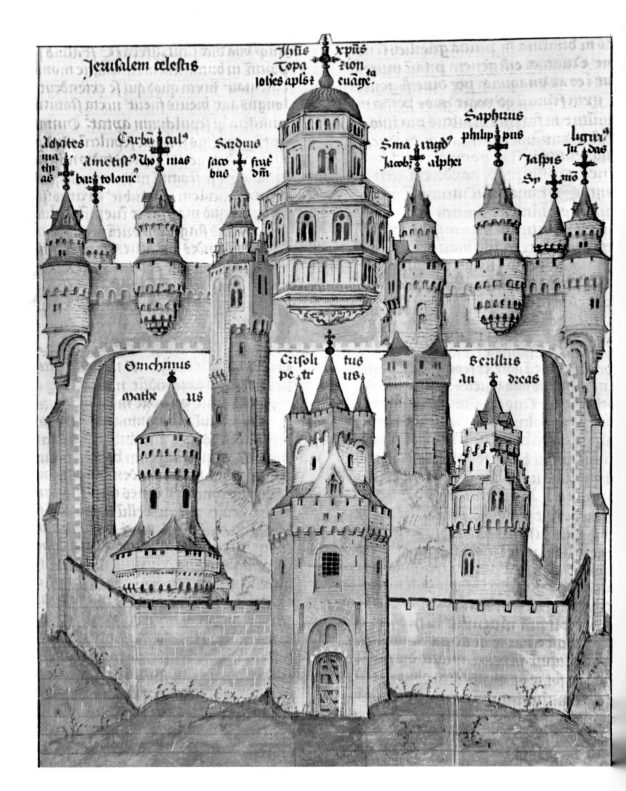

Jerusalem cœlestis

Ihūs xpūs
Topa zion ta
Iohes apls euāge.

Adytes
ma Ametist? Tho mas
thi bar tolome
as

Carbū cul?

Sardius
saco sīut
bus dm

Sma ingd?
Jacob; alphei

Saphirus
philip pus

ligur?
Iu das
Jaspis
Sy mō

Omichnius
mathe us

Crisoli tus
pe tr us

Berillus
an dreas

And when he was come near, he beheld the city and wept over it. LUKE 19:41

On this Sunday the Gospel returns to the subject of the Gospel for the First Sunday in Advent – the destruction of Jerusalem which Jesus knew to be approaching. It is the passage in the narrative of the entry of Jesus into Jerusalem on Palm Sunday, which Luke alone relates, that when He came within sight of the city He wept over it because it failed to recognize the time of its visitation and the things which belonged to its peace. And He foretold the terrible fate that would overtake the unprepared and unrepentant city at the hands of the Roman attackers, who would build a rampart round it to encircle the defenders and prevent them escaping from the slaughter and pillage with which a siege inevitably ended.

Then, as the Gospel proceeds, the story changes from Christ's lament over Jerusalem to His expulsion of the money-changers and traders from the precincts of the Temple. His sorrow was replaced by anger as He acted against the commercialism and materialism of the contemporary Jewish religion which was largely responsible for the fate hanging over the city, long accepted as the nation's capital and the centre of its faith. It was also a deliberate symbolic action on His part, setting forth His claim to be the Messiah by publicly fulfilling the prophecy of Malachi, 'The Lord whom ye see shall suddenly come to his temple, ... and he shall purify the sons of Levi (the priesthood), ... and they shall offer to the Lord offerings in righteousness'.

Jerusalem held for Christ, as for all Jews, a very special significance. It was not only the Holy City but it was the symbol of the nation, and its destruction in AD 70 was the beginning of nearly nineteen centuries of wandering for the chosen people.

The sacred centre of the Holy City was the Temple which Solomon had built and which served as the geographical centre of the Jewish religion. To defile this was a real scandal, and the presence of the traders underlined the degree to which Judaism had become a cult of rules and regulations rather than the expression of a real relationship with God.

Jerusalem's special significance for the Jews is carried on in the importance of the New Jerusalem for Christians. This twelfth-century miniature shows the heavenly city which takes the place of the earthly Jerusalem which has denied Christ its Lord. Within it are the mansions Jesus promised to prepare for His disciples – each one labelled with the owner's name.

Blessed, unhappy city! dearly loved
But still unkind! Art this day nothing moved?
Art senseless still? Oh, canst thou sleep
When God himself for thee doth weep?
Stiff-necked Jews! your fathers' breed
That served the calf, not Abraham's seed,
Had not the babes 'Hosanna' cried,
The stones had spoke what you denied.

HENRY VAUGHAN

THE TRANSFIGURATION

In their presence he was transfigured.

MARK 9:2

This festival on 6 August commemorates the event in the course of the ministry of Jesus in which He was visibly glorified in the presence of three chosen disciples – Peter, James and John. The evidence for the Transfiguration is very strong. It is related in the first three Gospels, where it is described as an actual historical event and with striking agreement as to detail. Six days after Peter had recognized that Jesus was the Messiah, He took the selected three with Him to a high mountain, where He prayed. As He did this, His face became radiant with a supernatural light, and there appeared Moses and Elijah who were talking to Him. They were speaking about the martyr's death which Jesus was about to undergo at Jerusalem. When it seemed that Jesus and Moses and Elijah were about to withdraw, Peter, in order to retain them,

suggested that he and his companions should construct three shelters (such as the Jews were accustomed to build at the Feast of Tabernacles and on the flat roofs of their houses in the hot season). Then a luminous cloud, the traditional symbol to the Israelites of God's presence, overshadowed them all, and from it came the Divine voice proclaiming, 'This is my Son, my Beloved; listen to Him'. The disciples were overcome with awe and yet experienced great joy at the same time. When Jesus had returned to the ordinary conditions of human life, He forbade the disciples to talk about their recent experience until the Son of Man should be risen from the dead.

There has been considerable disagreement about the place of the Transfiguration, which is not definitely located in the Gospels. They simply state that it occurred on a 'high mountain', and tradition has identified this with Mount Tabor, which became a place of pilgrimage in commemoration of the event, and in the sixth century three churches were built on its summit to correspond to the shelters of Peter; but it is unlikely that this was the place because it was inhabited, and Jesus and His disciples could not have gone there to be 'apart by themselves'. The event may have occurred on Mount Hermon or even on the Mount of Olives.

The significance of the Transfiguration is to indicate the testimony of the Law and the Prophets (the two great sections of the Jewish scriptures), as represented by Moses and Elijah, to the Messiahship of Jesus. Tradition held that both Moses and Elijah, who had not died ordinary deaths, would return when the Messiah came. The vision also provided a further Divine proclamation of His Sonship and foreshadowed His coming glory.

The festival was first observed in the Eastern Church, apparently originally as a local and unofficial commemoration, but it had become widely adopted by the end of the ninth century. It was probably first brought to the West much later by the Crusaders, and its general observance began in 1457 when Pope Callistus III ordered its universal observance to commemorate the victory gained over the Turks at Belgrade on 6 August 1456. It is now one of the greater festivals of the Roman Catholic Church. Its removal from the English Book of Common Prayer is an example of the desire in the sixteenth century to reduce the number of holy days during harvest-time, but nowadays it is generally observed throughout the Anglican Communion.

Bellini's Transfiguration depicts clearly the three different reactions of the disciples. One wants to get away – unwilling to face up to what he cannot grasp. Another kneels in rapt adoration, while the third is bowled over with shock. Yet, despite their reactions, the predominant feeling is one of a miracle taking place in the midst of ordinary life. Christ is glorified while men continue to work in the fields or chat at the roadside. Only His closest followers see Him transfigured.

Everyone who exalts himself will be humbled, but he who humbles himself will be exalted. LUKE 18:14

As on the two previous Sundays, the Gospel for this day is from St Luke and is the parable of the Pharisee and the tax-collector, a story about prayer. This time it is again, like the parable of the lost sheep on the Third Sunday after Pentecost, a well-known parable, which is also often misunderstood. The Pharisee has been likened to a modern, insincere churchgoer and cited as a reason for not attending church, but the parable is about two men who both 'went up into the temple to pray'. Nor is it correct, as is commonly done, to represent the Pharisee as a hypocrite. He was sincere in his piety, fasting regularly, and giving away a tenth of his whole income to support his religion.

The failure of the Pharisee is to be found in the introductory statement that Jesus told this parable 'to some who trusted in themselves that they were righteous and despised others'. The Pharisee, as a member of a group noted for its strict observance of the Hebrew religious law and ceremony, knew that he was a religious man and was proud of it, while he also despised the tax-collector because he was one of those officials, hated by the Jews as traitors, who were employed by the Roman government to collect the taxes imposed upon their race. He thanked God that he was not as other men 'or even as this tax-collector'.

The tax-collector, on the other hand, knew that he was a sinner and was humble. He beat his breast as a sign of penitence and cried, 'God, be merciful to me a sinner!' He knew that his only claim upon God for forgiveness was His mercy. Nothing that he had done could plead for him. He could only approach God in faith. And, Jesus said, he went down to his house justified and accepted by God.

The tax-collector's heart was set on God. He truly desired forgiveness. The priest thought of himself and his own perfections. In his view he had fulfilled the law and had therefore made himself ready for God's acceptance. Instead he was left to comfort himself while God reached out to the man who claimed nothing but asked merely to be forgiven.

Two went to pray! O, rather say
One went to brag, th'other to pray:
One stands up close and treads on high,
Where th'other dares not send his eye;
One nearer to God's altar trod,
The other to the altar's God.

RICHARD CRASHAW

Raphael's Transfiguration lifts Christ up to the company of the heroes of Israel. It is a private manifestation to His disciples of the fact that He is the promised one. Their realization of this truth comes slowly, bit by bit. Here God reveals the majesty of His Son to the closest of His companions.

PENTECOST XI

The ears of the deaf shall be unstopped, ... and the tongue of the dumb shall sing.
ISAIAH 35:5, 6

On this Sunday, the Gospel is concerned not with the teaching of Jesus, but with an act of healing by Him. Yet, as was recognized at the time, it is a symbolic action, a miracle which conveys teaching about Jesus Himself. It is the healing of the deaf stammerer, which took place in the half-heathen country of the Decapolis, lying mainly on the eastern bank of the River Jordan, and it is a miracle to be found only in St Mark's Gospel.

Naturally it has been chosen as the special Sunday to bring to mind the Church's work among the deaf and dumb and this day has sometimes been called Ephphatha Sunday, after the actual Aramaic word *Ephphatha*, meaning 'Be opened', which was used by Jesus on this occasion and recorded by Mark. He accompanied this injunction by appealing to the faith and understanding of the deaf man by sign-language. The crowd wanted Him 'to put his hand upon him', but, as Mark carefully describes, He touched his ears and tongue, indicating to him in the only possible way that he was to regain his hearing and speech. He also looked up to heaven to convey to the man a sign that the cure was to be a gift of God.

Mark draws attention also to the reaction of the crowd to the act of healing. Here there is a contrast with the healing of the blind beggar, which is the subject of the Gospel for Quinquagesima Sunday. On that occasion it was the man healed by Jesus who recognized Him as the Messiah; this time it is the onlookers who see the miracle as the sign of His messianic role. Their astonished words, 'He makes both the deaf to hear and the dumb to speak!' refer to the great messianic prophecy of Isaiah which they saw being fulfilled before their eyes. Christ was not yet ready for this 'messianic secret' to be revealed, but so great was their surprise that it was in vain that He charged them to be quiet.

Again it was His determined view that miracles of healing may bear witness to His role as Saviour but He would not allow them to be the means of drawing men to Him. He had come to change their hearts not to astonish them into the Kingdom of Heaven. His desire was to open souls to love, not to mystify them with magic.

> *Christ bids the dumb tongue speak, it speaks; the sound*
> *He charges to be quiet, it runs round:*
> *If in the first he used his finger's touch,*
> *His hand's whole strength here could not be too much.*
>
> RICHARD CRASHAW

This illustration, from a gradual, shows in simple and moving terms the healing of the deaf mute. The crowd's reaction and the pity and concern on the faces of the disciples point inwards to the central fact of Christ's power to heal.

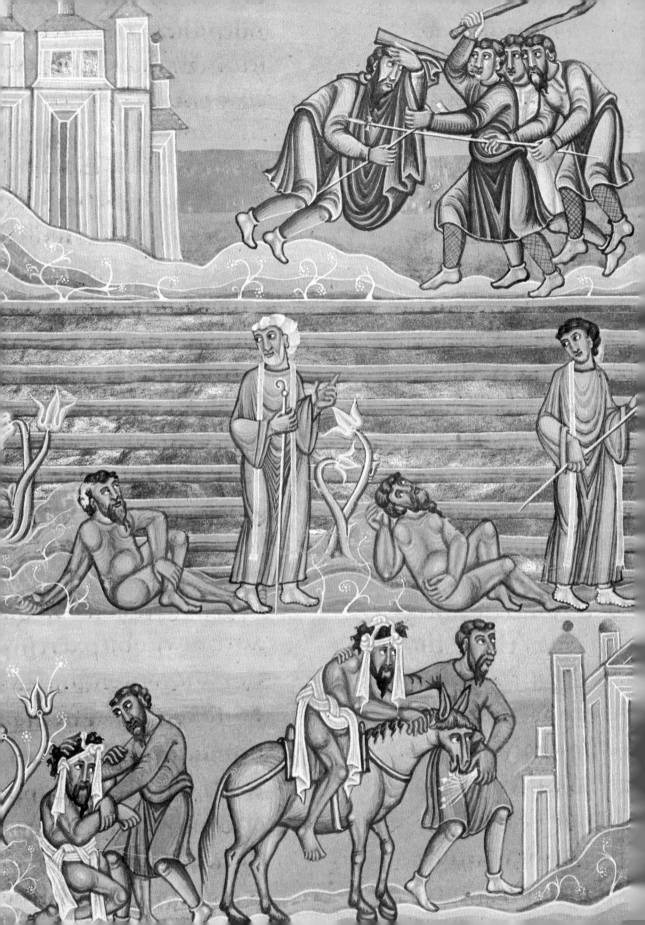

The parable of the good Samaritan, which forms the Gospel for this Sunday, is probably the best-known of all the parables of Jesus. He told the parable in answer to a scribe or lawyer who came to question Him in a hostile manner. The scribe asked, 'What shall I do to inherit eternal life?' And when Jesus told him he must obey the two great commandments enjoining love towards God and towards one's neighbour, he went on to ask 'And who is my neighbour?' Probably he hoped to trap Jesus into some debatable definition of neighbour and non-neighbour, but instead He told him this parable and let him find the answer himself.

It is a simple story about a traveller between Jerusalem and Jericho, attacked and robbed by brigands, who was ignored as he then lay helpless at the roadside by two men passing by, but eventually succoured by a Samaritan. The point of the story is heightened by the fact that the first two men were a priest and a Levite, who should, above all other men, have lived up to the precepts of the Jewish religion, while the Samaritan belonged to a race hated and despised by the Jews.

Yet it is more subtle than is often suggested, for the demands of the law were such that the priest hurrying on his way to Jerusalem to carry out his ceremonial duties in the Temple would be forbidden to look on a dead body without needing to be ceremonially purified; the Levite too would need cleansing. Thus in both cases the regulations of the law stood in the way of recognizing one's duty to one's neighbour.

When He had told the story, Jesus asked the scribe, 'Which of these three, do you think, proved neighbour to the man who fell among the robbers?' The scribe, not able to bring himself to use the word 'Samaritan', replied 'The one who showed mercy on him'. And Jesus said, 'Go thou and do likewise.' This was His final answer to the scribe's original question, 'What shall I do to inherit eternal life?'

What dost thou with my wounds, O thou that passest by,
Handling and turning them with an unwounded eye?
The calm that cools thine eye does shipwreck mine, for oh,
Unmoved to see one wretched, is to make him so.

RICHARD CRASHAW

Another medieval strip cartoon. The muggers with their clubs strike an all too modern note, while the steadily deteriorating condition of their victim reminds us that he might have died, left there by both priest and Levite. The pictures of the Samaritan with his first aid and the lift in to Jericho, are intensely practical even down to the food held out to encourage the donkey to move on as fast as possible. This snapshot technique is a masterly accompaniment to Our Lord's most vivid parable.

The simple impact of this fifteenth-century Dutch illustration is remarkable. Some of the lepers are showing themselves to the priest, while one returns alone to thank Jesus. All wear distinctive clothing which serves to show how separate they were from ordinary men. The wild and ragged background underline this isolation which kept lepers from the inhabited parts of Palestine. Above all it is the simplicity which gives a completeness to this illustration matching the direct message of the original parable.

Jesus said, Were there not ten cleansed? But where are the nine? LUKE 17:17

The Gospel for this Sunday is closely linked with that for the previous Sunday. It is true that it contains an act of healing by Jesus and not a parable, but it is (as with the Gospel for the Eleventh Sunday after Pentecost) a miracle with a meaning attached to it. That meaning is again to be found in the conduct of a Samaritan which is favourably contrasted with that of the others, who were Jews. The parable of the good Samaritan is followed by the incident of the grateful Samaritan.

The miracle, like that in the Gospel for the Third Sunday after the Epiphany, brought Jesus into contact again with the terrible disease of leprosy. This time, as Jesus was making His last journey to Jerusalem, travelling along the border between Samaria and Galilee, He was met by ten lepers who were gathered outside a village, for the law would not allow them to enter it. They would have chosen this desolate no-man's land between the two countries as everyone else avoided it. They came to Him in faith, and He tested their faith by telling them to go to the priests as if they were healed. Only the priests had the right to allow a leper back into the society from which his disease had excluded him. When they obeyed Him, they found themselves free of the disease. Their faith was rewarded, but only one of the ten returned to give thanks to Jesus, 'and he was a Samaritan'. Jesus commented, 'Was no one found to return and give praise to God except this foreigner?' Just as in the first story a Samaritan had exceeded the Jews in charity, so here one had done so in gratitude.

A final point shared by the Gospels for this and the previous Sunday, is that both are stories to be found only in St Luke's Gospel, and this is very characteristic of the Evangelist. While Matthew emphasizes Christ as the expected Redeemer of the House of Israel, Luke likes to depict Him as the Saviour of all mankind who accepts people as they are, whether Jew or Samaritan, and shows no favour to any race. His fascination with Christ's healing ministry may be a result of his training as a doctor. He certainly includes the points which would have been important to a medical man of the time and this gives a particular authenticity to the stories.

> *Unclean! unclean! But thou canst make me clean.*
> *Yet if thou clean'st me, Lord, see that I be*
> *Like that one grateful leper of the ten*
> *Who ran back praising thee.*

KATHARINE TYNAN HINKSON

PENTECOST XIV

Be careful for nothing; but in everything by prayer and supplication with
thanksgiving let your requests be made known unto God. And the peace of God, which
passeth all understanding, shall keep your hearts and minds through Jesus Christ.
PHILIPPIANS 4:6, 7

Though the exact date of these Sundays after Pentecost varies from year to year, according to the position of Easter, this Sunday comes towards the close of the summer and the time of harvest. It may well be that the Gospel for this Sunday was chosen to speak to people at that important and anxious season of the natural year when the condition of the crop may make all the difference to their lives in the months ahead.

Once again the Gospel is taken from the Sermon on the Mount. The passage belongs to that part in it where Jesus spoke about the attitude of the Christian disciple towards material things, which are described as 'mammon'. As He went about the countryside of Palestine he would have seen the birds flying freely about, the lilies blooming wild and magnificent and the grass, one day growing green in the fields and the next day cut down to be dried into hay; and from these He drew His condemnation of material things.

Anxiety, He said, is useless and faithless: useless because it cannot achieve anything – 'Which of you by being anxious can add one cubit to his span of life?'; and faithless because it means a lack of trust in God who feeds the birds and clothes the lilies and the grass. It is the Gentiles, those who do not serve God, that are anxious about these things. To the Christian the call is, 'Seek ye first the kingdom of God and his righteousness; and all these things shall be added unto you.' In the same way, the Lord's Prayer addresses first its petitions to God's glory and then only briefly asks for 'daily bread'. The service of the Kingdom brings its own reward and assigns all else to its proper place.

This spirit of a life led in trusting obedience to God has been a continual inspiration to those who have withdrawn from the world's demands. For St Francis, imparting the example of the natural world where animals and flowers took no thought for the morrow, provided a lesson for his followers which he never tired of using. It is the trust that holds nothing back; the trust that can only come from the human being who, unlike the rest of creation, can envisage the possibilities of material disaster; it is this trust of the twice born that God demands.

> *God will have all, or none; serve him, or fall*
> *Down before Baal, Bel or Belial:*
> *Either be hot, or cold: God doth despise,*
> *Abhor, and spew out all neutralities.*

> ROBERT HERRICK

PENTECOST XV

Our Saviour Jesus Christ, who hath abolished death and hath brought life and immortality to light through the gospel. II TIMOTHY I : 10

A story of great pathos and wonder, the raising from the dead of the widow's son at Nain by Jesus, is told in the Gospel for this day. It is another incident in the life of Jesus which is to be found in St Luke's Gospel alone, and he tells it with his usual literary skill, recounting it dramatically and vividly.

Luke says the incident occurred the day after Jesus had healed the slave of the Roman centurion at Capernaum as described in the Gospel for the Third Sunday after the Epiphany. He and the disciples went on through the countryside of Galilee towards the small town of Nain, and as they approached its walls, there came out through the gate a funeral procession headed by a widow, who was taking to the cemetery outside the town the body of her only son, a young man. Under Jewish law to her grief was added the threat of poverty for she would be left without legal inheritance and completely dependent on the charity of others. To this widow, Jesus said, 'Weep not', and to the young man, 'Arise'; and He restored the son to life and to his mother.

This incident, which shows Christ taking pity on the widowed and childless mother, is an example of Christ's compassion, and his care for the individual. There is no place in Christianity for the argument that with so many dying there is no point in saving one life. Every life is precious to God and even one widow's grief can call forth His mercy. This story also emphasizes that He came to bring life and immortality to mankind. The Gospel for this day recalls this miracle, which caused such amazement among the onlookers, as a reminder of the enduring centrality in Christian belief of the Easter message throughout the year. It is not just a general statement but a particular claim. Not just that there is a God who cares for the whole world but One who actually loves each one of us individually; who loves the widow's son in particular and not only mankind in general.

> *Christ said, 'Weep not,' but still she went on weeping.*
> *The mother thus, – how will the son obey?*
> *'Young man, arise;' lo! from the bier up-leaping,*
> *The dead proved quicker than the quick that day.*
>
> ANON

PENTECOST XVI

For everyone who exalts himself will be humbled, and he who humbles himself will be exalted. LUKE 14:11

This Sunday begins a series of Epistles taken from Paul's Epistle to the Ephesians, which continues, with only one interruption, until the Twenty-First Sunday after Pentecost. Taken together, these passages dwell upon the great central doctrinal theme of the Epistle to the Ephesians, the need for unity among all Christians who have 'one Lord, one faith, one baptism, one God and Father of all'. They look forward to the season of Advent with its thought of the coming of Christ to judge His Church.

The passage from the fourteenth chapter of St Luke's Gospel chosen as the Gospel for this day illustrates two Christian virtues. The first is humanity and arises from the occasion when Jesus healed a man afflicted with the dropsy on the Sabbath and met the disapproval of the Pharisees by making them realise that, if in an emergency they would show mercy to an animal which had met with a mishap on that day and needed rescuing, then it could not be unlawful to attend to the sick on the day of rest. The second part of the passage is the parable of the chief seats, the warning to a guest at a banquet not to take the chief seat at the table lest a more important man should arrive and he has to move lower down the table to make way for the newcomer. It is better for him to take the lowest seat, and then, if the host says, 'Friend, go up higher', he will rise in the esteem of his fellow-guests. Jesus is teaching here the same virtue of humility as in the story of the Pharisee and the tax-collector. There He urged humility in worship, here in everyday life.

He that is down need fear no fall,
He that is low, no pride:
He that is humble ever shall
Have God to be his guide.

I am content with what I have,
Little be it or much:
And, Lord, contentment still I crave,
Because Thou gavest such.

Fullness to such a burden is
That go on pilgrimage:
Here little, and hereafter bliss,
Is best for age to age.

JOHN BUNYAN

The Gospel for this Sunday is about the Tuesday of Holy Week, the last week spent by Jesus in Jerusalem before the Crucifixion. The passage is the close of the record in St Matthew's Gospel of the encounter between Jesus and the Pharisees which has led to this day being sometimes called 'the Day of Questions' or 'the Day of Gainsaying'. As Jesus was teaching in the Temple, the Pharisees came to Him with their subtle questions in the hope that 'they might entangle him in their talk'. They were busy trying to find some sort of excuse which would enable them to bring Jesus before Pilate with a convincing case to have Him executed.

The first question put to Jesus in this passage was by a scribe who asked, 'Which is the great commandment in the law?' Jesus, as when He told the parable of the good Samaritan, again referred to the two great commandments which come from the Old Testament books of Deuteronomy and Leviticus, and He here emphatically declared that 'on these two commandments hang all the Law and the Prophets'.

Then He turned to the Pharisees and asked them, 'What think ye of the Christ? Whose son is he?' They replied, 'The son of David', referring to the popular contemporary Jewish idea that the Messiah would come as a warrior-king who would establish the supremacy of His chosen people among the nations of the world. Jesus replied by quoting the opening words of Psalm 110, regarded by Jewish teachers as a messianic prophecy by David who calls him 'my Lord'. Jesus insisted that if David addresses the Messiah in this way, then He must be more than his son. This construction was to use the same methods of exposition as the scribes used in order to set before His questioners a higher and more spiritual conception of the Messiah. So the Gospel for this day also begins to look forward to Advent and its teaching about the coming of Christ and the establishment of His Kingdom. It points the sharp contrast between the Messiah of those with military or political hopes and the real Messiah who came to change men's hearts. It says once again that Christ is not the revolutionary leader but the personal Saviour.

> *'What think ye of Christ?' is the test*
> *To try both your state and your scheme;*
> *You cannot be right in the rest*
> *Unless you think rightly of him.*

> JOHN NEWTON

Rembrandt's drawing of the woman with an issue of
blood brings home the pathos of someone who suffers,
half comprehending, from a disease which makes life
intolerable and yet never kills. Christ's heart goes out
to her and she is healed.

PENTECOST XVIII

Be of good cheer, thy sins be forgiven thee. MATTHEW 9:2

This Sunday, since it follows an Ember week, originally had no Mass for the people, and the service for the day is therefore later in date than that for those other Sundays on which there was always a Mass. The sign of this is that the Epistle taken from the First Epistle to the Corinthians, breaks into the series of selections from the Epistle to the Ephesians.

The Gospel is the account in the ninth chapter of St Matthew of the healing of the paralyzed man together with Christ's own teaching about the symbolic meaning of His miracles. This man was brought to Jesus by his friends in faith, but He knew that his physical weakness had been produced by previous sin. He sought his confidence, therefore, by saying to him, 'Be of good cheer', as He did to the disciples at the stilling of the storm and to the woman with a haemorrhage, and then He told him, 'Your sins are forgiven', to bring him the assurance that he needed.

This immediately brought upon Jesus a charge of presumptuous blasphemy from some scribes. He replied, 'Why are you thinking evil? Which is easier, to say, Your sins have been forgiven or to say, Get up and walk?' He meant, of course, that the effectiveness of forgiving sins lacks outward proof, but the claim to heal can be proved true or false at once: indeed the paralyzed man straightaway got up and went home. Jesus was also pointing to the fact that if physical illness had come about because of some previous sin then the act of healing was tantamount to the forgiveness of sin because it eradicated the just reward of evil doing. Again Jesus is turning the scribes' methods of argument upon themselves. The physical cure attested the spiritual change; the visible act of healing was a sign of the invisible miracle of grace and forgiveness. The response of the man himself to the words of Jesus was the answer to the charge of blasphemy. He was well and if God had made him ill as a punishment for sin, as the scribes taught, then God must have forgiven him if he was now healed.

Either Jesus is a blasphemer, and the sense of sins forgiven, which many win at his hands, is a pernicious lie, or Jesus has power, in the name of God, to release men from their sin. We must decide one way or the other.

A.M.HUNTER, *The Gospel according to St Mark*

PENTECOST XIX

Let Christ Jesus himself be the garment that you wear. ROMANS 13:14

There is a strange incongruity in the Gospel for this Sunday. The story about the king who made a wedding feast for his son ends with the ignominious expulsion of a guest for not wearing a 'wedding garment'. However, it has already been stated that the invited guests refused to come, and those present had been hurriedly brought in from the 'highways' and were hardly likely to have proper clothes for the occasion!

Matthew has evidently mixed up two different parables. The first part of the story is from the parable of the great supper as told by Luke in the Gospel for the Second Sunday after Pentecost. The second part is the separate parable of the rejected guest. Though its beginning has been lost, its meaning is clear. There are those today who think they may enter the Christian fellowship without wearing the robe of righteousness; but they do not understand that their righteousness must exceed that of the scribes and Pharisees. They remain discourteous guests, nominal Christians, who have never sought to discover what discipleship means and what are its implications. They have not truly joined the company of the Good News of the Lord, the giver of the feast. They cannot realise what He meant when He said, 'He who finds his life will lose it, and he who loses his life for my sake will find it.' This is the meaning of the wearing of the wedding garment by those who are prepared to enter upon a new life and share a new experience with Him. It is the symbol of a total change of state – a change which is permanent and irreversible.

The Christian faith, if accepted, drives a wedge between its own adherents and the disciples of every other philosophy of religion, however lofty or soaring. And they will not see this; they will tell you that really your views and theirs are the same thing and only differ in words, which if only you were a little more highly trained, you would understand. Even among Christ's nominal servants, there are many who think that a little good-will is all that is needed to bridge the gulf, – a little amiability and mutual explanation, a more careful use of phrases, would soon accommodate Christianity to fashionable modes of speaking and thinking and destroy all causes of provocation. So they would. But they would destroy also its one inalienable attraction; that of being the romance among religions – a wonder and a beauty and a terror – no dull and drab system of thought, no mere symbolic idealism.

JOHN NEVILLE FIGGIS

Jesus Christ is the same yesterday and today, yea and for ever. HEBREWS 13:8

The Gospel for this Sunday is the account of the healing by Jesus of the son of the nobleman of Capernaum in St John's Gospel, where it is stated to be His second miracle in Galilee, His first being that told in the Gospel for the Second Sunday after the Epiphany. St John's Gospel was called by an early Christian writer the 'spiritual' Gospel, by which he meant that it was 'symbolical' or 'allegorical'; and to the Evangelist Christ's miracles are 'signs' revealing deep spiritual truth.

The healing of the nobleman's son, which is not recorded in any other gospel, has a likeness to the healing of the centurion's slave, told by Matthew in the passage forming the Gospel for the Third Sunday after the Epiphany. Both men had faith in Christ, but this story typically shows how the miracle reveals the nature and development of Christian faith. The nobleman first believed in Christ's healing powers because he journeyed the twenty miles or more from Capernaum to Cana to see Him; then, without any sign or proof, he believed in Christ's assurance that his son was alive; and, finally, when he found that Christ's promise was true, he believed in Him, with his whole house, as the Messiah of Israel. It is the way in which many come to Christ. Faith in the power of Christ leads first to faith in the promises of Christ and then to faith in the person of Christ. Intellectual knowledge of Christ is completed by ethical and spiritual knowledge of Him.

Men hear of what Christ has done for others and this brings them to an acceptance of the truth of what He says. True faith is one step on. It is faith in Jesus himself that finally convinces and saves. It is the faith which was summed up in Fr Ignatius' continual call to hold to just two words 'Jesus only'. The primacy of this faith in the Christian life is demonstrated by Cardinal Newman in *The Grammar of Assent*:

If religion is to be devotion and not a mere matter of sentiment, if it is to be made the ruling principle of our lives, if our actions, one by one, and our daily conduct, are to be consistently directed towards an Invisible Being, we need something higher than a mere balance of arguments to fix and control our minds. Sacrifice of wealth, name or position, faith and hope, self-conquest, communion with the spiritual world, presuppose a real hold and habitual intuition of the objects of Revelation, which is certitude under another name.

PENTECOST XXI

Be ye merciful, even as your Father is merciful. LUKE 6:36

'How often shall my brother sin against me, and I forgive him?', asked Peter of Christ, who replied by telling the parable of the unmerciful servant, which forms the Gospel for this day, to show that forgiveness and mercy must be without limit. It is a story in three stages or episodes.

First, there is the servant who owes the king, his master, a vast sum of money, but escapes severe punishment by successfully begging from the king forgiveness and annulment of the debt. Then, as he comes away from the king's presence, he meets a fellow-servant, who owes him a trifling sum; he demands instant payment of the debt, refuses to listen to his plea for mercy and orders him to be imprisoned until the money is forthcoming. Finally, the king, who has been informed of his servant's harsh behaviour by the other servants, is indignant that the man was not as merciful to his fellow-servant as he had been to him and sends him to prison until he should repay all that he owed.

The moral of the tale, the central thrust of the parable, is unmistakable. Men are judged according to the judgement they pronounce; they receive mercy according to the way they show mercy; they are forgiven even as they also forgive – 'forgive us our trespasses as we forgive them that trespass against us'. Moreover, the king in the parable had set an example of mercy which his servant ought to have followed. Christians must be merciful, not upon consideration of expediency, but because God is merciful; and Jesus set the example by praying that His enemies might be forgiven and by suffering on the Cross for all mankind.

My God, I love thee; not because
I hope for heaven thereby,
Nor yet because who love Thee not
Are lost eternally.

Not from the hope of gaining aught
Not seeking a reward
But as Thyself has loved me,
O ever-loving Lord.

    Ascribed to ST FRANCIS XAVIER

The Parable of the Unmerciful Servant
by Jan Sanders van Hemessen.

PENTECOST XXII

Render unto Caesar the things that are Caesar's; and unto God the things that are God's. MATTHEW 22:21

This Gospel tells again of an attempt to trap Jesus. The question He was asked, 'Is it lawful to give tribute to Caesar or not?', was a subtle, far-reaching one. It involved the widespread resentment among religious and patriotic Jews at having to pay taxes to the Imperial Roman government, the pagan power which had subjugated them.

Jesus made the questioners answer their own question by producing the tribute-money, the Roman silver coin bearing the Emperor's image and name, with which the Jews paid the poll-tax imposed upon them by the Romans since AD 6.

The coin represented the government that issued it. It represented therefore, the maintenance of law and order, the safeguarding of life, the administration of justice, the protection of trade and travel. If the Jews accepted these and benefited from them, then they were under a moral obligation to pay for what they had obtained. At the same time, He insisted that there were the things of God equally binding upon citizens. The early Christians recognized this twofold obedience required of them. They sought to be good citizens but they knew that in the end as Peter said, 'We must obey God rather than men'.

> *All we have is God's, and yet*
> *Caesar challenges a debt;*
> *Nor hath God a thinner share,*
> *Whatever Caesar's payments are;*
> *All is God's; and yet 'tis true*
> *All we have is Caesar's too.*
> *All is Caesar's: and what odds,*
> *As long as Caesar's self is God's?*
>
> RICHARD CRASHAW, *Give to Caesar – and to God*

The head of Tiberius Caesar on a coin minted in the time of Christ.

Giotto's painting of Pentecost shows the descent of
the Holy Spirit represented by the dove and the
tongues of flame.

PENTECOST XXIII

Thy faith hath made thee whole. MATTHEW 9:22

A double healing by Jesus forms the subject of the Gospel for this day, the healing of the daughter of Jairus, the ruler of a synagogue, and of the woman with a haemorrhage. This took place when, in the course of His ministry, He crossed from one side to the other of the Sea of Galilee. The rulers of a synagogue were the ten adult male Jews required by the law to control its affairs if a community were to establish and maintain a synagogue. The synagogue here may have been the one at Capernaum founded by the Roman centurion who loved the Jewish nation and whose daughter Jesus also healed.

The two stories of healing are interwoven with each other. Jairus besought Jesus to come to his dying daughter. As he went, the woman with a haemorrhage came with the crowd and touched His garment. Again He said, 'Be of good cheer', and gave her the assurance that her faith had healed her. When He reached the house of Jairus, He found the mourners already proclaiming the death of the child, but He insisted that she was not dead but sleeping and went in and took her by the hand; and she awoke. Mark has preserved the actual Aramaic words He used to her, *Talitha Cumi* – 'Little girl, wake up'.

These are miracles of deliverance from sickness and death. They symbolize that absolution from the weakening, deadening burden of sin for which the Collect for this day prays – 'that through thy bountiful goodness we may all be delivered from the bands of those sins, which by our frailty we have committed.'

> Talitha Cumi! *O thou Christ*
> *Hast kept the tryst?*
> *Laugh not, O maidens! this is He*
> *Of Galilee,*
> *Of Nazareth,*
> *The Christ that conquers death –*
> *Dost catch a breath,*
> *O Christ? O, Life!*
> Talitha Cumi! *See*
> *The tumult as of some sweet strife*
> *Strained tremulous up; up –*
> *'Give her to drink!' he saith –*
> *Yea, Lord, behold, a cup!*
>
> T.E.BROWN, *The Daughter of Jairus*

144

Heaven and earth shall pass away, but my words shall not pass away.

MATTHEW 24:35

This is also called the Last Sunday after Pentecost (and in the English Prayer Book the Sunday Next before Advent) because, however more or fewer than twenty-four Sundays after Pentecost there may be in a year, they always end with this one. By ancient practice, this Sunday has been regarded as a sort of eve of Advent which anticipates the great theme of that season.

The English Prayer Book follows the old Sarum rite in repeating for the Gospel for this Sunday the account in St John's Gospel of the feeding of the five thousand by Jesus, which forms the Gospel for the Fourth Sunday in Lent. The reason for this is probably that the account ends with the comment by the crowd, when they saw what Jesus had done, 'This is of a truth that Prophet that should come into the World', and so provides a theme for the approaching days of Advent.

The Roman Missal for its Gospel anticipates the words of Jesus which appear in the Gospel for the First Sunday in Advent, but using the version in St Luke's Gospel instead of that in St Matthew's Gospel. Over the preceding Sundays the teaching of Christ has been expounded. Now the Gospel looks to the future with its violence and uncertainty, its testing and judgement, and concludes with the assurance of Christ that His words will never pass away.

In England, this day is popularly known as 'Stir-up Sunday' from the opening words of the Collect for the day, 'Stir up we beseech thee, O Lord, the wills of thy faithful people . . .', which are said to remind housewives that they must now begin to make (and stir up) their Christmas puddings.

> *Yea, through life, death, through sorrow and through sinning,*
> *He shall suffice me, for he hath sufficed:*
> *Christ is the end, for Christ was the beginning,*
> *Christ the beginning, for the end is Christ.*
>
> F.W.H.MYERS, *St Paul*

I am Alpha and Omega – the beginning and the end.

On the scroll: Ecce quomodo
genuit. Fecinuat
tibi in[...] a filia
qui qua[...] te thronu
daturus[...] sanctorum
et neme agni anima
poterit.

the year of the saints

All the Saints in the Roman calendar are arranged on the day that they are remembered. Those who are beatified have the prefix Bl while full Saints are given their names without the prefix St. In all cases the date after each name refers to the date of death.

OPPOSITE The saints in heaven, a panel of a triptych by Orcagna.

The Circumcision of Christ (*Bellini*).

1 January

The Circumcision of Our Lord Jesus Christ and the Octave Day of His Nativity.

Concordius of Spoleto (175) M, Elvan and Mydwyn (2nd cent.), Thirty Soldiers martyred at Rome (*c*.304), Euphrosyne (?), Magnus (?), Gregory Nazianzen the Elder (374), Almachius (*c*.400), Beoc (5th or 6th cent.), Eugendus (*c*.510), Basil of Aix (521), Fulgentius of Ruspe (533), Justin of Chieti (*c*.540), Fanchea (*c*.585), Felix of Bourges (*c*.580), Connat (*c*.590), Maelrhys (6th cent.), Cuan (6th cent.), Clarus (*c*.660), William of Dijon (1031), Odilo of Cluny (1049), Bl Adalbero of Liége (1128), Bl Zdislava Berka (1252), Bl Hugolinus of Gualdo (1260), Bl Bonannus (*c*. 1320), Bl Joseph Mary Tommasi (1713), Bl Vincent Strambi (1824).

2 January

Abel, Many Martyrs who suffered in Rome (*c*.303), Argeus, Narcissus and Marcellinus (320), Isidore of Nitria (4th cent.), Isidore of Antioch (4th cent.), Siridion (?), Macarius the Younger (*c*.408), Martinian of Milan (*c*.435), Aspasius of Auch (*c*.560), Munchin of Limerick (?), Seiriol (6th cent.), Blidulf of Bobbio (*c*.630), Vincentian (*c*.730), Adalard of Corbie (827), Airaldus (1160), Bl Bentivoglio de Bonis (1232), Bl Stephana de Quinzanis (1530), Caspar (1836).

THE HOLY NAME OF JESUS

The Hebrews strongly believed that there was a close relation between a person and his name. The name revealed both his character and the significance of his life. So, in the New Testament, the name of Jesus, meaning 'God saves', is often used to represent Jesus Himself and His mission and message. Peter urged repentance 'in the name of Jesus', and Paul reminded the Corinthians that they were 'justified through the name of the Lord Jesus'.

The Church in the Middle Ages used the name of Jesus in blessings and exorcisms and the thirteenth century produced devotional hymns concentrating on the Holy Name – 'Jesu the very thought is sweet' and 'O Jesu, King most wonderful'. However, observance of the feast of the Holy Name of Jesus only began locally in the late Middle Ages. In 1530 it was officially recognized for the Franciscans, who had popularized the devotion. Innocent XIII fixed the date in 1721 for the whole Roman Catholic Church. Following a local use, it was observed in England in the late Middle Ages on 7 August, and since this is the date in the calendar of the Book of Common Prayer, it is commonly observed on this day in the Anglican Communion. Yet, whenever observed, the reason is constant; it commemorates the Christian belief so well expressed by John Donne, 'Cesar is not Cesar still, nor Alexander Alexander, but Jesus is Jesus still and shall be for ever'.

Jesu is in my heart, His sacred name
Is deeply carved there: but th'other week
A great affliction broke the little frame
Ev'n all to pieces; which I went to seek:
And first I found the corner where was J,
After where ES, and next where U was grav'd.
When I had got these parcels, instantly
I sat me down to spell them, and perceiv'd
That to my broken heart he was I ease you,
And to my whole is JESU.
GEORGE HERBERT

3 January

Daniel of Padua (168), Antheros (236), Theopemptus and Theonas (284), Peter Apselamus and Peter Absalo (291 and 311), Zosimus and Athanasius (303), Gordinus of Cappadocia (304), Cyrinus, Primus and Theogenes (320), Florentius of Vienne (p.374), Geneviève of Paris (c.500), Fintan of Doon (6th cent.), Finlugh (6th cent.), Blitmund of Bobbio (650), Bertilia of Marolles (c.705), Wenog (?).

4 January

Titus (c.96), Mavilus of Adrumetum (212), Hermes, Aggaeus and Caius (c.300), Priscus, Priscillian and Benedict (362), Drafosa, Aquilinus, Geminus, Eugene, Marcian, Quintus, Theodotus and Tryphon (c.484), Gregory of Langres (539), Ferreolus of Uzès (581), Pharaïldis of Ghent (c.740), Rigobert of Reims (c.745), Libentius of Hamburg (1013), Bl Palumbus of Subiaco (c.1070), Stephen du Bourg (1118), Bl Roger of Ellant (1160), Bl Angela of Foligno (1309), Bl Oringa of the Cross (1310), Bl Thomas Plumtree (1570).

5 January

Telesphorus (136), Martyrs of Egypt (303), Talida of

Antinoe (4th cent.), Syncletica (c.400), Apollinaris Syncletica (c.450), Simeon Stylites the Elder (459), Emiliana of Rome (6th cent.), Cera of Kilkeary (7th cent.), Conwoion of Redon (868), Gaudentius of Gnesen (c.1004), Gerlac of Valkenberg (c.1170), Bl Alacrinus of Casamari (1216), Paula (1368).

6 January

Balthasar, Caspar and Melchior (1st cent.), Martyrs in Africa (c.210), Macra of Reims (287), Hywyn of Averdaron (p.516), Melanius of Rennes (c.530), Merinus (6th cent.), Edeyrn (6th cent.), Eigrad (6th cent.), Schottin (6th cent.), Peter of Canterbury (c.606), Diman of Connor (658), Wiltrudis of Bergen (c.986), Frederick of St Vanne (1020), Erminold of Prufenning (1121), Guarinus (1150), Gertrude van Oosten (1358), John de Ribera (1611), Charles of Sezze (1670).

7 January

Crispin of Pavia (c.250), Clerus of Antioch (c.300), Felix and Januarius (?), Julian of Cagliari (?), Lucian of Antioch (312), Theodore of Egypt (4th cent.), Nicetas of Remesiana (c.414), Crispin II of Pavia (p.451), Valentine (c.470), Brannock (6th cent.), Cedd (664), Cronan Beg (7th cent.), Tillo of Solignac (702), Kentigerna (734), Emilian of Saujon (767), Wittikund of Westphalia (c.804), Aldericus (856), Reinold (960), Anastasius of Sens (977), Canute Lavard (1133), Bl Edward Waterson (1593).

8 January

Apollinaris the Apologist (c.180), Patiens of Metz (2nd cent.), Lucian, Maximian and Julian (c.290), Theophilus and Helladius, Carterius (304), Eugenian of Autun (4th cent.), Atticus of Constantinople (425), Severinus of Noricum (476), Severinus of Naples (?), Ergnad of Ulster (5th cent.), Maximus of Pavia (511), Frodobert (c.673), Erhard of Ratisbon (c.686), Albert of Cashel (7th cent.), Maurontus (c.700), Gudula of Brussels (712), Pega (c.719), Garibaldus (c.762), Athelm (923), Wulsin of Sherborne (1005), Laurence Giustiniani (1455).

9 January

Paschasia of Dijon (c.178), Epictetus, Jucundus, Secundus, Vitalis, Felix and Comp. (c.250), Marciana (c.303), Julian, Basilissa, Antony, Anastasius, Celsus, Marcionilla and Comp. (c.304), Vitalis, Revocatus and Fortunatus (?), Peter of Sebaste (c.391), Marcellinus of Ancona (c.566), Waningus of Fécamp (c.686), Adrian of Canterbury (710), Brithwald of Canterbury (731), Foellan (8th cent.), Honorius of Buzancais (1250), Bl Philip Berruyer (1260).

10 January

Nicanor (c.76), Petronius of Avignon (c.463), Marcian of Constantinople (c.480), John Camillus Bonus (c.660), Sethrida (c.660), Thomian of Armagh (c.660), Agatho (681), Peter Urseolus (987), Benincasa of Cava (1194), William of Bourges (1209), Bl Gregory X (1276).

11 January

Hyginus (c.142) Pope, Leucius of Brindisi (c.180), Alexander of Fermo (c. 250), Peter, Severus and Leucius (c.309), Palaemon (325), Ethenea and Fidelmia (433), Beandan (5th cent.), Honorata of Pavia (c.500), Theodosius the Cenobiarch (529), Anastasius of Castel Sant'Elia (c.570), Salvius of Amiens (c.625), Boadin (?), Vitalis of Gaza (c.625), Paldo, Taso and Tato (8th cent.).

12 January

Tatiana of Rome (c.230), Satyrus (267), Arcadius of Mauretania (c.302), Zoticus, Rogatus, Modestus, Castulus and Comp. (?), Tigrius and Eutropius (404), John of Ravenna (594), Elian ap Erbin (?5th cent.), Caesaria of Arles (c.530), Victorian of Asan (c.560), Probus of Verona (p.591), Benedict Biscop (690), Forty-two Martyrs of Ephesus (c.762), Aelred (1167), Martin of Leon (1203), BB John Gaspard Cratz, Emmanuel d' Abreu, Bartholomew Alvarez and Vincent Da Cunha (1737), Bl Paula Frassinetti (1882).

13 January

Andrew of Trèves? (?235), Forty Soldiers martyred at Rome (262), Hermylus and Stratonicus (315), Glaphyra (c.324), Agrecius of Trèves (c.333), Leontius of Caesarea (337), Viventius (c.400), Potitus (?), Erbin (?5th cent.), Elian (6th cent.), Gumersindus and Servusdei (850), Berno of Cluny (927), Bl Stephen of Liège (1061), Bl Hildemar of Arrouaise (1097–8), Bl Godfrey of Cappenberg (1127), Bl Ida of Argensolles (1226), Bl Ivetta (1228), Bl Veronica of Binasco (1497).

14 January

Felix of Nola (c.260), Felix of Rome (?), Isaias, Sabas and Comp. (309), Macrina the Elder (c.340), Barbasymas and Comp. (346), Hilary of Poitiers (368), Euphrasius (?), Martyrs of Raithu (c.510), Datius of Milan (552), Kentigern Mungo (603), Deusdedit of Canterbury (664), Bl Amadeus of Clermont (c.1150), Bl Odo of Novara (c. 1200), Bl Antony Pucci (1892).

15 January

Secundina (c.250), Maximus of Nola (p.250), Ephysius of Sardinia (303), Paul the Hermit (c.342), Macarius the Elder (390), Isidore the Egyptian (404), Alexander Akimetos (430), John Calabytes (c.450), Ita of Limerick (c.570), Maurus (c.580), Sawl (6th cent.), Lleudadd of Bardsey (6th cent.), Tarsicia of Rodez (c.600), Malard of Chartres (p.650), Emebert (c.710), Bonitus of Clermont (c.710), Ceolwulph (764), Blaithmaic of Jona (c.823), Peter of Castelnau (1208), Bl Francis Ferdinand de Capillas (1648).

16 January

Priscilla (1st cent.), Marcellus (309), Melas (c.385), James of Tarentaise (c.429), Honoratus of Arles (429), Valerius of Sorrento (c.453), Triverius (c.550), Honoratus of Fondi (6th cent.), Karantoc (?), Fulgentius of Ecija (c.633), Fursey of Lagny (c.648), Titian (650), Ferreolus of Grenoble (c.670), Dunchaid O'Braoin (988), Bl Jane of Bagno (1105), Henry (1127), Bl Conrad of Mondsee (1145), Berardus, Peter, Otto, Accursius and Adjutus (1220), Bl Gundisalvus (c.1259).

17 January

Speusippus, Eleusippus, Meleusippus and Leonilla (175), Genulfus and Genitus (3rd cent.), Anthony (325), Julian Sabas the Elder (377), Pior (c.395), Achillas and Amoes (4th cent.), Antony, Merulus and John (c.590), Nennius (6th cent.), Mildgytha (c.676), Sulpitius II Pius (647), Richimirus (c.715), Bl Joseph of Freising (764), Bl Roseline de Villeneuve (1329).

ST ANTHONY ABBOT

It was St Anthony Abbot who first brought together individual hermits into some kind of monastic community. He was an Egyptian who had inherited from his parents considerable wealth and took directly to

The temptation of St Anthony Abbot (*Jan de Cock*).

heart the commandment: 'go and sell what thou hast and give to the poor.' He went into the desert and there was considerably tempted by all kinds of suggestions to draw him back to the world. This has been a subject which has attracted many of the greatest painters.

St Anthony was a violent opponent of the heretical Arians of the fourth century and did a great deal to counter their influence in North Africa. He led a life of great abstinence and prayer, and it was he who began the long story of monasticism by binding hermits into a community.

18 January

Moseus and Ammonius (250), Prisca of Rome (*c*.270?), Archelais, Thecla and Susanna (293), Athenogenes (?), Volusian of Tours (496), Faustina and Liberata (*c*.580), Leobard of Tours (593), Diarmis

(6th cent.), Deicola of Lure (*c*.625), Day (?), Ulfrid (1029), Bl Beatrix II of Este (1262), Fazzio of Verona (1272), Bl Christina Ciccarelli (1543).

19 January

Germanicus of Smyrna (156), Pontian of Spoleto (169), Paul, Gerontius, Januarius, Saturninus, Successus, Julius, Catus, Pia and Germana (2nd cent.?), Marius, Martha, Abachum and Audifax (*c*.270), Messalina of Foligno (3rd cent.), Bassian of Lodi (413), Contestus of Bayeux (*c*.510), Lomer of Corbion (593), Firminus of Gabales (?), Branwallader (6th cent.?), Nathalan of Aberdeen (678), Remigius of Rouen (*c*.772), Catellus of Castellamare (9th cent.), Arsenius of Corfu (959), Canute IV of Denmark (1086), Wulstan of Worcester (1095), Henry of Upsala (*c*.1156), Bl Beatrix of Lens (p.1216), Bl Antony Fatati (1484), Bl

January

Andrew of Peschiera (1485), Bl Bernard of Corleone (1667), Bl Thomas of Cori (1729).

20 January

Fabian (250), Sebastian (c.288), Neophytus of Nicaea (310), Euthymius the Great (473), Molagga of Fermoy (c.664), Fechin of Fobhar (c.665), Maurus of Cesena (946), Bl Benedict Ricasoli (1107), Bl Desiderius of Therouanne (1194), Bl Daniel of Cambron (1232).

21 January

Publius of Malta (c.112), Fructuosus, Augurius and Eulogius (259), Patroclus of Troyes (c.275), Agnes of Rome (c.304), Epiphanius of Pavia (497), Brigid of Kilbride (6th cent.), Lawdog (6th cent.), Vimin of Holywood (6th cent.), Meinrad of Einsiedeln (861), Maccallin of Waulsort (978), Bl Edward Stransham (1586), BB Bartholomew Roe, Thomas Reynolds (1642), Bl Agnes de Beniganim (1696).

ST AGNES

St Agnes died at the age of 13 and, with St Lucy, St Cecilia and St Agatha, was one of the prototypes of Christian chastity. She was denounced as a Christian by a rejected suitor and refused to deny her faith by sacrificing to the Roman gods. St Ambrose said of her 'she went to the place of execution a virgin more willingly and beautiful as others go to the nuptial chamber as a bride'. Her name is mentioned in the Gregorian Canon. Her Acts were written a long time after her death and are therefore unreliable. Nevertheless, there were clearly a number of young Christians who refused either to marry with pagans or to sacrifice to heathen deities. At very least St Agnes stands to represent all these.

22 January

Vincent the Deacon (304), Vincent, Orontius and Victor (305), Vincent of Digne (380), Blaesilla of Rome (383), Gaudentius of Novara (c.418), Anastasius the Persian (628), Brithwold of Sarum (1045), Dominic of Sora (1031), Bl Walter of Himmerode (1222), Bl William Patenson (1592), Bl Francis Gil (1744), Bl Matthew Leziniana (1745), Vincent Pallotti (1850).

23 January

Parmenas (c.98), Asclas of Antinoe (c.287), Clement of

Ancyra (303), Emerentiana (304), Agathangelus (c.309), Severian and Aquila (?), Amasius of Teano (356), Eusebius of Mount Coryphe (4th cent.), Martyrius of Valeria (6th cent.), Ormond of Marié (6th cent.), John the Almoner (c.616), Ildephonsus of Toledo (667), Colman of Lismore (c.702), Barnard of Vienne (841), Lufthild of Cologne (c.850), Maimbod (c.880), Bl Bernard of Lippe (1217), Raymund de Peñafort (1275), Bl Margaret of Ravenna (1505), Bl Joseph Cafasso (1860).

24 January

Timothy (97), Babilas, Urban, Prilidian and Epolonius (c.250), Felician of Foligno (254), Zama of Bologna (c.268), Mardonius, Musonius, Eugene and Metellus (c.305), Macedonius Kritophagos (c.340), Artemius of Clermont (396), Thyrsus and Projectus (?), Guasacht (4th cent.), Exuperantius of Cingoli (5th cent.), Cadoc of Llancarvan (c.580), Suranus of Sora (c.580), Bertrand of St Quentin (7th cent.), Bl Felix O'Dullany (1202), Bl Marcolino of Forli (1397), Bl William Ireland, and Bl John Grove (1679).

ST TIMOTHY

Timothy was born at Lystra in Asia Minor. His father was a Greek and his mother, Eunice, a Jewess, who taught him the Hebrew Scriptures. Probably both he and his mother were converted during Paul's first visit to Lystra, because, by the time of the second visit he was already a 'disciple' who was 'well spoken of by the Christians' there. To Paul he was his 'beloved and faithful child in the Lord', and henceforward the lives of the two men were closely connected.

He was chosen by Paul to go with him on his second missionary journey and eighteen months later on the third journey, assisting the apostle to take Christianity from Palestine to Asia Minor and on into Europe. Among the tasks entrusted to Timothy was to go to Thessalonica to encourage the Christians under persecution and to Corinth to confirm the converts in their faith. He became one of Paul's closest friends and two of Paul's Epistles are addressed to him. When Paul was in custody in Rome, he summoned Timothy to his side. If Timothy ever got there, he may himself have been imprisoned since the Epistle to the Hebrews mentions him being 'set at liberty'.

Of the rest of Timothy's life, nothing is known with certainty. Traditionally he survived Paul by about thirty years, becoming the first Bishop of Ephesus (where Paul had appointed him as his representative)

152

A fifth-century mosaic of St Paul.

and suffering martyrdom on 22 January 97 when he was stoned by pagans after he had denounced the worship of Diana.

25 January

Ananias of Damascus (1st cent.), Donatus, Sabinus and Agape (?), Artemas of Puzzuoli (?), Publius of Zeugma (c.380), Bretannion of Tomi (c.380), Juventinus and Maximus (363), Apollo of Heliopolis (c.395), Dwynwen (c.460), Eochod (597), Racho of Autun (c.660), Praejectus of Clermont, and St Amarinus (676), Thordgith of Barking (c.700), Poppo of Stavelot (1048), Joel of Pulsano (1185), Peter Thomas (1366).

CONVERSION OF ST PAUL

St Paul is the most considerable figure in the history of the Christian church, apart from its Founder. It is not only that his writings provide a gloss upon the teachings of Christ which substantially influences all the development of the Church's doctrine but, also, that his personal missionary endeavours spread Christianity from being a Jewish sect to becoming a world-wide religion. In his martyrdom at Rome St Paul set the seal on Christianity as a missionary religion, not a nationalist cult. His life in general is remembered together with that of St Peter, but he has this special day because of the traumatic nature of his conversion on the road to Damascus. He had been a notable

opponent of Christianity; he was present at the stoning of Stephen, the first martyr; at the moment of his conversion he was travelling to Damascus in order to begin persecutions there. The direct and unexpected call which characterizes the moment when Saul became Paul has since always been seen as the prototype of sudden conversion. After he heard the words of Christ 'Saul, Saul, why persecutest thou me', he was blinded and taken in by the Christians in Damascus until he recovered and could escape from the city in a basket let down over the walls.

The characteristics of the conversion of St Paul are found in the lives of many other Christians. It fits so well psychologically with one who was imbued with so fierce an opposition to the church. Its outcome was to turn the energy used for destruction to a burning desire for converting the world.

And the Lord said, I am Jesus whom thou persecutest.
It is hard for thee to kick against the pricks.

26 January

Polycarp of Smyrna (*c.*156), Theogenes and Comp. (258), Athanasius (?), Paula of Rome (404), Conan of Iona (*c.*648), Theofrid of Corbie (*c.*690), Alphonsus of Astorga (9th cent.), Ansurius of Orense (925), Alberic of Citeaux (1109), Margaret of Hungary (1270).

27 January

Julian of Sora (*c.*150), Julian of Le Mans (3rd cent.), Devota of Corsica (*c.*303), Avitus (?), Datius, Reatrus and Comp., and Datius, Julian, Vincent and twenty-seven Comp. (?), John Chrysostom (407), Maurus of Bodon (*c.*555), Natalis (6th cent.), Lupus of Chalons (*c.*610), Vitalian (672), Emerius of Banoles (8th cent.), Candida of Banoles (8th cent.), Gamelbert of Michaelsbuch (*c.*800), Theodoric II of Orléans (1022), Bl John of Warneton (1130), Bl Michael Pini (1522), Bl John Mary Mzec (1887).

ST JOHN CHRYSOSTOM

John Chrysostom, a monk born in Antioch with an outstanding preaching ability, made his real mark as Archbishop of Constantinople. He was consecrated, much against his will, in 398 and threw himself into the reform of a lapsed and difficult diocese. He founded

The conversion of St Paul
(*Michelangelo*).

St John Chrysostom (*Cappella Palatina*).

hospitals, called back the Christian community to real fervour, and sent missionaries to the Goths and other heathens who lived in the unsettled areas of the Near-East. He made a considerable contribution to the liturgy of the Orthodox Church and, for that reason, it has been named after him. He was a man of sharp intellect and singled out the excesses of the Byzantine court for special attack. As a result he fell out with the Empress Eudoxia who intrigued with a disappointed claimant to the Archbishopric. John Chrysostom was exiled for a short time but the public outcry was so great that he had to be brought back to the city. Nevertheless, later on Eudoxia sent him to Pontus and he was so ill-treated on the journey there that he died. Nearly thirty years later his body was brought back in triumph to Constantinople and he was buried with great ceremony. St John Chrysostom is one of the first four Eastern Doctors of the Church and his writings remain one of the most important contributions to Christian theology.

28 January

Thyrsus, Leucius and Callinicus (251), Flavian of Città Vecchia (c.304), Leonidas and Comp. (304), Valerius of Saragossa (315), Martyrs of Alexandria (356), Palladius of Antioch (c.390), Cannera of Bantry (c.530), John of Reomay (c.544), James the Hermit (6th cent.), Bl Charlemagne (814), Antimus of Brantome (8th cent.), Paulinus of Aquileia (804), Glastian of Kinglassie (830), Odo of Beauvais (880), Bl Richard the Sacrist (p.1142), Bl Amadeus of Lausanne (1159), Richard of Vaucelles (1169), Julian of Cuenca (1208), Bl Bartholomew Aiutamicristo (1224), Bl Roger of Todi (1237), Peter Nolasco (1258), Bl James the Almsgiver (1304), Bl Mary of Pisa (1431), Bl Antony of Amandola (1450), Bl Giles of Lorenzana (1518), BB Jerome Lu and Laurence Wang (1858).

29 January

Sarbellius and Barbea (101), Constantius and Comp. (170), Sabinian of Troyes (c.275), Caesarius of Angoulême (?), Papias and Maurus (c.303), Valerius of Trèves (c.320), Blath of Kildare (523), Gildas the Wise (c.570), Sulpitius I Severus (591), Dallan Forgaill (598), Triphina of Brittany (6th cent.), Aquilinus of Milan (650), Voloc (c.724), Bl Charles of Sayn (1212), Francis of Sales (1622).

Charles I, King and Martyr (*Edward Bower*).

30 January

Barsimaeus (c.114), Matthias of Jerusalem (c.120), Agrippinus of Alexandria (c.180), Martina of Rome (228), Hippolytus of Antioch (p.250), Felician, Philippian and one hundred and twenty-four Comp. (?), Alexander (3rd cent.), Savina of Milan (311), Barses of Edessa (c.379), Armentarius of Antibes (p.450), Tudy (5th cent.), Bathildis, Queen (680), Aldegund of Maubeuge (684), Armentarius of Pavia (c.711), Bl Amnichad of Fulda (1043), Adelelmus of Burgos (c.1100), Bl Haberilla of Mehrerau (c.1100), Bl Gerard of Clairvaux (1138), Hyacintha of Mariscotti (1640), Bl Sebastian Velfré (1710).

KING CHARLES I

On this morning in 1649, Charles I was beheaded on a scaffold erected outside the Banqueting House of the royal palace of Whitehall in London before the vast crowd watching in outraged silence. His last words, 'I go from a corruptible to an incorruptible crown', were clearly an echo of St Paul's phrase in the Epistle for Septuagesima which he had heard on the Sunday during his trial.

He had been King of England since 1625, during which time he had been engaged in a bitter dispute over his powers with Parliament culminating in his defeat in the Civil War and the order by the House of Commons for his death.

After the monarchy had been restored in 1660, this day when the 'royal martyr' had suffered was placed in the calendar of the Book of Common Prayer. Charles I was commemorated by the Church of England because of the stand he took during the negotiations with his Puritan captors. In the words of Mandell Creighton, 'Had Charles been willing to abandon the Church and give up episcopacy, he might have saved his throne and his life. But on this point Charles stood firm; for this he died, and by dying saved it for the future.'

Charles I's name was deleted from the calendar in 1859 by an Order in Council, but many continue to remember him on this day. He is a local saint made by popular acclamation, and his epitaph might be the Earl of Warwick's words, 'God, I am assured, hath pardoned his failures and crowned him for his piety and sufferings'.

31 January

Metranus of Alexandria (*c*.250), Saturninus, Thyrsus and Victor (*c*.250), Tarcisius, Zoticus, Cyriacus and Comp. (?), Tryphena of Cyzicus (?), Cyrus and John (*c*.303), Geminian of Modena (348), Julius of Novara (p.390), Marcella of Rome (410), Melangell (*c*.590), Aedan of Ferns (632), Madoes (?), Adamnan of Coldinham (*c*.680), Bobinus of Troyes (*c*.766), Eusebius of St Gall (884), Athanasius of Modon (*c*.885), Ulphia of Amiens (995), Bl John Angelus (*c*.1050), Martin Manuel (1156), Bl Paula Gambara-Costa (1515), Bl Louise degli Albertoni (1533), Bl Francis Xavier Bianchi (1815), Bl Mary Christina (1836), John Bosco (1888).

1 February

Ignatius of Antioch (*c*.107), Pionius and Comp. (251), Severus of Ravenna (*c*.348), Paul of Trois-Chateaux (*c*.405), Jarlath of Armagh (*c*.480), Cinnia of Ulster (5th cent.), Crewenna (5th cent.), Brigid of Kildare (*c*.525), Kinnia (6th cent.), Darlugdach of Kildare (p.525), Sigebert III (656), Severus of Avranches (*c*.690), Brigid, Clarus of Seligenstadt (*c*.1048), Autbert of Landevenec (1129), John of the Grating (*c*.1170), Bl Reginald of Saint-Gilles (1220), Viridiana (1242), Bl Antony Manzoni (1267), Bl Eustochium Calefato (1468), Bl Henry Morse (1645).

2 February

Feast of the Purification of the Blessed Virgin Mary, Cornelius the Centurion (1st cent.), Apronian the Executioner (*c*.304), Fortunatus, Felician, Firmus and Candidus (?), Flosculus of Orléans (p.480), Feock (?), Laurence of Canterbury (619), Adalbald d'Ostrevant (652), Adeloga of Kitzingen (*c*.745), Martyrs of Ebsford: Bruno, Marquard and Comp. (880), Columbanus (959), Bl Peter Cambian (1365), Catherine dei Ricci (1590), Jane de Lestonnac (1640), Bl Theophanes Vénard (1861).

3 February

Celerinus of Carthage (p.250), Laurentinus, Ignatius and Celerina (3rd cent.), Blaise of Sebaste (*c*.316), Felix, Symphronius, Hippolytus and Comp. (?), Tigides and Remedius (?), Ia of Cornwall (450), Lupicinus and Felix (5th cent.), Laurence the Illuminator (576), Philip of Vienne (*c*.578), Caellainn (6th cent.), Hadelin of Dinant (*c*.690), Werburg of Chester (*c*.699), Berlinda of Meerbeke (702), Werburg of Mercia (*c*.785) Matron, Deodatus of Lagny (8th cent.), Anschar of Hamburg (865), Anatolius of Salins (9th cent.), Oliver of Portonuovo (*c*.1050), Margaret of England (1192), Bl Elinand of Froidmont (1237), Bl Odoric of Pordenone (1331), Bl Simon Fidati (1348), Bl Matthew of Girgenti (1450), Bl John Nelson (1578), Bl Stephen Bellesini (1840).

ST BLAISE

In a sense St Blaise's feast is better known than the Saint himself. It appears that St Blaise was Bishop of Sebaste in Armenia and was martyred in 316. Nothing else is known about his life except the tradition that he healed a boy dying from a thorn in his throat. As a result of this legend St Blaise has always been known as the patron of those with throat diseases. On his feast day those who look for a cure kneel before the altar and the priest blesses them, holding candles to their affected throats.

4 February

Aquilinus, Geminus, Gelasius, Magnus and Donatus (3rd cent.), Phileas and Comp. (*c*.304), Aldate (5th cent.), Eutychius of Rome (4th cent.), Aventinus of Chartres (*c*.520), Aventinus of Troyes (538), Theophilus the Penitent (*c*.538), Isidore of Pelusium (*c*.540), Vincent of Troyes (*c*.546), Modan (?6th cent.),

St Blaise.

Liephard (649), Vulgis of Lobbes (*c*.760), Nithard of Corbie (845), Rabanus Maurus (856), Nicholas Studites (863), Bl Simon of St-Bertin (1148), Gilbert of Sempringham (1189), Obitius of Brescia (*c*.1204), Andrew Corsini (1373), Jane of Valois (1504), Bl John Speed (1594), Joseph of Leonissa (1612), John de Britto (1693).

5 February

Agatha of Catania (*c*.250), Abraham of Arbela (*c*.345), Agricola of Tongres (420), Avitus of Vienne (*c*.519), Genuinus of Brixen (7th cent.), Bertulfus of Renty (705), Indract of Glastonbury (*c*.710), Modestus of Salzburg (*c*.722), Vodoaldus (*c*.725), Arcontius of Viviers (?8th cent.), Bl John Morosini (1012), Adelaide of Willich (*c*.1015), Agatha of Carinthia (1024), Martyrs of Japan: seven Franciscans, three Jesuits, eighteen lay people (1597).

ST AGATHA

St Agatha is another of the early Virgin Martyrs and her name is mentioned in the Gregorian Canon along with Lucy, Agnes and Cecilia. Again the Acts which are attributed to her are of a much later date and no real reliance can be placed on them. It was said that she was extremely beautiful and attracted the attentions of the Praetor of Sicily, Quintanius. As she refused to have anything to do with him, he put her into a brothel where again she would not submit. The Praetor then resorted to torture and the Apostle Peter appeared to her in prison and healed her wounds. As a result of the earthquake which took place at the same time, Quintanius was terrified by the unrest of the population and stopped the torture, but Agatha died in prison *c*.250.

6 February

Titus (1st cent.), Martyrs of Africa (*c*.210), Antholian of Auvergne (*c*.267), Dorothy of Caesarea (*c*.300), Theophilus of Caesarea (*c*.300), Silvanus, Luke and Mucius (312), Saturninus, Theophilus and Revocata (?), Mel of Armagh (*c*.490), Jacut and Guethenoc (5th cent.), Mun of Lough Ree (5th cent.), Vedast of Arras (539), Amandus of Moissac (644), Amandus of Elnone (*c*.676), Andrew of Elnone (*c*.690), Amandus of Nantes (7th cent.), Relindis of Eyck (*c*.750), Gerald of Ostia (1077), Guarinus of Palestrina (1159), Hildegund of Meer (1183), Didacus de Azevedo (1207), Bl Angelus of Furci (1372).

A lady as St Agatha (*Piombo*).

7 February

Augulus (*c*.303), Adaucus (304), Theodore Stratelates (319), Moses (*c*.372), Chrysolius the Armenian (4th cent.), Anatolius of Cahors (?), Juliana of Bologna (435), Laurence of Siponto (*c*.546), Tressan of Marauil (550), Fidelis of Mérida (*c*.570), Meldon of Péronne (6th cent.), Richard the King (722), Amulwinus of Lobbes (*c*.750), Luke the Younger (*c*.946), Romuald (1027), Bl Nivard of Vaucelles (p.1150), Bl Rizzerio (1236), Bl Antony of Stroncone (1461), Bl Thomas Sherwood (1578), BB James Sales and William Saultemouche (1593), Bl Giles Mary of St Joseph (1812).

8 February

Juventius of Pavia (1st cent.), Cointha of Alexandria (249), Paul, Lucius and Cyriacus (?), Dionysius, Aemilian and Sebastian (?), Martyrs of Constantinople (485), Honoratus of Milan (570), Martyrs in Persia (6th cent.), Kigwe (?), Oncho of Clonmore (*c*.600), Nicetius of Besançon (611), Paul of Verdun (*c*.649), Elfleda of Whitby (714), Meingold of Huy (*c*.892), Cuthman (9th cent.), Bl Mlada of Prague (994), Peter Igneus (*c*.1089), Stephen of Gradmont (1124), John of Matha (1213), Bl Isaias Boner (1471), Bl John Charles Cornay (1837), Bl Stephen Guénot (1861).

9 February

Apollonia of Alexandria (249), Nicephorus of Antioch (260), Primus and Fonatus (362), Ammonius and Alexander (?), Alexander and Comp. (?), Ammon, Emilian, Lassa and Comp. (?), Cyril of Alexandria (444), Nebridius of Egara (p.527), Sabinus of Canosa (*c*.566), Teilo of Llandaff (*c*.580), Eingan of Llanengan (6th cent.), Ansbert of Fontenelle (*c*.700), Cuaran the Wise (p.700), Alto of Altomunster (*c*.760), Cronan the Wise (8th cent.), Bl Marianus Scotus (1088), Bl Erizzo (1094), Raynald of Nocera (1225), Bl Albaro of Cordoba (*c*.1430).

10 February

Andrew and Aponius (1st cent.), Zoticus, Irenaeus, Hyacinth, Amantius and Comp. (120), Soteris of Rome (304), Silvanus of Terracina (?), Scholastica (*c*.550), Baldegundis (*c*.580), Desideratus of Clermont (6th cent.), Prothadius of Bescançon (624), Austreberta of Pavilly (704), Caedmon of Whitby (7th cent.), Erluph of Werden (830), Bl Salvius of Albelda (962), William of Maleval (1157), Bl Hugh of Fosse (1164), Bl Clare Agolanti (1346), Bl Paganus of Sicily (1423), Bl Eusebius of Murano (1501), Bl Alexander of Lugo (1645).

11 February

Calocerus of Ravenna (*c*.130), Martyrs of Africa (*c*.303), Saturninus, Dativus, Felix, Ampelius and Comp. (304), Lucius and Comp. (350), Jonas of Deméskenyanos (4th cent.), Lazarus of Milan (*c*.450), Castrensis of Capua (5th cent.), Severinus of Agaunum (*c*.507), Gobnata (?6th cent.), Gregory II (731), Benedict of Aniane (821), Paschal I (824), Theodora (867), Ardanus of Tournus (1058), Bl Helwisa of Coulombs (1066), Adolphus of Osnabruck (1224), Elisabeth Salviati (1519).

February

12 February

Eulalia of Barcelona (304), Modestus and Ammonius (?), Modestus and Julian (?), Julian the Hospitaller (?), Damian (?), Meletius of Antioch (381), Gaudentius of Verona (p.465), Ethelwold of Lindisfarne (c.740), Benedict Revelli (c.900), Antony Cauleas (901), Humbeline (1141), Goscelinus of Turin (1153), Ludan of Alsace (c.1202), Seven Holy Founders (13th and 14th cent.), BB Antony of Saxony, Gregory of Tragurio, Nicholas of Hungary, Thomas of Foligno and Ladislaus of Hungary (1369), BB James Fenn, John Nutter, John Munden and Thomas Henerford (1584), Bl Nicholas Saggio (1709).

13 February

Agabus the Prophet (1st cent.), Fusca V. and Maura (c.250), Polyeuctus of Melitene (c.259), Benignus of Todi (c.303), Julian of Lyons (?), Martinian of Caesarea (c.400), Stephen of Lyons (512), Modomnock O'Neil (c.550), Stephen of Rieti (c.590), Lucinus of Angers (c.618), Enogatus of Aleth (631), Huna of Ely (c.690), Dyfnog (7th cent.), Ermenilda of Ely (703), Aimo of Meda (c.790), Gosbert of Osnabruck (c.859), Fulcran of Lodève (1006), Beatrix d'Ornacieux (1309), Bl Christina of Spoleto (1458), Bl Eustochium of Padua (1469), Bl Archangela Girlani (1494), Bl John Lantrua (1816), Bl Paul Lieou (1818), Bl Paul Loc (1859).

14 February

Eleuchadius of Ravenna (112), Valentine of Rome (269), Valentine of Terni (c.269), Proculus, Ephebus and Apollonius (273), Vitalis, Felicula and Zeno (?), Dionysius and Ammonius (?), Cyrion, Bassian, Agatho and Moses (?), Bassus, Antony and Protolicus (?), Abraham of Harran (c.422), Maro of Beit-Marun (c.435), Nostrianus of Naples (c.450), Auxentius of Bithynia (c.470), Theodosius of Vaison (554), Conran (?), Antoninus of Sorrento (830), Bl Nicholas Palea (1255), Bl Angelus of Gualdo (1325), Bl Vincent of Siena (1442), Bl John Baptist of the Conception (1613).

ST VALENTINE

Another February saint whose festival is much better known than his life, St Valentine lived in the third century and was probably the Bishop of Terni in Italy. He was a doctor who was martyred during the persecutions of Claudius. He appears to have had no connec-

tion with young love at all and the custom of choosing a Valentine on this day is probably more closely linked with the time of the year as it was an old English belief that birds chose their mates on 14 February.

15 February

Faustinus and Jovita (c.121), Agape of Terni (c.273), Saturninus, Castulus, Magnus and Lucius (273), Craton and Comp. (c.273), Joseph of Antioch (?), Eusebius of Aschia (5th cent.), Dochow (?), Georgia of Clermont (c.500), Severus of Androcca (c.530), Quinidius of Vaison (c.579), Farannan (c.590) Ab, Faustus of Glanfeuil (6th cent.), Berach of Cluain (6th cent.), Decorosus of Capua (695), Walfrid della Gherardesca (c.765), Tanco of Werden (808), Winaman, Unaman and Sunaman (c.1040), Sigfrid of Wexlow (c.1045), Druthmar of Lorsch (1046), Bl Conrad of Baviera (1154), Bl Jordan of Saxony (1237), Bl Andrew Conti (1302), Bl Angelus of Borgo San Sepolcro (c.1306), Bl Julia of Certaldo (1367), Euseus of Serravalle (14th cent.), Bl Claude de la Colombière (1682).

16 February

Onesimus (c.90), Honestus of Nîmes (270), Juliana of Nicomedia (305), Porphyrius and Seleucius (309), Elias, Jeremias, Isaias, Samuel and Daniel (309), Julian of Egypt and Comp. (?), Faustinus of Brescia (381), Aganus of Airola (c.1050), Bl Philippa Mareri (1236), Bl Bernard Scammacca (1486).

17 February

St Polychronius (250), Donatus, Secundian, Romulus and Comp. (304), St Theodulus of Caesarea (308), St Julian of Caesarea (308), Faustinus and Comp. (?), Loman of Trim (c.450), Habet-Deus (c.500), Guevrock (6th cent.), Fortchern of Trim (6th cent.), Fintan of Clonenagh (603), Finan of Iona (661), Silvinus of Auchy (c.720), Benedict of Cagliari (p. 1112), Constabilis of Cava (1124), Bl Frowin of Bellevaux (1165), Evermod of Ratzeburg (1178), Bl Luke Belludi (1285), Bl William Richardson (1603), Bl Francis Regis Clet (1820).

18 February

Simeon of Jerusalem (*c.*107), Charalampias and Comp. (203), Leo and Paregorius (*c.*260), Maximus, Claudius, Praepedigna, Alexander and Cutias (295), Lucius, Silvanus, Rutilus, Classicus, Secundinus, Fructuosus and Maximus (?), Flavian of Constantinople (449), Helladius of Toledo (632), Colman of Lindisfarne (676), Angilbert of Centula (814), Theotonius of Coimbra (1166), Bl William Harrington (1594), Bl John Pibush (1601), Bl Agnes De (1841), Bl Andrew Nam-Thung (1855), Bl Agatha Lin (1858), BB John Peter Néel and Martin (1862).

19 February

Auxibius of Cyprus (1st cent.), Gabinus of Rome (*c.*295), Zambdas of Jerusalem (*c.*304), Publius, Julian, Marcellus and Comp. (?), Valerius of Antibes (p.450), Odran (*c.*452), Martyrs of Palestine (*c.*509), Barbatus of Benevento (682), Mansuetus of Milan (*c.*690), Beatus of Liébana (789), George of Lodève (*c.*884), Belina of Troyes (1135), Boniface of Lausanne (1265), Conrad of Piacenza (1354), Bl Lucy (1862).

20 February

Tyrannio, Silvanus, Peleus, Nilus and Zenobius (*c.*304), Martyrs of Tyre (302–10), Pothmius and Nemesius (?), Valerius of Conserans (?), Eleutherius of Byzantium (*c.*310), Sadoth and Comp. (*c.*342), Bolcan of Derkan (p.480), Falco of Maestricht (512), Flavian and Elias (*c.*512), Eleutherius of Tournai (532), Eucherius of Orléans (743), Leo of Catania (787), Colgan of Clonmacnoise (*c.*796), Wulfric (1154), Amata of Assisi (*c.*1250), Bl Peter of Treja (1304), Bl Elisabeth Bartholomea Picenardi (1468).

21 February

Felix of Metz (2nd cent.), Daniel and Verda (344), Verulus, Secundinus, Siricius, Felix, Servulus, Saturninus, Fortunatus and Comp. (*c.*434), Severian of Scythopolis (*c.*452), Paterius of Brescia (606), Bl Pepin of Landen (*c.*646), Gundebert of Senones (*c.*676), Germanus and Randoald (*c.*677), Avitus II of Clermont (689), Valerius of Astorga (695), Peter the Scribe (743), George of Amastris (*c.*825), Bl Nicholas of Vangadizza (*c.*1210), Bl Robert Southwell (1595), Bl Noel Pinot (1794).

22 February

Abilius of Alexandria (*c.*98), Aristion of Salamis (1st cent.), Papias of Hierapolis (*c.*120), Martyrs of Arabia (?), Paschasius of Vienne (*c.*312), Baradates (*c.*460), Thalasius and Limnaeus (5th cent.), Maximian of Ravenna (*c.*556), Elwin (6th cent.), Athanasius of Nicomedia (*c.*818), Bl John the Saxon (895), Raynerius of Beaulieu (*c.*967), Margaret of Cortona (1297), Bl Angelus Portasole (1334), Bl Didacus Carvalho and Comp. (1624).

23 February

Martha of Astorga (252), Polycarp of Rome (*c.*300), Sirenus of Sirmium (*c.*303), Martyrs of Sirmium (*c.*303), Romana of Todi (324), Florentius of Seville (*c.*485), Zebinus of Syria (5th cent.), Dositheus of Gaza (*c.*530), Felix of Brescia (*c.*650), Boswell of Melrose (*c.*664), Jurmin (7th cent.), Milburga of Wenlock (722), Medrald of Vendôme (*c.*850), Lazarus the Painter (*c.*867), Willigis of Mainz (1011), Ordonius of Sahagún (1066), Peter Damian (1072), Milo of Benevento (1076), Bl Nicholas of Prussia (1456).

24 February

Matthias (1st cent.), Montanus, Lucius, Julian, Victoricus, Flavian and Comp. (259), Sergius of Cappadocia (304), Primitiva (?), Modestus of Trèves (489), Praetextatus of Rouen (586), Ethelbert of Kent (616), Betto of Auxerre (918), Bl Robert of Arbrissel (1117), John Theristus (1129), Adela (1137), Bl Ida of Hohenfels (*c.*1195), Bl Mark dei Marconi (1510).

ST MATTHIAS

St Matthias was a substitute for Judas Iscariot. He was chosen as one of the two candidates to take the place of Christ's betrayer. The Apostles cast lots and Matthias became one of the twelve. Nothing is known for certain about his later life but he is thought to have preached in Cappadocia and round the Caspian Sea. Traditionally he is supposed to have worked among savages and was martyred in Colchis, the city of Jason's Golden Fleece.

25 February

Victorinus, Victor, Nicephorus, Claudian, Dioscorus, Serapion and Papias (284), Ananias and Comp. (*c.*298), Donatus, Justus, Herena and Comp. (3rd cent.), Caesarius of Nazianzus (369), Aldetrudis of

St Matthias with a pope (*Masolino*).

Maubeuge (*c*.696), Walburga of Eichstätt (779), Tarasius of Constantinople (806), Victor of St Gall (995), Gerland of Girgenti (1104), Bl Adelelmus of Engelberg (1131), Avertanus of Limoges (1380), Bl Constantius of Fabriano (1481), Bl Sebastian Aparicio (1600), Bl James Carvalho (1624).

26 February

Papias, Diodorus, Conon and Claudian (*c*.250), Nestor of Perge (251), Dionysius of Augsburg (*c*.303), Fortunatus, Felix and Comp. (?), Alexander of Alexandria (326), Fautinian of Bologna (4th cent.), Andrew of Florence (*c*.407), Porphyrius of Gaza (420), Quodvultdeus of Carthage (*c*.450), Agricola of Nevers (*c*.594), Victor of Arcis-sur-Aube (7th cent.), Bl Matilda of Spanheim (1154), Bl Leo of Saint-Bertin (1163), Bl Isabelle of France (1270).

27 February

Julian, Cronion Eunus, and Besas (250), Honorina (?), Alexander, Abundius, Antigonus and Fortunatus (?), Thalelaeus Epilautos (*c*.450), Leander of Seville (596), Baldomerus of Lyons (*c*.650), Basil and Procopius (*c*.750), John of Gorze (*c*.975), Bl Emmanuel of Cremona (1198), BB Mark Barkworth and Anne Linne (1601), Bl Augustus Chapdelaine (1856), Gabriel of Our Lady of Sorrows (1862).

28 February

Macarius, Rufinus, Justus and Theophilus (*c*.250), Martyrs of Alexandria (261), Caerealis, Populus, Caius and Serapion (?), Proterius of Alexandria (458), Romanus of Condat (*c*.460), Hilarus (468), Ruellinus of Tréguier (6th cent.), Llibio (6th cent.), Maidoc (?), Sillan of Bangor (*c*.610), Oswald of Worcester (992), Bl Villana de' Botti (1360), Bl Hedwig of Lithuania (1399), Bl Antonia of Florence (1472).

1 March

Eudocia of Heliopolis (*c*.117), Hermes and Adrian (*c*.290), Luperculus of Tarbes (*c*.300), Leo, Abundantius, Nicephorus, Donatus and Comp. (?), Felix III (492), David of Wales (5th–6th cent.), Albinus of Angers (*c*.554), Marnock of Annandale (*c*.625), Swithbert of Kaiserswerth (*c*.713), Siviard of St-Calais (*c*.729), Monan of St Andrew's (874), Leo of Rouen (*c*.900), Rudesind of Celanova (977), Bl Roger Le Fort (1367), Bl Bonavita (1375), Bl Christopher of Milan (1484), Bl Jane Mary Bonomo, Bl Peter Roque (1796), Two hundred and sixty Martyrs in Rome (269).

ST DAVID

Though David is famous as the patron saint of Wales, much uncertainty surrounds his life. Indeed the earliest biography of him was written to support the claims of the Welsh bishops to be independent of the Archbishop of Canterbury. According to legend, he was born of a noble family in South Wales and became a priest. Here he established an abbey at St David's which followed an extremely austere rule based upon that of the Egyptian monks.

The Welsh custom of wearing a leek on St David's Day is old and one legend says that the saint caused the Britons under King Cadwallader to adopt the leek as their badge to distinguish themselves from their Saxon enemies.

St David's Cathedral and Bishop's Palace (*Reconstruction by Alan Sorrell*).

The most picturesque of the legends surrounding St David is that which tells of his laying his handkerchief on the ground and how it became a hill upon which he could stand to address the crowds. David has become for the Welsh a symbol of nationhood thus carrying out even today some of the intentions of his first biographer!

This saint before the rest their patron still they hold ;
Whose birth their ancient bards to Cambria long
*   foretold,*
And seated here a see, his bishopric of yore,
Upon the furthest point of this unfruitful shore.

MICHAEL DRAYTON, *St David*

2 March

Roman Martyrs (219), Jovinus and Basileus (c.258), Paul, Heraclius, Secundilla and Januaria (c.305), Lucius, Absalom and Lorgius (?), Joavan of Leon (c.576), Martyrs of Campania (c.579), Fergna the White (637), Chad of Lichfield (673), Cynibild (7th cent.), Slebhene (767), Bl Charles the Good (1127), Bl Fulk of Neuilly (1201), Bl Agnes of Bohemia (1282), Bl Henry Suso (1365).

JOHN AND CHARLES WESLEY

The Wesley brothers, who are commemorated on this day by the Anglican Church of Canada, were the sons of an English clergyman who was Rector of Epworth in Lincolnshire. Both were ordained and went on a missionary journey to the American colony of Georgia. They were profoundly affected by the Moravian Brethren, who had established a 'religious society' in London, and in 1738 were brought, through them, to 'that faith whereby alone we are saved'.

March

After this conversion the brothers devoted themselves to evangelistic work. John was a man of great courage and persistence, a compelling preacher and an outstanding leader and organizer. He established the Methodist movement while Charles, who was a gentler character, became the most gifted and prolific hymn-writer in the English language.

During his fifty years of evangelism, John travelled 250,000 miles on horseback and preached 40,000 sermons, while Charles wrote over 5,500 hymns. Together they took the lead in inspiring one of the most important popular movements in the history of Christianity. The evangelical revival, of which the Wesley story is a part, struck out against the moribund Church of the eighteenth century and called for a new vision and enthusiasm. Only the exigencies of missionary work in America led John Wesley to break with the Church. His own views on the sacraments and the priesthood were High Church in character but he believed that the refusal of the Anglican bishops to consecrate a bishop in America was so great an impediment to the spread of Christianity that he made his own bishop and thereby began the Methodist Episcopal Church of America.

John Wesley.

3 March

Marinus and Asterius (262), Cleonicus, Eutropius and Basiliscus (c.298), Felix, Luciolus, Fortunatus, Marcia and Comp. (?), Hemiterius and Cheledonius (4th cent.), Camilla of Auxerre (c.437), Winwaloë of Landevennec (c.532), Titian of Brescia (c.536), Calupan of Meallet (575), Nonnita (6th cent.), Foila of Galway (6th cent.), Arthelais of Benevento (6th cent.), Owen of Lichfield (680), Sacer of Saggard (7th cent.), Lamalisse of Lamlash (7th cent.), Cele-Christ (c.728), Anselm of Nonantola (803), Cunegund (1039), Gervinus of St-Riquier (1075), Bl Serlo of Gloucester (1104), Bl Frederick of Mariengarten (1175), Bl Jacobinus de' Canepaci (1508).

4 March

Lucius I (c.254) Caius and Comp. (259), Nine hundred Martyrs in Rome (c.260), Archelaus, Cyril and Photius, Basil, Eugene, Agathodorus, Elpidius, Aetherius, Capiton, Ephrem, Nestor, and Arcadius (4th cent.), Gistilian of Menevia (6th cent.), Basinus of Treves (c.705), Adrian and Comp. (c.875), Felix of Rhuis (1038), Peter Pappacarbone (1123), Bl Humbert of Savoy (1188), Bl Romeo of Limoges (1310), Casimir of Poland (1483), Bl Christopher Bales (1590), Bl Placida Viel (1877).

5 March

Theophilus of Caesarea (c.195), Adrian and Eubulus (308), Eusebius and Comp. (?), Phocas of Antioch (c.320), Eusebius of Cremona (c.423), Gerasimus (c.475), Kieran of Ossory (5th cent.), Colman of Armagh (5th cent.), Caron of Tregaron (?), Piran of Padstow (5th or 6th cent.), Carthage the Elder (c.540), Virgilius of Arles (c.610), Clement of Syracuse (c.800), Dionysius Fugixima (1622), John-Joseph of the Cross (1734).

6 March

Marcian of Tortona (120), Perpetua, Felicitas, Saturus, Saturninus, Revocatus and Secundulus (203), Conon of Mandona (250), Victor, Victorinus, Claudian and Bassa (?), Basil of Bologna (335), Evagrius of Constantinople (c.380), Sezin of Guic-Sezni (c.529), Fridolin of Säckingen (c.650), Kyneburga, Kuneswide and Tibba (c.680), Baldred of Glasgow (756), Balther of Tinningham (756), Bilfrid of Lindisfarne (c.758),

Chrodegang of Metz (776), Cadroe of Waulsort (976), Bl Jordan of Pisa (1131), Ollegarius of Tarragona (1137), Bl Helen of Poland (1298), Cyril of Constantinople (1235), Colette (1447).

7 March

Eubulus of Caesarea (308), Paul the Simple (*c.*339), Gaudiosus of Brescia (*c.*445), Enodoch (*c.*520), Drausinus of Soissons (*c.*576), Deifer of Bodfari (6th cent.), Easterwine of Wearmouth (688), Paul of Prusa (840), Ardo of Aniane (843), Theophylact of Nicomedia (845), Bl Reinhard of Reinhausen (p.1170), Bl Volker of Siegburg (1132), Bl Frowin II of Engelberg (1178), Thomas Aquinas (1274), BB Jermyn Gardiner, John Larke and John Ireland (1544).

8 March

Pontius of Carthage (*c.*260), Philemon and Apollonius (*c.*305), Arianus, Theoticus and Comp. (*c.*311), Quintilis of Nicomedia (?), Cyril, Rogatus, Felix, Rogatus, Herenia, Felicitas, Urbanus, Sylvanus and Mamilius (?), Provinus of Como (*c.*420), Rhian (?), Beoadh (*c.*525), Senan (*c.*560), Felix of Dunwich (648), Julian of Toledo (690), Humphrey of Prum (871), Duthac of Ross (1065), Veremundus of Hirache (1092), Ogmund of Holar (1121), Stephen of Obazine (1154), Vincent Kadlubeck (1223), John of God (1550).

9 March

Cyrion and Candidus (?), Pacianus of Barcelona (*c.*390), Gregory of Nyssa (*c.*395), Bosa of York (686), Antony of Froidemont (10th cent.), Frances of Rome (1440), Catherine of Bologna (1463), Dom. Savio (1857).

10 March

Caius and Alexander (*c.*172), Codratus, Dionysius, Cyprian, Anectus, Paul and Crescens (*c.*258), Forty-two Martyrs of Persia (?), Victor (?), Forty Armenian Martyrs (320), Macarius of Jerusalem (*c.*353), Simplicius (483), Kessog of Lennox (*c.*560), Droctoveus of Paris (*c.*580), Anastasia the Patrician (6th cent.), Attalas of Bobbio (627), Emilian of Lagny (675), Himelin of Vissenaeken (*c.*750), Failbhe the Little (754), Bl Andrew of Strumi (1097), John of Vallombrosa (*c.*1380), Peter de Geremia (1452), John Ogilvie (1615).

The Apotheosis of St Thomas Aquinas (*Zurbaran*), the medieval philosopher who is remembered on 7 March.

11 March

Candidus, Piperion and Comp. (*c.*259), Heraclius and Zosimus (*c.*263), Alberta of Agen (*c.*286), Gorgonius and Firmus (3rd cent.), Martyrs of Antioch (*c.*300), Trophimus and Thalus (*c.*300), Firminus of Amiens (?), Constantine of Carthage (?), Constantine of Scotland (576), Sophronius of Jerusalem (*c.*369), Vigilius of Auxerre (685), Benedict Crispus (725), Aengus the Culdee (*c.*830), Euthimius of Sardis (840), Peter the Spaniard (?), Eulogius of Cordova (859), Firmian of Fermo (*c.*1020), Aurea of San Millán (*c.*1069), Amunia of San Millán (*c.*1069), Bl Christopher Macassoli (1485), Bl John Righi (1539), Teresa Margaret Redi (1770).

March

12 March

Egdunus and Comp. (303), Peter of Nicomedia (303), Mamilian of Rome (?), Paul Aurelian (*c*.575), Gregory the Great (604), Peter the Deacon (p.605), Mura McFeredach (*c*.645), Vindician of Cambrai (712), Theophanes of Mt Sigriana (818), Elphege the Elder (951), Bl Rusticus of Vallumbrosa (1092), Bernard of Carinola (1109), Seraphina of San Geminiano (1253), Bl Justina Bezzoli (1319), Bl Dionysius the Carthusian (1471), Bl Nicholas Owen (1606), Bl Joseph Tshang-Ta-Pong (1815).

St Gregory celebrates the Eucharist.

ST GREGORY THE GREAT

Gregory was born in Rome of wealthy parents. He became mayor before he was thirty, but resigned the office and became a monk in the Benedictine monastery which he had established in his ancestral home. In 590 he became Pope and resolved to convert England to Christianity. As a monk he had seen fair-haired slave-boys for sale in the market-place and, discovering that they were English, he said 'Non Angli sed Angeli' – 'not Angles but Angels'. He never forgot the incident and in 597 sent St Augustine and forty monks to England to begin her conversion. Gregory did much to regularize the music and services of the Church and was credited with the perfection of plainsong which is still called Gregorian Chant. Throughout his life he was particularly famous for his holiness and as a result is given the dove as a symbol of his inspiration by the Holy Spirit. Writing of St Gregory, the Venerable Bede said: 'We may, and ought to, call Gregory our apostle because he made our nation, till then given up to idols, the Church of Christ; so that though he is not an apostle to others, he is to us, for we are the seal of his apostleship in the Lord.'

13 March

Sabinus of Egypt (287), Theusitas, Horres, Theodora, Nymphora, Mark and Arabia (?), Macedonius, Patricia and Modesta (*c*.304), Christina of Persia (?), Euphrasia of Constantinople (*c*.420), Ramirus and Comp. (*c*.630), Mochocmoc of Leamokevoge (*c*.656), Gerald of Mayo (732), Nicephorus of Constantinople (828), Ansovinus of Camerino (840), Heldrad of Novalese (842), Rudericus and Salomon (857), Bl Peter II of Cava (1208), Bl Sancha of Cellas (1229), Bl Agnellus of Pisa (1236), Bl Boniface of Savoy (1270).

14 March

Forty-seven Roman Martyrs (*c*.67), Leo (?), Peter and Aphrodisius (5th cent.), Martyrs of Valeria (6th cent.), Diaconus (6th cent.), Kyrin (Boniface) (*c*.630), Talmach (7th cent.), Eutychius and Comp. (741), Matilda (968), Paulina of Zell (1107), Bl Arnold of Padua (1254), Bl James Capocci (1308), Bl Dominic Jorjes (1619), Bl Ambrose Fernández (1620).

15 March

Longinus the Centurion (1st cent.), Aristobulus (1st cent.), Menignus the Dyer (251), Nicander the

Physician (*c*.304), Matrona of Thessalonica (*c*.350), Mancius of Evora (5th cent.), Speciosus of Terracina (*c*.555), Probus of Rieti (*c*.571), Leocritia of Córdova (859), Sisebutus of Cardeña (1082), Malcodia of Asti (*c*.1090), Raymund of Fitero (1163), Bl William Hart (1583), Louise de Marillac (1660), Clement Mary Hofbauer (1820).

16 March

Hilary, Tatian, Felix, Largus and Denis (*c*.284), Papas of Lycaonia (*c*.300), Julian of Anazarbus (*c*.302), Abraham Kidunaia (*c*.366), Patrick of Auvergne (?), Agapitus of Ravenna (4th cent.), Abban of Kill-Abban (5th cent.), Finian Lobhar (*c*.560), Eusebia of Hamay (*c*.680), Dentlin (7th cent.), Megingaud of Würzburg (794), Gregory Makar (*c*.1000), Heribert of Cologne (1022), John Sordi (1183), Bl Torello of Poppi (1281), BB Robert Dalby and John Amias (1589), John de Brébeuf, Isaac Jogues, Antony Daniel, Gabriel Lalemant, Charles Garnier, Noel Chabanel, John Lalande and René Goupil (1642–9).

17 March

Joseph of Arimathaea (1st cent.), Ambrose of Alexandria (*c*.250), Alexander and Theodore (?), Martyrs of Seramis (390), Patrick of Ireland (*c*.461), Agricola of Chalon (580), Gertrude of Nivelles (659), Paul of Cyprus (777), Bl Stephen of Palestrina (1144), Bl John Sarkander (1620), Bl Peter Lieou (1834).

ST PATRICK

Patrick is the earliest of the British saints and the only one whose writings have survived. These record that he was born of a British landowning family who had probably been Roman citizens for at least two hundred years and Christian for nearly a century. When he was sixteen he was captured by pirates and sold as a slave to Ireland where he was a herdsman for six years before he escaped home. There he was told in a vision to return to evangelize his former captors. He studied for the priesthood on the Continent and was then sent to Ireland by the Pope in 431. Christianity had made hardly any headway among the many small kingdoms of Ireland and yet St Patrick managed in ten years to establish churches all over the land, converting the kings, and himself becoming the first Bishop of Armagh; to this day this is the premier see of all Ireland in both the Roman Catholic Church and the Church of Ireland. Lough Dergh in Ulster has become

The vision of St Joseph. (*Champaigne*).

the centre of pilgrimage for the faithful in memory of Patrick's prayer and penance done in the great cave there. As the patron saint of Ireland he was promised that he would judge the Irish on the last day.

May the strength of God pilot us.
May the power of God preserve us.
May the wisdom of God instruct us.
May the hand of God protect us.
May the way of God direct us.
May the shield of God defend us.
May the hosts of God guard us against
the snares of the Evil One and the temptations of the
world.
May Christ be with us. Christ before us.
Christ in us. Christ over us.
May thy salvation, O Lord, be always ours
this day and for evermore.

ST PATRICK

18 March

Alexander of Jerusalem (251), Martyrs of Nicomedia (c.300), Trophimus and Eucarpius (c.304), Narcissus and Felix (c.307), Cyril of Jerusalem (387), Frediano of Lucca (588), Egbert of Ripon (c.700), Edward the Martyr (979), Anselm of Lucca (1086), Bl Christianus of Mellifont (1186), Bl Fra Angelico (1455), Salvator of Horta (1567).

19 March

Joseph (1st cent.), Pancharius of Nicomedia (303), Quintus, Quintilla, Quartilla, Mark and Comp. (?), Apollonius and Leontius (?), John the Syrian (6th cent.), Leontius of Saintes (640), Adrian of Maestricht (c.668), Landoald and Amantius (c.668), Lactan (672), Alcmund (c.800), Bl Andrew de' Gallerani (1251), Gemus of Moyenmoutier (?).

ST JOSEPH

The few references in the first two chapters of St Matthew's and St Luke's Gospels provide the only information that we have about St Joseph, the spouse of the Blessed Virgin Mary. He is there described as 'a just man' – a pious Jew of Davidic descent – who worked as a carpenter in the village of Nazareth. One tradition holds that he was a widower well into middle-age before he married Mary and there is no further Gospel reference to him after the incident of Christ teaching in the Temple. This makes it likely that he

died before the ministry of Jesus began, and, as St Francis de Sales said, it would have been unthinkable for Christ to have commended His mother into the care of St John, had St Joseph, her husband, still been alive.

He has become the pattern of domestic holiness and a patron of those who work with their hands.

20 March

Archippus of Colossi (1st cent.), Alexandra, Caldia, Euphrasia, Matrona, Juliana, Euphemia, Theodosia, Derphuta and a sister of Derphuta (c.300), Photina, Joseph, Victor, Sebastian, Anatolius, Photius, Photis, Parasceve and Cyriaca (?), Paul, Cyril, Eugene and Comp. (?), Urbitius of Metz (c.420), Tetricus of Langres (572), Martin of Braga (580), Cuthbert of Lindisfarne (687), Herbert (687), Wulfram of Fontenelle (c.703), Benignus of Flay (725), Nicetas of Bithynia (c.735), Bl Remigius of Strassburg (783), John, Sergius and Comp. (796), Anastasius of St Sabas (c.797), William of Peñacorada (c.1042), Bl Eberhard (c.1150), BB Evangelist and Peregrinus (c.1250), Bl Ambrose Sassedoni (1287), Bl John of Parma (1289), Bl Maurice Csaky (1336), Bl Mark of Montegallo (1497), Bl John Baptist Spagnuolo (1516), Bl Hippolytus Galantini (1619).

King Alfred sees a vision of St Cuthbert, the bishop of Lindisfarne in the seventh century, whose missionary zeal earned him fame as 'the wonder-worker of Britain'.

21 March

Birillus of Catania (c.90), Philemon and Domninus (?),

Martyrs of Alexandria (342), Serapion of Thmuis (*c*.370), Lupicinus of Lauconne (*c*.480), Benedict (*c*.550), Enda of Arranmore (*c*.590), Bl Clementia of Oehren (1176), Bl Santuccia Terrebotti (1305), Bl Alphonsus de Rojas (1617).

22 March

Epaphroditus (1st cent.), Callinica and Basilissa (250), Paul of Narbonne (p.250), Saturninus and Comp. (?), Basil of Ancyra (362), Lea of Rome (384), Deogratias of Carthage (457), Octavianus and Comp. (484), Darerca (5th cent.), Failbhe of Iona (*c*.680), Trien of Killelga (5th cent.), Zachary (752), Bl Isnard de Chiampo (1244), Bl Benvenutus Scotivoli (1282), Bl Hugolinus Zefferini (*c*.1470), Nicholas von Flue (1487).

23 March

Nicon and Comp. (*c*.250), Fidelis (?), Julian (?), Theodolus of Antioch (?), Domitius, Pelagia, Aquila, Eparchius and Theodosia (361), Victorian, Frumentius and Comp. (484), Maidoc of Fiddown (5th cent.), Felix and Comp. (5th cent.), Benedict of Campania (*c*.550), Ethelwald of Lindisfarne (699), Felix of Montecassino (*c*.1000), Bl Peter of Gubbio (*c*.1350), Bl Sibyllina Biscossi (1367), Turibius de Mogrobejo (1600), Joseph Oriol (1702).

ST BENEDICT

St Benedict's life was sketched by St Gregory and can partly be inferred from the rule which he established for his monks. He has become one of the great inspira-

St Benedict clothing St Maurus and St Placidus (*Lorenzo Monano*).

tions of Western Christendom, partly because of the supreme influence of his monastic rule and the Benedictine Order and partly because, in the sixth century when the whole of the Christian world seemed to be crumbling as the remains of the Roman Empire fell to the Barbarians, Benedict led his followers out to create a community which allowed Christianity to survive the destruction of the old order. At Monte Cassino he began the real prototype of Western monasticism. His rule was planned for his own monks primarily, but from the first was seen by the Pope as of value for all the monks of the Empire. The Benedictine order spread throughout the known world and has been the basis of most of the reformed orders which succeeded it. Poverty, chastity, and stability were the earliest vows taken, for St Benedict recognized that, in a world on the brink of collapse, it was essential for men to have a strong and sure allegiance to a community. Therefore the monks promised to remain within the community to which they were professed. 'A monastery should, if possible, be so arranged that everything necessary – that is water, a mill, a garden, a bakery – may be available, and different trades be carried on within the monastery, so that there shall be no need for the monks to wander about outside. For this is not at all good for their souls.' (Rule of St Benedict LXVI.)

24 March

The Archangel Gabriel, Latinus of Brescia (115), Mark and Timothy (c.150), Agapitus of Synnada (3rd cent.), Epigmenius (c.300), Timolaus and Comp. (303), Romulus and Secundus (?), Seleucus (?), Pigmenius of Rome (362), Domangard of Maghera (c.500), Macartin of Clogher (c.505), Cairlon of Cashel (6th cent.), Caimin of Lough Derg (7th cent.), Hildelid of Barking (c.717), Aldemar the Wise (c.1080), William of Norwich (1144), Bl Bertha of Cavriglia (1163), Bl John del Bastone (1290), Catherine of Sweden (1381), Simeon of Trent (1475), Bl Didacus of Cádiz (1801).

ARCHANGEL GABRIEL

Together with Michael and Raphael, Gabriel is one of the three archangels designated by name in the Bible. The name means in Hebrew 'man of God', and as the messenger of divine comfort, he is accorded in Jewish theology a place second only to Michael.

St Benedict (*Piero della Francesca*).

Detail from the Annunciation (*Leonardo da Vinci*).

Twice in the Book of Daniel he appears to assist the prophet in the interpretation of his visions. Twice in St Luke's Gospel he comes to announce miraculous births – first the birth of John the Baptist to his father, Zechariah, the priest in the Temple, and second the coming of Jesus to the Virgin Mary. He is for this reason called the 'Angel of the Annunciation'.

Devotion to Gabriel seems to have begun in Roman times but it was only in 1921 that the Roman Catholic Church celebrated his feast universally on the 24 March, that is, the day before the Annunciation. In early Christian art he is depicted as bearing a sceptre, the staff of authority of a royal messenger. He has naturally become the patron saint of postal, telegraph and telephone workers.

The virgin was pure there was no nay;
The angel Gabriel to her did say,
'Thou shalt conceive a child this day,
The which shall be our dearest dear.'

Traditional Carol

25 March

Feast of the Annunciation of Our Lady, The Good Thief, Quirinus of Rome (*c.*269), Irenaeus of Sirmium (304), Two hundred and sixty-two Roman Martyrs (?), Dula the Slave (?), Pelagius of Laodicea (*c.* 381), Humbert of Marolles (*c.*680), Hermenland of Fontenelle (*c.*720), Barontius and Desiderius (*c.*725), Kennocha (1007), Bl Herman of Zähringen (1074), Harold of Gloucester (1168), Robert of Bury St Edmunds (1181), Bl Thomas of Costacciaro (1337), Bl James Bird (1593), Lucy Filippini (1732).

26 March

Castulus of Rome (288), Quadratus, Theodosius, Emmanuel and Comp. (*c.*304), Montanus and Maxima (304), Peter, Marcian, Jovinus, Thecla, Cassian and Comp. (?), Theodore, Irenaeus, Serapion and Armonius (310), Eutychius of Alexandria and Comp. (356), Felix of Trèves (*c.*400), Sincheall of Killeigh (5th cent.), Mochelloc of Kilmallock (*c.*639), Braulio of Saragossa (646), Garbhan (7th cent.), Ludger of Utrecht (809), Bertillo of Dijon (888), Felicitas of Padua (9th cent.), Basil the Younger (952), Alfwold of Sherborne (1058), Bl Melior of Vallombrosa (1198), Bl Peter Maginet (1435).

27 March

Philetas, Lydia, Macedo, Theoprepius, Amphilochius and Chronidas (*c*.121), Alexander (3rd cent.), Amator of Guarda (?), Zanitas, Lazarus, Marotas, Narses and Comp. (344), John of Lycopolis (394), Augusta of Treviso (?), Rupert of Salzburg (*c*.720), Romulus of Nimes (*c*.730), John Damascene (*c*.749), Suairlech of Fore (*c*.750), Alkeld (10th cent.), Matthew of Beauvais (*c*.1098), Gelasius of Armagh (1174), Bl William Tempier (1197).

28 March

Priscus, Malthus and Alexander (260), Rogatus, Successus and Comp. (?), Castor and Dorotheus (?), Spes of Campi (*c*.513), Gunthrammus (592), Gundelindis of Niedermunster (*c*.750), Tutilo of St Gall (*c*.915), Osburga of Coventry (*c*.1016), Conon of Nesi (1236), John of Capistrano (1456).

29 March

Secundus of Asti (119), Pastor, Victorinus and Comp. (*c*.311), Jonas, Barachisius and Comp. (327), Mark of Arethusa (*c*.362), Cyril of Heliopolis (*c*.362), Armogastes and Comp. (p.460), Gladys (5th cent.), Gundleus (*c*.500), Lasar (6th cent.), Firminus of Viviers (6th cent.), Eustace of Luxeuil (625), Bl Diemut of Wessobrunn (*c*.1130), Berthold of Mt Carmel (*c*.1195), Bl Hough of Vaucelles (1239), Ludolphus of Ratzeburg (1250), Bl Jane Mary de Maillé (1414).

30 March

Quirinus the Jailer (*c*.117), Regulus of Senlis (*c*.260), Domninus, Victor and Comp. (?), Mamertinus of Auxerre (*c*.462), Regulus of Scotland (4th cent.), Pastor of Orleans (6th cent.), Fergus of Downpatrick (6th cent.), John Climacus (605), Zosimus of Syracuse (*c*.660), Tola (*c*.733), Patto of Werden (*c*.788), Forannan of Waulsort (982), Clinius of Pontecorvo (?), Bl Joachim of Fiore (1202), Bl Dodo of Asch (1231), Bl Moricus (1236), Peter Regalado (1456), Bl Amadeus IX of Savoy (1472).

31 March

Amos (8th cent. BC), Balbina of Rome (*c*.130), Acacius Agathangelos (*c*.251), Theodulus, Anesius, Felix, Cornelia and Comp. (?), Benjamin the Deacon (*c*.421), Aldo of Hasnon (end 8th cent.), Guy of Pomposa (1046), Guy of Vicogne (1147), Machabeo of Armagh (1174), Bl Jane of Toulouse (1286), Daniel of Murano

(1411), Bl Mary Mamala (1453), Bl Bonaventure Tornielli (1491).

1 April

Theodora of Rome (132), Melito of Sardis (*c*.180), Venantius of Spalato (*c*.255), Victor and Stephen (?), Quintian and Irenaeus (?), Walericus of Leucone (*c*.622), Dodolinus of Vienne (7th cent.), Caidoc and Fricor (7th cent.), Macarius the Wonder-Worker (830), Cellach of Armagh (9th cent.), Cellagh II of Armagh (1129), Hugh of Grenoble (1132), Hugh of Bonnevaux (1194), Bl Nicholas of Neti (*c*.1220), Bl Gerard of Sassoferrato (1367), Catherine Tomás (1574).

2 April

Amphianus of Lycia (*c*.305), Theodosia of Tyre (308), Urban of Langres (*c*.390), Abundius of Como (469), Mary of Egypt (*c*.500), Bronach of Glen-Seichis (?), Nicetius of Lyons (573), Constantine II of Scotland (874), Bl Drogo of Baume (10th cent.), Bl Meingosus of Weingarten (*c*.1200), Francis of Paola (1507), Bl John Payne (1582), Bl Margaret Clitherow (1586), Bl Leopold of Gaiche (1815), Bl Dominic Tuoc (1839).

3 April

Pancras of Taormina (1st cent.), Sixtus I (127), Agape, Chionia and Irene (304), Vulpian of Tyre (*c*.304), Evagrius and Benignus (?), Nicetas of Medikion (824), Burgundofara (657), Attala of Taormina (*c*.800), Richard of Chichester (1253), Bl Gandulphus of Binasco (1260), Bl John of Penna (1271), Bl Alexandrina di Letto (1458).

4 April

Agathopedes and Theodulus (303), Zosimus of Palestine (5th cent.), Tigernach of Clogher (549), Gwerir of Liskeard (?), Isidore of Seville (636), Hildebert of Ghent (752), Plato of Sakkudion (813), Bl Aleth of Dijon (1105), Peter of Poitiers (1115), Bl Henry of Gheest (*c*.1190) Cist., St Benedict the Moor (1589).

5 April

Irene (304), Martyrs of Lesbos (?), Zeno (?), Martyrs of Africa (459), Probus and Grace (?), Becan of Kill-Beggan (6th cent.), Ethelburga of Lyminge (*c*.647), Gerald of Sauve-Majeure (1095), Albert of Monte-

St Vincent Ferrer (*Cossa*).

corvino (1127), Bl Sighardus of Bonlieu (1162), Vincent Ferrer (1418), Bl Peter Cerdán (1422), Bl Blaise of Auvergne (14th cent.), Bl Antony Fuster (14th cent.), Bl Crescentia Höss (1744).

ST VINCENT FERRER

It was St Vincent Ferrer who did most to heal the Great Schism which so disastrously split the Church in the late fourteenth century. He travelled throughout Western Europe preaching repentance and seeking an end to the division in the Church. His personal life was very strict and his preaching remarkably effective. He became the confessor to the Avignon pope and managed to get him to resign when the two other claimants also resigned so that Martin v could be elected as a Pope supported by all. St Vincent Ferrer is one of the greatest of the Dominicans and his public work as a teacher converted many, but his life was crowned by his success in ending the scandal of a divided Western Church.

6 April

Platonis and Comp. (*c.*308), Timothy and Diogenes (*c.*345), Marcellinus of Carthage (413), Ulched (?), Amandus of Bergamo (515), Eutychius of Constantinople (582), Winebald of Troyes (*c.*650), Gennard of Flay (720), Berthanc of Kirkwall (*c.*840), Prudentius Galindo (861), Notker Balbulus (912), Urban of Peñalba (*c.*940), Elstan of Winchester (981), William of Eskilsoe (1203), Bl Juliana of Cornillon (1258), Bl Catherine of Pallanza (1478), Bl Paul Tinh (1857).

7 April

Hegesippus (*c.*180), Calliopus (*c.*303), Bl Christian of Douai (?), Epiphanius, Donatus, Rufinus and Comp. (?), Cyriacus and Comp. (?), Pelagius of Alexandria (?), Peleusius of Alexandria (?), Saturninus of Verona (*c.*356), Aphraates of Antioch (4th cent.), Brynach (?5th cent.), Villicus of Metz (568), Llewellyn and Gwrnerth (6th cent.), Goran (6th cent.), Finan of Kinnitty (6th cent.), George the Younger (*c.*816), Gibardus of Luxeuil (*c.*888), Bl Eberhard of Schäffhausen (1078), Aybert of Crépin (1140), Bl Herman Joseph (1241), Bl Ursulina of Bologna (1410), Bl William Cufitella (1411), BB Henry Walpole, and Alexander Rawlins (1595), BB Edward Oldcorne and Ralph Ashley (1606).

April

8 April

Herodion, Asyncritus and Phlegon (1st cent.), Dionysius of Corinth (c.180), Concessa of Carthage (?), Januarius, Maxima and Macaria (?), Aedesius of Alexandria (c.306), Amantius of Como (440), Perpetuus of Tours (c.490), Redemptus of Ferentino (586), Walter of Pontoise (1099), Bl Clement of St Elpidio (1291), Bl Julian of St Augustine (1606), Bl Julia Billiart (1816).

9 April

Mary Cleophas (1st cent.), Prochorus of Nicomedia (1st cent.), Martyrs of Pannonia (?), Demetrius, Concessus, Hilary and Comp. (?), Hermogenes, Caius, Expeditus, Aristonicus, Rufus and Galata (?), Martyrs of Sirmium (c.303), Eupsychius of Caesarea (362), Acacius of Amida (p.421), Marcellus of Avignon (474), Madrun (5th cent.), Dotto (6th cent.), Waldetrudis of Mons (c.688), Hugh of Rouen (730), Theodore and Comp. (c.870), Hedda and Comp. (c.870), Casilda of Briviesca (c.1050), Gaucherius of Aureil (1140), Bl Ubald Adimari (1315), BB Thomas of Tolentino and Comp. (1321), Bl John of Vespignano (1331), Bl Reginald Montemarti (1348), Bl Antony Pavoni (1374).

10 April

Martyrs of Rome (c.115), Terence, Africanus, Pompeius and Comp. (250), Apollonius of Alexandria (?), Bademus of Perisa (c.380), Palladius of Auxerre (661), Beocca, Ethor and Comp. (c.870), Bede the Younger (883), Macarius of Antioch (1012), Fulbert of Chartres (1029), Paternus of Abdinghof (1058), Malchus of Waterford (1110), Bl Mark Fantucci (1479), Bl Antony Neyrot (1460), Michael of the Saints (1625).

11 April

Antipas of Pergamus (c.90), Philip of Gortyna (c.180), Eustorgius of Nicomedia (c.300), Domnio and Comp. (?), Leo I the Great (461), Machai of Bute (5th cent.), Aid of Achad-Finglas (?), Bassanuphius of Gaza (c.540), Isaac of Monteluco (c.550), Maedhog-Aedhan (6th cent.), Agericus of Tours (c.680), Godeberta of Noyon (c.700), Bl Waltmann of Cambrai (1138), BB Stephen and Hildebrand (1209), Bl Raynerius Inclusus (1237), Bl John of Cuppramontana (1303), Bl George Gervase (1608), Gemma Galgani (1903).

St Leo the Great.

ST LEO I

St Leo was Pope at a turbulent moment in the Church's history. The Catholic faith was attacked by all kinds of heresies, many of them centred around the exact nature of the person of Christ. How was he God and Man? The Manichaeans, Pelagians, Eutychians, and Nestorians, all had conflicting answers to this. St Leo clearly defined the orthodox statement about the nature of Christ and his definition was confirmed at the Council of Chalcedon in 451.

St Leo was also personally responsible for the safety of Rome in the face of two attacks by the barbarians. By his intervention, Atilla the Hun turned aside in his ravaging of Italy and later Leo managed also to get the Vandals to restrain their forces from destroying Rome. Leo was also responsible for the reform of the regulations for entry into the priesthood and he added to the Canon of the Mass words which emphasized the Christian doctrine that matter is not evil but made by God. In this he struck hard at the Manichaeans who saw all matter as evil – a heresy which arose again with the teachings of the Albigenses in France.

In all, for twenty-two years, Leo proved a wise and fearless leader of the Church of great personal sanctity and theological ability.

12 April

Vissia of Fermo (c.250), Victor of Braga (c.300), Julius I (352), Zeno of Vernoa (371), Sabas and Comp.

(372), Constantine of Gap (529), Wigbert of Friesland (690), Tetricus of Auxerre (707), Damian of Pavia (710), Guthlac of Croyland (714), Erkemboden of Thérouanne (714), Alferius of Cava (1050), Bl Peter of Montepiano (1098), Bl Meinhard of Yxkill (1196), Bl Andrew of Montereale (1480), Bl Angelus Carletti (1495).

13 April

Carpus, Papylus, Agathonica, Agathodorus and Comp. (150 or 250), Maximus, Dadas and Quintilianus (303), Ursus of Ravenna (396), Hermenegild (583), Guinoc of Scotland (*c*.838), Bl Ida of Boulogne (1113), Caradoc of Llandaff (1124), Bl Ida of Louvain (*c*.1300), Bl Margaret of Città di Castello (1320), Bl James of Certaldo (1392), BB John Lockwood and Edward Catherick (1642).

14 April

Justin the Philosopher (*c*.165), Tiburtius, Valerian and

Maximus (*c*.190), Fronto of Nitria (2nd cent.), Domnina and Another (?), Ardalion the Actor (*c*.300), Proculus of Terni (310), Thomais of Alexandria (476), Tassach of Raholp (*c*.495), Abundius the Sacristan (*c*.564), Lambert of Lyons (688), Bernard of Thiron (1117), Bl Lanuinus of Torre (1120), Benedict the Bridge-Builder (1184), Bl Conrad of Hildesheim (*c*.1235), Bl Ralph of Sisteron (1241), Peter González (1246), Antony, John and Eustace (1342), Bl Lydwina of Schiedam (1433).

15 April

Basilissa and Anastasia (*c*.62), Maro, Eutyches and Victorinus (*c*.99), Theodore and Pausilippus (*c*.130), Maximus and Olympiades (251), Crescens of Myra (?), Eutychius of Ferentino (?), Bl Laurentinus Sossius (485), Paternus of Vannes (*c*.500), Ruadan of Lothra (584), Silvester of Réome (*c*.625), Hunna of Alsace (679), Bl Nidger of Augsburg (*c*.829), Mundus of Argyle (*c*.962).

A torchlight ceremony at Lourdes.

16 April

Callistus, Charisius and Comp. (?), Eighteen Martyrs of Saragossa (*c.*304), Caius and Crementius (304), Encratia of Saragossa (*c.*304), Turibius of Astorga (*c.*460), Vasius of Saintes (*c.*500), Turibius of Palencia (*c.*528), Paternus of Wales (5th cent.), Paternus of Avranches (*c.*574), Paternus of Coutances (*c.*574), Fructuosus of Braga (665), Lambert of Saragossa (*c.*900), Bl Elias of Cologne (1042), Magnus (1116), Drogo of Sebourg (1186), Contardo of Este (1249), Bl Joachim Piccolomini (1305), Bl William Gnoffi (*c.*1317), Bl Archangelus Canetuli (1513), Benedict Joseph Labre (1783), Bernardette Soubirous (1879).

ST BERNARDETTE SOUBIROUS

There is no saint of modern times who has so captured the popular imagination as St Bernardette (1844–79), and to the grotto at Lourdes come more than a million pilgrims every year. The story is shatteringly simple. A little peasant girl, daughter of the local miller, came back home to prepare for her confirmation. For two years she had been working as a maid but now she was back with her parents and the rest of their family of six. It was a little way outside the village that the miracle happened. In a cave in the rock Bernardette saw a lady who came and visited her seventeen times in the course of the next six months. She said 'Je suis La Conception Immaculée', and near where she stood a spring began to run, in which many found healing properties.

The whole thing was a great embarrassment to the Church. Lourdes shared with Galilee the reputation of being impossibly provincial and unsophisticated. At a time in which the Church was trying to bring herself up to date and emerge into the nineteenth-century industrial world, she was not over-keen on miraculous visitations to peasant girls. Bernardette suffered a great deal from the continued hostile questioning from the authorities and the protracted attempts to discredit her firmly-held story. The transcript of some of these hearings shows how tough must have been the pressure on someone hardly prepared for such an ordeal. Gradually the sincerity of the girl and the unshakeable details of her story gained acceptance but her trials were not to end there.

She entered a nunnery at Nevers where she was very roughly treated by her superiors who were determined to ensure that she did not presume upon her miracle. It was for the saintliness of her life as Nevers that

Bernardette was acclaimed a Saint in 1933 but within her lifetime a great basilica was built above the grotto at Lourdes. The pilgrims who come there bear witness to the continuing appeal of this simple girl who was out playing with her friends when she saw her 'lady'.

17 April

Anicetus (160), Mappalicus and Comp. (250), Fortunatus and Marcian (?), Peter and Hermogenes (?), Innocent of Tortona (*c.*350), Pantagathus of Vienne (540), Donnan and Comp. (*c.*616), Landericus of Soignies (*c.*730), Wando of Fontenelle (*c.*756), Elias Paul and Isidore (856), Robert of Chaise-Dieu (1067), Bl Gervinus of Oudenburg (1117), Stephen Harding (1134), Bl Eberhard of Marchtal (1178), Bl James of Cerqueto (1367), Bl Clare Gambacorta (1419).

18 April

Eleutherius and Anthia (*c.*117), Corebus of Messina (*c.*117), Apollonius the Apologist (*c.*190), Calocerus of Brescia (?), Bitheus and Genocus (6th cent.), Laserian of Leighlin (639), Agia of Mons (*c.*714), Wicterp of Augsburg (749), Cogitosus of Kildare (8th cent.), Perfectus of Córdova (851), Gebuinus of Lyons (1080), Bl Idesbald of Dunes (1167), Galdinus of Milan (1176), Bl Andrew Hibernón (1602), Bl Mary of the Incarnation (1618).

19 April

Timon the Deacon (1st cent.), Socrates and Dionysius (275), Vincent of Collioure (*c.*304), Paphnutius of Jerusalem (?), Crescentius of Florence (*c.*396), Ursmar of Lobbes (713), George of Antioch (814), Gerold of Einsiedeln (978), Elphege the Martyr (1012), Leo IX (1054), Bl Burchard of Bellevaux, Bl Bernard the Penitent (1182), St Wernher (1275), Bl Conrad Miliani of Ascoli (1289), Bl James of Oldo (1404), Bl James Duckett (1602).

20 April

The Seven Angels who stand before the throne of God: Michael, Gabriel, Raphael, Shealtiel, Uriel, Jehudiel and Berachiel, Sulpicius and Servilian (*c.*117), Victor, Zoticus, Zeno, Acindynus, Caesareus, Severian, Chrysophorus, Theonas and Antoninus (*c.*303), Theodore

Trichinas (*c*.330), Marcellinus, Vincent and Domninus (*c*.374), Theotimus of Tomi (407), Marcian of Auxerre (*c*.470), Ceadwalla (689), Bl Harduin of Fontenelle (811), Hugh of Anzy-le-Duc (*c*.930), Bl Hildegund, or Joseph (1188), Bl Oda of Rivroelles (1158), Bl Dominic Vernagalli (1218), Bl John of Grace-Dieu (1280), Agnes of Montepulciano (1317), Bl Simon Rinalducci (1322), BB James Bell and John Finch (1584), BB Francis Page S.J. and Robert Watkinson (1602), Bl Margaret of Amelia (1666).

21 April

Apollo, Isacius and Crotates (*c*.302), Arator, Fortunatus, Felix, Silvius, and Vitalis (?), Simeon, Abdechalas, Ananias, Usthazanes, Pusicius and Comp. (341), Cyprian of Brescia (582), Anastasius I of Antioch (599), Beuno of Wales (*c*.630), Anastasius the Sinaite (*c*.678), Frodulphus of Barjon (*c*.750), Anselm of Canterbury (1109), Bl Walter of Mondsee (1158), Bl Fastred of Cambron (1163), Bl Bartholomew of Cervere (1466), Conrad of Parzham (1894).

ST ANSELM

In the eleventh century the principal centre of learning in Europe was the Abbey of Bec, in Normandy. It was there that in 1060, Anselm, the son of an Italian landowner, became a monk. He studied under his fellow-countryman Lanfranc and succeeded him as prior in 1063.

In 1078 he became the abbot, which meant that he had to travel often to England and there he renewed his friendship with Lanfranc who had been made Archbishop of Canterbury. As a result he succeeded his old master as Archbishop and then began a life of increasing strife as he tried to uphold the rights and powers of the Papacy over the English Church. This meant periods of exile and frequent visits to Rome but Anselm was still able to continue his studies and writings. This made him one of the most considerable philosophers and theologians of the Middle Ages as well as the writer of some important religious poetry. Anselm was canonised in 1492 and declared a Doctor of the Church in 1720. He is buried before the altar in the Chapel of St Anselm in Canterbury Cathedral.

And though our prayer is cold, because our charity is so little fervent, yet Thou art rich in mercy.

ST ANSELM

22 April

Soter (174), Epipodius and Alexander (178), Leonidas of Alexandria (202), Parmenius and Comp. (*c*.250), Caius (*c*.296), Azadanes and Azades (342), Mareas and Comp. (342), Abrosimus of Persia (342), Tarbula of Persia (345), Acepsimas of Hnaita (376), Abdiesus the Deacon (4th cent.), Aithalas of Persia (4th cent.), Leo of Sens (541), Rufus of Glendalough (?), Theodore of Sikion (613), Arwald and Arwald (686), Opportuna of Montreuil (*c*.770), Senorina of Basto (982), Bl Wolfhelm of Brauweiler (1091), Bl Francis Venimbene of Fabriano (1322).

23 April

Felix, Fortunatus and Achilleus (212), George the Martyr (*c*.300), Marolus of Milan (423), Iberius of Meath (5th cent.), Gerald of Toul (994), Adalbert of Prague (997), Bl Gerard of Orchimont (1138), Bl Giles of Assisi (1262), Bl Giles of Saumur (1266), Bl Helen Valentini (1458).

ST GEORGE THE MARTYR

Though his historical existence is now generally accepted, little is known with certainty of the life or even

St George.

of the martyrdom of George. He probably suffered at or near Lydda in Palestine, shortly before the accession of the Emperor Constantine.

The story of his rescuing a princess from a dragon seems to have originated in Italy during the late twelfth century. It may indeed, have been derived from the Classical Greek story of the slaying by Perseus of the sea-monster to save Andromeda at Arsuf or Joppa, both of which are cities near Lydda.

George seems to be known in England since at least the eighth century, but his special veneration came during the Crusades when Richard I's soldiers are said to have been inspired by visions of St George. From the fourteenth century 'St George's arms' – the red cross on the white background – became the badge for English fighting men and from the reign of Edward III St George displaced Edward the Confessor as the patron saint of England.

24 April

Alexander and Comp. (177), Sabas and Comp. (272), Eusebius, Neon, Leontius, Longinus and Comp. (?), Gregory of Elvira (*c*.400), Dyfnan (5th cent.), Deo-datus of Blois (*c*.525), Honorius of Brescia (*c*.586), Ivo of Huntingdonshire (?), Musa of Rome (6th cent.), Mellitus of Canterbury (624), Bova and Doda (*c*.680), Authaire of La Ferté (7th cent.), Egbert of Rathelmigisi (729), Bl Corona of Elche (?), William Firmatus (1103), Bl Francis Colmenario (1590), Fidelis of Sigmaringen (1622), Euphrasia Pelletier (1868).

25 April

Mark the Evangelist (75), Anianus of Alexandria (1st cent.), Philo and Agathopodes (*c*.150), Evodius, Hermogenes and Calistus (?), Phebadius of Agen (*c*.392), Stephen of Antioch (481), Macaille of Croghan (*c*.489), Erminus of Lobbes (737), Mella of Doire-Melle (*c*.780), Heribaldus of Auxerre (*c*.857), Robert of Syracuse (*c*.1000), Bl Boniface of Valperga (1243), BB Robert Anderton and William Marsden (1586).

ST MARK

John Mark was the cousin of Barnabas. His mother, Mary, made their home in Jerusalem a sanctuary for the disciples of Christ and it may be that it was there that they held the Last Supper. It seems that he was the young man so oddly described in St Mark's Gospel, as having rushed to rescue Jesus from the soldier of the High Priest. When the guard attempted to arrest him, he ran off leaving his only garment, a linen cloak, in the soldier's hands.

Mark accompanied Paul and Barnabas on their first Missionary journey but left them at Perga. There was clearly some friction between him and St Paul as he was not taken on the next journey. Later they seem to have been reconciled and he was certainly in Rome with Paul. Afterwards Mark was the disciple and interpreter of St Peter when he was in Rome and the same tradition suggests that he wrote his Gospel from the information given to him by Peter. It was his Gospel which is the earliest account that we have of the life of Christ.

At some time Mark seems to have visited Asia and is thought to have been martyred in Alexandria. It was from there that the Venetian traders stole his body and took it to their own city where very much later the basilica of St Mark was built to house it. As a result the Venetian Republic adopted the symbol of the lion as their emblem in honour of their patron St Mark.

St Catherine of Siena's mystical marriage (*Bartolomeo Cavarossi*).

St Mark (*Mantegna*).

26 April

Cletus (*c*.91), Peter of Braga (?), Marcellinus (304), Lucidius of Verona (?), Exuperantia of Troyes (?), Basileus of Amasea (319), Clarentius of Vienne (*c*.620), Trudpert of Munstethal (*c*.644), Richarius of Centula (*c*.645), Paschasius Radbert (*c*.851), John of Valence (1146), Franca Visalta (1218), Dominic and Gregory (1300), Bl Alda of Siena (1309).

27 April

Anthimus of Nicomedia (303), Castor and Stephen (?), Theodore of Tabenna (*c*.368), Liberalis of Ancona (*c*.400), Theophilus of Brescia (p.427), Tertullian of Bologna (*c*.490), Asicus of Elphin (*c*.490), Enoder (6th cent.), Winebald of Beverley (*c*.731), Floribert of Liége (746), John of Constantinople (813), Adelelmus of Flanders (1152), Zita of Lucca (1278), Peter Armengol (1304), Bl Antony de' Patrizi (1311), Bl James of Bitetto (*c*.1485), Bl Hosanna of Cattaro (1565), Peter Canisius (1597), Bl Mariana of Jesus (1624), Bl Laurence Hung (1856).

28 April

Mark of Galilee (92), Aphrodisius, Caralippus, Agapitus and Eusebius (1st cent.), Vitalis of Milan (?1st cent.), Valeria of Milan (?1st cent.), Patrick, Acatius, Menander and Polyenus (?), Pollio of Pannonia (*c*.304), Theodora v and Didymus (304), Artemius of Sens (609), Cronan of Roscrea (*c*.626), Pamphilus of Sulmona (*c*.700), Prudentius of Tarazona (p.700), Gerard the Pilgrim (?), Bl Adalbero of Augsburg (909), Bl Gerard of Bourgogne (1172), Bl Luchesius of Umbria (1260), Bl Louis Mary Grignon de Montfort (1716), Paul of the Cross (1775), BB Paul Khoan, Peter Hieu and John Baptist Thauh (1840), Peter Chanel (1889).

29 April

Torpes of Pisa (*c*.65), Martyrs of Corfu (1st cent.), Tychicus of Paphos (1st cent.), Agapius and Comp. (*c*.259), Severus of Naples (409), Dichu of Ulster (5th cent.), Paulinus of Brescia (*c*.545), Senan of North Wales (7th cent.), Fiachan of Lismore (7th cent.), Wilfrid the Younger (744), Gundebert (8th cent.), Ava of Dinant (p.845), Daniel of Gerona (9th cent.), Hugh the Great of Cluny (1109), Robert of Molesmes

(1110), Bl Theoger of Metz (1120), Bl Robert of Bruges (1157), Peter Martyr (1252).

30 April

Eutropius of Saintes (?), Aphrodisius and Comp. (?), Sophia of Fermo (*c*.250), Maximus of Ephesus (*c*.251), Marianus, James and Comp. (259), Laurence of Novara and Comp. (*c*.397), Donatus of Euraea (late 4th cent.), Pomponius of Naples (536), Desideratus of Gourdon (*c*.569), Cynwl of Wales (6th cent.), Erconwald of London (*c*.686), Hildegard (783), Swithbert the Younger (807), Amator, Peter and Louis (855), Genistus of Beaulieu (*c*.1100), Adjutor of Vernon (1131), Aimo of Savigny (1173), Catherine of Siena (1380), Louis von Bruck (1429), BB Francis Dickenson and Miles Gerard (1590), Bl Benedict of Urbino (1625), Joseph Benedict Cottolengo (1842).

ST CATHERINE OF SIENA

St Catherine began to experience visions as a child and when still only sixteen she took religious vows but remained at home. There she devoted herself to the care of the sick and the poor.

Catherine had an important influence on the political situation of the Church. She went to Avignon and persuaded the Pope to return to Rome and then she took a leading part in trying to heal the Great Schism by writing to leaders all over the West to canvass support for Urban vi against the anti-Pope who had gone off to Avignon again. She died in Rome at 33 while seeking to convince Urban to be more conciliatory towards his opponents.

Could you but know the beauty of but one immortal soul, you would think it little to give your life a hundred times over for its salvation.

CATHERINE OF SIENA

1 May

Jeremias (*c*.590 B.C), Philip (*c*.80) and James the Less (*c*.62), Andeolus of Smyrna (208), Orentius and Patientia (*c*.240), Acius and Aceolus (*c*.303), Isidora of Egypt (*c*.365), Grata of Bergamo (4th or 8th cent.), Amator of Auxerre (418), Orentius of Auch (*c*.439), Brieuc (*c*.510), Sigismund of Burgundy (523), Marculfus of Nanteuil (558), Ceallach of Killala (6th cent.), Asaph of Wales (*c*.600), Bertha of Avenay (p.680), Kevoca of Kyle (7th cent.), Evermarus of Tongres (*c*.700), Theodard of Narbonne (893), Aldebrandus of

Fossombrone (1219), Peregrinus Laziosi (1345), Panacea of Quarona (1383), BB Augustine Schöffler and John-Louis Bonnard (1851).

ST PHILIP THE APOSTLE AND ST JAMES THE LESS

Philip, the first disciple actually called to follow Jesus, was a friend of Peter and Andrew, coming like them from Bethsaida, near Nazareth. He is traditionally the young man who at first declined the call to discipleship in order to 'go and bury his father'. He brought his friend, Nathaniel, to Jesus and was present at the feeding of the five thousand, so that his symbol in medieval art was loaves.

Of James the Less, so-called to distinguish him from James the Greater, nothing definite is known except that he was one of the Twelve Apostles and the son of Alphaeus. His symbol was commonly the fuller's club with which he is said to have been beaten to death by the Jews.

The festival of Philip and James is also May Day, the ancient pagan celebration of the start of the summer. Most of the old customs connected with the first of May were not Christian. In some places religious services were held at dawn. A survival of this is the May Morning Service on Magdalen College Tower, Oxford when the choir assembles at six to sing hymns, and the bells are rung.

Philip saith unto him, Lord, show us the Father, and it sufficeth us.

JOHN 14:8

St Athanasius.

2 May

Exuperius, Zoe, Cyriacus and Theodulus (140), Felix of Seville (?), Saturninus, Neopolus, Germanus and Clestine (304), Valentine of Genoa (c.307), Athanasius of Alexandria (373), Germanus of Normandy (c.460), Vindemialis, Eugene and Longinus (c.485), Neachtain (5th cent.), Gluvias (6th cent.), Waldebert of Luxeuil (c.668), Ultan of Peronne (c.686), Bertinus the Younger (c.699), Wiborada of St Gall (925), Bl Conrad of Seldenburen (1126), Mafalda of Portugal (1252), Bl Joseph Luu (1854).

ST ATHANASIUS

'Father of Orthodoxy', 'Pillar of the Church' and 'Champion of Christ's Divinity' are all deserved titles for Athanasius. He was a native of Alexandria of which he was Bishop for over forty years from 328. He devoted the whole of his life to the confutation of the teachings of Arius, who denied the divinity of Christ.

His refusal to compromise made his life a sustained martyrdom, which he bore with humility but unswerving constancy to the truth as he saw it. He was five times exiled from Alexandria for a total of nearly twenty-two years. In the end he triumphed; Arianism was condemned as a herecy.

The most famous of his works is *Of the Incarnation of the Word of God*, in which he expounded how the Word of God, by His union with manhood, restored to fallen man the image of God, in which he had been created.

Anyone who wishes to understand the mind of the sacred writers must first cleanse his own life and approach the saints by copying their deeds. Thus united to them in the fellowship of life, he will both understand the things revealed to them by God and will receive that which is laid up for the saints in the kingdom of God.

ATHANASIUS, *The Incarnation*

3 May

Alexander I (c.113), Alexander, Eventius and Theo-

St Helena's vision of the True Cross (*Veronese*).

INVENTION OF THE CROSS

Soon after the Emperor Constantine proclaimed toleration for Christianity throughout the Roman Empire, his mother, Helena, was baptized; and in the year 326, though then nearly eighty years old, she made a pilgrimage to Jerusalem. There, according to a later tradition, she discovered the Cross on which Jesus had been crucified.

As a result part of the relic was preserved in a silver case in the Church of the Holy Sepulchre which was built by Constantine.

Churches throughout Christendom wanted pieces of the Cross, and a large part of the wood was distributed among them. Indeed the triumphant hymn, *The Royal Banners*, was written for the reception of a fragment at Poitiers in 569.

The royal banners forward go,
The Cross shines forth in mystic glow,
Where he, the Life, did death endure,
And by that death did life procure.

BISHOP VENANTIUS FORTUNATUS
(530–609)

4 May

Porphyrius of Camerino (250), Curcodomus of Auxerre (3rd cent.), Pelagia of Tarsus (*c*.300), Florian of Austria (304), Cyriacus of Ancona (?), Paulinus of Cologne (?), Silvanus and Comp. (*c*.311), Monica of Carthage (387), Nepotian of Attino (395), Venerius of Milan (409), Antony du Rocher (6th cent.), Ethelred of Bardney (716), Sacerdos of Limoges (*c*.720), Paulinus of Sinigaglia (826), Bl Hilsindis (1028), Godehard of Hildesheim (1038), Cunegund (p.1052), Bl Gregory Celli of Verucchio (1343), Bl Catherine of Parc-aux-Dames (13th cent.), Bl Michael Gedroye (1485), BB Carthusian Martyrs (1535–40), Martyrs of England (1535–1681).

THE ENGLISH MARTYRS

The religious turmoil of the sixteenth century produced martyrs for the cause of both the Reformation and the Counter-Reformation in England. The earliest Protestant martyrs suffered in Henry VIII's reign, among them Thomas Bilney, who was burnt at Norwich for heresy in 1531. Soon it was the turn of those who supported Rome and Sir Thomas More, Lord Chancellor of England, and John Fisher, Bishop of Rochester, were both executed in 1535 for opposing the Act of Succession. They were canonized by Pope

dulus (*c*.113), Timothy and Maura (298), Alexander and Antonina (313), Juvenal of Narni (369), Diodorus and Rhodopianus (early 5th cent.), Conleth of Kildare (*c*.519), Scannal (p.563), Adalsindis of Bèze (*c*.680), Philip of Zell (*c*.770), Ethelwin of Lindsey (8th cent.), Ansfridus of Utrecht (1010), Bl Ventura Spellucci (12th cent.), Bl Alexander of Foigny (1229), Bl Alexander Vincioli (1363).

P.Edmundus Campianus, et P. Alexander Briantus Angli S.I. pro
Fide suspensi et secti Londini in Anglia A. 1581. 1 Decembris.

P. Alexander Briantus Anglus Soc: IESV post crudelem in Equuleo sæ:
pius, ex summis pedum et manuum articulis, distensionem, cum P. Campiano
suspensus et dissectus in Anglia Londini A 1581. 1 Decembris.
C. Screta, d: M. Küsell F

The fate of the Catholic martyrs depicted in a Jesuit book of 1675.

Pius XI in 1935 and are commemorated on 9 July.

During the reign of Mary Tudor, when papal supremacy was restored over the Church of England, some three hundred people were burnt as heretics. They included Thomas Cranmer, Archbishop of Canterbury; Hugh Latimer, Bishop of Worcester; and Nicholas Ridley, Bishop of London; but many others were ordinary men and women who held to the Reformed religion.

The accession of Elizabeth I was followed by the restoration of royal supremacy and changes in worship and doctrine. Many Roman Catholic priests and laypeople were executed or died in prison. They were arrested on various charges, but the real reason was their refusal to deny their faith. Men like Edmund Campion and Edmund Arrowsmith died because they were priests and others suffered because they harboured priests or refused to accept the Elizabethan settlement. Often the motives for persecution were not purely religious but the fear of foreign domination. Nevertheless in canonizing the Roman Catholic martyrs in 1970, the Pope brought home the real courage and devoted loyalty of those who lived and died in England for their faith.

It is not our death that ever we feared, but we knew that we were not lords of our own lives.

EDMUND CAMPION at his trial

5 May

Irenaeus, Peregrinus and Irene (c.300), Jovinian of Auxerre (p.300), Euthymius of Alexandria (?), Silvanus of Rome (?), Maximus of Jerusalem (c.350), Nectarius of Vienne (375), Eulogius of Edessa (p.381), Brito of Trèves (386), Hilary of Arles (449), Nicetus of Vienne (p.449), Geruntius of Milan (c.470), Crescentiana (5th cent.), Hydroc (5th cent.), Gibrian (c.515), Theodore of Bologna (c.550), Sacerdos of Saguntum (c.560), Waldrada of Metz (c.620), Maurontus of Douai (701), Echa of Crayk (767), Angelus of Jerusalem (1220), Jutta of Kulmsee (1250), Bl John Haile (1535), Pius V (1572), Mary Magdalen Sophia Barat (1865).

6 May

Evodius of Antioch (c.67), Lucius of Cyrene (1st cent.), Heliodorus, Venustus and Comp. (3rd cent.), Theodotus of Cyprus (c.325), Protogenes of Syria (4th cent.),

The Martyrs' Memorial, Oxford, dedicated to the Anglican martyrs.

Benedicta of Rome (6th cent.), Eadbert of Lindisfarne (698), Petronax of Monte Cassino (*c*.747), Bl Bonizella Piccolomini (1300), Bl Prudentia Castori (1492), BB Antony Middleton and Edward Jones (1590).

7 May

Juvenal of Beneventum (*c*.132), Flavia Domitilla, Euphrosyna and Theodora (2nd cent.), Quadratus of Herbipolis (*c*.257), Flavius, Augustus and Augustine (*c*.300), Domitian of Huy (*c*.560), Michael Ulumbijski (6th cent.), Liudhard of Canterbury (*c*.600), Serenicus and Serenus (*c*.669), Placid of Autun (*c*.675), John of Beverley (721), Peter of Pavia (*c*.735), Bl Frederick of Hirsau (*c*.1070), Stanislaus of Cracow (1079), Villanus of Gubbio (1237), Bl Rose Venerini (1728).

8 May

Dionysius of Vienne (p.193), Acacius of Byzantium (*c*.303), Victor the Moor (303), Helladius of Auxerre (387), Odrian of Waterford (?), Desideratus of Bourges (6th cent.), Boniface IV (615), Ida of Nivelles (652), Benedict II (685), Wiro, Plechelm and Otger (*c*.739), Peter of Tarantaise (1175), Bl Amatus Ronconi (1292), Bl Angelus of Masaccio (1458).

9 May

Hermas of Rome (1st cent.), Pachomius of Tabenna (346), Gregory Nazianzen (390), John of Chalon (*c*.475), Beatus of Beatenberg (?), Gofor of Llanover (?), Tudy of Landevennec (5th cent.), Gerontius of Cervia (501), Sanctan of Kill-da-Les (6th cent.), Vincent of Montes (*c*.950), Gregory of Ostia (*c*.1044), Brynoth of Scara (1317), Bl Nicholas Albergati (1443), Bl Thomas Pickering (1679).

10 May

Aurelian of Limoges (1st or 3rd cent.), Calepodius, Palmatius, Simplicius, Felix, Blanda and Comp. (232), Gordian (*c*.362) and Epimachus (*c*.250), Alphius, Philadelphius and Cyrinus (251), Dioscorides of Smyrna (?), Quartus and Quintus (?), Comgall of Bangor (601), Cataldus of Taranto (7th cent.), Solangia of Bourges (*c*.880), Isidore the Farmer (1170), William of Pontoise (1192), Bl Beatrix d'Estell (1226), Antoninus of Florence (1459), Bl John of Avila (1569).

11 May

Evellius of Pisa (*c*.66), Anastasius and Comp. (251), Anastasius of Lérida (?), Anthimus of Rome (303), Maximus, Bassus and Fabius (304), Sisinius, Diocletius and Florentius (304), Principia of Rome (*c*.420), Mamertus of Vienne (475), Possessor of Verdun (*c*.485), Walbert of Hainault (*c*.678), Gangulphus of Burgundy (760), Fremund of Dunstable (9th cent.), Majolus of Cluny (994), Illuminatus of Sanseverino (*c*.1000), Walter of L'Esterp (1070), Gualfardus of Verona (1127), Illuminatus (*c*.1230), Bl Julian Cesarello de Valle (?), Bl Albert of Bergamo (1279), Bl Vivaldus (1300), Bl Benincasa of Montechiello (1426), Bl Aloysius Rabata (1490), BB James Walworth and John Rochester (1537), Francis de Geronimo (1716).

12 May

Nereus and Achilleus (*c*.100), Philip of Arirone (?), Dionysius of Asia (304), Epiphanius of Salamis (403), Pancras of Rome (*c*.304), Diomma of Kildimo (5th cent.), Modoald of Trèves (640), Rictrudis of Marchiennes (688), Germanus of Constantinople (732), Ethelhard of Canterbury (803), Dominic de la Calzada (*c*.1109), Bl Gemma of Goriano (1249), Bl Francis Patrizi (1328), Bl Imelda Lambertini (1333), Bl Jane of Portugal (1490), Bl John Stone (1538).

13 May

Glyceria of Trajanopolis (*c*.177), Mucius of Byzantium (304), Valerian of Auxerre (p.350), Onesimus of Soissons (*c*.361), Martyrs of Alexandria (372), Servatius of Tongres (384), John the Silent (558), Hermenegild (585), Agnes of Poitiers (588), Mael of Bardsey (6th cent.), Natalis of Milan (751), Anno of Verona (780), Merewenna of Rumsey (*c*.970), Bl Fortis Gabrielli (1040), Bl Gerard of Villamagna (1242), Bl Juliana of Norwich (*c*.1423), Robert Bellarmine (1621), Andrew Fournet (1834).

14 May

Justa, Justina and Henedina (*c*.130), Victor and Corona (*c*.176), Dyfan (2nd cent.), Pontius of Cimiez (*c*.258), Boniface of Tarsus (*c*.307), Boniface of Ferentino (6th cent.), Carthage the Younger (*c*.637), Erembert of Toulouse (*c*.672), Bl Tuto of Ratisbon (930), Halward of Oslo (*c*.1043), Bl Giles of Santarem (1265), Michael Garicoits (1863), Maria Mazzarello (1881).

15 May

Torquatus, Ctesiphon, Secundus, Indaletius, Caecilius, Hesychius, and Euphrasius (1st cent.), Isidore of Chios (*c*.250), Peter, Paul, Andrew and Dionysia (251), Cassius, Victorinus, Maximus, and Comp. (260), Caesarea (?), Simplicius of Sardinia (304), Achilles of Thessaly (*c*.330), Silvanus of Tabennisi (4th cent.), Dympna of Gheel (?), Hilary of Galeata (558), Colman McO'Laoighse (6th cent.), Gerebern (7th cent.), Britwin of Beverley (*c*.733), Rupert and Bertha (9th cent.), Nicholas the Mystic (925), Bl Leonard of Camaldoli (*c*.1250), Bl Andrew Abellón (1450), Bl Mary Magdalen Albrizzi (1465), John Baptist de la Salle (1719).

16 May

Fort of Bordeaux (?1st cent.), Peregrinus of Terni (*c*.138), Peregrinus of Auxerre (*c*.304), Aquilinus and Victorian (?), Felix and Gennadius (?), Maxima of Fréjus (?), Hilary of Pavia (376), Audas of Persia (420), Possidius of Calama (450), Primael of Quimper (*c*.450), Carantac of Wales (5th cent.), Fidolus of Aumont (*c*.540), Germerius of Toulouse (*c*.560), Domnolus of Le Mans (581), Brendan the Voyager (*c*.583), Carantock (6th cent.), Honoratus of Amiens (*c*.600), Annobert of Séez (p.689), Francoveus (7th cent.), Ubald Baldassini (1160), Adam of Fermo (p.1212), Simon Stock (1265), John Nepomucen (1393).

17 May

Andronicus and Junias (1st cent.), Restituta of Carthage (255 or 304), Adrio, Victor and Basilla (?), Heradius, Paul, Aquilinus and Comp. (303), Solochon and Comp. (305), Maden of Cornwall (*c*.545), Cathan (?), Maildulf of Malmesbury (673), Bl Rasso of Grafrath (953), Silaus of Lucca (1100), Thethmar of Neumünster (1152), Paschal Baylon (1592).

18 May

Venantius of Camerino (*c*.250), Theodotus, Thecusa, Alexandra, Claudia, Faina, Euphrasia, Matrona and Julitta (304), Felix of Spoleto (*c*.304), Dioscorus of Kynopolis (*c*.305), Potamon of Heraclea (*c*.340), Merililaun (8th cent.), Feredarius of Iona (p.863), Elgiva of Shaftesbury (971), Eric of Sweden (1160), Bl William de Naurose (1369), Bl Camilla Gentili (1486), Felix of Cantalice (1587).

May

19 May

Pudentiana of Rome (*c.*160), Pudens of Rome (2nd cent.), Calocerus and Parthenius (250), Philoterus of Nicomedia (303), Cyriaca and Comp. (307), Cyril of Trèves (5th cent.), Hadulph of Saint-Vaast (*c.*728), Bl Alcuin of York (804), Dunstan of Canterbury (988), BB Bellatanus and Savinus (?), Bl Humiliana de' Cerchi (1246), Peter Celestine (1296), Ivo Hélory (1303), Bl Augustine Novello (1309), Bl Peter de Dueñas (1397), Bl Peter Wright (1651), Bl Joaquina Vedruna de Mas (1854).

ST DUNSTAN

The son of a West Saxon nobleman, Dunstan abandoned the life of a courtier to become a monk at Glastonbury Abbey and about the year 943 he became its abbot. Under him the monastery was reformed and the original purity of the Benedictine rule restored. It soon became one of the chief religious and educational centres in the country.

In 957 Dunstan was made Bishop of Worcester, then Bishop of London and in 959 Archbishop of Canterbury. He embarked upon a thorough reform of the Church of England, which had suffered severely during the Viking raids of the previous century. He founded over forty new monasteries, among them the great abbeys of Peterborough, Ely and Thorney. The

restoration of monastic life, which seems to have practically disappeared in England by the middle of the tenth century, was almost entirely his work.

He zealously supported the cause of learning and made his own contribution to the artistic revival of the century. Dunstan has been adopted as the patron saint of goldsmiths, and there is a legend that, while he was making a chalice, the devil once appeared to tempt him. He showed himself in the guise of a beautiful maiden, but Dunstan recognized him and seized the maiden's nose with his red-hot tongs!

God forbid that for the sake of any mortal man or to save my own life, I should set aside the law which Christ my Lord, the Son of God, established in His Church.

DUNSTAN

20 May

Plautilla of Rome (*c.*67), Thalelaeus, Asterius, Alexander and Comp. (*c.*284), Basilla of Rome (304), Aquila of Egypt (311), Baudelius of Nimes (2nd or 3rd cent.), Hilary of Toulouse (4th cent.), Anastasius of Brescia (610), Austregisilus of Bourges (624), Theodore of Pavia (778), Ethelbert of East Anglia (793), Bl Guy de Gherardescha (1099), Bl Orlando of Vallumbrosa (1242), Bl Albert of Bologna (1245), Bernardine of Siena (1444), Bl Columba of Rieti (1501).

Glastonbury Abbey ruins.

The Venerable Bede presents a book to the Bishop of Lindisfarne.

21 May

Nicostratus, Antiochus and Comp. (303), Secundinus of Córdova (c.306), Polyeuctus, Victorius and Donatus (?), Timothy, Polius and Eutychius (?), Valens and Comp. (?), Secundus and Comp. (357), Hospitius of Cap-Saint-Hospice (c.580), Barrfoin of Killbarron (6th cent.), Gollen of Denbighshire (7th cent.), Isberga of Aire (c.800), Ageranus of Bèze (888), Theobald of Vienne (1001), Godric of Finchale (1170), Bl Benvenutus of Recanati (1289), Bl Catherine of Cardona (1577), Theophilus of Corte (1740).

22 May

Ausonius of Angoulême (1st or 3rd cent.), Marcian of Ravenna (c.127), Castus and Aemilius (c.250), Quiteria (?), Basiliscus of Comana (312), Faustinus, Timothy and Venustus (c.362), Helen of Auxerre (p.418), Julia of Corsica (5th cent.), Romanus of Subiaco (c.560), Fulk of Castrofurli (p.600), Conall of Inniscoel (7th cent.), Boethian of Pierrepont (7th cent.),

Aigulphus of Bourges (c.835), John of Parma (c.982), Bobo of Provence (c.985), Atto of Pistoia (1153), Peter Parenzi (1199), Humilitas of Faenza (1310), BB John of Cetina and Peter de Dueñas (1397), Rita of Cascia (1457), Bl John Forest (1538), BB Peter of the Assumption and John Baptist Machado (1617), Bl Matthias of Arima (1622), Bl Michael Ho-Dinh-Hy (1857).

23 May

Epitacius and Basileus (1st cent.), Euphebius of Naples (?), Desiderius of Langres (?), Martyrs of Cappadocia (303), Martyrs of Mesopotamia (c.307), Mercurialis of Forlì (c.406), Quintian, Lucius and Julian (c.430), Eutychius and Florentius (6th cent.), Goban of Old-Leighlin (6th or 7th cent.), Desiderius of Vienne (608), Syagrius of Nice (c.787), Michael of Synnada (c.820), Guibertus of Gembloux (962), Ivo of Chartres (1115), William of Rochester (1201), Bl Bartholomew Pucci-Franceschi (1330), Andrew Bobola (1657), Bl Crispin of Viterbo (1750), St John Baptist de Rossi (1764).

May

24 May

Joanna (1st cent.), Manahen (1st cent.), Susanna, Marciana, Palladia and Comp. (2nd cent.), Donatian and Rogatian (299), Afra of Brescia (?), Meletius (?), Robustian of Milan (?), Zoellus, Servilius, Felix, Sylvanus and Diocles (?), Vincent of Porto (?), Vincent of Lérins (c.445), Patrick of Bayeux (c.469), Bl John of Montfort (1177), Bl William of Dongelberg (c.1250), Gerard de Lunel (1298), Bl Philip Suzanni (1306), Bl John del Prado (1636).

25 May

Zachary of Vienne (c.106), Urban I (230), Pasicrates, Valention and Comp. (c.302), Dionysius of Milan (c.359), Maximus and Venerandus (c.384), Zenobius of Florence (c.390), Leo of Troyes (c.550), Injuriosus and Scholastica (c.550), Aldhelm of Sherborne (709), Dunchadh of Iona (717), Egilhard of Cornelimünster (881), Gennadius of Astorga (c.936), Gregory VII (1085), Bl Claritus Voglia (1348), Bl Peter Van (1857).

26 May

Alphaeus (1st cent.), Quadratus the Apologist (c.130), Simitrius and Comp. (c.159), Eleutherius (189), Fugatius and Damian (2nd cent.), Priscus and Comp. (c.272), Felicissimus, Heraclius and Paulinus (303), Quadratus of Africa (?), Becan of Cork (6th cent.), Augustine of Canterbury (604) (feast on the 28th), Odulvald of Melrose (698), Bl Regintrudis of Nonnberg (c.750), Guinizo of Montecassino (c.1050), Lambert Péloguin (1154), Berengarius of St Papoul (1093), Bl Eva of Liège (c.1266), Philip Neri (1595), Bl Mariana de Paredes (1645), Bl Peter Sanz (1747), BB John Hoan and Matthew Phun (1861).

ST PHILIP NERI

Known as the 'Second Apostle of Rome', Philip Neri was born in Florence in 1515. He refused the offer of a rich relative to make him a merchant and at the age of eighteen went to Rome, where for many years he cared for the poor, the sick, and the pilgrims who came to the city. He also spent many hours in solitary prayer in the catacombs.

Yet he was by no means a killjoy but enjoyed life and scandalized some religious people by encouraging the young to join in dances and games. In 1551 he was persuaded to become a priest and gathered around him a number of fellow-workers. The centre of their activities was a hall turned into an oratory for sermons, lectures, prayer meetings and music. There he held the popular services from which the word 'oratorio' comes. With the priests who joined him he founded a religious order, the Congregation of the Oratory. This was to carry on his work and it established oratories in Italy, France and Spain. In these there were preaching and services for the people, as well as the clubs and societies which have now become part of the life of all churches and parishes. Venerated as a saint during his lifetime, Philip Neri was canonized in 1622.

For one who truly loves God, there is nothing more difficult and painful than to remain alive.

PHILIP NERI

27 May

Restituta and Comp. (272), Julius of Dorostorum (c.302), Eutropius of Orange (p.475), John I (526), Ranulphus of Arras (c.700), The Venerable Bede (735), Bruno of Würzburg (1045), Frederick of Liège (1121), Bl James of Nocera (1300), Bl Bartholomaea Bagnesi (1577), Bl Matthew Gam (1847).

THE VENERABLE BEDE

His *History of the English Church and People*, from Caesar's invasion to the year 731, has earned Bede the title of the 'Father of English History'. At the age of seven, he was sent to the monastery of Wearmouth in Northumberland and transferred to Jarrow, probably when it was founded about the year 681. He spent the rest of his life there, 'always writing, always praying, always reading, always teaching'. He was ordained priest when he was about thirty, and this dignity, which was not common then among monks, led to him being styled Venerable, the usual title by which priests were then addressed.

His outward life was uneventful. He visited Lindisfarne and York, but it seems unlikely that he ever went beyond his native Northumberland. He was a most voluminous writer, completing more than forty works, and yet men wondered how a man so constant in prayer should have time even to study. 'All my life', he wrote, 'I have given all my labour to the study of the Scriptures; and amid the observance of monastic discipline and the daily duty of chanting in the church, I have ever delighted to learn or teach or write.'

He died on Ascension Eve, just after he had dictated the last sentence of his translation of St John's Gospel, with the *Gloria* on his lips. He was buried at Jarrow, but in the eleventh century his relics were transferred to Durham Cathedral near to St Cuthbert's shrine where they now remain.

28 May

Crescens, Dioscorides, Paul and Helladius (*c*.244), Heliconis of Thessalonica (*c*250), Emilius, Felix, Priamus and Lucian (?), Senator of Milan (480), Senator of Pavia (480), Caraunus of Chartres (5th cent.), Justus of Urgell (p.527), Germanus of Paris (576), Augustine of Canterbury (604), William of Gellone (812), Podius of Florence (1002), Bernard of Menthon (*c*.1081), Bl Lanfranc of Canterbury (1089), BB Stephen of Narbonne and Comp. (1242), Bl Margaret Pole (1541), BB John Shert, Thomas Ford and Robert Johnson (1582), Bl Paul Hanh (1859).

ST AUGUSTINE OF CANTERBURY

When Pope Gregory the Great sent Augustine and his forty fellow-monks to evangelize England, they were so alarmed by stories of its savage people that they sought to be recalled. Gregory, however, insisted that they must go, and they landed on the Isle of Thanet, off the coast of Kent, in 597. They were welcomed by the Christian wife of Ethelbert, King of Kent, and were allowed to live in Canterbury and use the ancient St Martin's Church, which had been built by Christians in Roman times.

After a few months, Ethelbert was baptized and his people with him. Augustine then went to Arles to be consecrated Archbishop of Canterbury and, on his return, built on the site of an old Roman basilica the monastery of Christ Church, which later became the Cathedral. He laboured for seven years among the people, who were at first antagonistic and suspicious, but the sincerity of his life slowly but surely attracted them to his faith. His final act, shortly before he died at Canterbury, was to consecrate two of his monks as bishops to extend the evangelization of England.

We pray Thee, O Lord, in all Thy mercy, that Thy wrath and anger may be turned away from this city and from Thy holy house, for we are sincere. Alleluia.

Prayer of Augustine and his monks
on entering Canterbury

29 May

Cyril of Caesarea (*c*.251), Conon, Father and Son (275), Restitutus of Rome (*c*.299), Maximus of Verona (6th cent.), Theodosia and Comp. (*c*.303), Maximinus of Trèves (*c*.349), Sisinius, Martyrius and Alexander (397), Eleutherius of Rocca d'Arce (?), Venantius of Lérins (*c*.400), Theodosia of Constantinople (745), John de Atarés (*c*.750), Votus, Felix and John (*c*.750), Gerald of Macon (927), Bl Ulric of Einsiedeln (p.978), Bl Gerardesca of Pisa (*c*.1260), Bl Peter Petroni (1361), Bl Richard Thirkeld (1583), Mary Magdalen de'Pazzi (1607).

30 May

Gabinus and Crispulus (*c*.130), Felix I (274), Sycus and Palatinus (?), Basil and Emmelia (*c*.370), Isaac of Constantinople (*c*.410), Exuperantius of Ravenna (418), Madelgisilus of Monstrelet (*c*.655), Anastasius of Pavia (680), Hubert of Brétigny (*c*.714), Walstan of Norfolk (1016), Ferdinand III (1252), Bl Andrew Franchi (1401), Joan of Arc (1431), Bl James Bertoni (1483), BB Laurence Richardson, Luke Kirby, Thomas Cottam S.J. and William Filby (1582), BB Maurus William Scott and Richard Newport (1612).

ST JOAN OF ARC

Joan was a peasant girl at Domremy in Lorraine and she grew up while large parts of France were ruled by the English and their allies, the Burgundians.

When she was seventeen, she heard the voices of St Catherine, St Michael, and St Margaret telling her that she had been chosen to help the King of France reconquer his kingdom. Eventually, by sheer persistence, she reached Charles VII and after much scrutiny of her claims, she was given a military command. Clad in a suit of white armour, she secured the relief of Orleans and persuaded Charles to be crowned at Rheims. Her action virtually saved France.

In 1430 she was captured by the Burgundians and sold to the English, who were determined to discredit her. She was brought before the court of the Bishop of Beauvais at Rouen and charged with witchcraft and heresy. The judges declared her visions 'false and diabolical' and handed her over to the English to be burnt at the stake. The sentence was carried out in the market-place at Rouen and her ashes were thrown into the Seine.

Twenty-five years later, at the request of her mother and brothers, her case was reviewed, and she was declared innocent. She was canonized in 1920 as a holy maiden and two years later was declared the second patron saint of France.

St Joan of Arc.

31 May

Petronilla of Rome (1st cent.), Crescentian of Sassari (*c*.130), Hermias of Cappadocia (170), Cantius, Cantian, Cantianilla and Protus (*c*.304), Lupicinus of Verona (5th cent.), Paschasius of Rome (*c*.512), Winnow, Mancus and Myrbad (6th cent.), Mechtildis of Diessen (1160), Bl Nicholas of Vaucelles (*c*.1163), Bl James Salomone (1314), Vitalis of Monte Subasio (1370), Bl Camilla Varani (1527), Angela de'Merici (1540), Bl Thomas Du (1839).

1 June

Thespesius of Cappadocia (*c*.230), Ischirion and Comp. (250), Felinus and Gratian (250), Reverianus, Paul and Comp. (272), Crescentian of Saldo (*c*.287), Firmus (*c*.290), Secundus of Amelia (304), Proculus of Bologna (*c*.304), Pamphilus and Comp. (309), Tegla of Denbighshire (?), Juventius (?), Clarus of Aquitaine (?), Fortunatus of Spoleto (*c*.400), Caprasius of Lérins (*c*.430), Ruadan of Cornwall (5th cent.), Herveus of Brittany (*c*.575), Wistan of Evesham (849), Simeon of Trèves (1035), Gaudentius of Ossero (1044), Atto of Oca (*c*.1044), Eneco of Oña (1057), Conrad of Trèves (1066), Bl Ermengardis (*c*.1147), Bl Theobald Roggeri (1150), BB Bernard, Mary and Gracia (*c*.1180), Bl Conrad of Hessen (13th cent.), Bl John Pelingotto (1304), Bl James of Strepar (1411), Bl Herculanus of Piegare (1541), Bl John Storey (1571), BB Alphonsus Navarrete, and Ferdinand of St Joseph Ayala and Comp. (1617), Bl Felix of Nicosia (1787).

2 June

Photinus, Sanctus, Vetius, Epagathus, Maturus, Ponticus, Biblides, Attalus, Alexander, Blandina and Comp. (177), Erasmus of Formiae (303), Marcellinus and Peter (304), Eugene I (657), Adalgis (*c*.686), Bodfan (7th cent.), Bl Guy of Acqui (1070), Stephen of Corvey (*c*.1075), Nicholas Peregrinus (1094), John de Ortega (*c*.1150), BB Sadoc and Comp. (1260).

3 June

Pergentinus and Laurentinus (251), Lucillian, Claudius, Hypatius, Paul and Dionysius (273), Paula of Nicomedia (*c*.273), Caecilius of Carthage (3rd cent.), Hilary of Carcassonne (4th cent.), Clotilde of France (545), Liphardus of Orleans (*c*.550), Oliva of Anagni (?), Cronan the Tanner (617), Kevin of Glendalough

(*c*.618), Genesius of Clermont (662), Glunshallaich (7th cent.), Isaac of Córdova (852), Bl Gausmarus of Savigny (984), Davinus of Lucca (1051), Albert of Como (*c*.1092), Morandus of Cluny (*c*.1115), Conus of Lucania (*c*.1200), Bl Andrew Caccioli (*c*.1264), BB Peregrinus I and Peregrinus II (*c*.1291), Bl John Grande (1600), BB Martyrs of Uganda (1887).

THE MARTYRS OF UGANDA

In the later years of the nineteenth century an amazing growth of the Christian Church took place in Uganda through Anglican and Roman Catholic missions which entered the country simultaneously, but within a few years some of the early converts had paid for their faith with their lives.

In 1884, Mwanga, a young man of eighteen, became King of the Baganda, the ruling people in the country. Moved to panic by Arab traders who told him that Europeans intended to annex his territory, he instituted a persecution of native Christians which lasted over two years.

Among those who perished were a number of converts of the White Fathers, boys and young men from thirteen to thirty years old, who were treated with terrible cruelty. It has been said that 'their courage rivalled that of the early martyrs'. One of them was Charles Luanga, an official at the King's court, who in 1934 was made the patron saint of African youth.

They were joined in their martyrdom by converts of the Church Missionary Society, which was led in Uganda by Alexander Mackay, 'Mackay of the Great Lake', who had been a Scottish engineer. Several of 'Mackay's boys', who were pages of the King, were thrown on to a fire, their arms being first hacked off that they might not struggle in the flames. Though the youngest was only eleven, they died singing a Christian hymn they had learnt from Mackay.

Daily, daily sing to Jesus;
Sing, my soul, His praises due.

4 June

Clateus of Brescia (*c*.64), Aretius and Dacian (?), Quirinus of Tivoli (?), Rutilus and Comp. (?), Saturnina of Arras (?), Quirinus of Croatia (308), Metrophanes of Byzantium (325), Optatus of Milevis (*c*.387), Nennoc (*c*.467), Petroc of Cornwall (*c*.594), Breaca of Cornwall (5th-6th cent.), Buriana of Cornwall (6th cent.), Croidan, Medan and Degan (6th cent.), Alexander of Verona (8th cent.), Adegrin of Baume

(939), Elsiar of Lavedan (*c.*1050), Walter of Fontenelle (1150), Cornelius McConchailleach (1176), Walter of Serviliano (*c.*1250), Bl Margaret of Vau-le-Duc (1277), Bl Boniface of Villiers (*c.*1280), Bl Francis Ronci (1294), Francis Caracciolo (1608), Bl Luke Loan (1840), Vincenza Gerosa (1846).

5 June

Florentius, Julian, Cyriacus, Marcellinus and Faustinus (250), Marcian, Nicanor, Apollonius and Comp. (*c.*304), Zenais, Cyria, Valeria and Marcia (?), Dorotheus of Tyre (*c.*362), Tudno of Caernarvon (6th cent.), Dorotheus the Archimandrite (*c.*640), Boniface and Comp. (755), Felix of Fritzlar (*c.*790), Sancho of Córdova (851), Bl Meinwerk of Paderborn (1036), Dorotheus the Younger (11th cent.), Franco of Asserigo (*c.*1275), Bl Ferdinand of Portugal (1443).

ST BONIFACE

Boniface totally changed the map of Europe. His continual battles against paganism and his establishment of a proper church structure, with bishoprics and religious houses, brought order as well as religion to Germany. Born in Crediton in 680 and christened Winfred, he felt called to evangelize Germany, 'the land of our fathers, whose inhabitants are of our own blood'. After several false starts he managed to get established in 719 in 'Roman Germany', Thuringia, the Rhineland and Bavaria, where Christianity still survived as a struggling faith. He faced paganism head-on by felling the Oak of Thor at Geismar, near Fritzlar, and by showing that the old gods had no power he won many converts from paganism. He brought over monks and nuns from England for the schools and monasteries he founded, and created at Fulda a northern rival to the Abbey of Monte Cassino. He had been the bishop responsible for Germany since 722 but in 747 the Pope made him Archbishop of Mainz, a position he finally resigned because he was drawn back to his first love and felt called to evangelize 'barbarian Germany', Frisia and Saxony, which was entirely pagan.

Already Boniface had earned his place as one of the founders of Christian Europe and his martyrdom in pursuit of his last great goal seems oddly like an afterthought. His band of missionaries began by reclaiming areas lost to Christianity but by 755 they had moved on into North East Frisland which had never been evangelized. They were remarkably successful and many people were baptized. Boniface therefore planned

St Boniface.

a confirmation at Dokkum. It was here that he and his companions had camped beside the river, where they were set upon by an armed mob and slaughtered.

St Boniface's body was taken to his abbey at Fulda and there became the centre of pilgrimage. He left behind a Germany tied into civilized Europe and his diocesan organization survives even today. 'The Apostle of Germany' certainly earns Christopher Dawson's judgement that he 'had a deeper influence on the history of Europe than any Englishman who ever lived'.

Let us not return evil for evil; the long-expected day has come, and the time of our departure is at hand. Strengthen yourselves in the Lord, and He will redeem your souls.

Boniface to his companions at their martyrdom

6 June

Philip the Deacon (1st cent.), Martyrs of Tarsus (*c.*290), Arthemius, Candida and Paulina (302), Amantius, Alexander and Comp. (?), John of Verona (4th cent.), Nilamnon of Egypt (404), Ceratus of

Grenoble (*c*.455), Eustorgius II of Milan (518), Jarlath of Tuam (*c*.550), Alexander of Fiesole (590), Cocca of Kilcock (?), Claudius of Besançon (*c*.699), Gudwall of Wales (7th cent.), Agobard of Lyons (840), Norbert (1134), Bl Falco of Cava (1146), Bl Gilbert of Neuffons (1152), Bl Gerard Tintorio (1207), Bertrand of Aquileia (1350), Bl Gundisalvus of Azebeyro (1466), Bl Laurence of Villamagna (1535), BB John Davy, Robert Salt and Walter Pierson (1537), Bl Felicia de Montmorency (1666).

7 June

Potamioena the Younger (*c*.304), Lycarion of Egypt (?), Paul of Constantinople (*c*.350), Colman of Dromore (6th cent.), Vulphy of Abbeville (*c*.643), Meriadec of Vannes (*c*.688), Aventinus of Bagnères (732), Deochar (847), Peter, Wallabonso, Sabinianus, Wistremundus, Habentius and Jeremias (851), Bl Odo of Massay (967), Gotteschalk (1066), Landulf Variglia (1134), Robert of Newminster (1159), Meriadec II of Vannes (1302), Bl Anne of St Bartholomew (1626), Antony Mary Gianelli (1846).

8 June

Maximinus of Aix (1st cent.), Calliope (*c*.250), Sallustian of Sardinia (?), Melania the Elder (*c*.400), Bron of Cassel (*c*.511), Gildard of Rouen (*c*.514), Heraclius of Sens (*c*.515), Victorinus (543), Severinus of Sanseverino (550), Medard of Noyon (*c*.558), Levan (6th cent.), Eustadiola of Moyen-Moutier (690), Clodulphus of Metz (696), Muirchu (7th cent.), Syra of Troyes (7th cent.), Robert of Frassinoro (p.1070), William of York (1154), Bl John Rainuzzi (*c*.1330), Bl Pacificus of Cerano (1482).

9 June

Vincent of Agen (*c*.292), Primus and Felician (*c*.297), Pelagia of Antioch (*c*.311), Julian of Syria (*c*.370), Maximian of Syracuse (594), Columba of Iona (597), Baithin of Iona (*c*.598), Cumian of Bobbio (1st half of 8th cent.), Richard of Andria (p.1196), BB Diana, Caecilia and Amiata (13th cent.), Bl Silvester Ventura (1348), Bl Henry the Shoemaker (1666), Bl Anne Mary Taigi (1837).

10 June

Crispulus and Restitutus (1st cent.), Getulius, Caerea-

St Margaret of Scotland.

lis, Amantius and Primitivus (*c*.120), Basilides, Tripos, Mandal and Comp. (275), Aresius, Rogatus and Comp. (?), Oliva of Palermo (?), Zachary of Nicomedia (?), Asterius of Petra (p.362), Timothy of Prussa (362), Maximus of Naples (4th cent.), Censurius of Auxerre (486), Maurinus of Cologne (?), Illadan of Rathlihen (6th cent.), Ithamar of Rochester (*c*.656), Landericus of Paris (*c*.661), Evermund of Fontenay (*c*.720), Landericus of Novalese (1050), Bardo of Mainz (1053), Margaret of Scotland (1093), Bogumilus of Gnesen (1182), Bl Amata of San Sisto (1270), Bl Henry of Treviso (1315), Bl Bonaventure Baduario (1386), Bl John Dominici (1419), Bl Mary Magdalen of Carpi (1546).

ST MARGARET OF SCOTLAND

Margaret's brother was Saxon heir to the English throne and after the Norman Conquest the family sought safety overseas. They were shipwrecked off the coast of Scotland where King Malcolm welcomed them and soon after fell in love with Margaret and married her. Her intention had been to become a nun but together with her husband she set about the improvement of the people of Scotland and brought up a family of eight, one of whom became the renowned Queen Maud of England. Her piety and concern for the poor was famous throughout the known world and of her the Bishop of St Andrew's said: 'All who waited on her, men as well as women, loved her, even while they feared her, and in fearing loved her.'

11 June

Barnabas (1st cent.), Felix and Fortunatus (296), Tochumra of Kilmore (?), Blitharius of Seganne (7th cent.), Herebald of Brittany (8th cent.), Bl Hugh of Marchiennes (1158), BB Peter Rodríguez, Damian Vaz and Comp. (1242), St Parisius of Treviso (1267), Bl Flora of Beaulieu (1347), Bl Paula Frasinetti (1882).

ST BARNABAS

Barnabas was a rich Levite from Cyprus, who was one of the 72 disciples of Christ. He introduced Paul to the Church and to the Apostles at whose feet he had, himself, laid all his wealth. He had lands in his native island which he had sold in order to do this and as a result was called Barnabas by the Christian Community. We do not know much about the rest of his life but he spent a part of it in missionary journeys with St Paul and may have been martyred in Cyprus.

The Church of Jerusalem sent him to Antioch from where he went to Tarsus to find Paul. Together they returned to Antioch and then back to Jerusalem where they were joined by John Mark only to set off again to

St Anthony of Padua (*G. van Herpil*).

Iconium. Because of this close connection with St Paul, Barnabas is counted as one of the Apostles.

12 June

Antonia (*c*.304), Basilides, Cyrinus, Nabor and Nazarius (?), Amphion of Cilicia (p.325), Olympius of Enos (p.343), Onuphrius of Egypt (*c*.400), Ternan of Culross (5th cent.), Cunera (?), Leo III (816), Odulphus of Stavoren (*c*.855), Gerebald of Châlons-sur-Seine (885), Marinus, Vimius and Zimius (p.1100), Christian of Clogher (1138), Bl Placid of Val d'Ocre (1248), Bl Stephen Bandelli (1450), John of Sahagún (1479), Bl Louis Naisen (1626).

13 June

Felicula of Rome (*c*.90), Aquilina of Syria (293), Fortunatus and Lucian (?), Triphyllius of Cyprus (*c*.370), Damhnade (?), Peregrinus of Aquila (*c*.600), Rambert (*c*.680), Fandilas of Peñamelaria (853), Eskill of Sweden (*c*.1080), Anthony of Padua (1231).

ST ANTHONY OF PADUA

Anthony first joined the Canons Regular at the age of fifteen and later moved to the Franciscans because he hoped to become a martyr in preaching Christianity to

St Barnabas.

St John in Prison (*left*) and Donatello's John the Baptist (*right*).

the Moslems. Instead, although he took ship for Africa, he was forced back to Italy and from there his Order sent him out preaching, so much so, that he became known as 'The Hammer of the Heretics'.

He was a great seeker after souls and is even now thought of as the saint most able to help in finding that which is lost.

The purity of his life and the effect of his sermons drew men and women to him wherever he went. It was however, not only his outward life which commanded such attention, Anthony was a man of deep spiritual experience and once he saw a vision of the Holy Family with which he has since been often pictured.

14 June

Eliseus (8th cent. BC), Marcian of Syracuse (*c*.255), Valerius and Rufinus (*c*.287), Mark of Lucera (*c*.328), Basil the Great (379), Quintian (?), Dogmael of Wales (5th–6th cent.), Etherius of Vienne (*c*.675), Psalmodius of Limoges (*c*.690), Nennus of Arran (7th cent.), Lotharius of Séez (*c*.756), Gerold of Fontenelle (806), Joseph the Hymnographer (845), Methodius the Confessor (847), Anastasius, Felix and Digna (853), Cearan the Devout (870), Bl Hartwig of Salzburg (1023), Bl Richard of St Vannes (1046), Elgar of Bardsey (*c*.1100), Bl Castora Gabrielli (1391).

June

ST BASIL THE GREAT

St Basil came from a family of saints. One set of grand-parents, his parents, his two brothers and one sister were all canonized. He himself was a great theologian, an outstanding preacher, and a founder of Eastern monasticism. He is reckoned one of the four doctors of the Eastern Church and he spent much of his life battling against the Arian heresy. He started a monastery in Pontus and as Bishop of Caesarea he continued his foundations adapting them so that they combined the advantages of contemplative and active life. His work on the Holy Ghost is still perhaps the greatest in Christian theology and his imprint on the Eastern Church continues to be strong.

15 June

Dulas of Cilicia (300), Hesychius of Dorostorum (c.302), Lybe, Leonis and Eutropia (303), Vitus, Modestus and Crescentia (?), Orsisius the Cenobite (c.380), Abraham of Saint-Cyrgues (c.480), Melan of Viviers (p.549), Vouga of Lesneven (6th cent.), Trillo of Wales (6th cent.), Landelinus of Lobbes (c.686), Domitian and Hadelinus of Lobbes (c.686), Constantine of Beauvais (c.706), Edburga of Winchester (960), Adelaide of La Cambre (1250), BB Thomas Green, Thomas Scryven and Thomas Reding (1537), St Germana Cousin (1601).

16 June

Ferreolus and Ferrutio (c.212), Quiricus and Julitta (304), Similian of Nantes (310), Actinea and Graecina (4th cent.), Tychon of Cyprus (c.450), Simplicius of Bourges (477), Cettin (5th cent.), Berthaldus (c.540), Aurelian of Arles (c.550), Colman McRoi (6th cent.), Curig of Wales (6th cent.), Ismael (6th cent.), Felix and Maurus (6th cent.), Aureus, Justina and Comp. (?), Benno of Meissen (1106), Bl Guy Vignotelli (c.1245), Lutgardis of Aywières (1246).

17 June

Nicander and Marcian (173 or 303?), Antidius of Besançon (c.265), Montanus of Gaeta (c.300), Isaurus, Innocent, Felix, Jeremias and Peregrinus (?), Manuel, Sabel and Ismael (362), Prior of Egypt (c.395), Bessarion of Egypt (c.400), Hypatius of Bithynia (c.450), Avitus of Micy (c.530), Himerius of Cremona (c.560), Briavel (?), Gundulphus of Bourges (6th cent.), Nectan of Hartland (6th cent.), Agrippinus of Como (615),

Botulph and Adulph (c.680), Molling of Wexford (697), Rambold of Ratisbon (1001), Raynerius of Pisa (1160), Bl Euphemia of Andechs (1180), Teresa of Portugal (1250), Bl Peter Gambacorta (1435), Bl Paul Burali d'Arezzo (1578), Emily de Vialan (1856).

18 June

Leontius, Hypatius and Theodulus (135?), Mark and Marcellian (c.287), Etherius of Nicomedia (c.303), Marina (?), Cyriacus and Paula (305), Ephrem the Syrian (c.379), Amandus of Bordeaux (c.431), Calogerus the Anchoret (c.486), Gregory, Demetrius and Calogerus (5th cent.), Fortunatus the Philosopher (c.569), Osmanna of Jouarre (c.700), Guy of Baume (p.940), Bl Jerome of Vallombrosa (1135), Elisabeth of Schönau (1164), Gerland of Caltagirone (13th cent.), Bl Marina of Spoleto (c.1300), Bl Hosanna of Mantua (1505), Gregory Barbarigo (1697).

19 June

Ursicinus of Ravenna (c.67), Zosimus of Spoleto (110), Gervase and Protase (?2nd cent.), Gaudentius and Culmatius (364), Innocent of Le Mans (559), Deodatus of Nevers (679), Deodatus of Jointures (c.680), Hildegrin of Châlons-sur-Marne (c.827), Bruno-Boniface (1009), Bl Odo of Cambrai (1113), Juliana Falconieri (1340), Bl Thomas Woodhouse (1573).

20 June

Novatus of Rome (c.151), Paul and Cyriacus (?), Macarius of Petra (c.350), Silverius (c.537), Florentina of Carthagena (c.636), Goban (c.670), Edburga of Caistor (late 7th cent.), Bain of Calais (c.710), Helia of Öhren (c.750), Adalbert of Magdeburg (981), John of Pulsano (1139), Benignus of Breslau (13th cent.), Bl Michelina of Pesaro (1356), BB Francis Pacheco and Comp. (1626), BB Thomas Whitbread and Comp. (1679).

21 June

Lazarus (1st cent.), Terence of Iconium (1st cent.), Urciscenus of Pavia (c.216), Cyriacus and Apollinaris (?), Rufinus and Martia (?), Martin of Tongres (c.350), Demetria (363), Eusebius of Samosata (c.379), Alban of Mainz (c.400), Corbmac of Durrow (6th cent.), Maine of Brittany (617), Leutfrid of Saint-Leufroy (738), Agofredus of Saint-Leufroy (p.738), Engelmund of Vebsen (*c*.739), Dominic of Comacchio (p.820), Ralph of Bourges (866), Bl Wolfrid of Hohentwiel (*c*.990), Raymund of Barbastro (1126), Aloysius Gonzaga (1591), Bl John Rigby (1600).

22 June

Flavius Clemens (*c*.96), Acacius and Comp. (?), Alban of Great Britain (3rd or 4th cent.), Nicaeas (*c*.414), Paulinus of Nola (431), John I of Naples (5th cent.), Aaron of Brittany (p.552), Consortia (?570), Rotrudis of Saint-Omer (*c*.869), John IV of Naples (835), Bl Lambert of Saint-Bertin (1125), Eberhard of Salzburg (1164), Bl Innocent V (1277).

23 June

Felix of Sutri (257), Agrippina of Rome (*c*.262), Zeno and Zenas (*c*.304), John of Rome (362), Moeliai of Nendrum (*c*.493), Etheldreda of Ely (679), Walhere of Dinant (?), Hidulphus of Lobbes (*c*.707), James of Toul (769), Libert of Cambrai (1076), Bl Felix of Citeaux (1113), Peter of Juilly (1136), Bl Lanfranc Beccaria (1194), Bl Mary of Oignies (1213), Bl Thomas Corsini (1343), Bl Peter James of Pesaro (*c*.1496), Bl Thomas Garnet (1608).

24 June

John the Baptist (1st cent.), Roman Martyrs under Nero (64), Faustus and Comp. (?), Amphibalus of Verulam (*c*.304), Orentius, Heros, Pharnacius, Firminus, Firmus, Cyriac and Longinus (*c*.304), Simplicius of Autun (*c*.360), Alena of Brussels (*c*.640), Agoard, Aglibert and Others (5th–7th cent.), Rumoldus of Malines (*c*.775), Theodulphus of Lobbes (776), Ivan of Bohemia (845), Henry of Auxerre (*c*.880), John of Tuy (9th cent.), Bl Erembert I of Kremsmünster (p.1050), Bl Raingardis of Marcingy (1135), Bartholomew of Durham (*c*.1193).

ST JOHN THE BAPTIST

St John was born six months before Christ in a village in Judea. His mother Elizabeth was well past childbearing age and could not believe the angel's word when he announced that she would have the child she had longed for. Her husband Zacharias was struck dumb, so that when John was born he could not say what he was to be called and had to write the name down. In choosing John, he surprised his friends as it appears not to have been a family name. It was, however, a name with a meaning and confirmed the Baptist's role as fore-runner of Christ. That perhaps had already been underlined when the Virgin Mary came from Nazareth to visit her cousin Elizabeth who welcomed her with the words 'Blessed art thou among women and blessed is the fruit of thy womb'.

John went into the wilderness, fulfilling the prophesy of Isaiah that there would be someone calling out for repentance and making the way ready for the Messiah. He clearly gathered together many adherents and, as Jesus later said, impressed them with his ascetic life and his words directed against the worldliness of his generation. It was to the wilderness and to Jordan that Christ came to be baptized. Despite the efforts of John, He insisted that the ancient prophecies should be fulfilled and the greater should be blessed by the lesser. Some time after the baptism of Christ, John was arrested and it was from prison that he sent his disciples to ask for confirmation that Jesus was indeed the One he had come to announce. His weakness after a long captivity was condemned by Jesus but his strength as a true prophet was commended. Soon afterwards, at the entreaties of Salome, John was beheaded on the orders of Herod.

25 June

Sosipater (2nd cent.), Febronia of Nisibis (304), Gallicanus of Ostia (*c*.362), Solomon of Brittany (434), Prosper of Aquitaine (*c*.463), Prosper of Reggio (*c*.466), Maximus of Turin (*c*.470), Gallicanus of Embrun (p.541), Moloc of Mortlach (*c*.572), Molonachus of Lismore (7th cent.), Eurosia of Jaca (714), Adalbert of Egmont (*c*.740), Gohardus of Nantes (843), Solomon III (874), William of Montevergine (1142), Bl Burchard of Mallersdorf (1122), Bl Henry Zdik (1150), Bl John the Spaniard (1160), Bl Guy Maramaldi (1391), BB Dominic Henares and Francis Chien (1838).

26 June

John and Paul (362), Vigilius of Trent (405), Maxentius of Poitou (*c*.515), David of Thessalonica (5th cent.), Babolenus of Fosses (*c*.677), Perseveranda of Poitiers (*c*.726), Salvius and Superius (*c*.768), Corbican (8th cent.), John of the Goths (*c*.800), Pelagius of Oviedo (925), Hermogius of Tuy (*c*.942), Bl Bartholomew de Vir (1157), Anthelmus of Belley (1178), BB Mary Magdalen Fontaine, Jane Gerard, Frances Lanel, and Teresa Fantou (1794).

June

St Peter and St Paul (*Crivelli*)

27 June

Crescens (2nd cent.), Zoilus and Comp. (*c*.301), Anectus (303), Deodatus of Nola (473), Samson Xenodochius (*c*.530), John of Chinon (6th cent.), Hadelin of Crespin (*c*.700), Arialdus of Milan (1066), Ladislas (1095), Bl Eppo of Mallersdorf (1143), Bl Benvenutus of Gubbio (1232), Ferdinand of Aragón (13th cent.), BB Joseph Heiu and Thomas Toan (1840).

28 June

Irenaeus of Lyons (*c*.202), Plutarch, Serenus, Heraclides, Heron, a second Serenus, Rhais, Potamioena and Marcella (202), Papias of Sicily (*c*.303), Crummine of Lackan (5th cent.), Austell of Cornwall (6th cent.), Benignus of Utrecht (6th cent.), Theodichildis of Jouarre (p.660), Paul I (767), Argymirus of Cordova (858), Egilo of Prüm (871), Heimrad of Hersfeld (1019), Bl Ekhard of Huysburg (1084), Almus of Balmerino (1270), Bl Paul Giustiniani (1528), Bl John Southworth (1654).

29 June

Peter and Paul (*c*.67), Mary (1st cent.), Marcellus and Anastasius (274), Syrus of Genoa (*c*.380), Benedicta of Sens (?), Cassius of Narni (558), Cocha of Ross-Benchuir (6th cent.), Salome and Judith (9th cent.), Gemma (1045).

ST PETER AND ST PAUL

On this day is celebrated the feast of two of Christ's Apostles. St Peter, said to be the first Bishop of Rome, impetuously close to our Lord and St Paul who for so long 'kicked against the pricks', but ultimately became the missionary father of the church.

St Peter was present at the crucial moments of Christ's life. It was he who needed the faith when he 'launched out into the deep' and walked upon the water, trusting His master. It was he who, in a sudden flash of genius, saw that Jesus was the Christ, the Son of the Living God. And it was to him that it was said 'Thou art Peter and upon this rock I will build My Church and the Gates of Hell shall not prevail against it'. Yet it was he who failed, at first, to believe when Christ called him out of the ship. It was he too, who denied his Lord three times and it was he for whom the Crucifixion was the end, so that he had to be found in order that he could hear of Christ's Resurrection. It is

The Visitation (*Flemish School*).

the mixture of strength and weakness; of human contradictions, in this fisherman from provincial Galilee, that comes so clearly out of the Gospels. After Easter and Pentecost, Peter was prominent in the Church and traditionally died as a martyr in Rome.

Linked with Peter is St Paul who saw himself as the 'least among the Apostles' because of his early opposition to Christianity and the way in which he fought to destroy it. His conversion on the road to Damascus lead to a life totally committed to spreading the faith. His letters remain as memorials of the directness with which he nurtured and sometimes chided the new Christian communities he had established. He too died in Rome sharing the martyr's crown. His influence upon Christianity must be counted as the greatest after Christ Himself.

30 June

Lucina of Rome (1st cent.), Astriclinian of Limoges (1st or 3rd cent.), Basilides of Egypt (205), Martial of Limoges (*c*.250), Caius and Leo (?), Ostianus of Viviers (?), Emiliana of Rome (?), Eurgain of Glamorgan (6th cent.), Bertrand of Le Mans (623), Clotsindis (*c*.700), Erentrudis of Nonnberg (*c*.718), Marcian of Pampeluna (*c*.757), Theobald of Salanigo (1066), Alrick (11th cent.), Bl Arnulf Cornibout (1228) Cist., Bl Philip Powel (1646), Bl Vincent Yen (1830).

1 July

Castus and Secundinus, Julius and Aaron with others (*c*.305), Domitian of Bebron (*c*.440), Schenute of Egypt (*c*.460), Theodoric of Mont d'Or (*c*.533), Carilefus of Anisole (*c*.536), Gall of Clermont (*c*.554), Leonorius of Pontual (*c*.570), Eparchius of Angoulême (581), Simeon Salus (p.588), Cewydd of Anglesey (6th cent.), Veep of Cornwall (6th cent.), Servan of Culross (?), Juthware (7th cent.), Arnulf of Mainz (1160), Bl Thomas Maxfield (1616).

THE PRECIOUS BLOOD

The image of the Precious Blood as a symbol for the Passion of Christ is a very old one and has always been very powerful in both Catholic and Protestant writings. This special feast is however of fairly recent date. It was promulgated for the Roman Catholic Church by Pope Pius IX in 1849 when he was still in exile from the Vatican. Naturally the Mass shares a great deal with those appointed for Passiontide and the centrality of the devotion is perhaps summed up in the words of

St John Chrysostom which are appointed to be read for Matins on this day. 'I say that the Church is founded in these things, whereof the substance came out of the Redeemer's side, namely, Baptism and the Mysteries of the Altar. It was therefore out of the side of Christ that the Church was created, just as it was out of the side of Adam that Eve was raised up to be his bride.'

2 July

Feast of the Visitation of the Blessed Virgin Mary, Acestes (1st cent.), Processus and Martinian (?), Ariston, Crescentian, Eutychian, Urban, Vitalis, Justus, Felicissimus, Felix, Marcia and Symphorosa (*c*.285), Monegundis (570), Oudaceus of Wales (*c*.600), Bl Reginald of Baume (*c*.1095), Lidanus of Sezze (1118), Otto of Bamberg (1139).

THE VISITATION OF THE BLESSED VIRGIN MARY

It is on this day that the Western Church commemorates the visit of Our Lady to her cousin Elizabeth, who was pregnant with St John the Baptist. It would have been a difficult journey which Mary undertook and the Visitation has always been seen as symbolic of the homely kindnesses associated with the Virgin. Just as Christ later will go to be baptized of John, even though infinitely greater than he, so His mother goes to visit Elizabeth whose child leaps in her womb as if in recognition. It is then that Elizabeth says the words which have now become an ever-repeated phrase in the Ave Maria 'Blessed art thou among women, and blessed is the fruit of thy womb'. She is obviously overcome at the importance of the visit and says 'And whence is this to me, that the mother of my Lord should come to me'. So the natural affections of cousins are caught up in the eternal mission in which they both share.

Perhaps the surprising thing is the late date at which the Visitation became a feast of the Church. It was the Franciscans who first observed it in the West and their devotion was confirmed at the Council of Basle. The Eastern Church has no such feast but it has struck a real chord among many people and St Francis de Sales and St Jeanne de Chantal chose it to name their new Order dedicated to the care of the sick and the poor.

3 July

Hyacinth of Cappadocia (*c*.120), Dathus of Ravenna

(190), Irenaeus and Mustiola (273), Anatolius of Alexandria (*c*.283), Mark, Mucian, an un-named boy and Paul (?), Tryphon and Comp. (?), Eulogius and Comp. (364–370), Heliodorus of Altinum (*c*.390), Anatolius of Constantinople (458), Germanus of the Isle of Man (*c*.474), Gunthiern of Brittany (*c*.500), Byblig of Wales (?), Bladus of the Isle of Man (?), Leo II (683), Cillene of Iona (*c*.752), Guthagon (8th cent.), Maelmuire O'Gorman (p.1167), Bl Raymund Lull (1315), Bernardinus Realini (1616), Bl Joseph Peter Vyen (1838), Bl Philip Minh (1853).

4 July

Osee (8th cent. BC), Aggaeus (*c*.516 BC), Namphanion and Comp. (*c*.180), Innocent, Sebastia and Comp. (?), Jucundian of Africa (?), Theodore of Cyrene (*c*.310), Sisoes of Egypt (*c*.429), Laurian of Seville (*c*.544), Finbar of Wexford (6th cent.), Bertha of Blangy (*c*.725), Andrew of Crete (740), Aurelian of Lyons (895), Odo the Good (959), Ulric of Augsburg (973), Bl Hatto of Ottobeuren (985), Procopius of Sazaba (1053), Bl William of Hirsau (1091), Albert Quadrelli (1179), Bl Henry of Albano (1188), Bl Peter of Luxemburg (1387), BB John Cornelius, Thomas Bosgrave and John Carey (1594), BB William Andleby, Edward Fulthrop, Thomas Warcop and Henry Abbot (1597).

5 July

Stephen of Reggio (1st cent.), Zoe of Rome (*c*.286), Cyrilla of Cyrene (*c*.300), Agatho and Triphina (306), Marinus, Theodotus and Sedolpha (?), Domitius of Phrygia (362), Athanasius of Jerusalem (452), Fragan and Gwen (5th cent.), Edana of West Ireland (?), Erfyl (?), Grace and Probus of Cornwall (?), Philomena of Sanseverino (*c*.500), Numerian of Trèves (*c*.666), Modwenna of Whitby (*c*.695), Modwenna of Polesworth (*c*.900), Athanasius the Athonite (920–1003), Bl Elias of Bourdeilles (1484), Antony Mary Zaccaria (1539).

6 July

Isaias (*c*.681 BC), Romulus and Comp. (*c*.90), Tranquillinus of Rome (286), Dominica of Campania (?), Rixius Varus (?), Noyala of Brittany (?), Moninne (518), Goar of Aquitaine (*c*.575), Sexburga of Ely (*c*.699), Godeleva of Ghistelles (1070), Bl Thomas Alfield (1585), BB Thirty-two Martyrs of Orange (1794), Bl Mary Rose (1797), Maria Goretti (1902).

7 July

Peregrinus, Lucian, Pompeius, Hesychius, Papius, Saturninus, Germanus and Astius (*c*.120), Pantaenus of Alexandria (*c*.216), Claudius, Nicostratus, Castorius, Victorinus and Symphorina (*c*.288), Apollonius of Brescia (?), Illidius of Clermont (385), Palladius of Ireland (432), Illtyd of Wales (*c*.505), Bonitus of Monte Cassino (*c*.582), Felix of Nantes (584), Medran and Odran (6th cent.), Ercongotha of Faremoutiers (660), Ethelburga of Faremoutiers (*c*.664), Ampelius of Milan (*c*.672), Hedda of Winchester (705), Willibald of Eichstätt (*c*.786), Maolruain of Tallagh (792), Angelelmus of Auxerre (828), Cyril and Methodius (869 and 885), Odo of Urgell (1122), Bl Benedict XI (1304), BB Roger Dickenson and Ralph Milner (1591), Bl Laurence Humphrey (*c*.1591).

8 July

Aquila and Priscilla (1st cent.), Auspicius of Trèves (p.130), Procopius of Scythopolis (303), Apollonius of Benevento (p.326), Auspicius of Toul (*c*.475), Morwenna of Cornwall (5th cent.), Landrada of Munsterbilsen (*c*.690), Kilian, Colman and Totnan (*c*.689), Withburga of Dereham (*c*.743), Arnold of Julich (p.800), Abrahamite Monks (830–840), Adrian III (885), Grimbald of Winchester (903), Edgar the Peaceful (975), Sunniva of Bergen (10th cent.), Bl Peter the Hermit (1115), Raymund of Toulouse (1118), Bl Eugene III (1153), Albert of Genoa (1239), Bl Benedict d'Alignan (1268), Elisabeth of Portugal (1336), Bl Mancius Araki (1626).

9 July

Anatolia and Audax (*c*.250), Cyril of Crete (250), Zeno and Comp. (*c*.300), Brictius of Martola (*c*.312), Patermuthius, Copras and Alexander (*c*.363), Agrippinus of Autun (538), Golvinus of Rennes (?7th cent.), Everildis of Everingham (late 7th cent.), Agilulph of Cologne (p.720), Benedict, Andrew, Barnabas and Justus (1008), Bl Jane Scopelli (1491), John Fisher and Thomas More (1535), Bl Adrian Fortescue (1539), Nineteen Martyrs of Gorkum (1572), Veronica Giuliani (1727), BB Martyrs of China II (1900).

ST THOMAS MORE

Sir Thomas More is the only saint of the Roman Church to have his martyrdom commemorated by a brass plaque in the Houses of Parliament. Just a

St Thomas More

little way down from a similar plaque reminding us of the death of King Charles I there is an inscription marking the place in Westminster Hall where Thomas More, Lord Chancellor of England and once Speaker of the House of Commons, was condemned to death for refusing to accept King Henry VIII as head of the Church.

More was a layman who had married twice and was on both occasions ideally happy. He was trained as a lawyer and in 1516 he published his book *Utopia* which won him recognition throughout Europe. He became a favourite of the King and of Cardinal Wolsey but could not accept the breaking of England's link with Rome. He was locked up in the Tower for fifteen months and finally beheaded in 1535. Nearly four hundred years later, at his canonization, Pius XI described him as the 'Martyr of the Papacy'.

10 July

Seven Brothers (c.150), Rufina and Secunda (257), Januarius, Marinus, Nabor and Felix (?), Leontius, Maurice, Daniel and Comp. (c.329), Apollonius of Sardis (early 4th cent.), Bianor and Sylvanus (4th cent.), Etto of Fescau (c.670), Paschasius of Nantes (c.680), Amelberga of Maubeuge (c.690), Amelberga of Munsterbilsen (c.770), Lantfrid, Waltram and

Elilantus (p.770), Peter of Perugia (1007), Bl Peter Tu (1840), BB Emmanuel Ruiz and Comp. (1860).

11 July

Pius I (c.154), Marcian of Iconium (243), Sidronius of Rome (c.270), Cindeus of Pamphilia (c.300), Sabinus and Cyprian (?), Januarius and Pelagia (320), Sabinus of Poitiers (5th cent.), Leontius the Younger (c.565), Drostan of Deer (c.610), Sigisbert and Placid (c.650 or 750?), Amabilis of Rouen (p.684), John of Bergamo (c.690), Hydulphus of Moyenmoutier (707), Abundius of Cordova (854), Olga of Russia (969), Turketil of Croyland (975), Bl Oliver Plunkett (1681), Bl Ignatius Delgado (1838).

12 July

Jason (1st cent.), Veronica (1st cent.), Hermagoras and Fortunatus (c.66), Proclus and Hilarion (115), Epiphana (?), Paulinus of Antioch and Comp. (?), Marciana of Toledo (c.303), Nabor and Felix (c.304), Paternian of Bologna (c.470), Viventiolus of Lyons (524), Proculus of Bologna (542), Menulphus of Quimper (7th cent.), Ansbald of Prüm (886), John the Georgian (c.1002), John Gualbert (1073), Leo I of Cava (1079), Benno of Osnabruck (1088), Bl Lambert of Morimond (1163), Bl Andrew of Rinn (1462), Bl David Gonson (1541), Bl John Jones (1598), BB Japanese Martyrs (1626), Bl Peter Khanh (1842).

13 July

Silas (1st cent.), Anacletus (1st cent.), Serapion of Macedonia (c.195), Myrope of Chios (c.251), Brigid and Maura (5th cent.), Dofgan of Wales (5th cent.), Eugene, Salutaris, Muritta and Comp. (505), Mildred of Thanet (c.700), Turiaf of Dol (c.750), Bl Berthold of Scheda (c.1214), Bl James of Voragine (c.1298), Bl Thomas Tunstal (1616), Bl Nicholas The (1838).

14 July

Phocas of Sinope (117), Heraclias of Alexandria (247), Cyrus of Carthage (?), Justus of Rome (?), Felix of Como (c.390), Idus of Leinster (5th cent.), Optatian of Brescia (c.505), Marcellinus of Oldensee (c.762), Libert of Saint-Trond (783), Ulric of Cluny (1093), William of Breteuil (1130), Bonaventure (1274), Bl Humbert of Romans (1277), Bl Caspar de Bono (1604), Francis Solano (1610), Bl Richard Langhorne (1679).

St Bonaventure (*Raphael*).

ST BONAVENTURE

St Bonaventure went to Paris to study at a time in which the newly discovered works of Aristotle were making a big impact in the intellectual world and calling into question many of the teachings of theologians. It was with his close friend St Thomas Aquinas that St Bonaventure helped to produce the synthesis which gave new intellectual and devotional life to the Church in the thirteenth century. Essentially concerned with devotion, he said of his crucifix 'This is the source of all my knowledge. I study only Jesus Christ and Him crucified.'

At thirty-six Bonaventure became Father Minister of the Franciscans and brought them all back to a common observance. Bonaventure was later made a cardinal-bishop and ended his life in effecting a temporary union between the Greek and Latin Churches at the council called by Pope Gregory X.

15 July

Eutropius, Zosima and Nonosa (*c*.273), Catulinus, Januarius, Florentius, Julia and Justa (?), Felix of Pavia (?), Philip, Zeno, Narseus and Comp. (?), Antiochus and Cyriacus (3rd cent.), James of Nisibis (*c*.340), Abudimus of Tenedos (4th cent.), Apronia of Troyes (5th or 6th cent.), Eternus of Evreux (p.660), Plechelm of Guelderland (*c*.730), Donald of Ogilvy (8th cent.), Benedict of Angers (*c*.820), Adalard the Younger (*c*.824), Haruch of Werden (*c*.830), Benildis of Cordova (853), Swithun of Winchester (862), Athanasius of Naples (872), Edith of Polesworth (?925), Vladimir of Russia (1015), Henry II (1024), David of Sweden (*c*.1080), Egino of Augsburg (1122), Baldwin of Rieti (1140), Bl Angelina of Marsciano (1435), Bl Bernard of Baden (1458), BB Ignatius de Azevedo and Comp. (1570), Pompilius Mary Pirotti (1756), Bl Peter Tuan (1838).

16 July

Feast of Our Lady of Mount Carmel, Faustus (250), Domnio of Bergamo (*c*.295), Vitalian of Capua (?), Valentine of Trèves (*c*.305), Eustace of Antioch (*c*.335), Helier of Tongres (6th cent.), Tenenan of Léon (*c*.635), Reneldis and Comp. (*c*.680), Generosus of Poitou (*c*.682), Vitalian of Osimo (776), Fulrad of St-Denis (784), Sisenandus of Cordova (851), Bl Irmengard of Chiemsee (866), Bl Milo of Selincourt (1159), BB Mary St-Henry and Mary Magdalen Justamond (1794), Mary Magdalen Postel (1846).

17 July

Scillitan Martyrs (180), Generosus of Tivoli (?), Hyacinth of Paphlagonia (?), Marcellina of Rome (*c*.398), Alexius of Rome (early 5th cent.), Cynllo of Wales (5th cent.), Theodosius of Auxerre (516), Ennodius of

Pavia (521), Theodota of Constantinople (*c.*735), Fredegand of Kerkelodor (*c.*740), Turninus of Antwerp (8th cent.), Kenelm (821), Leo IV (855), Seven Apostles of Bulgaria (7th-8th cent.), Andrew and Benedict (*c.*1020), Ansuerus and Comp. (p.1066), Nerses Lambronazzi (1198), Bl Benignus Visdomini (1236), Bl Ceslas of Poland (1242), BB Carmelite Nuns of Compiègne (1794).

18 July

Symphorosa and Comp. (*c.*135), Gundenis of Carthage (203), Marina of Orense (?), Maternus of Milan (*c.*307), Emilian of Bulgaria (362), Rufilius of Forlimpopoli (382), Philastrius of Brescia (*c.*387), Pambo of the Nitrian Desert (*c.*390), Goneri of Brittany (6th cent.), Arnulf of Metz (640), Edburga and Edith (*c.*650), Theneva of Glasgow (7th cent.), Frederick of Utrecht (838), Minnborinus of Cologne (986), Bruno of Segni (1123), Herveus of Anjou (1130), Bl Bertha of Marbais (1247), Bl Alanus of Sassovivo (1313), Bl Robert of Salentino (1341), Camillus de Lellis (1614), Bl Dominic Nicholas Dat (1838).

19 July

Epaphras (1st cent.), Martin of Trèves (*c.*210), Justa and Rufina (287), Felix of Verona (?), Macrina the Younger (*c.*380), Arsenius the Great (*c.*449), Symmachus (514), Ambrose Autpertus (*c.*778), Jerome of Pavia (787), Aurea of Cordova (856), Bl Bernard of Rodez (1079), Bl Stilla of Abenberg (*c.*1141), Stephen del Lupo (1191), Bl Hroznata of Bohemia (1217), Vincent de Paul (1660), Bl John Plesington (1679).

ST VINCENT DE PAUL

It took two oxen to pay for St Vincent's university course. His father was a peasant in Ranquine in southwest France and, as the fourth son, Vincent looked after the sheep until he went off to study theology at the University of Toulouse. He was ordained priest in 1600 at the extraordinarily early age of twenty, and five years later was sent to Marseilles on business. When returning to Narbonne by sea he was captured by pirates and kept as a slave in Tunis for two years until he escaped to Avignon.

From there he went to Paris and resolved to make his way in the world. He held several important benefices and was determined to do well. Then in 1617 his style of life changed and he resolved to devote himself completely to works of charity. He founded the Congrega-

tion of Priests of the Mission and the Sisters of Charity, the first order of women entirely devoted to the care of the sick and poor. He was canonized in 1737 and was later declared the patron saint of all charitable societies.

20 July

Elias (8th cent. BC), Joseph Barsabas (1st cent.), Margaret of Antioch (*c.*304), Sabinus, Julian, Maximus, Macrobius, Cassia, Paula and ten Comp. (?), Wilgefortis (?), Rheticus of Autun (334), Barhadbesciabas (355), Aurelius of Carthage (429), Severa of Villeneuve (*c.*680), Wulmar of Samer (689), Severa of Öhren (*c.*750), Ansegisus of Fontenelle (833), Paul of Cordova (851), Etheldwitha of Winchester (903), Jerome Emiliani (1537), Bl Gregory López (1596).

21 July

Daniel (5th cent. BC), Praxedes of Rome (2nd cent.), Zoticus of Cappadocia (204), Julia of Troyes (p.272), Claudius, Justus, Jucundinus and Comp. (273), Victor, Alexander, Felician and Longinus (304), Constantine of Montecassino (*c.*560), John of Edessa (6th cent.), Arbogast of Strassburg (*c.*678), John and Benignus (707), Wastrada of Utrecht (*c.*670), Bl Oddino Barrotti (1400).

22 July

Mary Magdalen (1st cent.), Syntyche of Philippi (1st cent.), Cyril of Antioch (*c.*300), Plato of Ancyra (*c.*306), Joseph of Palestine (*c.*356), Pancharius of Besançon (*c.*356), Movean of Inis-Coosery (?), Dabius of Scotland (?), Wandrille of Fontenelle (668), Meneleus (*c.*720), of Ménat, Theophilus of Cyprus (789), Bl Augustine Fangi (1493), Laurence of Brindisi (1619), BB Philip Evans S.J. and John Lloyd (1679).

ST MARY MAGDALENE

It was Mary Magdalene who, having watched with Our Lady at the Cross of Christ, came to his tomb early in the morning and, finding it empty, turned to the man she supposed was a gardener and asked where they had taken the body. He only said one word to her – Mary – and she knew it was her Master. She is first mentioned in the Gospels as having had 'seven devils' cast out of her by Jesus. She has been identified, with the 'woman who was a sinner', who anointed the feet of Jesus and with Mary, the sister of Martha and Lazarus, who also anointed Him. In the Eastern Church, the three Marys are commemorated separately and an early legend held that Mary Magdalene went with John the Evangelist to Ephesus and died there. In the West a later story said that she had gone to France with Martha and Lazarus, and her supposed tomb at Aix-en-Provence was a pilgrimage place for medieval pilgrims. She is the patron saint of penitents and of homes for fallen women.

When blessed Mary wiped her Saviour's feet –
Whose precepts she had trampled on before –
And wore them for a jewel on her head,
Showing His steps should be the street,
Wherein she thenceforth evermore
With pensive humbleness would live and tread.

GEORGE HERBERT, *Mary Magdalene*

23 July

Apollinaris of Ravenna (1st cent.), Trophimus and Theophilus (*c*.302), Phocas the Gardener (*c*.303), Apollonius and Eugene (?), Rasyphus of Rome (?), Primitiva of Rome (?), Liborius of Le Mans (390), John Cassian (*c*.433), Valerian of Cimiez (*c*.460), Rasyphus and Ravennus (5th cent.), Romula, Redempta and Herundo (*c*.580), Martyrs of Bulgaria (9th cent.), Anne of Constantinople (*c*.918), Bl Jane of Orvieto (1306).

24 July

Victor, Stercatius and Antinogenes (304), Meneus and Capito (?), Niceta and Aquilina (?), Christina of Tuscany (?), Vincent of Rome (?), Ursicinus of Sens (*c*.380), Dictinus of Astorga (420), Declan of Ardmore (5th cent.), Lewina of Berg (5th cent.), Menefrida of Cornwall (5th cent.), Germoc of Cornwall (6th cent.), Wulfhade and Ruffinus (675), Godo of Oye (*c*.690), Christiana of Termonde (7th cent.), Sigolena of Troclar (*c*.769), Aliprandus of Ciel d'Oro (8th cent.), Romanus and David (1010), Bl Christina the Astonishing (1224), Kinga of Poland (13th cent.), Bl Nicholas Hermansson (1391), Bl John of Tossignano (1446), Bl Louise of Savoy (1503), Bl John Boste (1594), Bl Antony Turriani (1694), Bl Joseph Fernández (1838).

25 July

James the Greater (*c*.43) Apostle, Christopher (?), Florentius and Felix (235), Cucufas of Barcelona (304), Paul of Gaza (308), Valentina and Comp. (308), Nissen of Wexford (5th cent.), Magnericus of Trèves (596),

Ebrulfus of Beauvais (*c*.600), Glodesind of Metz (*c*.608), Theodemir of Cordova (851), Fagildus of Compostella (1086).

ST JAMES THE GREATER

Called 'the Greater' to distinguish him from James the Less, whose feast day is on 1 May, this James was the son of Zebedee and the elder brother of John. Like his brother, he was a fisherman in Galilee with Zebedee, in partnership with Andrew and Peter. At the call of Jesus he 'forsook all and followed Him'. In the lists of the Apostles, he is coupled with John, which meant that, when the twelve were sent out two by two to preach the Kingdom of God, they went in company, and both were nicknamed Boanerges, 'Sons of Thunder', by Jesus because of their fiery spirit. They were among the privileged group of disciples present at the Transfiguration and Gethsemane. James was martyred, in Jerusalem in 43.

From the ninth century, a legend alleged that he had preached in Spain before his martyrdom and that his body had been taken to Compostella, a city in northwestern Spain. He became the patron saint of Spain,

St James the Greater (*Nardi di Cione*).

St Mary Magdalene (*Jan van Scorel*).

and his aid was invoked in the struggle which drove the Moors from the country. His shrine was, after Rome and Jerusalem, the most popular place of pilgrimage in Christendom and his symbol, a scallop-shell, became the badge of medieval pilgrims.

26 July

Anne (1st cent.), Erastus of Corinth (1st cent.), Hyacinth (*c*.110), Pastor of Rome (*c*.160), BB George Swallowell and John Ingram (1594), Bl William Ward (1641), Bl Bartholomaea Capitanio (1833).

27 July

Maurus, Pantaleemon and Sergius (*c*.117), Felix, Julia and Jucunda (?), Hermolaus, Hermippus and Hermocrates (*c*.300), Pantaleon the Physician (*c*.305), Seven Sleepers (250–362), Celestine I (432), Ecclesius of Ravenna (532), Etherius of Auxerre (573), Anthusa of Constantinople (8th cent.), George, Aurelius,

Natalia, Felix and Liliosa (*c*.852), Bl Berthold of Garsten (1142), Bl Conrad of Ottobeuren (1227), Theobald of Marly (1247), Bl Nevolo of Faenza (1280), Bl Lucy Bufalari (1350), BB Rudolph Acquaviva and Comp. (1583), Bl Mary Magdalen Martinengo (1737).

28 July

Nazarius and Celsus (*c*.68), Victor I (*c*.199), Peregrinus of Lyons (2nd cent.), Eustace of Galatia (?), Acacius of Miletus (*c*.310), Innocent I (417), Camelian (*c*.525), Samson of Brittany (*c*.565), Arduinus of Ceprano (7th cent.), Lucidus of Aquara (*c*.938), Botwid of Sweden (1100), Bl Antony della Chiesa (1459).

29 July

Martha (*c*.80), Serapia of Syria (119), Lucilla, Flora, Eugene, Antony, Theodore and Comp. (*c*.260),

St Dominic (*El Greco*).

Callinicus of Paphlagonia (3rd cent.), Simplicius, Faustinus and Beatrix (303), Felix II (366), Faustinus of Spello (4th cent.), Seraphina (*c*.426), Prosper of Orléans (*c*.453), Lupus of Troyes (478), Kilian (7th cent.), Olav of Norway (1030), Bl Urban II (1099), William of Saint-Brieuc (1234), Bl Beatrix of Valfleury (1268), BB Louis Bertrán and two Comp. (1629), BB Joseph Tshang, Hohn Baptist Lo and Martha Wang (1861).

ST MARTHA

The sister of Lazarus and Mary at Bethany, Martha received Jesus as He passed on His way to Jerusalem. Her character is strongly contrasted with that of her sister, Mary, who as a disciple, sat 'at the feet of Jesus', while she was 'cumbered about much serving' and complained about her sister's inactivity to Him. From this incident she is frequently regarded as representing the 'active' religious life in contrast with Mary who represents the 'contemplative' life.

Martha appears again after the resurrection of Lazarus from the dead, and when Jesus had supped at the house of Simon the Leper at Bethany, Martha 'served' the meal, while Mary poured the precious ointment on His head and feet.

In accordance with her supposed visit to southern France with her sister and brother, relics of Martha were believed to have been found at Tarascon in 1187. During the next century, the Franciscans assigned her a feast day, which was gradually adopted throughout the Western Church. She has been chosen as the patron saint of housewives and inn-keepers.

30 July

Abdon and Sennen (3rd or 4th cent.), Julitta of Caesarea (303), Maxima, Donatilla and Secunda (304), Rufinus of Assisi (?), Ursus of Auxerre (508), Ermengytha of Thanet (*c*.680), Tatwin of Canterbury (734), Olav of Sweden (*c*.950), Hatebrand of Olden-Klooster (1198), Bl Manes de Guzman (1230), Bl John Soreth (1471), Bl Archangelus of Calafatimi (1460), Bl Simon of Lipnicza (1482), Bl Peter of Mogliano (1490), BB Edward Powell, Richard Featherstone and Thomas Abel (1540), Bl Everard Hanse (1581).

31 July

Calimerius of Milan (*c*.190), Fabius of Mauritania (300), Democritus, Secundus and Dionysius (?), Firmus of Tagaste (?), Germanus of Auxerre (448), Neot

of Cornwall (*c*.880), Helen of Sköfde (*c*.1160), Bl John Colombini (1367), Ignatius of Loyola (1556), BB Emmanuel Phung and Peter Qui (1859).

ST IGNATIUS LOYOLA

Born of a noble Spanish family Ignatius Loyola served in the army until he was crippled in 1521 while fighting the French. During his convalescence, he read a life of Christ and stories about the saints, which made him resolve to devote himself henceforward to the service of Christ.

He was an original 'mature' student – graduating in Paris at the age of forty-three. He gathered around him a group of nine companions, and in 1537 they went to Rome as the Company of Jesus and offered their services to Pope Paul III. Three years later he approved the Society of Jesus which was organized on military lines with Ignatius as its first General. Its members promised complete obedience to him and the Pope.

By the time of Ignatius' death, the Jesuits were established throughout Europe and had also gone as successful missionaries to Asia, Africa and America. The first ten had become one thousand and the strongest instrument of the Counter-Reformation had been forged. Ignatius was canonized in 1622; and his *Spiritual Exercises*, designed to train his followers to conquer their passions and give themselves to God, are today prescribed for all preparing themselves for the priesthood in the Roman Catholic Church.

1 August

Faith, Hope and Charity (*c*.120) VV, Bonus, Faustus, Maurus and Comp. (257), Justin of Paris (*c*.290), Leontius, Attius, Alexander and Comp. (*c*.300), Felix of Gerona (303), Cyril, Aquila, Peter, Domitian, Rufus and Menander (?), Nemesius of Lisieux (?), Verus of Vienne (p.314), Rioch of Innisboffin (*c*.480), Sidwell (?), Friardus of Nantes (*c*.577), Kenneth of Wales (6th cent.), Peregrinus of Modena (643), Jonatus of Elnone (*c*.695), Almedha of Brecknock (9th cent.) Ethelwold of Winchester (984), Bl Albert of Vallombrosa (end 11th cent.), Bl Emeric of Aosta (1318), Bl Thomas Welbourne (1605), BB Bernard Due and Dominic Dien (1838).

2 August

Maximus of Padua (*c*.195), Rutilius of Africa (250), Stephen I (257), Theodota and her three Sons (304), Boetharius of Chartres (7th cent.), Etheldritha of

Croyland (834), Plegmund of Canterbury (914), Peter of Osma (1109), Alphonsus Mary Liguori (1787).

3 August

Nicodemus (1st cent.), Gamaliel (1st cent.), Abibas (1st cent.), Aspren of Naples (1st cent.), Lydia Purpuraria (1st cent.), Hermellus of Constantinople (?), Marana and Cyra (5th cent.), Euphronius of Autun (p.475), Trea of Ardtree (5th cent.), Senach of Clonard (6th cent.), Bl Gregory of Nonantula (933), Bl Benno of Metz (940), Peter of Anagni (1105), Waltheof of Melrose (1160), Bl Augustine Gazotich (1323), Bl Peter Julian Eymard (1868).

4 August

Perpetua of Rome (c.80), Aristarchus of Salonika (1st cent.), Agabius of Verona (c.250), Tertullinus of Rome (257), Protasius of Cologne (?), Eleutherius of Constantinople (before 310), Ia and Comp. (360), Euphronius of Tours (573), Luanus (622), Raynerius of Spalatro (1180), Dominic of Guzman (1221), Bl Cicco of Pesaro (1350), BB William Horne and Comp. (1540).

ST DOMINIC

Because both men established orders of friars, Dominic and Francis of Assisi are often thought of together. In fact, despite their mutual respect, their characters were fundamentally different and their Orders complemented each other. Francis always had a mistrust for learning as a distraction from devotion while Dominic saw in it an effective weapon in the battle to win men's minds to God. He demanded that the Church should be in the forefront of intellectual enquiry in order that it might control its course and confound the critics of Christianity. His experiences in Southern France with the Albigenses confirmed his view. Even though the Dominicans had little success in arguing with the heretics, they persevered often risking their lives to preach the orthodox faith. The Order was given papal approval and was soon established throughout Europe. It specialized in teaching and study and therefore supplied the leaders of Christian thought to the universities of the later Middle Ages. To them the thirteenth-century Renaissance owes most of its glory and their contribution to the development of doctrine is unique.

Dominic combined rare organizational abilities with a devotion and piety which was the inspiration to the many who joined him.

5 August

Dedication of the Church of Our Lady of the Snow, Addai and Mari (1st cent.?), Cantidius, Cantidian and Sobel (?), Memmius of Chalons-sur-Marne (c.300), Emygdius of Ascoli (c.303), Afra of Augsburg (c.304), Paris of Teano (346), Cassian of Autun (c.350), Eusignius of Antioch (362), Nonna of Nazianzen (374), Venantius of Viviers (544), Oswald of Northumbria (642), Abel of Reims (c.571), Theodore of Cambrai (863), Gormgal of Ardoilen (1016), Thomas of Dover (1295), Bl James Gerius (1345).

6 August

Transfiguration of Our Lord Jesus Christ, Sixtus II Pope and Comp. (258), Justus and Pastor (c.304), James the Syrian (p.500), Hormisdas (523), Stephen of Cardeña and Comp. (872), Bl Octavianus of Savona (c.1128).

7 August

Claudia (1st cent.), Fautus of Milan (c.190), Peter, Julian and Comp. (c.260), Carpophorus, Exanthus, Cassius, Severinus, Secundus and Licinius (c.290), Donatian of Chalons-sur-Marne (?), Donatus and Hilary (361), Domitius and Comp. (4th cent.), Victricius of Rouen (c.409), Donatus of Besançon (before 660), Bl Jordan Forzatei (1248), Albert of Trapani (1306), Bl Vincent of Aquila (1504), Cajetan of Tienne (1547), BB Agathangelus and Cassian (1638).

8 August

Fourteen Holy Helpers, Marinus of Cilicia (290), Eleutherius and Leonides (?), Cyriacus, Largus and Comp. (304), Myron the Wonder-Worker (c.350), Hormisdas of Persia (420), Severus of Gaul (p.445), Gunifort of Pavia (?), Leobald of Fleury (650), Mummolus of Fleury (c.678), Sigrada of Soissons (c.678), Ternatius of Besançon (c.680), Agilberta of Jouarre (c.680), Ellidius of Hirnant (7th cent.), Gedeon of Besançon (c.796), Ultan of Craik (8th cent.), Bl Rathard of Andechs (815), Emilian of Cyzicus (c.820), Altman of Passau (1091), Famianus of Gallese (1150), Bl Jane of Aza (c.1190), Bl John Felton (1570).

9 August

Secundian, Marcellian and Verian (250), Numidicus

and Comp. (252), Romanus Ostiarius (258), Firmus and Rusticus (*c.*290), Amor of Burgundy (?), Domitian of Chalons-sur-Marne (?), Autor of Metz (5th cent.), Bandaridus of Soissons (566), Phelim of Kilmore (6th cent.), Serenus of Marseilles (606), Nathy of Achonry (*c.*610), Julian, Marcian and Comp. (730), Maurilius of Rouen (1067), Bl Teuzzo of Florence (*c.*1072), Bl John of Salerno (1242), Bl John of Alvernia (1322), Bl Falco of Palena (1440), Bl John of Rieti (*c.*1530), John Baptist Vianney (1859).

ST JOHN BAPTIST VIANNEY

The Cure d'Ars was hard put to it to get ordained at all. It was the time of the French Revolution when he was brought up in a village near Lyons. The opportunities for Christian instruction were practically non-existent and even when Napoleon took over, he found himself recruited to the army and it was some time before he could get his release. Once out, he began to train for the priesthood and after many academic problems he was ordained and later went to Ars, a tiny village with a population of 230 almost all of whom had ceased to practice their religion.

St John Baptist Vianney transformed the situation by his zeal and his piety. He prayed with and for his flock and the change was so remarkable that his fame spread throughout Europe and America. His bishop said of him 'I do not know whether he is educated or not; what I do know is that the Holy Spirit makes a point of enlightening him'. Many others found the same and in the ten years before his death the Cure d'Ars was spending eighteen hours a day in the confessional and more than twenty thousand visitors a year were coming to see him and the village which he had transformed.

It is as a parish priest that he is remembered and he is the patron of all parochial clergy throughout the world.

10 August

Lawrence of Rome (258), Martyrs of Alexandria (260–267), Bassa, Paula and Agathonica (?), Asteria of Bergamo (*c.*307), Gerontius (?508), Blane of Scotland (6th cent.), Deusdedit of Rome (6th cent.), Thiento and Comp. (955), Bl Hugh de Montaigu (1136), Bl Conrad Nantwin (1268), Bl Amadeus of Portugal (1482).

ST LAWRENCE OF ROME

St Lawrence is one of the most famous of all martyrs. He was one of the seven deacons of Rome under the Pope Sixtus II and he had been brought there from his native Aragon. When Sixtus was killed as part of the persecution of the Church in the time of Valerian, Lawrence was ordered to bring forth the treasures of the Christians so that they could be confiscated. Instead he gathered together all the poor and the sick who had been helped by the alms which he had distributed and said, 'these are the treasures of the Church'. For this Lawrence was condemned to death and probably beheaded although the legend suggests that he was roasted alive on a gridiron.

The Cure d'Ars.

11 August

Alexander Carbonarius (250), Tiburtius of Rome (*c.*288), Susanna of Rome (295), Chomatius of Rome (3rd cent.), Rufinus and Comp. (?), Philomena of Mugnano (?), Digna of Todi (4th cent.), Taurinus of Evreux (*c.*412), Attracta of Drum (5th cent.), Lelia of Limerick (?), Equitius of Valeria (*c.*540), Gaugericus of Cambrai (*c.*625), BB John and Peter Becchetti (13th cent.), BB Laurence Nerucci, Augustine Cenini, Bartholomew Sonati and John Baptist Petrucci (1420), Bl Nicholas Appleine (1466), Bl Peter Faber (1546).

12 August

Antoninus of Rome (186), Euplius of Catania (304), Gracilian and Felicissima (c.304), Hilaria, Digna, Euprepia, Eunomia, Quiriacus, Largio, Crescentian, Nimmia, Juliana and Comp. (c.304), Anicetus, Photinus and Comp. (c.305), Macarius and Julian (?), Merewenna (?), Ust of Penzance (?), Cassian of Benevento (c.340), Eusebius of Milan (465), Porcarius and Comp. (c.732), Jambert of Canterbury (790), Clare of Assisi (1253), BB Michael Mi, James Nam and Antony Dich (1838).

13 August

Hippolytus, Concordia and Comp. (c.236), Centolla and Helen (c.304), Cassian of Imola (?), Cassian of Todi (4th cent.), Muredach of Killala (c.455), Herculanus of Brescia (c.550), Radegund of Poitiers (587), Junian of Chaulnay (587), Maximus Homologetes and Comp. (662), Wigbert of Fritzlar (c.746), Herulph of Langres (785), Ludolphus of New Corvey (983), Nerses Glaietsi (1173), Bl Gertrude of Altenberg (1297), Radegund of Augsburg (before 1300), Bl Francis of Pesaro (1530), Bl William Freeman (1595), John Berchmans (1621).

14 August

Eusebius of Palestine (3rd cent.), Demetrius of Africa (?), Ursicius of Nicomedia (304), Eusebius of Rome (c.357), Marcellus of Apamaea (389), Callistus of Todi (528), Fachanan of Ross (late 6th cent.), Werenfrid of Arnheim (c.780), Athanasia of Constantinople (860), Bl Eberhard of Einsiedeln (958), BB Antony Primaldi and Comp. (1480), Bl Sanctes Brancasino (1490), Bl Juliana Puricelli (1501).

15 August

Assumption of the B.V. Mary, Tarcisius of Rome (c.255), Napoleon of Alexandria (c.300), Alipius of Tagaste (c.430), Altfrid of Hildesheim (874), Arduinus of Rimini (1009), Arnulf of Soissons (1087), Rupert of Ottobeuren (1145), Limbania of Genoa (1294), Stanislaus Kostka (1568).

THE ASSUMPTION OF THE BLESSED VIRGIN MARY

The earliest record that we have of this doctrine comes in certain apocryphal writers of the fourth century.

From then it took two forms: either the Virgin never died at all but was taken straight into heaven, or that she died but her body was preserved from the corruption of death and she was then miraculously assumed into heaven. In either case, the Assumption is the natural corollary to the doctrine of the Immaculate Conception because if Our Lady was born without the stain of original sin then death which is the result of sin would not intervene and she would pass from this life to the next directly.

In the Eastern Church this day was kept in honour of her death from the sixth century but in the West it was not until over a hundred years later that the different festivals in honour of the Blessed Virgin were introduced. By the end of the eighth century the devotion was universal in the West and in the thirteenth it was made one of the major feasts of the Church. The Reformers objected to the Assumption as unscriptural and it was removed from the calendar of the 1549 English Prayer Book.

In the Roman Catholic Church, however, the devotion became increasingly popular and therefore there were growing requests for a definition of the dogma, which was made in 1950. In the Eastern Church the bodily assumption of the Virgin is generally accepted but there is no very precise definition and therefore it is usually known as the Kormesis or falling asleep – a phrase which is sometimes used in the Church of England.

Pardon, Lord, we besseech thee, the transgressions of thy servants; that we, who by our own deeds are unable to please thee, may be saved by the intercession of the Mother of thy Son our Lord.

Collect for the Feast of the Assumption

16 August

Joachim (1st cent. BC), Serena of Rome (c.290), Diomedes of Tarsus (300), Ambrose of Ferentino (c.303), Arsacius of Nicomedia (358), Simplician of Milan (400), Titus of Rome (c.410), Eleutherius of Auxerre (561), Armagillus of Brittany (c.570), Uguzo of Carvagna (?), Bl Ralph de la Futaye (1129), Bl Laurence Loricatus (1243), Roch of Montpellier (1337), Bl Angelus Agostini Mazzinghi (1438).

17 August

Myron of Cyzicus (c.250), Paul and Juliana (c.270), Mamas of Cappadocia (c.275), Straton, Philip and

Eutychian (*c*.301), Eusebius (310), Liberatus, Boniface, Servus, Rusticus, Rogatus, Septimus and Maximus (483), Anastasius of Terni (653), James the Deacon (7th cent.), Drithelm of Melrose (*c*.700), Bl Carloman of Austrasia (755), Amor of Amorbach (*c*.767), Theodulus of Grammont (*c*.840), Hiero of Holland (885), Benedicta and Caecilia (10th cent.), John of Monte Marano (1094), Bl Nicholas Politi (1167), Donatus of Ripacandida (1198), Hyacinth of Cracow (1257), Clare of Montefalco (1308).

18 August

Floridus, Laurus, Proculus and Maximus (2nd cent.), Agapitus of Palestrina (*c*.274), Hermas, Serapion and Polyaenus (?), Leo and Juliana (?), John and Crispus (*c*.303), Firminus of Metz (496), Dagaeus of Iniskin (*c*.560), Bl Milo of Fontenelle (*c*.730), Evan of Ayrshire (9th cent.), Bl Leonard of Cava (1255), Hugh of Lincoln (1255), Bl Raynald of Ravenna (1321), Bl Beatrix da Silva (1490), Bl Aimo Taparelli (1495).

19 August

Julius of Rome (*c*.190), Magnus of Anagni (*c*.250), Rufinus of Mantua (?), Andrew the Tribune and Comp. (*c*.303), Timothy, Thecla and Agapius (304–306), Sixtus III (440), Marianus of Entreaigues (*c*.515), Mochta of Louth (*c*.534), Donatus of Sisteron (*c*.535), Elaphius of Chalons-sur-Marne (580), Bertulfus of Bobbio (640), Magnus of Avignon (660), Calminius of Villars (*c*.690), Guenninus of Vannes (7th cent.), Namadia of Marsat (*c*.700), Sebald of Nuremberg (*c*.770), Credan of Evesham (*c*.780), Marinus of Besalú (*c*.800), Badulfus of Ainay (*c*.850), Bl Guerricus of Igny (*c*.1157), Bl Leo II of Cava (1295), Louis of Toulouse (1297), Bl Angelus of Acquapagana (1313), Bl Emily Bicchieri (1314), BB Louis Flores, Francis of St Mary, Peter Zúniga, Joachim Firaiama-Diaz and Comp. (1622), Bl Hugh Green (1642), John Eudes (1680).

20 August

Samuel (11th cent. BC), Severus, Mennon and Comp. (*c*.300), Porphyrius of Palestrina (?), Martyrs of Thrace (?), Amator of Rocamadour (?), Lucius and Comp. (311), Oswin (651), Haduin of Le Mans (*c*.662), Philibert of Jumièges (684), Edbert of York (768), Leovigild and Christopher (852), Bl Burchard of Worms (1026), Bernard of Clairvaux (1153),

Bernard of Valdeiglesias (p.1155), Ronald of Orkney (1158), Herbert Hoscam (1180), Bl Gobert of Villiers (1263), Manettus (1268), Bl Mary de Mattis (1866).

ST BERNARD OF CLAIRVAUX

Reform of the monasteries was in the air at the beginning of the twelfth century and the Cistercians had already been founded for fifteen years when St Bernard joined them at Citeaux. It was only then however that the movement began to grow and the thirty kinsmen whom he brought with him soon multiplied until, in Clairvaux alone, there were more than seven hundred monks. It was said that mothers would hide their sons when Bernard was about so effective was his challenge to join him.

Yet St Bernard was more than a monastic reformer and refounder. He occupied a unique place in the world of his time. His writings and advice were so influential that he was said to have 'carried the twelfth century on his shoulders'. He was prepared to take up matters which he felt to be wrong with anyone whoever they were. He reminded the Abbot of Cluny and the King of France of their duty and from Veselay he toured France and Germany preaching the Second Crusade which was to defend the remains of Christian Jerusalem against the Saracens.

Yet in his writings we can see the real measure of the man; there is a simplicity and humility which informs and illuminates the massive intellect and organizational ability which are so evident.

21 August

Euprepius of Verona (1st cent.), Cyriaca of Rome (249), Paternus of Egypt (*c*.255), Privatus of Mende (266), Anastasius Cornicularius (274), Luxorius, Cisellus and Camerinus (*c*.303), Bassa, Theogonius, Agapius and Fidelis (304), Quadratus (?), Bonosus and Maximian (362), Sidonius Apollinaris (*c*.488), Hardulph (?), Leontius the Elder (*c*.541), Avitus I of Clermont (*c*.600), Mary and Gratia (*c*.1180), Bl Gilbert of Valenciennes (1185), Bl Bernard Tolomeo (1348), BB Ambrose Piccolomini and Patrick de'Patrizi (*c*.1348), Jane Frances Fémiol de Chantal (1641), Bl Joseph Nien (1838).

22 August

Symphorian of Autun (*c*.180), Athanasius, Anthusa and Comp. (*c*.257), Agathonicus, Zoticus and Comp. (end 3rd cent.), Fabrician and Philibert (?), Hippolytus of Porto (?), Maurus and Comp. (?), Martial, Saturninus, Epictetus, Maprilis, Felix and Comp. (*c*.300), Neophytus of Nicaea (310), Timothy of Rome (311), Sigfrid of Wearmouth (688), Ethelgitha of Northumbria (*c*.720), Arnulf of Eynesbury (9th cent.), Andrew of Tuscany (*c*.880), Bl Lambert of Chézery (1151), BB William Lacey and Richard Kirkman (1582), BB John Wall and John Kemble (1679), Bl Bernard of Offida (1694).

23 August

Zaccheus of Jerusalem (*c*.116), Quiriacus, Maximus, Archelaus and Comp. (*c*.235), Timothy and Apollinaris (*c*.290), Minervus, Eleazar and Comp. (3rd cent.), Theonas of Alexandria (300), Claudius, Asterius, Neon, Donvina and Theonilla (303), Lupus (?), Restitutus, Donatus, Valerian, Fructuosa and Comp. (*c*.305), Maximus of Chinon (*c*.470), Tydfil of Glamorgan (*c*.480), Victor of Vita (*c*.505), Eugene of Tyrone (618), Flavian of Autun (7th cent.), Altigianus and Hilarinus (731), Ebba the Younger and Comp. (*c*.870), Bl Richildis of Hohenwart (*c*.1100), Philip Benizi (1285), Bl James of Mevania (1301).

24 August

Bartholomew (1st cent.), Romanus of Nepi (1st cent.), Eutychius of Phrygia (1st cent.), Ptolomy of Nepi (1st cent.), Massa Candida (*c*.260), Aurea of Ostia (*c*.260), Tation of Cladiopolis (*c*.304), Patrick the Elder (*c*.450), Yrchard of Scotland (5th cent.), George Limniotes (*c*.730), Bl Sandratus of Gladbach (986), Bl Alice Rich (*c*.1270), Bl Luke Mellini (*c*.1460).

ST BARTHOLOMEW

St Bartholomew's Day is better known than the Saint himself. The anniversary of the massacre of the Huguenot Protestants in Paris in 1572 and the eviction of the Nonconformist ministers who held Anglican benefices in 1662 – both these events are remembered while the 'son of Tolmai' – Bar Tolmai – exists only in lists of the twelve Apostles.

He may have been identical with Nathaniel who was a friend of St Philip to whom he said 'Can there be any good thing come out of Nazareth?' to which Philip answered 'Come and see'. Late traditions suggest that Bartholomew preached in India and Armenia and was martyred by being flayed alive. His alleged relics are to be found on the Isola di San Bartolomeo in the Tiber in Rome and he has given his name to very many churches.

St Bartholomew (*Leonardo da Vinci*).

25 August

Geruntius of Italica (*c*.100), Eusebius, Pontian, Vincent and Peregrinus (192), Nemesius and Lucilla (*c*.260), Genesius the Comedian (*c*.300), Genesius of Arles (*c*.303), Maginus of Tarragona (*c*.304), Julian the Syrian (?), Mennas of Constantinople (552), Aredius of Atane (591), Patritia of Naples (*c*.665), Ebba the Elder (683), Hunegund of Homblieres (*c*.690), Gregory of Utrecht (*c*.776), Marcian of Saignon (1010), Gurloës of Quimperlé (1057), Louis IX (1270), Thomas of Hereford (1282), BB Louis Sotelo, Michael Carvalho and Comp. (1627), Jane Antide Thouret (1828), Mary Michaela (1865).

KING LOUIS IX

Louis became a king when he would much rather have been a monk but, having accepted the throne with reluctance, he threw himself into the responsibilities of kingship so that he lived to be recognized as the embodiment of medieval ideals of monarchy. He was a man of his time, his reluctance to wage war was not

The Dormition of the Virgin (*Philip Goul*).

St Bernard in Prayer (*Sozg Bzeu*).

extended to preventing the crusade against the Albigenses. Nevertheless he was 'transfixed by pity for the unfortunate' and was prepared to tend lepers with his own hands.

Indeed, it was this willingness to do what he felt to be right without making a fuss about it which distinguished King Louis from other royal religious. He walked barefoot but wore soleless shoes so that his private penance would not be obvious.

To the world of the time his leadership in two Crusades was the clearest statement of his faith and he proved himself a brave and compassionate leader, finally dying for his cause at Tunis.

26 August

Simplicius, Constantius and Victorian (*c*.161), Zephyrinus (217), Irenaeus and Abundius (*c*.258), Gelasinus of Heliopolis (297), Alexander of Bergamo (297), Secundus of Ventimiglia (3rd cent.), Adrian of Nicomedia ˙(?), Rufinus of Capua (5th cent.), Elias of Syracuse (660), Bregwin of Canterbury (765), Felix of Pistoia (9th cent.), Pandwina of Ettisley (*c*.904), Victor of Cerezo (*c*.950), Bl Herluin of Bec (1078), Bl Vyevain of York (1285), Margaret of Faenza (1330), Bl John of Caramola (1339), Bl John Bassano (1445), Bl Timothy of Montecchio (1504), Bl Thomas Percy (1572).

27 August

Narnus of Bergamo (*c*.75), Rufus of Capua (1st cent.), Rufus and Carpophorus (295), Anthusa the Younger (?), Euthalia of Lentini (?), Honoratus, Fortunatus, Arontius, Sabinian (*c*.303), Marcellinus, Mannea, John, Serapion, Peter and Comp. (*c*.303), Poemon of Skete (*c*.450), Caesarius of Arles (542), Licerius of Conserans (*c*.548), Syagrius of Autun (600), Etherius of Lyons (602), Decuman of Wales (716), Ebbo of Sens (740), John of Pavia (813), Bl Agilo of Sithiu (957), Gebhard of Constance (995), Malrubius of Scotland (*c*.1040), Bl Ebbo of Hamberg (1162), Bl Angelus of Foligno (1312), Bl Margaret the Barefooted (1395), Bl Gabriel Mary (1532), Joseph Calasanctius (1648), Bl David Lewis (1679).

28 August

Hermes and Comp. (*c*.120), Pelagius of Istria (*c*.283), Fortunatus, Caius and Anthes (303), Julian of Auvergne (304), Helen (*c*.330), Alexander of Constantinople (340), Moses the Black (*c*.395), Augustine of Hippo (430), Vivian of Saintes (*c*.460), Ambrose of Saintes (p.475), Facundinus of Taino (*c*.620), Rumbold of Northumbria (*c*.650), Bl Adelindis of Buchau (*c*.930), Gorman of Sleswig (965), Bl Adelina of

Poulangy (1170), BB Hugh More, James Claxton, Robert Morton, Thomas Holford, Thomas Felton, William Dean and William Gunter (1588), Bl Edmund Arrowsmith (1628).

ST AUGUSTINE OF HIPPO

It is all too easy to believe that history is unaffected by great men and that things had to be as they were. Augustine gives the lie to such determinism. His battle against heresy in North Africa ensured the victory of the Catholic faith and his writings made a permanent contribution to the development of Christian thought. As a young man Augustine's famous phrase – 'Lord make me pure but not yet' summed up his easy life and it was the emptiness of everything in the face of the challenge of the barbarians determined to overthrow civilization, that finally made him commit himself. Augustine was baptised by St Ambrose and then he returned to Africa where he was ordained priest and later became the Bishop of Hippo. He lived frugally in a monastery and gave liberally to the poor.

Probably no other writer outside the Bible has exercised so much influence on the Church's thought. For centuries he dominated the intellectual attitudes of the West. His two great works – the *Confessions* – which told of his life before his conversion – and *City of God* –

which defended the Christian Church from the accusation that it was responsible for the decline of the Roman Empire – both have a vividness and power which has rarely been equalled. In the *City of God* is the supreme exposition of the fundamental opposition between the Church and the world. Neither the Church nor the world was the same after St Augustine's life – no epitaph can be more telling.

29 August

Sabina of Rome (*c*.127), Sabina of Troyes (*c*.275), Basilla of Smyrna (?), Candida of Rome (?), Nicaeas and Paul (?), Vitalis, Sator and Repositus (3rd or 4th cent.), Euthymius of Perugia (4th cent.), Adelphius of Metz (5th cent.), Sebbe (*c*.694), Medericus of Autun (*c*.700), Hypatius and Andrew (735), Velleicus of Kaiserswerth (8th cent.), Bl Alberic of Ocri (*c*.1050), Bl Philippa Guidoni (1335), Bl Richard Herst (1628).

30 August

Boniface and Thecla (*c*.250), Felix and Adauctus (*c*.304), Gaudentia and Comp. (?), Pammachius the Senator (410), Loarn of Downpatrick (5th cent.), Agilus of Rebais (650), Fiacre of Breuil (*c*.670), Pelagius, Arsenius and Silvanus (*c*.950), Fantinus of Calabria (p.980), Bononius of Locedio (1026), Peter of Trevi (*c*.1060), Bl Bronislava of Poland (1259), BB John Roche, Edward Shelley, Richard Leigh, Richard Martin and Margaret Ward (1588), Rose of Lima (1617).

31 August

Aristides the Athenian (*c*.133), Theodotus, Rufina and Amnia (*c*.270), Caesidius and Comp. (3rd cent.), Robustian and Mark (?), Paulinus of Trèves (358), Optatus of Auxerre (*c*.530), Babolenus of Bobbio (*c*.640), Aidan of Lindisfarne (651), Cuthburga of Wimborne (*c*.725), Amatus of Nusco (1093 or 1193), Raymund Nonnatus (1240), Dominic del Val (1250), Albertinus of Fonteavellana (1294), BB Servite Martyrs (1420), Bl Richard Bere (1537).

1 September

Anna the Prophetess (1st cent.), Priscus of Capua (*c*.66), Terentian (118), Verena of Zurich (3rd cent.), Sixtus of Reims (*c*.300), Ammon and Comp. (*c*.322), Victorius of Le Mans (*c*.490), Vincent and Laetus (5th

cent.), Priscus, Castrensis, Tammarus, Rosius, Secundus, Heraclius, Adjutor, Mark, Augustus, Elpidius, Canion and Vindonius (5th cent.), Lythan of Wales (?), Constantius of Aquino (*c*.520), Regulus of Tuscany (*c*.545), Silin of Brittany (6th cent.), Agia of Sens (6th cent.), Lupus of Sens (*c*.623), Nivard of Reims (*c*.670), Giles of Provence (*c*.712), Giles and Arcanus (*c*.1050), Bl Agnes of Venosa (*c*.1144), Bl Giles of Castañeda (*c*.1203), Bl Juliana of Collalto (1262), Bl Jane Soderini (1367), Bl Michael Ghebre (1855).

2 September

Diomedes, Julian, Philip, Eutychian, Hesychius, Leonides, Philadelphus, Menalippus and Pantagapes (?), Antoninus (?), Maxima of Rome (304), Justus of Lyons (390), Valentine of Strasbourg (4th cent.), Elpidius the Cappadocian (4th cent.), Castor of Apt (*c*.420), Elpidius of Lyons (422), Nonnosus of Mount Soracte (*c*.575), Heiu of Tadcaster (*c*.657), Agricola of Avignon (700), Lolanus of Scotland (*c*.1034), Stephen of Hungary (1038), William of Roeskilde (1067), Bl Margaret of Louvain (1225), Brocard of Mount Carmel (1231), BB Martyrs of September (1792).

3 September

Euphemia, Dorothy, Thecla and Erasma (1st cent.), Phoebe of Cenchreae (1st cent.), Zeno, Concordius and Theodore (302), Zeno and Chariton (*c*.303), Basilissa of Nicomedia (*c*.303), Aristaeus and Antoninus (?), Mansuetus of Toul (*c*.350), Ambrose of Sens (*c*.355), Macanisius (514), Auxanus of Milan (568), Maurilius of Cahors (580), Simeon Stylites the Younger (598), Natalis of Casale (6th cent.), Remaclus of Maestricht (*c*.663), Aigulphus of Lérins (676), Frugentius of Fleury (676), Hereswitha of Chelles (*c*.690), Regulus of Reims (698), Balin of Techsaxon (7th cent.), Sandila of Córdova (*c*.855), Martin of Hinokosa (1213), BB John of Perugia and Peter of Sassoferrato (1231), Bl Guala of Brescia (1244), Bl Andrew Dotti (1315), Bl Herman of Heidelberg (*c*.1326), Bl Degenhard of Niederaltaich (1374), BB Antony Ixida and Comp. (1632), Pius x (1914).

4 September

Moses (12th cent. BC), Candida the Elder (*c*.78), Hermione of Ephesus (*c*.117), Thamel and Comp. (*c*.125), Marcellus of Lyons (*c*.178), Marinus, Castus and Maximus (?), Rufinus, Silvanus and Vitalicus (?),

Marinus of San Marino (?), Marcellus of Trèves (?), Theodore, Oceanus, Ammianus and Julian (*c*.310), Silvinus of Verdun (*c*.420), Boniface I (423), Monessa of Ireland (456), Caletricus of Chartres (*c*.580), Ultan (7th cent.), Rhuddlad (7th cent.), Bl Ida of Herzfeld (*c*.813), Sulpitius of Bayeux (843), Bl Agnes of Bagno (*c*.1105), Rosalia of Palermo (1160), Rose of Viterbo (1252), Bl Catherine Mattei (1574).

5 September

Romulus the Courtier (*c*.112), Herculanus of Porto (*c*.180), Eudoxius, Zeno, Macarius and Comp. (2nd cent.), Victorinus (2nd cent.), Quintius, Arcontius and Donatus (?), Obdulia of Toledo (?), Macarius of Melitene (?), Urban, Theodore and Comp. (370), Genebald of Laon (*c*.555), Victorinus of Como (644), Bertinus of Sithiu (*c*.709), Albert of Butrio (1073), Alvitus of Leon (*c*.1073), Bl Albert of Pontida (1095), Vitus of Pontida (*c*.1095), Bl Jordan of Pulsano (1152), Bl Gentilis of Matelica (1340), Laurence Justinian (1455), Bl William Browne (1605), Bl Joseph Canh (1838).

6 September

Zachary (6th cent. BC), Onesiphorus and Porphyrius (*c*.80), Faustus, Macarius and Comp. (250), Augustine, Sanctian and Beata (273), Cottidus, Eugene and Comp. (?), Petronius of Verona (*c*.450), Arator of Verdun (*c*.460), Maccallin of Lusk (*c*.497), Donatian, Praesidius, Mansuetus, Germanus, Fusculus and Laetus (5th cent.), Eleutherius of Spoleto (*c*.590), Faustus of Syracuse (*c*.607), Chainoaldus (633), Magnus of Füssen (*c*.666), Felix and Augebert (7th cent.), Bl Bertrand of Garrigue (1230), Bl Peregrinus of Falerone (1240), Bl Liberatus da Loro (1258).

7 September

Eupsychius of Caesarea (*c*.130), Regina of Autun (*c*.286), John of Nicomedia (303), Anastasius the Fuller (304), Sozon of Cilicia (*c*.304), Evortius of Orléans (*c*.340), Grimonia of Picardy (4th cent.), Pamphilus of Capua (*c*.400), Augustalis of Gaul (*c*.450), Memorius and Comp. (451), Gratus of Aosta (*c*.470), Carissima of Albi (5th cent.), Clodoaldus of Nogent (*c*.560), Madalberta of Maubeuge (706), Hilduard of Dickelvenne (*c*.750), Alcmund of Hexham (781), Tilbert of Hexham (789), Faciolus of Poitiers (*c*.950), John of Lodi (1106), Stephen of Chatillon (1208), Eustace of

Flay (1211), BB Mark, Stephen and Melchior (1619), BB John Duckett and Ralph Corby (1644).

8 September

Nativity of the B.V. Mary, Ammon, Theophilus, Neoterius and Comp. (?), Timothy and Faustus (?), Adrian and Natalia (*c*.304), Eusebius, Nestabus, Zeno and Nestor (362), Nestor of Gaza (362), Kingsmark of Wales (5th cent.), Disibod of Bingen (*c*.700), Sergius I (701), Ina and Ethelburga (727), Corbinian of Freising (730), Adela of Messines (1071), Bl Alanus de Rupe (1475), Peter Claver (1654).

NATIVITY OF THE BLESSED VIRGIN MARY

The reason for the choice of this day to commemorate the birth of the Virgin Mary, is unknown but there is a legend which says that a concert of angels was heard in the air solemnizing the day as her birthday. Nothing is known from Scripture about the place, date or circumstances of her birth, except that she was a lineal descendant of the royal family of David.

The festival is mentioned in the Eastern Church

The Birth of the Virgin (*Master of Osservanza*).

September

during the eighth century, but it was not generally observed in the West until the eleventh century. In 1244 Pope Innocent III honoured it with an Octave because prayers to the Virgin Mary had brought about the end of the quarrel between the Papacy and the Emperor Frederick III. This had made possible the election of Pope Celestine IV in 1241. Later Gregory XI further granted the festival a vigil.

9 September

Dorotheus and Gorgonius (303), Rufinus and Rufinian (?), Hyacinth, Alexander and Tiburtius (?), Straton (?), Severian of Sebaste (322), Isaac the Great (c.440), Kieran the Younger (c.556), Ciarin of Clonmacnoise (c.556), Osmanna of Brieuc (c.650), Omer of Thérouanne (c.670), Bettelin of Croyland (8th cent.), Wulfhilda of Barking (980), Wilfrida of Wilton (c.988), Bl Gaufridus of Savigny (1139), Bl Mary de la Cabeza (c.1175), Bl Seraphina Sforza (1478).

10 September

Apelles, Lucius and Clement (1st cent.), Barypsebas of Dalmatia (1st cent.), Nemesian, Felix, Lucius, Another Felix, Litteus, Polyanus, Victor, Jader, Dativus and Comp. (257), Menodora, Metrodora and Nymphodora (306), Sosthenes and Victor (307), Agapius of Novara (c.420), Veranus of Bence (c.480), Pulcheria Augusta (453), Finian of Moville (c.575), Salvius of Albi (584), Candida the Younger (c.586), Theodard of Maestricht (c.670), Autbert of Avranches (p.709), Frithestan of Winchester (933), Peter de Mozonzo (c.1000), Cosmas of Aphrodisia (1160), Bl Serlo of Savigny (1158), Bl Ogerius of Locedio (1214), Nicholas of Tolentino (1305), BB Apollinaris Franco and Comp. (1622), Bl Ambrose Edward Barlow (1641).

11 September

Protus and Hyacinth (c.257), Felix and Regula (3rd

St Augustine of Hippo and the mystery of the Trinity (*Gaspard Dughet*).

cent.), Diodorus, Diomedes and Didymus (?), Paphnutius the Great (*c*.356), Theodora of Alexandria (491), Patiens of Lyons (*c*.491), Emilian of Vercelli (520), Daniel of Bangor (545), Vincent of León (*c*.554), Almirus of Gréez (*c*.560), Adelphius of Rémiremont (*c*.670), Bodo of Toul (p.670), Peter of Chavanon (1080), Bl Louis of Thuringia (1227), Sperandea of Cingoli (1276), Bl Matthew of Mount Massaccio (1303), BB Charles Spinola and Comp. (1622), Bl Bonaventure Grau (1684), Bl Gabriel Perboyre (1840).

12 September

Feast of the Most Holy Name of Mary, Curonotus of Iconium (*c*.258), Hieronides, Leontius, Serapion, Seleucus, Valerian and Straton (*c*.300), Autonomus of Bithynia (*c*.300), Macedonius, Theodulus and Tatian (362), Sacerdos of Lyons (551), Silvinus of Verona (*c*.550), Ailbe of Emly (6th cent.), Eanswida of Folkestone (*c*.640), Guy of Laken (*c*.1012), Bl Miro of Vich (1161), Bl Juvenal Ancina (1604), Bl Mary Victoria Fornari-Strata (1617), BB Thomas Zumárraga and Mancius of St Thomas (1622).

13 September

Philip (3rd cent.), Ligorius (?), Macrobius and Julian (*c*.321), Maurilius of Angers (*c*.430), Nectarius of Autun (*c*.550), Eulogius of Alexandria (607), Amatus of Rémiremont (*c*.630), Columbinus of Lure (*c*.680), Amatus of Sion in Valais (690), Barsenorius of Fécamp (7th cent.), Venerius of Tino Island (7th or 9th cent.), Bl Hedwig of Herford (*c*.887), Bl Martin III of Camaldoli (1259), Bl Francis of Calderola (1407).

14 September

Caerealis and Sallustia (251), Crescentian, Victor, Rosula and Generalis (*c*.258), Crescentius of Perugia (*c*.300), Maternus of Cologne (*c*.325), Cormac of Cashel (908), Notburga of Tyrol (1313), Bl Gabriel-John Tautin Dufresse (1815).

15 September

Feast of the Seven Sorrows of the B.V.Mary, Nicomedes of Rome (*c*.90), Melitina of Marcianopolis (middle of 2nd cent.), Valerian of Lyons (178), Maximus, Theodore and Scelpiodotus (*c*.310), Porphyrius the Actor (362), Nicetas the Goth (*c*.378), Albinus of Lyons (*c*.390), Mamilian of Palermo (460), Eutropia of

Auvergne (5th cent.), Aprus of Toul (507), John the Dwarf (*c*.540), Leobinus of Chartres (*c*.556), Joseph Abibos (*c*.590), Hernan of Brittany (6th cent.), Merinus of Benchor (*c*.620), Aichardus of Jumièges (*c*.687), Ritbert of Varennes (*c*.690), Ribert of Saint-Valéry (7th cent.), Emilas and Jeremias (852), Bl Aichardus of Clairvaux (*c*.1170), Bl Roland de' Medici (1386), Catherine of Genoa (1510).

ST CATHERINE OF GENOA

Despite the opposition of her spendthrift, pleasure-loving husband, to whom she was married in 1463, at the age of sixteen, Catherine persisted in a life of active charity. She devoted herself to the service of the sick and poor of Genoa. Eventually she won over her husband and together they managed a hospital in the city and she continued the work with her friends after his death.

Catherine was able to combine mysticism with a practical approach to religion. From 1475 she received communion almost daily, which in the later Middle Ages was very unusual, except for priests. She expressed her spiritual teaching in a book, *Life and Doctrine*, published in 1551, and the record of her spiritual revelations is one of the outstanding documents of Christian mysticism.

16 September

Sebastiana of Heraclea (1st cent.), Cornelius (253), Cyprian of Carthage (258), Dulcissima of Sutri (?), Lucy and Geminianus (*c*.300), Abundius, Abundantius, Marcian and John (*c*.303), Euphemia of Chalcedon (307), Ninian of Whithorn (*c*.432), Cunibert of Maroilles (*c*.680), Eugenia of Hohenburg (735), Rogelius and Servus-Dei (852), Ludmilla of Bohemia (921), Edith of Wilton (984), Stephen of Perugia (1026), Victor III (1087), Bl Vitalis of Savigny (1122), Bl Louis Allemand (1450), Bl Francis of Camporosso (1866).

17 September

Ariadne of Phrygia (*c*.130), Flocellus of Autun (2nd cent.), Justin (259), Narcissus and Crescentio (*c*.260), Valerian, Macrinus and Gordian (?), Agathoclia (?), Socrates and Stephen (*c*.304), Theodora of Rome (*c*.305), Satyrus of Milan (*c*.392), Rodingus of Beaulieu (*c*.690), Lambert of Liége (709), Columba of Córdova (853), Uni of Birka (936), Hildegard of Bingen (1179), Peter Arbués (1485), Bl Emmanuel Trieu (1797).

September

18 September

Sophia and Irene (*c.*200), Eumenes of Crete (3rd cent.), Ferreolus of Vienne (304), Methodius of Olympus (311), Eustorgius of Milan (p.331), Ferreolus of Limoges (4th cent.), Eustochius of Tours (461), Hygbald (*c.*690), Richardis (*c.*895), Simon of Crespy (*c.*1080), Bl Volcuin of Schem (1154), Bl Philip Oderisi (1285), Bl Simon of Genoa (1292), Bl John de Massias (1645), Joseph of Cupertino (1663), Bl Dominic Trach (1843).

19 September

Felix and Constania (1st cent.), Trophimus, Sabbatius and Dorymendon (*c.*277), Januarius and Comp. (304), Peleus, Nilus, Elias and Comp. (*c.*310), Susanna (662), Sequanus of Saint-Seine (*c.*580), Goeric of Metz (647), Theodore of Canterbury (690), Pomposa of Córdova (853), Arnulfus of Gap (1070), Mary de Cervellon (1290), Bl Hugh of Sassoferrato (*c.*1290), Bl Alphonsus de Orozco (1591), Emily de Rodat (1852).

20 September

Eustace, Theopistes, Agapitus and Theopistus (118), Theodore, Philippa and Comp. (220), Digna and Emerita (259), Candida of Carthage (*c.*300), Priscus of Phrygia (?), Dionysius and Privatus (?), Fausta and Evilasius (303), Glycerius of Milan (*c.*438), Agapitus I (536), Vincent Madelgarus (677), Eusebia of Marseilles and Comp. (*c.*731), Bl John Eustace (1481), Bl Thomas Johnson (1537), Bl Francis de Posadas (1713).

21 September

Jonas (*c.*761 BC), Matthew (1st cent.), Iphigenia (1st cent.), Alexander of Rome (2nd cent.), Eusebius of Phoenicia (?), Isaac of Cyprus (?), Meletius of Cyprus (?), Pamphilus of Rome (?), Mabyn (6th cent.), Gerulph of Flanders (*c.*746), Maura of Troyes (850), BB Francis Jaccard and Comp. (1838), BB Martyrs of Corea (1839–46).

ST MATTHEW

This is one of the most ancient festivals, being mentioned at Rome in the early fifth century. Matthew, who was also known as 'Levi', was evidently a Jew and was a wealthy tax-collector and customs official at Capernaum. These agents of the Romans were every-where hated, and treated by the Pharisees as public sinners. After he had been called by Jesus from the receipt of customs to be a disciple, he gave Him a great feast which roused the anger of the 'scribes and the Pharisees'. It was a challenge to public opinion for Jesus to associate with him in this way.

Since the name 'Matthew' probably means 'Gift of God', it was doubtless given to him as an additional name, perhaps by Jesus Himself. He is said to have made a collection of the sayings of Jesus in Hebrew and is traditionally the author of the Gospel bearing his name. Of his later career there is no trustworthy information, though he is supposed to have preached to the Jews. His relics are at Salerno.

Matthew by Christ called from the customs board
Disputes not whom he follows, what he leaves:
So life a loadstone draws his powerful word
That seeming just rejects, sinner receives.

HENRY CLIFFORD, EARL OF CUMBERLAND

22 September

Sanctinus of Meaux (*c.*300), Irais of Alexandria (*c.*300), Silvanus of Levroux (?), Jonas of Paris (?), Florentius of Mt Glonne (5th cent.), Felix III (530), Lauto of Coutances (568), Salaberga of Poulangey (*c.*665), Emmeramus of Ratisbon (*c.*690), Thomas of Villanueva (1555).

23 September

Linus (*c.*79), Xantippa and Polyxena (1st cent.), Thecla of Iconium (1st cent.), Constantius of Ancona (6th cent.), Cissa of Northumbria (late 7th cent.), Adamnan of Iona (704), Andrew, John, Peter and Antony (*c.*900), Bl Guy of Durnes (*c.*1157), Bl Peter Acotanto (*c.*1180), Bl Mark of Modena (1498), Bl Helen Duglioli (1520), Bl William Way (1588).

24 September

Our Lady of Ransom, Anathalon of Milan (1st cent.), Andochius, Thyrsus and Felix (2nd cent.), Paphnutius and Comp. (*c.*303), Martyrs of Chalcedon (304), Rusticus of Clermont (446), Geremarus of Flay (*c.*658), Cuniald and Gislar (7th cent.), Berchtun of Beverley (733), Gerard Sagredo (1046), Ysarn of Marseilles (1048), Bl Robert Flower (1218), Pacificus of Sanseverino (1721).

25 September

Cleophas (1st cent.), Herculanus (2nd cent.), Firminus of Amiens (2nd cent.), Bardomìan, Eucarpus and Comp. (?), Paul, Tatta, Sabinian, Maximus, Rufus and Eugene (?), Aurelia and Neomisia (?), Paphnutius of Egypt (*c.*480), Caian (5th cent.), Mewrog (?), Principius of Soissons (*c.*505), Solemnius of Chartres (*c.*511), Lupus of Lyons (542), Barr of Cork (6th cent.), Anacharius of Auxerre (604), Fymbert of Scotland (7th cent.), Ermenfridus of Cusance (*c.*670), Ceolfrid of Wearmouth (716), Egelred of Croyland (*c.*870), Bl Herman the Cripple (1054), Austindus of Auch (1068), Albert of Jerusalem (1214), Christopher of Guardia (*c.*1490), Bl Ladislas of Gielniow (1505), Bl Mark Criado (1569), Vincent Strombi (1824).

26 September

Callistratus and Comp. (*c.*300), Cyprian and Justina (?), Senator of Albanum (?), Eusebius of Bologna (*c.*400), Vigilius of Brescia (p.506), Meugant of Cornwall (6th cent.), Amantius of Città di Castello (*c.*600), Colman Elo (*c.*610), Nilus the Younger (1004), Bl Meginhard of Hersfeld (1059), John of Meda (1159), Bl Dalmatius Moner (1341), Bl Lucy of Caltagirone (1304), Martyrs of N. America (1642).

LANCELOT ANDREWES

On this day, the anniversary of his death, the American Episcopal Church remembers Lancelot Andrewes who was successively Bishop of Chichester, Ely and Winchester in the reign of King James I.

He was one of the most influential leaders in forming for the Church of England distinctive principles and beliefs. He opposed the prevailing Puritanism of the time as narrow and irrational. He wished Anglicanism, looking to sound learning for its authority, to be reasonable and yet respect past traditions. He insisted that at the Eucharist the communicants receive the true body and blood of Christ and thought that worship should be expressed in ordered ceremonial.

During his lifetime, he was known chiefly for his sermons, especially those he preached at court on the greater festivals of the Christian year. In these he showed himself a master of the short and even startling sentence – like 'Christ is no wild-cat'. He also took an important part in producing the Authorized Version of the Bible.

27 September

John Mark (1st cent.), Caius of Milan (1st cent.), Adheritus of Ravenna (2nd or 3rd cent.), Epicharis of Byzantium (*c.*300), Cosmas and Damian (*c.*303), Anthimus (*c.*303), Euprepius (*c.*303), Florentinus and Hilary (?), Fidentius and Terentius (?), Deodatus of Sora (?), Ceraunus of Paris (p.614), Sigebert of East Anglia (635), Barrog of Wales (7th cent.), Hiltrude of Liessies (*c.*790), Adolphus and John (*c.*850), Marcellus of St Gall (*c.*869), Bonfilius of Foligno (1125), Elzear of Provence (1323).

28 September

Privatus of Rome (223), Solomon of Genoa (p.269), Paternus of Auch (3rd cent.), Mark, Alphius, Alexander and Comp. (*c.*303), Martial, Laurence and Comp. (?), Stacteus (?), Maximus (?), Machan of Scotland (?), Exuperius of Toulouse (411), Eustochium of Rome (419), Silvinus of Brescia (444), Faustus of Riez (*c.*493), Conwall of Scotland (*c.*630), Annemundus of Lyons (657), Willigod and Martin (7th cent.), Tetta of Wimborne (*c.*772), Lioba of Bischoffsheim (*c.*779), Wenceslaus of Bohemia (935), Thiemo of Salzburg (1102), Bl Laurence of Rippafratta (1457), Bl Bernardinus of Feltre (1494), Bl Simon de Rojas (1624), BB Bartholomew Gutiérrez and Comp. (1630).

29 September

Michael the Archangel, Ripsime, Gaiana and Comp. (*c.*290), Eutychius, Plautus and Heracleas (?), Theodota of Philippopolis (*c.*318), Gudelia of Persia (*c.*340), Dadas, Casdoë and Gaboelas (368), Fraternus of Auxerre (*c.*450), Quiriacus of Palestine (*c.*550), Ludwin of Mettlach (713), Catholdus, Anno and Diethardus (late 8th cent.), Alaricus of Uffnan (975), Garcia of Arlanza (*c.*1073), Grimoaldus of Pontecorvo (p.1137), Bl John of Montmirail (1217), Bl Richard Rolle (1349), Bl Charles of Blois (1364), Bl John of Ghent (1439).

ST MICHAEL THE ARCHANGEL

Michael is mentioned several times in the Old Testament in the Book of Daniel, where he is described as the guardian of the Israelites, 'the prince which standeth for the people' in opposition to the prince-angels of Persia and of Greece. In the New Testament he is represented in the Epistle of St Jude as disputing with the devil over the body of Moses and in the Book of

Revelation as fighting in heaven against the dragon, 'him that is called the devil and Satan'.

The observance of this day originated in the dedication festival of a Basilica of St Michael in Rome. In the early seventeenth century, Pope Paul V instituted the festival of the Guardian Angels on 2 October. At the revision of the English Prayer Book in 1662, this day was renamed 'St Michael and All Angels', perhaps suggested by the new Roman festival.

30 September

Sophia of Rome (c.138), Victor and Ursus (c.286), Antoninus of Piacenza (3rd cent.), Gregory the Illuminator (c.330), Leopardus of Rome (362), Jerome of Rome (420), Midan (c.610), Honorius of Canterbury (653), Laurus of Brittany (7th cent.), Enghenedl of Wales (7th cent.), Bl Conrad of Zähringen (1227).

ST JEROME

Eusebius Hieronymous Sophronius, otherwise known as Jerome, was born at Strido in Dalmatia in 342. His parents were Christians and rich enough to send him to Rome where he studied to be a lawyer. There he led a life of pleasure until an illness changed his life and he retired as a monk to the Syrian desert. In 382 he returned to Rome as secretary to the Pope and became spiritual adviser to many Roman ladies until he had to

St Jerome (*Crivelli*).

leave because of the malicious slanders from his enemies.

He spent his last years at Bethlehem, translating the Scriptures into Latin, using Hebrew and Greek sources. His version of the Bible is known as the Vulgate and is still the authorized Latin text of the Roman Catholic Church. His text was used in the first printed Bible which was produced in Germany in 1455.

1 October

Platon of Tournai (c.286), Verissimus, Maxima and Julia (c.302), Priscus, Crescens and Evagrius (?), Aretas and Comp. (?), Aizan and Sazan (c.400), Albaud of Toul (c.520), Remigius of Reims (c.533), Romanus the Melodist (c.540), Melorius of Cornwall (c.540), Bavo of Ghent (654), Dodo of Wallers (c.750), Fidharleus of Rathin (762), Virila of Leyre (c.1000), Bl Nicholas of Forca-Palena (1449), Bl John of Dukla (1484), BB Edward Campion, Christopher Buxton, Robert Wilcox, Robert Widmerpool, Edward James, Ralph Crockett and John Robinson (1588).

2 October

Feast of the Guardian Angels, Primus, Cyril and Secundarius (?), Eleutherius and Comp. (c.303), Modestus of Sardinia (c.304), Leudomer of Chartres (c.585), Beregisus of St-Hubert (p.725), Gerinus of Arras (676), Leodegarius (678), Theophilus of Bulgaria (c.750), Ursicinus II of Chur (760).

3 October

Dionysius, Faustus, Caius, Peter, Paul and Comp. (257), Candidus of Rome (?), Hesychius of Gaza (c.380), Menna of Lorraine (c.395), Maximian of Numidia (404), Cyprian of Toulon (6th cent.), Ewald the Fair and Ewald the Dark (c.695), Widradus of Saulieu (747), Bl Utto of Metten (820), Gerard of Brogne (959), Froilan of León (1006), Ebontius of Barbastro (1104), Adalgott of Chur (1165), Bl Dominic Spadafora (1521), Teresa of Lisieux (1897).

ST TERESA OF LISIEUX

The life of St Teresa is summed up in her cry 'My God I choose all! I don't want to be a saint by halves.' She was consciously set upon perfection and the attraction of the directness and simplicity of her autobiography *Story of a Soul* meant that her following grew

St Matthew (*Book of Kells*).

remarkably quickly after her death, so much so that the Pope, Pius XI dispensed with the fifty years rule, and proclaimed her a saint in 1925.

She was one of the five daughters of a watchmaker in Lisieux. Teresa fought hard to be allowed to enter the Carmelite convent at the impossibly early age of fifteen. By the time she was 22 she had become the mistress of the novices and the prioress ordered St Teresa to write her autobiography. It reveals her humility, simplicity, and brave endurance of suffering. Hers was an expression of the faith of the simple – 'I do as a child who has not learned to read – I just tell Our Lord all I want and He understands.' She is often called the Little Flower – a name derived from the sub-title of her book and reminiscent of her famous saying 'I have never given the good Lord ought but love, and it is with love that He will repay. After my death I will let fall a shower of roses.' She died, aged twenty-four, in 1897.

4 October

Crispus and Caius (1st cent.), Hierotheus of Athens (?), Caius, Faustus, Eusebius, Chaeremon, Lucius and Comp. (3rd cent.), Domnina, Berenice and Prosdoce (303–10), Mark, Marcian and Comp. (304), Adauctus and Callisthene (c.312), Ammon the Great (c.350), Petronius of Bologna (c.445), Quintus of Tours (c.570), Aurea of Paris (666), Peter of Damascus (c.750), Francis of Assisi (1226), Bl Julian Majali (1470), Bl Francis Titelmans (1537).

ST FRANCIS OF ASSISI

The Francis who preached to the birds and loved the flowers is the same Francis who received the marks of Christ's crucifixion in his own hands and feet and who kissed and cared for the most repulsive of lepers. He can easily be thought of as the patron saint of the sentimental and yet it was the strength of his personality which drew to himself the great band of followers which became the largest religious order in the world. St Francis was born into the rich and comfortable background of a successful merchant of Assisi. As a young man he enjoyed himself and took little interest in the conduct of his father's business or in any other serious pursuits. It was only after his experience as a captive during the battles between Perugia and Assisi and his failure in his attempt to join the Pope's forces fighting against the Germans in Southern Italy that he was driven to accept his vocation to live with the poorest as one of themselves. It was his special insight

St Francis (*Sassetta*).

to take directly to heart the Gospel's demand of complete poverty. He would not allow his order to own property and the friars had to beg for their living.

The Franciscans were placed under the protection of the Pope and yet he would not accept any special treatment because of this. When his brothers asked that they might be allowed to preach wherever they wanted to without the permission of the local bishop, St Francis said: 'Let it be your singular privilege to have no privilege.'

5 October

Thraseas of Eumenia (c.170), Palmatius and Comp. (c.287), Marcellinus of Ravenna (3rd cent.), Alexander of Trèves (3rd cent.), Firmatus and Flaviana (?), Placid, Eutychius, Victorinus, Flavia, Donatus, Firmatus, Faustus and Comp. (?), Charitina (c.304), Apollinaris of Valence (c.520), Galla of Rome (c.550), Magdalveus of Verdun (c.776), Aurea of Amiens (8th cent.), Meinulf of Bödeken (c.859), Bl Aymard of Cluny (965), Attilanus of Zamora (1009), Bl Sanctes of Cori (1392), Bl Raymund of Capua (1399), Bl Felicia Meda (1444), BB John Hewett, William Hartley and Robert Sutton (1588).

6 October

Sagar of Laodicea (*c.*175), Martyrs of Trèves (287), Marcellus, Castus, Aemilius and Saturninus (?), Faith of Agen (?), Erotis of Greece (4th cent.), Romanus of Auxerre (*c.*564), Magnus of Città Nuova (*c.*660), Cumine the White (669), Ceollach (7th cent.), Pardulphus of Guéret (*c.*738), Epiphania of Pavia (*c.*800), Nicetas of Constantinople (*c.*838), Adalbero of Würzburg (1090), Bruno (1101), Mary Frances (1791), Bl Francis Trung (1858).

ST BRUNO

St Bruno's early career was that of an ecclesiastical high-flyer. By the age of twenty-seven he was the professor of Grammar at his old school in Rheims and very soon afterwards was made Chancellor of the diocese. It was then that he found that the archbishop, Manasses, was a profligate totally unsuitable to be a prince of the Church and Bruno had to denounce him. Manasses hounded him out of his prebend and Bruno ended up in Cologne. Again, preferment was offered and this time he refused it, deciding instead to go with six friends to ask St Hugh, the Bishop of Grenoble, for a distant place to set up a hermitage.

St Hugh set out to help his visitors as he had been told in a vision that they would build a church at La Grande Chartreuse and it was there that the one Order which has never needed reform was founded. The Carthusian's life was that of a hermit, conforming as far as is possible to St Benedict's rule. They ate no meat and only the roughest bread. If fish were given to them they would take it but never buy such a delicacy. They spent their days in prayer and manual work, reading and worship. They wore hair shirts and the simplest and poorest of habits. At last St Bruno was content. He had found his way to God. Yet soon he was on the move again for the Pope tested his obedience by demanding that he come to Rome and help in drawing up the plans for reform of the Church. St Bruno himself lived the life of a hermit in Rome until 1101 when he died. He has never been formally canonized as that is not sufficiently humble for the Carthusians but the Pope has allowed them to keep his feast day and in 1674 it became a feast day to be honoured throughout the Western Church.

7 October

Justina of Padua (*c.*300), Julia of Egypt (*c.*300), Sergius and Bacchus (303), Mark (336), Canog of Wales (*c.*492), Dubtach of Armagh (*c.*513), Palladius of Saintes (*c.*590), Helanus of Reims (6th cent.), Augustus of Bourges (6th cent.), Osyth of Chich (*c.*675), Adalgis of Novara (*c.*850), Bl Artaldus of Belley (1206), Bl Gerold of Cologne (13th cent.), Bl Matthew Carreri (1471).

8 October

Simeon Senex (1st cent.), Reparata of Palestine (*c.*250), Peter of Seville (?), Benedicta of Laon (?), Palatias and Laurentia (302), Nestor of Thessalonica (*c.*304), Artemon of Laodicea (*c.*305), Thais of Alexandria (*c.*348), Demetrius the Megalomartyr (early 4th cent.), Triduana (4th or 8th cent.), Keyna of Wales (5th cent.), Evodius of Rouen (5th cent.), Gratus of Chalons-sur-Saone (*c.*652), Ywi of Lindisfarne (*c.*690), Badilo of Leuze (*c.*870), Amor of Aquitaine (9th cent.), Martin Cid (1152), Bl Companius (12th cent.), Hugh Canefro (1230), Bl Mechtildis of Magdeburg (1282), Brigid of Sweden (1373).

9 October

Dionysius the Areopagite (1st cent.), Demetrius of Alexandria (231), Dionysius, Rusticus and Eleutherius (3rd cent.), Domninus of Parma (304), Publia of Antioch (*c.*370), Andronicus and Athanasia (5th cent.), Gislenus of St-Ghislain (*c.*680), Lambert and Valerius (*c.*680), Geminus of Sanpaterniano (*c.*815), Savinus of Lavedan (*c.*820), Deusdedit of Monte Cassino (836), Gunther of Niederaltaich (1045), Bl Aaron of Cracoa (1059), Alfanus of Salerno (1085), Goswin of Anchin (1165), Louis Bertran (1581), John Leonardi (1609).

10 October

Pinytus of Crete (p.180), Victor and Comp. (*c.*286), Gereon and Comp. (?), Clarus of Nantes (?), Cassius, Florentius and Comp. (303), Eulampius, Eulampia and Comp. (*c.*310), Cerbonius of Verona (*c.*400), Maharsapor of Persia (421), Patrician of Scotland (5th cent.), Cerbonius of Piombino (*c.*580), Tranca of Troyes (*c.*637), Paulinus of York (644), Aldericus of Sens (841), Paulinus of Capua (843), Fulk of Fontenelle (845), Gundisalvus of Las Junias (p.1135), Bl Hugh of Mâcon (1151), Daniel, Samuel, Angelus, Domnus, Leo, Nicholas and Hugolinus (1221), Francis Borgia (1572).

October

11 October

Zenais and Philonilla (1st cent.), Nicasius, Quirinus, Scubiculus and Pientia v (c.285), Emilian of Rennes (?), Anastasius, Placid, Genesius and Comp. (?), Tharacus, Probus and Andronicus (304), Sarmata the Hermit (357), Germanus of Besançon (c.390), Nectarius of Constantinople (397), Placidia of Verona (c.460), Gratus of Oloron (p. 506), Firminus of Uzes (553), Canice of Kilkenny (599), Ethelburga (c.678), Agilbert of Paris (c.685), Eufridus of Alba (7th cent.), Ansilio of Lagny (late 7th cent.), Juliana of Pavilly (c.750), Gummarus of Lier (c.774), Bruno the Great (965), John of Bridlington (1379), Bl James Griesinger (1491), Alexander Sauli (1593), Bl Peter Tuy (1833).

12 October

Monas of Milan (249), Maximilian of Lorch (284), Evagrius, Priscian and Comp. (?), Eustace (?), Pantalus of Basle (?), Edistius of Ravenna (c.303), Domnina of Anazarbus (303), Felix and Cyprian (c.484), Fiace (5th cent.), Salvinus of Verona (562), Edwin (633), Wilfrid of York (709), Herlindis and Relindis (c.745), Amicus and Amelius (773), Seraphinus of Ascoli-Piceno (1604), Bl Camillus Costanzi (1622).

13 October

Theophilus of Antioch (181), Carpus of Troas (1st cent.), Fyncana and Fyndoca (?), Faustus, Januarius and Martial (304), Florentius of Thessalonica (312), Venantius of Tours (5th cent.), Romulus of Genoa (p.641), Berthold of Cambrai (7th cent.), Comgan of Scotland (8th cent.), Simbert of Augsburg (c.809), Gerald of Aurillac (909), Colman of Stockerau (1012), Regimbald of Speyer (1039), Edward the Confessor

(1066), Chelidonia of Subiaco (1152), Maurice of Carnoet (1191), Bl Gerbrand of Bloemkamp (1218), Bl Mary Magdalen dei Panattieri (1503).

KING EDWARD THE CONFESSOR

Edward the Confessor (1003–66) was the last of the old English kings but perhaps the least English of them all. He was nearly forty when he came back to Britain which he had left as a young boy because of the danger from the Danish kings. It was a crucial point in the history of the country, torn between Scandinavian and Norman influences. After his exile in Normandy and his preference for the Normans, Edward prepared the way for the Conquest and thereby tied Britain to the mainstream of European affairs – political and cultural – when the danger was that she would have thrown in her lot with the more isolated Northern countries. It was therefore natural that later Norman kings should have encouraged English devotion to St Edward the Confessor whose memory gave expression to the nationalist feelings of the Saxons without danger to the Norman throne.

Yet the sanctity of the king was not a figment of political imagination. Edward was personally a devout and gentle man. He built a new abbey in London which, to distinguish it from St Paul's, was called Westminster and his concern for the poor was real and renowned. Edward was popularly thought a saint long before his official canonization and his shrine in Westminster Abbey became a centre of pilgrimage during the Middle Ages. It was one of the two left undisturbed by the Reformation.

14 October

Callistus I (c.222), Saturninus and Lupus (?), Fortunata of Caesarea (303), Carponius, Evaristus and Priscian (303), Gaudentius of Rimini (c.360), Donatian of Reims (390), Manehildis of Champagne (c.490), Fortunatus of Todi (537), Rusticus of Trèves (574), Manakus of Wales (6th cent.), Angadresima of Beauvais (c.695), Burchard of Würzburg (c.754), Bernard of Arce (9th cent.), Dominic Loricatus (1060).

15 October

Agileus of Carthage (c.300), Martyrs of Germany (303). Severus of Trèves (c.455), Cannatus of Marseilles (5th cent.), Antiochus of Lyons (5th cent.), Leonard of

St Francis tells the Pope of his new Order (*Giotto*).

St Bruno's vision (*Mola*).

Vandoeuvre (c.570), Sabinus of Catania (c.760), Thecla of Kitzingen (c.790), Euthymius the Thessalonian (886), Bl Odilo of Stavelot (p.954), Callistus of Huesca (1003), Aurelia of Strassburg (1027), Bl Willa of Nonnberg (c.1050), Teresa of Avila (1582).

ST TERESA OF AVILA

St Teresa (1515–82) is perhaps the greatest of all women mystics and shares with St John of the Cross in the rediscovery of the contemplative life. When first she joined the nunnery at Avila, she joined one of the fashionable centres of the town's life. She had had a normal upbringing although her mother had died when she was young and her father had taken on the job of restraining her rather fanciful nature. He had resisted Teresa's desire to join the Carmelites but she

St Teresa in Ecstasy (*Bernini*).

greatest of many examples of the effect of her spiritual understanding. She was perhaps the rarest of women to be canonized – a mystical writer who ranks among the greatest.

16 October

Eliphius of Toul (362), Bolonia (362), Florentinus of Trèves (4th cent.), Saturninus, Nereus and Comp. (*c*.450), Dulcidius of Agen (*c*.450), Martinian, Saturian and Comp. (458), Conogan of Quimper (460), Junian (5th cent.), Gall (*c*.640), Magnobodus of Angers (*c*.670), Baldwin of Laon (*c*.680), Kiara of Kilkeary (*c*.680), Mummolinus of Noyon (*c*.686), Bercharius of Moutier-en-Der (696), Balderic of Montfaucon (7th cent.), Eremberta of Wierre (late 7th cent.), Vitalis of Noirmoutier (*c*.740), Ambrose of Cahors (p.772), Lullus of Mainz (787), Anastasius of Cluny (1085), Bertrand of Comminges (1123), Gerald of Clairvaux (1177), Hedwig (1243), Gerard Majella (1755).

17 October

Heron of Antioch (*c*.136), Solina of Gascony (*c*.290), Mamelta of Persia (*c*.344), Florentius of Orange (*c*.526), Victor of Capua (554), Louthiern of Cornwall (6th cent.), Colman of Kilroot (6th cent.), Ethelbert and Ethelred (670), Berarius I of Le Mans (*c*.680), Anstrudis of Laon (688), Nothelm of Canterbury (*c*.740), Rudolph of Gubbio (*c*.1066), Bl Gilbert the Theologian (1167), Bl Balthassar of Chiavari (1492), Bl Richard Gwyn (1584), Margaret Mary Alacoque (1690), BB Ursuline Nuns (1794), Bl Francis Isidore Gagelin (1833).

HENRY MARTYN

The American Episcopal Church has chosen this day to commemorate Henry Martyn, the young English clergyman who gave up his Cambridge fellowship in order to preach to the people of India. He went out to Calcutta in 1805 during the Napoleonic wars as a chaplain to the East India Company. Martyn was determined to be a missionary among the indigenous population instead of among European officials. Taking Francis Xavier as his ideal, he established schools for the Indians and preached to the Hindus and Moslems. He also used his gifts of scholarship, translating the New Testament into Hindustani and Persian. He then set out for Persia but he was worn out and he died before he could finish his translation work.

Henry Martyn became one of the best remembered

won him over and fell easily into the unreformed life of the nunnery. Constant promptings of conscience culminated in a real moment of decision. Her reading of St Augustine and her contemplation of a picture of the Passion produced a determination to live the religious life more completely. Despite every attempt to stop her, Teresa began a new house in Avila where nuns would live to a much stricter Rule. They became known as the Discalced Carmelites because they went almost barefoot in rough sandals. The community was tiny compared with the over-large number of sisters in the ordinary Carmelite house, and Teresa always limited the number to twenty-one – 'Experience has taught me what a house full of women is like. God preserve us from such a state.'

Despite the continuing opposition to the new foundations, the Discalced Carmelites were given approval in 1580 and St Teresa continued her active work, dying in harness on her way home from her new house at Burgos. It is however her spiritual insight – which is continued today in her books – *The Way of Perfection, Foundations* and the *Interior Castle* – which represents her major contribution to the Church. Her influence on St John of the Cross was only the first and missionaries in India and one of his Moslem converts became the first Indian to become an Anglican priest.

18 October

Luke (1st cent.), Asclepiades of Antioch (217), Athenodorus of Pontus (c.269), Justus of Beauvais (287), Tryphonia of Rome (3rd cent.), Gwen of Wales (c.492), Gwen (5th cent.), Brothen and Gwendolen (6th cent.), Monon of Scotland (c.645).

ST LUKE

How St Luke was converted to Christianity is not known but he does appear to have been neither a Jew nor one of Jesus' original disciples. However, he is clearly a figure in the early Church almost from the beginning and he accompanied St Paul on part of the second missionary journey and afterwards went with him to Rome where he stayed during Paul's imprisonment. It is generally accepted that Luke was the author of the third Gospel and also of the Acts of the Apostles and St Paul mentions him in Colossians as 'the beloved physician'. Yet we have no knowledge of what happened later in his life or how he met his death.

Luke is the patron saint of doctors and also of artists. There is no scriptural reason for the second ascription but in the Middle Ages a picture in the Santa Maggiore of the Virgin Mary was claimed as his work. His symbol of the ox was suggested because his Gospel begins with the story of the priest sacrificing in the Temple and the ox is the symbol of sacrifice. Thus all that we really know of Luke comes from accounts in the New Testament. Even his day was not chosen for any biographical reason but only because it was on 18 October 537 that his relics were transferred from Thebes in Boetia to Constantinople, where they were preserved in the Church of the Apostles which was built soon afterwards.

19 October

Altinus of Orleans (1st or 4th cent.), Ptolemy and Lucius (c.165), Veronicus, Pelagia and Comp. (?), Varus of Upper Egypt (307), Cleopatra of Syria (319), Eusterius of Salerno (5th cent.), Lupus of Soissons (c.540), Veranus of Cavaillon (590), Ethbin of Kildare (c.600), Aquilinus of Evreux (695), Desiderius of Lonrey (c.705), Theofrid of Carmery (728), Frideswide of Oxford (c.735), Laura of Córdova (864), Eadnot of Dorchester (1016), Bl Thomas Hélye (1257), Peter of Alcántara (1562), Bl Philip Howard (1595).

20 October

Maximus of Aquila (c.250), Martha, Saula and Comp. (?), Caprasius of Agen (303), Barsabas and Comp. (c.342), Artemius (363), Bradan and Orora (?), Irene of Santarem (c.653), Sindulphus of Reims (660), Acca of Hexham (742), Vitalis of Salzburg (745), Andrew the Calabyte (766), Aidan of Mayo (768), Bernard of Bagnorea (p.800), Aderald of Troyes (1004), Bl William of Savigny (c.1122), Adelina of Moriton (1125), John Cantius (1473), BB Francis Serrano and Francis Diaz (1648), Bertilla Boscardin (1922).

21 October

Asterius of Ostia (c.223), Dasius, Zoticus, Caius and Comp. (c.303), Hilarion of Gaza (c.371), Viator of Lyons (c.390), Malchus of Chalcis (c.390), Ursula and Comp. (before 4th cent.), Agatho of Egypt (4th cent.), Cilinia of Laon (p.458), Wendelinus (c.607), Finian of Taghmon (c.635), Tuda of Lindisfarne (664), Condedus of Fontenelle (c.690), Maurontus of Marseilles (c.804), Hugh of Ambronay (9th or 10th cent.), Gebizo of Monte Cassino (c.1087), Berthold of Parma (1111), Bl Imana of Loss (1270), Bl Gundisalvus of Lagos (1422), Bl Peter Capucci (1445).

22 October

Mary Salome (1st cent.), Mark of Jerusalem (c.156), Abercius of Hierapolis (c.167), Philip of Fermo (c.270), Alexander, Heraclius and Comp. (?), Philip, Severus, Eusebius and Hermes (304), Mellonius of Rouen (314), Nepotian of Clermont (c.388), Cordula (c.453), Verecundus of Verona (522), Simplicius of Monte Cassino (c.570), Maroveus of Precipiano (c.650), Nunctus of Mérida (668), Moderan of Berceto (c.730), Benedict of Macerac (845), Nunilo and Alodia (851), Donatus of Fiesole (874), Bertharius of Monte Cassino (c.884), Bl Paul Doi Buong (1833).

23 October

Servandus and Germanus (c.305), Theodore of Antioch (362), Verus of Salerno (4th cent.), Amo of Toul (4th cent.), Severinus of Cologne (c.403), Severinus of Bordeaux (c.420), Clether of Wales (c.520), Severinus Boëthius (525), John of Syracuse (c.609), Romanus of Rouen (639), Benedict of Sebaste (c.654), Syra of Faremoutiers (c.660), Leothadius of Moissae (718), Oda of Amay (c.723), Domitius of

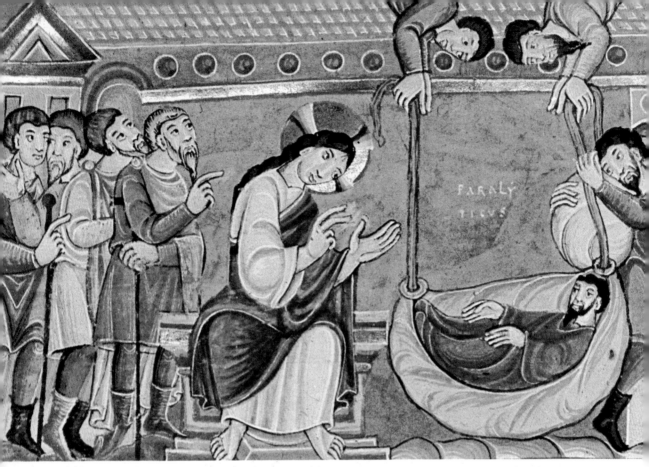

St Luke the Physician's story of Christ's healing of the man let down through the roof (*Echternach: Codex Aureo*).

Amiens (8th cent.), Ignatius of Constantinople (877), Elfleda of Glastonbury (*c*.936), Allucio of Pescia (1134), Bl Bertrand of Grandselve (1149), Bl Henry of Cologne (1225), Bl John Buoni (1249), Bl Bartholomew of Braganza (1271), Bl Thomas Thwing (1680).

24 October

Raphael the Archangel, Felix, Audactus, Januarius, Fortunatus and Septimus (303), Proclus of Constantinople (447), Evergislus of Cologne (5th cent.), Martyrs of Nagran (523), Maglorius of Wales (*c*.586), Cadfarch of Wales (6th cent.), Martin of Vertou (601), Marcius of Mt Massico (*c*.679), Fromundus of Coutances (p.690), Bernard Calvó (1243), Bl John Angelo Porro (1504), Bl Joseph Thi (1860), Antony Mary Claret (1870).

25 October

Tabitha or Dorcas (1st cent.), Minias of Florence (*c*.250), Theodosius, Lucius, Mark and Peter (269), Chrysanthus and Daria (283), Crispin and Crispinian (*c*.287), Cyrinus of Rome (3rd cent.), Marcellinus, Claudius, Cyrinus and Antoninus (3rd cent.), Fronto and George (?), Protus and Januarius (303), Martyrius and Marcian (351), Gaudentius of Brescia (*c*.410), Lupus of Bayeux (5th cent.), Hilary of Mende (535), Dulcardus of Micy (584), Hildemarca of Fécamp (*c*.670), Goeznoveus of Leon (675), Guesnoveus of Quimper (675), Fructus, Valentine and Engratia (*c*.715), Bl Theodoric of St-Hubert (1087), Bl Albert of Sassoferrato (1330), Bl Thaddeus McCarthy (1497).

26 October

Evaristus (*c*.197), Lucian, Florius and Comp. (*c*.250), Rogatian and Felicissimus (256), Rusticus of Narbonne (*c*.462), Alanus and Aldrus (5th cent.), Quadragesimus of Policastro (*c*.590), Aneurin and Gwinoc (6th cent.), Gibitrudis of Faremoutiers (*c*.655), Eadfrid of Leominster (*c*.675), Eata of Hexham (*c*.686), Gaudiosus of Salerno (7th cent.), Humbert of Fritzlar (7th or 8th cent.), Sigibald of Metz (*c*.740), Cuthbert of Canterbury (758), Albinus of Buraburg (p.760), Bean of Aberdeen (p.1012), Bl Adalgott of Dissentis (1031), Fulk of Pavia (1229), Bl Damian dei Fulcheri (1484), Bl Bonaventure of Potenza (1711), Bl Dominic Doan (1839).

St Simon and St Jude
(*Saxlingham Church,
Norfolk*).

27 October

Florentius of Burgundy (3rd cent.), Vincent, Sabina and Christeta (303), Capitolina and Erotheis (304), Abraham the Child (367), Frumentius of Ethiopia (*c*.380), Gaudiosus of Naples (*c*.455), Namatius of Clermont (p.462), Elesbaan (*c*.555), Otteran of Iona (*c*.563), Abban of Wexford (6th cent.), Cyriacus of Constantinople (606), Desiderius of Auxerre (*c*.625), Colman of Senboth-Fola (*c*.632), Bl Goswin of Chemnion (1203), Bl Antonia of Brescia (1507).

28 October

Simon the Zealot and Jude Thaddaeus (1st cent.), Anastasia and Cyril (*c*.253), Cyrilla of Rome (*c*.270), Ferrutius of Mainz (?), Fidelis of Como (*c*.304), Honoratus of Vercelli (*c*.410), Salvius of Normandy (6th cent.), Abraham of Ephesus (6th cent.), Faro of Meaux (*c*.675), Godwin of Stavelot (*c*.690), Dorbhene of Iona (713), Anglinus of Stavelot (*c*.768), Alberic of Stavelot (779), Remigius of Lyons (875), Eadsin of Canterbury (1050), Bl John Dat (1798), Bl Joachim Royo (1848).

ST SIMON AND ST JUDE

It may be that these two saints were both considered among the brethren of Our Lord. We know very little about them from the Gospels and we have no real reason to account for the fact that they are always referred to jointly in the ecclesiastical calendar. Both were numbered among the twelve Apostles and Simon is called the Canaanean by Matthew and Mark and the Zealot or Zealotes by Luke. The first is a translation of the second which itself suggests that Simon may have been a member of the extreme nationalists – the Zealots – who were later to inspire the disastrous revolt against the Romans in AD 70 which culminated in the destruction of Jerusalem.

Jude is called Lebbaeus, Thaddaeus and Judas, not Iscariot. His only recorded act is in asking Jesus in the Upper Room when He would manifest Himself to them and not to the world. St Luke does call him 'Judas of James' which would suggest that he was the son of James but he has more generally been identified with Jude 'brother of James', one of the brethren of the Lord and the author of the Epistle of Jude.

29 October

Narcissus of Jerusalem (*c*.222), Maximilian of Lorch (284), Eusebia of Bergamo (late 3rd cent.), Donatus of Corfù (?), Hyacinth, Quintus, Felician and Lucius (?), John of Autun (?), Zenobius of Antioch (310), Kennera of Scotland (5th cent.), Terence of Metz (520), Theuderius of Vienne (*c*.575), Ermelinda of Meldaert (*c*.595), Colman of Kilmacduagh (632), Sigolinus of Stavelot (670), Bond of Sens (7th cent.), Anne, or Euphemian (820), Elfleda of Ramsey (*c*.1000), Stephen of Caiazzo (1023), Bl Berengarius of Formbach (1108), Bl Wirnto of Göttweig (1127), Bl Paula of Montaldo (1514), BB Martyrs of Douai (16th and 17th cent.).

30 October

Artemas of Lystra (1st cent.), Serapion of Antioch (199), Eutropia of Africa (*c*.253), Zenobius and Zenobia (285–90), Marcellus of Tangier (298), Julian, Eunus, Macarius and Comp. (?), Claudius, Lupercus and Victorius (*c*.300), Saturninus of Cagliari (303), Maximus of Cumae (304), Asterius of Amasea (*c*.400), Theonestus of Altino (425), Lucanus of Lagny (5th cent.), Germanus of Capua (*c*.545), Talarica of Scotland (6th cent.), Arilda of Gloucestershire (?), Herbert of Tours (?), Egelnoth the Good (1038), Nanterius of St-Mihiel (*c*.1044), Gerard of Potenza (1119), Bl Bernard de la Tour (1258), Bl Benvenuta Bojani (1292), Dorothy of Montau (1394), Bl John Slade (1583), Bl Angelus of Acri (1739).

31 October

Ampliatus, Urban and Narcissus (1st cent.), Stachys of Byzantium (1st cent.), Quintinus of Amiens (287), Erth of Cornwall (6th cent.), Foillan of Fosses (*c*.655), Antoninus Fontana (660), Bega (681), Notburga of Cologne (*c*.714), Arnulfus of Novalese (p.840), Wolfgang of Ratisbon (994), Bl Christopher of Romagnola (1272), Bl Thomas Bellaci (1447), Alphonsus Rodríguez (1617).

1 November

Feast of All Saints, Austremonius of Clermont (1st or 3rd cent.), Benignus of Dijon (3rd cent.), Caesarius and Julian (?), Caesarius, Decius and Comp., Mary the Slave (*c*.300), Cyrenia and Juliana (306), John and James (*c*.344), Mathurin of Sens (388), Marcellus of Paris (*c*.430), Amabilis of Auvergne (475), Dingad of Wales (5th cent.), Cledwyn of Wales (5th cent.), Pabiali of Wales (5th or 6th cent.), Vigor of Bayeux (*c*.537), Cadfan of Wales (early 6th cent.), Ceitho of Wales (6th cent.), Licinius of Angers (*c*.616), Caesarius of Clermont (p.627), Floribert of Ghent (*c*.660), Genesius of Fontenelle (*c*.679), Severinus of Tiboli (*c*.699), Germanus of Montfort (*c*.1000), Salaun of Brittany (1358), Bl Conradin of Brescia (1429), BB Paul Navarro and Comp. (1622), BB Jerome Hermosilla, Peter Almató and Valentine Berrio-Ochoa (1861).

ALL SAINTS

This festival is kept in the Western Church to commemorate all Christian saints and martyrs particularly those who are not otherwise remembered. At Antioch in Chrysostom's time a festival of 'all the martyrs' was celebrated on the First Sunday after Pentecost. This was especially important when persecution meant that so many were killed that it was no longer possible to commemorate them all individually. On 13 May 608, Pope Boniface IV dedicated to Christian worship the old Roman Pantheon. This was the circular temple built by the Emperor Hadrian in the second century AD in honour of all the gods. With its new Christian guise it became the Church of St Mary and All Martyrs, and its dedication day became an annual commemoration of 'All Saints'. The transference of the feast to 1 November seems to have taken place when Pope Gregory III (d.741) chose the date to dedicate the Chapel of All Saints in the basilica of St Peter. Its universal observance on that day was ordered by Pope Gregory IV (d.844).

In Britain, All Saints was formerly known as All Hallows Day. Hallowe'en (the night before), was believed to be the time when witches, devils, fairies and other imps of earth and air held their annual holiday. The night was long observed, especially in northern England and Scotland, by fireside revelries concerned with divination of the future. Traditionally children bob for apples on Hallowe'en. Hands firmly behind their backs they try to bite the apples floating in a pail of water or fastened to a hanging cross supporting lighted candles.

Once it was true that many dioceses had a special day on which to commemorate all their local saints but now these are abolished and only Ireland with its special feasts of All Saints of Ireland on 6 November has this custom. However, there are a number of religious orders who celebrate a feast of the saints in their own order on a special day.

2 November

Commemoration of All the Souls of the Faithful Departed, Publius, Victor, Hermas and Papias (?), George of Vienne (?), Victorinus of Pettau (*c*.303), Justus of Trieste (303), Carterius, Styriacus, Tobias, Eudoxius, Aagpius and Comp. (*c*.315), Theodotus of Laodicea (334), Acindynus, Pegasius, Aphthonius, Elpidephorus and Anempodistus (345), Eustochium of Tarsus (362), Marcian of Chalcis (387), Ambrose of Agaune (523), Cumgar of Devon (6th or 8th cent.), Baya and Maura (10th cent.), Amicus of Monte Cassino (*c*.1045), Jorandus of Kergrist (1340), Bl Thomas of Walden (1430), Bl John Bodey (1583).

ALL SOULS

Regular Christian commemorations of the dead are mentioned as early as the third century by several writers. In the Eastern Church, Saturday was a special day of prayer for the dead, especially the Saturday before Lent and before Pentecost. In the Western Church the commemoration of the souls of the faithful departed on the day after All Saints Day is said to have been instituted by St Odilo, Abbot of Cluny, in 998, when he commanded its annual celebration in all the Benedictine monasteries of his congregation.

Priests of the Roman Catholic Church are allowed to celebrate three Masses on this day, the only other day on which this privilege is permitted being Christmas Day. The Mass on All Souls Day, like a Mass at the burial of the dead, contains the famous sequence known by its opening words as *Dies Irae* (Day of Wrath), probably written by a Franciscan friar of the thirteenth century and not originally intended for use in services as it is written in the first person singular:

Think, good Jesu, my salvation
Caused Thy wondrous Incarnation;
Leave me not to reprobation.

3 November

Quartus (1st cent.), Germanus, Theophilus, Caesareus and Vitalis (250), Papulus of Toulouse (*c*.300), Innumerable Martyrs of Saragossa (*c*.304), Valentine and Hilary (*c*.304), Florus of Lodeve (389), Acepsimas of Cyrrhus (5th cent.), Valentinian of Salerno (*c*.500), Domnus of Vienne (527), Guenhael of Landevenec (*c*.550), Sylvia of Rome (*c*.572), Gaudiosus of Tarazona (*c*.585), Elerius of Wales (6th cent.), Winifred of Wales (*c*.680), Cristiolus of Wales (7th cent.), Vulgan-

ius of Arras (*c*.704), Hubert of Liége (727), Pirminius of Reichenau (753), Acheric and William (*c*.860), Englatius of Scotland (966), Hermengaudius of Urgell (1035), Malachy O'More (1148), Bl Berthold of Engelberg (1197), Bl Alpais of Cudot (1211), Bl Ida of Toggenburg (1226), Bl Raynerius of Arezzo (1304), Bl Simon Ballachi (1319), Bl Peter-Francis Neron (1860).

4 November

Philologus and Patrobas (1st cent.), Porphyrius of Ephesus (171), Nicander and Hermas (?), Vitalis and Agricola (*c*.304), Pierius of Alexandria (*c*.310), John Zedazneli (6th cent.), Modesta of Öhren (*c*.680), Proculus of Autun (p.717), Joannicius of Mt Olympus (846), Clarus of Rouen (*c*.875), Birnstan of Winchester (*c*.934), Gregory of Burtscheid (999), Emeric of Hungary (1031), Gerard of Bazonches (1123), Bl Helen Enselmini (1242), Bl Henry of Zwiefalten (p.1250), Bl Frances d'Amboise (1485), Charles Borromeo (1584), Bl Theodore Guenot (1861).

ST CHARLES BORROMEO

Few circumstances could have been more propitious for a great Prince of the Church than those into which Charles Borromeo was born. His father was an aristocrat from a family already well entrenched in the ecclesiastical establishment. His mother was a Medici. At twelve Charles Borromeo began his studies for the priesthood and was given the Benedictine Abbey of SS Gratinian and Felinus. At twenty-one his uncle became Pope and at twenty-two he was made Cardinal-deacon and administrator of the see of Milan. During the pontificate of Paul IV he governed the Church, so much did his uncle rely upon him, and he therefore played an important part in the reconstituted Council of Trent and in the whole course of the counter-Reformation. Altogether a likely start for an ecclesiastical politician, but hardly for a saint. Yet when the death of his patron allowed him to return as Archbishop to Milan, Charles Borromeo began his great work as an authentic father in God. Using his wealth to relieve poverty and build churches, he lived simply. His visitations purged his diocese of unworthy priests and reorganized the monasteries. He invented Sunday schools by establishing the Institutes of Christian Doctrine and he founded an order of secular priests – the Oblates of St Ambrose. The unreformed Church made him a Cardinal at twenty-two but his canonization came from the devotion of the ordinary people

among whom he had worked, worn himself out, and died.

5 November

Zachary (1st cent.), Elisabeth (1st cent.), Felix and Eusebius (1st cent.), Galation and Epistemis (252), Domninus, Theotimus, Philotheus, Sylvanus and Comp. (?), Domninus of Grenoble (4th cent.), Dominator of Brescia (c.495), Fibitius of Trèves (c.500), Magnus of Milan (525), Laetus of Orleans (533), Kanten of Wales (6th cent.), Kea (6th cent.), Augustine and Paulinus (6th cent.), Bertilla of Chelles (c.705), Spinulus of Moyen-moutier (707), Hermenegild of Salcedo (953), Gerald of Beziers (1123), Bl Raynerius of Todi (c.1586), Bl Martin Porres (1639), Bl Gomidas Keumurjian (1707).

6 November

Felix of Thynissa (?), Atticus of Phrygia (?), Pinnock (?), Leonard of Noblac (c.559), Leonianus of Autun (c.570), Felix of Fondi (6th cent.), Severus of Barcelona (633), Ten Martyrs of Antioch (637), Edwen of Anglesey (7th cent.), Efflam of Brittany (c.700), Winoc of Wormhoult (717), Appian of Commachio (c.800), Erlafrid of Hirsau (p.830), Demetrian of Cyprus (c.912), Stephen of Apt (1046), Bl Simon of Aulne (1215), Leonard of Reresby (13th cent.), Bl Christina of Stommeln (1312), Bl Nonius Alvarez (1431), Bl Margaret of Lorraine (1521).

7 November

Prosdocimus of Padua (c.100), Amaranthus of Albi (3rd cent.), Hieron, Nicander, Hesychius and Comp. (c.300), Auctus, Taurion and Thessalonica (?), Achillas of Alexandria (313), Melasippus, Antony and Carina (360), Rufus of Metz (c.400), Herculanus of Perugia (549), Tremorus of Brittany (6th cent.), Raverannus of Séez (682), Gertrude of Remiremont (c.690), Florentius of Strassburg (c.693), Amarand of Albi (p.700), Willibrord of Echternach (739), Blinlivet of Quimperlé (9th cent.), Ernest of Zwiefalten (1148), Bl Lucy of Settefonti (12th cent.), Engelbert of Cologne (1225), Bl Antony Baldinucci (1717), BB Hyacinth Castañeda and Comp. (1773), Bl John Baptist Cou (1840).

St Charles Borromeo (*Stefano Moderno*).

8 November

Four Crowned Martyrs (*c*.305), Maurus of Verdun (383), Clarus of Marmoutier (397), Cuby of Caernarvon (6th cent.), Deusdedit I (618), Tysilio of Wales (*c*.640), Willehad of Bremen (*c*.790), Wiomad of Trèves (*c*.790), Moroc of Scotland (9th cent.), Gregory of Einsiedeln (996), Gervadius of Elgin (10th cent.), Godfrey of Amiens (1115), Bl Columbus of Toulouse (1229), BB Joseph Nghi, Martin Tinh and Martin Tho (1840).

9 November

Agrippinus of Naples (2nd or 3rd cent.), Ursinus of Bourges (3rd cent.), Orestes of Cappadocia (304), Theodore Tyro (*c*.306), Alexander of Salonica (4th cent.), Benignas of Ireland (*c*.468), Pabo of Brittany (*c*.510), Vitonus of Verdun (*c*.525), Eustiola and Sopatra (7th cent.), Bl George Napper (1610).

10 November

Tryphena and Tryphosa (1st cent.), Probus of Ravenna (*c*.175), Tryphon, Respicius and Nympha (251), Demetrius, Anianus, Eustosius and Comp. (?), Leo of Melun (?), Tiberius, Modestus and Florence (303), Monitor of Orleans (*c*.490), Justus of Canterbury (627), Elaeth of Anglesey (6th cent.), Aedh McBricc (6th cent.), Hadelin of Séez (*c*.910), Guerembaldus of Hirsau (965), Theoctiste of Lesbos (10th cent.), John of Ratzeburg (1066), Bl Andrew of Baudiment (1142), Bl Andrew Avellino (1608).

11 November

Mennas of Egypt (*c*.295), **Athenodorus of Mesopotamia** (*c*.304), Valentine, Felician and Victorinus (*c*.305), Martin of Tours (397), Cynfran of Wales (5th cent.), Veranus of Lyons (5th cent.), Rhedius of Wales (?), Mennas of Santomena (6th cent.), Bertuin of Malonne (*c*.698), Theodore Studites (826), Bartholomew of Rossano (1065), Bl Bartholomew of Marmoutier (1067), Bl Alradus of Isenhagen (*c*.1250), Bl Agnes of Bavaria (1532), Bl Joseph Pignatelli (1811).

ST MARTIN OF TOURS

Four thousand French churches are dedicated to St Martin and more than five hundred French villages bear his name. Once he was the most popular saint of the West and he still remains one of the patrons of France. St Martin was born on the Danube in the Roman province of Pannonia. His parents were pagans and his father an old campaigner. Martin became a catechumen and continued his interest in Christianity when he followed his father into the Imperial Army. While stationed in Amiens he met a poor man begging alms in the freezing winter. Martin cut his own cloak in two and gave it to the wretch. Later he had a vision of Christ, clad in the cloak, and this finally brought him to be baptized. During the Barbarian invasion of Gaul he became a conscientious objector and refused to fight. The conclusion of an armistice saved him from punishment and he went off to Poitiers where St Hilary, the bishop, ordained him deacon. In 371 he was forcibly conveyed to the cathedral of Tours and made bishop. He continued to live simply and was joined by a company of monks many of whom became bishops in neighbouring dioceses, so renowned was

St Martin of Tours shares his cloak with a beggar (*Spanish*).

the community as a seminary. St Martin set a high standard in pastoral work and interceded with the civil authorities to save the lives of prisoners of war and through a prolonged battle managed to get a number of heretics reprieved. His insistence that heresy should not be punished by death but by public excommunication showed an understanding of Christianity rare at this time and made many doubt his orthodoxy. He is said to have died of exhaustion and two thousand monks followed his funeral procession at Tours.

12 November

Aurelius and Publius (2nd cent.), Rufus of Avignon (c.200), Renatus of Angers (c.422), Nilus the Elder (c.430), Evodius of Le Puy (p.560), Aemilian of La Cogolla (574), Machar of Iona (6th cent.), Imerius of Immertal (c.610), Cunibert of Trèves (c.633), Livinus of Alsot (c.650), Martin I (655), Cumian Fada (662), Cadwallador of Wales (c.662), Paternus of St-Pierre-le-Vif (c.729), Lebuin of Deventer (c.773), Namphasius of Marcillac (c.800), Yvar of Reculver (c.830), Benedict, John, Matthew, Isaac and Christinus (1005), Anastasius of Pannonhalma (c.1030), Bl John Cini 'della Pace' (1433), Bl Gabriel Ferretti (1456), Didacus of Alcalá (1463) (Feast on the 13th), Bl Christopher of Portugal (c.1500), Josaphat of Poland (1623).

13 November

Antoninus, Zebinas, Germanus and Ennatha (297), Valentine, Solutor and Victor (c.305), Mitrius of Aix (314), Arcadius, Paschasius, Probus, Eutychian and Paulillus (437), Brice of Tours (444), Quintian of Rodez (c.527), Dalmatius of Rodez (580), Devinicus of Caithness (6th cent.), Columbia of Cornwall (?), Eugene II of Toledo (657), Maxellendis of Caudry (c.670), Gredifael of Wales (7th cent.), Chillien of Aubigny (7th cent.), Caillin of Ferns (7th cent.), Nicholas the Great (867), Abbo of Fleury (1004), Homobonus of Cremona (1197), Siardus of Mariengaarden (1230), Bl Mark of Scala (c.1280).

14 November

Veneranda of Gaul (2nd cent.), Serapion of Alexandria (252), Venerandus of Troyes (275), Clementinus, Theodotus and Philomenus (?), Hypatius of Gangra (p.325), Jucundus of Bologna (c.485), Modanic of Aberdeen (?), Dubricius of Wales (c.545), Sidonius of St-Saens (c.690), Alberic of Utrecht (784), Laurence

O'Toole (1180), Serapion of Algiers (1240), Bl John Licci (1511).

15 November

Felix of Nola (287), Secundus, Fidentian and Varicus (?), Eugene (?), Gurias and Samonas (306), Abibus of Edessa (322), Luperius of Verona (6th or 8th cent.), Malo of Brittany (621), Desiderius of Cahors (655), Machudd of Llanfechell (7th cent.), Paduinus of Le Mans (c.703), Arnulfus of Toul (871), Findan of Rheinau (879), Albert the Great (1280), Leopold the Good (1136), BB Richard Whiting, Roger James and John Thorne (1539), BB Hugh Faringdon, John Eynon and John Rugg (1539), Bl Lucy Brocolelli (1544), Bl Caius of Corea (1624).

16 November

Rufinus, Mark and Valerius and Comp. (?), Fidentius of Padua (?), Elpidius, Marcellus, Eustochius and Comp. (362), Eucherius of Lyons (450), Afan of Wales (6th cent.), Gobrian of Vannes (725), Othmar of St-Gall (759), Africus of Comminges (7th cent.), Alfrick of Canterbury (1006), Bl Simeon of Cava (1141), Edmund Rich (1242), Agnes of Assisi (1253), Gertrude the Great (c.1302), Bl Louis Morbioli (1495), Bl Gratia of Cattaro (1509).

17 November

Dionysius of Alexandria (265), Gregory Thaumaturgus (c.270), Alphaeus and Zacchaeus (303), Acisclus and Victoria (304), Eugene of Florence (422), Anianus of Orleans (453), Namasius of Vienne (c.559), Gregory of Tours (596), Hilda of Whitby (680), Hugh of Noara (p.1172), Hugh of Lincoln (1200), Bl Salomea of Poland (1268), Bl Jane of Segna (1307), BB Martyrs of Paraguay (1628).

18 November

Hesychius of Antioch (c.303), Romanus and Barulas (304), Maximus of Mainz (378), Oriculus and Comp. (c.430), Nazarius of Lérins (c.450), Mawes (6th cent.), Keverne (6th cent.), Mummolus of Lagny (c.690), Amandus and Anselm (8th cent.), Fergus (p.721), Constant (777), Thomas of Antioch (782), Odo of Cluny (942), Burginus and Guilminus (p.1065), Bl Andrew Trong (1835), Bl Rose-Philippine Duchesne (1852).

19 November

Abdias (9th cent. BC), Exuperius, Severinus and Felician (170), Pontian (*c*.236), Maximus of Rome (*c*.255), Barlaam of Caesarea (*c*.304), Azas and Comp. (*c*.304), Nerses the Great (373), Crispin of Ecoja (4th cent.), Faustus of Alexandria (4th cent.), Anastasius II (498), Ermenburga of Thanet (*c*.650), Medana of Galloway (8th cent.), Bl Tuto of Ottobeuren (815), James of Sasseau (*c*.865), Atto of Tordino (p.1010), Elisabeth of Hungary (1231), Mechtildis of Hackeborn (1298), BB Martyrs of Annam (1754–1861, 1820–41).

ST ELISABETH OF HUNGARY

A Hungarian princess, Elisabeth was sent to Germany and married at the age of fourteen to Louis IV of Thuringia. Their marriage was an idyllically happy one but her generosity to the poor and her holy life of prayer and penance, made her famous. The much loved story of her finding a leper and putting him in her own bed exemplifies this. Her husband, usually patient and supportive in her devotion, sprang out of bed and berated her – only to see the leper as if he were Christ, bleeding at hands, feet, and side. In 1227 St Elisabeth's husband went on the Crusade and died of the plague. His brother drove her out and she settled at Marburg, where she made an unwise choice of a spiritual director – Conrad of Marburg – who treated her with great severity, compelling her to give up her children and undergo whippings at his hands. At the same time she lived very austerely and nursed the sick in a hospital she built there. Her continued work for the poor, and self-denial brought her an early death at the age of twenty-three. She was canonized in 1235, one of the witnesses in her cause being Conrad of Marburg.

20 November

Eustace, Thespesius and Anatolius (235), Octavius, Solutor and Adventor (297), Bassius, Dionysius, Agapitus and Comp. (?), Ampelius and Caius (*c*.302), Dasius of Dorostorum (*c*.303), Agapius of Caesarea (*c*.306), Nerses and Comp. (343), Benignus of Milan (*c*.477), Maxentia of Beauvais (?), Silvester of Chalons-sur-Saone (*c*.525), Simplicius of Verona (*c*.535), Eval of Cornwall (6th cent.), Autbodus of Laon (690), Eudo of Cormery (*c*.760), Edmund (870), Gregory Decapolites (9th cent.), Leo of Nonantula (1000), Bernward of Hildesheim (1022), Felix of Valois (1212), Bl Ambrose Traversari (1439), Bl Francis Xavier Can (1837).

21 November

Feast of the Presentation of the B.V.Mary, Rufus of Rome (*c*.90), Heliodorus and Comp. (*c*.270), Demetrius and Honorius (?), Celsus and Clement (?), Honorius, Eutychius and Stephen (*c*.300), Gelasius I (496), Digain of Cornwall (5th cent.), Columbanus of Luxeuil (615), Columbanus Junior (p.616), Maurus of Verona (*c*.600), Amelberga of Susteren (p.900), Hilary of Volturno (*c*.1045), Bl Nicholas Giustiniani (p.1180).

THE PRESENTATION OF THE BLESSED VIRGIN MARY

This feast began in the East in the seventh century and in the West during the late Middle Ages. It commemorates the day when the Apochryphal Gospel says that Our Lady was brought to the Temple at the age of three to be dedicated there until her marriage. Whatever the historical truth, the day points to the total offering of the Virgin as the mother of Christ.

22 November

Philemon and Appia (*c*.70), Caecilia of Rome (2nd–3rd cent.), Maurus of Africa (*c*.284), Mark of Antioch (*c*.305), Pragmatius of Autun (*c*.520), Dayniol the Younger (621), Savinian of Menat (*c*.720), Bl Christian of Auxerre (*c*.873), Trigidia of Oña (*c*.925), Bl Eugenia of Matera (*c*.1093), Bl Benedict de Ponte (13th cent.).

23 November

Clement of Rome (*c*.100), Felicitas of Rome (165),

A miracle of St Elizabeth of Hungary (*Piero*).

Christ of St John of the Cross (*Salvador Dali*).

Clement of Metz (?), Lucretia of Merida (306), Sisinius of Cyzicus (p.325), Paternian of Fermo (*c.*343), Amphilochius of Iconium (p.392), Paulinus of Wales (*c.*505), Gregory of Girgenti (*c.*638), Wilfretudis of Nivelle (p.670), Trudo of St-Trond (*c.*695), Rachildis of St-Gall (*c.*946), Bl Margaret of Savoy (1464).

24 November

Firmina of Amelia (*c.*303), Felicissimus of Perugia (*c.*303), Chrysogonus of Aquileia (*c.*304), Crescentian of Rome (309), Protasius of Milan (352), Alexander of Corinth (361), Romanus of Le Mans (385), Kenan of Damleag (*c.*500), Portianus of Miranda (533), Colman of Cloyne (*c.*600), Leopardinus of Vivaris (7th cent.), Bieuzy of Brittany (7th cent.), Eanfleda of Whitby (*c.*700), Marinus of Maurienne (731), Flora and Mary (856), Bl Balsamus of Cava (1232), Bl Conrad of Frisach (1239), John of the Cross (1591), BB Peter Dumoulin-Borie and Comp. (1838), BB Martyrs of China and Cochin-China (1823–56).

ST JOHN OF THE CROSS

Described as the 'Prince of Mystics' and the 'Doctor of Nothingness', John de Yepes was born at Fontiberos in Old Castile, the son of a poor weaver. He entered a Carmelite monastery in 1563, but was so dissatisfied with its laxity that he would have become a Carthusian had he not met Teresa of Avila, who persuaded him to join her first reformed house for friars where he became known as John of the Cross. He was a man of deep devotion whose mystical insights led him through a period of joy and then plunged him into a terrible time when he felt he had been forsaken by God. His book *The Dark Night of the Soul* tells of this period. Later his spiritual conflict was to be paralleled by a physical one. Battles between the reformed and unreformed Carmelites had broken out and so John was seized by the unreformed friars and imprisoned in one of their monasteries, where he was frequently flogged and fed only on bread, water and salt fish. After nine months he escaped and was made the prior of several reformed Carmelite houses. His own moderation led to ill-feeling between him and his over-zealous superiors who sent him to one of their poorest monasteries where he fell ill and died in obscurity. His death changed the popular attitude and his fame spread widely. St Teresa had regarded him as one of the most pure souls, and his mystical works – *The Ascent of Mt Carmel, The Living Flame of Love*, as well as *The Dark Night of the Soul* were seen as major spiritual writings. He was canonized in 1726 and declared a Doctor of the Church in 1926.

25 November

Moses of Rome (*c.*250), Mercurius of Caesarea (*c.*250), Erasmus of Antioch (?), Catherine of Alexandria (*c.*310), Mesrob the Teacher (441), Jucunda of Reggio (466), Lavanus of Gascony (7th cent.), Alnoth of Stowe (*c.*700), Imma of Karlburg (*c.*752), Adalbert and Guido of Casauria (*c.*1045), Bl Bernold of Otto-beuren (*c.*1050), Bl Ekbert of Münsterschwarzach (1075), Bl Conrad of Heisterbach (*c.*1200), Bl Elisabeth the Good (1420).

ST CATHERINE OF ALEXANDRIA

The traditional story of Catherine of Alexandria is that she was one of the most beautiful and learned women of her time in Egypt and was martyred for her faith. She became one of the most venerated of women saints in the Middle Ages, but the facts of her life are doubtful, and she is not mentioned before the tenth century. According to legend, the Emperor Maximilian was attracted by her and when she refused his advances, he assembled fifty heathen philosophers to overcome her scruples; but she defeated them in argument and made an unanswerable defence of Christian faith and morals. For this she was tortured by being tied to a revolving spiked wheel and then flogged and beheaded. Devotion to her seems to have started in the great monastery on Mount Sinai, which claims her relics. Her fame was brought to Europe by the Crusaders, and her feast was proclaimed for the Western Church by Pope John XXII in 1335. The Catherine-wheel firework and the Catherine or Rose window, with its radiating design, were named after her. Formerly it was the custom for her statue in churches to be crowned on this day by maidens who wished to have a good husband.

Ah, foolish crowd! This world's thick vapours whelm,
Your eyes unworthy of that glorious show,
Blind to His splendour, bent upon His shame.

JOSIAH CONDER, *Hymns*

26 November

Amator of Autun (3rd cent.), Peter of Alexandria (311), Faustus, Didius, Ammonius, Phileas, Hesychius, Pachomius, Theodore and Comp. (*c*.311), Marcellus of Nicomedia (349), Stylianus of Adrianopolis (390), Siricius (399), Basolus of Verzy (*c*.620), Egelwine of Athelney (7th cent.), Martin of Arades (726), Conrad of Constance (975), Nicon Metanoite (998), Bellinus of Padua (1151), Bl Pontius of Faucigny (1178), Bl Walter of Aulnes (*c*.1180), Silvester Gozzolini (1267), Bl Albert of Haigerloch (1311), Bl James Benfatti (1338), Bl Redemptus of the Cross (1638), Leonard of Port Maurice (1751).

27 November

Basileus, Auxilius and Saturninus (?), Barlaam and Josaphat (?), Facundus and Primitivus (*c*.300), Hirenarchus, Acacius and Comp. (*c*.305), Valerian of Aquileia (389), James Intercisus (421), John Angeloptes (433), Seachnall of Dunshauglin (457), Maximus of Riez (460), Severinus of Paris (*c*.540), Siffred of Carpentras (540), Gallgo of Wales (6th cent.), Acharius of Noyon (640), Bilhild of Altenmünster (*c*.710), Virgilius of Salzburg (784), Apollinaris of Monte Cassino (828), Edwold of Cerne (9th cent.), Albert of Louvain (1192), Bl Angelus Sinesio (*c*.1386), Bl Bernardinus of Fossa (1503), BB Antony Kimura and Comp. (1619), Bl Humilis of Bisignano (1637).

28 November

Sosthenes (1st cent.), Rufus and Comp. (304), Valerian, Urban, Crescens, Eustace, Cresconius, Crescentian, Felix, Hortulanus and Florentian (5th cent.), Papinianus and Mansuetus (5th cent.), Fionnchu of Bangor (6th cent.), Stephen, Basil, Peter, Andrew and Comp. (764), Hippolytus of St-Claude (*c*.775), James della Marca (1475), Bl Calimerius of Montechiaro (1521), Joseph Pignatelli (1811), Catherine Labouré (1876).

29 November

Paramon and Comp. (250), Saturninus of Toulouse (*c*.257), Philomenus of Ancyra (275), Blaise and Demetrius (?), Saturninus and Sisinius (*c*.309), Illuminata of Todi (*c*.320), Brendan of Birr (*c*.562), Sadwen of Wales (6th cent.), Hardoin of Brittany (7th cent.), Walderic of Murrhardt (p.817), Radbod of Utrecht (918), Gulstan of Rhuys (*c*.1010), Bl Jutta of

Crucifixion of St Andrew (*Venetian missal*).

Heiligenthal (*c*.1250), Bl Frederick of Ratisbon (1329), Bl Nicolino Magalotti (1370), Bl Cuthbert Mayne (1577), BB Dionysius and Redemptus (1638).

30 November

Andrew (1st cent.), Maura of Constantinople (?), Justina of Constantinople (?), Castulus and Euprepis (?), Sapor, Isaac and Comp. (339), Constantius of Rome (5th cent.), Trojan of Saintes (533), Truwal of Treguier (*c*.564), Zosimus the Wonder-Worker (6th cent.), Arnold of Gemblours (1155), Bl Joscius of St-Bertin (1186), Bl Andrew of Antioch (1348), Bl William de Paulo (1423), Bl Joseph Marchand (1835).

ST ANDREW

The elder brother of Peter and like him a fisherman, Andrew was a disciple of John the Baptist before he heard of Jesus, turning to follow Him when he heard the Baptist say, 'Behold, the Lamb of God'. Tradition holds that he evangelized the districts around the Black Sea and was crucified at Patras in Achaia in Greece and hung alive on the cross for two days, exhorting the spectators all the while. However, the idea that the cross was in the form of an X is not found before the fourteenth century. His alleged relics were taken by Constantine to Constantinople, but were stolen from there and now rest at Amalfi in southern Italy. Another legend suggests that the relics were brought by St Regulus to Kilrymont in Scotland, which was renamed St Andrews, and this was why Andrew became the patron saint of Scotland.

1 December

Nahum (*c*.660 BC), Castritian of Milan (137), Diodorus, Marianus and Comp. (283), Lucius, Rogatus, Cassian and Candida (?), Ananias of Arbela (?), Olympiades of Rome (303), Ansanus the Baptizer (304), Natalia of Nicomedia (*c*.311), Ursicinus of Brescia (347), Evasius of Asti (*c*.362), Leontius of Fréjus (*c*.432), Candres of Maestricht (5th cent.), Proculus of Narni (*c*.542), Constantian of Javron (570), Agericus of Verdun (591), Eligius of Noyon (660), Grwst of Wales (7th cent.), Bl John of Vercelli (1283), Bl Christian of Perugia (13th cent.), Bl Antony Bonfadini (1482), Bl John Beche (1539), BB Alexander Briant S.J. and Ralph Sherwin (1581), Bl Richard Langley (1586).

2 December

Pontian and Comp. (*c*.259), Eusebius, Marcellus,

Hippolytus, Maximus, Adria, Paulina, Neon, Mary, Martana and Aurelia (254–59), Lupus of Verona (?), Evasius of Brescia (?), Bibiana of Rome (?), Chromatius of Aquileia (*c*.406), Severus, Securus, Januarius and Victorinus (*c*.450), Silvanus of Troas (*c*.450), Nonnus of Edessa (*c*.458), Trumwin of Whitby (*c*.700), Bl Oderisius of Monte Cassino (1105), Bl Richard of Schonthal (1219), Bl John Ruysbroeck (1231), Bl John Armero (1566).

3 December

Sophonias (7th cent. BC), Lucius (*c*.200), Claudius, Hilaria, Jason, Maurus and Comp. (*c*.283), Cassian of Tangier (298), Claudius, Crispin, Magna, John and Stephen (?), Agricola of Hungary (?), Ethernan of Scotland (?), Mirocles of Milan (318), Ambicus, Victor and Julius (4th cent.), Birinus of Dorchester (*c*.650), Attalia of Strassburg (741), Sola of Solnhofen (794), Abbo of Auxerre (*c*.860), Galganus of Monte Siepe (1181), Bl Bernard of Toulouse (1320), Francis Xavier (1552), Bl Edward Coleman (1678).

ST FRANCIS XAVIER

St Francis was born into a noble family in Spain and was one of the earliest disciples of St Ignatius by whom he was sent as a missionary to the East. His life is a constant story of travel to parts where the Church had not reached before. He started in Goa where the Portuguese had already made a colony and where Christianity was confined to the traders and state officials. They set an appalling example of the Faith to the Indians and St Francis wrote back to the King asking that he should do more to safeguard Portugal's reputation.

Having established missions in India, Francis went on to China and took Christianity also to Japan. Wherever he went he was remarkable both for his personal humility and for his insistence that all people of every race are equally the children of God. He had a remarkable facility in languages and was able to translate the scriptures and preach in many of the local tongues. He died in Canton and his body was taken to Goa where his shrine is still honoured. St Francis Xavier was made co-patron of foreign missions.

4 December

Clement of Alexandria (*c*.217), Meletius of Pontus (*c*.295), Barbara of Nicomedia (?), Maruthas of Mesopotamia (*c*.415), Felix of Bologna (429), Peter Chrysologus (*c*.450), Bertoara (p.614), Ada of Le Mans (late

St Nicholas of Myra.

7th cent.), Theophanes and Comp. (*c*.810), Maurus of Pecs (*c*.1070), Annon of Cologne (1075), Osmund of Salisbury (1099), Bernard degli Uberti (1133), Bl Mary of St Martin (1240), Bl Christian of Prussia (1245), Bl Francis Gálvez (1623).

5 December

Bassus of Nice (*c*.257), Anastasius (?), Julius, Potamin, Crispin, Felix, Gratus and Comp. (302), Dalmatius of Pavia (304), Crispina of Numidia (304), Pelinus of Corfinium (361), Sabbas of Palestine (532), Cawrdaf of Wales (*c*.560), Nicetius of Trèves (566), Justinian of S. Wales (6th cent.), Firminus of Verdun (6th cent.), Sigiranus of Lonrey (*c*.655), Gerbold of Bayeux

(*c*.690), John the Wonder-Worker (*c*.750), Basilissa of Oehren (*c*.780), Bl John Gradenigo (1025), Gerald of Braga (1109), Bl Nicholas Tavigli (1391), Bl Bartholomew Fanti (1495), Bl John Almond (1612), BB Jerome de Angelis S.J. and Comp. (1623).

6 December

Nicholas of Myra (*c*.350), Polychronius (4th cent.), Asella of Rome (*c*.406), Dionysia, Dativa, Leontia, Tertius, Aemilian, Boniface and Comp. (484), Majoricus of Africa (*c*.490), Auxilius, Isserninus and Secundinus (5th cent.), Abraham of Kratia (*c*.558), Gertrude the Elder (649), Gerard of Joigny (1109), Peter Pascual (1300), Bl Joseph Khang (1861).

ST NICHOLAS OF MYRA

There is very little which is known about Nicholas with any certainty. He was a holy Bishop of Myra in the fourth century and he may well have been martyred in the persecutions of Diocletian. Some account of how he was transmuted into Father Christmas can be found in the section on the Christmas season but most of the legends with which he is associated are untrue. He is supposed to have saved three girls from prostitution by throwing three bags of money into their home at night so they would have a dowry and could get married. The bags have been changed into the pawnbrokers' three balls and thus St Nicholas has become the patron of money-lenders. In the East he is the patron of sailors and in Russia, Greece, Apulia, Sicily, and Lorraine he is accounted their patron saint. Devotion to St Nicholas has been prodigious and it is sad that so little of the legend has historical foundation.

7 December

Agatho (250), Eutychian (283), Polycarp and Theodore (?), Urban of Teano (*c*.356), Victor of Piacenza (375), Ambrose of Milan (397), Martin of Saujon (*c*.400), Servus of Africa (483), Anianus of Chartres (5th cent.), Buithe of Scotland (521), Humbert of Igny (1148).

8 December

Feast of the Immaculate Conception of Our Lady, Eucharius of Trèves (1st cent.), Sophronius of Cyprus (6th cent.), Romaricus of Remiremont (653), Patapius of Constantinople (7th cent.), Gunthildis of Wimborne (*c*.748), Bl Jane of Cáceres (1383).

THE IMMACULATE CONCEPTION OF OUR LADY

The dogma of the Immaculate Conception asserts that 'from the first moment of her conception, the Blessed Virgin Mary was, by the singular grace and privilege of Almighty God, and in view of the merits of Jesus Christ, Saviour of Mankind, kept free from all stain of original sin'.

The observance of feast of the conception of the Virgin Mary on this day was known in the East from the seventh century and had spread to the West by the eleventh century. The dogma of the Immaculate Conception was a matter of controversy for hundreds of years. The Franciscans were great supporters while in general the Dominicans opposed it. The argument continued after the Council of Basle had accepted it as a pious opinion in 1439 and in 1482 Pope Sixtus IV forbade supporters of the contrary opinion to censure their opponents. From the sixteenth century belief in the dogma became general in the Roman Catholic Church and in 1854 Pope Pius IX proclaimed it an article of faith in the Bull Ineffabilis Deus.

O God who by the immaculate conception of the Virgin, didst prepare for thy Son an habitation worthy of Him; grant us, by her intercession, faithfully to keep our hearts and bodies immaculate for thee, who didst preserve her from all stain.

Collect for the Feast of the Immaculate Conception

9 December

Syrus of Pavia (1st cent.), Julian of Apamaea (3rd cent.), Restitutus of Carthage (?), Valeria of Limoges (?), Peter, Successus, Bassianus, Primitivus and Comp. (?), Leocadia of Toledo (c.303), Seven Martyrs of Samosata (c.311), Proculus of Verona (c.320), Gorgonia of Cappadocia (c.375), Cyprian of Perigeux (586), Budoc of Dol (7th cent.), Balda of Jourre (late 7th cent.), Ethelgiva of Shaftesbury (896), Bl Enguerrammus the Wise (1045), Bl Severus of Prague (1067), Bl Delphina of Languedoc (1358), Peter Fourier (1640).

10 December

Carpophorus and Abundius (290–300), Nercurius and Comp. (c.300), Eulalia of Merida (304), Julia of Merida (304), Mennas, Hermogenes and Eugraphus (c.312), Miltiades (314), Gemellus of Ancyra (362), Sindulphus of Vienne (c.669), Deusdedit of Brescia (c.700),

Thomas of Farfa (c.720), Lucerius of Farfa (739), Gregory III (741), Guitmarus of Centula (p.756), Hildemar of Beauvais (p.844), Bl Albert of Sassovivom (p.1102), Bl Fulgentius of Afflighem (1122), Florentius of Carracedo (1156), Bl Peter Tecelano (1287), Bl Edmund Campion (1581), BB Eustace White and Comp. (1591), BB Edmund Gennings and Swithun Wells (1591), BB Thomas Somers and John Roberts, (1610), Bl Sebastian Montañol (1616).

11 December

Victoricus, Fuscian and Gentian (c.287), Trason, Pontian and Praetextatus (c.302), Barsabas of Persia (c.342), Damasus (384), Eutychius of Cádiz (4th cent.), Sabinus of Piacenza (420), Daniel the Stylite (493), Peris of Wales (?), Cian of Wales (6th cent.), Fidweten of Redon (c.888), Bl David of Himmerode (1179), Bl Franco Lippi (1291), Bl Hugolinus Magalotti (1373).

12 December

Ammonaria, Mercuria, Dionysia and a second Ammonaria (c.250), Synesius of Rome (725), Maxentius, Constantius, Crescentius, Justin and Comp. (c.287), Hermogenes, Donatus and Comp. (?), Abra of Poitiers (c.360), Cury of Cornwall (401), Corentinus of Quimper (c.490), Columba of Tyrdaglas (548), Finian of Clonard (c.552), Cormac (6th cent.), Colman of Glendalough (659), Edburga of Thanet (751), Agatha of Wimborne (c.790), Vicelinus of Lübeck (1154), Bl Jerome Ranuzzi (1455), Bl Thomas Holland (1642), Bl Simon Hoa (1840).

13 December

Antiochus of Sardinia (c.110), Eustratius, Auxentius, Eugene, Mardarius and Orestes (c.302), Lucy of Syracuse (304), Jodocus of Brittany (668), Autbert of Cambrai (c.669), Edburga of Lyminge (7th cent.), Ottilia of Hohenburg (c.720), Bl Tassilo of Bavaria (p. 794), BB Einhildis and Roswinda (8th cent.), Bl Wifred of Marseilles (1021), Elisabeth-Rose (1130), Bl Pontius of Balmey (1140), Bl John Marinoni (1562), Bl Antoni Grassi (1671).

14 December

Heron, Arsenius, Isidore and Dioscorus (250), Justus and Abundius (283), Pompeius of Pavia (c.290),

The Immaculate Conception (*Velazquez*).

Matronianus of Milan (?), Drusus, Zosimus and Theodore (?), Spiridion of Cyprus (*c.*348), Viator of Bergamo (*c.*378), Nicasius, Eutropia and Comp. (*c.*407), Fingar, Phiala and Comp. (5th cent.), Agnellus of Naples (*c.*596), Venantius Fortunatus (*c.*605), Bl John Bread-and-Water (p.1150), Bl Bartholomew Buonpedoni (1300), Bl Conrad of Offida (1306), Bl Bonaventure Buonacorsi (1313).

15 December

Irenaeus, Antony, Theodore, Saturninus, Victor and Comp. (*c.*258), Faustinus, Lucius, Candidus, Caelian, Mark, Januarius and Fortunatus (?), Nino of Georgia (*c.*320), Valerian of Abbenza (457), Maximinus of Micy (*c.*520), Florentius of Bangor (7th cent.), Urbitius of Nocito (*c.*805), Paul of Latros (956), Bl Adalbero of Metz (1005), Bl Julia of Arezzo (?), Bl Marinus of Cava (1170), Bl Sigfrid, Maria di Rosa (1855).

16 December

Ananias, Azarias and Misael (7th cent. BC), Albina of Gaeta (250), Valentine, Concordius, Navalis and Agricola (*c.*305), Eusebius of Vercelli (*c.*370), Irenion

St Thomas touches the Risen Christ.

of Gaza (389), Bean of Leinster (?), Ado of Vienne (875), Nicholas Chrysoberges (996), Adelaide (999), Bl Raynald de Bar (1151), Bl Sebastian Maggi (1494), Bl Mary of the Angels (1717).

17 December

Lazarus (1st cent.), Olympias of Constantinople (408), Maxentiolus of Cunault (5th cent.), Tydecho of Wales (6th cent.), Briach of Guingamp (*c.*627), Florian, Calanicus and Comp. (*c.*637), Judicael (658), Begga of Andenne (698), Sturmius of Fulda (779), Eigil of Fulda (822), Wivina of Alost (*c.*1170), Bl Cherubinus Testa (1479), Bl Philippine Duchesne (1852).

18 December

Rufus and Zosimus (*c.*107), Moses of Africa (*c.*250), Quintus, Simplicius and Comp. (*c.*255), Theotimus and Basilian (?), Victurus, Victor, Victorinus, Adjutor, Quartus and Comp. (?), Auxentius of Mopsuestia (p.321), Gatian of Tours (*c.*337), Bodagisil (588), Flannan of Killaloe (7th cent.), Desideratus of Fontenelle (*c.*700), Winebald of Heidenheim (761), BB Augustine Moi, Peter Duong, Peter Truat and Paul Mi (1838).

19 December

Nemesius of Alexandria (250), Timothy of Africa (*c.*250), Fausta of Sirmium (3rd cent.), Darius, Zosimus, Paul and Secundus (?), Avitus of Micy (?), Manirus of Scotland (?), Cyriacus, Paulillus, Secundus, Anastasius, Syndimius and Comp. (303), Meuris and Thaea (*c.*307), Anastasius I (401), Gregory of Auxerre (*c.*540), Samthana of Meath (6th cent.), Ribert of St-Oyend (*c.*790), Bernard Paleara (1122), Bl Macarius the Scot (1153), Bl William of Fenoli (*c.*1205), Bl Urban V (1370), Bl Caecilia of Ferrara (1511), BB Thomas De and Comp. (1839).

20 December

Ammon, Zeno, Ptolemy, Ingen and Theophilus (249), Julius of Gelduba (?), Liberatus and Bajulus (?), Philogonius of Antioch (324), Eugene and Macarius (362), Ursicinus of Cahors (*c.*535), Dominic of Brescia (*c.*612), Ursicinus of St-Ursanne (*c.*625), Dominic of Silos (1073), Bl Gundisalvus of Silos (*c.*1073), Bl Peter de la Cadireta (1277), Bl Peter Massalenus (1453), Bl Peter Thi (1839).

21 December

Thomas (1st cent.), Themistocles of Lycia (253), Honoratus of Toulouse (3rd cent.), John and Festus (?) Severinus of Trèves (*c*.300), Glycerius of Nicomedia (303), Anastasius II the Younger (609), Baudacarius of Bobbio (650), Bl Adrian of Dalmatia (13th cent.).

ST THOMAS THE APOSTLE

One of the twelve Apostles, Thomas is mentioned in all four Gospels, but only in St John's Gospel are specific episodes of his discipleship described. When the other disciples tried to dissuade Christ from going to Bethany as they feared his life was in danger, Thomas offered to die with Him. 'Let us also go, that we may die with him.' Just before Christ went to his Crucifixion, St Thomas interrupted Him with the question, 'Lord we know not whither thou goest, and how can we know the way?' However, he is best remembered as the disciple who doubted the Resurrection until he touched the wounds of the Risen Christ. He has, because of this, become known as 'Doubting Thomas', but he was the first to call Jesus, 'My Lord and my God'.

A very old tradition holds that, after Pentecost, Thomas went as a missionary in South India where he was martyred. Another tradition says that, in order to reach India, he allowed himself to be sold to an Indian merchant as a slave and worked as a carpenter. His symbol in art, therefore, has been a carpenter's rule.

22 December

Chaeremon and Comp. (p.250), Demetrius, Honoratus and Florus (?), Zeno of Nicomedia (303), Flavian of Acquapendente (362), Amaethlu of Wales (6th cent.), Hunger of Utrecht (866), Amaswinthus of Malaga (982), Bl Marianus Scotus (1086), Bl Jutta of Dissibodenberg (1136), Bl Adam of Saxony (*c*.1210), Frances Xavier Cabrini (1917).

23 December

Victoria (and Anatolia) (250), Theodulus, Saturninus, Euporus, Gelasius, Eunician, Zeticus, Cleomenes, Agathopus, Basilides and Evaristus (250), Martyrs of Crete (?), Migdonius and Mardonius (303), Servulus of Rome (*c*.590), Dagobert II (679), Frithbert of Hexham (766), Mazota of Abernethy (8th cent.), Vintila of Orense (890), Bl Hartmann of Brixen (1164), Bl John Cirita (*c*.1164), Thorlac Thornalli (1193), Bl Hermann of Scheda (*c*.1200), Nicholas Factor (1583).

St Stephen (*Crivelli*)

24 December

Adam and Eve, Forty Maidens martyred at Antioch (250), Lucian, Metrobius, Paul, Zenobius, Theotimus and Drusus (?), Euthymius of Nicomedia (303), Gregory of Spoleto (*c*.304), Delphinus of Bordeaux (404), Venerandus of Clermont (423), Tarsilla of Rome (*c*.581), Caranus of Scotland (7th cent.), Irmina of Oehren (708), Adela of Pfalzel (*c*.730), Alberic of Gladbach (10th cent.), Bruno of Ottobeuren (*c*.1050).

25 December

Eugenia of Rome (*c*.257), Anastasia of Sirmium (*c*.304), Adalsindis of Hamay (*c*.715), Alburga of Wilton (*c*.800), Bl Matthew of Albano (1134), Peter the

December

Venerable (1156), Bl Fulk of Toulouse (1231), Bl Jacopone da Todi (1306).

26 December

Stephen the Deacon (33), Dionysius (269), Archelaus of Mesopotamia (c.278), Marinus of Rome (283), Zeno of Gaza (p.399), Zosimus (418), Tathai of Wales (5th cent.), Theodore the Sacristan (6th cent.), Maethlu of Anglesey (6th cent.), BB Margaret and Ida (p.1150), Christina of Markgate (1160), Bl Daniel of Villiers (late 12th cent.), Bl Paganus of Lecco (1274), Bl Andrew Dung (1839), Bl Vincentia Lopez (1890).

ST STEPHEN THE DEACON

Probably a Hellenistic Jew, Stephen was the first of the seven deacons appointed by the Apostles to assist in the distribution of alms. He was 'full of faith and power' and 'did great wonders and miracles among the people'.

His success aroused the hostility of the Jews, who accused him of blasphemy. In his defence he denounced them for having killed Christ, who was the prophet announced by Moses. This so enraged them that they

sentenced him to be stoned to death, and he became the first Christian martyr. He died confessing Christ and asking forgiveness for his persecutors. His death made a deep impression on Saul, the future Paul the Apostle, who was present there as a witness.

He was one of the most popular saints of the Middle Ages and his statue was honoured in many churches.

27 December

John (c.100), Maximus of Alexandria (282), Fabiola of Rome (c.400), Nicarete of Constantinople (c.405), Theodore M. and Theophanes (c.841 and c.845), Bl Hesso of Beinwil (1133), Bl Walto of Wessobrunn (1156), Bl Adelheidis of Tennenbach (1273), Bl Bonaventure Tolomei (1348).

ST JOHN THE EVANGELIST

The son of Zebedee and younger brother of James, John was a Galilean fisherman and probably a native of Bethsaida. His mother was Salome, who may have been the sister of the mother of Jesus. He was present with Peter and James on the mountain of the Transfiguration and with Peter was sent to prepare the Last

OPPOSITE The Slaughter of the Innocents (*English psalter*).

St John the Evangelist (*Lorenzo Ghiberti*).

Supper in the Upper Room in Jerusalem. He is traditionally identified with 'the disciple whom Jesus loved', and from the Cross, Jesus gave His mother into his keeping. After the death of Jesus, he was prominent in the Church of Jerusalem.

He is supposed to have been a young man when he first followed Jesus and to have lived to a great age and died at Ephesus, his last message to those around him being, 'Little children, love one another'. When asked why he repeated these words when he was too old to preach anything more, he replied that they were Christ's words and if followed were enough for anyone. Tradition has held him to be the author of the fourth Gospel, of the three Epistles bearing his name, and of the Book of Revelation in the New Testament. On the Isle of Patmos, the Greek Church preserves the cave in which St John is thought to have written the Apocalypse. In Christian art St John the Divine's emblem has been an eagle because, like the eagle, he looked on 'the sun of glory'.

28 December

The Holy Innocents (1st cent.), Troadius of Pontus (250), Eutychius and Domitian (?), Castor, Victor and Rogatian (?), Indes, Domna, Agapes and Theophila (303), Caesarius of Armenia (309), Domnio of Rome (4th cent.), Romulus and Conindrus (c.450), Maughold of Ireland (c.488), Gowan of Wales (5th cent.), Antony of Lérins (c.520), Bl Otto of Heidelberg (1344), Bl Caspar del Bufalo (1837).

THE HOLY INNOCENTS

This festival was at one time known as Childermas and commemorates King Herod's slaughter of all the boy-children in Judea in order to ensure that Christ did not become a threat to his throne. In the Eastern Church the feast is kept one day later and is known as the festival of the 'fourteen thousand holy children'.

In the Roman rite, the mass said on this day is a penitential one, celebrated in purple vestments as a symbol of the idea that the children, though martyrs, had to wait until Christ's Ascension when He opened heaven to all believers. If, however, the feast falls on a Sunday then red, the colour of martyrs, is used.

In some cathedrals and abbey churches during the Middle Ages, it was the custom for children to take part in the festivities in honour of the Holy Innocents. Choir-boys used to be allowed to sit in the canons' stalls and one of them, wearing a bishop's robes, was often allowed to give the blessing at the end of the

service. Other children did not fare so well as it was the custom to whip them in order that they would remember the story of Herod's cruelty. Almost everywhere the day was thought to be one of ill-omen. People would not wear new clothes or enter into any major undertaking. In England it was formerly known as Childermas Day, and was a day of mourning when the churches rang a muffled peal of bells.

29 December

Trophimus of Arles (c.280), Dominic, Victor, Primian, Lybosus, Saturninus, Crescentius, Secundus and Honoratus (?), Callistus, Felix and Boniface (?), Marcellus Akimetes (c.485), Ebrulfus of Ouche (596), Albert of Gambron (7th cent.), Girald of Fontenelle (1031), Thomas à Becket (1170), Bl William Howard (1680).

ST THOMAS À BECKET

The son of a London sheriff of Norman descent, Thomas studied in Paris and then became a member of the household of Theobald, Archbishop of Canterbury, who made him his archdeacon in 1154. He became the intimate friend of King Henry II and was soon made Chancellor of England. Thomas had an undoubted taste for magnificence and lived a sumptuous life. He was good-looking, athletic, and thoroughly enjoyed himself. Yet when the King decided that he should became Archbishop of Canterbury he refused saying, 'Should God permit me to be Archbishop I should lose your majesty's favour'. Henry would not be put off and so Thomas, not yet a priest, was ordained and consecrated Archbishop.

From that time on he devoted himself to the work of the Church, living a careful and restrained life in keeping with his new responsibilities. He quarrelled with the King over the rights of the clergy to be tried in Church courts but this was the instance of a more general argument as to whether the State or the Church should have jurisdiction in spiritual matters. The fight was as bitter as the former friendship had been close and Becket had to leave England for France for six years. On his return he was seized in his cathedral at Canterbury and murdered by four knights.

The people of England were shocked and miracles were soon reported from his tomb. In 1173 the Pope canonized him and the next year Henry did penance at his tomb, being whipped by monks from the abbey. In 1220 his shrine was moved to the choir of the cathedral and it remained as a great centre of pil-

The Pilgrim Steps leading to the scene of the martyrdom of St Thomas (*Canterbury Cathedral*).

grimage until it was destroyed by Henry VIII.

30 December

Liberius of Ravenna (*c.*200), Eugene of Milan (?), Sabinus, Exuperantius, Marcellus, Venustian and Comp. (303), Anysia of Salonika (304), Anysius of Salonika (*c.*407), Mansuetus, Severus, Appian, Donatus, Honorius and Comp. (*c.*483), Egwin of Worcester (717), Raynerius of Aquila (1077), Bl Ralph of Vaucelles (1152), Bl Mattia dei Nazarei (1213), Bl Margaret Colonna (1284), Bl Gerard Cagnoli (1345), Bl John Alcober (1748).

31 December

Hermes of Rome (*c.*270), Columba of Sens (273), Stephen, Pontian, Attalus, Fabian, Cornelius, Sextus, Flos, Quintian, Minervinus and Simplician (?), Donata, Paulina, Rustica, Nominanda, Serotina, Hilaria and Comp. (?), Sabinian and Potentian (*c.*300), Silvester I (335), Zoticus of Constantinople (*c.*350), Melania the Younger and Pinian (5th cent.), Barbatian of Ravenna (5th cent.), Bl Peter of Subiaco (1003), Offa of Benevento (*c.*1070), Bl Walembert of Cambrai (1141), Bl Wisinto of Kremsmünster (*c.*1250), John Francis Régis (1640), Bl Catherine Labouré (1876).

Holy is the true light, and passing wonderful, lending radiance to them that endured in the heat of the conflict: from Christ they inherit a home of unfading splendour wherein they rejoice with gladness evermore.

SALISBURY ANTIPHONER

patron saints

ST AGNES (21 January)
Betrothed couples, gardeners and maidens
ST AMBROSE (7 December)
Beekeepers and domestic animals
ST ANDREW (30 November)
Scotland, fishermen and sailors
ST ANTHONY (17 January)
Lost things
ST AUGUSTINE (28 August)
Theologians
ST BARBARA (4 December)
Builders and firework makers
ST BENEDICT (21 March)
Coppersmiths and schoolboys
ST BERNARD OF CLAIRVAUX (20 August)
Beekeepers
ST BONIFACE (5 June)
Brewers and tailors
ST CATHERINE (25 November)
Philosophers and spinsters
ST CECILIA (22 November)
Musicians
ST CHRISTOPHER (25 July)
Sailors and travellers
ST CORNELIUS (16 September)
Cattle and domestic animals
ST CUTHBERT (20 March)
Shepherds and seafarers
ST DAVID (1 March)
Wales
ST DOROTHY (6 February)
Brides and gardeners
ST DUNSTAN (19 May)
Blacksmiths, goldsmiths and the blind
ST ELIGIUS (1 December)
Smiths and metal workers
ST ELISABETH OF HUNGARY (19 November)
Bakers and beggars
ST FRANCIS (4 October)
Animals
ST GABRIEL (ARCHANGEL) (24 March)
Postmen
ST GEORGE (23 April)
England, cavalrymen, chivalry and soldiers
ST GILES (1 September)
Beggars, blacksmiths and cripples

ST GREGORY THE GREAT (12 March)
Musicians
ST JEROME (30 September)
Students
ST JOHN THE EVANGELIST (27 September)
Booksellers, painters, printers and publishers
ST JOSEPH (19 March)
Carpenters, engineers and the family
ST JUDE (28 October)
The desperate
ST LAWRENCE (10 August)
Cooks, cutters, armouries and schoolboys
ST LUKE (18 October)
Doctors, goldsmiths and sculptors
ST MARGARET (20 July)
Women (especially maidens), nurses and peasants
ST MARK (25 April)
Venice, glaziers and notaries
ST MARTIN OF TOURS (11 November)
Beggars, innkeepers and tailors
ST MATTHEW (21 September)
Bankers and tax collectors
ST MICHAEL, ARCHANGEL (29 September)
Artists and soldiers
ST NICHOLAS (6 December)
Children and captives
ST PATRICK (17 March)
Ireland
ST PAUL (30 June)
Musicians
ST PETER (29 June)
Bakers, butchers and clockmakers
ST RAPHAEL, ARCHANGEL (24 October)
Guardian angels
ST SEBASTIAN (20 January)
Armourers, ironmongers and potters
ST TERESA OF AVILA (15 October)
Those in need of grace
ST THOMAS (21 December)
Architects, carpenters and geometricians
ST URSULA (21 October)
Maidens, drapers and teachers
ST ZITA (27 April)
Domestic servants

glossarial index

Abbot. The title of the head of a large monastery belonging to the Benedictine order or one of the orders derived from it, such as the Cistercians. An influential abbot in English history was St Dunstan, who was Abbot of Glastonbury in the tenth century. 186.

Agatha, St. 152, 158.

Agnus Dei. The words, beginning 'O Lamb of God', recited thrice by the priest in the Latin Mass shortly before the Communion. It was introduced into the service in the seventh century. 86.

Albert, Prince. 22.

Albigenses. The name, probably derived from the city of Albi, to a heretical sect which appeared in the south of France during the twelfth century, who believed that there were two independent principles, good and evil, spirit and matter, in Creation. After St Dominic had failed to convert them by preaching, a crusade was organised against them which led to their extirpation. 174, 209, 214.

Alexander II, Pope. 104.

Alexander III, Pope. 8.

Alexandria. Formerly the capital of Egypt and founded by Alexander the Great in 331 BC, it was a centre of Greek and Jewish learning and then became the home of a school of Christian theology said to have been founded by St Mark. 178.

Altar. The name for the table on which the Eucharist is celebrated. 72, 74, 78.

Ambrose, St. 152, 215, 241.

Andrew, St. 205, 240.

Andrewes, Lancelot. 221.

Anselm, St. 177.

Anthony, St. 150–1.

Anthony of Padua, St. 194.

Antioch. This Syrian city, the third in the Roman Empire, had a very early Christian community, and there the disciples of Christ were first called 'Christians'. It had an important theological school at which St John Chrysostom was educated. 155.

Aquinas, St Thomas. 115, 203.

Archangels. In later Jewish thought angels and archangels became prominent as intermediaries between God and man, and the early Christian Church adopted this idea. Though Michael alone is mentioned in the New Testament as 'the Archangel', Christian tradition has commonly accorded the title to Gabriel and Raphael also. 171, 221.

Arians. Heretics in the early fourth century, who denied the true divinity of Jesus Christ, so-called after their leader, Arius. 151, 196.

Arrowsmith, Edmund. 183.

Atilla the Hun. 174.

Athanasius, St. 181.

Augustine of Canterbury, St. 166, 189.

Augustine of Hippo, St. 96, 215, 228.

Avignon. A town in the south of France in which the popes resided from 1309 to 1377, and where, during the Great Schism of 1378–1417, two antipopes, Clement VII and Benedict XIII, resided. 173, 180.

Barbarossa, Emperor Frederick, 33.

Barabas, St. 178, 194.

Bartholomew, St. 213.

Basil, St. 196.

Basilica. A building used by the Romans as a law court and place of business, which was adopted by the early Christians as the form for their churches, some of which remain in Rome. 64, 65, 222.

Becket, Thomas à. 105, 248.

Bede, Venerable. 8, 166, 188–9.

Benedict, St. 169–70.

Bernard of Clairvaux, St. 212.

Bernadette, St. 176.

Bethany. The village of Martha and Mary and Lazarus about two miles from Jerusalem on the slopes of the Mount of Olives. 96, 208.

Bethsaida. A town on the shore of the Sea of Galilee, the home of Philip, Andrew and Peter. 240, 246.

Bilney, Thomas. 182.

Blaise, St. 157.

Blood, Precious. 200.

Bonaventure, St. 203.

Boniface, St. 22, 192.

Boniface IV. Pope. 232.

Borromeo, Charles. 233.

Bradford, William. 11.

Bruno, St. 225.

Byrom, John. 114.

Caesar. The family name of the Roman dictator, Gaius Julius Caesar, used as a title for the Roman emperors who followed him. 142, 149.

Calvin, John. The sixteenth-century reformer, who established a Puritan Church at Geneva in Switzerland with simplified worship and a system of government in which laymen took part. 11.

Campion, Edmund. 183.

Cana. A village in Galilee. 37, 139.

Canon. The word originally meant a rod or measure and so came to be used of a set of rules, such as, for instance, the fixed and unchanging part of the Mass. 152, 174.

Canons Regular. Canons are clergy living under the rules of a cathedral or some other church, and the Canons Regular were an order of canons founded in the eleventh century. 194.

Capernaum. 63, 133, 139, 144, 240.

Canterbury. Since the arrival of St Augustine, this city has been the seat of the Archbishop of Canterbury. 177, 186, 189, 248.

Carling Sunday. 67.

Carmelites. The order of Carmelites was founded for monks in the twelfth century and for nuns in the fifteenth century. Both orders were reformed in the sixteenth century by St

Teresa and St John of the Cross. 227, 238.

Carthusians. 225.

Catacombs. Roman law protected all catacombs or underground burial places from violation, and so the early Christians met for safety in those outside Rome in the time of the persecutions. 90, 188,

Catechumens. Converts in the early Church undergoing instruction before Baptism. 51, 78, 86.

Catherine of Alexandria, St. 238–9.

Catherine of Siena, St. 180.

Cecilia, St. 152.

Celestine IV, Pope. 218.

Centurion. An officer in the Roman army, commanding a century or company of a hundred men. 144.

Chalcedon, Council of. 174.

Chalice. The cup used to contain the wine consecrated in the Eucharist; the plate used for the bread is the paten. 74.

Charlemagne. 25.

Charles I (of England). 10, 157, 202.

Charles VII (of France). 189.

Chaucer, Geoffrey. 33.

Chrysostom, St John. 21, 52, 155–6, 200, 232.

Circumcision. A Jewish rite of iniation for male children on the eighth day after birth. 31.

Cistercians. The members of the reformed Benedictine order, which placed special emphasis on seclusion, plain living and manual labour. 27.

Clement V, Pope. 65.

Collop Monday. 58.

Constantine, Emperor. The Roman Emperor who made Christianity the official religion of the Empire. 7, 78, 178, 182.

Constantinople. Established by Constantine in AD 330 as his capital on the site of the Greek city of Byzantium. 40, 155.

Counter-Reformation. The sixteenth-century movement, which opposed the Protestant Reformation and reformed the Roman Catholic Church. 183, 208, 233.

Cranmer, Thomas. 10, 183.

Cross, Holy. 65, 78, 81, 90, 182.

Crucifixion. 21. 51, 204.

Crusades. The military expeditions undertaken by the Christians of Europe between the eleventh and thirteenth centuries to recover the Holy Land from the Moslems. 178, 212, 214, 239.

Curé d'Ars. 210.

Cuthbert, St. 168.

David, St. 162.

Deacons. The Apostles appointed seven men, including Stephen and Philip, as deacons or 'servants' to serve the poor and distribute alms. Later they became important administrative officials under the Pope in Rome. In the modern Roman Catholic Church and Anglican Communion ordination as a deacon is merely the first stage in preparation for the priesthood. 210, 246.

Decapolis. A region consisting of ten allied cities, Greek in population, east of the Jordan in northern Palestine. 126.

Diocletian, Emperor. 241.

Dominic, St. 209.

Dostoevsky. 61.

Drayton, Michael. 163.

Dunstan, St. 186.

Easter. 7, 52, 78, 85–7.

Edward the Confessor. 178, 227.

Edward I (of England). 87.

Edward III (of England). 178.

Elijah. 18, 52, 122.

Elisabeth of Hungary, St. 237.

Elizabeth I (of England). 74, 95.

Ember Days. 19, 63, 104, 137.

Ephphatha Sunday. 126.

Eucharist. The Christian service, also called the Holy Communion, the Lord's Supper or the Mass, which was instituted by Christ on the night before He was betrayed. 74, 78, 81, 221.

Fasting. 7, 51–2, 77.

Fisher, John. 182.

Francis of Assisi, St. 22, 132, 224.

Friars. Members of religious orders, taking the same vows as monks, but engaging in works of charity or preaching instead of remaining within a monastery. The most important orders of friars were the Franciscans and Dominicans. 22, 132.

Gabriel, Archangel. 171.

Galilee. The northern part of Palestine, extending from the Jordan to the Mediterranean and including such places as Nazareth, Capernaum and Bethsaida. In it Jesus spent nearly all His earlier life and most of His ministry. 42, 131, 205, 240.

Gaul. A province of the Roman Empire, which included most of modern France, Belgium and northern Italy. 31, 33.

George, St. 177–8.

Gethsemane. The garden, in the valley between Jerusalem and the Mount of Olives, to which Jesus retired with His disciples after the Last Supper and in which occurred His agony and betrayal. 205.

Glastonbury. 186.

Gloria in Excelsis. The opening Latin words of the hymn, 'Glory be to God on high', which originated in the Eastern Church and was introduced into the Roman Mass in the early sixth century. 188.

Gloria Patri. The first Latin words of the ascription of praise to the Trinity which was first used at the end of psalms in the fourth century. 104, 188.

Gregory the Great, Pope. 52, 166, 169, 189.

Gregory III, Pope. 232.

Gregory IX, Pope. 218.

Gregory X, Pope. 203.

Green Thursday. 76.

Gruber, Franz. 22.

UNIT CONVERSION FACTORS

Length

1 m = 100 cm = 1000 mm = 10^6 μm = 10^9 nm

1 km = 1000 m = 0.6214 mi

1 m = 3.281 ft = 39.37 in.

1 cm = 0.3937 in.

1 in. = 2.540 cm

1 ft = 30.48 cm

1 yd = 91.44 cm

1 mi = 5280 ft = 1.609 km

1 Å = 10^{-10} m = 10^{-8} cm = 10^{-1} nm

1 nautical mile = 6080 ft

1 light year = 9.461×10^{15} m

Area

1 cm^2 = 0.155 $in.^2$

1 m^2 = 10^4 cm^2 = 10.76 ft^2

1 $in.^2$ = 6.452 cm^2

1 ft = 144 $in.^2$ = 0.0929 m^2

Volume

1 liter = 1000 cm^3 = 10^{-3} m^3 = 0.03531 ft^3 = 61.02 $in.^3$

1 ft^3 = 0.02832 m^3 = 28.32 liters = 7.477 gallons

1 gallon = 3.788 liters

Time

1 min = 60 s

1 h = 3600 s

1 d = 86,400 s

1 y = 365.24 d = 3.156×10^7 s

Angle

1 rad = 57.30° = 180°/π

1° = 0.01745 rad = π/180 rad

1 revolution = 360° = 2π rad

1 rev/min (rpm) = 0.1047 rad/s

Speed

1 m/s = 3.281 ft/s

1 ft/s = 0.3048 m/s

1 mi/min = 60 mi/h = 88 ft/s

1 km/h = 0.2778 m/s = 0.6214 mi/h

1 mi/h = 1.466 ft/s = 0.4470 m/s = 1.609 km/h

1 furlong/fortnight = 1.662×10^{-4} m/s

Acceleration

1 m/s^2 = 100 cm/s^2 = 3.281 ft/s

1 cm/s^2 − 0.01 m/s^2 = 0.03281 ft/s^2

1 ft/s^2 = 0.3048 m/s^2 = 30.48 cm/s^2

1 mi/h · s = 1.467 ft/s^2

Mass

1 kg = 10^3 g = 0.0685 slug

1 g = 6.85×10^{-5} slug

1 slug = 14.59 kg

1 u = 1.661×10^{-27} kg

1 kg has a weight of 2.205 lb when g = 9.80 m/s^2

Force

1 N = 10^5 dyn = 0.2248 lb

1 lb = 4.448 N = 4.448×10^5 dyn

Pressure

1 Pa = 1 N/m^2 = $1.450 \times 10^{-4}$$lb/in.^2$ = 0.209 lb/ft^2

1 bar = 10^5 Pa

1 $lb/in.^2$ = 6895 Pa

1 lb/ft^2 = 47.88 Pa

1 atm = 1.013×10^5 Pa = 1.013 bar

     = 14.7 $lb/in.^2$ = 2117 lb/ft^2

1 mm Hg = 1 torr = 133.3 Pa

Energy

1 J = 10^7ergs = 0.239 cal

1 cal = 4.186 J (based on 15° calorie)

1 ft · lb = 1.356 J

1 Btu = 1055 J = 252 cal = 778 ft · lb

1 eV = 1.602×10^{-19} J

1 kWh = 3.600×10^6 J

Mass–Energy Equivalence

1 kg $\leftrightarrow$ 8.988×10^{16} J

1 u $\leftrightarrow$ 931.5 MeV

1 eV $\leftrightarrow$ 1.074×10^{-9} u

Power

1 W = 1 J/s

1 hp = 746 W = 550 ft · lb/s

1 Btu/h = 0.293 W

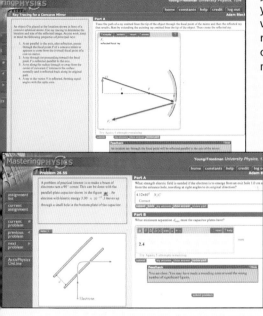
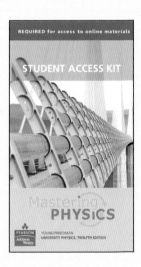

PROBLEM-SOLVING STRATEGIES

Extended Edition includes Chapters 1–44. Standard Edition includes Chapters 1–37.
Three-volume edition: Volume 1 includes Chapters 1–20, Volume 2 includes Chapters 21–37,
and Volume 3 includes Chapters 37–44.

ACTIVPHYSICS ONLINE™ ACTIVITIES

Act|v
ONLINE
Phys|cs   www.mastering physics.com

VOLUME 2
CUSTOM EDITION FOR UCLA

SEARS AND ZEMANSKY'S

UNIVERSITY PHYSICS

HUGH D. YOUNG
ROGER A. FREEDMAN

CONTRIBUTING AUTHOR A. LEWIS FORD

Taken from:

Sears and Zemansky's University Physics, Volume Two, Twelfth Edition
by Hugh D. Young and Roger A. Freedman; contributing author, A. Lewis Ford

Cover Art: "Chadstone," by Jessica Lamarre.

Taken from:

Sears and Zemansky's University Physics, Volume Two, Twelfth Edition
by Hugh D. Young and Roger A. Freedman; contributing author, A. Lewis Ford
Copyright © 2008 by Pearson Education, Inc.
Published by Addison Wesley
Boston, Massachusetts 02116

This special edition published in cooperation with Pearson Custom Publishing.

Printed in the United States of America

10 9 8 7 6 5 4 3 2 1

ISBN 0-536-48936-X

2007460099

SS

Please visit our web site at *www.pearsoncustom.com*

PEARSON CUSTOM PUBLISHING
501 Boylston Street, Suite 900, Boston, MA 02116
A Pearson Education Company

BRIEF CONTENTS

ABOUT THE AUTHORS

Hugh D. Young is Emeritus Professor of Physics at Carnegie Mellon University in Pittsburgh, PA. He attended Carnegie Mellon for both undergraduate and graduate study and earned his Ph.D. in fundamental particle theory under the direction of the late Richard Cutkosky. He joined the faculty of Carnegie Mellon in 1956 and has also spent two years as a Visiting Professor at the University of California at Berkeley.

Prof. Young's career has centered entirely around undergraduate education. He has written several undergraduate-level textbooks, and in 1973 he became a co-author with Francis Sears and Mark Zemansky for their well-known introductory texts. With their deaths, he assumed full responsibility for new editions of these books until joined by Prof. Freedman for *University Physics*.

Prof. Young is an enthusiastic skier, climber, and hiker. He also served for several years as Associate Organist at St. Paul's Cathedral in Pittsburgh, and has played numerous organ recitals in the Pittsburgh area. Prof. Young and his wife Alice usually travel extensively in the summer, especially in Europe and in the desert canyon country of southern Utah.

Roger A. Freedman is a Lecturer in Physics at the University of California, Santa Barbara. Dr. Freedman was an undergraduate at the University of California campuses in San Diego and Los Angeles, and did his doctoral research in nuclear theory at Stanford University under the direction of Professor J. Dirk Walecka. He came to UCSB in 1981 after three years teaching and doing research at the University of Washington.

At UCSB, Dr. Freedman has taught in both the Department of Physics and the College of Creative Studies, a branch of the university intended for highly gifted and motivated undergraduates. He has published research in nuclear physics, elementary particle physics, and laser physics. In recent years, he has helped to develop computer-based tools for learning introductory physics and astronomy.

When not in the classroom or slaving over a computer, Dr. Freedman can be found either flying (he holds a commercial pilot's license) or driving with his wife, Caroline, in their 1960 Nash Metropolitan convertible.

A. Lewis Ford is Professor of Physics at Texas A&M University. He received a B.A. from Rice University in 1968 and a Ph.D. in chemical physics from the University of Texas at Austin in 1972. After a one-year postdoc at Harvard University, he joined the Texas A&M physics faculty in 1973 and has been there ever since. Professor Ford's research area is theoretical atomic physics, with a specialization in atomic collisions. At Texas A&M he has taught a variety of undergraduate and graduate courses, but primarily introductory physics.

HOW TO SUCCEED IN PHYSICS BY REALLY TRYING

Mark Hollabaugh *Normandale Community College*

Physics encompasses the large and the small, the old and the new. From the atom to galaxies, from electrical circuitry to aerodynamics, physics is very much a part of the world around us. You probably are taking this introductory course in calculus-based physics because it is required for subsequent courses you plan to take in preparation for a career in science or engineering. Your professor wants you to learn physics and to enjoy the experience. He or she is very interested in helping you learn this fascinating subject. That is part of the reason your professor chose this textbook for your course. That is also the reason Drs. Young and Freedman asked me to write this introductory section. We want you to succeed!

The purpose of this section of *University Physics* is to give you some ideas that will assist your learning. Specific suggestions on how to use the textbook will follow a brief discussion of general study habits and strategies.

Preparation for This Course

If you had high school physics, you will probably learn concepts faster than those who have not because you will be familiar with the language of physics. If English is a second language for you, keep a glossary of new terms that you encounter and make sure you understand how they are used in physics. Likewise, if you are farther along in your mathematics courses, you will pick up the mathematical aspects of physics faster. Even if your mathematics is adequate, you may find a book such as Arnold D. Pickar's *Preparing for General Physics: Math Skill Drills and Other Useful Help (Calculus Version)* to be useful. Your professor may actually assign sections of this math review to assist your learning.

Learning to Learn

Each of us has a different learning style and a preferred means of learning. Understanding your own learning style will help you to focus on aspects of physics that may give you difficulty and to use those components of your course that will help you overcome the difficulty. Obviously you will want to spend more time on those aspects that give you the most trouble. If you learn by hearing, lectures will be very important. If you learn by explaining, then working with other students will be useful to you. If solving problems is difficult for you, spend more time learning how to solve problems. Also, it is important to understand and develop good study habits. Perhaps the most important thing you can do for yourself is to set aside adequate, regularly scheduled study time in a distraction-free environment.

Answer the following questions for yourself:
- Am I able to use fundamental mathematical concepts from algebra, geometry and trigonometry? (If not, plan a program of review with help from your professor.)
- In similar courses, what activity has given me the most trouble? (Spend more time on this.) What has been the easiest for me? (Do this first; it will help to build your confidence.)

- Do I understand the material better if I read the book before or after the lecture? (You may learn best by skimming the material, going to lecture, and then undertaking an in-depth reading.)
- Do I spend adequate time in studying physics? (A rule of thumb for a class like this is to devote, on the average, 2.5 hours out of class for each hour in class. For a course meeting 5 hours each week, that means you should spend about 10 to 15 hours per week studying physics.)
- Do I study physics every day? (Spread that 10 to 15 hours out over an entire week!) At what time of the day am I at my best for studying physics? (Pick a specific time of the day and stick to it.)
- Do I work in a quiet place where I can maintain my focus? (Distractions will break your routine and cause you to miss important points.)

Working with Others

Scientists or engineers seldom work in isolation from one another but rather work cooperatively. You will learn more physics and have more fun doing it if you work with other students. Some professors may formalize the use of cooperative learning or facilitate the formation of study groups. You may wish to form your own informal study group with members of your class who live in your neighborhood or dorm. If you have access to e-mail, use it to keep in touch with one another. Your study group is an excellent resource when reviewing for exams.

Lectures and Taking Notes

An important component of any college course is the lecture. In physics this is especially important because your professor will frequently do demonstrations of physical principles, run computer simulations, or show video clips. All of these are learning activities that will help you to understand the basic principles of physics. Don't miss lectures, and if for some reason you do, ask a friend or member of your study group to provide you with notes and let you know what happened.

Take your class notes in outline form, and fill in the details later. It can be very difficult to take word for word notes, so just write down key ideas. Your professor may use a diagram from the textbook. Leave a space in your notes and just add the diagram later. After class, edit your notes, filling in any gaps or omissions and noting things you need to study further. Make references to the textbook by page, equation number, or section number.

Make sure you ask questions in class, or see your professor during office hours. Remember the only "dumb" question is the one that is not asked. Your college may also have teaching assistants or peer tutors who are available to help you with difficulties you may have.

Examinations

Taking an examination is stressful. But if you feel adequately prepared and are well-rested, your stress will be lessened. Preparing for an exam is a continual process; it begins the moment the last exam is over. You should immediately go over the exam and understand any mistakes you made. If you worked a problem and made substantial errors, try this: Take a piece of paper and divide it down the middle with a line from top to bottom. In one column, write the proper solution to the problem. In the other column, write what you did and why, if you know, and why your solution was incorrect. If you are uncertain why you made your mistake, or how to avoid making it again, talk with your professor. Physics continually builds on fundamental ideas and it is important to correct any misunderstandings immediately. Warning: While cramming at the last minute may get you through the present exam, you will not adequately retain the concepts for use on the next exam.

PREFACE

This book is the product of more than half a century of leadership and innovation in physics education. When the first edition of University Physics by Francis W. Sears and Mark W. Zemansky was published in 1949, it was revolutionary among calculus-based physics textbooks in its emphasis on the fundamental principles of physics and how to apply them. The success of University Physics with generations of (several million) students and educators around the world is a testament to the merits of this approach, and to the many innovations it has introduced subsequently.

In preparing this new Twelfth Edition, we have further enhanced and developed *University Physics* to assimilate the best ideas from education research with enhanced problem-solving instruction, pioneering visual and conceptual pedagogy, the first systematically enhanced problems, and the most pedagogically proven and widely used online homework and tutorial system in the world.

New to This Edition

- **Problem solving.** The acclaimed, research-based **four-step problem-solving framework** (Identify, Set Up, Execute, and Evaluate) is now used throughout every Worked Example, chapter-specific Problem-Solving Strategy, and every Solution in the Instructor and Student Solutions Manuals. Worked Examples now incorporate black-and-white Pencil Sketches to focus students on this critical step—one that research shows students otherwise tend to skip when illustrated with highly rendered figures.

- **Instruction followed by practice.** A streamlined and systematic learning path of instruction followed by practice includes **Learning Goals** at the start of each chapter and **Visual Chapter Summaries** that consolidate each concept in words, math, and figures. Popular **Test Your Understanding** conceptual questions at the end of each section now use **multiple-choice and ranking formats** to allow students to instantly check their knowledge.

- **Instructional power of figures.** The instructional power of figures is enhanced using the research-proven technique of **"annotation"** (chalkboard-style commentary integrated into the figure to guide the student in interpreting the figure) and by **streamlined use of color and detail** (in mechanics, for example, color is used to focus the student on the object of interest while the rest of the image is in grayscale and without distracting detail).

- **Enhanced end-of-chapter problems.** Renowned for providing the most wide-ranging and best-tested problems available, the Twelfth Edition goes still further: It provides **the first library of physics problems systematically enhanced** based on student performance nationally. Using this analysis, more than 800 new problems make up the entire library of 3700.

- **MasteringPhysics™** (www.masteringphysics.com). Launched with the Eleventh Edition, MasteringPhysics is now the most widely adopted, educationally proven, and technically advanced online homework and tutorial system in the world. For the Twelfth Edition, MasteringPhysics provides a wealth of new content and technological enhancements. In addition to a library of more than 1200 tutorials and all the end-of-chapter problems, MasteringPhysics

Standard, Extended,
and Three-Volume Editions

With MasteringPhysics™:
- **Standard Edition:** Chapters 1–37
  (ISBN-13: 978-0-321-50161-5)
  (ISBN-10: 0-321-50161-6)
- **Extended Edition:** Chapters 1–44
  (ISBN-13: 978-0-8053-2187-6)
  (ISBN-10: 0-8053-2187-X)
- **Volume 1:** Chapters 1–20
  (ISBN-13: 978-0-321-50056-4)
  (ISBN-10: 0-321-50056-3)
- **Volume 2:** Chapters 21–37
  (ISBN-13: 978-0-321-50039-7)
  (ISBN-10: 0-321-50039-3)
- **Volume 3:** Chapters 37–44
  (ISBN-13: 978-0-321-50040-3)
  (ISBN-10: 0-321-50040-7)

Without MasteringPhysics™:
- **Standard Edition:** Chapters 1–37
  (ISBN-13: 978-0-321-50147-9)
  (ISBN-10: 0-321-50147-0)
- **Extended Edition:** Chapters 1–44
  (ISBN-13: 978-0-321-50121-9)
  (ISBN-10: 0-321-50121-7)
- **Volume 1:** Chapters 1–20
  (ISBN-13: 978-0-321-50062-5)
  (ISBN-10: 0-321-50062-8)
- **Volume 2:** Chapters 21–37
  (ISBN-13: 978-0-321-50076-2)
  (ISBN-10: 0-321-50076-8)
- **Volume 3:** Chapters 37–44
  (ISBN-13: 978-0-321-50077-9)
  (ISBN-10: 0-321-50077-6)

now also provides specific tutorials for every Problem-Solving Strategy and key Test Your Understanding questions from each chapter. Answer types include algebraic, numerical, and multiple-choice answers, as well as ranking, sorting, graph drawing, vector drawing, and ray tracing.

Key Features of *University Physics*

A Guide for the Student Many physics students experience difficulty simply because they don't know how to use their textbook. The section entitled "How to Succeed in Physics by Really Trying," which precedes this preface, is a "user's manual" to all the features of this book. This section, written by Professor Mark Hollabaugh (Normandale Community College), also gives a number of helpful study hints. *Every* student should read this section!

Chapter Organization The first section of each chapter is an *Introduction* that gives specific examples of the chapter's content and connects it with what has come before. There are also a *Chapter Opening Question* and a list of *Learning Goals* to make the reader think about the subject matter of the chapter ahead. (To find the answer to the question, look for the **?** icon.) Most sections end with a *Test Your Understanding Question,* which can be conceptual or quantitative in nature. At the end of the last section of the chapter is a *Visual Chapter Summary* of the most important principles in the chapter, as well as a list of *Key Terms* with reference to the page number where each term is introduced. The answers to the Chapter Opening Question and Test Your Understanding Questions follow the Key Terms.

Questions and Problems At the end of each chapter is a collection of *Discussion Questions* that probe and extend the student's conceptual understanding. Following these are *Exercises,* which are single-concept problems keyed to specific sections of the text; *Problems,* usually requiring one or two nontrivial steps; and *Challenge Problems,* intended to challenge the strongest students. The problems include applications to such diverse fields as astrophysics, biology, and aerodynamics. Many problems have a conceptual part in which students must discuss and explain their results. The new questions, exercises, and problems for this edition were created and organized by Wayne Anderson (Sacramento City College), Laird Kramer (Florida International University), and Charlie Hibbard.

Problem-Solving Strategies and Worked Examples Throughout the book, *Problem-Solving Strategy* boxes provide students with specific tactics for solving particular types of problems. They address the needs of any students who have ever felt that they "understand the concepts but can't do the problems."

All Problem-Solving Strategy boxes follow the ISEE approach (Identify, Set Up, Execute, and Evaluate) to solving problems. This approach helps students see how to begin with a seemingly complex situation, identify the relevant physical concepts, decide what tools are needed to solve the problem, carry out the solution, and then evaluate whether the result makes sense.

Each Problem-Solving Strategy box is followed by one or more worked-out *Examples* that illustrate the strategy. Many other worked-out Examples are found in each chapter. Like the Problem-Solving Strategy boxes, all of the quantitative Examples use the ISEE approach. Several of the examples are purely qualitative and are labeled as *Conceptual Examples;* see, for instance, Conceptual Examples 6.5 (Comparing kinetic energies, p. 191), 8.1 (Momentum versus kinetic energy, p. 251) and 20.7 (A reversible adiabatic process, p. 693).

"Caution" paragraphs Two decades of physics education research have revealed a number of conceptual pitfalls that commonly plague beginning physics students. These include the ideas that force is required for motion, that electric current is "used up" as it goes around a circuit, and that the product of an object's mass and its acceleration is itself a force. The "Caution" paragraphs alert students to these and other pitfalls, and explain why the wrong way to think about a certain situation (which may have occurred to the student first) is indeed wrong. (See, for example, pp. 118, 159, and 559.)

Notation and units Students often have a hard time keeping track of which quantities are vectors and which are not. We use boldface italic symbols with an arrow on top for vector quantities, such as $\vec{v}$, $\vec{a}$, and $\vec{F}$; unit vectors such as $\hat{i}$, have a caret on top. Boldface $+$, $-$, $\times$, and $=$ signs are used in vector equations to emphasize the distinction between vector and scalar mathematical operations.

SI units are used exclusively (English unit conversions are included where appropriate). The joule is used as the standard unit of energy of all forms, including heat.

Flexibility The book is adaptable to a wide variety of course outlines. There is plenty of material for a three-semester or a five-quarter course. Most instructors will find that there is too much material for a one-year course, but it is easy to tailor the book to a variety of one-year course plans by omitting certain chapters or sections. For example, any or all of the chapters on fluid mechanics, sound and hearing, electromagnetic waves, or relativity can be omitted without loss of continuity. In any case, no instructor should feel constrained to work straight through the entire book.

Instructor Supplements

The **Instructor Solutions Manuals,** prepared by A. Lewis Ford (Texas A&M University), contain complete and detailed solutions to all end-of-chapter problems. All solutions follow consistently the same Identify/Set Up/Execute/Evaluate problem-solving framework used in the textbook. The *Instructor Solutions Manual for Volume 1* (ISBN 0-321-49968-9) covers Chapters 1–20, and the *Instructor Solutions Manual for Volumes 2 and 3* (ISBN 0-321-49210-2) covers Chapters 21–44.

The cross-platform **Media Manager CD-ROM** (ISBN 0-321-49916-6) provides a comprehensive library of more than 220 applets from ActivPhysics OnLine™ as well as all line figures from the textbook in JPEG format. In addition, all the key equations, Problem-Solving Strategies, tables, and chapter summaries are provided in editable Word format. In-class weekly multiple-choice questions for use with various Classroom Response Systems (CRS) are also provided, based on the Test Your Understanding questions in the text. The CD-ROM also provides the Instructor Solutions Manual in convenient editable Word format and as PDFs.

MasteringPhysics™ (www.masteringphysics.com) is the most advanced, educationally effective, and widely used physics homework and tutorial system in the world. It provides instructors with a library of extensively pretested end-of-chapter problems and rich, Socratic tutorials that incorporate a wide variety of answer types, wrong-answer feedback, and adaptive help (comprising hints or simpler sub-problems upon request). MasteringPhysics™ allows instructors to quickly build wide-ranging homework assignments of just the right difficulty and duration and provides them with efficient tools to analyze class trends—or the work of any student—in unprecedented detail and to compare the results either with the national average or with the performance of previous classes.

Five Easy Lessons: Strategies for Successful Physics Teaching (ISBN 0-8053-8702-1) by Randall D. Knight (California Polytechnic State University, San Luis

Obispo) is packed with creative ideas on how to enhance any physics course. It is an invaluable companion for both novice and veteran physics instructors.

The **Transparency Acetates** (ISBN 0-321-50034-2) contain more than 200 key figures from *University Physics,* Twelfth Edition, in full color.

The **Printed Test Bank** (ISBN 0-321-50035-0) provides more than 2000 multiple-choice questions.

The **Computerized Test Bank** (ISBN 0-321-50126-8) includes all of the questions from the Printed Test Bank on a cross-platform CD-ROM. More than half the questions have numerical values that can be randomly assigned for each student.

Student Supplements

The **Study Guide,** by James R. Gaines, William F. Palmer, and Laird Kramer, reinforces the text's emphasis on problem-solving strategies and student misconceptions. The *Study Guide for Volume 1* (ISBN 0-321-50033-4) covers Chapters 1–20, and the *Study Guide for Volumes 2 and 3* (ISBN 0-321-50037-7) covers Chapters 21–44.

The **Student Solutions Manual,** by A. Lewis Ford (Texas A&M University), contains detailed, step-by-step solutions to more than half of the odd-numbered end-of-chapter problems from the textbook. All solutions follow consistently the same Identify/Set Up/Execute/Evaluate problem-solving framework used in the textbook. The *Student Solutions Manual for Volume 1* (ISBN 0-321-50063-6) covers Chapters 1–20, and the *Student Solutions Manual for Volumes 2 and 3* (ISBN 0-321-50038-5) covers Chapters 21–44.

 MasteringPhysics™ (www.masteringphysics.com) is the most advanced, widely used, and educationally proven physics tutorial system in the world. It is the result of eight years of detailed studies of how real students work physics problems, and of precisely where they need help. Studies show that students who use MasteringPhysics™ significantly improve their scores on final exams and conceptual tests such as the Force Concept Inventory. MasteringPhysics™ achieves this by providing students with instantaneous feedback specific to their wrong answers, simpler sub-problems upon request when they get stuck, and partial credit for their method. This individualized, 24/7 tutor system is recommended by nine out of ten students to their peers as the most effective and time-efficient way to study.

 ActivPhysics OnLine™ (www.masteringphysics.com), now included in the self-study area of MasteringPhysics, provides the most comprehensive library of applets and applet-based tutorials available. ActivPhysics OnLine was created by the educational pioneer Alan Van Heuvelen of Rutgers. Throughout *University Physics,* Twelfth Edition, in-margin icons direct the student to specific applets in ActivPhysics OnLine in for additional interactive help.

ActivPhysics OnLine™ **Workbooks, Volume 1** (0-8053-9060-X) and **Volume 2** (0-8053-9061-8) by Alan Van Heuvelen, Rutgers, and Paul d'Alessandris, Monroe Community College, provide a range of tutorials that use the critically acclaimed ActivPhysics OnLine applets to help students develop understanding and confidence. In particular, they focus on developing intuition, making predictions, testing assumptions experimentally, drawing effective diagrams, understanding key equations both qualitatively and quantitatively, and interpreting graphical information. These workbooks can be used for labs, homework, or self-study.

The **Addison-Wesley Tutor Center** (www.aw.com/tutorcenter) provides one-on-one tutoring via telephone, fax, e-mail, or interactive website. Qualified instructors answer questions and provide instruction with examples, problems, and other content from *University Physics,* Twelfth Edition, as well as help with Mastering-Physics™.

Acknowledgments

We would like to thank the hundreds of reviewers and colleagues who have offered valuable comments and suggestions over the life of this textbook. The continuing success of *University Physics* is due in large measure to their contributions.

Edward Adelson (Ohio State University), Ralph Alexander (University of Missouri at Rolla), J. G. Anderson, R. S. Anderson, Wayne Anderson (Sacramento City College), Alex Azima (Lansing Community College), Dilip Balamore (Nassau Community College), Harold Bale (University of North Dakota), Arun Bansil (Northeastern University), John Barach (Vanderbilt University), J. D. Barnett, H. H. Barschall, Albert Bartlett (University of Colorado), Paul Baum (CUNY, Queens College), Frederick Becchetti (University of Michigan), B. Bederson, David Bennum (University of Nevada, Reno), Lev I. Berger (San Diego State University), Robert Boeke (William Rainey Harper College), S. Borowitz, A. C. Braden, James Brooks (Boston University), Nicholas E. Brown (California Polytechnic State University, San Luis Obispo), Tony Buffa (California Polytechnic State University, San Luis Obispo), A. Capecelatro, Michael Cardamone (Pennsylvania State University), Duane Carmony (Purdue University), Troy Carter (UCLA), P. Catranides, John Cerne (SUNY at Buffalo), Roger Clapp (University of South Florida), William M. Cloud (Eastern Illinois University), Leonard Cohen (Drexel University), W. R. Coker (University of Texas, Austin), Malcolm D. Cole (University of Missouri at Rolla), H. Conrad, David Cook (Lawrence University), Gayl Cook (University of Colorado), Hans Courant (University of Minnesota), Bruce A. Craver (University of Dayton), Larry Curtis (University of Toledo), Jai Dahiya (Southeast Missouri State University), Steve Detweiler (University of Florida), George Dixon (Oklahoma State University), Donald S. Duncan, Boyd Edwards (West Virginia University), Robert Eisenstein (Carnegie Mellon University), Amy Emerson Missourn (Virginia Institute of Technology), William Faissler (Northeastern University), William Fasnacht (U.S. Naval Academy), Paul Feldker (St. Louis Community College), Carlos Figueroa (Cabrillo College), L. H. Fisher, Neil Fletcher (Florida State University), Robert Folk, Peter Fong (Emory University), A. Lewis Ford (Texas A&M University), D. Frantszog, James R. Gaines (Ohio State University), Solomon Gartenhaus (Purdue University), Ron Gautreau (New Jersey Institute of Technology), J. David Gavenda (University of Texas, Austin), Dennis Gay (University of North Florida), James Gerhart (University of Washington), N. S. Gingrich, J. L. Glathart, S. Goodwin, Rich Gottfried (Frederick Community College), Walter S. Gray (University of Michigan), Paul Gresser (University of Maryland), Benjamin Grinstein (UC San Diego), Howard Grotch (Pennsylvania State University), John Gruber (San Jose State University), Graham D. Gutsche (U.S. Naval Academy), Michael J. Harrison (Michigan State University), Harold Hart (Western Illinois University), Howard Hayden (University of Connecticut), Carl Helrich (Goshen College), Laurent Hodges (Iowa State University), C. D. Hodgman, Michael Hones (Villanova University), Keith Honey (West Virginia Institute of Technology), Gregory Hood (Tidewater Community College), John Hubisz (North Carolina State University), M. Iona, John Jaszczak (Michigan Technical University), Alvin Jenkins (North Carolina State University), Robert P. Johnson (UC Santa Cruz), Lorella Jones (University of Illinois), John Karchek (GMI Engineering & Management Institute), Thomas Keil (Worcester Polytechnic Institute), Robert Kraemer (Carnegie Mellon University), Jean P. Krisch (University of Michigan), Robert A. Kromhout, Andrew Kunz (Marquette University), Charles Lane (Berry College), Thomas N. Lawrence (Texas State University), Robert J. Lee, Alfred Leitner (Rensselaer Polytechnic University), Gerald P. Lietz (De Paul University), Gordon Lind (Utah State University), S. Livingston, Elihu Lubkin (University of Wisconsin, Milwaukee), Robert Luke (Boise State University), David Lynch (Iowa State University), Michael Lysak (San Bernardino Valley College), Jeffrey Mallow (Loyola University), Robert Mania (Kentucky State University), Robert Marchina (University of Memphis), David Markowitz (University of Connecticut), R. J. Maurer, Oren Maxwell (Florida International University), Joseph L. McCauley (University of Houston), T. K. McCubbin, Jr. (Pennsylvania State University), Charles McFarland (University of Missouri at Rolla), James Mcguire (Tulane University), Lawrence McIntyre (University of Arizona), Fredric Messing (Carnegie-Mellon University), Thomas Meyer (Texas A&M University), Andre Mirabelli (St. Peter's College, New Jersey), Herbert Muether (S.U.N.Y., Stony Brook), Jack Munsee (California State University, Long Beach), Lorenzo Narducci (Drexel University), Van E. Neie (Purdue University), David A. Nordling (U. S. Naval Academy), Benedict Oh (Pennsylvania State University), L. O. Olsen, Jim Pannell (DeVry Institute of Technology), W. F. Parks (University of Missouri), Robert Paulson (California State University, Chico), Jerry Peacher (University of Missouri at Rolla), Arnold Perlmutter (University of Miami), Lennart Peterson (University of Florida), R. J. Peterson (University of Colorado, Boulder), R. Pinkston, Ronald Poling (University of Minnesota), J. G. Potter, C. W. Price (Millersville University), Francis Prosser (University of Kansas), Shelden H. Radin, Michael Rapport (Anne Arundel Community College), R. Resnick, James A. Richards, Jr., John S. Risley (North Carolina State University), Francesc Roig (University of California, Santa Barbara), T. L. Rokoske, Richard Roth (Eastern Michigan University), Carl Rotter (University of West Virginia), S. Clark Rowland (Andrews University), Rajarshi Roy (Georgia Institute of Technology), Russell A. Roy (Santa Fe Community College), Dhiraj Sardar (University of Texas, San Antonio), Bruce Schumm (UC Santa Cruz), Melvin Schwartz (St. John's University), F. A. Scott, L. W. Seagondollar, Paul Shand (University of

Northern Iowa), Stan Shepherd (Pennsylvania State University), Douglas Sherman (San Jose State), Bruce Sherwood (Carnegie Mellon University), Hugh Siefkin (Greenville College), Tomasz Skwarnicki (Syracuse University), C. P. Slichter, Charles W. Smith (University of Maine, Orono), Malcolm Smith (University of Lowell), Ross Spencer (Brigham Young University), Julien Sprott (University of Wisconsin), Victor Stanionis (Iona College), James Stith (American Institute of Physics), Chuck Stone (North Carolina A&T State University), Edward Strother (Florida Institute of Technology), Conley Stutz (Bradley University), Albert Stwertka (U.S. Merchant Marine Academy), Martin Tiersten (CUNY, City College), David Toot (Alfred University), Somdev Tyagi (Drexel University), F. Verbrugge, Helmut Vogel (Carnegie Mellon University), Robert Webb (Texas A & M), Thomas Weber (Iowa State University), M. Russell Wehr, (Pennsylvania State University), Robert Weidman (Michigan Technical University), Dan Whalen (UC San Diego), Lester V. Whitney, Thomas Wiggins (Pennsylvania State University), David Willey (University of Pittsburgh, Johnstown), George Williams (University of Utah), John Williams (Auburn University), Stanley Williams (Iowa State University), Jack Willis, Suzanne Willis (Northern Illinois University), Robert Wilson (San Bernardino Valley College), L. Wolfenstein, James Wood (Palm Beach Junior College), Lowell Wood (University of Houston), R. E. Worley, D. H. Ziebell (Manatee Community College), George O. Zimmerman (Boston University)

In addition, we both have individual acknowledgments we would like to make.

I want to extend my heartfelt thanks to my colleagues at Carnegie Mellon, especially Professors Robert Kraemer, Bruce Sherwood, Ruth Chabay, Helmut Vogel, and Brian Quinn, for many stimulating discussions about physics pedagogy and for their support and encouragement during the writing of several successive editions of this book. I am equally indebted to the many generations of Carnegie Mellon students who have helped me learn what good teaching and good writing are, by showing me what works and what doesn't. It is always a joy and a privilege to express my gratitude to my wife Alice and our children Gretchen and Rebecca for their love, support, and emotional sustenance during the writing of several successive editions of this book. May all men and women be blessed with love such as theirs. — H. D. Y.

I would like to thank my past and present colleagues at UCSB, including Rob Geller, Carl Gwinn, Al Nash, Elisabeth Nicol, and Francesc Roig, for their wholehearted support and for many helpful discussions. I owe a special debt of gratitude to my early teachers Willa Ramsay, Peter Zimmerman, William Little, Alan Schwettman, and Dirk Walecka for showing me what clear and engaging physics teaching is all about, and to Stuart Johnson for inviting me to become a co-author of *University Physics* beginning with the 9th edition. I want to express special thanks to the editorial staff at Addison Wesley and their partners: to Adam Black for his editorial vision; to Margot Otway for her superb graphic sense and careful development of this edition; to Peter Murphy and Carol Reitz for their careful reading of the manuscript; to Wayne Anderson, Charlie Hibbard, Laird Kramer, and Larry Stookey for their work on the end-of-chapter problems; and to Laura Kenney, Chandrika Madhavan, Nancy Tabor, and Pat McCutcheon for keeping the editorial and production pipeline flowing. I want to thank my father for his continued love and support and for keeping a space open on his bookshelf for this book. Most of all, I want to express my gratitude and love to my wife Caroline, to whom I dedicate my contribution to this book. Hey, Caroline, the new edition's done at last — let's go flying! — R. A. F.

Please Tell Us What You Think!

We welcome communications from students and professors, especially concerning errors or deficiencies that you find in this edition. We have devoted a lot of time and effort to writing the best book we know how to write, and we hope it will help you to teach and learn physics. In turn, you can help us by letting us know what still needs to be improved! Please feel free to contact us either electronically or by ordinary mail. Your comments will be greatly appreciated.

October 2006

Hugh D. Young
Department of Physics
Carnegie Mellon University
Pittsburgh, PA 15213
hdy@andrew.cmu.edu

Roger A. Freedman
Department of Physics
University of California, Santa Barbara
Santa Barbara, CA 93106-9530
airboy@physics.ucsb.edu
http://www.physics.ucsb.edu/~airboy/

DETAILED CONTENTS

MODERN PHYSICS

APPENDICES

ELECTRIC CHARGE AND ELECTRIC FIELD

21

? Water makes life possible: The cells of your body could not function without water in which to dissolve essential biological molecules. What electrical properties of water make it such a good solvent?

Back in Chapter 5, we briefly mentioned the four kinds of fundamental forces. To this point the only one of these forces that we have examined in any detail is gravity. Now we are ready to examine the force of *electromagnetism*, which encompasses both electricity and magnetism. Our exploration of electromagnetic phenomena will occupy our attention for most of the remainder of this book.

Electromagnetic interactions involve particles that have a property called *electric charge*, an attribute that is as fundamental as mass. Just as objects with mass are accelerated by gravitational forces, so electrically charged objects are accelerated by electric forces. The annoying electric spark you feel when you scuff your shoes across a carpet and then reach for a metal doorknob is due to charged particles leaping between your finger and the doorknob. Electric currents, such as those in a flashlight or a television, are simply streams of charged particles flowing within wires in response to electric forces. Even the forces that hold atoms together to form solid matter, and that keep the atoms of solid objects from passing through each other, are fundamentally due to electric interactions between the charged particles within atoms.

We begin our study of electromagnetism in this chapter by examining the nature of electric charge. We'll find that electric charge is quantized and that it obeys a conservation principle. We then turn to a discussion of the interactions of electric charges that are at rest in our frame of reference, called *electrostatic* interactions. Such interactions are of tremendous importance in chemistry and biology and have many technological applications. Electrostatic interactions are governed by a simple relationship known as *Coulomb's law* and are most conveniently described by using the concept of *electric field*. In later chapters we'll expand our discussion to include electric charges in motion. This will lead us to an understanding of magnetism and, remarkably, of the nature of light.

While the key ideas of electromagnetism are conceptually simple, applying them to practical problems will make use of many of your mathematical skills, especially your knowledge of geometry and integral calculus. For this reason you may find this chapter and those that follow to be more mathematically demanding than earlier chapters. The reward for your extra effort will be a deeper understanding of principles that are at the heart of modern physics and technology.

21.1 Electric Charge

The ancient Greeks discovered as early as 600 B.C. that after they rubbed amber with wool, the amber could attract other objects. Today we say that the amber has acquired a net **electric charge,** or has become *charged.* The word "electric" is derived from the Greek word *elektron,* meaning amber. When you scuff your shoes across a nylon carpet, you become electrically charged, and you can charge a comb by passing it through dry hair.

Plastic rods and fur (real or fake) are particularly good for demonstrating **electrostatics,** the interactions between electric charges that are at rest (or nearly so). Figure 21.1a shows two plastic rods and a piece of fur. After we charge each rod by rubbing it with the piece of fur, we find that the rods repel each other.

When we rub glass rods with silk, the glass rods also become charged and repel each other (Fig. 21.1b). But a charged plastic rod *attracts* a charged glass rod; furthermore, the plastic rod and the fur attract each other, and the glass rod and the silk attract each other (Fig. 21.1c).

These experiments and many others like them have shown that there are exactly two kinds of electric charge: the kind on the plastic rod rubbed with fur and the kind on the glass rod rubbed with silk. Benjamin Franklin (1706–1790) suggested calling these two kinds of charge *negative* and *positive,* respectively, and these names are still used. The plastic rod and the silk have negative charge; the glass rod and the fur have positive charge.

Two positive charges or two negative charges repel each other. A positive charge and a negative charge attract each other.

21.1 Experiments in electrostatics. (a) Negatively charged objects repel each other. (b) Positively charged objects repel each other. (c) Positively charged objects and negatively charged objects attract each other.

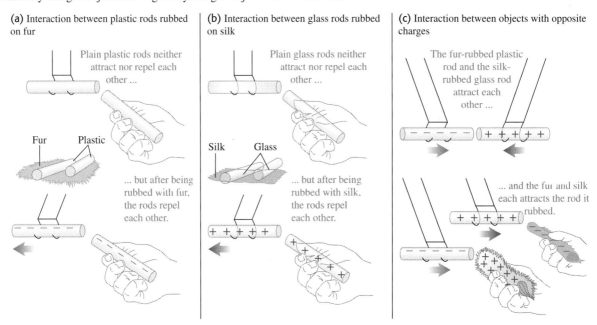

(a) Interaction between plastic rods rubbed on fur

Plain plastic rods neither attract nor repel each other ...

Fur   Plastic

... but after being rubbed with fur, the rods repel each other.

(b) Interaction between glass rods rubbed on silk

Plain glass rods neither attract nor repel each other ...

Silk   Glass

... but after being rubbed with silk, the rods repel each other.

(c) Interaction between objects with opposite charges

The fur-rubbed plastic rod and the silk-rubbed glass rod attract each other ...

... and the fur and silk each attracts the rod it rubbed.

21.2 Schematic diagram of the operation of a laser printer.

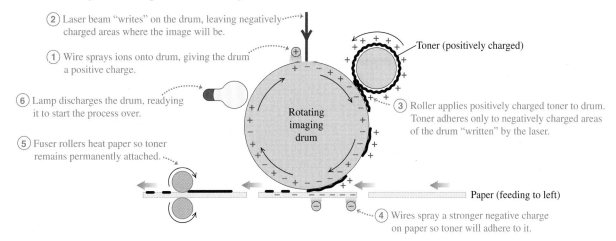

② Laser beam "writes" on the drum, leaving negatively charged areas where the image will be.

① Wire sprays ions onto drum, giving the drum a positive charge.

⑥ Lamp discharges the drum, readying it to start the process over.

⑤ Fuser rollers heat paper so toner remains permanently attached.

Rotating imaging drum

Toner (positively charged)

③ Roller applies positively charged toner to drum. Toner adheres only to negatively charged areas of the drum "written" by the laser.

Paper (feeding to left)

④ Wires spray a stronger negative charge on paper so toner will adhere to it.

CAUTION **Electric attraction and repulsion** The attraction and repulsion of two charged objects are sometimes summarized as "Like charges repel, and opposite charges attract." But keep in mind that the phrase "like charges" does *not* mean that the two charges are exactly identical, only that both charges have the same algebraic *sign* (both positive or both negative). "Opposite charges" means that both objects have an electric charge, and those charges have different signs (one positive and the other negative). ▮

One technological application of forces between charged bodies is in a laser printer (Fig. 21.2). Initially the printer's light-sensitive imaging drum is given a positive charge. As the drum rotates, a laser beam shines on selected areas of the drum, leaving those areas with a *negative* charge. Positively charged particles of toner adhere only to the areas of the drum "written" by the laser. When a piece of paper is placed in contact with the drum, the toner particles stick to the paper and form an image.

Electric Charge and the Structure of Matter

When you charge a rod by rubbing it with fur or silk as in Fig. 21.1, there is no visible change in the appearance of the rod. What, then, actually happens to the rod when you charge it? To answer this question, we must look more closely at the structure and electric properties of atoms, the building blocks of ordinary matter of all kinds.

The structure of atoms can be described in terms of three particles: the negatively charged **electron**, the positively charged **proton,** and the uncharged **neutron** (Fig. 21.3). The proton and neutron are combinations of other entities called *quarks,* which have charges of $\pm\frac{1}{3}$ and $\pm\frac{2}{3}$ times the electron charge. Isolated quarks have not been observed, and there are theoretical reasons to believe that it is impossible in principle to observe a quark in isolation.

The protons and neutrons in an atom make up a small, very dense core called the **nucleus,** with dimensions of the order of 10^{-15} m. Surrounding the nucleus are the electrons, extending out to distances of the order of 10^{-10} m from the nucleus. If an atom were a few kilometers across, its nucleus would be the size of a tennis ball. The negatively charged electrons are held within the atom by the attractive electric forces exerted on them by the positively charged nucleus. (The protons and neutrons are held within the stable atomic nuclei by an attractive interaction, called the *strong nuclear force,* that overcomes the electric repulsion of the protons. The strong nuclear force has a short range, and its effects do not extend far beyond the nucleus.)

21.3 The structure of an atom. The particular atom depicted here is lithium (see Fig. 21.4a).

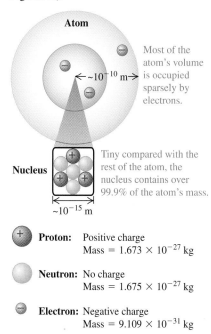

Atom

Most of the atom's volume is occupied sparsely by electrons.

← ~10^{-10} m →

Nucleus

Tiny compared with the rest of the atom, the nucleus contains over 99.9% of the atom's mass.

~10^{-15} m

⊕ **Proton:** Positive charge
Mass = 1.673×10^{-27} kg

◯ **Neutron:** No charge
Mass = 1.675×10^{-27} kg

⊖ **Electron:** Negative charge
Mass = 9.109×10^{-31} kg

The charges of the electron and proton are equal in magnitude.

21.4 (a) A neutral atom has as many electrons as it does protons. (b) A positive ion has a deficit of electrons. (c) A negative ion has an excess of electrons. (The electron "shells" are a schematic representation of the actual electron distribution, a diffuse cloud many times larger than the nucleus.)

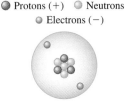

Protons (+)   Neutrons
Electrons (−)

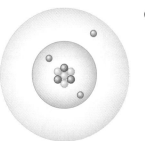 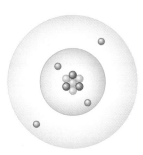

(a) Neutral lithium atom (Li):	(b) Positive lithium ion (Li⁺):	(c) Negative lithium ion (Li⁻):
3 protons (3+)	3 protons (3+)	3 protons (3+)
4 neutrons	4 neutrons	4 neutrons
3 electrons (3−)	2 electrons (2−)	4 electrons (4−)
Electrons equal protons: Zero net charge	Fewer electrons than protons: Positive net charge	More electrons than protons: Negative net charge

The masses of the individual particles, to the precision that they are presently known, are

$$\text{Mass of electron} = m_e = 9.1093826(16) \times 10^{-31}\ \text{kg}$$

$$\text{Mass of proton} = m_p = 1.67262171(29) \times 10^{-27}\ \text{kg}$$

$$\text{Mass of neutron} = m_n = 1.67492728(29) \times 10^{-27}\ \text{kg}$$

The numbers in parentheses are the uncertainties in the last two digits. Note that the masses of the proton and neutron are nearly equal and are roughly 2000 times the mass of the electron. Over 99.9% of the mass of any atom is concentrated in its nucleus.

The negative charge of the electron has (within experimental error) *exactly* the same magnitude as the positive charge of the proton. In a neutral atom the number of electrons equals the number of protons in the nucleus, and the net electric charge (the algebraic sum of all the charges) is exactly zero (Fig. 21.4a). The number of protons or electrons in a neutral atom of an element is called the **atomic number** of the element. If one or more electrons are removed, the remaining positively charged structure is called a **positive ion** (Fig. 21.4b). A **negative ion** is an atom that has *gained* one or more electrons (Fig. 21.4c). This gaining or losing of electrons is called **ionization.**

When the total number of protons in a macroscopic body equals the total number of electrons, the total charge is zero and the body as a whole is electrically neutral. To give a body an excess negative charge, we may either *add negative* charges to a neutral body or *remove positive* charges from that body. Similarly, we can create an excess positive charge by either *adding positive* charge or *removing negative* charge. In most cases, negatively charged (and highly mobile) electrons are added or removed, and a "positively charged body" is one that has lost some of its normal complement of electrons. When we speak of the charge of a body, we always mean its *net* charge. The net charge is always a very small fraction (typically no more than 10^{-12}) of the total positive charge or negative charge in the body.

Electric Charge Is Conserved

Implicit in the foregoing discussion are two very important principles. First is the **principle of conservation of charge:**

> **The algebraic sum of all the electric charges in any closed system is constant.**

If we rub together a plastic rod and a piece of fur, both initially uncharged, the rod acquires a negative charge (since it takes electrons from the fur) and the fur acquires a positive charge of the *same* magnitude (since it has lost as many electrons as the rod has gained). Hence the total electric charge on the two bodies together does not change. In any charging process, charge is not created or destroyed; it is merely *transferred* from one body to another.

Conservation of charge is thought to be a *universal* conservation law. No experimental evidence for any violation of this principle has ever been observed. Even in high-energy interactions in which particles are created and destroyed, such as the creation of electron–positron pairs, the total charge of any closed system is exactly constant.

The second important principle is:

The magnitude of charge of the electron or proton is a natural unit of charge.

Every observable amount of electric charge is always an integer multiple of this basic unit. We say that charge is *quantized*. A familiar example of quantization is money. When you pay cash for an item in a store, you have to do it in one-cent increments. Cash can't be divided into amounts smaller than one cent, and electric charge can't be divided into amounts smaller than the charge of one electron or proton. (The quark charges, $\pm\frac{1}{3}$ and $\pm\frac{2}{3}$ of the electron charge, are probably not observable as isolated charges.) Thus the charge on any macroscopic body is always either zero or an integer multiple (negative or positive) of the electron charge.

Understanding the electric nature of matter gives us insight into many aspects of the physical world (Fig. 21.5). The chemical bonds that hold atoms together to form molecules are due to electric interactions between the atoms. They include the strong ionic bonds that hold sodium and chlorine atoms together to make table salt and the relatively weak bonds between the strands of DNA that record your body's genetic code. The normal force exerted on you by the chair in which you're sitting arises from electric forces between charged particles in the atoms of your seat and in the atoms of your chair. The tension force in a stretched string and the adhesive force of glue are likewise due to the electric interactions of atoms.

Test Your Understanding of Section 21.1   (a) Strictly speaking, does the plastic rod in Fig. 21.1 weigh more, less, or the same after rubbing it with fur? (b) What about the glass rod after rubbing it with silk? What about (c) the fur and (d) the silk? ∎

21.5 Most of the forces on this water skier are electric. Electric interactions between adjacent molecules give rise to the force of the water on the ski, the tension in the tow rope, and the resistance of the air on the skier's body. Electric interactions also hold the atoms of the skier's body together. Only one wholly nonelectric force acts on the skier: the force of gravity.

21.2 Conductors, Insulators, and Induced Charges

Some materials permit electric charge to move easily from one region of the material to another, while others do not. For example, Fig. 21.6a shows a copper wire supported by a nylon thread. Suppose you touch one end of the wire to a charged plastic rod and attach the other end to a metal ball that is initially uncharged; you then remove the charged rod and the wire. When you bring another charged body up close to the ball (Figs. 21.6b and 21.6c), the ball is attracted or repelled, showing that the ball has become electrically charged. Electric charge has been transferred through the copper wire between the ball and the surface of the plastic rod.

The copper wire is called a **conductor** of electricity. If you repeat the experiment using a rubber band or nylon thread in place of the wire, you find that *no* charge is transferred to the ball. These materials are called **insulators.** Conductors permit the easy movement of charge through them, while insulators do not. (The supporting nylon threads shown in Fig. 21.6 are insulators, which prevents charge from leaving the metal ball and copper wire.)

As an example, carpet fibers on a dry day are good insulators. As you walk across a carpet, the rubbing of your shoes against the fibers causes charge to build

21.6 Copper is a good conductor of electricity; nylon is a good insulator. (a) The copper wire conducts charge between the metal ball and the charged plastic rod to charge the ball negatively. Afterward, the metal ball is (b) repelled by a negatively charged plastic rod and (c) attracted to a positively charged glass rod.

(a)

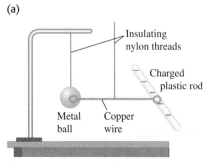

The wire conducts charge from the negatively charged plastic rod to the metal ball.

(b)

(c)

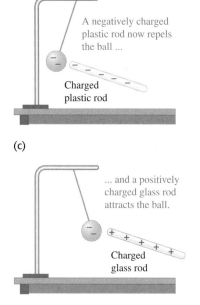

up on you, and this charge remains on you because it can't flow through the insulating fibers. If you then touch a conducting object such as a doorknob, a rapid charge transfer takes place between your finger and the doorknob, and you feel a shock. One way to prevent this is to wind some of the carpet fibers around conducting cores so that any charge that builds up on you can be transferred harmlessly to the carpet. Another solution is to coat the carpet fibers with an antistatic layer that does not easily transfer electrons to or from your shoes; this prevents any charge from building up on you in the first place.

Most metals are good conductors, while most nonmetals are insulators. Within a solid metal such as copper, one or more outer electrons in each atom become detached and can move freely throughout the material, just as the molecules of a gas can move through the spaces between the grains in a bucket of sand. The motion of these negatively charged electrons carries charge through the metal. The other electrons remain bound to the positively charged nuclei, which themselves are bound in nearly fixed positions within the material. In an insulator there are no, or very few, free electrons, and electric charge cannot move freely through the material. Some materials called *semiconductors* are intermediate in their properties between good conductors and good insulators.

Charging by Induction

We can charge a metal ball using a copper wire and an electrically charged plastic rod, as in Fig. 21.6a. In this process, some of the excess electrons on the rod are transferred from it to the ball, leaving the rod with a smaller negative charge. There is a different technique in which the plastic rod can give another body a charge of *opposite* sign without losing any of its own charge. This process is called charging by **induction.**

Figure 21.7 shows an example of charging by induction. An uncharged metal ball is supported on an insulating stand (Fig. 21.7a). When you bring a negatively charged rod near it, without actually touching it (Fig. 21.7b), the free electrons in the metal ball are repelled by the excess electrons on the rod, and they shift toward the right, away from the rod. They cannot escape from the ball because the supporting stand and the surrounding air are insulators. So we get excess negative charge at the right surface of the ball and a deficiency of negative charge (that is, a net positive charge) at the left surface. These excess charges are called **induced charges.**

Not all of the free electrons move to the right surface of the ball. As soon as any induced charge develops, it exerts forces toward the *left* on the other free electrons. These electrons are repelled by the negative induced charge on the right and attracted toward the positive induced charge on the left. The system reaches an equilibrium state in which the force toward the right on an electron, due to the charged rod, is just balanced by the force toward the left due to the induced charge. If we remove the charged rod, the free electrons shift back to the left, and the original neutral condition is restored.

21.7 Charging a metal ball by induction.

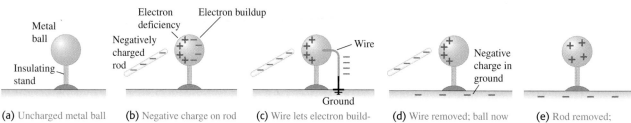

(a) Uncharged metal ball

(b) Negative charge on rod repels electrons, creating zones of negative and positive **induced charge**.

(c) Wire lets electron build-up (induced negative charge) flow into ground.

(d) Wire removed; ball now has only an electron-deficient region of positive charge.

(e) Rod removed; electrons rearrange themselves, ball has overall electron deficiency (net positive charge).

21.8 The charges within the molecules of an insulating material can shift slightly. As a result, a comb with either sign of charge attracts a neutral insulator. By Newton's third law the neutral insulator exerts an equal-magnitude attractive force on the comb.

(a) A charged comb picking up uncharged pieces of plastic

(b) How a negatively charged comb attracts an insulator

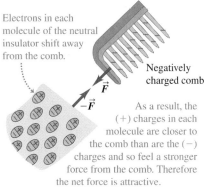

Electrons in each molecule of the neutral insulator shift away from the comb.

Negatively charged comb

$\vec{F}$

$-\vec{F}$

As a result, the (+) charges in each molecule are closer to the comb than are the (−) charges and so feel a stronger force from the comb. Therefore the net force is attractive.

(c) How a positively charged comb attracts an insulator

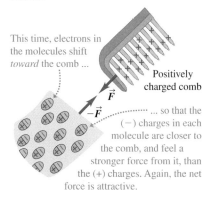

This time, electrons in the molecules shift *toward* the comb ...

Positively charged comb

$\vec{F}$

$-\vec{F}$

... so that the (−) charges in each molecule are closer to the comb, and feel a stronger force from it, than the (+) charges. Again, the net force is attractive.

What happens if, while the plastic rod is nearby, you touch one end of a conducting wire to the right surface of the ball and the other end to the earth (Fig. 21.7c)? The earth is a conductor, and it is so large that it can act as a practically infinite source of extra electrons or sink of unwanted electrons. Some of the negative charge flows through the wire to the earth. Now suppose you disconnect the wire (Fig. 21.7d) and then remove the rod (Fig. 21.7e); a net positive charge is left on the ball. The charge on the negatively charged rod has not changed during this process. The earth acquires a negative charge that is equal in magnitude to the induced positive charge remaining on the ball.

Charging by induction would work just as well if the mobile charges in the ball were positive charges instead of negatively charged electrons, or even if both positive and negative mobile charges were present. In a metallic conductor the mobile charges are always negative electrons, but it is often convenient to describe a process *as though* the moving charges were positive. In ionic solutions and ionized gases, both positive and negative charges are mobile.

Electric Forces on Uncharged Objects

Finally, we note that a charged body can exert forces even on objects that are *not* charged themselves. If you rub a balloon on the rug and then hold the balloon against the ceiling, it sticks, even though the ceiling has no net electric charge. After you electrify a comb by running it through your hair, you can pick up uncharged bits of paper or plastic with the comb (Fig. 21.8a). How is this possible?

This interaction is an induced-charge effect. Even in an insulator, electric charges can shift back and forth a little when there is charge nearby. This is shown in Fig. 21.8b; the negatively charged plastic comb causes a slight shifting of charge within the molecules of the neutral insulator, an effect called *polarization*. The positive and negative charges in the material are present in equal amounts, but the positive charges are closer to the plastic comb and so feel an attraction that is stronger than the repulsion felt by the negative charges, giving a net attractive force. (In Section 21.3 we will study how electric forces depend on distance.) Note that a neutral insulator is also attracted to a *positively* charged comb (Fig. 21.8c). Now the charges in the insulator shift in the opposite direction; the negative charges in the insulator are closer to the comb and feel an attractive force that is stronger than the repulsion felt by the positive charges in the insulator. Hence a charged object of *either* sign exerts an attractive force on an uncharged insulator.

The attraction between a charged object and an uncharged one has many important practical applications, including the electrostatic painting process used in the automobile industry (Fig. 21.9). A metal object to be painted is connected to the earth ("ground" in Fig. 21.9), and the paint droplets are given an electric charge as they exit the sprayer nozzle. Induced charges of the opposite sign

21.9 The electrostatic painting process (compare Figs. 21.7b and 21.7c).

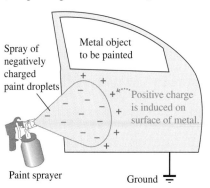

Spray of negatively charged paint droplets

Metal object to be painted

Positive charge is induced on surface of metal.

Paint sprayer

Ground

appear in the object as the droplets approach, just as in Fig. 21.7b, and they attract the droplets to the surface. This process minimizes overspray from clouds of stray paint particles and gives a particularly smooth finish.

Test Your Understanding of Section 21.2 You have two lightweight metal spheres, each hanging from an insulating nylon thread. One of the spheres has a net negative charge, while the other sphere has no net charge. (a) If the spheres are close together but do not touch, will they (i) attract each other, (ii) repel each other, or (iii) exert no force on each other? (b) You now allow the two spheres to touch. Once they have touched, will the two spheres (i) attract each other, (ii) repel each other, or (iii) exert no force on each other?

21.3 Coulomb's Law

Charles Augustin de Coulomb (1736–1806) studied the interaction forces of charged particles in detail in 1784. He used a torsion balance (Fig. 21.10a) similar to the one used 13 years later by Cavendish to study the much weaker gravitational interaction, as we discussed in Section 12.1. For **point charges,** charged bodies that are very small in comparison with the distance r between them, Coulomb found that the electric force is proportional to $1/r^2$. That is, when the distance r doubles, the force decreases to $\frac{1}{4}$ of its initial value; when the distance is halved, the force increases to four times its initial value.

The electric force between two point charges also depends on the quantity of charge on each body, which we will denote by q or Q. To explore this dependence, Coulomb divided a charge into two equal parts by placing a small charged spherical conductor into contact with an identical but uncharged sphere; by symmetry, the charge is shared equally between the two spheres. (Note the essential role of the principle of conservation of charge in this procedure.) Thus he could obtain one-half, one-quarter, and so on, of any initial charge. He found that the forces that two point charges q_1 and q_2 exert on each other are proportional to each charge and therefore are proportional to the *product* $q_1 q_2$ of the two charges.

Thus Coulomb established what we now call **Coulomb's law:**

The magnitude of the electric force between two point charges is directly proportional to the product of the charges and inversely proportional to the square of the distance between them.

21.10 (a) Measuring the electric force between point charges. (b) The electric forces between point charges obey Newton's third law: $\vec{F}_{1\text{ on }2} = -\vec{F}_{2\text{ on }1}$.

(a) A torsion balance of the type used by Coulomb to measure the electric force

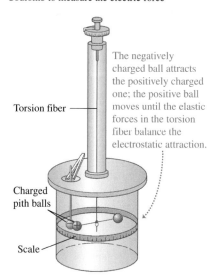

Torsion fiber

The negatively charged ball attracts the positively charged one; the positive ball moves until the elastic forces in the torsion fiber balance the electrostatic attraction.

Charged pith balls

Scale

(b) Interactions between point charges

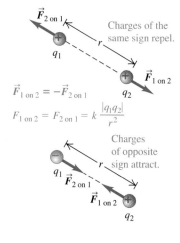

$\vec{F}_{2\text{ on }1}$

q_1

Charges of the same sign repel.

r

$\vec{F}_{1\text{ on }2}$

q_2

$\vec{F}_{1\text{ on }2} = -\vec{F}_{2\text{ on }1}$

$$F_{1\text{ on }2} = F_{2\text{ on }1} = k\frac{|q_1 q_2|}{r^2}$$

Charges of opposite sign attract.

q_1

$\vec{F}_{2\text{ on }1}$

r

$\vec{F}_{1\text{ on }2}$

q_2

In mathematical terms, the magnitude F of the force that each of two point charges q_1 and q_2 a distance r apart exerts on the other can be expressed as

$$F = k\frac{|q_1 q_2|}{r^2} \tag{21.1}$$

where k is a proportionality constant whose numerical value depends on the system of units used. The absolute value bars are used in Eq. (21.1) because the charges q_1 and q_2 can be either positive or negative, while the force magnitude F is always positive.

The directions of the forces the two charges exert on each other are always along the line joining them. When the charges q_1 and q_2 have the same sign, either both positive or both negative, the forces are repulsive; when the charges have opposite signs, the forces are attractive (Fig. 21.10b). The two forces obey Newton's third law; they are always equal in magnitude and opposite in direction, even when the charges are not equal in magnitude.

The proportionality of the electric force to $1/r^2$ has been verified with great precision. There is no reason to suspect that the exponent is different from precisely 2. Thus the form of Eq. (21.1) is the same as that of the law of gravitation. But electric and gravitational interactions are two distinct classes of phenomena. Electric interactions depend on electric charges and can be either attractive or repulsive, while gravitational interactions depend on mass and are always attractive (because there is no such thing as negative mass).

Fundamental Electric Constants

The value of the proportionality constant k in Coulomb's law depends on the system of units used. In our study of electricity and magnetism we will use SI units exclusively. The SI electric units include most of the familiar units such as the volt, the ampere, the ohm, and the watt. (There is *no* British system of electric units.) The SI unit of electric charge is called one **coulomb** (1 C). In SI units the constant k in Eq. (21.1) is

$$k = 8.987551787 \times 10^9 \ \text{N} \cdot \text{m}^2/\text{C}^2 \cong 8.988 \times 10^9 \ \text{N} \cdot \text{m}^2/\text{C}^2$$

The value of k is known to such a large number of significant figures because this value is closely related to the speed of light in vacuum. (We will show this in Chapter 32 when we study electromagnetic radiation.) As we discussed in Section 1.3, this speed is *defined* to be exactly $c = 2.99792458 \times 10^8$ m/s. The numerical value of k is defined in terms of c to be precisely

$$k = (10^{-7} \ \text{N} \cdot \text{s}^2/\text{C}^2)c^2$$

You should check this expression to confirm that k has the right units.

In principle we can measure the electric force F between two equal charges q at a measured distance r and use Coulomb's law to determine the charge. Thus we could regard the value of k as an operational definition of the coulomb. For reasons of experimental precision it is better to define the coulomb instead in terms of a unit of electric *current* (charge per unit time), the *ampere*, equal to 1 coulomb per second. We will return to this definition in Chapter 28.

In SI units we usually write the constant k in Eq. (21.1) as $1/4\pi\epsilon_0$, where ϵ_0 ("epsilon-nought" or "epsilon-zero") is another constant. This appears to complicate matters, but it actually simplifies many formulas that we will encounter in later chapters. From now on, we will usually write Coulomb's law as

$$F = \frac{1}{4\pi\epsilon_0} \frac{|q_1 q_2|}{r^2} \qquad \text{(Coulomb's law: force between} \atop \text{two point charges)} \tag{21.2}$$

The constants in Eq. (21.2) are approximately

$$\epsilon_0 = 8.854 \times 10^{-12}\,\text{C}^2/\text{N} \cdot \text{m}^2 \quad \text{and} \quad \frac{1}{4\pi\epsilon_0} = k = 8.988 \times 10^9\,\text{N} \cdot \text{m}^2/\text{C}^2$$

In examples and problems we will often use the approximate value

$$\frac{1}{4\pi\epsilon_0} = 9.0 \times 10^9\,\text{N} \cdot \text{m}^2/\text{C}^2$$

which is within about 0.1% of the correct value.

As we mentioned in Section 21.1, the most fundamental unit of charge is the magnitude of the charge of an electron or a proton, which is denoted by e. The most precise value available as of the writing of this book is

$$e = 1.60217653(14) \times 10^{-19}\,\text{C}$$

One coulomb represents the negative of the total charge of about 6×10^{18} electrons. For comparison, a copper cube 1 cm on a side contains about 2.4×10^{24} electrons. About 10^{19} electrons pass through the glowing filament of a flashlight bulb every second.

In electrostatics problems (that is, problems that involve charges at rest), it's very unusual to encounter charges as large as 1 coulomb. Two 1-C charges separated by 1 m would exert forces on each other of magnitude 9×10^9 N (about 1 million tons)! The total charge of all the electrons in a copper one-cent coin is even greater, about 1.4×10^5 C, which shows that we can't disturb electric neutrality very much without using enormous forces. More typical values of charge range from about 10^{-9} to about 10^{-6} C. The microcoulomb ($1\,\mu\text{C} = 10^{-6}\,\text{C}$) and the nanocoulomb ($1\,\text{nC} = 10^{-9}\,\text{C}$) are often used as practical units of charge.

Example 21.1   Electric force versus gravitational force

An α particle ("alpha") is the nucleus of a helium atom. It has mass $m = 6.64 \times 10^{-27}$ kg and charge $q = +2e = 3.2 \times 10^{-19}$ C. Compare the force of the electric repulsion between two α particles with the force of gravitational attraction between them.

SOLUTION

IDENTIFY: This problem involves Newton's law for the gravitational force F_g between particles (see Section 12.1) and Coulomb's law for the electric force F_e between point charges. We are asked to compare these forces, so our target variable is the *ratio* of these two forces, F_e/F_g.

SET UP: Figure 21.11 shows our sketch. The magnitude of the repulsive electric force is given by Eq. (21.2):

$$F_e = \frac{1}{4\pi\epsilon_0}\frac{q^2}{r^2}$$

The magnitude F_g of the attractive gravitational force is given by Eq. (12.1):

$$F_g = G\frac{m^2}{r^2}$$

EXECUTE: The ratio of the electric force to the gravitational force is

$$\frac{F_e}{F_g} = \frac{1}{4\pi\epsilon_0 G}\frac{q^2}{m^2} = \frac{9.0 \times 10^9\,\text{N} \cdot \text{m}^2/\text{C}^2}{6.67 \times 10^{-11}\,\text{N} \cdot \text{m}^2/\text{kg}^2}\frac{(3.2 \times 10^{-19}\,\text{C})^2}{(6.64 \times 10^{-27}\,\text{kg})^2}$$

$$= 3.1 \times 10^{35}$$

EVALUATE: This astonishingly large number shows that the gravitational force in this situation is completely negligible in comparison to the electric force. This is always true for interactions of atomic and subatomic particles. (Notice that this result doesn't depend on the distance r between the two α particles.) But within objects the size of a person or a planet, the positive and negative charges are nearly equal in magnitude, and the net electric force is usually much *smaller* than the gravitational force.

21.11 Our sketch for this problem.

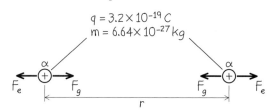

Superposition of Forces

Coulomb's law as we have stated it describes only the interaction of two *point* charges. Experiments show that when two charges exert forces simultaneously on a third charge, the total force acting on that charge is the *vector sum* of the forces that the two charges would exert individually. This important property, called the **principle of superposition of forces,** holds for any number of charges. By using this principle, we can apply Coulomb's law to *any* collection of charges. Several of the examples at the end of this section show applications of the superposition principle.

Strictly speaking, Coulomb's law as we have stated it should be used only for point charges *in a vacuum.* If matter is present in the space between the charges, the net force acting on each charge is altered because charges are induced in the molecules of the intervening material. We will describe this effect later. As a practical matter, though, we can use Coulomb's law unaltered for point charges in air. At normal atmospheric pressure, the presence of air changes the electric force from its vacuum value by only about one part in 2000.

Problem-Solving Strategy 21.1 **Coulomb's Law**

IDENTIFY *the relevant concepts:* Coulomb's law comes into play whenever you need to know the electric force acting between charged particles.

SET UP *the problem* using the following steps:

1. Make a drawing showing the locations of the charged particles, and label each particle with its charge. This step is particularly important if more than two charged particles are present.
2. If three or more charges are present and they do not all lie on the same line, set up an xy-coordinate system.
3. Often you will need to find the electric force on just one particle. If so, identify that particle.

EXECUTE *the solution* as follows:

1. For each particle that exerts a force on the particle of interest, calculate the magnitude of that force using Eq.(21.2).
2. Sketch the electric force vectors acting on the particle(s) of interest due to each of the other particles (that is, make a free-body diagram). Remember that the force exerted by particle 1 on particle 2 points from particle 2 toward particle 1 if the two charges have opposite signs, but points from particle 2 directly away from particle 1 if the charges have the same sign.
3. Calculate the total electric force on the particle(s) of interest. Remember that the electric force, like any force, is a *vector.* When the forces acting on a charge are caused by two or more other charges, the total force on the charge is the *vector sum* of the individual forces. You may want to go back and review the vector algebra in Sections 1.7 through 1.9. It's often helpful to use components in an xy-coordinate system. Be sure to use correct vector notation; if a symbol represents a vector quantity, put an arrow over it. If you get sloppy with your notation, you will also get sloppy with your thinking.

4. As always, using consistent units is essential. With the value of $k = 1/4\pi\epsilon_0$ given above, distances *must* be in meters, charge in coulombs, and force in newtons. If you are given distances in centimeters, inches, or furlongs, don't forget to convert! When a charge is given in microcoulombs (μC) or nanocoulombs (nC), remember that $1\ \mu C = 10^{-6}$ C and 1 nC $= 10^{-9}$ C.
5. Some examples and problems in this and later chapters involve a continuous distribution of charge along a line or over a surface. In these cases the vector sum described in step 3 becomes a vector integral, usually carried out by use of components. We divide the total charge distribution into infinitesimal pieces, use Coulomb's law for each piece, and then integrate to find the vector sum. Sometimes this process can be done without explicit use of integration.
6. In many situations the charge distribution will be *symmetrical.* For example, you might be asked to find the force on a charge Q in the presence of two other identical charges q, one above and to the left of Q and the other below and to the left of Q. If the distances from Q to each of the other charges are the same, the force on Q from each charge has the same magnitude; if each force vector makes the same angle with the horizontal axis, adding these vectors to find the net force is particularly easy. Whenever possible, exploit any symmetries to simplify the problem-solving process.

EVALUATE *your answer:* Check whether your numerical results are reasonable, and confirm that the direction of the net electric force agrees with the principle that like charges repel and opposite charges attract.

Example 21.2 Force between two point charges

Two point charges, $q_1 = +25$ nC and $q_2 = -75$ nC, are separated by a distance of 3.0 cm (Fig. 21.12a). Find the magnitude and direction of (a) the electric force that q_1 exerts on q_2; and (b) the electric force that q_2 exerts on q_1.

SOLUTION

IDENTIFY: This problem asks for the electric forces that two charges exert on each other, so we will need to use Coulomb's law.

SET UP: We use Eq. (21.2) to calculate the magnitude of the force that each particle exerts on the other. We use Newton's third law to relate the forces that the two particles exert on each other.

EXECUTE: (a) After we convert charge to coulombs and distance to meters, the magnitude of the force that q_1 exerts on q_2 is

$$F_{1\text{ on }2} = \frac{1}{4\pi\epsilon_0}\frac{|q_1 q_2|}{r^2}$$

$$= (9.0 \times 10^9 \, \text{N} \cdot \text{m}^2/\text{C}^2)\frac{|(+25 \times 10^{-9} \, \text{C})(-75 \times 10^{-9} \, \text{C})|}{(0.030 \, \text{m})^2}$$

$$= 0.019 \, \text{N}$$

Since the two charges have opposite signs, the force is attractive; that is, the force that acts on q_2 is directed toward q_1 along the line joining the two charges, as shown in Fig. 21.12b.

21.12 What force does q_1 exert on q_2, and what force does q_2 exert on q_1? Gravitational forces are negligible.

(a) The two charges

q_1 q_2

(b) Free-body diagram for charge q_2

$\vec{F}_{1\text{ on }2}$ q_2

(c) Free-body diagram for charge q_1

q_1 $\vec{F}_{2\text{ on }1}$

(b) Newton's third law applies to the electric force. Even though the charges have different magnitudes, the magnitude of the force that q_2 exerts on q_1 is the *same* as the magnitude of the force that q_1 exerts on q_2:

$$F_{2\text{ on }1} = 0.019 \, \text{N}$$

Newton's third law also states that the direction of the force that q_2 exerts on q_1 is exactly opposite the direction of the force that q_1 exerts on q_2; this is shown in Fig. 21.12c.

EVALUATE: Note that the force on q_1 is directed toward q_2, as it must be, since charges of opposite sign attract each other.

Example 21.3 Vector addition of electric forces on a line

Two point charges are located on the positive x-axis of a coordinate system. Charge $q_1 = 1.0$ nC is 2.0 cm from the origin, and charge $q_2 = -3.0$ nC is 4.0 cm from the origin. What is the total force exerted by these two charges on a charge $q_3 = 5.0$ nC located at the origin? Gravitational forces are negligible.

SOLUTION

IDENTIFY: Here there are *two* electric forces acting on the charge q_3, and we must add these forces to find the total force.

SET UP: Figure 21.13a shows the coordinate system. Our target variable is the net electric force exerted *on* charge q_3 by the other two charges. This is the vector sum of the forces due to q_1 and q_2 individually.

EXECUTE: Figure 21.13b is a free-body diagram for charge q_3. Note that q_3 is repelled by q_1 (which has the same sign) and attracted to q_2 (which has the opposite sign). Converting charge to coulombs and distance to meters, we use Eq. (21.2) to find the magnitude $F_{1\text{ on }3}$ of the force of q_1 on q_3:

$$F_{1\text{ on }3} = \frac{1}{4\pi\epsilon_0}\frac{|q_1 q_3|}{r^2}$$

$$= (9.0 \times 10^9 \, \text{N} \cdot \text{m}^2/\text{C}^2)\frac{(1.0 \times 10^{-9} \, \text{C})(5.0 \times 10^{-9} \, \text{C})}{(0.020 \, \text{m})^2}$$

$$= 1.12 \times 10^{-4} \, \text{N} = 112 \, \mu\text{N}$$

This force has a negative x-component because q_3 is repelled (that is, pushed in the negative x-direction) by q_1.

The magnitude $F_{2\text{ on }3}$ of the force of q_2 on q_3 is

$$F_{2\text{ on }3} = \frac{1}{4\pi\epsilon_0}\frac{|q_2 q_3|}{r^2}$$

$$= (9.0 \times 10^9 \, \text{N} \cdot \text{m}^2/\text{C}^2)\frac{(3.0 \times 10^{-9} \, \text{C})(5.0 \times 10^{-9} \, \text{C})}{(0.040 \, \text{m})^2}$$

$$= 8.4 \times 10^{-5} \, \text{N} = 84 \, \mu\text{N}$$

This force has a positive x-component because q_3 is attracted (that is, pulled in the positive x-direction) by q_2. The sum of the x-components is

$$F_x = -112 \, \mu\text{N} + 84 \, \mu\text{N} = -28 \, \mu\text{N}$$

There are no y- or z-components. Thus the total force on q_3 is directed to the left, with magnitude 28 μN $= 2.8 \times 10^{-5}$ N.

EVALUATE: To check the magnitudes of the individual forces, note that q_2 has three times as much charge (in magnitude) as q_1 but is twice as far from q_3. From Eq. (21.2) this means that $F_{2\text{ on }3}$ must be $3/2^2 = \frac{3}{4}$ as large as $F_{1\text{ on }3}$. Indeed, our results show that this ratio is $(84 \, \mu\text{N})/(112 \, \mu\text{N}) = 0.75$. The direction of the net force also makes sense: $\vec{F}_{1\text{ on }3}$ is opposite to and has a larger magnitude than $\vec{F}_{2\text{ on }3}$, so the net force is in the direction of $\vec{F}_{1\text{ on }3}$.

21.13 Our sketches for this problem.

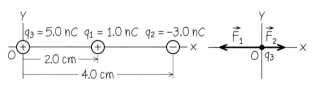

(a) Our diagram of the situation

$q_3 = 5.0$ nC $q_1 = 1.0$ nC $q_2 = -3.0$ nC

2.0 cm

4.0 cm

(b) Free-body diagram for q_3

$\vec{F}_1$ $\vec{F}_2$ q_3

Example 21.4 **Vector addition of electric forces in a plane**

Two equal positive point charges $q_1 = q_2 = 2.0\ \mu$C are located at $x = 0$, $y = 0.30$ m and $x = 0$, $y = -0.30$ m, respectively. What are the magnitude and direction of the total (net) electric force that these charges exert on a third point charge $Q = 4.0\ \mu$C at $x = 0.40$ m, $y = 0$?

SOLUTION

IDENTIFY: As in Example 21.3, we have to compute the force that each charge exerts on Q and then find the vector sum of the forces.

SET UP: Figure 21.14 shows the situation. Since the three charges do not all lie on a line, the best way to calculate the forces that q_1 and q_2 exert on Q is to use components.

21.14 Our sketch for this problem.

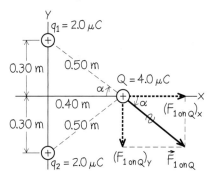

EXECUTE: Figure 21.14 shows the force on Q due to the upper charge q_1. From Coulomb's law the magnitude F of this force is

$$F_{1\text{ on }Q} = (9.0 \times 10^9\ \text{N}\cdot\text{m}^2/\text{C}^2)\frac{(4.0 \times 10^{-6}\ \text{C})(2.0 \times 10^{-6}\ \text{C})}{(0.50\ \text{m})^2}$$

$$= 0.29\ \text{N}$$

The angle α is below the x-axis, so the components of this force are given by

$$(F_{1\text{ on }Q})_x = (F_{1\text{ on }Q})\cos\alpha = (0.29\ \text{N})\frac{0.40\ \text{m}}{0.50\ \text{m}} = 0.23\ \text{N}$$

$$(F_{1\text{ on }Q})_y = -(F_{1\text{ on }Q})\sin\alpha = -(0.29\ \text{N})\frac{0.30\ \text{m}}{0.50\ \text{m}} = -0.17\ \text{N}$$

The lower charge q_2 exerts a force with the same magnitude but at an angle α *above* the x-axis. From symmetry we see that its x-component is the same as that due to the upper charge, but its y-component has the opposite sign. So the components of the total force $\vec{F}$ on Q are

$$F_x = 0.23\ \text{N} + 0.23\ \text{N} = 0.46\ \text{N}$$
$$F_y = -0.17\ \text{N} + 0.17\ \text{N} = 0$$

The total force on Q is in the $+x$-direction, with magnitude 0.46 N.

EVALUATE: The total force on Q is in a direction that points neither directly away from q_1 nor directly away from q_2. Rather, this direction is a compromise that points away from the *system* of charges q_1 and q_2. Can you see that the total force would *not* be in the $+x$-direction if q_1 and q_2 were not equal or if the geometrical arrangement of the changes were not so symmetrical?

Test Your Understanding of Section 21.3 Suppose that charge q_2 in Example 21.4 were $-2.0\ \mu$C. In this case, the total electric force on Q would be (i) in the positive x-direction; (ii) in the negative x-direction; (iii) in the positive y-direction; (iv) in the negative y-direction; (v) zero; (vi) none of these.

21.4 Electric Field and Electric Forces

When two electrically charged particles in empty space interact, how does each one know the other is there? What goes on in the space between them to communicate the effect of each one to the other? We can begin to answer these questions, and at the same time reformulate Coulomb's law in a very useful way, by using the concept of *electric field*.

Electric Field

To introduce this concept, let's look at the mutual repulsion of two positively charged bodies A and B (Fig. 21.15a). Suppose B has charge q_0, and let $\vec{F}_0$ be the electric force of A on B. One way to think about this force is as an "action-at-a-distance" force—that is, as a force that acts across empty space without needing any matter (such as a push rod or a rope) to transmit it through the intervening space. (Gravity can also be thought of as an "action-at-a-distance" force.) But a more fruitful way to visualize the repulsion between A and B is as a two-stage process. We first envision that body A, as a result of the charge that it carries, somehow *modifies the properties of the space around it*. Then body B, as

21.15 A charged body creates an electric field in the space around it.

(a) *A and B exert electric forces on each other.*

(b) *Remove body B ...*

... and label its former position as *P*.

(c) *Body A sets up an electric field $\vec{E}$ at point P.*

$$\vec{E} = \frac{\vec{F}_0}{q_0}$$

$\vec{E}$ is the force per unit charge exerted by A on a test charge at P.

a result of the charge that *it* carries, senses how space has been modified at its position. The response of body B is to experience the force $\vec{F}_0$.

To elaborate how this two-stage process occurs, we first consider body A by itself: We remove body B and label its former position as point P (Fig. 21.15b). We say that the charged body A produces or causes an **electric field** at point P (and at all other points in the neighborhood). This electric field is present at P even if there is no charge at P; it is a consequence of the charge on body A only. If a point charge q_0 is then placed at point P, it experiences the force $\vec{F}_0$. We take the point of view that this force is exerted on q_0 *by the field* at P (Fig. 21.15c). Thus the electric field is the intermediary through which A communicates its presence to q_0. Because the point charge q_0 would experience a force at *any* point in the neighborhood of A, the electric field that A produces exists at all points in the region around A.

We can likewise say that the point charge q_0 produces an electric field in the space around it and that this electric field exerts the force $-\vec{F}_0$ on body A. For each force (the force of A on q_0 and the force of q_0 on A), one charge sets up an electric field that exerts a force on the second charge. We emphasize that this is an *interaction* between *two* charged bodies. A single charge produces an electric field in the surrounding space, but this electric field cannot exert a net force on the charge that created it; this is an example of the general principle that a body cannot exert a net force on itself, as discussed in Section 4.3. (If this principle wasn't valid, you would be able to lift yourself to the ceiling by pulling up on your belt!)

The electric force on a charged body is exerted by the electric field created by *other* charged bodies.

To find out experimentally whether there is an electric field at a particular point, we place a small charged body, which we call a **test charge,** at the point (Fig. 21.15c). If the test charge experiences an electric force, then there is an electric field at that point. This field is produced by charges other than q_0.

Force is a vector quantity, so electric field is also a vector quantity. (Note the use of vector signs as well as boldface letters and plus, minus, and equals signs in the following discussion.) We define the *electric field* $\vec{E}$ at a point as the electric force $\vec{F}_0$ experienced by a test charge q_0 at the point, divided by the charge q_0. That is, the electric field at a certain point is equal to the *electric force per unit charge* experienced by a charge at that point:

$$\vec{E} = \frac{\vec{F}_0}{q_0} \qquad \text{(definition of electric field as electric force per unit charge)} \qquad (21.3)$$

21.16 The force $\vec{F}_0 = q_0\vec{E}$ exerted on a point charge q_0 placed in an electric field $\vec{E}$.

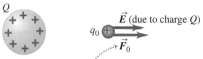

The force on a positive test charge q_0 points in the direction of the electric field.

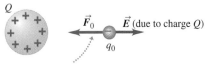

The force on a negative test charge q_0 points opposite to the electric field.

In SI units, in which the unit of force is 1 N and the unit of charge is 1 C, the unit of electric field magnitude is 1 newton per coulomb $\left(1 \text{ N/C}\right)$.

If the field $\vec{E}$ at a certain point is known, rearranging Eq. (21.3) gives the force $\vec{F}_0$ experienced by a point charge q_0 placed at that point. This force is just equal to the electric field $\vec{E}$ produced at that point by charges other than q_0, multiplied by the charge q_0:

$$\vec{F}_0 = q_0\vec{E} \qquad \text{(force exerted on a point charge } q_0 \text{ by an electric field } \vec{E}) \qquad (21.4)$$

The charge q_0 can be either positive or negative. If q_0 is *positive,* the force $\vec{F}_0$ experienced by the charge is the same direction as $\vec{E}$; if q_0 is *negative,* $\vec{F}_0$ and $\vec{E}$ are in opposite directions (Fig. 21.16).

While the electric field concept may be new to you, the basic idea—that one body sets up a field in the space around it and a second body responds to that field—is one that you've actually used before. Compare Eq. (21.4) to the familiar expression for the gravitational force $\vec{F}_g$ that the earth exerts on a mass m_0:

$$\vec{F}_g = m_0 \vec{g} \qquad (21.5)$$

In this expression, $\vec{g}$ is the acceleration due to gravity. If we divide both sides of Eq. (21.5) by the mass m_0, we obtain

$$\vec{g} = \frac{\vec{F}_g}{m_0}$$

Thus $\vec{g}$ can be regarded as the gravitational force per unit mass. By analogy to Eq. (21.3), we can interpret $\vec{g}$ as the *gravitational field.* Thus we treat the gravitational interaction between the earth and the mass m_0 as a two-stage process: The earth sets up a gravitational field $\vec{g}$ in the space around it, and this gravitational field exerts a force given by Eq. (21.5) on the mass m_0 (which we can regard as a *test mass*). In this sense, you've made use of the field concept every time you've used Eq. (21.5) for the force of gravity. The gravitational field $\vec{g}$, or gravitational force per unit mass, is a useful concept because it does not depend on the mass of the body on which the gravitational force is exerted; likewise, the electric field $\vec{E}$, or electric force per unit charge, is useful because it does not depend on the charge of the body on which the electric force is exerted.

CAUTION $\vec{F}_0 = q_0 \vec{E}_0$ **is for *point* test charges only**   The electric force experienced by a test charge q_0 can vary from point to point, so the electric field can also be different at different points. For this reason, Eq. (21.4) can be used only to find the electric force on a *point* charge. If a charged body is large enough in size, the electric field $\vec{E}$ may be noticeably different in magnitude and direction at different points on the body, and calculating the net electric force on the body can become rather complicated.

We have so far ignored a subtle but important difficulty with our definition of electric field: In Fig. 21.15 the force exerted by the test charge q_0 on the charge distribution on body A may cause this distribution to shift around. This is especially true if body A is a conductor, on which charge is free to move. So the electric field around A when q_0 is present may not be the same as when q_0 is absent. But if q_0 is very small, the redistribution of charge on body A is also very small. So to make a completely correct definition of electric field, we take the *limit* of Eq. (21.3) as the test charge q_0 approaches zero and as the disturbing effect of q_0 on the charge distribution becomes negligible:

$$\vec{E} = \lim_{q_0 \to 0} \frac{\vec{F}_0}{q_0}$$

In practical calculations of the electric field $\vec{E}$ produced by a charge distribution, we will consider the charge distribution to be fixed, and so we will not need this limiting process.

Electric Field of a Point Charge

If the source distribution is a point charge q, it is easy to find the electric field that it produces. We call the location of the charge the **source point,** and we call the point P where we are determining the field the **field point.** It is also useful to introduce a *unit vector* $\hat{r}$ that points along the line from source point to field point (Fig. 21.17a). This unit vector is equal to the displacement vector $\vec{r}$ from the source point to the field point, divided by the distance $\hat{r} = |\vec{r}|$ between these two points; that is, $\hat{r} = \vec{r}/r$. If we place a small test charge q_0 at the field point P, at a distance r from the source point, the magnitude F_0 of the force is given by Coulomb's law, Eq. (21.2):

$$F_0 = \frac{1}{4\pi\epsilon_0} \frac{|qq_0|}{r^2}$$

21.17 The electric field $\vec{E}$ produced at point P by an isolated point charge q at S. Note that in both **(b)** and **(c)**, $\vec{E}$ is *produced* by q [see Eq. (21.7)] but *acts on* the charge q_0 at point P [see Eq. (21.4)].

(a)

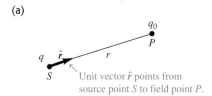

Unit vector $\hat{r}$ points from source point S to field point P.

(b)

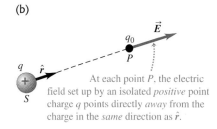

At each point P, the electric field set up by an isolated *positive* point charge q points directly *away* from the charge in the *same* direction as $\hat{r}$.

(c)

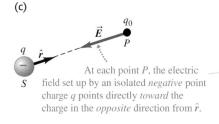

At each point P, the electric field set up by an isolated *negative* point charge q points directly *toward* the charge in the *opposite* direction from $\hat{r}$.

21.18 A point charge q produces an electric field $\vec{E}$ at *all* points in space. The field strength decreases with increasing distance.

(a) The field produced by a positive point charge points *away from* the charge.

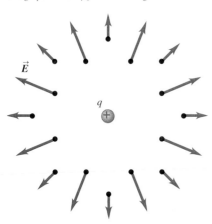

(b) The field produced by a negative point charge points *toward* the charge.

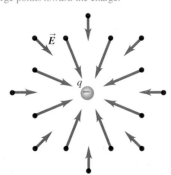

From Eq. (21.3) the magnitude E of the electric field at P is

$$E = \frac{1}{4\pi\epsilon_0}\frac{|q|}{r^2} \qquad \text{(magnitude of electric field of a point charge)} \quad \text{(21.6)}$$

Using the unit vector $\hat{r}$, we can write a *vector* equation that gives both the magnitude and direction of the electric field $\vec{E}$:

$$\vec{E} = \frac{1}{4\pi\epsilon_0}\frac{q}{r^2}\hat{r} \qquad \text{(electric field of a point charge)} \quad \text{(21.7)}$$

By definition, the electric field of a point charge always points *away from* a positive charge (that is, in the same direction as $\hat{r}$; see Fig. 21.17b) but *toward* a negative charge (that is, in the direction opposite $\hat{r}$; see Fig. 21.17c).

We have emphasized calculating the electric field $\vec{E}$ at a certain point. But since $\vec{E}$ can vary from point to point, it is not a single vector quantity but rather an *infinite* set of vector quantities, one associated with each point in space. This is an example of a **vector field.** Figure 21.18 shows a number of the field vectors produced by a positive or negative point charge. If we use a rectangular (x, y, z) coordinate system, each component of $\vec{E}$ at any point is in general a function of the coordinates (x, y, z) of the point. We can represent the functions as $E_x(x, y, z)$, $E_y(x, y, z)$, and $E_z(x, y, z)$. Vector fields are an important part of the language of physics, not just in electricity and magnetism. One everyday example of a vector field is the velocity $\vec{v}$ of wind currents; the magnitude and direction of $\vec{v}$, and hence its vector components, vary from point to point in the atmosphere.

In some situations the magnitude and direction of the field (and hence its vector components) have the same values everywhere throughout a certain region; we then say that the field is *uniform* in this region. An important example of this is the electric field inside a *conductor.* If there is an electric field within a conductor, the field exerts a force on every charge in the conductor, giving the free charges a net motion. By definition an electrostatic situation is one in which the charges have *no* net motion. We conclude that *in electrostatics the electric field at every point within the material of a conductor must be zero.* (Note that we are not saying that the field is necessarily zero in a *hole* inside a conductor.)

With the concept of electric field, our description of electric interactions has two parts. First, a given charge distribution acts as a source of electric field. Second, the electric field exerts a force on any charge that is present in the field. Our analysis often has two corresponding steps: first, calculating the field caused by a source charge distribution; second, looking at the effect of the field in terms of force and motion. The second step often involves Newton's laws as well as the principles of electric interactions. In the next section we show how to calculate fields caused by various source distributions, but first here are some examples of calculating the field due to a point charge and of finding the force on a charge due to a given field $\vec{E}$.

Example 21.5 **Electric-field magnitude for a point charge**

What is the magnitude of the electric field at a field point 2.0 m from a point charge $q = 4.0$ nC? (The point charge could represent any small charged object with this value of q, provided the dimensions of the object are much less than the distance from the object to the field point.)

SET UP: We are given the magnitude of the charge and the distance from the object to the field point, so we use Eq. (21.6) to calculate the field magnitude E.

EXECUTE: From Eq. (21.6),

SOLUTION

IDENTIFY: This problem uses the expression for the electric field due to a point charge.

$$E = \frac{1}{4\pi\epsilon_0}\frac{|q|}{r^2} = (9.0 \times 10^9 \text{ N} \cdot \text{m}^2/\text{C}^2)\frac{4.0 \times 10^{-9} \text{ C}}{(2.0 \text{ m})^2}$$
$$= 9.0 \text{ N/C}$$

EVALUATE: To check our result, we use the definition of electric field as the electric force per unit charge. We can first use Coulomb's law, Eq. (21.2), to find the magnitude F_0 of the force on a test charge q_0 placed 2.0 m from q:

$$F_0 = \frac{1}{4\pi\epsilon_0} \frac{|qq_0|}{r^2} = (9.0 \times 10^9 \text{ N} \cdot \text{m}^2/\text{C}^2)\frac{4.0 \times 10^{-9} \text{ C}|q_0|}{(2.0 \text{ m})^2}$$

$$= (9.0 \text{ N/C})|q_0|$$

Then, from Eq. (21.3), the magnitude of $\vec{E}$ is

$$E = \frac{F_0}{|q_0|} = 9.0 \text{ N/C}$$

Because q is positive, the *direction* of $\vec{E}$ at this point is along the line from q toward q_0, as shown in Fig. 21.17b. However, the magnitude and direction of $\vec{E}$ do not depend on the sign of q_0. Do you see why not?

Example 21.6   Electric-field vector for a point charge

A point charge $q = -8.0$ nC is located at the origin. Find the electric-field vector at the field point $x = 1.2$ m, $y = -1.6$ m.

SOLUTION

IDENTIFY: In this problem we are asked to find the electric-field *vector* $\vec{E}$ due to a point charge. Hence we need to find either the components of $\vec{E}$ or its magnitude and direction.

SET UP: Figure 21.19 shows the situation. The electric field is given in vector form by Eq. (21.7). To use this equation, we first find the distance r from the source point S (the position of the charge q) to the field point P, as well as the unit vector $\hat{r}$ that points in the direction from S to P.

21.19 Our sketch for this problem.

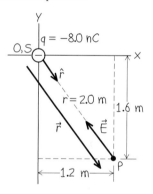

EXECUTE: The distance from the charge at the source point S (which in this example is at the origin O) to the field point P is

$$r = \sqrt{x^2 + y^2} = \sqrt{(1.2 \text{ m})^2 + (-1.6 \text{ m})^2} = 2.0 \text{ m}$$

The unit vector $\hat{r}$ is directed from the source point to the field point. This is equal to the displacement vector $\vec{r}$ from the source point to the field point (shown shifted to one side in Fig. 21.19 so as not to obscure the other vectors), divided by its magnitude r:

$$\hat{r} = \frac{\vec{r}}{r} = \frac{x\hat{i} + y\hat{j}}{r}$$

$$= \frac{(1.2 \text{ m})\hat{i} + (-1.6 \text{ m})\hat{i}}{2.0 \text{ m}} = 0.60\hat{i} - 0.80\hat{j}$$

Hence the electric-field vector is

$$\vec{E} = \frac{1}{4\pi\epsilon_0} \frac{q}{r^2} \hat{r}$$

$$= (9.0 \times 10^9 \text{ N} \cdot \text{m}^2/\text{C}^2)\frac{(-8.0 \times 10^{-9} \text{ C})}{(2.0 \text{ m})^2}(0.60\hat{i} - 0.80\hat{j})$$

$$= (-11 \text{ N/C})\hat{i} + (14 \text{ N/C})\hat{j}$$

EVALUATE: Since q is negative, $\vec{E}$ points from the field point to the charge (the source point), in the direction opposite to $\hat{r}$ (compare Fig. 21.17c). We leave the calculation of the magnitude and direction of $\vec{E}$ to you (see Exercise 21.36).

Example 21.7   Electron in a uniform field

When the terminals of a battery are connected to two large parallel conducting plates, the resulting charges on the plates cause an electric field $\vec{E}$ in the region between the plates that is very nearly uniform. (We will see the reason for this uniformity in the next section. Charged plates of this kind are used in common electrical devices called *capacitors,* to be discussed in Chapter 24.) If the plates are horizontal and separated by 1.0 cm and the plates are connected to a 100-volt battery, the magnitude of the field is $E = 1.00 \times 10^4$ N/C. Suppose the direction of $\vec{E}$ is vertically upward, as shown by the vectors in Fig. 21.20. (a) If an electron is released from rest at the upper plate, what is its acceleration? (b) What speed and kinetic energy does the electron acquire while traveling 1.0 cm to the lower plate? (c) How much time is

21.20 A uniform electric field between two parallel conducting plates connected to a 100-volt battery. (The separation of the plates is exaggerated in this figure relative to the dimensions of the plates.)

Continued

required for it to travel this distance? An electron has charge $-e = -1.60 \times 10^{-19}$ C and mass $m = 9.11 \times 10^{-31}$ kg.

SOLUTION

IDENTIFY: This example involves several concepts: the relationship between electric field and electric force, the relationship between force and acceleration, the definition of kinetic energy, and the kinematic relationships among acceleration, distance, velocity, and time.

SET UP: Figure 21.20 shows our coordinate system. We are given the electric field, so we use Eq. (21.4) to find the force on the electron and Newton's second law to find its acceleration. Because the field is uniform between the plates, the force and acceleration are constant and we can use the constant-acceleration formulas from Chapter 3 to find the electron's velocity and travel time. We find the kinetic energy using the definition $K = \frac{1}{2}mv^2$.

EXECUTE: (a) Note that $\vec{E}$ is upward (in the $+y$-direction) but $\vec{F}$ is downward because the charge of the electron is negative. Thus F_y is negative. Because F_y is constant, the electron moves with constant acceleration a_y given by

$$a_y = \frac{F_y}{m} = \frac{-eE}{m} = \frac{(-1.60 \times 10^{-19}\,\text{C})(1.00 \times 10^4\,\text{N/C})}{9.11 \times 10^{-31}\,\text{kg}}$$

$$= -1.76 \times 10^{15}\,\text{m/s}^2$$

This is an enormous acceleration! To give a 1000-kg car this acceleration, we would need a force of about 2×10^{18} N (about 2×10^{14} tons). The gravitational force on the electron is completely negligible compared to the electric force.

(b) The electron starts from rest, so its motion is in the y-direction only (the direction of the acceleration). We can find the electron's speed at any position using the constant-acceleration formula $v_y^2 = v_{0y}^2 + 2a_y(y - y_0)$. We have $v_{0y} = 0$ and $y_0 = 0$, so the speed $|v_y|$ when $y = -1.0$ cm $= -1.0 \times 10^{-2}$ m is

$$|v_y| = \sqrt{2a_y y} = \sqrt{2(-1.76 \times 10^{15}\,\text{m/s}^2)(-1.0 \times 10^{-2}\,\text{m})}$$

$$= 5.9 \times 10^6\,\text{m/s}$$

The velocity is downward, so its y-component is $v_y = -5.9 \times 10^6$ m/s. The electron's kinetic energy is

$$K = \frac{1}{2}mv^2 = \frac{1}{2}(9.11 \times 10^{-31}\,\text{kg})(5.9 \times 10^6\,\text{m/s})^2$$

$$= 1.6 \times 10^{-17}\,\text{J}$$

(c) From the constant-acceleration formula $v_y = v_{0y} + a_y t$, we find that the time required is very brief:

$$t = \frac{v_y - v_{0y}}{a_y} = \frac{(-5.9 \times 10^6\,\text{m/s}) - (0\,\text{m/s})}{-1.76 \times 10^{15}\,\text{m/s}^2}$$

$$= 3.4 \times 10^{-9}\,\text{s}$$

(We could also have found the time by solving the equation $y = y_0 + v_{0y}t + \frac{1}{2}a_y t^2$ for t.)

EVALUATE: This example shows that in problems about subatomic particles such as electrons, many quantities—including acceleration, speed, kinetic energy, and time—will have *very* different values from what we have seen for ordinary objects such as baseballs and automobiles.

Example 21.8   An electron trajectory

If we launch an electron into the electric field of Example 21.7 with an initial horizontal velocity v_0 (Fig. 21.21), what is the equation of its trajectory?

SOLUTION

IDENTIFY: We found the electron's acceleration in Example 21.7. Our goal is to find the trajectory that corresponds to that acceleration.

SET UP: The acceleration is constant and in the negative y-direction (there is no acceleration in the x-direction). Hence we can use the kinematic equations from Chapter 3 for two-dimensional motion with constant acceleration.

EXECUTE: We have $a_x = 0$ and $a_y = (-e)E/m$. At $t = 0$, $x_0 = y_0 = 0$, $v_{0x} = v_0$, and $v_{0y} = 0$; hence at time t,

$$x = v_0 t \quad \text{and} \quad y = \frac{1}{2}a_y t^2 = -\frac{1}{2}\frac{eE}{m}t^2$$

Eliminating t between these equations, we get

$$y = -\frac{1}{2}\frac{eE}{mv_0^2}x^2$$

EVALUATE: This is the equation of a parabola, just like the trajectory of a projectile launched horizontally in the earth's gravitational field (discussed in Section 3.3). For a given initial velocity of the electron, the curvature of the trajectory depends on the field magnitude E. If we reverse the signs of the charges on the two plates in Fig. 21.21, the direction of $\vec{E}$ reverses, and the electron trajectory will curve up, not down. Hence we can "steer" the electron by varying the charges on the plates. The electric field between charged conducting plates can be used in this way to control the trajectory of electron beams in oscilloscopes.

21.21 The parabolic trajectory of an electron in a uniform electric field.

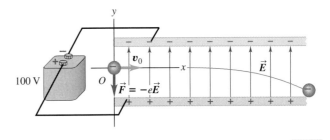

Test Your Understanding of Section 21.4 (a) A negative point charge moves along a straight-line path directly toward a stationary positive point charge. Which aspect(s) of the electric force on the negative point charge will remain constant as it moves? (i) magnitude; (ii) direction; (iii) both magnitude and direction; (iv) neither magnitude nor direction. (b) A negative point charge moves along a circular orbit around a positive point charge. Which aspect(s) of the electric force on the negative point charge will remain constant as it moves? (i) magnitude; (ii) direction; (iii) both magnitude and direction; (iv) neither magnitude nor direction.

21.5 Electric-Field Calculations

Equation (21.7) gives the electric field caused by a single point charge. But in most realistic situations that involve electric fields and forces, we encounter charge that is *distributed* over space. The charged plastic and glass rods in Fig. 21.1 have electric charge distributed over their surfaces, as does the imaging drum of a laser printer (Fig. 21.2). In this section we'll learn to calculate electric fields caused by various distributions of electric charge. Calculations of this kind are of tremendous importance for technological applications of electric forces. To determine the trajectories of electrons in a TV tube, of atomic nuclei in an accelerator for cancer radiotherapy, or of charged particles in a semiconductor electronic device, you have to know the detailed nature of the electric field acting on the charges.

The Superposition of Electric Fields

To find the field caused by a charge distribution, we imagine the distribution to be made up of many point charges $q_1, q_2, q_3, \ldots$. (This is actually quite a realistic description, since we have seen that charge is carried by electrons and protons that are so small as to be almost pointlike.) At any given point P, each point charge produces its own electric field $\vec{E}_1, \vec{E}_2, \vec{E}_3, \ldots$, so a test charge q_0 placed at P experiences a force $\vec{F}_1 = q_0\vec{E}_1$ from charge q_1, a force $\vec{F}_2 = q_0\vec{E}_2$ from charge q_2, and so on. From the principle of superposition of forces discussed in Section 21.3, the *total* force $\vec{F}_0$ that the charge distribution exerts on q_0 is the vector sum of these individual forces:

$$\vec{F}_0 = \vec{F}_1 + \vec{F}_2 + \vec{F}_3 + \cdots = q_0\vec{E}_1 + q_0\vec{E}_2 + q_0\vec{E}_3 + \cdots$$

The combined effect of all the charges in the distribution is described by the *total* electric field $\vec{E}$ at point P. From the definition of electric field, Eq. (21.3), this is

$$\vec{E} = \frac{\vec{F}_0}{q_0} = \vec{E}_1 + \vec{E}_2 + \vec{E}_3 + \cdots$$

The total electric field at P is the vector sum of the fields at P due to each point charge in the charge distribution (Fig. 21.22). This is the **principle of superposition of electric fields.**

When charge is distributed along a line, over a surface, or through a volume, a few additional terms are useful. For a line charge distribution (such as a long, thin, charged plastic rod), we use λ (the Greek letter lambda) to represent the **linear charge density** (charge per unit length, measured in C/m). When charge is distributed over a surface (such as the surface of the imaging drum of a laser printer), we use σ (sigma) to represent the **surface charge density** (charge per unit area, measured in C/m^2). And when charge is distributed through a volume, we use ρ (rho) to represent the **volume charge density** (charge per unit volume, C/m^3).

Some of the calculations in the following examples may look fairly intricate; in electric-field calculations a certain amount of mathematical complexity is in the nature of things. After you've worked through the examples one step at a time, the process will seem less formidable. We will use many of the calculational techniques in these examples in Chapter 28 to calculate the *magnetic* fields caused by charges in motion.

21.22 Illustrating the principle of superposition of electric fields.

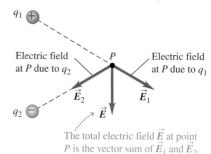

The total electric field $\vec{E}$ at point P is the vector sum of $\vec{E}_1$ and $\vec{E}_2$.

Problem-Solving Strategy 21.2 **Electric-Field Calculations**

IDENTIFY *the relevant concepts:* Use the principle of superposition whenever you need to calculate the electric field due to a charge distribution (two or more point charges, a distribution over a line, surface, or volume, or a combination of these).

SET UP *the problem* using the following steps:
1. Make a drawing that clearly shows the locations of the charges and your choice of coordinate axes.
2. On your drawing, indicate the position of the *field point* (the point at which you want to calculate the electric field $\vec{E}$). Sometimes the field point will be at some arbitrary position along a line. For example, you may be asked to find $\vec{E}$ at any point on the x-axis.

EXECUTE *the solution* as follows:
1. Be sure to use a consistent set of units. Distances must be in meters and charge must be in coulombs. If you are given centimeters or nanocoulombs, don't forget to convert.
2. When adding up the electric fields caused by different parts of the charge distribution, remember that electric field is a vector, so you *must* use vector addition. Don't simply add together the magnitudes of the individual fields; the directions are important, too.
3. Take advantage of any symmetries in the charge distribution. For example, if a positive charge and a negative charge of equal magnitude are placed symmetrically with respect to the field point, they produce electric fields of the same magnitude but with mirror-image directions. Exploiting these symmetries will simplify your calculations.

4. Most often you will use components to compute vector sums. Use the methods you learned in Chapter 1; review them if necessary. Use proper vector notation; distinguish carefully between scalars, vectors, and components of vectors. Be certain the components are consistent with your choice of coordinate axes.
5. In working out the directions of $\vec{E}$ vectors, be careful to distinguish between the *source point* and the *field point*. The field produced by a point charge always points from source point to field point if the charge is positive; it points in the opposite direction if the charge is negative.
6. In some situations you will have a continuous distribution of charge along a line, over a surface, or through a volume. Then you must define a small element of charge that can be considered as a point, find its electric field at point *P*, and find a way to add the fields of all the charge elements. Usually it is easiest to do this for each component of $\vec{E}$ separately, and often you will need to evaluate one or more integrals. Make certain the limits on your integrals are correct; especially when the situation has symmetry, make sure you don't count the charge twice.

EVALUATE *your answer:* Check that the direction of $\vec{E}$ is reasonable. If your result for the electric-field magnitude *E* is a function of position (say, the coordinate *x*), check your result in any limits for which you know what the magnitude should be. When possible, check your answer by calculating it in a different way.

Example 21.9 **Field of an electric dipole**

Point charges q_1 and q_2 of +12 nC and −12 nC, respectively, are placed 0.10 m apart (Fig. 21.23). This combination of two charges with equal magnitude and opposite sign is called an *electric dipole.* (Such combinations occur frequently in nature. For example, in Figs. 21.8b and 21.8c, each molecule in the neutral insulator is an electric dipole. We'll study dipoles in more detail in Section 21.7.) Compute the electric field caused by q_1, the field caused by q_2, and the total field (a) at point *a*; (b) at point *b*; and (c) at point *c*.

SOLUTION

IDENTIFY: We need to find the total electric field at three different points due to two point charges. We will use the principle of superposition: $\vec{E} = \vec{E}_1 + \vec{E}_2$.

SET UP: Figure 21.23 shows the coordinate system and the locations of the three field points *a*, *b*, and *c*.

21.23 Electric field at three points, *a*, *b*, and *c*, set up by charges q_1 and q_2, which form an electric dipole.

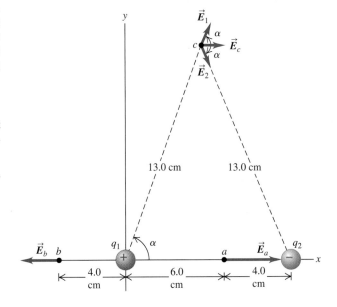

EXECUTE: (a) At point a the field $\vec{E}_1$ caused by the positive charge q_1 and the field $\vec{E}_2$ caused by the negative charge q_2 are both directed toward the right. The magnitudes of $\vec{E}_1$ and $\vec{E}_2$ are

$$E_1 = \frac{1}{4\pi\epsilon_0}\frac{|q_1|}{r^2} = (9.0 \times 10^9 \text{ N} \cdot \text{m}^2/\text{C}^2)\frac{12 \times 10^{-9} \text{ C}}{(0.060 \text{ m})^2}$$

$$= 3.0 \times 10^4 \text{ N/C}$$

$$E_2 = \frac{1}{4\pi\epsilon_0}\frac{|q_2|}{r^2} = (9.0 \times 10^9 \text{ N} \cdot \text{m}^2/\text{C}^2)\frac{12 \times 10^{-9} \text{ C}}{(0.040 \text{ m})^2}$$

$$= 6.8 \times 10^4 \text{ N/C}$$

The components of $\vec{E}_1$ and $\vec{E}_2$ are

$$E_{1x} = 3.0 \times 10^4 \text{ N/C} \qquad E_{1y} = 0$$
$$E_{2x} = 6.8 \times 10^4 \text{ N/C} \qquad E_{2y} = 0$$

Hence at point a the total electric field $\vec{E}_a = \vec{E}_1 + \vec{E}_2$ has components

$$(E_a)_x = E_{1x} + E_{2x} = (3.0 + 6.8) \times 10^4 \text{ N/C}$$
$$(E_a)_y = E_{1y} + E_{2y} = 0$$

At point a the total field has magnitude 9.8×10^4 N/C and is directed toward the right, so

$$\vec{E}_a = (9.8 \times 10^4 \text{ N/C})\hat{\imath}$$

(b) At point b the field $\vec{E}_1$ due to q_1 is directed toward the left, while the field $\vec{E}_2$ due to q_2 is directed toward the right. The magnitudes of $\vec{E}_1$ and $\vec{E}_2$ are

$$E_1 = \frac{1}{4\pi\epsilon_0}\frac{|q_1|}{r^2} = (9.0 \times 10^9 \text{ N} \cdot \text{m}^2/\text{C}^2)\frac{12 \times 10^{-9} \text{ C}}{(0.040 \text{ m})^2}$$

$$= 6.8 \times 10^4 \text{ N/C}$$

$$E_2 = \frac{1}{4\pi\epsilon_0}\frac{|q_2|}{r^2} = (9.0 \times 10^9 \text{ N} \cdot \text{m}^2/\text{C}^2)\frac{12 \times 10^{-9} \text{ C}}{(0.140 \text{ m})^2}$$

$$= 0.55 \times 10^4 \text{ N/C}$$

The components of $\vec{E}_1$, $\vec{E}_2$, and the total field $\vec{E}_b$ at point b are

$$E_{1x} = -6.8 \times 10^4 \text{ N/C} \qquad E_{1y} = 0$$
$$E_{2x} = 0.55 \times 10^4 \text{ N/C} \qquad E_{2y} = 0$$
$$(E_b)_x = E_{1x} + E_{2x} = (-6.8 + 0.55) \times 10^4 \text{ N/C}$$
$$(E_b)_y = E_{1y} + E_{2y} = 0$$

That is, the electric field at b has magnitude 6.2×10^4 N/C and is directed toward the left, so

$$\vec{E}_b = (-6.2 \times 10^4 \text{ N/C})\hat{\imath}$$

(c) At point c, both $\vec{E}_1$ and $\vec{E}_2$ have the same magnitude, since this point is equidistant from both charges and the charge magnitudes are the same:

$$E_1 = E_2 = \frac{1}{4\pi\epsilon_0}\frac{|q|}{r^2} = (9.0 \times 10^9 \text{ N} \cdot \text{m}^2/\text{C}^2)\frac{12 \times 10^{-9} \text{ C}}{(0.130 \text{ m})^2}$$

$$= 6.39 \times 10^3 \text{ N/C}$$

The directions of $\vec{E}_1$ and $\vec{E}_2$ are shown in Fig 21.23. The x-components of both vectors are the same:

$$E_{1x} = E_{2x} = E_1\cos\alpha = (6.39 \times 10^3 \text{ N/C})\left(\frac{5}{13}\right)$$

$$= 2.46 \times 10^3 \text{ N/C}$$

From symmetry the y-components E_{1y} and E_{2y} are equal and opposite and so add to zero. Hence the components of the total field $\vec{E}_c$ are

$$(E_c)_x = E_{1x} + E_{2x} = 2(2.46 \times 10^3 \text{ N/C}) = 4.9 \times 10^3 \text{ N/C}$$
$$(E_c)_y = E_{1y} + E_{2y} = 0$$

So at point c the total electric field has magnitude 4.9×10^3 N/C and is directed toward the right, so

$$\vec{E}_c = (4.9 \times 10^3 \text{ N/C})\hat{\imath}$$

Does it surprise you that the field at point c is parallel to the line between the two charges?

EVALUATE: An alternative way to find the electric field at c is to use the vector expression for the field of a point charge, Eq. (21.7). The displacement vector $\vec{r}_1$ from q_1 to point c, a distance $r = 13.0$ cm away, is

$$\vec{r}_1 = r\cos\alpha\,\hat{\imath} + r\sin\alpha\,\hat{\jmath}$$

Hence the unit vector that points from q_1 to c is

$$\hat{r}_1 = \frac{\vec{r}_1}{r} = \cos\alpha\,\hat{\imath} + \sin\alpha\,\hat{\jmath}$$

and the field due to q_1 at point c is

$$\vec{E}_1 = \frac{1}{4\pi\epsilon_0}\frac{q_1}{r^2}\hat{r}_1 = \frac{1}{4\pi\epsilon_0}\frac{q_1}{r^2}(\cos\alpha\,\hat{\imath} + \sin\alpha\,\hat{\jmath})$$

By symmetry the unit vector $\hat{r}_2$ that points from q_2 to point c has the opposite x-component but the same y-component, so the field at c due to q_2 is

$$\vec{E}_2 = \frac{1}{4\pi\epsilon_0}\frac{q_2}{r^2}\hat{r}_2 = \frac{1}{4\pi\epsilon_0}\frac{q_2}{r^2}(-\cos\alpha\,\hat{\imath} + \sin\alpha\,\hat{\jmath})$$

Since $q_2 = -q_1$, the total field at c is

$$\vec{E}_c = \vec{E}_1 + \vec{E}_2$$

$$= \frac{1}{4\pi\epsilon_0}\frac{q_1}{r^2}(\cos\alpha\,\hat{\imath} + \sin\alpha\,\hat{\jmath}) + \frac{1}{4\pi\epsilon_0}\frac{(-q_1)}{r^2}(-\cos\alpha\,\hat{\imath} + \sin\alpha\,\hat{\jmath})$$

$$= \frac{1}{4\pi\epsilon_0}\frac{q_1}{r^2}(2\cos\alpha\,\hat{\imath})$$

$$= (9.0 \times 10^9 \text{ N} \cdot \text{m}^2/\text{C}^2)\frac{12 \times 10^{-9} \text{ C}}{(0.13 \text{ m})^2}\left[2\left(\frac{5}{13}\right)\right]\hat{\imath}$$

$$= (4.9 \times 10^3 \text{ N/C})\hat{\imath}$$

as before.

Example 21.10   Field of a ring of charge

A ring-shaped conductor with radius a carries a total charge Q uniformly distributed around it (Fig. 21.24). Find the electric field at a point P that lies on the axis of the ring at a distance x from its center.

SOLUTION

IDENTIFY: This is a problem in the superposition of electric fields. The new wrinkle is that the charge is distributed continuously around the ring rather than in a number of point charges.

SET UP: The field point is an arbitrary point on the x-axis in Fig. 21.24. Our target variable is the electric field at such a point as a function of the coordinate x.

EXECUTE: As shown in Fig. 21.24, we imagine the ring divided into infinitesimal segments of length ds. Each segment has charge dQ and acts as a point-charge source of electric field. Let $d\vec{E}$ be the electric field from one such segment; the net electric field at P is then the sum of all contributions $d\vec{E}$ from all the segments that make up the ring. (This same technique works for any situation in which charge is distributed along a line or a curve.)

The calculation of $\vec{E}$ is greatly simplified because the field point P is on the symmetry axis of the ring. Consider two segments at the top and bottom of the ring: The contributions $d\vec{E}$ to the field at P from these segments have the same x-component but opposite y-components. Hence the total y-component of field due to this pair of segments is zero. When we add up the contributions from all such pairs of segments, the total field $\vec{E}$ will have only a component along the ring's symmetry axis (the x-axis), with no component perpendicular to that axis (that is, no y-component or z-component). So the field at P is described completely by its x-component E_x.

21.24 Calculating the electric field on the axis of a ring of charge. In this figure, the charge is assumed to be positive.

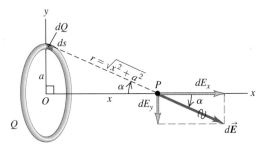

To calculate E_x, note that the square of the distance r from a ring segment to the point P is $r^2 = x^2 + a^2$. Hence the magnitude of this segment's contribution $d\vec{E}$ to the electric field at P is

$$dE = \frac{1}{4\pi\epsilon_0}\frac{dQ}{x^2 + a^2}$$

Using $\cos\alpha = x/r = x/(x^2 + a^2)^{1/2}$, the x-component dE_x of this field is

$$dE_x = dE\cos\alpha = \frac{1}{4\pi\epsilon_0}\frac{dQ}{x^2 + a^2}\frac{x}{\sqrt{x^2 + a^2}}$$

$$= \frac{1}{4\pi\epsilon_0}\frac{x\,dQ}{(x^2 + a^2)^{3/2}}$$

To find the *total* x-component E_x of the field at P, we integrate this expression over all segments of the ring:

$$E_x = \int \frac{1}{4\pi\epsilon_0}\frac{x\,dQ}{(x^2 + a^2)^{3/2}}$$

Since x does not vary as we move from point to point around the ring, all the factors on the right side except dQ are constant and can be taken outside the integral. The integral of dQ is just the total charge Q, and we finally get

$$\vec{E} = E_x\hat{\imath} = \frac{1}{4\pi\epsilon_0}\frac{Qx}{(x^2 + a^2)^{3/2}}\hat{\imath} \qquad (21.8)$$

EVALUATE: Our result for $\vec{E}$ shows that at the center of the ring $(x = 0)$ the field is zero. We should expect this; charges on opposite sides of the ring would push in opposite directions on a test charge at the center, and the forces would add to zero. When the field point P is much farther from the ring than its size (that is, $x \gg a$), the denominator in Eq. (21.8) becomes approximately equal to x^3, and the expression becomes approximately

$$\vec{E} = \frac{1}{4\pi\epsilon_0}\frac{Q}{x^2}\hat{\imath}$$

In other words, when we are so far from the ring that its size a is negligible in comparison to the distance x, its field is the same as that of a point charge. To an observer far from the ring, the ring would appear like a point, and the electric field reflects this.

In this example we used a *symmetry argument* to conclude that $\vec{E}$ had only an x-component at a point on the ring's axis of symmetry. We'll use symmetry arguments many times in this and subsequent chapters. Keep in mind, however, that such arguments can be used only in special cases. At a point in the xy-plane that is not on the x-axis in Fig. 21.24, the symmetry argument doesn't apply, and the field has in general both x- and y-components.

Example 21.11   Field of a line of charge

Positive electric charge Q is distributed uniformly along a line with length $2a$, lying along the y-axis between $y = -a$ and $y = +a$. (This might represent one of the charged rods in Fig. 21.1.) Find the electric field at point P on the x-axis at a distance x from the origin.

SOLUTION

IDENTIFY: As in Example 21.10, our target variable is the electric field due to a continuous distribution of charge.

SET UP: Figure 21.25 shows the situation. We need to find the electric field at P as a function of the coordinate x. The x-axis is the perpendicular bisector of the charged line, so as in Example 21.10 we will be able to make use of a symmetry argument.

EXECUTE: We divide the line charge into infinitesimal segments, each of which acts as a point charge; let the length of a typical segment at height y be dy. If the charge is distributed uniformly, the linear charge density λ at any point on the line is equal to $Q/2a$ (the total charge divided by the total length). Hence the charge dQ in a segment of length dy is

$$dQ = \lambda dy = \frac{Q dy}{2a}$$

The distance r from this segment to P is $(x^2 + y^2)^{1/2}$, so the magnitude of field dE at P due to this segment is

$$dE = \frac{1}{4\pi\epsilon_0} \frac{dQ}{r^2} = \frac{Q}{4\pi\epsilon_0} \frac{dy}{2a(x^2 + y^2)}$$

We represent this field in terms of its x- and y-components:

$$dE_x = dE \cos\alpha \qquad dE_y = -dE \sin\alpha$$

We note that $\sin\alpha = y/(x^2 + y^2)^{1/2}$ and $\cos\alpha = x/(x^2 + y^2)^{1/2}$; combining these with the expression for dE, we find

$$dE_x = \frac{Q}{4\pi\epsilon_0} \frac{x \, dy}{2a(x^2 + y^2)^{3/2}}$$

$$dE_y = -\frac{Q}{4\pi\epsilon_0} \frac{y \, dy}{2a(x^2 + y^2)^{3/2}}$$

To find the total field components E_x and E_y, we integrate these expressions, noting that to include all of Q, we must integrate from $y = -a$ to $y = +a$. We invite you to work out the details of the integration; an integral table is helpful. The final results are

$$E_x = \frac{1}{4\pi\epsilon_0} \frac{Qx}{2a} \int_{-a}^{a} \frac{dy}{(x^2 + y^2)^{3/2}} = \frac{Q}{4\pi\epsilon_0} \frac{1}{x\sqrt{x^2 + a^2}}$$

$$E_y = -\frac{1}{4\pi\epsilon_0} \frac{Q}{2a} \int_{-a}^{a} \frac{y \, dy}{(x^2 + y^2)^{3/2}} = 0$$

or, in vector form,

$$\vec{E} = \frac{1}{4\pi\epsilon_0} \frac{Q}{x\sqrt{x^2 + a^2}} \hat{i} \qquad (21.9)$$

EVALUATE: Using a symmetry argument as in Example 21.10, we could have guessed that E_y would be zero; if we place a positive test charge at P, the upper half of the line of charge pushes downward on it, and the lower half pushes up with equal magnitude.

21.25 Our sketch for this problem.

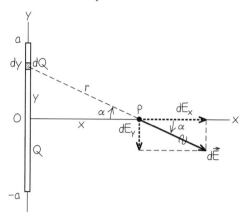

To explore our result, let's first see what happens in the limit that x is much larger than a. Then we can neglect a in the denominator of Eq. (21.9), and our result becomes

$$\vec{E} = \frac{1}{4\pi\epsilon_0} \frac{Q}{x^2} \hat{i}$$

This means that if point P is very far from the line charge in comparison to the length of the line, the field at P is the same as that of a point charge. We found a similar result for the charged ring in Example 21.10.

To further explore our exact result for $\vec{E}$, Eq. (21.9), let's express it in terms of the linear charge density $\lambda = Q/2a$. Substituting $Q = 2a\lambda$ into Eq. (21.9) and simplifying, we get

$$\vec{E} = \frac{1}{2\pi\epsilon_0} \frac{\lambda}{x\sqrt{(x^2/a^2) + 1}} \hat{i} \qquad (21.10)$$

Now we can answer the question: What is $\vec{E}$ at a distance x from a *very* long line of charge? To find the answer we take the *limit* of Eq. (21.10) as a becomes very large. In this limit, the term x^2/a^2 in the denominator becomes much smaller than unity and can be thrown away. We are left with

$$\vec{E} = \frac{\lambda}{2\pi\epsilon_0 x} \hat{i}$$

The field magnitude depends only on the distance of point P from the line of charge. So at any point P at a perpendicular distance r from the line in any direction, $\vec{E}$ has magnitude

$$E = \frac{\lambda}{2\pi\epsilon_0 r} \qquad \text{(infinite line of charge)}$$

Thus the electric field due to an infinitely long line of charge is proportional to $1/r$ rather than to $1/r^2$ as for a point charge. The direction of $\vec{E}$ is radially outward from the line if λ is positive and radially inward if λ is negative.

There's really no such thing in nature as an infinite line of charge. But when the field point is close enough to the line, there's very little difference between the result for an infinite line and the real-life finite case. For example, if the distance r of the field point from the center of the line is 1% of the length of the line, the value of E differs from the infinite-length value by less than 0.02%.

Example 21.12 Field of a uniformly charged disk

Find the electric field caused by a disk of radius R with a uniform positive surface charge density (charge per unit area) σ, at a point along the axis of the disk a distance x from its center. Assume that x is positive.

SOLUTION

IDENTIFY: This example is similar to Examples 21.10 and 21.11 in that our target variable is the electric field along a symmetry axis of a continuous charge distribution.

SET UP: Figure 21.26 shows the situation. We can represent the charge distribution as a collection of concentric rings of charge dQ, as shown in Fig. 21.26. From Example 21.10 we know the field of a single ring on its axis of symmetry, so all we have to do is add the contributions of the rings.

EXECUTE: A typical ring has charge dQ, inner radius r, and outer radius $r + dr$ (Fig. 21.26). Its area dA is approximately equal to its width dr times its circumference $2\pi r$, or $dA = 2\pi r\, dr$. The charge per unit area is $\sigma = dQ/dA$, so the charge of the ring is $dQ = \sigma\, dA = \sigma\, (2\pi r\, dr)$, or

$$dQ = 2\pi\sigma r\, dr$$

We use this in place of Q in the expression for the field due to a ring found in Example 21.10, Eq. (21.8), and also replace the ring radius a with r. The field component dE_x at point P due to charge dQ is

$$dE_x = \frac{1}{4\pi\epsilon_0}\frac{dQ}{r^2} = \frac{1}{4\pi\epsilon_0}\frac{(2\pi\sigma r\, dr)x}{(x^2 + r^2)^{3/2}}$$

21.26 Our sketch for this problem.

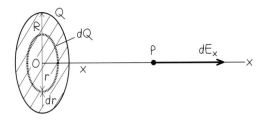

To find the total field due to all the rings, we integrate dE_x over r from $r = 0$ to $r = R$ (*not* from $-R$ to R):

$$E_x = \int_0^R \frac{1}{4\pi\epsilon_0}\frac{(2\pi\sigma r\, dr)x}{(x^2 + r^2)^{3/2}} = \frac{\sigma x}{2\epsilon_0}\int_0^R \frac{r\, dr}{(x^2 + r^2)^{3/2}}$$

Remember that x is a constant during the integration and that the integration variable is r. The integral can be evaluated by use of the substitution $z = x^2 + r^2$. We'll let you work out the details; the result is

$$E_x = \frac{\sigma x}{2\epsilon_0}\left[-\frac{1}{\sqrt{x^2 + R^2}} + \frac{1}{x}\right]$$
$$= \frac{\sigma}{2\epsilon_0}\left[1 - \frac{1}{\sqrt{(R^2/x^2) + 1}}\right] \quad (21.11)$$

The electric field due to the ring has no components perpendicular to the axis. Hence at point P in Fig. 21.26, $dE_y = dE_z = 0$ for each ring, and the total field has $E_y = E_z = 0$.

EVALUATE Suppose we keep increasing the radius R of the disk, simultaneously adding charge so that the surface charge density σ (charge per unit area) is constant. In the limit that R is much larger than the distance x of the field point from the disk, the term $1/\sqrt{(R^2/x^2) + 1}$ in Eq. (21.11) becomes negligibly small, and we get

$$E = \frac{\sigma}{2\epsilon_0} \quad (21.12)$$

Our final result does not contain the distance x from the plane. Hence the electric field produced by an *infinite* plane sheet of charge is *independent of the distance from the sheet*. The field direction is everywhere perpendicular to the sheet, away from it. There is no such thing as an infinite sheet of charge, but if the dimensions of the sheet are much larger than the distance x of the field point P from the sheet, the field is very nearly given by Eq. (21.11).

If P is to the *left* of the plane $(x < 0)$, the result is the same except that the direction of $\vec{E}$ is to the left instead of the right. If the surface charge density is negative, the directions of the fields on both sides of the plane are toward it rather than away from it.

Example 21.13 Field of two oppositely charged infinite sheets

Two infinite plane sheets are placed parallel to each other, separated by a distance d (Fig. 21.27). The lower sheet has a uniform positive surface charge density σ, and the upper sheet has a uniform negative surface charge density $-\sigma$ with the same magnitude. Find the electric field between the two sheets, above the upper sheet, and below the lower sheet.

SOLUTION

IDENTIFY: From Example 21.12 we know the electric field due to a single infinite plane sheet of charge. Our goal is to find the electric field due to *two* such sheets.

SET UP: We use the principle of superposition to combine the electric fields produced by the two sheets, as shown in Fig. 21.27.

21.27 Finding the electric field due to two oppositely charged infinite sheets. The sheets are seen edge-on; only a portion of the infinite sheets can be shown!

y

Sheet 2 $-\sigma$

$\vec{E}_1\uparrow$ $\vec{E}_2\downarrow$ $\vec{E} = \vec{E}_1 + \vec{E}_2 = 0$

x

d $\vec{E}_1\uparrow$ $\vec{E}_2\uparrow$ $\uparrow\vec{E} = \vec{E}_1 + \vec{E}_2$

Sheet 1 $+\sigma$

$\vec{E}_1\downarrow$ $\vec{E}_2\uparrow$ $\vec{E} = \vec{E}_1 + \vec{E}_2 = 0$

EXECUTE: Let sheet 1 be the lower sheet of positive charge, and let sheet 2 be the upper sheet of negative charge; the fields due to each sheet are $\vec{E}_1$ and $\vec{E}_2$, respectively. From Eq. (21.12) of Example 21.12, both $\vec{E}_1$ and $\vec{E}_2$ have the same magnitude at all points, no matter how far from either sheet:

$$E_1 = E_2 = \frac{\sigma}{2\epsilon_0}$$

At all points, the direction of $\vec{E}_1$ is away from the positive charge of sheet 1, and the direction of $\vec{E}_2$ is toward the negative charge of sheet 2. These fields and the x- and y-axes are shown in Fig. 21.27.

CAUTION   Electric fields are not "flows" You may be surprised that $\vec{E}_1$ is unaffected by the presence of sheet 2 and that $\vec{E}_2$ is unaffected by the presence of sheet 1. Indeed, you may have thought that the field of one sheet would be unable to "penetrate" the other sheet. You might conclude this if you think of the electric field as some kind of physical substance that "flows" into or out of charges. But in fact there is no such substance, and the electric fields $\vec{E}_1$ and $\vec{E}_2$ depend only on the individual charge distributions that create them. The *total* field is just the vector sum of $\vec{E}_1$ and $\vec{E}_2$. ∎

At points between the sheets, $\vec{E}_1$ and $\vec{E}_2$ reinforce each other; at points above the upper sheet or below the lower sheet, $\vec{E}_1$ and $\vec{E}_2$ cancel each other. Thus the total field is

$$\vec{E} = \vec{E}_1 + \vec{E}_2 = \begin{cases} 0 & \text{above the upper sheet} \\ \frac{\sigma}{\epsilon_0}\hat{\jmath} & \text{between the sheets} \\ 0 & \text{below the lower sheet} \end{cases}$$

Because we considered the sheets to be infinite, our result does not depend on the separation d.

EVALUATE: Note that the field between the oppositely charged sheets is uniform. We used this in Examples 21.7 and 21.8, in which two large parallel conducting plates were connected to the terminals of a battery. The battery causes the two plates to become oppositely charged, giving a field between the plates that is essentially uniform if the plate separation is much smaller than the dimensions of the plates. In Chapter 23 we will examine how a battery can produce such separation of positive and negative charge. An arrangement of two oppositely charged conducting plates is called a *capacitor;* these devices prove to be of tremendous practical utility and are the principal subject of Chapter 24.

Test Your Understanding of Section 21.5   Suppose that the line of charge in Fig. 21.25 (Example 21.11) had charge $+Q$ distributed uniformly between $y = 0$ and $y = +a$ and had charge $-Q$ distributed uniformly between $y = 0$ and $y = -a$. In this situation, the electric field at P would be (i) in the positive x-direction; (ii) in the negative x-direction; (iii) in the positive y-direction; (iv) in the negative y-direction; (v) zero; (vi) none of these.

21.6 Electric Field Lines

The concept of an electric field can be a little elusive because you can't see an electric field directly. Electric field *lines* can be a big help for visualizing electric fields and making them seem more real. An **electric field line** is an imaginary line or curve drawn through a region of space so that its tangent at any point is in the direction of the electric-field vector at that point. Figure 21.28 shows the basic idea. (We used a similar concept in our discussion of fluid flow in Section 14.5. A *streamline* is a line or curve whose tangent at any point is in the direction of the velocity of the fluid at that point. However, the similarity between electric field lines and fluid streamlines is a mathematical one only; there is nothing "flowing" in an electric field.) The English scientist Michael Faraday (1791–1867) first introduced the concept of field lines. He called them "lines of force," but the term "field lines" is preferable.

Electric field lines show the direction of $\vec{E}$ at each point, and their spacing gives a general idea of the *magnitude* of $\vec{E}$ at each point. Where $\vec{E}$ is strong, we draw lines bunched closely together; where $\vec{E}$ is weaker, they are farther apart. At any particular point, the electric field has a unique direction, so only one field line can pass through each point of the field. In other words, *field lines never intersect.*

Figure 21.29 shows some of the electric field lines in a plane containing (a) a single positive charge; (b) two equal-magnitude charges, one positive and one negative (a dipole); and (c) two equal positive charges. Diagrams such as these are sometimes called *field maps;* they are cross sections of the actual three-dimensional patterns. The direction of the total electric field at every point in each diagram is along the tangent to the electric field line passing through the point. Arrowheads indicate the direction of the $\vec{E}$-field vector along each field

21.28 The direction of the electric field at any point is tangent to the field line through that point.

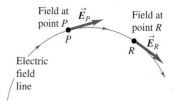

21.29 Electric field lines for three different charge distributions. In general, the magnitude of $\vec{E}$ is different at different points along a given field line.

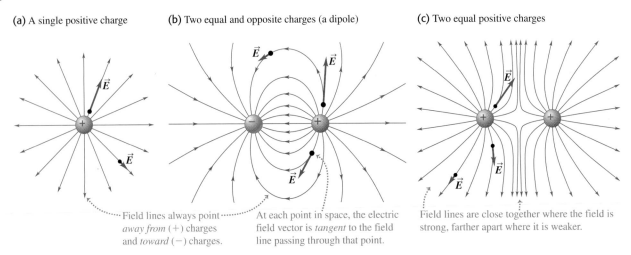

(a) A single positive charge

(b) Two equal and opposite charges (a dipole)

(c) Two equal positive charges

Field lines always point *away from* (+) charges and *toward* (−) charges.

At each point in space, the electric field vector is *tangent* to the field line passing through that point.

Field lines are close together where the field is strong, farther apart where it is weaker.

line. The actual field vectors have been drawn at several points in each pattern. Notice that in general, the magnitude of the electric field is different at different points on a given field line; a field line is *not* a curve of constant electric-field magnitude!

Figure 21.29 shows that field lines are directed *away* from positive charges (since close to a positive point charge, $\vec{E}$ points away from the charge) and *toward* negative charges (since close to a negative point charge, $\vec{E}$ points toward the charge). In regions where the field magnitude is large, such as between the positive and negative charges in Fig. 21.29b, the field lines are drawn close together. In regions where the field magnitude is small, such as between the two positive charges in Fig. 21.29c, the lines are widely separated. In a *uniform* field, the field lines are straight, parallel, and uniformly spaced, as in Fig. 21.20.

Figure 21.30 is a view from above of a demonstration setup for visualizing electric field lines. In the arrangement shown here, the tips of two positively charged wires are inserted in a container of insulating liquid, and some grass seeds are floated on the liquid. The grass seeds are electrically neutral insulators, but the electric field of the two charged wires causes *polarization* of the grass seeds; there is a slight shifting of the positive and negative charges within the molecules of each seed, like that shown in Fig. 21.8. The positively charged end of each grass seed is pulled in the direction of $\vec{E}$ and the negatively charged end is pulled opposite $\vec{E}$. Hence the long axis of each grass seed tends to orient parallel to the electric field, in the direction of the field line that passes through the position of the seed (Fig. 21.30b).

21.30 (a) Electric field lines produced by two equal point charges. The pattern is formed by grass seeds floating on a liquid above two charged wires. Compare this pattern with Fig. 21.29c. (b) The electric field causes polarization of the grass seeds, which in turn causes the seeds to align with the field.

(a)

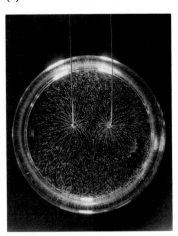

(b)

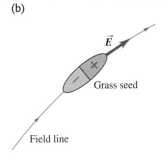

Grass seed

Field line

CAUTION **Electric field lines are not the same as trajectories** It's a common misconception that if a charged particle of charge q is in motion where there is an electric field, the particle must move along an electric field line. Because $\vec{E}$ at any point is tangent to the field line that passes through that point, it is indeed true that the *force* $\vec{F} = q\vec{E}$ on the particle, and hence the particle's acceleration, are tangent to the field line. But we learned in Chapter 3 that when a particle moves on a curved path, its acceleration *cannot* be tangent to the path. So in general, the trajectory of a charged particle is *not* the same as a field line. ▌

Test Your Understanding of Section 21.6 Suppose the electric field lines in a region of space are straight lines. If a charged particle is released from rest in that region, will the trajectory of the particle be along a field line?

21.7 Electric Dipoles

An **electric dipole** is a pair of point charges with equal magnitude and opposite sign (a positive charge q and a negative charge $-q$) separated by a distance d. We introduced electric dipoles in Example 21.9 (Section 21.5); the concept is worth exploring further because many physical systems, from molecules to TV antennas, can be described as electric dipoles. We will also use this concept extensively in our discussion of dielectrics in Chapter 24.

Figure 21.31 a shows a molecule of water (H_2O), which in many ways behaves like an electric dipole. The water molecule as a whole is electrically neutral, but the chemical bonds within the molecule cause a displacement of charge; the result is a net negative charge on the oxygen end of the molecule and a net positive charge on the hydrogen end, forming an electric dipole. The effect is equivalent to shifting one electron only about 4×10^{-11} m (about the radius of a hydrogen atom), but the consequences of this shift are profound. Water is an excellent solvent for ionic substances such as table salt (sodium chloride, NaCl) precisely because the water molecule is an electric dipole (Fig. 21.31b). When dissolved in water, salt dissociates into a positive sodium ion (Na^+) and a negative chlorine ion (Cl^-), which tend to be attracted to the negative and positive ends, respectively, of water molecules; this holds the ions in solution. If water molecules were not electric dipoles, water would be a poor solvent, and almost all of the chemistry that occurs in aqueous solutions would be impossible. This includes all of the biochemical reactions that occur in all of the life on earth. In a very real sense, your existence as a living being depends on electric dipoles!

We examine two questions about electric dipoles. First, what forces and torques does an electric dipole experience when placed in an external electric field (that is, a field set up by charges outside the dipole)? Second, what electric field does an electric dipole itself produce?

Force and Torque on an Electric Dipole

To start with the first question, let's place an electric dipole in a *uniform* external electric field $\vec{E}$, as shown in Fig. 21.32. The forces $\vec{F}_+$ and $\vec{F}_-$ on the two charges both have magnitude qE, but their directions are opposite, and they add to zero. *The net force on an electric dipole in a uniform external electric field is zero.*

However, the two forces don't act along the same line, so their *torques* don't add to zero. We calculate torques with respect to the center of the dipole. Let the angle between the electric field $\vec{E}$ and the dipole axis be ϕ; then the lever arm for both $\vec{F}_+$ and $\vec{F}_-$ is $(d/2)\sin\phi$. The torque of $\vec{F}_+$ and the torque of $\vec{F}_-$ both have the same magnitude of $(qE)(d/2)\sin\phi$, and both torques tend to rotate the dipole clockwise (that is, $\vec{\tau}$ is directed into the page in Fig. 21.32). Hence the magnitude of the net torque is twice the magnitude of either individual torque:

$$\tau = (qE)(d\sin\phi) \tag{21.13}$$

where $d\sin\phi$ is the perpendicular distance between the lines of action of the two forces.

The product of the charge q and the separation d is the magnitude of a quantity called the **electric dipole moment,** denoted by p:

$$p = qd \quad \text{(magnitude of electric dipole moment)} \tag{21.14}$$

The units of p are charge times distance $(C \cdot m)$. For example, the magnitude of the electric dipole moment of a water molecule is $p = 6.13 \times 10^{-30}\ C \cdot m$.

CAUTION **The symbol p has multiple meanings** Be careful not to confuse dipole moment with momentum or pressure. There aren't as many letters in the alphabet as there are physical quantities, so some letters are used several times. The context usually makes it clear what we mean, but be careful. ▮

21.31 (a) A water molecule is an example of an electric dipole. (b) Each test tube contains a solution of a different substance in water. The large electric dipole moment of water makes it an excellent solvent.

(a) A water molecule, showing positive charge as red and negative charge as blue

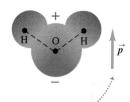

The electric dipole moment $\vec{p}$ is directed from the negative end to the positive end of the molecule.

(b) Various substances dissolved in water

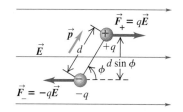

21.32 The net force on this electric dipole is zero, but there is a torque directed into the page that tends to rotate the dipole clockwise.

We further define the electric dipole moment to be a *vector* quantity $\vec{p}$. The magnitude of $\vec{p}$ is given by Eq. (21.14), and its direction is along the dipole axis from the negative charge to the positive charge as shown in Fig. 21.32.

In terms of p, Eq. (21.13) for the magnitude τ of the torque exerted by the field becomes

$$\tau = pE \sin\phi \qquad \text{(magnitude of the torque on an electric dipole)} \quad (21.15)$$

Since the angle ϕ in Fig. 21.32 is the angle between the directions of the vectors $\vec{p}$ and $\vec{E}$, this is reminiscent of the expression for the magnitude of the *vector product* discussed in Section 1.10. (You may want to review that discussion.) Hence we can write the torque on the dipole in vector form as

$$\vec{\tau} = \vec{p} \times \vec{E} \qquad \text{(torque on an electric dipole, in vector form)} \quad (21.16)$$

You can use the right-hand rule for the vector product to verify that in the situation shown in Fig. 21.32, $\vec{\tau}$ is directed into the page. The torque is greatest when $\vec{p}$ and $\vec{E}$ are perpendicular and is zero when they are parallel or antiparallel. The torque always tends to turn $\vec{p}$ to line it up with $\vec{E}$. The position $\phi = 0$, with $\vec{p}$ parallel to $\vec{E}$, is a position of stable equilibrium, and the position $\phi = \pi$, with $\vec{p}$ and $\vec{E}$ antiparallel, is a position of unstable equilibrium. The polarization of a grass seed in the apparatus of Fig. 21.30b gives it an electric dipole moment; the torque exerted by $\vec{E}$ then causes the seed to align with $\vec{E}$ and hence with the field lines.

Potential Energy of an Electric Dipole

When a dipole changes direction in an electric field, the electric-field torque does *work* on it, with a corresponding change in potential energy. The work dW done by a torque τ during an infinitesimal displacement $d\phi$ is given by Eq. (10.19): $dW = \tau \, d\phi$. Because the torque is in the direction of decreasing ϕ, we must write the torque as $\tau = -pE \sin\phi$, and

$$dW = \tau \, d\phi = -pE \sin\phi \, d\phi$$

In a finite displacement from ϕ_1 to ϕ_2 the total work done on the dipole is

$$W = \int_{\phi_1}^{\phi_2} (-pE \sin\phi) \, d\phi$$
$$= pE \cos\phi_2 - pE \cos\phi_1$$

The work is the negative of the change of potential energy, just as in Chapter 7: $W = U_1 - U_2$. So we see that a suitable definition of potential energy U for this system is

$$U(\phi) = -pE \cos\phi \qquad (21.17)$$

In this expression we recognize the *scalar product* $\vec{p} \cdot \vec{E} = pE\cos\phi$, so we can also write

$$U = -\vec{p} \cdot \vec{E} \qquad \text{(potential energy for a dipole in an electric field)} \quad (21.18)$$

The potential energy has its minimum value $U = -pE$ (i.e., its most negative value) at the stable equilibrium position, where $\phi = 0$ and $\vec{p}$ is parallel to $\vec{E}$. The potential energy is maximum when $\phi = \pi$ and $\vec{p}$ is antiparallel to $\vec{E}$; then $U = +pE$. At $\phi = \pi/2$, where $\vec{p}$ is perpendicular to $\vec{E}$, U is zero. We could of course define U differently so that it is zero at some other orientation of $\vec{p}$, but our definition is simplest.

Equation (21.18) gives us another way to look at the effect shown in Fig. 21.30. The electric field $\vec{E}$ gives each grass seed an electric dipole moment, and the grass seed then aligns itself with $\vec{E}$ to minimize the potential energy.

Example 21.14 Force and torque on an electric dipole

Figure 21.33a shows an electric dipole in a uniform electric field with magnitude 5.0×10^5 N/C directed parallel to the plane of the figure. The charges are $\pm 1.6 \times 10^{-19}$ C; both lie in the plane and are separated by 0.125 nm $= 0.125 \times 10^{-9}$ m. (Both the charge magnitude and the distance are typical of molecular quantities.) Find (a) the net force exerted by the field on the dipole; (b) the magnitude and direction of the electric dipole moment; (c) the magnitude and direction of the torque; (d) the potential energy of the system in the position shown.

SOLUTION

IDENTIFY: This problem uses the ideas of this section about an electric dipole placed in an electric field.

SET UP: We use the relationship $\vec{F} = q\vec{E}$ for each point charge to find the force on the dipole as a whole. Equation (21.14) tells us

21.33 (a) An electric dipole. (b) Directions of the electric dipole moment, electric field, and torque.

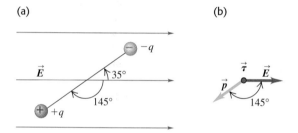

the dipole moment, Eq. (21.16) tells us the torque on the dipole, and Eq. (21.18) tells us the potential energy of the system.

EXECUTE: (a) Since the field is uniform, the forces on the two charges are equal and opposite, and the total force is zero.

(b) The magnitude p of the electric dipole moment $\vec{p}$ is

$$p = qd = (1.6 \times 10^{-19}\,\text{C})(0.125 \times 10^{-9}\,\text{m})$$
$$= 2.0 \times 10^{-29}\,\text{C}\cdot\text{m}$$

The direction of $\vec{p}$ is from the negative to the positive charge, 145° clockwise from the electric-field direction (Fig. 21.33b).

(c) The magnitude of the torque is

$$\tau = pE \sin\phi = (2.0 \times 10^{-29}\,\text{C})(5.0 \times 10^5\,\text{N/C})(\sin 145°)$$
$$= 5.7 \times 10^{-24}\,\text{N}\cdot\text{m}$$

From the right-hand rule for vector products (see Section 1.10), the direction of the torque $\vec{\tau} = \vec{p} \times \vec{E}$ is out of the page. This corresponds to a counterclockwise torque that tends to align $\vec{p}$ with $\vec{E}$.

(d) The potential energy is

$$U = -pE\cos\phi$$
$$= -(2.0 \times 10^{-29}\,\text{C}\cdot\text{m})(5.0 \times 10^5\,\text{N/C})(\cos 145°)$$
$$= 8.2 \times 10^{-24}\,\text{J}$$

EVALUATE: The dipole moment, torque, and potential energy are all exceedingly small. Don't be surprised by this result: Remember that we are looking at a single molecule, which is a very small object indeed!

In this discussion we have assumed that $\vec{E}$ is uniform, so there is no net force on the dipole. If $\vec{E}$ is not uniform, the forces at the ends may not cancel completely, and the net force may not be zero. Thus a body with zero net charge but an electric dipole moment can experience a net force in a nonuniform electric field. As we mentioned in Section 21.1, an uncharged body can be polarized by an electric field, giving rise to a separation of charge and an electric dipole moment. This is how uncharged bodies can experience electrostatic forces (see Fig. 21.8).

Field of an Electric Dipole

Now let's think of an electric dipole as a *source* of electric field. What does the field look like? The general shape of things is shown by the field map of Fig. 21.29b. At each point in the pattern the total $\vec{E}$ field is the vector sum of the fields from the two individual charges, as in Example 21.9 (Section 21.5). Try drawing diagrams showing this vector sum for several points.

To get quantitative information about the field of an electric dipole, we have to do some calculating, as illustrated in the next example. Notice the use of the principle of superposition of electric fields to add up the contributions to the field of the individual charges. Also notice that we need to use approximation techniques even for the relatively simple case of a field due to two charges. Field calculations often become very complicated, and computer analysis is typically used to determine the field due to an arbitrary charge distribution.

Example 21.15 Field of an electric dipole, revisited

In Fig. 21.34 an electric dipole is centered at the origin, with $\vec{p}$ in the direction of the $+y$-axis. Derive an approximate expression for the electric field at a point on the y-axis for which y is much larger than d. Use the binomial expansion of $(1 + x)^n$—that is, $(1 + x)^n \cong 1 + nx + n(n - 1)x^2/2 + \cdots$ —for the case $|x| < 1$. (This problem illustrates a useful calculational technique.)

SOLUTION

IDENTIFY: We use the principle of superposition: The total electric field is the vector sum of the field produced by the positive charge and the field produced by the negative charge.

SET UP: At the field point shown in Fig. 21.34, the field of the positive charge has a positive (upward) y-component and the field of the negative charge has a negative (downward) y-component. We add these components to find the total field and then apply the approximation that y is much greater than d.

21.34 Finding the electric field of an electric dipole at a point on its axis.

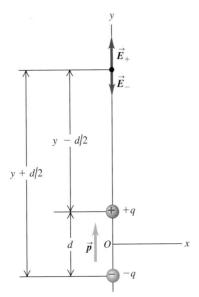

EXECUTE: The total y-component E_y of electric field from the two charges is

$$E_y = \frac{q}{4\pi\epsilon_0}\left[\frac{1}{(y - d/2)^2} - \frac{1}{(y + d/2)^2}\right]$$
$$= \frac{q}{4\pi\epsilon_0 y^2}\left[\left(1 - \frac{d}{2y}\right)^{-2} - \left(1 + \frac{d}{2y}\right)^{-2}\right]$$

We used this same approach in Example 21.9 (Section 21.5). Now comes the approximation. When y is much greater than d—that is, when we are far away from the dipole compared to its size—the quantity $d/2y$ is much smaller than 1. With $n = -2$ and $d/2y$ playing the role of x in the binomial expansion, we keep only the first two terms. The terms we discard are much smaller than those we keep, and we have

$$\left(1 - \frac{d}{2y}\right)^{-2} \cong 1 + \frac{d}{y} \quad \text{and} \quad \left(1 + \frac{d}{2y}\right)^{-2} \cong 1 - \frac{d}{y}$$

Hence E_y is given approximately by

$$E \cong \frac{q}{4\pi\epsilon_0 y^2}\left[1 + \frac{d}{y} - \left(1 - \frac{d}{y}\right)\right]$$
$$= \frac{qd}{2\pi\epsilon_0 y^3}$$
$$= \frac{p}{2\pi\epsilon_0 y^3}$$

EVALUATE: An alternative route to this expression is to put the fractions in the E_y expression over a common denominator and combine, then approximate the denominator $(y - d/2)^2(y + d/2)^2$ as y^4. We leave the details to you (see Exercise 21.65).

For points P off the coordinate axes, the expressions are more complicated, but at *all* points far away from the dipole (in any direction) the field drops off as $1/r^3$. We can compare this with the $1/r^2$ behavior of a point charge, the $1/r$ behavior of a long line charge, and the independence of r for a large sheet of charge. There are charge distributions for which the field drops off even more quickly. An *electric quadrupole* consists of two equal dipoles with opposite orientation, separated by a small distance. The field of a quadrupole at large distances drops off as $1/r^4$.

Test Your Understanding of Section 21.7 An electric dipole is placed in a region of uniform electric field $\vec{E}$, with the electric dipole moment $\vec{p}$, pointing in the direction opposite to $\vec{E}$. Is the dipole (i) in stable equilibrium, (ii) in unstable equilibrium, or (iii) neither? (*Hint:* You many want to review Section 7.5.)

Electric charge, conductors, and insulators: The fundamental quantity in electrostatics is electric charge. There are two kinds of charge, positive and negative. Charges of the same sign repel each other; charges of opposite sign attract. Charge is conserved; the total charge in an isolated system is constant.

All ordinary matter is made of protons, neutrons, and electrons. The positive protons and electrically neutral neutrons in the nucleus of an atom are bound together by the nuclear force; the negative electrons surround the nucleus at distances much greater than the nuclear size. Electric interactions are chiefly responsible for the structure of atoms, molecules, and solids.

Conductors are materials that permit electric charge to move easily within them. Insulators permit charge to move much less readily. Most metals are good conductors; most nonmetals are insulators.

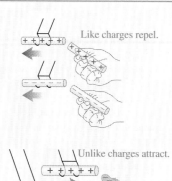

Coulomb's law: Coulomb's law is the basic law of interaction for point electric charges. For charges q_1 and q_2 separated by a distance r, the magnitude of the force on either charge is proportional to the product $q_1 q_2$ and inversely proportional to r^2. The force on each charge is along the line joining the two charges—repulsive if q_1 and q_2 have the same sign, attractive if they have opposite signs. The forces form an action–reaction pair and obey Newton's third law. In SI units the unit of electric charge is the coulomb, abbreviated C. (See Examples 21.1 and 21.2.)

The principle of superposition of forces states that when two or more charges each exert a force on a charge, the total force on that charge is the vector sum of the forces exerted by the individual charges. (See Examples 21.3 and 21.4.)

$$F = \frac{1}{4\pi\epsilon_0}\frac{|q_1 q_2|}{r^2} \tag{21.2}$$

$$\frac{1}{4\pi\epsilon_0} = 8.988 \times 10^9 \ \text{N} \cdot \text{m}^2/\text{C}^2$$

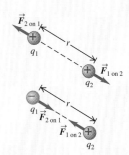

Electric field: Electric field $\vec{E}$, a vector quantity, is the force per unit charge exerted on a test charge at any point, provided the test charge is small enough that it does not disturb the charges that cause the field. The electric field produced by a point charge is directed radially away from or toward the charge. (See Examples 21.5–21.8.)

$$\vec{E} = \frac{\vec{F}_0}{q_0} \tag{21.3}$$

$$\vec{E} = \frac{1}{4\pi\epsilon_0}\frac{q}{r^2}\hat{r} \tag{21.7}$$

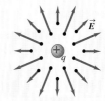

Superposition of electric fields: The principle of superposition of electric fields states that the electric field $\vec{E}$ of any combination of charges is the vector sum of the fields caused by the individual charges. To calculate the electric field caused by a continuous distribution of charge, divide the distribution into small elements, calculate the field caused by each element, and then carry out the vector sum or each component sum, usually by integrating. Charge distributions are described by linear charge density λ, surface charge density σ, and volume charge density ρ. (See Examples 21.9–21.13.)

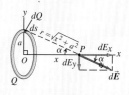

Electric field lines: Field lines provide a graphical representation of electric fields. At any point on a field line, the tangent to the line is in the direction of $\vec{E}$ at that point. The number of lines per unit area (perpendicular to their direction) is proportional to the magnitude of $\vec{E}$ at the point.

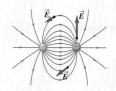

Electric dipoles: An electric dipole is a pair of electric charges of equal magnitude q but opposite sign, separated by a distance d. The electric dipole moment $\vec{p}$ is defined to have magnitude $p = qd$. The direction of $\vec{p}$ is from negative toward positive charge. An electric dipole in an electric field $\vec{E}$ experiences a torque $\vec{\tau}$ equal to the vector product of $\vec{p}$ and $\vec{E}$. The magnitude of the torque depends on the angle ϕ between $\vec{p}$ and $\vec{E}$. The potential energy U for an electric dipole in an electric field also depends on the relative orientation of $\vec{p}$ and $\vec{E}$. (See Examples 21.14 and 21.15.)

$$\tau = pE \sin \phi \qquad (21.15)$$
$$\vec{\tau} = \vec{p} \times \vec{E} \qquad (21.16)$$
$$U = -\vec{p} \cdot \vec{E} \qquad (21.18)$$

Key Terms

electric charge, *710*
electrostatics, *710*
electron, *711*
proton, *711*
neutron, *711*
nucleus, *711*
atomic number, *712*
positive ion, *712*
negative ion, *712*
ionization, *712*
principle of conservation of charge, *712*

conductor, *713*
insulator, *713*
induction, *714*
induced charge, *714*
point charge, *716*
Coulomb's law, *716*
coulomb, *717*
principle of superposition of forces, *719*
electric field, *722*
test charge, *722*
source point, *723*

field point, *723*
vector field, *724*
principle of superposition of electric fields, *727*
linear charge density, *727*
surface charge density, *727*
volume charge density, *727*
electric field line, *733*
electric dipole, *735*
electric dipole moment, *735*

Answer to Chapter Opening Question ?

Water molecules have a permanent electric dipole moment: One end of the molecule has a positive charge and the other end has a negative charge. These ends attract negative and positive ions, respectively, holding the ions apart in solution. Water is less effective as a solvent for materials whose molecules do not ionize (called *nonionic* substances), such as oils.

Answers to Test Your Understanding Questions

21.1 Answers: (a) the plastic rod weighs more, (b) the glass rod weighs less, (c) the fur weighs a little less, (d) the silk weighs a little less The plastic rod gets a negative charge by taking electrons from the fur, so the rod weighs a little more and the fur weighs a little less after the rubbing. By contrast, the glass rod gets a positive charge by giving electrons to the silk. Hence, after they are rubbed together, the glass rod weighs a little less and the silk weighs a little more. The weight change is *very* small: The number of electrons transferred is a small fraction of a mole, and a mole of electrons has a mass of only $(6.02 \times 10^{23}\text{ electrons})(9.11 \times 10^{-31}\text{ kg/electron}) = 5.48 \times 10^{-7}\text{ kg} = 0.548$ milligram!

21.2 Answers: (a) (i), (b) (ii) Before the two spheres touch, the negatively charged sphere exerts a repulsive force on the electrons in the other sphere, causing zones of positive and negative induced charge (see Fig. 21.7b). The positive zone is closer to the negatively charged sphere than the negative zone, so there is a net force of attraction that pulls the spheres together, like the comb and insulator in Fig. 21.8b. Once the two metal spheres touch, some of the excess electrons on the negatively charged sphere will flow onto the other sphere (because metals are conductors). Then both spheres will have a net negative charge and will repel each other.

21.3 Answer: (iv) The force exerted by q_1 on Q is still as in Example 21.4. The magnitude of the force exerted by q_2 on Q is still equal to $F_{1\text{ on }Q}$, but the direction of the force is now *toward* q_2 at an angle α below the x-axis. Hence the x-components of the two forces cancel while the (negative) y-components add together, and the total electric force is in the negative y-direction.

21.4 Answers: (a) (ii), (b) (i) The electric field $\vec{E}$ produced by a positive point charge points directly away from the charge (see Fig. 21.18a) and has a magnitude that depends on the distance r from the charge to the field point. Hence a second, negative point charge $q < 0$ will feel a force $\vec{F} = q\vec{E}$ that points directly toward the positive charge and has a magnitude that depends on the distance r between the two charges. If the negative charge moves directly toward the positive charge, the direction of the force remains the same (along the line of the negative charge's motion) but the force magnitude increases as the distance r decreases. If the negative charge moves in a circle around the positive charge, the force magnitude stays the same (because the distance r is constant) but the force direction changes (when the negative charge is on the right side of the positive charge, the force is to the left; when the negative charge is on the left side of the positive charge, the force is to the right).

21.5 Answer: (iv) Think of a pair of segments of length dy, one at coordinate $y > 0$ and the other at coordinate $-y < 0$. The upper segment has a positive charge and produces an electric field $d\vec{E}$ at P that points away from the segment, so this $d\vec{E}$ has a positive x-component and a negative y-component, like the vector $d\vec{E}$ in Fig. 21.25. The lower segment has the same amount of negative charge. It produces a $d\vec{E}$ that has the same magnitude but points *toward* the lower segment, so it has a negative x-component and a negative y-component. By symmetry, the two x-components are equal but opposite, so they cancel. Thus the total electric field has only a negative y-component.

21.6 Answer: yes If the field lines are straight, $\vec{E}$ must point in the same direction throughout the region. Hence the force $\vec{F} = q\vec{E}$ on a particle of charge q is always in the same direction. A particle released from rest accelerates in a straight line the direction of $\vec{F}$, and so its trajectory is a straight line that will be along a field line.

21.7 Answer: (ii) Equations (21.17) and (21.18) tell is that the potential energy for a dipole in an electric field is $U = -\vec{p} \cdot \vec{E} = -pE\cos\phi$, where ϕ is the angle between the directions of $\vec{p}$ and $\vec{E}$. If $\vec{p}$ and $\vec{E}$ point in opposite directions, so that $\phi = 180°$, we have $\cos\phi = -1$ and $U = +pE$. This is the maximum value that U can have. From our discussion of energy diagrams in Section 7.5, it follows that this is a situation of unstable equilibrium.

Another way to see this is from Eq. (21.15), which tells us that the magnitude of the torque on an electric dipole is $\tau = pE\sin\phi$.

This is zero if $\phi = 180°$, so there is no torque, and if left undisturbed the dipole will not rotate. However, if the dipole is disturbed slightly so that ϕ is a little less than $180°$, there will be a nonzero torque that tries to rotate the dipole toward $\phi = 0$ so that $\vec{p}$ and $\vec{E}$ point in the same direction. Hence if the dipole is disturbed from the equilibrium orientation at $\phi = 180°$, it moves farther away from that orientation—which is the hallmark of unstable equilbrium.

You can show that the situation in which $\vec{p}$ and $\vec{E}$ point in the same direction $(\phi = 0)$ is a case of *stable* equilibrium: The potential energy is minimum, and if the dipole is displaced slightly there is a torque that tries to return it to the original orientation (a *restoring* torque).

PROBLEMS

For instructor-assigned homework, go to **www.masteringphysics.com**

Discussion Questions

Q21.1. If you peel two strips of transparent tape off the same roll and immediately let them hang near each other, they will repel each other. If you then stick the sticky side of one to the shiny side of the other and rip them apart, they will attract each other. Give a plausible explanation, involving transfer of electrons between the strips of tape, for this sequence of events.

Q21.2. Two metal spheres are hanging from nylon threads. When you bring the spheres close to each other, they tend to attract. Based on this information alone, discuss all the possible ways that the spheres could be charged. Is it possible that after the spheres touch, they will cling together? Explain.

Q21.3. The electric force between two charged particles becomes weaker with increasing distance. Suppose instead that the electric force were *independent* of distance. In this case, would a charged comb still cause a neutral insulator to become polarized as in Fig. 21.8? Why or why not? Would the neutral insulator still be attracted to the comb? Again, why or why not?

Q21.4. Your clothing tends to cling together after going through the dryer. Why? Would you expect more or less clinging if all your clothing were made of the same material (say, cotton) than if you dried different kinds of clothing together? Again, why? (You may want to experiment with your next load of laundry.)

Q21.5. An uncharged metal sphere hangs from a nylon thread. When a positively charged glass rod is brought close to the metal sphere, the sphere is drawn toward the rod. But if the sphere touches the rod, it suddenly flies away from the rod. Explain why the sphere is first attracted and then repelled.

Q21.6. The free electrons in a metal are gravitationally attracted toward the earth. Why, then, don't they all settle to the bottom of the conductor, like sediment settling to the bottom of a river?

Q21.7. Some of the free electrons in a good conductor (such as a piece of copper) move at speeds of 10^6 m/s or faster. Why don't these electrons fly out of the conductor completely?

Q21.8. Good electrical conductors, such as metals, are typically good conductors of heat; electrical insulators, such as wood, are typically poor conductors of heat. Explain why there should be a relationship between electrical conduction and heat conduction in these materials.

Q21.9. Defend this statement: "If there were only one electrically charged particle in the entire universe, the concept of electric charge would be meaningless."

Q21.10. Two identical metal objects are mounted on insulating stands. Describe how you could place charges of opposite sign but exactly equal magnitude on the two objects.

Q21.11. You can use plastic food wrap to cover a container by stretching the material across the top and pressing the overhanging material against the sides. What makes it stick? (*Hint:* The answer involves the electric force.) Does the food wrap stick to itself with equal tenacity? Why or why not? Does it work with metallic containers? Again, why or why not?

Q21.12. If you walk across a nylon rug and then touch a large metal object such as a doorknob, you may get a spark and a shock. Why does this tend to happen more on dry days than on humid days? (*Hint:* See Fig. 21.31.) Why are you less likely to get a shock if you touch a *small* metal object, such as a paper clip?

Q21.13. You have a negatively charged object. How can you use it to place a net negative charge on an insulated metal sphere? To place a net positive charge on the sphere?

Q21.14. When two point charges of equal mass and charge are released on a frictionless table, each has an initial acceleration a_0. If instead you keep one fixed and release the other one, what will be its initial acceleration: a_0, $2a_0$, or $a_0/2$? Explain.

Q21.15. A point charge of mass m and charge Q and another point charge of mass m but charge $2Q$ are released on a frictionless table. If the charge Q has an initial acceleration a_0, what will be the acceleration of $2Q$: a_0, $2a_0$, $4a_0$, $a_0/2$, or $a_0/4$? Explain.

Q21.16. A proton is placed in a uniform electric field and then released. Then an electron is placed at this same point and released. Do these two particles experience the same force? The same acceleration? Do they move in the same direction when released?

Q21.17. In Example 21.1 (Section 21.3) we saw that the electric force between two α particles is of the order of 10^{35} times as strong as the gravitational force. So why do we readily feel the gravity of the earth but no electrical force from it?

Q21.18. What similarities do electrical forces have with gravitational forces? What are the most significant differences?

Q21.19. At a distance R from a point charge its electric field is E_0. At what distance (in terms of R) from the point charge would the electric field be $\frac{1}{3}E_0$

Q21.20. Atomic nuclei are made of protons and neutrons. This shows that there must be another kind of interaction in addition to gravitational and electric forces. Explain.

Q21.21. Sufficiently strong electric fields can cause atoms to become positively ionized—that is, to lose one or more electrons. Explain how this can happen. What determines how strong the field must be to make this happen?

Q21.22. The electric fields at point P due to the positive charges q_1 and q_2 are shown in Fig. 21.35. Does the fact that they cross each other violate the statement in Section 21.6 that electric field lines never cross? Explain.

Figure **21.35**
Question Q21.22.

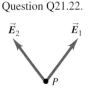

Q21.23. The air temperature and the velocity of the air have different values at different places in the earth's atmosphere. Is the air velocity a vector field? Why or why not? Is the air temperature a vector field? Again, why or why not?

Exercises

Section 21.3 Coulomb's Law

21.1. Excess electrons are placed on a small lead sphere with mass 8.00 g so that its net charge is -3.20×10^{-9} C. (a) Find the number of excess electrons on the sphere. (b) How many excess electrons are there per lead atom? The atomic number of lead is 82, and its atomic mass is 207 g/mol.

21.2. Lightning occurs when there is a flow of electric charge (principally electrons) between the ground and a thundercloud. The maximum rate of charge flow in a lightning bolt is about 20,000 C/s; this lasts for 100 μs or less. How much charge flows between the ground and the cloud in this time? How many electrons flow during this time?

21.3. Estimate how many electrons there are in your body. Make any assumptions you feel are necessary, but clearly state what they are. (*Hint:* Most of the atoms in your body have equal numbers of electrons, protons, and neutrons.) What is the combined charge of all these electrons?

21.4. Particles in a Gold Ring.   You have a pure (24-karat) gold ring with mass 17.7 g. Gold has an atomic mass of 197 g/mol and an atomic number of 79. (a) How many protons are in the ring, and what is their total positive charge? (b) If the ring carries no net charge, how many electrons are in it?

21.5. An average human weighs about 650 N. If two such generic humans each carried 1.0 coulomb of excess charge, one positive and one negative, how far apart would they have to be for the electric attraction between them to equal their 650-N weight?

21.6. Two small spheres spaced 20.0 cm apart have equal charge. How many excess electrons must be present on each sphere if the magnitude of the force of repulsion between them is 4.57×10^{-21} N?

21.7. Two small plastic spheres are given positive electrical charges. When they are 15.0 cm apart, the repulsive force between them has magnitude 0.220 N. What is the charge on each sphere (a) if the two charges are equal and (b) if one sphere has four times the charge of the other?

21.8. Two small aluminum spheres, each having mass 0.0250 kg, are separated by 80.0 cm. (a) How many electrons does each sphere contain? (The atomic mass of aluminum is 26.982 g/mol, and its atomic number is 13.) (b) How many electrons would have to be removed from one sphere and added to the other to cause an attractive force between the spheres of magnitude 1.00×10^{4} N (roughly 1 ton)? Assume that the spheres may be treated as point charges. (c) What fraction of all the electrons in each sphere does this represent?

21.9. Two very small 8.55-g spheres, 15.0 cm apart from center to center, are charged by adding equal numbers of electrons to each of them. Disregarding all other forces, how many electrons would you have to add to each sphere so that the two spheres will accelerate at 25.0g when released? Which way will they accelerate?

21.10. (a) Assuming that only gravity is acting on it, how far does an electron have to be from a proton so that its acceleration is the same as that of a freely falling object at the earth's surface? (b) Suppose the earth were made only of protons but had the same size and mass it presently has. What would be the acceleration of an electron released at the surface? Is it necessary to consider the gravitational attraction as well as the electrical force? Why or why not?

21.11. In an experiment in space, one proton is held fixed and another proton is released from rest a distance of 2.50 mm away. (a) What is the initial acceleration of the proton after it is released? (b) Sketch qualitative (no numbers!) acceleration–time and velocity–time graphs of the released proton's motion.

21.12. A negative charge $-0.550\ \mu$C exerts an upward 0.200-N force on an unknown charge 0.300 m directly below it. (a) What is the unknown charge (magnitude and sign)? (b) What are the magnitude and direction of the force that the unknown charge exerts on the -0.550-μC charge?

21.13. Three point charges are arranged on a line. Charge $q_3 = +5.00$ nC and is at the origin. Charge $q_2 = -3.00$ nC and is at $x = +4.00$ cm. Charge q_1 is at $x = +2.00$ cm. What is q_1 (magnitude and sign) if the net force on q_3 is zero?

21.14. In Example 21.4, suppose the point charge on the y-axis at $y = -0.30$ m has negative charge $-2.0\ \mu$C, and the other charges remain the same. Find the magnitude and direction of the net force on Q. How does your answer differ from that in Example 21.3? Explain the differences.

21.15. In Example 21.3, calculate the net force on charge q_1.

21.16. In Example 21.4, what is the net force (magnitude and direction) on charge q_1 exerted by the other two charges?

21.17. Three point charges are arranged along the x-axis. Charge $q_1 = +3.00\ \mu$C is at the origin, and charge $q_2 = -5.00\ \mu$C is at $x = 0.200$ m. Charge $q_3 = -8.00\ \mu$C. Where is q_3 located if the net force on q_1 is 7.00 N in the $-x$-direction?

21.18. Repeat Exercise 21.17, for $q_3 = +8.00\ \mu$C.

21.19. Two point charges are located on the y-axis as follows: charge $q_1 = -1.50$ nC at $y = -0.600$ m, and charge $q_2 = +3.20$ nC at the origin $(y = 0)$. What is the total force (magnitude and direction) exerted by these two charges on a third charge $q_3 = +5.00$ nC located at $y = -0.400$ m?

21.20. Two point charges are placed on the x-axis as follows: Charge $q_1 = +4.00$ nC is located at $x = 0.200$ m, and charge $q_2 = +5.00$ nC is at $x = -0.300$ m. What are the magnitude and direction of the total force exerted by these two charges on a negative point charge $q_3 = -6.00$ nC that is placed at the origin?

21.21. A positive point charge q is placed on the $+y$-axis at $y = a$, and a negative point charge $-q$ is placed on the $-y$-axis at $y = -a$. A negative point charge $-Q$ is located at some point on the $+x$-axis. (a) In a free-body diagram, show the forces that act on the charge $-Q$. (b) Find the x- and y-components of the net force that the two charges q and $-q$ exert on $-Q$. (Your answer should involve only k, q, Q, a and the coordinate x of the third charge.) (c) What is the net force on the charge $-Q$ when it is at the origin $(x = 0)$? (d) Graph the y-component of the net force on the charge $-Q$ as a function of x for values of x between $-4a$ and $+4a$.

21.22. Two positive point charges q are placed on the y-axis at $y = a$ and $y = -a$. A negative point charge $-Q$ is located at some point on the $+x$-axis. (a) In a free-body diagram, show the forces that act on the charge $-Q$. (b) Find the x- and y-components of the net force that the two positive charges exert on $-Q$. (Your answer should involve only k, q, Q, a and the coordinate x of the third charge.) (c) What is the net force on the charge $-Q$ when it is at the origin $(x = 0)$? (d) Graph the x-component of the net force on the charge $-Q$ as a function of x for values of x between $-4a$ and $+4a$.

21.23. Four identical charges Q are placed at the corners of a square of side L. (a) In a free-body diagram, show all of the forces that act on one of the charges. (b) Find the magnitude and direction of the total force exerted on one charge by the other three charges.

21.24. Two charges, one of 2.50 μC and the other of -3.50 μC, are placed on the x-axis, one at the origin and the other at $x = 0.600$ m, as shown in Fig. 21.36. Find the position on the x-axis where the net force on a small charge $+q$ would be zero.

Figure **21.36** Exercise 21.24.

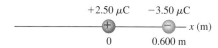

Section 21.4 Electric Field and Electric Forces

21.25. A proton is placed in a uniform electric field of 2.75 $\times$ 10^3 N/C. Calculate: (a) the magnitude of the electric force felt by the proton; (b) the proton's acceleration; (c) the proton's speed after 1.00 μs in the field, assuming it starts from rest.

21.26. A particle has charge -3.00 nC. (a) Find the magnitude and direction of the electric field due to this particle at a point 0.250 m directly above it. (b) At what distance from this particle does its electric field have a magnitude of 12.0 N/C?

21.27. A proton is traveling horizontally to the right at 4.50 $\times$ 10^6 m/s. (a) Find the magnitude and direction of the weakest electric field that can bring the proton uniformly to rest over a distance of 3.20 cm. (b) How much time does it take the proton to stop after entering the field? (c) What minimum field (magnitude and direction) would be needed to stop an electron under the conditions of part (a)?

21.28. An electron is released from rest in a uniform electric field. The electron accelerates vertically upward, traveling 4.50 m in the first 3.00 μs after it is released. (a) What are the magnitude and direction of the electric field? (b) Are we justified in ignoring the effects of gravity? Justify your answer quantitatively.

21.29. (a) What must the charge (sign and magnitude) of a 1.45-g particle be for it to remain stationary when placed in a downward-directed electric field of magnitude 650 N/C? (b) What is the magnitude of an electric field in which the electric force on a proton is equal in magnitude to its weight?

21.30. (a) What is the electric field of an iron nucleus at a distance of 6.00 $\times$ 10^{-10} m from the nucleus? The atomic number of iron is 26. Assume that the nucleus may be treated as a point charge. (b) What is the electric field of a proton at a distance of 5.29 $\times$ 10^{-11} m from the proton? (This is the radius of the electron orbit in the Bohr model for the ground state of the hydrogen atom.)

21.31. Two point charges are separated by 25.0 cm (Fig. 21.37). Find the net electric field these charges produce at (a) point A and

Figure **21.37** Exercise 21.31.

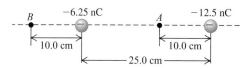

(b) point B. (c) What would be the manitude and direction of the electric force this combination of charges would produce on a proton at A?

21.32. Electric Field of the Earth. The earth has a net electric charge that causes a field at points near its surface equal to 150 N/C and directed in toward the center of the earth. (a) What magnitude and sign of charge would a 60-kg human have to acquire to overcome his or her weight by the force exerted by the earth's electric field? (b) What would be the force of repulsion between two people each with the charge calculated in part (a) and separated by a distance of 100 m? Is use of the earth's electric field a feasible means of flight? Why or why not?

21.33. An electron is projected with an initial speed $v_0 = 1.60 \times 10^6$ m/s into the uniform field between the parallel plates in Fig. 21.38. Assume that the field between the plates is uniform and directed vertically downward, and that the field outside the plates is zero. The electron enters the field at a point midway between the plates. (a) If the electron just misses the upper plate as it emerges from the field, find the magnitude of the electric field. (b) Suppose that in Fig. 21.38 the electron is replaced by a proton with the same initial speed v_0. Would the proton hit one of the plates? If the proton would not hit one of the plates, what would be the magnitude and direction of its vertical displacement as it exits the region between the plates? (c) Compare the paths traveled by the electron and the proton and explain the differences. (d) Discuss whether it is reasonable to ignore the effects of gravity for each particle.

Figure **21.38**
Exercise 21.33.

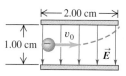

21.34. Point charge $q_1 = -5.00$ nC is at the origin and point charge $q_2 = +3.00$ nC is on the x-axis at $x = 3.00$ cm. Point P is on the y-axis at $y = 4.00$ cm. (a) Calculate the electric fields $\vec{E}_1$ and $\vec{E}_2$ at point P due to the charges q_1 and q_2. Express your results in terms of unit vectors (see Example 21.6). (b) Use the results of part (a) to obtain the resultant field at P, expressed in unit vector form.

21.35. In Exercise 21.33, what is the speed of the electron as it emerges from the field?

21.36. (a) Calculate the magnitude and direction (relative to the $+x$-axis) of the electric field in Example 21.6. (b) A -2.5-nC point charge is placed at the point P in Fig. 21.19. Find the magnitude and direction of (i) the force that the -8.0-nC charge at the origin exerts on this charge and (ii) the force that this charge exerts on the -8.0-nC charge at the origin.

21.37. (a) For the electron in Examples 21.7 and 21.8, compare the weight of the electron to the magnitude of the electric force on the electron. Is it appropriate to ignore the gravitational force on the electron in these examples? Explain. (b) A particle with charge $+e$ is placed at rest between the charged plates in Fig. 21.20. What must the mass of this object be if it is to remain at rest? Give your answer in kilograms and in multiples of the electron mass. (c) Does the answer to part (b) depend on where between the plates the object is placed? Why or why not?

21.38. A uniform electric field exists in the region between two oppositely charged plane parallel plates. A proton is released from rest at the surface of the positively charged plate and strikes the surface of the opposite plate, 1.60 cm distant from the first, in a time interval of 1.50×10^{-6} s. (a) Find the magnitude of the electric field. (b) Find the speed of the proton when it strikes the negatively charged plate.

21.39. A point charge is at the origin. With this point charge as the source point, what is the unit vector $\hat{r}$ in the direction of (a) the field point at $x = 0$, $y = -1.35$ m; (b) the field point at $x = 12.0$ cm, $y = 12.0$ cm; (c) the field point at $x = -1.10$ m, $y = 2.60$ m? Express your results in terms of the unit vectors $\hat{\imath}$ and $\hat{\jmath}$.

21.40. A $+8.75$-μC point charge is glued down on a horizontal frictionless table. It is tied to a -6.50-μC point charge by a light, nonconducting 2.50-cm wire. A uniform electric field of magnitude 1.85×10^8 N/C is directed parallel to the wire, as shown in Fig. 21.39. (a) Find the tension in the wire. (b) What would the tension be if both charges were negative?

Figure **21.39** Exercise 21.40.

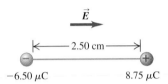

$\vec{E}$

$\longleftarrow$ 2.50 cm $\longrightarrow$

$-6.50\ \mu$C $8.75\ \mu$C

21.41. (a) An electron is moving east in a uniform electric field of 1.50 N/C directed to the west. At point A, the velocity of the electron is 4.50×10^5 m/s toward the east. What is the speed of the electron when it reaches point B, 0.375 m east of point A? (b) A proton is moving in the uniform electric field of part (a). At point A, the velocity of the proton is 1.90×10^4 m/s, east. What is the speed of the proton at point B?

21.42. Electric Field in the Nucleus. Protons in the nucleus are of the order of 10^{-15} m (1 fm) apart. (a) What is the magnitude of the electric field produced by a proton at a distance of 1.50 fm from it? (b) How does this field compare in magnitude to the field in Example 21.7?

Section 21.5 Electric-Field Calculations

21.43. Two positive point charges q are placed on the x-axis, one at $x = a$ and one at $x = -a$. (a) Find the magnitude and direction of the electric field at $x = 0$. (b) Derive an expression for the electric field at points on the x-axis. Use your result to graph the x-component of the electric field as a function of x, for values of x between $-4a$ and $+4a$.

21.44. Two particles having charges $q_1 = 0.500$ nC and $q_2 = 8.00$ nC are separated by a distance of 1.20 m. At what point along the line connecting the two charges is the total electric field due to the two charges equal to zero?

21.45. A $+2.00$-nC point charge is at the origin, and a second -5.00-nC point charge is on the x-axis at $x = 0.800$ m. (a) Find the electric field (magnitude and direction) at each of the following points on the x-axis: (i) $x = 0.200$ m; (ii) $x = 1.20$ m; (iii) $x = -0.200$ m. (b) Find the net electric force that the two charges would exert on an electron placed at each point in part (a).

21.46. Repeat Exercise 21.44, but now let $q_1 = -4.00$ nC.

21.47. Three negative point charges lie along a line as shown in Fig. 21.40. Find the magnitude and direction of the electric field this combination of charges produces at point P, which lies 6.00 cm. from the -2.00-μC charge measured perpendiular to the line connecting the three charges.

21.48. A positive point charge q is placed at $x = a$, and a negative point charge $-q$ is placed at $x = -a$. (a) Find the magnitude and direction of the electric field at $x = 0$.

Figure **21.40**
Exercise 21.47.

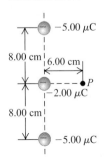

$-5.00\ \mu$C

8.00 cm 6.00 cm

$-2.00\ \mu$C P

8.00 cm

$-5.00\ \mu$C

(b) Derive an expression for the electric field at points on the x-axis. Use your result to graph the x-component of the electric field as a function of x, for values of x between $-4a$ and $+4a$.

21.49. In a rectangular coordinate system a positive point charge $q = 6.00 \times 10^{-9}$ C is placed at the point $x = +0.150$ m, $y = 0$, and an identical point charge is placed at $x = -0.150$ m, $y = 0$. Find the x- and y-components, the magnitude, and the direction of the electric field at the following points: (a) the origin; (b) $x = 0.300$ m, $y = 0$; (c) $x = 0.150$ m, $y = -0.400$ m; (d) $x = 0$, $y = 0.200$ m.

21.50. A point charge $q_1 = -4.00$ nC is at the point $x = 0.600$ m, $y = 0.800$ m, and a second point charge $q_2 = +6.00$ nC is at the point $x = 0.600$ m, $y = 0$. Calculate the magnitude and direction of the net electric field at the origin due to these two point charges.

21.51. Repeat Exercise 21.49 for the case where the point charge at $x = +0.150$ m, $y = 0$ is positive and the other is negative, each with magnitude 6.00×10^{-9} C.

21.52. A very long, straight wire has charge per unit length 1.50×10^{-10} C/m. At what distance from the wire is the electric-field magnitude equal to 2.50 N/C?

21.53. Positive electric charge is distributed along the y-axis with charge per unit length λ. (a) Consider the case where charge is distributed only between the points $y = a$ and $y = -a$. For points on the $+x$-axis, graph the x-component of the electric field as a function of x for values of x between $x = a/2$ and $x = 4a$. (b) Consider instead the case where charge is distributed along the entire y-axis with the same charge per unit length λ. Using the same graph as in part (a), plot the x-component of the electric field as a function of x for values of x between $x = a/2$ and $x = 4a$. Label which graph refers to which situation.

21.54. A straight, nonconducting plastic wire 8.50 cm long carries a charge density of $+175$ nC/m distributed uniformly along its length. It is lying on a horizontal tabletop. (a) Find the magnitude and direction of the electric field this wire produces at a point 6.00 cm directly above its midpoint. (b) If the wire is now bent into a circle lying flat on the table, find the magnitude and direction of the electric field it produces at a point 6.00 cm directly above its center.

21.55. A ring-shaped conductor with radius $a = 2.50$ cm has a total positive charge $Q = +0.125$ nC uniformly distributed around it, as shown in Fig. 21.24. The center of the ring is at the origin of coordinates O. (a) What is the electric field (magnitude and direction) at point P, which is on the x-axis at $x = 40.0$ cm? (b) A point charge $q = -2.50$ μC is placed at the point P described in part (a). What are the magnitude and direction of the force exerted by the charge q on the ring?

21.56. A charge of -6.50 nC is spread uniformly over the surface of one face of a nonconducting disk of radius 1.25 cm. (a) Find the magnitude and direction of the electric field this disk produces at a point P on the axis of the disk a distance of 2.00 cm from its center. (b) Suppose that the charge were all pushed away from the center and distributed uniformly on the outer rim of the disk. Find the magnitude and direction of the electric field at point P. (c) If the charge is all brought to the center of the disk, find the magnitude and direction of the electric field at point P. (d) Why is the field in part (a) stronger than the field in part (b)? Why is the field in part (c) the strongest of the three fields?

21.57. Two horizontal, infinite, plane sheets of charge are separated by a distance d. The lower sheet has negative charge with uniform surface charge density $-\sigma < 0$. The upper sheet has positive charge with uniform surface charge density $\sigma > 0$. What is the electric field (magnitude, and direction if the field is nonzero) (a) above the upper sheet, (b) below the lower sheet, (c) between the sheets?

Section 21.6 Electric Field Lines

21.58. Infinite sheet A carries a positive uniform charge density σ, and sheet B, which is to the right of A and parallel to it, carries a uniform negative charge density -2σ. (a) Sketch the electric field lines for this pair of sheets. Include the region between the sheets as well as the regions to the left of A and to the right of B. (b) Repeat part (a) for the case in which sheet B carries a charge density of $+2\sigma$.

21.59. Suppose the charge shown in Fig. 21.29a is fixed in position. A small, positively charged particle is then placed at some point in the figure and released. Will the trajectory of the particle follow an electric field line? Why or why not? Suppose instead that the particle is placed at some point in Fig. 21.29b and released (the positive and negative charges shown in the figure are fixed in position). Will its trajectory follow an electric field line? Again, why or why not? Explain any differences between your answers for the two different situations.

21.60. Sketch the electric field lines for a disk of radius R with a positive uniform surface charge density σ. Use what you know about the electric field very close to the disk and very far from the disk to make your sketch.

21.61. (a) Sketch the electric field lines for an infinite line of charge. You may find it helpful to show the field lines in a plane containing the line of charge in one sketch and the field lines in a plane perpendicular to the line of charge in a second sketch. (b) Explain how your sketches show (i) that the magnitude E of the electric field depends only on the distance r from the line of charge and (ii) that E decreases like $1/r$.

21.62. Figure 21.41 shows some of the electric field lines due to three point charges arranged along the vertical axis. All three charges have the same magnitude. (a) What are the signs of the three charges? Explain your reasoning. (b) At what point(s) is the magnitude of the electric field the smallest? Explain your reasoning. Explain how the fields produced by each individual point charge combine to give a small net field at this point or points.

Figure **21.41** Exercise 21.62.

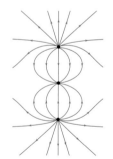

Section 21.7 Electric Dipoles

21.63. Point charges $q_1 = -4.5$ nC and $q_2 = +4.5$ nC are separated by 3.1 mm, forming an electric dipole. (a) Find the electric dipole moment (magnitude and direction). (b) The charges are in a uniform electric field whose direction makes an angle of $36.9°$ with the line connecting the charges. What is the magnitude of this field if the torque exerted on the dipole has magnitude 7.2×10^{-9} N·m?

21.64. The ammonia molecule (NH_3) has a dipole moment of 5.0×10^{-30} C·m. Ammonia molecules in the gas phase are placed in a uniform electric field $\vec{E}$ with magnitude 1.6×10^6 N/C. (a) What is the change in electric potential energy when the dipole moment of a molecule changes its orientation with respect to $\vec{E}$ from parallel to perpendicular? (b) At what absolute temperature T

is the average translational kinetic energy $\frac{3}{2}kT$ of a molecule equal to the change in potential energy calculated in part (a)? (*Note:* Above this temperature, thermal agitation prevents the dipoles from aligning with the electric field.)

21.65. In Example 21.15, the approximate result $E \cong p/2\pi\epsilon_0 y^3$ was derived for the electric field of a dipole at points on the dipole axis. (a) Rederive this result by putting the fractions in the expression for E_y over a common denominator, as described in Example 21.15. (b) Explain why the approximate result also gives the correct approximate expression for E_y for $y < 0$.

21.66. The dipole moment of the water molecule (H_2O) is 6.17×10^{-30} C·m. Consider a water molecule located at the origin whose dipole moment $\vec{p}$ points in the $+x$-direction. A chlorine ion (Cl^-), of charge -1.60×10^{-19} C, is located at $x = 3.00 \times 10^{-9}$ m. Find the magnitude and direction of the electric force that the water molecule exerts on the chlorine ion. Is this force attractive or repulsive? Assume that x is much larger than the separation d between the charges in the dipole, so that the approximate expression for the electric field along the dipole axis derived in Example 21.15 can be used.

21.67. Surface Tension. The surface of a polar liquid, such as water, can be viewed as a series of dipoles strung together in the stable arrangement in which the dipole moment vectors are parallel to the surface and all point in the same direction. Suppose now that something presses inward on the surface, distorting the dipoles as shown in Fig. 21.42. (a) Show that the two slanted dipoles exert a net upward force on the dipole between them, and hence oppose the downward external force. (b) Show that the dipoles attract each other and hence resist being separated. The force between dipoles opposes penetration of the liquid's surface and is a simple model for surface tension (see Section 14.3 and Fig. 14.15).

Figure **21.42** Exercise 21.67.

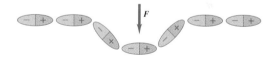

21.68. Consider the electric dipole of Example 21.15. (a) Derive an expression for the magnitude of the electric field produced by the dipole at a point on the x-axis in Fig. 21.34. What is the direction of this electric field? (b) How does the electric field at points on the x-axis depend on x when x is very large?

21.69. Torque on a Dipole. An electric dipole with dipole moment $\vec{p}$ is in a uniform electric field $\vec{E}$. (a) Find the orientations of the dipole for which the torque on the dipole is zero. (b) Which of the orientations in part (a) is stable, and which is unstable? (*Hint:* Consider a small displacement away from the equilibrium position and see what happens.) (c) Show that for the stable orientation in part (b), the dipole's own electric field tends to oppose the external field.

21.70. A dipole consisting of charges $\pm e$, 220 nm apart, is placed between two very large (essentially infinite) sheets carrying equal but opposite charge densities of $125\ \mu C/m^2$. (a) What is the maximum potential energy this dipole can have due to the sheets, and how should it be oriented relative to the sheets to attain this value? (b) What is the maximum torque the sheets can exert on the dipole, and how should it be oriented relative to the sheets to attain this value? (c) What net force do the two sheets exert on the dipole?

21.71. Three charges are at the corners of an isosceles triangle as shown in Fig. 21.43. The ± 5.00-μC charges form a dipole. (a) Find the force (magnitude and direction) the -10.00-μC charge exerts on the dipole. (b) For an axis perpendicular to the line connecting the ± 5.00-μC charges at the midpoint of this line, find the torque (magnitude and direction) exerted on the dipole by the -10.00-μC charge.

Figure **21.43** Exercise 21.71.

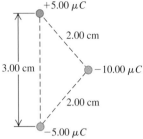

Problems

21.72. A charge $q_1 = +5.00$ nC is placed at the origin of an xy-coordinate system, and a charge $q_2 = -2.00$ nC is placed on the positive x-axis at $x = 4.00$ cm. (a) If a third charge $q_3 = +6.00$ nC is now placed at the point $x = 4.00$ cm, $y = 3.00$ cm, find the x- and y-components of the total force exerted on this charge by the other two. (b) Find the magnitude and direction of this force.

21.73. Two positive point charges Q are held fixed on the x-axis at $x = a$ and $x = -a$. A third positive point charge q, with mass m, is placed on the x-axis away from the origin at a coordinate x such that $|x| \ll a$. The charge q, which is free to move along the x-axis, is then released. (a) Find the frequency of oscillation of the charge q. (*Hint:* Review the definition of simple harmonic motion in Section 13.2. Use the binomial expansion $(1 + z)^n = 1 + nz + n(n-1)z^2/2 + \cdots$, valid for the case $|z| < 1$.) (b) Suppose instead that the charge q were placed on the y-axis at a coordinate y such that $|y| \ll a$, and then released. If this charge is free to move anywhere in the xy-plane, what will happen to it? Explain your answer.

21.74. Two identical spheres with mass m are hung from silk threads of length L, as shown in Fig. 21.44. Each sphere has the same charge, so $q_1 = q_2 = q$. The radius of each sphere is very small compared to the distance between the spheres, so they may be treated as point charges. Show that if the angle θ is small, the equilibrium separation d between the spheres is $d = (q^2 L/2\pi\epsilon_0 mg)^{1/3}$. (*Hint:* If θ is small, then $\tan\theta \cong \sin\theta$.)

21.75. Two small spheres with mass $m = 15.0$ g are hung by silk threads of length $L = 1.20$ m from a common point (Fig. 21.44). When the spheres are given equal quantities of negative charge, so that $q_1 = q_2 = q$, each thread hangs at $\theta = 25.0°$ from the vertical. (a) Draw a diagram showing the forces on each sphere. Treat the spheres as point charges. (b) Find the magnitude of q. (c) Both threads are now shortened to length $L = 0.600$ m, while the charges q_1 and q_2 remain unchanged. What new angle will each thread make with the vertical? (*Hint:* This part of the problem can be solved numerically by using trial values for θ and adjusting the values of θ until a self-consistent answer is obtained.)

21.76. Two identical spheres are each attached to silk threads of length $L = 0.500$ m and hung from a common point (Fig. 21.44). Each sphere has mass $m = 8.00$ g. The radius of each sphere is

Figure **21.44** Problems 21.74, 21.75, and 21.76.

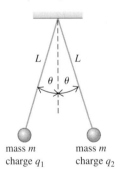

very small compared to the distance between the spheres, so they may be treated as point charges. One sphere is given positive charge q_1, and the other a different positive charge q_2; this causes the spheres to separate so that when the spheres are in equilibrium, each thread makes an angle $\theta = 20.0°$ with the vertical. (a) Draw a free-body diagram for each sphere when in equilibrium, and label all the forces that act on each sphere. (b) Determine the magnitude of the electrostatic force that acts on each sphere, and determine the tension in each thread. (c) Based on the information you have been given, what can you say about the magnitudes of q_1 and q_2? Explain your answers. (d) A small wire is now connected between the spheres, allowing charge to be transferred from one sphere to the other until the two spheres have equal charges; the wire is then removed. Each thread now makes an angle of $30.0°$ with the vertical. Determine the original charges. (*Hint:* The total charge on the pair of spheres is conserved.)

21.77. Sodium chloride (NaCl, ordinary table salt) is made up of positive sodium ions (Na^+) and negative chloride ions (Cl^-). (a) If a point charge with the same charge and mass as all the Na^+ ions in 0.100 mol of NaCl is 2.00 cm from a point charge with the same charge and mass as all the Cl^- ions, what is the magnitude of the attractive force between these two point charges? (b) If the positive point charge in part (a) is held in place and the negative point charge is released from rest, what is its initial acceleration? (See Appendix D for atomic masses.) (c) Does it seem reasonable that the ions in NaCl could be separated in this way? Why or why not? (In fact, when sodium chloride dissolves in water, it breaks up into Na^+ and Cl^- ions. However, in this situation there are additional electric forces exerted by the water molecules on the ions.)

21.78. Two point charges q_1 and q_2 are held in place 4.50 cm apart. Another point charge $Q = -1.75$ μC of mass 5.00 g is initially located 3.00 cm from each of these charges (Fig. 21.45) and released from rest. You observe that the initial acceleration of Q is 324 m/s² upward, parallel to the line connecting the two point charges. Find q_1 and q_2.

Figure **21.45** Problem 21.78.

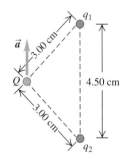

21.79. Three identical point charges q are placed at each of three corners of a square of side L. Find the magnitude and direction of the net force on a point charge $-3q$ placed (a) at the center of the square and (b) at the vacant corner of the square. In each case, draw a free-body diagram showing the forces exerted on the $-3q$ charge by each of the other three charges.

21.80. Three point charges are placed on the y-axis: a charge q at $y = a$, a charge $-2q$ at the origin, and a charge q at $y = -a$. Such an arrangement is called an electric quadrupole. (a) Find the magnitude and direction of the electric field at points on the positive x-axis. (b) Use the binomial expansion to find an approximate expression for the electric field valid for $x \gg a$. Contrast this behavior to that of the electric field of a point charge and that of the electric field of a dipole.

21.81. Strength of the Electric Force. Imagine two 1.0-g bags of protons, one at the earth's north pole and the other at the south pole. (a) How many protons are in each bag? (b) Calculate the gravitational attraction and the electrical repulsion that each bag exerts on the other. (c) Are the forces in part (b) large enough for you to feel if you were holding one of the bags?

21.82. Electric Force Within the Nucleus. Typical dimensions of atomic nuclei are of the order of 10^{-15} m (1 fm). (a) If two protons in a nucleus are 2.0 fm apart, find the magnitude of the electric force each one exerts on the other. Express the answer in newtons and in pounds. Would this force be large enough for a person to feel? (b) Since the protons repel each other so strongly, why don't they shoot out of the nucleus?

21.83. If Atoms Were Not Neutral . . . Because the charges on the electron and proton have the same absolute value, atoms are electrically neutral. Suppose this were not precisely true, and the absolute value of the charge of the electron were less than the charge of the proton by 0.00100%. (a) Estimate what the net charge of this textbook would be under these circumstances. Make any assumptions you feel are justified, but state clearly what they are. (*Hint:* Most of the atoms in this textbook have equal numbers of electrons, protons, and neutrons.) (b) What would be the magnitude of the electric force between two textbooks placed 5.0 m apart? Would this force be attractive or repulsive? Estimate what the acceleration of each book would be if the books were 5.0 m apart and there were no nonelectrical forces on them. (c) Discuss how the fact that ordinary matter is stable shows that the absolute values of the charges on the electron and proton must be identical to a *very* high level of accuracy.

21.84. Two tiny balls of mass m carry equal but opposite charges of magnitude q. They are tied to the same ceiling hook by light strings of length L. When a horizontal uniform electric field E is turned on, the balls hang with an angle θ between the strings (Fig. 21.46). (a) Which ball (the right or the left) is positive, and which is negative? (b) Find the angle θ between the strings in terms of E, q, m, and g. (c) As the electric field is gradually increased in strength, what does your result from part (b) give for the largest possible angle θ?

Figure **21.46** Problem 21.84.

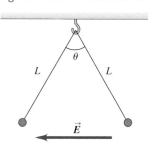

21.85. Two small, copper spheres each have radius 1.00 mm. (a) How many atoms does each sphere contain? (b) Assume that each copper atom contains 29 protons and 29 electrons. We know that electrons and protons have charges of exactly the same magnitude, but let's explore the effect of small differences (see also Problem 21.83). If the charge of a proton is $+e$ and the magnitude of the charge of an electron is 0.100% smaller, what is the net charge of each sphere and what force would one sphere exert on the other if they were separated by 1.00 m?

21.86. Operation of an Inkjet Printer. In an inkjet printer, letters are built up by squirting drops of ink at the paper from a rapidly moving nozzle. The ink drops, which have a mass of 1.4×10^{-8} g each, leave the nozzle and travel toward the paper at 20 m/s, passing through a charging unit that gives each drop a positive charge q by removing some electrons from it. The drops then pass between parallel deflecting plates 2.0 cm long where there is a uniform vertical electric field with magnitude 8.0×10^4 N/C. If a drop is to be deflected 0.30 mm by the time it reaches the end of the deflection plates, what magnitude of charge must be given to the drop?

21.87. A proton is projected into a uniform electric field that points vertically upward and has magnitude E. The initial velocity of the proton has a magnitude v_0 and is directed at an angle α below the horizontal. (a) Find the maximum distance h_{max} that the proton descends vertically below its initial elevation. You can ignore

gravitational forces. (b) After what horizontal distance d does the proton return to its original elevation? (c) Sketch the trajectory of the proton. (d) Find the numerical values of h_{max} and d if $E = 500$ N/C, $v_0 = 4.00 \times 10^5$ m/s, and $\alpha = 30.0°$.

21.88. A negative point charge $q_1 = -4.00$ nC is on the x-axis at $x = 0.60$ m. A second point charge q_2 is on the x-axis at $x = -1.20$ m. What must the sign and magnitude of q_2 be for the net electric field at the origin to be (a) 50.0 N/C in the $+x$-direction and (b) 50.0 N/C in the $-x$-direction?

21.89. Positive charge Q is distributed uniformly along the x-axis from $x = 0$ to $x = a$. A positive point charge q is located on the positive x-axis at $x = a + r$, a distance r to the right of the end of Q (Fig. 21.47). (a) Calculate the x- and y-components of the electric field produced by the charge distribution Q at points on the positive x-axis where $x > a$. (b) Calculate the force (magnitude and direction) that the charge distribution Q exerts on q. (c) Show that if $r \gg a$, the magnitude of the force in part (b) is approximately $Qq/4\pi\epsilon_0 r^2$. Explain why this result is obtained.

Figure **21.47** Problem 21.89.

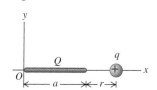

21.90. Positive charge Q is distributed uniformly along the positive y-axis between $y = 0$ and $y = a$. A negative point charge $-q$ lies on the positive x-axis, a distance x from the origin (Fig. 21.48). (a) Calculate the x- and y-components of the electric field produced by the charge distribution Q at points on the positive x-axis. (b) Calculate the x- and y-components of the force that the charge distribution Q exerts on q. (c) Show that if $x \gg a$, $F_x \cong -Qq/4\pi\epsilon_0 x^2$ and $F_y \cong +Qqa/8\pi\epsilon_0 x^3$. Explain why this result is obtained.

Figure **21.48** Problem 21.90.

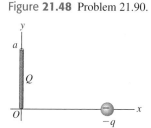

21.91. A charged line like that shown in Fig. 21.25 extends from $y = 2.50$ cm to $y = -2.50$ cm. The total charge distributed uniformly along the line is -9.00 nC. (a) Find the electric field (magnitude and direction) on the x-axis at $x = 10.0$ cm. (b) Is the magnitude of the electric field you calculated in part (a) larger or smaller than the electric field 10.0 cm from a point charge that has the same total charge as this finite line of charge? In terms of the approximation used to derive $E = Q/4\pi\epsilon_0 x^2$ for a point charge from Eq. (21.9), explain why this is so. (c) At what distance x does the result for the finite line of charge differ by 1.0% from that for the point charge?

21.92. A Parallel Universe. Imagine a parallel universe in which the electric force has the same properties as in our universe but there is no gravity. In this parallel universe, the sun carries charge Q, the earth carries charge $-Q$, and the electric attraction between them keeps the earth in orbit. The earth in the parallel universe has the same mass, the same orbital radius, and the same orbital period as in our universe. Calculate the value of Q. (Consult Appendix F as needed.)

21.93. A uniformly charged disk like the disk in Fig. 21.26 has radius 2.50 cm and carries a total charge of 4.0×10^{-12} C. (a) Find the electric field (magnitude and direction) on the x-axis at $x = 20.0$ cm. (b) Show that for $x \gg R$, Eq. (21.11) becomes $E = Q/4\pi\epsilon_0 x^2$, where Q is the total charge on the disk. (c) Is the magnitude of the electric field you calculated in part (a) larger or smaller than the electric field 20.0 cm from a point charge that has the same total charge as this disk? In terms of the approximation used in part (b) to derive $E = Q/4\pi\epsilon_0 x^2$ for a point charge from Eq. (21.11), explain why this is so. (d) What is the percent difference between the electric fields produced by the finite disk and by a point charge with the same charge at $x = 20.0$ cm and at $x = 10.0$ cm?

21.94. (a) Let $f(x)$ be an even function of x so that $f(x) = f(-x)$. Show that $\int_{-a}^{a} f(x)\,dx = 2\int_{0}^{a} f(x)\,dx$. (*Hint:* Write the integral from $-a$ to a as the sum of the integral from $-a$ to 0 and the integral from 0 to a. In the first integral, make the change of variable $x' = -x$.) (b) Let $g(x)$ be an odd function of x so that $g(x) = -g(-x)$. Use the method given in the hint for part (a) to show that $\int_{-a}^{a} g(x)\,dx = 0$. (c) Use the result of part (b) to show why E_y in Example 21.11 (Section 21.5) is zero.

21.95. Positive charge $+Q$ is distributed uniformly along the $+x$-axis from $x = 0$ to $x = a$. Negative charge $-Q$ is distributed uniformly along the $-x$-axis from $x = 0$ to $x = -a$. (a) A positive point charge q lies on the positive y-axis, a distance y from the origin. Find the force (magnitude and direction) that the positive and negative charge distributions together exert on q. Show that this force is proportional to y^{-3} for $y \gg a$. (b) Suppose instead that the positive point charge q lies on the positive x-axis, a distance $x > a$ from the origin. Find the force (magnitude and direction) that the charge distribution exerts on q. Show that this force is proportional to x^{-3} for $x \gg a$.

21.96. Positive charge Q is uniformly distributed around a semicircle of radius a (Fig. 21.49). Find the electric field (magnitude and direction) at the center of curvature P.

Figure **21.49** Problem 21.96.

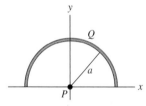

21.97. Negative charge $-Q$ is distributed uniformly around a quarter-circle of radius a that lies in the first quadrant, with the center of curvature at the origin. Find the x- and y-components of the net electric field at the origin.

21.98. A small sphere with mass m carries a positive charge q and is attached to one end of a silk fiber of length L. The other end of the fiber is attached to a large vertical insulating sheet that has a positive surface charge density σ. Show that when the sphere is in equilibrium, the fiber makes an angle equal to arctan $(q\sigma/2mg\epsilon_0)$ with the vertical sheet.

21.99. Two 1.20-m nonconducting wires meet at a right angle. One segment carries $+2.50\ \mu\text{C}$ of charge distributed uniformly along its length, and the other carries $-2.50\ \mu\text{C}$ distributed uniformly along it, as shown in Fig. 21.50. (a) Find the magnitude and direction of the electric field these wires produce at point P, which is 60.0 cm from each wire. (b) If an electron is released at P, what are the magnitude and direction of the net force that these wires exert on it?

Figure **21.50** Problem 21.99.

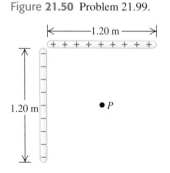

21.100. Two very large parallel sheets are 5.00 cm apart. Sheet A carries a uniform surface charge density of $-9.50\mu\text{C}/\text{m}^2$, and sheet B, which is to the right of A, carries a uniform charge of

$-11.6\ \mu\text{C}/\text{m}^2$. Assume the sheets are large enough to be treated as infinite. Find the magnitude and direction of the net electric field these sheets produce at a point (a) 4.00 cm to the right of sheet A; (b) 4.00 cm to the left of sheet A; (c) 4.00 cm to the right of sheet B.

21.101. Repeat Problem 21.100 for the case where sheet B is positive.

21.102. Two very large horizontal sheets are 4.25 cm apart and carry equal but opposite uniform surface charge densities of magnitude σ. You want to use these sheets to hold stationary in the region between them an oil droplet of mass 324 μg that carries an excess of five electrons. Assuming that the drop is in vacuum, (a) which way should the electric field between the plates point, and (b) what should σ be?

21.103. An infinite sheet with positive charge per unit area σ lies in the xy-plane. A second infinite sheet with negative charge per unit area $-\sigma$ lies in the yz-plane. Find the net electric field at all points that do not lie in either of these planes. Express your answer in terms of the unit vectors $\hat{\imath}$, $\hat{\jmath}$, and $\hat{k}$.

21.104. A thin disk with a circular hole at its center, called an *annulus*, has inner radius R_1 and outer radius R_2 (Fig. 21.51). The disk has a uniform positive surface charge density σ on its surface. (a) Determine the total electric charge on the annulus. (b) The annulus lies in the yz-plane, with its center at the origin. For an arbitrary point on the x-axis (the axis of the annulus), find the magnitude and direction of the electric field $\vec{E}$. Consider points both above and below the annulus in Fig. 21.51. (c) Show that at points on the x-axis that are sufficiently close to the origin, the magnitude of the electric field is approximately proportional to the distance between the center of the annulus and the point. How close is "sufficiently close"? (d) A point particle with mass m and negative charge $-q$ is free to move along the x-axis (but cannot move off the axis). The particle is originally placed at rest at $x = 0.01R_1$ and released. Find the frequency of oscillation of the particle. (*Hint:* Review Section 13.2. The annulus is held stationary.)

Figure **21.51** Problem 21.104.

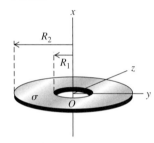

Challenge Problems

21.105. Three charges are placed as shown in Fig. 21.52. The magnitude of q_1 is 2.00 μC, but its sign and the value of the charge q_2 are not known. Charge q_3 is $+4.00\ \mu$C, and the net force $\vec{F}$ on q_3 is entirely in the negative x-direction. (a) Considering the different possible signs of q_1 and there are four possible force diagrams representing the forces $\vec{F}_1$ and $\vec{F}_2$ that q_1 and q_2 exert on q_3. Sketch these four possible force configurations. (b) Using the sketches from part (a) and the direction of $\vec{F}$, deduce the signs of the charges q_1 and q_2. (c) Calculate the magnitude of q_2. (d) Determine F, the magnitude of the net force on q_3.

Figure **21.52** Challenge Problem 21.105.

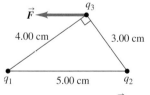

21.106. Two charges are placed as shown in Fig. 21.53. The magnitude of q_1 is 3.00 μC, but its sign and the value of the charge q_2 are not known. The direction of the net electric field $\vec{E}$ at point P is

entirely in the negative y-direction. (a) Considering the different possible signs of q_1 and q_2, there are four possible diagrams that could represent the electric fields $\vec{E}_1$ and $\vec{E}_2$ produced by q_1 and q_2. Sketch the four possible electric field configurations. (b) Using the sketches from part (a) and the direction of $\vec{E}$, deduce the signs of q_1 and q_2. (c) Determine the magnitude of $\vec{E}$.

Figure **21.53** Challenge Problem 21.106.

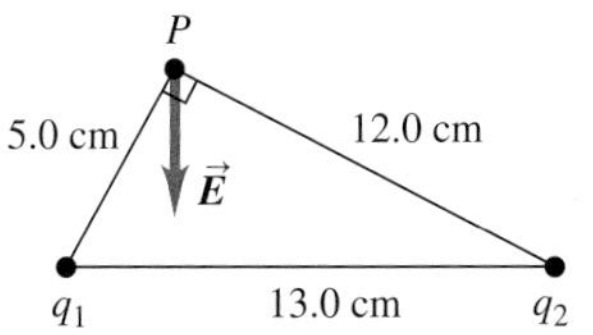

21.107. Two thin rods of length L lie along the x-axis, one between $x = a/2$ and $x = a/2 + L$ and the other between $x = -a/2$ and

$x = -a/2 - L$. Each rod has positive charge Q distributed uniformly along its length. (a) Calculate the electric field produced by the second rod at points along the positive x-axis. (b) Show that the magnitude of the force that one rod exerts on the other is

$$F = \frac{Q^2}{4\pi\epsilon_0 L^2}\ln\left[\frac{(a+L)^2}{a(a+2L)}\right]$$

(c) Show that if $a \gg L$, the magnitude of this force reduces to $F = Q^2/4\pi\epsilon_0 a^2$. (*Hint:* Use the expansion $\ln(1 + z) = z - z^2/2 + z^3/3 - \cdots$, valid for $|z| \ll 1$. Carry *all* expansions to at least order L^2/a^2.) Interpret this result.

22 GAUSS'S LAW

LEARNING GOALS

By studying this chapter, you will learn:

- How you can determine the amount of charge within a closed surface by examining the electric field on the surface.

- What is meant by electric flux, and how to calculate it.

- How Gauss's law relates the electric flux through a closed surface to the charge enclosed by the surface.

- How to use Gauss's law to calculate the electric field due to a symmetrical charge distribution.

- Where the charge is located on a charged conductor.

? This child acquires an electric charge by touching the charged metal sphere. The charged hairs on the child's head repel and stand out. If the child stands *inside* a large, charged metal sphere, will her hair stand on end?

O ften, there are both an easy way and a hard way to do a job; the easy way may involve nothing more than using the right tools. In physics, an important tool for simplifying problems is the *symmetry properties* of systems. Many physical systems have symmetry; for example, a cylindrical body doesn't look any different after you've rotated it around its axis, and a charged metal sphere looks just the same after you've turned it about any axis through its center.

Gauss's law is part of the key to using symmetry considerations to simplify electric-field calculations. For example, the field of a straight-line or plane-sheet charge distribution, which we derived in Section 21.5 using some fairly strenuous integrations, can be obtained in a few lines with the help of Gauss's law. But Gauss's law is more than just a way to make certain calculations easier. Indeed, it is a fundamental statement about the relationship between electric charges and electric fields. Among other things, Gauss's law can help us understand how electric charge distributes itself over conducting bodies.

Here's what Gauss's law is all about. Given any general distribution of charge, we surround it with an imaginary surface that encloses the charge. Then we look at the electric field at various points on this imaginary surface. Gauss's law is a relationship between the field at *all* the points on the surface and the total charge enclosed within the surface. This may sound like a rather indirect way of expressing things, but it turns out to be a tremendously useful relationship. Above and beyond its use as a calculational tool, Gauss's law can help us gain deeper insights into electric fields. We will make use of these insights repeatedly in the next several chapters as we pursue our study of electromagnetism.

22.1 Charge and Electric Flux

In Chapter 21 we asked the question, "Given a charge distribution, what is the electric field produced by that distribution at a point *P*?" We saw that the answer could be found by representing the distribution as an assembly of point charges,

The discussion of Gauss's law in this section is based on and inspired by the innovative ideas of Ruth W. Chabay and Bruce A. Sherwood in *Electric and Magnetic Interactions* (John Wiley & Sons, 1994).

each of which produces an electric field $\vec{E}$ given by Eq. (21.7). The total field at P is then the vector sum of the fields due to all the point charges.

But there is an alternative relationship between charge distributions and electric fields. To discover this relationship, let's stand the question of Chapter 21 on its head and ask, "If the electric field pattern is known in a given region, what can we determine about the charge distribution in that region?"

Here's an example. Consider the box shown in Fig. 22.1a, which may or may not contain electric charge. We'll imagine that the box is made of a material that has no effect on any electric fields; it's of the same breed as the massless rope and the frictionless incline. Better still, let the box represent an *imaginary* surface that may or may not enclose some charge. We'll refer to the box as a **closed surface** because it completely encloses a volume. How can you determine how much (if any) electric charge lies within the box?

Knowing that a charge distribution produces an electric field and that an electric field exerts a force on a test charge, you move a test charge q_0 around the vicinity of the box. By measuring the force $\vec{F}$ experienced by the test charge at different positions, you make a three-dimensional map of the electric field $\vec{E} = \vec{F}/q_0$ outside the box. In the case shown in Fig. 22.1b, the map turns out to be the same as that of the electric field produced by a positive point charge (Fig. 21.29a). From the details of the map, you can find the exact value of the point charge inside the box.

To determine the contents of the box, we actually need to measure $\vec{E}$ only on the *surface* of the box. In Fig. 22.2a there is a single positive point charge inside the box, and in Fig. 22.2b there are two such charges. The field patterns on the surfaces of the boxes are different in detail, but in both cases the electric field points out of the box. Figures 22.2c and 22.2d show cases with one and two negative point charges, respectively, inside the box. Again, the details of $\vec{E}$ on the surface of the box are different, but in both cases the field points into the box.

Activ
ONLINE
Physics

11.7   Electric Flux

22.1 How can you measure the charge inside a box without opening it?

(a) A box containing an unknown amount of charge

(b) Using a test charge outside the box to probe the amount of charge inside the box

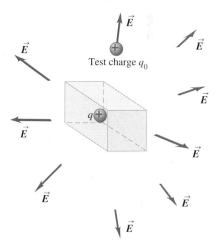

22.2 The electric field on the surface of boxes containing (a) a single positive point charge, (b) two positive point charges, (c) a single negative point charge, or (d) two negative point charges.

(a) Positive charge inside box, outward flux

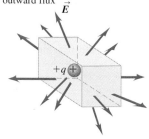

(b) Positive charges inside box, outward flux

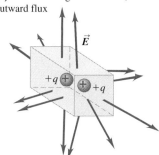

(c) Negative charge inside box, inward flux

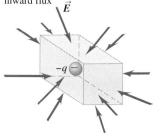

(d) Negative charges inside box, inward flux

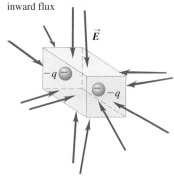

Electric Flux and Enclosed Charge

In Section 21.4 we mentioned the analogy between electric-field vectors and the velocity vectors of a fluid in motion. This analogy can be helpful, even though an electric field does not actually "flow." Using this analogy, in Figs. 22.2a and 22.2b, in which the electric field vectors point out of the surface, we say that there is an outward **electric flux.** (The word "flux" comes from a Latin word meaning "flow.") In Figs. 22.2c and 22.2d the $\vec{E}$ vectors point into the surface, and the electric flux is *inward.*

Figure 22.2 suggests a simple relationship: Positive charge inside the box goes with an outward electric flux through the box's surface, and negative charge inside goes with an inward electric flux. What happens if there is *zero* charge inside the box? In Fig. 22.3a the box is empty and $\vec{E} = 0$ everywhere, so there is no electric flux into or out of the box. In Fig. 22.3b, one positive and one negative point charge of equal magnitude are enclosed within the box, so the *net* charge inside the box is zero. There is an electric field, but it "flows into" the box on half of its surface and "flows out of" the box on the other half. Hence there is no *net* electric flux into or out of the box.

The box is again empty in Fig. 22.3c. However, there is charge present *outside* the box; the box has been placed with one end parallel to a uniformly charged infinite sheet, which produces a uniform electric field perpendicular to the sheet (as we learned in Example 21.12 of Section 21.5). On one end of the box, $\vec{E}$ points into the box; on the opposite end, $\vec{E}$ points out of the box; and on the sides, $\vec{E}$ is parallel to the surface and so points neither into nor out of the box. As in Fig. 22.3b, the inward electric flux on one part of the box exactly compensates for the outward electric flux on the other part. So in all of the cases shown in Fig. 22.3, there is no *net* electric flux through the surface of the box, and no *net* charge is enclosed in the box.

Figures 22.2 and 22.3 demonstrate a connection between the *sign* (positive, negative, or zero) of the *net* charge enclosed by a closed surface and the sense (outward, inward, or none) of the net electric flux through the surface. There is also a connection between the *magnitude* of the net charge inside the closed surface and the *strength* of the net "flow" of $\vec{E}$ over the surface. In both Figs. 22.4a and 22.4b there is a single point charge inside the box, but in Fig. 22.4b the magnitude of the charge is twice as great, and so $\vec{E}$ is everywhere twice as great in magnitude as in Fig. 22.4a. If we keep in mind the fluid-flow analogy, this means that the net outward electric flux is also twice as great in Fig. 22.4b as in Fig. 22.4a. This suggests that the net electric flux through the surface of the box is *directly proportional* to the magnitude of the net charge enclosed by the box.

22.3 Three cases in which there is zero *net* charge inside a box and no net electric flux through the surface of the box. (a) An empty box with $\vec{E} = 0$. (b) A box containing one positive and one equal-magnitude negative point charge. (c) An empty box immersed in a uniform electric field.

(a) No charge inside box, zero flux

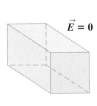

(b) Zero *net* charge inside box, inward flux cancels outward flux.

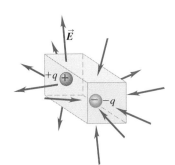

(c) No charge inside box, inward flux cancels outward flux.

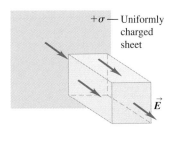

This conclusion is independent of the size of the box. In Fig. 22.4c the point charge $+q$ is enclosed by a box with twice the linear dimensions of the box in Fig.22.4a. The magnitude of the electric field of a point charge decreases with distance according to $1/r^2$, so the average magnitude of $\vec{E}$ on each face of the large box in Fig. 22.4c is just $\frac{1}{4}$ of the average magnitude on the corresponding face in Fig. 22.4a. But each face of the large box has exactly four times the area of the corresponding face of the small box. Hence the outward electric flux is the *same* for the two boxes if we *define* electric flux as follows: For each face of the box, take the product of the average perpendicular component of $\vec{E}$ and the area of that face; then add up the results from all faces of the box. With this definition the net electric flux due to a single point charge inside the box is independent of the size of the box and depends only on the net charge inside the box.

We have seen that there is a relationship between the net amount of charge inside a closed surface and the electric flux through that surface. For the special cases of a closed surface in the shape of a rectangular box and charge distributions made up of point charges or infinite charged sheets, we have found:

1. Whether there is a net outward or inward electric flux through a closed surface depends on the sign of the enclosed charge.
2. Charges *outside* the surface do not give a net electric flux through the surface.
3. The net electric flux is directly proportional to the net amount of charge enclosed within the surface but is otherwise independent of the size of the closed surface.

These observations are a qualitative statement of *Gauss's law.*

Do these observations hold true for other kinds of charge distributions and for closed surfaces of arbitrary shape? The answer to these questions will prove to be yes. But to explain why this is so, we need a precise mathematical statement of what we mean by electric flux. This is developed in the next section.

Test Your Understanding of Section 22.1   If all of the dimensions of the box in Fig. 22.2a are increased by a factor of 3, what effect will this change have on the electric flux through the box? (i) The flux will be $3^2 = 9$ times greater; (ii) the flux will be 3 times greater; (iii) the flux will be unchanged; (iv) the flux will be $\left(\frac{1}{3}\right)$ as great; (v) the flux will be $\left(\frac{1}{3}\right)^2 = \frac{1}{9}$ as great; (vi) not enough information is given to decide. ∎

22.2 Calculating Electric Flux

In the preceding section we introduced the concept of *electric flux*. Qualitatively, the electric flux through a surface is a description of whether the electric field $\vec{E}$ points into or out of the surface. We used this to give a rough qualitative statement of Gauss's law: The net electric flux through a closed surface is directly proportional to the net charge inside that surface. To be able to make full use of this law, we need to know how to *calculate* electric flux. To do this, let's again make use of the analogy between an electric field $\vec{E}$ and the field of velocity vectors $\vec{v}$ in a flowing fluid. (Again, keep in mind that this is only an analogy; an electric field is *not* a flow.)

Flux: Fluid-Flow Analogy

Figure 22.5 shows a fluid flowing steadily from left to right. Let's examine the volume flow rate dV/dt (in, say, cubic meters per second) through the wire rectangle with area A. When the area is perpendicular to the flow velocity $\vec{v}$ (Fig. 22.5a) and the flow velocity is the same at all points in the fluid, the volume flow rate dV/dt is the area A multiplied by the flow speed v:

$$\frac{dV}{dt} = vA$$

22.4 (a) A box enclosing a positive point charge $+q$. (b) Doubling the charge causes the magnitude of $\vec{E}$ to double, and it doubles the electric flux through the surface. (c) If the charge stays the same but the dimensions of the box are doubled, the flux stays the same. The magnitude of $\vec{E}$ on the surface decreases by a factor of $\frac{1}{4}$, but the area through which $\vec{E}$ "flows" increases by a factor of 4.

(a) A box containing a charge

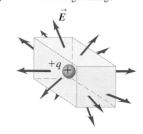

(b) Doubling the enclosed charge doubles the flux.

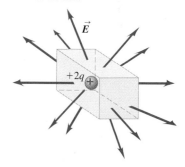

(c) Doubling the box dimensions *does not change* the flux.

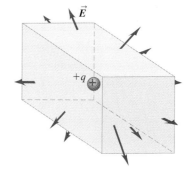

22.5 The volume flow rate of fluid through the wire rectangle (a) is vA when the area of the rectangle is perpendicular to $\vec{v}$ and (b) is $vA\cos\phi$ when the rectangle is tilted at an angle ϕ.

(a) A wire rectangle in a fluid

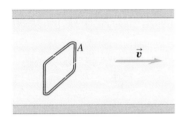

(b) The wire rectangle tilted by an angle ϕ

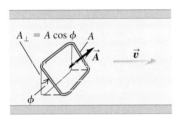

When the rectangle is tilted at an angle ϕ (Fig. 22.5b) so that its face is not perpendicular to $\vec{v}$, the area that counts is the silhouette area that we see when we look in the direction of $\vec{v}$. This area, which is outlined in red and labeled $A_\perp$ in Fig. 22.5b, is the *projection* of the area A onto a surface perpendicular to $\vec{v}$. Two sides of the projected rectangle have the same length as the original one, but the other two are foreshortened by a factor of $\cos\phi$, so the projected area $A_\perp$ is equal to $A\cos\phi$. Then the volume flow rate through A is

$$\frac{dV}{dt} = vA\cos\phi$$

If $\phi = 90°$, $dV/dt = 0$; the wire rectangle is edge-on to the flow, and no fluid passes through the rectangle.

Also, $v\cos\phi$ is the component of the vector $\vec{v}$ perpendicular to the plane of the area A. Calling this component $v_\perp$, we can rewrite the volume flow rate as

$$\frac{dV}{dt} = v_\perp A$$

We can express the volume flow rate more compactly by using the concept of *vector area $\vec{A}$*, a vector quantity with magnitude A and a direction perpendicular to the plane of the area we are describing. The vector area $\vec{A}$ describes both the size of an area and its orientation in space. In terms of $\vec{A}$, we can write the volume flow rate of fluid through the rectangle in Fig. 22.5b as a scalar (dot) product:

$$\frac{dV}{dt} = \vec{v} \cdot \vec{A}$$

Flux of a Uniform Electric Field

Using the analogy between electric field and fluid flow, we now define electric flux in the same way as we have just defined the volume flow rate of a fluid; we simply replace the fluid velocity $\vec{v}$ by the electric field $\vec{E}$. The symbol that we use for electric flux is Φ_E (the capital Greek letter phi; the subscript E is a reminder that this is *electric* flux). Consider first a flat area A perpendicular to a uniform electric field $\vec{E}$ (Fig. 22.6a). We define the electric flux through this area to be the product of the field magnitude E and the area A:

$$\Phi_E = EA$$

Roughly speaking, we can picture Φ_E in terms of the field lines passing through A. Increasing the area means that more lines of $\vec{E}$ pass through the area, increasing the flux; stronger field means more closely spaced lines of $\vec{E}$ and therefore more lines per unit area, so again the flux increases.

If the area A is flat but not perpendicular to the field $\vec{E}$, then fewer field lines pass through it. In this case the area that counts is the silhouette area that we see when looking in the direction of $\vec{E}$. This is the area $A_\perp$ in Fig. 22.6b and is equal to $A\cos\phi$ (compare to Fig. 22.5b). We generalize our definition of electric flux for a uniform electric field to

$$\Phi_E = EA\cos\phi \qquad \text{(electric flux for uniform } \vec{E}\text{, flat surface)} \qquad (22.1)$$

Since $E\cos\phi$ is the component of $\vec{E}$ perpendicular to the area, we can rewrite Eq. (22.1) as

$$\Phi_E = E_\perp A \qquad \text{(electric flux for uniform } \vec{E}\text{, flat surface)} \qquad (22.2)$$

In terms of the vector area $\vec{A}$ perpendicular to the area, we can write the electric flux as the scalar product of $\vec{E}$ and $\vec{A}$:

$$\Phi_E = \vec{E} \cdot \vec{A} \qquad \text{(electric flux for uniform } \vec{E}\text{, flat surface)} \qquad (22.3)$$

22.6 A flat surface in a uniform electric field. The electric flux Φ_E through the surface equals the scalar product of the electric field $\vec{E}$ and the area vector $\vec{A}$.

(a) Surface is face-on to electric field:
- $\vec{E}$ and $\vec{A}$ are parallel (the angle between $\vec{E}$ and $\vec{A}$ is $\phi = 0$).
- The flux $\Phi_E = \vec{E} \cdot \vec{A} = EA$.

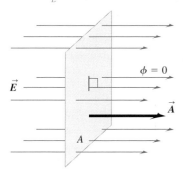

(b) Surface is tilted from a face-on orientation by an angle ϕ:
- The angle between $\vec{E}$ and $\vec{A}$ is ϕ.
- The flux $\Phi_E = \vec{E} \cdot \vec{A} = EA \cos \phi$.

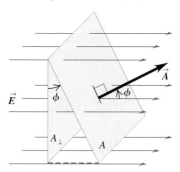

(c) Surface is edge-on to electric field:
- $\vec{E}$ and $\vec{A}$ are perpendicular (the angle between $\vec{E}$ and $\vec{A}$ is $\phi = 90°$).
- The flux $\Phi_E = \vec{E} \cdot \vec{A} = EA \cos 90° = 0$.

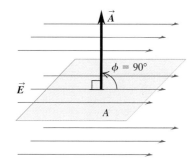

Equations (22.1), (22.2), and (22.3) express the electric flux for a *flat* surface and a *uniform* electric field in different but equivalent ways. The SI unit for electric flux is $1 \, \text{N} \cdot \text{m}^2/\text{C}$. Note that if the area is edge-on to the field, $\vec{E}$ and $\vec{A}$ are perpendicular and the flux is zero (Fig. 22.6c).

We can represent the direction of a vector area $\vec{A}$ by using a *unit vector $\hat{n}$* perpendicular to the area; $\hat{n}$ stands for "normal." Then

$$\vec{A} = A\hat{n} \qquad (22.4)$$

A surface has two sides, so there are two possible directions for $\hat{n}$ and $\vec{A}$. We must always specify which direction we choose. In Section 22.1 we related the charge inside a *closed* surface to the electric flux through the surface. With a closed surface we will always choose the direction of $\hat{n}$ to be *outward,* and we will speak of the flux *out of* a closed surface. Thus what we called "outward electric flux" in Section 22.1 corresponds to a *positive* value of Φ_E, and what we called "inward electric flux" corresponds to a *negative* value of Φ_E.

Flux of a Nonuniform Electric Field

What happens if the electric field $\vec{E}$ isn't uniform but varies from point to point over the area A? Or what if A is part of a curved surface? Then we divide A into many small elements dA, each of which has a unit vector $\hat{n}$ perpendicular to it and a vector area $d\vec{A} = \hat{n} \, dA$. We calculate the electric flux through each element and integrate the results to obtain the total flux:

$$\Phi_E = \int E\cos\phi \, dA = \int E_\perp \, dA = \int \vec{E} \cdot d\vec{A} \qquad \begin{array}{l}\text{(general definition} \\ \text{of electric flux)}\end{array} \qquad (22.5)$$

We call this integral the **surface integral** of the component $E_\perp$ over the area, or the surface integral of $\vec{E} \cdot d\vec{A}$. The various forms of the integral all express the same thing in different terms. In specific problems, one form is sometimes more convenient than another. Example 22.3 at the end of this section illustrates the use of Eq. (22.5).

In Eq. (22.5) the electric flux $\int E_\perp \, dA$ is equal to the *average* value of the perpendicular component of the electric field, multiplied by the area of the surface. This is the same definition of electric flux that we were led to in Section 22.1, now expressed more mathematically. In the next section we will see the connection between the total electric flux through *any* closed surface, no matter what its shape, and the amount of charge enclosed within that surface.

Example 22.1 | Electric flux through a disk

A disk with radius 0.10 m is oriented with its normal unit vector $\hat{n}$ at an angle of 30° to a uniform electric field $\vec{E}$ with magnitude 2.0×10^3 N/C (Fig. 22.7). (Since this isn't a closed surface, it has no "inside" or "outside." That's why we have to specify the direction of $\hat{n}$ in the figure.) (a) What is the electric flux through the disk? (b) What is the flux through the disk if it is turned so that its normal is perpendicular to $\vec{E}$? (c) What is the flux through the disk if its normal is parallel to $\vec{E}$?

SOLUTION

IDENTIFY: This problem is about a flat surface in a uniform electric field, so we can apply the ideas of this section.

SET UP: The orientation of the disk is like that of the rectangle in Fig. 22.6b. We calculate the electric flux using Eq. (22.1).

EXECUTE: (a) The area is $A = \pi(0.10 \text{ m})^2 = 0.0314 \text{ m}^2$ and the angle between $\vec{E}$ and $\vec{A} = A\hat{n}$ is $\phi = 30°$, so

$$\Phi_E = EA\cos\phi = (2.0 \times 10^3 \text{ N/C})(0.0314 \text{ m}^2)(\cos 30°)$$
$$= 54 \text{ N} \cdot \text{m}^2/\text{C}$$

(b) The normal to the disk is now perpendicular to $\vec{E}$, so $\phi = 90°$, $\cos\phi = 0$, and $\Phi_E = 0$. There is no flux through the disk.

(c) The normal to the disk is parallel to $\vec{E}$, so $\phi = 0$, $\cos\phi = 1$, and the flux has its maximum possible value. From Eq. (22.1),

$$\Phi_E = EA\cos\phi = (2.0 \times 10^3 \text{ N/C})(0.0314 \text{ m}^2)(1)$$
$$= 63 \text{ N} \cdot \text{m}^2/\text{C}$$

EVALUATE: As a check on our results, note that the answer to part (a) is smaller than the answer to part (c). Is this as it should be?

22.7 The electric flux Φ_E through a disk depends on the angle between its normal $\hat{n}$ and the electric field $\vec{E}$.

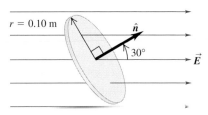

Example 22.2 | Electric flux through a cube

A cube of side L is placed in a region of uniform electric field $\vec{E}$. Find the electric flux through each face of the cube and the total flux through the cube when (a) it is oriented with two of its faces perpendicular to the field $\vec{E}$, as in Fig. 22.8a; and (b) when the cube is turned by an angle θ, as in Fig. 22.8b.

SOLUTION

IDENTIFY: In this problem we are to find the electric flux through each face of the cube as well as the total flux (the sum of the fluxes through the six faces).

SET UP: Since $\vec{E}$ is uniform and each of the six faces of the cube is a flat surface, we find the flux through each face using Eqs. (22.3) and (22.4). We then calculate the total flux through the cube by adding the six individual fluxes.

EXECUTE: (a) The unit vectors for each face ($\hat{n}_1$ through $\hat{n}_6$) are shown in the figure; the direction of each unit vector is *outward* from the closed surface of the cube. The angle between $\vec{E}$ and $\hat{n}_1$ is 180°; the angle between $\vec{E}$ and $\hat{n}_2$ is 0°; and the angle between $\vec{E}$ and each of the other four unit vectors is 90°. Each face of the cube has area L^2, so the fluxes through each of the faces are

$$\Phi_{E1} = \vec{E} \cdot \hat{n}_1 A = EL^2\cos 180° = -EL^2$$
$$\Phi_{E2} = \vec{E} \cdot \hat{n}_2 A = EL^2\cos 0° = +EL^2$$
$$\Phi_{E3} = \Phi_{E4} = \Phi_{E5} = \Phi_{E6} = EL^2\cos 90° = 0$$

The flux is negative on face 1, where $\vec{E}$ is directed into the cube, and positive on face 2, where $\vec{E}$ is directed out of the cube. The *total* flux through the cube is the sum of the fluxes through the six faces:

$$\Phi_E = \Phi_{E1} + \Phi_{E2} + \Phi_{E3} + \Phi_{E4} + \Phi_{E5} + \Phi_{E6}$$
$$= -EL^2 + EL^2 + 0 + 0 + 0 + 0 = 0$$

22.8 Electric flux of a uniform field $\vec{E}$ through a cubical box of side L in two orientations.

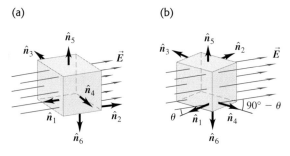

(b) The fluxes through faces 1 and 3 are negative, since $\vec{E}$ is directed into those faces; the field is directed out of faces 2 and 4, so the fluxes through those faces are positive. We find

$$\Phi_{E1} = \vec{E} \cdot \hat{n}_1 A = EL^2\cos(180° - \theta) = -EL^2\cos\theta$$
$$\Phi_{E2} = \vec{E} \cdot \hat{n}_2 A = +EL^2\cos\theta$$
$$\Phi_{E3} = \vec{E} \cdot \hat{n}_3 A = EL^2\cos(90° + \theta) = -EL^2\sin\theta$$
$$\Phi_{E4} = \vec{E} \cdot \hat{n}_4 A = EL^2\cos(90° - \theta) = +EL^2\sin\theta$$
$$\Phi_{E5} = \Phi_{E6} = EL^2\cos 90° = 0$$

The total flux $\Phi_E = \Phi_{E1} + \Phi_{E2} + \Phi_{E3} + \Phi_{E4} + \Phi_{E5} + \Phi_{E6}$ through the surface of the cube is again zero.

EVALUATE: It's no surprise that the total flux is zero for both orientations. We came to this same conclusion in our discussion of Fig. 22.3c in Section 22.1. There we observed that there was zero net flux of a uniform electric field through a closed surface that contains no electric charge.

Example 22.3 **Electric flux through a sphere**

A positive point charge $q = 3.0\ \mu\text{C}$ is surrounded by a sphere with radius 0.20 m centered on the charge (Fig. 22.9). Find the electric flux through the sphere due to this charge.

SOLUTION

IDENTIFY: Here the surface is not flat and the electric field is not uniform, so we must use the general definition of electric flux.

SET UP: We use Eq. (22.5) to calculate the electric flux (our target variable). Because the sphere is centered on the point charge, at any point on the spherical surface, $\vec{E}$ is directed out of the sphere perpendicular to the surface. The positive direction for both $\hat{n}$ and $E_\perp$ is outward, so $E_\perp = E$ and the flux through a surface element dA is $\vec{E} \cdot d\vec{A} = E\,dA$. This greatly simplifies the integral in Eq. (22.5).

EXECUTE: At any point on the sphere the magnitude of $\vec{E}$ is

$$E = \frac{q}{4\pi\epsilon_0 r^2} = (9.0 \times 10^9\ \text{N}\cdot\text{m}^2/\text{C}^2)\frac{3.0 \times 10^{-6}\ \text{C}}{(0.20\ \text{m})^2}$$

$$= 6.75 \times 10^5\ \text{N/C}$$

Because E is the same at every point, it can be taken outside the integral $\Phi_E = \int E\,dA$ in Eq. (22.5). What remains is the integral $\int dA$, which is just the total area $A = 4\pi r^2$ of the spherical surface. Thus the total flux out of the sphere is

$$\Phi_E = EA = (6.75 \times 10^5\ \text{N/C})(4\pi)(0.20\ \text{m})^2$$

$$= 3.4 \times 10^5\ \text{N}\cdot\text{m}^2/\text{C}$$

22.9 Electric flux through a sphere centered on a point charge.

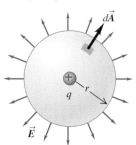

EVALUATE: Notice that we divided by $r^2 = (0.20\ \text{m})^2$ to find E, then multiplied by $r^2 = (0.20\ \text{m})^2$ to find Φ_E; hence the radius r of the sphere cancels out of the result for Φ_E. We would have obtained the same flux with a sphere of radius 2.0 m or 200 m. We came to essentially the same conclusion in our discussion of Fig. 22.4 in Section 22.1, where we considered rectangular closed surfaces of two different sizes enclosing a point charge. There we found that the flux of $\vec{E}$ was independent of the size of the surface; the same result holds true for a spherical surface. Indeed, the flux through *any* surface enclosing a single point charge is independent of the shape or size of the surface, as we'll soon see.

Test Your Understanding of Section 22.2 Rank the following surfaces in order from most positive to most negative electric flux. (i) a flat rectangular surface with vector area $\vec{A} = (6.0\ \text{m}^2)\hat{\imath}$ in a uniform electric field $\vec{E} = (4.0\ \text{N/C})\hat{\jmath}$; (ii) a flat circular surface with vector area $\vec{A} = (3.0\ \text{m}^2)\hat{\jmath}$ in a uniform electric field $\vec{E} = (4.0\ \text{N/C})\hat{\imath} + (2.0\ \text{N/C})\hat{\jmath}$; (iii) a flat square surface with vector area $\vec{A} = (3.0\ \text{m}^2)\hat{\imath} + (7.0\ \text{m}^2)\hat{\jmath}$ in a uniform electric field $\vec{E} = (4.0\ \text{N/C})\hat{\imath} - (2.0\ \text{N/C})\hat{\jmath}$; (iv) a flat oval surface with vector area $\vec{A} = (3.0\ \text{m}^2)\hat{\imath} - (7.0\ \text{m}^2)\hat{\jmath}$ in a uniform electric field $\vec{E} = (4.0\ \text{N/C})\hat{\imath} - (2.0\ \text{N/C})\hat{\jmath}$. ∎

22.3 Gauss's Law

Gauss's law is an alternative to Coulomb's law. While completely equivalent to Coulomb's law, Gauss's law provides a different way to express the relationship between electric charge and electric field. It was formulated by Carl Friedrich Gauss (1777–1855), one of the greatest mathematicians of all time. Many areas of mathematics bear the mark of his influence, and he made equally significant contributions to theoretical physics (Fig. 22.10).

Point Charge Inside a Spherical Surface

Gauss's law states that the total electric flux through any closed surface (a surface enclosing a definite volume) is proportional to the total (net) electric charge inside the surface. In Section 22.1 we observed this relationship qualitatively for certain special cases; now we'll develop it more rigorously. We'll start with the field of a single positive point charge q. The field lines radiate out equally in all directions. We place this charge at the center of an imaginary spherical surface with radius R. The magnitude E of the electric field at every point on the surface is given by

$$E = \frac{1}{4\pi\epsilon_0}\frac{q}{R^2}$$

22.10 Carl Friedrich Gauss helped develop several branches of mathematics, including differential geometry, real analysis, and number theory. The "bell curve" of statistics is one of his inventions. Gauss also made state-of-the-art investigations of the earth's magnetism and calculated the orbit of the first asteroid to be discovered.

22.11 Projection of an element of area dA of a sphere of radius R onto a concentric sphere of radius $2R$. The projection multiplies each linear dimension by 2, so the area element on the larger sphere is $4\,dA$.

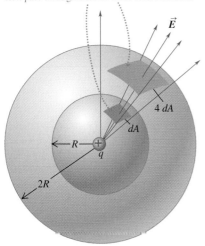

The same number of field lines and the same flux pass through both of these area elements.

At each point on the surface, $\vec{E}$ is perpendicular to the surface, and its magnitude is the same at every point, just as in Example 22.3 (Section 22.2). The total electric flux is the product of the field magnitude E and the total area $A = 4\pi R^2$ of the sphere:

$$\Phi_E = EA = \frac{1}{4\pi\epsilon_0}\frac{q}{R^2}(4\pi R^2) = \frac{q}{\epsilon_0} \tag{22.6}$$

The flux is independent of the radius R of the sphere. It depends only on the charge q enclosed by the sphere.

We can also interpret this result in terms of field lines. Figure 22.11 shows two spheres with radii R and $2R$ centered on the point charge q. Every field line that passes through the smaller sphere also passes through the larger sphere, so the total flux through each sphere is the same.

What is true of the entire sphere is also true of any portion of its surface. In Fig. 22.11 an area dA is outlined on the sphere of radius R and then projected onto the sphere of radius $2R$ by drawing lines from the center through points on the boundary of dA. The area projected on the larger sphere is clearly $4\,dA$. But since the electric field due to a point charge is inversely proportional to r^2, the field magnitude is $\frac{1}{4}$ as great on the sphere of radius $2R$ as on the sphere of radius R. Hence the electric flux is the same for both areas and is independent of the radius of the sphere.

Point Charge Inside a Nonspherical Surface

This projection technique shows us how to extend this discussion to nonspherical surfaces. Instead of a second sphere, let us surround the sphere of radius R by a surface of irregular shape, as in Fig. 22.12a. Consider a small element of area dA on the irregular surface; we note that this area is *larger* than the corresponding element on a spherical surface at the same distance from q. If a normal to dA makes an angle ϕ with a radial line from q, two sides of the area projected onto the spherical surface are foreshortened by a factor $\cos\phi$ (Fig. 22.12b). The other two sides are unchanged. Thus the electric flux through the spherical surface element is equal to the flux $E\,dA\cos\phi$ through the corresponding irregular surface element.

We can divide the entire irregular surface into elements dA, compute the electric flux $E\,dA\cos\phi$ for each, and sum the results by integrating, as in Eq. (22.5). Each of the area elements projects onto a corresponding spherical surface element. Thus the *total* electric flux through the irregular surface, given by any of the forms of Eq. (22.5), must be the same as the total flux through a sphere, which Eq. (22.6) shows is equal to q/ϵ_0. Thus, for the irregular surface,

$$\Phi_E = \oint \vec{E} \cdot d\vec{A} = \frac{q}{\epsilon_0} \tag{22.7}$$

22.12 Calculating the electric flux through a nonspherical surface.

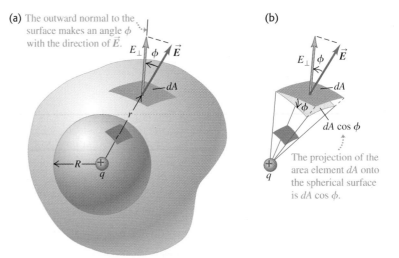

(a) The outward normal to the surface makes an angle ϕ with the direction of $\vec{E}$.

$E_\perp$ ϕ $\vec{E}$

dA

r

R q

(b)

$E_\perp$ ϕ $\vec{E}$

dA

ϕ

$dA\cos\phi$

q

The projection of the area element dA onto the spherical surface is $dA\cos\phi$.

Equation (22.7) holds for a surface of *any* shape or size, provided only that it is a *closed* surface enclosing the charge q. The circle on the integral sign reminds us that the integral is always taken over a *closed* surface.

The area elements $d\vec{A}$ and the corresponding unit vectors $\hat{n}$ always point *out of* the volume enclosed by the surface. The electric flux is then positive in areas where the electric field points out of the surface and negative where it points inward. Also, $E_\perp$ is positive at points where $\vec{E}$ points out of the surface and negative at points where $\vec{E}$ points into the surface.

If the point charge in Fig. 22.12 is negative, the $\vec{E}$ field is directed radially *inward;* the angle ϕ is then greater than 90°, its cosine is negative, and the integral in Eq. (22.7) is negative. But since q is also negative, Eq. (22.7) still holds.

For a closed surface enclosing *no* charge,

$$\Phi_E = \oint \vec{E} \cdot d\vec{A} = 0$$

This is the mathematical statement that when a region contains no charge, any field lines caused by charges *outside* the region that enter on one side must leave again on the other side. (In Section 22.1 we came to the same conclusion by considering the special case of a rectangular box in a uniform field.) Figure 22.13 illustrates this point. *Electric field lines can begin or end inside a region of space only when there is charge in that region.*

General Form of Gauss's Law

Now comes the final step in obtaining the general form of Gauss's law. Suppose the surface encloses not just one point charge q but several charges q_1, q_2, q_3, ... The total (resultant) electric field $\vec{E}$ at any point is the vector sum of the $\vec{E}$ fields of the individual charges. Let Q_{encl} be the *total* charge enclosed by the surface: $Q_{encl} = q_1 + q_2 + q_3 + \cdots$. Also let $\vec{E}$ be the *total* field at the position of the surface area element $d\vec{A}$, and let $E_\perp$ be its component perpendicular to the plane of that element (that is, parallel to $d\vec{A}$). Then we can write an equation like Eq. (22.7) for each charge and its corresponding field and add the results. When we do, we obtain the general statement of Gauss's law:

$$\Phi_E = \oint \vec{E} \cdot d\vec{A} = \frac{Q_{encl}}{\epsilon_0} \qquad \text{(Gauss's law)} \qquad (22.8)$$

The total electric flux through a closed surface is equal to the total (net) electric charge inside the surface, divided by ϵ_0.

CAUTION Gaussian surfaces are imaginary Remember that the closed surface in Gauss's law is *imaginary;* there need not be any material object at the position of the surface. We often refer to a closed surface used in Gauss's law as a **Gaussian surface.** ▮

Using the definition of Q_{encl} and the various ways to express electric flux given in Eq. (22.5), we can express Gauss's law in the following equivalent forms:

$$\Phi_E = \oint E \cos\phi \, dA = \oint E_\perp \, dA = \oint \vec{E} \cdot d\vec{A} = \frac{Q_{encl}}{\epsilon_0} \qquad \begin{array}{l}\text{(various forms} \\ \text{of Gauss's law)}\end{array} \qquad (22.9)$$

As in Eq. (22.5), the various forms of the integral all express the same thing, the total electric flux through the Gaussian surface, in different terms. One form is sometimes more convenient than another.

As an example, Fig. 22.14a shows a spherical Gaussian surface of radius r around a positive point charge $+q$. The electric field points out of the Gaussian surface, so at every point on the surface $\vec{E}$ is in the same direction as $d\vec{A}$, $\phi = 0$, and

22.13 A point charge *outside* a closed surface that encloses no charge. If an electric field line from the external charge enters the surface at one point, it must leave at another.

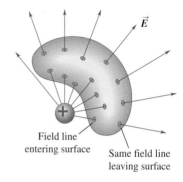

Field line entering surface

Same field line leaving surface

$\vec{E}$

22.14 Spherical Gaussian surfaces around (a) a positive point charge and (b) a negative point charge.

(a) Gaussian surface around positive charge: positive (outward) flux

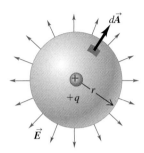

(b) Gaussian surface around negative charge: negative (inward) flux

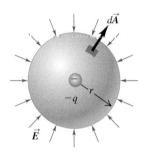

$E_\perp$ is equal to the field magnitude $E = q/4\pi\epsilon_0 r^2$. Since E is the same at all points on the surface, we can take it outside the integral in Eq. (22.9). Then the remaining integral is $\int dA = A = 4\pi r^2$, the area of the sphere. Hence Eq. (22.9) becomes

$$\Phi_E = \oint E_\perp \, dA = \oint \frac{q}{4\pi\epsilon_0 r^2} \, dA = \frac{q}{4\pi\epsilon_0 r^2} \oint dA = \frac{q}{4\pi\epsilon_0 r^2} 4\pi r^2 = \frac{q}{\epsilon_0}$$

The enclosed charge Q_{encl} is just the charge $+q$, so this agrees with Gauss's law. If the Gaussian surface encloses a *negative* point charge as in Fig. 22.14b, then $\vec{E}$ points *into* the surface at each point in the direction opposite $d\vec{A}$. Then $\phi = 180°$ and $E_\perp$ is equal to the negative of the field magnitude: $E_\perp = -E = -|-q|/4\pi\epsilon_0 r^2 = -q/4\pi\epsilon_0 r^2$. Equation (22.9) then becomes

$$\Phi_E = \oint E_\perp \, dA = \oint \left(\frac{-q}{4\pi\epsilon_0 r^2} \right) dA = \frac{-q}{4\pi\epsilon_0 r^2} \oint dA = \frac{-q}{4\pi\epsilon_0 r^2} 4\pi r^2 = \frac{-q}{\epsilon_0}$$

This again agrees with Gauss's law because the enclosed charge in Fig. 22.14b is $Q_{encl} = -q$.

In Eqs. (22.8) and (22.9), Q_{encl} is always the algebraic sum of all the positive and negative charges enclosed by the Gaussian surface, and $\vec{E}$ is the *total* field at each point on the surface. Also note that in general, this field is caused partly by charges inside the surface and partly by charges outside. But as Fig. 22.13 shows, the outside charges do *not* contribute to the total (net) flux through the surface. So Eqs. (22.8) and (22.9) are correct even when there are charges outside the surface that contribute to the electric field at the surface. When $Q_{encl} = 0$, the total flux through the Gaussian surface must be zero, even though some areas may have positive flux and others may have negative flux (see Fig. 22.3b).

Gauss's law is the definitive answer to the question we posed at the beginning of Section 22.1: "If the electric field pattern is known in a given region, what can we determine about the charge distribution in that region?" It provides a relationship between the electric field on a closed surface and the charge distribution within that surface. But in some cases we can use Gauss's law to answer the reverse question: "If the charge distribution is known, what can we determine about the electric field that the charge distribution produces?" Gauss's law may seem like an unappealing way to address this question, since it may look as though evaluating the integral in Eq. (22.8) is a hopeless task. Sometimes it is, but other times it is surprisingly easy. Here's an example in which *no* integration is involved at all; we'll work out several more examples in the next section.

Conceptual Example 22.4   **Electric flux and enclosed charge**

Figure 22.15 shows the field produced by two point charges $+q$ and $-q$ of equal magnitude but opposite sign (an electric dipole). Find the electric flux through each of the closed surfaces A, B, C, and D.

SOLUTION

The definition of electric flux given in Eq. (22.5) involves a surface integral, and so it might seem that integration is called for. But Gauss's law says that the total electric flux through a closed surface is equal to the total enclosed charge divided by ϵ_0. By inspection of Fig. 22.15, surface A (shown in red) encloses the positive charge, so $Q_{encl} = +q$; surface B (shown in blue) encloses the negative charge, so $Q_{encl} = -q$; surface C (shown in yellow), which encloses *both* charges, has $Q_{encl} = +q + (-q) = 0$; and surface D (shown in purple), which has no charges enclosed within it, also has $Q_{encl} = 0$. Hence without having to do any integration, we can

22.15 The net number of field lines leaving a closed surface is proportional to the total charge enclosed by that surface.

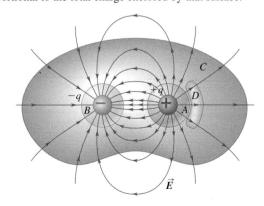

conclude that the total fluxes for the various surfaces are $\Phi_E = +q/\epsilon_0$ for surface A, $\Phi_E = -q/\epsilon_0$ for surface B, and $\Phi_E = 0$ for both surface C and surface D.

These results depend only on the charges enclosed within each Gaussian surface, not on the precise shapes of the surfaces. For example, compare surface C to the rectangular surface shown in Fig. 22.3b, which also encloses both charges of an electric dipole. In that case as well, we concluded that the net flux of $\vec{E}$ was zero; the inward flux on one part of the surface exactly compensates for the outward flux on the remainder of the surface.

We can draw similar conclusions by examining the electric field lines. Surface A encloses only the positive charge; in Fig. 22.15, 18 lines are depicted crossing A in an outward direction. Surface B encloses only the negative charge; it is crossed by these same 18 lines, but in an inward direction. Surface C encloses *both* charges. It is intersected by lines at 16 points; at 8 intersections the lines are outward, and at 8 they are inward. The *net* number of lines crossing in an outward direction is zero, and the net charge inside the surface is also zero. Surface D is intersected at 6 points; at 3 points the lines are outward, and at the other 3 they are inward. The net number of lines crossing in an outward direction and the total charge enclosed are both zero. There are points on the surfaces where $\vec{E}$ is not perpendicular to the surface, but this doesn't affect the counting of the field lines.

Test Your Understanding of Section 22.3   Figure 22.16 shows six point charges that all lie in the same plane. Five Gaussian surfaces—S_1, S_2, S_3, S_4, and S_5—each enclose part of this plane, and Fig. 22.16 shows the intersection of each surface with the plane. Rank these five surfaces in order of the electric flux through them, from most positive to most negative.

22.16 Five Gaussian surfaces and six point charges.

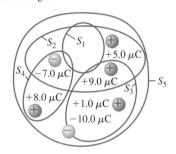

22.4 Applications of Gauss's Law

Gauss's law is valid for *any* distribution of charges and for *any* closed surface. Gauss's law can be used in two ways. If we know the charge distribution, and if it has enough symmetry to let us evaluate the integral in Gauss's law, we can find the field. Or if we know the field, we can use Gauss's law to find the charge distribution, such as charges on conducting surfaces.

In this section we present examples of both kinds of applications. As you study them, watch for the role played by the symmetry properties of each system. We will use Gauss's law to calculate the electric fields caused by several simple charge distributions; the results are collected in a table in the chapter summary.

In practical problems we often encounter situations in which we want to know the electric field caused by a charge distribution on a conductor. These calculations are aided by the following remarkable fact: *When excess charge is placed on a solid conductor and is at rest, it resides entirely on the surface, not in the interior of the material.* (By *excess* we mean charges other than the ions and free electrons that make up the neutral conductor.) Here's the proof. We know from Section 21.4 that in an electrostatic situation (with all charges at rest) the electric field $\vec{E}$ at every point in the interior of a conducting material is zero. If $\vec{E}$ were *not* zero, the excess charges would move. Suppose we construct a Gaussian surface inside the conductor, such as surface A in Fig. 22.17. Because $\vec{E} = 0$ everywhere on this surface, Gauss's law requires that the net charge inside the surface is zero. Now imagine shrinking the surface like a collapsing balloon until it encloses a region so small that we may consider it as a point P; then the charge at that point must be zero. We can do this anywhere inside the conductor, so *there can be no excess charge at any point within a solid conductor; any excess charge must reside on the conductor's surface.* (This result is for a *solid* conductor. In the next section we'll discuss what can happen if the conductor has cavities in its interior.) We will make use of this fact frequently in the examples that follow.

22.17 Under electrostatic conditions (charges not in motion), any excess charge on a solid conductor resides entirely on the conductor's surface.

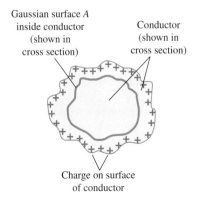

Gaussian surface A inside conductor (shown in cross section)

Conductor (shown in cross section)

Charge on surface of conductor

Problem-Solving Strategy 22.1   Gauss's Law

IDENTIFY *the relevant concepts:* Gauss's law is most useful in situations where the charge distribution has spherical or cylindrical symmetry or is distributed uniformly over a plane. In these situations we determine the direction of $\vec{E}$ from the symmetry of the charge distribution. If we are given the charge distribution, we can use Gauss's law to find the magnitude of $\vec{E}$. Alternatively, if we are given the field, we can use Gauss's law to determine the details of the charge distribution. In either case, begin your analysis by asking the question: What is the symmetry?

SET UP *the problem* using the following steps:
1. Select the surface that you will use with Gauss's law. We often call it a *Gaussian surface*. If you are trying to find the field at a particular point, then that point must lie on your Gaussian surface.
2. The Gaussian surface does not have to be a real physical surface, such as a surface of a solid body. Often the appropriate surface is an imaginary geometric surface; it may be in empty space, embedded in a solid body, or both.
3. Usually you can evaluate the integral in Gauss's law (without using a computer) only if the Gaussian surface and the charge distribution have some symmetry property. If the charge distribution has cylindrical or spherical symmetry, choose the Gaussian surface to be a coaxial cylinder or a concentric sphere, respectively.

EXECUTE *the solution* as follows:
1. Carry out the integral in Eq. (22.9). This may look like a daunting task, but the symmetry of the charge distribution and your careful choice of a Gaussian surface make it straightforward.

2. Often you can think of the closed Gaussian surface as being made up of several separate surfaces, such as the sides and ends of a cylinder. The integral $\oint E_\perp \, dA$ over the entire closed surface is always equal to the sum of the integrals over all the separate surfaces. Some of these integrals may be zero, as in points 4 and 5 below.
3. If $\vec{E}$ is *perpendicular* (normal) at every point to a surface with area A, if it points *outward* from the interior of the surface, and if it also has the same *magnitude* at every point on the surface, then $E_\perp = E = $ constant, and $\int E_\perp \, dA$ over that surface is equal to EA. If instead $\vec{E}$ is perpendicular and *inward*, then $E_\perp = -E$ and $\int E_\perp \, dA = -EA$.
4. If $\vec{E}$ is *tangent* to a surface at every point, then $E_\perp = 0$ and the integral over that surface is zero.
5. If $\vec{E} = 0$ at every point on a surface, the integral is zero.
6. In the integral $\oint E_\perp \, dA$, $E_\perp$ is always the perpendicular component of the *total* electric field at each point on the closed Gaussian surface. In general, this field may be caused partly by charges within the surface and partly by charges outside it. Even when there is *no* charge within the surface, the field at points on the Gaussian surface is not necessarily zero. In that case, however, the *integral* over the Gaussian surface—that is, the total electric flux through the Gaussian surface—is always zero.
7. Once you have evaluated the integral, use Eq. (22.9) to solve for your target variable.

EVALUATE *your answer:* Often your result will be a *function* that describes how the magnitude of the electric field varies with position. Examine this function with a critical eye to see whether it makes sense.

Example 22.5   Field of a charged conducting sphere

We place positive charge q on a solid conducting sphere with radius R (Fig. 22.18). Find $\vec{E}$ at any point inside or outside the sphere.

SOLUTION

IDENTIFY: As we discussed earlier in this section, all the charge must be on the surface of the sphere. The system has spherical symmetry.

SET UP: To take advantage of the symmetry, we take as our Gaussian surface an imaginary sphere of radius r centered on the conductor. To calculate the field outside the conductor, we take r to be greater than the conductor's radius R; to calculate the field inside, we take r to be less than R. In either case, the point where we want to calculate $\vec{E}$ lies on the Gaussian surface.

EXECUTE: The role of symmetry deserves careful discussion before we do any calculations. When we say that the system is spherically symmetric, we mean that if we rotate it through any angle about any axis through the center, the system after rotation is indistinguishable from the original unrotated system. The charge is free to move on the conductor, and there is nothing about the con-

22.18 Calculating the electric field of a conducting sphere with positive charge q. Outside the sphere, the field is the same as if all of the charge were concentrated at the center of the sphere.

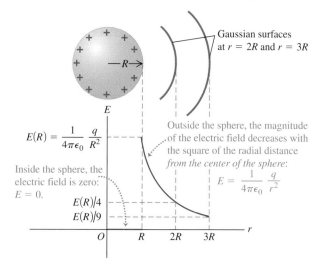

ductor that would make it tend to concentrate more in some regions than others. So we conclude that the charge is distributed *uniformly* over the surface.

Symmetry also shows that the direction of the electric field must be *radial*, as shown in Fig. 22.18. If we again rotate the system, the field pattern of the rotated system must be identical to that of the original system. If the field had a component at some point that was perpendicular to the radial direction, that component would have to be different after at least some rotations. Thus there can't be such a component, and the field must be radial. For the same reason the magnitude E of the field can depend only on the distance r from the center and must have the same value at all points on a spherical surface concentric with the conductor.

Our choice of a sphere as a Gaussian surface takes advantage of these symmetry properties. We first consider the field outside the conductor, so we choose $r > R$. The entire conductor is within the Gaussian surface, so the enclosed charge is q. The area of the Gaussian surface is $4\pi r^2$; $\vec{E}$ is uniform over the surface and perpendicular to it at each point. The flux integral $\oint E_\perp \, dA$ in Gauss's law is therefore just $E(4\pi r^2)$, and Eq. (22.8) gives

$$E(4\pi r^2) = \frac{q}{\epsilon_0} \quad \text{and}$$

$$E = \frac{1}{4\pi\epsilon_0} \frac{q}{r^2} \quad \text{(outside a charged conducting sphere)}$$

This expression for the field at any point *outside* the sphere $(r > R)$ is the same as for a point charge; the field due to the charged sphere is the same as though the entire charge were concentrated at its center. Just outside the surface of the sphere, where $r = R$,

$$E = \frac{1}{4\pi\epsilon_0} \frac{q}{R^2}$$

(at the surface of a charged conducting sphere)

CAUTION **Flux can be positive or negative** Remember that we have chosen the charge q to be *positive*. If the charge is negative, the electric field is radially *inward* instead of radially outward, and the electric flux through the Gaussian surface is negative. The electric field magnitudes outside and at the surface of the sphere are given by the same expressions as above, except that q denotes the *magnitude* (absolute value) of the charge. ∎

To find $\vec{E}$ inside the conductor, we use a spherical Gaussian surface with radius $r < R$. The spherical symmetry again tells us that $E(4\pi r^2) = Q_{encl}/\epsilon_0$. But because all of the charge is on the surface of the conductor, our Gaussian surface (which lies entirely within the conductor) encloses *no* charge. So $Q_{encl} = 0$ and, therefore, the electric field inside the conductor is zero.

EVALUATE: We already knew that $\vec{E} = 0$ inside the conductor, as it must be inside any solid conductor when the charges are at rest. Figure 22.18 shows E as a function of the distance r from the center of the sphere. Note that in the limit as $R \rightarrow 0$, the sphere becomes a point charge; there is then only an "outside," and the field is everywhere given by $E = q/4\pi\epsilon_0 r^2$. Thus we have deduced Coulomb's law from Gauss's law. (In Section 22.3 we deduced Gauss's law from Coulomb's law, so this completes the demonstration of their logical equivalence.)

We can also use this method for a conducting spherical *shell* (a spherical conductor with a concentric spherical hole in the center) if there is no charge inside the hole. We use a spherical Gaussian surface with radius r less than the radius of the hole. If there *were* a field inside the hole, it would have to be radial and spherically symmetric as before, so $E = Q_{encl}/4\pi\epsilon_0 r^2$. But now there is no enclosed charge, so $Q_{encl} = 0$ and $E = 0$ inside the hole.

Can you use this same technique to find the electric field in the interspace between a charged sphere and a concentric hollow conducting sphere that surrounds it?

Example 22.6   Field of a line charge

Electric charge is distributed uniformly along an infinitely long, thin wire. The charge per unit length is λ (assumed positive). Find the electric field. (This is an approximate representation of the field of a uniformly charged *finite* wire, provided that the distance from the field point to the wire is much less than the length of the wire.)

SOLUTION

IDENTIFY: The system has *cylindrical* symmetry. The field must point away from the positive charges. To determine the direction of $\vec{E}$ more precisely, as well as how its magnitude can depend on position, we use symmetry as in Example 22.5.

SET UP: Cylindrical symmetry means that we can rotate the system through any angle about its axis, and we can shift it by any amount along the axis; in each case the resulting system is indistinguishable from the original. Hence $\vec{E}$ at each point can't change when either of these operations is carried out. The field can't have any component parallel to the wire; if it did, we would have to explain why the field lines that begin on the wire pointed in one direction parallel to the wire and not the other. Also, the field can't have any component tangent to a circle in a plane perpendicular to the wire with its center on the wire. If it did, we would have to explain why the component pointed in one direction around the

wire rather than the other. All that's left is a component radially outward from the wire at each point. So the field lines outside a uniformly charged, infinite wire are *radial* and lie in planes perpendicular to the wire. The field *magnitude* can depend only on the radial distance from the wire.

These symmetry properties suggest that we use as a Gaussian surface a *cylinder* with arbitrary radius r and arbitrary length l, with its ends perpendicular to the wire (Fig. 22.19).

22.19 A coaxial cylindrical Gaussian surface is used to find the electric field outside an infinitely long, charged wire.

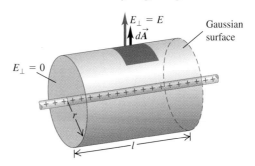

Continued

EXECUTE: We break the surface integral for the flux Φ_E into an integral over each flat end and one over the curved side walls. There is no flux through the ends because $\vec{E}$ lies in the plane of the surface and $E_\perp = 0$. To find the flux through the side walls, note that $\vec{E}$ is perpendicular to the surface at each point, so $E = E_\perp$; by symmetry, E has the same value everywhere on the walls. The area of the side walls is $2\pi rl$. (To make a paper cylinder with radius r and height l, you need a paper rectangle with width $2\pi r$, height l, and area $2\pi rl$.) Hence the total flux Φ_E through the entire cylinder is the sum of the flux through the side walls, which is $(E)(2\pi rl)$, and the zero flux through the two ends. Finally, we need the total enclosed charge, which is the charge per unit length multiplied by the length of wire inside the Gaussian surface, or $Q_{encl} = \lambda l$. From Gauss's law, Eq. (22.8),

$$\Phi_E = (E)(2\pi rl) = \frac{\lambda l}{\epsilon_0} \quad \text{and}$$

$$E = \frac{1}{2\pi\epsilon_0} \frac{\lambda}{r} \quad \text{(field of an infinite line of charge)}$$

This is the same result that we found in Example 21.11 (Section 21.5) by much more laborious means.

We have assumed that λ is *positive*. If it is *negative*, $\vec{E}$ is directed radially inward toward the line of charge, and in the above expression for the field magnitude E we must interpret λ as the *magnitude* (absolute value) of the charge per unit length.

EVALUATE: Note that although the *entire* charge on the wire contributes to the field, only the part of the total charge that is within the Gaussian surface is considered when we apply Gauss's law. This may seem strange; it looks as though we have somehow obtained the right answer by ignoring part of the charge and the field of a *short* wire of length l would be the same as that of a very long wire. But we *do* include the entire charge on the wire when we make use of the *symmetry* of the problem. If the wire is short, the symmetry with respect to shifts along the axis is not present, and the field is not uniform in magnitude over our Gaussian surface. Gauss's law is then no longer useful and *cannot* be used to find the field; the problem is best handled by the integration technique used in Example 21.11.

We can use a Gaussian surface like that in Fig. 22.19 to show that the field at points outside a long, uniformly charged cylinder is the same as though all the charge were concentrated on a line along its axis. We can also calculate the electric field in the space between a charged cylinder and a coaxial hollow conducting cylinder surrounding it. We leave these calculations to you (see Problems 22.37 and 22.40).

Example 22.7 Field of an infinite plane sheet of charge

Find the electric field caused by a thin, flat, infinite sheet on which there is a uniform positive charge per unit area σ.

SOLUTION

IDENTIFY: The field must point away from the positively charged sheet. As in Examples 22.5 and 22.6, before doing calculations we use the symmetry (in this case, *planar* symmetry) to learn more about the direction and position dependence of $\vec{E}$.

SET UP: Planar symmetry means that the charge distribution doesn't change if we slide it in any direction parallel to the sheet. From this we conclude that at each point, $\vec{E}$ is perpendicular to the sheet. The symmetry also tells us that the field must have the same magnitude E at any given distance on either side of the sheet. To take advantage of these symmetry properties, we use as our Gaussian surface a cylinder with its axis perpendicular to the sheet of charge, with ends of area A (Fig. 22.20).

EXECUTE: The charged sheet passes through the middle of the cylinder's length, so the cylinder ends are equidistant from the sheet. At each end of the cylinder, $\vec{E}$ is perpendicular to the surface and $E_\perp$ is equal to E; hence the flux through each end is $+EA$.

Because $\vec{E}$ is perpendicular to the charged sheet, it is parallel to the curved *side* walls of the cylinder, so $E_\perp$ at these walls is zero and there is no flux through these walls. The total flux integral in Gauss's law is then $2EA$ (EA from each end and zero from the side walls). The net charge within the Gaussian surface is the charge per unit area multiplied by the sheet area enclosed by the surface, or $Q_{encl} = \sigma A$. Hence Gauss's law, Eq. (22.8), gives

$$2EA = \frac{\sigma A}{\epsilon_0} \quad \text{and}$$

$$E = \frac{\sigma}{2\epsilon_0} \quad \text{(field of an infinite sheet of charge)}$$

This is the same result that we found in Example 21.12 (Section 21.5) using a much more complex calculation. The field is uniform and directed perpendicular to the plane of the sheet. Its magnitude is *independent* of the distance from the sheet. The field lines are therefore straight, parallel to each other, and perpendicular to the sheet.

If the charge density is negative, $\vec{E}$ is directed *toward* the sheet, the flux through the Gaussian surface in Fig. 22.20 is negative, and σ in the expression $E = \sigma/2\epsilon_0$ denotes the magnitude (absolute value) of the charge density.

22.20 A cylindrical Gaussian surface is used to find the field of an infinite plane sheet of charge.

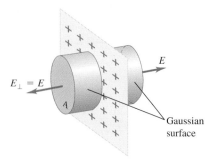

$E_\perp = E$

E

Gaussian surface

EVALUATE: The assumption that the sheet is infinitely large is an idealization; nothing in nature is really infinitely large. But the result $E = \sigma/2\epsilon_0$ is a good approximation for points that are close to the sheet (compared to the sheet's dimensions) and not too near its edges. At such points, the field is very nearly uniform and perpendicular to the plane.

Example 22.8   **Field between oppositely charged parallel conducting plates**

Two large plane parallel conducting plates are given charges of equal magnitude and opposite sign; the charge per unit area is $+\sigma$ for one and $-\sigma$ for the other. Find the electric field in the region between the plates.

SOLUTION

IDENTIFY: The field between and around the plates is approximately as shown in Fig. 22.21a. Because opposite charges attract, most of the charge accumulates at the opposing faces of the plates. A small amount of charge resides on the *outer* surfaces of the plates, and there is some spreading or "fringing" of the field at the edges. But if the plates are very large in comparison to the distance between them, the amount of charge on the outer surfaces is negligibly small, and the fringing can be neglected except near the edges. In this case we can assume that the field is uniform in the interior region between plates, as in Fig. 22.21b, and that the charges are distributed uniformly over the opposing surfaces.

SET UP: To exploit this symmetry, we can use the shaded Gaussian surfaces S_1, S_2, S_3, and S_4. These surfaces are cylinders with ends of area A like the one shown in perspective in Fig. 22.20; they are shown in a side view in Fig. 22.21b. One end of each surface lies within one of the conducting plates.

EXECUTE: For the surface labeled S_1, the left-hand end is within plate 1 (the positive plate). Since the field is zero within the volume of any solid conductor under electrostatic conditions, there is no electric flux through this end. The electric field between the plates is perpendicular to the right-hand end, so on that end, $E_\perp$ is

equal to E and the flux is EA; this is positive, since $\vec{E}$ is directed out of the Gaussian surface. There is no flux through the side walls of the cylinder, since these walls are parallel to $\vec{E}$. So the total flux integral in Gauss's law is EA. The net charge enclosed by the cylinder is σA, so Eq. (22.8) yields

$$EA = \frac{\sigma A}{\epsilon_0} \quad \text{and} \quad E = \frac{\sigma}{\epsilon_0} \quad \begin{array}{l}\text{(field between oppositely} \\ \text{charged conducting plates)}\end{array}$$

The field is uniform and perpendicular to the plates, and its magnitude is independent of the distance from either plate. This same result can be obtained by using the Gaussian surface S_4; furthermore, the surfaces S_2 and S_3 can be used to show that $E = 0$ to the left of plate 1 and to the right of plate 2. We leave these calculations to you (see Exercise 22.27).

EVALUATE: We obtained the same results in Example 21.13 (Section 21.5) by using the principle of superposition of electric fields. The fields due to the two sheets of charge (one on each plate) are $\vec{E}_1$ and $\vec{E}_2$; from Example 22.7, both of these have magnitude $\sigma/2\epsilon_0$. The total (resultant) electric field at any point is the vector sum $\vec{E} = \vec{E}_1 + \vec{E}_2$. At points a and c in Fig. 22.21b, $\vec{E}_1$ and $\vec{E}_2$ have opposite directions, and their resultant is zero. This is also true at every point within the material of each plate, consistent with the requirement that with charges at rest there can be no field within a solid conductor. At any point b between the plates, $\vec{E}_1$ and $\vec{E}_2$ have the same direction; their resultant has magnitude $E = \sigma/\epsilon_0$, just as we found above using Gauss's law.

22.21 Electric field between oppositely charged parallel plates.

(a) Realistic drawing

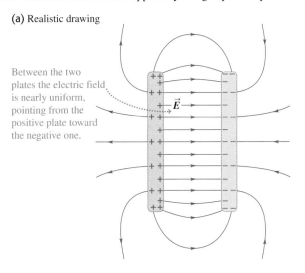

Between the two plates the electric field is nearly uniform, pointing from the positive plate toward the negative one.

(b) Idealized model

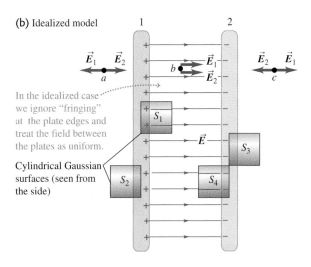

In the idealized case we ignore "fringing" at the plate edges and treat the field between the plates as uniform.

Cylindrical Gaussian surfaces (seen from the side)

Example 22.9   Field of a uniformly charged sphere

Positive electric charge Q is distributed uniformly *throughout the volume* of an *insulating* sphere with radius R. Find the magnitude of the electric field at a point P a distance r from the center of the sphere.

SOLUTION

IDENTIFY: As in Example 22.5, the system is spherically symmetric. Hence we can use the conclusions of that example about the direction and magnitude of $\vec{E}$.

SET UP: To make use of the symmetry, we choose as our Gaussian surface a sphere with radius r, concentric with the charge distribution.

EXECUTE: From symmetry the magnitude E of the electric field has the same value at every point on the Gaussian surface, and the direction of $\vec{E}$ is radial at every point on the surface, so $E_\perp = E$. Hence the total electric flux through the Gaussian surface is the product of E and the total area of the surface $A = 4\pi r^2$, that is, $\Phi_E = 4\pi r^2 E$.

The amount of charge enclosed within the Gaussian surface depends on the radius r. Let's first find the field magnitude *inside* the charged sphere of radius R; the magnitude E is evaluated at the radius of the Gaussian surface, so we choose $r < R$. The volume charge density ρ is the charge Q divided by the volume of the entire charged sphere of radius R:

$$\rho = \frac{Q}{4\pi R^3/3}$$

22.22 The magnitude of the electric field of a uniformly charged insulating sphere. Compare this with the field for a conducting sphere (Fig. 22.18).

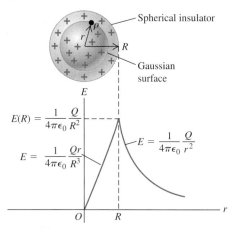

The volume V_{encl} enclosed by the Gaussian surface is $\frac{4}{3}\pi r^3$, so the total charge Q_{encl} enclosed by that surface is

$$Q_{encl} = \rho V_{encl} = \left(\frac{Q}{4\pi R^3/3}\right)\left(\frac{4}{3}\pi r^3\right) = Q\frac{r^3}{R^3}$$

Then Gauss's law, Eq. (22.8), becomes

$$4\pi r^2 E = \frac{Q}{\epsilon_0}\frac{r^3}{R^3} \quad \text{or}$$

$$E = \frac{1}{4\pi\epsilon_0}\frac{Qr}{R^3} \quad \text{(field inside a uniformly charged sphere)}$$

The field magnitude is proportional to the distance r of the field point from the center of the sphere. At the center $(r = 0)$, $E = 0$.

To find the field magnitude *outside* the charged sphere, we use a spherical Gaussian surface of radius $r > R$. This surface encloses the entire charged sphere, so $Q_{encl} = Q$, and Gauss's law gives

$$4\pi r^2 E = \frac{Q}{\epsilon_0} \quad \text{or}$$

$$E = \frac{1}{4\pi\epsilon_0}\frac{Q}{r^2} \quad \text{(field outside a uniformly charged sphere)}$$

For *any* spherically symmetric charged body the electric field outside the body is the same as though the entire charge were concentrated at the center. (We made this same observation in Example 22.5.)

Figure 22.22 shows a graph of E as a function of r for this problem. For $r < R$, E is directly proportional to r, and for $r > R$, E varies as $1/r^2$. If the charge is negative instead of positive, $\vec{E}$ is radially *inward* and Q in the expressions for E is interpreted as the magnitude (absolute value) of the charge.

EVALUATE: Notice that if we set $r = R$ in either of the two expressions for E (inside or outside the sphere), we get the same result $E = Q/4\pi\epsilon_0 R^2$ for the magnitude of the field at the surface of the sphere. This is because the magnitude E is a *continuous* function of r. By contrast, for the charged conducting sphere of Example 22.5 the electric-field magnitude is *discontinuous* at $r = R$ (it jumps from $E = 0$ just inside the sphere to $E = Q/4\pi\epsilon_0 R^2$ just outside the sphere). In general, the electric field $\vec{E}$ is discontinuous in magnitude, direction, or both wherever there is a *sheet* of charge, such as at the surface of a charged conducting sphere (Example 22.5), at the surface of an infinite charged sheet (Example 22.7), or at the surface of a charged conducting plate (Example 22.8).

The general technique used in this example can be applied to *any* spherically symmetric distribution of charge, whether it is uniform or not. Such charge distributions occur within many atoms and atomic nuclei, which is why Gauss's law is a useful tool in atomic and nuclear physics.

Example 22.10   Field of a hollow charged sphere

A thin-walled, hollow sphere of radius 0.250 m has an unknown amount of charge distributed uniformly over its surface. At a distance of 0.300 m from the center of the sphere, the electric field points directly toward the center of the sphere and has magnitude 1.80×10^2 N/C. How much charge is on the sphere?

SOLUTION

IDENTIFY: The charge distribution is spherically symmetric. As in Examples 22.5 and 22.9, it follows that the electric field is radial everywhere and its magnitude is a function only of the radial distance r from the center of the sphere.

SET UP: We again use a spherical Gaussian surface that is concentric with the charge distribution and that passes through the point of interest at $r = 0.300$ m.

EXECUTE: The charge distribution is the same as if the charge were on the surface of a 0.250-m-radius conducting sphere. Hence we can borrow the results of Example 22.5. A key difference from that example is that because the electric field here is directed toward the sphere, the charge must be *negative*. Furthermore, because the electric field is directed into the Gaussian surface, $E_\perp = -E$ and the flux is $\oint E_\perp \, dA = -E(4\pi r^2)$.

By Gauss's law, the flux is equal to the charge q on the sphere (all of which is enclosed by the Gaussian surface) divided by ϵ_0. Solving for q, we find

$$q = -E(4\pi\epsilon_0 r^2) = -(1.80 \times 10^2 \text{ N/C})(4\pi)$$
$$\times (8.854 \times 10^{-12} \text{ C}^2/\text{N} \cdot \text{m}^2)(0.300 \text{ m})^2$$
$$= -8.01 \times 10^{-10} \text{ C} = -0.801 \text{ nC}$$

EVALUATE: To determine the charge, we had to know the electric field at *all* points on the Gaussian surface so that we could calculate the flux integral. This was possible here because the charge distribution is highly symmetric. If the charge distribution is irregular or lacks symmetry, however, Gauss's law is not very useful for calculating the charge distribution from the field, or vice versa.

Test Your Understanding of Section 22.4 You place a known amount of charge Q on the irregularly shaped conductor shown in Fig. 22.17. If you know the size and shape of the conductor, can you use Gauss's law to calculate the electric field at an arbitrary position outside the conductor?

22.5 Charges on Conductors

We have learned that in an electrostatic situation (in which there is no net motion of charge) the electric field at every point within a conductor is zero and that any excess charge on a solid conductor is located entirely on its surface (Fig. 22.23a). But what if there is a *cavity* inside the conductor (Fig. 22.23b)? If there is no charge within the cavity, we can use a Gaussian surface such as A (which lies completely within the material of the conductor) to show that the *net* charge on the *surface of the cavity* must be zero, because $\vec{E} = 0$ everywhere on the Gaussian surface. In fact, we can prove in this situation that there can't be any charge *anywhere* on the cavity surface. We will postpone detailed proof of this statement until Chapter 23.

Suppose we place a small body with a charge q inside a cavity within a conductor (Fig. 22.23c). The conductor is uncharged and is insulated from the charge q. Again $\vec{E} = 0$ everywhere on surface A, so according to Gauss's law the *total* charge inside this surface must be zero. Therefore there must be a charge $-q$ distributed on the surface of the cavity, drawn there by the charge q inside the cavity. The *total* charge on the conductor must remain zero, so a charge $+q$ must appear either on its outer surface or inside the material. But we showed in Section 22.4 that in an electrostatic situation there can't be any excess charge within the material of a conductor. So we conclude that the charge $+q$ must appear on the outer surface. By the same reasoning, if the conductor originally had a charge q_C, then the total charge on the outer surface must be $q_C + q$ after the charge q is inserted into the cavity.

22.23 Finding the electric field within a charged conductor.

(a) Solid conductor with charge q_C

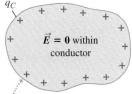

The charge q_C resides entirely on the surface of the conductor. The situation is electrostatic, so $\vec{E} = 0$ within the conductor.

(b) The same conductor with an internal cavity

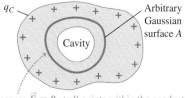

Because $\vec{E} = 0$ at all points within the conductor, the electric field at all points on the Gaussian surface must be zero.

(c) An isolated charge q placed in the cavity

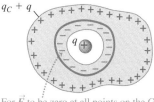

For $\vec{E}$ to be zero at all points on the Gaussian surface, the surface of the cavity must have a total charge $-q$.

Conceptual Example 22.11 **A conductor with a cavity**

A solid conductor with a cavity carries a total charge of $+7$ nC. Within the cavity, insulated from the conductor, is a point charge of -5 nC. How much charge is on each surface (inner and outer) of the conductor?

SOLUTION

Figure 22.24 shows the situation. If the charge in the cavity is $q = -5$ nC, the charge on the inner cavity surface must be $-q = -(-5 \text{ nC}) = +5$ nC. The conductor carries a *total* charge of $+7$ nC, none of which is in the interior of the material. If $+5$ nC is on the inner surface of the cavity, then there must be $(+7 \text{ nC}) - (+5 \text{ nC}) = +2$ nC on the outer surface of the conductor.

22.24 Our sketch for this problem. There is zero electric field inside the bulk conductor and hence zero flux through the Gaussian surface shown, so the charge on the cavity wall must be the opposite of the point charge.

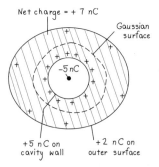

Net charge $= +7$ nC

Gaussian surface

-5 nC

$+5$ nC on cavity wall

$+2$ nC on outer surface

Testing Gauss's Law Experimentally

We can now consider a historic experiment, shown in Fig. 22.25. We mount a conducting container, such as a metal pail with a lid, on an insulating stand. The container is initially uncharged. Then we hang a charged metal ball from an insulating thread (Fig. 22.25a), lower it into the pail, and put the lid on (Fig. 22.25b). Charges are induced on the walls of the container, as shown. But now we let the ball *touch* the inner wall (Fig. 22.25c). The surface of the ball becomes, in effect, part of the cavity surface. The situation is now the same as Fig. 22.23b; if Gauss's law is correct, the net charge on the cavity surface must be zero. Thus the ball must lose all its charge. Finally, we pull the ball out; we find that it has indeed lost all its charge.

This experiment was performed in the 19th century by the English scientist Michael Faraday, using a metal icepail with a lid, and it is called **Faraday's ice-pail experiment.** (Similar experiments were carried out in the 18th century by Benjamin Franklin in America and Joseph Priestley in England, although with much less precision.) The result confirms the validity of Gauss's law and therefore of Coulomb's law. Faraday's result was significant because Coulomb's experimental method, using a torsion balance and dividing of charges, was not very precise; it is very difficult to confirm the $1/r^2$ dependence of the electrostatic force with great precision by direct force measurements. By contrast, experiments like Faraday's test the validity of Gauss's law, and therefore of Coulomb's law, with much greater precision.

22.25 (a) A charged conducting ball suspended by an insulating thread outside a conducting container on an insulating stand. (b) The ball is lowered into the container, and the lid is put on. (c) The ball is touched to the inner surface of the container.

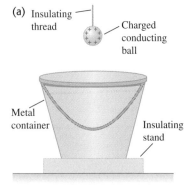

(a) Insulating thread — Charged conducting ball

Metal container — Insulating stand

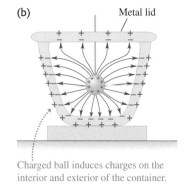

(b) Metal lid

Charged ball induces charges on the interior and exterior of the container.

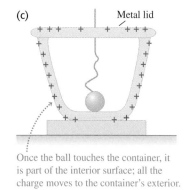

(c) Metal lid

Once the ball touches the container, it is part of the interior surface; all the charge moves to the container's exterior.

A modern version of Faraday's experiment is shown in Fig. 22.26. The details of the box labeled "Power supply" aren't important; its job is to place charge on the outer sphere and remove it, on demand. The inner box with a dial is a sensitive *electrometer,* an instrument that can detect motion of extremely small amounts of charge between the outer and inner spheres. If Gauss's law is correct, there can never be any charge on the inner surface of the outer sphere. If so, there should be no flow of charge between spheres while the outer sphere is being charged and discharged. The fact that no flow is actually observed is a very sensitive confirmation of Gauss's law and therefore of Coulomb's law. The precision of the experiment is limited mainly by the electrometer, which can be astonishingly sensitive. Experiments have shown that the exponent 2 in the $1/r^2$ of Coulomb's law does not differ from precisely 2 by more than 10^{-16}. So there is no reason to suspect that it is anything other than exactly 2.

The same principle behind Faraday's icepail experiment is used in a *Van de Graaff electrostatic generator* (Fig. 22.27). The charged conducting sphere of Fig. 22.26 is replaced by a charged belt that continuously carries charge to the inside of a conducting shell, only to have it carried away to the outside surface of the shell. As a result, the charge on the shell and the electric field around it can become very large very rapidly. The Van de Graaff generator is used as an accelerator of charged particles and for physics demonstrations.

This principle also forms the basis for *electrostatic shielding.* Suppose we have a very sensitive electronic instrument that we want to protect from stray electric fields that might cause erroneous measurements. We surround the instrument with a conducting box, or we line the walls, floor, and ceiling of the room with a conducting material such as sheet copper. The external electric field redistributes the free electrons in the conductor, leaving a net positive charge on the outer

22.26 The outer spherical shell can be alternately charged and discharged by the power supply. If there were any flow of charge between the inner and outer shells, it would be detected by the electrometer inside the inner shell.

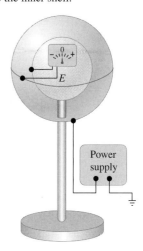

22.27 Cutaway view of the essential parts of a Van de Graaff electrostatic generator. The electron sink at the bottom draws electrons from the belt, giving it a positive charge; at the top the belt attracts electrons away from the conducting shell, giving the shell a positive charge.

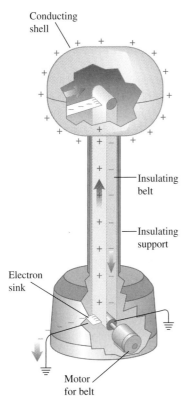

22.28 (a) A conducting box (a Faraday cage) immersed in a uniform electric field. The field of the induced charges on the box combines with the uniform field to give zero total field inside the box. (b) Electrostatic shielding can protect you from a dangerous electric discharge.

(a)

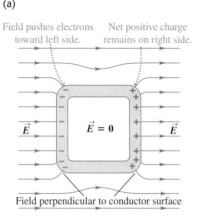

Field pushes electrons toward left side.   Net positive charge remains on right side.

$\vec{E}$ $\vec{E} = 0$ $\vec{E}$

Field perpendicular to conductor surface

(b)

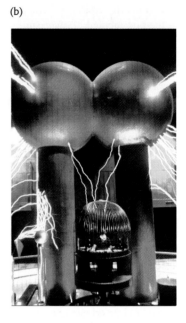

surface in some regions and a net negative charge in others (Fig. 22.28). This charge distribution causes an additional electric field such that the *total* field at every point inside the box is zero, as Gauss's law says it must be. The charge distribution on the box also alters the shapes of the field lines near the box, as the figure shows. Such a setup is often called a *Faraday cage*. The same physics tells you that one of the safest places to be in a lightning storm is inside an automobile; if the car is struck by lightning, the charge tends to remain on the metal skin of the vehicle, and little or no electric field is produced inside the passenger compartment.

Field at the Surface of a Conductor

Finally, we note that there is a direct relationship between the $\vec{E}$ field at a point just outside any conductor and the surface charge density σ at that point. In general, σ varies from point to point on the surface. We will show in Chapter 23 that at any such point, the direction of $\vec{E}$ is always *perpendicular* to the surface (see Fig. 22.28a).

To find a relationship between σ at any point on the surface and the perpendicular component of the electric field at that point, we construct a Gaussian surface in the form of a small cylinder (Fig. 22.29). One end face, with area A, lies within the conductor and the other lies just outside. The electric field is zero at all points within the conductor. Outside the conductor the component of $\vec{E}$ perpendicular to the side walls of the cylinder is zero, and over the end face the perpendicular component is equal to $E_\perp$. (If σ is positive, the electric field points out of the conductor and $E_\perp$ is positive; if σ is negative, the field points inward and $E_\perp$ is negative.) Hence the total flux through the surface is $E_\perp A$. The charge enclosed within the Gaussian surface is σA, so from Gauss's law,

22.29 The field just outside a charged conductor is perpendicular to the surface, and its perpendicular component $E_\perp$ is equal to σ/ϵ_0.

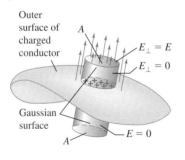

Outer surface of charged conductor

A

$E_\perp = E$

$E_\perp = 0$

Gaussian surface

$E = 0$

A

$$E_\perp A = \frac{\sigma A}{\epsilon_0} \qquad \text{and} \qquad E_\perp = \frac{\sigma}{\epsilon_0} \qquad \begin{array}{l}\text{(field at the surface}\\ \text{of a conductor)}\end{array} \qquad (22.10)$$

We can check this with the results we have obtained for spherical, cylindrical, and plane surfaces.

We showed in Example 22.8 that the field magnitude between two infinite flat oppositely charged conducting plates also equals σ/ϵ_0. In this case the field magnitude is the same at *all* distances from the plates, but in all other cases it decreases with increasing distance from the surface.

Conceptual Example 22.12   Field at the surface of a conducting sphere

Verify Eq. (22.10) for a conducting sphere with radius R and total charge q.

SOLUTION

In Example 22.5 (Section 22.4) we showed that the electric field just outside the surface is

$$E = \frac{1}{4\pi\epsilon_0}\frac{q}{R^2}$$

The surface charge density is uniform and equal to q divided by the surface area of the sphere:

$$\sigma = \frac{q}{4\pi R^2}$$

Comparing these two expressions, we see that $E = \sigma/\epsilon_0$, as Eq. (22.10) states.

Example 22.13   Electric field of the earth

The earth (a conductor) has a net electric charge. The resulting electric field near the surface can be measured with sensitive electronic instruments; its average value is about 150 N/C, directed toward the center of the earth. (a) What is the corresponding surface charge density? (b) What is the *total* surface charge of the earth?

SOLUTION

IDENTIFY: We are given the electric field magnitude at the surface of the conducting earth, and we are asked to calculate the surface charge density and the total charge on the entire surface of the earth.

SET UP: Given the perpendicular electric field, we determine the surface charge density σ using Eq. (22.10). The total surface charge on the earth is then the product of σ and the earth's surface area.

EXECUTE: (a) We know from the direction of the field that σ is negative (corresponding to $\vec{E}$ being directed *into* the surface, so $E_\perp$ is negative). From Eq. (22.10),

$$\sigma = \epsilon_0 E_\perp = (8.85 \times 10^{-12}\ \mathrm{C^2/N \cdot m^2})(-150\ \mathrm{N/C})$$
$$= -1.33 \times 10^{-9}\ \mathrm{C/m^2} = -1.33\ \mathrm{nC/m^2}$$

(b) The earth's surface area is $4\pi R_E^2$, where $R_E = 6.38 \times 10^6$ m is the radius of the earth (see Appendix F). The total charge Q is the product $4\pi R_E^2 \sigma$, or

$$Q = 4\pi(6.38 \times 10^6\ \mathrm{m})^2(-1.33 \times 10^{-9}\ \mathrm{C/m^2})$$
$$= -6.8 \times 10^5\ \mathrm{C} = -680\ \mathrm{kC}$$

EVALUATE: You can check our result in part (b) using the result of Example 22.5. Solving for Q, we find

$$Q = 4\pi\epsilon_0 R^2 E_\perp$$
$$= \frac{1}{9.0 \times 10^9\ \mathrm{N \cdot m^2/C^2}}(6.38 \times 10^6\ \mathrm{m})^2(-150\ \mathrm{N/C})$$
$$= -6.8 \times 10^5\ \mathrm{C}$$

One electron has a charge of -1.60×10^{-19} C. Hence this much excess negative electric charge corresponds to there being $(-6.8 \times 10^5\ \mathrm{C})/(-1.60 \times 10^{-19}\ \mathrm{C}) = 4.2 \times 10^{24}$ excess electrons on the earth, or about 7 moles of excess electrons. This is compensated by an equal *deficiency* of electrons in the earth's upper atmosphere, so the combination of the earth and its atmosphere is electrically neutral.

Test Your Understanding of Section 22.5   A hollow conducting sphere has no net charge. There is a positive point charge q at the center of the spherical cavity within the sphere. You connect a conducting wire from the outside of the sphere to ground. Will you measure an electric field outside the sphere?

Electric flux: Electric flux is a measure of the "flow" of electric field through a surface. It is equal to the product of an area element and the perpendicular component of $\vec{E}$, integrated over a surface. (See Examples 22.1–22.3.)

$$\Phi_E = \int E\cos\phi\, dA$$

$$= \int E_\perp\, dA = \int \vec{E}\cdot d\vec{A} \qquad (22.5)$$

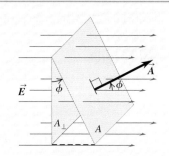

Gauss's law: Gauss's law states that the total electric flux through a closed surface, which can be written as the surface integral of the component of $\vec{E}$ normal to the surface, equals a constant times the total charge Q_{encl} enclosed by the surface. Gauss's law is logically equivalent to Coulomb's law, but its use greatly simplifies problems with a high degree of symmetry. (See Examples 22.4–22.10.)

When excess charge is placed on a conductor and is at rest, it resides entirely on the surface, and $\vec{E} = 0$ everywhere in the material of the conductor. (See Examples 22.11–22.13.)

$$\Phi_E = \oint E\cos\phi\, dA$$

$$= \oint E_\perp\, dA = \oint \vec{E}\cdot d\vec{A}$$

$$= \frac{Q_{encl}}{\epsilon_0} \qquad (22.8),\ (22.9)$$

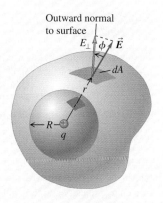

Outward normal to surface

Electric field of various symmetric charge distributions: The following table lists electric fields caused by several symmetric charge distributions. In the table, q, Q, λ, and σ refer to the *magnitudes* of the quantities.

Charge Distribution	Point in Electric Field	Electric Field Magnitude
Single point charge q	Distance r from q	$E = \dfrac{1}{4\pi\epsilon_0}\dfrac{q}{r^2}$
Charge q on surface of conducting sphere with radius R	Outside sphere, $r > R$	$E = \dfrac{1}{4\pi\epsilon_0}\dfrac{q}{r^2}$
	Inside sphere, $r < R$	$E = 0$
Infinite wire, charge per unit length λ	Distance r from wire	$E = \dfrac{1}{2\pi\epsilon_0}\dfrac{\lambda}{r}$
Infinite conducting cylinder with radius R, charge per unit length λ	Outside cylinder, $r > R$	$E = \dfrac{1}{2\pi\epsilon_0}\dfrac{\lambda}{r}$
	Inside cylinder, $r < R$	$E = 0$
Solid insulating sphere with radius R, charge Q distributed uniformly throughout volume	Outside sphere, $r > R$	$E = \dfrac{1}{4\pi\epsilon_0}\dfrac{Q}{r^2}$
	Inside sphere, $r < R$	$E = \dfrac{1}{4\pi\epsilon_0}\dfrac{Qr}{R^3}$
Infinite sheet of charge with uniform charge per unit area σ	Any point	$E = \dfrac{\sigma}{2\epsilon_0}$
Two oppositely charged conducting plates with surface charge densities $+\sigma$ and $-\sigma$	Any point between plates	$E = \dfrac{\sigma}{\epsilon_0}$

Key Terms

Answer to Chapter Opening Question   **?**

No. The electric field inside a cavity within a conductor is zero, so there is no electric effect on the child. (See Section 22.5.)

Answers to Test Your Understanding Questions

22.1 Answer: (iii)   Each part of the surface of the box will be three times farther from the charge $+q$, so the electric field will be $\left(\frac{1}{3}\right)^2 = \frac{1}{9}$ as strong. But the area of the box will increase by a factor of $3^2 = 9$. Hence the electric flux will be multiplied by a factor of $\left(\frac{1}{9}\right)(9) = 1$. In other words, the flux will be unchanged.

22.2 Answer: (iv), (ii), (i), (iii)   In each case the electric field in uniform, so the flux is $\Phi_E = \vec{E} \cdot \vec{A}$. We use the relationships for the scalar products of unit vectors: $\hat{\imath} \cdot \hat{\imath} = \hat{\jmath} \cdot \hat{\jmath} = 1$, $\hat{\imath} \cdot \hat{\jmath} = 0$. In case (i) we have $\Phi_E = (4.0 \text{ N/C})(6.0 \text{ m}^2)\hat{\imath} \cdot \hat{\jmath} = 0$ (the electric field and vector area are perpendicular, so there is zero flux). In case (ii) we have $\Phi_E [(4.0 \text{ N/C})\hat{\imath} + (2.0 \text{ N/C})\hat{\jmath}] \cdot (3.0 \text{ m}^2)\hat{\jmath} = (2.0 \text{ N/C}) \cdot (3.0 \text{ m}^2) = 6.0 \text{ N} \cdot \text{m}^2/\text{C}$. Similarly, in case (iii) we have $\Phi_E = [(4.0 \text{ N/C})\hat{\imath} - (2.0 \text{ N/C})\hat{\jmath}] \cdot [(3.0 \text{ m}^2)\hat{\imath} + (7.0 \text{ m}^2)\hat{\jmath}] = (4.0 \text{ N/C})(3.0 \text{ m}^2) - (2.0 \text{ N/C})(7.0 \text{ m}^2) = -2 \text{ N} \cdot \text{m}^2/\text{C}$, and in case (iv) we have $\Phi_E = [(4.0 \text{ N/C})\hat{\imath} - (2.0 \text{ N/C})\hat{\jmath}] \cdot [(3.0 \text{ m}^2)\hat{\imath} - (7.0 \text{ m}^2)\hat{\jmath}] = (4.0 \text{ N/C})(3.0 \text{ m}^2) + (2.0 \text{ N/C}) \cdot (7.0 \text{ m}^2) = 26 \text{ N} \cdot \text{m}^2/\text{C}$.

22.3 Answer: S_2, S_5, S_4, S_1 and S_3 (tie)   Gauss's law tells us that the flux through a closed surface is proportional to the amount of charge enclosed within that surface. So an ordering of these surfaces by their fluxes is the same as an ordering by the amount of enclosed charge. Surface S_1 encloses no charge, surface S_2 encloses $9.0 \ \mu\text{C} + 5.0 \ \mu\text{C} + (-7.0 \ \mu\text{C}) = 7.0 \ \mu\text{C}$, surface S_3 encloses $9.0 \ \mu\text{C} + 1.0 \ \mu\text{C} + (-10.0 \ \mu\text{C}) = 0$, surface S_4 encloses $8.0 \ \mu\text{C} + (-7.0 \ \mu\text{C}) = 1.0 \ \mu\text{C}$, and surface S_5 encloses $8.0 \ \mu\text{C} + (-7.0 \ \mu\text{C}) + (-10.0 \ \mu\text{C}) + (1.0 \ \mu\text{C}) + (9.0 \ \mu\text{C}) + (5.0 \ \mu\text{C}) = 6.0 \ \mu\text{C}$.

22.4 Answer: no   You might be tempted to draw a Gaussian surface that is an enlarged version of the conductor, with the same shape and placed so that it completely encloses the conductor. While you know the flux through this Gaussian surface (by Gauss's law, it's $\Phi_E = Q/\epsilon_0$), the direction of the electric field need not be perpendicular to the surface and the magnitude of the field need not be the same at all points on the surface. It's not possible to do the flux integral $\oint E_\perp \, dA$, and we can't calculate the electric field. Gauss's law is useful for calculating the electric field only when the charge distribution is *highly* symmetric.

22.5 Answer: no   Before you connect the wire to the sphere, the presence of the point charge will induce a charge $-q$ on the inner surface of the hollow sphere and a charge q on the outer surface (the net charge on the sphere is zero). There will be an electric field outside the sphere due to the charge on the outer surface. Once you touch the conducting wire to the sphere, however, electrons will flow from ground to the outer surface of the sphere to neutralize the charge there (see Fig. 21.7c). As a result the sphere will have no charge on its outer surface and no electric field outside.

PROBLEMS

For instructor-assigned homework, go to **www.masteringphysics.com**

Discussion Questions

Q22.1. A rubber balloon has a single point charge in its interior. Does the electric flux through the balloon depend on whether or not it is fully inflated? Explain your reasoning.

Q22.2. Suppose that in Fig. 22.15 both charges were positive. What would be the fluxes through each of the four surfaces in the example?

Q22.3. In Fig. 22.15, suppose a third point charge were placed outside the purple Gaussian surface *C*. Would this affect the electric flux through any of the surfaces *A*, *B*, *C*, or *D* in the figure? Why or why not?

Q22.4. A certain region of space bounded by an imaginary closed surface contains no charge. Is the electric field always zero everywhere on the surface? If not, under what circumstances is it zero on the surface?

Q22.5. A spherical Gaussian surface encloses a point charge q. If the point charge is moved from the center of the sphere to a point away from the center, does the electric field at a point on the surface change? Does the total flux through the Gaussian surface change? Explain.

Q22.6. You find a sealed box on your doorstep. You suspect that the box contains several charged metal spheres packed in insulat-

ing material. How can you determine the total net charge inside the box without opening the box? Or isn't this possible?

Q22.7. During the flow of electric current in a conducting wire, one or more electrons from each atom are free to move along the wire, somewhat like water flowing through a pipe. Would you expect to find an electric field outside a wire carrying such a steady flow of electrons? Explain.

Q22.8. If the electric field of a point charge were proportional to $1/r^3$ instead of $1/r^2$, would Gauss's law still be valid? Explain your reasoning. (*Hint:* Consider a spherical Gaussian surface centered on a single point charge.)

Q22.9. Suppose the disk in Example 22.1 (Section 22.2), instead of having its normal vector oriented at just two or three particular angles to the electric field, began to rotate continuously, so that its normal vector was first parallel to the field, then perpendicular to it, then opposite to it, and so on. Sketch a graph of the resulting electric flux versus time, for an entire rotation of 360°.

Q22.10. In a conductor, one or more electrons from each atom are free to roam throughout the volume of the conductor. Does this contradict the statement that any excess charge on a solid conductor must reside on its surface? Why or why not?

Q22.11. You charge up the van de Graaff generator shown in Fig. 22.27, and then bring an identical but uncharged hollow conducting sphere near it, without letting the two spheres touch. Sketch the distribution of charges on the second sphere. What is the net flux through the second sphere? What is the electric field inside the second sphere?

Q22.12. The magnitude of $\vec{E}$ at the surface of an irregularly shaped solid conductor must be greatest in regions where the surface curves most sharply, such as point A in Fig. 22.30, and must be least in flat regions such as point B in Fig. 22.30. Explain why this must be so by considering how electric field lines must be arranged near a conducting surface. How does the surface charge density compare at points A and B ? Explain.

Figure **22.30**
Question Q22.12.

Q22.13. A lightning rod is a rounded copper rod mounted on top of a building and welded to a heavy copper cable running down into the ground. Lightning rods are used to protect houses and barns from lightning; the lightning current runs through the copper rather than through the building. Why? Why should the end of the rod be rounded? (*Hint:* The answer to Discussion Question Q22.12 may be helpful.)

Q22.14. A solid conductor has a cavity in its interior. Would the presence of a point charge inside the cavity affect the electric field outside the conductor? Why or why not? Would the presence of a point charge outside the conductor affect the electric field inside the cavity? Again, why or why not?

Q22.15. Explain this statement: "In a static situation, the electric field at the surface of a conductor can have no component parallel to the surface because this would violate the condition that the charges on the surface are at rest." Would this same statement be valid for the electric field at the surface of an *insulator?* Explain your answer and the reason for any differences between the cases of a conductor and an insulator.

Q22.16. A solid copper sphere has a net positive charge. The charge is distributed uniformly over the surface of the sphere, and the electric field inside the sphere is zero. Then a negative point charge outside the sphere is brought close to the surface of the sphere. Is all the net charge on the sphere still on its surface? If so, is this charge still distributed uniformly over the surface? If it is not uniform, how is it distributed? Is the electric field inside the sphere still zero? In each case justify your answers.

Q22.17. Some modern aircraft are made primarily of composite materials that do not conduct electricity. The U.S. Federal Aviation Administration requires that such aircraft have conducting wires embedded in their surfaces to provide protection when flying near thunderstorms. Explain the physics behind this requirement.

Exercises

Section 22.2 Calculating Electric Flux

22.1. A flat sheet of paper of area 0.250 m² is oriented so that the normal to the sheet is at an angle of 60° to a uniform electric field of magnitude 14 N/C. (a) Find the magnitude of the electric flux through the sheet. (b) Does the answer to part (a) depend on the shape of the sheet? Why or why not? (c) For what angle ϕ between the normal to the sheet and the electric field is the magnitude of the flux through the sheet (i) largest and (ii) smallest? Explain your answers.

22.2. A flat sheet is in the shape of a rectangle with sides of lengths 0.400 m and 0.600 m. The sheet is immersed in a uniform electric field of magnitude 75.0 N/C that is directed at 20° from the plane of the sheet (Fig. 22.31). Find the magnitude of the electric flux through the sheet.

Figure **22.31** Exercise 22.2.

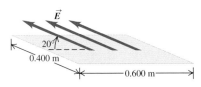

22.3. You measure an electric field of 1.25×10^6 N/C at a distance of 0.150 m from a point charge. (a) What is the electric flux through a sphere at that distance from the charge? (b) What is the magnitude of the charge?

22.4. A cube has sides of length $L = 0.300$ m. It is placed with one corner at the origin as shown in Fig. 22.32. The electric field is not uniform but is given by $\vec{E} = (-5.00\ \text{N}/\text{C} \cdot \text{m})x\hat{i} + (3.00\ \text{N}/\text{C} \cdot \text{m})z\hat{k}$. (a) Find the electric flux through each of the six cube faces S_1, S_2, S_3, S_4, S_5, and S_6. (b) Find the total electric charge inside the cube.

Figure **22.32** Exercises 22.4 and 22.6; Problem 22.32.

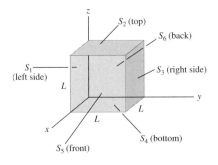

22.5. A hemispherical surface with radius r in a region of uniform electric field $\vec{E}$ has its axis aligned parallel to the direction of the field. Calculate the flux through the surface.

22.6. The cube in Fig. 22.32 has sides of length $L = 10.0$ cm. The electric field is uniform, has magnitude $E = 4.00 \times 10^3$ N/C, and is parallel to the xy-plane at an angle of 36.9° measured from the $+x$-axis toward the $+y$-axis. (a) What is the electric flux through each of the six cube faces S_1, S_2, S_3, S_4, S_5, and S_6? (b) What is the total electric flux through all faces of the cube?

22.7. It was shown in Example 21.11 (Section 21.5) that the electric field due to an infinite line of charge is perpendicular to the line and has magnitude $E = \lambda/2\pi\epsilon_0 r$. Consider an imaginary cylinder with radius $r = 0.250$ m and length $l = 0.400$ m that has an infinite line of positive charge running along its axis. The charge per unit length on the line is $\lambda = 6.00\ \mu\text{C}/\text{m}$. (a) What is the electric flux through the cylinder due to this infinite line of charge? (b) What is the flux through the cylinder if its radius is increased to $r = 0.500$ m? (c) What is the flux through the cylinder if its length is increased to $l = 0.800$ m?

Section 22.3 Gauss's Law

22.8. The three small spheres shown in Fig. 22.33 carry charges $q_1 = 4.00$ nC, $q_2 = -7.80$ nC, and $q_3 = 2.40$ nC. Find the net electric flux through each of the following closed surfaces shown in cross section in the figure: (a) S_1; (b) S_2; (c) S_3; (d) S_4; (e) S_5. (f) Do your answers to parts (a)–(e) depend on how the charge is distributed over each small sphere? Why or why not?

Figure **22.33** Exercise 22.8.

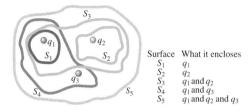

Surface	What it encloses
S_1	q_1
S_2	q_2
S_3	q_1 and q_2
S_4	q_1 and q_3
S_5	q_1 and q_2 and q_3

22.9. A charged paint is spread in a very thin uniform layer over the surface of a plastic sphere of diameter 12.0 cm, giving it a charge of $-15.0 \ \mu$C. Find the electric field (a) just inside the paint layer; (b) just outside the paint layer; (c) 5.00 cm outside the surface of the paint layer.

22.10. A point charge $q_1 = 4.00$ nC is located on the x-axis at $x = 2.00$ m, and a second point charge $q_2 = -6.00$ nC is on the y-axis at $y = 1.00$ m. What is the total electric flux due to these two point charges through a spherical surface centered at the origin and with radius (a) 0.500 m, (b) 1.50 m, (c) 2.50 m?

22.11. In a certain region of space, the electric field $\vec{E}$ is uniform. (a) Use Gauss's law to prove that this region of space must be electrically neutral; that is, the volume charge density ρ must be zero. (b) Is the converse true? That is, in a region of space where there is no charge, must $\vec{E}$ be uniform? Explain.

22.12. (a) In a certain region of space, the volume charge density ρ has a uniform positive value. Can $\vec{E}$ be uniform in this region? Explain. (b) Suppose that in this region of uniform positive ρ there is a "bubble" within which $\rho = 0$. Can $\vec{E}$ be uniform within this bubble? Explain.

22.13. A 9.60-μC point charge is at the center of a cube with sides of length 0.500 m. (a) What is the electric flux through one of the six faces of the cube? (b) How would your answer to part (a) change if the sides were 0.250 m long? Explain.

22.14. Electric Fields in an Atom. The nuclei of large atoms, such as uranium, with 92 protons, can be modeled as spherically symmetric spheres of charge. The radius of the uranium nucleus is approximately 7.4×10^{-15} m. (a) What is the electric field this nucleus produces just outside its surface? (b) What magnitude of electric field does it produce at the distance of the electrons, which is about 1.0×10^{-10} m? (c) The electrons can be modeled as forming a uniform shell of negative charge. What net electric field do they produce at the location of the nucleus?

22.15. A point charge of $+5.00 \ \mu$C is located on the x-axis at $x = 4.00$ m, next to a spherical surface of radius 3.00 m centered at the origin. (a) Calculate the magnitude of the electric field at $x = 3.00$ m. (b) Calculate the magnitude of the electric field at $x = -3.00$ m. (c) According to Gauss's law, the net flux through the sphere is zero because it contains no charge. Yet the field due to the external charge is much stronger on the near side of the sphere (i.e., at $x = 3.00$ m) than on the far side (at $x = -3.00$ m). How, then, can the flux into the sphere (on the near side) equal the flux out of it (on the far side)? Explain. A sketch will help.

Section 22.4 Applications of Gauss's Law and Section 22.5 Charges on Conductors

22.16. A solid metal sphere with radius 0.450 m carries a net charge of 0.250 nC. Find the magnitude of the electric field (a) at a point 0.100 m outside the surface of the sphere and (b) at a point inside the sphere, 0.100 m below the surface.

22.17. On a humid day, an electric field of 2.00×10^4 N/C is enough to produce sparks about an inch long. Suppose that in your physics class, a van de Graaff generator (see Fig. 22.27) with a sphere radius of 15.0 cm is producing sparks 6 inches long. (a) Use Gauss's law to calculate the amount of charge stored on the surface of the sphere before you bravely discharge it with your hand. (b) Assume all the charge is concentrated at the center of the sphere, and use Coulomb's law to calculate the electric field at the surface of the sphere.

22.18. Some planetary scientists have suggested that the planet Mars has an electric field somewhat similar to that of the earth, producing a net electric flux of 3.63×10^{16} N · m²/C at the planet's surface. Calculate: (a) the total electric charge on the planet; (b) the electric field at the planet's surface (refer to the astronomical data inside the back cover); (c) the charge density on Mars, assuming all the charge is uniformly distributed over the planet's surface.

22.19. How many excess electrons must be added to an isolated spherical conductor 32.0 cm in diameter to produce an electric field of 1150 N/C just outside the surface?

22.20. The electric field 0.400 m from a very long uniform line of charge is 840 N/C. How much charge is contained in a 2.00-cm section of the line?

22.21. A very long uniform line of charge has charge per unit length $4.80 \ \mu$C/m and lies along the x-axis. A second long uniform line of charge has charge per unit length $-2.40 \ \mu$C/m and is parallel to the x-axis at $y = 0.400$ m. What is the net electric field (magnitude and direction) at the following points on the y-axis: (a) $y = 0.200$ m and (b) $y = 0.600$ m?

22.22. (a) At a distance of 0.200 cm from the center of a charged conducting sphere with radius 0.100 cm, the electric field is 480 N/C. What is the electric field 0.600 cm from the center of the sphere? (b) At a distance of 0.200 cm from the axis of a very long charged conducting cylinder with radius 0.100 cm, the electric field is 480 N/C. What is the electric field 0.600 cm from the axis of the cylinder? (c) At a distance of 0.200 cm from a large uniform sheet of charge, the electric field is 480 N/C. What is the electric field 1.20 cm from the sheet?

22.23. A hollow, conducting sphere with an outer radius of 0.250 m and an inner radius of 0.200 m has a uniform surface charge density of $+6.37 \times 10^{-6}$ C/m². A charge of $-0.500 \ \mu$C is now introduced into the cavity inside the sphere. (a) What is the new charge density on the outside of the sphere? (b) Calculate the strength of the electric field just outside the sphere. (c) What is the electric flux through a spherical surface just inside the inner surface of the sphere?

22.24. A point charge of $-2.00 \ \mu$C is located in the center of a spherical cavity of radius 6.50 cm inside an insulating charged solid. The charge density in the solid is $\rho = 7.35 \times 10^{-4}$ C/m³. Calculate the electric field inside the solid at a distance of 9.50 cm from the center of the cavity.

22.25. The electric field at a distance of 0.145 m from the surface of a solid insulating sphere with radius 0.355 m is 1750 N/C. (a) Assuming the sphere's charge is uniformly distributed, what is the charge density inside it? (b) Calculate the electric field inside the sphere at a distance of 0.200 m from the center.

22.26. A conductor with an inner cavity, like that shown in Fig. 22.23c, carries a total charge of +5.00 nC. The charge within the cavity, insulated from the conductor, is −6.00 nC. How much charge is on (a) the inner surface of the conductor and (b) the outer surface of the conductor?

22.27. Apply Gauss's law to the Gaussian surfaces S_2, S_3, and S_4 in Fig. 22.21b to calculate the electric field between and outside the plates.

22.28. A square insulating sheet 80.0 cm on a side is held horizontally. The sheet has 7.50 nC of charge spread uniformly over its area. (a) Calculate the electric field at a point 0.100 mm above the center of the sheet. (b) Estimate the electric field at a point 100 m above the center of the sheet. (c) Would the answers to parts (a) and (b) be different if the sheet were made of a conducting material? Why or why not?

22.29. An infinitely long cylindrical conductor has radius R and uniform surface charge density σ. (a) In terms of σ and R, what is the charge per unit length λ for the cylinder? (b) In terms of σ, what is the magnitude of the electric field produced by the charged cylinder at a distance $r > R$ from its axis? (c) Express the result of part (b) in terms of λ and show that the electric field outside the cylinder is the same as if all the charge were on the axis. Compare your result to the result for a line of charge in Example 22.6 (Section 22.4).

22.30. Two very large, nonconducting plastic sheets, each 10.0 cm thick, carry uniform charge densities σ_1, σ_2, σ_3, and σ_4 on their surfaces, as shown in Fig. 22.34. These surface charge densities have the values $\sigma_1 = -6.00\ \mu C/m^2$, $\sigma_2 = +5.00\ \mu C/m^2$, $\sigma_3 = +2.00\ \mu C/m^2$, and $\sigma_4 = +4.00\ \mu C/m^2$. Use Gauss's law to find the magnitude and direction of the electric field at the following points, far from the edges of these sheets: (a) point A, 5.00 cm from the left face of the left-hand sheet; (b) point B, 1.25 cm from the inner surface of the right-hand sheet; (c) point C, in the middle of the right-hand sheet.

Figure 22.34
Exercise 22.30.

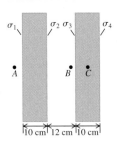

22.31. A negative charge $-Q$ is placed inside the cavity of a hollow metal solid. The outside of the solid is grounded by connecting a conducting wire between it and the earth. (a) Is there any excess charge induced on the inner surface of the piece of metal? If so, find its sign and magnitude. (b) Is there any excess charge on the outside of the piece of metal? Why or why not? (c) Is there an electric field in the cavity? Explain. (d) Is there an electric field within the metal? Why or why not? Is there an electric field outside the piece of metal? Explain why or why not. (e) Would someone outside the solid measure an electric field due to the charge $-Q$? Is it reasonable to say that the grounded conductor has *shielded* the region from the effects of the charge $-Q$? In principle, could the same thing be done for gravity? Why or why not?

Problems

22.32. A cube has sides of length L. It is placed with one corner at the origin as shown in Fig. 22.32. The electric field is uniform and given by $\vec{E} = -B\hat{i} + C\hat{j} - D\hat{k}$, where B, C, and D are positive constants. (a) Find the electric flux through each of the six cube faces S_1, S_2, S_3, S_4, S_5, and S_6. (b) Find the electric flux through the entire cube.

22.33. The electric field $\vec{E}$ in Fig. 22.35 is everywhere parallel to the x-axis, so the components E_y and E_z are zero. The x-component of the field E_x depends on x but not on y and z. At points in the yz-plane (where $x = 0$), $E_x = 125\ N/C$. (a) What is the electric flux through surface I in Fig. 22.35? (b) What is the electric flux through surface II? (c) The volume shown in the figure is a small section of a very large insulating slab 1.0 m thick. If there is a total charge of -24.0 nC within the volume shown, what are the magnitude and direction of $\vec{E}$ at the face opposite surface I? (d) Is the electric field produced only by charges within the slab, or is the field also due to charges outside the slab? How can you tell?

Figure 22.35
Problem 22.33.

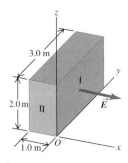

22.34. A flat, square surface with sides of length L is described by the equations

$$x = L \qquad (0 \leq y \leq L, 0 \leq z \leq L)$$

(a) Draw this square and show the x-, y-, and z-axes. (b) Find the electric flux through the square due to a positive point charge q located at the origin $(x = 0, y = 0, z = 0)$. (Hint: Think of the square as part of a cube centered on the origin.)

22.35. The electric field $\vec{E}_1$ at one face of a parallelepiped is uniform over the entire face and is directed out of the face. At the opposite face, the electric field $\vec{E}_2$ is also uniform over the entire face and is directed into that face (Fig. 22.36). The two faces in question are inclined at 30.0° from the horizontal, while $\vec{E}_1$ and $\vec{E}_2$ are both horizontal; $\vec{E}_1$ has a magnitude of $2.50 \times 10^4\ N/C$, and $\vec{E}_2$ has a magnitude of $7.00 \times 10^4\ N/C$. (a) Assuming that no other electric field lines cross the surfaces of the parallelepiped, determine the net charge contained within. (b) Is the electric field produced only by the charges within the parallelepiped, or is the field also due to charges outside the parallelepiped? How can you tell?

Figure 22.36
Problem 22.35.

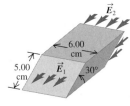

22.36. A long line carrying a uniform linear charge density $+50.0\ \mu C/m$ runs parallel to and 10.0 cm from the surface of a large, flat plastic sheet that has a uniform surface charge density of $-100\ \mu C/m^2$ on one side. Find the location of all points where an α particle would feel no force due to this arrangement of charged objects.

22.37. The Coaxial Cable. A long coaxial cable consists of an inner cylindrical conductor with radius a and an outer coaxial cylinder with inner radius b and outer radius c. The outer cylinder is mounted on insulating supports and has no net charge. The inner cylinder has a uniform positive charge per unit length λ. Calculate the electric field (a) at any point between the cylinders a distance r from the axis and (b) at any point outside the outer cylinder. (c) Graph the magnitude of the electric field as a function of the distance r from the axis of the cable, from $r = 0$ to $r = 2c$. (d) Find the charge per unit length on the inner surface and on the outer surface of the outer cylinder.

22.38. A very long conducting tube (hollow cylinder) has inner radius a and outer radius b. It carries charge per unit length $+\alpha$, where α is a positive constant with units of C/m. A line of charge lies along the axis of the tube. The line of charge has charge per unit length $+\alpha$. (a) Calculate the electric field in terms of α and the distance r from the axis of the tube for (i) $r < a$; (ii) $a < r < b$; (iii) $r > b$. Show your results in a graph of E as a function of r. (b) What is the charge per unit length on (i) the inner surface of the tube and (ii) the outer surface of the tube?

22.39. Repeat Problem 22.38, but now let the conducting tube have charge per unit length $-\alpha$. As in Problem 22.38, the line of charge has charge per unit length $+\alpha$.

22.40. A very long, solid cylinder with radius R has positive charge uniformly distributed throughout it, with charge per unit volume ρ. (a) Derive the expression for the electric field inside the volume at a distance r from the axis of the cylinder in terms of the charge density ρ. (b) What is the electric field at a point outside the volume in terms of the charge per unit length λ in the cylinder? (c) Compare the answers to parts (a) and (b) for $r = R$. (d) Graph the electric-field magnitude as a function of r from $r = 0$ to $r = 3R$.

22.41. A small sphere with a mass of 0.002 g and carrying a charge of 5.00×10^{-8} C hangs from a thread near a very large, charged conducting sheet, as shown in Fig. 22.37. The charge density on the sheet is 2.50×10^{-9} C/m². Find the angle of the thread.

Figure **22.37**
Problem 22.41.

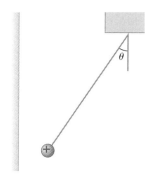

22.42. A Sphere in a Sphere. A solid conducting sphere carrying charge q has radius a. It is inside a concentric hollow conducting sphere with inner radius b and outer radius c. The hollow sphere has no net charge. (a) Derive expressions for the electric-field magnitude in terms of the distance r from the center for the regions $r < a$, $a < r < b$, $b < r < c$, and $r > c$. (b) Graph the magnitude of the electric field as a function of r from $r = 0$ to $r = 2c$. (c) What is the charge on the inner surface of the hollow sphere? (d) On the outer surface? (e) Represent the charge of the small sphere by four plus signs. Sketch the field lines of the system within a spherical volume of radius $2c$.

22.43. A solid conducting sphere with radius R that carries positive charge Q is concentric with a very thin insulating shell of radius $2R$ that also carries charge Q. The charge Q is distributed uniformly over the insulating shell. (a) Find the electric field (magnitude and direction) in each of the regions $0 < r < R$, $R < r < 2R$, and $r > 2R$. (b) Graph the electric-field magnitude as a function of r.

22.44. A conducting spherical shell with inner radius a and outer radius b has a positive point charge Q located at its center. The total charge on the shell is $-3Q$, and it is insulated from its surroundings (Fig. 22.38). (a) Derive expressions for the electric-field magnitude in terms of the distance r from the center for the regions $r < a$, $a < r < b$, and $r > b$. (b) What is the surface charge density on the inner surface of the conducting shell? (c) What is the surface charge density on the outer surface of the conducting shell? (d) Sketch the electric field lines and the location of all charges. (e) Graph the electric-field magnitude as a function of r.

Figure **22.38**
Problem 22.44.

22.45. Concentric Spherical Shells. A small conducting spherical shell with inner radius a and outer radius b is concentric with a larger conducting spherical shell with inner radius c and outer radius d (Fig. 22.39). The inner shell has total charge $+2q$, and the outer shell has charge $+4q$. (a) Calculate the electric field (magnitude and direction) in terms of q and the distance r from the common center of the two shells for (i) $r < a$; (ii) $a < r < b$; (iii) $b < r < c$; (iv) $c < r < d$; (v) $r > d$. Show your results in a graph of the radial component of $\vec{E}$ as a function of r. (b) What is the total charge on the (i) inner surface of the small shell; (ii) outer surface of the small shell; (iii) inner surface of the large shell; (iv) outer surface of the large shell?

Figure **22.39**
Problem 22.45.

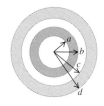

22.46. Repeat Problem 22.45, but now let the outer shell have charge $-2q$. As in Problem 22.45, the inner shell has charge $+2q$.

22.47. Repeat Problem 22.45, but now let the outer shell have charge $-4q$. As in Problem 22.45, the inner shell has charge $+2q$.

22.48. A solid conducting sphere with radius R carries a positive total charge Q. The sphere is surrounded by an insulating shell with inner radius R and outer radius $2R$. The insulating shell has a uniform charge density ρ. (a) Find the value of ρ so that the net charge of the entire system is zero. (b) If ρ has the value found in part (a), find the electric field (magnitude and direction) in each of the regions $0 < r < R$, $R < r < 2R$, and $r > 2R$. Show your results in a graph of the radial component of $\vec{E}$ as a function of r. (c) As a general rule, the electric field is discontinuous only at locations where there is a thin sheet of charge. Explain how your results in part (b) agree with this rule.

22.49. Negative charge $-Q$ is distributed uniformly over the surface of a thin spherical insulating shell with radius R. Calculate the force (magnitude and direction) that the shell exerts on a positive point charge q located (a) a distance $r > R$ from the center of the shell (outside the shell) and (b) a distance $r < R$ from the center of the shell (inside the shell).

22.50. (a) How many excess electrons must be distributed uniformly within the volume of an isolated plastic sphere 30.0 cm in diameter to produce an electric field of 1150 N/C just outside the surface of the sphere? (b) What is the electric field at a point 10.0 cm outside the surface of the sphere?

22.51. A single isolated, large conducting plate (Fig. 22.40) has a charge per unit area σ on its surface. Because the plate is a conductor, the electric field at its surface is perpendicular to the surface and has magnitude $E = \sigma/\epsilon_0$. (a) In Example 22.7 (Section 22.4) it was shown that the field caused by a large, uniformly charged sheet with charge per unit area σ has magnitude $E = \sigma/2\epsilon_0$, exactly *half* as much as for a charged conducting plate. Why is there a difference? (b) Regarding the charge distribution on the conducting plate as being two sheets of charge (one on each surface), each with charge per unit area σ, use the result of Example 22.7 and the principle of superposition to show that $E = 0$ inside the plate and $E = \sigma/\epsilon_0$ outside the plate.

Figure **22.40** Problem 22.51.

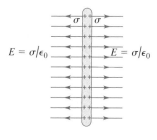

$E = \sigma/\epsilon_0$ $E = \sigma/\epsilon_0$

22.52. Thomson's Model of the Atom. In the early years of the 20th century, a leading model of the structure of the atom was that of the English physicist J. J. Thomson (the discoverer of the electron). In Thomson's model, an atom consisted of a sphere of positively charged material in which were embedded negatively charged electrons, like chocolate chips in a ball of cookie dough. Consider such an atom consisting of one electron with mass m and charge $-e$, which may be regarded as a point charge, and a uniformly charged sphere of charge $+e$ and radius R. (a) Explain why the equilibrium position of the electron is at the center of the nucleus. (b) In Thomson's model, it was assumed that the positive material provided little or no resistance to the motion of the electron. If the electron is displaced from equilibrium by a distance less than R, show that the resulting motion of the electron will be simple harmonic, and calculate the frequency of oscillation. (*Hint:* Review the definition of simple harmonic motion in Section 13.2. If it can be shown that the net force on the electron is of this form, then it follows that the motion is simple harmonic. Conversely, if the net force on the electron does not follow this form, the motion is not simple harmonic.) (c) By Thomson's time, it was known that excited atoms emit light waves of only certain frequencies. In his model, the frequency of emitted light is the same as the oscillation frequency of the electron or electrons in the atom. What would the radius of a Thomson-model atom have to be for it to produce red light of frequency 4.57×10^{14} Hz? Compare your answer to the radii of real atoms, which are of the order of 10^{-10} m (see Appendix F for data about the electron). (d) If the electron were displaced from equilibrium by a distance greater than R, would the electron oscillate? Would its motion be simple harmonic? Explain your reasoning. (*Historical note:* In 1910, the atomic nucleus was discovered, proving the Thomson model to be incorrect. An atom's positive charge is not spread over its volume as Thomson supposed, but is concentrated in the tiny nucleus of radius 10^{-14} to 10^{-15} m.)

22.53. Thomson's Model of the Atom, Continued. Using Thomson's (outdated) model of the atom described in Problem 22.52, consider an atom consisting of two electrons, each of charge $-e$, embedded in a sphere of charge $+2e$ and radius R. In equilibrium, each electron is a distance d from the center of the atom (Fig. 22.41). Find the distance d in terms of the other properties of the atom.

Figure 22.41 Problem 22.53.

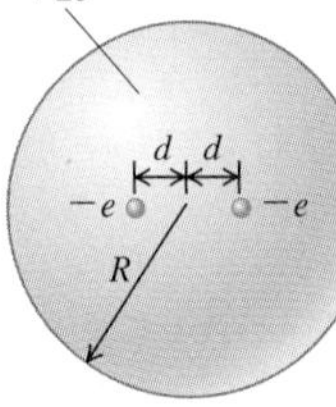

22.54. A Uniformly Charged Slab. A slab of insulating material has thickness $2d$ and is oriented so that its faces are parallel to the yz-plane and given by the planes $x = d$ and $x = -d$. The y- and z-dimensions of the slab are very large compared to d and may be treated as essentially infinite. The slab has a uniform positive charge density ρ. (a) Explain why the electric field due to the slab is zero at the center of the slab ($x = 0$). (b) Using Gauss's law, find the electric field due to the slab (magnitude and direction) at all points in space.

22.55. A Nonuniformly Charged Slab. Repeat Problem 22.54, but now let the charge density of the slab be given by $\rho(x) = \rho_0(x/d)^2$, where ρ_0 is a positive constant.

22.56. Can Electric Forces Alone Give Stable Equilibrium? In Chapter 21, several examples were given of calculating the force exerted on a point charge by other point charges in its surroundings. (a) Consider a positive point charge $+q$. Give an example of how you would place two other point charges of your choosing so that the net force on charge $+q$ will be zero. (b) If the net force on charge $+q$ is zero, then that charge is in equilibrium. The equilibrium will be *stable* if, when the charge $+q$ is displaced slightly in *any* direction from its position of equilibrium, the net force on the charge pushes it back toward the equilibrium position. For this to be the case, what must the direction of the electric field

$\vec{E}$ be due to the other charges at points surrounding the equilibrium position of $+q$? (c) Imagine that the charge $+q$ is moved very far away, and imagine a small Gaussian surface centered on the position where $+q$ was in equilibrium. By applying Gauss's law to this surface, show that it is *impossible* to satisfy the condition for stability described in part (b). In other words, a charge $+q$ cannot be held in stable equilibrium by electrostatic forces alone. This result is known as *Earnshaw's theorem*. (d) Parts (a)–(c) referred to the equilibrium of a positive point charge $+q$. Prove that Earnshaw's theorem also applies to a negative point charge $-q$.

22.57. A nonuniform, but spherically symmetric, distribution of charge has a charge density $\rho(r)$ given as follows:

$$\rho(r) = \rho_0 \left(1 - r/R\right) \quad \text{for } r \le R$$
$$\rho(r) = 0 \quad \text{for } r \ge R$$

where $\rho_0 = 3Q/\pi R^3$ is a positive constant. (a) Show that the total charge contained in the charge distribution is Q. (b) Show that the electric field in the region $r \ge R$ is identical to that produced by a point charge Q at $r = 0$. (c) Obtain an expression for the electric field in the region $r \le R$. (d) Graph the electric-field magnitude E as a function of r. (e) Find the value of r at which the electric field is maximum, and find the value of that maximum field.

22.58. A nonuniform, but spherically symmetric, distribution of charge has a charge density $\rho(r)$ given as follows:

$$\rho(r) = \rho_0 \left(1 - 4r/3R\right) \quad \text{for } r \le R$$
$$\rho(r) = 0 \quad \text{for } r \ge R$$

where ρ_0 is a positive constant. (a) Find the total charge contained in the charge distribution. (b) Obtain an expression for the electric field in the region $r \ge R$. (c) Obtain an expression for the electric field in the region $r \le R$. (d) Graph the electric-field magnitude E as a function of r. (e) Find the value of r at which the electric field is maximum, and find the value of that maximum field.

22.59. Gauss's Law for Gravitation. The gravitational force between two point masses separated by a distance r is proportional to $1/r^2$, just like the electric force between two point charges. Because of this similarity between gravitational and electric interactions, there is also a Gauss's law for gravitation. (a) Let $\vec{g}$ be the acceleration due to gravity caused by a point mass m at the origin, so that $\vec{g} = -(Gm/r^2)\hat{r}$. Consider a spherical Gaussian surface with radius r centered on this point mass, and show that the flux of $\vec{g}$ through this surface is given by

$$\oint \vec{g} \cdot d\vec{A} = -4\pi Gm$$

(b) By following the same logical steps used in Section 22.3 to obtain Gauss's law for the electric field, show that the flux of $\vec{g}$ through *any* closed surface is given by

$$\oint \vec{g} \cdot d\vec{A} = -4\pi GM_{encl}$$

where M_{encl} is the total mass enclosed within the closed surface.

22.60. Applying Gauss's Law for Gravitation. Using Gauss's law for gravitation (derived in part (b) of Problem 22.59), show that the following statements are true: (a) For any spherically symmetric mass distribution with total mass M, the acceleration due to gravity outside the distribution is the same as though all the mass were concentrated at the center. (*Hint:* See Example 22.5 in Section 22.4.) (b) At any point inside a spherically symmetric shell of mass, the acceleration due to gravity is zero. (*Hint:* See Example 22.5.) (c) If we could drill a hole through a spherically symmetric planet to its center, and if the density were uniform, we would find that the magnitude of $\vec{g}$ is directly proportional to the distance r from the center. (*Hint:* See Example 22.9 in Section 22.4.) We proved these results in Section 12.6 using some fairly strenuous analysis; the proofs using Gauss's law for gravitation are *much* easier.

22.61. (a) An insulating sphere with radius a has a uniform charge density ρ. The sphere is not centered at the origin but at $\vec{r} = \vec{b}$. Show that the electric field inside the sphere is given by $\vec{E} = \rho(\vec{r} - \vec{b})/3\epsilon_0$. (b) An insulating sphere of radius R has a spherical hole of radius a located within its volume and centered a distance b from the center of the sphere, where $a < b < R$ (a cross section of

Figure **22.42**
Problem 22.61.

Charge density ρ

the sphere is shown in Fig. 22.42). The solid part of the sphere has a uniform volume charge density ρ. Find the magnitude and direction of the electric field $\vec{E}$ inside the hole, and show that $\vec{E}$ is uniform over the entire hole. [*Hint:* Use the principle of superposition and the result of part (a).]

22.62. A very long, solid insulating cylinder with radius R has a cylindrical hole with radius a bored along its entire length. The axis of the hole is a distance b from the axis of the cylinder, where $a < b < R$ (Fig. 22.43). The solid material of the cylinder has a uniform volume charge density ρ. Find the magnitude and direction of the electric field $\vec{E}$ inside the hole, and show that $\vec{E}$ is uniform over the entire hole. (*Hint:* See Problem 22.61.)

Figure **22.43**
Problem 22.62.

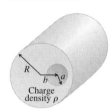

Charge density ρ

22.63. Positive charge Q is distributed uniformly over each of two spherical volumes with radius R. One sphere of charge is centered at the origin and the other at $x = 2R$ (Fig. 22.44). Find the magnitude and direction of the net electric field due to these two distributions of charge at the following points on the x-axis: (a) $x = 0$; (b) $x = R/2$; (c) $x = R$; (d) $x = 3R$.

Figure **22.44**   Problem 22.63.

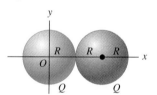

22.64. Repeat Problem 22.63, but now let the left-hand sphere have positive charge Q and let the right-hand sphere have negative charge $-Q$.

22.65. Electric Field Inside a Hydrogen Atom. A hydrogen atom is made up of a proton of charge $+Q = 1.60 \times 10^{-19}$ C and an electron of charge $-Q = -1.60 \times 10^{-19}$ C. The proton may be regarded as a point charge at $r = 0$, the center of the atom. The motion of the electron causes its charge to be "smeared out" into a spherical distribution around the proton, so that the electron is equivalent to a charge per unit volume of

$$\rho(r) = -\frac{Q}{\pi a_0^3} e^{-2r/a_0}$$

where $a_0 = 5.29 \times 10^{-11}$ m is called the *Bohr radius.* (a) Find the total amount of the hydrogen atom's charge that is enclosed within a sphere with radius r centered on the proton. Show that as $r \to \infty$, the enclosed charge goes to zero. Explain this result. (b) Find the electric field (magnitude and direction) caused by the charge of the hydrogen atom as a function of r. (c) Graph the electric-field magnitude E as a function of r.

Challenge Problems

22.66. A region in space contains a total positive charge Q that is distributed spherically such that the volume charge density $\rho(r)$ is given by

$$\rho(r) = \alpha \qquad \text{for } r \le R/2$$
$$\rho(r) = 2\alpha(1 - r/R) \quad \text{for } R/2 \le r \le R$$
$$\rho(r) = 0 \qquad \text{for } r \ge R$$

Here α is a positive constant having units of C/m^3. (a) Determine α in terms of Q and R. (b) Using Gauss's law, derive an expression for the magnitude of $\vec{E}$ as a function of r. Do this separately for all three regions. Express your answers in terms of the total charge Q. Be sure to check that your results agree on the boundaries of the regions. (c) What fraction of the total charge is contained within the region $r \le R/2$? (d) If an electron with charge $q' = -e$ is oscillating back and forth about $r = 0$ (the center of the distribution) with an amplitude less than $R/2$, show that the motion is simple harmonic. (*Hint:* Review the discussion of simple harmonic motion in Section 13.2. If, and only if, the net force on the electron is proportional to its displacement from equilibrium, then the motion is simple harmonic.) (e) What is the period of the motion in part (d)? (f) If the amplitude of the motion described in part (e) is greater than $R/2$, is the motion still simple harmonic? Why or why not?

22.67. A region in space contains a total positive charge Q that is distributed spherically such that the volume charge density $\rho(r)$ is given by

$$\rho(r) = 3\alpha r/(2R) \qquad \text{for } r \le R/2$$
$$\rho(r) = \alpha[1 - (r/R)^2] \quad \text{for } R/2 \le r \le R$$
$$\rho(r) = 0 \qquad \text{for } r \ge R$$

Here α is a positive constant having units of C/m^3. (a) Determine α in terms of Q and R. (b) Using Gauss's law, derive an expression for the magnitude of the electric field as a function of r. Do this separately for all three regions. Express your answers in terms of the total charge Q. (c) What fraction of the total charge is contained within the region $R/2 \le r \le R$? (d) What is the magnitude of $\vec{E}$ at $r = R/2$? (e) If an electron with charge $q' = -e$ is released from rest at any point in any of the three regions, the resulting motion will be oscillatory but not simple harmonic. Why? (See Challenge Problem 22.66.)

23

ELECTRIC POTENTIAL

LEARNING GOALS

By studying this chapter, you will learn:

- How to calculate the electric potential energy of a collection of charges.

- The meaning and significance of electric potential.

- How to calculate the electric potential that a collection of charges produces at a point in space.

- How to use equipotential surfaces to visualize how the electric potential varies in space.

- How to use electric potential to calculate the electric field.

? In one type of welding, electric charge flows between the welding tool and the metal pieces that are to be joined together. This produces a glowing arc whose high temperature fuses the pieces together. Why must the tool be held close to the pieces being welded?

This chapter is about energy associated with electrical interactions. Every time you turn on a light, a CD player, or an electric appliance, you are making use of electrical energy, an indispensable ingredient of our technological society. In Chapters 6 and 7 we introduced the concepts of *work* and *energy* in the context of mechanics; now we'll combine these concepts with what we've learned about electric charge, electric forces, and electric fields. Just as the energy concept made it possible to solve some kinds of mechanics problems very simply, using energy ideas makes it easier to solve a variety of problems in electricity.

When a charged particle moves in an electric field, the field exerts a force that can do *work* on the particle. This work can always be expressed in terms of electric potential energy. Just as gravitational potential energy depends on the height of a mass above the earth's surface, electric potential energy depends on the position of the charged particle in the electric field. We'll describe electric potential energy using a new concept called *electric potential,* or simply *potential.* In circuits, a difference in potential from one point to another is often called *voltage.* The concepts of potential and voltage are crucial to understanding how electric circuits work and have equally important applications to electron beams used in cancer radiotherapy, high-energy particle accelerators, and many other devices.

23.1 Electric Potential Energy

The concepts of work, potential energy, and conservation of energy proved to be extremely useful in our study of mechanics. In this section we'll show that these concepts are just as useful for understanding and analyzing electrical interactions.

Let's begin by reviewing three essential points from Chapters 6 and 7. First, when a force $\vec{F}$ acts on a particle that moves from point a to point b, the work $W_{a \to b}$ done by the force is given by a *line integral:*

$$W_{a \to b} = \int_a^b \vec{F} \cdot d\vec{l} = \int_a^b F \cos\phi \, dl \qquad \text{(work done by a force)} \qquad (23.1)$$

where $d\vec{l}$ is an infinitesimal displacement along the particle's path and ϕ is the angle between $\vec{F}$ and $d\vec{l}$ at each point along the path.

Second, if the force $\vec{F}$ is *conservative,* as we defined the term in Section 7.3, the work done by $\vec{F}$ can always be expressed in terms of a **potential energy** U. When the particle moves from a point where the potential energy is U_a to a point where it is U_b, the change in potential energy is $\Delta U = U_b - U_a$ and the work $W_{a\rightarrow b}$ done by the force is

$$W_{a\rightarrow b} = U_a - U_b = -(U_b - U_a) = -\Delta U \qquad \text{(work done by a conservative force)} \qquad (23.2)$$

When $W_{a\rightarrow b}$ is positive, U_a is greater than U_b, ΔU is negative, and the potential energy *decreases.* That's what happens when a baseball falls from a high point (a) to a lower point (b) under the influence of the earth's gravity; the force of gravity does positive work, and the gravitational potential energy decreases (Fig. 23.1). When a tossed ball is moving upward, the gravitational force does negative work during the ascent, and the potential energy increases.

Third, the work–energy theorem says that the change in kinetic energy $\Delta K = K_b - K_a$ during any displacement is equal to the *total* work done on the particle. If the only work done on the particle is done by conservative forces, then Eq. (23.2) gives the total work, and $K_b - K_a = -(U_b - U_a)$. We usually write this as

$$K_a + U_a = K_b + U_b \qquad (23.3)$$

That is, the total mechanical energy (kinetic plus potential) is *conserved* under these circumstances.

Electric Potential Energy in a Uniform Field

Let's look at an electrical example of these basic concepts. In Fig. 23.2 a pair of charged parallel metal plates sets up a uniform, downward electric field with magnitude E. The field exerts a downward force with magnitude $F = q_0 E$ on a positive test charge q_0. As the charge moves downward a distance d from point a to point b, the force on the test charge is constant and independent of its location. So the work done by the electric field is the product of the force magnitude and the component of displacement in the (downward) direction of the force:

$$W_{a\rightarrow b} = Fd = q_0 Ed \qquad (23.4)$$

This work is positive, since the force is in the same direction as the net displacement of the test charge.

The y-component of the electric force, $F_y = -q_0 E$, is constant, and there is no x- or z-component. This is exactly analogous to the gravitational force on a mass m near the earth's surface; for this force, there is a constant y-component $F_y = -mg$ and the x- and z-components are zero. Because of this analogy, we can conclude that the force exerted on q_0 by the uniform electric field in Fig. 23.2 is *conservative,* just as is the gravitational force. This means that the work $W_{a\rightarrow b}$ done by the field is independent of the path the particle takes from a to b. We can represent this work with a *potential-energy* function U, just as we did for gravitational potential energy in Section 7.1. The potential energy for the gravitational force $F_y = -mg$ was $U = mgy$; hence the potential energy for the electric force $F_y = -q_0 E$ is

$$U = q_0 Ey \qquad (23.5)$$

When the test charge moves from height y_a to height y_b, the work done on the charge by the field is given by

$$W_{a\rightarrow b} = -\Delta U = -(U_b - U_a) = -(q_0 Ey_b - q_0 Ey_a) = q_0 E(y_a - y_b) \quad (23.6)$$

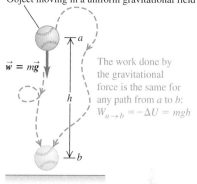

23.1 The work done on a baseball moving in a uniform gravitational field.

Object moving in a uniform gravitational field

The work done by the gravitational force is the same for any path from a to b: $W_{a\rightarrow b} = -\Delta U = mgh$

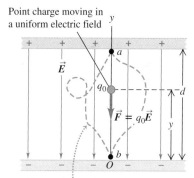

23.2 The work done on a point charge moving in a uniform electric field. Compare with Fig. 23.1.

Point charge moving in a uniform electric field

The work done by the electric force is the same for any path from a to b: $W_{a\rightarrow b} = -\Delta U = q_0 Ed$

23.3 A positive charge moving (a) in the direction of the electric field $\vec{E}$ and (b) in the direction opposite $\vec{E}$.

(a) Positive charge moves in the direction of $\vec{E}$:
• Field does *positive* work on charge.
• *U decreases.*

(b) Positive charge moves opposite $\vec{E}$:
• Field does *negative* work on charge.
• *U increases.*

When y_a is greater than y_b (Fig. 23.3a), the positive test charge q_0 moves downward, in the same direction as $\vec{E}$; the displacement is in the same direction as the force $\vec{F} = q_0\vec{E}$, so the field does positive work and U decreases. [In particular, if $y_a - y_b = d$ as in Fig. 23.2, Eq. (23.6) gives $W_{a \to b} = q_0Ed$, in agreement with Eq. (23.4).] When y_a is less than y_b (Fig. 23.3b), the positive test charge q_0 moves upward, in the opposite direction to $\vec{E}$; the displacement is opposite the force, the field does negative work, and U increases.

If the test charge q_0 is *negative,* the potential energy increases when it moves with the field and decreases when it moves against the field (Fig. 23.4).

Whether the test charge is positive or negative, the following general rules apply: U *increases* if the test charge q_0 moves in the direction *opposite* the electric force $\vec{F} = q_0\vec{E}$ (Figs. 23.3b and 23.4a); U *decreases* if q_0 moves in the *same* direction as $\vec{F} = q_0\vec{E}$ (Figs. 23.3a and 23.4b). This is the same behavior as for gravitational potential energy, which increases if a mass m moves upward (opposite the direction of the gravitational force) and decreases if m moves downward (in the same direction as the gravitational force).

CAUTION **Electric potential energy** The relationship between electric potential energy change and motion in an electric field is an important one that we'll use often. It's also a relationship that takes a little effort to truly understand. Take the time to review the preceding paragraph thoroughly and to study Figs. 23.3 and 23.4 carefully. Doing so now will help you tremendously later! ■

Electric Potential Energy of Two Point Charges

The idea of electric potential energy isn't restricted to the special case of a uniform electric field. Indeed, we can apply this concept to a point charge in *any* electric field caused by a static charge distribution. Recall from Chapter 21 that

23.4 A negative charge moving (a) in the direction of the electric field $\vec{E}$ and (b) in the direction opposite $\vec{E}$. Compare with Fig. 23.3.

(a) Negative charge moves in the direction of $\vec{E}$:
• Field does *negative* work on charge.
• *U increases.*

(b) Negative charge moves opposite $\vec{E}$:
• Field does *positive* work on charge.
• *U decreases.*

we can represent any charge distribution as a collection of point charges. Therefore it's useful to calculate the work done on a test charge q_0 moving in the electric field caused by a single, stationary point charge q.

We'll consider first a displacement along the *radial* line in Fig. 23.5, from point a to point b. The force on q_0 is given by Coulomb's law, and its radial component is

$$F_r = \frac{1}{4\pi\epsilon_0}\frac{qq_0}{r^2} \tag{23.7}$$

If q and q_0 have the same sign ($+$ or $-$) the force is repulsive and F_r is positive; if the two charges have opposite signs, the force is attractive and F_r is negative. The force is *not* constant during the displacement, and we have to integrate to calculate the work $W_{a\to b}$ done on q_0 by this force as q_0 moves from a to b. We find

$$W_{a\to b} = \int_{r_a}^{r_b} F_r\,dr = \int_{r_a}^{r_b}\frac{1}{4\pi\epsilon_0}\frac{qq_0}{r^2}\,dr = \frac{qq_0}{4\pi\epsilon_0}\left(\frac{1}{r_a}-\frac{1}{r_b}\right) \tag{23.8}$$

The work done by the electric force for this particular path depends only on the endpoints.

In fact, the work is the same for *all possible* paths from a to b. To prove this, we consider a more general displacement (Fig. 23.6) in which a and b do not lie on the same radial line. From Eq. (23.1) the work done on q_0 during this displacement is given by

$$W_{a\to b} = \int_{r_a}^{r_b} F\cos\phi\,dl = \int_{r_a}^{r_b}\frac{1}{4\pi\epsilon_0}\frac{qq_0}{r^2}\cos\phi\,dl$$

But the figure shows that $\cos\phi\,dl = dr$. That is, the work done during a small displacement $d\vec{l}$ depends only on the change dr in the distance r between the charges, which is the *radial component* of the displacement. Thus Eq. (23.8) is valid even for this more general displacement; the work done on q_0 by the electric field $\vec{E}$ produced by q depends only on r_a and r_b, not on the details of the path. Also, if q_0 returns to its starting point a by a different path, the total work done in the round-trip displacement is zero (the integral in Eq. (23.8) is from r_a back to r_a). These are the needed characteristics for a conservative force, as we defined it in Section 7.3. Thus the force on q_0 is a *conservative* force.

We see that Eqs. (23.2) and (23.8) are consistent if we define $qq_0/4\pi\epsilon_0 r_a$ to be the potential energy U_a when q_0 is at point a, a distance r_a from q, and we define $qq_0/4\pi\epsilon_0 r_b$ to be the potential energy U_b when q_0 is at point b, a distance r_b from

23.5 Test charge q_0 moves along a straight line extending radially from charge q. As it moves from a to b, the distance varies from r_a to r_b.

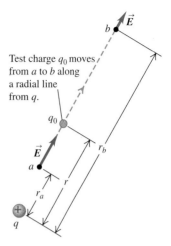

Test charge q_0 moves from a to b along a radial line from q.

23.6 The work done on charge q_0 by the electric field of charge q does not depend on the path taken, but only on the distances r_a and r_b.

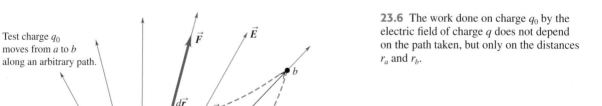

Test charge q_0 moves from a to b along an arbitrary path.

23.7 Graphs of the potential energy U of two point charges q and q_0 versus their separation r.

(a) q and q_0 have the same sign.

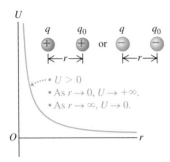

- $U > 0$
- As $r \to 0$, $U \to +\infty$.
- As $r \to \infty$, $U \to 0$.

(b) q and q_0 have opposite signs.

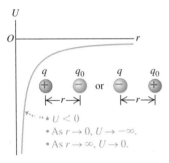

- $U < 0$
- As $r \to 0$, $U \to -\infty$.
- As $r \to \infty$, $U \to 0$.

q. Thus the potential energy U when the test charge q_0 is at *any* distance r from charge q is

$$U = \frac{1}{4\pi\epsilon_0}\frac{qq_0}{r} \quad \text{(electric potential energy of two point charges } q \text{ and } q_0) \tag{23.9}$$

Note that we have *not* assumed anything about the signs of q and q_0; Eq. (23.9) is valid for any combination of signs. The potential energy is positive if the charges q and q_0 have the same sign (Fig. 23.7a) and negative if they have opposite signs (Fig. 23.7b).

CAUTION **Electric potential energy vs. electric force** Be careful not to confuse Eq. (23.9) for the potential energy of two point charges with the similar expression in Eq. (23.7) for the radial component of the electric force that one charge exerts on the other. The potential energy U is proportional to $1/r$, while the force component F_r is proportional to $1/r^2$. ∎

Potential energy is always defined relative to some reference point where $U = 0$. In Eq. (23.9), U is zero when q and q_0 are infinitely far apart and $r = \infty$. Therefore U represents the work that would be done on the test charge q_0 by the field of q if q_0 moved from an initial distance r to infinity. If q and q_0 have the same sign, the interaction is repulsive, this work is positive, and U is positive at any finite separation (Fig. 23.7a). If the charges have opposite signs, the interaction is attractive, the work done is negative, and U is negative (Fig. 23.7b).

We emphasize that the potential energy U given by Eq. (23.9) is a *shared* property of the two charges q and q_0; it is a consequence of the *interaction* between these two bodies. If the distance between the two charges is changed from r_a to r_b, the change in potential energy is the same whether q is held fixed and q_0 is moved or q_0 is held fixed and q is moved. For this reason, we never use the phrase "the electric potential energy *of* a point charge." (Likewise, if a mass m is at a height h above the earth's surface, the gravitational potential energy is a shared property of the mass m and the earth. We emphasized this in Sections 7.1 and 12.3.)

Gauss's law tells us that the electric field outside any spherically symmetric charge distribution is the same as though all the charge were concentrated at the center. Therefore Eq. (23.9) also holds if the test charge q_0 is outside any spherically symmetric charge distribution with total charge q at a distance r from the center.

Example 23.1 **Conservation of energy with electric forces**

A positron (the antiparticle of the electron) has a mass of 9.11×10^{-31} kg and a charge $+e = +1.60 \times 10^{-19}$ C. Suppose a positron moves in the vicinity of an alpha particle, which has a charge $+2e = 3.20 \times 10^{-19}$ C. The alpha particle is more than 7000 times as massive as the positron, so we assume that it is at rest in some inertial frame of reference. When the positron is 1.00×10^{-10} m from the alpha particle, it is moving directly away from the alpha particle at a speed of 3.00×10^6 m/s. (a) What is the positron's speed when the two particles are 2.00×10^{-10} m apart? (b) What is the positron's speed when it is very far away from the alpha particle? (c) How would the situation change if the moving particle were an electron (same mass as the positron but opposite charge)?

SOLUTION

IDENTIFY: The electric force between the positron and the alpha particle is conservative, so mechanical energy (kinetic plus potential) is conserved.

SET UP: The kinetic and potential energies at any two points a and b are related by Eq. (23.3), $K_a + U_a = K_b + U_b$, and the potential energy at any distance r is given by Eq. (23.9). We are given complete information about the system at a point a where the two charges are 1.00×10^{-10} m apart. We use Eqs. (23.3) and (23.9) to find the speed at two different values of r in parts (a) and (b), and for the case where the charge $+e$ is replaced by $-e$ in part (c).

EXECUTE: (a) In this part, $r_b = 2.00 \times 10^{-10}$ m and we want to find the final speed v_b of the positron. This appears in the expression for the final kinetic energy, $K_b = \frac{1}{2}mv_b^2$; solving the energy-conservation equation for K_b, we have

$$K_b = K_a + U_a - U_b$$

The values of the energies on the right-hand side of this expression are

$$K_a = \frac{1}{2}mv_a^2 = \frac{1}{2}(9.11 \times 10^{-31} \text{ kg})(3.00 \times 10^6 \text{ m/s})^2$$

$$= 4.10 \times 10^{-18} \text{ J}$$

$$U_a = \frac{1}{4\pi\epsilon_0} \frac{qq_0}{r_a}$$

$$= (9.0 \times 10^9 \text{ N} \cdot \text{m}^2/\text{C}^2)\frac{(3.20 \times 10^{-19} \text{ C})(1.60 \times 10^{-19} \text{ C})}{1.00 \times 10^{-10} \text{ m}}$$

$$= 4.61 \times 10^{-18} \text{ J}$$

$$U_b = (9.0 \times 10^9 \text{ N} \cdot \text{m}^2/\text{C}^2)\frac{(3.20 \times 10^{-19} \text{ C})(1.60 \times 10^{-19} \text{ C})}{2.00 \times 10^{-10} \text{ m}}$$

$$= 2.30 \times 10^{-18} \text{ J}$$

Hence the final kinetic energy is

$$K_b = \frac{1}{2}mv_b^2 = K_a + U_a - U_b$$

$$= 4.10 \times 10^{-18} \text{ J} + 4.61 \times 10^{-18} \text{ J} - 2.30 \times 10^{-18} \text{ J}$$

$$= 6.41 \times 10^{-18} \text{ J}$$

and the final speed of the positron is

$$v_b = \sqrt{\frac{2K_b}{m}} = \sqrt{\frac{2(6.41 \times 10^{-18} \text{ J})}{9.11 \times 10^{-31} \text{ kg}}} = 3.8 \times 10^6 \text{ m/s}$$

The force is repulsive, so the positron speeds up as it moves away from the stationary alpha particle.

(b) When the final positions of the positron and alpha particle are very far apart, the separation r_b approaches infinity and the final potential energy U_b approaches zero. Then the final kinetic energy of the positron is

$$K_b = K_a + U_a - U_b = 4.10 \times 10^{-18} \text{ J} + 4.61 \times 10^{-18} \text{ J} - 0$$

$$= 8.71 \times 10^{-18} \text{ J}$$

and its final speed is

$$v_b = \sqrt{\frac{2K_b}{m}} = \sqrt{\frac{2(8.71 \times 10^{-18} \text{ J})}{9.11 \times 10^{-31} \text{ kg}}} = 4.4 \times 10^6 \text{ m/s}$$

Comparing to part (a), we see that as the positron moves from $r = 2.00 \times 10^{-10}$ m to infinity, the additional work done on it by the electric field of the alpha particle increases the speed by only about 16%. This is because the electric force decreases rapidly with distance.

(c) If the moving charge is negative, the force on it is attractive rather than repulsive, and we expect it to slow down rather than speed up. The only difference in the above calculations is that both potential-energy quantities are negative. From part (a), at a distance $r_b = 2.00 \times 10^{-10}$ m we have

$$K_b = K_a + U_a - U_b$$

$$= 4.10 \times 10^{-18} \text{ J} + (-4.61 \times 10^{-18} \text{ J}) - (-2.30 \times 10^{-18} \text{ J})$$

$$= 1.79 \times 10^{-18} \text{ J}$$

$$v_b = \sqrt{\frac{2K_b}{m}} = 2.0 \times 10^6 \text{ m/s}$$

From part (b), at $r_b = \infty$ the kinetic energy of the electron would seem to be

$$K_b = K_a + U_a - U_b$$

$$= 4.10 \times 10^{-18} \text{ J} + (-4.61 \times 10^{-18} \text{ J}) - 0$$

$$= -5.1 \times 10^{-19} \text{ J}$$

But kinetic energies can *never* be negative! This result means that the electron can never reach $r_b = \infty$; the attractive force brings the electron to a halt at a finite distance from the alpha particle. The electron will then begin to move back toward the alpha particle. You can solve for the distance r_b at which the electron comes momentarily to rest by setting K_b equal to zero in the equation for conservation of mechanical energy.

EVALUATE: It's useful to compare our calculations with Fig. 23.7. In parts (a) and (b), the charges have the same sign; since $r_b > r_a$, the potential energy U_b is less than U_a. In part (c), the charges have opposite signs; since $r_b > r_a$, the potential energy U_b is greater (that is, less negative) than U_a.

Electric Potential Energy with Several Point Charges

Suppose the electric field $\vec{E}$ in which charge q_0 moves is caused by *several* point charges $q_1, q_2, q_3, \ldots$ at distances $r_1, r_2, r_3, \ldots$ from q_0, as in Fig. 23.8. For example, q_0 could be a positive ion moving in the presence of other ions (Fig. 23.9). The total electric field at each point is the *vector sum* of the fields due to the individual charges, and the total work done on q_0 during any displacement is the sum of the contributions from the individual charges. From Eq. (23.9) we conclude that the potential energy associated with the test charge q_0 at point a in Fig. 23.8 is the *algebraic* sum (*not* a vector sum):

23.8 The potential energy associated with a charge q_0 at point a depends on the other charges q_1, q_2, and q_3 and on their distances r_1, r_2, and r_3 from point a.

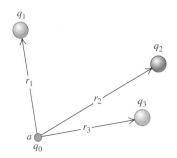

$$U = \frac{q_0}{4\pi\epsilon_0}\left(\frac{q_1}{r_1} + \frac{q_2}{r_2} + \frac{q_3}{r_3} + \cdots\right) = \frac{q_0}{4\pi\epsilon_0}\sum_i \frac{q_i}{r_i} \qquad \begin{array}{l}\text{(point charge } q_0 \\ \text{and collection} \qquad (23.10)\\ \text{of charges } q_i)\end{array}$$

When q_0 is at a different point b, the potential energy is given by the same expression, but $r_1, r_2, \ldots$ are the distances from $q_1, q_2, \ldots$ to point b. The work

23.9 This ion engine for spacecraft uses electric forces to eject a stream of positive xenon ions (Xe^+) at speeds in excess of 30 km/s. The thrust produced is very low (about 0.09 newton) but can be maintained continuously for days, in contrast to chemical rockets, which produce a large thrust for a short time (see Fig. 8.33). Such ion engines have been used for maneuvering interplanetary spacecraft.

done on charge q_0 when it moves from a to b along any path is equal to the difference $U_a - U_b$ between the potential energies when q_0 is at a and at b.

We can represent *any* charge distribution as a collection of point charges, so Eq. (23.10) shows that we can always find a potential-energy function for *any* static electric field. It follows that **for every electric field due to a static charge distribution, the force exerted by that field is conservative.**

Equations (23.9) and (23.10) define U to be zero when all the distances $r_1, r_2, \ldots$ are infinite—that is, when the test charge q_0 is very far away from all the charges that produce the field. As with any potential-energy function, the point where $U = 0$ is arbitrary; we can always add a constant to make U equal zero at any point we choose. In electrostatics problems it's usually simplest to choose this point to be at infinity. When we analyze electric circuits in Chapters 25 and 26, other choices will be more convenient.

Equation (23.10) gives the potential energy associated with the presence of the test charge q_0 in the $\vec{E}$ field produced by $q_1, q_2, q_3, \ldots$. But there is also potential energy involved in assembling these charges. If we start with charges $q_1, q_2, q_3, \ldots$ all separated from each other by infinite distances and then bring them together so that the distance between q_i and q_j is r_{ij}, the *total* potential energy U is the sum of the potential energies of interaction for each pair of charges. We can write this as

$$U = \frac{1}{4\pi\epsilon_0} \sum_{i<j} \frac{q_i q_j}{r_{ij}} \tag{23.11}$$

This sum extends over all *pairs* of charges; we don't let $i = j$ (because that would be an interaction of a charge with itself), and we include only terms with $i < j$ to make sure that we count each pair only once. Thus, to account for the interaction between q_3 and q_4, we include a term with $i = 3$ and $j = 4$ but not a term with $i = 4$ and $j = 3$.

Interpreting Electric Potential Energy

As a final comment, here are two viewpoints on electric potential energy. We have defined it in terms of the work done *by the electric field* on a charged particle moving in the field, just as in Chapter 7 we defined potential energy in terms of the work done by gravity or by a spring. When a particle moves from point a to point b, the work done on it by the electric field is $W_{a \to b} = U_a - U_b$. Thus the potential-energy difference $U_a - U_b$ equals *the work that is done by the electric force when the particle moves from a to b*. When U_a is greater than U_b, the field does positive work on the particle as it "falls" from a point of higher potential energy (a) to a point of lower potential energy (b).

An alternative but equivalent viewpoint is to consider how much work we would have to do to "raise" a particle from a point b where the potential energy is U_b to a point a where it has a greater value U_a (pushing two positive charges closer together, for example). To move the particle slowly (so as not to give it any kinetic energy), we need to exert an additional external force $\vec{F}_{ext}$ that is equal and opposite to the electric-field force and does positive work. The potential-energy difference $U_a - U_b$ is then defined as *the work that must be done by an external force to move the particle slowly from b to a against the electric force*. Because $\vec{F}_{ext}$ is the negative of the electric-field force and the displacement is in the opposite direction, this definition of the potential difference $U_a - U_b$ is equivalent to that given above. This alternative viewpoint also works if U_a is less than U_b, corresponding to "lowering" the particle; an example is moving two positive charges away from each other. In this case, $U_a - U_b$ is again equal to the work done by the external force, but now this work is negative.

We will use both of these viewpoints in the next section to interpret what is meant by electric *potential,* or potential energy per unit charge.

Example 23.2   A system of point charges

Two point charges are located on the x-axis, $q_1 = -e$ at $x = 0$ and $q_2 = +e$ at $x = a$. (a) Find the work that must be done by an external force to bring a third point charge $q_3 = +e$ from infinity to $x = 2a$. (b) Find the total potential energy of the system of three charges.

SOLUTION

IDENTIFY: This problem involves the relationship between the work done to move a point charge and the change in potential energy. It also involves the expression for the potential energy of a collection of point charges.

SET UP: Figure 23.10 shows the final arrangement of the three charges. To find the work required to bring q_3 in from infinity, we use Eq. (23.10) to find the potential energy associated with q_3 in the presence of q_1 and q_2. We then use Eq. (23.11) to find the total potential energy of the system.

23.10 Our sketch of the situation after the third charge has been brought in from infinity.

$$q_1 = -e \qquad q_2 = +e \qquad q_3 = +e$$
$$\ominus \qquad\qquad \oplus \qquad\qquad \oplus \qquad\quad x$$
$$x = 0 \qquad\quad x = a \qquad\quad x = 2a$$

EXECUTE: (a) The work that must be done on q_3 by an external force $\vec{F}_{\text{ext}}$ is equal to the difference between two quantities: the potential energy U associated with q_3 when it is at $x = 2a$ and the potential energy when it is infinitely far away. The second of these is zero, so the work that must be done is equal to U. The distances between the charges are $r_{13} = 2a$ and $r_{23} = a$, so from Eq. (23.10),

$$W = U = \frac{q_3}{4\pi\epsilon_0}\left(\frac{q_1}{r_{13}} + \frac{q_2}{r_{23}}\right) = \frac{+e}{4\pi\epsilon_0}\left(\frac{-e}{2a} + \frac{+e}{a}\right) = \frac{+e^2}{8\pi\epsilon_0 a}$$

If q_3 is brought in from infinity along the $+x$-axis, it is attracted by q_1 but is repelled more strongly by q_2; hence positive work must be done to push q_3 to the position at $x = 2a$.

(b) The total potential energy of the assemblage of three charges is given by Eq. (23.11):

$$U = \frac{1}{4\pi\epsilon_0}\sum_{i<j}\frac{q_i q_j}{r_{ij}} = \frac{1}{4\pi\epsilon_0}\left(\frac{q_1 q_2}{r_{12}} + \frac{q_1 q_3}{r_{13}} + \frac{q_2 q_3}{r_{23}}\right)$$

$$= \frac{1}{4\pi\epsilon_0}\left(\frac{(-e)(e)}{a} + \frac{(-e)(e)}{2a} + \frac{(e)(e)}{a}\right) = \frac{-e^2}{8\pi\epsilon_0 a}$$

EVALUATE: Since our result in part (b) is negative, the system has lower potential energy than it would if the three charges were infinitely far apart. An external force would have to do *negative* work to bring the three charges from infinity to assemble this entire arrangement and would have to do *positive* work to move the three charges back to infinity.

Test Your Understanding of Section 23.1   Consider the system of three point charges in Example 21.4 (Section 21.3) and shown in Fig. 21.14. (a) What is the sign of the total potential energy of this system? (i) positive; (ii) negative; (iii) zero. (b) What is the sign of the total amount of work you would have to do to move these charges infinitely far from each other? (i) positive; (ii) negative; (iii) zero.

23.2 Electric Potential

In Section 23.1 we looked at the potential energy U associated with a test charge q_0 in an electric field. Now we want to describe this potential energy on a "per unit charge" basis, just as electric field describes the force per unit charge on a charged particle in the field. This leads us to the concept of *electric potential,* often called simply *potential.* This concept is very useful in calculations involving energies of charged particles. It also facilitates many electric-field calculations because electric potential is closely related to the electric field $\vec{E}$. When we need to determine an electric field, it is often easier to determine the potential first and then find the field from it.

Potential is *potential energy per unit charge.* We define the potential V at any point in an electric field as the potential energy U *per unit charge* associated with a test charge q_0 at that point:

$$V = \frac{U}{q_0} \quad\text{or}\quad U = q_0 V \qquad\qquad (23.12)$$

Potential energy and charge are both scalars, so potential is a scalar quantity. From Eq. (23.12) its units are found by dividing the units of energy by those of charge. The SI unit of potential, called one **volt** (1 V) in honor of the Italian

Actlv
Physlcs
ONLINE

11.13 Electrical Potential Energy and Potential

scientist and electrical experimenter Alessandro Volta (1745–1827), equals 1 joule per coulomb:

$$1 \text{ V} = 1 \text{ volt} = 1 \text{ J/C} = 1 \text{ joule/coulomb}$$

Let's put Eq. (23.2), which equates the work done by the electric force during a displacement from a to b to the quantity $-\Delta U = -(U_b - U_a)$, on a "work per unit charge" basis. We divide this equation by q_0, obtaining

$$\frac{W_{a \to b}}{q_0} = -\frac{\Delta U}{q_0} = -\left(\frac{U_b}{q_0} - \frac{U_a}{q_0}\right) = -(V_b - V_a) = V_a - V_b \quad (23.13)$$

where $V_a = U_a/q_0$ is the potential energy per unit charge at point a and similarly for V_b. We call V_a and V_b the *potential at point a* and *potential at point b*, respectively. Thus the work done per unit charge by the electric force when a charged body moves from a to b is equal to the potential at a minus the potential at b.

The difference $V_a - V_b$ is called the *potential of a with respect to b*; we sometimes abbreviate this difference as $V_{ab} = V_a - V_b$ (note the order of the subscripts). This is often called the potential difference between a and b, but that's ambiguous unless we specify which is the reference point. In electric circuits, which we will analyze in later chapters, the potential difference between two points is often called **voltage** (Fig. 23.11). Equation (23.13) then states; V_{ab}, **the potential of a with respect to b, equals the work done by the electric force when a UNIT charge moves from a to b.**

Another way to interpret the potential difference V_{ab} in Eq. (23.13) is to use the alternative viewpoint mentioned at the end of Section 23.1. In that viewpoint, $U_a - U_b$ is the amount of work that must be done by an *external* force to move a particle of charge q_0 slowly from b to a against the electric force. The work that must be done *per unit charge* by the external force is then $(U_a - U_b)/q_0 = V_a - V_b = V_{ab}$. In other words: V_{ab}, **the potential of a with respect to b, equals the work that must be done to move a UNIT charge slowly from b to a against the electric force.**

An instrument that measures the difference of potential between two points is called a *voltmeter*. In Chapter 26 we will discuss the principle of the common type of moving-coil voltmeter. There are also much more sensitive potential-measuring devices that use electronic amplification. Instruments that can measure a potential difference of 1 μV are common, and sensitivities down to 10^{-12} V can be attained.

23.11 The voltage of this battery equals the difference in potential $V_{ab} = V_a - V_b$ between its positive terminal (point a) and its negative terminal (point b).

Point a

ENERGY PLUS

ALKALINE

LONGER LASTING POWER

Point b

$V_{ab} = 1.5$ volts

Calculating Electric Potential

To find the potential V due to a single point charge q, we divide Eq. (23.9) by q_0:

$$V = \frac{U}{q_0} = \frac{1}{4\pi\epsilon_0}\frac{q}{r} \qquad \text{(potential due to a point charge)} \qquad (23.14)$$

where r is the distance from the point charge q to the point at which the potential is evaluated. If q is positive, the potential that it produces is positive at all points; if q is negative, it produces a potential that is negative everywhere. In either case, V is equal to zero at $r = \infty$, an infinite distance from the point charge. Note that potential, like electric field, is independent of the test charge q_0 that we use to define it.

Similarly, we divide Eq. (23.10) by q_0 to find the potential due to a collection of point charges:

$$V = \frac{U}{q_0} = \frac{1}{4\pi\epsilon_0}\sum_i \frac{q_i}{r_i} \qquad \text{(potential due to a collection of point charges)} \qquad (23.15)$$

In this expression, r_i is the distance from the ith charge, q_i, to the point at which V is evaluated. Just as the electric field due to a collection of point charges is the *vector* sum of the fields produced by each charge, the electric potential due to a collection of point charges is the *scalar* sum of the potentials due to each charge. When we have a continuous distribution of charge along a line, over a surface, or through a volume, we divide the charge into elements dq, and the sum in Eq. (23.15) becomes an integral:

$$V = \frac{1}{4\pi\epsilon_0} \int \frac{dq}{r} \qquad \text{(potential due to a continuous distribution of charge)} \qquad (23.16)$$

where r is the distance from the charge element dq to the field point where we are finding V. We'll work out several examples of such cases. The potential defined by Eqs. (23.15) and (23.16) is zero at points that are infinitely far away from *all* the charges. Later we'll encounter cases in which the charge distribution itself extends to infinity. We'll find that in such cases we cannot set $V = 0$ at infinity, and we'll need to exercise care in using and interpreting Eqs. (23.15) and (23.16).

CAUTION   What is electric potential? Before getting too involved in the details of how to calculate electric potential, you should stop and remind yourself what potential is. The electric *potential* at a certain point is the potential energy that would be associated with a *unit* charge placed at that point. That's why potential is measured in joules per coulomb, or volts. Keep in mind, too, that there doesn't have to be a charge at a given point for a potential V to exist at that point. (In the same way, an electric field can exist at a given point even if there's no charge there to respond to it.) ▮

Finding Electric Potential from Electric Field

When we are given a collection of point charges, Eq. (23.15) is usually the easiest way to calculate the potential V. But in some problems in which the electric field is known or can be found easily, it is easier to determine V from $\vec{E}$. The force $\vec{F}$ on a test charge q_0 can be written as $\vec{F} = q_0\vec{E}$, so from Eq. (23.1) the work done by the electric force as the test charge moves from a to b is given by

$$W_{a\to b} = \int_a^b \vec{F} \cdot d\vec{l} = \int_a^b q_0 \vec{E} \cdot d\vec{l}$$

If we divide this by q_0 and compare the result with Eq. (23.13), we find

$$V_a - V_b = \int_a^b \vec{E} \cdot d\vec{l} = \int_a^b E\cos\phi\, dl \qquad \text{(potential difference as an integral of } \vec{E}) \qquad (23.17)$$

The value of $V_a - V_b$ is independent of the path taken from a to b, just as the value of $W_{a\to b}$ is independent of the path. To interpret Eq. (23.17), remember that $\vec{E}$ is the electric force per unit charge on a test charge. If the line integral $\int_a^b \vec{E} \cdot d\vec{l}$ is positive, the electric field does positive work on a positive test charge as it moves from a to b. In this case the electric potential energy decreases as the test charge moves, so the potential energy per unit charge decreases as well; hence V_b is less than V_a and $V_a - V_b$ is positive.

As an illustration, consider a positive point charge (Fig. 23.12a). The electric field is directed away from the charge, and $V = q/4\pi\epsilon_0 r$ is positive at any finite distance from the charge. If you move away from the charge, in the direction of $\vec{E}$, you move toward lower values of V; if you move toward the charge, in the direction opposite $\vec{E}$, you move toward greater values of V. For the negative point charge in Fig. 23.12b, $\vec{E}$ is directed toward the charge and $V = q/4\pi\epsilon_0 r$ is negative at any finite distance from the charge. In this case, if you move toward the charge, you are moving in the direction of $\vec{E}$ and in the direction of decreasing (more negative) V. Moving away from the charge, in the direction opposite $\vec{E}$,

23.12 If you move in the direction of $\vec{E}$, electric potential V decreases; if you move in the direction opposite $\vec{E}$, V increases.

(a) A positive point charge

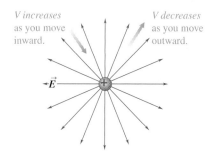

(b) A negative point charge

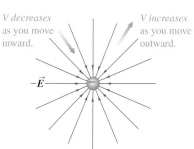

moves you toward increasing (less negative) values of V. The general rule, valid for *any* electric field, is: Moving *with* the direction of $\vec{E}$ means moving in the direction of *decreasing* V, and moving *against* the direction of $\vec{E}$ means moving in the direction of *increasing* V.

Also, a positive test charge q_0 experiences an electric force in the direction of $\vec{E}$, toward lower values of V; a negative test charge experiences a force opposite $\vec{E}$, toward higher values of V. Thus a positive charge tends to "fall" from a high-potential region to a lower-potential region. The opposite is true for a negative charge.

Notice that Eq. (23.17) can be rewritten as

$$V_a - V_b = -\int_b^a \vec{E} \cdot d\vec{l} \tag{23.18}$$

This has a negative sign compared to the integral in Eq. (23.17), and the limits are reversed; hence Eqs. (23.17) and (23.18) are equivalent. But Eq. (23.18) has a slightly different interpretation. To move a unit charge slowly against the electric force, we must apply an *external* force per unit charge equal to $-\vec{E}$, equal and opposite to the electric force per unit charge $\vec{E}$. Equation (23.18) says that $V_a - V_b = V_{ab}$, the potential of a with respect to b, equals the work done per unit charge by this external force to move a unit charge from b to a. This is the same alternative interpretation we discussed under Eq. (23.13).

Equations (23.17) and (23.18) show that the unit of potential difference $(1\ \text{V})$ is equal to the unit of electric field $(1\ \text{N/C})$ multiplied by the unit of distance $(1\ \text{m})$. Hence the unit of electric field can be expressed as 1 *volt per meter* $(1\ \text{V/m})$, as well as 1 N/C:

$$1\ \text{V/m} = 1\ \text{volt/meter} = 1\ \text{N/C} = 1\ \text{newton/coulomb}$$

In practice, the volt per meter is the usual unit of electric-field magnitude.

Electron Volts

The magnitude e of the electron charge can be used to define a unit of energy that is useful in many calculations with atomic and nuclear systems. When a particle with charge q moves from a point where the potential is V_b to a point where it is V_a, the change in the potential energy U is

$$U_a - U_b = q(V_a - V_b) = qV_{ab}$$

If the charge q equals the magnitude e of the electron charge, 1.602×10^{-19} C, and the potential difference is $V_{ab} = 1$ V, the change in energy is

$$U_a - U_b = (1.602 \times 10^{-19}\ \text{C})(1\ \text{V}) = 1.602 \times 10^{-19}\ \text{J}$$

This quantity of energy is defined to be 1 **electron volt** $(1\ \text{eV})$:

$$1\ \text{eV} = 1.602 \times 10^{-19}\ \text{J}$$

The multiples meV, keV, MeV, GeV, and TeV are often used.

CAUTION **Electron volts vs. volts** Remember that the electron volt is a unit of energy, *not* a unit of potential or potential difference! ▮

When a particle with charge e moves through a potential difference of 1 volt, the change in potential *energy* is 1 eV. If the charge is some multiple of e—say Ne—the change in potential energy in electron volts is N times the potential difference in volts. For example, when an alpha particle, which has charge $2e$, moves between two points with a potential difference of 1000 V, the change in potential energy is $2(1000\ \text{eV}) = 2000\ \text{eV}$. To confirm this, we write

$$U_a - U_b = qV_{ab} = (2e)(1000\ \text{V}) = (2)(1.602 \times 10^{-19}\ \text{C})(1000\ \text{V})$$
$$= 3.204 \times 10^{-16}\ \text{J} = 2000\ \text{eV}$$

Although we have defined the electron volt in terms of *potential* energy, we can use it for *any* form of energy, such as the kinetic energy of a moving particle. When we speak of a "one-million-electron-volt proton," we mean a proton with a kinetic energy of one million electron volts (1 MeV), equal to $(10^6)(1.602 \times 10^{-19} \text{ J}) = 1.602 \times 10^{-13} \text{ J}$ (Fig. 23.13).

23.13 This accelerator at the Fermi National Accelerator Laboratory in Illinois gives protons a kinetic energy of 400 MeV $(4 \times 10^8 \text{ eV})$. Additional acceleration stages increase their kinetic energy to 980 GeV, or 0.98 TeV $(9.8 \times 10^{11} \text{ eV})$.

Example 23.3   Electric force and electric potential

A proton (charge $+e = 1.602 \times 10^{-19} \text{ C}$) moves in a straight line from point a to point b inside a linear accelerator, a total distance $d = 0.50 \text{ m}$. The electric field is uniform along this line, with magnitude $E = 1.5 \times 10^7 \text{ V/m} = 1.5 \times 10^7 \text{ N/C}$ in the direction from a to b. Determine (a) the force on the proton; (b) the work done on it by the field; (c) the potential difference $V_a - V_b$.

SOLUTION

IDENTIFY: This problem uses the relationship between electric field (which we are given) and electric force (which is one of our target variables). It also uses the relationship among force, work, and potential energy difference.

SET UP: We are given the electric field, so it is straightforward to find the electric force on the proton. Calculating the work done on the proton by this force is also straightforward because $\vec{E}$ is uniform, which means that the force is constant. Once the work is known, we find the potential difference using Eq. (23.13).

EXECUTE: (a) The force on the proton is in the same direction as the electric field, and its magnitude is

$$F = qE = (1.602 \times 10^{-19} \text{ C})(1.5 \times 10^7 \text{ N/C})$$
$$= 2.4 \times 10^{-12} \text{ N}$$

(b) The force is constant and in the same direction as the displacement, so the work done on the proton is

$$W_{a \to b} = Fd = (2.4 \times 10^{-12} \text{ N})(0.50 \text{ m}) = 1.2 \times 10^{-12} \text{ J}$$

$$= (1.2 \times 10^{-12} \text{ J})\frac{1 \text{ eV}}{1.602 \times 10^{-19} \text{ J}}$$

$$= 7.5 \times 10^6 \text{ eV} = 7.5 \text{ MeV}$$

(c) From Eq. (23.13) the potential difference is the work per unit charge, which is

$$V_a - V_b = \frac{W_{a \to b}}{q} = \frac{1.2 \times 10^{-12} \text{ J}}{1.602 \times 10^{-19} \text{ C}} = 7.5 \times 10^6 \text{ J/C}$$
$$= 7.5 \times 10^6 \text{ V} = 7.5 \text{ MV}$$

We can get this same result even more easily by remembering that 1 electron volt equals 1 volt multiplied by the charge e. Since the work done is 7.5×10^6 eV and the charge is e, the potential difference is $(7.5 \times 10^6 \text{ eV})/e = 7.5 \times 10^6 \text{ V}$.

EVALUATE: We can check our result in part (c) by using Eq. (23.17) or (23.18) to calculate an integral of the electric field. The angle ϕ between the constant field $\vec{E}$ and the displacement is zero, so Eq. (23.17) becomes

$$V_a - V_b = \int_a^b E \cos\phi \, dl = \int_a^b E \, dl = E \int_a^b dl$$

The integral of dl from a to b is just the distance d, so we again find

$$V_a - V_b = Ed = (1.5 \times 10^7 \text{ V/m})(0.50 \text{ m}) = 7.5 \times 10^6 \text{ V}$$

Example 23.4   Potential due to two point charges

An electric dipole consists of two point charges, $q_1 = +12$ nC and $q_2 = -12$ nC, placed 10 cm apart (Fig. 23.14). Compute the potentials at points a, b, and c by adding the potentials due to either charge, as in Eq. (23.15).

SOLUTION

IDENTIFY: This is the same arrangement of charges as in Example 21.9 (Section 21.5). In that example we calculated electric *field* at each point by doing a *vector* sum. Our target variable in this problem is the electric *potential* V at three points.

SET UP: To find V at each point, we do the *algebraic* sum in Eq. (23.15):

$$V = \frac{1}{4\pi\epsilon_0} \sum_i \frac{q_i}{r_i}$$

EXECUTE: At point a the potential due to the positive charge q_1 is

$$\frac{1}{4\pi\epsilon_0} \frac{q_1}{r_1} = (9.0 \times 10^9 \text{ N} \cdot \text{m}^2/\text{C}^2)\frac{12 \times 10^{-9} \text{ C}}{0.060 \text{ m}}$$

$$= 1800 \text{ N} \cdot \text{m}/\text{C}$$

$$= 1800 \text{ J/C} = 1800 \text{ V}$$

and the potential due to the negative charge q_2 is

$$\frac{1}{4\pi\epsilon_0} \frac{q_2}{r_2} = (9.0 \times 10^9 \text{ N} \cdot \text{m}^2/\text{C}^2)\frac{(-12 \times 10^{-9} \text{ C})}{0.040 \text{ m}}$$

$$= -2700 \text{ N} \cdot \text{m}/\text{C}$$

$$= -2700 \text{ J/C} = -2700 \text{ V}$$

The potential V_a at point a is the sum of these:

$$V_a = 1800 \text{ V} + (-2700 \text{ V}) = -900 \text{ V}$$

By similar calculations you can show that at point b the potential due to the positive charge is $+2700$ V, the potential due to the negative charge is -770 V, and

$$V_b = 2700 \text{ V} + (-770 \text{ V}) = 1930 \text{ V}$$

23.14 What are the potentials at points a, b, and c due to this electric dipole?

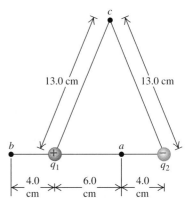

At point c the potential due to the positive charge is

$$\frac{1}{4\pi\epsilon_0} \frac{q_1}{r_1} = (9.0 \times 10^9 \text{ N} \cdot \text{m}^2/\text{C}^2)\frac{12 \times 10^{-9} \text{ C}}{0.13 \text{ m}} = 830 \text{ V}$$

The potential due to the negative charge is -830 V, and the total potential is zero:

$$V_c = 830 \text{ V} + (-830 \text{ V}) = 0$$

The potential is also equal to zero at infinity (infinitely far from both charges).

EVALUATE: Comparing this example with Example 21.9 shows that it's much easier to calculate electric potential (a scalar) than electric field (a vector). We'll take advantage of this simplification whenever possible.

Example 23.5   Potential and potential energy

Compute the potential energy associated with a point charge of $+4.0$ nC if it is placed at points a, b, and c in Fig. 23.14.

SOLUTION

IDENTIFY: We know the value of the electric potential at each of these points, and we need to find the potential energy for a point charge placed at each point.

SET UP: For any point charge q, the associated potential energy is $U = qV$. We use the values of V from Example 23.4.

EXECUTE: At point a,

$$U_a = qV_a = (4.0 \times 10^{-9} \text{ C})(-900 \text{ J/C}) = -3.6 \times 10^{-6} \text{ J}$$

At point b,

$$U_b = qV_b = (4.0 \times 10^{-9} \text{ C})(1930 \text{ J/C}) = 7.7 \times 10^{-6} \text{ J}$$

At point c,

$$U_c = qV_c = 0$$

All of these values correspond to U and V being zero at infinity.

EVALUATE: Note that *no* net work is done on the 4.0-nC charge if it moves from point c to infinity *by any path*. In particular, let the path be along the perpendicular bisector of the line joining the other two charges q_1 and q_2 in Fig. 23.14. As shown in Example 21.9 (Section 21.5), at points on the bisector the direction of $\vec{E}$ is perpendicular to the bisector. Hence the force on the 4.0-nC charge is perpendicular to the path, and no work is done in any displacement along it.

Example 23.6   Finding potential by integration

By integrating the electric field as in Eq. (23.17), find the potential at a distance r from a point charge q.

SOLUTION

IDENTIFY: This problem asks us to find the electric potential from the electric field.

SET UP: To find the potential V at a distance r from the point charge, we let point a in Eq. (23.17) be at distance r and let point b be at infinity (Fig. 23.15). As usual, we choose the potential to be zero at an infinite distance from the charge.

EXECUTE: To carry out the integral, we can choose any path we like between points a and b. The most convenient path is a straight radial line as shown in Fig. 23.15, so that $d\vec{l}$ is in the radial direction and has magnitude dr. If q is positive, $\vec{E}$ and $d\vec{l}$ are always parallel, so $\phi = 0$ and Eq. (23.17) becomes

$$V - 0 = \int_r^\infty E\,dr = \int_r^\infty \frac{q}{4\pi\epsilon_0 r^2}\,dr$$

$$= -\frac{q}{4\pi\epsilon_0 r}\Big|_r^\infty = 0 - \left(-\frac{q}{4\pi\epsilon_0 r}\right)$$

$$V = \frac{q}{4\pi\epsilon_0 r}$$

This agrees with Eq. (23.14). If q is negative, $\vec{E}$ is radially inward while $d\vec{l}$ is still radially outward, so $\phi = 180°$. Since $\cos 180° = -1$, this adds a minus sign to the above result. However, the field magnitude E is always positive, and since q is negative, we must write $E = |q|/4\pi\epsilon_0 r = -q/4\pi\epsilon_0 r$, giving another minus sign. The two minus signs cancel, and the above result for V is valid for point charges of either sign.

23.15 Calculating the potential by integrating $\vec{E}$ for a single point charge.

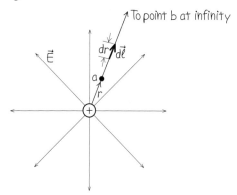

EVALUATE: We can get the same result by using Eq. (21.7) for the electric field, which is valid for either sign of q, and writing $d\vec{l} = \hat{r}\,dr$:

$$V - 0 = V = \int_r^\infty \vec{E}\cdot d\vec{l}$$

$$= \int_r^\infty \frac{1}{4\pi\epsilon_0}\frac{q}{r^2}\hat{r}\cdot\hat{r}\,dr = \int_r^\infty \frac{q}{4\pi\epsilon_0 r^2}\,dr$$

$$V = \frac{q}{4\pi\epsilon_0 r}$$

Example 23.7   Moving through a potential difference

In Fig. 23.16 a dust particle with mass $m = 5.0 \times 10^{-9}$ kg $= 5.0\ \mu$g and charge $q_0 = 2.0$ nC starts from rest at point a and moves in a straight line to point b. What is its speed v at point b?

SOLUTION

IDENTIFY: This problem involves the change in speed and hence kinetic energy of the particle, so we can use an energy approach. This problem would be difficult to solve without using energy techniques, since the force that acts on the particle varies in magnitude as the particle moves from a to b.

SET UP: Only the conservative electric force acts on the particle, so mechanical energy is conserved:

$$K_a + U_a = K_b + U_b$$

EXECUTE: For this situation, $K_a = 0$ and $K_b = \frac{1}{2}mv^2$. We get the potential energies (U) from the potentials (V) using Eq. (23.12):

23.16 The particle moves from point a to point b; its acceleration is not constant.

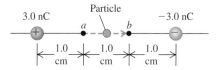

$U_a = q_0 V_a$ and $U_b = q_0 V_b$. Substituting these into the energy-conservation equation and solving for v, we find

$$0 + q_0 V_a = \frac{1}{2}mv^2 + q_0 V_b$$

$$v = \sqrt{\frac{2q_0(V_a - V_b)}{m}}$$

Continued

We calculate the potentials using Eq. (23.15), just as we did in Example 23.4:

$$V_a = (9.0 \times 10^9 \text{ N} \cdot \text{m}^2/\text{C}^2)$$

$$\times \left(\frac{3.0 \times 10^{-9} \text{ C}}{0.010 \text{ m}} + \frac{(-3.0 \times 10^{-9} \text{ C})}{0.020 \text{ m}} \right) = 1350 \text{ V}$$

$$V_b = (9.0 \times 10^9 \text{ N} \cdot \text{m}^2/\text{C}^2)$$

$$\times \left(\frac{3.0 \times 10^{-9} \text{ C}}{0.020 \text{ m}} + \frac{(-3.0 \times 10^{-9} \text{ C})}{0.010 \text{ m}} \right) = -1350 \text{ V}$$

$$V_a - V_b = (1350 \text{ V}) - (-1350 \text{ V}) = 2700 \text{ V}$$

Finally,

$$v = \sqrt{\frac{2(2.0 \times 10^{-9} \text{ C})(2700 \text{ V})}{5.0 \times 10^{-9} \text{ kg}}} = 46 \text{ m/s}$$

EVALUATE: Our result makes sense: The positive test charge gains speed as it moves away from the positive charge and toward the negative charge. To check unit consistency in the final line of the calculation, note that $1 \text{ V} = 1 \text{ J/C}$, so the numerator under the radical has units of J or $\text{kg} \cdot \text{m}^2/\text{s}^2$.

We can use exactly this same method to find the speed of an electron accelerated across a potential difference of 500 V in an oscilloscope tube or 20 kV in a TV picture tube. The end-of-chapter problems include several examples of such calculations.

Test Your Understanding of Section 23.2 If the electric *potential* at a certain point is zero, does the electric *field* at that point have to be zero? (*Hint:* Consider point *c* in Example 23.4 and Example 21.9.)

23.3 Calculating Electric Potential

When calculating the potential due to a charge distribution, we usually follow one of two routes. If we know the charge distribution, we can use Eq. (23.15) or (23.16). Or if we know how the electric field depends on position, we can use Eq. (23.17), defining the potential to be zero at some convenient place. Some problems require a combination of these approaches.

As you read through these examples, compare them with the related examples of calculating electric *field* in Section 21.5. You'll see how much easier it is to calculate scalar electric potentials than vector electric fields. The moral is clear: Whenever possible, solve problems using an energy approach (using electric potential and electric potential energy) rather than a dynamics approach (using electric fields and electric forces).

Problem-Solving Strategy 23.1 **Calculating Electric Potential**

IDENTIFY *the relevant concepts:* Remember that potential is *potential energy per unit charge.* Understanding this statement can get you a long way.

SET UP *the problem* using the following steps:
1. Make a drawing that clearly shows the locations of the charges (which may be point charges or a continuous distribution of charge) and your choice of coordinate axes.
2. Indicate on your drawing the position of the point at which you want to calculate the electric potential V. Sometimes this position will be an arbitrary one (say, a point a distance r from the center of a charged sphere).

EXECUTE *the solution* as follows:
1. To find the potential due to a collection of point charges, use Eq. (23.15). If you are given a continuous charge distribution, devise a way to divide it into infinitesimal elements and then use Eq. (23.16). Carry out the integration, using appropriate limits to include the entire charge distribution. In the integral, be careful about which geometric quantities vary and which are held constant.
2. If you are given the electric field, or if you can find it using any of the methods presented in Chapter 21 or 22, it may be easier

to use Eq. (23.17) or (23.18) to calculate the potential difference between points *a* and *b*. When appropriate, make use of your freedom to define V to be zero at some convenient place, and choose this place to be point *b*. (For point charges, this will usually be at infinity. For other distributions of charge—especially those that themselves extend to infinity—it may be convenient or necessary to define V_b to be zero at some finite distance from the charge distribution. This is just like defining U to be zero at ground level in gravitational problems.) Then the potential at any other point, say *a*, can by found from Eq. (23.17) or (23.18) with $V_b = 0$.

3. Remember that potential is a *scalar* quantity, not a *vector*. It doesn't have components! However, you may have to use components of the vectors $\vec{E}$ and $d\vec{l}$ when you use Eq. (23.17) or (23.18).

EVALUATE *your answer:* Check whether your answer agrees with your intuition. If your result gives V as a function of position, make a graph of this function to see whether it makes sense. If you know the electric field, you can make a rough check of your result for V by verifying that V decreases if you move in the direction of $\vec{E}$.

Example 23.8   **A charged conducting sphere**

A solid conducting sphere of radius R has a total charge q. Find the potential everywhere, both outside and inside the sphere.

SOLUTION

IDENTIFY: We used Gauss's law in Example 22.5 (Section 22.4) to find the electric field at all points for this charge distribution. We can use that result to determine the potential at all points.

SET UP: We choose the origin at the center of the sphere. Since we know E at all values of the distance r from the center of the sphere, we can determine V as a function of r.

EXECUTE: From Example 22.5, at all points *outside* the sphere the field is the same as if the sphere were removed and replaced by a point charge q. We take $V = 0$ at infinity, as we did for a point charge. Then the potential at a point outside the sphere at a distance r from its center is the same as the potential due to a point charge q at the center:

$$V = \frac{1}{4\pi\epsilon_0}\frac{q}{r}$$

The potential at the surface of the sphere is $V_{surface} = q/4\pi\epsilon_0 R$.

Inside the sphere, $\vec{E}$ is zero everywhere; otherwise, charge would move within the sphere. Hence if a test charge moves from any point to any other point inside the sphere, no work is done on that charge. This means that the potential is the same at every point inside the sphere and is equal to its value $q/4\pi\epsilon_0 R$ at the surface.

EVALUATE: Figure 23.17 shows the field and potential as a function of r for a positive charge q. In this case the electric field points

radially away from the sphere. As you move away from the sphere, in the direction of $\vec{E}$, V decreases (as it should). The electric field at the surface has magnitude $E_{surface} = |q|/4\pi\epsilon_0 R^2$.

23.17 Electric field magnitude E and potential V at points inside and outside a positively charged spherical conductor.

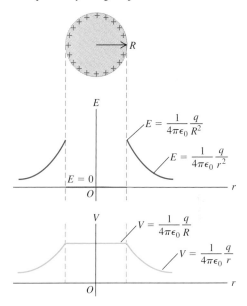

Ionization and Corona Discharge

The results of Example 23.8 have numerous practical consequences. One consequence relates to the maximum potential to which a conductor in air can be raised. This potential is limited because air molecules become *ionized,* and air becomes a conductor, at an electric-field magnitude of about 3×10^6 V/m. Assume for the moment that q is positive. When we compare the expressions in Example 23.8 for the potential $V_{surface}$ and field magnitude $E_{surface}$ at the surface of a charged conducting sphere, we note that $V_{surface} = E_{surface}R$. Thus, if E_m represents the electric-field magnitude at which air becomes conductive (known as the *dielectric strength* of air), then the maximum potential V_m to which a spherical conductor can be raised is

$$V_m = RE_m$$

For a conducting sphere 1 cm in radius in air, $V_m = (10^{-2}\,\text{m})(3 \times 10^6\,\text{V/m}) = 30{,}000$ V. No amount of "charging" could raise the potential of a conducting sphere of this size in air higher than about 30,000 V; attempting to raise the potential further by adding extra charge would cause the surrounding air to become ionized and conductive, and the extra added charge would leak into the air.

To attain even higher potentials, high-voltage machines such as Van de Graaff generators use spherical terminals with very large radii (see Fig. 22.27 and the photograph that opens Chapter 22). For example, a terminal of radius $R = 2$ m has a maximum potential $V_m = (2\,\text{m})(3 \times 10^6\,\text{V/m}) = 6 \times 10^6\,\text{V} = 6$ MV. Such machines are sometimes placed in pressurized tanks filled with a gas such as sulfur hexafluoride (SF_6) that has a larger value of E_m than does air and, therefore, can withstand even larger fields without becoming conductive.

23.18 The metal mast at the top of the Empire State Building acts as a lightning rod. It is struck by lightning as many as 500 times each year.

Our result in Example 23.8 also explains what happens with a charged conductor with a very *small* radius of curvature, such as a sharp point or thin wire. Because the maximum potential is proportional to the radius, even relatively small potentials applied to sharp points in air produce sufficiently high fields just outside the point to ionize the surrounding air, making it become a conductor. The resulting current and its associated glow (visible in a dark room) are called *corona*. Laser printers and photocopying machines use corona from fine wires to spray charge on the imaging drum (see Fig. 21.2).

A large-radius conductor is used in situations where it's important to *prevent* corona. An example is the metal ball at the end of a car radio antenna, which prevents the static that would be caused by corona. Another example is the blunt end of a metal lightning rod (Fig. 23.18). If there is an excess charge in the atmosphere, as happens during thunderstorms, a substantial charge of the opposite sign can build up on this blunt end. As a result, when the atmospheric charge is discharged through a lightning bolt, it tends to be attracted to the charged lightning rod rather than to other nearby structures that could be damaged. (A conducting wire connecting the lightning rod to the ground then allows the acquired charge to dissipate harmlessly.) A lightning rod with a sharp end would allow less charge buildup and hence would be less effective.

Example 23.9 Oppositely charged parallel plates

Find the potential at any height y between the two oppositely charged parallel plates discussed in Section 23.1 (Fig. 23.19).

SOLUTION

IDENTIFY: From Section 23.1 we know the electric *potential energy* U for a test charge q_0 as a function of y. Our goal here is to find the electric *potential* V due to the charges on the plates as a function of y.

SET UP: From Eq. (23.5), $U = q_0 Ey$ at a point a distance y above the bottom plate. We use this expression to determine the potential V at such a point.

EXECUTE: The potential $V(y)$ at coordinate y is the potential energy per unit charge:

$$V(y) = \frac{U(y)}{q_0} = \frac{q_0 Ey}{q_0} = Ey$$

We have chosen $U(y)$, and therefore $V(y)$, to be zero at point b, where $y = 0$. Even if we choose the potential to be different from zero at b, it is still true that

$$V(y) - V_b = Ey$$

The potential decreases as we move in the direction of $\vec{E}$ from the upper to the lower plate. At point a, where $y = d$ and $V(y) = V_a$,

$$V_a - V_b = Ed \quad \text{and} \quad E = \frac{V_a - V_b}{d} = \frac{V_{ab}}{d}$$

where V_{ab} is the potential of the positive plate with respect to the negative plate. That is, the electric field equals the potential difference between the plates divided by the distance between them. For a given potential difference V_{ab}, the smaller the distance d between the two plates, the greater the magnitude E of the electric field. (This relationship between E and V_{ab} holds *only* for the planar geometry we have described. It does *not* work for situations such as concentric cylinders or spheres in which the electric field is not uniform.)

23.19 The charged parallel plates from Fig. 23.2

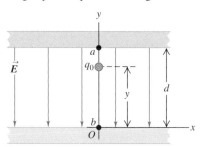

EVALUATE: Our result tells us how to measure the charge density on the charges on the two plates in Fig. 23.19. In Example 22.8 (Section 22.4), we derived the expression $E = \sigma/\epsilon_0$ for the electric field E between two conducting plates having surface charge densities $+\sigma$ and $-\sigma$. Setting this expression equal to $E = V_{ab}/d$ gives

$$\sigma = \frac{\epsilon_0 V_{ab}}{d}$$

The surface charge density on the positive plate is directly proportional to the potential difference between the plates, and its value σ can be determined by measuring V_{ab}. This technique is useful because no instruments are available that read surface charge density directly. On the negative plate the surface charge density is $-\sigma$.

CAUTION *"Zero potential" is arbitrary* You might think that if a conducting body has zero potential, it must necessarily also have zero net charge. But that just isn't so! As an example, the plate at $y = 0$ in Fig. 23.19 has zero potential ($V = 0$) but has a nonzero charge per unit area $-\sigma$. Remember that there's nothing particularly special about the place where potential is zero; we can *define* this place to be wherever we want it to be.

Example 23.10 An infinite line charge or charged conducting cylinder

Find the potential at a distance r from a very long line of charge with linear charge density (charge per unit length) λ.

SOLUTION

IDENTIFY: One approach to this problem is to divide the line of charge into infinitesimal elements, as we did in Example 21.11 (Section 21.5) to find the electric field produced by such a line. We could then integrate as in Eq. (23.16) to find the net potential V. In this case, however, our task is greatly simplified because we already know the electric field.

SET UP: In both Example 21.11 and Example 22.6 (Section 22.4), we found that the electric field at a distance r from a long straight-line charge (Fig. 23.20a) has only a radial component, given by

$$E_r = \frac{1}{2\pi\epsilon_0}\frac{\lambda}{r}$$

We use this expression to find the potential by integrating $\vec{E}$ as in Eq. (23.17).

EXECUTE: Since the field has only a radial component, the scalar product $\vec{E} \cdot d\vec{l}$ is equal to $E_r dr$. Hence the potential of any point a with respect to any other point b, at radial distances r_a and r_b from the line of charge, is

$$V_a - V_b = \int_a^b \vec{E} \cdot d\vec{l} = \int_a^b E_r dr = \frac{\lambda}{2\pi\epsilon_0}\int_{r_a}^{r_b}\frac{dr}{r} = \frac{\lambda}{2\pi\epsilon_0}\ln\frac{r_b}{r_a}$$

If we take point b at infinity and set $V_b = 0$, we find that V_a is *infinite*:

$$V_a = \frac{\lambda}{2\pi\epsilon_0}\ln\frac{\infty}{r_a} = \infty$$

This shows that if we try to define V to be zero at infinity, then V must be infinite at *any* finite distance from the line charge. This is *not* a useful way to define V for this problem! The difficulty is that the charge distribution itself extends to infinity.

To get around this difficulty, remember that we can define V to be zero at any point we like. We set $V_b = 0$ at point b at an arbi-

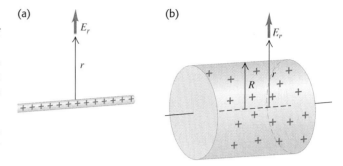

23.20 Electric field outside **(a)** a long positively charged wire and **(b)** a long, positively charged cylinder.

trary radial distance r_0. Then the potential $V = V_a$ at point a at a radial distance r is given by $V - 0 = (\lambda/2\pi\epsilon_0)\ln(r_0/r)$, or

$$V = \frac{\lambda}{2\pi\epsilon_0}\ln\frac{r_0}{r}$$

EVALUATE: According to our result, if λ is positive, then V decreases as r increases. This is as it should be: V decreases as we move in the direction of $\vec{E}$.

From Example 22.6, the expression for E_r with which we started also applies outside a long charged conducting cylinder with charge per unit length λ (Fig. 23.20b). Hence our result also gives the potential for such a cylinder, but only for values of r (the distance from the cylinder axis) equal to or greater than the radius R of the cylinder. If we choose r_0 to be the cylinder radius R, so that $V = 0$ when $r = R$, then at any point for which $r > R$,

$$V = \frac{\lambda}{2\pi\epsilon_0}\ln\frac{R}{r}$$

Inside the cylinder, $\vec{E} = 0$, and V has the same value (zero) as on the cylinder's surface.

Example 23.11 A ring of charge

Electric charge is distributed uniformly around a thin ring of radius a, with total charge Q (Fig. 23.21). Find the potential at a point P on the ring axis at a distance x from the center of the ring.

SOLUTION

IDENTIFY: We already know the electric field at all points along the x-axis from Example 21.10 (Section 21.5), so we could solve the problem by integrating $\vec{E}$ as in Eq. (23.17) to find V along this axis. Alternatively, we could divide the ring up into infinitesimal segments and use Eq. (23.16) to find V.

SET UP: Figure 23.21 shows that it's far easier to find V on the axis by using the infinitesimal-segment approach. That's because

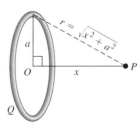

23.21 All the charge in a ring of charge Q is the same distance r from a point P on the ring axis.

Continued

all parts of the ring (that is, all elements of the charge distribution) are the same distance r from point P.

EXECUTE: Figure 23.21 shows that the distance from each charge element dq on the ring to the point P is $r = \sqrt{x^2 + a^2}$. Hence we can take the factor $1/r$ outside the integral in Eq. (23.16), and

$$V = \frac{1}{4\pi\epsilon_0}\int\frac{dq}{r} = \frac{1}{4\pi\epsilon_0}\frac{1}{\sqrt{x^2 + a^2}}\int dq = \frac{1}{4\pi\epsilon_0}\frac{Q}{\sqrt{x^2 + a^2}}$$

Potential is a *scalar* quantity; there is no need to consider components of vectors in this calculation, as we had to do when we found the electric field at P. So the potential calculation is a lot simpler than the field calculation.

EVALUATE: When x is much larger than a, the above expression for V becomes approximately equal to $V = Q/4\pi\epsilon_0 x$. This corresponds to the potential of a point charge Q at distance x. So when we are very far away from a charged ring, it looks like a point charge. (We drew a similar conclusion about the electric field of a ring in Example 21.10.)

These results for V can also be found by integrating the expression for E_x found in Example 21.10 (see Problem 23.69).

Example 23.12   A line of charge

Electric charge Q is distributed uniformly along a line or thin rod of length $2a$. Find the potential at a point P along the perpendicular bisector of the rod at a distance x from its center.

SOLUTION

IDENTIFY: This is the same situation as in Example 21.11 (Section 21.5), where we found an expression for the electric field $\vec{E}$ at an arbitrary point on the x-axis. We could integrate $\vec{E}$ using Eq. (23.17) to find V. Instead, we'll integrate over the charge distribution using Eq. (23.16) to get a bit more experience with this approach.

SET UP: Figure 23.22 shows the situation. Unlike the situation in Example 23.11, each charge element dQ is a different distance from point P.

EXECUTE: As in Example 21.11, the element of charge dQ corresponding to an element of length dy on the rod is given by $dQ = (Q/2a)dy$. The distance from dQ to P is $\sqrt{x^2 + y^2}$, and the contribution dV that it makes to the potential at P is

$$dV = \frac{1}{4\pi\epsilon_0}\frac{Q}{2a}\frac{dy}{\sqrt{x^2 + y^2}}$$

To get the potential at P due to the entire rod, we integrate dV over the length of the rod from $y = -a$ to $y = a$:

$$V = \frac{1}{4\pi\epsilon_0}\frac{Q}{2a}\int_{-a}^{a}\frac{dy}{\sqrt{x^2 + y^2}}$$

23.22 Our sketch for this problem.

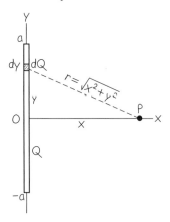

You can look up the integral in a table. The final result is

$$V = \frac{1}{4\pi\epsilon_0}\frac{Q}{2a}\ln\left(\frac{\sqrt{a^2 + x^2} + a}{\sqrt{a^2 + x^2} - a}\right)$$

EVALUATE: We can check our result by letting x approach infinity. In this limit the point P is infinitely far from all of the charge, so we expect V to approach zero; we invite you to verify that it does so.

As in Example 23.11, this problem is simpler than finding $\vec{E}$ at point P because potential is a scalar quantity and no vector calculations are involved.

Test Your Understanding of Section 23.3   If the electric *field* at a certain point is zero, does the electric *potential* at that point have to be zero? (*Hint:* Consider the center of the ring in Example 23.11 and Example 21.10.)

23.4 Equipotential Surfaces

Field lines (see Section 21.6) help us visualize electric fields. In a similar way, the potential at various points in an electric field can be represented graphically by *equipotential surfaces*. These use the same fundamental idea as topographic maps like those used by hikers and mountain climbers (Fig. 23.23). On a topographic map, contour lines are drawn through points that are all at the same elevation. Any number of these could be drawn, but typically only a few contour lines are shown at equal spacings of elevation. If a mass m is moved over the terrain along such a contour line, the gravitational potential energy mgy does not change because the elevation y is constant. Thus contour lines on a topographic map are really curves of constant gravitational potential energy. Contour lines are close together in regions where the terrain is steep and there are large changes in elevation over a small horizontal distance; the contour lines are farther apart where the terrain is gently sloping. A ball allowed to roll downhill will experience the greatest downhill gravitational force where contour lines are closest together.

By analogy to contour lines on a topographic map, an **equipotential surface** is a three-dimensional surface on which the *electric potential V* is the same at every point. If a test charge q_0 is moved from point to point on such a surface, the *electric* potential energy q_0V remains constant. In a region where an electric field is present, we can construct an equipotential surface through any point. In diagrams we usually show only a few representative equipotentials, often with equal potential differences between adjacent surfaces. No point can be at two different potentials, so equipotential surfaces for different potentials can never touch or intersect.

23.23 Contour lines on a topographic map are curves of constant elevation and hence of constant gravitational potential energy.

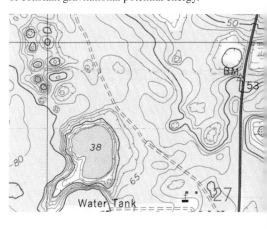

Equipotential Surfaces and Field Lines

Because potential energy does not change as a test charge moves over an equipotential surface, the electric field can do no work on such a charge. It follows that $\vec{E}$ must be perpendicular to the surface at every point so that the electric force $q_0\vec{E}$ is always perpendicular to the displacement of a charge moving on the surface. **Field lines and equipotential surfaces are always mutually perpendicular.** In general, field lines are curves, and equipotentials are curved surfaces. For the special case of a *uniform* field, in which the field lines are straight, parallel, and equally spaced, the equipotentials are parallel *planes* perpendicular to the field lines.

Figure 23.24 shows three arrangements of charges. The field lines in the plane of the charges are represented by red lines, and the intersections of the equipotential surfaces with this plane (that is, cross sections of these surfaces) are shown as blue lines. The actual equipotential surfaces are three-dimensional. At each crossing of an equipotential and a field line, the two are perpendicular.

In Fig. 23.24 we have drawn equipotentials so that there are equal potential differences between adjacent surfaces. In regions where the magnitude of $\vec{E}$ is large, the equipotential surfaces are close together because the field does a rela-

23.24 Cross sections of equipotential surfaces (blue lines) and electric field lines (red lines) for assemblies of point charges. There are equal potential differences between adjacent surfaces. Compare these diagrams to those in Fig. 21.29, which showed only the electric field lines.

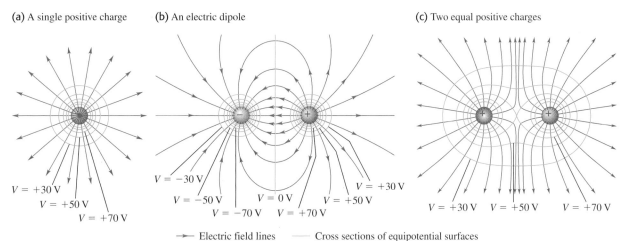

(a) A single positive charge

(b) An electric dipole

(c) Two equal positive charges

$V = +30\text{ V}$
$V = +50\text{ V}$
$V = +70\text{ V}$

$V = -30\text{ V}$
$V = -50\text{ V}$
$V = 0\text{ V}$
$V = +30\text{ V}$
$V = +50\text{ V}$
$V = -70\text{ V}$
$V = +70\text{ V}$

$V = +30\text{ V}$ $V = +50\text{ V}$ $V = +70\text{ V}$

→ Electric field lines   — Cross sections of equipotential surfaces

23.25 When charges are at rest, a conducting surface is always an equipotential surface. Field lines are perpendicular to a conducting surface.

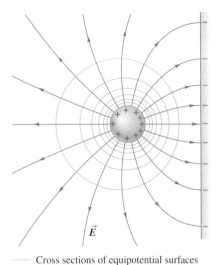

Cross sections of equipotential surfaces

23.26 At all points on the surface of a conductor, the electric field must be perpendicular to the surface. If $\vec{E}$ had a tangential component, a net amount of work would be done on a test charge by moving it around a loop as shown here—which is impossible because the electric force is conservative.

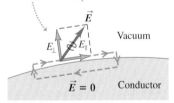

An impossible electric field
If the electric field just outside a conductor had a tangential component $E_\parallel$, a charge could move in a loop with net work done.

$\vec{E}$

$E_\perp$ $E_\parallel$ Vacuum

$\vec{E} = 0$ Conductor

23.27 A cavity in a conductor. If the cavity contains no charge, every point in the cavity is at the same potential, the electric field is zero everywhere in the cavity, and there is no charge anywhere on the surface of the cavity.

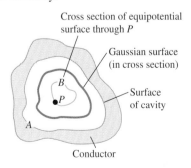

Cross section of equipotential surface through P

Gaussian surface (in cross section)

B
P

Surface of cavity

A

Conductor

tively large amount of work on a test charge in a relatively small displacement. This is the case near the point charge in Fig. 23.24a or between the two point charges in Fig. 23.24b; note that in these regions the field lines are also closer together. This is directly analogous to the downhill force of gravity being greatest in regions on a topographic map where contour lines are close together. Conversely, in regions where the field is weaker, the equipotential surfaces are farther apart; this happens at larger radii in Fig. 23.24a, to the left of the negative charge or the right of the positive charge in Fig. 23.24b, and at greater distances from both charges in Fig.23.24c. (It may appear that two equipotential surfaces intersect at the center of Fig.23.24c, in violation of the rule that this can never happen. In fact this is a single figure-8–shaped equipotential surface.)

CAUTION *E need not be constant over an equipotential surface* On a given equipotential surface, the potential V has the same value at every point. In general, however, the electric-field magnitude E is *not* the same at all points on an equipotential surface. For instance, on the equipotential surface labeled "$V = -30$ V" in Fig. 23.24b, the magnitude E is less to the left of the negative charge than it is between the two charges. On the figure-8–shaped equipotential surface in Fig. 23.24c, $E = 0$ at the middle point halfway between the two charges; at any other point on this surface, E is nonzero. ∎

Equipotentials and Conductors

Here's an important statement about equipotential surfaces: **When all charges are at rest, the surface of a conductor is always an equipotential surface.** Since the electric field $\vec{E}$ is always perpendicular to an equipotential surface, we can prove this statement by proving that **when all charges are at rest, the electric field just outside a conductor must be perpendicular to the surface at every point** (Fig. 23.25). We know that $\vec{E} = 0$ everywhere inside the conductor; otherwise, charges would move. In particular, at any point just inside the surface the component of $\vec{E}$ tangent to the surface is zero. It follows that the tangential component of $\vec{E}$ is also zero just *outside* the surface. If it were not, a charge could move around a rectangular path partly inside and partly outside (Fig. 23.26) and return to its starting point with a net amount of work having been done on it. This would violate the conservative nature of electrostatic fields, so the tangential component of $\vec{E}$ just outside the surface must be zero at every point on the surface. Thus $\vec{E}$ is perpendicular to the surface at each point, proving our statement.

Finally, we can now prove a theorem that we quoted without proof in Section 22.5. The theorem is as follows: In an electrostatic situation, if a conductor contains a cavity and if no charge is present inside the cavity, then there can be no net charge *anywhere* on the surface of the cavity. This means that if you're inside a charged conducting box, you can safely touch any point on the inside walls of the box without being shocked. To prove this theorem, we first prove that *every point in the cavity is at the same potential*. In Fig. 23.27 the conducting surface A of the cavity is an equipotential surface, as we have just proved. Suppose point P in the cavity is at a different potential; then we can construct a different equipotential surface B including point P.

Now consider a Gaussian surface, shown in Fig. 23.27, between the two equipotential surfaces. Because of the relationship between $\vec{E}$ and the equipotentials, we know that the field at every point between the equipotentials is from A toward B, or else at every point it is from B toward A, depending on which equipotential surface is at higher potential. In either case the flux through this Gaussian surface is certainly not zero. But then Gauss's law says that the charge enclosed by the Gaussian surface cannot be zero. This contradicts our initial assumption that there is *no* charge in the cavity. So the potential at P cannot be different from that at the cavity wall.

The entire region of the cavity must therefore be at the same potential. But for this to be true, *the electric field inside the cavity must be zero everywhere.*

Finally, Gauss's law shows that the electric field at any point on the surface of a conductor is proportional to the surface charge density σ at that point. We conclude that *the surface charge density on the wall of the cavity is zero at every point.* This chain of reasoning may seem tortuous, but it is worth careful study.

CAUTION **Equipotential surfaces vs. Gaussian surfaces** Don't confuse equipotential surfaces with the Gaussian surfaces we encountered in Chapter 22. Gaussian surfaces have relevance only when we are using Gauss's law, and we can choose *any* Gaussian surface that's convenient. We are *not* free to choose the shape of equipotential surfaces; the shape is determined by the charge distribution.

Test Your Understanding of Section 23.4 Would the shapes of the equipotential surfaces in Fig. 23.24 change if the sign of each charge were reversed?

23.5 Potential Gradient

Electric field and potential are closely related. Equation (23.17), restated here, expresses one aspect of that relationship:

$$V_a - V_b = \int_a^b \vec{E} \cdot d\vec{l}$$

Act|v
Physics ONLINE

11.12.3 Electric Potential, Field, and Force

If we know $\vec{E}$ at various points, we can use this equation to calculate potential differences. In this section we show how to turn this around; if we know the potential V at various points, we can use it to determine $\vec{E}$. Regarding V as a function of the coordinates (x, y, z) of a point in space, we will show that the components of $\vec{E}$ are directly related to the *partial derivatives* of V with respect to x, y, and z.

In Eq. (23.17), $V_a - V_b$ is the potential of a with respect to b—that is, the change of potential encountered on a trip from b to a. We can write this as

$$V_a - V_b = \int_b^a dV = -\int_a^b dV$$

where dV is the infinitesimal change of potential accompanying an infinitesimal element $d\vec{l}$ of the path from b to a. Comparing to Eq. (23.17), we have

$$-\int_a^b dV = \int_a^b \vec{E} \cdot d\vec{l}$$

These two integrals must be equal for *any* pair of limits a and b, and for this to be true the *integrands* must be equal. Thus, for *any* infinitesimal displacement $d\vec{l}$,

$$-dV = \vec{E} \cdot d\vec{l}$$

To interpret this expression, we write $\vec{E}$ and $d\vec{l}$ in terms of their components: $\vec{E} = \hat{\imath}\, E_x + \hat{\jmath}\, E_y + \hat{k}\, E_z$ and $d\vec{l} = \hat{\imath}\, dx + \hat{\jmath}\, dy + \hat{k}\, dz$. Then we have

$$-dV = E_x dx + E_y dy + E_z dz$$

Suppose the displacement is parallel to the x-axis, so $dy = dz = 0$. Then $-dV = E_x dx$ or $E_x = -(dV/dx)_{y, z \text{ constant}}$, where the subscript reminds us that only x varies in the derivative; recall that V is in general a function of x, y, and z. But this is just what is meant by the partial derivative $\partial V/\partial x$. The y- and z-components of $\vec{E}$ are related to the corresponding derivatives of V in the same way, so we have

$$E_x = -\frac{\partial V}{\partial x} \qquad E_y = -\frac{\partial V}{\partial y} \qquad E_z = -\frac{\partial V}{\partial z} \qquad \begin{array}{l}\text{(components of } \vec{E} \\ \text{in terms of } V)\end{array} \qquad \text{(23.19)}$$

This is consistent with the units of electric field being V/m. In terms of unit vectors we can write $\vec{E}$ as

$$\vec{E} = -\left(\hat{i}\frac{\partial V}{\partial x} + \hat{j}\frac{\partial V}{\partial y} + \hat{k}\frac{\partial V}{\partial z}\right) \qquad (\vec{E} \text{ in terms of } V) \qquad (23.20)$$

In vector notation the following operation is called the **gradient** of the function f:

$$\vec{\nabla}f = \left(\hat{i}\frac{\partial}{\partial x} + \hat{j}\frac{\partial}{\partial y} + \hat{k}\frac{\partial}{\partial z}\right)f \qquad (23.21)$$

The operator denoted by the symbol $\vec{\nabla}$ is called "grad" or "del." Thus in vector notation,

$$\vec{E} = -\vec{\nabla}V \qquad (23.22)$$

This is read "$\vec{E}$ is the negative of the gradient of V" or "$\vec{E}$ equals negative grad V." The quantity $\vec{\nabla}V$ is called the *potential gradient.*

At each point, the potential gradient points in the direction in which V *increases* most rapidly with a change in position. Hence at each point the direction of $\vec{E}$ is the direction in which V *decreases* most rapidly and is always perpendicular to the equipotential surface through the point. This agrees with our observation in Section 23.2 that moving in the direction of the electric field means moving in the direction of decreasing potential.

Equation (23.22) doesn't depend on the particular choice of the zero point for V. If we were to change the zero point, the effect would be to change V at every point by the same amount; the derivatives of V would be the same.

If $\vec{E}$ is radial with respect to a point or an axis and r is the distance from the point or the axis, the relationship corresponding to Eqs. (23.19) is

$$E_r = -\frac{\partial V}{\partial r} \qquad \text{(radial electric field)} \qquad (23.23)$$

Often we can compute the electric field caused by a charge distribution in either of two ways: directly, by adding the $\vec{E}$ fields of point charges, or by first calculating the potential and then taking its gradient to find the field. The second method is often easier because potential is a *scalar* quantity, requiring at worst the integration of a scalar function. Electric field is a *vector* quantity, requiring computation of components for each element of charge and a separate integration for each component. Thus, quite apart from its fundamental significance, potential offers a very useful computational technique in field calculations. Below, we present two examples in which a knowledge of V is used to find the electric field.

We stress once more that if we know $\vec{E}$ as a function of position, we can calculate V using Eq. (23.17) or (23.18), and if we know V as a function of position, we can calculate $\vec{E}$ using Eq. (23.19), (23.20), or (23.23). Deriving V from $\vec{E}$ requires integration, and deriving $\vec{E}$ from V requires differentiation.

Example 23.13 Potential and field of a point charge

From Eq. (23.14) the potential at a radial distance r from a point charge q is $V = q/4\pi\epsilon_0 r$. Find the vector electric field from this expression for V.

SOLUTION

IDENTIFY: This problem uses the relationship between the electric potential as a function of position and the electric field vector.

SET UP: By symmetry, the electric field has only a radial component E_r. We use Eq. (23.23) to find this component.

EXECUTE: From Eq. (23.23),

$$E_r = -\frac{\partial V}{\partial r} = -\frac{\partial}{\partial r}\left(\frac{1}{4\pi\epsilon_0}\frac{q}{r}\right) = \frac{1}{4\pi\epsilon_0}\frac{q}{r^2}$$

so the vector electric field is

$$\vec{E} = \hat{r}E_r = \frac{1}{4\pi\epsilon_0}\frac{q}{r^2}\hat{r}$$

EVALUATE: Our result agrees with Eq. (21.7), as it must.

An alternative approach is to ignore the radial symmetry, write the radial distance as $r = \sqrt{x^2 + y^2 + z^2}$, and take the derivatives of V with respect to x, y, and z as in Eq. (23.20). We find

$$\frac{\partial V}{\partial x} = \frac{\partial}{\partial x}\left(\frac{1}{4\pi\epsilon_0}\frac{q}{\sqrt{x^2+y^2+z^2}}\right) = -\frac{1}{4\pi\epsilon_0}\frac{qx}{(x^2+y^2+z^2)^{3/2}}$$

$$= -\frac{qx}{4\pi\epsilon_0 r^3}$$

and similarly

$$\frac{\partial V}{\partial y} = -\frac{qy}{4\pi\epsilon_0 r^3} \qquad \frac{\partial V}{\partial z} = -\frac{qz}{4\pi\epsilon_0 r^3}$$

From Eq. (23.20), the electric field is

$$\vec{E} = -\left[\hat{i}\left(-\frac{qx}{4\pi\epsilon_0 r^3}\right) + \hat{j}\left(-\frac{qy}{4\pi\epsilon_0 r^3}\right) + \hat{k}\left(-\frac{qz}{4\pi\epsilon_0 r^3}\right)\right]$$

$$= \frac{1}{4\pi\epsilon_0}\frac{q}{r^2}\left(\frac{x\hat{i}+y\hat{j}+z\hat{k}}{r}\right) = \frac{1}{4\pi\epsilon_0}\frac{q}{r^2}\hat{r}$$

This approach gives us the same answer, but with a bit more effort. Clearly it's best to exploit the symmetry of the charge distribution whenever possible.

Example 23.14 Potential and field of a ring of charge

In Example 23.11 (Section 23.3) we found that for a ring of charge with radius a and total charge Q, the potential at a point P on the ring axis a distance x from the center is

$$V = \frac{1}{4\pi\epsilon_0}\frac{Q}{\sqrt{x^2+a^2}}$$

Find the electric field at P.

SOLUTION

IDENTIFY: We are given V as a function of x along the x-axis, and we wish to find the electric field at a point on this axis.

SET UP: From the symmetry of the charge distribution shown in Fig. 23.21, the electric field along the symmetry axis of the ring can have only an x-component. We find it using the first of Eqs. (23.19).

EXECUTE: The x-component of the electric field is

$$E_x = -\frac{\partial V}{\partial x} = \frac{1}{4\pi\epsilon_0}\frac{Qx}{(x^2+a^2)^{3/2}}$$

EVALUATE: This agrees with the result that we obtained in Example 21.10 (Section 21.5).

CAUTION Don't use expressions where they don't apply In this example, V does not appear to be a function of y or z, but it would *not* be correct to conclude that $\partial V/\partial y = \partial V/\partial z = 0$ and $E_y = E_z = 0$ everywhere. The reason is that our expression for V is valid *only for points on the x-axis*, where $y = z = 0$. Hence our expression for E_x is likewise valid on the x-axis only. If we had the complete expression for V valid at *all* points in space, then we could use it to find the components of $\vec{E}$ at any point using Eq. (23.19).

Test Your Understanding of Section 23.5 In a certain region of space the potential is given by $V = A + Bx + Cy^3 + Dxy$, where A, B, C, and D are positive constants. Which of these statements about the electric field $\vec{E}$ in this region of space is correct? (There may be more than one correct answer.) (i) Increasing the value of A will increase the value of $\vec{E}$ at all points; (ii) increasing the value of A will decrease the value of $\vec{E}$ at all points; (iii) $\vec{E}$ has no z-component; (iv) the electric field is zero at the origin $(x = 0, y = 0, z = 0)$.

Electric potential energy: The electric force caused by any collection of charges at rest is a conservative force. The work W done by the electric force on a charged particle moving in an electric field can be represented by the change in a potential-energy function U.

The electric potential energy for two point charges q and q_0 depends on their separation r. The electric potential energy for a charge q_0 in the presence of a collection of charges q_1, q_2, q_3 depends on the distance from q_0 to each of these other charges. (See Examples 23.1 and 23.2.)

$$W_{a \to b} = U_a - U_b \tag{23.2}$$

$$U = \frac{1}{4\pi\epsilon_0} \frac{qq_0}{r} \tag{23.9}$$
(two point charges)

$$U = \frac{q_0}{4\pi\epsilon_0}\left(\frac{q_1}{r_1} + \frac{q_2}{r_2} + \frac{q_3}{r_3} + \cdots\right)$$
$$= \frac{q_0}{4\pi\epsilon_0}\sum_i \frac{q_i}{r_i} \tag{23.10}$$
(q_0 in presence of other point charges)

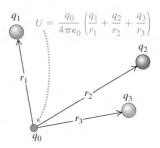

Electric potential: Potential, denoted by V, is potential energy per unit charge. The potential difference between two points equals the amount of work that would be required to move a unit positive test charge between those points. The potential V due to a quantity of charge can be calculated by summing (if the charge is a collection of point charges) or by integrating (if the charge is a distribution). (See Examples 23.3, 23.4, 23.5, 23.7, 23.11, and 23.12.)

The potential difference between two points a and b, also called the potential of a with respect to b, is given by the line integral of $\vec{E}$. The potential at a given point can be found by first finding $\vec{E}$ and then carrying out this integral. (See Examples 23.6, 23.8, 23.9, and 23.10.)

$$V = \frac{U}{q_0} = \frac{1}{4\pi\epsilon_0}\frac{q}{r} \tag{23.14}$$
(due to a point charge)

$$V = \frac{U}{q_0} = \frac{1}{4\pi\epsilon_0}\sum_i \frac{q_i}{r_i} \tag{23.15}$$
(due to a collection of point charges)

$$V = \frac{1}{4\pi\epsilon_0}\int \frac{dq}{r} \tag{23.16}$$
(due to a charge distribution)

$$V_a - V_b = \int_a^b \vec{E}\cdot d\vec{l} = \int_a^b E\cos\phi\, dl \tag{23.17}$$

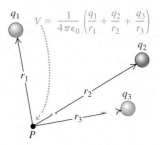

Equipotential surfaces: An equipotential surface is a surface on which the potential has the same value at every point. At a point where a field line crosses an equipotential surface, the two are perpendicular. When all charges are at rest, the surface of a conductor is always an equipotential surface and all points in the interior of a conductor are at the same potential. When a cavity within a conductor contains no charge, the entire cavity is an equipotential region and there is no surface charge anywhere on the surface of the cavity.

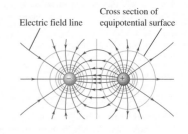

Cross section of
Electric field line   equipotential surface

Finding electric field from electric potential: If the potential V is known as a function of the coordinates x, y, and z, the components of electric field $\vec{E}$ at any point are given by partial derivatives of V. (See Examples 23.13 and 23.14.)

$$E_x = -\frac{\partial V}{\partial x} \quad E_y = -\frac{\partial V}{\partial y} \quad E_z = -\frac{\partial V}{\partial z} \tag{23.19}$$

$$\vec{E} = -\left(\hat{i}\frac{\partial V}{\partial x} + \hat{j}\frac{\partial V}{\partial y} + \hat{k}\frac{\partial V}{\partial z}\right) \tag{23.20}$$
(vector form)

Key Terms

(electric) potential energy, *781*
(electric) potential, *787*
volt, *787*

voltage, *788*
electron volt, *790*

equipotential surface, *799*
gradient, *802*

Answer to Chapter Opening Question ?

A large, constant potential difference V_{ab} is maintained between the welding tool (a) and the metal pieces to be welded (b). From Example 23.9 (Section 23.3) the electric field between two conductors separated by a distance d has magnitude $E = V_{ab}/d$. Hence d must be small in order for the field magnitude E to be large enough to ionize the gas between the conductors a and b (see Section 23.3) and produce an arc through this gas.

Answers to Test Your Understanding Questions

23.1 Answers: (a) (i), (b) (ii) The three charges q_1, q_2, and q_3 are all positive, so all three of the terms in the sum in Eq. (23.11)—$q_1q_2/r_{12}, q_1q_3/r_{13}$, and q_2q_3/r_{23}—are positive. Hence the total electric potential energy U is positive. This means that it would take positive work to bring the three charges from infinity to the positions shown in Fig. 21.14, and hence *negative* work to move the three charges from these positions back to infinity.

23.2 Answer: no If $V = 0$ at a certain point, $\vec{E}$ does *not* have to be zero at that point. An example is point c in Figs. 21.23 and 23.14, for which there is an electric field in the $+x$-direction (see Example 21.9 in Section 21.5) even though $V = 0$ (see Example 23.4). This isn't a surprising result because V and $\vec{E}$ are quite different quantities: V is the net amount of work required to bring a unit charge from infinity to the point in question, whereas $\vec{E}$ is the electric force that acts on a unit charge when it arrives at that point.

23.3 Answer: no If $\vec{E} = 0$ at a certain point, V does *not* have to be zero at that point. An example is point O at the center of the charged ring in Figs. 21.24 and 23.21. From Example 21.10 (Section 21.5), the electric field is zero at O because the electric-field contributions from different parts of the ring completely cancel. From Example 23.11, however, the potential at O is *not* zero: This point corresponds to $x = 0$, so $V = (1/4\pi\epsilon_0)(Q/a)$. This value of V corresponds to the work that would have to be done to move a unit positive test charge along a path from infinity to point O; it is nonzero because the charged ring repels the test charge, so positive work must be done to move the test charge toward the ring.

23.4 Answer: no If the positive charges in Fig. 23.24 were replaced by negative charges, and vice versa, the equipotential surfaces would be the same but the sign of the potential would be reversed. For example, the surfaces in Fig. 23.24b with potential $V = +30$ V and $V = -50$ V would have potential $V = -30$ V and $V = +50$ V, respectively.

23.5 Answer: (iii) From Eqs. (23.19), the components of the electric field are $E_x = -\partial V/\partial x = B + Dy$, $E_y = -\partial V/\partial y = 3Cy^2 + Dx$, and $E_z = -\partial V/\partial z = 0$. The value of A has no effect, which means that we can add a constant to the electric potential at all points without changing $\vec{E}$ or the potential difference between two points. The potential does not depend on z, so the z-component of $\vec{E}$ is zero. Note that at the origin the electric field is not zero because it has a nonzero x-component: $E_x = B$, $E_y = 0$, $E_z = 0$.

PROBLEMS

For instructor-assigned homework, go to **www.masteringphysics.com**

Discussion Questions

Q23.1. A student asked, "Since electrical potential is always proportional to potential energy, why bother with the concept of potential at all?" How would you respond?

Q23.2. The potential (relative to a point at infinity) midway between two charges of equal magnitude and opposite sign is zero. Is it possible to bring a test charge from infinity to this midpoint in such a way that no work is done in any part of the displacement? If so, describe how it can be done. If it is not possible, explain why.

Q23.3. Is it possible to have an arrangement of two point charges separated by a finite distance such that the electric potential energy of the arrangement is the same as if the two charges were infinitely far apart? Why or why not? What if there are three charges? Explain your reasoning.

Q23.4. Since potential can have any value you want depending on the choice of the reference level of zero potential, how does a voltmeter know what to read when you connect it between two points?

Q23.5. If $\vec{E}$ is zero everywhere along a certain path that leads from point A to point B, what is the potential difference between those two points? Does this mean that $\vec{E}$ is zero everywhere along *any* path from A to B? Explain.

Q23.6. If $\vec{E}$ is zero throughout a certain region of space, is the potential necessarily also zero in this region? Why or why not? If not, what *can* be said about the potential?

Q23.7. If you carry out the integral of the electric field $\int \vec{E} \cdot d\vec{l}$ for a *closed* path like that shown in Fig. 23.28, the integral will *always* be equal to zero, independent of the shape of the path and independent of where charges may be located relative to the path. Explain why.

Figure **23.28** Question Q23.7.

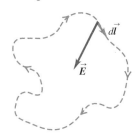

Q23.8. The potential difference between the two terminals of an AA battery (used in flashlights and portable stereos) is 1.5 V. If two AA batteries are placed end to end with the positive terminal of one battery touching the negative terminal of the other, what is the potential difference between the terminals at the exposed ends of the combination? What if the two positive terminals are touching each other? Explain your reasoning.

Q23.9. It is easy to produce a potential difference of several thousand volts between your body and the floor by scuffing your shoes across a nylon carpet. When you touch a metal doorknob, you get a mild shock. Yet contact with a power line of comparable voltage would probably be fatal. Why is there a difference?

Q23.10. If the electric potential at a single point is known, can $\vec{E}$ at that point be determined? If so, how? If not, why not?

Q23.11. Because electric field lines and equipotential surfaces are always perpendicular, two equipotential surfaces can never cross; if they did, the direction of $\vec{E}$ would be ambiguous at the crossing points. Yet two equipotential surfaces appear to cross at the center of Fig. 23.24c. Explain why there is no ambiguity about the direction of $\vec{E}$ in this particular case.

Q23.12. The electric field due to a very large sheet of charge is independent of the distance from the sheet, yet the fields due to the individual point charges on the sheet all obey an inverse-square law. Why doesn't the field of the sheet get weaker at greater distances?

Q23.13. We often say that if point A is at a higher potential than point B, A is at positive potential and B is at negative potential. Does it necessarily follow that a point at positive potential is positively charged, or that a point at negative potential is negatively charged? Illustrate your answers with clear, simple examples.

Q23.14. A conducting sphere is to be charged by bringing in positive charge a little at a time until the total charge is Q. The total work required for this process is alleged to be proportional to Q^2. Is this correct? Why or why not?

Q23.15. Three pairs of parallel metal plates $(A, B, \text{and } C)$ are connected as shown in Fig. 23.29, and a battery maintains a potential of 1.5 V across ab. What can you say about the potential difference across each pair of plates? Why?

Figure 23.29 Question Q23.15.

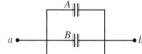

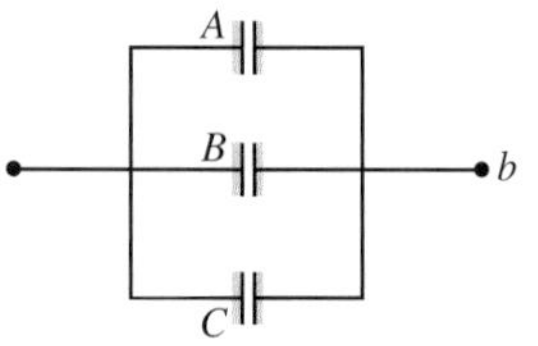

Q23.16. A conducting sphere is placed between two charged parallel plates such as those shown in Fig. 23.2. Does the electric field inside the sphere depend on precisely where between the plates the sphere is placed? What about the electric potential inside the sphere? Do the answers to these questions depend on whether or not there is a net charge on the sphere? Explain your reasoning.

Q23.17. A conductor that carries a net charge Q has a hollow, empty cavity in its interior. Does the potential vary from point to point within the material of the conductor? What about within the cavity? How does the potential inside the cavity compare to the potential within the material of the conductor?

Q23.18. A high-voltage dc power line falls on a car, so the entire metal body of the car is at a potential of 10,000 V with respect to the ground. What happens to the occupants (a) when they are sitting in the car and (b) when they step out of the car? Explain your reasoning.

Q23.19. When a thunderstorm is approaching, sailors at sea sometimes observe a phenomenon called "St. Elmo's fire," a bluish flickering light at the tips of masts. What causes this? Why does it occur at the tips of masts? Why is the effect most pronounced when the masts are wet? (*Hint:* Seawater is a good conductor of electricity.)

Q23.20. A positive point charge is placed near a very large conducting plane. A professor of physics asserted that the field caused by this configuration is the same as would be obtained by removing the plane and placing a negative point charge of equal magnitude in the mirror-image position behind the initial position of the plane. Is this correct? Why or why not? (*Hint:* Inspect Fig. 23.24b.)

Q23.21. In electronics it is customary to define the potential of ground (thinking of the earth as a large conductor) as zero. Is this consistent with the fact that the earth has a net electric charge that is not zero? (Refer to Exercise 21.32.)

Exercises

Section 23.1 Electric Potential Energy

23.1. A point charge $q_1 = +2.40\ \mu\text{C}$ is held stationary at the origin. A second point charge $q_2 = -4.30\ \mu\text{C}$ moves from the point $x = 0.150$ m, $y = 0$ to the point $x = 0.250$ m, $y = 0.250$ m. How much work is done by the electric force on q_2?

23.2. A point charge q_1 is held stationary at the origin. A second charge q_2 is placed at point a, and the electric potential energy of the pair of charges is $+5.4 \times 10^{-8}$ J. When the second charge is moved to point b, the electric force on the charge does -1.9×10^{-8} J of work. What is the electric potential energy of the pair of charges when the second charge is at point b?

23.3. Energy of the Nucleus. How much work is needed to assemble an atomic nucleus containing three protons (such as Be) if we model it as an equilateral triangle of side 2.00×10^{-15} m with a proton at each vertex? Assume the protons started from very far away.

23.4. (a) How much work would it take to push two protons very slowly from a separation of 2.00×10^{-10} m (a typical atomic distance) to 3.00×10^{-15} m (a typical nuclear distance)? (b) If the protons are both released from rest at the closer distance in part (a), how fast are they moving when they reach their original separation?

23.5. A small metal sphere, carrying a net charge of $q_1 = -2.80\ \mu\text{C}$, is held in a stationary position by insulating supports. A second small metal sphere, with a net charge of $q_2 = -7.80\ \mu\text{C}$ and mass 1.50 g, is projected toward q_1. When the two spheres are 0.800 m apart, q_2 is moving toward q_1 with speed 22.0 m/s (Fig. 23.30). Assume that the two spheres can be treated as point charges. You can ignore the force of gravity. (a) What is the speed of q_2 when the spheres are 0.400 m apart? (b) How close does q_2 get to q_1?

Figure 23.30 Exercise 23.5.

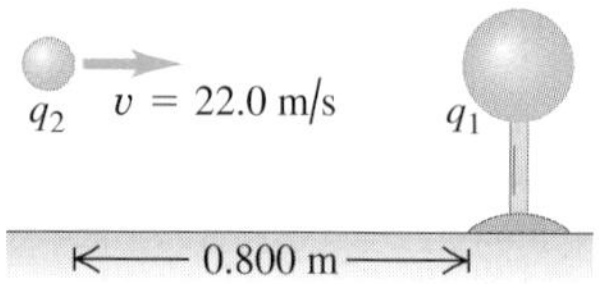

23.6. How far from a -7.20-μC point charge must a $+2.30$-μC point charge be placed for the electric potential energy U of the pair of charges to be -0.400 J? (Take U to be zero when the charges have infinite separation.)

23.7. A point charge $Q = +4.60\ \mu\text{C}$ is held fixed at the origin. A second point charge $q = +1.20\ \mu\text{C}$ with mass of 2.80×10^{-4} kg is placed on the x-axis, 0.250 m from the origin. (a) What is the electric potential energy U of the pair of charges? (Take U to be zero when the charges have infinite separation.) (b) The second point charge is released from rest. What is its speed when its distance from the origin is (i) 0.500 m; (ii) 5.00 m; (iii) 50.0 m?

23.8. Three equal 1.20-μC point charges are placed at the corners of an equilateral triangle whose sides are 0.500 m long. What is the potential energy of the system? (Take as zero the potential energy of the three charges when they are infinitely far apart.)

23.9. A point charge $q_1 = 4.00$ nC is placed at the origin, and a second point charge $q_2 = -3.00$ nC is placed on the x-axis at $x = +20.0$ cm. A third point charge $q_3 = 2.00$ nC is to be placed on the x-axis between q_1 and q_2. (Take as zero the potential energy of the three charges when they are infinitely far apart.) (a) What is the potential energy of the system of the three charges if q_3 is placed at $x = +10.0$ cm? (b) Where should q_3 be placed to make the potential energy of the system equal to zero?

23.10. Four electrons are located at the corners of a square 10.0 nm on a side, with an alpha particle at its midpoint. How much work is needed to move the alpha particle to the midpoint of one of the sides of the square?

23.11. Three point charges, which initially are infinitely far apart, are placed at the corners of an equilateral triangle with sides d. Two of the point charges are identical and have charge q. If zero net work is required to place the three charges at the corners of the triangle, what must the value of the third charge be?

23.12. Two protons are aimed directly toward each other by a cyclotron accelerator with speeds of 1000 km/s, measured relative to the earth. Find the maximum electrical force that these protons will exert on each other.

Section 23.2 Electric Potential

23.13. A uniform electric field is directed due east. Point B is 2.00 m west of point A, point C is 2.00 m east of point A, and point D is 2.00 m south of A. For each point, B, C, and D, is the potential at that point larger, smaller, or the same as at point A? Give the reasoning behind your answers.

23.14. Identical point charges $q = +5.00$ μC are placed at opposite corners of a square. The length of each side of the square is 0.200 m. A point charge $q_0 = -2.00$ μC is placed at one of the empty corners. How much work is done on q_0 by the electric force when q_0 is moved to the other empty corner?

23.15. A small particle has charge -5.00 μC and mass 2.00×10^{-4} kg. It moves from point A, where the electric potential is $V_A = +200$ V, to point B, where the electric potential is $V_B = +800$ V. The electric force is the only force acting on the particle. The particle has speed 5.00 m/s at point A. What is its speed at point B? Is it moving faster or slower at B than at A? Explain.

23.16. A particle with a charge of $+4.20$ nC is in a uniform electric field $\vec{E}$ directed to the left. It is released from rest and moves to the left; after it has moved 6.00 cm, its kinetic energy is found to be $+1.50 \times 10^{-6}$ J. (a) What work was done by the electric force? (b) What is the potential of the starting point with respect to the end point? (c) What is the magnitude of $\vec{E}$?

23.17. A charge of 28.0 nC is placed in a uniform electric field that is directed vertically upward and has a magnitude of 4.00×10^4 V/m. What work is done by the electric force when the charge moves (a) 0.450 m to the right; (b) 0.670 m upward; (c) 2.60 m at an angle of 45.0° downward from the horizontal?

23.18. Two stationary point charges $+3.00$ nC and $+2.00$ nC are separated by a distance of 50.0 cm. An electron is released from rest at a point midway between the two charges and moves along the line connecting the two charges. What is the speed of the electron when it is 10.0 cm from the $+3.00$-nC charge?

23.19. A point charge has a charge of 2.50×10^{-11} C. At what distance from the point charge is the electric potential (a) 90.0 V and (b) 30.0 V? Take the potential to be zero at an infinite distance from the charge.

23.20. Two charges of equal magnitude Q are held a distance d apart. Consider only points on the line passing through both charges. (a) If the two charges have the same sign, find the location of all points (if there are any) at which (i) the potential (relative to infinity) is zero (is the electric field zero at these points?), and (ii) the electric field is zero (is the potential zero at these points?). (b) Repeat part (a) for two charges having opposite signs.

23.21. Two point charges $q_1 = +2.40$ nC and $q_2 = -6.50$ nC are 0.100 m apart. Point A is midway between them; point B is 0.080 m from q_1 and 0.060 m from q_2 (Fig. 23.31). Take the electric potential to be zero at infinity. Find (a) the potential at point A; (b) the potential at point B; (c) the work done by the electric field on a charge of 2.50 nC that travels from point B to point A.

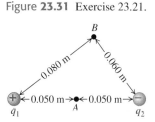
Figure **23.31** Exercise 23.21.

23.22. Two positive point charges, each of magnitude q, are fixed on the y-axis at the points $y = +a$ and $y = -a$. Take the potential to be zero at an infinite distance from the charges. (a) Show the positions of the charges in a diagram. (b) What is the potential V_0 at the origin? (c) Show that the potential at any point on the x-axis is

$$V = \frac{1}{4\pi\epsilon_0} \frac{2q}{\sqrt{a^2 + x^2}}$$

(d) Graph the potential on the x-axis as a function of x over the range from $x = -4a$ to $x = +4a$. (e) What is the potential when $x \gg a$? Explain why this result is obtained.

23.23. A positive charge $+q$ is located at the point $x = 0$, $y = -a$, and a negative charge $-q$ is located at the point $x = 0$, $y = +a$. (a) Show the positions of the charges in a diagram. (b) Derive an expression for the potential V at points on the x-axis as a function of the coordinate x. Take V to be zero at an infinite distance from the charges. (c) Graph V at points on the x-axis as a function of x over the range from $x = -4a$ to $x = +4a$. (d) What is the answer to part (b) if the two charges are interchanged so that $+q$ is at $y = +a$ and $-q$ is at $y = -a$?

23.24. Consider the arrangement of charges described in Exercise 23.23. (a) Derive an expression for the potential V at points on the y-axis as a function of the coordinate y. Take V to be zero at an infinite distance from the charges. (b) Graph V at points on the y-axis as a function of y over the range from $y = -4a$ to $y = +4a$. (c) Show that for $y \gg a$, the potential at a point on the positive y-axis is given by $V = -(1/4\pi\epsilon_0)2qa/y^2$. (d) What are the answers to parts (a) and (c) if the two charges are interchanged so that $+q$ is at $y = +a$ and $-q$ is at $y = -a$?

23.25. A positive charge q is fixed at the point $x = 0$, $y = 0$, and a negative charge $-2q$ is fixed at the point $x = a$, $y = 0$. (a) Show the positions of the charges in a diagram. (b) Derive an expression for the potential V at points on the x-axis as a function of the coordinate x. Take V to be zero at an infinite distance from the charges. (c) At which positions on the x-axis is $V = 0$? (d) Graph V at points on the x-axis as a function of x in the range from $x = -2a$ to $x = +2a$. (e) What does the answer to part (b) become when $x \gg a$? Explain why this result is obtained.

23.26. Consider the arrangement of point charges described in Exercise 23.25. (a) Derive an expression for the potential V at points on the y-axis as a function of the coordinate y. Take V to be zero at an infinite distance from the charges. (b) At which positions on the y-axis is $V = 0$? (c) Graph V at points on the y-axis as a function of y in the range from $y = -2a$ to $y = +2a$. (d) What does the answer to part (a) become when $y \gg a$? Explain why this result is obtained.

23.27. Before the advent of solid-state electronics, vacuum tubes were widely used in radios and other devices. A simple type of vacuum tube known as a *diode* consists essentially of two electrodes within a highly evacuated enclosure. One electrode, the *cathode,* is maintained at a high temperature and emits electrons from its surface. A potential difference of a few hundred volts is maintained between the cathode and the other electrode, known as the *anode,* with the anode at the higher potential. Suppose that in a particular vacuum tube the potential of the anode is 295 V higher than that of the cathode. An electron leaves the surface of the cathode with zero initial speed. Find its speed when it strikes the anode.

23.28. At a certain distance from a point charge, the potential and electric-field magnitude due to that charge are 4.98 V and 12.0 V/m, respectively. (Take the potential to be zero at infinity.) (a) What is the distance to the point charge? (b) What is the magnitude of the charge? (c) Is the electric field directed toward or away from the point charge?

23.29. A uniform electric field has magnitude E and is directed in the negative x-direction. The potential difference between point a (at $x = 0.60$ m) and point b (at $x = 0.90$ m) is 240 V. (a) Which point, a or b, is at the higher potential? (b) Calculate the value of E. (c) A negative point charge $q = -0.200$ μC is moved from b to a. Calculate the work done on the point charge by the electric field.

23.30. For each of the following arrangements of two point charges, find all the points along the line passing through both charges for which the electric potential V is zero (take $V = 0$ infinitely far from the charges) and for which the electric field E is zero: (a) charges $+Q$ and $+2Q$ separated by a distance d, and (b) charges $-Q$ and $+2Q$ separated by a distance d. (c) Are both V and E zero at the same places? Explain.

23.31. (a) An electron is to be accelerated from 3.00×10^6 m/s to 8.00×10^6 m/s. Through what potential difference must the electron pass to accomplish this? (b) Through what potential difference must the electron pass if it is to be slowed from 8.00×10^6 m/s to a halt?

Section 23.3 Calculating Electric Potential

23.32. A total electric charge of 3.50 nC is distributed uniformly over the surface of a metal sphere with a radius of 24.0 cm. If the potential is zero at a point at infinity, find the value of the potential at the following distances from the center of the sphere: (a) 48.0 cm; (b) 24.0 cm; (c) 12.0 cm.

23.33. A uniformly charged thin ring has radius 15.0 cm and total charge $+24.0$ nC. An electron is placed on the ring's axis a distance 30.0 cm from the center of the ring and is constrained to stay on the axis of the ring. The electron is then released from rest. (a) Describe the subsequent motion of the electron. (b) Find the speed of the electron when it reaches the center of the ring.

23.34. An infinitely long line of charge has linear charge density 5.00×10^{-12} C/m. A proton (mass 1.67×10^{-27} kg, charge $+1.60 \times 10^{-19}$ C) is 18.0 cm from the line and moving directly toward the line at 1.50×10^3 m/s. (a) Calculate the proton's initial kinetic energy. (b) How close does the proton get to the line of charge? (*Hint:* See Example 23.10.)

23.35. A very long wire carries a uniform linear charge density λ. Using a voltmeter to measure potential difference, you find that when one probe of the meter is placed 2.50 cm from the wire and the other probe is 1.00 cm farther from the wire, the meter reads 575 V. (a) What is λ? (b) If you now place one probe at 3.50 cm from the wire and the other probe 1.00 cm farther away, will the voltmeter read 575 V? If not, will it read more or less than 575 V? Why? (c) If you place both probes 3.50 cm from the wire but 17.0 cm from each other, what will the voltmeter read?

23.36. A very long insulating cylinder of charge of radius 2.50 cm carries a uniform linear density of 15.0 nC/m. If you put one probe of a voltmeter at the surface, how far from the surface must the other probe be placed so that the voltmeter reads 175 V?

23.37. A very long insulating cylindrical shell of radius 6.00 cm carries charge of linear density 8.50 μC/m spread uniformly over its outer surface. What would a voltmeter read if it were connected between (a) the surface of the cylinder and a point 4.00 cm above the surface, and (b) the surface and a point 1.00 cm from the central axis of the cylinder?

23.38. A ring of diameter 8.00 cm is fixed in place and carries a charge of $+5.00$ μC uniformly spread over its circumference. (a) How much work does it take to move a tiny $+3.00$-μC charged ball of mass 1.50 g from very far away to the center of the ring? (b) Is it necessary to take a path along the axis of the ring? Why? (c) If the ball is slightly displaced from the center of the ring, what will it do and what is the maximum speed it will reach?

23.39. Two very large, parallel metal plates carry charge densities of the same magnitude but opposite signs (Fig. 23.32). Assume they are close enough together to be treated as ideal infinite plates. Taking the potential to be zero at the left surface of the negative plate, sketch a graph of the potential as a function of x. Include *all* regions from the left of the plates to the right of the plates.

Figure **23.32** Exercise 23.39.

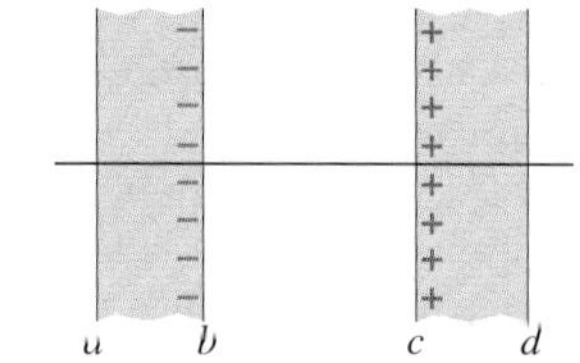

23.40. Two large, parallel conducting plates carrying opposite charges of equal magnitude are separated by 2.20 cm. (a) If the surface charge density for each plate has magnitude 47.0 nC/m², what is the magnitude of $\vec{E}$ in the region between the plates? (b) What is the potential difference between the two plates? (c) If the separation between the plates is doubled while the surface charge density is kept constant at the value in part (a), what happens to the magnitude of the electric field and to the potential difference?

23.41. Two large, parallel, metal plates carry opposite charges of equal magnitude. They are separated by 45.0 mm, and the potential difference between them is 360 V. (a) What is the magnitude of the electric field (assumed to be uniform) in the region between the plates? (b) What is the magnitude of the force this field exerts on a particle with charge $+2.40$ nC? (c) Use the results of part (b) to compute the work done by the field on the particle as it moves from the higher-potential plate to the lower. (d) Compare the result of part (c) to the change of potential energy of the same charge, computed from the electric potential.

23.42. (a) How much excess charge must be placed on a copper sphere 25.0 cm in diameter so that the potential of its center, relative to infinity, is 1.50 kV? (b) What is the potential of the sphere's surface relative to infinity?

23.43. (a) Show that V for a spherical shell of radius R, that has charge q distributed uniformly over its surface, is the same as V for a solid conductor with radius R and charge q. (b) You rub an inflated balloon on the carpet and it acquires a potential that is 1560 V lower than its potential before it became charged. If the charge is uniformly distributed over the surface of the balloon and if the radius of the balloon is 15 cm, what is the net charge on the balloon? (c) In light of its 1200-V potential difference relative to you, do you think this balloon is dangerous? Explain.

23.44. The electric field at the surface of a charged, solid, copper sphere with radius 0.200 m is 3800 N/C, directed toward the center of the sphere. What is the potential at the center of the sphere, if we take the potential to be zero infinitely far from the sphere?

Section 23.4 Equipotential Surfaces and
Section 23.5 Potential Gradient

23.45. A potential difference of 480 V is established between large, parallel, metal plates. Let the potential of one plate be 480 V and the other be 0 V. The plates are separated by $d = 1.70$ cm. (a) Sketch the equipotential surfaces that correspond to 0, 120, 240, 360, and 480 V. (b) In your sketch, show the electric field lines. Does your sketch confirm that the field lines and equipotential surfaces are mutually perpendicular?

23.46. A very large plastic sheet carries a uniform charge density of -6.00 nC/m^2 on one face. (a) As you move away from the sheet along a line perpendicular to it, does the potential increase or decrease? How do you know, without doing any calculations? Does your answer depend on where you choose the reference point for potential? (b) Find the spacing between equipotential surfaces that differ from each other by 1.00 V. What type of surfaces are these?

23.47. In a certain region of space, the electric potential is $V(x, y, z) = Axy - Bx^2 + Cy$, where $A, B,$ and C are positive constants. (a) Calculate the x-, y-, and z-components of the electric field. (b) At which points is the electric field equal to zero?

23.48. The potential due to a point charge Q at the origin may be written as

$$V = \frac{Q}{4\pi\epsilon_0 r} = \frac{Q}{4\pi\epsilon_0\sqrt{x^2 + y^2 + z^2}}$$

(a) Calculate $E_x, E_y,$ and E_z using Eqs. (23.19). (b) Show that the results of part (a) agrees with Eq. (21.7) for the electric field of a point charge.

23.49. A metal sphere with radius r_a is supported on an insulating stand at the center of a hollow, metal, spherical shell with radius r_b. There is charge $+q$ on the inner sphere and charge $-q$ on the outer spherical shell. (a) Calculate the potential $V(r)$ for (i) $r < r_a$; (ii) $r_a < r < r_b$; (iii) $r > r_b$. (Hint: The net potential is the sum of the potentials due to the individual spheres.) Take V to be zero when r is infinite. (b) Show that the potential of the inner sphere with respect to the outer is

$$V_{ab} = \frac{q}{4\pi\epsilon_0}\left(\frac{1}{r_a} - \frac{1}{r_b}\right)$$

(c) Use Eq. (23.23) and the result from part (a) to show that the electric field at any point between the spheres has magnitude

$$E(r) = \frac{V_{ab}}{(1/r_a - 1/r_b)}\frac{1}{r^2}$$

(d) Use Eq. (23.23) and the result from part (a) to find the electric field at a point outside the larger sphere at a distance r from the center, where $r > r_b$. (e) Suppose the charge on the outer sphere is not $-q$ but a negative charge of different magnitude, say $-Q$. Show that the answers for parts (b) and (c) are the same as before but the answer for part (d) is different.

23.50. A metal sphere with radius $r_a = 1.20$ cm is supported on an insulating stand at the center of a hollow, metal, spherical shell with radius $r_b = 9.60$ cm. Charge $+q$ is put on the inner sphere and charge $-q$ on the outer spherical shell. The magnitude of q is chosen to make the potential difference between the spheres 500 V, with the inner sphere at higher potential. (a) Use the result of Exercise 23.49(b) to calculate q. (b) With the help of the result of Exercise 23.49(a), sketch the equipotential surfaces that correspond to 500, 400, 300, 200, 100, and 0 V. (c) In your sketch, show the electric field lines. Are the electric field lines and equipo-

tential surfaces mutually perpendicular? Are the equipotential surfaces closer together when the magnitude of $\vec{E}$ is largest?

23.51. A very long cylinder of radius 2.00 cm carries a uniform charge density of 1.50 nC/m. (a) Describe the shape of the equipotential surfaces for this cylinder. (b) Taking the reference level for the zero of potential to be the surface of the cylinder, find the radius of equipotential surfaces having potentials of 10.0 V, 20.0 V, and 30.0 V. (c) Are the equipotential surfaces equally spaced? If not, do they get closer together or farther apart as r increases?

Problems

23.52. Figure 23.33 shows the potential of a charge distribution as a function of x. Sketch a graph of the electric field E_x over the region shown.

Figure **23.33** Problem 23.52.

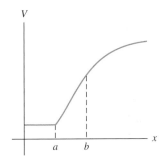

23.53. A particle with charge $+7.60$ nC is in a uniform electric field directed to the left. Another force, in addition to the electric force, acts on the particle so that when it is released from rest, it moves to the right. After it has moved 8.00 cm, the additional force has done 6.50×10^{-5} J of work and the particle has 4.35×10^{-5} J of kinetic energy. (a) What work was done by the electric force? (b) What is the potential of the starting point with respect to the end point? (c) What is the magnitude of the electric field?

23.54. In the *Bohr model* of the hydrogen atom, a single electron revolves around a single proton in a circle of radius r. Assume that the proton remains at rest. (a) By equating the electric force to the electron mass times its acceleration, derive an expression for the electron's speed. (b) Obtain an expression for the electron's kinetic energy, and show that its magnitude is just half that of the electric potential energy. (c) Obtain an expression for the total energy, and evaluate it using $r = 5.29 \times 10^{-11}$ m. Give your numerical result in joules and in electron volts.

23.55. A vacuum tube diode (see Exercise 23.27) consists of concentric cylindrical electrodes, the negative cathode and the positive anode. Because of the accumulation of charge near the cathode, the electric potential between the electrodes is not a linear function of the position, even with planar geometry, but is given by

$$V(x) = Cx^{4/3}$$

where x is the distance from the cathode and C is a constant, characteristic of a particular diode and operating conditions. Assume that the distance between the cathode and anode is 13.0 mm and the potential difference between electrodes is 240 V. (a) Determine the value of C. (b) Obtain a formula for the electric field between the electrodes as a function of x. (c) Determine the force on an electron when the electron is halfway between the electrodes.

23.56. Two oppositely charged identical insulating spheres, each 50.0 cm in diameter and carrying a uniform charge of magnitude 175 μC, are placed

Figure **23.34** Problem 23.56.

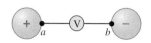

1.00 m apart center to center (Fig. 23.34). (a) If a voltmeter is connected between the nearest points (a and b) on their surfaces, what will it read? (b) Which point, a or b, is at the higher potential? How can you know this without any calculations?

23.57. An Ionic Crystal. Figure 23.35 shows eight point charges arranged at the corners of a cube with sides of length d. The values of the charges are $+q$ and $-q$, as shown. This is a model of one cell of a cubic ionic crystal. In sodium chloride (NaCl), for instance, the positive ions are Na$^+$ and the negative ions are Cl$^-$. (a) Calculate the potential energy U of this arrangement. (Take as zero the

Figure **23.35** Problem 23.57.

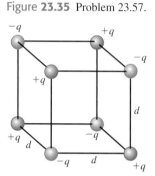

potential energy of the eight charges when they are infinitely far apart.) (b) In part (a), you should have found that $U < 0$. Explain the relationship between this result and the observation that such ionic crystals exist in nature.

23.58. (a) Calculate the potential energy of a system of two small spheres, one carrying a charge of 2.00 μC and the other a charge of -3.50 μC, with their centers separated by a distance of 0.250 m. Assume zero potential energy when the charges are infinitely separated. (b) Suppose that one of the spheres is held in place and the other sphere, which has a mass of 1.50 g, is shot away from it. What minimum initial speed would the moving sphere need in order to escape completely from the attraction of the fixed sphere? (To escape, the moving sphere would have to reach a velocity of zero when it was infinitely distant from the fixed sphere.)

23.59. The H$_2^+$ Ion. The H$_2^+$ ion is composed of two protons, each of charge $+e = 1.60 \times 10^{-19}$ C, and an electron of charge $-e$ and mass 9.11×10^{-31} kg. The separation between the protons is 1.07×10^{-10} m. The protons and the electron may be treated as point charges. (a) Suppose the electron is located at the point midway between the two protons. What is the potential energy of the interaction between the electron and the two protons? (Do not include the potential energy due to the interaction between the two protons.) (b) Suppose the electron in part (a) has a velocity of magnitude 1.50×10^6 m/s in a direction along the perpendicular bisector of the line connecting the two protons. How far from the point midway between the two protons can the electron move? Because the masses of the protons are much greater than the electron mass, the motions of the protons are very slow and can be ignored. (*Note:* A realistic description of the electron motion requires the use of quantum mechanics, not Newtonian mechanics.)

23.60. A small sphere with mass 1.50 g hangs by a thread between two parallel vertical plates 5.00 cm apart (Fig. 23.36). The plates are insulating and have uniform surface charge densities $+\sigma$ and $-\sigma$. The charge on the sphere is $q = 8.90 \times 10^{-6}$ C. What potential difference between the plates will cause the thread to assume an angle of 30.0° with the vertical?

Figure **23.36** Problem 23.60.

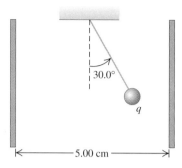

23.61. Coaxial Cylinders. A long metal cylinder with radius a is supported on an insulating stand on the axis of a long, hollow, metal tube with radius b. The positive charge per unit length on the inner cylinder is λ, and there is an equal negative charge per unit length on the outer cylinder. (a) Calculate the potential $V(r)$ for (i) $r < a$; (ii) $a < r < b$; (iii) $r > b$. (*Hint:* The net potential is the sum of the potentials due to the individual conductors.) Take $V = 0$ at $r = b$. (b) Show that the potential of the inner cylinder with respect to the outer is

$$V_{ab} = \frac{\lambda}{2\pi\epsilon_0}\ln\frac{b}{a}$$

(c) Use Eq. (23.23) and the result from part (a) to show that the electric field at any point between the cylinders has magnitude

$$E(r) = \frac{V_{ab}}{\ln(b/a)}\frac{1}{r}$$

(d) What is the potential difference between the two cylinders if the outer cylinder has no net charge?

23.62. A *Geiger counter* detects radiation such as alpha particles by using the fact that the radiation ionizes the air along its path. A thin wire lies on the axis of a hollow metal cylinder and is insulated from it (Fig. 23.37). A large potential difference is established between the wire and the outer cylinder, with the wire at higher potential; this sets up a strong electric field directed radially outward. When ionizing radiation enters the device, it ionizes a few air molecules. The free electrons produced are accelerated by the electric field toward the wire and, on the way there, ionize many more air molecules. Thus a current pulse is produced that can be detected by appropriate electronic circuitry and converted to an audible "click." Suppose the radius of the central wire is 145 μm and the radius of the hollow cylinder is 1.80 cm. What potential difference between the wire and the cylinder produces an

Figure **23.37** Problem 23.62.

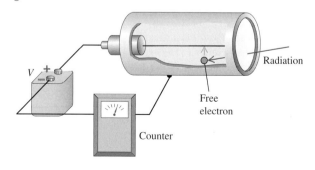

electric field of 2.00×10^4 V/m at a distance of 1.20 cm from the axis of the wire? (The wire and cylinder are both very long in comparison to their radii, so the results of Problem 23.61 apply.)

23.63. Deflection in a CRT. Cathode-ray tubes (CRTs) are often found in oscilloscopes and computer monitors. In Fig. 23.38 an electron with an initial speed of 6.50×10^6 m/s is projected along the axis midway between the deflection plates of a cathode-ray tube. The uniform electric field between the plates has a magnitude of 1.10×10^3 V/m and is upward. (a) What is the force (magnitude and direction) on the electron when it is between the plates? (b) What is the acceleration of the electron (magnitude and direction) when acted on by the force in part (a)? (c) How far below the axis has the electron moved when it reaches the end of the plates? (d) At what angle with the axis is it moving as it leaves the plates? (e) How far below the axis will it strike the fluorescent screen S?

Figure **23.38** Problem 23.63.

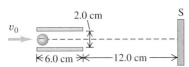

23.64. Deflecting Plates of an Oscilloscope. The vertical deflecting plates of a typical classroom oscilloscope are a pair of parallel square metal plates carrying equal but opposite charges. Typical dimensions are about 3.0 cm on a side, with a separation of about 5.0 mm. The plates are close enough that we can ignore fringing at the ends. Under these conditions: (a) how much charge is on each plate, and (b) how strong is the electric field between the plates? (c) If an electron is ejected at rest from the negative plates, how fast is it moving when it reaches the positive plate?

23.65. *Electrostatic precipitators* use electric forces to remove pollutant particles from smoke, in particular in the smokestacks of coal-burning power plants. One form of precipitator consists of a vertical, hollow, metal cylinder with a thin wire, insulated from the cylinder, running along its axis (Fig. 23.39). A large potential difference is established between the wire and the outer cylinder, with the wire at lower potential. This sets up a strong radial electric field directed inward. The field produces a region of ionized air near the wire. Smoke enters the precipitator at the bottom, ash and dust in it pick up electrons, and the charged pollutants are accelerated

Figure **23.39** Problem 23.65.

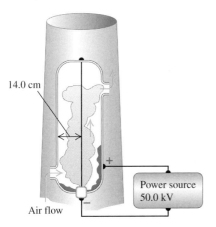

toward the outer cylinder wall by the electric field. Suppose the radius of the central wire is 90.0 μm, the radius of the cylinder is 14.0 cm, and a potential difference of 50.0 kV is established between the wire and the cylinder. Also assume that the wire and cylinder are both very long in comparison to the cylinder radius, so the results of Problem 23.61 apply. (a) What is the magnitude of the electric field midway between the wire and the cylinder wall? (b) What magnitude of charge must a 30.0-μg ash particle have if the electric field computed in part (a) is to exert a force ten times the weight of the particle?

23.66. A disk with radius R has uniform surface charge density σ. (a) By regarding the disk as a series of thin concentric rings, calculate the electric potential V at a point on the disk's axis a distance x from the center of the disk. Assume that the potential is zero at infinity. (*Hint:* Use the result of Example 23.11 in Section 23.3.) (b) Calculate $-\partial V/\partial x$. Show that the result agrees with the expression for E_x calculated in Example 21.12 (Section 21.5).

23.67. (a) From the expression for E obtained in Problem 22.40, find the expressions for the electric potential V as a function of r, both inside and outside the cylinder. Let $V = 0$ at the surface of the cylinder. In each case, express your result in terms of the charge per unit length λ of the charge distribution. (b) Graph V and E as functions of r from $r = 0$ to $r = 3R$.

23.68. Alpha particles ($mass = 6.7 \times 10^{-27}$ kg, charge $= +2e$) are shot directly at a gold foil target. We can model the gold nucleus as a uniform sphere of charge and assume that the gold does not move. (a) If the radius of the gold nucleus is 5.6×10^{-15} m, what minimum speed do the alpha particles need when they are far away to reach the surface of the gold nucleus? (Ignore relativistic effects.) (b) Give good physical reasons why we can ignore the effects of the orbital electrons when the alpha particle is (i) outside the electron orbits and (ii) inside the electron orbits.

23.69. For the ring of charge described in Example 23.11 (Section 23.3), integrate the expression for E_x found in Example 21.10 (Section 21.5) to find the potential at point P on the ring's axis. Assume that $V = 0$ at infinity. Compare your result to that obtained in Example 23.11 using Eq. (23.16).

23.70. A thin insulating rod is bent into a semicircular arc of radius a, and a total electric charge Q is distributed uniformly along the rod. Calculate the potential at the center of curvature of the arc if the potential is assumed to be zero at infinity.

23.71. Self-Energy of a Sphere of Charge. A solid sphere of radius R contains a total charge Q distributed uniformly throughout its volume. Find the energy needed to assemble this charge by bringing infinitesimal charges from far away. This energy is called the "self-energy" of the charge distribution. (*Hint:* After you have assembled a charge q in a sphere of radius r, how much energy would it take to add a spherical shell of thickness dr having charge dq? Then integrate to get the total energy.)

23.72. (a) From the expression for E obtained in Example 22.9 (Section 22.4), find the expression for the electric potential V as a function of r both inside and outside the uniformly charged sphere. Assume that $V = 0$ at infinity. (b) Graph V and E as functions of r from $r = 0$ to $r = 3R$.

23.73. A solid insulating sphere with radius R has charge Q uniformly distributed throughout its volume. (a) Use the results of Problem 23.72 to find the magnitude of the potential difference between the surface of the sphere and its center. (b) Which is at higher potential, the surface or the center, if (i) Q is positive and (ii) Q is negative?

23.74. An insulating spherical shell with inner radius 25.0 cm and outer radius 60.0 cm carries a charge of $+150.0\ \mu C$ uniformly distributed over its outer surface (see Exercise 23.43). Point a is at the center of the shell, point b is on the inner surface, and point c is on the outer surface. (a) What will a voltmeter read if it is connected between the following points: (i) a and b; (ii) b and c; (iii) c and infinity; (iv) a and c? (b) Which is at higher potential: (i) a or b; (ii) b or c; (iii) a or c? (c) Which, if any, of the answers would change sign if the charges were $-150\ \mu C$?

23.75. Exercise 23.43 shows that, outside a spherical shell with uniform surface charge, the potential is the same as if all the charge were concentrated into a point charge at the center of the sphere. (a) Use this result to show that for two uniformly charged insulating shells, the force they exert on each other and their mutual electrical energy are the same as if all the charge were concentrated at their centers. (*Hint:* See Section 12.6.) (b) Does this same result hold for solid insulating spheres, with charge distributed uniformly throughout their volume? (c) Does this same result hold for the force between two charged conducting shells? Between two charged solid conductors? Explain.

23.76. Two plastic spheres, each carrying charge uniformly distributed throughout its interior, are initially placed in contact and then released. One sphere is 60.0 cm in diameter, has mass 50.0 g and contains $-10.0\ \mu C$ of charge. The other sphere is 40.0 cm in diameter, has mass 150.0 g, and contains $-30.0\ \mu C$ of charge. Find the maximum acceleration and the maximum speed achieved by each sphere (relative to the fixed point of their initial location in space), assuming that no other forces are acting on them. (*Hint:* The uniformly distributed charges behave as though they were concentrated at the centers of the two spheres.)

23.77. Use the electric field calculated in Problem 22.43 to calculate the potential difference between the solid conducting sphere and the thin insulating shell.

23.78. Consider a solid conducting sphere inside a hollow conducting sphere, with radii and charges specified in Problem 22.42. Take $V = 0$ as $r \rightarrow \infty$. Use the electric field calculated in Problem 22.42 to calculate the potential V at the following values of r: (a) $r = c$ (at the outer surface of the hollow sphere); (b) $r = b$ (at the inner surface of the hollow sphere); (c) $r = a$ (at the surface of the solid sphere); (d) $r = 0$ (at the center of the solid sphere).

23.79. Electric charge is distributed uniformly along a thin rod of length a, with total charge Q. Take the potential to be zero at infinity. Find the potential at the following points (Fig. 23.40): (a) point P, a distance x to the right of the rod, and (b) point R, a distance y above the right-hand end of the rod. (c) In parts (a) and (b), what does your result reduce to as x or y becomes much larger than a?

Figure **23.40** Problem 23.79.

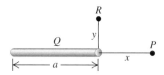

23.80. (a) If a spherical raindrop of radius 0.650 mm carries a charge of -1.20 pC uniformly distributed over its volume, what is the potential at its surface? (Take the potential to be zero at an infinite distance from the raindrop.) (b) Two identical raindrops, each with radius and charge specified in part (a), collide and merge into one larger raindrop. What is the radius of this larger drop, and what is the potential at its surface, if its charge is uniformly distributed over its volume?

23.81. Two metal spheres of different sizes are charged such that the electric potential is the same at the surface of each. Sphere A has a radius three times that of sphere B. Let Q_A and Q_B be the charges on the two spheres, and let E_A and E_B be the electric-field magnitudes at the surfaces of the two spheres. What are (a) the ratio Q_B/Q_A and (b) the ratio E_B/E_A?

23.82. An alpha particle with kinetic energy 11.0 MeV makes a head-on collision with a lead nucleus at rest. What is the distance of closest approach of the two particles? (Assume that the lead nucleus remains stationary and that it may be treated as a point charge. The atomic number of lead is 82. The alpha particle is a helium nucleus, with atomic number 2.)

23.83. A metal sphere with radius R_1 has a charge Q_1. Take the electric potential to be zero at an infinite distance from the sphere. (a) What are the electric field and electric potential at the surface of the sphere? This sphere is now connected by a long, thin conducting wire to another sphere of radius R_2 that is several meters from the first sphere. Before the connection is made, this second sphere is uncharged. After electrostatic equilibrium has been reached, what are (b) the total charge on each sphere; (c) the electric potential at the surface of each sphere (d) the electric field at the surface of each sphere? Assume that the amount of charge on the wire is much less than the charge on each sphere.

23.84. Use the charge distribution and electric field calculated in Problem 22.57. (a) Show that for $r \geq R$ the potential is identical to that produced by a point charge Q. (Take the potential to be zero at infinity.) (b) Obtain an expression for the electric potential valid in the region $r \leq R$.

23.85. Nuclear Fusion in the Sun. The source of the sun's energy is a sequence of nuclear reactions that occur in its core. The first of these reactions involves the collision of two protons, which fuse together to form a heavier nucleus and release energy. For this process, called *nuclear fusion,* to occur, the two protons must first approach until their surfaces are essentially in contact. (a) Assume both protons are moving with the same speed and they collide head-on. If the radius of the proton is 1.2×10^{-15} m, what is the minimum speed that will allow fusion to occur? The charge distribution within a proton is spherically symmetric, so the electric field and potential outside a proton are the same as if it were a point charge. The mass of the proton is 1.67×10^{-27} kg. (b) Another nuclear fusion reaction that occurs in the sun's core involves a collision between two helium nuclei, each of which has 2.99 times the mass of the proton, charge $+2e$, and radius 1.7×10^{-15} m. Assuming the same collision geometry as in part (a), what minimum speed is required for this fusion reaction to take place if the nuclei must approach a center-to-center distance of about 3.5×10^{-15} m? As for the proton, the charge of the helium nucleus is uniformly distributed throughout its volume. (c) In Section 18.3 it was shown that the average translational kinetic energy of a particle with mass m in a gas at absolute temperature T is $\frac{3}{2}kT$, where k is the Boltzmann constant (given in Appendix F). For two protons with kinetic energy equal to this average value to be able to undergo the process described in part (a), what absolute temperature is required? What absolute temperature is required for two average helium nuclei to be able to undergo the process described in part (b)? (At these temperatures, atoms are completely ionized, so nuclei and electrons move separately.) (d) The temperature in the sun's core is about 1.5×10^7 K. How does this compare to the temperatures calculated in part (c)? How can the reactions described in parts (a) and (b) occur at all in the interior of the sun? (*Hint:* See the discussion of the distribution of molecular speeds in Section 18.5.)

23.86. The electric potential V in a region of space is given by

$$V(x, y, z) = A(x^2 - 3y^2 + z^2)$$

where A is a constant. (a) Derive an expression for the electric field $\vec{E}$ at any point in this region. (b) The work done by the field when a $1.50\text{-}\mu\text{C}$ test charge moves from the point $(x, y, z) = (0, 0, 0.250 \text{ m})$ to the origin is measured to be 6.00×10^{-5} J. Determine A. (c) Determine the electric field at the point $(0, 0, 0.250$ m). (d) Show that in every plane parallel to the xz-plane the equipotential contours are circles. (e) What is the radius of the equipotential contour corresponding to $V = 1280$ V and $y = 2.00$ m?

23.87. Nuclear Fission. The unstable nucleus of uranium-236 can be regarded as a uniformly charged sphere of charge $Q = +92e$ and radius $R = 7.4 \times 10^{-15}$ m. In nuclear fission, this can divide into two smaller nuclei, each with half the charge and half the volume of the original uranium-236 nucleus. This is one of the reactions that occurred in the nuclear weapon that exploded over Hiroshima, Japan, in August 1945. (a) Find the radii of the two "daughter" nuclei of charge $+46e$. (b) In a simple model for the fission process, immediately after the uranium-236 nucleus has undergone fission, the "daughter" nuclei are at rest and just touching, as shown in Fig. 23.41. Calculate the kinetic energy that each of the "daughter" nuclei will have when they are very far apart. (c) In this model the sum of the kinetic energies of the two "daughter" nuclei, calculated in part (b), is the energy released by the fission of one uranium-236 nucleus. Calculate the energy released by the fission of 10.0 kg of uranium-236. The atomic mass of uranium-236 is 236 u, where $1 \text{ u} = 1$ atomic mass unit $= 1.66 \times 10^{-24}$ kg. Express your answer both in joules and in kilotons of TNT (1 kiloton of TNT releases 4.18×10^{12} J when it explodes). (d) In terms of this model, discuss why an atomic bomb could just as well be called an "electric bomb."

Figure 23.41 Problem 23.87.

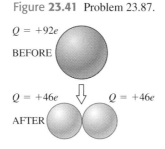

$Q = +92e$

BEFORE

$Q = +46e$ ⇩ $Q = +46e$

AFTER

Challenge Problems

23.88. In a certain region, a charge distribution exists that is spherically symmetric but nonuniform. That is, the volume charge density $\rho(r)$ depends on the distance r from the center of the distribution but not on the spherical polar angles θ and ϕ. The electric potential $V(r)$ due to this charge distribution is

$$V(r) = \begin{cases} \dfrac{\rho_0 a^2}{18\epsilon_0}\left[1 - 3\left(\dfrac{r}{a}\right)^2 + 2\left(\dfrac{r}{a}\right)^3 \right] & \text{for } r \le a \\ 0 & \text{for } r \ge a \end{cases}$$

where ρ_0 is a constant having units of C/m^3 and a is a constant having units of meters. (a) Derive expressions for $\vec{E}$ for the regions $r \le a$ and $r \ge a$. [*Hint:* Use Eq. (23.23).] Explain why $\vec{E}$ has only a radial component. (b) Derive an expression for $\rho(r)$ in each of the two regions $r \le a$ and $r \ge a$. [*Hint:* Use Gauss's law for two spherical shells, one of radius r and the other of radius $r + dr$. The charge contained in the infinitesimal spherical shell of radius dr is $dq = 4\pi r^2 \rho(r)dr$.] (c) Show that the net charge contained in the volume of a sphere of radius greater than or equal to a is zero. [*Hint:* Integrate the expressions derived in part (b) for $\rho(r)$ over a spherical volume of radius greater than or equal to a.] Is this result consistent with the electric field for $r > a$ that you calculated in part (a)?

23.89. In experiments in which atomic nuclei collide, head-on collisions like that described in Problem 23.82 do happen, but "near misses" are more common. Suppose the alpha particle in Problem 23.82 was not "aimed" at the center of the lead nucleus, but had an initial nonzero angular momentum (with respect to the stationary lead nucleus) of magnitude $L = p_0 b$, where p_0 is the magnitude of the initial momentum of the alpha particle and $b = 1.00 \times 10^{-17}$ m. What is the distance of closest approach? Repeat for $b = 1.00 \times 10^{-13}$ m and $b = 1.00 \times 10^{-14}$ m.

23.90. A hollow, thin-walled insulating cylinder of radius R and length L (like the cardboard tube in a roll of toilet paper) has charge Q uniformly distributed over its surface. (a) Calculate the electric potential at all points along the axis of the tube. Take the origin to be at the center of the tube, and take the potential to be zero at infinity. (b) Show that if $L \ll R$, the result of part (a) reduces to the potential on the axis of a ring of charge of radius R (See Example 23.11 in Section 23.3). (c) Use the result of part (a) to find the electric field at all points along the axis of the tube.

23.91. The Millikan Oil-Drop Experiment. The charge of an electron was first measured by the American physicist Robert Millikan during 1909–1913. In his experiment, oil is sprayed in very fine drops (around 10^{-4} mm in diameter) into the space between two parallel horizontal plates separated by a distance d. A potential difference V_{AB} is maintained between the parallel plates, causing a downward electric field between them. Some of the oil drops acquire a negative charge because of frictional effects or because of ionization of the surrounding air by x rays or radioactivity. The drops are observed through a microscope. (a) Show that an oil drop of radius r at rest between the plates will remain at rest if the magnitude of its charge is

$$q = \frac{4\pi}{3} \frac{\rho r^3 g d}{V_{AB}}$$

where ρ is the density of the oil. (Ignore the buoyant force of the air.) By adjusting V_{AB} to keep a given drop at rest, the charge on that drop can be determined, provided its radius is known. (b) Millikan's oil drops were much too small to measure their radii directly. Instead, Millikan determined r by cutting off the electric field and measuring the *terminal speed* v_t of the drop as it fell. (We discussed the concept of terminal speed in Section 5.3.) The viscous force F on a sphere of radius r moving with speed v through a fluid with viscosity η is given by Stokes's law: $F = 6\pi\eta rv$. When the drop is falling at v_t, the viscous force just balances the weight $w = mg$ of the drop. Show that the magnitude of the charge on the drop is

$$q = 18\pi \frac{d}{V_{AB}}\sqrt{\frac{\eta^3 v_t^3}{2\rho g}}$$

Within the limits of their experimental error, every one of the thousands of drops that Millikan and his coworkers measured had a charge equal to some small integer multiple of a basic charge e. That is, they found drops with charges of $\pm 2e$, $\pm 5e$, and so on, but none with values such as $0.76e$ or $2.49e$. A drop with charge $-e$ has acquired one extra electron; if its charge is $-2e$, it has acquired two extra electrons, and so on. (c) A charged oil drop in a Millikan oil-drop apparatus is observed to fall 1.00 mm at constant speed in 39.3 s if $V_{AB} = 0$. The same drop can be held at rest between two plates separated by 1.00 mm if $V_{AB} = 9.16$ V. How many excess electrons has the drop acquired, and what is the radius of the drop? The viscosity of air is $1.81 \times 10^{-5} \text{ N} \cdot \text{s}/\text{m}^2$, and the density of the oil is $824 \text{ kg}/\text{m}^3$.

23.92. Two point charges are moving to the right along the x-axis. Point charge 1 has charge $q_1 = 2.00\,\mu C$, mass $m_1 = 6.00 \times 10^{-5}$ kg, and speed v_1. Point charge 2 is to the right of q_1 and has charge $q_2 = -5.00\,\mu C$, mass $m_2 = 3.00 \times 10^{-5}$ kg, and speed v_2. At a particular instant, the charges are separated by a distance of 9.00 mm and have speeds $v_1 = 400$ m/s and $v_2 = 1300$ m/s. The only forces on the particles are the forces they exert on each other. (a) Determine the speed v_{cm} of the center of mass of the system. (b) The *relative energy* E_{rel} of the system is defined as the total energy minus the kinetic energy contributed by the motion of the center of mass:

$$E_{rel} = E - \frac{1}{2}(m_1 + m_2)v_{cm}^2$$

where $E = \frac{1}{2}m_1 v_1^2 + \frac{1}{2}m_2 v_2^2 + q_1 q_2/4\pi\epsilon_0 r$ is the total energy of the system and r is the distance between the charges. Show that $E_{rel} = \frac{1}{2}\mu v^2 + q_1 q_2/4\pi\epsilon_0 r$, where $\mu = m_1 m_2/(m_1 + m_2)$ is called the *reduced mass* of the system and $v = v_2 - v_1$ is the relative speed of the moving particles. (c) For the numerical values given above, calculate the numerical value of E_{rel}. (d) Based on the result of part (c), for the conditions given above, will the particles escape from one another? Explain. (e) If the particles do escape, what will be their final relative speed when $r \to \infty$? If the particles do not escape, what will be their distance of maximum separation? That is, what will be the value of r when $v = 0$? (f) Repeat parts (c)–(e) for $v_1 = 400$ m/s and $v_2 = 1800$ m/s when the separation is 9.00 mm.

CAPACITANCE AND DIELECTRICS

24

? The energy used in a camera's flash unit is stored in a capacitor, which consists of two closely spaced conductors that carry opposite charges. If the amount of charge on the conductors is doubled, by what factor does the stored energy increase?

LEARNING GOALS

By studying this chapter, you will learn:

• The nature of capacitors, and how to calculate a quantity that measures their ability to store charge.

• How to analyze capacitors connected in a network.

• How to calculate the amount of energy stored in a capacitor.

• What dielectrics are, and how they make capacitors more effective.

When you set an old-fashioned spring mousetrap or pull back the string of an archer's bow, you are storing mechanical energy as elastic potential energy. A capacitor is a device that stores *electric* potential energy and electric charge. To make a capacitor, just insulate two conductors from each other. To store energy in this device, transfer charge from one conductor to the other so that one has a negative charge and the other has an equal amount of positive charge. Work must be done to move the charges through the resulting potential difference between the conductors, and the work done is stored as electric potential energy.

Capacitors have a tremendous number of practical applications in devices such as electronic flash units for photography, pulsed lasers, air bag sensors for cars, and radio and television receivers. We'll encounter many of these applications in later chapters (particularly Chapter 31, in which we'll see the crucial role played by capacitors in the alternating-current circuits that pervade our technological society). In this chapter, however, our emphasis is on the fundamental properties of capacitors. For a particular capacitor, the ratio of the charge on each conductor to the potential difference between the conductors is a constant, called the *capacitance*. The capacitance depends on the sizes and shapes of the conductors and on the insulating material (if any) between them. Compared to the case in which there is only vacuum between the conductors, the capacitance increases when an insulating material (a *dielectric*) is present. This happens because a redistribution of charge, called *polarization,* takes place within the insulating material. Studying polarization will give us added insight into the electrical properties of matter.

Capacitors also give us a new way to think about electric potential energy. The energy stored in a charged capacitor is related to the electric field in the space between the conductors. We will see that electric potential energy can be regarded as being stored *in the field itself.* The idea that the electric field is itself a storehouse of energy is at the heart of the theory of electromagnetic waves and our modern understanding of the nature of light, to be discussed in Chapter 32.

24.1 Any two conductors a and b insulated from each another form a capacitor.

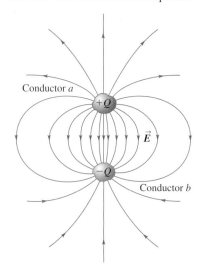

Conductor a

$+Q$

$\vec{E}$

$-Q$

Conductor b

Act|v
Physics

11.11.6   Electric Potential: Qualitative
            Introduction
11.12.1 and 11.12.3
            Electric Potential, Field and, Force

24.1 Capacitors and Capacitance

Any two conductors separated by an insulator (or a vacuum) form a **capacitor** (Fig. 24.1). In most practical applications, each conductor initially has zero net charge and electrons are transferred from one conductor to the other; this is called *charging* the capacitor. Then the two conductors have charges with equal magnitude and opposite sign, and the *net* charge on the capacitor as a whole remains zero. We will assume throughout this chapter that this is the case. When we say that a capacitor has charge Q, or that a charge Q is *stored* on the capacitor, we mean that the conductor at higher potential has charge $+Q$ and the conductor at lower potential has charge $-Q$ (assuming that Q is positive). Keep this in mind in the following discussion and examples.

In circuit diagrams a capacitor is represented by either of these symbols:

$$\dashv\vdash \qquad \dashv\!\!\leftarrow$$

In either symbol the vertical lines (straight or curved) represent the conductors and the horizontal lines represent wires connected to either conductor. One common way to charge a capacitor is to connect these two wires to opposite terminals of a battery. Once the charges Q and $-Q$ are established on the conductors, the battery is disconnected. This gives a fixed *potential difference* V_{ab} between the conductors (that is, the potential of the positively charged conductor a with respect to the negatively charged conductor b) that is just equal to the voltage of the battery.

The electric field at any point in the region between the conductors is proportional to the magnitude Q of charge on each conductor. It follows that the potential difference V_{ab} between the conductors is also proportional to Q. If we double the magnitude of charge on each conductor, the charge density at each point doubles, the electric field at each point doubles, and the potential difference between conductors doubles; however, the *ratio* of charge to potential difference does not change. This ratio is called the **capacitance** C of the capacitor:

$$C = \frac{Q}{V_{ab}} \qquad \text{(definition of capacitance)} \qquad (24.1)$$

The SI unit of capacitance is called one **farad** (1 F), in honor of the 19th-century English physicist Michael Faraday. From Eq. (24.1), one farad is equal to one *coulomb per volt* ($1\ \text{C}/\text{V}$):

$$1\ \text{F} = 1\ \text{farad} = 1\ \text{C}/\text{V} = 1\ \text{coulomb}/\text{volt}$$

CAUTION **Capacitance vs. coulombs** Don't confuse the symbol C for capacitance (which is always in italics) with the abbreviation C for coulombs (which is never italicized). ∎

The greater the capacitance C of a capacitor, the greater the magnitude Q of charge on either conductor for a given potential difference V_{ab} and hence the greater the amount of stored energy. (Remember that potential is potential energy per unit charge.) Thus *capacitance is a measure of the ability of a capacitor to store energy*. We will see that the value of the capacitance depends only on the shapes and sizes of the conductors and on the nature of the insulating material between them. (The above remarks about capacitance being independent of Q and V_{ab} do not apply to certain special types of insulating materials. We won't discuss these materials in this book, however.)

Calculating Capacitance: Capacitors in Vacuum

We can calculate the capacitance C of a given capacitor by finding the potential difference V_{ab} between the conductors for a given magnitude of charge Q and then using Eq. (24.1). For now we'll consider only *capacitors in vacuum;* that is, we'll assume that the conductors that make up the capacitor are separated by empty space.

The simplest form of capacitor consists of two parallel conducting plates, each with area A, separated by a distance d that is small in comparison with their dimensions (Fig. 24.2a). When the plates are charged, the electric field is almost completely localized in the region between the plates (Fig. 24.2b). As we discussed in Example 22.8 (Section 22.4), the field between such plates is essentially *uniform,* and the charges on the plates are uniformly distributed over their opposing surfaces. We call this arrangement a **parallel-plate capacitor.**

We worked out the electric-field magnitude E for this arrangement in Example 21.13 (Section 21.5) using the principle of superposition of electric fields and again in Example 22.8 (Section 22.4) using Gauss's law. It would be a good idea to review those examples. We found that $E = \sigma/\epsilon_0$, where σ is the magnitude (absolute value) of the surface charge density on each plate. This is equal to the magnitude of the total charge Q on each plate divided by the area A of the plate, or $\sigma = Q/A$, so the field magnitude E can be expressed as

$$E = \frac{\sigma}{\epsilon_0} = \frac{Q}{\epsilon_0 A}$$

The field is uniform and the distance between the plates is d, so the potential difference (voltage) between the two plates is

$$V_{ab} = Ed = \frac{1}{\epsilon_0}\frac{Qd}{A}$$

From this we see that the capacitance C of a parallel-plate capacitor in vacuum is

$$C = \frac{Q}{V_{ab}} = \epsilon_0 \frac{A}{d} \quad \begin{array}{l}\text{(capacitance of a parallel-plate}\\ \text{capacitor in vacuum)}\end{array} \quad (24.2)$$

The capacitance depends only on the geometry of the capacitor; it is directly proportional to the area A of each plate and inversely proportional to their separation d. The quantities A and d are constants for a given capacitor, and ϵ_0 is a universal constant. Thus in vacuum the capacitance C is a constant independent of the charge on the capacitor or the potential difference between the plates. If one of the capacitor plates is flexible, the capacitance C changes as the plate separation d changes. This is the operating principle of a condenser microphone (Fig. 24.3).

When matter is present between the plates, its properties affect the capacitance. We will return to this topic in Section 24.4. Meanwhile, we remark that if the space contains air at atmospheric pressure instead of vacuum, the capacitance differs from the prediction of Eq. (24.2) by less than 0.06%.

In Eq. (24.2), if A is in square meters and d in meters, C is in farads. The units of ϵ_0 are $C^2/N \cdot m^2$, so we see that

$$1 \text{ F} = 1 \text{ C}^2/N \cdot m = 1 \text{ C}^2/J$$

Because $1 \text{ V} = 1 \text{ J}/C$ (energy per unit charge), this is consistent with our definition $1 \text{ F} = 1 \text{ C}/V$. Finally, the units of ϵ_0 can be expressed as $1 \text{ C}^2/N \cdot m^2 = 1 \text{ F}/m$, so

$$\epsilon_0 = 8.85 \times 10^{-12} \text{ F}/m$$

24.2 A charged parallel-plate capacitor.

(a) Arrangement of the capacitor plates

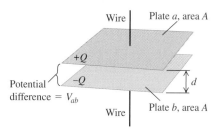

(b) Side view of the electric field $\vec{E}$

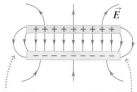

When the separation of the plates is small compared to their size, the fringing of the field is slight.

24.3 Inside a condenser microphone is a capacitor with one rigid plate and one flexible plate. The two plates are kept at a constant potential difference V_{ab}. Sound waves cause the flexible plate to move back and forth, varying the capacitance C and causing charge to flow to and from the capacitor in accordance with the relationship $C = Q/V_{ab}$. Thus a sound wave is converted to a charge flow that can be amplified and recorded digitally.

24.4 A commercial capacitor is labeled with the value of its capacitance. For these capacitors, $C = 2200 \ \mu\text{F}$, $1000 \ \mu\text{F}$, and $470 \ \mu\text{F}$.

This relationship is useful in capacitance calculations, and it also helps us to verify that Eq. (24.2) is dimensionally consistent.

One farad is a very large capacitance, as the following example shows. In many applications the most convenient units of capacitance are the *microfarad* $(1 \ \mu\text{F} = 10^{-6} \ \text{F})$ and the *picofarad* $(1 \ \text{pF} = 10^{-12} \ \text{F})$. For example, the flash unit in a point-and-shoot camera uses a capacitor of a few hundred microfarads (Fig. 24.4), while capacitances in a radio tuning circuit are typically from 10 to 100 picofarads.

For *any* capacitor in vacuum, the capacitance C depends only on the shapes, dimensions, and separation of the conductors that make up the capacitor. If the conductor shapes are more complex than those of the parallel-plate capacitor, the expression for capacitance is more complicated than in Eq. (24.2). In the following examples we show how to calculate C for two other conductor geometries.

Example 24.1   Size of a 1-F capacitor

A parallel-plate capacitor has a capacitance of 1.0 F. If the plates are 1.0 mm apart, what is the area of the plates?

SOLUTION

IDENTIFY: This problem uses the relationship among the capacitance, plate separation, and plate area (our target variable) for a parallel-plate capacitor.

SET UP: We are given the values of C and d for a parallel-plate capacitor, so we use Eq. (24.2) and solve for the target variable A.

EXECUTE: From Eq. (24.2), the area A is

$$A = \frac{Cd}{\epsilon_0} = \frac{(1.0 \ \text{F})(1.0 \times 10^{-3} \ \text{m})}{8.85 \times 10^{-12} \ \text{F/m}}$$
$$= 1.1 \times 10^8 \ \text{m}^2$$

EVALUATE: This corresponds to a square about 10 km (about 6 miles) on a side! This area is about a third larger than Manhattan Island. Clearly this is not a very practical design for a capacitor.

In fact, it's now possible to make 1-F capacitors a few centimeters on a side. The trick is to have an appropriate substance between the plates rather than a vacuum. We'll explore this further in Section 24.4.

Example 24.2   Properties of a parallel-plate capacitor

The plates of a parallel-plate capacitor in vacuum are 5.00 mm apart and 2.00 m² in area. A potential difference of 10,000 V $(10.0 \ \text{kV})$ is applied across the capacitor. Compute (a) the capacitance; (b) the charge on each plate; and (c) the magnitude of the electric field in the space between them.

SOLUTION

IDENTIFY: We are given the plate area A, the plate spacing d, and the potential difference V_{ab} for this parallel-plate capacitor. Our target variables are the capacitance C, charge Q, and electric-field magnitude E.

SET UP: We use Eq. (24.2) to calculate C and then find the charge Q on each plate using the given potential difference V_{ab} and Eq. (24.1). Once we have Q, we find the electric field between the plates using the relationship $E = Q/\epsilon_0 A$.

EXECUTE: (a) From Eq. (24.2),

$$C = \epsilon_0 \frac{A}{d} = \frac{(8.85 \times 10^{-12} \ \text{F/m})(2.00 \ \text{m}^2)}{5.00 \times 10^{-3} \ \text{m}}$$
$$= 3.54 \times 10^{-9} \ \text{F} = 0.00354 \ \mu\text{F}$$

(b) The charge on the capacitor is

$$Q = CV_{ab} = (3.54 \times 10^{-9} \ \text{C/V})(1.00 \times 10^4 \ \text{V})$$
$$= 3.54 \times 10^{-5} \ \text{C} = 35.4 \ \mu\text{C}$$

The plate at higher potential has charge $+35.4 \ \mu\text{C}$ and the other plate has charge $-35.4 \ \mu\text{C}$.

(c) The electric-field magnitude is

$$E = \frac{\sigma}{\epsilon_0} = \frac{Q}{\epsilon_0 A} = \frac{3.54 \times 10^{-5} \ \text{C}}{(8.85 \times 10^{-12} \ \text{C}^2/\text{N} \cdot \text{m}^2)(2.00 \ \text{m}^2)}$$
$$= 2.00 \times 10^6 \ \text{N/C}$$

EVALUATE: An alternative way to get the result in part (c) is to recall that the electric field is equal in magnitude to the potential gradient [Eq. (23.22)]. Since the field between the plates is uniform,

$$E = \frac{V_{ab}}{d} = \frac{1.00 \times 10^4 \ \text{V}}{5.00 \times 10^{-3} \ \text{m}} = 2.00 \times 10^6 \ \text{V/m}$$

(Remember that the newton per coulomb and the volt per meter are equivalent units.)

Example 24.3 **A spherical capacitor**

Two concentric spherical conducting shells are separated by vacuum. The inner shell has total charge $+Q$ and outer radius r_a, and the outer shell has charge $-Q$ and inner radius r_b (Fig. 24.5). (The inner shell is attached to the outer shell by thin insulating rods that have negligible effect on the capacitance.) Find the capacitance of this spherical capacitor.

SOLUTION

IDENTIFY: This isn't a parallel-plate capacitor, so we can't use the relationships developed for that particular geometry. Instead, we'll go back to the fundamental definition of capacitance: the magnitude of the charge on either conductor divided by the potential difference between the conductors.

SET UP: We use Gauss's law to find the electric field between the spherical conductors. From this value we determine the potential difference V_{ab} between the two conductors; we then use Eq. (24.1) to find the capacitance $C = Q/V_{ab}$.

EXECUTE: Using the same procedure as in Example 22.5 (Section 22.4), we take as our Gaussian surface a sphere with radius r between the two spheres and concentric with them. Gauss's law, Eq. (22.8), states that the electric flux through this surface is equal to the total charge enclosed within the surface, divided by ϵ_0:

$$\oint \vec{E} \cdot d\vec{A} = \frac{Q_{encl}}{\epsilon_0}$$

By symmetry, $\vec{E}$ is constant in magnitude and parallel to $d\vec{A}$ at every point on this surface, so the integral in Gauss's law is equal

to $(E)(4\pi r^2)$. The total charge enclosed is $Q_{encl} = Q$, so we have

$$(E)(4\pi r^2) = \frac{Q}{\epsilon_0}$$

$$E = \frac{Q}{4\pi\epsilon_0 r^2}$$

The electric field between the spheres is just that due to the charge on the inner sphere; the outer sphere has no effect. We found in Example 22.5 that the charge on a conducting sphere produces zero field *inside* the sphere, which also tells us that the outer conductor makes no contribution to the field between the conductors.

The above expression for E is the same as that for a point charge Q, so the expression for the potential can also be taken to be the same as for a point charge, $V = Q/4\pi\epsilon_0 r$. Hence the potential of the inner (positive) conductor at $r = r_a$ with respect to that of the outer (negative) conductor at $r = r_b$ is

$$V_{ab} = V_a - V_b = \frac{Q}{4\pi\epsilon_0 r_a} - \frac{Q}{4\pi\epsilon_0 r_b}$$

$$= \frac{Q}{4\pi\epsilon_0}\left(\frac{1}{r_a} - \frac{1}{r_b}\right) = \frac{Q}{4\pi\epsilon_0}\frac{r_b - r_a}{r_a r_b}$$

Finally, the capacitance is

$$C = \frac{Q}{V_{ab}} = 4\pi\epsilon_0 \frac{r_a r_b}{r_b - r_a}$$

As an example, if $r_a = 9.5$ cm and $r_b = 10.5$ cm,

$$C = 4\pi(8.85 \times 10^{-12}\text{ F/m})\frac{(0.095\text{ m})(0.105\text{ m})}{0.010\text{ m}}$$

$$= 1.1 \times 10^{-10}\text{ F} = 110\text{ pF}$$

EVALUATE: We can relate this result to the capacitance of a parallel-plate capacitor. The quantity $4\pi r_a r_b$ is intermediate between the areas $4\pi r_a^2$ and $4\pi r_b^2$ of the two spheres; in fact, it's the *geometric mean* of these two areas, which we can denote by A_{gm}. The distance between spheres is $d = r_b - r_a$, so we can rewrite the above result as $C = \epsilon_0 A_{gm}/d$. This is exactly the same form as for parallel plates: $C = \epsilon_0 A/d$. The point is that if the distance between spheres is very small in comparison to their radii, they behave like parallel plates with the same area and spacing.

24.5 A spherical capacitor.

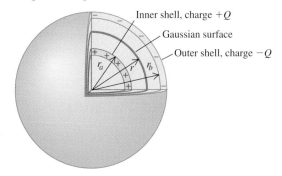

Inner shell, charge $+Q$

Gaussian surface

Outer shell, charge $-Q$

Example 24.4 **A cylindrical capacitor**

A long cylindrical conductor has a radius r_a and a linear charge density $+\lambda$. It is surrounded by a coaxial cylindrical conducting shell with inner radius r_b and linear charge density $-\lambda$ (Fig. 24.6). Calculate the capacitance per unit length for this capacitor, assuming that there is vacuum in the space between cylinders.

SOLUTION

IDENTIFY: As in Example 24.3, we use the fundamental definition of capacitance.

SET UP: We first find expressions for the potential difference V_{ab} between the cylinders and the charge Q in a length L of the cylinders; we then find the capacitance of a length L using Eq. (24.1). Our target variable is this capacitance divided by L.

EXECUTE: To find the potential difference between the cylinders, we use a result that we worked out in Example 23.10 (Section 23.3). There we found that at a point outside a charged

Continued

24.6 A long cylindrical capacitor. The linear charge density λ is assumed to be positive in this figure. The magnitude of charge in a length L of either cylinder is λL.

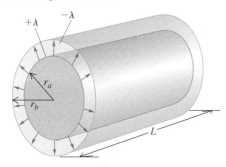

cylinder a distance r from the axis, the potential due to the cylinder is

$$V = \frac{\lambda}{2\pi\epsilon_0} \ln \frac{r_0}{r}$$

where r_0 is the (arbitrary) radius at which $V = 0$. We can use this same result for the potential *between* the cylinders in the present problem because, according to Gauss's law, the charge on the outer cylinder doesn't contribute to the field between cylinders (see Example 24.3). In our case, we take the radius r_0 to be r_b, the radius of the inner surface of the outer cylinder, so that the outer conducting cylinder is at $V = 0$. Then the potential at the outer surface of the inner cylinder (where $r = r_a$) is just equal to the

potential V_{ab} of the inner (positive) cylinder a with respect to the outer (negative) cylinder b, or

$$V_{ab} = \frac{\lambda}{2\pi\epsilon_0} \ln \frac{r_b}{r_a}$$

This potential difference is positive (assuming that λ is positive, as in Fig. 24.6) because the inner cylinder is at higher potential than the outer.

The total charge Q in a length L is $Q = \lambda L$, so from Eq. (24.1) the capacitance C of a length L is

$$C = \frac{Q}{V_{ab}} = \frac{\lambda L}{\dfrac{\lambda}{2\pi\epsilon_0} \ln \dfrac{r_b}{r_a}} = \frac{2\pi\epsilon_0 L}{\ln\left(r_b/r_a\right)}$$

The capacitance per unit length is

$$\frac{C}{L} = \frac{2\pi\epsilon_0}{\ln\left(r_b/r_a\right)}$$

Substituting $\epsilon_0 = 8.85 \times 10^{-12}$ F/m $= 8.85$ pF/m, we get

$$\frac{C}{L} = \frac{55.6 \text{ pF/m}}{\ln\left(r_b/r_a\right)}$$

EVALUATE: We see that the capacitance of the coaxial cylinders is determined entirely by the dimensions, just as for the parallel-plate case. Ordinary coaxial cables are made like this but with an insulating material instead of vacuum between the inner and outer conductors. A typical cable for TV antennas and VCR connections has a capacitance per unit length of 69 pF/m.

Test Your Understanding of Section 24.1 A capacitor has vacuum in the space between the conductors. If you double the amount of charge on each conductor, what happens to the capacitance? (i) It increases; (ii) it decreases; (iii) it remains the same; (iv) the answer depends on the size or shape of the conductors.

24.2 Capacitors in Series and Parallel

24.7 An assortment of commercially available capacitors.

Capacitors are manufactured with certain standard capacitances and working voltages (Fig. 24.7). However, these standard values may not be the ones you actually need in a particular application. You can obtain the values you need by combining capacitors; many combinations are possible, but the simplest combinations are a series connection and a parallel connection.

Capacitors in Series

Figure 24.8a is a schematic diagram of a **series connection.** Two capacitors are connected in series (one after the other) by conducting wires between points a and b. Both capacitors are initially uncharged. When a constant positive potential difference V_{ab} is applied between points a and b, the capacitors become charged; the figure shows that the charge on *all* conducting plates has the same magnitude. To see why, note first that the top plate of C_1 acquires a positive charge Q. The electric field of this positive charge pulls negative charge up to the bottom plate of C_1 until all of the field lines that begin on the top plate end on the bottom plate. This requires that the bottom plate have charge $-Q$. These negative charges had to come from the top plate of C_2, which becomes positively charged with charge $+Q$. This positive charge then pulls negative charge $-Q$ from the connection at point b onto the bottom plate of C_2. The total charge on the lower plate of C_1 and the upper plate of C_2 together must always be zero because these plates aren't connected to anything except each other. Thus *in a series connection the magnitude of charge on all plates is the same.*

Referring to Fig. 24.8a, we can write the potential differences between points a and c, c and b, and a and b as

$$V_{ac} = V_1 = \frac{Q}{C_1} \qquad V_{cb} = V_2 = \frac{Q}{C_2}$$

$$V_{ab} = V = V_1 + V_2 = Q\left(\frac{1}{C_1} + \frac{1}{C_2}\right)$$

and so

$$\frac{V}{Q} = \frac{1}{C_1} + \frac{1}{C_2} \tag{24.3}$$

Following a common convention, we use the symbols V_1, V_2, and V to denote the potential *differences* V_{ac} (across the first capacitor), V_{cb} (across the second capacitor), and V_{ab} (across the entire combination of capacitors), respectively.

The **equivalent capacitance** C_{eq} of the series combination is defined as the capacitance of a *single* capacitor for which the charge Q is the same as for the combination, when the potential difference V is the same. In other words, the combination can be replaced by an *equivalent capacitor* of capacitance C_{eq}. For such a capacitor, shown in Fig. 24.8b,

$$C_{eq} = \frac{Q}{V} \quad \text{or} \quad \frac{1}{C_{eq}} = \frac{V}{Q} \tag{24.4}$$

Combining Eqs. (24.3) and (24.4), we find

$$\frac{1}{C_{eq}} = \frac{1}{C_1} + \frac{1}{C_2}$$

We can extend this analysis to any number of capacitors in series. We find the following result for the *reciprocal* of the equivalent capacitance:

$$\frac{1}{C_{eq}} = \frac{1}{C_1} + \frac{1}{C_2} + \frac{1}{C_3} + \cdots \qquad \text{(capacitors in series)} \tag{24.5}$$

The reciprocal of the equivalent capacitance of a series combination equals the sum of the reciprocals of the individual capacitances. In a series connection the equivalent capacitance is always *less than* any individual capacitance.

CAUTION **Capacitors in series** The magnitude of charge is the same on all plates of all the capacitors in a series combination; however, the potential differences of the individual capacitors are *not* the same unless their individual capacitances are the same. The potential differences of the individual capacitors add to give the total potential difference across the series combination: $V_{total} = V_1 + V_2 + V_3 + \cdots$. ▮

Capacitors in Parallel

The arrangement shown in Fig. 24.9a is called a **parallel connection.** Two capacitors are connected in parallel between points a and b. In this case the upper plates of the two capacitors are connected by conducting wires to form an equipotential surface, and the lower plates form another. Hence *in a parallel connection the potential difference for all individual capacitors is the same* and is equal to $V_{ab} = V$. The charges Q_1 and Q_2 are not necessarily equal, however,

24.8 A series connection of two capacitors.

(a) Two capacitors in series

Capacitors in series:
• The capacitors have the same charge Q.
• Their potential differences add:
  $V_{ac} + V_{cb} = V_{ab}$.

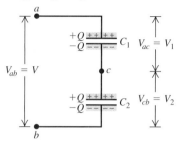

(b) The equivalent single capacitor

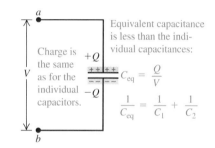

Equivalent capacitance is less than the individual capacitances:

$$C_{eq} = \frac{Q}{V}$$

$$\frac{1}{C_{eq}} = \frac{1}{C_1} + \frac{1}{C_2}$$

24.9 A parallel connection of two capacitors.

(a) Two capacitors in parallel

Capacitors in parallel:
• The capacitors have the same potential V.
• The charge on each capacitor depends on its capacitance: $Q_1 = C_1 V$, $Q_2 = C_2 V$.

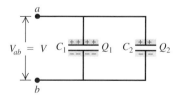

(b) The equivalent single capacitor

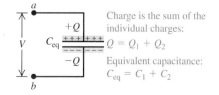

Charge is the sum of the individual charges:
$$Q = Q_1 + Q_2$$
Equivalent capacitance:
$$C_{eq} = C_1 + C_2$$

since charges can reach each capacitor independently from the source (such as a battery) of the voltage V_{ab}. The charges are

$$Q_1 = C_1 V \quad \text{and} \quad Q_2 = C_2 V$$

The *total* charge Q of the combination, and thus the total charge on the equivalent capacitor, is

$$Q = Q_1 + Q_2 = (C_1 + C_2)V$$

so

$$\frac{Q}{V} = C_1 + C_2 \tag{24.6}$$

The parallel combination is equivalent to a single capacitor with the same total charge $Q = Q_1 + Q_2$ and potential difference V as the combination (Fig. 24.9b). The equivalent capacitance of the combination, C_{eq}, is the same as the capacitance Q/V of this single equivalent capacitor. So from Eq. (24.6),

$$C_{eq} = C_1 + C_2$$

In the same way we can show that for any number of capacitors in parallel,

$$C_{eq} = C_1 + C_2 + C_3 + \cdots \quad \text{(capacitors in parallel)} \tag{24.7}$$

The equivalent capacitance of a parallel combination equals the *sum* of the individual capacitances. In a parallel connection the equivalent capacitance is always *greater than* any individual capacitance.

CAUTION   Capacitors in parallel The potential differences are the same for all the capacitors in a parallel combination; however, the charges on individual capacitors are *not* the same unless their individual capacitances are the same. The charges on the individual capacitors add to give the total charge on the parallel combination: $Q_{total} = Q_1 + Q_2 + Q_3 + \cdots$. [Compare these statements to those in the "Caution" paragraph following Eq. (24.5).]

Problem-Solving Strategy 24.1   Equilibrium Capacitance

IDENTIFY *the relevant concepts:* The concept of equivalent capacitance is useful whenever two or more capacitors are connected.

SET UP *the problem* using the following steps:
1. Make a drawing of the capacitor arrangement.
2. Identify whether the capacitors are connected in series or in parallel. With more complicated combinations, you can sometimes identify parts that are simple series or parallel connections.
3. Keep in mind that when we say a capacitor has charge Q, we always mean that the plate at higher potential has charge $+Q$ and the other plate has charge $-Q$.

EXECUTE *the solution* as follows:
1. When capacitors are connected in series, as in Fig. 24.8a, they always have the same charge, assuming that they were uncharged before they were connected. The potential differences are *not* equal unless the capacitances are equal. The total potential difference across the combination is the sum of the individual potential differences.

2. When capacitors are connected in parallel, as in Fig. 24.9a, the potential difference V is always the same for all of the individual capacitors. The charges on the individual capacitors are *not* equal unless the capacitances are equal. The total charge on the combination is the sum of the individual charges.
3. For more complicated combinations, find the parts that are simple series or parallel connections and replace them with their equivalent capacitances, in a step-by-step reduction. If you then need to find the charge or potential difference for an individual capacitor, you may have to retrace your path to the original capacitors.

EVALUATE *your answer:* Check whether your result makes sense. If the capacitors are connected in series, the equivalent capacitance C_{eq} must be *smaller* than any of the individual capacitances. By contrast, if the capacitors are connected in parallel, C_{eq} must be *greater* than any of the individual capacitances.

Example 24.5   Capacitors in series and in parallel

In Figs. 24.8 and 24.9, let $C_1 = 6.0\ \mu F$, $C_2 = 3.0\ \mu F$, and $V_{ab} = 18$ V. Find the equivalent capacitance, and find the charge and potential difference for each capacitor when the two capacitors are connected (a) in series and (b) in parallel.

SOLUTION

IDENTIFY: This problem uses the ideas discussed in this section about capacitor connections.

SET UP: In both parts, one of the target variables is the equivalent capacitance C_{eq}. For the series combination in part (a), it is given by Eq. (24.5); for the parallel combination in part (b), C_{eq} is given by Eq. (24.6). In each part we find the charge and potential difference using the definition of capacitance, Eq. (24.1), and the rules outlined in the Problem-Solving Strategy 24.1.

EXECUTE: (a) Using Eq. (24.5) for the equivalent capacitance of the series combination (Fig. 24.8a), we find

$$\frac{1}{C_{eq}} = \frac{1}{C_1} + \frac{1}{C_2} = \frac{1}{6.0\ \mu F} + \frac{1}{3.0\ \mu F} \qquad C_{eq} = 2.0\ \mu F$$

The charge Q on each capacitor in series is the same as the charge on the equivalent capacitor:

$$Q = C_{eq}V = (2.0\ \mu F)(18\ V) = 36\ \mu C$$

The potential difference across each capacitor is inversely proportional to its capacitance:

$$V_{ac} = V_1 = \frac{Q}{C_1} = \frac{36\ \mu C}{6.0\ \mu F} = 6.0\ V$$

$$V_{cb} = V_2 = \frac{Q}{C_2} = \frac{36\ \mu C}{3.0\ \mu F} = 12.0\ V$$

(b) To find the equivalent capacitance of the parallel combination (Fig. 24.9a), we use Eq. (24.6):

$$C_{eq} = C_1 + C_2 = 6.0\ \mu F + 3.0\ \mu F = 9.0\ \mu F$$

The potential difference across each of the two capacitors in parallel is the same as that across the equivalent capacitor, 18 V. The charges Q_1 and Q_2 are directly proportional to the capacitances C_1 and C_2, respectively:

$$Q_1 = C_1 V = (6.0\ \mu F)(18\ V) = 108\ \mu C$$
$$Q_2 = C_2 V = (3.0\ \mu F)(18\ V) = 54\ \mu C$$

EVALUATE: Note that the equivalent capacitance C_{eq} for the series combination in part (a) is indeed less than either C_1 or C_2, while for the parallel combination in part (b) the equivalent capacitance is indeed greater than either C_1 or C_2.

It's instructive to compare the potential differences and charges in each part of the example. For two capacitors in series, as in part (a), the charge is the same on either capacitor and the *larger* potential difference appears across the capacitor with the *smaller* capacitance. Furthermore, $V_{ac} + V_{cb} = V_{ab} = 18$ V, as it must. By contrast, for two capacitors in parallel, as in part (b), each capacitor has the same potential difference and the *larger* charge appears on the capacitor with the *larger* capacitance. Can you show that the total charge $Q_1 + Q_2$ on the parallel combination is equal to the charge $Q = C_{eq}V$ on the equivalent capacitor?

Example 24.6   A capacitor network

Find the equivalent capacitance of the combination shown in Fig. 24.10a.

SOLUTION

IDENTIFY: The five capacitors in Fig. 24.10a are neither all in series nor all in parallel. We can, however, identify portions of the

arrangement that *are* either in series or parallel, which we combine to find the net equivalent capacitance.

SET UP: We use Eq. (24.5) to analyze portions of the network that are series connections and Eq. (24.7) to analyze portions that are parallel connections.

24.10 (a) A capacitor network between points a and b. (b) The 12-μF and 6-μF capacitors in series in (a) are replaced by an equivalent 4-μF capacitor. (c) The 3-μF, 11-μF, and 4-μF capacitors in parallel in (b) are replaced by an equivalent 18-μF capacitor. (d) Finally, the 18-μF and 9-μF capacitors in series in (c) are replaced by an equivalent 6-μF capacitor.

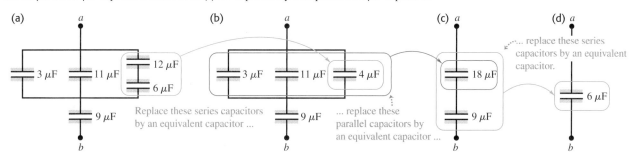

Continued

EXECUTE: We first replace the 12-μF and 6-μF series combination by its equivalent capacitance; calling that C', we use Eq. (24.5):

$$\frac{1}{C'} = \frac{1}{12\ \mu\text{F}} + \frac{1}{6\ \mu\text{F}} \qquad C' = 4\ \mu\text{F}$$

This gives us the equivalent combination shown in Fig. 24.10b. Next we find the equivalent capacitance of the three capacitors in parallel, using Eq. (24.7). Calling their equivalent capacitance C'', we have

$$C'' = 3\ \mu\text{F} + 11\ \mu\text{F} + 4\ \mu\text{F} = 18\ \mu\text{F}$$

This gives us the simpler equivalent combination shown in Fig. 24.10c. Finally, we find the equivalent capacitance C_{eq} of these two capacitors in series (Fig. 24.10d):

$$\frac{1}{C_{\text{eq}}} = \frac{1}{18\ \mu\text{F}} + \frac{1}{9\ \mu\text{F}} \qquad C_{\text{eq}} = 6\ \mu\text{F}$$

EVALUATE: The equivalent capacitance of the network is 6 μF; that is, if a potential difference V_{ab} is applied across the terminals of the network, the net charge on the network is 6 μF times V_{ab}. How is this net charge related to the charges on the individual capacitors in Fig. 24.10a?

Test Your Understanding of Section 24.2 You want to connect a 4-μF capacitor and an 8-μF capacitor. (a) With which type of connection will the 4-μF capacitor have a greater *potential difference* across it than the 8-μF capacitor? (i) series; (ii) parallel; (iii) either series or parallel; (iv) neither series nor parallel. (b) With which type of connection will the 4-μF capacitor have a greater *charge* than the 8-μF capacitor? (i) series; (ii) parallel; (iii) either series or parallel; (iv) neither series nor parallel.

24.3 Energy Storage in Capacitors and Electric-Field Energy

Many of the most important applications of capacitors depend on their ability to store energy. The electric potential energy stored in a charged capacitor is just equal to the amount of work required to charge it—that is, to separate opposite charges and place them on different conductors. When the capacitor is discharged, this stored energy is recovered as work done by electrical forces.

We can calculate the potential energy U of a charged capacitor by calculating the work W required to charge it. Suppose that when we are done charging the capacitor, the final charge is Q and the final potential difference is V. From Eq. (24.1) these quantities are related by

$$V = \frac{Q}{C}$$

Let q and v be the charge and potential difference, respectively, at an intermediate stage during the charging process; then $v = q/C$. At this stage the work dW required to transfer an additional element of charge dq is

$$dW = v\ dq = \frac{q\ dq}{C}$$

The total work W needed to increase the capacitor charge q from zero to a final value Q is

$$W = \int_0^W dW = \frac{1}{C} \int_0^Q q\ dq = \frac{Q^2}{2C} \qquad \text{(work to charge a capacitor)} \quad (24.8)$$

This is also equal to the total work done by the electric field on the charge when the capacitor discharges. Then q *decreases* from an initial value Q to zero as the elements of charge dq "fall" through potential differences v that vary from V down to zero.

If we define the potential energy of an *uncharged* capacitor to be zero, then W in Eq. (24.8) is equal to the potential energy U of the charged capacitor. The final stored charge is $Q = CV$, so we can express U (which is equal to W) as

$$U = \frac{Q^2}{2C} = \frac{1}{2}CV^2 = \frac{1}{2}QV \qquad \text{(potential energy stored in a capacitor)} \quad (24.9)$$

When Q is in coulombs, C in farads (coulombs per volt), and V in volts (joules per coulomb), U is in joules.

The last form of Eq. (24.9), $U = \frac{1}{2}QV$, shows that the total work W required to charge the capacitor is equal to the total charge Q multiplied by the *average* potential difference $\frac{1}{2}V$ during the charging process.

The expression $U = \frac{1}{2}(Q^2/C)$ in Eq. (24.9) shows that a charged capacitor is the electrical analog of a stretched spring with elastic potential energy $U = \frac{1}{2}kx^2$. The charge Q is analogous to the elongation x, and the *reciprocal* of the capacitance, $1/C$, is analogous to the force constant k. The energy supplied to a capacitor in the charging process is analogous to the work we do on a spring when we stretch it.

Equations (24.8) and (24.9) tell us that capacitance measures the ability of a capacitor to store both energy and charge. If a capacitor is charged by connecting it to a battery or other source that provides a fixed potential difference V, then increasing the value of C gives a greater charge $Q = CV$ and a greater amount of stored energy $U = \frac{1}{2}CV^2$. If instead the goal is to transfer a given quantity of charge Q from one conductor to another, Eq. (24.8) shows that the work W required is inversely proportional to C; the greater the capacitance, the easier it is to give a capacitor a fixed amount of charge.

Applications of Capacitors: Energy Storage

Most practical applications of capacitors take advantage of their ability to store and release energy. In electronic flash units used by photographers, the energy stored in a capacitor (see Fig. 24.4) is released by depressing the camera's shutter button. This provides a conducting path from one capacitor plate to the other through the flash tube. Once this path is established, the stored energy is rapidly converted into a brief but intense flash of light. An extreme example of the same principle is the Z machine at Sandia National Laboratories in New Mexico, which is used in experiments in controlled nuclear fusion (Fig. 24.11). A bank of charged capacitors releases more than a million joules of energy in just a few billionths of a second. For that brief space of time, the power output of the Z machine is 2.9×10^{14} W, or about 80 times the electric output of all the electric power plants on earth combined!

In other applications, the energy is released more slowly. Springs in the suspension of an automobile, help smooth out the ride by absorbing the energy from sudden jolts and releasing that energy gradually; in an analogous way, a capacitor in an electronic circuit can smooth out unwanted variations in voltage due to power surges. And just as the presence of a spring gives a mechanical system a natural frequency at which it responds most strongly to an applied periodic force, so the presence of a capacitor gives an electric circuit a natural frequency for current oscillations. This idea is used in tuned circuits such as those in radio and television receivers, which respond to broadcast signals at one particular frequency and ignore signals at other frequencies. We'll discuss these circuits in detail in Chapter 31.

The energy-storage properties of capacitors also have some undesirable practical effects. Adjacent pins on the underside of a computer chip act like a capacitor, and the property that makes capacitors useful for smoothing out voltage variations acts to retard the rate at which the potentials of the chip's pins can be changed. This tendency limits how rapidly the chip can perform computations, an effect that becomes more important as computer chips become smaller and are pushed to operate at faster speeds.

24.11 The Z machine uses a large number of capacitors in parallel to give a tremendous equivalent capacitance C (see Section 24.2). Hence a large amount of energy $U = \frac{1}{2}CV^2$ can be stored with even a modest potential difference V. The arcs shown here are produced when the capacitors discharge their energy into a target, which is no larger than a spool of thread. This heats the target to a temperature higher than 2×10^9 K.

Electric-Field Energy

We can charge a capacitor by moving electrons directly from one plate to another. This requires doing work against the electric field between the plates. Thus we can think of the energy as being stored *in the field* in the region between the plates. To develop this relationship, let's find the energy *per unit volume* in the space between the plates of a parallel-plate capacitor with plate area A and separation d. We call this the **energy density,** denoted by u. From Eq. (24.9) the total stored potential energy is $\frac{1}{2}CV^2$ and the volume between the plates is just Ad; hence the energy density is

$$u = \text{Energy density} = \frac{\frac{1}{2}CV^2}{Ad} \qquad (24.10)$$

From Eq. (24.2) the capacitance C is given by $C = \epsilon_0 A/d$. The potential difference V is related to the electric field magnitude E by $V = Ed$. If we use these expressions in Eq. (24.10), the geometric factors A and d cancel, and we find

$$u = \frac{1}{2}\epsilon_0 E^2 \qquad \text{(electric energy density in a vacuum)} \qquad (24.11)$$

Although we have derived this relationship only for a parallel-plate capacitor, it turns out to be valid for any capacitor in vacuum and indeed *for any electric field configuration in vacuum.* This result has an interesting implication. We think of vacuum as space with no matter in it, but vacuum can nevertheless have electric fields and therefore energy. Thus "empty" space need not be truly empty after all. We will use this idea and Eq. (24.11) in Chapter 32 in connection with the energy transported by electromagnetic waves.

CAUTION **Electrical-field energy is electric potential energy** It's a common misconception that electric-field energy is a new kind of energy, different from the electric potential energy described before. This is *not* the case; it is simply a different way of interpreting electric potential energy. We can regard the energy of a given system of charges as being a shared property of all the charges, or we can think of the energy as being a property of the electric field that the charges create. Either interpretation leads to the same value of the potential energy. ∎

Example 24.7 Transferring charge and energy between capacitors

In Fig. 24.12 we charge a capacitor of capacitance $C_1 = 8.0\ \mu\text{F}$ by connecting it to a source of potential difference $V_0 = 120\ \text{V}$ (not shown in the figure). The switch S is initially open. Once C_1 is charged, the source of potential difference is disconnected. (a) What is the charge Q_0 on C_1 if switch S is left open? (b) What is the energy stored in C_1 if switch S is left open? (c) The capacitor of capacitance $C_2 = 4.0\ \mu\text{F}$ is initially uncharged. After we close switch S, what is the potential difference across each capacitor, and what is the charge on each capacitor? (d) What is the total energy of the system after we close switch S?

SOLUTION

IDENTIFY: Initially we have a single capacitor with a given potential difference between its plates. After the switch is closed, one wire connects the upper plates of the two capacitors and another wire connects the lower plates; in other words, the capacitors are connected in parallel.

SET UP: In parts (a) and (b) we find the charge and stored energy for capacitor C_1 using Eqs. (24.1) and (24.9), respectively. In part (c) we use the character of the parallel connection to determine how the charge Q_0 is shared between the two capacitors. In part (d) we again use Eq. (24.9) to find the energy stored in capacitors C_1 and C_2; the total energy is the sum of these values.

24.12 When the switch S is closed, the charged capacitor C_1 is connected to an uncharged capacitor C_2. The center part of the switch is an insulating handle; charge can flow only between the two upper terminals and between the two lower terminals.

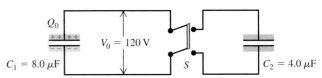

EXECUTE: (a) The charge Q_0 on C_1 is

$$Q_0 = C_1 V_0 = (8.0\ \mu\text{F})(120\ \text{V}) = 960\ \mu\text{C}$$

(b) The energy initially stored in the capacitor is

$$U_{\text{initial}} = \frac{1}{2}Q_0 V_0 = \frac{1}{2}(960 \times 10^{-6}\ \text{C})(120\ \text{V}) = 0.058\ \text{J}$$

(c) When the switch is closed, the positive charge Q_0 becomes distributed over the upper plates of both capacitors and the negative charge $-Q_0$ is distributed over the lower plates of both capacitors. Let Q_1 and Q_2 be the magnitudes of the final charges on the two capacitors. From conservation of charge,

$$Q_1 + Q_2 = Q_0$$

In the final state, when the charges are no longer moving, both upper plates are at the same potential; they are connected by a conducting wire and so form a single equipotential surface. Both lower plates are also at the same potential, different from that of the upper plates. The final potential difference V between the plates is therefore the same for both capacitors, as we would expect for a parallel connection. The capacitor charges are

$$Q_1 = C_1 V \qquad Q_2 = C_2 V$$

When we combine these with the preceding equation for conservation of charge, we find

$$V = \frac{Q_0}{C_1 + C_2} = \frac{960 \ \mu C}{8.0 \ \mu F + 4.0 \ \mu F} = 80 \ V$$

$$Q_1 = 640 \ \mu C \qquad Q_2 = 320 \ \mu C$$

(d) The final energy of the system is the sum of the energies stored in each capacitor:

$$U_{\text{final}} = \frac{1}{2} Q_1 V + \frac{1}{2} Q_2 V = \frac{1}{2} Q_0 V$$

$$= \frac{1}{2} (960 \times 10^{-6} \ C)(80 \ V) = 0.038 \ J$$

EVALUATE: The final energy is less than the original energy $U_{\text{initial}} = 0.058 \ J$; the difference has been converted to energy of some other form. The conductors become a little warmer because of their resistance, and some energy is radiated as electromagnetic waves. We'll study the circuit behavior of capacitors in detail in Chapters 26 and 31.

Example 24.8 Electric-field energy

Suppose you want to store 1.00 J of electric potential energy in a volume of 1.00 m^3 in vacuum. (a) What is the magnitude of the required electric field? (b) If the field magnitude is 10 times larger, how much energy is stored per cubic meter?

SOLUTION

IDENTIFY: We use the relationship between the electric-field magnitude E and the energy density u, which equals the electric-field energy divided by the volume occupied by the field.

SET UP: In part (a) we use the given information to find u, then we use Eq. (24.11) to find the required value of E. This same equation gives us the relationship between changes in E and the corresponding changes in u.

EXECUTE: (a) The desired energy density is $u = 1.00 \ J/m^3$. We solve Eq. (24.11) for E:

$$E = \sqrt{\frac{2u}{\epsilon_0}} = \sqrt{\frac{2(1.00 \ J/m^3)}{8.85 \times 10^{-12} \ C^2/N \cdot m^2}}$$

$$= 4.75 \times 10^5 \ N/C = 4.75 \times 10^5 \ V/m$$

(b) Equation (24.11) shows that u is proportional to E^2. If E increases by a factor of 10, u increases by a factor of $10^2 = 100$, and the energy density is 100 J/m^3.

EVALUATE: The value of E found in part (a) is sizable, corresponding to a potential difference of nearly a half million volts over a distance of 1 meter. We will see in Section 24.4 that the field magnitudes in practical insulators can be as great as this or even larger.

Example 24.9 Two ways to calculate energy stored in a capacitor

The spherical capacitor described in Example 24.3 (Section 24.1) has charges $+Q$ and $-Q$ on its inner and outer conductors. Find the electric potential energy stored in the capacitor (a) by using the capacitance C found in Example 24.3 and (b) by integrating the electric-field energy density.

SOLUTION

IDENTIFY: This problem asks us to think about the energy stored in a capacitor, U, in two different ways: in terms of the work done to put the charges on the two conductors, $U = Q^2/2C$, and in terms of the energy in the electric field between the two conductors. Both descriptions are equivalent, so both must give us the same answer for U.

SET UP: In Example 24.3 we found the capacitance C and the field magnitude E between the conductors. We find the stored energy U in part (a) using the expression for C in Eq. (24.9). In part (b) we use the expression for E in Eq. (24.11) to find the electric-field energy density u between the conductors. The field magnitude depends on the distance r from the center of the capacitor, so u also depends on r. Hence we cannot find U by simply multiplying u by the volume between the conductors; instead, we must integrate u over this volume.

EXECUTE: (a) From Example 24.3, the spherical capacitor has capacitance

$$C = 4\pi\epsilon_0 \frac{r_a r_b}{r_b - r_a}$$

where r_a and r_b are the radii of the inner and outer conducting spheres. From Eq. (24.9) the energy stored in this capacitor is

$$U = \frac{Q^2}{2C} = \frac{Q^2}{8\pi\epsilon_0} \frac{r_b - r_a}{r_a r_b}$$

(b) The electric field in the volume between the two conducting spheres has magnitude $E = Q/4\pi\epsilon_0 r^2$. The electric field is zero inside the inner sphere and is also zero outside the inner surface of the outer sphere, because a Gaussian surface with radius $r < r_a$ or $r > r_b$ encloses zero net charge. Hence the energy density is nonzero only in the space between the spheres $(r_a < r < r_b)$. In this region,

$$u = \frac{1}{2}\epsilon_0 E^2 = \frac{1}{2}\epsilon_0 \left(\frac{Q}{4\pi\epsilon_0 r^2}\right)^2 = \frac{Q^2}{32\pi^2 \epsilon_0 r^4}$$

The energy density is *not* uniform; it decreases rapidly with increasing distance from the center of the capacitor. To find the

Continued

total electric-field energy, we integrate u (the energy per unit volume) over the volume between the inner and outer conducting spheres. Dividing this volume up into spherical shells of radius r, surface area $4\pi r^2$, thickness dr, and volume $dV = 4\pi r^2\, dr$, we have

$$U = \int u\, dV = \int_{r_a}^{r_b}\left(\frac{Q^2}{32\pi^2\epsilon_0 r^4}\right)4\pi r^2\, dr$$

$$= \frac{Q^2}{8\pi\epsilon_0}\int_{r_a}^{r_b}\frac{dr}{r^2} = \frac{Q^2}{8\pi\epsilon_0}\left(-\frac{1}{r_b} + \frac{1}{r_a}\right)$$

$$= \frac{Q^2}{8\pi\epsilon_0}\frac{r_b - r_a}{r_a r_b}$$

EVALUATE: We obtain the same result for U with either approach, as we must. We emphasize that electric potential energy can be regarded as being associated with either the *charges,* as in part (a), or the *field,* as in part (b); regardless of which viewpoint you choose, the amount of stored energy is the same.

Test Your Understanding of Section 24.3   You want to connect a 4-μF capacitor and an 8-μF capacitor. With which type of connection will the 4-μF capacitor have a greater amount of *stored energy* than the 8-μF capacitor? (i) series; (ii) parallel; (iii) either series or parallel; (iv) neither series nor parallel.

24.4 Dielectrics

24.13 A common type of capacitor uses dielectric sheets to separate the conductors.

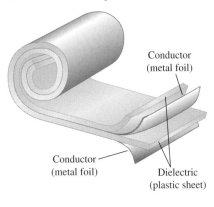

Conductor (metal foil)

Conductor (metal foil)

Dielectric (plastic sheet)

Most capacitors have a nonconducting material, or **dielectric,** between their conducting plates. A common type of capacitor uses long strips of metal foil for the plates, separated by strips of plastic sheet such as Mylar. A sandwich of these materials is rolled up, forming a unit that can provide a capacitance of several microfarads in a compact package (Fig. 24.13).

Placing a solid dielectric between the plates of a capacitor serves three functions. First, it solves the mechanical problem of maintaining two large metal sheets at a very small separation without actual contact.

Second, using a dielectric increases the maximum possible potential difference between the capacitor plates. As we described in Section 23.3, any insulating material, when subjected to a sufficiently large electric field, experiences a partial ionization that permits conduction through it. This is called **dielectric breakdown.** Many dielectric materials can tolerate stronger electric fields without breakdown than can air. Thus using a dielectric allows a capacitor to sustain a higher potential difference V and so store greater amounts of charge and energy.

Third, the capacitance of a capacitor of given dimensions is *greater* when there is a dielectric material between the plates than when there is vacuum. We can demonstrate this effect with the aid of a sensitive *electrometer,* a device that measures the potential difference between two conductors without letting any appreciable charge flow from one to the other. Figure 24.14a shows an electrometer connected across a charged capacitor, with magnitude of charge Q on each plate and potential difference V_0. When we insert an uncharged sheet of dielectric, such as glass, paraffin, or polystyrene, between the plates, experiment shows that the potential difference *decreases* to a smaller value V (Fig. 24.14b). When we remove the dielectric, the potential difference returns to its original value V_0, showing that the original charges on the plates have not changed.

The original capacitance C_0 is given by $C_0 = Q/V_0$, and the capacitance C with the dielectric present is $C = Q/V$. The charge Q is the same in both cases, and V is less than V_0, so we conclude that the capacitance C with the dielectric present is *greater* than C_0. When the space between plates is completely filled by the dielectric, the ratio of C to C_0 (equal to the ratio of V_0 to V) is called the **dielectric constant** of the material, K:

$$K = \frac{C}{C_0} \qquad \text{(definition of dielectric constant)} \qquad (24.12)$$

When the charge is constant, $Q = C_0 V_0 = CV$ and $C/C_0 = V_0/V$. In this case, Eq. (24.12) can be rewritten as

$$V = \frac{V_0}{K} \qquad \text{(when } Q \text{ is constant)} \qquad (24.13)$$

With the dielectric present, the potential difference for a given charge Q is *reduced* by a factor K.

The dielectric constant K is a pure number. Because C is always greater than C_0, K is always greater than unity. Some representative values of K are given in Table 24.1. For vacuum, $K = 1$ by definition. For air at ordinary temperatures and pressures, K is about 1.0006; this is so nearly equal to 1 that for most purposes an air capacitor is equivalent to one in vacuum. Note that while water has a very large value of K, it is usually not a very practical dielectric for use in capacitors. The reason is that while pure water is a very poor conductor, it is also an excellent ionic solvent. Any ions that are dissolved in the water will cause charge to flow between the capacitor plates, so the capacitor discharges.

Table 24.1 Values of Dielectric Constant K at 20°C

Material	K	Material	K
Vacuum	1	Polyvinyl chloride	3.18
Air (1 atm)	1.00059	Plexiglas	3.40
Air (100 atm)	1.0548	Glass	5–10
Teflon	2.1	Neoprene	6.70
Polyethylene	2.25	Germanium	16
Benzene	2.28	Glycerin	42.5
Mica	3–6	Water	80.4
Mylar	3.1	Strontium titanate	310

No real dielectric is a perfect insulator. Hence there is always some *leakage current* between the charged plates of a capacitor with a dielectric. We tacitly ignored this effect in Section 24.2 when we derived expressions for the equivalent capacitances of capacitors in series, Eq. (24.5), and in parallel, Eq. (24.7). But if a leakage current flows for a long enough time to substantially change the charges from the values we used to derive Eqs. (24.5) and (24.7), those equations may no longer be accurate.

Induced Charge and Polarization

When a dielectric material is inserted between the plates while the charge is kept constant, the potential difference between the plates decreases by a factor K. Therefore the electric field between the plates must decrease by the same factor. If E_0 is the vacuum value and E is the value with the dielectric, then

$$E = \frac{E_0}{K} \qquad \text{(when } Q \text{ is constant)} \qquad (24.14)$$

Since the electric-field magnitude is smaller when the dielectric is present, the surface charge density (which causes the field) must be smaller as well. The surface charge on the conducting plates does not change, but an *induced* charge of the opposite sign appears on each surface of the dielectric (Fig. 24.15). The dielectric was originally electrically neutral and is still neutral; the induced surface charges arise as a result of *redistribution* of positive and negative charge within the dielectric material, a phenomenon called **polarization.** We first encountered polarization in Section 21.2, and we suggest that you reread the discussion of Fig. 21.8. We will assume that the induced surface charge is *directly proportional* to the electric-field magnitude E in the material; this is indeed the case for many common dielectrics. (This direct proportionality is analogous to

24.14 Effect of a dielectric between the plates of a parallel-plate capacitor. **(a)** With a given charge, the potential difference is V_0. **(b)** With the same charge but with a dielectric between the plates, the potential difference V is smaller than V_0.

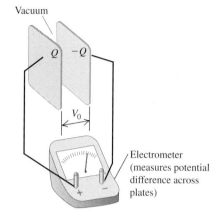

24.15 Electric field lines with **(a)** vacuum between the plates and **(b)** dielectric between the plates.

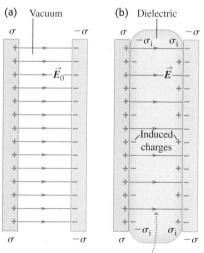

For a given charge density σ, the induced charges on the dielectric's surfaces reduce the electric field between the plates.

Hooke's law for a spring.) In that case, K is a constant for any particular material. When the electric field is very strong or if the dielectric is made of certain crystalline materials, the relationship between induced charge and the electric field can be more complex; we won't consider such cases here.

We can derive a relationship between this induced surface charge and the charge on the plates. Let's denote the magnitude of the charge per unit area induced on the surfaces of the dielectric (the induced surface charge density) by σ_i. The magnitude of the surface charge density on the capacitor plates is σ, as usual. Then the *net* surface charge on each side of the capacitor has magnitude $(\sigma - \sigma_i)$, as shown in Fig. 24.15b. As we found in Example 21.13 (Section 21.5) and in Example 22.8 (Section 22.4), the field between the plates is related to the net surface charge density by $E = \sigma_{net}/\epsilon_0$. Without and with the dielectric, respectively, we have

$$E_0 = \frac{\sigma}{\epsilon_0} \qquad E = \frac{\sigma - \sigma_i}{\epsilon_0} \tag{24.15}$$

Using these expressions in Eq. (24.14) and rearranging the result, we find

$$\sigma_i = \sigma\left(1 - \frac{1}{K}\right) \qquad \text{(induced surface charge density)} \tag{24.16}$$

This equation shows that when K is very large, σ_i is nearly as large as σ. In this case, σ_i nearly cancels σ, and the field and potential difference are much smaller than their values in vacuum.

The product $K\epsilon_0$ is called the **permittivity** of the dielectric, denoted by ϵ:

$$\epsilon = K\epsilon_0 \qquad \text{(definition of permittivity)} \tag{24.17}$$

In terms of ϵ we can express the electric field within the dielectric as

$$E = \frac{\sigma}{\epsilon} \tag{24.18}$$

The capacitance when the dielectric is present is given by

$$C = KC_0 = K\epsilon_0\frac{A}{d} = \epsilon\frac{A}{d} \qquad \begin{array}{l}\text{(parallel-plate capacitor,}\\ \text{dielectric between plates)}\end{array} \tag{24.19}$$

We can repeat the derivation of Eq. (24.11) for the energy density u in an electric field for the case in which a dielectric is present. The result is

$$u = \frac{1}{2}K\epsilon_0E^2 = \frac{1}{2}\epsilon E^2 \qquad \text{(electric energy density in a dielectric)} \tag{24.20}$$

In empty space, where $K = 1$, $\epsilon = \epsilon_0$ and Eqs. (24.19) and (24.20) reduce to Eqs. (24.2) and (24.11), respectively, for a parallel-plate capacitor in vacuum. For this reason, ϵ_0 is sometimes called the "permittivity of free space" or the "permittivity of vacuum." Because K is a pure number, ϵ and ϵ_0 have the same units, $C^2/N \cdot m^2$ or F/m.

Equation (24.19) shows that extremely high capacitances can be obtained with plates that have a large surface area A and are separated by a small distance d by a dielectric with a large value of K. In an *electrolytic double-layer capacitor,* tiny carbon granules adhere to each plate: The value of A is the combined surface area of the granules, which can be tremendous. The plates with granules attached are separated by a very thin dielectric sheet. A capacitor of this kind can have a capacitance of 5000 farads yet fit in the palm of your hand (compare Example 24.1 in Section 24.1).

Several practical devices make use of the way in which a capacitor responds to a change in dielectric constant. One example is an electric stud finder, used by home repair workers to locate metal studs hidden behind a wall's surface. It consists of a metal plate with associated circuitry. The plate acts as one half of a capacitor, with the wall acting as the other half. If the stud finder moves over a metal stud, the effective dielectric constant for the capacitor changes, changing the capacitance and triggering a signal.

Problem-Solving Strategy 24.2   Dielectrics

IDENTIFY *the relevant concepts:* The relationships in this section are useful whenever there is an electric field in a dielectric, such as a dielectric between charged capacitor plates. Typically you will be asked to relate the potential difference between the plates, the electric field in the capacitor, the charge density on the capacitor plates, and the induced charge density on the surfaces of the capacitor.

SET UP *the problem* using the following steps:
1. Make a drawing of the situation.
2. Identify the target variables, and choose which of the key equations of this section will help you find those variables.

EXECUTE *the solution* as follows:
1. In problems such as the next example, it is easy to get lost in a blizzard of formulas. Ask yourself at each step what kind of quantity each symbol represents. For example, distinguish

clearly between charges and charge densities, and between electric fields and electric potential differences.
2. As you calculate, continually check for consistency of units. This effort is a bit more complex with electrical quantities than it was in mechanics. Distances must always be in meters. Remember that a microfarad is 10^{-6} farad, and so on. Don't confuse the numerical value of ϵ_0 with the value of $1/4\pi\epsilon_0$. There are several alternative sets of units for electric-field magnitude, including N/C and V/m. The units of ϵ_0 are $C^2/N \cdot m^2$ or F/m.

EVALUATE *your answer:* When you check numerical values, remember that with a dielectric present, (a) the capacitance is always greater than without a dielectric; (b) for a given amount of charge on the capacitor, the electric field and potential difference are less than without a dielectric; and (c) the induced surface charge density σ_i on the dielectric is always less in magnitude than the charge density σ on the capacitor plates.

Example 24.10   A capacitor with and without a dielectric

Suppose the parallel plates in Fig. 24.15 each have an area of 2000 cm² (2.00×10^{-1} m²) and are 1.00 cm (1.00×10^{-2} m) apart. The capacitor is connected to a power supply and charged to a potential difference $V_0 = 3000$ V $= 3.00$ kV. It is then disconnected from the power supply, and a sheet of insulating plastic material is inserted between the plates, completely filling the space between them. We find that the potential difference decreases to 1000 V while the charge on each capacitor plate remains constant. Compute (a) the original capacitance C_0; (b) the magnitude of charge Q on each plate; (c) the capacitance C after the dielectric is inserted; (d) the dielectric constant K of the dielectric; (e) the permittivity ϵ of the dielectric; (f) the magnitude of the induced charge Q_i on each face of the dielectric; (g) the original electric field E_0 between the plates; and (h) the electric field E after the dielectric is inserted.

SOLUTION

IDENTIFY: This problem uses most of the relationships we have discussed for capacitors and dielectrics.

SET UP: Most of the target variables can be obtained in several different ways. The methods used below are a representative sample; we encourage you to think of others and compare your results.

EXECUTE: (a) With vacuum between the plates, we use Eq. (24.19) with $K = 1$:

$$C_0 = \epsilon_0 \frac{A}{d} = (8.85 \times 10^{-12}\ \text{F/m}) \frac{2.00 \times 10^{-1}\ \text{m}^2}{1.00 \times 10^{-2}\ \text{m}}$$

$$= 1.77 \times 10^{-10}\ \text{F} = 177\ \text{pF}$$

(b) Using the definition of capacitance, Eq. (24.1),

$$Q = C_0 V_0 = (1.77 \times 10^{-10}\ \text{F})(3.00 \times 10^3\ \text{V})$$

$$= 5.31 \times 10^{-7}\ \text{C} = 0.531\ \mu\text{C}$$

(c) When the dielectric is inserted, the charge remains the same but the potential decreases to $V = 1000$ V. Hence from Eq. (24.1), the new capacitance is

$$C = \frac{Q}{V} = \frac{5.31 \times 10^{-7}\ \text{C}}{1.00 \times 10^3\ \text{V}} = 5.31 \times 10^{-10}\ \text{F} = 531\ \text{pF}$$

(d) From Eq. (24.12), the dielectric constant is

$$K = \frac{C}{C_0} = \frac{5.31 \times 10^{-10}\ \text{F}}{1.77 \times 10^{-10}\ \text{F}} = \frac{531\ \text{pF}}{177\ \text{pF}} = 3.00$$

Alternatively, from Eq. (24.13),

$$K = \frac{V_0}{V} = \frac{3000\ \text{V}}{1000\ \text{V}} = 3.00$$

(e) Using K from part (d) in Eq. (24.17), the permittivity is

$$\epsilon = K\epsilon_0 = (3.00)(8.85 \times 10^{-12}\ \text{C}^2/\text{N} \cdot \text{m}^2)$$

$$= 2.66 \times 10^{-11}\ \text{C}^2/\text{N} \cdot \text{m}^2$$

(f) Multiplying Eq. (24.15) by the area of each plate gives the induced charge $Q_i = \sigma_i A$ in terms of the charge $Q = \sigma A$ on each plate:

$$Q_i = Q\left(1 - \frac{1}{K}\right) = (5.31 \times 10^{-7}\ \text{C})\left(1 - \frac{1}{3.00}\right)$$

$$= 3.54 \times 10^{-7}\ \text{C}$$

Continued

(g) Since the electric field between the plates is uniform, its magnitude is the potential difference divided by the plate separation:

$$E_0 = \frac{V_0}{d} = \frac{3000 \text{ V}}{1.00 \times 10^{-2} \text{ m}} = 3.00 \times 10^5 \text{ V/m}$$

(h) With the new potential difference after the dielectric is inserted,

$$E = \frac{V}{d} = \frac{1000 \text{ V}}{1.00 \times 10^{-2} \text{ m}} = 1.00 \times 10^5 \text{ V/m}$$

or, from Eq. (24.17),

$$E = \frac{\sigma}{\epsilon} = \frac{Q}{\epsilon A} = \frac{5.31 \times 10^{-7} \text{ C}}{(2.66 \times 10^{-11} \text{ C}^2/\text{N} \cdot \text{m}^2)(2.00 \times 10^{-1} \text{ m}^2)}$$

$$= 1.00 \times 10^5 \text{ V/m}$$

or, from Eq. (24.15),

$$E = \frac{\sigma - \sigma_i}{\epsilon_0} = \frac{Q - Q_i}{\epsilon_0 A}$$

$$= \frac{(5.31 - 3.54) \times 10^{-7} \text{ C}}{(8.85 \times 10^{-12} \text{ C}^2/\text{N} \cdot \text{m}^2)(2.00 \times 10^{-1} \text{ m}^2)}$$

$$= 1.00 \times 10^5 \text{ V/m}$$

or, from Eq. (24.14),

$$E = \frac{E_0}{K} = \frac{3.00 \times 10^5 \text{ V/m}}{3.00} = 1.00 \times 10^5 \text{ V/m}$$

EVALUATE: It's always useful to check the results by finding them in more than one way, as we did in parts (d) and (h). Our results show that inserting the dielectric increased the capacitance by a factor of $K = 3.00$ and reduced the electric field between the plates by a factor of $1/K = 1/3.00$. It did so by developing induced charges on the faces of the dielectric of magnitude $Q(1 - 1/K) = Q(1 - 1/3.00) = 0.667Q$.

Example 24.11 Energy storage with and without a dielectric

Find the total energy stored in the electric field of the capacitor in Example 24.10 and the energy density, both before and after the dielectric sheet is inserted.

SOLUTION

IDENTIFY: In this problem we have to extend the analysis of Example 24.10 to include the ideas of energy stored in a capacitor and electric-field energy.

SET UP: We use Eq. (24.9) to find the stored energy before and after the dielectric is inserted, and Eq. (24.20) to find the energy density.

EXECUTE: Let the original energy be U_0 and let the energy with the dielectric in place be U. From Eq. (24.9),

$$U_0 = \frac{1}{2}C_0 V_0^2 = \frac{1}{2}(1.77 \times 10^{-10} \text{ F})(3000 \text{ V})^2 = 7.97 \times 10^{-4} \text{ J}$$

$$U = \frac{1}{2}CV^2 = \frac{1}{2}(5.31 \times 10^{-10} \text{ F})(1000 \text{ V})^2 = 2.66 \times 10^{-4} \text{ J}$$

The final energy is one-third of the original energy.

The energy density without the dielectric is given by Eq. (24.20) with $K = 1$:

$$u_0 = \frac{1}{2}\epsilon_0 E_0^2 = \frac{1}{2}(8.85 \times 10^{-12} \text{ C}^2/\text{N} \cdot \text{m}^2)(3.0 \times 10^5 \text{ N/C})^2$$

$$= 0.398 \text{ J/m}^3$$

With the dielectric in place,

$$u = \frac{1}{2}\epsilon E^2 = \frac{1}{2}(2.66 \times 10^{-11} \text{ C}^2/\text{N} \cdot \text{m}^2)(1.00 \times 10^5 \text{ N/C})^2$$

$$= 0.133 \text{ J/m}^3$$

The energy density with the dielectric is one-third of the original energy density.

EVALUATE: We can check our answer for u_0 by noting that the volume between the plates is $V = (0.200 \text{ m})^2(0.0100 \text{ m}) = 0.00200 \text{ m}^3$. Since the electric field is uniform between the plates, u_0 is uniform as well and the energy density is just the stored energy divided by the volume:

$$u_0 = \frac{U_0}{V} = \frac{7.97 \times 10^{-4} \text{ J}}{0.00200 \text{ m}^3} = 0.398 \text{ J/m}^3$$

which agrees with our earlier answer. You should use the same approach to check the value for U, the energy density with the dielectric.

We can generalize the results of this example. When a dielectric is inserted into a capacitor while the charge on each plate remains the same, the permittivity ϵ increases by a factor of K (the dielectric constant), the electric field decreases by a factor of $1/K$, and the energy density $u = \frac{1}{2}\epsilon E^2$ decreases by a factor of $1/K$. Where did the energy go? The answer lies in the fringing field at the edges of a real parallel-plate capacitor. As Fig. 24.16 shows, that field tends to pull the dielectric into the space between the plates, doing work on it as it does so. We could attach a spring to the left end of the dielectric in Fig. 24.16 and use this force to stretch the spring. Because work is done by the field, the field energy density decreases.

24.16 The fringing field at the edges of the capacitor exerts forces $\vec{F}_{-i}$ and $\vec{F}_{+i}$ on the negative and positive induced surface charges of a dielectric, pulling the dielectric into the capacitor.

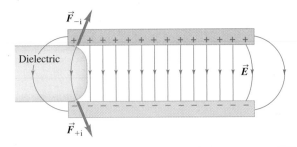

Dielectric Breakdown

We mentioned earlier that when any dielectric material is subjected to a sufficiently strong electric field, *dielectric breakdown* takes place and the dielectric becomes a conductor (Fig. 24.17). This occurs when the electric field is so strong that electrons are ripped loose from their molecules and crash into other molecules, liberating even more electrons. This avalanche of moving charge, forming a spark or arc discharge, often starts quite suddenly.

Because of dielectric breakdown, capacitors always have maximum voltage ratings. When a capacitor is subjected to excessive voltage, an arc may form through a layer of dielectric, burning or melting a hole in it. This arc creates a conducting path (a short circuit) between the conductors. If a conducting path remains after the arc is extinguished, the device is rendered permanently useless as a capacitor.

The maximum electric-field magnitude that a material can withstand without the occurrence of breakdown is called its **dielectric strength.** This quantity is affected significantly by temperature, trace impurities, small irregularities in the metal electrodes, and other factors that are difficult to control. For this reason we can give only approximate figures for dielectric strengths. The dielectric strength of dry air is about 3×10^6 V/m. Values of dielectric strength for a few common insulating materials are shown in Table 24.2. Note that the values are all substantially greater than the value for air. For example, a layer of polycarbonate 0.01 mm thick (about the smallest practical thickness) has 10 times the dielectric strength of air and can withstand a maximum voltage of about $(3 \times 10^7 \text{ V/m})(1 \times 10^{-5} \text{ m}) = 300$ V.

24.17 A very strong electric field caused dielectric breakdown in a block of Plexiglas. The resulting flow of charge etched this pattern into the block.

Table 24.2 Dielectric Constant and Dielectric Strength of Some Insulating Materials

Material	Dielectric Constant, K	Dielectric Strength, E_m (V/m)
Polycarbonate	2.8	3×10^7
Polyester	3.3	6×10^7
Polypropylene	2.2	7×10^7
Polystyrene	2.6	2×10^7
Pyrex glass	4.7	1×10^7

Test Your Understanding of Section 24.4 The space between the plates of an isolated parallel-plate capacitor is filled by a slab of dielectric with dielectric constant K. The two plates of the capacitor have charges Q and $-Q$. You pull out the dielectric slab. If the charges do not change, how does the energy in the capacitor change when you remove the slab? (i) It increases; (ii) it decreases; (iii) it remains the same.

*24.5 Molecular Model of Induced Charge

In Section 24.4 we discussed induced surface charges on a dielectric in an electric field. Now let's look at how these surface charges can arise. If the material were a *conductor,* the answer would be simple. Conductors contain charge that is free to move, and when an electric field is present, some of the charge redistributes itself on the surface so that there is no electric field inside the conductor. But an ideal dielectric has *no* charges that are free to move, so how can a surface charge occur?

To understand this, we have to look again at rearrangement of charge at the *molecular* level. Some molecules, such as H_2O and N_2O, have equal amounts of positive and negative charges but a lopsided distribution, with excess positive charge concentrated on one side of the molecule and negative charge on the other. As we described in Section 21.7, such an arrangement is called an *electric dipole,* and the molecule is called a *polar molecule.* When no electric field is present in a gas or liquid with polar molecules, the molecules are oriented randomly (Fig. 24.18a). When they are placed in an electric field, however, they tend

24.18 Polar molecules **(a)** without and **(b)** with an applied electric field $\vec{E}$.

(a)

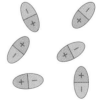

In the absence of an electric field, polar molecules orient randomly.

(b)

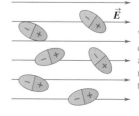

When an electric field is applied, the molecules tend to align with it.

24.19 Nonpolar molecules **(a)** without and **(b)** with an applied electric field $\vec{E}$.

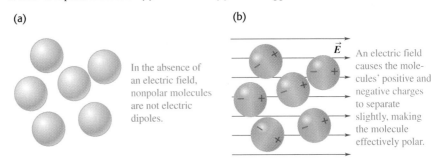

(a)

In the absence of an electric field, nonpolar molecules are not electric dipoles.

(b)

An electric field causes the molecules' positive and negative charges to separate slightly, making the molecule effectively polar.

to orient themselves as in Fig. 24.18b, as a result of the electric-field torques described in Section 21.7. Because of thermal agitation, the alignment of the molecules with $\vec{E}$ is not perfect.

Even a molecule that is *not* ordinarily polar *becomes* a dipole when it is placed in an electric field because the field pushes the positive charges in the molecules in the direction of the field and pushes the negative charges in the opposite direction. This causes a redistribution of charge within the molecule (Fig. 24.19). Such dipoles are called *induced* dipoles.

With either polar or nonpolar molecules, the redistribution of charge caused by the field leads to the formation of a layer of charge on each surface of the dielectric material (Fig. 24.20). These layers are the surface charges described in Section 24.4; their surface charge density is denoted by σ_i. The charges are *not* free to move indefinitely, as they would be in a conductor, because each charge is bound to a molecule. They are in fact called **bound charges** to distinguish them from the **free charges** that are added to and removed from the conducting capacitor plates. In the interior of the material the net charge per unit volume remains zero. As we have seen, this redistribution of charge is called *polarization*, and we say that the material is *polarized*.

The four parts of Fig. 24.21 show the behavior of a slab of dielectric when it is inserted in the field between a pair of oppositely charged capacitor plates. Figure 24.21a shows the original field. Figure 24.21b is the situation after the dielectric has been inserted but before any rearrangement of charges has occurred.

24.20 Polarization of a dielectric in an electric field $\vec{E}$ gives rise to thin layers of bound charges on the surfaces, creating surface charge densities σ_i and $-\sigma_i$. The sizes of the molecules are greatly exaggerated for clarity.

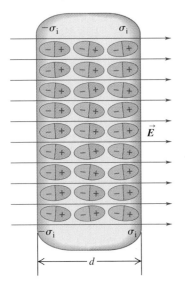

24.21 **(a)** Electric field of magnitude E_0 between two charged plates. **(b)** Introduction of a dielectric of dielectric constant K. **(c)** The induced surface charges and their field. **(d)** Resultant field of magnitude E_0/K.

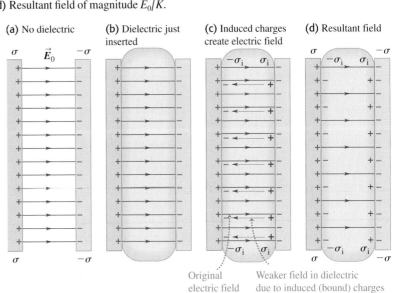

(a) No dielectric

(b) Dielectric just inserted

(c) Induced charges create electric field

(d) Resultant field

Original electric field

Weaker field in dielectric due to induced (bound) charges

Figure 24.21c shows by thinner arrows the additional field set up in the dielectric by its induced surface charges. This field is *opposite* to the original field, but it is not great enough to cancel the original field completely because the charges in the dielectric are not free to move indefinitely. The resultant field in the dielectric, shown in Fig. 24.21d, is therefore decreased in magnitude. In the field-line representation, some of the field lines leaving the positive plate go through the dielectric, while others terminate on the induced charges on the faces of the dielectric.

As we discussed in Section 21.2, polarization is also the reason a charged body, such as an electrified plastic rod, can exert a force on an *uncharged* body such as a bit of paper or a pith ball. Figure 24.22 shows an uncharged dielectric sphere B in the radial field of a positively charged body A. The induced positive charges on B experience a force toward the right, while the force on the induced negative charges is toward the left. The negative charges are closer to A, and thus are in a stronger field, than are the positive charges. The force toward the left is stronger than that toward the right, and B is attracted toward A, even though its net charge is zero. The attraction occurs whether the sign of A's charge is positive or negative (see Fig. 21.8). Furthermore, the effect is not limited to dielectrics; an uncharged conducting body would be attracted in the same way.

24.22 A neutral sphere B in the radial electric field of a positively charged sphere A is attracted to the charge because of polarization.

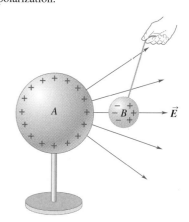

Test Your Understanding of Section 24.5   A parallel-plate capacitor has charges Q and $-Q$ on its two plates. A dielectric slab with $K = 3$ is then inserted into the space between the plates as shown in Fig. 24.21. Rank the following electric-field magnitudes in order from largest to smallest. (i) the field before the slab is inserted; (ii) the resultant field after the slab is inserted; (iii) the field due to the bound charges.

*24.6 Gauss's Law in Dielectrics

We can extend the analysis of Section 24.4 to reformulate Gauss's law in a form that is particularly useful for dielectrics. Figure 24.23 is a close-up view of the left capacitor plate and left surface of the dielectric in Fig. 24.15b. Let's apply Gauss's law to the rectangular box shown in cross section by the purple line; the surface area of the left and right sides is A. The left side is embedded in the conductor that forms the left capacitor plate, and so the electric field everywhere on that surface is zero. The right side is embedded in the dielectric, where the electric field has magnitude E, and $E_\perp = 0$ everywhere on the other four sides. The total charge enclosed, including both the charge on the capacitor plate and the induced charge on the dielectric surface, is $Q_{encl} = (\sigma - \sigma_i)A$, so Gauss's law gives

$$EA = \frac{(\sigma - \sigma_i)A}{\epsilon_0} \qquad (24.21)$$

This equation is not very illuminating as it stands because it relates two unknown quantities: E inside the dielectric and the induced surface charge density σ_i. But now we can use Eq. (24.16), developed for this same situation, to simplify this equation by eliminating σ_i. Equation (24.16) is

$$\sigma_i = \sigma\left(1 - \frac{1}{K}\right) \quad \text{or} \quad \sigma - \sigma_i = \frac{\sigma}{K}$$

Combining this with Eq. (24.21), we get

$$EA = \frac{\sigma A}{K\epsilon_0} \quad \text{or} \quad KEA = \frac{\sigma A}{\epsilon_0} \qquad (24.22)$$

Equation (24.22) says that the flux of $K\vec{E}$, not $\vec{E}$, through the Gaussian surface in Fig. 24.23 is equal to the enclosed *free* charge σA divided by ϵ_0. It turns out

24.23 Gauss's law with a dielectric. This figure shows a close-up of the left-hand capacitor plate in Fig. 24.15b. The Gaussian surface is a rectangular box that lies half in the conductor and half in the dielectric.

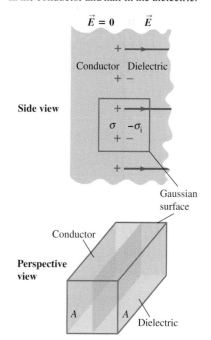

that for *any* Gaussian surface, whenever the induced charge is proportional to the electric field in the material, we can rewrite Gauss's law as

$$\oint K\vec{E} \cdot d\vec{A} = \frac{Q_{\text{encl-free}}}{\epsilon_0} \qquad \text{(Gauss's law in a dielectric)} \qquad (24.23)$$

where $Q_{\text{encl-free}}$ is the total *free* charge (not bound charge) enclosed by the Gaussian surface. The significance of these results is that the right sides contain only the *free* charge on the conductor, not the bound (induced) charge. In fact, although we have not proved it, Eq. (24.23) remains valid even when different parts of the Gaussian surface are embedded in dielectrics having different values of K, provided that the value of K in each dielectric is independent of the electric field (usually the case for electric fields that are not too strong) and that we use the appropriate value of K for each point on the Gaussian surface.

Example 24.12 A spherical capacitor with dielectric

In the spherical capacitor of Example 24.3 (Section 24.1), the volume between the concentric spherical conducting shells is filled with an insulating oil with dielectric constant K. Use Gauss's law to find the capacitance.

SOLUTION

IDENTIFY: This is essentially the same problem as Example 24.3. The only difference is the presence of the dielectric.

SET UP: As we did in Example 24.3, we use a spherical Gaussian surface of radius r between the two spheres. Since a dielectric is present, we use Gauss's law in the form of Eq. (24.23).

EXECUTE: The spherical symmetry of the problem is not changed by the presence of the dielectric, so we have

$$\oint K\vec{E} \cdot d\vec{A} = \oint KE\, dA = KE \oint dA = (KE)(4\pi r^2) = \frac{Q}{\epsilon_0}$$

$$E = \frac{Q}{4\pi K\epsilon_0 r^2} = \frac{Q}{4\pi\epsilon r^2}$$

where $\epsilon = K\epsilon_0$ is the permittivity of the dielectric (introduced in Section 24.4). Compared to the case in which there is vacuum between the conducting shells, the electric field is reduced by a factor of $1/K$. The potential difference V_{ab} between the shells is likewise reduced by a factor of $1/K$, and so the capacitance $C = Q/V_{ab}$ is *increased* by a factor of K, just as for a parallel-plate capacitor when a dielectric is inserted. Using the result for the vacuum case in Example 24.3, we find that the capacitance with the dielectric is

$$C = \frac{4\pi K\epsilon_0 r_a r_b}{r_b - r_a} = \frac{4\pi\epsilon r_a r_b}{r_b - r_a}$$

EVALUATE: In this case the dielectric completely fills the volume between the two conductors, so the capacitance is just K times the value with no dielectric. The result is more complicated if the dielectric only partially fills this volume (see Challenge Problem 24.76).

Test Your Understanding of Section 24.6 A single point charge q is imbedded in a dielectric of dielectric constant K. At a point inside the dielectric a distance r from the point charge, what is the magnitude of the electric field? (i) $q/4\pi\epsilon_0 r^2$; (ii) $Kq/4\pi\epsilon_0 r^2$; (iii) $q/4\pi K\epsilon_0 r^2$; (iv) none of these.

Capacitors and capacitance: A capacitor is any pair of conductors separated by an insulating material. When the capacitor is charged, there are charges of equal magnitude Q and opposite sign on the two conductors, and the potential V_{ab} of the positively charged conductor with respect to the negatively charged conductor is proportional to Q. The capacitance C is defined as the ratio of Q to V_{ab}. The SI unit of capacitance is the farad (F): $1\,\text{F} = 1\,\text{C}/\text{V}$.

A parallel-plate capacitor consists of two parallel conducting plates, each with area A, separated by a distance d. If they are separated by vacuum, the capacitance depends only on A and d. For other geometries, the capacitance can be found by using the definition $C = Q/V_{ab}$. (See Examples 24.1–24.4.)

$$C = \frac{Q}{V_{ab}} \qquad (24.1)$$

$$C = \frac{Q}{V_{ab}} = \epsilon_0 \frac{A}{d} \qquad (24.2)$$

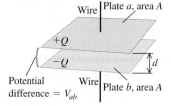

Capacitors in series and parallel: When capacitors with capacitances $C_1, C_2, C_3, \ldots$ are connected in series, the reciprocal of the equivalent capacitance C_{eq} equals the sum of the reciprocals of the individual capacitances. When capacitors are connected in parallel, the equivalent capacitance C_{eq} equals the sum of the individual capacitances. (See Examples 24.5 and 24.6.)

$$\frac{1}{C_{eq}} = \frac{1}{C_1} + \frac{1}{C_2} + \frac{1}{C_3} + \cdots \qquad (24.5)$$
(capacitors in series)

$$C_{eq} = C_1 + C_2 + C_3 + \cdots \qquad (24.7)$$
(capacitors in parallel)

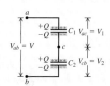

Energy in a capacitor: The energy U required to charge a capacitor C to a potential difference V and a charge Q is equal to the energy stored in the capacitor. This energy can be thought of as residing in the electric field between the conductors; the energy density u (energy per unit volume) is proportional to the square of the electric-field magnitude. (See Examples 24.7–24.9.)

$$U = \frac{Q^2}{2C} = \frac{1}{2}CV^2 = \frac{1}{2}QV \qquad (24.9)$$

$$u = \frac{1}{2}\epsilon_0 E^2 \qquad (24.11)$$

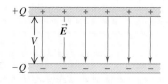

Dielectrics: When the space between the conductors is filled with a dielectric material, the capacitance increases by a factor K, called the dielectric constant of the material. The quantity $\epsilon = K\epsilon_0$ is called the permittivity of the dielectric. For a fixed amount of charge on the capacitor plates, induced charges on the surface of the dielectric decrease the electric field and potential difference between the plates by the same factor K. The surface charge results from polarization, a microscopic rearrangement of charge in the dielectric. (See Example 24.10.)

Under sufficiently strong fields, dielectrics become conductors, a situation called dielectric breakdown. The maximum field that a material can withstand without breakdown is called its dielectric strength.

In a dielectric, the expression for the energy density is the same as in vacuum but with ϵ_0 replaced by $\epsilon = K\epsilon$. (See Example 24.11.)

Gauss's law in a dielectric has almost the same form as in vacuum, with two key differences: $\vec{E}$ is replaced by $K\vec{E}$ and Q_{encl} is replaced by $Q_{encl\text{-}free}$, which includes only the free charge (not bound charge) enclosed by the Gaussian surface. (See Example 24.12.)

$$C = KC_0 = K\epsilon_0 \frac{A}{d} = \epsilon \frac{A}{d} \qquad (24.19)$$
(parallel-plate capacitor filled with dielectric)

$$u = \frac{1}{2}K\epsilon_0 E^2 = \frac{1}{2}\epsilon E^2 \qquad (24.20)$$

$$\oint K\vec{E} \cdot d\vec{A} = \frac{Q_{encl\text{-}free}}{\epsilon_0} \qquad (24.23)$$

Dielectric between plates

Key Terms

capacitor, *816*
capacitance, *816*
farad, *816*
parallel-plate capacitor, *817*
series connection, *820*
equivalent capacitance, *821*

parallel connection, *821*
energy density, *826*
dielectric, *828*
dielectric breakdown, *828*
dielectric constant, *828*
polarization, *829*

permittivity, *830*
dielectric strength, *833*
bound charge, *834*
free charge, *834*

Answer to Chapter Opening Question ?

Equation (24.9) shows that the energy stored in a capacitor with capacitance C and charge Q is $U = Q^2/2C$. If the charge Q is doubled, the stored energy increases by a factor of $2^2 = 4$. Note that if the value of Q is too great, the electric-field magnitude inside the capacitor will exceed the dielectric strength of the material between the plates and dielectric breakdown will occur (see Section 24.4). This puts a practical limit on the amount of energy that can be stored.

Answers to Test Your Understanding Questions

24.1 Answer: (iii) The capacitance does not depend on the value of the charge Q. Doubling the value of Q causes the potential difference V_{ab} to double, so the capacitance $C = Q/V_{ab}$ remains the same. These statements are true no matter what the geometry of the capacitor.

24.2 Answers: (a) (i), (b) (iv) In a series connection the two capacitors carry the same charge Q but have different potential differences $V_{ab} = Q/C$; the capacitor with the smaller capacitance C has the greater potential difference. In a parallel connection the two capacitors have the same potential difference V_{ab} but carry different charges $Q = CV_{ab}$; the capacitor with the larger capacitance C has the greater charge. Hence a 4-μF capacitor will have a greater potential difference than an 8-μF capacitor if the two are connected in series. The 4-μF capacitor cannot carry more charge than the 8-μF capacitor no matter how they are connected: In a series connection they will carry the same charge, and in a parallel connection the 8-μF capacitor will carry more charge.

24.3 Answer: (i) Capacitors connected in series carry the same charge Q. To compare the amount of energy stored, we use the expression $U = Q^2/2C$ from Eq. (24.9); it shows that the capacitor with the *smaller* capacitance ($C = 4 \,\mu$F) has more stored energy in a series combination. By contrast, capacitors in parallel have the same potential difference V, so to compare them we use $U = \frac{1}{2}CV^2$ from Eq. (24.9). It shows that in a parallel combination, the capacitor with the *larger* capacitance ($C = 8 \,\mu$F) has more stored energy. (If we had instead used $U = \frac{1}{2}CV^2$ to analyze the series combination, we would have to account for the different potential differences across the two capacitors. Likewise, using $U = Q^2/2C$ to study the parallel combination would require us to account for the different charges on the capacitors.)

24.4 Answers: (i) Here Q remains the same, so we use $U = Q^2/2C$ from Eq. (24.9) for the stored energy. Removing the dielectric lowers the capacitance by a factor of $1/K$; since U is inversely proportional to C, the stored energy *increases* by a factor of K. It takes work to pull the dielectric slab out of the capacitor because the fringing field tries to pull the slab back in (Fig. 24.16). The work that you do goes into the energy stored in the capacitor.

24.5 Answer: (i), (iii), (ii) Equation (24.14) says that if E_0 is the initial electric-field magnitude (before the dielectric slab is inserted), then the resultant field magnitude after the slab is inserted is $E_0/K = E_0/3$. The magnitude of the resultant field equals the difference between the initial field magnitude and the magnitude E_i of the field due to the bound charges (see Fig. 24.21). Hence $E_0 - E_i = E_0/3$ and $E_i = 2E_0/3$.

24.6 Answer: (iii) Equation (24.23) shows that this situation is the same as an isolated point charge in vacuum but with $\vec{E}$ replaced by $K\vec{E}$. Hence KE at the point of interest is equal to $q/4\pi\epsilon_0 r^2$, and so $E = q/4\pi K\epsilon_0 r^2$. As in Example 24.12, filling the space with a dielectric reduces the electric field by a factor of $1/K$.

PROBLEMS

For instructor-assigned homework, go to **www.masteringphysics.com**

Discussion Questions

Q24.1. Equation (24.2) shows that the capacitance of a parallel-plate capacitor becomes larger as the plate separation d decreases. However, there is a practical limit to how small d can be made, which places limits on how large C can be. Explain what sets the limit on d. (*Hint:* What happens to the magnitude of the electric field as $d \rightarrow 0$?)

Q24.2. Suppose several different parallel-plate capacitors are charged up by a constant-voltage source. Thinking of the actual movement and position of the charges on an atomic level, why does it make sense that the capacitances are proportional to the surface areas of the plates? Why does it make sense that the capacitances are *inversely* proportional to the distance between the plates?

Q24.3. Suppose the two plates of a capacitor have different areas. When the capacitor is charged by connecting it to a battery, do the charges on the two plates have equal magnitude, or may they be different? Explain your reasoning.

Q24.4. At the Fermi National Accelerator Laboratory (Fermilab) in Illinois, protons are accelerated around a ring 2 km in radius to speeds that approach that of light. The energy for this is stored in capacitors the size of a house. When these capacitors are being charged, they make a very loud creaking sound. What is the origin of this sound?

Q24.5. In the parallel-plate capacitor of Fig. 24.2, suppose the plates are pulled apart so that the separation d is much larger than the size of the plates. (a) Is it still accurate to say that the electric field between the plates is uniform? Why or why not? (b) In the situation shown in Fig. 24.2, the potential difference between the plates is $V_{ab} = Qd/\epsilon_0 A$. If the plates are pulled apart as described above, is V_{ab} more or less than this formula would indicate? Explain your reasoning. (c) With the plates pulled apart as described above, is the capacitance more than, less than, or the same as that given by Eq. (24.2)? Explain your reasoning.

Q24.6. A parallel-plate capacitor is charged by being connected to a battery and is kept connected to the battery. The separation between the plates is then doubled. How does the electric field change? The charge on the plates? The total energy? Explain your reasoning.

Q24.7. A parallel-plate capacitor is charged by being connected to a battery and is then disconnected from the battery. The separation between the plates is then doubled. How does the electric field change? The potential difference? The total energy? Explain your reasoning.

Q24.8. Two parallel-plate capacitors, identical except that one has twice the plate separation of the other, are charged by the same voltage source. Which capacitor has a stronger electric field between the plates? Which capacitor has a greater charge? Which has greater energy density? Explain your reasoning.

Q24.9. The charged plates of a capacitor attract each other, so to pull the plates farther apart requires work by some external force. What becomes of the energy added by this work? Explain your reasoning.

Q24.10. The two plates of a capacitor are given charges $\pm Q$. The capacitor is then disconnected from the charging device so that the charges on the plates can't change, and the capacitor is immersed in a tank of oil. Does the electric field between the plates increase, decrease, or stay the same? Explain your reasoning. How can this field be measured?

Q24.11. As shown in Table 24.1, water has a very large dielectric constant $K = 80.4$. Why do you think water is not commonly used as a dielectric in capacitors?

Q24.12. Is dielectric strength the same thing as dielectric constant? Explain any differences between the two quantities. Is there a simple relationship between dielectric strength and dielectric constant (see Table 24.2)?

Q24.13. A capacitor made of aluminum foil strips separated by Mylar film was subjected to excessive voltage, and the resulting dielectric breakdown melted holes in the Mylar. After this, the capacitance was found to be about the same as before, but the breakdown voltage was much less. Why?

Q24.14. Suppose you bring a slab of dielectric close to the gap between the plates of a charged capacitor, preparing to slide it between the plates. What force will you feel? What does this force tell you about the energy stored between the plates once the dielectric is in place, compared to before the dielectric is in place?

Q24.15. The freshness of fish can be measured by placing a fish between the plates of a capacitor and measuring the capacitance. How does this work? (*Hint:* As time passes, the fish dries out. See Table 24.1.)

Q24.16. *Electrolytic* capacitors use as their dielectric an extremely thin layer of nonconducting oxide between a metal plate and a conducting solution. Discuss the advantage of such a capacitor over one constructed using a solid dielectric between the metal plates.

Q24.17. In terms of the dielectric constant K, what happens to the electric flux through the Gaussian surface shown in Fig. 24.23 when the dielectric is inserted into the previously empty space between the plates? Explain.

Q24.18. A parallel-plate capacitor is connected to a power supply that maintains a fixed potential difference between the plates. (a) If a sheet of dielectric is then slid between the plates, what happens to (i) the electric field between the plates, (ii) the magnitude of charge on each plate, and (iii) the energy stored in the capacitor? (b) Now suppose that before the dielectric is inserted, the charged capacitor is disconnected from the power supply. In this case, what happens to (i) the electric field between the plates, (ii) the magnitude of charge on each plate, (iii) the energy stored in the capacitor? Explain any differences between the two situations.

Q24.19. Liquid dielectrics that have polar molecules (such as water) always have dielectric constants that decrease with increasing temperature. Why?

Q24.20. A conductor is an extreme case of a dielectric, since if an electric field is applied to a conductor, charges are free to move within the conductor to set up "induced charges." What is the dielectric constant of a perfect conductor? Is it $K = 0$, $K \to \infty$, or something in between? Explain your reasoning.

Exercises

Section 24.1 Capacitors and Capacitance

24.1. A capacitor has a capacitance of $7.28\ \mu F$. What amount of charge must be placed on each of its plates to make the potential difference between its plates equal to 25.0 V?

24.2. The plates of a parallel-plate capacitor are 3.28 mm apart, and each has an area of 12.2 cm^2. Each plate carries a charge of magnitude 4.35×10^{-8} C. The plates are in vacuum. (a) What is the capacitance? (b) What is the potential difference between the plates? (c) What is the magnitude of the electric field between the plates?

24.3. A parallel-plate air capacitor of capacitance 245 pF has a charge of magnitude $0.148\ \mu C$ on each plate. The plates are 0.328 mm apart. (a) What is the potential difference between the plates? (b) What is the area of each plate? (c) What is the electric-field magnitude between the plates? (d) What is the surface charge density on each plate?

24.4. Capacitance of an Oscilloscope. Oscilloscopes have parallel metal plates inside them to deflect the electron beam. These plates are called the *deflecting plates*. Typically, they are squares 3.0 cm on a side and separated by 5.0 mm, with vacuum in between. What is the capacitance of these deflecting plates and hence of the oscilloscope? (*Note:* This capacitance can sometimes have an effect on the circuit you are trying to study and must be taken into consideration in your calculations.)

24.5. A 10.0-μF parallel-plate capacitor with circular plates is connected to a 12.0-V battery. (a) What is the charge on each plate? (b) How much charge would be on the plates if their separation were doubled while the capacitor remained connected to the battery? (c) How much charge would be on the plates if the capacitor were connected to the 12.0-V battery after the radius of each plate was doubled without changing their separation?

24.6. A 10.0-μF parallel-plate capacitor is connected to a 12.0-V battery. After the capacitor is fully charged, the battery is disconnected without loss of any of the charge on the plates. (a) A voltmeter is connected across the two plates without discharging them. What does it read? (b) What would the voltmeter read if (i) the plate separation were doubled; (ii) the radius of each plate were doubled and, but their separation was unchanged?

24.7. How far apart would parallel pennies have to be to make a 1.00-pF capacitor? Does your answer suggest that you are justified in treating these pennies as infinite sheets? Explain.

24.8. A 5.00-pF, parallel-plate, air-filled capacitor with circular plates is to be used in a circuit in which it will be subjected to potentials of up to 1.00×10^2 V. The electric field between the plates is to be no greater than 1.00×10^4 N/C. As a budding electrical engineer for Live-Wire Electronics, your tasks are to (a) design the capacitor by finding what its physical dimensions and separation must be; (b) find the maximum charge these plates can hold.

24.9. A capacitor is made from two hollow, coaxial, iron cylinders, one inside the other. The inner cylinder is negatively charged and the outer is positively charged; the magnitude of the charge on each is 10.0 pC. The inner cylinder has radius 0.50 mm, the outer one has radius 5.00 mm, and the length of each cylinder is 18.0 cm. (a) What is the capacitance? (b) What applied potential difference is necessary to produce these charges on the cylinders?

24.10. A cylindrical capacitor consists of a solid inner conducting core with radius 0.250 cm, surrounded by an outer hollow conducting tube. The two conductors are separated by air, and the length of the cylinder is 12.0 cm. The capacitance is 36.7 pF. (a) Calculate the inner radius of the hollow tube. (b) When the capacitor is charged to 125 V, what is the charge per unit length λ on the capacitor?

24.11. A cylindrical capacitor has an inner conductor of radius 1.5 mm and an outer conductor of radius 3.5 mm. The two conductors are separated by vacuum, and the entire capacitor is 2.8 m long. (a) What is the capacitance per unit length? (b) The potential of the inner conductor is 350 mV higher than that of the outer conductor. Find the charge (magnitude and sign) on both conductors.

24.12. A spherical capacitor is formed from two concentric, spherical, conducting shells separated by vacuum. The inner sphere has radius 15.0 cm and the capacitance is 116 pF. (a) What is the radius of the outer sphere? (b) If the potential difference between the two spheres is 220 V, what is the magnitude of charge on each sphere?

24.13. A spherical capacitor contains a charge of 3.30 nC when connected to a potential difference of 220 V. If its plates are separated by vacuum and the inner radius of the outer shell is 4.00 cm, calculate: (a) the capacitance; (b) the radius of the inner sphere; (c) the electric field just outside the surface of the inner sphere.

Section 24.2 Capacitors in Series and Parallel

24.14. For the system of capacitors shown in Fig. 24.24, find the equivalent capacitance (a) between b and c, and (b) between a and c.

Figure **24.24** Exercise 24.14.

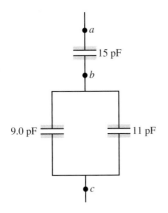

24.15. In Fig. 24.25, each capacitor has $C = 4.00 \,\mu$F and $V_{ab} = +28.0$ V. Calculate (a) the charge on each capacitor; (b) the potential difference across each capacitor; (c) the potential difference between points a and d.

24.16. In Fig. 24.8a, let $C_1 = 3.00 \,\mu$F, $C_2 = 5.00 \,\mu$F, and $V_{ab} = +52.0$ V. Calculate (a) the charge on each capacitor and (b) the potential difference across each capacitor.

Figure **24.25** Exercise 24.15.

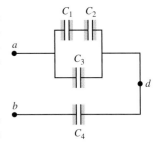

24.17. In Fig. 24.9a, let $C_1 = 3.00 \,\mu$F, $C_2 = 5.00 \,\mu$F, and $V_{ab} = +52.0$ V. Calculate (a) the charge on each capacitor and (b) the potential difference across each capacitor.

24.18. In Fig. 24.26, $C_1 = 6.00 \,\mu$F, $C_2 = 3.00 \,\mu$F, and $C_3 = 5.00 \,\mu$F. The capacitor network is connected to an applied potential V_{ab}. After the charges on the capacitors have reached their final values, the charge on C_2 is 40.0 μC. (a) What are the charges on capacitors C_1 and C_3? (b) What is the applied voltage V_{ab}?

Figure **24.26** Exercises 24.18 and 24.19.

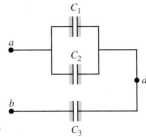

24.19. In Fig. 24.26, $C_1 = 3.00 \,\mu$F and $V_{ab} = 120$ V. The charge on capacitor C_1 is 150 μC. Calculate the voltage across the other two capacitors.

24.20. Two parallel-plate vacuum capacitors have plate spacings d_1 and d_2 and equal plate areas A. Show that when the capacitors are connected in series, the equivalent capacitance is the same as for a single capacitor with plate area A and spacing $d_1 + d_2$.

24.21. Two parallel-plate vacuum capacitors have areas A_1 and A_2 and equal plate spacings d. Show that when the capacitors are connected in parallel, the equivalent capacitance is the same as for a single capacitor with plate area $A_1 + A_2$ and spacing d.

24.22. Figure 24.27 shows a system of four capacitors, where the potential difference across ab is 50.0 V. (a) Find the equivalent capacitance of this system between a and b. (b) How much charge is stored by this combination of capacitors? (c) How much charge is stored in each of the 10.0-μF and the 9.0-μF capacitors?

Figure **24.27** Exercise 24.22.

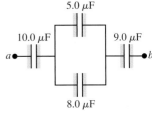

24.23. Suppose the 3-μF capacitor in Fig. 24.10a were removed and replaced by a different one, and that this changed the equivalent capacitance between points a and b to 8 μF. What would be the capacitance of the replacement capacitor?

Section 24.3 Energy Storage in Capacitors and Electric-Field Energy

24.24. A parallel-plate air capacitor has a capacitance of 920 pF. The charge on each plate is 2.55 μC. (a) What is the potential difference between the plates? (b) If the charge is kept constant, what will be the potential difference between the plates if the separation is doubled? (c) How much work is required to double the separation?

24.25. A 5.80-μF, parallel-plate, air capacitor has a plate separation of 5.00 mm and is charged to a potential difference of 400 V. Calculate the energy density in the region between the plates, in units of J/m^3.

24.26. An air capacitor is made from two flat parallel plates 1.50 mm apart. The magnitude of charge on each plate is 0.0180 μC when the potential difference is 200 V. (a) What is the capacitance? (b) What is the area of each plate? (c) What maximum voltage can be applied without dielectric breakdown? (Dielectric breakdown for air occurs at an electric-field strength of 3.0 × 10^6 V/m.) (d) When the charge is 0.0180 μC, what total energy is stored?

24.27. A 450-μF capacitor is charged to 295 V. Then a wire is connected between the plates. How many joules of thermal energy are produced as the capacitor discharges if all of the energy that was stored goes into heating the wire?

24.28. A capacitor of capacitance C is charged to a potential difference V_0. The terminals of the charged capacitor are then connected to those of an uncharged capacitor of capacitance $C/2$. Compute (a) the original charge of the system; (b) the final potential difference across each capacitor; (c) the final energy of the system; (d) the decrease in energy when the capacitors are connected. (e) Where did the "lost" energy go?

24.29. A parallel-plate vacuum capacitor with plate area A and separation x has charges $+Q$ and $-Q$ on its plates. The capacitor is disconnected from the source of charge, so the charge on each plate remains fixed. (a) What is the total energy stored in the capacitor? (b) The plates are pulled apart an additional distance dx. What is the change in the stored energy? (c) If F is the force with which the plates attract each other, then the change in the stored energy must equal the work $dW = Fdx$ done in pulling the plates apart. Find an expression for F. (d) Explain why F is *not* equal to QE, where E is the electric field between the plates.

24.30. A parallel-plate vacuum capacitor has 8.38 J of energy stored in it. The separation between the plates is 2.30 mm. If the separation is decreased to 1.15 mm, what is the energy stored (a) if the capacitor is disconnected from the potential source so the charge on the plates remains constant, and (b) if the capacitor remains connected to the potential source so the potential difference between the plates remains constant?

24.31. (a) How much charge does a battery have to supply to a 5.0-μF capacitor to create a potential difference of 1.5 V across its plates? How much energy is stored in the capacitor in this case? (b) How much charge would the battery have to supply to store 1.0 J of energy in the capacitor? What would be the potential across the capacitor in that case?

24.32. For the capacitor network shown in Fig. 24.28, the potential difference across ab is 36 V. Find (a) the total charge stored in this network; (b) the charge on each capacitor; (c) the total energy stored in the network; (d) the energy stored in each capacitor; (e) the potential differences across each capacitor.

Figure **24.28** Exercise 24.32.

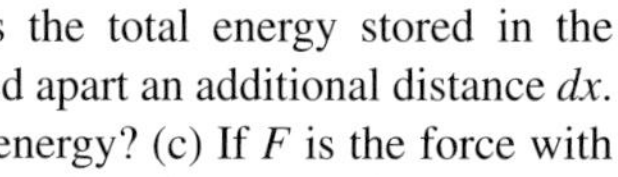

150 nF   120 nF

a ——||——||—— b

24.33. For the capacitor network shown in Fig. 24.29, the potential difference across ab is 220 V. Find (a) the total charge stored in this network; (b) the charge on each capacitor; (c) the total energy stored in the network; (d) the energy

Figure **24.29** Exercise 24.33

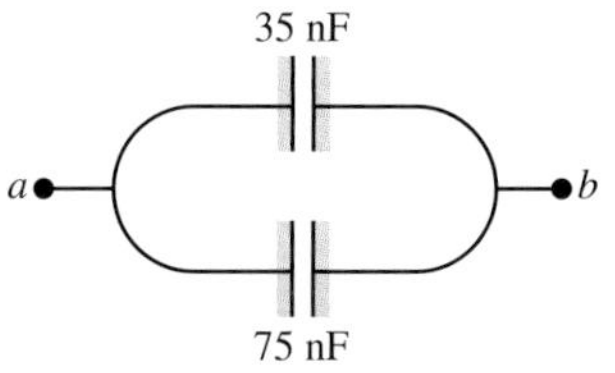

35 nF

a ——(||)—— b

75 nF

stored in each capacitor; (e) the potential difference across each capacitor.

24.34. A 0.350-m-long cylindrical capacitor consists of a solid conducting core with a radius of 1.20 mm and an outer hollow conducting tube with an inner radius of 2.00 mm. The two conductors are separated by air and charged to a potential difference of 6.00 V. Calculate (a) the charge per length for the capacitor; (b) the total charge on the capacitor; (c) the capacitance; (d) the energy stored in the capacitor when fully charged.

24.35. A cylindrical air capacitor of length 15.0 m stores 3.20 × 10^{-9} J of energy when the potential difference between the two conductors is 4.00 V. (a) Calculate the magnitude of the charge on each conductor. (b) Calculate the ratio of the radii of the inner and outer conductors.

24.36. A capacitor is formed from two concentric spherical conducting shells separated by vacuum. The inner sphere has radius 12.5 cm, and the outer sphere has radius 14.8 cm. A potential difference of 120 V is applied to the capacitor. (a) What is the energy density at $r = 12.6$ cm, just outside the inner sphere? (b) What is the energy density at $r = 14.7$ cm, just inside the outer sphere? (c) For a parallel-plate capacitor the energy density is uniform in the region between the plates, except near the edges of the plates. Is this also true for a spherical capacitor?

24.37. You have two identical capacitors and an external potential source. (a) Compare the total energy stored in the capacitors when they are connected to the applied potential in series and in parallel. (b) Compare the maximum amount of charge stored in each case. (c) Energy storage in a capacitor can be limited by the maximum electric field between the plates. What is the ratio of the electric field for the series and parallel combinations?

Section 24.4 Dielectrics

24.38. A parallel-plate capacitor has capacitance $C_0 = 5.00$ pF when there is air between the plates. The separation between the plates is 1.50 mm. (a) What is the maximum magnitude of charge Q that can be placed on each plate if the electric field in the region between the plates is not to exceed 3.00 × 10^4 V/m? (b) A dielectric with $K = 2.70$ is inserted between the plates of the capacitor, completely filling the volume between the plates. Now what is the maximum magnitude of charge on each plate if the electric field between the plates is not to exceed 3.00 × 10^4 V/m?

24.39. Two parallel plates have equal and opposite charges. When the space between the plates is evacuated, the electric field is $E = 3.20 × 10^5$ V/m. When the space is filled with dielectric, the electric field is $E = 2.50 × 10^5$ V/m. (a) What is the charge density on each surface of the dielectric? (b) What is the dielectric constant?

24.40. A budding electronics hobbyist wants to make a simple 1.0-nF capacitor for tuning her crystal radio, using two sheets of aluminum foil as plates, with a few sheets of paper between them as a dielectric. The paper has a dielectric constant of 3.0, and the thickness of one sheet of it is 0.20 mm. (a) If the sheets of paper measure 22 × 28 cm and she cuts the aluminum foil to the same dimensions, how many sheets of paper should she use between her plates to get the proper capacitance? (b) Suppose for convenience she wants to use a single sheet of posterboard, with the same dielectric constant but a thickness of 12.0 mm, instead of the paper. What area of aluminum foil will she need for her plates to get her 1.0 nF of capacitance? (c) Suppose she goes high-tech and finds a sheet of Teflon of the same thickness as the posterboard to use as a dielectric. Will she need a larger or smaller area of Teflon than of posterboard? Explain.

24.41. The dielectric to be used in a parallel-plate capacitor has a dielectric constant of 3.60 and a dielectric strength of 1.60×10^7 V/m. The capacitor is to have a capacitance of 1.25×10^{-9} F and must be able to withstand a maximum potential difference of 5500 V. What is the minimum area the plates of the capacitor may have?

24.42. Show that Eq. (24.20) holds for a parallel-plate capacitor with a dielectric material between the plates. Use a derivation analogous to that used for Eq. (24.11).

24.43. A capacitor has parallel plates of area 12 cm^2 separated by 2.0 mm. The space between the plates is filled with polystyrene (see Table 24.2). (a) Find the permittivity of polystyrene. (b) Find the maximum permissible voltage across the capacitor to avoid dielectric breakdown. (c) When the voltage equals the value found in part (b), find the surface charge density on each plate and the induced surface-charge density on the surface of the dielectric.

24.44. A constant potential difference of 12 V is maintained between the terminals of a 0.25-μF, parallel-plate, air capacitor. (a) A sheet of Mylar is inserted between the plates of the capacitor, completely filling the space between the plates. When this is done, how much additional charge flows onto the positive plate of the capacitor (see Table 24.1)? (b) What is the total induced charge on either face of the Mylar sheet? (c) What effect does the Mylar sheet have on the electric field between the plates? Explain how you can reconcile this with the increase in charge on the plates, which acts to *increase* the electric field.

24.45. When a 360-nF air capacitor $\left(1 \text{ nF} = 10^{-9} \text{ F}\right)$ is connected to a power supply, the energy stored in the capacitor is 1.85×10^{-5} J. While the capacitor is kept connected to the power supply, a slab of dielectric is inserted that completely fills the space between the plates. This increases the stored energy by 2.32×10^{-5} J. (a) What is the potential difference between the capacitor plates? (b) What is the dielectric constant of the slab?

24.46. A parallel-plate capacitor has capacitance $C = 12.5$ pF when the volume between the plates is filled with air. The plates are circular, with radius 3.00 cm. The capacitor is connected to a battery and a charge of magnitude 25.0 pC goes onto each plate. With the capacitor still connected to the battery, a slab of dielectric is inserted between the plates, completely filling the space between the plates. After the dielectric has been inserted, the charge on each plate has magnitude 45.0 pC. (a) What is the dielectric constant K of the dielectric? (b) What is the potential difference between the plates before and after the dielectric has been inserted? (c) What is the electric field at a point midway between the plates before and after the dielectric has been inserted?

24.47. A 12.5-μF capacitor is connected to a power supply that keeps a constant potential difference of 24.0 V across the plates. A piece of material having a dielectric constant of 3.75 is placed between the plates, completely filling the space between them. (a) How much energy is stored in the capacitor before and after the dielectric is inserted? (b) By how much did the energy change during the insertion? Did it increase or decrease?

*Section 24.6 Gauss's Law in Dielectrics

*24.48. A parallel-plate capacitor has plates with area 0.0225 m^2 separated by 1.00 mm of Teflon. (a) Calculate the charge on the plates when they are charged to a potential difference of 12.0 V. (b) Use Gauss's law (Eq. 24.23) to calculate the electric field inside the Teflon. (c) Use Gauss's law to calculate the electric field if the voltage source is disconnected and the Teflon is removed.

*24.49. A parallel-plate capacitor has the volume between its plates filled with plastic with dielectric constant K. The magnitude

of the charge on each plate is Q. Each plate has area A, and the distance between the plates is d. (a) Use Gauss's law as stated in Eq. (24.23) to calculate the magnitude of the electric field in the dielectric. (b) Use the electric field determined in part (a) to calculate the potential difference between the two plates. (c) Use the result of part (b) to determine the capacitance of the capacitor. Compare your result to Eq. (24.12).

Problems

24.50. A parallel-plate air capacitor is made by using two plates 16 cm square, spaced 4.7 mm apart. It is connected to a 12-V battery. (a) What is the capacitance? (b) What is the charge on each plate? (c) What is the electric field between the plates? (d) What is the energy stored in the capacitor? (e) If the battery is disconnected and then the plates are pulled apart to a separation of 9.4 mm, what are the answers to parts (a)–(d)?

24.51. Suppose the battery in Problem 24.50 remains connected while the plates are pulled apart. What are the answers then to parts (a)–(d) after the plates have been pulled apart?

24.52. Cell Membranes. Cell membranes (the walled enclosure around a cell) are typically about 7.5 nm thick. They are partially permeable to allow charged material to pass in and out, as needed. Equal but opposite charge densities build up on the inside and outside faces of such a membrane, and these charges prevent additional charges from passing through the cell wall. We can model a cell membrane as a parallel-plate capacitor, with the membrane itself containing proteins embedded in an organic material to give the membrane a dielectric constant of about 10. (See Fig. 24.30.) (a) What is the capacitance per square centimeter of such a cell wall? (b) In its normal resting state, a cell has a potential difference of 85 mV across its membrane. What is the electric field inside this membrane?

Figure **24.30**
Problem 24.52.

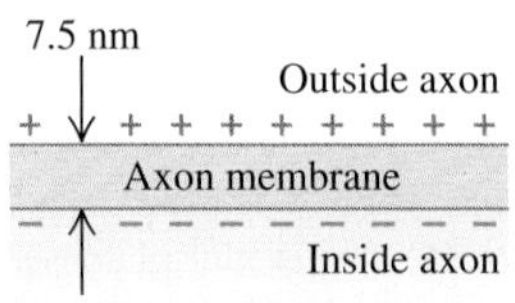

24.53. Electronic flash units for cameras contain a capacitor for storing the energy used to produce the flash. In one such unit, the flash lasts for $\frac{1}{675}$ s with an average light power output of 2.70×10^5 W. (a) If the conversion of electrical energy to light is 95% efficient (the rest of the energy goes to thermal energy), how much energy must be stored in the capacitor for one flash? (b) The capacitor has a potential difference between its plates of 125 V when the stored energy equals the value calculated in part (a). What is the capacitance?

24.54. In one type of computer keyboard, each key holds a small metal plate that serves as one plate of a parallel-plate, air-filled capacitor. When the key is depressed, the plate separation decreases and the capacitance increases. Electronic circuitry detects the change in capacitance and thus detects that the key has been pressed. In one particular keyboard, the area of each metal plate is 42.0 mm^2, and the separation between the plates is 0.700 mm before the key is depressed. (a) Calculate the capacitance before the key is depressed. (b) If the circuitry can detect a change in capacitance of 0.250 pF, how far must the key be depressed before the circuitry detects its depression?

24.55. Consider a cylindrical capacitor like that shown in Fig. 24.6. Let $d = r_b - r_a$ be the spacing between the inner and outer conductors. (a) Let the radii of the two conductors be only slightly different, so that $d \ll r_a$. Show that the result derived in Example 24.4 (Section 24.1) for the capacitance of a cylindrical capacitor then reduces to Eq. (24.2), the equation for the capacitance of a parallel-plate capacitor, with A being the surface area of each cylinder. Use the result that $\ln(1+z) \cong z$ for $|z| \ll 1$. (b) Even though the earth is essentially spherical, its surface appears flat to us because its radius is so large. Use this idea to explain why the result of part (a) makes sense from a purely geometrical standpoint.

24.56. In Fig. 24.9a, let $C_1 = 9.0 \, \mu\text{F}$, $C_2 = 4.0 \, \mu\text{F}$, and $V_{ab} = 28$ V. Suppose the charged capacitors are disconnected from the source and from each other, and then reconnected to each other with plates of *opposite* sign together. By how much does the energy of the system decrease?

24.57. For the capacitor network shown in Fig. 24.31, the potential difference across ab is 12.0 V. Find (a) the total energy stored in this network and (b) the energy stored in the 4.80-μF capacitor.

Figure **24.31** Problem 24.57.

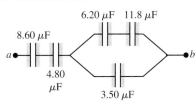

6.20 μF   11.8 μF

8.60 μF

a

4.80 μF

3.50 μF

b

24.58. Several 0.25-μF capacitors are available. The voltage across each is not to exceed 600 V. You need to make a capacitor with capacitance 0.25 μF to be connected across a potential difference of 960 V. (a) Show in a diagram how an equivalent capacitor with the desired properties can be obtained. (b) No dielectric is a perfect insulator that would not permit the flow of any charge through its volume. Suppose that the dielectric in one of the capacitors in your diagram is a moderately good conductor. What will happen in this case when your combination of capacitors is connected across the 960-V potential difference?

24.59. In Fig. 24.32, $C_1 = C_5 = 8.4 \, \mu\text{F}$ and $C_2 = C_3 = C_4 = 4.2 \, \mu\text{F}$. The applied potential is $V_{ab} = 220$ V. (a) What is the equivalent capacitance of the network between points a and b? (b) Calculate the charge on each capacitor and the potential difference across each capacitor.

Figure **24.32** Problem 24.59.

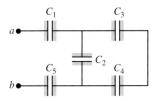

C_1 C_3

a

C_2
C_5 C_4

b

Figure **24.33** Problem 24.60.

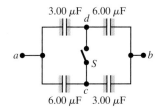

3.00 μF   6.00 μF
d

a b
S

c
6.00 μF   3.00 μF

24.60. The capacitors in Fig. 24.33 are initially uncharged and are connected, as in the diagram, with switch S open. The applied potential difference is $V_{ab} = +210$ V. (a) What is the potential difference V_{cd}? (b) What is the potential difference across each capacitor after switch S is closed? (c) How much charge flowed through the switch when it was closed?

24.61. Three capacitors having capacitances of 8.4, 8.4, and 4.2 μF are connected in series across a 36-V potential difference. (a) What is the charge on the 4.2-μF capacitor? (b) What is the total energy stored in all three capacitors? (c) The capacitors are disconnected from the potential difference without allowing them to discharge.

They are then reconnected in parallel with each other, with the positively charged plates connected together. What is the voltage across each capacitor in the parallel combination? (d) What is the total energy now stored in the capacitors?

24.62. Capacitance of a Thundercloud. The charge center of a thundercloud, drifting 3.0 km above the earth's surface, contains 20 C of negative charge. Assuming the charge center has a radius of 1.0 km, and modeling the charge center and the earth's surface as parallel plates, calculate: (a) the capacitance of the system; (b) the potential difference between charge center and ground; (c) the average strength of the electric field between cloud and ground; (d) the electrical energy stored in the system.

24.63. In Fig. 24.34, each capacitance C_1 is 6.9 μF, and each capacitance C_2 is 4.6 μF. (a) Compute the equivalent capacitance of the network between points a and b. (b) Compute the charge on each of the three capacitors nearest a and b when $V_{ab} = 420$ V. (c) With 420 V across a and b, compute V_{cd}.

Figure **24.34** Problem 24.63.

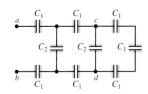

a C_1 C_1 c C_1

C_2 C_2 C_1

b C_1 C_1 d C_1

24.64. Each combination of capacitors between points a and b in Fig. 24.35 is first connected across a 120-V battery, charging the combination to 120 V. These combinations are then connected to make the circuits shown. When the switch S is thrown, a surge of charge for the discharging capacitors flows to trigger the signal device. How much charge flows through the signal device?

Figure **24.35** Problem 24.64.

(a)

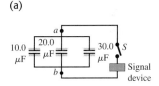

a

10.0 μF   20.0 μF   30.0 μF S

b

Signal device

(b)

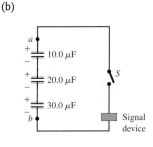

a

10.0 μF

20.0 μF S

30.0 μF

b

Signal device

24.65. A parallel-plate capacitor with only air between the plates is charged by connecting it to a battery. The capacitor is then disconnected from the battery, without any of the charge leaving the plates. (a) A voltmeter reads 45.0 V when placed across the capacitor. When a dielectric is inserted between the plates, completely filling the space, the voltmeter reads 11.5 V. What is the dielectric constant of this material? (b) What will the voltmeter read if the dielectric is now pulled partway out so it fills only one-third of the space between the plates?

24.66. An air capacitor is made by using two flat plates, each with area A, separated by a distance d. Then a metal slab having thickness a (less than d) and the same shape and size as the plates is inserted between them, parallel to the plates and not touching either plate (Fig. 24.36). (a) What is the capacitance of this arrangement? (b) Express the capacitance as a multiple of the capacitance C_0 when the metal slab is not present. (c) Discuss what happens to the capacitance in the limits $a \to 0$ and $a \to d$.

Figure **24.36** Problem 24.66.

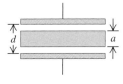

d a

24.67. Capacitance of the Earth. (a) Discuss how the concept of capacitance can also be applied to a *single* conductor. (*Hint:* In the relationship $C = Q/V_{ab}$, think of the second conductor as being located at infinity.) (b) Use Eq. (24.1) to show that $C = 4\pi\epsilon_0 R$ for a solid conducting sphere of radius R. (c) Use your result in part (b) to calculate the capacitance of the earth, which is a good conductor of radius 6380 km. Compare to typical capacitors used in electronic circuits that have capacitances ranging from 10 pF to 100 μF.

24.68. A solid conducting sphere of radius R carries a charge Q. Calculate the electric-field energy density at a point a distance r from the center of the sphere for (a) $r < R$ and (b) $r > R$. (c) Calculate the total electric-field energy associated with the charged sphere. (*Hint:* Consider a spherical shell of radius r and thickness dr that has volume $dV = 4\pi r^2\, dr$, and find the energy stored in this volume. Then integrate from $r = 0$ to $r \to \infty$.) (d) Explain why the result of part (c) can be interpreted as the amount of work required to assemble the charge Q on the sphere. (e) By using Eq. (24.9) and the result of part (c), show that the capacitance of the sphere is as given in Problem 24.67.

24.69. Earth-Ionosphere Capacitance. The earth can be considered as a single-conductor capacitor (see Problem 24.67). It can also be considered in combination with a charged layer of the atmosphere, the ionosphere, as a spherical capacitor with two plates, the surface of the earth being the negative plate. The ionosphere is at a level of about 70 km, and the potential difference between earth and ionosphere is about 350,000 V. Calculate: (a) the capacitance of this system; (b) the total charge on the capacitor; (c) the energy stored in the system.

24.70. The inner cylinder of a long, cylindrical capacitor has radius r_a and linear charge density $+\lambda$. It is surrounded by a coaxial cylindrical conducting shell with inner radius r_b and linear charge density $-\lambda$ (see Fig. 24.6). (a) What is the energy density in the region between the conductors at a distance r from the axis? (b) Integrate the energy density calculated in part (a) over the volume between the conductors in a length L of the capacitor to obtain the total electric-field energy per unit length. (c) Use Eq. (24.9) and the capacitance per unit length calculated in Example 24.4 (Section 24.1) to calculate U/L. Does your result agree with that obtained in part (b)?

24.71. A parallel-plate capacitor has the space between the plates filled with two slabs of dielectric, one with constant K_1 and one with constant K_2 (Fig. 24.37). Each slab has thickness $d/2$, where d is the plate separation. Show that the capacitance is

Figure **24.37**
Problem 24.71.

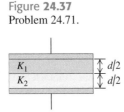

$$C = \frac{2\epsilon_0 A}{d}\left(\frac{K_1 K_2}{K_1 + K_2}\right)$$

24.72. A parallel-plate capacitor has the space between the plates filled with two slabs of dielectric, one with constant K_1 and one with constant K_2 (Fig. 24.38). The thickness of each slab is the same as the plate separation d, and each slab fills half of the volume between the plates. Show that the capacitance is

Figure **24.38**
Problem 24.72.

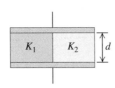

$$C = \frac{\epsilon_0 A(K_1 + K_2)}{2d}$$

Challenge Problems

24.73. Capacitors in networks cannot always be grouped into simple series or parallel combinations. As an example, Fig. 24.39a shows three capacitors C_x, C_y, and C_z in a *delta network,* so called because of its triangular shape. This network has *three* terminals a, b, and c and hence cannot be transformed into a single equivalent capacitor. It can be shown that as far as any effect on the external circuit is concerned, a delta network is equivalent to what is called a *Y network.* For example, the delta network of Fig. 24.39a can be replaced by the Y network of Fig. 24.39b. (The name "Y network" also refers to the shape of the network.) (a) Show that the transformation equations that give C_1, C_2, and C_3 in terms of C_x, and C_y, and C_z are

$$C_1 = (C_x C_y + C_y C_z + C_z C_x)/C_x$$
$$C_2 = (C_x C_y + C_y C_z + C_z C_x)/C_y$$
$$C_3 = (C_x C_y + C_y C_z + C_z C_x)/C_z$$

(*Hint:* The potential difference V_{ac} must be the same in both circuits, as V_{bc} must be. Also, the charge q_1 that flows from point a along the wire as indicated must be the same in both circuits, as must q_2. Obtain a relationship for V_{ac} as a function of q_1 and q_2 and the capacitances for each network, and obtain a separate relationship for V_{bc} as a function of the charges for each network. The coefficients of corresponding charges in corresponding equations must be the same for both networks.) (b) For the network shown in Fig. 24.39c, determine the equivalent capacitance between the terminals at the left end of the network. (*Hint:* Use the delta-Y transformation derived in part (a). Use points a, b, and c to form the delta, and transform the delta into a Y. The capacitors can then be combined using the relationships for series and parallel combinations of capacitors.) (c) Determine the charges of, and the potential differences across, each capacitor in Fig. 24.39c.

Figure **24.39** Challenge Problem 24.73.

(a)
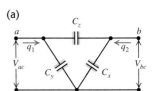

(b)
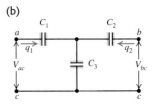

(c)
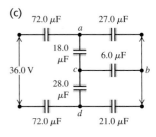

24.74. The parallel-plate air capacitor in Fig. 24.40 consists of two horizontal conducting plates of equal area A. The bottom plate rests on a fixed support, and the top plate is suspended by four

Figure **24.40** Challenge Problem 24.74.

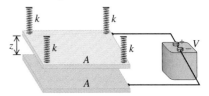

springs with spring constant k, positioned at each of the four corners of the top plate as shown in the figure. When uncharged, the plates are separated by a distance z_0. A battery is connected to the plates and produces a potential difference V between them. This causes the plate separation to decrease to z. Neglect any fringing effects. (a) Show that the electrostatic force between the charged plates has a magnitude $\epsilon_0 A V^2/2z^2$. (*Hint:* See Exercise 24.29.) (b) Obtain an expression that relates the plate separation z to the potential difference V. The resulting equation will be cubic in z. (c) Given the values $A = 0.300$ m^2, $z_0 = 1.20$ mm, $k = 25.0$ N/m, and $V = 120$ V, find the two values of z for which the top plate will be in equilibrium. (*Hint:* You can solve the cubic equation by plugging a trial value of z into the equation and then adjusting your guess until the equation is satisfied to three significant figures. Locating the roots of the cubic equation graphically can help you pick starting values of z for this trial-and-error procedure. One root of the cubic equation has a nonphysical negative value.) (d) For each of the two values of z found in part (c), is the equilibrium stable or unstable? For stable equilibrium a small displacement of the object will give rise to a net force tending to return the object to the equilibrium position. For unstable equilibrium a small displacement gives rise to a net force that takes the object farther away from equilibrium.

24.75. Two square conducting plates with sides of length L are separated by a distance D. A dielectric slab with constant K with dimensions $L \times L \times D$ is inserted a distance x into the space between the plates, as shown in Fig. 24.41. (a) Find the capacitance C of this system (see Problem 24.72). (b) Suppose that the capacitor is connected to a battery that maintains a constant potential difference V between the plates. If the dielectric slab is inserted an additional distance dx into the space between the plates, show that the change in stored energy is

Figure **24.41** Challenge Problem 24.75.

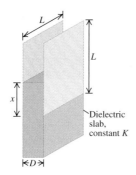

$$dU = +\frac{(K-1)\epsilon_0 V^2 L}{2D}dx$$

(c) Suppose that before the slab is moved by dx, the plates are disconnected from the battery, so that the charges on the plates remain constant. Determine the magnitude of the charge on each plate, and then show that when the slab is moved dx farther into the space between the plates, the stored energy changes by an amount that is the *negative* of the expression for dU given in part (b). (d) If F is the force exerted on the slab by the charges on the plates, then dU should equal the work done *against* this force to move the slab a distance dx. Thus $dU = -F\,dx$. Show that applying this expression to the result of part (b) suggests that the electric force on the slab pushes it *out* of the capacitor, while the result of part (c) suggests that the force pulls the slab *into* the capacitor. (e) Figure 24.16 shows that the force in fact pulls the slab into the capacitor. Explain why the result of part (b) gives an incorrect answer for the direction of this force, and calculate the magnitude

of the force. (This method does not require knowledge of the nature of the fringing field.)

24.76. An isolated spherical capacitor has charge $+Q$ on its inner conductor (radius r_a) and charge $-Q$ on its outer conductor (radius r_b). Half of the volume between the two conductors is then filled with a liquid dielectric of constant K, as shown in cross section in Fig. 24.42. (a) Find the capacitance of the half-filled capacitor. (b) Find the magnitude of $\vec{E}$ in the volume between the two conductors as a function of the distance r from the center of the capacitor. Give answers for both the upper and lower halves of this volume. (c) Find the surface density of free charge on the upper and lower halves of the inner and outer conductors. (d) Find the surface density of bound charge on the inner $(r = r_a)$ and outer $(r = r_b)$ surfaces of the dielectric. (e) What is the surface density of bound charge on the flat surface of the dielectric? Explain.

Figure **24.42** Challenge Problem 24.76.

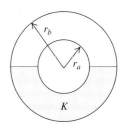

24.77. Three square metal plates A, B, and C, each 12.0 cm on a side and 1.50 mm thick, are arranged as in Fig. 24.43. The plates are separated by sheets of paper 0.45 mm thick and with dielectric constant 4.2. The outer plates are connected together and connected to point b. The inner plate is connected to point a. (a) Copy the diagram and show by plus and minus signs the charge distribution on the plates when point a is maintained at a positive potential relative to point b. (b) What is the capacitance between points a and b?

Figure **24.43** Challenge Problem 24.77.

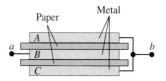

24.78. A fuel gauge uses a capacitor to determine the height of the fuel in a tank. The effective dielectric constant K_{eff} changes from a value of 1 when the tank is empty to a value of K, the dielectric constant of the fuel, when the tank is full. The appropriate electronic circuitry can determine the effective dielectric constant of the combined air and fuel between the capacitor plates. Each of the two rectangular plates has a width w and a length

Figure **24.44** Challenge Problem 24.78.

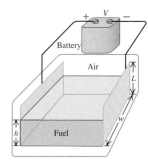

L (Fig. 24.44). The height of the fuel between the plates is h. You can ignore any fringing effects. (a) Derive an expression for K_{eff} as a function of h. (b) What is the effective dielectric constant for a tank $\frac{1}{4}$ full, $\frac{1}{2}$ full, and $\frac{3}{4}$ full if the fuel is gasoline $(K = 1.95)$? (c) Repeat part (b) for methanol $(K = 33.0)$. (d) For which fuel is this fuel gauge more practical?

25

CURRENT, RESISTANCE, AND ELECTROMOTIVE FORCE

LEARNING GOALS

By studying this chapter, you will learn:

- The meaning of electric current, and how charges move in a conductor.

- What is meant by the resistivity and conductivity of a substance.

- How to calculate the resistance of a conductor from its dimensions and its resistivity.

- How an electromotive force (emf) makes it possible for current to flow in a circuit.

- How to do calculations involving energy and power in circuits.

? In a flashlight, is the amount of current that flows out of the bulb less than, greater than, or equal to the amount of current that flows into the bulb?

In the past four chapters we studied the interactions of electric charges *at rest;* now we're ready to study charges *in motion.* An *electric current* consists of charges in motion from one region to another. When this motion takes place within a conducting path that forms a closed loop, the path is called an *electric circuit.*

Fundamentally, electric circuits are a means for conveying *energy* from one place to another. As charged particles move within a circuit, electric potential energy is transferred from a source (such as a battery or generator) to a device in which that energy is either stored or converted to another form: into sound in a stereo system or into heat and light in a toaster or light bulb. From a technological standpoint, electric circuits are useful because they allow energy to be transported without any moving parts (other than the moving charged particles themselves). Electric circuits are at the heart of flashlights, CD players, computers, radio and television transmitters and receivers, and household and industrial power distribution systems. The nervous systems of animals and humans are specialized electric circuits that carry vital signals from one part of the body to another.

In Chapter 26 we will see how to analyze electric circuits and will examine some practical applications of circuits. Before we can do so, however, you must understand the basic properties of electric currents. These properties are the subject of this chapter. We'll begin by describing the nature of electric conductors and considering how they are affected by temperature. We'll learn why a short, fat, cold copper wire is a better conductor than a long, skinny, hot steel wire. We'll study the properties of batteries and see how they cause current and energy transfer in a circuit. In this analysis we will use the concepts of current, potential difference (or voltage), resistance, and electromotive force. Finally, we'll look at electric current in a material from a microscopic viewpoint.

25.1 Current

A **current** is any motion of charge from one region to another. In this section we'll discuss currents in conducting materials. The vast majority of technological applications of charges in motion involve currents of this kind.

In electrostatic situations (discussed in Chapters 21 through 24) the electric field is zero everywhere within the conductor, and there is *no* current. However, this does not mean that all charges within the conductor are at rest. In an ordinary metal such as copper or alumium, some of the electrons are free to move within the conducting material. These free electrons move randomly in all directions, somewhat like the molecules of a gas but with much greater speeds, of the order of 10^6 m/s. The electrons nonetheless do not escape from the conducting material, because they are attracted to the positive ions of the material. The motion of the electrons is random, so there is no *net* flow of charge in any direction and hence no current.

Now consider what happens if a constant, steady electric field $\vec{E}$ is established inside a conductor. (We'll see later how this can be done.) A charged particle (such as a free electron) inside the conducting material is then subjected to a steady force $\vec{F} = q\vec{E}$. If the charged particle were moving in *vacuum,* this steady force would cause a steady acceleration in the direction of $\vec{F}$, and after a time the charged particle would be moving in that direction at high speed. But a charged particle moving in a *conductor* undergoes frequent collisions with the massive, nearly stationary ions of the material. In each such collision the particle's direction of motion undergoes a random change. The net effect of the electric field $\vec{E}$ is that in addition to the random motion of the charged particles within the conductor, there is also a very slow net motion or *drift* of the moving charged particles as a group in the direction of the electric force $\vec{F} = q\vec{E}$ (Fig. 25.1). This motion is described in terms of the **drift velocity** $\vec{v}_d$ of the particles. As a result, there is a net current in the conductor.

While the random motion of the electrons has a very fast average speed of about 10^6 m/s, the drift speed is very slow, often on the order of 10^{-4} m/s. Given that the electrons move so slowly, you may wonder why the light comes on immediately when you turn on the switch of a flashlight. The reason is that the electric field is set up in the wire with a speed approaching the speed of light, and electrons start to move all along the wire at very nearly the same time. The time that it takes any individual electron to get from the switch to the light bulb isn't really relevant. A good analogy is a group of soldiers standing at attention when the sergeant orders them to start marching; the order reaches the soldiers' ears at the speed of sound, which is much faster than their marching speed, so all the soldiers start to march essentially in unison.

The Direction of Current Flow

The drift of moving charges through a conductor can be interpreted in terms of work and energy. The electric field $\vec{E}$ does work on the moving charges. The resulting kinetic energy is transferred to the material of the conductor by means of collisions with the ions, which vibrate about their equilibrium positions in the crystalline structure of the conductor. This energy transfer increases the average vibrational energy of the ions and therefore the temperature of the material. Thus much of the work done by the electric field goes into heating the conductor, *not* into making the moving charges move ever faster and faster. This heating is sometimes useful, as in an electric toaster, but in many situations is simply an unavoidable by-product of current flow.

In different current-carrying materials, the charges of the moving particles may be positive or negative. In metals the moving charges are always (negative) electrons, while in an ionized gas (plasma) or an ionic solution the moving

25.1 If there is no electric field inside a conductor, an electron moves randomly from point P_1 to point P_2 in a time Δt. If an electric field $\vec{E}$ is present, the electric force $\vec{F} = q\vec{E}$ imposes a small drift (greatly exaggerated here) that takes the electron to point P'_2, a distance $v_d\Delta t$ from P_2 in the direction of the force.

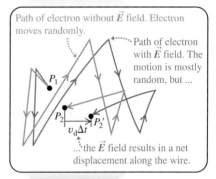

Conductor without internal $\vec{E}$ field

Path of electron without $\vec{E}$ field. Electron moves randomly.

Path of electron with $\vec{E}$ field. The motion is mostly random, but ...

P_1

P_2

$v_d\Delta t$

P'_2

... the $\vec{E}$ field results in a net displacement along the wire.

Conductor with internal $\vec{E}$ field

$\vec{E}$ $\vec{F} = q\vec{E}$ $\vec{E}$

An electron has a negative charge q, so the force on it due to the $\vec{E}$ field is in the direction opposite to $\vec{E}$.

25.2 The same current can be produced by (a) positive charges moving in the direction of the electric field $\vec{E}$ or (b) the same number of negative charges moving at the same speed in the direction opposite to $\vec{E}$.

(a)

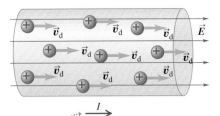

A **conventional current** is treated as a flow of positive charges, regardless of whether the free charges in the conductor are positive, negative, or both.

(b)

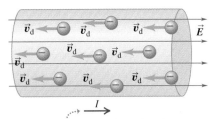

In a metallic conductor, the moving charges are electrons — but the *current* still points in the direction positive charges would flow.

25.3 The current I is the time rate of charge transfer through the cross-sectional area A. The random component of each moving charged particle's motion averages to zero, and the current is in the same direction as $\vec{E}$ whether the moving charges are positive (as shown here) or negative (see Fig. 25.2b).

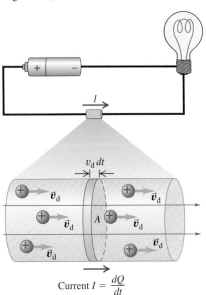

Current $I = \dfrac{dQ}{dt}$

charges may include both electrons and positively charged ions. In a semiconductor material such as germanium or silicon, conduction is partly by electrons and partly by motion of *vacancies,* also known as *holes;* these are sites of missing electrons and act like positive charges.

Fig. 25.2 shows segments of two different current-carrying materials. In Fig. 25.2a the moving charges are positive, the electric force is in the same direction as $\vec{E}$, and the drift velocity $\vec{v}_d$ is from left to right. In Fig. 25.2b the charges are negative, the electric force is opposite to $\vec{E}$, and the drift velocity $\vec{v}_d$ is from right to left. In both cases there is a net flow of positive charge from left to right, and positive charges end up to the right of negative ones. We *define* the current, denoted by I, to be in the direction in which there is a flow of *positive* charge. Thus we describe currents as though they consisted entirely of positive charge flow, even in cases in which we know that the actual current is due to electrons. Hence the current is to the right in both Figs. 25.2a and 25.2b. This choice or convention for the direction of current flow is called **conventional current.** While the direction of the conventional current is *not* necessarily the same as the direction in which charged particles are actually moving, we'll find that the sign of the moving charges is of little importance in analyzing electric circuits.

Fig. 25.3 shows a segment of a conductor in which a current is flowing. We consider the moving charges to be *positive,* so they are moving in the same direction as the current. We define the current through the cross-sectional area A to be *the net charge flowing through the area per unit time.* Thus, if a net charge dQ flows through an area in a time dt, the current I through the area is

$$I = \frac{dQ}{dt} \qquad \text{(definition of current)} \qquad (25.1)$$

CAUTION **Current is not a vector** Although we refer to the *direction* of a current, current as defined by Eq. (25.1) is *not* a vector quantity. In a current-carrying wire, the current is always along the length of the wire, regardless of whether the wire is straight or curved. No single vector could describe motion along a curved path, which is why current is not a vector. We'll usually describe the direction of current either in words (as in "the current flows clockwise around the circuit") or by choosing a current to be positive if it flows in one direction along a conductor and negative if it flows in the other direction.

The SI unit of current is the **ampere;** one ampere is defined to be *one coulomb per second* $(1\text{ A} = 1\text{ C/s})$. This unit is named in honor of the French scientist André Marie Ampère (1775–1836). When an ordinary flashlight (D-cell size) is turned on, the current in the flashlight is about 0.5 to 1 A; the current in the wires of a car engine's starter motor is around 200 A. Currents in radio and television circuits are usually expressed in *milliamperes* $(1\text{ mA} = 10^{-3}\text{ A})$ or *microamperes* $(1\ \mu\text{A} = 10^{-6}\text{ A})$, and currents in computer circuits are expressed in *nanoamperes* $(1\text{ nA} = 10^{-9}\text{ A})$ or *picoamperes* $(1\text{ pA} = 10^{-12}\text{ A})$.

Current, Drift Velocity, and Current Density

We can express current in terms of the drift velocity of the moving charges. Let's consider again the situation of Fig. 25.3, a conductor with cross-sectional area A and an electric field $\vec{E}$ directed from left to right. To begin with, we'll assume that the free charges in the conductor are positive; then the drift velocity is in the same direction as the field.

Suppose there are n moving charged particles per unit volume. We call n the **concentration** of particles; its SI unit is m^{-3}. Assume that all the particles move with the same drift velocity with magnitude v_d. In a time interval dt, each particle moves a distance $v_d\, dt$. The particles that flow out of the right end of the shaded cylinder with length $v_d\, dt$ during dt are the particles that were within this cylinder at the beginning of the interval dt. The volume of the cylinder is $Av_d\, dt$, and the number of particles within it is $nAv_d\,dt$. If each particle has a charge q, the charge dQ that flows out of the end of the cylinder during time dt is

$$dQ = q(nAv_d\,dt) = nqv_dA\,dt$$

and the current is

$$I = \frac{dQ}{dt} = nqv_dA$$

The current *per unit cross-sectional area* is called the **current density** J:

$$J = \frac{I}{A} = nqv_d$$

The units of current density are amperes per square meter (A/m^2).

If the moving charges are negative rather than positive, as in Fig. 25.2b, the drift velocity is opposite to $\vec{E}$. But the *current* is still in the same direction as $\vec{E}$ at each point in the conductor. Hence the current I and current density J don't depend on the sign of the charge, and so in the above expressions for I and J we replace the charge q by its absolute value $|q|$:

$$I = \frac{dQ}{dt} = n|q|v_dA \qquad \text{(general expression for current)} \qquad (25.2)$$

$$J = \frac{I}{A} = n|q|v_d \qquad \text{(general expression for current density)} \qquad (25.3)$$

The current in a conductor is the product of the concentration of moving charged particles, the magnitude of charge of each such particle, the magnitude of the drift velocity, and the cross-sectional area of the conductor.

We can also define a *vector* current density $\vec{J}$ that includes the direction of the drift velocity:

$$\vec{J} = nq\vec{v}_d \qquad \text{(vector current density)} \qquad (25.4)$$

There are *no* absolute value signs in Eq. (25.4). If q is positive, $\vec{v}_d$ is in the same direction as $\vec{E}$; if q is negative, $\vec{v}_d$ is opposite to $\vec{E}$. In either case, $\vec{J}$ is in the same direction as $\vec{E}$. Equation (25.3) gives the *magnitude* J of the vector current density $\vec{J}$.

CAUTION **Current density vs. current** Note that current density $\vec{J}$ is a vector, but current I is not. The difference is that the current density $\vec{J}$ describes how charges flow at a certain point, and the vector's direction tells you about the direction of the flow at that point. By contrast, the current I describes how charges flow through an extended object such as a wire. For example, I has the same value at all points in the circuit of Fig. 25.3, but $\vec{J}$ does not: the current density is directed downward in the left-hand side of the loop and upward in the right-hand side. The magnitude of $\vec{J}$ can also vary around a circuit. In Fig. 25.3 the current density magnitude $J = I/A$ is less in the battery (which has a large cross-sectional area A) than in the wires (which have a small cross-sectional area). ▮

In general, a conductor may contain several different kinds of moving charged particles having charges $q_1, q_2, \ldots$, concentrations $n_1, n_2, \ldots$, and drift velocities with magnitudes $v_{d1}, v_{d2}, \ldots$. An example is current flow in an ionic solution (Fig. 25.4). In a sodium chloride solution, current can be carried by both positive sodium ions and negative chlorine ions; the total current I is found by adding up the currents due to each kind of charged particle, using Eq. (25.2). Likewise, the total vector current density $\vec{J}$ is found by using Eq. (25.4) for each kind of charged particle and adding the results.

We will see in Section 25.4 that it is possible to have a current that is *steady* (that is, one that is constant in time) only if the conducting material forms a

25.4 Part of the electric circuit that includes this light bulb passes through a beaker with a solution of sodium chloride. The current in the solution is carried by both positive charges (Na^+ ions) and negative charges (Cl^- ions).

closed loop, called a *complete circuit.* In such a steady situation, the total charge in every segment of the conductor is constant. Hence the rate of flow of charge *out* at one end of a segment at any instant equals the rate of flow of charge *in* at the other end of the segment, and *the current is the same at all cross sections of the circuit.* We'll make use of this observation when we analyze electric circuits later in this chapter.

In many simple circuits, such as flashlights or cordless electric drills, the direction of the current is always the same; this is called *direct current.* But home appliances such as toasters, refrigerators, and televisions use *alternating current,* in which the current continuously changes direction. In this chapter we'll consider direct current only. Alternating current has many special features worthy of detailed study, which we'll examine in Chapter 31.

Example 25.1 | **Current density and drift velocity in a wire**

An 18-gauge copper wire (the size usually used for lamp cords) has a nominal diameter of 1.02 mm. This wire carries a constant current of 1.67 A to a 200-watt lamp. The density of free electrons is 8.5×10^{28} electrons per cubic meter. Find the magnitudes of (a) the current density and (b) the drift velocity.

SOLUTION

IDENTIFY: This problem uses the relationships among current, current density, and drift velocity.

SET UP: We are given the current and the dimensions of the wire, so we use Eq. (25.3) to find the magnitude J of the current density. We then use Eq. (25.3) again to find the drift speed v_d from J and the concentration of electrons.

EXECUTE: (a) The cross-sectional area is

$$A = \frac{\pi d^2}{4} = \frac{\pi (1.02 \times 10^{-3} \text{ m})^2}{4} = 8.17 \times 10^{-7} \text{ m}^2$$

The magnitude of the current density is

$$J = \frac{I}{A} = \frac{1.67 \text{ A}}{8.17 \times 10^{-7} \text{ m}^2} = 2.04 \times 10^6 \text{ A/m}^2$$

(b) Solving Eq. (25.3) for the drift velocity magnitude v_d, we find

$$v_d = \frac{J}{n|q|} = \frac{2.04 \times 10^6 \text{ A/m}^2}{(8.5 \times 10^{28} \text{ m}^{-3})|-1.60 \times 10^{-19} \text{ C}|}$$

$$= 1.5 \times 10^{-4} \text{ m/s} = 0.15 \text{ mm/s}$$

EVALUATE: At this speed an electron would require 6700 s, or about 1 hr 50 min, to travel the length of a wire 1 m long. The speeds of random motion of the electrons are of the order of 10^6 m/s. So in this example the drift speed is around 10^{10} times slower than the speed of random motion. Picture the electrons as bouncing around frantically, with a very slow and sluggish drift!

Test Your Understanding of Section 25.1 Suppose we replaced the wire in Example 25.1 with 12-gauge copper wire, which has twice the diameter of 18-gauge wire. If the current remains the same, what effect would this have on the magnitude of the drift velocity v_d? (i) none—v_d would be unchanged; (ii) v_d would be twice as great; (iii) v_d would be four times greater; (iv) v_d would be half as great; (v) v_d would be one-fourth as great.

25.2 Resistivity

The current density $\vec{J}$ in a conductor depends on the electric field $\vec{E}$ and on the properties of the material. In general, this dependence can be quite complex. But for some materials, especially metals, at a given temperature, $\vec{J}$ is nearly *directly proportional* to $\vec{E}$, and the ratio of the magnitudes of E and J is constant. This relationship, called Ohm's law, was discovered in 1826 by the German physicist Georg Simon Ohm (1787–1854). The word "law" should actually be in quotation marks, since **Ohm's law,** like the ideal-gas equation and Hooke's law, is an *idealized model* that describes the behavior of some materials quite well but is not a general description of *all* matter. In the following discussion we'll assume that Ohm's law is valid, even though there are many situations in which it is not. The situation is comparable to our representation of the behavior of the static and kinetic friction forces; we treated these friction forces as being directly proportional to the normal force, even though we knew that this was at best an approximate description.

Table 25.1 Resistivities at Room Temperature $(20\ °C)$

	Substance	$\rho\,(\Omega\cdot m)$		Substance	$\rho\,(\Omega\cdot m)$
Conductors			**Semiconductors**		
Metals	Silver	1.47×10^{-8}		Pure carbon (graphite)	3.5×10^{-5}
	Copper	1.72×10^{-8}		Pure germanium	0.60
	Gold	2.44×10^{-8}		Pure silicon	2300
	Aluminum	2.75×10^{-8}	**Insulators**		
	Tungsten	5.25×10^{-8}		Amber	5×10^{14}
	Steel	20×10^{-8}		Glass	10^{10}–10^{14}
	Lead	22×10^{-8}		Lucite	$>10^{13}$
	Mercury	95×10^{-8}		Mica	10^{11}–10^{15}
Alloys	Manganin (Cu 84%, Mn 12%, Ni 4%)	44×10^{-8}		Quartz (fused)	75×10^{16}
	Constantan (Cu 60%, Ni 40%)	49×10^{-8}		Sulfur	10^{15}
	Nichrome	100×10^{-8}		Teflon	$>10^{13}$
				Wood	10^{8}–10^{11}

We define the **resistivity** ρ of a material as the ratio of the magnitudes of electric field and current density:

$$\rho = \frac{E}{J} \qquad \text{(definition of resistivity)} \qquad (25.5)$$

The greater the resistivity, the greater the field needed to cause a given current density, or the smaller the current density caused by a given field. From Eq. (25.5) the units of ρ are $(V/m)/(A/m^2) = V\cdot m/A$. As we will discuss in the next section, 1 V/A is called one *ohm* (1 Ω; we use the Greek letter Ω, or omega, which is alliterative with "ohm"). So the SI units for ρ are $\Omega\cdot m$ (ohm-meters). Table 25.1 lists some representative values of resistivity. A perfect conductor would have zero resistivity, and a perfect insulator would have an infinite resistivity. Metals and alloys have the smallest resistivities and are the best conductors. The resistivities of insulators are greater than those of the metals by an enormous factor, on the order of 10^{22}.

The reciprocal of resistivity is **conductivity.** Its units are $(\Omega\cdot m)^{-1}$. Good conductors of electricity have larger conductivity than insulators. Conductivity is the direct electrical analog of thermal conductivity. Comparing Table 25.1 with Table 17.5 (Thermal Conductivities), we note that good electrical conductors, such as metals, are usually also good conductors of heat. Poor electrical conductors, such as ceramic and plastic materials, are also poor thermal conductors. In a metal the free electrons that carry charge in electrical conduction also provide the principal mechanism for heat conduction, so we should expect a correlation between electrical and thermal conductivity. Because of the enormous difference in conductivity between electrical conductors and insulators, it is easy to confine electric currents to well-defined paths or circuits (Fig. 25.5). The variation in *thermal* conductivity is much less, only a factor of 10^3 or so, and it is usually impossible to confine heat currents to that extent.

Semiconductors have resistivities intermediate between those of metals and those of insulators. These materials are important because of the way their resistivities are affected by temperature and by small amounts of impurities.

A material that obeys Ohm's law reasonably well is called an *ohmic* conductor or a *linear* conductor. For such materials, at a given temperature, ρ is a *constant* that does not depend on the value of E. Many materials show substantial departures from Ohm's-law behavior; they are *nonohmic,* or *nonlinear.* In these materials, J depends on E in a more complicated manner.

Analogies with fluid flow can be a big help in developing intuition about electric current and circuits. For example, in the making of wine or maple syrup, the product is sometimes filtered to remove sediments. A pump forces the fluid through the filter under pressure; if the flow rate (analogous to J) is proportional to the pressure difference between the upstream and downstream sides (analogous to E), the behavior is analogous to Ohm's law.

25.5 The copper "wires," or traces, on this circuit board are printed directly onto the surface of the dark-colored insulating board. Even though the traces are very close to each other (only about a millimeter apart), the board has such a high resistivity (and low conductivity) compared to the copper that no current can flow between the traces.

Conducting paths
(traces)

25.6 Variation of resistivity ρ with absolute temperature T for (a) a normal metal, (b) a semiconductor, and (c) a superconductor. In (a) the linear approximation to ρ as a function of T is shown as a green line; the approximation agrees exactly at $T = T_0$, where $\rho = \rho_0$.

(a) ρ

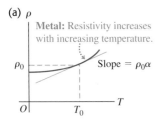

Metal: Resistivity increases with increasing temperature.

Slope = $\rho_0\alpha$

(b) ρ

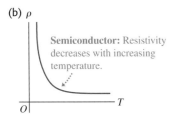

Semiconductor: Resistivity decreases with increasing temperature.

(c) ρ

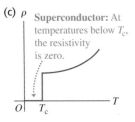

Superconductor: At temperatures below T_c, the resistivity is zero.

Resistivity and Temperature

The resistivity of a *metallic* conductor nearly always increases with increasing temperature, as shown in Fig. 25.6a. As temperature increases, the ions of the conductor vibrate with greater amplitude, making it more likely that a moving electron will collide with an ion as in Fig. 25.1; this impedes the drift of electrons through the conductor and hence reduces the current. Over a small temperature range (up to 100 C° or so), the resistivity of a metal can be represented approximately by the equation

$$\rho(T) = \rho_0[1 + \alpha(T - T_0)] \qquad \text{(temperature dependence of resistivity)} \qquad (25.6)$$

where ρ_0 is the resistivity at a reference temperature T_0 (often taken as 0°C or 20°C) and $\rho(T)$ is the resistivity at temperature T, which may be higher or lower than T_0. The factor α is called the **temperature coefficient of resistivity.** Some representative values are given in Table 25.2. The resistivity of the alloy manganin is practically independent of temperature.

Table 25.2 Temperature Coefficients of Resistivity (Approximate Values Near Room Temperature)

Material	$\alpha\,[(\degree C)^{-1}]$	Material	$\alpha\,[(\degree C)^{-1}]$
Aluminum	0.0039	Lead	0.0043
Brass	0.0020	Manganin	0.00000
Carbon (graphite)	−0.0005	Mercury	0.00088
Constantan	0.00001	Nichrome	0.0004
Copper	0.00393	Silver	0.0038
Iron	0.0050	Tungsten	0.0045

The resistivity of graphite (a nonmetal) *decreases* with increasing temperature, since at higher temperatures, more electrons are "shaken loose" from the atoms and become mobile; hence the temperature coefficient of resistivity of graphite is negative. This same behavior occurs for semiconductors (Fig. 25.6b). Measuring the resistivity of a small semiconductor crystal is therefore a sensitive measure of temperature; this is the principle of a type of thermometer called a *thermistor.*

Some materials, including several metallic alloys and oxides, show a phenomenon called *superconductivity.* As the temperature decreases, the resistivity at first decreases smoothly, like that of any metal. But then at a certain critical temperature T_c a phase transition occurs and the resistivity suddenly drops to zero, as shown in Fig. 25.6c. Once a current has been established in a superconducting ring, it continues indefinitely without the presence of any driving field.

Superconductivity was discovered in 1911 by the Dutch physicist Heike Kamerlingh Onnes (1853–1926). He discovered that at very low temperatures, below 4.2 K, the resistivity of mercury suddenly dropped to zero. For the next 75 years, the highest T_c attained was about 20 K. This meant that superconductivity occurred only when the material was cooled using expensive liquid helium, with a boiling-point temperature of 4.2 K, or explosive liquid hydrogen, with a boiling point of 20.3 K. But in 1986 Karl Müller and Johannes Bednorz discovered an oxide of barium, lanthanum, and copper with a T_c of nearly 40 K, and the race was on to develop "high-temperature" superconducting materials.

By 1987 a complex oxide of yttrium, copper, and barium had been found that has a value of T_c well above the 77 K boiling temperature of liquid nitrogen, a refrigerant that is both inexpensive and safe. The current (2006) record for T_c at atmospheric pressure is 138 K, and materials that are superconductors at room temperature may become a reality. The implications of these discoveries for power-distribution systems, computer design, and transportation are enormous. Meanwhile, superconducting electromagnets cooled by liquid helium are used in particle accelerators and some experimental magnetic-levitation railroads. Superconductors have other exotic properties that require an understanding of magnetism to explore; we will discuss these further in Chapter 29.

Test Your Understanding of Section 25.2   You maintain a constant electric field inside a piece of semiconductor while lowering the semiconductor's temperature. What happens to the current density in the semiconductor? (i) It increases; (ii) it decreases; (iii) it remains the same.

25.3 Resistance

For a conductor with resistivity ρ, the current density $\vec{J}$ at a point where the electric field is $\vec{E}$ is given by Eq. (25.5), which we can write as

$$\vec{E} = \rho \vec{J} \tag{25.7}$$

When Ohm's law is obeyed, ρ is constant and independent of the magnitude of the electric field, so $\vec{E}$ is directly proportional to $\vec{J}$. Often, however, we are more interested in the total current in a conductor than in $\vec{J}$ and more interested in the potential difference between the ends of the conductor than in $\vec{E}$. This is so largely because current and potential difference are much easier to measure than are $\vec{J}$ and $\vec{E}$.

Suppose our conductor is a wire with uniform cross-sectional area A and length L, as shown in Fig. 25.7. Let V be the potential difference between the higher-potential and lower-potential ends of the conductor, so that V is positive. The *direction* of the current is always from the higher-potential end to the lower-potential end. That's because current in a conductor flows in the direction of $\vec{E}$, no matter what the sign of the moving charges (Fig. 25.2), and because $\vec{E}$ points in the direction of *decreasing* electric potential (see Section 23.2). As the current flows through the potential difference, electric potential energy is lost; this energy is transferred to the ions of the conducting material during collisions.

We can also relate the *value* of the current I to the potential difference between the ends of the conductor. If the magnitudes of the current density $\vec{J}$ and the electric field $\vec{E}$ are uniform throughout the conductor, the total current I is given by $I = JA$, and the potential difference V between the ends is $V = EL$. When we solve these equations for J and E, respectively, and substitute the results in Eq. (25.7), we obtain

$$\frac{V}{L} = \frac{\rho I}{A} \quad \text{or} \quad V = \frac{\rho L}{A} I \tag{25.8}$$

This shows that when ρ is constant, the total current I is proportional to the potential difference V.

The ratio of V to I for a particular conductor is called its **resistance** R:

$$R = \frac{V}{I} \tag{25.9}$$

Comparing this definition of R to Eq. (25.8), we see that the resistance R of a particular conductor is related to the resistivity ρ of its material by

$$R = \frac{\rho L}{A} \quad \text{(relationship between resistance and resistivity)} \tag{25.10}$$

If ρ is constant, as is the case for ohmic materials, then so is R.

The equation

$$V = IR \quad \text{(relationship among voltage, current, and resistance)} \tag{25.11}$$

is often called Ohm's law, but it is important to understand that the real content of Ohm's law is the direct proportionality (for some materials) of V to I or of J to E. Equation (25.9) or (25.11) *defines* resistance R for *any* conductor, whether or not it obeys Ohm's law, but only when R is constant can we correctly call this relationship Ohm's law.

25.7 A conductor with uniform cross section. The current density is uniform over any cross section, and the electric field is constant along the length.

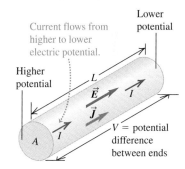

25.8 A long fire hose offers substantial resistance to water flow. To make water pass through the hose rapidly, the upstream end of the hose must be at much higher pressure than the end where the water emerges. In an analogous way, there must be a large potential difference between the ends of a long wire in order to cause a substantial electric current through the wire.

Interpreting Resistance

Equation (25.10) shows that the resistance of a wire or other conductor of uniform cross section is directly proportional to its length and inversely proportional to its cross-sectional area. It is also proportional to the resistivity of the material of which the conductor is made.

The flowing-fluid analogy is again useful. In analogy to Eq. (25.10), a narrow water hose offers more resistance to flow than a fat one, and a long hose has more resistance than a short one (Fig. 25.8). We can increase the resistance to flow by stuffing the hose with cotton or sand; this corresponds to increasing the resistivity. The flow rate is approximately proportional to the pressure difference between the ends. Flow rate is analogous to current, and pressure difference is analogous to potential difference ("voltage"). Let's not stretch this analogy too far, though; the water flow rate in a pipe is usually *not* proportional to its cross-sectional area (see Section 14.6).

The SI unit of resistance is the **ohm,** equal to one volt per ampere $(1 \, \Omega = 1 \, \text{V}/\text{A})$. The *kilohm* $(1 \, \text{k}\Omega = 10^3 \, \Omega)$ and the *megohm* $(1 \, \text{M}\Omega = 10^6 \, \Omega)$ are also in common use. A 100-m length of 12-gauge copper wire, the size usually used in household wiring, has a resistance at room temperature of about $0.5 \, \Omega$. A 100-W, 120-V light bulb has a resistance (at operating temperature) of $140 \, \Omega$. If the same current I flows in both the copper wire and the light bulb, the potential difference $V = IR$ is much greater across the light bulb, and much more potential energy is lost per charge in the light bulb. This lost energy is converted by the light bulb filament into light and heat. You don't want your household wiring to glow white-hot, so its resistance is kept low by using wire of low resistivity and large cross-sectional area.

Because the resistivity of a material varies with temperature, the resistance of a specific conductor also varies with temperature. For temperature ranges that are not too great, this variation is approximately a linear relationship, analogous to Eq. (25.6):

$$R(T) = R_0[1 + \alpha(T - T_0)] \qquad (25.12)$$

In this equation, $R(T)$ is the resistance at temperature T and R_0 is the resistance at temperature T_0, often taken to be 0°C or 20°C. The *temperature coefficient of resistance* α is the same constant that appears in Eq. (25.6) if the dimensions L and A in Eq. (25.10) do not change appreciably with temperature; this is indeed the case for most conducting materials (see Problem 25.67). Within the limits of validity of Eq. (25.12), the *change* in resistance resulting from a temperature change $T - T_0$ is given by $R_0\alpha(T - T_0)$.

A circuit device made to have a specific value of resistance between its ends is called a **resistor.** Resistors in the range 0.01 to $10^7 \, \Omega$ can be bought off the shelf. Individual resistors used in electronic circuitry are often cylindrical, a few millimeters in diameter and length, with wires coming out of the ends. The resistance may be marked with a standard code using three or four color bands near one end (Fig. 25.9), according to the scheme shown in Table 25.3. The first two bands (starting with the band nearest an end) are digits, and the third is a power-of-10 multiplier, as shown in Fig. 25.9. For example, green–violet–red means $57 \times 10^2 \Omega$, or $5.7 \, \text{k}\Omega$. The fourth band, if present, indicates the precision (tolerance) of the value; no band means $\pm 20\%$, a silver band $\pm 10\%$, and a gold band $\pm 5\%$. Another important characteristic of a resistor is the maximum *power* it can dissipate without damage. We'll return to this point in Section 25.5.

For a resistor that obeys Ohm's law, a graph of current as a function of potential difference (voltage) is a straight line (Fig. 25.10a). The slope of the line is $1/R$. If the sign of the potential difference changes, so does the sign of the current produced; in Fig. 25.7 this corresponds to interchanging the higher- and lower-potential ends of the conductor, so the electric field, current density, and current

Table 25.3 Color Codes for Resistors

Color	Value as Digit	Value as Multiplier
Black	0	1
Brown	1	10
Red	2	10^2
Orange	3	10^3
Yellow	4	10^4
Green	5	10^5
Blue	6	10^6
Violet	7	10^7
Gray	8	10^8
White	9	10^9

25.9 This resistor has a resistance of $5.7 \, \text{k}\Omega$ with a precision (tolerance) of $\pm 10\%$.

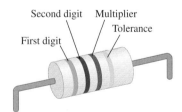

Second digit   Multiplier

Tolerance

First digit

25.10 Current–voltage relationships for two devices. Only for a resistor that obeys Ohm's law as in (a) is current I proportional to voltage V.

(a)

Ohmic resistor (e.g., typical metal wire): At a given temperature, current is proportional to voltage.

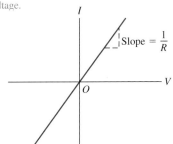

Slope $= \dfrac{1}{R}$

(b)

Semiconductor diode: a nonohmic resistor

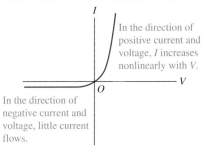

In the direction of positive current and voltage, I increases nonlinearly with V.

In the direction of negative current and voltage, little current flows.

all reverse direction. In devices that do not obey Ohm's law, the relationship of voltage to current may not be a direct proportion, and it may be different for the two directions of current. Figure 25.10b shows the behavior of a semiconductor *diode*, a device used to convert alternating current to direct current and to perform a wide variety of logic functions in computer circuitry. For positive potentials V of the anode (one of two terminals of the diode) with respect to the cathode (the other terminal), I increases exponentially with increasing V; for negative potentials the current is extremely small. Thus a positive potential difference V causes a current to flow in the positive direction, but a potential difference of the other sign causes little or no current. Hence a diode acts like a one-way valve in a circuit.

Example 25.2   Electric field, potential difference, and resistance in a wire

The 18-gauge copper wire in Example 25.1 (Section 25.1) has a diameter of 1.02 mm and a cross-sectional area of $8.20 \times 10^{-7} \text{ m}^2$. It carries a current of 1.67 A. Find (a) the electric-field magnitude in the wire; (b) the potential difference between two points in the wire 50.0 m apart; (c) the resistance of a 50.0-m length of this wire.

SOLUTION

IDENTIFY: We are given the values of cross-sectional area A and current I. Our target variables are the electric-field magnitude E, potential difference V, and resistance R.

SET UP: The magnitude of the current density is $J = I/A$ and the resistivity ρ is given in Table 25.1. We find the electric-field magnitude by using Eq. (25.5), $E = \rho J$. Once we have found E, the potential difference is simply the product of E and the length of the wire. We find the resistance by using Eq. (25.11).

EXECUTE: (a) From Table 25.1, the resistivity of copper is $1.72 \times 10^{-8} \ \Omega \cdot \text{m}$. Hence, using Eq. (25.5),

$$E = \rho J = \frac{\rho I}{A} = \frac{(1.72 \times 10^{-8} \ \Omega \cdot \text{m})(1.67 \text{ A})}{8.20 \times 10^{-7} \text{ m}^2}$$

$$= 0.0350 \text{ V/m}$$

(b) The potential difference is given by

$$V = EL = (0.0350 \text{ V/m})(50.0 \text{ m}) = 1.75 \text{ V}$$

(c) From Eq. (25.11) the resistance of a 50.0-m length of this wire is

$$R = \frac{V}{I} = \frac{1.75 \text{ V}}{1.67 \text{ A}} = 1.05 \ \Omega$$

EVALUATE: To check our result in part (c), we calculate the resistance using Eq. (25.10):

$$R = \frac{\rho L}{A} = \frac{(1.72 \times 10^{-8} \ \Omega \cdot \text{m})(50.0 \text{ m})}{8.20 \times 10^{-7} \text{ m}^2} = 1.05 \ \Omega$$

We emphasize that the resistance of the wire is *defined* to be the ratio of voltage to current. If the wire is made of nonohmic material, then R is different for different values of V but is always given by $R = V/I$. Resistance is also always given by $R = \rho L/A$; if the material is nonohmic, ρ is not constant but depends on E (or, equivalently, on $V = EL$).

Example 25.3 Temperature dependence of resistance

Suppose the resistance of the wire in Example 25.2 is 1.05 Ω at a temperature of 20°C. Find the resistance at 0°C and at 100°C.

SOLUTION

IDENTIFY: This example concerns how resistance (the target variable) depends on temperature. As Table 25.2 shows, this temperature dependence differs for different substances.

SET UP: Our target variables are the values of the wire resistance R at two temperatures, $T = 0°C$ and $T = 100°C$. To find these values we use Eq. (25.12). Note that we are given the resistance $R_0 = 1.05 \Omega$ at a reference temperature $T_0 = 20°C$, and we know from Example 25.2 that the wire is made of copper.

EXECUTE: From Table 25.2 the temperature coefficient of resistivity of copper is $\alpha = 0.00393\ (C°)^{-1}$. From Eq. (25.12), the resistance at $T = 0°C$ is

$$R = R_0[1 + \alpha(T - T_0)]$$
$$= (1.05\ \Omega)\{1 + [0.00393\ (C°)^{-1}][0°C - 20°C]\}$$
$$= 0.97\ \Omega$$

At $T = 100°C$,

$$R = (1.05\ \Omega)\{1 + [0.00393\ (C°)^{-1}][100°C - 20°C]\}$$
$$= 1.38\ \Omega$$

EVALUATE: The resistance at 100°C is greater than that at 0°C by a factor of $(1.38\ \Omega)/(0.97\ \Omega) = 1.42$. In other words, raising the temperature of ordinary copper wire from 0°C to 100°C increases its resistance by 42%. From Eq. (25.11), $V = IR$, this means that 42% more voltage V is required to produce the same current I at 100°C than at 0°C. This is a substantial effect that must be taken into account in designing electric circuits that are to operate over a wide range of temperatures.

Example 25.4 Calculating resistance

The hollow cylinder shown in Fig. 25.11 has length L and inner and outer radii a and b. It is made of a material with resistivity ρ. A potential difference is set up between the inner and outer surfaces of the cylinder (each of which is an equipotential surface) so that current flows radially through the cylinder. What is the resistance to this radial current flow?

SOLUTION

IDENTIFY: Figure 25.11 shows that the current flows radially from the inside of the conductor toward the outside, *not* along the length of the conductor as in Fig. 25.7. Hence we must use the ideas of this section to derive a new formula for resistance (our target variable) appropriate for radial current flow.

SET UP: We can't use Eq. (25.10) directly because the cross section through which the charge travels is *not* constant; it varies from $2\pi a L$ at the inner surface to $2\pi b L$ at the outer surface. Instead, we calculate the resistance to radial current flow through a thin cylindrical shell of inner radius r and thickness dr. We then combine the resistances for all such shells between the inner and outer radii of the cylinder.

EXECUTE: The area A for the shell is $2\pi r L$, the surface area that the current encounters as it flows outward. The length of the current path through the shell is dr. The resistance dR of this shell, between inner and outer surfaces, is that of a conductor with length dr and area $2\pi r L$:

$$dR = \frac{\rho\ dr}{2\pi r L}$$

The current has to pass successively through all such shells between the inner and outer radii a and b. From Eq. (25.11) the potential difference across one shell is $dV = I\ dR$, and the total potential difference between the inner and outer surfaces is the sum of the potential differences for all shells. The total current is

the same through each shell, so the total resistance is the sum of the resistances of all the shells. If the area $2\pi r L$ were constant, we could just integrate dr from $r = a$ to $r = b$ to get the total length of the current path. But the area increases as the current passes through shells of greater radius, so we have to integrate the above expression for dR. The total resistance is thus given by

$$R = \int dR = \frac{\rho}{2\pi L} \int_a^b \frac{dr}{r} = \frac{\rho}{2\pi L} \ln \frac{b}{a}$$

EVALUATE: The conductor geometry shown in Fig. 25.11 plays an important role in your body's nervous system. Each neuron, or nerve cell, has a long extension called a nerve fiber or *axon*. An axon has a cylindrical membrane shaped much like the resistor in Fig. 25.11, with one conducting fluid inside the membrane and another outside it. Ordinarily all of the inner fluid is at the same potential, so no current tends to flow along the length of the axon. If the axon is stimulated at a certain point along its length, however, charged ions flow radially across the cylindrical membrane at that point, as in Fig. 25.11. This flow causes a potential difference between that point and other points along the length of the axon, which makes a nerve signal flow along that length.

25.11 Finding the resistance for radial current flow.

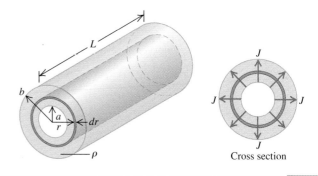

Cross section

Test Your Understanding of Section 25.3   Suppose you increase the voltage across the copper wire in Examples 25.2 and 25.3. The increased voltage causes more current to flow, which makes the temperature of the wire increase. (The same thing happens to the coils of an electric oven or a toaster when a voltage is applied to them. We'll explore this issue in more depth in Section 25.5.) If you double the voltage across the wire, the current in the wire increases. By what factor does it increase? (i) 2; (ii) greater than 2; (iii) less than 2.

25.4 Electromotive Force and Circuits

For a conductor to have a steady current, it must be part of a path that forms a closed loop or **complete circuit.** Here's why. If you establish an electric field $\vec{E}_1$ inside an isolated conductor with resistivity ρ that is *not* part of a complete circuit, a current begins to flow with current density $\vec{J} = \vec{E}_1/\rho$ (Fig. 25.12a). As a result a net positive charge quickly accumulates at one end of the conductor and a net negative charge accumulates at the other end (Fig. 25.12b). These charges themselves produce an electric field $\vec{E}_2$ in the direction opposite to $\vec{E}_1$, causing the total electric field and hence the current to decrease. Within a very small fraction of a second, enough charge builds up on the conductor ends that the total electric field $\vec{E} = \vec{E}_1 + \vec{E}_2 = 0$ inside the conductor. Then $\vec{J} = 0$ as well, and the current stops altogether (Fig. 25.12c). So there can be no steady motion of charge in such an *incomplete* circuit.

To see how to maintain a steady current in a *complete* circuit, we recall a basic fact about electric potential energy: If a charge q goes around a complete circuit and returns to its starting point, the potential energy must be the same at the end of the round trip as at the beginning. As described in Section 25.3, there is always a *decrease* in potential energy when charges move through an ordinary conducting material with resistance. So there must be some part of the circuit in which the potential energy *increases.*

The problem is analogous to an ornamental water fountain that recycles its water. The water pours out of openings at the top, cascades down over the terraces and spouts (moving in the direction of decreasing gravitational potential energy), and collects in a basin in the bottom. A pump then lifts it back to the top (increasing the potential energy) for another trip. Without the pump, the water would just fall to the bottom and stay there.

Electromotive Force

In an electric circuit there must be a device somewhere in the loop that acts like the water pump in a water fountain (Fig. 25.13). In this device a charge travels "uphill," from lower to higher potential energy, even though the electrostatic force is trying to push it from higher to lower potential energy. The direction of current in such a device is from lower to higher potential, just the opposite of what happens in an ordinary conductor. The influence that makes current flow from lower to higher potential is called **electromotive force** (abbreviated **emf** and pronounced "ee-em-eff"). This is a poor term because emf is *not* a force but an energy-per-unit-charge quantity, like potential. The SI unit of emf is the same as that for potential, the volt $(1\ \text{V} = 1\ \text{J/C})$. A typical flashlight battery has an emf of 1.5 V; this means that the battery does 1.5 J of work on every coulomb of charge that passes through it. We'll use the symbol $\mathcal{E}$ (a script capital E) for emf.

Every complete circuit with a steady current must include some device that provides emf. Such a device is called a **source of emf.** Batteries, electric generators, solar cells, thermocouples, and fuel cells are all examples of sources of emf. All such devices convert energy of some form (mechanical, chemical, thermal, and so on) into electric potential energy and transfer it into the circuit to which the device is connected. An *ideal* source of emf maintains a constant potential

25.12 If an electric field is produced inside a conductor that is *not* part of a complete circuit, current flows for only a very short time.

(a) An electric field $\vec{E}_1$ produced inside an isolated conductor causes a current.

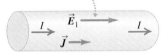

(b) The current causes charge to build up at the ends.

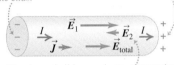

The charge buildup produces an opposing field $\vec{E}_2$, thus reducing the current.

(c) After a very short time $\vec{E}_2$ has the same magnitude as $\vec{E}_1$; then the total field is $\vec{E}_{\text{total}} = 0$ and the current stops completely.

25.13 Just as a water fountain requires a pump, an electric circuit requires a source of electromotive force to sustain a steady current.

12.1 DC Series Circuits (Qualitative)

25.14 Schematic diagram of a source of emf in an "open-circuit" situation. The electric-field force $\vec{F}_e = q\vec{E}$ and the non-electrostatic force $\vec{F}_n$ are shown for a positive charge q.

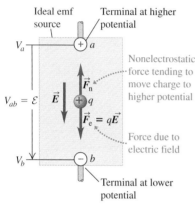

Ideal emf source Terminal at higher potential

V_a

Nonelectrostatic force tending to move charge to higher potential

$V_{ab} = \mathcal{E}$ $\vec{E}$

$\vec{F}_n$

q

$\vec{F}_e = q\vec{E}$

Force due to electric field

V_b

Terminal at lower potential

When the emf source is not part of a closed circuit, $F_n = F_e$ and there is no net motion of charge between the terminals.

25.15 Schematic diagram of an ideal source of emf in a complete circuit. The electric-field force $\vec{F}_e = q\vec{E}$ and the non-electrostatic force $\vec{F}_n$ are shown for a positive charge q The current is in the direction from a to b in the external circuit and from b to a within the source.

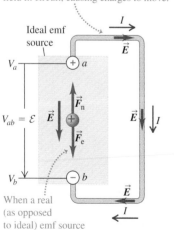

Potential across terminals creates electric field in circuit, causing charges to move.

Ideal emf source

V_a

I

$\vec{E}$

$V_{ab} = \mathcal{E}$ $\vec{E}$

$\vec{F}_n$

$\vec{F}_e$

$\vec{E}$ I

V_b

$\vec{E}$

When a real (as opposed to ideal) emf source is connected to a circuit, V_{ab} and thus F_e fall, so that $F_n > F_e$ and $\vec{F}_n$ does work on the charges.

I

difference between its terminals, independent of the current through it. We define electromotive force quantitatively as the magnitude of this potential difference. As we will see, such an ideal source is a mythical beast, like the frictionless plane and the massless rope. We will discuss later how real-life sources of emf differ in their behavior from this idealized model.

Fig. 25.14 is a schematic diagram of an ideal source of emf that maintains a potential difference between conductors a and b, called the *terminals* of the device. Terminal a, marked $+$, is maintained at *higher* potential than terminal b, marked $-$. Associated with this potential difference is an electric field $\vec{E}$ in the region around the terminals, both inside and outside the source. The electric field inside the device is directed from a to b, as shown. A charge q within the source experiences an electric force $\vec{F}_e = q\vec{E}$. But the source also provides an additional influence, which we represent as a nonelectrostatic force $\vec{F}_n$. This force, operating inside the device, pushes charge from b to a in an "uphill" direction against the electric force $\vec{F}_e$. Thus $\vec{F}_n$ maintains the potential difference between the terminals. If $\vec{F}_n$ were not present, charge would flow between the terminals until the potential difference was zero. The origin of the additional influence $\vec{F}_n$ depends on the kind of source. In a generator it results from magnetic-field forces on moving charges. In a battery or fuel cell it is associated with diffusion processes and varying electrolyte concentrations resulting from chemical reactions. In an electrostatic machine such as a Van de Graaff generator (see Fig. 22.27), an actual mechanical force is applied by a moving belt or wheel.

If a positive charge q is moved from b to a inside the source, the nonelectrostatic force $\vec{F}_n$ does a positive amount of work $W_n = q\mathcal{E}$ on the charge. This displacement is *opposite* to the electrostatic force $\vec{F}_e$, so the potential energy associated with the charge *increases* by an amount equal to qV_{ab}, where $V_{ab} = V_a - V_b$ is the (positive) potential of point a with respect to point b. For the ideal source of emf that we've described, $\vec{F}_e$ and $\vec{F}_n$ are equal in magnitude but opposite in direction, so the total work done on the charge q is zero; there is an increase in potential energy but *no* change in the kinetic energy of the charge. It's like lifting a book from the floor to a high shelf at constant speed. The increase in potential energy is just equal to the non-electrostatic work W_n, so $q\mathcal{E} = qV_{ab}$, or

$$V_{ab} = \mathcal{E} \qquad \text{(ideal source of emf)} \qquad (25.13)$$

Now let's make a complete circuit by connecting a wire with resistance R to the terminals of a source (Fig. 25.15). The potential difference between terminals a and b sets up an electric field within the wire; this causes current to flow around the loop from a toward b, from higher to lower potential. Where the wire bends, equal amounts of positive and negative charge persist on the "inside" and "outside" of the bend. These charges exert the forces that cause the current to follow the bends in the wire.

From Eq. (25.11) the potential difference between the ends of the wire in Fig. 25.15 is given by $V_{ab} = IR$. Combining with Eq. (25.13), we have

$$\mathcal{E} = V_{ab} = IR \qquad \text{(ideal source of emf)} \qquad (25.14)$$

That is, when a positive charge q flows around the circuit, the potential *rise* $\mathcal{E}$ as it passes through the ideal source is numerically equal to the potential *drop* $V_{ab} = IR$ as it passes through the remainder of the circuit. Once $\mathcal{E}$ and R are known, this relationship determines the current in the circuit.

CAUTION **Current is not "used up" in a circuit** It's a common misconception that in a closed circuit, current is something that squirts out of the positive terminal of a battery and is consumed or "used up" by the time it reaches the negative terminal. In fact the current is the *same* at every point in a simple loop circuit like that in Fig. 25.15, even if the thickness of the wires is different at different points in the circuit. This happens because charge is conserved (that is, it can be neither created nor destroyed) and because charge cannot accumulate in the circuit devices we have described. If charge did accumulate, the potential differences would change with time. It's like the flow of water in an ornamental fountain; water flows out of the top of the fountain at the same rate at which it reaches the bottom, no matter what the dimensions of the fountain. None of the water is "used up" along the way! ▮

Internal Resistance

Real sources of emf in a circuit don't behave in exactly the way we have described; the potential difference across a real source in a circuit is *not* equal to the emf as in Eq. (25.14). The reason is that charge moving through the material of any real source encounters *resistance*. We call this the **internal resistance** of the source, denoted by r. If this resistance behaves according to Ohm's law, r is constant and independent of the current I. As the current moves through r, it experiences an associated drop in potential equal to Ir. Thus, when a current is flowing through a source from the negative terminal b to the positive terminal a, the potential difference V_{ab} between the terminals is

$$V_{ab} = \mathcal{E} - Ir \qquad \text{(terminal voltage, source with internal resistance)} \qquad (25.15)$$

The potential V_{ab}, called the **terminal voltage,** is less than the emf $\mathcal{E}$ because of the term Ir representing the potential drop across the internal resistance r. Expressed another way, the increase in potential energy qV_{ab} as a charge q moves from b to a within the source is now less than the work $q\mathcal{E}$ done by the nonelectrostatic force $\vec{F}_n$, since some potential energy is lost in traversing the internal resistance.

A 1.5-V battery has an emf of 1.5 V, but the terminal voltage V_{ab} of the battery is equal to 1.5 V only if no current is flowing through it so that $I = 0$ in Eq. (25.15). If the battery is part of a complete circuit through which current is flowing, the terminal voltage will be less than 1.5 V. *For a real source of emf, the terminal voltage equals the emf only if no current is flowing through the source* (Fig. 25.16). Thus we can describe the behavior of a source in terms of two properties: an emf $\mathcal{E}$, which supplies a constant potential difference independent of current, in series with an internal resistance r.

The current in the external circuit connected to the source terminals a and b is still determined by $V_{ab} = IR$. Combining this with Eq. (25.15), we find

$$\mathcal{E} - Ir = IR \quad \text{or} \quad I = \frac{\mathcal{E}}{R + r} \qquad \text{(current, source with internal resistance)} \qquad (25.16)$$

That is, the current equals the source emf divided by the *total* circuit resistance $(R + r)$.

CAUTION **A battery is not a "current source"** You might have thought that a battery or other source of emf always produces the same current, no matter what circuit it's used in. But as Eq. (25.16) shows, the current that a source of emf produces in a given circuit depends on the resistance R of the external circuit (as well as on the internal resistance r of the source). The greater the resistance, the less current the source will produce. It's analogous to pushing an object through a thick, viscous liquid such as oil or molasses; if you exert a certain steady push (emf), you can move a small object at high speed (small R, large I) or a large object at low speed (large R, small I). ▮

Symbols for Circuit Diagrams

An important part of analyzing any electric circuit is drawing a schematic *circuit diagram.* Table 25.4 shows the usual symbols used in circuit diagrams. We will use these symbols extensively in this chapter and the next. We usually assume that the wires that connect the various elements of the circuit have negligible resistance; from Eq. (25.11), $V = IR$, the potential difference between the ends of such a wire is zero.

25.16 The emf of this battery—that is, the terminal voltage when it's not connected to anything—is 12 V. But because the battery has internal resistance, the terminal voltage of the battery is less than 12 V when it is supplying current to a light bulb.

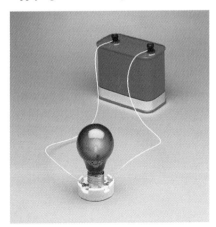

Table 25.4 includes two *meters* that are used to measure the properties of circuits. Idealized meters do not disturb the circuit in which they are connected. A **voltmeter,** introduced in Section 23.2, measures the potential difference between its terminals; an idealized voltmeter has infinitely large resistance and measures potential difference without having any current diverted through it. An ammeter measures the current passing through it; an idealized **ammeter** has zero resistance and has no potential difference between its terminals. Because meters act as part of the circuit in which they are connected, these properties are important to remember.

Table 25.4 Symbols for Circuit Diagrams

————————	Conductor with negligible resistance
——R—/\/\/\——	Resistor
——+ $\mathcal{E}$——	Source of emf (longer vertical line always represents the positive terminal, usually the terminal with higher potential)
or —/\/\—$\mathcal{E}$+— —/\/\—+ $\mathcal{E}$—	Source of emf with internal resistance r (r can be placed on either side)
——(V)——	Voltmeter (measures potential difference between its terminals)
——(A)——	Ammeter (measures current through it)

Conceptual Example 25.5   **A source in an open circuit**

Fig. 25.17 shows a source (a battery) with an emf $\mathcal{E}$ of 12 V and an internal resistance r of 2 Ω. (For comparison, the internal resistance of a commercial 12-V lead storage battery is only a few thousandths of an ohm.) The wires to the left of a and to the right of the ammeter A are not connected to anything. Determine the readings of the idealized voltmeter V and the idealized ammeter A.

25.17 A source of emf in an open circuit.

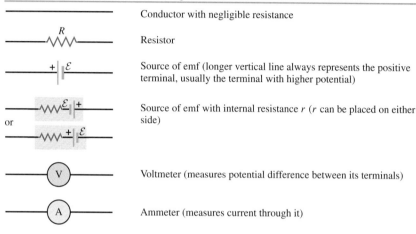

SOLUTION

There is no current because there is no complete circuit. (There is no current through our idealized voltmeter, with its infinitely large resistance.) Hence the ammeter A reads $I = 0$. Because there is no current through the battery, there is no potential difference across its internal resistance. From Eq. (25.15) with $I = 0$, the potential

difference V_{ab} across the battery terminals is equal to the emf. So the voltmeter reads $V_{ab} = \mathcal{E} = 12$ V. The terminal voltage of a real, nonideal source equals the emf *only* if there is no current flowing through the source, as in this example.

Example 25.6   **A source in a complete circuit**

Using the battery in Conceptual Example 25.5, we add a 4-Ω resistor to form the complete circuit shown in Fig. 25.18. What are the voltmeter and ammeter readings now?

SOLUTION

IDENTIFY Our first target variable is the current I through the circuit $aa'b'b$ (equal to the ammeter reading). The second is the potential difference V_{ab} (equal to the voltmeter reading).

SET UP: We find I using Eq. (25.16). To find V_{ab}, we note that we can regard this either as the potential difference across the source or as the potential difference around the circuit through the external resistor.

25.18 A source of emf in a complete circuit.

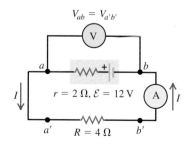

EXECUTE: The ideal ammeter has zero resistance, so the resistance external to the source is $R = 4\ \Omega$. From Eq. (25.16), the current through the circuit $aa'b'b$ is

$$I = \frac{\mathcal{E}}{R + r} = \frac{12\ \text{V}}{4\ \Omega + 2\Omega} = 2\ \text{A}$$

The ammeter A reads $I = 2$ A.

Our idealized conducting wires have zero resistance, and the idealized ammeter A also has zero resistance. So there is no potential difference between points a and a' or between points b and b'; that is, $V_{ab} = V_{a'b'}$. We can find V_{ab} by considering a and b either as the terminals of the resistor or as the terminals of the source. Considering them as terminals of the resistor, we use Ohm's law ($V = IR$):

$$V_{a'b'} = IR = (2\ \text{A})(4\ \Omega) = 8\ \text{V}$$

Considering them as the terminals of the source, we have

$$V_{ab} = \mathcal{E} - Ir = 12\ \text{V} - (2\ \text{A})(2\ \Omega) = 8\ \text{V}$$

Either way, we conclude that the voltmeter reads $V_{ab} = 8$ V.

EVALUATE: With a current flowing through the source, the terminal voltage V_{ab} is less than the emf. The smaller the internal resistance r, the less the difference between V_{ab} and $\mathcal{E}$.

Conceptual Example 25.7   Using voltmeters and ammeters

The voltmeter and ammeter in Example 25.6 are moved to different positions in the circuit. What are the voltmeter and ammeter readings in the situations shown in (a) Fig. 25.19a and (b) Fig. 25.19b?

25.19 Different placements of a voltmeter and an ammeter in a complete circuit.

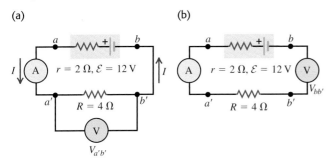

(a)   (b)

$V_{a'b'}$

SOLUTION

(a) The voltmeter now measures the potential difference between points a' and b'. But as mentioned in Example 25.6, $V_{ab} = V_{a'b'}$, so the voltmeter reads the same as in Example 25.6: $V_{a'b'} = 8$ V.

CAUTION   **Current in a simple loop**   You might be tempted to conclude that the ammeter in Fig. 25.19a, which is located "upstream" of the resistor, would have a higher reading than the one located "downstream" of the resistor in Fig. 25.18. But this conclusion is based on the misconception that current is somehow "used up" as it moves through a resistor. As charges move through a resistor, there is a decrease in electric potential energy, but there is *no* change in the current. *The current in a simple loop is the same at every point.* An ammeter placed as in Fig. 25.19a reads the same as one placed as in Fig. 25.18: $I = 2$ A. ▪

(b) There is no current through the voltmeter because it has infinitely large resistance. Since the voltmeter is now part of the circuit, there is no current at all in the circuit, and the ammeter reads $I = 0$.

The voltmeter measures the potential difference $V_{bb'}$ between points b and b'. Since $I = 0$, the potential difference across the resistor is $V_{a'b'} = IR = 0$, and the potential difference between the ends a and a' of the idealized ammeter is also zero. So $V_{bb'}$ is equal to V_{ab}, the terminal voltage of the source. As in Conceptual Example 25.5, there is no current flowing, so the terminal voltage equals the emf, and the voltmeter reading is $V_{ab} = \mathcal{E} = 12$ V.

This example shows that ammeters and voltmeters are circuit elements, too. Moving the voltmeter from the position in Fig. 25.19a to that in Fig. 25.19b changes the current and potential differences in the circuit—in this case rather dramatically. If you want to measure the potential difference between two points in a circuit without disturbing the circuit, use a voltmeter as in Figs. 25.18 or 25.19a, *not* as in Fig. 25.19b.

Example 25.8   A source with a short circuit

Using the same battery as in the preceding three examples, we now replace the 4-Ω resistor with a zero-resistance conductor. What are the meter readings now?

SOLUTION

IDENTIFY: Our target variables are I and V_{ab}, the same as in Example 25.6. The only difference from that example is that the external resistance is now $R = 0$.

SET UP: Figure 25.20 shows the new circuit. There is now a zero-resistance path between points a and b (through the lower loop in Fig. 25.20). Hence the potential difference between these points must be zero, which we can use to help solve the problem.

25.20 Our sketch for this problem.

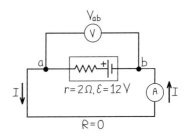

Continued

EXECUTE: We must have $V_{ab} = IR = I(0) = 0$, no matter what the current. Knowing this, we can find the current I from Eq. (25.15):

$$V_{ab} = \mathcal{E} - Ir = 0$$

$$I = \frac{\mathcal{E}}{r} = \frac{12\ \text{V}}{2\ \Omega} = 6\ \text{A}$$

The ammeter reads $I = 6$ A and the voltmeter reads $V_{ab} = 0$.

EVALUATE: The current has a different value than in Example 25.6, even though the same battery is used. A source does *not* deliver the same current in all situations; the amount of current depends on the internal resistance r and on the resistance of the external circuit.

The situation in this example is called a *short circuit.* The terminals of the battery are connected directly to each other, with no external resistance. The short-circuit current is equal to the emf $\mathcal{E}$ divided by the internal resistance r. *Warning:* A short circuit can be an extremely dangerous situation. An automobile battery or a household power line has very small internal resistance (much less than in these examples), and the short-circuit current can be great enough to melt a small wire or cause a storage battery to explode. Don't try it!

Potential Changes Around a Circuit

The net change in potential energy for a charge q making a round trip around a complete circuit must be zero. Hence the net change in *potential* around the circuit must also be zero; in other words, the algebraic sum of the potential differences and emfs around the loop is zero. We can see this by rewriting Eq. (25.16) in the form

$$\mathcal{E} - Ir - IR = 0$$

A potential gain of $\mathcal{E}$ is associated with the emf, and potential drops of Ir and IR are associated with the internal resistance of the source and the external circuit, respectively. Fig. 25.21 is a graph showing how the potential varies as we go around the complete circuit of Fig. 25.18. The horizontal axis doesn't necessarily represent actual distances, but rather various points in the loop. If we take the potential to be zero at the negative terminal of the battery, then we have a rise $\mathcal{E}$ and a drop Ir in the battery and an additional drop IR in the external resistor, and as we finish our trip around the loop, the potential is back where it started.

In this section we have considered only situations in which the resistances are ohmic. If the circuit includes a nonlinear device such as a diode (see Fig. 25.10b), Eq. (25.16) is still valid but cannot be solved algebraically because R is not a constant. In such a situation, the current I can be found by using numerical techniques (see Challenge Problem 25.84).

Finally, we remark that Eq. (25.15) is not always an adequate representation of the behavior of a source. The emf may not be constant, and what we have

25.21 Potential rises and drops in a circuit.

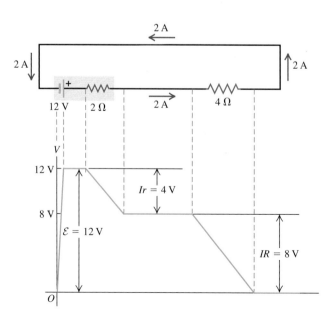

described as an internal resistance may actually be a more complex voltage–current relationship that doesn't obey Ohm's law. Nevertheless, the concept of internal resistance frequently provides an adequate description of batteries, generators, and other energy converters. The principal difference between a fresh flashlight battery and an old one is not in the emf, which decreases only slightly with use, but in the internal resistance, which may increase from less than an ohm when the battery is fresh to as much as 1000 Ω or more after long use. Similarly, a car battery can deliver less current to the starter motor on a cold morning than when the battery is warm, not because the emf is appreciably less but because the internal resistance increases with decreasing temperature. Cold-climate dwellers take a number of measures to avoid this loss, from using special battery warmers to soaking the battery in warm water on very cold mornings.

Test Your Understanding of Section 25.4   Rank the following circuits in order from highest to lowest current. (i) a 1.4-Ω resistor connected to a 1.5-V battery that has an internal resistance of 0.10 Ω; (ii) a 1.8-Ω resistor connected to a 4.0-V battery that has a terminal voltage of 3.6 V but an unknown internal resistance; (iii) an unknown resistor connected to a 12.0-V battery that has an internal resistance of 0.20 Ω and a terminal voltage of 11.0 V.

25.5 Energy and Power in Electric Circuits

Let's now look at some energy and power relationships in electric circuits. The box in Fig. 25.22 represents a circuit element with potential difference $V_a - V_b = V_{ab}$ between its terminals and current I passing through it in the direction from a toward b. This element might be a resistor, a battery, or something else; the details don't matter. As charge passes through the circuit element, the electric field does work on the charge. In a source of emf, additional work is done by the force $\vec{F}_n$ that we mentioned in Section 25.4.

As an amount of charge q passes through the circuit element, there is a change in potential energy equal to qV_{ab}. For example, if $q > 0$ and $V_{ab} = V_a - V_b$ is positive, potential energy decreases as the charge "falls" from potential V_a to lower potential V_b. The moving charges don't gain *kinetic* energy, because the rate of charge flow (that is, the current) out of the circuit element must be the same as the rate of charge flow into the element. Instead, the quantity qV_{ab} represents electrical energy transferred into the circuit element. This situation occurs in the coils of a toaster or electric oven, in which electrical energy is converted to thermal energy.

It may happen that the potential at b is higher than that at a. In this case V_{ab} is negative, and a net transfer of energy *out* of the circuit element occurs. The element then acts as a source, delivering electrical energy into the circuit to which it is attached. This is the usual situation for a battery, which converts chemical energy into electrical energy and delivers it to the external circuit. Thus qV_{ab} can denote either a quantity of energy delivered to a circuit element or a quantity of energy extracted from that element.

In electric circuits we are most often interested in the *rate* at which energy is either delivered to or extracted from a circuit element. If the current through the element is I, then in a time interval dt an amount of charge $dQ = I\, dt$ passes through the element. The potential energy change for this amount of charge is $V_{ab}\, dQ = V_{ab} I\, dt$. Dividing this expression by dt, we obtain the *rate* at which energy is transferred either into or out of the circuit element. The time rate of energy transfer is *power*, denoted by P, so we write

$$P = V_{ab}I \qquad \text{(rate at which energy is delivered to or extracted from a circuit element)} \qquad (25.17)$$

25.22 The power input to the circuit element between a and b is $P = (V_a - V_b)I = V_{ab}I$.

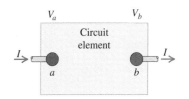

The unit of V_{ab} is one volt, or one joule per coulomb, and the unit of I is one ampere, or one coulomb per second. Hence the unit of $P = V_{ab}I$ is one watt, as it should be:

$$(1 \text{ J/C})(1 \text{ C/s}) = 1 \text{ J/s} = 1 \text{ W}$$

Let's consider a few special cases.

Power Inout to a Pure Resistance

If the circuit element in Fig. 25.22 is a resistor, the potential difference is $V_{ab} = IR$. From Eq. (25.17) the electrical power delivered to the resistor by the circuit is

$$P = V_{ab}I = I^2R = \frac{V_{ab}^2}{R} \qquad \text{(power delivered to a resistor)} \qquad (25.18)$$

In this case the potential at a (where the current enters the resistor) is always higher than that at b (where the current exits). Current enters the higher-potential terminal of the device, and Eq. (25.18) represents the rate of transfer of electric potential energy *into* the circuit element.

What becomes of this energy? The moving charges collide with atoms in the resistor and transfer some of their energy to these atoms, increasing the internal energy of the material. Either the temperature of the resistor increases or there is a flow of heat out of it, or both. In any of these cases we say that energy is *dissipated* in the resistor at a rate I^2R. Every resistor has a *power rating*, the maximum power the device can dissipate without becoming overheated and damaged. In practical applications the power rating of a resistor is often just as important a characteristic as its resistance value. Of course, some devices, such as electric heaters, are designed to get hot and transfer heat to their surroundings. But if the power rating is exceeded, even such a device may melt or even explode.

Power Output of a Source

The upper rectangle in Fig. 25.23a represents a source with emf $\mathcal{E}$ and internal resistance r, connected by ideal (resistanceless) conductors to an external circuit represented by the lower box. This could describe a car battery connected to one of the car's headlights (Fig. 25.23b). Point a is at higher potential than point b, so $V_a > V_b$ and V_{ab} is positive. Note that the current I is *leaving* the source at the higher-potential terminal (rather than entering there). Energy is being delivered to the external circuit, and the rate of its delivery to the circuit is given by Eq. (25.17):

$$P = V_{ab}I$$

For a source that can be described by an emf $\mathcal{E}$ and an internal resistance r, we may use Eq. (25.15):

$$V_{ab} = \mathcal{E} - Ir$$

Multiplying this equation by I, we find

$$P = V_{ab}I = \mathcal{E}I - I^2r \qquad (25.19)$$

What do the terms $\mathcal{E}I$ and I^2r mean? In Section 25.4 we defined the emf $\mathcal{E}$ as the work per unit charge performed on the charges by the nonelectrostatic force as the charges are pushed "uphill" from b to a in the source. In a time dt, a charge $dQ = I\,dt$ flows through the source; the work done on it by this nonelectrostatic force is $\mathcal{E}\,dQ = \mathcal{E}I\,dt$. Thus $\mathcal{E}I$ is the *rate* at which work is done on the circulating charges by whatever agency causes the nonelectrostatic force in the source. This term represents the rate of conversion of nonelectrical energy to electrical energy within the source. The term I^2r is the rate at which electrical energy is

25.23 Energy conversion in a simple circuit.

(a) Diagrammatic circuit

- The emf source converts nonelectrical to electrical energy at a rate $\mathcal{E}I$.
- Its internal resistance *dissipates* energy at a rate I^2r.
- The difference $\mathcal{E}I - I^2r$ is its power output.

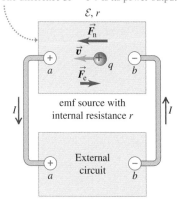

(b) A real circuit of the type shown in (a)

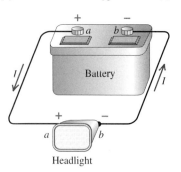

Headlight

dissipated in the internal resistance of the source. The difference $\mathcal{E}I - I^2r$ is the *net* electrical power output of the source—that is, the rate at which the source delivers electrical energy to the remainder of the circuit.

Power Input to a Source

Suppose that the lower rectangle in Fig. 25.23a is itself a source, with an emf *larger* than that of the upper source and with its emf opposite to that of the upper source. Fig. 25.24 shows a practical example, an automobile battery (the upper circuit element) being charged by the car's alternator (the lower element). The current I in the circuit is then *opposite* to that shown in Fig. 25.23; the lower source is pushing current backward through the upper source. Because of this reversal of current, instead of Eq. (25.15) we have for the upper source

$$V_{ab} = \mathcal{E} + Ir$$

and instead of Eq. (25.19), we have

$$P = V_{ab}I = \mathcal{E}I + I^2R \qquad (25.20)$$

Work is being done *on*, rather than *by*, the agent that causes the nonelectrostatic force in the upper source. There is a conversion of electrical energy into nonelectrical energy in the upper source at a rate $\mathcal{E}I$. The term I^2r in Eq. (25.20) is again the rate of dissipation of energy in the internal resistance of the upper source, and the sum $\mathcal{E}I + I^2r$ is the total electrical power *input* to the upper source. This is what happens when a rechargeable battery (a storage battery) is connected to a charger. The charger supplies electrical energy to the battery; part of it is converted to chemical energy, to be reconverted later, and the remainder is dissipated (wasted) in the battery's internal resistance, warming the battery and causing a heat flow out of it. If you have a power tool or laptop computer with a rechargeable battery, you may have noticed that it gets warm while it is charging.

25.24 When two sources are connected in a simple loop circuit, the source with the larger emf delivers energy to the other source.

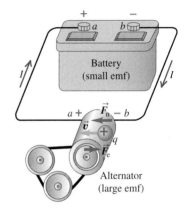

Problem-Solving Strategy 25.1 **Power and Energy in Circuits**

IDENTIFY *the relevant concepts:*
The ideas of electric power input and output can be applied to any electric circuit. In most cases you'll know when these concepts are needed because the problem will ask you explicitly to consider power or energy.

SET UP *the problem* using the following steps:
1. Make a drawing of the circuit.
2. Identify the circuit elements, including sources of emf and resistors. In later chapters we will add other kinds of circuit elements, including capacitors and inductors (described in Chapter 30).
3. Determine the target variables. Typically they will be the power input or output for each circuit element, or the total amount of energy put into or taken out of a circuit element in a given time.

EXECUTE *the solution* as follows:
1. A source of emf $\mathcal{E}$ delivers power $\mathcal{E}I$ into a circuit when the current I runs through the source from $-$ to $+$. The energy is converted from chemical energy in a battery, from mechanical energy in a generator, or whatever. In this case the source has a *positive* power output to the circuit or, equivalently, a *negative* power input to the source.
2. A source of emf takes power $\mathcal{E}I$ from a circuit—that is, it has a negative power output or, equivalently, a positive power input—when current passes through the source in the direction from $+$

to $-$. This occurs in charging a storage battery, when electrical energy is converted back to chemical energy. In this case the source has a *negative* power output to the circuit or, equivalently, a *positive* power input to the source.
3. No matter what the direction of the current through a resistor, there is always a *positive* power input to the resistor. It removes energy from a circuit at a rate given by $VI = I^2R = V^2/R$, where V is the potential difference across the resistor.
4. There is also a *positive* power input to the internal resistance r of a source, irrespective of the direction of the current. The internal resistance always removes energy from the circuit, converting it into heat at a rate I^2r.
5. You may need to calculate the total energy delivered to or extracted from a circuit element in a given amount of time. If the power into or out of a circuit element is constant, this integral is just the product of power and elapsed time. (In Chapter 26 we will encounter situations in which the power is not constant. In such cases, calculating the total energy requires an integral.)

EVALUATE *your answer:* Check your results, including a check that energy is conserved. This conservation can be expressed in either of two forms: "net power input = net power output" or "the algebraic sum of the power inputs to the circuit elements is zero."

Example 25.9 Power input and output in a complete circuit

For the situation that we analyzed in Example 25.6, find the rate of energy conversion (chemical to electrical) and the rate of dissipation of energy in the battery and the net power output of the battery.

SOLUTION

IDENTIFY: Our target variables are the power output of the source of emf, the power input to the internal resistance, and the net power output of the source.

SET UP: Fig. 25.25 shows the circuit. We use Eq. (25.17) to find the power input or output of a circuit element and Eq. (25.19) to find the source's net power output.

25.25 Our sketch for this problem.

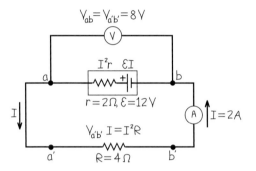

EXECUTE: From Example 25.6 the current in the circuit is $I = 2$ A. The rate of energy conversion in the battery is

$$\mathcal{E}I = (12\text{ V})(2\text{ A}) = 24\text{ W}$$

The rate of dissipation of energy in the battery is

$$I^2r = (2\text{ A})^2(2\text{ }\Omega) = 8\text{ W}$$

The electrical power *output* of the source is the difference between these: $\mathcal{E}I - I^2r = 16$ W.

EVALUATE: The power output is also given by the terminal voltage $V_{ab} = 8$ V (calculated in Example 25.6) multiplied by the current:

$$V_{ab}I = (8\text{ V})(2\text{ A}) = 16\text{ W}$$

The electrical power input to the resistor is

$$V_{a'b'}I = (8\text{ V})(2\text{ A}) = 16\text{ W}$$

This equals the rate of dissipation of electrical energy in the resistor:

$$I^2R = (2\text{ A})^2(4\text{ }\Omega) = 16\text{ W}$$

Note that our results agree with Eq. (25.19), which states that $V_{ab}I = \mathcal{E}I - I^2R$; the left side of this equation equals 16 W, and the right side equals 24 W − 8 W = 16 W. This verifies the consistency of the various power quantities.

Example 25.10 Increasing the resistance

Suppose the 4-Ω resistor in Fig. 25.25 is replaced by an 8-Ω resistor. How does this affect the electrical power dissipated in the resistor?

SOLUTION

IDENTIFY: Our target variable is the power dissipated in the resistor to which the source of emf is connected.

SET UP: The situation is the same as that in Example 25.9, but with a different value of the external resistance R.

EXECUTE: According to Eq. (25.18), the power dissipated in the resistor is given by $P = I^2R$. If you were in a hurry, you might conclude that since R now has twice the value that it had in Example 25.9, the power should also be twice as great, or 2(16 W) = 32 W. Or you might instead try to use the formula $P = V_{ab}^2/R$; this formula would lead you to conclude that the power should be one-half as great as in the preceding example, or (16 W)/2 = 8 W. Which answer is correct?

In fact, *both* of these conclusions are *incorrect*. The first is incorrect because changing the resistance R also changes the current in the circuit (remember, a source of emf does *not* generate the same current in all situations). The second conclusion is also incorrect because the potential difference V_{ab} across the resistor changes when the current changes. To get the correct answer, we first use the same technique as in Example 25.6 to find the current:

$$I = \frac{\mathcal{E}}{R + r} = \frac{12\text{ V}}{8\text{ }\Omega + 2\text{ }\Omega} = 1.2\text{ A}$$

The greater resistance causes the current to decrease. The potential difference across the resistor is

$$V_{ab} = IR = (1.2\text{ A})(8\text{ }\Omega) = 9.6\text{ V}$$

which is greater than that with the 4-Ω resistor. We can then find the power dissipated in the resistor in either of two ways:

$$P = I^2R = (1.2\text{ A})^2(8\text{ }\Omega) = 12\text{ W}\quad\text{or}$$
$$P = \frac{V_{ab}^2}{R} = \frac{(9.6\text{ V})^2}{8\text{ }\Omega} = 12\text{ W}$$

EVALUATE: Increasing the resistance R causes a *reduction* in the power input to the resistor. In the expression $P = I^2R$ the decrease in current is more important than the increase in resistance; in the expression $P = V_{ab}^2/R$ the increase in resistance is more important than the increase in V_{ab}. This same principle applies to ordinary light bulbs; a 50-W light bulb has a greater resistance than does a 100-W light bulb.

Can you show that replacing the 4-Ω resistor with an 8-Ω resistor decreases both the rate of energy conversion (chemical to electrical) in the battery and the rate of energy dissipation in the battery?

| Example 25.11 | **Power in a short circuit** |

For the circuit that we analyzed in Example 25.8, find the rates of energy conversion and energy dissipation in the battery and the net power output of the battery.

SOLUTION

IDENTIFY: Our target variables are again the power inputs and outputs associated with the battery.

SET UP: Fig. 25.26 shows the circuit. This is once again the same situation as in Example 25.9, but now the external resistance R is zero.

EXECUTE: We found in Example 25.8 that the current in this situation is $I = 6$ A. The rate of energy conversion (chemical to electrical) in the battery is

$$\mathcal{E}I = (12 \text{ V})(6 \text{ A}) = 72 \text{ W}$$

The rate of dissipation of energy in the battery is

$$I^2r = (6 \text{ A})^2(2 \text{ }\Omega) = 72 \text{ W}$$

The net power output of the source, given by $V_{ab}I$, is zero because the terminal voltage V_{ab} is zero.

25.26 Our sketch for this problem.

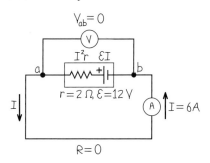

EVALUATE: With ideal wires and an ideal ammeter so that $R = 0$, *all* of the converted energy is dissipated within the source. This is why a short-circuited battery is quickly ruined and in some cases may even explode.

Test Your Understanding of Section 25.5   Rank the following circuits in order from highest to lowest values of the net power output of the battery. (i) a 1.4-Ω resistor connected to a 1.5-V battery that has an internal resistance of 0.10 Ω; (ii) a 1.8-Ω; resistor connected to a 4.0-V battery that has a terminal voltage of 3.6 V but an unknown internal resistance; (iii) an unknown resistor connected to a 12.0-V battery that has an internal resistance of 0.20 Ω; and a terminal voltage of 11.0 V.

*25.6 Theory of Metallic Conduction

We can gain additional insight into electrical conduction by looking at the microscopic origin of conductivity. We'll consider a very simple model that treats the electrons as classical particles and ignores their quantum-mechanical, wavelike behavior in solids. Using this model, we'll derive an expression for the resistivity of a metal. Even though this model is not entirely correct conceptually, it will still help you to develop an intuitive idea of the microscopic basis of conduction.

In the simplest microscopic model of conduction in a metal, each atom in the metallic crystal gives up one or more of its outer electrons. These electrons are then free to move through the crystal, colliding at intervals with the stationary positive ions. The motion of the electrons is analogous to the motion of molecules of a gas moving through a porous bed of sand, and they are often referred to as an "electron gas."

If there is no electric field, the electrons move in straight lines between collisions, the directions of their velocities are random, and on average they never get anywhere (Fig. 25.27a). But if an electric field is present, the paths curve slightly because of the acceleration caused by electric-field forces. Figure 25.27b shows a few paths of an electron in an electric field directed from right to left. As we mentioned in Section 25.1, the average speed of random motion is of the order of 10^6 m/s, while the average drift speed is *much* slower, of the order of 10^{-4} m/s.

25.27 Random motions of an electron in a metallic crystal **(a)** with zero electric field and **(b)** with an electric field that causes drift. The curvatures of the paths are greatly exaggerated.

(a) Typical trajectory for an electron in a metallic crystal *without* an internal $\vec{E}$ field

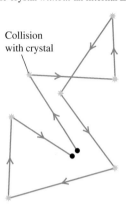

(a) Typical trajectory for an electron in a metallic crystal *with* an internal $\vec{E}$ field

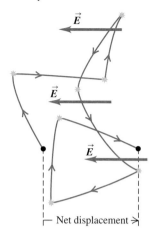

25.28 The motion of a ball rolling down an inclined plane and bouncing off pegs in its path is analogous to the motion of an electron in a metallic conductor with an electric field present.

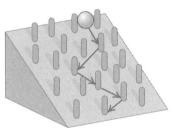

The average time between collisions is called the **mean free time,** denoted by τ. Figure 25.28 shows a mechanical analog of this electron motion.

We would like to derive from this model an expression for the resistivity ρ of a material, defined by Eq. (25.5):

$$\rho = \frac{E}{J} \tag{25.21}$$

where E and J are the magnitudes of electric field and current density. The current density $\vec{J}$ is in turn given by Eq. (25.4):

$$\vec{J} = nq\vec{v}_{\rm d} \tag{25.22}$$

where n is the number of free electrons per unit volume, q is the charge of each, and $\vec{v}_{\rm d}$ is their average drift velocity. (We also know that $q = -e$ in an ordinary metal; we'll use that fact later.)

We need to relate the drift velocity $\vec{v}_{\rm d}$ to the electric field $\vec{E}$. The value of $\vec{v}_{\rm d}$ is determined by a steady-state condition in which, on average, the velocity *gains* of the charges due to the force of the $\vec{E}$ field are just balanced by the velocity *losses* due to collisions.

To clarify this process, let's imagine turning on the two effects one at a time. Suppose that before time $t = 0$ there is no field. The electron motion is then completely random. A typical electron has velocity $\vec{v}_0$ at time $t = 0$, and the value of $\vec{v}_0$ averaged over many electrons (that is, the initial velocity of an average electron) is zero: $(\vec{v}_0)_{\rm av} = \mathbf{0}$. Then at time $t = 0$ we turn on a constant electric field $\vec{E}$. The field exerts a force $\vec{F} = q\vec{E}$ on each charge, and this causes an acceleration $\vec{a}$ in the direction of the force, given by

$$\vec{a} = \frac{\vec{F}}{m} = \frac{q\vec{E}}{m}$$

where m is the electron mass. *Every* electron has this acceleration.

We wait for a time τ, the average time between collisions, and then "turn on" the collisions. An electron that has velocity $\vec{v}_0$ at time $t = 0$ has a velocity at time $t = \tau$ equal to

$$\vec{v} = \vec{v}_0 + \vec{a}\tau$$

The velocity $\vec{v}_{av}$ of an *average* electron at this time is the sum of the averages of the two terms on the right. As we have pointed out, the initial velocity $\vec{v}_0$ is zero for an average electron, so

$$\vec{v}_{av} = \vec{a}\tau = \frac{q\tau}{m}\vec{E} \qquad (25.23)$$

After time $t = \tau$, the tendency of the collisions to decrease the velocity of an average electron (by means of randomizing collisions) just balances the tendency of the $\vec{E}$ field to increase this velocity. Thus the velocity of an average electron, given by Eq. (25.23), is maintained over time and is equal to the drift velocity $\vec{v}_d$:

$$\vec{v}_d = \frac{q\tau}{m}\vec{E}$$

Now we substitute this equation for the drift velocity $\vec{v}_d$ into Eq. (25.22):

$$\vec{J} = nq\vec{v}_d = \frac{nq^2\tau}{m}\vec{E}$$

Comparing this with Eq. (25.21), which we can rewrite as $\vec{J} = \vec{E}/\rho$, and substituting $q = -e$, we see that the resistivity ρ is given by

$$\rho = \frac{m}{ne^2\tau} \qquad (25.24)$$

If n and τ are independent of $\vec{E}$, then the resistivity is independent of $\vec{E}$ and the conducting material obeys Ohm's law.

Turning the interactions on one at a time may seem artificial. But the derivation would come out the same if each electron had its own clock and the $t = 0$ times were different for different electrons. If τ is the average time between collisions, then $\vec{v}_d$ is still the average electron drift velocity, even though the motions of the various electrons aren't actually correlated in the way we postulated.

What about the temperature dependence of resistivity? In a perfect crystal with no atoms out of place, a correct quantum-mechanical analysis would let the free electrons move through the crystal with no collisions at all. But the atoms vibrate about their equilibrium positions. As the temperature increases, the amplitudes of these vibrations increase, collisions become more frequent, and the mean free time τ decreases. So this theory predicts that the resistivity of a metal increases with temperature. In a superconductor, roughly speaking, there are no inelastic collisions, τ is infinite, and the resistivity ρ is zero.

In a pure semiconductor such as silicon or germanium, the number of charge carriers per unit volume, n, is not constant but increases very rapidly with increasing temperature. This increase in n far outweighs the decrease in the mean free time, and in a semiconductor the resistivity always decreases rapidly with increasing temperature. At low temperatures, n is very small, and the resistivity becomes so large that the material can be considered an insulator.

Electrons gain energy between collisions through the work done on them by the electric field. During collisions they transfer some of this energy to the atoms of the material of the conductor. This leads to an increase in the material's internal energy and temperature; that's why wires carrying current get warm. If the electric field in the material is large enough, an electron can gain enough energy between collisions to knock off electrons that are normally bound to atoms in the material. These can then knock off more electrons, and so on, possibly leading to an avalanche of current. This is the microscopic basis of dielectric breakdown in insulators.

Example 25.12   Mean free time in copper

Calculate the mean free time between collisions in copper at room temperature.

SOLUTION

IDENTIFY: This problem uses the ideas developed in this section.

SET UP: We can find an expression for mean free time τ in terms of n, ρ, e, and m by rearranging Eq. (25.24). From Example 25.1 and Table 25.1, for copper $n = 8.5 \times 10^{28}$ m^{-3} and $\rho = 1.72 \times 10^{-8}$ $\Omega \cdot$ m. Also, $e = 1.60 \times 10^{-19}$ C and $m = 9.11 \times 10^{-31}$ kg for electrons.

EXECUTE: From Eq. (25.24), we get

$$\tau = \frac{m}{ne^2\rho}$$

$$= \frac{9.11 \times 10^{-31} \text{ kg}}{(8.5 \times 10^{28} \text{ m}^{-3})(1.60 \times 10^{-19} \text{ C})^2(1.72 \times 10^{-8}\ \Omega \cdot \text{m})}$$

$$= 2.4 \times 10^{-14} \text{ s}$$

EVALUATE: Taking the reciprocal of this time, we find that each electron averages about 4×10^{13} collisions every second!

Test Your Understanding of Section 25.6   Which of the following factors will, if increased, make it more difficult to produce a certain amount of current in a conductor? (There may be more than one correct answer.) (i) the mass of the moving charged particles in the conductor; (ii) the number of moving charged particles per cubic meter; (iii) the amount of charge on each moving particle; (iv) the average time between collisions for a typical moving charged particle.

Current and current density: Current is the amount of charge flowing through a specified area, per unit time. The SI unit of current is the ampere, equal to one coulomb per second ($1\ \text{A} = 1\ \text{C/s}$). The current I through an area A depends on the concentration n and charge q of the charge carriers, as well as on the magnitude of their drift velocity $\vec{v}_d$. The current density is current per unit cross-sectional area. Current is conventionally described in terms of a flow of positive charge, even when the actual charge carriers are negative or of both signs. (See Example 25.1.)

$$I = \frac{dQ}{dt} = n|q|v_d A \qquad (25.2)$$

$$\vec{J} = nq\vec{v}_d \qquad (25.4)$$

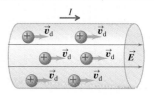

Resistivity: The resistivity ρ of a material is the ratio of the magnitudes of electric field and current density. Good conductors have small resistivity; good insulators have large resistivity. Ohm's law, obeyed approximately by many materials, states that ρ is a constant independent of the value of E. Resistivity usually increases with temperature; for small temperature changes this variation is represented approximately by Eq. (25.6), where α is the temperature coefficient of resistivity.

$$\rho = \frac{E}{J} \qquad (25.5)$$

$$\rho(T) = \rho_0[1 + \alpha(T - T_0)] \qquad (25.6)$$

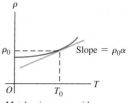

Metal: ρ increases with increasing T.

Resistors: For materials obeying Ohm's law, the potential difference V across a particular sample of material is proportional to the current I through the material. The ratio $V/I = R$ is the resistance of the sample. The SI unit of resistance is the ohm ($1\ \Omega = 1\ \text{V/A}$). The resistance of a cylindrical conductor is related to its resistivity ρ, length L, and cross-sectional area A. (See Examples 25.2–25.4.)

$$V = IR \qquad (25.11)$$

$$R = \frac{\rho L}{A} \qquad (25.10)$$

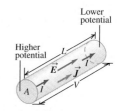

Circuits and emf: A complete circuit has a continuous current-carrying path. A complete circuit carrying a steady current must contain a source of electromotive force (emf) $\mathcal{E}$. The SI unit of electromotive force is the volt (1 V). An ideal source of emf maintains a constant potential difference, independent of current through the device, but every real source of emf has some internal resistance r. The terminal potential difference V_{ab} then depends on current. (See Examples 25.5–25.8.)

$$V_{ab} = \mathcal{E} - Ir \qquad (25.15)$$
(source with internal resistance)

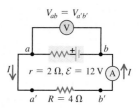

Energy and power in circuits: A circuit element with a potential difference $V_a - V_b = V_{ab}$ and a current I puts energy into a circuit if the current direction is from lower to higher potential in the device, and it takes energy out of the circuit if the current is opposite. The power P (rate of energy transfer) is equal to the product of the potential difference and the current. A resistor always takes electrical energy out of a circuit. (See Examples 25.9–25.11.)

$$P = V_{ab}I \qquad (25.17)$$
(general circuit element)

$$P = V_{ab}I = I^2R = \frac{V_{ab}^2}{R} \qquad (25.18)$$
(power into a resistor)

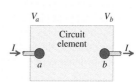

Conduction in metals: The microscopic basis of conduction in metals is the motion of electrons that move freely through the metallic crystal, bumping into ion cores in the crystal. In a crude classical model of this motion, the resistivity of the material can be related to the electron mass, charge, speed of random motion, density, and mean free time between collisions. (See Example 25.12.)

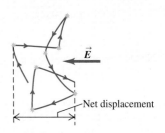

Net displacement

Key Terms

current, *847*	resistivity, *851*	electromotive force (emf), *857*
drift velocity, *847*	conductivity, *851*	source of emf, *857*
conventional current, *848*	temperature coefficient of resistivity, *852*	internal resistance, *859*
ampere, *848*	resistance, *853*	terminal voltage, *859*
concentration, *848*	ohm, *854*	voltmeter, *860*
current density, *849*	resistor, *854*	ammeter, *860*
Ohm's law, *850*	complete circuit, *857*	mean free time, *868*

Answer to Chapter Opening Question ?

The current out equals the current in. In other words, charge must enter the bulb at the same rate as it exits the bulb. It is not "used up" or consumed as it flows through the bulb.

Answers to Test Your Understanding Questions

25.1 Answer: (v) Doubling the diameter increases the cross-sectional area A by a factor of 4. Hence the current density magnitude $J = I/A$ is reduced to $\frac{1}{4}$ of the value in Example 25.1, and the magnitude of the drift velocity $v_d = J/n|q|$ is reduced by the same factor. The new magnitude is $v_d = (0.15 \text{ mm/s})/4 = 0.038 \text{ mm/s}$. This behavior is the same as that of an incompressible fluid, which slows down when it moves from a narrow pipe to a broader one (see Section 14.4).

25.2 Answer (ii) Figure 25.6b shows that the resistivity ρ of a semiconductor increases as the temperature decreases. From Eq. (25.5), the magnitude of the current density is $J = E/\rho$, so the current density decreases as the temperature drops and the resistivity increases.

25.3 Answer (iii) Solving Eq. (25.11) for the current shows that $I = V/R$. If the resistance R of the wire remained the same, doubling the voltage V would make the current I double as well. However, we saw in Example 25.3 that the resistance is *not* constant: As the current increases and the temperature increases, R increases as well. Thus doubling the voltage produces a current that is *less* than double the original current. An ohmic conductor is one for which $R = V/I$ has the same value no matter what the voltage, so the

wire is *nonohmic*. (In many practical problems the temperature change of the wire is so small that it can be ignored, so we can safely regard the wire as being ohmic. We do so in almost all examples in this book.)

25.4 Answer: (iii), (ii), (i) For circuit (i), we find the current from Eq. (25.16): $I = \mathcal{E}/(R + r) = (1.5 \text{ V})/(1.4 \,\Omega + 0.10 \,\Omega) = 1.0 \text{ A}$. For circuit (ii), we note that the terminal voltage $V_{ab} = 3.6 \text{ V}$ equals the voltage IR across the 1.8-Ω resistor: $V_{ab} = IR$, so $I = V_{ab}/R = (3.6 \text{ V})/(1.8 \,\Omega) = 2.0 \text{ A}$. For circuit (iii), we use Eq. (25.15) for the terminal voltage: $V_{ab} = \mathcal{E} - Ir$, so $I = (\mathcal{E} - V_{ab})/r = (12.0 \text{ V} - 11.0 \text{ V})/(0.20 \,\Omega) = 5.0 \text{ A}$.

25.5 Answer: (iii), (ii), (i) These are the same circuits that we analyzed in Test Your Understanding of Section 25.4. In each case the net power output of the battery is $P = V_{ab}I$, where V_{ab} is the battery terminal voltage. For circuit (i), we found that $I = 1.0 \text{ A}$, so $V_{ab} = \mathcal{E} - Ir = 1.5 \text{ V} - (1.0 \text{ A})(0.10 \,\Omega) = 1.4 \text{ V}$, so $P = (1.4 \text{ V})(1.0 \text{ A}) = 1.4 \text{ W}$. For circuit (ii), we have $V_{ab} = 3.6 \text{ V}$ and found that $I = 2.0 \text{ A}$, so $P = (3.6 \text{ V})(2.0 \text{ A}) = 7.2 \text{ W}$. For circuit (iii), we have $V_{ab} = 11.0 \text{ V}$ and found that $I = 5.0 \text{ A}$, so $P = (11.0 \text{ V})(5.0 \text{ A}) = 55 \text{ A}$.

25.6 Answer: (i) The difficulty of producing a certain amount of current increases as the resistivity ρ increases. From Eq. (25.24), $\rho = m/ne^2\tau$, so increasing the mass m will increase the resistivity. That's because a more massive charged particle will respond more sluggishly to an applied electric field and hence drift more slowly. To produce the same current, a greater electric field would be needed. (Increasing n, e, or τ; would decrease the resistivity and make it easier to produce a given current.)

PROBLEMS

For instructor-assigned homework, go to **www.masteringphysics.com** (MP)

Discussion Questions

Q25.1. The definition of resistivity $(\rho = E/J)$ implies that an electric field exists inside a conductor. Yet we saw in Chapter 21

that there can be no electric field inside a conductor. Is there a contradiction here? Explain.

Q25.2. A cylindrical rod has resistance R. If we triple its length and diameter, what is its resistance, in terms of R?

Q25.3. A cylindrical rod has resistivity ρ. If we triple its length and diameter, what is its resistivity, in terms of ρ?

Q25.4. Two copper wires with different diameters are joined end to end. If a current flows in the wire combination, what happens to electrons when they move from the larger-diameter wire into the smaller-diameter wire? Does their drift speed increase, decrease, or stay the same? If the drift speed changes, what is the force that causes the change? Explain your reasoning.

Q25.5. When is a 1.5-V AAA battery *not* actually a 1.5-V battery? That is, when do its terminals provide a potential difference of less than 1.5 V?

Q25.6. Can the potential difference between the terminals of a battery ever be opposite in direction to the emf? If it can, give an example. If it cannot, explain why not.

Q25.7. A rule of thumb used to determine the internal resistance of a source is that it is the open-circuit voltage divided by the short-circuit current. Is this correct? Why or why not?

Q25.8. Batteries are always labeled with their emf; for instance, an AA flashlight battery is labeled "1.5 volts." Would it also be appropriate to put a label on batteries stating how much current they provide? Why or why not?

Q25.9. We have seen that a coulomb is an enormous amount of charge; it is virtually impossible to place a charge of 1 C on an object. Yet, a current of 10 A, 10 C/s, is quite reasonable. Explain this apparent discrepancy.

Q25.10. Electrons in an electric circuit pass through a resistor. The wire on either side of the resistor has the same diameter. (a) How does the drift speed of the electrons before entering the resistor compare to the speed after leaving the resistor? Explain your reasoning. (b) How does the potential energy for an electron before entering the resistor compare to the potential energy after leaving the resistor? Explain your reasoning.

Q25.11. Current causes the temperature of a real resistor to increase. Why? What effect does this heating have on the resistance? Explain.

Q25.12. Which of the graphs in Fig. 25.29 best illustrates the current I in a real resistor as a function of the potential difference V across it? Explain. (*Hint*: See Discussion Question Q25.11.)

Figure **25.29** Question Q25.12.

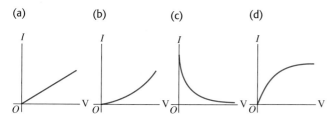

Q25.13. Why does an electric light bulb nearly always burn out just as you turn on the light, almost never while the light is shining?

Q25.14. A light bulb glows because it has resistance. The brightness of a light bulb increases with the electrical power dissipated in the bulb. (a) In the circuit shown in Fig. 25.30a, the two bulbs A

Figure **25.30** Question Q25.14.

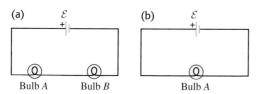

and B are identical. Compared to bulb A, does bulb B glow more brightly, just as brightly, or less brightly? Explain your reasoning. (b) Bulb B is removed from the circuit and the circuit is completed as shown in Fig. 25.30b. Compared to the brightness of bulb A in Fig. 25.30a, does bulb A now glow more brightly, just as brightly, or less brightly? Explain your reasoning.

Q25.15. (See Discussion Question Q25.14.) An ideal ammeter A is placed in a circuit with a battery and a light bulb as shown in Fig. 25.31a, and the ammeter reading is noted. The circuit is then reconnected as in Fig. 25.31b, so that the positions of the ammeter and light bulb are reversed. (a) How does the ammeter reading in the situation shown in Fig. 25.31a compare to the reading in the situation shown in Fig. 25.31b? Explain your reasoning. (b) In which situation does the light bulb glow more brightly? Explain your reasoning.

Figure **25.31** Question Q25.15.

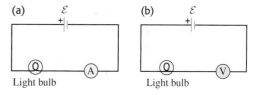

Q25.16. (See Discussion Question Q25.14.) Will a light bulb glow more brightly when it is connected to a battery as shown in Fig. 25.32a, in which an ideal ammeter A is placed in the circuit, or when it is connected as shown in Fig. 25.32b, in which an ideal voltmeter V is placed in the circuit? Explain your reasoning.

Figure **25.32** Question Q25.16.

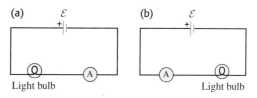

Q25.17. The energy that can be extracted from a storage battery is always less than the energy that goes into it while it is being charged. Why?

Q25.18. Eight flashlight batteries in series have an emf of about 12 V, similar to that of a car battery. Could they be used to start a car with a dead battery? Why or why not?

Q25.19. Small aircraft often have 24-V electrical systems rather than the 12-V systems in automobiles, even though the electrical power requirements are roughly the same in both applications. The explanation given by aircraft designers is that a 24-V system weighs less than a 12-V system because thinner wires can be used. Explain why this is so.

Q25.20. Long-distance, electric-power, transmission lines always operate at very high voltage, sometimes as much as 750 kV. What are the advantages of such high voltages? What are the disadvantages?

Q25.21. Ordinary household electric lines in North America usually operate at 120 V. Why is this a desirable voltage, rather than a value considerably larger or smaller? On the other hand, automobiles usually have 12-V electrical systems. Why is this a desirable voltage?

Q25.22. A fuse is a device designed to break a circuit, usually by melting when the current exceeds a certain value. What characteristics should the material of the fuse have?

Q25.23. High-voltage power supplies are sometimes designed intentionally to have rather large internal resistance as a safety precaution. Why is such a power supply with a large internal resistance safer than a supply with the same voltage but lower internal resistance?

Q25.24. The text states that good thermal conductors are also good electrical conductors. If so, why don't the cords used to connect toasters, irons, and similar heat-producing appliances get hot by conduction of heat from the heating element?

Exercises

Section 25.1 Current

25.1. A current of 3.6 A flows through an automobile headlight. How many coulombs of charge flow through the headlight in 3.0 h?

25.2. A silver wire 2.6 mm in diameter transfers a charge of 420 C in 80 min. Silver contains 5.8×10^{28} free electrons per cubic meter. (a) What is the current in the wire? (b) What is the magnitude of the drift velocity of the electrons in the wire?

25.3. A 5.00-A current runs through a 12-gauge copper wire (diameter 2.05 mm) and through a light bulb. Copper has 8.5×10^{28} free electrons per cubic meter. (a) How many electrons pass through the light bulb each second? (b) What is the current density in the wire? (c) At what speed does a typical electron pass by any given point in the wire? (d) If you were to use wire of twice the diameter, which of the above answers would change? Would they increase or decrease?

25.4. An 18-gauge wire (diameter 1.02 mm) carries a current with a current density of 1.50×10^6 A/m^2. Calculate (a) the current in the wire and (b) the drift velocity of electrons in the wire.

25.5. Copper has 8.5×10^{28} free electrons per cubic meter. A 71.0-cm length of 12-gauge copper wire that is 2.05 mm in diameter carries 4.85 A of current. (a) How much time does it take for an electron to travel the length of the wire? (b) Repeat part (a) for 6-gauge copper wire (diameter 4.12 mm) of the same length that carries the same current. (c) Generally speaking, how does changing the diameter of a wire that carries a given amount of current affect the drift velocity of the electrons in the wire?

25.6. Consider the 18-gauge wire in Example 25.1. How many atoms are in 1.00 m^3 of copper? With the density of free electrons given in the example, how many free electrons are there per copper atom?

25.7. The current in a wire varies with time according to the relationship $I = 55$ A $- (0.65$ A/s$^2)t^2$. (a) How many coulombs of charge pass a cross section of the wire in the time interval between $t = 0$ and $t = 8.0$ s? (b) What constant current would transport the same charge in the same time interval?

25.8. Current passes through a solution of sodium chloride. In 1.00 s, 2.68×10^{16} Na$^+$ ions arrive at the negative electrode and 3.92×10^{16} Cl$^-$ ions arrive at the positive electrode. (a) What is the current passing between the electrodes? (b) What is the direction of the current?

25.9. Assume that in silver metal there is one free electron per silver atom. Compute the free electron density for silver, and compare it to the value given in Exercise 25.2.

Section 25.2 Resistivity and Section 25.3 Resistance

25.10. (a) At room temperature what is the strength of the electric field in a 12-gauge copper wire (diameter 2.05 mm) that is needed to cause a 2.75-A current to flow? (b) What field would be needed if the wire were made of silver instead?

25.11. A 1.50-m cylindrical rod of diameter 0.500 cm is connected to a power supply that maintains a constant potential difference of 15.0 V across its ends, while an ammeter measures the current through it. You observe that at room temperature (20.0°C) the ammeter reads 18.5 A, while at 92.0°C it reads 17.2 A. You can ignore any thermal expansion of the rod. Find (a) the resistivity and (b) the temperature coefficient of resistivity at 20°C for the material of the rod.

25.12. A copper wire has a square cross section 2.3 mm on a side. The wire is 4.0 m long and carries a current of 3.6 A. The density of free electrons is 8.5×10^{28}/m^3. Find the magnitudes of (a) the current density in the wire and (b) the electric field in the wire. (c) How much time is required for an electron to travel the length of the wire?

25.13. In an experiment conducted at room temperature, a current of 0.820 A flows through a wire 3.26 mm in diameter. Find the magnitude of the electric field in the wire if the wire is made of (a) tungsten; and (b) aluminum.

25.14. A wire 6.50 m long with diameter of 2.05 mm has a resistance of 0.0290 Ω. What material is the wire most likely made of?

25.15. A cylindrical tungsten filament 15.0 cm long with a diameter of 1.00 mm is to be used in a machine for which the temperature will range from room temperature (20°C) up to 120°C. It will carry a current of 12.5 A at all temperatures (consult Tables 25.1 and 25.2). (a) What will be the maximum electric field in this filament, and (b) what will be its resistance with that field? (c) What will be the maximum potential drop over the full length of the filament?

25.16. What length of copper wire, 0.462 mm in diameter, has a resistance of 1.00 Ω?

25.17. In household wiring, copper wire 2.05 mm in diameter is often used. Find the resistance of a 24.0-m length of this wire.

25.18. What diameter must a copper wire have if its resistance is to be the same as that of an equal length of aluminum wire with diameter 3.26 mm?

25.19. You need to produce a set of cylindrical copper wires 3.50 m long that will have a resistance of 0.125 Ω each. What will be the mass of each of these wires?

25.20. A tightly coiled spring having 75 coils, each 3.50 cm in diameter, is made of insulated metal wire 3.25 mm in diameter. An ohmmeter connected across its opposite ends reads 1.74 Ω. What is the resistivity of the metal?

25.21. An aluminum cube has sides of length of 1.80 m. What is the resistance between two opposite faces of the cube?

25.22. A battery-powered light bulb has a tungsten filament. When the switch connecting the bulb to the battery is first turned on and the temperature of the bulb is 20°C, the current in the bulb is 0.860 A. After the bulb has been on for 30 s, the current is 0.220 A. What is then the temperature of the filament?

25.23. A rectangular solid of pure germanium measures 12 cm × 12 cm × 25 cm. Assuming that each of its faces is an equipotential surface, what is the resistance between opposite faces that are (a) farthest apart and (b) closest together?

25.24. You apply a potential difference of 4.50 V between the ends of a wire that is 2.50 m in length and 0.654 mm in radius. The resulting current through the wire is 17.6 A. What is the resistivity of the wire?

25.25. A current-carrying gold wire has diameter 0.84 mm. The electric field in the wire is 0.49 V/m. What are (a) the current carried by the wire; (b) the potential difference between two points in the wire 6.4 m apart; (c) the resistance of a 6.4-m length of this wire?

25.26. The potential difference between points in a wire 75.0 cm apart is 0.938 V when the current density is 4.40×10^7 A/m². What are (a) the magnitude of $\vec{E}$ in the wire and (b) the resistivity of the material of which the wire is made?

25.27. (a) What is the resistance of a Nichrome wire at 0.0°C if its resistance is 100.00 Ω at 11.5°C? (b) What is the resistance of a carbon rod at 25.8°C if its resistance is 0.0160 Ω at 0.0°C?

25.28. A carbon resistor is to be used as a thermometer. On a winter day when the temperature is 4.0°C, the resistance of the carbon resistor is 217.3 Ω. What is the temperature on a spring day when the resistance is 215.8 Ω? (Take the reference temperature T_0 to be 4.0°C.)

25.29. A strand of wire has resistance 5.60 μΩ. Find the net resistance of 120 such strands if they are (a) placed side by side to form a cable of the same length as a single strand, and (b) connected end to end to form a wire 120 times as long as a single strand.

25.30. A hollow aluminum cylinder is 2.50 m long and has an inner radius of 3.20 cm and an outer radius of 4.60 cm. Treat each surface (inner, outer, and the two end faces) as an equipotential surface. At room temperature, what will an ohmmeter read if it is connected between (a) the opposite faces and (b) the inner and outer surfaces?

Section 25.4 Electromotive Force and Circuits

25.31. A copper transmission cable 100 km long and 10.0 cm in diameter carries a current of 125 A. (a) What is the potential drop across the cable? (b) How much electrical energy is dissipated as thermal energy every hour?

25.32. Consider the circuit shown in Fig. 25.33. The terminal voltage of the 24.0-V battery is 21.2 V. What are (a) the internal resistance r of the battery and (b) the resistance R of the circuit resistor?

Figure **25.33** Exercise 25.32.

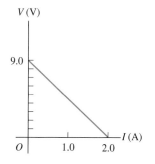

25.33. An idealized voltmeter is connected across the terminals of a battery while the current is varied. Figure 25.34 shows a graph of the voltmeter reading V as a function of the current I through the battery. Find (a) the emf $\mathcal{E}$ and (b) the internal resistance of the battery.

Figure **25.34** Exercise 25.33.

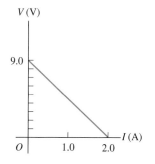

25.34. An idealized ammeter is connected to a battery as shown in Fig. 25.35. Find (a) the reading of the ammeter, (b) the current through the 4.00-Ω resistor, (c) the terminal voltage of the battery.

Figure **25.35** Exercise 25.34.

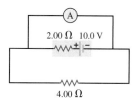

25.35. An ideal voltmeter V is connected to a 2.0-Ω resistor and a battery with emf 5.0 V and internal resistance 0.5 Ω as shown in Fig. 25.36. (a) What is the current in the 2.0-Ω resistor? (b) What is the terminal voltage of the battery? (c) What is the reading on the voltmeter? Explain your answers.

Figure **25.36** Exercise 25.35.

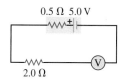

25.36. The circuit shown in Fig. 25.37 contains two batteries, each with an emf and an internal resistance, and two resistors. Find (a) the current in the circuit (magnitude *and* direction); (b) the terminal voltage V_{ab} of the 16.0-V battery; (c) the potential difference V_{ac} of point *a* with respect to point *c*. (d) Using Fig. 25.21 as a model, graph the potential rises and drops in this circuit.

Figure **25.37** Exercises 25.36, 25.38, 25.39, and 25.48.

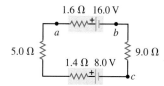

25.37. When switch *S* in Fig. 25.38 is open, the voltmeter V of the battery reads 3.08 V. When the switch is closed, the voltmeter reading drops to 2.97 V, and the ammeter A reads 1.65 A. Find the emf, the internal resistance of the battery, and the circuit resistance *R*. Assume that the two meters are ideal, so they don't affect the circuit.

25.38. In the circuit of Fig. 25.37, the 5.0-Ω resistor is removed and replaced

Figure **25.38**
Exercise 25.37.

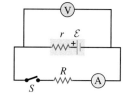

by a resistor of unknown resistance R. When this is done, an ideal voltmeter connected across the points b and c reads 1.9 V. Find (a) the current in the circuit and (b) the resistance R. (c) Graph the potential rises and drops in this circuit (see Fig. 25.21).

25.39. In the circuit shown in Fig. 25.37, the 16.0-V battery is removed and reinserted with the opposite polarity, so that its negative terminal is now next to point a. Find (a) the current in the circuit (magnitude *and* direction); (b) the terminal voltage V_{ba} of the 16.0-V battery; (c) the potential difference V_{ac} of point a with respect to point c. (d) Graph the potential rises and drops in this circuit (see Fig. 25.21).

25.40. The following measurements were made on a Thyrite resistor:

$I(A)$	0.50	1.00	2.00	4.00
$V_{ab}(V)$	2.55	3.11	3.77	4.58

(a) Graph V_{ab} as a function of I. (b) Does Thyrite obey Ohm's law? How can you tell? (c) Graph the resistance $R = V_{ab}/I$ as a function of I.

25.41. The following measurements of current and potential difference were made on a resistor constructed of Nichrome wire:

$I(A)$	0.50	1.00	2.00	4.00
$V_{ab}(V)$	1.94	3.88	7.76	15.52

(a) Graph V_{ab} as a function of I. (b) Does Nichrome obey Ohm's law? How can you tell? (c) What is the resistance of the resistor in ohms?

Section 25.5 Energy and Power in Electric Circuits

25.42. A resistor with a 15.0-V potential difference across its ends develops thermal energy at a rate of 327 W. (a) What is its resistance? (b) What is the current in the resistor?

25.43. Light Bulbs. The power rating of a light bulb (such as a 100-W bulb) is the power it dissipates when connected across a 120-V potential difference. What is the resistance of (a) a 100-W bulb and (b) a 60-W bulb? (c) How much current does each bulb draw in normal use?

25.44. If a "75-W" bulb (see Problem 25.43) is connected across a 220-V potential difference (as is used in Europe), how much power does it dissipate?

25.45. European Light Bulb. In Europe the standard voltage in homes is 220 V instead of the 120 V used in the United States. Therefore a "100-W" European bulb would be intended for use with a 220-V potential difference (see Problem 25.44). (a) If you bring a "100-W" European bulb home to the United States, what should be its U.S. power rating? (b) How much current will the 100-W European bulb draw in normal use in the United States?

25.46. A battery-powered global positioning system (GPS) receiver operating on 9.0 V draws a current of 0.13 A. How much electrical energy does it consume during 1.5 h?

25.47. Consider a resistor with length L, uniform cross-sectional area A, and uniform resistivity ρ that is carrying a current with uniform current density J. Use Eq. (25.18) to find the electrical power dissipated per unit volume, p. Express your result in terms of (a) E and J; (b) J and ρ; (c) E and ρ.

25.48. Consider the circuit of Fig. 25.37. (a) What is the total rate at which electrical energy is dissipated in the 5.00-Ω and 9.00-Ω resistors? (b) What is the power output of the 16.0-V battery? (c) At what rate is electrical energy being converted to other forms in the 8.0-V battery? (d) Show that the power output of the 16.0-V

battery equals the overall rate of dissipation of electrical energy in the rest of the circuit.

25.49. The capacity of a storage battery, such as those used in automobile electrical systems, is rated in ampere-hours $(A \cdot h)$. A 50-A $\cdot$ h battery can supply a current of 50 A for 1.0 h, or 25 A for 2.0 h, and so on. (a) What total energy can be supplied by a 12-V, 60-A $\cdot$ h battery if its internal resistance is negligible? (b) What volume (in liters) of gasoline has a total heat of combustion equal to the energy obtained in part (a)? (See Section 17.6; the density of gasoline is 900 kg/m^3.) (c) If a generator with an average electrical power output of 0.45 kW is connected to the battery, how much time will be required for it to charge the battery fully?

25.50. In the circuit analyzed in Example 25.9 the 4.0-Ω resistor is replaced by a 8.0-Ω resistor, as in Example 25.10. (a) Calculate the rate of conversion of chemical energy to electrical energy in the battery. How does your answer compare to the result calculated in Example 25.9? (b) Calculate the rate of electrical energy dissipation in the internal resistance of the battery. How does your answer compare to the result calculated in Example 25.9? (c) Use the results of parts (a) and (b) to calculate the net power output of the battery. How does your result compare to the electrical power dissipated in the 8.0-Ω resistor as calculated for this circuit in Example 25.10?

25.51. A 25.0-Ω bulb is connected across the terminals of a 12.0-V battery having 3.50 Ω of internal resistance. What percentage of the power of the battery is dissipated across the internal resistance and hence is not available to the bulb?

25.52. An idealized voltmeter is connected across the terminals of a 15.0-V battery, and a 75.0-Ω appliance is also connected across its terminals. If the voltmeter reads 11.3 V: (a) how much power is being dissipated by the appliance, and (b) what is the internal resistance of the battery?

25.53. In the circuit in Fig. 25.39, find (a) the rate of conversion of internal (chemical) energy to electrical energy within the battery; (b) the rate of dissipation of electrical energy in the battery; (c) the rate of dissipation of electrical energy in the external resistor.

Figure **25.39** Exercise 25.53.

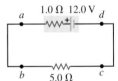

25.54. A typical small flashlight contains two batteries, each having an emf of 1.5 V, connected in series with a bulb having resistance 17 Ω. (a) If the internal resistance of the batteries is negligible, what power is delivered to the bulb? (b) If the batteries last for 5.0 h, what is the total energy delivered to the bulb? (c) The resistance of real batteries increases as they run down. If the initial internal resistance is negligible, what is the combined internal resistance of both batteries when the power to the bulb has decreased to half its initial value? (Assume that the resistance of the bulb is constant. Actually, it will change somewhat when the current through the filament changes, because this changes the temperature of the filament and hence the resistivity of the filament wire.)

25.55. A "540-W" electric heater is designed to operate from 120-V lines. (a) What is its resistance? (b) What current does it draw? (c) If the line voltage drops to 110 V, what power does the heater take? (Assume that the resistance is constant. Actually, it will change because of the change in temperature.) (d) The heater coils are metallic, so that the resistance of the heater decreases with decreasing temperature. If the change of resistance with temperature is taken into account, will the electrical power consumed by the heater be larger or smaller than what you calculated in part (c)? Explain.

*Section 25.6 Theory of Metallic Conduction

*25.56. Pure silicon contains approximately 1.0×10^{16} free electrons per cubic meter. (a) Referring to Table 25.1, calculate the mean free time τ for silicon at room temperature. (b) Your answer in part (a) is much greater than the mean free time for copper given in Example 25.12. Why, then, does pure silicon have such a high resistivity compared to copper?

Problems

25.57. An electrical conductor designed to carry large currents has a circular cross section 2.50 mm in diameter and is 14.0 m long. The resistance between its ends is 0.104 Ω. (a) What is the resistivity of the material? (b) If the electric-field magnitude in the conductor is 1.28 V/m, what is the total current? (c) If the material has 8.5×10^{28} free electrons per cubic meter, find the average drift speed under the conditions of part (b).

25.58. A plastic tube 25.0 m long and 4.00 cm in diameter is dipped into a silver solution, depositing a layer of silver 0.100 mm thick uniformly over the outer surface of the tube. If this coated tube is then connected across a 12.0-V battery, what will be the current?

25.59. On your first day at work as an electrical technician, you are asked to determine the resistance per meter of a long piece of wire. The company you work for is poorly equipped. You find a battery, a voltmeter, and an ammeter, but no meter for directly measuring resistance (an ohmmeter). You put the leads from the voltmeter across the terminals of the battery, and the meter reads 12.6 V. You cut off a 20.0-m length of wire and connect it to the battery, with an ammeter in series with it to measure the current in the wire. The ammeter reads 7.00 A. You then cut off a 40.0-m length of wire and connect it to the battery, again with the ammeter in series to measure the current. The ammeter reads 4.20 A. Even though the equipment you have available to you is limited, your boss assures you of its high quality: The ammeter has very small resistance, and the voltmeter has very large resistance. What is the resistance of 1 meter of wire?

25.60. A 2.0-mm length of wire is made by welding the end of a 120-cm-long silver wire to the end of an 80-cm-long copper wire. Each piece of wire is 0.60 mm in diameter. The wire is at room temperature, so the resistivities are as given in Table 25.1. A potential difference of 5.0 V is maintained between the ends of the 2.0-m composite wire. (a) What is the current in the copper section? (b) What is the current in the silver section? (c) What is the magnitude of $\vec{E}$ in the copper? (d) What is the magnitude of $\vec{E}$ in the silver? (e) What is the potential difference between the ends of the silver section of wire?

25.61. A 3.00-m length of copper wire at 20°C has a 1.20-m-long section with diameter 1.60 mm and a 1.80-m-long section with diameter 0.80 mm. There is a current of 2.5 mA in the 1.60-mm-diameter section. (a) What is the current in the 0.80-mm-diameter section? (b) What is the magnitude of $\vec{E}$ in the 1.60-mm-diameter section? (c) What is the magnitude of $\vec{E}$ in the 0.80-mm-diameter section? (d) What is the potential difference between the ends of the 3.00-m length of wire?

25.62. Critical Current Density in Superconductors. One problem with some of the newer high-temperature superconductors is getting a large enough current density for practical use without causing the resistance to reappear. The maximum current density for which the material will remain a superconductor is called the critical current density of the material. In 1987, IBM research labs had produced thin films with critical current densities of 1.0×10^5 A/cm^2. (a) How much current could an 18-gauge wire (see Example 25.1 in Section 25.1) of this material carry and still remain superconducting? (b) Researchers are trying to develop superconductors with critical current densities of 1.0×10^6 A/cm^2. What diameter cylindrical wire of such a material would be needed to carry 1000 A without losing its superconductivity?

25.63. A material of resistivity ρ is formed into a solid, truncated cone of height h and radii r_1 and r_2 at either end (Fig. 25.40). (a) Calculate the resistance of the cone between the two flat end faces. (*Hint:* Imagine slicing the cone into very many thin disks, and calculate the resistance of one such disk.) (b) Show that your result agrees with Eq. (25.10) when $r_1 = r_2$.

Figure 25.40
Problem 25.63.

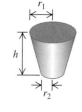

25.64. The region between two concentric conducting spheres with radii a and b is filled with a conducting material with resistivity ρ. (a) Show that the resistance between the spheres is given by

$$ R = \frac{\rho}{4\pi}\left(\frac{1}{a} - \frac{1}{b}\right) $$

(b) Derive an expression for the current density as a function of radius, in terms of the potential difference V_{ab} between the spheres. (c) Show that the result in part (a) reduces to Eq. (25.10) when the separation $L = b - a$ between the spheres is small.

25.65. Leakage in a Dielectric. Two parallel plates of a capacitor have equal and opposite charges Q. The dielectric has a dielectric constant K and a resistivity ρ. Show that the "leakage" current I carried by the dielectric is given by $I = Q/K\epsilon_0\rho$.

25.66. In the circuit shown in Fig. 25.41, R is a variable resistor whose value can range from 0 to ∞, and a and b are the terminals of a battery having an emf $\mathcal{E} = 15.0$ V and an internal resistance of 4.00 Ω. The ammeter and voltmeter are both idealized meters. As R varies over its full range of values, what will be the largest and smallest readings of (a) the voltmeter and (b) the ammeter? (c) Sketch qualitative graphs of the readings of both meters as functions of R, as R ranges from 0 to ∞.

Figure 25.41 Problem 25.66.

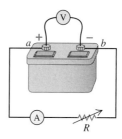

25.67. The temperature coefficient of resistance α in Eq. (25.12) equals the temperature coefficient of resistivity α in Eq. (25.6) only if the coefficient of thermal expansion is small. A cylindrical column of mercury is in a vertical glass tube. At 20°C, the length of the mercury column is 12.0 cm. The diameter of the mercury column is 1.6 mm and doesn't change with temperature because glass has a small coefficient of thermal expansion. The coefficient of volume expansion of the mercury is given in Table 17.2, its resistivity at 20°C is given in Table 25.1, and its temperature coefficient of resistivity is given in Table 25.2. (a) At 20°C, what is the resistance between the ends of the mercury column? (b) The mercury column is heated to 60°C. What is the change in its resistivity? (c) What is the change in its length? Explain why the coefficient of volume expansion, rather than the coefficient of linear expansion, determines the change in length. (d) What is the change in its resistance? (*Hint:* Since the percentage changes in ρ and L are small, you may find it helpful to derive from Eq. (25.10) an equation for ΔR in terms of $\Delta\rho$ and ΔL) (e) What is the temperature coefficient of resistance α for the mercury column, as defined in Eq. (25.12)? How does this value compare with the temperature coefficient of resistivity? Is the effect of the change in length important?

25.68. (a) What is the potential difference V_{ad} in the circuit of Fig. 25.42? (b) What is the terminal voltage of the 4.00-V battery? (c) A battery with emf 10.30z V and internal resistance 0.50 Ω is inserted in the circuit at d, with its negative terminal connected to the negative terminal of the 8.00-V battery. What is the difference of potential V_{bc} between the terminals of the 4.00-V battery now?

Figure **25.42** Problem 25.68.

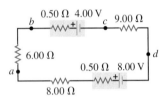

25.69. The potential difference across the terminals of a battery is 8.4 V when there is a current of 1.50 A in the battery from the negative to the positive terminal. When the current is 3.50 A in the reverse direction, the potential difference becomes 9.4 V. (a) What is the internal resistance of the battery? (b) What is the emf of the battery?

25.70. A person with body resistance between his hands of 10 kΩ accidentally grasps the terminals of a 14-kV power supply. (a) If the internal resistance of the power supply is 2000 Ω, what is the current through the person's body? (b) What is the power dissipated in his body? (c) If the power supply is to be made safe by increasing its internal resistance, what should the internal resistance be for the maximum current in the above situation to be 1.00 mA or less?

25.71. The average bulk resistivity of the human body (apart from surface resistance of the skin) is about 5.0 $\Omega \cdot$ m. The conducting path between the hands can be represented approximately as a cylinder 1.6 m long and 0.10 m in diameter. The skin resistance can be made negligible by soaking the hands in salt water. (a) What is the resistance between the hands if the skin resistance is negligible? (b) What potential difference between the hands is needed for a lethal shock current of 100 mA? (Note that your result shows that small potential differences produce dangerous currents when the skin is damp.) (c) With the current in part (b), what power is dissipated in the body?

25.72. A typical cost for electric power is 12.0¢ per kilowatt-hour. (a) Some people leave their porch light on all the time. What is the yearly cost to keep a 75-W bulb burning day and night? (b) Sup-

pose your refrigerator uses 400 W of power when it's running, and it runs 8 hours a day. What is the yearly cost of operating your refrigerator?

25.73. A 12.6-V car battery with negligible internal resistance is connected to a series combination of a 3.2-Ω resistor that obeys Ohm's law and a thermistor that does not obey Ohm's law but instead has a current–voltage relationship $V = \alpha I + \beta I^2$, with $\alpha = 3.8\ \Omega$ and $\beta = 1.3\ \Omega/$A. What is the current through the 3.2-Ω resistor?

25.74. A cylindrical copper cable 1.50 km long is connected across a 220.0-V potential difference. (a) What should be its diameter so that it produces heat at a rate of 50.0 W? (b) What is the electric field inside the cable under these conditions?

25.75. A Nonideal Ammeter. Unlike the idealized ammeter described in Section 25.4, any real ammeter has a nonzero resistance. (a) An ammeter with resistance R_A is connected in series with a resistor R and a battery of emf $\mathcal{E}$ and internal resistance r. The current measured by the ammeter is I_A. Find the current through the circuit if the ammeter is removed so that the battery and the resistor form a complete circuit. Express your answer in terms of I_A, r, R_A, and R. The more "ideal" the ammeter, the smaller the difference between this current and the current I_A. (b) If $R = 3.80\ \Omega$, $\mathcal{E} = 7.50$ V, and $r = 0.45\ \Omega$, find the maximum value of the ammeter resistance R_A so that I_A is within 1.0% of the current in the circuit when the ammeter is absent. (c) Explain why your answer in part (b) represents a *maximum* value.

25.76. A 1.50-m cylinder of radius 1.10 cm is made of a complicated mixture of materials. Its resistivity depends on the distance x from the left end and obeys the formula $\rho(x) = a + bx^2$, where a and b are constants. At the left end, the resistivity is $2.25 \times 10^{-8}\ \Omega \cdot$ m, while at the right end it is $8.50 \times 10^{-8}\ \Omega \cdot$ m. (a) What is the resistance of this rod? (b) What is the electric field at its midpoint if it carries a 1.75-A current? (c) If we cut the rod into two 75.0-cm halves, what is the resistance of each half?

25.77. According to the U.S. National Electrical Code, copper wire used for interior wiring of houses, hotels, office buildings, and industrial plants is permitted to carry no more than a specified maximum amount of current. The table below shows the maximum current I_{max} for several common sizes of wire with varnished cambric insulation. The "wire gauge" is a standard used to describe the diameter of wires. Note that the larger the diameter of the wire, the *smaller* the wire gauge.

Wire gauge	Diameter (cm)	I_{max} (A)
14	0.163	18
12	0.205	25
10	0.259	30
8	0.326	40
6	0.412	60
5	0.462	65
4	0.519	85

(a) What considerations determine the maximum current-carrying capacity of household wiring? (b) A total of 4200 W of power is to be supplied through the wires of a house to the household electrical appliances. If the potential difference across the group of appliances is 120 V, determine the gauge of the thinnest permissible wire that can be used. (c) Suppose the wire used in this house is of the gauge found in part (b) and has total length 42.0 m. At what rate is energy dissipated in the wires? (d) The house is built in a community where the consumer cost of electric energy is $0.11 per kilowatt-hour. If the house were built with wire of the next larger diameter than that found in part (b), what would be the savings in electricity costs in one year? Assume that the appliances are kept on for an average of 12 hours a day.

25.78. A toaster using a Nichrome heating element operates on 120 V. When it is switched on at 20°C, the heating element carries an initial current of 1.35 A. A few seconds later the current reaches the steady value of 1.23 A. (a) What is the final temperature of the element? The average value of the temperature coefficient of resistivity for Nichrome over the temperature range is $4.5 \times 10^{-4} \, (\text{C}°)^{-1}$. (b) What is the power dissipated in the heating element initially and when the current reaches a steady value?

25.79. In the circuit of Fig. 25.43, find (a) the current through the 8.0-Ω resistor and (b) the total rate of dissipation of electrical energy in the 8.0-Ω resistor and in the internal resistance of the batteries. (c) In one of the batteries, chemical energy is being converted into electrical energy. In which one is this happening, and at what rate? (d) In one of the batteries, electrical energy is being converted into chemical energy. In which one is this happening, and at what rate? (e) Show that the overall rate of production of electrical energy equals the overall rate of consumption of electrical energy in the circuit.

Figure **25.43** Problem 25.79.

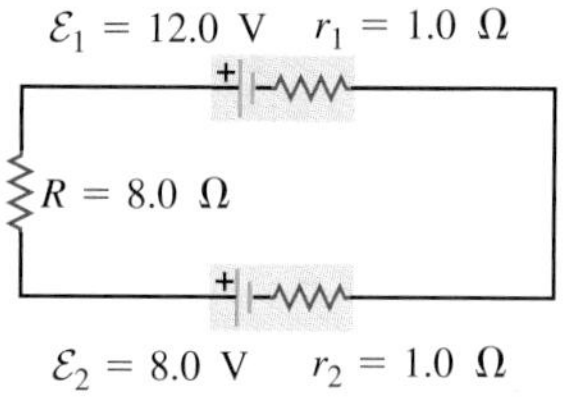

$$\mathcal{E}_1 = 12.0 \text{ V} \quad r_1 = 1.0 \, \Omega$$

$R = 8.0 \, \Omega$

$$\mathcal{E}_2 = 8.0 \text{ V} \quad r_2 = 1.0 \, \Omega$$

25.80. A lightning bolt strikes one end of a steel lightning rod, producing a 15,000-A current burst that lasts for 65 μs. The rod is 2.0 m long and 1.8 cm in diameter, and its other end is connected to the ground by 35 m of 8.0-mm-diameter copper wire. (a) Find the potential difference between the top of the steel rod and the lower end of the copper wire during the current burst. (b) Find the total energy deposited in the rod and wire by the current burst.

25.81. A 12.0-V battery has an internal resistance of 0.24 Ω and a capacity of 50.0 A · h (see Exercise 25.49). The battery is charged by passing a 10-A current through it for 5.0 h. (a) What is the terminal voltage during charging? (b) What total electrical energy is supplied to the battery during charging? (c) What electrical energy is dissipated in the internal resistance during charging? (d) The battery is now completely discharged through a resistor, again with a constant current of 10 A. What is the external circuit resistance? (e) What total electrical energy is supplied to the external resistor? (f) What total electrical energy is dissipated in the internal resistance? (g) Why are the answers to parts (b) and (e) not the same?

25.82. Repeat Problem 25.81 with charge and discharge currents of 30 A. The charging and discharging times will now be 1.7 h rather than 5.0 h. What differences in performance do you see?

Challenge Problems

25.83. The *Tolman-Stewart experiment* in 1916 demonstrated that the free charges in a metal have negative charge and provided a quantitative measurement of their charge-to-mass ratio, $|q|/m$. The experiment consisted of abruptly stopping a rapidly rotating spool of wire and measuring the potential difference that this produced

between the ends of the wire. In a simplified model of this experiment, consider a metal rod of length L that is given a uniform acceleration $\vec{a}$ to the right. Initially the free charges in the metal lag behind the rod's motion, thus setting up an electric field $\vec{E}$ in the rod. In the steady state this field exerts a force on the free charges that makes them accelerate along with the rod. (a) Apply $\Sigma \vec{F} = m\vec{a}$ to the free charges to obtain an expression for $|q|/m$ in terms of the magnitudes of the induced electric field $\vec{E}$ and the acceleration $\vec{a}$. (b) If all the free charges in the metal rod have the same acceleration, the electric field $\vec{E}$ is the same at all points in the rod. Use this fact to rewrite the expression for $|q|/m$ in terms of the potential V_{bc} between the ends of the rod (Fig. 25.44). (c) If the free charges have negative charge, which end of the rod, b or c, is at higher potential? (d) If the rod is 0.50 m long and the free charges are electrons (charge $q = -1.60 \times 10^{-19}$ C, mass 9.11×10^{-31} kg), what magnitude of acceleration is required to produce a potential difference of 1.0 mV between the ends of the rod? (e) Discuss why the actual experiment used a rotating spool of thin wire rather than a moving bar as in our simplified analysis.

Figure **25.44** Challenge Problem 25.83.

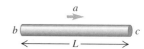

25.84. The current–voltage relationship of a semiconductor diode is given by

$$I = I_S \left[\exp\left(\frac{eV}{kT}\right) - 1 \right]$$

where I and V are the current through and the voltage across the diode, respectively. I_S is a constant characteristic of the device, e is the magnitude of the electron charge, k is the Boltzmann constant, and T is the Kelvin temperature. Such a diode is connected in series with a resistor with $R = 1.00 \, \Omega$ and a battery with $\mathcal{E} = 2.00$ V. The polarity of the battery is such that the current through the diode is in the forward direction (Fig. 25.45). The battery has negligible internal resistance. (a) Obtain an equation for V. Note that you cannot solve for V algebraically. (b) The value of V must be obtained by using a numerical method. One approach is to try a value of V, see how the left- and right-hand sides of the equation compare for this V, and use this to refine your guess for V. Using $I_S = 1.50$ mA and $T = 293$ K, obtain a solution (accurate to three significant figures) for the voltage drop V across the diode and the current I through it.

Figure **25.45** Challenge Problem 25.84.

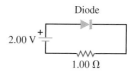

25.85. The resistivity of a semiconductor can be modified by adding different amounts of impurities. A rod of semiconducting material of length L and cross-sectional area A lies along the x-axis between $x = 0$ and $x = L$. The material obeys Ohm's law, and its resistivity varies along the rod according to $\rho(x) = \rho_0 \exp(-x/L)$. The end of the rod at $x = 0$ is at a potential V_0 greater than the end at $x = L$. (a) Find the total resistance of the rod and the current in the rod. (b) Find the electric-field magnitude

$E(x)$ in the rod as a function of x. (c) Find the electric potential $V(x)$ in the rod as a function of x. (d) Graph the functions $\rho(x)$, $E(x)$, and $V(x)$ for values of x between $x = 0$ and $x = L$.

25.86. A source with emf $\mathcal{E}$ and internal resistance r is connected to an external circuit. (a) Show that the power output of the source is maximum when the current in the circuit is one-half the short-circuit current of the source. (b) If the external circuit consists of a resistance R, show that the power output is maximum when $R = r$ and that the maximum power is $\mathcal{E}^2/4r$.

25.87. The temperature coefficient of resistivity α is given by

$$\alpha = \frac{1}{\rho}\frac{d\rho}{dT}$$

where ρ is the resistivity at the temperature T. Equation (25.6) then follows if α is assumed constant and much smaller than $(T - T_0)^{-1}$. (a) If α is not constant but is given by $\alpha = -n/T$, where T is the Kelvin temperature and n is a constant, show that the resistivity is given by $\rho = a/T^n$, where a is a constant. (b) From Fig. 25.10, you can see that such a relationship might be used as a rough approximation for a semiconductor. Using the values of ρ and α for carbon from Tables 25.1 and 25.2, determine a and n. (In Table 25.1, assume that "room temperature" means 293 K.) (c) Using your result from part (b), determine the resistivity of carbon at $-196°C$ and $300°C$. (Remember to express T in kelvins.)

DIRECT-CURRENT CIRCUITS

26

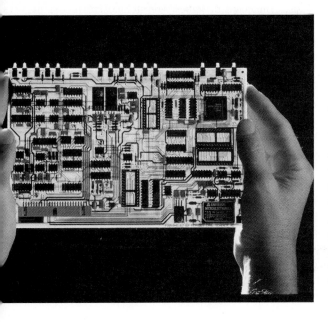

? In a complex circuit like the one on this circuit board, is it possible to connect several resistors with different resistances so that they all have the same potential difference? If so, will the current be the same through all of the resistors?

LEARNING GOALS

By studying this chapter, you will learn:

- How to analyze circuits with multiple resistors in series or parallel.

- Rules that you can apply to any circuit with more than one loop.

- How to use an ammeter, voltmeter, ohmmeter, or potentiometer in a circuit.

- How to analyze circuits that include both a resistor and a capacitor.

- How electric power is distributed in the home.

I f you look inside your TV, your computer, or your stereo receiver or under the hood of a car, you will find circuits of much greater complexity than the simple circuits we studied in Chapter 25. Whether connected by wires or integrated in a semiconductor chip, these circuits often include several sources, resistors, and other circuit elements, such as capacitors, transformers, and motors, interconnected in a *network*.

In this chapter we study general methods for analyzing such networks, including how to find unknown voltages, currents, and properties of circuit elements. We'll learn how to determine the equivalent resistance for several resistors connected in series or in parallel. For more general networks we need two rules called *Kirchhoff's rules*. One is based on the principle of conservation of charge applied to a junction; the other is derived from energy conservation for a charge moving around a closed loop. We'll discuss instruments for measuring various electrical quantities. We also look at a circuit containing resistance and capacitance, in which the current varies with time.

Our principal concern in this chapter is with **direct-current** (dc) circuits, in which the direction of the current does not change with time. Flashlights and automobile wiring systems are examples of direct-current circuits. Household electrical power is supplied in the form of **alternating current** (ac), in which the current oscillates back and forth. The same principles for analyzing networks apply to both kinds of circuits, and we conclude this chapter with a look at household wiring systems. We'll discuss alternating-current circuits in detail in Chapter 31.

26.1 Resistors in Series and Parallel

Resistors turn up in all kinds of circuits, ranging from hair dryers and space heaters to circuits that limit or divide current or reduce or divide a voltage. Such circuits often contain several resistors, so it's appropriate to consider *combinations* of resistors. A simple example is a string of light bulbs used for holiday decorations;

Activ
ONLINE
Physics

12.1 DC Series Circuits (Qualitative)

26.1 Four different ways of connecting three resistors.

(a) R_1, R_2, and R_3 in series

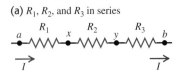

(b) R_1, R_2, and R_3 in parallel

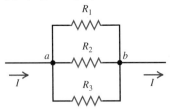

(c) R_1 in series with parallel combination of R_2 and R_3

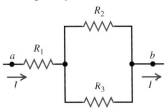

(d) R_1 in parallel with series combination of R_2 and R_3

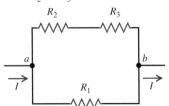

each bulb acts as a resistor, and from a circuit-analysis perspective the string of bulbs is simply a combination of resistors.

Suppose we have three resistors with resistances R_1, R_2, and R_3. Figure 26.1 shows four different ways in which they might be connected between points a and b. When several circuit elements such as resistors, batteries, and motors are connected in sequence as in Fig. 26.1a, with only a single current path between the points, we say that they are connected in **series**. We studied *capacitors* in series in Section 24.2; we found that, because of conservation of charge, capacitors in series all have the same charge if they are initially uncharged. In circuits we're often more interested in the *current,* which is charge flow per unit time.

The resistors in Fig. 26.1b are said to be connected in **parallel** between points a and b. Each resistor provides an alternative path between the points. For circuit elements that are connected in parallel, the *potential difference* is the same across each element. We studied capacitors in parallel in Section 24.2.

In Fig. 26.1c, resistors R_2 and R_3 are in parallel, and this combination is in series with R_1. In Fig. 26.1d, R_2 and R_3 are in series, and this combination is in parallel with R_1.

For any combination of resistors we can always find a *single* resistor that could replace the combination and result in the same total current and potential difference. For example, a string of holiday light bulbs could be replaced by a single, appropriately chosen light bulb that would draw the same current and have the same potential difference between its terminals as the original string of bulbs. The resistance of this single resistor is called the **equivalent resistance** of the combination. If any one of the networks in Fig. 26.1 were replaced by its equivalent resistance R_{eq}, we could write

$$V_{ab} = IR_{eq} \quad \text{or} \quad R_{eq} = \frac{V_{ab}}{I}$$

where V_{ab} is the potential difference between terminals a and b of the network and I is the current at point a or b. To compute an equivalent resistance, we assume a potential difference V_{ab} across the actual network, compute the corresponding current I, and take the ratio V_{ab}/I.

Resistors in Series

We can derive general equations for the equivalent resistance of a series or parallel combination of resistors. If the resistors are in *series,* as in Fig. 26.1a, the current I must be the same in all of them. (As we discussed in Section 25.4, current is *not* "used up" as it passes through a circuit.) Applying $V = IR$ to each resistor, we have

$$V_{ax} = IR_1 \qquad V_{xy} = IR_2 \qquad V_{yb} = IR_3$$

The potential differences across each resistor need not be the same (except for the special case in which all three resistances are equal). The potential difference V_{ab} across the entire combination is the sum of these individual potential differences:

$$V_{ab} = V_{ax} + V_{xy} + V_{yb} = I(R_1 + R_2 + R_3)$$

and so

$$\frac{V_{ab}}{I} = R_1 + R_2 + R_3$$

The ratio V_{ab}/I is, by definition, the equivalent resistance R_{eq}. Therefore

$$R_{eq} = R_1 + R_2 + R_3$$

It is easy to generalize this to any number of resistors:

$$R_{eq} = R_1 + R_2 + R_3 + \cdots \quad \text{(resistors in series)} \quad (26.1)$$

The equivalent resistance of *any number* of resistors in series equals the sum of their individual resistances.

The equivalent resistance is *greater than* any individual resistance.

Let's compare this result with Eq. (24.5) for *capacitors* in series. Resistors in series add directly because the voltage across each is directly proportional to its resistance and to the common current. Capacitors in series add reciprocally because the voltage across each is directly proportional to the common charge but *inversely* proportional to the individual capacitance.

Resistors in Parallel

If the resistors are in *parallel,* as in Fig. 26.1b, the current through each resistor need not be the same. But the potential difference between the terminals of each resistor must be the same and equal to V_{ab} (Fig. 26.2). (Remember that the potential difference between any two points does not depend on the path taken between the points.) Let's call the currents in the three resistors I_1, I_2, and I_3. Then from $I = V/R$,

$$I_1 = \frac{V_{ab}}{R_1} \qquad I_2 = \frac{V_{ab}}{R_2} \qquad I_3 = \frac{V_{ab}}{R_3}$$

In general, the current is different through each resistor. Because charge is not accumulating or draining out of point *a,* the total current *I* must equal the sum of the three currents in the resistors:

$$I = I_1 + I_2 + I_3 = V_{ab}\left(\frac{1}{R_1} + \frac{1}{R_2} + \frac{1}{R_3}\right) \quad \text{or}$$

$$\frac{I}{V_{ab}} = \frac{1}{R_1} + \frac{1}{R_2} + \frac{1}{R_3}$$

But by the definition of the equivalent resistance R_{eq}, $I/V_{ab} = 1/R_{eq}$, so

$$\frac{1}{R_{eq}} = \frac{1}{R_1} + \frac{1}{R_2} + \frac{1}{R_3}$$

Again it is easy to generalize to *any number* of resistors in parallel:

$$\frac{1}{R_{eq}} = \frac{1}{R_1} + \frac{1}{R_2} + \frac{1}{R_3} + \cdots \qquad \text{(resistors in parallel)} \qquad (26.2)$$

For *any number* of resistors in parallel, the *reciprocal* of the equivalent resistance equals the *sum of the reciprocals* of their individual resistances.

The equivalent resistance is always *less than* any individual resistance.

We can compare this result with Eq. (24.7) for *capacitors* in parallel. Resistors in parallel add reciprocally because the current in each is proportional to the common voltage across them and *inversely* proportional to the resistance of each. Capacitors in parallel add directly because the charge on each is proportional to the common voltage across them and *directly* proportional to the capacitance of each.

For the special case of *two* resistors in parallel,

$$\frac{1}{R_{eq}} = \frac{1}{R_1} + \frac{1}{R_2} = \frac{R_1 + R_2}{R_1 R_2} \quad \text{and}$$

$$R_{eq} = \frac{R_1 R_2}{R_1 + R_2} \qquad \text{(two resistors in parallel)} \qquad (26.3)$$

?

26.2 A car's headlights are connected in parallel. Hence each headlight is exposed to the full potential difference supplied by the car's electrical system, giving maximum brightness. Another advantage is that if one headlight burns out, the other one keeps shining (see Example 26.2).

Activ
Physics ONLINE

12.2   DC Parallel Circuits

Because $V_{ab} = I_1 R_1 = I_2 R_2$, it follows that

$$\frac{I_1}{I_2} = \frac{R_2}{R_1} \qquad \text{(two resistors in parallel)} \qquad (26.4)$$

This shows that the currents carried by two resistors in parallel are *inversely proportional* to their resistances. More current goes through the path of least resistance.

Problem-Solving Strategy 26.1   Resistors in Series and Parallel

IDENTIFY *the relevant concepts:*   Many resistor networks are made up of resistors in series, in parallel, or a combination of the two. The key concept is that such a network can be replaced by a single equivalent resistor.

SET UP *the problem* using the following steps:
1. Make a drawing of the resistor network.
2. Determine whether the resistors are connected in series or parallel. Note that you can often consider networks such as those in Figs. 26.1c and 26.1d as combinations of series and parallel arrangements.
3. Determine what the target variables are. They could include the equivalent resistance of the network, the potential difference across each resistor, or the current through each resistor.

EXECUTE *the solution* as follows:
1. Use Eq. (26.1) or (26.2) to find the equivalent resistance for a series or a parallel combination, respectively.
2. If the network is more complex, try reducing it to series and parallel combinations. For example, in Fig. 26.1c we first replace the parallel combination of R_2 and R_3 with its equivalent resistance; this then forms a series combination with R_1. In

Fig. 26.1d, the combination of R_2 and R_3 in series forms a parallel combination with R_1.
3. When calculating potential differences, remember that when resistors are connected in series, the total potential difference across the combination equals the sum of the individual potential differences. When resistors are connected in parallel, the potential difference is the same for every resistor and equals the potential difference across the parallel combination.
4. Keep in mind the analogous statements for current. When resistors are connected in series, the current is the same through every resistor and equals the current through the series combination. When resistors are connected in parallel, the total current through the combination equals the sum of the currents through the individual resistors.

EVALUATE *your answer:*   Check whether your results are consistent. If resistors are connected in series, the equivalent resistance should be greater than that of any individual resistor; if they are connected in parallel, the equivalent resistance should be less than that of any individual resistor.

Example 26.1   Equivalent resistance

Compute the equivalent resistance of the network in Fig. 26.3a, and find the current in each resistor. The source of emf has negligible internal resistance.

SOLUTION

IDENTIFY: This network of three resistors is a *combination* of series and parallel resistances, just as in Fig. 26.1c. The 6-Ω and

26.3 Steps in reducing a combination of resistors to a single equivalent resistor and finding the current in each resistor.

(a)

$\mathcal{E} = 18\text{ V}, r = 0$

$6\,\Omega$

$a \quad 4\,\Omega \quad c$

$3\,\Omega$

b

(b)

18 V

$a \quad 4\,\Omega \quad c \quad 2\,\Omega \quad b$

(c)

18 V

$a \quad 6\,\Omega \quad b$

(d)

18 V

18 V

$a \quad 6\,\Omega \quad b$

3 A

(e)

18 V

$12\text{ V} \qquad 6\text{ V}$

$a \quad 4\,\Omega \quad c \quad 2\,\Omega \quad b$

$3\text{ A} \qquad 3\text{ A}$

(f)

$\mathcal{E} = 18\text{ V}, r = 0$

$6\,\Omega$

12 V

$a \quad 4\,\Omega \quad c \quad 1\text{ A} \quad 6\text{ V} \quad b$

3 A

$3\,\Omega$

2 A

3-Ω resistors are in parallel, and their combination is in series with the 4-Ω resistor.

SET UP: We first determine the equivalent resistance R_{eq} of this network as a whole. Given this value, we find the current in the emf, which is the same as the current in the 4-Ω resistor. This same current is split between the 6-Ω and 3-Ω resistors; we determine how much goes into each resistor by using the principle that the potential difference must be the same across these two resistors (because they are connected in parallel).

EXECUTE: Figures 26.3b and 26.3c show successive steps in reducing the network to a single equivalent resistance. From Eq.(26.2) the 6-Ω and 3-Ω resistors in parallel in Fig. 26.3a are equivalent to the single 2-Ω resistor in Fig. 26.3b:

$$\frac{1}{R_{eq}} = \frac{1}{6\ \Omega} + \frac{1}{3\ \Omega} = \frac{1}{2\ \Omega}$$

[You can find the same result using Eq. (26.3).] From Eq. (26.1) the series combination of this 2-Ω resistor with the 4-Ω resistor is equivalent to the single 6-Ω resistor in Fig. 26.3c.

To find the current in each resistor of the original network, we reverse the steps by which we reduced the network. In the circuit shown in Fig. 26.3d (identical to Fig. 26.3c), the current is $I = V_{ab}/R = (18\ \text{V})/(6\ \Omega) = 3$ A. So the current in the 4-Ω and 2-Ω resistors in Fig. 26.3e (identical to Fig. 26.3b) is also 3 A. The potential difference V_{cb} across the 2-Ω resistor is therefore $V_{cb} = IR = (3\ \text{A})(2\ \Omega) = 6$ V. This potential difference must also be 6 V in Fig. 26.3f (identical to Fig. 26.3a). Using $I = V_{cb}/R$, the currents in the 6-Ω and 3-Ω resistors in Fig. 26.3f are $(6\ \text{V})/(6\ \Omega) = 1$ A and $(6\ \text{V})/(3\ \Omega) = 2$ A, respectively.

EVALUATE: Note that for the two resistors in parallel between points c and b in Fig. 26.3f, there is twice as much current through the 3-Ω resistor as through the 6-Ω resistor; more current goes through the path of least resistance, in accordance with Eq. (26.4). Note also that the total current through these two resistors is 3 A, the same as it is through the 4-Ω resistor between points a and c.

Example 26.2 Series versus parallel combinations

Two identical light bulbs are to be connected to a source with $\mathcal{E} = 8$ V and negligible internal resistance. Each light bulb has a resistance $R = 2\ \Omega$. Find the current through each bulb, the potential difference across each bulb, and the power delivered to each bulb and to the entire network if the bulbs are connected (a) in series and (b) in parallel. (c) Suppose one of the bulbs burns out; that is, its filament breaks and current can no longer flow through it. What happens to the other bulb in the series case? In the parallel case?

SOLUTION

IDENTIFY: The light bulbs are just resistors in simple series and parallel connections.

SET UP: Figures 26.4a and 26.4b show our sketches of the series and parallel circuits, respectively. Once we have found the current

26.4 Our sketches for this problem.

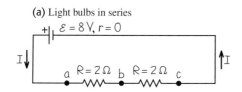

(a) Light bulbs in series

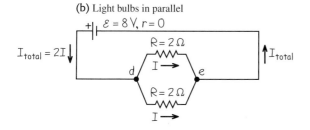

(b) Light bulbs in parallel

through each light bulb, we can find the power delivered to each bulb using Eq. (25.18), $P = I^2R = V^2/R$.

EXECUTE: (a) From Eq. (26.1) the equivalent resistance of the two bulbs between points a and c in Fig. 26.4a is the sum of their individual resistances:

$$R_{eq} = 2R = 2(2\ \Omega) = 4\ \Omega$$

The current is the same through either light bulb in series:

$$I = \frac{V_{ac}}{R_{eq}} = \frac{8\ \text{V}}{4\ \Omega} = 2\ \text{A}$$

Since the bulbs have the same resistance, the potential difference is the same across each bulb:

$$V_{ab} = V_{bc} = IR = (2\ \text{A})(2\ \Omega) = 4\ \text{V}$$

This is one-half of the 8-V terminal voltage of the source. From Eq.(25.18), the power delivered to each light bulb is

$$P = I^2R = (2\ \text{A})^2(2\ \Omega) = 8\ \text{W} \qquad \text{or}$$

$$P = \frac{V_{ab}^2}{R} = \frac{V_{bc}^2}{R} = \frac{(4\ \text{V})^2}{2\ \Omega} = 8\ \text{W}$$

The total power delivered to both bulbs is $P_{total} = 2P = 16$ W. Alternatively, we can find the total power by using the equivalent resistance $R_{eq} = 4\ \Omega$, through which the current is $I = 2$ A and across which the potential difference is $V_{ac} = 8$ V:

$$P_{total} = I^2R_{eq} = (2\ \text{A})^2(4\ \Omega) = 16\ \text{W} \qquad \text{or}$$

$$P_{total} = \frac{V_{ac}^2}{R_{eq}} = \frac{(8\ \text{V})^2}{4\ \Omega} = 16\ \text{W}$$

(b) If the light bulbs are in parallel, as in Fig. 26.4b, the potential difference V_{de} across each bulb is the same and equal to 8 V,

Continued

the terminal voltage of the source. Hence the current through each light bulb is

$$I = \frac{V_{de}}{R} = \frac{8 \text{ V}}{2 \text{ }\Omega} = 4 \text{ A}$$

and the power delivered to each bulb is

$$P = I^2R = (4 \text{ A})^2(2 \text{ }\Omega) = 32 \text{ W} \quad \text{or}$$

$$P = \frac{V_{de}^2}{R} = \frac{(8 \text{ V})^2}{2 \text{ }\Omega} = 32 \text{ W}$$

Both the potential difference across each bulb and the current through each bulb are twice as great as in the series case. Hence the power delivered to each bulb is *four* times greater, and each bulb glows more brightly than in the series case. If the goal is to produce the maximum amount of light from each bulb, a parallel arrangement is superior to a series arrangement.

The total power delivered to the parallel network is $P_{total} = 2P = 64 \text{ W}$, four times greater than in the series case. The increased power compared to the series case isn't obtained "for free"; energy is extracted from the source four times more rapidly in the parallel case than in the series case. If the source is a battery, it will be used up four times as fast.

We can also find the total power by using the equivalent resistance R_{eq}, given by Eq. (26.2):

$$\frac{1}{R_{eq}} = 2\left(\frac{1}{2 \text{ }\Omega}\right) = 1 \text{ }\Omega^{-1} \quad \text{or} \quad R_{eq} = 1 \text{ }\Omega$$

The total current through the equivalent resistor is $I_{total} = 2I = 2(4 \text{ A}) = 8 \text{ A}$, and the potential difference across the equivalent resistor is 8 V. Hence the total power is

$$P_{total} = I^2R_{eq} = (8 \text{ A})^2(1 \text{ }\Omega) = 64 \text{ W} \quad \text{or}$$

$$P_{total} = \frac{V_{de}^2}{R} = \frac{(8 \text{ V})^2}{1 \text{ }\Omega} = 64 \text{ W}$$

The potential difference across the equivalent resistance is the same for both the series and parallel cases, but for the parallel case the value of R_{eq} is less, and so $P_{total} = V^2/R_{eq}$ is greater.

(c) In the series case the same current flows through both bulbs. If one of the bulbs burns out, there will be no current at all in the circuit, and neither bulb will glow.

In the parallel case the potential difference across either bulb remains equal to 8 V even if one of the bulbs burns out. Hence the current through the functional bulb remains equal to 4 A, and the power delivered to that bulb remains equal to 32 W, the same as before the other bulb burned out. This is another of the merits of a parallel arrangement of light bulbs: If one fails, the other bulbs are unaffected. This principle is used in household wiring systems, which we'll discuss in Section 26.5.

EVALUATE: Our calculation isn't completely accurate, because the resistance $R = V/I$ of real light bulbs is *not* a constant independent of the potential difference V across the bulb. (The resistance of the filament increases with increasing operating temperature and hence with increasing V.) But it is indeed true that light bulbs connected in series across a source glow less brightly than when connected in parallel across the same source (Fig. 26.5).

26.5 When connected to the same source, two light bulbs in series (shown at top) draw less power and glow less brightly than when they are in parallel (shown at bottom).

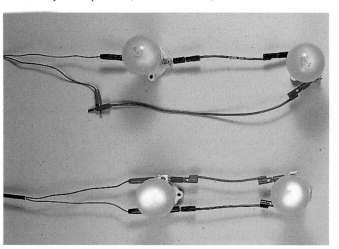

26.2 Kirchhoff's Rules

Many practical resistor networks cannot be reduced to simple series-parallel combinations. Figure 26.6a shows a dc power supply with emf $\mathcal{E}_1$ charging a battery with a smaller emf $\mathcal{E}_2$ and feeding current to a light bulb with resistance R. Figure 26.6b is a "bridge" circuit, used in many different types of measurement and control systems. (One important application of a "bridge" circuit is described in Problem 26.79.) We don't need any new principles to compute the currents in these networks, but there are some techniques that help us handle such problems systematically. We will describe the techniques developed by the German physicist Gustav Robert Kirchhoff (1824–1887).

First, here are two terms that we will use often. A **junction** in a circuit is a point where three or more conductors meet. Junctions are also called *nodes* or *branch points*. A **loop** is any closed conducting path. In Fig. 26.6a points *a* and *b* are junctions, but points *c* and *d* are not; in Fig. 26.6b the points *a*, *b*, *c*, and *d* are junctions, but points *e* and *f* are not. The blue lines in Figs. 26.6a and 26.6b show some possible loops in these circuits.

Kirchhoff's rules are the following two statements:

Kirchhoff's junction rule: *The algebraic sum of the currents into any junction is zero.* That is,

$$\sum I = 0 \qquad \text{(junction rule, valid at any junction)} \qquad (26.5)$$

Kirchhoff's loop rule: *The algebraic sum of the potential differences in any loop, including those associated with emfs and those of resistive elements, must equal zero.* That is,

$$\sum V = 0 \qquad \text{(loop rule, valid for any closed loop)} \qquad (26.6)$$

The junction rule is based on *conservation of electric charge.* No charge can accumulate at a junction, so the total charge entering the junction per unit time must equal the total charge leaving per unit time (Fig. 26.7a). Charge per unit time is current, so if we consider the currents entering a junction to be positive and those leaving to be negative, the algebraic sum of currents into a junction must be zero. It's like a T branch in a water pipe (Fig. 26.7b); if you have 1 liter per minute coming in one pipe, you can't have 3 liters per minute going out the other two pipes. We may as well confess that we used the junction rule (without saying so) in Section 26.1 in the derivation of Eq. (26.2) for resistors in parallel.

The loop rule is a statement that the electrostatic force is *conservative.* Suppose we go around a loop, measuring potential differences across successive circuit elements as we go. When we return to the starting point, we must find that the *algebraic sum* of these differences is zero; otherwise, we could not say that the potential at this point has a definite value.

Sign Conventions for the Loop Rule

In applying the loop rule, we need some sign conventions. Problem-Solving Strategy 26.2 describes in detail how to use these, but here's a quick overview. We first assume a direction for the current in each branch of the circuit and mark it on a diagram of the circuit. Then, starting at any point in the circuit, we imagine traveling around a loop, adding emfs and *IR* terms as we come to them. When we travel through a source in the direction from − to +, the emf is considered to be *positive;* when we travel from + to −, the emf is considered to be *negative* (Fig. 26.8a). When we travel through a resistor in the *same* direction as the assumed current, the *IR* term is *negative* because the current goes in the direction of decreasing potential. When we travel through a resistor in the direction *opposite* to the assumed current, the *IR* term is *positive* because this represents a rise of potential (Fig. 26.8b).

26.6 Two networks that cannot be reduced to simple series-parallel combinations of resistors.

(a)

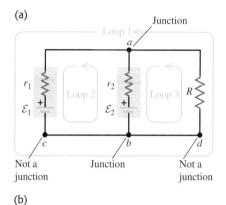

(b)

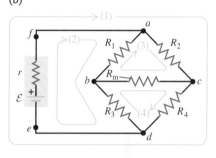

26.7 (a) Kirchhoff's junction rule states that as much current flows into a junction as flows out of it. (b) A water-pipe analogy.

(a) Kirchhoff's junction rule

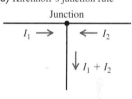

(b) Water-pipe analogy for Kirchhoff's junction rule

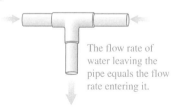

The flow rate of water leaving the pipe equals the flow rate entering it.

26.8 Use these sign conventions when you apply Kirchhoff's loop rule. In each part of the figure "Travel" is the direction that we imagine going around the loop, which is not necessarily the direction of the current.

(a) Sign conventions for emfs

$+\mathcal{E}$: Travel direction from − to +:	$-\mathcal{E}$: Travel direction from + to −:
— Travel →	← Travel —
$\mathcal{E}$	$\mathcal{E}$

(b) Sign conventions for resistors

$+IR$: Travel *opposite* to current direction:	$-IR$: Travel *in* current direction:
— Travel →	← Travel —
R	R

Kirchhoff's two rules are all we need to solve a wide variety of network problems. Usually, some of the emfs, currents, and resistances are known, and others are unknown. We must always obtain from Kirchhoff's rules a number of independent equations equal to the number of unknowns so that we can solve the equations simultaneously. Often the hardest part of the solution is not understanding the basic principles but keeping track of algebraic signs!

Problem-Solving Strategy 26.2   Kirchhoff's Rules

IDENTIFY *the relevant concepts:* Kirchhoff's rules are important tools for analyzing any circuit more complicated than a single loop.

SET UP *the problem* using the following steps:
1. Draw a *large* circuit diagram so you have plenty of room for labels. Label all quantities, known and unknown, including an assumed direction for each unknown current and emf. Often you will not know in advance the actual direction of an unknown current or emf, but this doesn't matter. If the actual direction of a particular quantity is opposite to your assumption, the result will come out with a negative sign. If you use Kirchhoff's rules correctly, they will give you the directions as well as the magnitudes of unknown currents and emfs.
2. When you label currents, it is usually best to use the junction rule immediately to express the currents in terms of as few quantities as possible. For example, Fig. 26.9a shows a circuit correctly labeled; Fig. 26.9b shows the same circuit, relabeled by applying the junction rule to point *a* to eliminate I_3.
3. Determine which quantities are the target variables.

EXECUTE *the solution* as follows:
1. Choose any closed loop in the network and designate a direction (clockwise or counterclockwise) to travel around the loop when applying the loop rule. The direction doesn't have to be the same as any assumed current direction.
2. Travel around the loop in the designated direction, adding potential differences as you cross them. Remember that a posi-

tive potential difference corresponds to an increase in potential and a negative potential difference corresponds to a decrease in potential. An emf is counted as positive when you traverse it from ($-$) to ($+$), and negative when you go from ($+$) to ($-$). An *IR* term is negative if you travel through the resistor in the same direction as the assumed current and positive if you pass through it in the opposite direction. Figure 26.8 summarizes these sign conventions.
3. Equate the sum in Step 2 to zero.
4. If necessary, choose another loop to get a different relationship among the unknowns, and continue until you have as many independent equations as unknowns or until every circuit element has been included in at least one of the chosen loops.
5. Solve the equations simultaneously to determine the unknowns. This step involves algebra, not physics, but it can be fairly complex. Be careful with algebraic manipulations; one sign error will prove fatal to the entire solution.
6. You can use this same bookkeeping system to find the potential V_{ab} of any point *a* with respect to any other point *b*. Start at *b* and add the potential changes you encounter in going from *b* to *a*, using the same sign rules as in Step 2. The algebraic sum of these changes is $V_{ab} = V_a - V_b$.

EVALUATE *your answer:* Check all the steps in your algebra. A useful strategy is to consider a loop other than the ones you used to solve the problem; if the sum of potential drops around this loop isn't zero, you made an error somewhere in your calculations. As always, ask yourself whether the answers make sense.

26.9 Applying the junction rule to point *a* reduces the number of unknown currents from three to two.

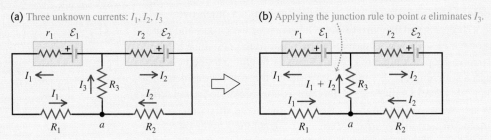

(a) Three unknown currents: I_1, I_2, I_3

(b) Applying the junction rule to point *a* eliminates I_3.

Example 26.3   A single-loop circuit

The circuit shown in Fig. 26.10a contains two batteries, each with an emf and an internal resistance, and two resistors. Find (a) the current in the circuit, (b) the potential difference V_{ab}, and (c) the power output of the emf of each battery.

SOLUTION

IDENTIFY: This single-loop circuit has no junctions, so we don't need Kirchhoff's junction rule to solve for the target variables.

SET UP: To apply the loop rule to the single loop, we first assume a direction for the current; let's assume a counterclockwise direction, as shown in Fig. 26.10a.

EXECUTE: (a) Starting at *a* and going counterclockwise, we add potential increases and decreases and equate the sum to zero, as in Eq. (26.6). The resulting equation is

$$-I(4\,\Omega) - 4\,\text{V} - I(7\,\Omega) + 12\,\text{V} - I(2\,\Omega) - I(3\,\Omega) = 0$$

Collecting terms containing I and solving for I, we find

$$8 \text{ V} = I(16 \ \Omega) \qquad \text{and} \qquad I = 0.5 \text{ A}$$

The result for I is positive, showing that our assumed current direction is correct. For an exercise, try assuming the opposite direction for I; you should then get $I = -0.5$ A, indicating that the actual current is opposite to this assumption.

(b) To find V_{ab}, the potential at a with respect to b, we start at b and add potential changes as we go toward a. There are two possible paths from b to a; taking the lower one first, we find

$$V_{ab} = (0.5 \text{ A})(7 \ \Omega) + 4 \text{ V} + (0.5 \text{ A})(4 \ \Omega) = 9.5 \text{ V}$$

Point a is at 9.5 V higher potential than b. All the terms in this sum, including the IR terms, are positive because each represents an *increase* in potential as we go from b toward a. If we use the upper path instead, the resulting equation is

$$V_{ab} = 12 \text{ V} - (0.5 \text{ A})(2 \ \Omega) - (0.5 \text{ A})(3 \ \Omega) = 9.5 \text{ V}$$

Here the IR terms are negative because our path goes in the direction of the current, with potential decreases through the resistors. The result is the same as for the lower path, as it must be in order for the total potential change around the complete loop to be zero. In each case, potential rises are taken to be positive and drops are taken to be negative.

(c) The power output of the emf of the 12-V battery is

$$P = \mathcal{E}I = (12 \text{ V})(0.5 \text{ A}) = 6 \text{ W}$$

and the power output of the emf of the 4-V battery is

$$P = \mathcal{E}I = (-4 \text{ V})(0.5 \text{ A}) = -2 \text{ W}$$

The negative sign in $\mathcal{E}$ for the 4-V battery appears because the current actually runs from the higher-potential side of the battery to the lower-potential side. The negative value of P means that we are *storing* energy in that battery, and it is being *recharged* by the 12-V battery.

EVALUATE: By applying the expression $P = I^2R$ to each of the four resistors in Fig. 26.10a, you should be able to show that the total power dissipated in all four resistors is 4 W. Of the 6 W provided by the emf of the 12-V battery, 2 W goes into storing energy in the 4-V battery and 4 W is dissipated in the resistances.

The circuit shown in Fig. 26.10a is very much like that used when a 12-V automobile battery is used to recharge a run-down battery in another automobile (Fig. 26.10b). The 3-Ω and 7-Ω resistors in Fig. 26.10a represent the resistances of the jumper cables and of the conducting path through the automobile with the run-down battery. (The values of the resistances in actual automobiles and jumper cables are different from those used in this example.)

26.10 (a) In this example we travel around the loop in the same direction as the assumed current, so all the IR terms are negative. The potential decreases as we travel from + to − through the bottom emf but increases as we travel from − to + through the top emf. (b) A real-life example of a circuit of this kind.

(a)

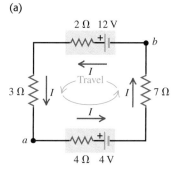

(b)

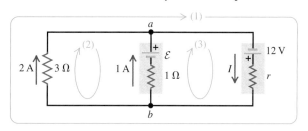

Example 26.4   Charging a battery

In the circuit shown in Fig. 26.11, a 12-V power supply with unknown internal resistance r is connected to a run-down rechargeable battery with unknown emf $\mathcal{E}$ and internal resistance $1 \ \Omega$ and to an indicator light bulb of resistance $3 \ \Omega$ carrying a current of 2 A. The current through the run-down battery is 1 A in the direction shown. Find the unknown current I, the internal resistance r, and the emf $\mathcal{E}$.

26.11 In this circuit a power supply charges a run-down battery and lights a bulb. An assumption has been made about the polarity of the emf $\mathcal{E}$ of the run-down battery. Is this assumption correct?

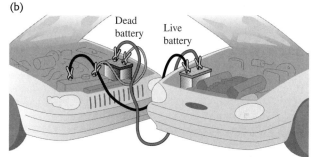

SOLUTION

IDENTIFY: This circuit has more than one loop, so we must apply both the junction rule and the loop rule.

SET UP: We assume the direction of the current through the 12-V power supply to be as shown. There are three target variables, so we need three equations.

EXECUTE: First we apply the junction rule, Eq. (26.5), to point a. We find

$$-I + 1 \text{ A} + 2 \text{ A} = 0 \qquad \text{so} \qquad I = 3 \text{ A}$$

Continued

To determine r, we apply the loop rule, Eq. (26.6), to the outer loop labeled (1); we find

$$12 \text{ V} - (3 \text{ A})r - (2 \text{ A})(3 \text{ }\Omega) = 0 \quad \text{so} \quad r = 2 \text{ }\Omega$$

The terms containing the resistances r and 3 Ω are negative because our loop traverses those elements in the same direction as the current and hence finds potential *drops*. If we had chosen to traverse loop (1) in the opposite direction, every term would have had the opposite sign, and the result for r would have been the same.

To determine $\mathcal{E}$, we apply the loop rule to loop (2):

$$-\mathcal{E} + (1 \text{ A})(1 \text{ }\Omega) - (2 \text{ A})(3 \text{ }\Omega) = 0 \quad \text{so} \quad \mathcal{E} = -5 \text{ V}$$

The term for the 1-Ω resistor is positive because in traversing it in the direction opposite to the current, we find a potential *rise*. The negative value for $\mathcal{E}$ shows that the actual polarity of this emf is opposite to the assumption made in Fig. 26.11; the positive terminal of this source is really on the right side. As in Example 26.3, the battery is being recharged.

EVALUATE: We can check our result for $\mathcal{E}$ by using loop (3), obtaining the equation

$$12 \text{ V} - (3 \text{ A})(2 \text{ }\Omega) - (1 \text{ A})(1 \text{ }\Omega) + \mathcal{E} = 0$$

from which we again find $\mathcal{E} = -5 \text{ V}$.

As an additional consistency check, we note that $V_{ba} = V_b - V_a$ equals the voltage across the 3-Ω resistance, which is $(2 \text{ A})(3 \text{ }\Omega) = 6 \text{ V}$. Going from a to b by the top branch, we encounter potential differences $+12 \text{ V} - (3 \text{ A})(2 \text{ }\Omega) = +6 \text{ V}$, and going by the middle branch we find $-(-5 \text{ V}) + (1 \text{ A})(1 \text{ }\Omega) = +6 \text{ V}$. The three ways of getting V_{ba} give the same results. Make sure that you understand all the signs in these calculations.

Example 26.5 Power in a battery-charging circuit

In the circuit of Example 26.4 (shown in Fig. 26.11), find the power delivered by the 12-V power supply and by the battery being recharged, and find the power dissipated in each resistor.

SOLUTION

IDENTIFY: We use the results of Section 25.5, in which we found that the power delivered *from* an emf to a circuit is $\mathcal{E}I$ and the power delivered *to* a resistor from a circuit is $V_{ab}I = I^2R$.

SET UP: We know the values of each emf, each current, and each resistance from Example 26.4.

EXECUTE: The power output from the emf of the power supply is

$$P_{\text{supply}} = \mathcal{E}_{\text{supply}}I_{\text{supply}} = (12 \text{ V})(3 \text{ A}) = 36 \text{ W}$$

The power dissipated in the power supply's internal resistance r is

$$P_{r\text{-supply}} = I_{\text{supply}}{}^2 r_{\text{supply}} = (3 \text{ A})^2(2 \text{ }\Omega) = 18 \text{ W}$$

so the power supply's *net* power output is $P_{\text{net}} = 36 \text{ W} - 18 \text{ W} = 18 \text{ W}$. Alternatively, from Example 26.4 the terminal voltage of the battery is $V_{ba} = 6 \text{ V}$, so the net power output is

$$P_{\text{net}} = V_{ba}I_{\text{supply}} = (6 \text{ V})(3 \text{ A}) = 18 \text{ W}$$

The power output of the emf $\mathcal{E}$ of the battery being charged is

$$P_{\text{emf}} = \mathcal{E}I_{\text{battery}} = (-5 \text{ V})(1 \text{ A}) = -5 \text{ W}$$

This is negative because the 1-A current runs through the battery from the higher-potential side to the lower-potential side. (As we mentioned in Example 26.4, the polarity assumed for this battery in Fig. 26.11 was wrong.) We are storing energy in the battery as we charge it. Additional power is dissipated in the battery's internal resistance; this power is

$$P_{r\text{-battery}} = I_{\text{battery}}{}^2 r_{\text{battery}} = (1 \text{ A})^2(1 \text{ }\Omega) = 1 \text{ W}$$

The total power input to the battery is thus $1 \text{ W} + |-5 \text{ W}| = 6 \text{ W}$. Of this, 5 W represents useful energy stored in the battery; the remainder is wasted in its internal resistance.

The power dissipated in the light bulb is

$$P_{\text{bulb}} = I_{\text{bulb}}{}^2 R_{\text{bulb}} = (2 \text{ A})^2(3 \text{ }\Omega) = 12 \text{ W}$$

EVALUATE: As a check, note that all of the power from the supply is accounted for. Of the 18 W of net power from the power supply, 5 W goes to recharge the battery, 1 W is dissipated in the battery's internal resistance, and 12 W is dissipated in the light bulb.

Example 26.6 A complex network

Figure 26.12 shows a "bridge" circuit of the type described at the beginning of this section (see Fig. 26.6b). Find the current in each resistor and the equivalent resistance of the network of five resistors.

SOLUTION

IDENTIFY: This network cannot be represented in terms of series and parallel combinations. Hence we must use Kirchhoff's rules to find the values of the target variables.

SET UP: There are five different currents to determine, but by applying the junction rule to junctions a and b, we can represent them in terms of three unknown currents, as shown in the figure. The current in the battery is $I_1 + I_2$.

26.12 A network circuit with several resistors.

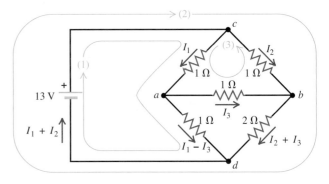

EXECUTE: We apply the loop rule to the three loops shown, obtaining the following three equations:

$$13 \text{ V} - I_1(1 \, \Omega) - (I_1 - I_3)(1 \, \Omega) = 0 \quad (1)$$
$$-I_2(1 \, \Omega) - (I_2 + I_3)(2 \, \Omega) + 13 \text{ V} = 0 \quad (2)$$
$$-I_1(1 \, \Omega) - I_3(1 \, \Omega) + I_2(1 \, \Omega) = 0 \quad (3)$$

This is a set of three simultaneous equations for the three unknown currents. They may be solved by various methods; one straightforward procedure is to solve the third equation for I_2, obtaining $I_2 = I_1 + I_3$, and then substitute this expression into the second equation to eliminate I_2. When this is done, we are left with the two equations

$$13 \text{ V} = I_1(2 \, \Omega) - I_3(1 \, \Omega) \quad (1')$$
$$13 \text{ V} = I_1(3 \, \Omega) + I_3(5 \, \Omega) \quad (2')$$

Now we can eliminate I_3 by multiplying Eq. (1') by 5 and adding the two equations. We obtain

$$78 \text{ V} = I_1(13 \, \Omega) \qquad I_1 = 6 \text{ A}$$

We substitute this result back into Eq. (1') to obtain $I_3 = -1$ A, and finally, from Eq. (3) we find $I_2 = 5$ A. The negative value of I_3 tells us that its direction is opposite to our initial assumption.

The total current through the network is $I_1 + I_2 = 11$ A, and the potential drop across it is equal to the battery emf—namely, 13 V. The equivalent resistance of the network is

$$R_{eq} = \frac{13 \text{ V}}{11 \text{ A}} = 1.2 \, \Omega$$

EVALUATE: You can check the results $I_1 = 6$ A, $I_2 = 5$ A, and $I_3 = -1$ A by substituting these values into the three equations (1), (2), and (3). What do you find?

Example 26.7 **A potential difference within a complex network**

In the circuit of Example 26.6 (Fig. 26.12), find the potential difference V_{ab}.

SOLUTION

IDENTIFY: Our target variable is $V_{ab} = V_a - V_b$, which is the potential at point a with respect to point b.

SET UP: To find V_{ab}, we start at point b and follow a path to point a, adding potential rises and drops as we go. We can follow any of several paths from b to a; the value of V_{ab} must be independent of which path we choose, which gives us a natural way to check our result.

EXECUTE: The simplest path to follow is through the center 1-Ω resistor. We have found $I_3 = -1$ A, showing that the actual current direction in this branch is from right to left. Thus, as we go

from b to a, there is a *drop* of potential with magnitude $IR = (1 \text{ A})(1 \, \Omega) = 1$ V, and $V_{ab} = -1$ V. That is, the potential at point a is 1 V less than that at point b.

EVALUATE: To test our result, let's try a path from b to a that goes through the lower two resistors. The currents through these are

$$I_2 + I_3 = 5 \text{ A} + (-1 \text{ A}) = 4 \text{ A} \quad \text{and}$$
$$I_1 - I_3 = 6 \text{ A} - (-1 \text{ A}) = 7 \text{ A}$$

and so

$$V_{ab} = -(4 \text{ A})(2 \, \Omega) + (7 \text{ A})(1 \, \Omega) = -1 \text{ V}$$

We suggest that you try some other paths from b to a to verify that they also give this result.

Test Your Understanding of Section 26.2 Subtract Eq. (1) from Eq. (2) in Example 26.6. To which loop in Fig. 26.12 does this equation correspond? Would this equation have simplified the solution of Example 26.6?

26.3 Electrical Measuring Instruments

We've been talking about potential difference, current, and resistance for two chapters, so it's about time we said something about how to *measure* these quantities. Many common devices, including car instrument panels, battery chargers, and inexpensive electrical instruments, measure potential difference (voltage), current, or resistance using a **d'Arsonval galvanometer** (Fig. 26.13). In the following discussion we'll often call it just a *meter*. A pivoted coil of fine wire is placed in the magnetic field of a permanent magnet (Fig. 26.14). Attached to the coil is a spring, similar to the hairspring on the balance wheel of a watch. In the equilibrium position, with no current in the coil, the pointer is at zero. When there is a current in the coil, the magnetic field exerts a torque on the coil that is proportional to the current. (We'll discuss this magnetic interaction in detail in Chapter 27.) As the coil turns, the spring exerts a restoring torque that is proportional to the angular displacement.

Thus the angular deflection of the coil and pointer is directly proportional to the coil current, and the device can be calibrated to measure current. The maximum deflection, typically 90° or so, is called *full-scale deflection*. The essential electrical characteristics of the meter are the current I_{fs} required for

26.13 This ammeter (top) and voltmeter (bottom) are both d'Arsonval galvanometers. The difference has to do with their internal connections (see Fig. 26.15).

26.14 A d'Arsonval galvanometer, showing a pivoted coil with attached pointer, a permanent magnet supplying a magnetic field that is uniform in magnitude, and a spring to provide restoring torque, which opposes magnetic-field torque.

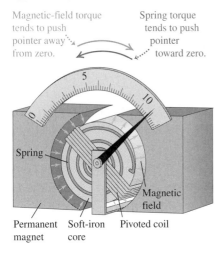

Magnetic-field torque tends to push pointer away from zero.

Spring torque tends to push pointer toward zero.

Spring

Magnetic field

Permanent magnet

Soft-iron core

Pivoted coil

Act|v
ONLINE
Phys|cs

12.4 Using Ammeters and Voltmeters

full-scale deflection (typically on the order of 10 μA to 10 mA) and the resistance R_c of the coil (typically on the order of 10 to 1000 Ω).

The meter deflection is proportional to the *current* in the coil. If the coil obeys Ohm's law, the current is proportional to the *potential difference* between the terminals of the coil, and the deflection is also proportional to this potential difference. For example, consider a meter whose coil has a resistance $R_c = 20.0$ Ω and that deflects full scale when the current in its coil is $I_{fs} = 1.00$ mA. The corresponding potential difference for full-scale deflection is

$$V = I_{fs}R_c = (1.00 \times 10^{-3}\ \text{A})(20.0\ \Omega) = 0.0200\ \text{V}$$

Ammeters

A current-measuring instrument is usually called an **ammeter** (or milliammeter, microammeter, and so forth, depending on the range). *An ammeter always measures the current passing through it.* An *ideal* ammeter, discussed in Section 25.4, would have *zero* resistance, so including it in a branch of a circuit would not affect the current in that branch. Real ammeters always have some finite resistance, but it is always desirable for an ammeter to have as little resistance as possible.

We can adapt any meter to measure currents that are larger than its full-scale reading by connecting a resistor in parallel with it (Fig. 26.15a) so that some of the current bypasses the meter coil. The parallel resistor is called a **shunt resistor** or simply a *shunt,* denoted as R_{sh}.

Suppose we want to make a meter with full-scale current I_{fs} and coil resistance R_c into an ammeter with full-scale reading I_a. To determine the shunt resistance R_{sh} needed, note that at full-scale deflection the total current through the parallel combination is I_a, the current through the coil of the meter is I_{fs}, and the current through the shunt is the difference $I_a - I_{fs}$. The potential difference V_{ab} is the same for both paths, so

$$I_{fs}R_c = (I_a - I_{fs})R_{sh} \quad \text{(for an ammeter)} \tag{26.7}$$

26.15 Using the same meter to measure (a) current and (b) voltage.

(a) A moving-coil ammeter

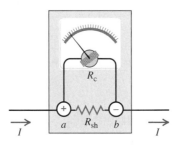

R_c

a R_{sh} b

I I

(b) A moving-coil voltmeter

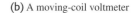

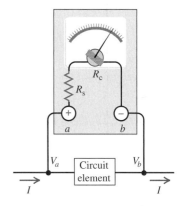

R_c

R_s

a b

V_a Circuit element V_b

I I

Example 26.8 **Designing an ammeter**

What shunt resistance is required to make the 1.00-mA, 20.0-Ω meter described above into an ammeter with a range of 0 to 50.0 mA?

SOLUTION

IDENTIFY: Since the meter is being used as an ammeter, its internal connections are as shown in Fig. 26.15a. Our target variable is the shunt resistance R_{sh}.

SET UP: We want the ammeter to be able to handle a maximum current $I_a = 50.0$ mA $= 50.0 \times 10^{-3}$ A. The resistance of the coil

is $R_c = 20.0$ Ω, and the meter shows full-scale deflection when the current through the coil is $I_{fs} = 1.00 \times 10^{-3}$ A. We find the shunt resistance R_{sh} using Eq. (26.7).

EXECUTE: Solving Eq. (26.7) for R_{sh}, we find

$$R_{sh} = \frac{I_{fs}R_c}{I_a - I_{fs}} = \frac{(1.00 \times 10^{-3}\ \text{A})(20.0\ \Omega)}{50.0 \times 10^{-3}\ \text{A} - 1.00 \times 10^{-3}\ \text{A}}$$

$$= 0.408\ \Omega$$

EVALUATE: It's useful to consider the equivalent resistance R_{eq} of the ammeter as a whole. From Eq. (26.2),

$$\frac{1}{R_{eq}} = \frac{1}{R_c} + \frac{1}{R_{sh}} = \frac{1}{20.0\ \Omega} + \frac{1}{0.408\ \Omega}$$

$$R_{eq} = 0.400\ \Omega$$

The shunt resistance is so small in comparison to the meter resistance that the equivalent resistance is very nearly equal to the shunt resistance. The result is a low-resistance instrument with the desired range of 0 to 50.0 mA. At full-scale deflection, $I = I_a = 50.0$ mA, the current through the galvanometer is 1.00 mA, the current through the shunt resistor is 49.0 mA, and $V_{ab} = 0.0200$ V. If the current I is *less* than 50.0 mA, the coil current and the deflection are proportionally less, but the resistance R_{eq} is still 0.400 Ω.

Voltmeters

This same basic meter may also be used to measure potential difference or *voltage*. A voltage-measuring device is called a **voltmeter** (or millivoltmeter, and so forth, depending on the range). A voltmeter always measures the potential difference between two points, and its terminals must be connected to these points. (Example 25.7 in Section 25.4 described what can happen if a voltmeter is connected incorrectly.) As we discussed in Section 25.4, an ideal voltmeter would have *infinite* resistance, so connecting it between two points in a circuit would not alter any of the currents. Real voltmeters always have finite resistance, but a voltmeter should have large enough resistance that connecting it in a circuit does not change the other currents appreciably.

For the meter described in Example 26.8 the voltage across the meter coil at full-scale deflection is only $I_{fs}R_c = (1.00 \times 10^{-3}\ \text{A})(20.0\ \Omega) = 0.0200$ V. We can extend this range by connecting a resistor R_s in *series* with the coil (Fig. 26.15b). Then only a fraction of the total potential difference appears across the coil itself, and the remainder appears across R_s. For a voltmeter with full-scale reading V_V, we need a series resistor R_s in Fig. 26.15b such that

$$V_V = I_{fs}(R_c + R_s) \qquad \text{(for a voltmeter)} \qquad (26.8)$$

Example 26.9 Designing a voltmeter

How can we make a galvanometer with $R_c = 20.0\ \Omega$ and $I_{fs} = 1.00$ mA into a voltmeter with a maximum range of 10.0 V?

SOLUTION

IDENTIFY: Since this meter is being used as a voltmeter, its internal connections are as shown in Fig. 26.15b. Our target variable is the series resistance R_s.

SET UP: The maximum allowable voltage across the voltmeter is $V_V = 10.0$ V. We want this to occur when the current through the coil (of resistance $R_c = 20.0\ \Omega$) is $I_{fs} = 1.00 \times 10^{-3}$ A. We find the series resistance R_s with Eq.(26.8).

EXECUTE: From Eq. (26.8),

$$R_s = \frac{V_V}{I_{fs}} - R_c = \frac{10.0\ \text{V}}{0.00100\ \text{A}} - 20.0\ \Omega = 9980\ \Omega$$

EVALUATE: At full-scale deflection, $V_{ab} = 10.0$ V, the voltage across the meter is 0.0200 V, the voltage across R_s is 9.98 V, and the current through the voltmeter is 0.00100 A. In this case most of the voltage appears across the series resistor. The equivalent meter resistance is $R_{eq} = 20.0\ \Omega + 9980\ \Omega = 10,000\ \Omega$. Such a meter is described as a "1000 ohms-per-volt meter," referring to the ratio of resistance to full-scale deflection. In normal operation the current through the circuit element being measured (I in Fig. 26.15b) is much greater than 0.00100 A, and the resistance between points a and b in the circuit is much less than 10,000 Ω. So the voltmeter draws off only a small fraction of the current and disturbs only slightly the circuit being measured.

Ammeters and Voltmeters in Combination

A voltmeter and an ammeter can be used together to measure *resistance* and *power*. The resistance R of a resistor equals the potential difference V_{ab} between its terminals divided by the current I; that is, $R = V_{ab}/I$. The power input P to any circuit element is the product of the potential difference across it and the current through it: $P = V_{ab}I$. In principle, the most straightforward way to measure R or P is to measure V_{ab} and I simultaneously.

With practical ammeters and voltmeters this isn't quite as simple as it seems. In Fig. 26.16a, ammeter A reads the current I in the resistor R. Voltmeter V, however, reads the *sum* of the potential difference V_{ab} across the resistor and the potential difference V_{bc} across the ammeter. If we transfer the voltmeter terminal from c to b, as in Fig. 26.16b, then the voltmeter reads the potential difference V_{ab} correctly, but the ammeter now reads the *sum* of the current I in the resistor and the current I_V in the voltmeter. Either way, we have to correct the reading of one instrument or the other unless the corrections are small enough to be negligible.

26.16 Ammeter–voltmeter method for measuring resistance.

(a)

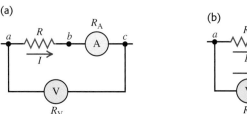

(b)

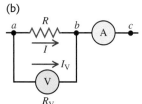

Example 26.10 Measuring resistance I

Suppose we want to measure an unknown resistance R using the circuit of Fig. 26.16a. The meter resistances are $R_V = 10,000 \, \Omega$ (for the voltmeter) and $R_A = 2.00 \, \Omega$ (for the ammeter). If the voltmeter reads 12.0 V and the ammeter reads 0.100 A, what are the resistance R and the power dissipated in the resistor?

SOLUTION

IDENTIFY: The ammeter reads the current $I = 0.100$ A through the resistor, and the voltmeter reads the potential difference between a and c. If the ammeter were *ideal* (that is, if $R_A = 0$), there would be zero potential difference between b and c, the voltmeter reading $V = 12.0$ V would be equal to the potential difference V_{ab} across the resistor, and the resistance would simply be equal to $R = V/I = (12.0 \text{ V})/(0.100 \text{ A}) = 120 \, \Omega$. The ammeter is *not* ideal, however (its resistance is $R_A = 2.00 \, \Omega$), so the voltmeter reading V is actually the sum of the potential differences V_{bc} (across the ammeter) and V_{ab} (across the resistor).

SET UP: We use Ohm's law to find the voltage V_{bc} across the ammeter from its known current and resistance. Then we solve for V_{ab} and the resistance R. Given these, we are able to calculate the power P into the resistor.

EXECUTE: From Ohm's law, $V_{bc} = IR_A = (0.100 \text{ A})(2.00 \, \Omega) = 0.200$ V and $V_{ab} = IR$. The sum of these is $V = 12.0$ V, so the potential difference across the resistor is $V_{ab} = V - V_{bc} = (12.0 \text{ V}) - (0.200 \text{ V}) = 11.8$ V. Hence the resistance is

$$R = \frac{V_{ab}}{I} = \frac{11.8 \text{ V}}{0.100 \text{ A}} = 118 \, \Omega$$

The power dissipated in this resistor is

$$P = V_{ab}I = (11.8 \text{ V})(0.100 \text{ A}) = 1.18 \text{ W}$$

EVALUATE: You can confirm this result for the power by using the alternative formula $P = I^2R$. Do you get the same answer?

Example 26.11 Measuring resistance II

Suppose the meters of Example 26.10 are connected to a different resistor in the circuit shown in Fig. 26.16b, and the readings obtained on the meters are the same as in Example 26.10. What is the value of this new resistance R, and what is the power dissipated in the resistor?

SOLUTION

IDENTIFY: In Example 26.10 the ammeter read the actual current through the resistor, but the voltmeter reading was not the same as the potential difference across the resistor. Now the situation is reversed: The voltmeter reading $V = 12.0$ V shows the actual potential difference V_{ab} across the resistor, but the ammeter reading $I_A = 0.100$ A is *not* equal to the current I through the resistor.

SET UP: Applying the junction rule at b in Fig. 26.16b shows that $I_A = I + I_V$, where I_V is the current through the voltmeter. We find I_V from the given values of V and the voltmeter resistance R_V, and we use this value to find the resistor current I. We then determine the resistance R from I and the voltmeter reading, and calculate the power as in Example 26.10.

EXECUTE: We have $I_V = V/R_V = (12.0 \text{ V})/(10,000 \, \Omega) = 1.20$ mA. The actual current I in the resistor is $I = I_A - I_V = 0.100 \text{ A} - 0.0012 \text{ A} = 0.0988$ A, and the resistance is

$$R = \frac{V_{ab}}{I} = \frac{12.0 \text{ V}}{0.0988 \text{ A}} = 121 \, \Omega$$

The power dissipated in the resistor is

$$P = V_{ab}I = (12.0 \text{ V})(0.0988 \text{ A}) = 1.19 \text{ W}$$

EVALUATE: Our results for R and P are not too different than the results of Example 26.10, in which the meters are connected in a different way. That's because the ammeter and voltmeter are nearly ideal: Compared to the resistance R under test, the ammeter resistance R_A is very small and the voltmeter resistance R_V is very large. Nonetheless, the results of the two examples *are* different, which shows that you must account for how ammeters and voltmeters are used when interpreting their readings.

Ohmmeters

An alternative method for measuring resistance is to use a d'Arsonval meter in an arrangement called an **ohmmeter.** It consists of a meter, a resistor, and a source (often a flashlight battery) connected in series (Fig. 26.17). The resistance R to be measured is connected between terminals x and y.

The series resistance R_s is variable; it is adjusted so that when terminals x and y are short-circuited (that is, when $R = 0$), the meter deflects full scale. When nothing is connected to terminals x and y, so that the circuit between x and y is *open* (that is, when $R \rightarrow \infty$), there is no current and hence no deflection. For any intermediate value of R the meter deflection depends on the value of R, and the meter scale can be calibrated to read the resistance R directly. Larger currents correspond to smaller resistances, so this scale reads backward compared to the scale showing the current.

In situations in which high precision is required, instruments containing d'Arsonval meters have been supplanted by electronic instruments with direct digital readouts. These are more precise, stable, and mechanically rugged than d'Arsonval meters. Digital voltmeters can be made with extremely high internal resistance, of the order of 100 MΩ. Figure 26.18 shows a digital *multimeter,* an instrument that can measure voltage, current, or resistance over a wide range.

The Potentiometer

The *potentiometer* is an instrument that can be used to measure the emf of a source without drawing any current from the source; it also has a number of other useful applications. Essentially, it balances an unknown potential difference against an adjustable, measurable potential difference.

The principle of the potentiometer is shown schematically in Fig. 26.19a. A resistance wire ab of total resistance R_{ab} is permanently connected to the terminals of a source of known emf $\mathcal{E}_1$. A sliding contact c is connected through the galvanometer G to a second source whose emf $\mathcal{E}_2$ is to be measured. As contact c is moved along the resistance wire, the resistance R_{cb} between points c and b varies; if the resistance wire is uniform, R_{cb} is proportional to the length of wire between c and b. To determine the value of $\mathcal{E}_2$, contact c is moved until a position is found at which the galvanometer shows no deflection; this corresponds to zero current passing through $\mathcal{E}_2$. With $I_2 = 0$, Kirchhoff's loop rule gives

$$\mathcal{E}_2 = IR_{cb}$$

With $I_2 = 0$, the current I produced by the emf $\mathcal{E}_1$ has the same value no matter what the value of the emf $\mathcal{E}_2$. We calibrate the device by replacing $\mathcal{E}_2$ by a source of known emf; then any unknown emf $\mathcal{E}_2$ can be found by measuring the length of wire cb for which $I_2 = 0$ (see Exercise 26.35). Note that for this to work, V_{ab} must be greater than $\mathcal{E}_2$.

The term *potentiometer* is also used for any variable resistor, usually having a circular resistance element and a sliding contact controlled by a rotating shaft and knob. The circuit symbol for a potentiometer is shown in Fig. 26.19b.

Test Your Understanding of Section 26.3 You want to measure the current through and the potential difference across the 2-Ω resistor shown in Fig. 26.12 (Example 26.6 in Section 26.2). (a) How should you connect an ammeter and a voltmeter to do this? (i) ammeter and voltmeter both in series with the 2-Ω resistor; (ii) ammeter in series with the 2-Ω resistor and voltmeter connected between points b and d; (iii) ammeter connected between points b and d and voltmeter in series with the 2-Ω resistor; (iv) ammeter and voltmeter both connected between points b and d. (b) What resistances should these meters have? (i) Ammeter and voltmeter resistances should both be much greater than 2 Ω; (ii) ammeter resistance should be much greater than 2 Ω and voltmeter resistance should be much less than 2 Ω; (iii) ammeter resistance should be much less than 2 Ω and voltmeter resistance should be much greater than 2 Ω; (iv) ammeter and voltmeter resistances should both be much less than 2 Ω.

26.17 Ohmmeter circuit. The resistor R_s has a variable resistance, as is indicated by the arrow through the resistor symbol. To use the ohmmeter, first connect x directly to y and adjust R_s until the meter reads zero. Then connect x and y across the resistor R and read the scale.

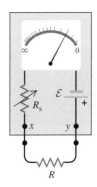

26.18 This digital multimeter can be used as a voltmeter (red arc), ammeter (yellow arc), or ohmmeter (green arc).

26.19 (a) Potentiometer circuit. (b) Circuit symbol for a potentiometer (variable resistor).

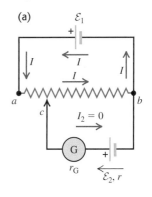

(b)

26.20 This colored x-ray image shows a pacemaker surgically implanted in a patient with a malfunctioning sinoatrial node, the part of the heart that generates the electrical signal to trigger heartbeats. To compensate, the pacemaker (located near the collarbone) sends a pulsed electrical signal along the lead to the heart to maintain regular beating.

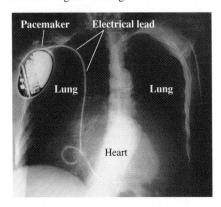

26.21 Charging a capacitor. (a) Just before the switch is closed, the charge q is zero. (b) When the switch closes (at $t = 0$), the current jumps from zero to $\mathcal{E}/R$. As time passes, q approaches Q_f and the current i approaches zero.

(a) Capacitor initially uncharged

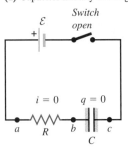

(b) Charging the capacitor

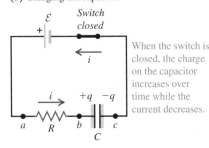

When the switch is closed, the charge on the capacitor increases over time while the current decreases.

26.4 *R-C* Circuits

In the circuits we have analyzed up to this point, we have assumed that all the emfs and resistances are *constant* (time independent) so that all the potentials, currents, and powers are also independent of time. But in the simple act of charging or discharging a capacitor we find a situation in which the currents, voltages, and powers *do* change with time.

Many important devices incorporate circuits in which a capacitor is alternately charged and discharged. These include heart pacemakers (Fig. 26.20), flashing traffic lights, automobile turn signals, and electronic flash units. Understanding what happens in such circuits is thus of great practical importance.

Charging a Capacitor

Figure 26.21 shows a simple circuit for charging a capacitor. A circuit such as this that has a resistor and a capacitor in series is called an ***R-C* circuit.** We idealize the battery (or power supply) to have a constant emf $\mathcal{E}$ and zero internal resistance $(r = 0)$, and we neglect the resistance of all the connecting conductors.

We begin with the capacitor initially uncharged (Fig. 26.21a); then at some initial time $t = 0$ we close the switch, completing the circuit and permitting current around the loop to begin charging the capacitor (Fig. 26.21b). For all practical purposes, the current begins at the same instant in every conducting part of the circuit, and at each instant the current is the same in every part.

CAUTION **Lowercase means time-varying** Up to this point we have been working with constant potential differences (voltages), currents, and charges, and we have used *capital* letters V, I, and Q, respectively, to denote these quantities. To distinguish between quantities that vary with time and those that are constant, we will use *lowercase* letters v, i, and q for time-varying voltages, currents, and charges, respectively. We suggest that you follow this same convention in your own work.

Because the capacitor in Fig. 26.21 is initially uncharged, the potential difference v_{bc} across it is zero at $t = 0$. At this time, from Kirchhoff's loop law, the voltage v_{ab} across the resistor R is equal to the battery emf $\mathcal{E}$. The initial $(t = 0)$ current through the resistor, which we will call I_0, is given by Ohm's law: $I_0 = v_{ab}/R = \mathcal{E}/R$.

As the capacitor charges, its voltage v_{bc} increases and the potential difference v_{ab} across the resistor decreases, corresponding to a decrease in current. The sum of these two voltages is constant and equal to $\mathcal{E}$. After a long time the capacitor becomes fully charged, the current decreases to zero, and the potential difference v_{ab} across the resistor becomes zero. Then the entire battery emf $\mathcal{E}$ appears across the capacitor and $v_{bc} = \mathcal{E}$.

Let q represent the charge on the capacitor and i the current in the circuit at some time t after the switch has been closed. We choose the positive direction for the current to correspond to positive charge flowing onto the left-hand capacitor plate, as in Fig. 26.21b. The instantaneous potential differences v_{ab} and v_{bc} are

$$v_{ab} = iR \qquad v_{bc} = \frac{q}{C}$$

Using these in Kirchhoff's loop rule, we find

$$\mathcal{E} - iR - \frac{q}{C} = 0 \tag{26.9}$$

The potential drops by an amount iR as we travel from a to b and by q/C as we travel from b to c. Solving Eq. (26.9) for i, we find

$$i = \frac{\mathcal{E}}{R} - \frac{q}{RC} \tag{26.10}$$

At time $t = 0$, when the switch is first closed, the capacitor is uncharged, and so $q = 0$. Substituting $q = 0$ into Eq. (26.10), we find that the *initial* current I_0 is given by $I_0 = \mathcal{E}/R$, as we have already noted. If the capacitor were not in the circuit, the last term in Eq. (26.10) would not be present; then the current would be *constant* and equal to $\mathcal{E}/R$.

As the charge q increases, the term q/RC becomes larger and the capacitor charge approaches its final value, which we will call Q_f. The current decreases and eventually becomes zero. When $i = 0$, Eq. (26.10) gives

$$\frac{\mathcal{E}}{R} = \frac{Q_f}{RC} \qquad Q_f = C\mathcal{E} \tag{26.11}$$

Note that the final charge Q_f does not depend on R.

The current and the capacitor charge are shown as functions of time in Fig. 26.22. At the instant the switch is closed $(t = 0)$, the current jumps from zero to its initial value $I_0 = \mathcal{E}/R$; after that, it gradually approaches zero. The capacitor charge starts at zero and gradually approaches the final value given by Eq. (26.11), $Q_f = C\mathcal{E}$.

We can derive general expressions for the charge q and current i as functions of time. With our choice of the positive direction for current (Fig. 26.21b), i equals the rate at which positive charge arrives at the left-hand (positive) plate of the capacitor, so $i = dq/dt$. Making this substitution in Eq. (26.10), we have

$$\frac{dq}{dt} = \frac{\mathcal{E}}{R} - \frac{q}{RC} = -\frac{1}{RC}(q - C\mathcal{E})$$

We can rearrange this to

$$\frac{dq}{q - C\mathcal{E}} = -\frac{dt}{RC}$$

and then integrate both sides. We change the integration variables to q' and t' so that we can use q and t for the upper limits. The lower limits are $q' = 0$ and $t' = 0$:

$$\int_0^q \frac{dq'}{q' - C\mathcal{E}} = -\int_0^t \frac{dt'}{RC}$$

When we carry out the integration, we get

$$\ln\left(\frac{q - C\mathcal{E}}{-C\mathcal{E}}\right) = -\frac{t}{RC}$$

Exponentiating both sides (that is, taking the inverse logarithm) and solving for q, we find

$$\frac{q - C\mathcal{E}}{-C\mathcal{E}} = e^{-t/RC}$$

$$q = C\mathcal{E}(1 - e^{-t/RC}) = Q_f(1 - e^{-t/RC}) \qquad \begin{array}{l}\text{(R-C circuit,}\\ \text{charging capacitor)}\end{array} \tag{26.12}$$

The instantaneous current i is just the time derivative of Eq. (26.12):

$$i = \frac{dq}{dt} = \frac{\mathcal{E}}{R}e^{-t/RC} = I_0 e^{-t/RC} \qquad \begin{array}{l}\text{(R-C circuit,}\\ \text{charging capacitor)}\end{array} \tag{26.13}$$

The charge and current are both *exponential* functions of time. Figure 26.22a is a graph of Eq. (26.13) and Fig. 26.22b is a graph of Eq. (26.12).

26.22 Current i and capacitor charge q as functions of time for the circuit of Fig. 26.21. The initial current is I_0 and the initial capacitor charge is zero. The current asymptotically approaches zero and the capacitor charge asymptotically approaches a final value of Q_f.

(a) Graph of current versus time for a charging capacitor

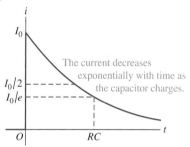

The current decreases exponentially with time as the capacitor charges.

(b) Graph of capacitor charge versus time for a charging capacitor

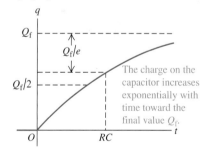

The charge on the capacitor increases exponentially with time toward the final value Q_f.

26.23 Discharging a capacitor. (a) Before the switch is closed at time $t = 0$, the capacitor charge is Q_0 and the current is zero. (b) At time t after the switch is closed, the capacitor charge is q and the current is i. The actual current direction is opposite to the direction shown; i is negative. After a long time, q and i both approach zero.

(a) Capacitor initially charged

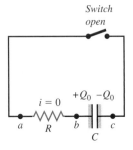

(b) Discharging the capacitor

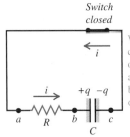

26.24 Current i and capacitor charge q as functions of time for the circuit of Fig. 26.23. The initial current is I_0 and the initial capacitor charge is Q_0. Both i and q asymptotically approach zero.

(a) Graph of current versus time for a discharging capacitor

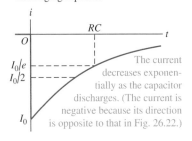

(b) Graph of capacitor charge versus time for a discharging capacitor

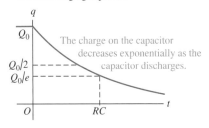

Time Constant

After a time equal to RC, the current in the R-C circuit has decreased to $1/e$ (about 0.368) of its initial value. At this time, the capacitor charge has reached $(1 - 1/e) = 0.632$ of its final value $Q_f = C\mathcal{E}$. The product RC is therefore a measure of how quickly the capacitor charges. We call RC the **time constant,** or the **relaxation time,** of the circuit, denoted by τ:

$$\tau = RC \qquad \text{(time constant for } R\text{-}C \text{ circuit)} \tag{26.14}$$

When τ is small, the capacitor charges quickly; when it is larger, the charging takes more time. If the resistance is small, it's easier for current to flow, and the capacitor charges more quickly. If R is in ohms and C in farads, τ is in seconds.

In Fig. 26.22a the horizontal axis is an *asymptote* for the curve. Strictly speaking, i never becomes exactly zero. But the longer we wait, the closer it gets. After a time equal to 10 RC, the current has decreased to 0.000045 of its initial value. Similarly, the curve in Fig. 26.22b approaches the horizontal dashed line labeled Q_f as an asymptote. The charge q never attains exactly this value, but after a time equal to $10RC$, the difference between q and Q_f is only 0.000045 of Q_f. We invite you to verify that the product RC has units of time.

Discharging a Capacitor

Now suppose that after the capacitor in Fig. 26.21b has acquired a charge Q_0, we remove the battery from our R-C circuit and connect points a and c to an open switch (Fig. 26.23a). We then close the switch and at the same instant reset our stopwatch to $t = 0$; at that time, $q = Q_0$. The capacitor then *discharges* through the resistor, and its charge eventually decreases to zero.

Again let i and q represent the time-varying current and charge at some instant after the connection is made. In Fig. 26.23b we make the same choice of the positive direction for current as in Fig. 26.21b. Then Kirchhoff's loop rule gives Eq. (26.10) but with $\mathcal{E} = 0$; that is,

$$i = \frac{dq}{dt} = -\frac{q}{RC} \tag{26.15}$$

The current i is now negative; this is because positive charge q is leaving the left-hand capacitor plate in Fig. 26.23b, so the current is in the direction opposite to that shown in the figure. At time $t = 0$, when $q = Q_0$, the initial current is $I_0 = -Q_0/RC$.

To find q as a function of time, we rearrange Eq. (26.15), again change the names of the variables to q' and t', and integrate. This time the limits for q' are Q_0 to q. We get

$$\int_{Q_0}^{q} \frac{dq'}{q'} = -\frac{1}{RC} \int_0^t dt'$$

$$\ln \frac{q}{Q_0} = -\frac{t}{RC}$$

$$q = Q_0 e^{-t/RC} \qquad \text{(}R\text{-}C \text{ circuit, discharging capacitor)} \tag{26.16}$$

The instantaneous current i is the derivative of this with respect to time:

$$i = \frac{dq}{dt} = -\frac{Q_0}{RC} e^{-t/RC} = I_0 e^{-t/RC} \qquad \begin{matrix} \text{(}R\text{-}C \text{ circuit,} \\ \text{discharging capacitor)} \end{matrix} \tag{26.17}$$

The current and the charge are graphed in Fig. 26.24; both quantities approach zero exponentially with time. Comparing these results with Eqs. (26.12) and (26.13), we note that the expressions for the current are identical, apart from the sign of I_0.

The capacitor charge approaches zero asymptotically in Eq. (26.16), while the *difference* between q and Q approaches zero asymptotically in Eq. (26.12).

Energy considerations give us additional insight into the behavior of an *R-C* circuit. While the capacitor is charging, the instantaneous rate at which the battery delivers energy to the circuit is $P = \mathcal{E}i$. The instantaneous rate at which electrical energy is dissipated in the resistor is i^2R and the rate at which energy is stored in the capacitor is $iv_{bc} = iq/C$. Multiplying Eq. (26.9) by i, we find

$$\mathcal{E}i = i^2R + \frac{iq}{C} \qquad (26.18)$$

This means that of the power $\mathcal{E}i$ supplied by the battery, part (i^2R) is dissipated in the resistor and part (iq/C) is stored in the capacitor.

The *total* energy supplied by the battery during charging of the capacitor equals the battery emf $\mathcal{E}$ multiplied by the total charge Q_f, or $\mathcal{E}Q_f$. The total energy stored in the capacitor, from Eq. (24.9), is $Q_f\mathcal{E}/2$. Thus, of the energy supplied by the battery, *exactly half* is stored in the capacitor, and the other half is dissipated in the resistor. It is a little surprising that this half-and-half division of energy doesn't depend on C, R, or $\mathcal{E}$. This result can also be verified in detail by taking the integral over time of each of the power quantities in Eq. (26.18). We leave this calculation for your amusement (see Problem 26.87).

Example 26.12   **Charging a capacitor**

A resistor with resistance 10 MΩ is connected in series with a capacitor with capacitance 1.0 μF and a battery with emf 12.0 V. Before the switch is closed at time $t = 0$, the capacitor is uncharged. (a) What is the time constant? (b) What fraction of the final charge is on the plates at time $t = 46$ s? (c) What fraction of the initial current remains at $t = 46$ s?

SOLUTION

IDENTIFY: This is the same situation as shown in Fig. 26.21, with $R = 10$ MΩ, $C = 1.0$ μF, and $\mathcal{E} = 12.0$ V. The charge and current vary with time as shown in Fig. 26.22. Our target variables are (a) the time constant, (b) the charge q at $t = 46$ s divided by the final charge Q_f, and (c) the current i at $t = 46$ s divided by the initial current i_0.

SET UP: For a capacitor being charged, the charge is given by Eq. (26.12) and the current by Eq. (26.13). Equation (26.14) gives the time constant.

EXECUTE: (a) From Eq. (26.14), the time constant is

$$\tau = RC = (10 \times 10^6 \ \Omega)(1.0 \times 10^{-6} \ \text{F}) = 10 \ \text{s}$$

(b) From Eq. (26.12),

$$\frac{q}{Q_f} = 1 - e^{-t/RC} = 1 - e^{-(46 \ \text{s})/(10 \ \text{s})} = 0.99$$

The capacitor is 99% charged after a time equal to 4.6 *RC*, or 4.6 time constants.

(c) From Eq. (26.13),

$$\frac{i}{I_0} = e^{-4.6} = 0.010$$

After 4.6 time constants the current has decreased to 1.0% of its initial value.

EVALUATE: The time constant is relatively long because the resistance is very large. The circuit charges more rapidly if a smaller resistance is used.

Example 26.13   **Discharging a capacitor**

The resistor and capacitor described in Example 26.12 are reconnected as shown in Fig. 26.23. The capacitor is originally given a charge of 5.0 μC and then discharged by closing the switch at $t = 0$. (a) At what time will the charge be equal to 0.50 μC? (b) What is the current at this time?

SOLUTION

IDENTIFY: Now the capacitor is being discharged, so the charge q and current i vary with time as shown in Fig. 26.24. Our target

variables are (a) the value of t at which $q = 0.50$ μC and (b) the value of i at this time.

SET UP: The charge is given by Eq. (26.16) and the current by Eq. (26.17).

EXECUTE: (a) Solving Eq. (26.16) for the time t gives

$$t = -RC \ln \frac{q}{Q_0}$$

$$= -(10 \times 10^6 \ \Omega)(1.0 \times 10^{-6} \ \text{F}) \ln \frac{0.50 \ \mu\text{C}}{5.0 \ \mu\text{C}} = 23 \ \text{s}$$

Continued

This is 2.3 times the time constant $\tau = RC = 10$ s.

(b) From Eq. (26.17), with $Q_0 = 5.0 \ \mu C = 5.0 \times 10^{-6}$ C,

$$i = -\frac{Q_0}{RC} e^{-t/RC} = -\frac{5.0 \times 10^{-6} \text{ C}}{10 \text{ s}} e^{-2.3} = -5.0 \times 10^{-8} \text{ A}$$

The current has the opposite sign when the capacitor is discharging than when it is charging.

EVALUATE: We could have saved the effort required to calculate $e^{-t/RC}$ by noticing that at the time in question, $q = 0.10Q_0$; from Eq. (26.16) this means $e^{-t/RC} = 0.10$.

Test Your Understanding of Section 26.4 The energy stored in a capacitor is equal to $q^2/2C$. When a capacitor is discharged, what fraction of the initial energy remains after an elapsed time of one time constant? (i) $1/e$; (ii) $1/e^2$; (iii) $1 - 1/e$; (iv) $(1 - 1/e)^2$; (v) answer depends on how much energy was stored initially.

26.5 Power Distribution Systems

We conclude this chapter with a brief discussion of practical household and automotive electric-power distribution systems. Automobiles use direct-current (dc) systems, while nearly all household, commercial, and industrial systems use alternating current (ac) because of the ease of stepping voltage up and down with transformers. Most of the same basic wiring concepts apply to both. We'll talk about alternating-current circuits in greater detail in Chapter 31.

The various lamps, motors, and other appliances to be operated are always connected in *parallel* to the power source (the wires from the power company for houses, or from the battery and alternator for a car). If appliances were connected in series, shutting one appliance off would shut them all off (see Example 26.2 in Section 26.1). The basic idea of house wiring is shown in Fig. 26.25. One side of the "line," as the pair of conductors is called, is called the *neutral* side; it is always connected to "ground" at the entrance panel. For houses, *ground* is an actual electrode driven into the earth (which is usually a good conductor) or sometimes connected to the household water pipes. Electricians speak of the "hot" side and the "neutral" side of the line. Most modern house wiring systems have *two* hot lines with opposite polarity with respect to the neutral. We'll return to this detail later.

Household voltage is nominally 120 V in the United States and Canada, and often 240 V in Europe. (For alternating current, which varies sinusoidally with time, these numbers represent the *root-mean-square* voltage, which is $1/\sqrt{2}$ times the peak voltage. We'll discuss this further in Section 31.1.) The amount of current I drawn by a given device is determined by its power input P, given by Eq. (25.17): $P = VI$. Hence $I = P/V$. For example, the current in a 100-W light bulb is

$$I = \frac{P}{V} = \frac{100 \text{ W}}{120 \text{ V}} = 0.83 \text{ A}$$

26.25 Schematic diagram of part of a house wiring system. Only two branch circuits are shown; an actual system might have four to thirty branch circuits. Lamps and appliances may be plugged into the outlets. The grounding wires, which normally carry no current, are not shown.

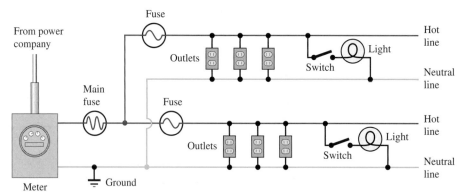

The power input to this bulb is actually determined by its resistance R. Using Eq. (25.18), which states that $P = VI = I^2R = V^2/R$ for a resistor, the resistance of this bulb at operating temperature is

$$R = \frac{V}{I} = \frac{120 \text{ V}}{0.83 \text{ A}} = 144 \ \Omega \qquad \text{or} \qquad R = \frac{V^2}{P} = \frac{(120 \text{ V})^2}{100 \text{ W}} = 144 \ \Omega$$

Similarly, a 1500-W waffle iron draws a current of $(1500 \text{ W})/(120 \text{ V}) = 12.5$ A and has a resistance, at operating temperature, of 9.6 Ω. Because of the temperature dependence of resistivity, the resistances of these devices are considerably less when they are cold. If you measure the resistance of a 100-W light bulb with an ohmmeter (whose small current causes very little temperature rise), you will probably get a value of about 10 Ω. When a light bulb is turned on, this low resistance causes an initial surge of current until the filament heats up. That's why a light bulb that's ready to burn out nearly always does so just when you turn it on.

Circuit Overloads and Short Circuits

The maximum current available from an individual circuit is limited by the resistance of the wires. As we discussed in Section 25.5, the I^2R power loss in the wires causes them to become hot, and in extreme cases this can cause a fire or melt the wires. Ordinary lighting and outlet wiring in houses usually uses 12-gauge wire. This has a diameter of 2.05 mm and can carry a maximum current of 20 A safely (without overheating). Larger sizes such as 8-gauge (3.26 mm) or 6-gauge (4.11 mm) are used for high-current appliances such as electric ranges and clothes dryers, and 2-gauge (6.54 mm) or larger is used for the main power lines entering a house.

Protection against overloading and overheating of circuits is provided by fuses or circuit breakers. A *fuse* contains a link of lead–tin alloy with a very low melting temperature; the link melts and breaks the circuit when its rated current is exceeded (Fig. 26.26a). A *circuit breaker* is an electromechanical device that performs the same function, using an electromagnet or a bimetallic strip to "trip" the breaker and interrupt the circuit when the current exceeds a specified value (Fig. 26.26b). Circuit breakers have the advantage that they can be reset after they are tripped, while a blown fuse must be replaced. However, fuses are somewhat more reliable in operation than circuit breakers are.

If your system has fuses and you plug too many high-current appliances into the same outlet, the fuse blows. *Do not* replace the fuse with one of larger rating; if you do, you risk overheating the wires and starting a fire. The only safe solution is to distribute the appliances among several circuits. Modern kitchens often have three or four separate 20-A circuits.

Contact between the hot and neutral sides of the line causes a *short circuit*. Such a situation, which can be caused by faulty insulation or by any of a variety of mechanical malfunctions, provides a very low-resistance current path, permitting a very large current that would quickly melt the wires and ignite their insulation if the current were not interrupted by a fuse or circuit breaker (see Example 25.11 in Section 25.5). An equally dangerous situation is a broken wire that interrupts the current path, creating an *open circuit*. This is hazardous because of the sparking that can occur at the point of intermittent contact.

In approved wiring practice, a fuse or breaker is placed *only* in the hot side of the line, never in the neutral side. Otherwise, if a short circuit should develop because of faulty insulation or other malfunction, the ground-side fuse could blow. The hot side would still be live and would pose a shock hazard if you touched the live conductor and a grounded object such as a water pipe. For similar reasons the wall switch for a light fixture is always in the hot side of the line, never the neutral side.

Further protection against shock hazard is provided by a third conductor called the *grounding wire,* included in all present-day wiring. This conductor

26.26 (a) Excess current will melt the thin wire of lead–tin alloy that runs along the length of a fuse, inside the transparent housing. (b) The switch on this circuit breaker will flip if the maximum allowable current is exceeded.

(a)

(b)

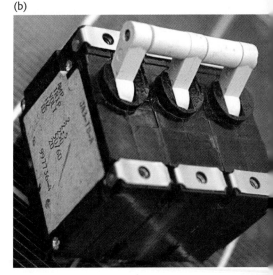

26.27 (a) If a malfunctioning electric drill is connected to a wall socket via a two-prong plug, a person may receive a shock. (b) When the drill malfunctions when connected via a three-prong plug, a person touching it receives no shock, because electric charge flows through the ground wire (shown in green) to the third prong and into the ground rather than into the person's body. If the ground current is appreciable, the fuse blows.

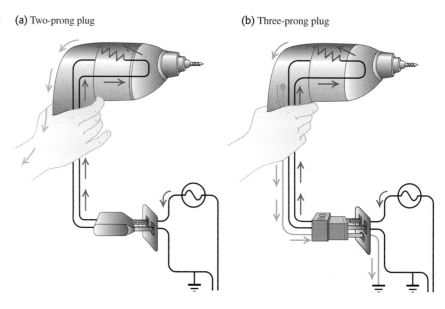

(a) Two-prong plug

(b) Three-prong plug

corresponds to the long round or U-shaped prong of the three-prong connector plug on an appliance or power tool. It is connected to the neutral side of the line at the entrance panel. The grounding wire normally carries no current, but it connects the metal case or frame of the device to ground. If a conductor on the hot side of the line accidentally contacts the frame or case, the grounding conductor provides a current path, and the fuse blows. Without the ground wire, the frame could become "live,"—that is, at a potential 120 V above ground. Then if you touched it and a water pipe (or even a damp basement floor) at the same time, you could get a dangerous shock (Fig. 26.27). In some situations, especially outlets located outdoors or near a sink or other water pipes, a special kind of circuit breaker called a *ground-fault interrupter* (GFI or GFCI) is used. This device senses the difference in current between the hot and neutral conductors (which is normally zero) and trips when this difference exceeds some very small value, typically 5 mA.

Household and Automotive Wiring

Most modern household wiring systems actually use a slight elaboration of the system described above. The power company provides *three* conductors (Fig. 26.28). One is neutral; the other two are both at 120 V with respect to the neutral but with opposite polarity, giving a voltage between them of 240 V. The power company calls this a *three-wire line,* in contrast to the 120-V two-wire (plus ground wire) line described above. With a three-wire line, 120-V lamps and appliances can be connected between neutral and either hot conductor, and high-power devices requiring 240 V, such as electric ranges and clothes dryers, are connected between the two hot lines.

To help prevent wiring errors, household wiring uses a standardized color code in which the hot side of a line has black insulation (black and red for the two sides of a 240-V line), the neutral side has white insulation, and the grounding conductor is bare or has green insulation. But in electronic devices and equipment the ground or neutral side of the line is usually black. Beware! (Our illustrations do not follow this standard code but use red for the hot line and blue for neutral.)

All of the above discussion can be applied directly to automobile wiring. The voltage is about 13 V (direct current); the power is supplied by the battery and by the alternator, which charges the battery when the engine is running. The neutral

26.28 Diagram of a typical 120–240-V wiring system in a kitchen. Grounding wires are not shown. For each line, the hot side is shown in red, and the neutral line is shown in blue. (Different colors are used in actual household wiring.)

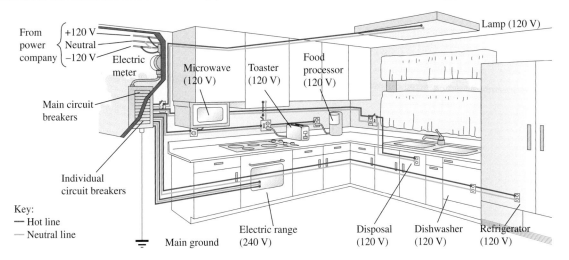

side of each circuit is connected to the body and frame of the vehicle. For this low voltage a separate grounding conductor is not required for safety. The fuse or circuit breaker arrangement is the same in principle as in household wiring. Because of the lower voltage (less energy per charge), more current (a greater number of charges per second) is required for the same power; a 100-W headlight bulb requires a current of about $(100 \text{ W})/(13 \text{ V}) = 8 \text{ A}$.

Although we spoke of *power* in the above discussion, what we buy from the power company is *energy*. Power is energy transferred per unit time, so energy is average power multiplied by time. The usual unit of energy sold by the power company is the kilowatt-hour $(1 \text{ kW} \cdot \text{h})$:

$$1 \text{ kW} \cdot \text{h} = (10^3 \text{ W})(3600 \text{ s}) = 3.6 \times 10^6 \text{ W} \cdot \text{s} = 3.6 \times 10^6 \text{ J}$$

One kilowatt-hour typically costs 2 to 10 cents, depending on the location and quantity of energy purchased. To operate a 1500-W (1.5-kW) waffle iron continuously for 1 hour requires 1.5 kW · h of energy; at 10 cents per kilowatt-hour, the energy cost is 15 cents. The cost of operating any lamp or appliance for a specified time can be calculated in the same way if the power rating is known. However, many electric cooking utensils (including waffle irons) cycle on and off to maintain a constant temperature, so the average power may be less than the power rating marked on the device.

Example 26.14 | A kitchen circuit

An 1800-W toaster, a 1.3-kW electric frying pan, and a 100-W lamp are plugged into the same 20-A, 120-V circuit. (a) What current is drawn by each device, and what is the resistance of each device? (b) Will this combination blow the fuse?

SOLUTION

IDENTIFY: When plugged into the same circuit, the three devices are in parallel. The voltage across each device is $V = 120 \text{ V}$.

SET UP: We find the current I drawn by each device using the relationship $P = VI$, where P is the power input of the device. To find the resistance R for each device we use the relationship $P = V^2/R$.

EXECUTE: (a) To simplify the calculation of current and resistance, we note that $I = P/V$ and $R = V^2/P$. Hence

$$I_{\text{toaster}} = \frac{1800 \text{ W}}{120 \text{ V}} = 15 \text{ A} \qquad R_{\text{toaster}} = \frac{(120 \text{ V})^2}{1800 \text{ W}} = 8 \text{ }\Omega$$

$$I_{\text{frying pan}} = \frac{1300 \text{ W}}{120 \text{ V}} = 11 \text{ A} \qquad R_{\text{frying pan}} = \frac{(120 \text{ V})^2}{1300 \text{ W}} = 11 \text{ }\Omega$$

$$I_{\text{lamp}} = \frac{100 \text{ W}}{120 \text{ V}} = 0.83 \text{ A} \qquad R_{\text{lamp}} = \frac{(120 \text{ V})^2}{100 \text{ W}} = 144 \text{ }\Omega$$

For constant voltage the device with the *least* resistance (in this case the toaster) draws the most current and receives the most power.

Continued

(b) The total current through the line is the sum of the currents drawn by the three devices:

$$I = I_{\text{toaster}} + I_{\text{frying pan}} + I_{\text{lamp}} = 15\text{ A} + 11\text{ A} + 0.83\text{ A} = 27\text{ A}$$

This exceeds the 20-A rating of the line, and the fuse will indeed blow.

EVALUATE: We could also find the current by first finding the equivalent resistance of the three devices in parallel:

$$\frac{1}{R_{\text{eq}}} = \frac{1}{R_{\text{toaster}}} + \frac{1}{R_{\text{frying pan}}} + \frac{1}{R_{\text{lamp}}}$$

$$= \frac{1}{8\ \Omega} + \frac{1}{11\ \Omega} + \frac{1}{144\ \Omega} = 0.22\ \Omega^{-1}$$

$$R_{\text{eq}} = 4.5\ \Omega$$

The total current is then $I = V/R_{\text{eq}} = (120\text{ V})/(4.5\ \Omega) = 27\text{ A}$, as before. A third way to determine I is to use $I = P/V$ and simply divide the total power delivered to all three devices by the voltage:

$$I = \frac{P_{\text{toaster}} + P_{\text{frying pan}} + P_{\text{lamp}}}{V} = \frac{1800\text{ W} + 1300\text{ W} + 100\text{ W}}{120\text{ V}}$$

$$= 27\text{ A}$$

Current demands like these are encountered in everyday life in kitchens, which is why modern kitchens have more than one 20-A circuit. In actual practice, the toaster and frying pan should be connected to different circuits; the current in each circuit would then be safely below the 20-A rating.

Test Your Understanding of Section 26.5   To prevent the fuse in Example 26.14 from blowing, a home electrician replaces the fuse with one rated at 40 A. Is this a reasonable thing to do?

Resistors in series and parallel: When several resistors $R_1, R_2, R_3, \ldots$, are connected in series, the equivalent resistance R_{eq} is the sum of the individual resistances. The same *current* flows through all the resistors in a series connection. When several resistors are connected in parallel, the reciprocal of the equivalent resistance R_{eq} is the sum of the reciprocals of the individual resistances. All resistors in a parallel connection have the same *potential difference* between their terminals. (See Examples 26.1 and 26.2.)

$$R_{eq} = R_1 + R_2 + R_3 + \cdots \quad (26.1)$$
(resistors in series)

$$\frac{1}{R_{eq}} = \frac{1}{R_1} + \frac{1}{R_2} + \frac{1}{R_3} + \cdots \quad (26.2)$$
(resistors in parallel)

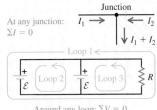

Kirchhoff's rules: Kirchhoff's junction rule is based on conservation of charge. It states that the algebraic sum of the currents into any junction must be zero. Kirchhoff's loop rule is based on conservation of energy and the conservative nature of electrostatic fields. It states that the algebraic sum of potential differences around any loop must be zero. Careful use of consistent sign rules is essential in applying Kirchhoff's rules. (See Examples 26.3–26.7)

$$\sum I = 0 \quad \text{(junction rule)} \quad (26.5)$$

$$\sum V = 0 \quad \text{(loop rule)} \quad (26.6)$$

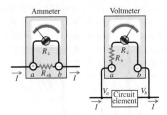

Electrical measuring instruments: In a d'Arsonval galvanometer, the deflection is proportional to the current in the coil. For a larger current range, a shunt resistor is added, so some of the current bypasses the meter coil. Such an instrument is called an ammeter. If the coil and any additional series resistance included obey Ohm's law, the meter can also be calibrated to read potential difference or voltage. The instrument is then called a voltmeter. A good ammeter has very low resistance; a good voltmeter has very high resistance. (See Examples 26.8–26.11.)

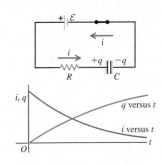

R-C circuits: When a capacitor is charged by a battery in series with a resistor, the current and capacitor charge are not constant. The charge approaches its final value asymptotically and the current approaches zero asymptotically. The charge and current in the circuit are given by Eqs. (26.12) and (26.13). After a time $\tau = RC$, the charge has approached within $1/e$ of its final value. This time is called the time constant or relaxation time of the circuit. When the capacitor discharges, the charge and current are given as functions of time by Eqs. (26.16) and (26.17). The time constant is the same for charging and discharging. (See Examples 26.12 and 26.13.)

Capacitor charging:
$$\begin{aligned} q &= C\mathcal{E}\left(1 - e^{-t/RC}\right) \\ &= Q_f\left(1 - e^{-t/RC}\right) \end{aligned} \quad (26.12)$$

$$\begin{aligned} i &= \frac{dq}{dt} = \frac{\mathcal{E}}{R}e^{-t/RC} \\ &= I_0 e^{-t/RC} \end{aligned} \quad (26.13)$$

Capacitor discharging:
$$q = Q_0 e^{-t/RC} \quad (26.16)$$

$$\begin{aligned} i &= \frac{dq}{dt} = -\frac{Q_0}{RC}e^{-t/RC} \\ &= I_0 e^{-t/RC} \end{aligned} \quad (26.17)$$

Household wiring: In household wiring systems, the various electrical devices are connected in parallel across the power line, which consists of a pair of conductors, one "hot" and the other "neutral." An additional "ground" wire is included for safety. The maximum permissible current in a circuit is determined by the size of the wires and the maximum temperature they can tolerate. Protection against excessive current and the resulting fire hazard is provided by fuses or circuit breakers. (See Example 26.14.)

Key Terms

direct current, *881*
alternating current, *881*
series, *882*
parallel, *882*
equivalent resistance, *882*
junction, *887*

loop, *887*
Kirchhoff's junction rule, *887*
Kirchhoff's loop rule, *887*
d'Arsonval galvanometer, *891*
ammeter, *892*
shunt resistor, *892*

voltmeter, *893*
ohmmeter, *895*
R-C circuit, *896*
time constant (relaxation time), *898*

Answer to Chapter Opening Question ?

The potential difference V is the same across resistors connected in parallel. However, there is a different current I through each resistor if the resistances R are different: $I = V/R$.

Answers to Test Your Understanding Questions

26.1 answer: (a), (c), (d), (b) Here's why: The three resistors in Fig. 26.1a are in series, so $R_{eq} = R + R + R = 3R$. In Fig. 26.1b the three resistors are in parallel, so $1/R_{eq} = 1/R + 1/R + 1/R = 3/R$ and $R_{eq} = R/3$. In Fig. 26.1c the second and third resistors are in parallel, so their equivalent resistance R_{23} is given by $1/R_{23} = 1/R + 1/R = 2/R$; hence $R_{23} = R/2$. This combination is in series with the first resistor, so the three resistors together have equivalent resistance $R_{eq} = R + R/2 = 3R/2$. In Fig. 26.1d the second and third resistors are in series, so their equivalent resistance is $R_{23} = R + R = 2R$. This combination is in parallel with the first resistor, so the equivalent resistance of the three-resistor combination is given by $1/R_{eq} = 1/R + 1/2R = 3/2R$. Hence $R_{eq} = 2R/3$.

26.2 answer: loop *cbdac* Equation (2) minus Eq. (1) gives $-I_2(1\ \Omega) - (I_2 + I_3)(2\ \Omega) + (I_1 - I_3)(1\ \Omega) + I_1(1\ \Omega) = 0$.

We can obtain this equation by applying the loop rule around the path from c to b to d to a to c in Fig. 26.12. This isn't a new equation, so it would not have helped with the solution of Example 26.6.

26.3 answers: (a) (ii), (b) (iii) An ammeter must always be placed in series with the circuit element of interest, and a voltmeter must always be placed in parallel. Ideally the ammeter would have zero resistance and the voltmeter would have infinite resistance so that their presence would have no effect on either the resistor current or the voltage. Neither of these idealizations is possible, but the ammeter resistance should be much less than 2 Ω and the voltmeter resistance should be much greater than 2 Ω.

26.4 answer: (ii) After one time constant, $t = RC$ and the initial charge Q_0 has decreased to $Q_0 e^{-t/RC} = Q_0 e^{-RC/RC} = Q_0 e^{-1} = Q_0/e$. Hence the stored energy has decreased from $Q_0^2/2C$ to $(Q_0/e)^2/2C = Q_0^2/2Ce^2$, a fraction $1/e^2 = 0.135$ of its initial value. This result doesn't depend on the initial value of the energy.

26.5 answer: no This is a very dangerous thing to do. The fuse will allow currents up to 40 A, double the rated value of the wiring. The amount of power $P = I^2R$ dissipated in a section of wire can therefore be up to four times the rated value, so the wires could get very warm and start a fire.

PROBLEMS

For instructor-assigned homework, go to **www.masteringphysics.com**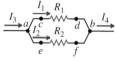

Discussion Questions

Q26.1. In which 120-V light bulb does the filament have greater resistance: a 60-W bulb or a 120-W bulb? If the two bulbs are connected to a 120-V line in series, through which bulb will there be the greater voltage drop? What if they are connected in parallel? Explain your reasoning.

Q26.2. Two 120-V light bulbs, one 25-W and one 200-W, were connected in series across a 240-V line. It seemed like a good idea at the time, but one bulb burned out almost immediately. Which one burned out, and why?

Q26.3. You connect a number of identical light bulbs to a flashlight battery. (a) What happens to the brightness of each bulb as more and more bulbs are added to the circuit if you connect them (i) in series and (ii) in parallel? (b) Will the battery last longer if the bulbs are in series or in parallel? Explain your reasoning.

Q26.4. In the circuit shown in Fig. 26.29, three identical light bulbs are connected to a flashlight battery. How do the brightnesses of the bulbs compare? Which light bulb has the greatest current passing through it? Which light bulb has the greatest potential difference between its terminals? What happens if bulb *A* is unscrewed? Bulb *B*? Bulb *C*? Explain your reasoning.

Figure **26.29**
Question Q26.4.

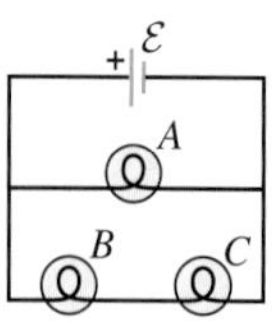

Q26.5. If two resistors R_1 and R_2 $(R_2 > R_1)$ are connected in series as shown in Fig. 26.30, which of the following must be true? In each case justify your answer. (a) $I_1 = I_2 = I_3$. (b) The current is greater in R_1 than in R_2. (c) The electrical power consumption is the same for both resistors. (d) The electrical power consumption is greater in R_2 than in R_1. (e) The potential drop is the same across both resistors. (f) The potential at point a is the same as at point c. (g) The potential at point b is lower than at point c. (h) The potential at point c is lower than at point b.

Figure **26.30**
Question Q26.5.

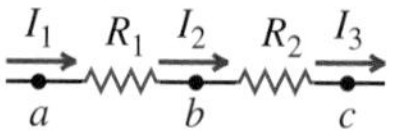

Q26.6. If two resistors R_1 and R_2 $(R_2 > R_1)$ are connected in parallel as shown in Fig. 26.31, which of the following must be true? In each case justify your answer. (a) $I_1 = I_2$. (b) $I_3 = I_4$. (c) The current is greater in R_1 than in R_2. (d) The rate of electrical energy consumption is the same for both resistors. (e) The rate of electrical energy consumption is greater in R_2 than in R_1. (f) $V_{cd} = V_{ef} = V_{ab}$. (g) Point c is at higher potential than point d. (h) Point f is at higher potential than point e. (i) Point c is at higher potential than point e.

Figure **26.31**
Question Q26.6.

Q26.7. Why do the lights on a car become dimmer when the starter is operated?

Q26.8. A resistor consists of three identical metal strips connected as shown in Fig. 26.32. If one of the strips is cut out, does the ammeter reading increase, decrease, or stay the same? Why?

Figure **26.32** Question Q26.8.

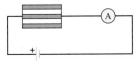

Q26.9. A light bulb is connected in the circuit shown in Fig. 26.33. If we close the switch S, does the bulb's brightness increase, decrease, or remain the same? Explain why.

Figure **26.33** Question Q26.9.

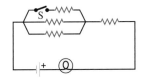

Q26.10. A real battery, having nonnegligible internal resistance, is connected across a light bulb as shown in Fig. 26.34. When the switch S is closed, what happens to the brightness of the bulb? Why?

Figure **26.34** Question Q26.10.

Q26.11. If the battery in Discussion Question Q26.10 is ideal with no internal resistance, what will happen to the brightness of the bulb when S is closed? Why?

Q26.12. For the circuit shown in Fig. 26.35 what happens to the brightness of the bulbs when the switch S is closed if the battery (a) has no internal resistance and (b) has nonnegligible internal resistance? Explain why.

Figure **26.35** Question Q26.12.

Q26.13. Is it possible to connect resistors together in a way that cannot be reduced to some combination of series and parallel combinations? If so, give examples. If not, state why not.

Q26.14. The direction of current in a battery can be reversed by connecting it to a second battery of greater emf with the positive terminals of the two batteries together. When the direction of current is reversed in a battery, does its emf also reverse? Why or why not?

Q26.15. In a two-cell flashlight, the batteries are usually connected in series. Why not connect them in parallel? What possible advantage could there be in connecting several identical batteries in parallel?

Q26.16. Electric rays (genus *Torpedo*) deliver electric shocks to stun their prey and to discourage predators. (In ancient Rome, physicians practiced a primitive form of electroconvulsive therapy by placing electric rays on their patients to cure headaches and gout.) Figure 26.36a shows *Torpedo* as seen from below. The voltage is produced by thin, waferlike cells called *electrocytes,* each of which acts like a battery with an emf of about 10^{-4} V. Stacks of electrocytes are arranged side by side on the underside of *Torpedo* (Fig. 26.36b); in such a stack, the positive face of each electrocyte

touches the negative face of the next electrocyte (Fig. 26.36c). What is the advantage of stacking the electrocytes? Of having the stacks side by side?

Figure **26.36** Question Q26.16.

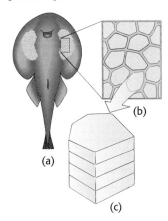

Q26.17. The emf of a flashlight battery is roughly constant with time, but its internal resistance increases with age and use. What sort of meter should be used to test the freshness of a battery?

Q26.18. Is it possible to have a circuit in which the potential difference across the terminals of a battery in the circuit is zero? If so, give an example. If not, explain why not.

Q26.19. Verify that the time constant RC has units of time.

Q26.20. For very large resistances it is easy to construct R-C circuits that have time constants of several seconds or minutes. How might this fact be used to measure very large resistances, those that are too large to measure by more conventional means?

Q26.21. Whan a capacitor, battery, and resistor are connected in series, does the resistor affect the maximum charge stores on the capacitor? Why or why not? What purpose does the resistor serve?

Q26.22. The greater the diameter of the wire used in household wiring, the greater the maximum current that can safely be carried by the wire. Why is this? Does the maximum permissible current depend on the length of the wire? Does it depend on what the wire is made of? Explain your reasoning.

Exercises

Section 26.1 Resistors in Series and Parallel

26.1. A uniform wire of resistance R is cut into three equal lengths. One of these is formed into a circle and connected between the other two (Fig. 26.37). What is the resistance between the opposite ends a and b?

Figure **26.37** Exercise 26.1.

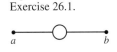

26.2. A machine part has a resistor X protruding from an opening in the side. This resistor is connected to three other resistors, as shown in Fig. 26.38. An ohmmeter connected across a and b reads $2.00\ \Omega$. What is the resistance of X?

Figure **26.38** Exercise 26.2.

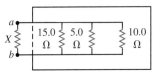

26.3. (a) Prove that when two resistors are connected in parallel, the equivalent resistance of the combination is always smaller than that of the smaller resistor. (b) Generalize your result from part (a) for N resistors.

26.4. A 32-Ω resistor and a 20-Ω resistor are connected in parallel, and the combination is connected across a 240-V dc line. (a) What is the resistance of the parallel combination? (b) What is the total current through the parallel combination? (c) What is the current through each resistor?

26.5. A triangular array of resistors is shown in Fig. 26.39. What current will this array draw from a 35.0-V battery having negligible internal resistance if we connect it across (a) ab; (b) bc; (c) ac? (d) If the battery has an internal resistance of 3.00 Ω, what current will the array draw if the battery is connected across bc?

Figure **26.39** Exercise 26.5.

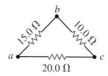

26.6. For the circuit shown in Fig. 26.40 both meters are idealized, the battery has no appreciable internal resistance, and the ammeter reads 1.25 A. (a) What does the voltmeter read? (b) What is the emf $\mathcal{E}$ of the battery?

Figure **26.40** Exercise 26.6.

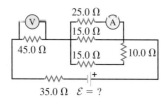

35.0 Ω $\mathcal{E} = ?$

26.7. For the circuit shown in Fig. 26.41 find the reading of the idealized ammeter if the battery has an internal resistance of 3.26 Ω.

Figure **26.41** Exercise 26.7.

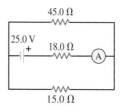

26.8. Three resistors having resistances of 1.60 Ω, 2.40 Ω, and 4.80 Ω are connected in parallel to a 28.0-V battery that has negligible internal resistance. Find (a) the equivalent resistance of the combination; (b) the current in each resistor; (c) the total current through the battery; (d) the voltage across each resistor; (e) the power dissipated in each resistor. (f) Which resistor dissipates the most power: the one with the greatest resistance or the least resistance? Explain why this should be.

26.9. Now the three resistors of Exercise 26.8 are connected in series to the same battery. Answer the same questions for this situation.

26.10. Power Rating of a Resistor. The *power rating* of a resistor is the maximum power the resistor can safely dissipate without too great a rise in temperature and hence damage to the resistor. (a) If the power rating of a 15-kΩ resistor is 5.0 W, what is the maximum allowable potential difference across the terminals of the resistor? (b) A 9.0-kΩ resistor is to be connected across a 120-V potential difference. What power rating is required? (c) A 100.0-Ω and a 150.0-Ω resistor, both rated at 2.00 W, are connected in series across a variable potential difference. What is the greatest this potential difference can be without overheating either resistor, and what is the rate of heat generated in each resistor under these conditions?

26.11. Compute the equivalent resistance of the network in Fig. 26.42, and find the current in each resistor. The battery has negligible internal resistance.

Figure **26.42** Exercise 26.11.

26.12. Compute the equivalent resistance of the network in Fig. 26.43, and find the current in each resistor. The battery has negligible internal resistance.

Figure **26.43** Exercise 26.12.

26.13. In the circuit of Fig. 26.44, each resistor represents a light bulb. Let $R_1 = R_2 = R_3 = R_4 = 4.50\ \Omega$ and $\mathcal{E} = 9.00$ V. (a) Find the current in each bulb. (b) Find the power dissipated in each bulb. Which bulb or bulbs glow the brightest? (c) Bulb R_4 is now removed from the circuit, leaving a break in the wire at its position. Now what is the current in each of the remaining bulbs R_1, R_2, and R_3? (d) With bulb R_4 removed, what is the power dissipated in each of the remaining bulbs? (e) Which light bulb(s) glow brighter as a result of removing R_4? Which bulb(s) glow less brightly? Discuss why there are different effects on different bulbs.

Figure **26.44** Exercise 26.13.

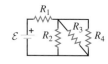

26.14. Consider the circuit shown in Fig. 26.45. The current through the 6.00-Ω resistor is 4.00 A, in the direction shown. What are the currents through the 25.0-Ω and 20.0-Ω resistors?

Figure **26.45** Exercise 26.14.

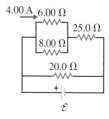

26.15. In the circuit shown in Fig. 26.46, the voltage across the 2.00-Ω resistor is 12.0 V. What are the emf of the battery and the current through the 6.00-Ω resistor?

26.16. A Three-Way Light Bulb. A three-way light bulb has three brightness settings (low, medium, and high) but only two filaments. (a) A particular three-way light bulb connected across a 120-V line can dissipate 60 W, 120 W, or 180 W. Describe how the two filaments are arranged in the bulb, and calculate the resistance of each filament. (b) Suppose the filament with the higher resistance burns out. How much power will the bulb dissipate on each of the three brightness settings? What will be the brightness (low, medium, or high) on each setting?

Figure **26.46** Exercise 26.15.

(c) Repeat part (b) for the situation in which the filament with the lower resistance burns out.

26.17. Light Bulbs in Series and in Parallel. Two light bulbs have resistances of 400 Ω and 800 Ω. If the two light bulbs are connected in series across a 120-V line, find (a) the current through each bulb; (b) the power dissipated in each bulb; (c) the total power dissipated in both bulbs. The two light bulbs are now connected in parallel across the 120-V line. Find (d) the current through each bulb; (e) the power dissipated in each bulb; (f) the total power dissipated in both bulbs. (g) In each situation, which of the two bulbs glows the brightest? (h) In which situation is there a greater total light output from both bulbs combined?

26.18. Light Bulbs in Series. A 60-W, 120-V light bulb and a 200-W, 120-V light bulb are connected in series across a 240-V line. Assume that the resistance of each bulb does not vary with current. (*Note:* This description of a light bulb gives the power it dissipates when connected to the stated potential difference; that is, a 25-W, 120-V light bulb dissipates 25 W when connected to a 120-V line.) (a) Find the current through the bulbs. (b) Find the power dissipated in each bulb. (c) One bulb burns out very quickly. Which one? Why?

26.19. In the circuit in Fig. 26.47, a 20.0-Ω resistor is inside 100 g of pure water that is surrounded by insulating styrofoam. If the water is initially at 10.0°C, how long will it take for its temperature to rise to 58.0°C?

Figure 26.47
Exercise 26.19.

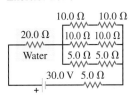

26.20. In the circuit shown in Fig. 26.48, the rate at which R_1 is dissipating electrical energy is 20.0 W. (a) Find R_1 and R_2. (b) What is the emf of the battery? (c) Find the current through both R_2 and the 10.0-Ω resistor. (d) Calculate the total electrical power consumption in all the resistors and the electrical power delivered by the battery. Show that your results are consistent with conservation of energy.

Figure 26.48
Exercise 26.20.

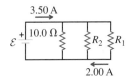

Section 26.2 Kirchhoff's Rules

26.21. In the circuit shown in Fig. 26.49 find (a) the current in resistor R; (b) the resistance R; (c) the unknown emf $\mathcal{E}$. (d) If the circuit is broken at point x, what is the current in resistor R?

Figure 26.49
Exercise 26.21.

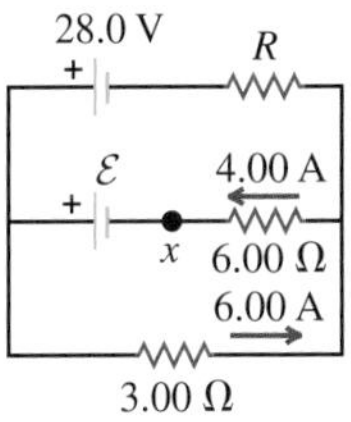

26.22. Find the emfs $\mathcal{E}_1$ and $\mathcal{E}_2$ in the circuit of Fig. 26.50, and find the potential difference of point b relative to point a.

Figure 26.50 Exercise 26.22.

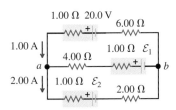

26.23. In the circuit shown in Fig. 26.51, find (a) the current in the 3.00-Ω resistor; (b) the unknown emfs $\mathcal{E}_1$ and $\mathcal{E}_2$; (c) the resistance R. Note that three currents are given.

Figure 26.51 Exercise 26.23.

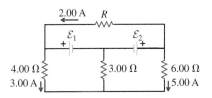

26.24. In the circuit shown in Fig. 26.52, find (a) the current in each branch and (b) the potential difference V_{ab} of point a relative to point b.

26.25. The 10.00-V battery in Fig. 26.52 is removed from the circuit and reinserted with the opposite polarity, so that its positive terminal is now next to point a. The rest of the circuit is as shown in the figure. Find (a) the current in each branch and (b) the potential difference V_{ab} of point a relative to point b.

Figure 26.52
Exercises 26.24, 26.25, and 26.26.

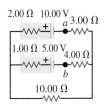

26.26. The 5.00-V battery in Fig. 26.52 is removed from the circuit and replaced by a 20.00-V battery, with its negative terminal next to point b. The rest of the circuit is as shown in the figure. Find (a) the current in each branch and (b) the potential difference V_{ab} of point a relative to point b.

26.27. In the circuit shown in Fig. 26.53 the batteries have negligible internal resistance and the meters are both idealized. With the switch S open, the voltmeter reads 15.0 V. (a) Find the emf $\mathcal{E}$ of the battery. (b) What will the ammeter read when the switch is closed?

Figure 26.53 Exercise 26.27.

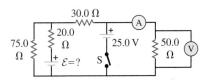

26.28. In the circuit shown in Fig. 26.54 both batteries have insignificant internal resistance and the idealized ammeter reads 1.50 A in the direction shown. Find the emf $\mathcal{E}$ of the battery. Is the polarity shown correct?

Figure 26.54 Exercise 26.28.

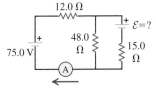

26.29. In the circuit shown in Fig. 26.55 all meters are idealized and the batteries have no appreciable internal resistance. (a) Find the reading of the voltmeter with the switch S open. Which point is at a higher potential: a or b? (b) With the switch closed, find the reading of the voltmeter and the ammeter. Which way (up or down) does the current flow through the switch?

Figure 26.55
Exercise 26.29.

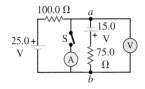

26.30. In the circuit shown in Fig. 26.12 (Example 26.6) the 2-Ω resistor is replaced by a 1-Ω resistor, and the center 1-Ω resistor (through which the current is I_3) is replaced by a resistor of unknown resistance R. The rest of the circuit is as shown in the figure. (a) Calculate the current in each resistor. Draw a diagram of the circuit, and label each resistor with the current through it. (b) Calculate the equivalent resistance of the network. (c) Calculate the potential difference V_{ab}. (d) Your answers in parts (a), (b), and (c) do not depend on the value of R. Explain why.

Section 26.3 Electrical Measuring Instruments

26.31. The resistance of a galvanometer coil is 25.0 Ω, and the current required for full-scale deflection is 500 μA. (a) Show in a diagram how to convert the galvanometer to an ammeter reading 20.0 mA full scale, and compute the shunt resistance. (b) Show how to convert the galvanometer to a voltmeter reading 500 mV full scale, and compute the series resistance.

26.32. The resistance of the coil of a pivoted-coil galvanometer is 9.36 Ω, and a current of 0.0224 A causes it to deflect full scale. We want to convert this galvanometer to an ammeter reading 20.0 A full scale. The only shunt available has a resistance of 0.0250 Ω. What resistance R must be connected in series with the coil (Fig. 26.56)?

Figure **26.56**
Exercise 26.32.

Shunt

26.33. A circuit consists of a series combination of 6.00-kΩ and 5.00-kΩ resistors connected across a 50.0-V battery having negligible internal resistance. You want to measure the true potential difference (that is, the potential difference without the meter present) across the 5.00-kΩ resistor using a voltmeter having an internal resistance of 10.0 kΩ. (a) What potential difference does the voltmeter measure across the 5.00-kΩ resistor? (b) What is the *true* potential difference across this resistor when the meter is not present? (c) By what percentage is the voltmeter reading in error from the true potential difference?

26.34. A galvanometer having a resistance of 25.0 Ω has a 1.00-Ω shunt resistance installed to convert it to an ammeter. It is then used to measure the current in a circuit consisting of a 15.0-Ω resistor connected across the terminals of a 25.0-V battery having no appreciable internal resistance. (a) What current does the ammeter measure? (b) What should be the *true* current in the circuit (that is, the current without the ammeter present)? (c) By what percentage is the ammeter reading in error from the *true* current?

26.35. Consider the potentiometer circuit of Fig. 26.19a. The resistor between a and b is a uniform wire with length l, with a sliding contact c at a distance x from b. An unknown emf $\mathcal{E}_2$ is measured by sliding the contact until the galvanometer G reads zero. (a) Show that under this condition the unknown emf is given by $\mathcal{E}_2 = (x/l)\mathcal{E}_1$. (b) Why is the internal resistance of the galvanometer not important? (c) Suppose $\mathcal{E}_1 = 9.15$ V and $l = 1.000$ m. The galvanometer G reads zero when $x = 0.365$ m. What is the emf $\mathcal{E}_2$?

26.36. In the ohmmeter of Fig. 26.17, the coil of the meter has resistance $R_c = 15.0$ Ω and the current required for full-scale deflection is $I_{fs} = 3.60$ mA. The source is a flashlight battery with $\mathcal{E} = 1.50$ V and negligible internal resistance. The ohmmeter is to show a meter deflection of one-half of full scale when connected to a resistor with $R = 600$ Ω. What series resistance R_s is required?

26.37. In the ohmmeter in Fig. 26.57 M is a 2.50-mA meter of resistance 65.0 Ω. (A 2.50-mA meter deflects full scale when the current through it is 2.50 mA.) The battery B has an emf of 1.52 V and negligible internal resistance. R is chosen so that when the terminals a and b are shorted $(R_x = 0)$, the meter reads full scale. When a and b are open $(R_x = \infty)$, the meter reads zero. (a) What is the resistance of the resistor R? (b) What current indi-

Figure **26.57**
Exercise 26.37.

cates a resistance R_x of 200 Ω? (c) What values of R_x correspond to meter deflections of $\frac{1}{4}$, $\frac{1}{2}$, and $\frac{3}{4}$ of full scale if the deflection is proportional to the current through the galvanometer?

Section 26.4 R-C Circuits

26.38. A 4.60-μF capacitor that is initially uncharged is connected in series with a 7.50-kΩ resistor and an emf source with $\mathcal{E} = 125$ V and negligible internal resistance. Just after the circuit is completed, what are (a) the voltage drop across the capacitor; (b) the voltage drop across the resistor; (c) the charge on the capacitor; (d) the current through the resistor? (e) A long time after the circuit is completed (after many time constants) what are the values of the quantities in parts (a)–(d)?

26.39. A capacitor is charged to a potential of 12.0 V and is then connected to a voltmeter having an internal resistance of 3.40 MΩ. After a time of 4.00 s the voltmeter reads 3.0 V. What are (a) the capacitance and (b) the time constant of the circuit?

26.40. A 12.4-μF capacitor is connected through a 0.895-MΩ resistor to a constant potential difference of 60.0 V. (a) Compute the charge on the capacitor at the following times after the connections are made: 0, 5.0 s, 10.0 s, 20.0 s, and 100.0 s. (b) Compute the charging currents at the same instants. (c) Graph the results of parts (a) and (b) for t between 0 and 20 s.

26.41. In the circuit shown in Fig. 26.58 both capacitors are initially charged to 45.0 V. (a) How long after closing the switch S will the potential across each capacitor be reduced to 10.0 V, and (b) what will be the current at that time?

Figure **26.58**
Exercise 26.41.

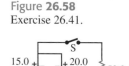

26.42. A resistor and a capacitor are connected in series to an emf source. The time constant for the circuit is 0.870 s. (a) A second capacitor, identical to the first, is added in series. What is the time constant for this new circuit? (b) In the original circuit a second capacitor, identical to the first, is connected in parallel with the first. What is the time constant for this new circuit?

26.43. An emf source with $\mathcal{E} = 120$ V, a resistor with $R = 80.0$ Ω, and a capacitor with $C = 4.00$ μF are connected in series. As the capacitor charges, when the current in the resistor is 0.900 A, what is the magnitude of the charge on each plate of the capacitor?

26.44. A 1.50-μF capacitor is charging through a 12.0-Ω resistor using a 10.0-V battery. What will be the current when the capacitor has acquired $\frac{1}{4}$ of its maximum charge? Will it be $\frac{1}{4}$ of the maximum current?

26.45. In the circuit shown in Fig. 26.59 each capacitor initially has a charge of magnitude 3.50 nC on its plates. After the switch S is closed, what will be the current in the circuit at the instant that the capacitors have lost 80.0% of their initial stored energy?

Figure **26.59**
Exercise 26.45.

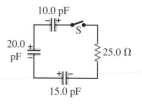

26.46. A 12.0-μF capacitor is charged to a potential of 50.0 V and then discharged through a 175-Ω resistor How long does it take the capacitor to lose (a) half of its charge and (b) half of its stored energy?

26.47. In the circuit in Fig. 26.60 the capacitors are all initially uncharged, the battery has no internal resistance, and the ammeter is idealized. Find the reading of the ammeter (a) just after the switch S is closed and (b) after the switch has been closed for a very long time

Figure **26.60** Exercise 26.47.

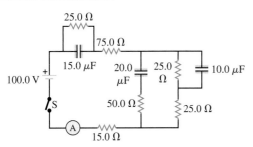

26.48. In the circuit shown in Fig. 26.61, $C = 5.90\ \mu F$, $\mathcal{E} = 28.0\ V$, and the emf has negligible resistance. Initially the capacitor is uncharged and the switch S is in position 1. The switch is then moved to position 2, so that the capacitor begins to charge. (a) What will be the charge on the capacitor a long time after the switch is moved to position 2? (b) After the switch has been in position 2 for 3.00 ms, the charge on the capacitor is measured to be 110 μC. What is the value of the resistance R? (c) How long after the switch is moved to position 2 will the charge on the capacitor be equal to 99.0% of the final value found in part (a)?

Figure **26.61** Exercises 26.48 and 26.49.

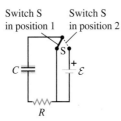

26.49. A capacitor with $C = 1.50 \times 10^{-5}\ F$ is connected as shown in Fig. 26.61 with a resistor with $R = 980\ \Omega$ and an emf source with $\mathcal{E} = 18.0\ V$ and negligible internal resistance. Initially the capacitor is uncharged and the switch S is in position 1. The switch is then moved to position 2, so that the capacitor begins to charge. After the switch has been in position 2 for 10.0 ms, the switch is moved back to position 1 so that the capacitor begins to discharge. (a) Compute the charge on the capacitor just *before* the switch is thrown from position 2 back to position 1. (b) Compute the voltage drops across the resistor and across the capacitor at the instant described in part (a). (c) Compute the voltage drops across the resistor and across the capacitor just *after* the switch is thrown from position 2 back to position 1. (d) Compute the charge on the capacitor 10.0 ms after the switch is thrown from position 2 back to position 1.

Section 26.5 Power Distribution Systems

26.50. The heating element of an electric dryer is rated at 4.1 kW when connected to a 240-V line. (a) What is the current in the heating element? Is 12-gauge wire large enough to supply this current? (b) What is the resistance of the dryer's heating element at its operating temperature? (c) At 11 cents per kWh, how much does it cost per hour to operate the dryer?

26.51. A 1500-W electric heater is plugged into the outlet of a 120-V circuit that has a 20-A circuit breaker. You plug an electric hair dryer into the same outlet. The hair dryer has power settings of 600, 900, 1200 W, and 1500 W. You start with the hair dryer on the 600-W setting and increase the power setting until the circuit breaker trips. What power setting caused the breaker to trip?

26.52. How many 90-W, 120-V light bulbs can be connected to a 20-A, 120-V circuit without tripping the circuit breaker? (See the note in Exercise 26.18.)

26.53. The heating element of an electric stove consists of a heater wire embedded within an electrically insulating material, which in turn is inside a metal casing. The heater wire has a resistance of 20 Ω at room temperature $(23.0°C)$ and a temperature coefficient of resistivity $\alpha = 2.8 \times 10^{-3}(C°)^{-1}$. The heating element operates from a 120-V line. (a) When the heating element is first turned on, what current does it draw and what electrical power does it dissipate? (b) When the heating element has reached an operating temperature of 280°C $(536°F)$, what current does it draw and what electrical power does it dissipate?

Problems

26.54. A 400-Ω, 2.4-W resistor is needed, but only several 400-Ω, 1.2-W resistors are available (see Exercise 26.10). (a) What two different combinations of the available units give the required resistance and power rating? (b) For each of the resistor networks from part (a), what power is dissipated in each resistor when 2.4 W is dissipated by the combination?

26.55. A 20.0-m-long cable consists of a solid-inner, cylindrical, nickel core 10.0 cm in diameter surrounded by a solid-outer cylindrical shell of copper 10.0 cm in inside diameter and 20.0 cm in outside diameter. The resistivity of nickel is $7.8 \times 10^{-8}\ \Omega \cdot m$. (a) What is the resistance of this cable? (b) If we think of this cable as a single material, what is its equivalent resistivity?

26.56. Two identical 1.00-Ω wires are laid side by side and soldered together so they touch each other for half of their lengths. What is the equivalent resistance of this combination?

26.57. The two identical light bulbs in Example 26.2 (Section 26.1) are connected in parallel to a different source, one with $\mathcal{E} = 8.0\ V$ and internal resistance 0.8 Ω. Each light bulb has a resistance $R = 2.0\ \Omega$ (assumed independent of the current through the bulb). (a) Find the current through each bulb, the potential difference across each bulb, and the power delivered to each bulb. (b) Suppose one of the bulbs burns out, so that its filament breaks and current no longer flows through it. Find the power delivered to the remaining bulb. Does the remaining bulb glow more or less brightly after the other bulb burns out than before?

26.58. Each of the three resistors in Fig. 26.62 has a resistance of 2.4 Ω and can dissipate a maximum of 36 W without becoming excessively heated. What is the maximum power the circuit can dissipate?

Figure **26.62** Problem 26.58.

26.59. If an ohmmeter is connected between points a and b in each of the circuits shown in Fig. 26.63, what will it read?

Figure **26.63** Problem 26.59.

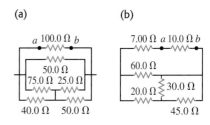

26.60. For the circuit shown in Fig. 26.64 a 20.0-Ω resistor is embedded in a large block of ice at 0.00°C, and the battery has negligible internal resistance. At what rate (in g/s) is this circuit melting the ice? (The latent heat of fusion for ice is $3.34 \times 10^5\ J/kg$.)

Figure 26.64 Problem 26.60.

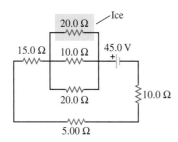

26.61. Calculate the three currents I_1, I_2, and I_3 indicated in the circuit diagram shown in Fig. 26.65.

Figure 26.65 Problem 26.61.

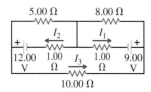

26.62. What must the emf $\mathcal{E}$ in Fig. 26.66 be in order for the current through the 7.00-Ω resistor to be 1.80 A? Each emf source has negligible internal resistance.

Figure 26.66 Problem 26.62.

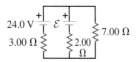

26.63. Find the current through each of the three resistors of the circuit shown in Fig. 26.67. The emf sources have negligible internal resistance.

26.64. (a) Find the current through the battery and each resistor in the circuit shown in Fig. 26.68. (b) What is the equivalent resistance of the resistor network?

Figure 26.67
Problem 26.63.

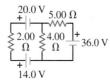

Figure 26.68 Problem 26.64.

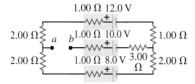

26.65. (a) Find the potential of point a with respect to point b in Fig. 26.69. (b) If points a and b are connected by a wire with negligible resistance, find the current in the 12.0-V battery.

Figure 26.69 Problem 26.65.

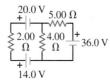

26.66. Consider the circuit shown in Fig. 26.70: (a) What must the emf $\mathcal{E}$ of the battery be in order for a current of 2.00 A to flow through the 5.00-V battery as shown? Is the polarity of the battery correct as shown? (b) How long does it take for 60.0 J of thermal energy to be produced in the 10.0-Ω resistor?

Figure 26.70 Problem 26.66.

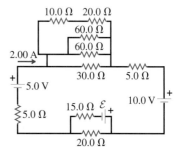

26.67. In the circuit shown in Fig. 26.71 the current through the 12.0-V battery is measured to be 70.6 mA in the direction shown. What is the terminal voltage V_{ab} of the 24.0-V battery?

Figure 26.71 Problem 26.67.

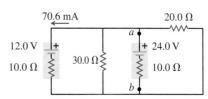

26.68. In the circuit shown in Fig. 26.72 all the resistors are rated at a maximum power of 1.00 W. What is the maximum emf $\mathcal{E}$ that the battery can have without burning up any of the resistors?

Figure 26.72 Problem 26.68.

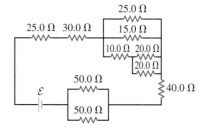

26.69. In the circuit shown in Fig. 26.73, the current in the 20.0-V battery is 5.00 A in the direction shown and the voltage across the 8.00-Ω resistor is 16.0 V, with the lower end of the resistor at higher potential. Find (a) the emf (including its polarity) of the battery X; (b) the current I through the 200.0-V battery (including its direction); (c) the resistance R.

Figure 26.73 Problem 26.69.

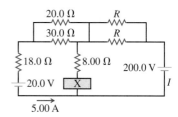

26.70. Three identical resistors are connected in series. When a certain potential difference is applied across the combination, the total power dissipated is 27 W. What power would be dissipated if the three resistors were connected in parallel across the same potential difference?

26.71. A resistor R_1 consumes electrical power P_1 when connected to an emf $\mathcal{E}$. When resistor R_2 is connected to the same emf, it consumes electrical power P_2. In terms of P_1 and P_2, what is the total electrical power consumed when they are both connected to this emf source (a) in parallel and (b) in series?

26.72. The capacitor in Fig. 26.74 is initially uncharged. The switch is closed at $t = 0$. (a) Immediately after the switch is closed, what is the current through each resistor? (b) What is the final charge on the capacitor?

Figure **26.74** Problem 26.72.

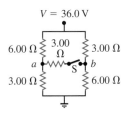

$R_1 = 8.00\ \Omega$

$+|\mathcal{E} = 42.0\ \text{V}$
$R_2 = $
$6.00\ \Omega$

$R_3 = 3.00\ \Omega$

$C = 4.00\ \mu\text{F}$

26.73. Figure 26.75 employs a convention often used in circuit diagrams. The battery (or other power supply) is not shown explicitly. It is understood that the point at the top, labeled "36.0 V," is connected to the positive terminal of a 36.0-V battery having negligible internal resistance, and that the "ground" symbol at the bottom is connected to the negative terminal of the battery. The circuit is completed through the battery, even though it is not shown on the diagram. (a) What is the potential difference V_{ab}, the potential of point a relative to point b, when the switch S is open? (b) What is the current through switch S when it is closed? (c) What is the equivalent resistance when switch S is closed?

Figure **26.75**
Problem 26.73.

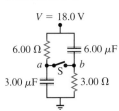

$V = 36.0\ \text{V}$

$6.00\ \Omega$ $3.00\ \Omega$ $3.00\ \Omega$
a S b
$3.00\ \Omega$ $6.00\ \Omega$

26.74. (See Problem 26.73.) (a) What is the potential of point a with respect to point b in Fig. 26.76 when switch S is open? (b) Which point, a or b, is at the higher potential? (c) What is the final potential of point b with respect to ground when switch S is closed? (d) How much does the charge on each capacitor change when S is closed?

Figure **26.76**
Problem 26.74.

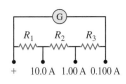

$V = 18.0\ \text{V}$

$6.00\ \Omega$ $6.00\ \mu\text{F}$
a S b
$3.00\ \mu\text{F}$ $3.00\ \Omega$

26.75. A Multirange Ammeter. The resistance of the moving coil of the galvanometer G in Fig. 26.77 is 48.0 Ω, and the galvanometer deflects full scale with a current of 0.0200 A. When the meter is connected to the circuit being measured, one connection is made to the post marked + and the other to the post marked with the desired current range. Find the magnitudes of the resistances R_1, R_2, and R_3 required to convert the galvanometer to a multirange ammeter deflecting full scale with currents of 10.0 A, 1.00 A, and 0.100 A.

Figure **26.77**
Problem 26.75.

G

R_1 R_2 R_3

$+$ 10.0 A 1.00 A 0.100 A

26.76. A Multirange Voltmeter. Figure 26.78 shows the internal wiring of a "three-scale" voltmeter whose binding posts are marked $+$, 3.00 V, 15.0 V, and 150 V. When the meter is connected to the circuit being meas-

Figure **26.78**
Problem 26.76.

R_G R_1 R_2 R_3

$+$ 3.00 V 15.0 V 150 V

ured, one connection is made to the post marked $+$ and the other to the post marked with the desired voltage range. The resistance of the moving coil, R_G, is 40.0 Ω, and a current of 1.00 mA in the coil causes it to deflect full scale. Find the resistances R_1, R_2, and R_3, and the overall resistance of the meter on each of its ranges.

26.77. Point a in Fig. 26.79 is maintained at a constant potential of 400 V above ground. (See Problem 26.73.) (a) What is the reading of a voltmeter with the proper range and with resistance $5.00 \times 10^4\ \Omega$ when connected between point b and ground? (b) What is the reading of a voltmeter with resistance $5.00 \times 10^6\ \Omega$? (c) What is the reading of a voltmeter with infinite resistance?

Figure **26.79**
Problem 26.77.

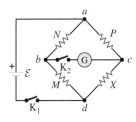

$100\ \text{k}\Omega$ $200\ \text{k}\Omega$
a b

26.78. A 150-V voltmeter has a resistance of 30,000 Ω. When connected in series with a large resistance R across a 110-V line, the meter reads 68 V. Find the resistance R.

26.79. The Wheatstone Bridge. The circuit shown in Fig. 26.80, called a *Wheatstone bridge*, is used to determine the value of an unknown resistor X by comparison with three resistors M, N, and P whose resistances can be varied. For each setting, the resistance of each resistor is precisely known. With switches K_1 and K_2 closed, these resistors are varied until the current in the galvanometer G is zero; the bridge is then said to be *balanced*. (a) Show that under this condition the unknown resistance is given by $X = MP/N$. (This method permits very high precision in comparing resistors.) (b) If the galvanometer G shows zero deflection when $M = 850.0\ \Omega$, $N = 15.00\ \Omega$, and $P = 33.48\ \Omega$, what is the unknown resistance X?

Figure **26.80**
Problem 26.79.

N a P
b K_2 G c
$+\ \mathcal{E}$
M X
K_1 d

26.80. A certain galvanometer has a resistance of 65.0 Ω and deflects full scale with a current of 1.50 mA in its coil. This is to be replaced with a second galvanometer that has a resistance of 38.0 Ω and deflects full scale with a current of 3.60 μA in its coil. Devise a circuit incorporating the second galvanometer such that the equivalent resistance of the circuit equals the resistance of the first galvanometer, and the second galvanometer deflects full scale when the current through the circuit equals the full-scale current of the first galvanometer.

26.81. A 224-Ω resistor and a 589-Ω resistor are connected in series across a 90.0-V line. (a) What is the voltage across each resistor? (b) A voltmeter connected across the 224-Ω resistor reads 23.8 V. Find the voltmeter resistance. (c) Find the reading of the same voltmeter if it is connected across the 589-Ω resistor. (d) The readings on this voltmeter are lower than the "true" voltages (that is, without the voltmeter present). Would it be possible to design a voltmeter that gave readings *higher* than the "true" voltages? Explain.

26.82. A .2.36-μF capacitor that is initially uncharged is connected in series with a 4.26-Ω resistor and an emf source with $\mathcal{E} = 120\ \text{V}$ and negligible internal resistance. (a) Just after the connection is made, what are (i) the rate at which electrical energy is being dissipated in the resistor; (ii) the rate at which the electrical energy stored in the capacitor is increasing; (iii) the electrical power output of the source? How do the answers to parts (i), (ii), and (iii) compare? (b) Answer the same questions as in part (a) at a long time after the connection is made. (c) Answer the same questions as in part (a) at the instant when the charge on the capacitor is one-half its final value.

26.83. A capacitor that is initially uncharged is connected in series with a resistor and an emf source with $\mathcal{E} = 110$ V and negligible internal resistance. Just after the circuit is completed, the current through the resistor is 6.5×10^{-5} A. The time constant for the circuit is 6.2 s. What are the resistance of the resistor and the capacitance of the capacitor?

26.84. A resistor with $R = 850\ \Omega$ is connected to the plates of a charged capacitor with capacitance $C = 4.62\ \mu$F. Just before the connection is made, the charge on the capacitor is 8.10 mC. (a) What is the energy initially stored in the capacitor? (b) What is the electrical power dissipated in the resistor just after the connection is made? (c) What is the electrical power dissipated in the resistor at the instant when the energy stored in the capacitor has decreased to half the value calculated in part (a)?

26.85. Strictly speaking, Eq. (26.16) implies that an *infinite* amount of time is required to discharge a capacitor completely. Yet for practical purposes, a capacitor may be considered to be fully discharged after a finite length of time. To be specific, consider a capacitor with capacitance C connected to a resistor R to be fully discharged if its charge q differs from zero by no more than the charge of one electron. (a) Calculate the time required to reach this state if $C = 0.920\ \mu$F, $R = 670\ k\Omega$, and $Q_0 = 7.00\ \mu$C. How many time constants is this? (b) For a given Q_0, is the time required to reach this state always the same number of time constants, independent of the values of C and R? Why or why not?

26.86. An *R-C* circuit has a time constant RC. (a) If the circuit is discharging, how long will it take for its stored energy to be reduced to $1/e$ of its initial value? (b) If it is charging, how long will it take for the stored energy to reach $1/e$ of its maximum value?

26.87. The current in a charging capacitor is given by Eq. (26.13). (a) The instantaneous power supplied by the battery is $\mathcal{E}i$. Integrate this to find the total energy supplied by the battery. (b) The instantaneous power dissipated in the resistor is i^2R. Integrate this to find the total energy dissipated in the resistor. (c) Find the final energy stored in the capacitor, and show that this equals the total energy supplied by the battery less the energy dissipated in the resistor, as obtained in parts (a) and (b). (d) What fraction of the energy supplied by the battery is stored in the capacitor? How does this fraction depend on R?

26.88. (a) Using Eq. (26.17) for the current in a discharging capacitor, derive an expression for the instantaneous power $P = i^2R$ dissipated in the resistor. (b) Integrate the expression for P to find the total energy dissipated in the resistor, and show that this is equal to the total energy initially stored in the capacitor.

Challenge Problems

26.89. According to the theorem of superposition, the response (current) in a circuit is proportional to the stimulus (voltage) that causes it. This is true even if there are multiple sources in a circuit. This theorem can be used to analyze a circuit without resorting to Kirchhoff's rules by considering the currents in the circuit to be the superposition of currents caused by each source independently. In this way the circuit can be analyzed by computing equivalent resistances rather than by using the (sometimes) more cumbersome method of Kirchhoff's rules. Furthermore, with the superposition theorem it is possible to

Figure **26.81** Challenge Problem 26.89.

examine how the modification of a source in one part of the circuit will affect the currents in all parts of the circuit without having to use Kirchhoff's rules to recalculate all of the currents. Consider the circuit shown in Fig. 26.81. If the circuit were redrawn with the 55.0-V and 57.0-V sources replaced by short circuits, the circuit could be analyzed by the method of equivalent resistances without resorting to Kirchhoff's rules, and the current in each branch could be found in a simple manner. Similarly, if the circuit with the 92.0-V and the 55.0-V sources were replaced by short circuits, the circuit could again be analyzed in a simple manner. Finally, if the 92.0-V and the 57.0-V sources were replaced with a short circuit, the circuit could once again be analyzed simply. By superimposing the respective currents found in each of the branches by using the three simplified circuits, we can find the actual current in each branch. (a) Using Kirchhoff's rules, find the branch currents in the 140.0-Ω, 210.0-Ω, and 35.0-Ω resistors. (b) Using a circuit similar to the circuit of Fig. 26.81, but with the 55.0-V and 57.0-V sources replaced by a short circuit, determine the currents in each resistance. (c) Repeat part (b) by replacing the 92.0-V and 55.0-V sources by short circuits, leaving the 57.0-V source intact. (d) Repeat part (b) by replacing the 92.0-V and 57.0-V sources by short circuits, leaving the 55.0-V source intact. (e) Verify the superposition theorem by taking the currents calculated in parts (b), (c), and (d) and comparing them with the currents calculated in part (a). (f) If the 57.0-V source is replaced by an 80.0-V source, what will be the new currents in all branches of the circuit? [*Hint:* Using the superposition theorem, recalculate the partial currents calculated in part (c) using the fact that those currents are proportional to the source that is being replaced. Then superpose the new partial currents with those found in parts (b) and (d).]

26.90. A Capacitor Burglar Alarm. The capacitance of a capacitor can be affected by dielectric material that, although not inside the capacitor, is near enough to the capacitor to be polarized by the fringing electric field that exists near a charged capacitor. This effect is usually of the order of picofarads (pF), but it can be used with appropriate electronic circuitry to detect a change in the dielectric material surrounding the capacitor. Such a dielectric material might be the human body, and the effect described above might be used in the design of a burglar alarm. Consider the simplified circuit shown in Fig. 26.82. The voltage source has emf $\mathcal{E} = 1000$ V, and the capacitor has capacitance $C = 10.0$ pF. The electronic circuitry for detecting the current, represented as an ammeter in the diagram, has negligible resistance and is capable of detecting a current that persists at a level of at least 1.00 μA for at least 200 μs after the capacitance has changed abruptly from C to C'. The burglar alarm is designed to be activated if the capacitance changes by 10%. (a) Determine the charge on the 10.0-pF capacitor when it is fully charged. (b) If the capacitor is fully charged before the intruder is detected, assuming that the time taken for the capacitance to change by 10% is short enough to be ignored, derive an equation that expresses the current through the resistor R as a function of the time t since the capacitance has changed. (c) Determine the range of values of the resistance R that will meet the design specifications of the burglar alarm. What happens if R is too small? Too large? (*Hint:* You will not be able to solve this part analytically but must use numerical methods. Express R as a logarithmic function of R plus known quantities. Use a trial value of R and calculate from the expression

Figure **26.82** Challenge Problem 26.90.

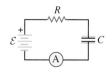

a new value. Continue to do this until the input and output values of R agree to within three significant figures.)

26.91. An Infinite Network.   As shown in Fig. 26.83, a network of resistors of resistances R_1 and R_2 extends to infinity toward the right. Prove that the total resistance R_T of the infinite network is equal to

$$R_T = R_1 + \sqrt{R_1^2 + 2R_1R_2}$$

(*Hint:* Since the network is infinite, the resistance of the network to the right of points c and d is also equal to R_T.)

Figure **26.83** Challenge Problems 26.91 and 26.93.

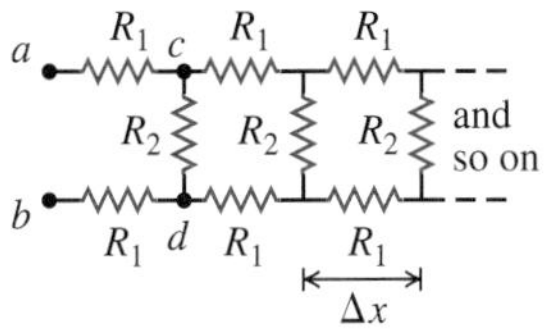

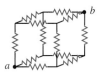

26.92. Suppose a resistor R lies along each edge of a cube (12 resistors in all) with connections at the corners. Find the equivalent resistance between two diagonally opposite corners of the cube (points a and b in Fig. 26.84).

Figure **26.84** Challenge Problem 26.92.

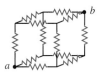

26.93. Attenuator Chains and Axons.   The infinite network of resistors shown in Fig. 26.83 is known as an *attenuator chain,* since this chain of resistors causes the potential difference between the upper and lower wires to decrease, or attenuate, along the length of the chain. a) Show that if the potential difference between the points a and b in Fig. 26.83 is V_{ab}, then the potential difference between points c and d is $V_{cd} = V_{ab}/(1 + \beta)$, where $\beta = 2R_1(R_T + R_2)/R_TR_2$ and R_T, the

total resistance of the network, is given in Challenge Problem 26.91. (See the hint given in that problem.) (b) If the potential difference between terminals a and b at the left end of the infinite network is V_0, show that the potential difference between the upper and lower wires n segments from the left end is $V_n = V_0/(1 + \beta)^n$. If $R_1 = R_2$, how many segments are needed to decrease the potential difference V_n to less than 1.0% of V_0? (c) An infinite attenuator chain provides a model of the propagation of a voltage pulse along a nerve fiber, or axon. Each segment of the network in Fig. 26.83 represents a short segment of the axon of length Δx. The resistors R_1 represent the resistance of the fluid inside and outside the membrane wall of the axon. The resistance of the membrane to current flowing through the wall is represented by R_2. For an axon segment of length $\Delta x = 1.0 \, \mu m$, $R_1 = 6.4 \times 10^3 \, \Omega$ and $R_2 = 8.0 \times 10^8 \, \Omega$ (the membrane wall is a good insulator). Calculate the total resistance R_T and β for an infinitely long axon. (This is a good approximation, since the length of an axon is much greater than its width; the largest axons in the human nervous system are longer than 1 m but only about 10^{-7} m in radius.) (d) By what fraction does the potential difference between the inside and outside of the axon decrease over a distance of 2.0 mm? (e) The attenuation of the potential difference calculated in part (d) shows that the axon cannot simply be a passive, current-carrying electrical cable; the potential difference must periodically be reinforced along the axon's length. This reinforcement mechanism is slow, so a signal propagates along the axon at only about 30 m/s. In situations where faster response is required, axons are covered with a segmented sheath of fatty myelin. The segments are about 2 mm long, separated by gaps called the *nodes of Ranvier.* The myelin increases the resistance of a 1.0-μm-long segment of the membrane to $R_2 = 3.3 \times 10^{12} \, \Omega$. For such a myelinated axon, by what fraction does the potential difference between the inside and outside of the axon decrease over the distance from one node of Ranvier to the next? This smaller attenuation means the propagation speed is increased.

27 MAGNETIC FIELD AND MAGNETIC FORCES

LEARNING GOALS

By studying this chapter, you will learn:

- The properties of magnets, and how magnets interact with each other.

- The nature of the force that a moving charged particle experiences in a magnetic field.

- How magnetic field lines are different from electric field lines.

- How to analyze the motion of a charged particle in a magnetic field.

- Some practical applications of magnetic fields in chemistry and physics.

- How to analyze magnetic forces on current-carrying conductors.

- How current loops behave when placed in a magnetic field.

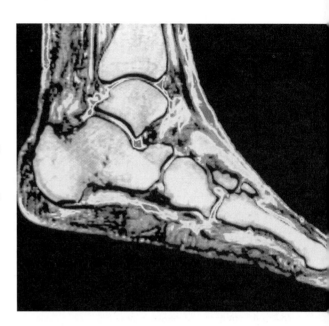

? Magnetic resonance imaging (MRI) makes it possible to see details of soft tissue (such as in the foot shown here) that aren't visible in x-ray images. Yet soft tissue isn't a magnetic material (it's not attracted to a magnet). How does MRI work?

Everybody uses magnetic forces. They are at the heart of electric motors, TV picture tubes, microwave ovens, loudspeakers, computer printers, and disk drives. The most familiar aspects of magnetism are those associated with permanent magnets, which attract unmagnetized iron objects and can also attract or repel other magnets. A compass needle aligning itself with the earth's magnetism is an example of this interaction. But the *fundamental* nature of magnetism is the interaction of moving electric charges. Unlike electric forces, which act on electric charges whether they are moving or not, magnetic forces act only on *moving* charges.

Although electric and magnetic forces are very different from each other, we use the idea of a *field* to describe both kinds of force. We saw in Chapter 21 that the electric force arises in two stages: (1) a charge produces an electric field in the space around it, and (2) a second charge responds to this field. Magnetic forces also arise in two stages. First, a *moving* charge or a collection of moving charges (that is, an electric current) produces a *magnetic* field. Next, a second current or moving charge responds to this magnetic field, and so experiences a magnetic force.

In this chapter we study the second stage in the magnetic interaction—that is, how moving charges and currents *respond* to magnetic fields. In particular, we will see how to calculate magnetic forces and torques, and we will discover why magnets can pick up iron objects like paper clips. In Chapter 28 we will complete our picture of the magnetic interaction by examining how moving charges and currents *produce* magnetic fields.

27.1 Magnetism

Magnetic phenomena were first observed at least 2500 years ago in fragments of magnetized iron ore found near the ancient city of Magnesia (now Manisa, in western Turkey). These fragments were examples of what are now called

permanent magnets; you probably have several permanent magnets on your refrigerator door at home. Permanent magnets were found to exert forces on each other as well as on pieces of iron that were not magnetized. It was discovered that when an iron rod is brought in contact with a natural magnet, the rod also becomes magnetized. When such a rod is floated on water or suspended by a string from its center, it tends to line itself up in a north-south direction. The needle of an ordinary compass is just such a piece of magnetized iron.

Before the relationship of magnetic interactions to moving charges was understood, the interactions of permanent magnets and compass needles were described in terms of *magnetic poles.* If a bar-shaped permanent magnet, or *bar magnet,* is free to rotate, one end points north. This end is called a *north pole* or *N pole;* the other end is a *south pole* or *S pole.* Opposite poles attract each other, and like poles repel each other (Fig. 27.1). An object that contains iron but is not itself magnetized (that is, it shows no tendency to point north or south) is attracted by *either* pole of a permanent magnet (Fig. 27.2). This is the attraction that acts between a magnet and the unmagnetized steel door of a refrigerator. By analogy to electric interactions, we describe the interactions in Figs. 27.1 and 27.2 by saying that a bar magnet sets up a *magnetic field* in the space around it and a second body responds to that field. A compass needle tends to align with the magnetic field at the needle's position.

The earth itself is a magnet. Its north geographic pole is close to a magnetic *south* pole, which is why the north pole of a compass needle points north. The earth's magnetic axis is not quite parallel to its geographic axis (the axis of rotation), so a compass reading deviates somewhat from geographic north. This deviation, which varies with location, is called *magnetic declination* or *magnetic variation.* Also, the magnetic field is not horizontal at most points on the earth's surface; its angle up or down is called *magnetic inclination.* At the magnetic poles the magnetic field is vertical.

Figure 27.3 is a sketch of the earth's magnetic field. The lines, called *magnetic field lines,* show the direction that a compass would point at each location; they are discussed in detail in Section 27.3. The direction of the field at any point can

27.1 (a) Two bar magnets attract when opposite poles (N and S, or S and N) are next to each other. (b) The bar magnets repel when like poles (N and N, or S and S) are next to each other.

(a) Opposite poles attract.

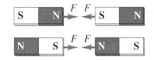

(b) Like poles repel.

27.2 (a) Either pole of a bar magnet attracts an unmagnetized object that contains iron, such as a nail. (b) A real-life example of this effect.

(a)

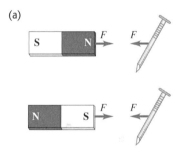

27.3 A sketch of the earth's magnetic field. The field, which is caused by currents in the earth's molten core, changes with time; geologic evidence shows that it reverses direction entirely at irregular intervals of about a half million years.

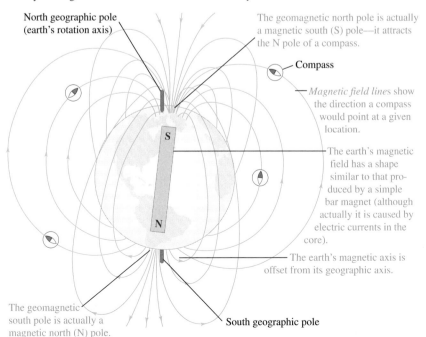

North geographic pole (earth's rotation axis)

Compass

The geomagnetic north pole is actually a magnetic south (S) pole—it attracts the N pole of a compass.

Magnetic field lines show the direction a compass would point at a given location.

The earth's magnetic field has a shape similar to that produced by a simple bar magnet (although actually it is caused by electric currents in the core).

The earth's magnetic axis is offset from its geographic axis.

The geomagnetic south pole is actually a magnetic north (N) pole.

South geographic pole

(b)

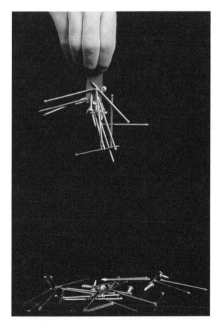

27.4 Breaking a bar magnet. Each piece has a north and south pole, even if the pieces are different sizes. (The smaller the piece, the weaker its magnetism.)

In contrast to electric charges, magnetic poles always come in pairs and can't be isolated.

Breaking a magnet in two ...

... yields two magnets, not two isolated poles.

27.5 In Oersted's experiment, a compass is placed directly over a horizontal wire (here viewed from above). When the compass is placed directly under the wire, the compass deflection is reversed.

(a)

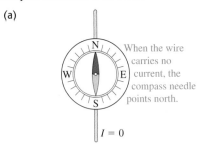

When the wire carries no current, the compass needle points north.

$I = 0$

(b)

When the wire carries a current, the compass needle deflects. The direction of deflection depends on the direction of the current.

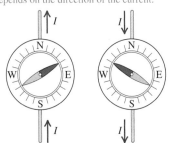

be defined as the direction of the force that the field would exert on a magnetic north pole. In Section 27.2 we'll describe a more fundamental way to define the direction and magnitude of a magnetic field.

Magnetic Poles Versus Electric Charge

The concept of magnetic poles may appear similar to that of electric charge, and north and south poles may seem analogous to positive and negative charge. But the analogy can be misleading. While isolated positive and negative charges exist, there is *no* experimental evidence that a single isolated magnetic pole exists; poles always appear in pairs. If a bar magnet is broken in two, each broken end becomes a pole (Fig. 27.4). The existence of an isolated magnetic pole, or **magnetic monopole,** would have sweeping implications for theoretical physics. Extensive searches for magnetic monopoles have been carried out, but so far without success.

The first evidence of the relationship of magnetism to moving charges was discovered in 1820 by the Danish scientist Hans Christian Oersted. He found that a compass needle was deflected by a current-carrying wire, as shown in Fig. 27.5. Similar investigations were carried out in France by André Ampère. A few years later, Michael Faraday in England and Joseph Henry in the United States discovered that moving a magnet near a conducting loop can cause a current in the loop. We now know that the magnetic forces between two bodies shown in Figs. 27.1 and 27.2 are fundamentally due to interactions between moving electrons in the atoms of the bodies. (There are also *electric* interactions between the two bodies, but these are far weaker than the magnetic interactions because the two bodies are electrically neutral.) Inside a magnetized body such as a permanent magnet, there is a *coordinated* motion of certain of the atomic electrons; in an unmagnetized body these motions are not coordinated. (We'll describe these motions further in Section 27.7, and see how the interactions shown in Figs. 27.1 and 27.2 come about.)

Electric and magnetic interactions prove to be intimately connected. Over the next several chapters we will develop the unifying principles of electromagnetism, culminating in the expression of these principles in *Maxwell's equations.* These equations represent the synthesis of electromagnetism, just as Newton's laws of motion are the synthesis of mechanics, and like Newton's laws they represent a towering achievement of the human intellect.

Test Your Understanding of Section 27.1 Suppose you cut off the part of the compass needle shown in Fig. 27.5a that is painted gray. You discard this part, drill a hole in the remaining red part, and place the red part on the pivot at the center of the compass. Will the red part still swing east and west when a current is applied as in Fig. 27.5b?

27.2 Magnetic Field

To introduce the concept of magnetic field properly, let's review our formulation of *electric* interactions in Chapter 21, where we introduced the concept of *electric* field. We represented electric interactions in two steps:

1. A distribution of electric charge at rest creates an electric field $\vec{E}$ in the surrounding space.
2. The electric field exerts a force $\vec{F} = q\vec{E}$ on any other charge q that is present in the field.

We can describe magnetic interactions in a similar way:

1. A moving charge or a current creates a **magnetic field** in the surrounding space (in addition to its *electric* field).
2. The magnetic field exerts a force $\vec{F}$ on any other moving charge or current that is present in the field.

In this chapter we'll concentrate on the *second* aspect of the interaction: Given the presence of a magnetic field, what force does it exert on a moving charge or a current? In Chapter 28 we will come back to the problem of how magnetic fields are *created* by moving charges and currents.

Like electric field, magnetic field is a *vector field*—that is, a vector quantity associated with each point in space. We will use the symbol $\vec{B}$ for magnetic field. At any position the direction of $\vec{B}$ is defined as the direction in which the north pole of a compass needle tends to point. The arrows in Fig. 27.3 suggest the direction of the earth's magnetic field; for any magnet, $\vec{B}$ points out of its north pole and into its south pole.

Magnetic Forces on Moving Charges

There are four key characteristics of the magnetic force on a moving charge. First, its magnitude is proportional to the magnitude of the charge. If a 1-μC charge and a 2-μC charge move through a given magnetic field with the same velocity, experiments show that the force on the 2-μC charge is twice as great as the force on the 1-μC charge. Second, the magnitude of the force is also proportional to the magnitude, or "strength," of the field; if we double the magnitude of the field (for example, by using two identical bar magnets instead of one) without changing the charge or its velocity, the force doubles.

A third characteristic is that the magnetic force depends on the particle's velocity. This is quite different from the electric-field force, which is the same whether the charge is moving or not. A charged particle at rest experiences *no* magnetic force. And fourth, we find by experiment that the magnetic force $\vec{F}$ *does not* have the same direction as the magnetic field $\vec{B}$ but instead is always *perpendicular* to both $\vec{B}$ and the velocity $\vec{v}$. The magnitude F of the force is found to be proportional to the component of $\vec{v}$ perpendicular to the field; when that component is zero (that is, when $\vec{v}$ and $\vec{B}$ are parallel or antiparallel), the force is zero.

Figure 27.6 shows these relationships. The direction of $\vec{F}$ is always perpendicular to the plane containing $\vec{v}$ and $\vec{B}$. Its magnitude is given by

$$F = |q|v_{\perp}B = |q|vB\sin\phi \qquad (27.1)$$

where $|q|$ is the magnitude of the charge and ϕ is the angle measured from the direction of $\vec{v}$ to the direction of $\vec{B}$, as shown in the figure.

This description does not specify the direction of $\vec{F}$ completely; there are always two directions, opposite to each other, that are both perpendicular to the plane of $\vec{v}$ and $\vec{B}$. To complete the description, we use the same right-hand rule that we used to define the vector product in Section 1.10. (It would be a good idea to review that section before you go on.) Draw the vectors $\vec{v}$ and $\vec{B}$ with their tails together, as in Fig. 27.7a. Imagine turning $\vec{v}$ until it points in the direction of $\vec{B}$ (turning through the smaller of the two possible angles). Wrap the fingers of your right hand around the line perpendicular to the plane of $\vec{v}$ and $\vec{B}$ so that they curl around with the sense of rotation from $\vec{v}$ to $\vec{B}$. Your thumb then points in the direction of the force $\vec{F}$ on a *positive* charge. (Alternatively, the direction of the force $\vec{F}$ on a positive charge is the direction in which a right-hand-thread screw would advance if turned the same way.)

This discussion shows that the force on a charge q moving with velocity $\vec{v}$ in a magnetic field $\vec{B}$ is given, both in magnitude and in direction, by

$$\vec{F} = q\vec{v} \times \vec{B} \qquad \text{(magnetic force on a moving charged particle)} \quad (27.2)$$

This is the first of several vector products we will encounter in our study of magnetic-field relationships. It's important to note that Eq. (27.2) was *not* deduced theoretically; it is an observation based on *experiment*.

13.4   Magnetic Force on a Particle

27.6 The magnetic force $\vec{F}$ acting on a positive charge q moving with velocity $\vec{v}$ is perpendicular to both $\vec{v}$ and the magnetic field $\vec{B}$. For given values of the speed v and magnetic field strength B, the force is greatest when $\vec{v}$ and $\vec{B}$ are perpendicular.

(a)

A charge moving **parallel** to a magnetic field experiences **zero** **magnetic** **force**.

(b)

A charge moving at an angle ϕ to a magnetic field experiences a magnetic force with magnitude $F = |q|v_{\perp}B = |q|vB\sin\phi$.

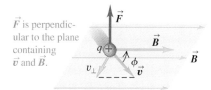

$\vec{F}$ is perpendicular to the plane containing $\vec{v}$ and $\vec{B}$.

(c)

A charge moving **perpendicular** to a magnetic field experiences a maximal magnetic force with magnitude $F_{max} = qvB$.

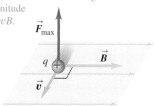

27.7 Finding the direction of the magnetic force on a moving charged particle.

(a)

Right-hand rule for the direction of magnetic force on a **positive** charge moving in a magnetic field:

① Place the $\vec{v}$ and $\vec{B}$ vectors tail to tail.

② Imagine turning $\vec{v}$ toward $\vec{B}$ in the $\vec{v}$-$\vec{B}$ plane (through the smaller angle).

③ The force acts along a line perpendicular to the $\vec{v}$-$\vec{B}$ plane. Curl the fingers of your *right hand* around this line in the same direction you rotated $\vec{v}$. Your thumb now points in the direction the force acts.

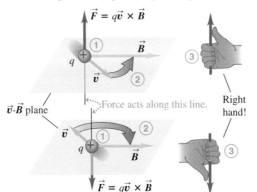

(b)

If the charge is negative, the direction of the force is *opposite* to that given by the right-hand rule.

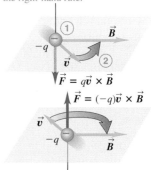

Equation (27.2) is valid for both positive and negative charges. When q is negative, the direction of the force $\vec{F}$ is opposite to that of $\vec{v} \times \vec{B}$ (Fig. 27. 7b). If two charges with equal magnitude and opposite sign move in the same $\vec{B}$ field with the same velocity (Fig. 27.8), the forces have equal magnitude and opposite direction. Figures 27.6, 27.7, and 27.8 show several examples of the relationships of the directions of $\vec{F}$, $\vec{v}$, and $\vec{B}$ for both positive and negative charges. Be sure you understand the relationships shown in these figures.

Equation (27.1) gives the magnitude of the magnetic force $\vec{F}$ in Eq. (27.2). We can express this magnitude in a different but equivalent way. Since ϕ is the angle between the directions of vectors $\vec{v}$ and $\vec{B}$, we may interpret $B\sin\phi$ as the component of $\vec{B}$ perpendicular to $\vec{v}$—that is, $B_\perp$. With this notation the force magnitude is

$$F = |q|vB_\perp \tag{27.3}$$

This form is sometimes more convenient, especially in problems involving *currents* rather than individual particles. We will discuss forces on currents later in this chapter.

From Eq. (27.1) the *units* of B must be the same as the units of F/qv. Therefore the SI unit of B is equivalent to $1 \text{ N} \cdot \text{s}/\text{C} \cdot \text{m}$, or, since one ampere is one coulomb per second $(1 \text{ A} = 1 \text{ C}/\text{s})$, $1 \text{ N}/\text{A} \cdot \text{m}$. This unit is called the **tesla** (abbreviated T), in honor of Nikola Tesla (1857–1943), the prominent Serbian-American scientist and inventor:

$$1 \text{ tesla} = 1 \text{ T} = 1 \text{ N}/\text{A} \cdot \text{m}$$

Another unit of B, the **gauss** $(1 \text{ G} = 10^{-4} \text{ T})$, is also in common use. Instruments for measuring magnetic field are sometimes called *gaussmeters*.

The magnetic field of the earth is of the order of 10^{-4} T or 1 G. Magnetic fields of the order of 10 T occur in the interior of atoms and are important in the analysis of atomic spectra. The largest steady magnetic field that can be produced at present in the laboratory is about 45 T. Some pulsed-current electromagnets can produce fields of the order of 120 T for short time intervals of the order of a millisecond. The magnetic field at the surface of a neutron star is believed to be of the order of 10^8 T.

27.8 Two charges of the same magnitude but opposite sign moving with the same velocity in the same magnetic field. The magnetic forces on the charges are equal in magnitude but opposite in direction.

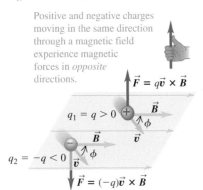

Positive and negative charges moving in the same direction through a magnetic field experience magnetic forces in *opposite* directions.

Measuring Magnetic Fields with Test Charges

To explore an unknown magnetic field, we can measure the magnitude and direction of the force on a *moving* test charge and then use Eq. (27.2) to determine $\vec{B}$. The electron beam in a cathode-ray tube, such as that used in a television set, is a convenient device for making such measurements. The electron gun shoots out a narrow beam of electrons at a known speed. If there is no force to deflect the beam, it strikes the center of the screen.

If a magnetic field is present, in general the electron beam is deflected. But if the beam is parallel or antiparallel to the field, then $\phi = 0$ or π in Eq. (27.1) and $F = 0$; there is no force, and hence no deflection. If we find that the electron beam is not deflected when its direction is parallel to a certain axis as in Fig. 27.9a, the $\vec{B}$ vector must point either up or down along that axis.

If we then turn the tube 90° (Fig. 27.9b), $\phi = \pi/2$ in Eq. (27.1) and the magnetic force is maximum; the beam is deflected in a direction perpendicular to the plane of $\vec{B}$ and $\vec{v}$. The direction and magnitude of the deflection determine the direction and magnitude of $\vec{B}$. We can perform additional experiments in which the angle between $\vec{B}$ and $\vec{v}$ is between zero and 90° to confirm Eq. (27.1) or (27.3) and the accompanying discussion. We note that the electron has a negative charge; the force in Fig. 27.9b is opposite in direction to the force on a positive charge.

When a charged particle moves through a region of space where *both* electric and magnetic fields are present, both fields exert forces on the particle. The total force $\vec{F}$ is the vector sum of the electric and magnetic forces:

$$\vec{F} = q(\vec{E} + \vec{v} \times \vec{B}) \qquad (27.4)$$

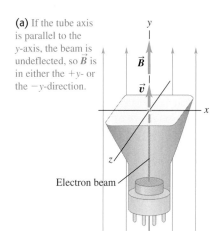

(a) If the tube axis is parallel to the y-axis, the beam is undeflected, so $\vec{B}$ is in either the $+y$- or the $-y$-direction.

Electron beam

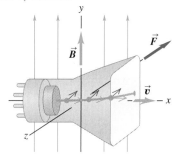

(b) If the tube axis is parallel to the x-axis, the beam is deflected in the $-z$-direction, so $\vec{B}$ is in the $+y$-direction.

27.9 Determining the direction of a magnetic field using a cathode-ray tube. Because electrons have a negative charge, the magnetic force $\vec{F} = q\vec{v} \times \vec{B}$ in part (b) points opposite to the direction given by the right-hand rule (see Fig. 27.7b).

Problem-Solving Strategy 27.1 **Magnetic Forces**

IDENTIFY *the relevant concepts:* The right-hand rule allows you to determine the magnetic force on a moving charged particle.

SET UP *the problem* using the following steps:
1. Draw the velocity vector $\vec{v}$ and magnetic field $\vec{B}$ with their tails together so that you can visualize the plane in which these two vectors lie.
2. Identify the angle ϕ between the two vectors.
3. Identify the target variables. This may be the magnitude and direction of the force, or it may be the magnitude or direction of $\vec{v}$ or $\vec{B}$.

EXECUTE *the solution* as follows:
1. Express the magnetic force using Eq. (27.2), $\vec{F} = q\vec{v} \times \vec{B}$. The magnitude of the force is given by Eq. (27.1), $F = qvB\sin\phi$.

2. Remember that $\vec{F}$ is perpendicular to the plane of the vectors $\vec{v}$ and $\vec{B}$. The direction of $\vec{v} \times \vec{B}$ is determined by the right-hand rule; keep referring to Fig. 27.7 until you're sure you understand this rule. If q is negative, the force is *opposite* to $\vec{v} \times \vec{B}$.

EVALUATE *your answer:* Whenever you can, solve the problem in two ways. Do it directly from the geometric definition of the vector product. Then find the components of the vectors in some convenient axis system and calculate the vector product algebraically from the components. Verify that the results agree.

| Example 27.1 | **Magnetic force on a proton** |

A beam of protons ($q = 1.6 \times 10^{-19}$ C) moves at 3.0×10^5 m/s through a uniform magnetic field with magnitude 2.0 T that is directed along the positive z-axis, as in Fig. 27.10. The velocity of each proton lies in the xz-plane at an angle of $30°$ to the $+z$-axis. Find the force on a proton.

SOLUTION

IDENTIFY: This problem uses the expression for the magnetic force on a moving charged particle.

SET UP: Figure 27.10 shows that the vectors $\vec{v}$ and $\vec{B}$ lie in the xz-plane. The angle between these vectors is $30°$. The target variables are the magnitude and direction of the force $\vec{F}$.

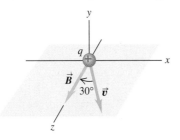

27.10 Directions of $\vec{v}$ and $\vec{B}$ for a proton in a magnetic field.

EXECUTE: The charge is positive, so the force is in the same direction as the vector product $\vec{v} \times \vec{B}$. From the right-hand rule, this direction is along the negative y-axis. The magnitude of the force, from Eq. (27.1), is

$$F = qvB\sin\phi$$
$$= (1.6 \times 10^{-19}\,\text{C})(3.0 \times 10^5\,\text{m/s})(2.0\,\text{T})(\sin 30°)$$
$$= 4.8 \times 10^{-14}\,\text{N}$$

EVALUATE: We check our result by evaluating the force using vector language and Eq. (27.2). We have

$$\vec{v} = (3.0 \times 10^5\,\text{m/s})(\sin 30°)\hat{\imath} + (3.0 \times 10^5\,\text{m/s})(\cos 30°)\hat{k}$$
$$\vec{B} = (2.0\,\text{T})\hat{k}$$
$$\vec{F} = q\vec{v} \times \vec{B}$$
$$= (1.6 \times 10^{-19}\,\text{C})(3.0 \times 10^5\,\text{m/s})(2.0\,\text{T})$$
$$\times (\sin 30°\,\hat{\imath} + \cos 30°\hat{k}) \times \hat{k}$$
$$= (-4.8 \times 10^{-14}\,\text{N})\hat{\jmath}$$

(Recall that $\hat{\imath} \times \hat{k} = -\hat{\jmath}$ and $\hat{k} \times \hat{k} = \mathbf{0}$.) We again find that the force is in the negative y direction with magnitude 4.8×10^{-14} N.

If the beam consists of *electrons* rather than protons, the charge is negative ($q = -1.6 \times 10^{-19}$ C) and the direction of the force is reversed. The force is now directed along the *positive* y-axis, but the magnitude is the same as before, $F = 4.8 \times 10^{-14}$ N.

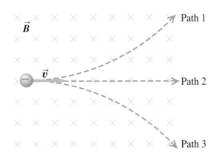

Test Your Understanding of Section 27.2 The figure at left shows a uniform magnetic field $\vec{B}$ directed into the plane of the paper (shown by the blue $\times$'s). A particle with a negative charge moves in the plane. Which of the three paths—1, 2, or 3—does the particle follow?

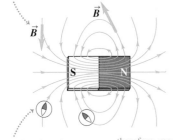

27.11 The magnetic field lines of a permanent magnet. Note that the field lines pass through the interior of the magnet.

At each point, the field line is tangent to the magnetic field vector $\vec{B}$.

The more densely the field lines are packed, the stronger the field is at that point.

At each point, the field lines point in the same direction a compass would . . .

. . . therefore, magnetic field lines point *away from* N poles and *toward* S poles.

27.3 Magnetic Field Lines and Magnetic Flux

We can represent any magnetic field by **magnetic field lines,** just as we did for the earth's magnetic field in Fig. 27.3. The idea is the same as for the electric field lines we introduced in Section 21.6. We draw the lines so that the line through any point is tangent to the magnetic field vector $\vec{B}$ at that point (Fig. 27.11). Just as with electric field lines, we draw only a few representative lines; otherwise, the lines would fill up all of space. Where adjacent field lines are close together, the field magnitude is large; where these field lines are far apart, the field magnitude is small. Also, because the direction of $\vec{B}$ at each point is unique, field lines never intersect.

CAUTION **Magnetic field lines are not "lines of force"** Magnetic field lines are sometimes called "magnetic lines of force," but that's not a good name for them; unlike electric field lines, they *do not* point in the direction of the force on a charge (Fig. 27.12). Equation (27.2) shows that the force on a moving charged particle is always perpendicular to the magnetic field, and hence to the magnetic field line that passes through the particle's position. The direction of the force depends on the particle's velocity and the sign of its charge, so just looking at magnetic field lines cannot in itself tell you the direction of the force on an arbitrary moving charged particle. Magnetic field lines *do* have the direction that a compass needle would point at each location; this may help you to visualize them.

Figures 27.11 and 27.13 show magnetic field lines produced by several common sources of magnetic field. In the gap between the poles of the magnet shown in Fig. 27.13a, the field lines are approximately straight, parallel, and equally spaced, showing that the magnetic field in this region is approximately *uniform* (that is, constant in magnitude and direction).

Because magnetic-field patterns are three-dimensional, it's often necessary to draw magnetic field lines that point into or out of the plane of a drawing. To do this we use a dot (·) to represent a vector directed out of the plane and a cross (×) to represent a vector directed into the plane (Fig. 27.13b). Here's a good way to remember these conventions: Think of a dot as the head of an arrow coming directly toward you, and think of a cross as the feathers of an arrow flying directly away from you.

Iron filings, like compass needles, tend to align with magnetic field lines. Hence they provide an easy way to visualize field lines (Fig. 27.14).

27.12 Magnetic field lines are *not* "lines of force."

Magnetic field lines are *not* "lines of force." The force on a charged particle is not along the direction of a field line.

The direction of the magnetic force depends on the velocity $\vec{v}$, as expressed by the magnetic force law $\vec{F} = q\vec{v} \times \vec{B}$.

27.13 Magnetic field lines produced by several common sources of magnetic field.

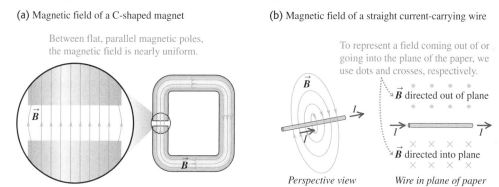

(a) Magnetic field of a C-shaped magnet

Between flat, parallel magnetic poles, the magnetic field is nearly uniform.

(b) Magnetic field of a straight current-carrying wire

To represent a field coming out of or going into the plane of the paper, we use dots and crosses, respectively.

$\vec{B}$ directed out of plane

$\vec{B}$ directed into plane

Perspective view   *Wire in plane of paper*

(c) Magnetic fields of a current-carrying loop and a current-carrying coil (solenoid)

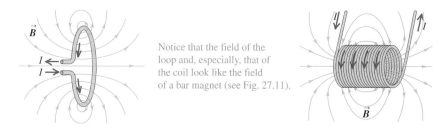

Notice that the field of the loop and, especially, that of the coil look like the field of a bar magnet (see Fig. 27.11).

27.14 (a) Like little compass needles, iron filings line up tangent to magnetic field lines. (b) Drawing of the field lines for the situation shown in (a).

(a)   (b)

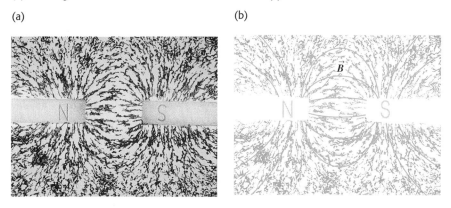

Magnetic Flux and Gauss's Law for Magnetism

27.15 The magnetic flux through an area element dA is defined to be $d\Phi_B = B_\perp dA$.

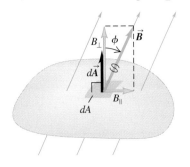

We define the **magnetic flux** Φ_B through a surface just as we defined electric flux in connection with Gauss's law in Section 22.2. We can divide any surface into elements of area dA (Fig. 27.15). For each element we determine $B_\perp$, the component of $\vec{B}$ normal to the surface at the position of that element, as shown. From the figure, $B_\perp = B\cos\phi$, where ϕ is the angle between the direction of $\vec{B}$ and a line perpendicular to the surface. (Be careful not to confuse ϕ with Φ_B.) In general, this component varies from point to point on the surface. We define the magnetic flux $d\Phi_B$ through this area as

$$d\Phi_B = B_\perp dA = B\cos\phi\, dA = \vec{B} \cdot d\vec{A} \tag{27.5}$$

The *total* magnetic flux through the surface is the sum of the contributions from the individual area elements:

$$\Phi_B = \int B_\perp dA = \int B\cos\phi\, dA = \int \vec{B} \cdot d\vec{A} \quad \text{(magnetic flux through a surface)} \tag{27.6}$$

(This equation uses the concepts of vector area and surface integral that we introduced in Section 22.2; you may want to review that discussion.)

Magnetic flux is a *scalar* quantity. In the special case in which $\vec{B}$ is uniform over a plane surface with total area A, $B_\perp$ and ϕ are the same at all points on the surface, and

$$\Phi_B = B_\perp A = BA\cos\phi \tag{27.7}$$

If $\vec{B}$ happens to be perpendicular to the surface, then $\cos\phi = 1$ and Eq. (27.7) reduces to $\Phi_B = BA$. We will use the concept of magnetic flux extensively during our study of electromagnetic induction in Chapter 29.

The SI unit of magnetic flux is equal to the unit of magnetic field (1 T) times the unit of area (1 m^2). This unit is called the **weber** (1 Wb), in honor of the German physicist Wilhelm Weber (1804–1891):

$$1\text{ Wb} = 1\text{ T} \cdot \text{m}^2$$

Also, $1\text{ T} = 1\text{ N}/\text{A} \cdot \text{m}$, so

$$1\text{ Wb} = 1\text{ T} \cdot \text{m}^2 = 1\text{ N} \cdot \text{m}/\text{A}$$

In Gauss's law the total *electric* flux through a closed surface is proportional to the total electric charge enclosed by the surface. For example, if the closed surface encloses an electric dipole, the total electric flux is zero because the total charge is zero. (You may want to review Section 22.3 on Gauss's law.) By analogy, if there were such a thing as a single magnetic charge (magnetic monopole), the total *magnetic* flux through a closed surface would be proportional to the total magnetic charge enclosed. But we have mentioned that no magnetic monopole has ever been observed, despite intensive searches. We conclude:

The total magnetic flux through a closed surface is always zero.

Symbolically,

$$\oint \vec{B} \cdot d\vec{A} = 0 \quad \text{(magnetic flux through any closed surface)} \tag{27.8}$$

This equation is sometimes called *Gauss's law for magnetism*. You can verify it by examining Figs. 27.11 and 27.13; if you draw a closed surface anywhere in any of the field maps shown in those figures, you will see that every field line that enters the surface also exits from it; the net flux through the surface is zero. It also follows from Eq. (27.8) that magnetic field lines always form closed loops.

CAUTION **Magnetic field lines have no ends** Unlike electric field lines that begin and end on electric charges, magnetic field lines *never* have end points; such a point would indicate the presence of a monopole. You might be tempted to draw magnetic field lines that begin at the north pole of a magnet and end at a south pole. But as Fig. 27.11 shows, the field lines of a magnet actually continue through the interior of the magnet. Like all other magnetic field lines, they form closed loops.

For Gauss's law, which always deals with *closed* surfaces, the vector area element $d\vec{A}$ in Eq. (27.6) always points *out of* the surface. However, some applications of *magnetic* flux involve an *open* surface with a boundary line; there is then an ambiguity of sign in Eq. (27.6) because of the two possible choices of direction for $d\vec{A}$. In these cases we choose one of the two sides of the surface to be the "positive" side and use that choice consistently.

If the element of area dA in Eq. (27.5) is at right angles to the field lines, then $B_\perp = B$; calling the area $dA_\perp$, we have

$$B = \frac{d\Phi_B}{dA_\perp} \tag{27.9}$$

That is, the magnitude of magnetic field is equal to *flux per unit area* across an area at right angles to the magnetic field. For this reason, magnetic field $\vec{B}$ is sometimes called **magnetic flux density.**

Example 27.2   Magnetic flux calculations

Figure 27.16a shows a perspective view of a flat surface with area 3.0 cm² in a uniform magnetic field. If the magnetic flux through this area is 0.90 mWb, calculate the magnitude of the magnetic field and find the direction of the area vector.

SOLUTION

IDENTIFY: In many problems we are asked to calculate the flux of a given magnetic field through a given area. In this example, how-

27.16 (a) A flat area A in a uniform magnetic field $\vec{B}$. (b) The area vector $\vec{A}$ makes a 60° angle with $\vec{B}$. (If we had chosen $\vec{A}$ to point in the opposite direction, ϕ would have been 120° and the magnetic flux Φ_B would have been negative.)

(a) Perspective view

(b) Our sketch of the problem (edge-on view)

ever, we are given the flux, the area, and the direction of the magnetic field. Our target variables are the field magnitude and the direction of the area vector.

SET UP: Because the magnetic field is uniform, B and ϕ are the same at all points on the surface. Hence we can use Eq. (27.7): $\Phi_B = BA\cos\phi$. Our target variable is B.

EXECUTE: The area A is 3.0×10^{-4} m²; the direction of $\vec{A}$ is perpendicular to the surface, so ϕ could be either 60° or 120°. But Φ_B, B, and A are all positive, so $\cos\phi$ must also be positive. This rules out 120°, so $\phi = 60°$, and we find

$$B = \frac{\Phi_B}{A\cos\phi} = \frac{0.90 \times 10^{-3}\,\text{Wb}}{(3.0 \times 10^{-4}\,\text{m}^2)(\cos 60°)} = 6.0\,\text{T}$$

The area vector $\vec{A}$ is perpendicular to the area in the direction shown in Fig. 27.16b.

EVALUATE: A good way to check our result is to calculate the product $BA\cos\phi$ to make sure that it is equal to the given value of the magnetic flux Φ_B. Is it?

Test Your Understanding of Section 27.3   Imagine moving along the axis of the current-carrying loop in Fig. 27.13c, starting at a point well to the left of the loop and ending at a point well to the right of the loop. (a) How would the magnetic field strength vary as you moved along this path? (i) It would be the same at all points along the path; (ii) it would increase and then decrease; (iii) it would decrease and then increase. (b) Would the magnetic field direction vary as you moved along the path?

27.4 Motion of Charged Particles in a Magnetic Field

When a charged particle moves in a magnetic field, it is acted on by the magnetic force given by Eq. (27.2), and the motion is determined by Newton's laws. Figure 27.17 shows a simple example. A particle with positive charge q is at

27.17 A charged particle moves in a plane perpendicular to a uniform magnetic field $\vec{B}$.

(a) The orbit of a charged particle in a uniform magnetic field

A charge moving at right angles to a uniform $\vec{B}$ field moves in a circle at constant speed because $\vec{F}$ and $\vec{v}$ are always perpendicular to each other.

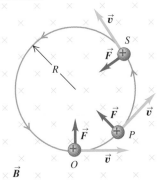

(b) An electron beam (seen as a blue arc) curving in a magnetic field

27.18 The general case of a charged particle moving in a uniform magnetic field $\vec{B}$. The magnetic field does no work on the particle, so its speed and kinetic energy remain constant.

This particle's motion has components both parallel ($v_{\parallel}$) and perpendicular ($v_{\perp}$) to the magnetic field, so it moves in a helical path.

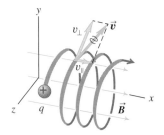

point O, moving with velocity $\vec{v}$ in a uniform magnetic field $\vec{B}$ directed into the plane of the figure. The vectors $\vec{v}$ and $\vec{B}$ are perpendicular, so the magnetic force $\vec{F} = q\vec{v} \times \vec{B}$ has magnitude $F = qvB$ and a direction as shown in the figure. The force is *always* perpendicular to $\vec{v}$, so it cannot change the *magnitude* of the velocity, only its direction. To put it differently, the magnetic force never has a component parallel to the particle's motion, so the magnetic force can never do *work* on the particle. This is true even if the magnetic field is not uniform.

Motion of a charged particle under the action of a magnetic field alone is always motion with constant speed.

Using this principle, we see that in the situation shown in Fig. 27.17a the magnitudes of both $\vec{F}$ and $\vec{v}$ are constant. At points such as P and S the directions of force and velocity have changed as shown, but their magnitudes are the same. The particle therefore moves under the influence of a constant-magnitude force that is always at right angles to the velocity of the particle. Comparing these conditions with the discussion of circular motion in Sections 3.4 and 5.4, we see that the particle's path is a *circle*, traced out with constant speed v. The centripetal acceleration is v^2/R and the only force acting is the magnetic force, so from Newton's second law,

$$F = |q|vB = m\frac{v^2}{R} \tag{27.10}$$

where m is the mass of the particle. Solving Eq. (27.10) for the radius R of the circular path, we find

$$R = \frac{mv}{|q|B} \qquad \text{(radius of a circular orbit in a magnetic field)} \tag{27.11}$$

We can also write this as $R = p/|q|B$, where $p = mv$ is the magnitude of the particle's momentum. If the charge q is negative, the particle moves *clockwise* around the orbit in Fig. 27.17a.

The angular speed ω of the particle can be found from Eq. (9.13), $v = R\omega$. Combining this with Eq. (27.11), we get

$$\omega = \frac{v}{R} = v\frac{|q|B}{mv} = \frac{|q|B}{m} \tag{27.12}$$

The number of revolutions per unit time is $f = \omega/2\pi$. This frequency f is independent of the radius R of the path. It is called the **cyclotron frequency;** in a particle accelerator called a *cyclotron,* particles moving in nearly circular paths are given a boost twice each revolution, increasing their energy and their orbital radii but not their angular speed or frequency. Similarly, one type of *magnetron,* a common source of microwave radiation for microwave ovens and radar systems, emits radiation with a frequency equal to the frequency of circular motion of electrons in a vacuum chamber between the poles of a magnet.

If the direction of the initial velocity is *not* perpendicular to the field, the velocity *component* parallel to the field is constant because there is no force parallel to the field. Then the particle moves in a helix (Fig. 27.18). The radius of the helix is given by Eq. (27.11), where v is now the component of velocity perpendicular to the $\vec{B}$ field.

Motion of a charged particle in a nonuniform magnetic field is more complex. Figure 27.19 shows a field produced by two circular coils separated by some distance. Particles near either coil experience a magnetic force toward the center of the region; particles with appropriate speeds spiral repeatedly from one end of the region to the other and back. Because charged particles can be trapped in such a magnetic field, it is called a *magnetic bottle.* This technique is used to confine very hot plasmas with temperatures of the order of 10^6 K. In a similar way the

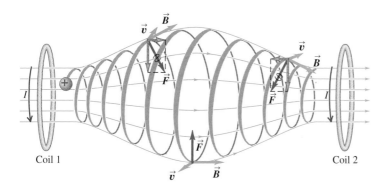

27.19 A magnetic bottle. Particles near either end of the region experience a magnetic force toward the center of the region. This is one way of containing an ionized gas that has a temperature of the order of 10^6 K, which would vaporize any material container.

(a)

(b)

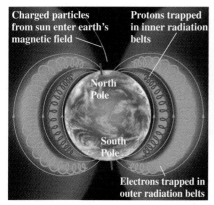

27.20 (a) The Van Allen radiation belts around the earth. Near the poles, charged particles from these belts can enter the atmosphere, producing the aurora borealis ("northern lights") and aurora australis ("southern lights"). (b) A photograph of the aurora borealis.

27.21 This bubble chamber image shows the result of a high-energy gamma ray (which does not leave a track) that collides with an electron in a hydrogen atom. This electron flies off to the right at high speed. Some of the energy in the collision is transformed into a second electron and a positron (a positively charged electron). A magnetic field is directed into the plane of the image, which makes the positive and negative particles curve off in different directions.

earth's nonuniform magnetic field traps charged particles coming from the sun in doughnut-shaped regions around the earth, as shown in Fig. 27.20. These regions, called the *Van Allen radiation belts,* were discovered in 1958 using data obtained by instruments aboard the Explorer I satellite.

Magnetic forces on charged particles play an important role in studies of elementary particles. Figure 27.21 shows a chamber filled with liquid hydrogen and with a magnetic field directed into the plane of the photograph. A high-energy gamma ray dislodges an electron from a hydrogen atom, sending it off at high speed and creating a visible track in the liquid hydrogen. The track shows the electron curving downward due to the magnetic force. The energy of the collision also produces another electron and a *positron* (a positively charged electron). Because of their opposite charges, the trajectories of the electron and the positron curve in opposite directions. As these particles plow through the liquid hydrogen, they collide with other charged particles, losing energy and speed. As a result, the radius of curvature decreases as suggested by Eq. (27.11). (The electron's speed is comparable to the speed of light, so Eq. (27.11) isn't directly applicable here.) Similar experiments allow physicists to determine the mass and charge of newly discovered particles.

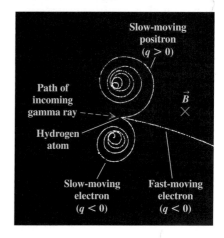

Slow-moving positron ($q > 0$)

Path of incoming gamma ray

Hydrogen atom

$\vec{B}$

Slow-moving electron ($q < 0$)

Fast-moving electron ($q < 0$)

Problem-Solving Strategy 27.2   Motion in Magnetic Fields

(MP)

IDENTIFY *the relevant concepts:* In analyzing the motion of a charged particle in electric and magnetic fields, you will apply Newton's second law of motion, $\sum \vec{F} = m\vec{a}$, with the net force given by $\sum \vec{F} = q(\vec{E} + \vec{v} \times \vec{B})$. Often other forces such as gravity can be neglected. Many of the problems are similar to the trajectory and circular-motion problems in Sections 3.3, 3.4, and 5.4; it would be a good idea to review those sections.

SET UP *the problem* using the following steps:
1. Determine the target variable(s).
2. Often the use of components is the most efficient approach. Choose a coordinate system and then express all vector quantities (including $\vec{E}$, $\vec{B}$, $\vec{v}$, $\vec{F}$, and $\vec{a}$) in terms of their components in this system.

Continued

EXECUTE *the solution* as follows:

1. If the particle moves perpendicular to a uniform magnetic field, the trajectory is a circle with a radius and angular speed given by Eqs. (27.11) and (27.12), respectively.
2. If your calculation involves a more complex trajectory, use $\Sigma \vec{F} = m\vec{a}$ in component form: $\Sigma F_x = ma_x$, and so forth. This

approach is particularly useful when both electric and magnetic fields are present.

EVALUATE *your answer:* Check whether your results are reasonable.

Example 27.3   Electron motion in a microwave oven

A magnetron in a microwave oven emits electromagnetic waves with frequency $f = 2450$ MHz. What magnetic field strength is required for electrons to move in circular paths with this frequency?

SOLUTION

IDENTIFY: The problem refers to circular motion as shown in Fig. 27.17a. Our target variable is the field magnitude B.

SET UP: We use Eq. (27.12) to relate the angular speed in circular motion to the mass and charge of the particle and the magnetic field strength B.

EXECUTE: The angular speed that corresponds to the frequency f is $\omega = 2\pi f = (2\pi)(2450 \times 10^6 \text{ s}^{-1}) = 1.54 \times 10^{10} \text{ s}^{-1}$. From Eq. (27.12),

$$B = \frac{m\omega}{|q|} = \frac{(9.11 \times 10^{-31} \text{ kg})(1.54 \times 10^{10} \text{ s}^{-1})}{1.60 \times 10^{-19} \text{ C}}$$

$$= 0.0877 \text{ T}$$

EVALUATE: This is a moderate field strength, easily produced with a permanent magnet. Incidentally, 2450-MHz electromagnetic waves are strongly absorbed by water molecules, so they are useful for heating and cooking food.

Example 27.4   Helical particle motion

In a situation like that shown in Fig. 27.18, the charged particle is a proton ($q = 1.60 \times 10^{-19}$ C, $m = 1.67 \times 10^{-27}$ kg) and the uniform magnetic field is directed along the x-axis with magnitude 0.500 T. Only the magnetic force acts on the proton. At $t = 0$ the proton has velocity components $v_x = 1.50 \times 10^5$ m/s, $v_y = 0$, and $v_z = 2.00 \times 10^5$ m/s. (a) At $t = 0$, find the force on the proton and its acceleration. (b) Find the radius of the helical path, the angular speed of the proton, and the *pitch* of the helix (the distance traveled along the helix axis per revolution).

SOLUTION

IDENTIFY: The force is given by $\vec{F} = q\vec{v} \times \vec{B}$ and the acceleration is given by Newton's second law. The force is perpendicular to the velocity, so the speed of the proton does not change. Hence the radius of the helical trajectory is just as given by Eq. (27.11) for circular motion, but with v replaced by the component of velocity perpendicular to $\vec{B}$. The angular speed is given by Eq. (27.12).

SET UP: We use the coordinate system shown in Fig. 27.18. Given the angular speed, we can determine the time required for one revolution; given the velocity parallel to the magnetic field, we can determine the distance traveled along the helix in this time.

EXECUTE: (a) Since $v_y = 0$, the velocity vector is $\vec{v} = v_x\hat{\imath} + v_z\hat{k}$. Using Eq. (27.2) and recalling that $\hat{\imath} \times \hat{\imath} = 0$ and $\hat{k} \times \hat{\imath} = \hat{\jmath}$, we find

$$\vec{F} = q\vec{v} \times \vec{B} = q(v_x\hat{\imath} + v_z\hat{k}) \times B\hat{\imath} = qv_zB\hat{\jmath}$$

$$= (1.60 \times 10^{-19} \text{ C})(2.00 \times 10^5 \text{ m/s})(0.500 \text{ T})\hat{\jmath}$$

$$= (1.60 \times 10^{-14} \text{ N})\hat{\jmath}$$

(To check unit consistency, recall from Section 27.2 that $1 \text{ T} = 1 \text{ N/A} \cdot \text{m} = 1 \text{ N} \cdot \text{s/C} \cdot \text{m}$.) This may seem like a very weak force, but the resulting acceleration is tremendous because the proton mass is so small:

$$\vec{a} = \frac{\vec{F}}{m} = \frac{1.60 \times 10^{-14} \text{ N}}{1.67 \times 10^{-27} \text{ kg}}\hat{\jmath} = (9.58 \times 10^{12} \text{ m/s}^2)\hat{\jmath}$$

(b) At $t = 0$ the component of velocity perpendicular to $\vec{B}$ is v_z, so

$$R = \frac{mv_z}{|q|B} = \frac{(1.67 \times 10^{-27} \text{ kg})(2.00 \times 10^5 \text{ m/s})}{(1.60 \times 10^{-19} \text{ C})(0.500 \text{ T})}$$

$$= 4.18 \times 10^{-3} \text{ m} = 4.18 \text{ mm}$$

From Eq. (27.12) the angular speed is

$$\omega = \frac{|q|B}{m} = \frac{(1.60 \times 10^{-19} \text{ C})(0.500 \text{ T})}{1.67 \times 10^{-27} \text{ kg}} = 4.79 \times 10^7 \text{ rad/s}$$

The time required for one revolution (the period) is $T = 2\pi/\omega = 2\pi/(4.79 \times 10^7 \text{ s}^{-1}) = 1.31 \times 10^{-7}$ s. The pitch is the distance traveled along the x-axis during this time, or

$$v_xT = (1.50 \times 10^5 \text{ m/s})(1.31 \times 10^{-7} \text{ s})$$

$$= 0.0197 \text{ m} = 19.7 \text{ mm}$$

EVALUATE: The pitch of the helix is almost five times greater than the radius. This helical trajectory is much more "stretched out" than that shown in Fig. 27.18.

Test Your Understanding of Section 27.4 (a) If you double the speed of the charged particle in Fig. 27.17a while keeping the magnetic field the same (as well as the charge and the mass), how does this affect the radius of the trajectory? (i) The radius is unchanged; (ii) the radius is twice as large; (iii) the radius is four times as large; (iv) the radius is $\frac{1}{2}$ as large; (v) the radius is $\frac{1}{4}$ as large. (b) How does this affect the time required for one complete circular orbit? (i) The time is unchanged; (ii) the time is twice as long; (iii) the time is four times as long; (iv) the time is $\frac{1}{2}$ as long; (v) the time is $\frac{1}{4}$ as long.

27.5 Applications of Motion of Charged Particles

This section describes several applications of the principles introduced in this chapter. Study them carefully, watching for applications of Problem-Solving Strategy 27.2 (Section 27.4).

Velocity Selector

In a beam of charged particles produced by a heated cathode or a radioactive material, not all particles move with the same speed. Many applications, however, require a beam in which all the particle speeds are the same. Particles of a specific speed can be selected from the beam using an arrangement of electric and magnetic fields called a *velocity selector*. In Fig. 27.22a a charged particle with mass m, charge q, and speed v enters a region of space where the electric and magnetic fields are perpendicular to the particle's velocity and to each other. The electric field $\vec{E}$ is to the left, and the magnetic field $\vec{B}$ is into the plane of the figure. If q is positive, the electric force is to the left, with magnitude qE, and the magnetic force is to the right, with magnitude qvB. For given field magnitudes E and B, for a particular value of v the electric and magnetic forces will be equal in magnitude; the total force is then zero, and the particle travels in a straight line with constant velocity. For zero total force, $\Sigma F_y = 0$, we need $-qE + qvB = 0$; solving for the speed v for which there is no deflection, we find

$$v = \frac{E}{B} \tag{27.13}$$

Only particles with speeds equal to E/B can pass through without being deflected by the fields (Fig. 27.22b). By adjusting E and B appropriately, we can select particles having a particular speed for use in other experiments. Because q divides out in Eq. (27.13), a velocity selector for positively charged particles also works for electrons or other negatively charged particles.

Thomson's e/m Experiment

In one of the landmark experiments in physics at the end of the 19th century, J. J. Thomson (1856–1940) used the idea just described to measure the ratio of charge to mass for the electron. For this experiment, carried out in 1897 at the Cavendish Laboratory in Cambridge, England, Thomson used the apparatus shown in Fig. 27.23. In a highly evacuated glass container, electrons from the hot cathode are accelerated and formed into a beam by a potential difference V between the two anodes A and A'. The speed v of the electrons is determined by the accelerating potential V. The kinetic energy $\frac{1}{2}mv^2$ equals the loss of electric potential energy eV, where e is the magnitude of the electron charge:

$$\frac{1}{2}mv^2 = eV \quad \text{or} \quad v = \sqrt{\frac{2eV}{m}} \tag{27.14}$$

27.22 (a) A velocity selector for charged particles uses perpendicular $\vec{E}$ and $\vec{B}$ fields. Only charged particles with $v = E/B$ move through undeflected. (b) The electric and magnetic forces on a positive charge. The forces are reversed if the charge is negative.

(a) Schematic diagram of velocity selector

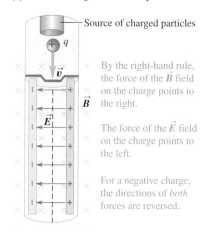

Source of charged particles

By the right-hand rule, the force of the $\vec{B}$ field on the charge points to the right.

The force of the $\vec{E}$ field on the charge points to the left.

For a negative charge, the directions of *both* forces are reversed.

(b) Free-body diagram for a positive particle

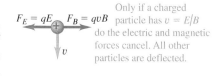

Only if a charged particle has $v = E/B$ do the electric and magnetic forces cancel. All other particles are deflected.

$F_E = qE \qquad F_B = qvB$

Act|v
Phys|cs
ONLINE

13.8 Velocity Selector

27.23 Thomson's apparatus for measuring the ratio e/m for the electron.

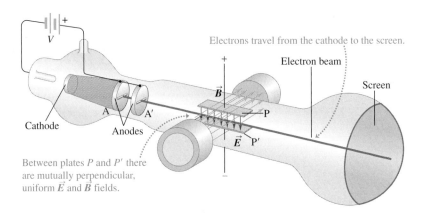

Electrons travel from the cathode to the screen.

Electron beam

Screen

$\vec{B}$

A   A'

P

Cathode

Anodes

$\vec{E}$ P'

Between plates P and P' there are mutually perpendicular, uniform $\vec{E}$ and $\vec{B}$ fields.

The electrons pass between the plates P and P' and strike the screen at the end of the tube, which is coated with a material that fluoresces (glows) at the point of impact. The electrons pass straight through the plates when Eq. (27.13) is satisfied; combining this with Eq. (27.14), we get

$$\frac{E}{B} = \sqrt{\frac{2eV}{m}} \quad \text{so} \quad \frac{e}{m} = \frac{E^2}{2VB^2} \quad (27.15)$$

All the quantities on the right side can be measured, so the ratio e/m of charge to mass can be determined. It is *not* possible to measure e or m separately by this method, only their ratio.

The most significant aspect of Thomson's e/m measurements was that he found a *single value* for this quantity. It did not depend on the cathode material, the residual gas in the tube, or anything else about the experiment. This independence showed that the particles in the beam, which we now call electrons, are a common constituent of all matter. Thus Thomson is credited with discovery of the first subatomic particle, the electron. He also found that the *speed* of the electrons in the beam was about one-tenth the speed of light, much greater than any previously measured speed of a material particle.

The most precise value of e/m available as of this writing is

$$e/m = 1.75882012(15) \times 10^{11} \text{ C/kg}$$

In this expression, (15) indicates the likely uncertainty in the last two digits, 12.

Fifteen years after Thomson's experiments, the American physicist Robert Millikan succeeded in measuring the charge of the electron precisely (see Challenge Problem 23.91). This value, together with the value of e/m, enables us to determine the *mass* of the electron. The most precise value available at present is

$$m = 9.1093826(16) \times 10^{-31} \text{ kg}$$

27.24 Bainbridge's mass spectrometer utilizes a velocity selector to produce particles with uniform speed v. In the region of magnetic field B', particles with greater mass $(m_2 > m_1)$ travel in paths with larger radius $(R_2 > R_1)$.

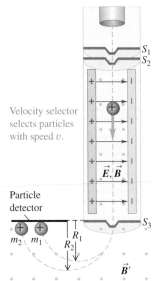

S_1
S_2

Velocity selector selects particles with speed v.

$\vec{E}, \vec{B}$

Particle detector

S_3

m_2 m_1

R_1
R_2

$\vec{B}'$

Magnetic field separates particles by mass; the greater a particle's mass, the larger is the radius of its path.

Mass Spectrometers

Techniques similar to Thomson's e/m experiment can be used to measure masses of ions and thus measure atomic and molecular masses. In 1919, Francis Aston (1877–1945), a student of Thomson's, built the first of a family of instruments called **mass spectrometers.** A variation built by Bainbridge is shown in Fig. 27.24. Positive ions from a source pass through the slits S_1 and S_2, forming a narrow beam. Then the ions pass through a velocity selector with crossed $\vec{E}$ and $\vec{B}$ fields, as we have described, to block all ions except those with speeds v equal to E/B. Finally, the ions pass into a region with a magnetic field $\vec{B}'$ perpendicular to the figure, where they move in circular arcs with radius R determined by Eq. (27.11): $R = mv/qB'$. Ions with different masses strike the detector (in

Bainbridge's design, a photographic plate) at different points, and the values of R can be measured. We assume that each ion has lost one electron, so the net charge of each ion is just $+e$. With everything known in this equation except m, we can compute the mass m of the ion.

One of the earliest results from this work was the discovery that neon has two species of atoms, with atomic masses 20 and 22 g/mol. We now call these species **isotopes** of the element. Later experiments have shown that many elements have several isotopes, atoms that are identical in their chemical behavior but different in mass owing to differing numbers of neutrons in their nuclei. This is just one of the many applications of mass spectrometers in chemistry and physics.

ActivPhysics ONLINE

13.7   Mass Spectrometer

Example 27.5   An e/m experiment

You set out to reproduce Thomson's e/m experiment with an accelerating potential of 150 V and a deflecting electric field of magnitude 6.0×10^6 N/C. (a) At what fraction of the speed of light do the electrons move? (b) What magnitude of magnetic field will you need? (c) With this magnetic field, what will happen to the electron beam if you increase the accelerating potential above 150 V?

SOLUTION

IDENTIFY: This is the same situation as depicted in Fig. 27.23.

SET UP: We use Eq. (27.14) to determine the speed of the electrons and Eq. (27.13) to determine the requisite magnetic field.

EXECUTE: (a) From Eq. (27.14), the electron speed v is related to the accelerating potential by:

$$v = \sqrt{2(e/m)V} = \sqrt{2(1.76 \times 10^{11}\ \text{C/kg})(150\ \text{V})}$$

$$= 7.27 \times 10^6\ \text{m/s}$$

$$\frac{v}{c} = \frac{7.27 \times 10^6\ \text{m/s}}{3.00 \times 10^8\ \text{m/s}} = 0.024$$

The electrons are traveling at 2.4% of the speed of light.

(b) From Eq. (27.13),

$$B = \frac{E}{v} = \frac{6.00 \times 10^6\ \text{N/C}}{7.27 \times 10^6\ \text{m/s}} = 0.83\ \text{T}$$

(c) Increasing the accelerating potential V increases the electron speed v. In Fig. 27.23 this doesn't change the upward electric force eE, but it increases the downward magnetic force evB. Therefore the electron beam will be bent *downward* and will hit the end of the tube below the undeflected position.

EVALUATE: The required magnetic field is relatively large. If the maximum available magnetic field B is less than 0.83 T, the electric field strength E would have to be reduced to maintain the desired ratio E/B in Eq. (27.15).

Example 27.6   Finding leaks in a vacuum system

There is almost no helium in ordinary air, so helium sprayed near a leak in a vacuum system will quickly show up in the output of a vacuum pump connected to such a system. You are designing a leak detector that uses a mass spectrometer to detect He^+ ions (charge $+e = +1.60 \times 10^{-19}$ C, mass 6.65×10^{-27} kg). The ions emerge from the velocity selector with a speed of 1.00×10^5 m/s. They are curved in a semicircular path by a magnetic field B' and are detected at a distance of 10.16 cm from the slit S_3 in Fig. 27.24. Calculate the magnitude of the magnetic field B'.

SOLUTION

IDENTIFY: The motion of the ion after it passes through slit S_3 in Fig. 27.24 is just motion in a circular path as described in Section 27.4 (see Fig. 27.17).

SET UP: We use Eq. (27.11) to relate the magnetic field strength B' (the target variable) to the radius of curvature of the path and to the mass, charge, and speed of the ion.

EXECUTE: The distance given is the *diameter* of the semicircular path shown in Fig. 27.24, so the radius is $R = \frac{1}{2}(10.16 \times 10^{-2}\ \text{m}) = 5.08 \times 10^{-2}$ m. From Eq. (27.11), $R = mv/qB'$, we get

$$B' = \frac{mv}{qR} = \frac{(6.65 \times 10^{-27}\ \text{kg})(1.00 \times 10^5\ \text{m/s})}{(1.60 \times 10^{-19}\ \text{C})(5.08 \times 10^{-2}\ \text{m})}$$

$$= 0.0817\ \text{T}$$

EVALUATE: Helium leak detectors are actual devices that are widely used for diagnosing problems with high-vacuum systems. Our result shows that only a small magnetic field is required, which makes it possible to build relatively compact leak detectors.

Test Your Understanding of Section 27.5 In Example 27.6 He$^+$ ions with charge $+e$ move at 1.00×10^5 m/s in a straight line through a velocity selector. Suppose the He$^+$ ions were replaced with He^{2+} ions, in which both electrons have been removed from the helium atom and the ion charge is $+2e$. At what speed must the He^{2+} ions travel through the same velocity selector in order to move in a straight line? (i) about 4.00×10^5 m/s; (ii) about 2.00×10^5 m/s; (iii) 1.00×10^5 m/s; (iv) about 0.50×10^5 m/s; (v) about 0.25×10^5 m/s.

27.6 Magnetic Force on a Current-Carrying Conductor

27.25 Forces on a moving positive charge in a current-carrying conductor.

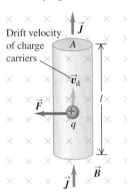

What makes an electric motor work? The forces that make it turn are forces that a magnetic field exerts on a conductor carrying a current. The magnetic forces on the moving charges within the conductor are transmitted to the material of the conductor, and the conductor as a whole experiences a force distributed along its length. The moving-coil galvanometer that we described in Section 26.3 also uses magnetic forces on conductors.

We can compute the force on a current-carrying conductor starting with the magnetic force $\vec{F} = q\vec{v} \times \vec{B}$ on a single moving charge. Figure 27.25 shows a straight segment of a conducting wire, with length l and cross-sectional area A; the current is from bottom to top. The wire is in a uniform magnetic field $\vec{B}$, perpendicular to the plane of the diagram and directed *into* the plane. Let's assume first that the moving charges are positive. Later we'll see what happens when they are negative.

The drift velocity $\vec{v}_d$ is upward, perpendicular to $\vec{B}$. The average force on each charge is $\vec{F} = q\vec{v}_d \times \vec{B}$, directed to the left as shown in the figure; since $\vec{v}_d$ and $\vec{B}$ are perpendicular, the magnitude of the force is $F = qv_dB$.

We can derive an expression for the *total* force on all the moving charges in a length l of conductor with cross-sectional area A using the same language we used in Eqs. (25.2) and (25.3) of Section 25.1. The number of charges per unit volume is n; a segment of conductor with length l has volume Al and contains a number of charges equal to nAl. The total force $\vec{F}$ on *all* the moving charges in this segment has magnitude

$$F = (nAl)(qv_dB) = (nqv_dA)(lB) \qquad (27.16)$$

From Eq. (25.3) the current density is $J = nqv_d$. The product JA is the total current I, so we can rewrite Eq. (27.16) as

$$F = IlB \qquad (27.17)$$

If the $\vec{B}$ field is not perpendicular to the wire but makes an angle ϕ with it, we handle the situation the same way we did in Section 27.2 for a single charge. Only the component of $\vec{B}$ perpendicular to the wire (and to the drift velocities of the charges) exerts a force; this component is $B_{\perp} = B\sin\phi$. The magnetic force on the wire segment is then

$$F = IlB_{\perp} = IlB\sin\phi \qquad (27.18)$$

27.26 A straight wire segment of length $\vec{l}$ carries a current I in the direction of $\vec{l}$. The magnetic force on this segment is perpendicular to both $\vec{l}$ and the magnetic field $\vec{B}$.

Force $\vec{F}$ on a straight wire carrying a positive current and oriented at an angle ϕ to a magnetic field $\vec{B}$:

• Magnitude is $F = IlB_{\perp} = IlB\sin\phi$.

• Direction of $\vec{F}$ is given by the right-hand rule.

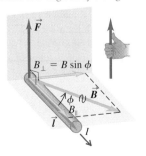

The force is always perpendicular to both the conductor and the field, with the direction determined by the same right-hand rule we used for a moving positive charge (Fig. 27.26). Hence this force can be expressed as a vector product, just like the force on a single moving charge. We represent the segment of wire with a vector $\vec{l}$ along the wire in the direction of the current; then the force $\vec{F}$ on this segment is

$$\vec{F} = I\vec{l} \times \vec{B} \qquad \text{(magnetic force on a straight wire segment)} \qquad (27.19)$$

Figure 27.27 illustrates the directions of $\vec{B}$, $\vec{l}$, and $\vec{F}$ for several cases.

   If the conductor is not straight, we can divide it into infinitesimal segments $d\vec{l}$. The force $d\vec{F}$ on each segment is

$$d\vec{F} = I\,d\vec{l} \times \vec{B} \qquad \text{(magnetic force on an infinitesimal wire section)} \qquad (27.20)$$

Then we can integrate this expression along the wire to find the total force on a conductor of any shape. The integral is a *line integral,* the same mathematical operation we have used to define work (Section 6.3) and electric potential (Section 23.2).

> **CAUTION** **Current is not a vector** Recall from Section 25.1 that the current I is not a vector. The direction of current flow is described by $d\vec{l}$, not I. If the conductor is curved, the current I is the same at all points along its length, but $d\vec{l}$ changes direction so that it is always tangent to the conductor. ∎

   Finally, what happens when the moving charges are negative, such as electrons in a metal? Then in Fig. 27.25 an upward current corresponds to a downward drift velocity. But because q is now negative, the direction of the force $\vec{F}$ is the same as before. Thus Eqs. (27.17) through (27.20) are valid for *both* positive and negative charges and even when *both* signs of charge are present at once. This happens in some semiconductor materials and in ionic solutions.

   A common application of the magnetic forces on a current-carrying wire is found in loudspeakers (Fig. 27.28). The radial magnetic field created by the permanent magnet exerts a force on the voice coil that is proportional to the current in the coil; the direction of the force is either to the left or to the right, depending on the direction of the current. The signal from the amplifier causes the current to oscillate in direction and magnitude. The coil and the speaker cone to which it is attached respond by oscillating with an amplitude proportional to the amplitude of the current in the coil. Turning up the volume knob on the amplifier increases the current amplitude and hence the amplitudes of the cone's oscillation and of the sound wave produced by the moving cone.

27.27 Magnetic field $\vec{B}$, length $\vec{l}$, and force $\vec{F}$ vectors for a straight wire carrying a current I.

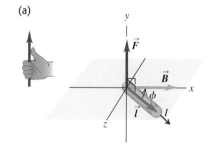
(a)

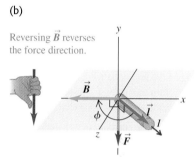
(b)

Reversing $\vec{B}$ reverses the force direction.

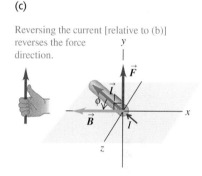
(c)

Reversing the current [relative to (b)] reverses the force direction.

27.28 (a) Components of a loudspeaker. (b) The permanent magnet creates a magnetic field that exerts forces on the current in the voice coil; for a current I in the direction shown, the force is to the right. If the electric current in the voice coil oscillates, the speaker cone attached to the voice coil oscillates at the same frequency.

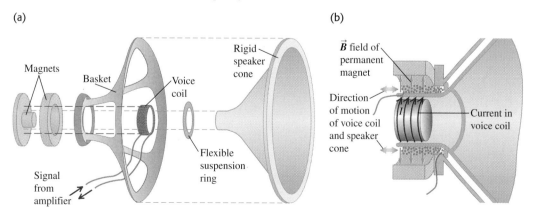
(a)

Magnets
Basket
Voice coil
Rigid speaker cone
Flexible suspension ring
Signal from amplifier

(b)

$\vec{B}$ field of permanent magnet
Direction of motion of voice coil and speaker cone
Current in voice coil

Example 27.7 Magnetic force on a straight conductor

A straight horizontal copper rod carries a current of 50.0 A from west to east in a region between the poles of a large electromagnet. In this region there is a horizontal magnetic field toward the northeast (that is, 45° north of east) with magnitude 1.20 T. (a) Find the magnitude and direction of the force on a 1.00-m section of rod. (b) While keeping the rod horizontal, how should it be oriented to maximize the magnitude of the force? What is the force magnitude in this case?

SOLUTION

IDENTIFY: This is a straight wire segment in a uniform magnetic field, which is the same situation as shown in Fig. 27.26. Our target variables are the force $\vec{F}$ on the rod segment and the angle ϕ for which the force magnitude is greatest.

SET UP: Figure 27.29 shows the situation. We can find the magnitude of the magnetic force using Eq. (27.18) and the direction from the right-hand rule. Alternatively, we can find the force vector (magnitude and direction) using Eq. (27.19).

EXECUTE: (a) The angle ϕ between the directions of current and field is 45°. From Eq. (27.18) we obtain

$$F = IlB\sin\phi = (50.0\text{ A})(1.00\text{ m})(1.20\text{ T})(\sin 45°) = 42.4\text{ N}$$

27.29 Our sketch of the copper rod as seen from overhead.

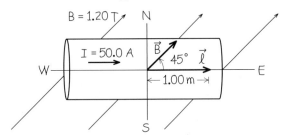

The *direction* of the force is perpendicular to the plane of the current and the field, both of which lie in the horizontal plane. Thus the force must be vertical; the right-hand rule shows that it is vertically *upward* (out of the plane of the figure).

Alternatively, we can use a coordinate system with the *x*-axis pointing east, the *y*-axis north, and the *z*-axis up. Then we have

$$\vec{l} = (1.00\text{ m})\hat{i} \qquad \vec{B} = (1.20\text{ T})[(\cos 45°)\hat{i} + (\sin 45°)\hat{j}]$$

$$\vec{F} = I\vec{l} \times \vec{B}$$

$$= (50\text{ A})(1.00\text{ m})\hat{i} \times (1.20\text{ T})[(\cos 45°)\hat{i} + (\sin 45°)\hat{j}]$$

$$= (42.4\text{ N})\hat{k}$$

If the conductor is in mechanical equilibrium under the action of its weight and the upward magnetic force, its weight is 42.4 N and its mass is

$$m = \frac{w}{g} = \frac{42.4\text{ N}}{9.8\text{ m/s}^2} = 4.33\text{ kg}$$

(b) The magnitude of the force is maximum if $\phi = 90°$ so that $\vec{l}$ and $\vec{B}$ are perpendicular. To have the force still be upward, we rotate the rod clockwise by 45° from its orientation in Fig. 27.29 so that the current runs toward the southeast. Then the magnetic force has magnitude

$$F = IlB = (50.0\text{ A})(1.00\text{ m})(1.20\text{ T}) = 60.0\text{ N}$$

and the mass of a rod that can be held up against gravity is $m = w/g = (60.0\text{ N})/(9.8\text{ m/s}^2) = 6.12\text{ kg}$.

EVALUATE: This is a simple example of magnetic levitation. Magnetic levitation is also used in special high-speed trains. Conventional electromagnetic technology is used to suspend the train over the tracks; the elimination of rolling friction allows the train to achieve speeds in excess of 400 km/h (250 mi/h).

Example 27.8 Magnetic force on a curved conductor

In Fig. 27.30 the magnetic field $\vec{B}$ is uniform and perpendicular to the plane of the figure, pointing out. The conductor has a straight segment with length L perpendicular to the plane of the figure on the right, with the current opposite to $\vec{B}$; followed by a semicircle with radius R; and finally another straight segment with length L

27.30 What is the total magnetic force on the conductor?

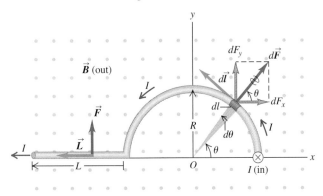

parallel to the *x*-axis, as shown. The conductor carries a current I. Find the total magnetic force on these three segments of wire.

SOLUTION

IDENTIFY: Two of the three segments of wire are straight and the magnetic field is uniform, so we can find the force on these using the ideas of this section. We can analyze the curved segment by first dividing it into a large number of infinitesimal straight segments. We find the force on one such segment and then integrate to find the force on the curved segment as a whole.

SET UP: We find the force on the straight segments using Eq. (27.19) and the force on an infinitesimal part of the curved segment using Eq. (27.20). The total magnetic force on all three segments is the vector sum of the forces on each individual segment.

EXECUTE: Let's do the easy parts (the straight segments) first. There is *no* force on the segment on the right perpendicular to the plane of the figure because it is antiparallel to $\vec{B}$; $\vec{L} \times \vec{B} = \mathbf{0}$, or $\phi = 180°$ and $\sin\phi = 0$. For the straight segment on the left, $\vec{L}$ points to the left (in the direction of the current), perpendicular to

$\vec{B}$. The force has magnitude $F = ILB$, and its direction is up (the $+y$-direction in the figure).

The fun part is the semicircle. The figure shows a segment $d\vec{l}$ with length $dl = R\,d\theta$, at angle θ. The direction of $d\vec{l} \times \vec{B}$ is radially outward from the center; make sure you can verify this direction. Because $d\vec{l}$ and $\vec{B}$ are perpendicular, the magnitude dF of the force on the segment $d\vec{l}$ is just $dF = I\,dl\,B$, so we have

$$dF = I(R\,d\theta)B$$

The components of the force $d\vec{F}$ on segment $d\vec{l}$ are

$$dF_x = IR\,d\theta\,B\cos\theta \qquad dF_y = IR\,d\theta\,B\sin\theta$$

To find the components of the total force, we integrate these expressions, letting θ vary from 0 to π to take in the whole semicircle. We find

$$F_x = IRB\int_0^\pi \cos\theta\,d\theta = 0$$

$$F_y = IRB\int_0^\pi \sin\theta\,d\theta = 2IRB$$

Finally, adding the forces on the straight and semicircular segments, we find the total force:

$$F_x = 0 \qquad F_y = IB(L + 2R)$$

or

$$\vec{F} = IB(L + 2R)\hat{\jmath}$$

EVALUATE: We could have predicted from symmetry that the x-component of force on the semicircle would be zero. On the right half of the semicircle the x-component of the force is positive (to the right) and on the left half it is negative (to the left); the positive and negative contributions to the integral cancel.

Note that the net force on all three segments together is the same force that would be exerted if we replaced the semicircle with a straight segment along the x-axis. Do you see why?

Test Your Understanding of Section 27.6   The figure at right shows a top view of two conducting rails on which a conducting bar can slide. A uniform magnetic field is directed perpendicular to the plane of the figure as shown. A battery is to be connected to the two rails so that when the switch is closed, current will flow through the bar and cause a magnetic force to push the bar to the right. In which orientation, A or B, should the battery be placed in the circuit?

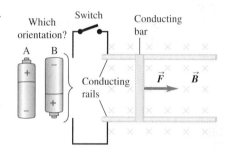

27.7 Force and Torque on a Current Loop

Current-carrying conductors usually form closed loops, so it is worthwhile to use the results of Section 27.6 to find the *total* magnetic force and torque on a conductor in the form of a loop. Many practical devices make use of the magnetic force or torque on a conducting loop, including loudspeakers (see Fig. 27.28) and galvanometers (see Section 26.3). Hence the results of this section are of substantial practical importance. These results will also help us understand the behavior of bar magnets described in Section 27.1.

As an example, let's look at a rectangular current loop in a uniform magnetic field. We can represent the loop as a series of straight line segments. We will find that the total *force* on the loop is zero but that there can be a net *torque* acting on the loop, with some interesting properties.

Figure 27.31a shows a rectangular loop of wire with side lengths a and b. A line perpendicular to the plane of the loop (i.e., a *normal* to the plane) makes an angle ϕ with the direction of the magnetic field $\vec{B}$, and the loop carries a current I. The wires leading the current into and out of the loop and the source of emf are omitted to keep the diagram simple.

The force $\vec{F}$ on the right side of the loop (length a) is to the right, in the $+x$-direction as shown. On this side, $\vec{B}$ is perpendicular to the current direction, and the force on this side has magnitude

$$F = IaB \tag{27.21}$$

A force $-\vec{F}$ with the same magnitude but opposite direction acts on the opposite side of the loop, as shown in the figure.

The sides with length b make an angle $(90° - \phi)$ with the direction of $\vec{B}$. The forces on these sides are the vectors $\vec{F}'$ and $-\vec{F}'$; their magnitude F' is given by

$$F' = IbB\sin(90° - \phi) = IbB\cos\phi$$

The lines of action of both forces lie along the y-axis.

13.6   Magnetic Torque on a Loop

27.31 Finding the torque on a current-carrying loop in a uniform magnetic field.

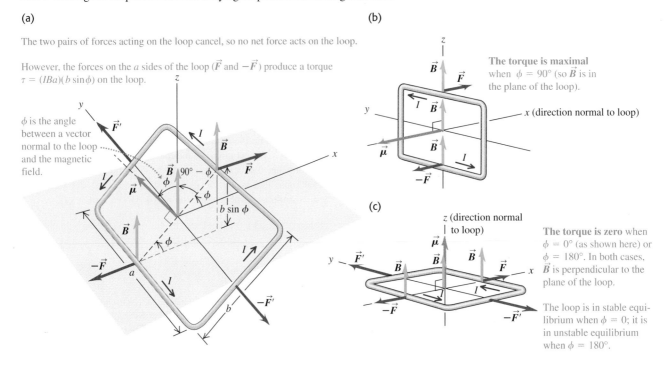

(a)

The two pairs of forces acting on the loop cancel, so no net force acts on the loop.

However, the forces on the a sides of the loop ($\vec{F}$ and $-\vec{F}$) produce a torque $\tau = (IBa)(b\sin\phi)$ on the loop.

ϕ is the angle between a vector normal to the loop and the magnetic field.

(b)

The torque is maximal when $\phi = 90°$ (so $\vec{B}$ is in the plane of the loop).

x (direction normal to loop)

(c)

z (direction normal to loop)

The torque is zero when $\phi = 0°$ (as shown here) or $\phi = 180°$. In both cases, $\vec{B}$ is perpendicular to the plane of the loop.

The loop is in stable equilibrium when $\phi = 0$; it is in unstable equilibrium when $\phi = 180°$.

The *total* force on the loop is zero because the forces on opposite sides cancel out in pairs.

The net force on a current loop in a uniform magnetic field is zero. However, the net torque is not in general equal to zero.

(You may find it helpful at this point to review the discussion of torque in Section 10.1.) The two forces $\vec{F}'$ and $-\vec{F}'$ in Fig. 27.31a lie along the same line and so give rise to zero net torque with respect to any point. The two forces $\vec{F}$ and $-\vec{F}$ lie along different lines, and each gives rise to a torque about the y-axis. According to the right-hand rule for determining the direction of torques, the vector torques due to $\vec{F}$ and $-\vec{F}$ are both in the $+y$-direction; hence the net vector torque $\vec{\tau}$ is in the $+y$-direction as well. The moment arm for each of these forces (equal to the perpendicular distance from the rotation axis to the line of action of the force) is $(b/2)\sin\phi$, so the torque due to each force has magnitude $F(b/2)\sin\phi$. If we use Eq. (27.21) for F, the magnitude of the net torque is

$$\tau = 2F(b/2)\sin\phi = (IBa)(b\sin\phi) \qquad (27.22)$$

The torque is greatest when $\phi = 90°$, $\vec{B}$ is in the plane of the loop, and the normal to this plane is perpendicular to $\vec{B}$ (Fig. 27.31b). The torque is zero when ϕ is $0°$ or $180°$ and the normal to the loop is parallel or antiparallel to the field (Fig. 27.31c). The value $\phi = 0°$ is a stable equilibrium position because the torque is zero there, and when the loop is rotated slightly from this position, the resulting torque tends to rotate it back toward $\phi = 0°$. The position $\phi = 180°$ is an *unstable* equilibrium position; if displaced slightly from this position, the loop tends to move farther away from $\phi = 180°$. Figure 27.31 shows rotation about the y-axis, but because the net force on the loop is zero, Eq. (27.22) for the torque is valid for *any* choice of axis.

The area A of the loop is equal to ab, so we can rewrite Eq. (27.22) as

$$\tau = IBA\sin\phi \qquad \text{(magnitude of torque on a current loop)} \qquad (27.23)$$

The product IA is called the **magnetic dipole moment** or **magnetic moment** of the loop, for which we use the symbol μ (the Greek letter mu):

$$\mu = IA \qquad (27.24)$$

It is analogous to the electric dipole moment introduced in Section 21.7. In terms of μ, the magnitude of the torque on a current loop is

$$\tau = \mu B \sin\phi \qquad (27.25)$$

where ϕ is the angle between the normal to the loop (the direction of the vector area $\vec{A}$) and $\vec{B}$. The torque tends to rotate the loop in the direction of *decreasing* ϕ—that is, toward its stable equilibrium position in which the loop lies in the xy-plane perpendicular to the direction of the field $\vec{B}$ (Fig. 27.31c). A current loop, or any other body that experiences a magnetic torque given by Eq. (27.25), is also called a **magnetic dipole.**

Magnetic Torque: Vector Form

We can also define a vector magnetic moment $\vec{\mu}$ with magnitude IA: this is shown in Fig. 27.31. The direction of $\vec{\mu}$ is defined to be perpendicular to the plane of the loop, with a sense determined by a right-hand rule, as shown in Fig. 27.32. Wrap the fingers of your right hand around the perimeter of the loop in the direction of the current. Then extend your thumb so that it is perpendicular to the plane of the loop; its direction is the direction $\vec{\mu}$ (and of the vector area $\vec{A}$ of the loop). The torque is greatest when $\vec{\mu}$ and $\vec{B}$ are perpendicular and is zero when they are parallel or antiparallel. In the stable equilibrium position, $\vec{\mu}$ and $\vec{B}$ are parallel.

Finally, we can express this interaction in terms of the torque vector $\vec{\tau}$, which we used for *electric*-dipole interactions in Section 21.7. From Eq. (27.25) the magnitude of $\vec{\tau}$ is equal to the magnitude of $\vec{\mu} \times \vec{B}$, and reference to Fig. 27.31 shows that the directions are also the same. So we have

$$\vec{\tau} = \vec{\mu} \times \vec{B} \qquad \text{(vector torque on a current loop)} \qquad (27.26)$$

This result is directly analogous to the result we found in Section 21.7 for the torque exerted by an *electric* field $\vec{E}$ on an *electric* dipole with dipole moment $\vec{p} \cdot \vec{\tau} = \vec{p} \times \vec{E}$.

Potential Energy for a Magnetic Dipole

When a magnetic dipole changes orientation in a magnetic field, the field does work on it. In an infinitesimal angular displacement $d\phi$ the work dW is given by $\tau d\phi$, and there is a corresponding change in potential energy. As the above discussion suggests, the potential energy is least when $\vec{\mu}$ and $\vec{B}$ are parallel and greatest when they are antiparallel. To find an expression for the potential energy U as a function of orientation, we can make use of the beautiful symmetry between the electric and magnetic dipole interactions. The torque on an *electric* dipole in an *electric* field is $\vec{\tau} = \vec{p} \times \vec{E}$; we found in Section 21.7 that the corresponding potential energy is $U = -\vec{p} \cdot \vec{E}$. The torque on a *magnetic* dipole in a *magnetic* field is $\vec{\tau} = \vec{\mu} \times \vec{B}$, so we can conclude immediately that the corresponding potential energy is

$$U = -\vec{\mu} \cdot \vec{B} = -\mu B \cos\phi \qquad \text{(potential energy for a magnetic dipole)} \qquad (27.27)$$

With this definition, U is zero when the magnetic dipole moment is perpendicular to the magnetic field.

Magnetic Torque: Loops and Coils

Although we have derived Eqs. (27.21) through (27.27) for a rectangular current loop, all these relationships are valid for a plane loop of any shape at all. Any planar loop may be approximated as closely as we wish by a very large number of

27.32 The right-hand rule determines the direction of the magnetic moment of a current-carrying loop. This is also the direction of the loop's area vector $\vec{A}$; $\vec{\mu} = I\vec{A}$ is a vector equation.

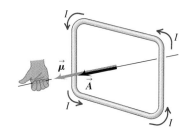

27.33 The collection of rectangles exactly matches the irregular plane loop in the limit as the number of rectangles approaches infinity and the width of each rectangle approaches zero.

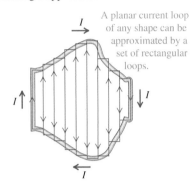

A planar current loop of any shape can be approximated by a set of rectangular loops.

27.34 The torque $\vec{\tau} = \vec{\mu} \times \vec{B}$ on this solenoid in a uniform magnetic field is directed straight into the page. An actual solenoid has many more turns, wrapped closely together.

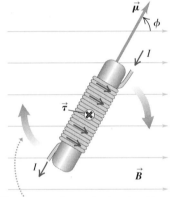

ϕ

$\vec{\mu}$

I

$\vec{\tau}$

I

$\vec{B}$

The torque tends to make the solenoid rotate clockwise in the plane of the page, aligning magnetic moment $\vec{\mu}$ with field $\vec{B}$.

rectangular loops, as shown in Fig. 27.33. If these loops all carry equal currents in the same clockwise sense, then the forces and torques on the sides of two loops adjacent to each other cancel, and the only forces and torques that do not cancel are due to currents around the boundary. Thus all the above relationships are valid for a plane current loop of any shape, with the magnetic moment $\vec{\mu}$ given by $\vec{\mu} = I\vec{A}$.

We can also generalize this whole formulation to a coil consisting of N planar loops close together; the effect is simply to multiply each force, the magnetic moment, the torque, and the potential energy by a factor of N.

An arrangement of particular interest is the **solenoid**, a helical winding of wire, such as a coil wound on a circular cylinder (Fig. 27.34). If the windings are closely spaced, the solenoid can be approximated by a number of circular loops lying in planes at right angles to its long axis. The total torque on a solenoid in a magnetic field is simply the sum of the torques on the individual turns. For a solenoid with N turns in a uniform field B, the magnetic moment is $\mu = NIA$ and

$$\tau = NIAB\sin\phi \qquad (27.28)$$

where ϕ is the angle between the axis of the solenoid and the direction of the field. The magnetic moment vector $\vec{\mu}$ is along the solenoid axis. The torque is greatest when the solenoid axis is perpendicular to the magnetic field and zero when they are parallel. The effect of this torque is to tend to rotate the solenoid into a position where its axis is parallel to the field. Solenoids are also useful as *sources* of magnetic field, as we'll discuss in Chapter 28.

The d'Arsonval galvanometer, described in Section 26.3, makes use of a magnetic torque on a coil carrying a current. As Fig. 26.14 shows, the magnetic field is not uniform but is *radial,* so the side thrusts on the coil are always perpendicular to its plane. Thus the angle ϕ in Eq. (27.28) is always 90°, and the magnetic torque is directly proportional to the current, no matter what the orientation of the coil. A restoring torque proportional to the angular displacement of the coil is provided by two hairsprings, which also serve as current leads to the coil. When current is supplied to the coil, it rotates along with its attached pointer until the restoring spring torque just balances the magnetic torque. Thus the pointer deflection is proportional to the current.

An important medical application of the torque on a magnetic dipole is **?** *magnetic resonance imaging* (MRI). A patient is placed in a magnetic field **!** of about 1.5 T, more than 10^4 times stronger than the earth's field. The nucleus of each hydrogen atom in the tissue to be imaged has a magnetic dipole moment, which experiences a torque that aligns it with the applied field. The tissue is then illuminated with radio waves of just the right frequency to flip these magnetic moments out of alignment. The extent to which these radio waves are absorbed in the tissue is proportional to the amount of hydrogen present. Hence hydrogen-rich soft tissue looks quite different from hydrogen-deficient bone, which makes MRI ideal for analyzing details in soft tissue that cannot be seen in x-ray images (see the image that opens this chapter).

Example 27.9 **Magnetic torque on a circular coil**

A circular coil 0.0500 m in radius, with 30 turns of wire, lies in a horizontal plane. It carries a current of 5.00 A in a counterclockwise sense when viewed from above. The coil is in a uniform magnetic field directed toward the right, with magnitude 1.20 T. Find the magnitudes of the magnetic moment and the torque on the coil.

SOLUTION

IDENTIFY: This problem uses the definition of magnetic moment and the expression for the torque on a magnetic dipole in a magnetic field.

SET UP: Figure 27.35 shows the situation. The magnitude μ of the magnetic moment of a single turn of wire is given in terms of the

27.35 Our sketch for this problem.

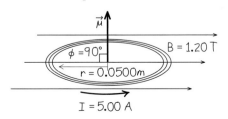

$\vec{\mu}$

$\phi = 90°$

$B = 1.20$ T

$r = 0.0500$ m

$I = 5.00$ A

current and coil area by Eq. (27.24). For N turns, the magnetic moment is N times greater. The magnitude τ of the torque is found using Eq. (27.25).

EXECUTE: The area of the coil is

$$A = \pi r^2 = \pi (0.0500 \text{ m})^2 = 7.85 \times 10^{-3} \text{ m}^2$$

The magnetic moment of each turn of the coil is

$$\mu = IA = (5.00 \text{ A})(7.85 \times 10^{-3} \text{ m}^2) = 3.93 \times 10^{-2} \text{ A} \cdot \text{m}^2$$

and the total magnetic moment of all 30 turns is

$$\mu_{\text{total}} = (30)(3.93 \times 10^{-2} \text{ A} \cdot \text{m}^2) = 1.18 \text{ A} \cdot \text{m}^2$$

The angle ϕ between the direction of $\vec{B}$ and the direction of $\vec{\mu}$ (which is along the normal to the plane of the coil) is 90°. From Eq. (27.25),

$$\tau = \mu_{\text{total}}B \sin \phi = (1.18 \text{ A} \cdot \text{m}^2)(1.20 \text{ T})(\sin 90°)$$
$$= 1.41 \text{ N} \cdot \text{m}$$

Alternatively, from Eq. (27.23), the torque on each turn of the coil is

$$\tau = IBA \sin \phi = (5.00 \text{ A})(1.20 \text{ T})(7.85 \times 10^{-3} \text{ m}^2)(\sin 90°)$$
$$= 0.0471 \text{ N} \cdot \text{m}$$

and the total torque on the coil is

$$\tau = (30)(0.0471 \text{ N} \cdot \text{m}) = 1.41 \text{ N} \cdot \text{m}$$

EVALUATE: The torque tends to rotate the right side of the coil down and the left side up, into a position where the normal to its plane is parallel to $\vec{B}$.

Example 27.10 Potential energy for a coil in a magnetic field

If the coil in Example 27.9 rotates from its initial position to a position where its magnetic moment is parallel to $\vec{B}$, what is the change in potential energy?

SOLUTION

IDENTIFY: The initial position is as shown in Fig. 27.35. In the final position, the coil is rotated 90° clockwise so that $\vec{\mu}$ and $\vec{B}$ are parallel ($\phi = 0$).

SET UP: We calculate the potential energy for each orientation using Eq. (27.27). We then take the difference between the final and initial values to find the change in potential energy.

EXECUTE: From Eq. (27.27), the initial potential energy U_1 is

$$U_1 = -\mu_{\text{total}}B \cos \phi_1 = -(1.18 \text{ A} \cdot \text{m}^2)(1.20 \text{ T})(\cos 90°) = 0$$

and the final potential energy U_2 is

$$U_2 = -\mu_{\text{total}}B \cos \phi_2 = -(1.18 \text{ A} \cdot \text{m}^2)(1.20 \text{ T})(\cos 0°)$$
$$= -1.41 \text{ J}$$

The change in potential energy is $\Delta U = U_2 - U_1 = -1.41 \text{ J}$.

EVALUATE: The potential energy decreases because the rotation is in the direction of the magnetic torque.

Magnetic Dipole in a Nonuniform Magnetic Field

We have seen that a current loop (that is, a magnetic dipole) experiences zero net force in a uniform magnetic field. Figure 27.36 shows two current loops in the *nonuniform* $\vec{B}$ field of a bar magnet; in both cases the net force on the loop is *not* zero. In Fig. 27.36a the magnetic moment $\vec{\mu}$ is in the direction opposite to the field, and the force $d\vec{F} = I \, d\vec{l} \times \vec{B}$ on a segment of the loop has both a radial component and a component to the right. When these forces are summed to find the net force $\vec{F}$ on the loop, the radial components cancel so that the net force is to the right, away from the magnet. Note that in this case the force is toward the region where the field lines are farther apart and the field magnitude B is less. The polarity of the bar magnet is reversed in Fig. 27.36b, so $\vec{\mu}$ and $\vec{B}$ are parallel; now the net force on the loop is to the left, toward the region of greater field magnitude near the magnet. Later in this section we'll use these observations to explain why bar magnets can pick up unmagnetized iron objects.

Magnetic Dipoles and How Magnets Work

The behavior of a solenoid in a magnetic field (see Fig. 27.34) resembles that of a bar magnet or compass needle; if free to turn, both the solenoid and the magnet orient themselves with their axes parallel to the $\vec{B}$ field. In both cases this is due to the interaction of moving electric charges with a magnetic field; the difference is that in a bar magnet the motion of charge occurs on the microscopic scale of the atom.

Think of an electron as being like a spinning ball of charge. In this analogy the circulation of charge around the spin axis is like a current loop, and so the electron has a net magnetic moment. (This analogy, while helpful, is inexact; an electron

27.36 Forces on current loops in a nonuniform $\vec{B}$ field. In each case the axis of the bar magnet is perpendicular to the plane of the loop and passes through the center of the loop.

(a) Net force on this coil is away from north pole of magnet.

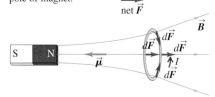

(b) Net force on same coil is toward south pole of magnet.

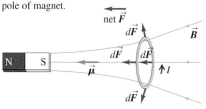

27.37 (a) An unmagnetized piece of iron. (Only a few representative atomic moments are shown.) (b) A magnetized piece of iron (bar magnet). The net magnetic moment of the bar magnet points from its south pole to its north pole. (c) A bar magnet in a magnetic field.

(a) Unmagnetized iron: magnetic moments are oriented randomly.

$\vec{\mu}_{atom}$

(b) In a bar magnet, the magnetic moments are aligned.

$\vec{\mu}$ N

S

(c) A magnetic field creates a torque on the bar magnet that tends to align its dipole moment with the $\vec{B}$ field.

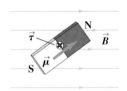

$\vec{\tau}$ N
$\vec{B}$
S $\vec{\mu}$

27.38 A bar magnet attracts an unmagnetized iron nail in two steps. First, the $\vec{B}$ field of the bar magnet gives rise to a net magnetic moment in the nail. Second, because the field of the bar magnet is not uniform, this magnetic dipole is attracted toward the magnet. The attraction is the same whether the nail is closer to (a) the magnet's north pole or (b) the magnet's south pole.

(a)

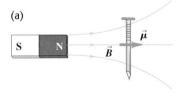

S N
$\vec{\mu}$
$\vec{B}$

(b)

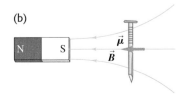

N S
$\vec{\mu}$
$\vec{B}$

isn't really a spinning sphere. A full explanation of the origin of an electron's magnetic moment involves quantum mechanics, which is beyond our scope here.) In an iron atom a substantial fraction of the electron magnetic moments align with each other, and the atom has a nonzero magnetic moment. (By contrast, the atoms of most elements have little or no net magnetic moment.) In an unmagnetized piece of iron there is no overall alignment of the magnetic moments of the atoms; their vector sum is zero, and the net magnetic moment is zero (Fig. 27.37a). But in an iron bar magnet the magnetic moments of many of the atoms are parallel, and there is a substantial net magnetic moment $\vec{\mu}$ (Fig. 27.37b). If the magnet is placed in a magnetic field $\vec{B}$, the field exerts a torque given by Eq. (27.26) that tends to align $\vec{\mu}$ with $\vec{B}$ (Fig. 27.37c). A bar magnet tends to align with a $\vec{B}$ field so that a line from the south pole to the north pole of the magnet is in the direction of $\vec{B}$; hence the real significance of a magnet's north and south poles is that they represent the head and tail, respectively, of the magnet's dipole moment $\vec{\mu}$.

The torque experienced by a current loop in a magnetic field also explains how an unmagnetized iron object like that in Fig. 27.37a becomes magnetized. If an unmagnetized iron paper clip is placed next to a powerful magnet, the magnetic moments of the paper clip's atoms tend to align with the $\vec{B}$ field of the magnet. When the paper clip is removed, its atomic dipoles tend to remain aligned, and the paper clip has a net magnetic moment. The paper clip can be demagnetized by being dropped on the floor or heated; the added internal energy jostles and re-randomizes the atomic dipoles.

The magnetic-dipole picture of a bar magnet explains the attractive and repulsive forces between bar magnets shown in Fig. 27.1. The magnetic moment $\vec{\mu}$ of a bar magnet points from its south pole to its north pole, so the current loops in Figs. 27.36a and 27.36b are both equivalent to a magnet with its north pole on the left. Hence the situation in Fig. 27.36a is equivalent to two bar magnets with their north poles next to each other; the resultant force is repulsive, just as in Fig. 27.1b. In Fig. 27.36b we again have the equivalent of two bar magnets end to end, but with the south pole of the left-hand magnet next to the north pole of the right-hand magnet. The resultant force is attractive, as in Fig. 27.1a.

Finally, we can explain how a magnet can attract an unmagnetized iron object (see Fig. 27.2). It's a two-step process. First, the atomic magnetic moments of the iron tend to align with the $\vec{B}$ field of the magnet, so the iron acquires a net magnetic dipole moment $\vec{\mu}$ parallel to the field. Second, the nonuniform field of the magnet attracts the magnetic dipole. Figure 27.38a shows an example. The north pole of the magnet is closer to the nail (which contains iron), and the magnetic dipole produced in the nail is equivalent to a loop with a current that circulates in a direction opposite to that shown in Fig. 27.36a. Hence the net magnetic force on the nail is opposite to the force on the loop in Fig. 27.36a, and the nail is attracted toward the magnet. Changing the polarity of the magnet, as in Fig. 27.38b, reverses the directions of both $\vec{B}$ and $\vec{\mu}$. The situation is now equivalent to that shown in Fig. 27.36b; like the loop in that figure, the nail is attracted toward the magnet. Hence a previously unmagnetized object containing iron is attracted to *either* pole of a magnet. By contrast, objects made of brass, aluminum, or wood hardly respond at all to a magnet; the atomic magnetic dipoles of these materials, if present at all, have less tendency to align with an external field.

Our discussion of how magnets and pieces of iron interact has just scratched the surface of a diverse subject known as *magnetic properties of materials*. We'll discuss these properties in more depth in Section 28.8.

Test Your Understanding of Section 27.7 Figure 27.13c depicts the magnetic field lines due to a circular current-carrying loop. (a) What is the direction of the magnetic moment of this loop? (b) Which side of the loop is equivalent to the north pole of a magnet, and which side is equivalent to the south pole?

*27.8 The Direct-Current Motor

Electric motors play an important role in contemporary society. In a motor a magnetic torque acts on a current-carrying conductor, and electric energy is converted to mechanical energy. As an example, let's look at a simple type of direct-current (dc) motor, shown in Fig. 27.39.

The moving part of the motor is the *rotor,* a length of wire formed into an open-ended loop and free to rotate about an axis. The ends of the rotor wires are attached to circular conducting segments that form a *commutator.* In Fig. 27.39a, each of the two commutator segments makes contact with one of the terminals, or *brushes,* of an external circuit that includes a source of emf. This causes a current to flow into the rotor on one side, shown in red, and out of the rotor on the other side, shown in blue. Hence the rotor is a current loop with a magnetic moment $\vec{\mu}$. The rotor lies between opposing poles of a permanent magnet, so there is a magnetic field $\vec{B}$ that exerts a torque $\vec{\tau} = \vec{\mu} \times \vec{B}$ on the rotor. For the rotor orientation shown in Fig. 27.39a the torque causes the rotor to turn counterclockwise, in the direction that will align $\vec{\mu}$ with $\vec{B}$.

In Fig. 27.39b the rotor has rotated by 90° from its orientation in Fig. 27.39a. If the current through the rotor were constant, the rotor would now be in its equilibrium orientation; it would simply oscillate around this orientation. But here's where the commutator comes into play; each brush is now in contact with *both* segments of the commutator. There is no potential difference between the commutators, so at this instant no current flows through the rotor, and the magnetic moment is zero. The rotor continues to rotate counterclockwise because of its inertia, and current again flows through the rotor as in Fig. 27.39c. But now current enters on the *blue* side of the rotor and exits on the *red* side, just the opposite of the situation in Fig. 27.39a. While the direction of the current has reversed with respect to the rotor, the rotor itself has rotated 180° and the magnetic moment $\vec{\mu}$ is in the same direction with respect to the magnetic field. Hence the magnetic torque $\vec{\tau}$ is in the same direction in Fig. 27.39c as in Fig. 27.39a. Thanks to the commutator, the current reverses after every 180° of rotation, so the torque is always in the direction to rotate the rotor counterclockwise. When the motor has come "up to speed," the average magnetic torque is just balanced by an opposing torque due to air resistance, friction in the rotor bearings, and friction between the commutator and brushes.

The simple motor shown in Fig. 27.39 has only a single turn of wire in its rotor. In practical motors, the rotor has many turns; this increases the magnetic

27.39 Schematic diagram of a simple dc motor. The rotor is a wire loop that is free to rotate about an axis; the rotor ends are attached to the two curved conductors that form the commutator. (The rotor halves are colored red and blue for clarity.) The commutator segments are insulated from one another.

(a) Brushes are aligned with commutator segments.

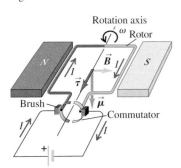

(b) Rotor has turned 90°.

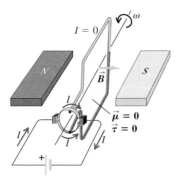

(c) Rotor has turned 180°.

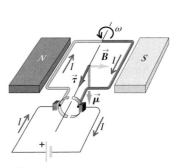

- Current flows into the red side of the rotor and out of the blue side.
- Therefore the magnetic torque causes the rotor to spin counterclockwise.

- Each brush is in contact with both commutator segments, so the current bypasses the rotor altogether.
- No magnetic torque acts on the rotor.

- The brushes are again aligned with commutator segments. This time the current flows into the blue side of the rotor and out of the red side.
- Therefore the magnetic torque again causes the rotor to spin counterclockwise.

27.40 This motor from a computer disk drive has 12 current-carrying coils. They interact with permanent magnets on the turntable (not shown) to make the turntable rotate. (This design is the reverse of the design in Fig. 27.39, in which the permanent magnets are stationary and the coil rotates.) Because there are multiple coils, the magnetic torque is very nearly constant and the turntable spins at a very constant rate.

Coils

moment and the torque so that the motor can spin larger loads. The torque can also be increased by using a stronger magnetic field, which is why many motor designs use electromagnets instead of a permanent magnet. Another drawback of the simple design in Fig. 27.39 is that the magnitude of the torque rises and falls as the rotor spins. This can be remedied by having the rotor include several independent coils of wire oriented at different angles (Fig. 27.40).

Power for Electric Motors

Because a motor converts electric energy to mechanical energy or work, it requires electric energy input. If the potential difference between its terminals is V_{ab} and the current is I, then the power input is $P = V_{ab}I$. Even if the motor coils have negligible resistance, there must be a potential difference between the terminals if P is to be different from zero. This potential difference results principally from magnetic forces exerted on the currents in the conductors of the rotor as they rotate through the magnetic field. The associated electromotive force $\mathcal{E}$ is called an *induced* emf; it is also called a *back* emf because its sense is opposite to that of the current. In Chapter 29 we will study induced emfs resulting from motion of conductors in magnetic fields.

In a *series* motor the rotor is connected in series with the electromagnet that produces the magnetic field; in a *shunt* motor they are connected in parallel. In a series motor with internal resistance r, V_{ab} is greater than $\mathcal{E}$, and the difference is the potential drop Ir across the internal resistance. That is,

$$V_{ab} = \mathcal{E} + Ir \tag{27.29}$$

Because the magnetic force is proportional to velocity, $\mathcal{E}$ is *not* constant but is proportional to the speed of rotation of the rotor.

Example 27.11   A series dc motor

A dc motor with its rotor and field coils connected in series has an internal resistance of 2.00 Ω. When running at full load on a 120-V line, it draws a current of 4.00 A. (a) What is the emf in the rotor? (b) What is the power delivered to the motor? (c) What is the rate of dissipation of energy in the resistance of the motor? (d) What is the mechanical power developed? (e) What is the efficiency of the motor? (f) What happens if the machine the motor is driving jams and the rotor suddenly stops turning?

SOLUTION

IDENTIFY: This problem uses the ideas of power and potential drop in a series dc motor.

SET UP: We are given the internal resistance $r = 2.00$ Ω, the voltage $V_{ab} = 120$ V across the motor, and the current $I = 4.00$ A through the motor. We use Eq. (27.29) to determine the emf $\mathcal{E}$ from these quantities. The power delivered to the motor is $V_{ab}I$, the rate of energy dissipation is I^2r, and the power output by the motor is the difference between the power input and the power dissipated. The efficiency e is the ratio of mechanical power output to electric power input.

EXECUTE: (a) From Eq. (27.29), $V_{ab} = \mathcal{E} + Ir$, we have

$$120 \text{ V} = \mathcal{E} + (4.0 \text{ A})(2.0 \text{ Ω}) \quad \text{and so} \quad \mathcal{E} = 112 \text{ V}$$

(b) The power delivered to the motor from the source is

$$P_{input} = V_{ab}I = (120 \text{ V})(4.0 \text{ A}) = 480 \text{ W}$$

(c) The power dissipated in the resistance r is

$$P_{dissipated} = I^2r = (4.0 \text{ A})^2(2.0 \text{ Ω}) = 32 \text{ W}$$

(d) The mechanical power output is the electric power input minus the rate of dissipation of energy in the motor's resistance (assuming that there are no other power losses):

$$P_{output} = P_{input} - P_{dissipated} = 480 \text{ W} - 32 \text{ W} = 448 \text{ W}$$

(e) The efficiency e is the ratio of mechanical power output to electric power input:

$$e = \frac{P_{output}}{P_{input}} = \frac{448 \text{ W}}{480 \text{ W}} = 0.93 = 93\%$$

(f) With the rotor stalled, the back emf $\mathcal{E}$ (which is proportional to rotor speed) goes to zero. From Eq. (27.29) the current becomes

$$I = \frac{V_{ab}}{r} = \frac{120 \text{ V}}{2.0 \text{ Ω}} = 60 \text{ A}$$

and the power dissipated in the resistance r becomes

$$P_{dissipated} = I^2r = (60 \text{ A})^2(2 \text{ Ω}) = 7200 \text{ W}$$

EVALUATE: If this massive overload doesn't blow a fuse or trip a circuit breaker, the coils will quickly melt. When the motor is first turned on, there's a momentary surge of current until the motor picks up speed. This surge causes greater-than-usual voltage drops $(V = IR)$ in the power lines supplying the current. Similar effects are responsible for the momentary dimming of lights in a house when an air conditioner or dishwasher motor starts.

Test Your Understanding of Section 27.8   In the circuit shown in Fig. 27.39, you
add a switch in series with the source of emf so that the current can be turned on and off.
When you close the switch and allow current to flow, will the rotor begin to turn no matter what its original orientation?

*27.9 The Hall Effect

The reality of the forces acting on the moving charges in a conductor in a magnetic field is strikingly demonstrated by the *Hall effect,* an effect analogous to the
transverse deflection of an electron beam in a magnetic field in vacuum. (The
effect was discovered by the American physicist Edwin Hall in 1879 while he
was still a graduate student.) To describe this effect, let's consider a conductor in
the form of a flat strip, as shown in Fig. 27.41. The current is in the direction of
the $+x$-axis and there is a uniform magnetic field $\vec{B}$ perpendicular to the plane
of the strip, in the $+y$-direction. The drift velocity of the moving charges (charge
magnitude $|q|$) has magnitude v_{d}. Figure 27.41a shows the case of negative
charges, such as electrons in a metal, and Fig. 27.41b shows positive charges. In
both cases the magnetic force is upward, just as the magnetic force on a conductor is the same whether the moving charges are positive or negative. In either
case a moving charge is driven toward the *upper* edge of the strip by the magnetic
force $F_z = |q|v_{\mathrm{d}}B$.

If the charge carriers are electrons, as in Fig. 27.41a, an excess negative
charge accumulates at the upper edge of the strip, leaving an excess positive
charge at its lower edge. This accumulation continues until the resulting transverse electrostatic field $\vec{E}_{\mathrm{e}}$ becomes large enough to cause a force (magnitude
$|q|E_{\mathrm{e}}$) that is equal and opposite to the magnetic force (magnitude $|q|v_{\mathrm{d}}B$).
After that, there is no longer any net transverse force to deflect the moving
charges. This electric field causes a transverse potential difference between
opposite edges of the strip, called the *Hall voltage* or the *Hall emf.* The polarity
depends on whether the moving charges are positive or negative. Experiments
show that for metals the upper edge of the strip in Fig. 27.41a *does* become negatively charged, showing that the charge carriers in a metal are indeed negative
electrons.

However, if the charge carriers are *positive,* as in Fig. 27.41b, then *positive*
charge accumulates at the upper edge, and the potential difference is *opposite* to
the situation with negative charges. Soon after the discovery of the Hall effect in
1879, it was observed that some materials, particularly some *semiconductors,*
show a Hall emf opposite to that of the metals, as if their charge carriers were
positively charged. We now know that these materials conduct by a process
known as *hole conduction.* Within such a material there are locations, called
holes, that would normally be occupied by an electron but are actually empty. A
missing negative charge is equivalent to a positive charge. When an electron
moves in one direction to fill a hole, it leaves another hole behind it. The hole
migrates in the direction opposite to that of the electron.

In terms of the coordinate axes in Fig. 27.41b, the electrostatic field $\vec{E}_{\mathrm{e}}$ for the
positive-q case is in the $-z$-direction; its z-component E_z is negative. The magnetic field is in the $+y$-direction, and we write it as B_y. The magnetic force (in the
$+z$-direction) is $qv_{\mathrm{d}}B_y$. The current density J_x is in the $+x$-direction. In the steady
state, when the forces qE_z and $qv_{\mathrm{d}}B_y$ are equal in magnitude and opposite in
direction,

$$qE_z + qv_{\mathrm{d}}B_y = 0 \quad \text{or} \quad E_z = -v_{\mathrm{d}}B_y$$

This confirms that when q is positive, E_z is negative. The current density J_x is

$$J_x = nqv_{\mathrm{d}}$$

27.41 Forces on charge carriers in a conductor in a magnetic field.

(a) Negative charge carriers (electrons)

The charge carriers are pushed toward the top
of the strip ...

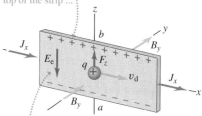

... so point a is at a higher potential than point b.

(b) Positive charge carriers

The charge carriers are again pushed toward the
top of the strip ...

... so the polarity of the potential difference is
opposite to that for negative charge carriers.

Eliminating v_d between these equations, we find

$$nq = \frac{-J_x B_y}{E_z} \qquad \text{(Hall effect)} \qquad (27.30)$$

Note that this result (as well as the entire derivation) is valid for both positive and negative q. When q is negative, E_z is positive, and conversely.

We can measure J_x, B_y, and E_z, so we can compute the product nq. In both metals and semiconductors, q is equal in magnitude to the electron charge, so the Hall effect permits a direct measurement of n, the concentration of current-carrying charges in the material. The *sign* of the charges is determined by the polarity of the Hall emf, as we have described.

The Hall effect can also be used for a direct measurement of electron drift speed v_d in metals. As we saw in Chapter 25, these speeds are very small, often of the order of 1 mm/s or less. If we move the entire conductor in the opposite direction to the current with a speed equal to the drift speed, then the electrons are at rest with respect to the magnetic field, and the Hall emf disappears. Thus the conductor speed needed to make the Hall emf vanish is equal to the drift speed.

Example 27.12 Using the Hall effect

You place a slab of copper, 2.0 mm thick and 1.50 cm wide, in a uniform magnetic field with magnitude 0.40 T, as shown in Fig. 27.41a. When you run a 75-A current in the $+x$-direction, you find by careful measurement that the potential at the bottom of the slab is 0.81 μV higher than at the top. From this measurement, determine the concentration of mobile electrons in copper.

SOLUTION

IDENTIFY: This problem describes a Hall-effect experiment.

SET UP: We use Eq. (27.30) to determine the mobile electron concentration n.

EXECUTE: First we find the current density J_x and the electric field E_z:

$$J_x = \frac{I}{A} = \frac{75\ \text{A}}{(2.0 \times 10^{-3}\ \text{m})(1.50 \times 10^{-2}\ \text{m})} = 2.5 \times 10^6\ \text{A/m}^2$$

$$E_z = \frac{V}{d} = \frac{0.81 \times 10^{-6}\ \text{V}}{1.5 \times 10^{-2}\ \text{m}} = 5.4 \times 10^{-5}\ \text{V/m}$$

Then, from Eq. (27.30),

$$n = \frac{-J_x B_y}{q E_z} = \frac{-(2.5 \times 10^6\ \text{A/m}^2)(0.40\ \text{T})}{(-1.60 \times 10^{-19}\ \text{C})(5.4 \times 10^{-5}\ \text{V/m})}$$
$$= 11.6 \times 10^{28}\ \text{m}^{-3}$$

EVALUATE: The actual value of n for copper is $8.5 \times 10^{28}\ \text{m}^{-3}$, which shows that the simple model of the Hall effect in this section, ignoring quantum effects and electron interactions with the ions, must be used with caution. This example also shows that with good conductors, the Hall emf is very small even with large current densities. Hall-effect devices for magnetic-field measurements and other purposes use semiconductor materials, for which moderate current densities give much larger Hall emfs.

Test Your Understanding of Section 27.9 A copper wire of square cross section is oriented vertically. The four sides of the wire face north, south, east, and west. There is a uniform magnetic field directed from east to west, and the wire carries current downward. Which side of the wire is at the highest electric potential? (i) north side; (ii) south side; (iii) east side; (iv) west side.

Magnetic forces: Magnetic interactions are fundamentally interactions between moving charged particles. These interactions are described by the vector magnetic field, denoted by $\vec{B}$. A particle with charge q moving with velocity $\vec{v}$ in a magnetic field $\vec{B}$ experiences a force $\vec{F}$ that is perpendicular to both $\vec{v}$ and $\vec{B}$. The SI unit of magnetic field is the tesla $(1\ \text{T} = 1\ \text{N}/\text{A} \cdot \text{m})$. (See Example 27.1.)

$$\vec{F} = q\vec{v} \times \vec{B} \tag{27.2}$$

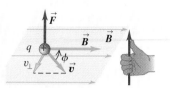

Magnetic field and flux: A magnetic field can be represented graphically by magnetic field lines. At each point a magnetic field line is tangent to the direction of $\vec{B}$ at that point. Where field lines are close together the field magnitude is large, and vice versa. Magnetic flux Φ_B through an area is defined in an analogous way to electric flux. The SI unit of magnetic flux is the weber $(1\ \text{Wb} = 1\ \text{T} \cdot \text{m}^2)$. The net magnetic flux through any closed surface is zero (Gauss's law for magnetism). As a result, magnetic field lines always close on themselves. (See Example 27.2.)

$$\Phi_B = \int B_\perp \, dA$$
$$= \int B \cos\phi \, dA \tag{27.6}$$
$$= \int \vec{B} \cdot d\vec{A}$$

$$\oint \vec{B} \cdot d\vec{A} = 0 \quad \text{(closed surface)} \tag{27.8}$$

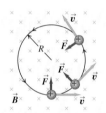

Motion in a magnetic field: The magnetic force is always perpendicular to $\vec{v}$; a particle moving under the action of a magnetic field alone moves with constant speed. In a uniform field, a particle with initial velocity perpendicular to the field moves in a circle with radius R that depends on the magnetic field strength B and the particle mass m, speed v, and charge q. (See Examples 27.3 and 27.4.)

Crossed electric and magnetic fields can be used as a velocity selector. The electric and magnetic forces exactly cancel when $v = E/B$. (See Examples 27.5 and 27.6.)

$$R = \frac{mv}{|q|B} \tag{27.11}$$

Magnetic force on a conductor: A straight segment of a conductor carrying current I in a uniform magnetic field $\vec{B}$ experiences a force $\vec{F}$ that is perpendicular to both $\vec{B}$ and the vector $\vec{l}$, which points in the direction of the current and has magnitude equal to the length of the segment. A similar relationship gives the force $d\vec{F}$ on an infinitesimal current-carrying segment $d\vec{l}$ (See Examples 27.7 and 27.8.)

$$\vec{F} = I\vec{l} \times \vec{B} \tag{27.19}$$

$$d\vec{F} = I \, d\vec{l} \times \vec{B} \tag{27.20}$$

Magnetic torque: A current loop with area A and current I in a uniform magnetic field $\vec{B}$ experiences no net magnetic force, but does experience a magnetic torque of magnitude τ. The vector torque $\vec{\tau}$ can be expressed in terms of the magnetic moment $\vec{\mu} = I\vec{A}$ of the loop, as can the potential energy U of a magnetic moment in a magnetic field $\vec{B}$. The magnetic moment of a loop depends only on the current and the area; it is independent of the shape of the loop. (See Examples 27.9 and 27.10.)

$$\tau = IBA \sin\phi \tag{27.23}$$

$$\vec{\tau} = \vec{\mu} \times \vec{B} \tag{27.26}$$

$$U = -\vec{\mu} \cdot \vec{B} = -\mu B \cos\phi \tag{27.27}$$

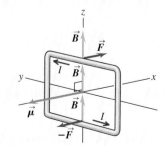

Electric motors: In a dc motor a magnetic field exerts a torque on a current in the rotor. Motion of the rotor through the magnetic field causes an induced emf called a back emf. For a series motor, in which the rotor coil is in parallel with coils that produce the magnetic field, the terminal voltage is the sum of the back emf and the drop Ir across the internal resistance. (See Example 27.11.)

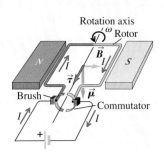

The Hall effect: The Hall effect is a potential difference perpendicular to the direction of current in a conductor, when the conductor is placed in a magnetic field. The Hall potential is determined by the requirement that the associated electric field must just balance the magnetic force on a moving charge. Hall-effect measurements can be used to determine the sign of charge carriers and their concentration n. (See Example 27.12.)

$$nq = \frac{-J_x B_y}{E_z} \qquad (27.30)$$

Key Terms

permanent magnet, *917*
magnetic monopole, *918*
magnetic field, *918*
tesla, *920*
gauss, *920*
magnetic field line, *922*

magnetic flux, *923*
weber, *924*
magnetic flux density, *925*
cyclotron frequency, *926*
mass spectrometer, *930*
isotope, *931*

magnetic dipole moment, *937*
magnetic moment, *937*
magnetic dipole, *937*
solenoid, *938*

Answer to Chapter Opening Question ?

In MRI the nuclei of hydrogen atoms within soft tissue act like miniature current loops whose magnetic moments align with an applied field. See Section 27.7 for details.

Answers to Test Your Understanding Questions

27.1 Answer: yes When a magnet is cut apart, each part has a north and south pole (see Fig. 27.4). Hence the small red part behaves much like the original, full-sized compass needle.

27.2 Answer: path 3 Applying the right-hand rule to the vectors $\vec{v}$ (which points to the right) and $\vec{B}$ (which points into the plane of the figure) says that the force $\vec{F} = q\vec{v} \times \vec{B}$ on a *positive* charge would point *upward*. Since the charge is *negative,* the force points *downward* and the particle follows a trajectory that curves downward.

27.3 Answer: (a) (ii), (b) no The magnitude of $\vec{B}$ would increase as you moved to the right, reaching a maximum as you pass through the plane of the loop. As you moved beyond the plane of the loop, the field magnitude would decrease. You can tell this from the spacing of the field lines: The closer the field lines, the stronger the field. The direction of the field would be to the right at all points along the path, since the path is along a field line and the direction of $\vec{B}$ at any point is tangent to the field line through that point.

27.4 Answers: (a) (ii), (b) (i) The radius of the orbit as given by Eq. (27.11) is directly proportional to the speed, so doubling the particle speed causes the radius to double as well. The particle has twice as far to travel to complete one orbit but is traveling at double the speed, so the time for one orbit is unchanged. This result

also follows from Eq. (27.12), which states that the angular speed ω is independent of the linear speed v. Hence the time per orbit, $T = 2\pi/\omega$, likewise does not depend on v.

27.5 Answer: (iii) From Eq. (27.13), the speed $v = E/B$ at which particles travel straight through the velocity selector does not depend on the magnitude or sign of the charge or the mass of the particle. All that is required is that the particles (in this case, ions) have a nonzero charge.

27.6 Answer: A This orientation will cause current to flow clockwise around the circuit and hence through the conducting bar in the direction from the top to the bottom of the figure. From the right-hand rule, the magnetic force $\vec{F} = I\vec{l} \times \vec{B}$ on the bar will then point to the right.

27.7 Answers: (a) to the right; (b) north pole on the right, south pole on the left If you wrap the fingers of your right hand around the coil in the direction of the current, your right thumb points to the right (perpendicular to the plane of the coil). This is the direction of the magnetic moment $\vec{\mu}$. The magnetic moment points from the south pole to the north pole, so the right side of the loop is equivalent to a north pole and the left side is equivalent to a south pole.

27.8 Answer: no The rotor will not begin to turn when the switch is closed if the rotor is initially oriented as shown in Fig. 27.39b. In this case there is no current through the rotor and hence no magnetic torque. This situation can be remedied by using multiple rotor coils oriented at different angles around the rotation axis. With this arrangement, there is always a magnetic torque no matter what the orientation.

27.9 Answer: (ii) The mobile charge carriers in copper are negatively charged electrons, which move upward through the wire to give a downward current. From the right-hand rule, the force on a positively charged particle moving upward in a westward-pointing magnetic field would be to the south; hence the force on a negatively charged particle is to the north. The result is an

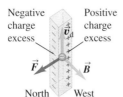

excess of negative charge on the north side of the wire, leaving an excess of positive charge—and hence a higher electric potential—on the south side.

PROBLEMS

For instructor-assigned homework, go to **www.masteringphysics.com**

Discussion Questions

Q27.1. Can a charged particle move through a magnetic field without experiencing any force? If so, how? If not, why not?

Q27.2. At any point in space, the electric field $\vec{E}$ is defined to be in the direction of the electric force on a positively charged particle at that point. Why don't we similarly define the magnetic field $\vec{B}$ to be in the direction of the magnetic force on a moving, positively charged particle?

Q27.3. Section 27.2 describes a procedure for finding the direction of the magnetic force using your right hand. If you use the same procedure, but with your left hand, will you get the correct direction for the force? Explain.

Q27.4. The magnetic force on a moving charged particle is always perpendicular to the magnetic field $\vec{B}$. Is the trajectory of a moving charged particle always perpendicular to the magnetic field lines? Explain your reasoning.

Q27.5. A charged particle is fired into a cubical region of space where there is a uniform magnetic field. Outside this region, there is no magnetic field. Is it possible that the particle will remain inside the cubical region? Why or why not?

Q27.6. If the magnetic force does no work on a charged particle, how can it have any effect on the particle's motion? Are there other examples of forces that do no work but have a significant effect on a particle's motion?

Q27.7. A charged particle moves through a region of space with constant velocity (magnitude and direction). If the external magnetic field is zero in this region, can you conclude that the external electric field in the region is also zero? Explain. (By "external" we mean fields other than those produced by the charged particle.) If the external electric field is zero in the region, can you conclude that the external magnetic field in the region is also zero?

Q27.8. How might a loop of wire carrying a current be used as a compass? Could such a compass distinguish between north and south? Why or why not?

Q27.9. How could the direction of a magnetic field be determined by making only *qualitative* observations of the magnetic force on a straight wire carrying a current?

Q27.10. A loose, floppy loop of wire is carrying current I. The loop of wire is placed on a horizontal table in a uniform magnetic field $\vec{B}$ perpendicular to the plane of the table. This causes the loop of wire to expand into a circular shape while still lying on the table. In a diagram, show all possible orientations of the current I and magnetic field $\vec{B}$ that could cause this to occur. Explain your reasoning.

Q27.11. Several charges enter a uniform magnetic field directed into the page, (a) What path would a positive charge q moving with a velocity of magnitude v follow through the field? (b) What path would a positive charge q moving with a velocity of magnitude $2v$ follow through the field? (c) What path would a negative charge $-q$ moving with a velocity of magnitude v follow through the field? (d) What path would a neutral particle follow through the field?

Q27.12. Each of the lettered points at the corners of the cube in Fig. 27.42 represents a positive charge q moving with a velocity of magnitude v in the direction indicated. The region in the figure is in a uniform magnetic field $\vec{B}$, parallel to the x-axis and directed toward the right. Which charges experience a force due to $\vec{B}$? What is the direction of the force on each charge?

Figure **27.42** Question Q27.12.

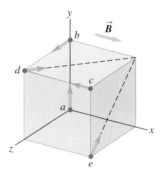

Q27.13. A student claims that if lightning strikes a metal flagpole, the force exerted by the earth's magnetic field on the current in the pole can be large enough to bend it. Typical lightning currents are of the order of 10^4 to 10^5 A. Is the student's opinion justified? Explain your reasoning.

Q27.14. Bubble Chamber I. Certain types of bubble chambers are filled with liquid hydrogen. When a particle (such as an electron or a proton) passes through the liquid, it leaves a track of bubbles, which can be photographed to show the path of the particle. The apparatus is immersed in a known magnetic field, which causes the particle to curve. Figure 27.43 is a trace of a bubble-chamber image showing the path of an electron. (a) How could you determine the *sign* of the charge of a particle from a photograph of its path? (b) How can physicists determine the *momentum* and the *speed* of this electron by using measurements made on the photograph, given that the magnetic field is known and is perpendicular to the plane of the figure? (c) The electron is obviously spiraling into smaller and smaller circles. What properties of the electron must be changing to cause this behavior? Why does this happen? (d) What would be the path of a neutron in a bubble chamber? Why?

Figure **27.43** Question Q27.14.

Q27.15. An ordinary loudspeaker such as that shown in Fig. 27.28 should not be placed next to a computer monitor or TV screen. Why not?

Q27.16. Bubble Chamber II. Figure 27.44 show the paths of several particles in a bubble chamber. (See Discussion Question Q27.14.) The two spirals near the top of the photo come from two particles that were created at the same instant due to a high-energy gamma ray. (a) What can you conclude about the *signs* of the charges of these two particles, assuming that the magnetic field is perpendicular to the plane of the photograph and pointing into the paper? (b) Which of the two particles (the right one or the left one) had more initial momentum? How do you know? (c) Why do the paths spiral inward? What causes this to happen?

Figure **27.44** Question Q27.16.

Q27.17. If an emf is produced in a dc motor, would it be possible to use the motor somehow as a generator or source, taking power out of it rather than putting power into it? How might this be done?

Q27.18. When the polarity of the voltage applied to a dc motor is reversed, the direction of motion does *not* reverse. Why not? How *could* the direction of motion be reversed?

Q27.19. In a Hall-effect experiment, is it possible that *no* transverse potential difference will be observed? Under what circumstances might this happen?

Q27.20. Hall-effect voltages are much greater for relatively poor conductors (such as germanium) than for good conductors (such as copper), for comparable currents, fields, and dimensions. Why?

Q27.21. Could an accelerator be built in which *all* the forces on the particles, for steering and for increasing speed, are magnetic forces? Why or why not?

Q27.22. The magnetic force acting on a charged particle can never do work because at every instant the force is perpendicular to the velocity. The torque exerted by a magnetic field can do work on a current loop when the loop rotates. Explain how these seemingly contradictory statements can be reconciled.

Exercises

Section 27.2 Magnetic Field

27.1. A particle with a charge of -1.24×10^{-8} C is moving with instantaneous velocity $\vec{v} = (4.19 \times 10^4 \text{ m/s})\hat{\imath} + (-3.85 \times 10^4 \text{ m/s})\hat{\jmath}$. What is the force exerted on this particle by a magnetic field (a) $\vec{B} = (1.40 \text{ T})\hat{\imath}$ and (b) $\vec{B} = (1.40 \text{ T})\hat{k}$?

27.2. A particle of mass 0.195 g carries a charge of -2.50×10^{-8} C. The particle is given an initial horizontal velocity that is due north and has magnitude 4.00×10^4 m/s. What are the magnitude and direction of the minimum magnetic field that will keep the particle moving in the earth's gravitational field in the same horizontal, northward direction?

27.3. In a 1.25-T magnetic field directed vertically upward, a particle having a charge of magnitude 8.50 μC and initially moving northward at 4.75 km/s is deflected toward the east. (a) What is the sign of the charge of this particle? Make a sketch to illustrate how you found your answer. (b) Find the magnetic force on the particle.

27.4. A particle with mass 1.81×10^{-3} kg and a charge of 1.22×10^{-8} C has, at a given instant, a velocity $\vec{v} = (3.00 \times 10^4 \text{ m/s})\hat{\jmath}$. What are the magnitude and direction of the particle's acceleration produced by a uniform magnetic field $\vec{B} = (1.63 \text{ T})\hat{\imath} + (0.980 \text{ T})\hat{\jmath}$?

27.5. An electron experiences a magnetic force of magnitude 4.60×10^{-15} N when moving at an angle of 60.0° with respect to a magnetic field of magnitude 3.50×10^{-3} T. Find the speed of the electron.

27.6. An electron moves at 2.50×10^6 m/s through a region in which there is a magnetic field of unspecified direction and magnitude 7.40×10^{-2} T. (a) What are the largest and smallest possible magnitudes of the acceleration of the electron due to the magnetic field? (b) If the actual acceleration of the electron is one-fourth of the largest magnitude in part (a), what is the angle between the electron velocity and the magnetic field?

27.7. A particle with charge 7.80 μC is moving with velocity $\vec{v} = -(3.80 \times 10^3 \text{ m/s})\hat{\jmath}$. The magnetic force on the particle is measured to be $\vec{F} = +(7.60 \times 10^{-3}\text{N})\hat{\imath} - (5.20 \times 10^{-3} \text{ N})\hat{k}$. (a) Calculate all the components of the magnetic field you can from this information. (b) Are there components of the magnetic field that are not determined by the measurement of the force? Explain. (c) Calculate the scalar product $\vec{B} \cdot \vec{F}$ What is the angle between $\vec{B}$ and $\vec{F}$?

27.8. A particle with charge -5.60 nC is moving in a uniform magnetic field $\vec{B} = -(1.25 \text{ T})\hat{k}$. The magnetic force on the particle is measured to be $\vec{F} = -(3.40 \times 10^{-7} \text{ N})\hat{\imath} + (7.40 \times 10^{-7} \text{ N})\hat{\jmath}$. (a) Calculate all the components of the velocity of the particle that you can from this information. (b) Are there components of the velocity that are not determined by the measurement of the force? Explain. (c) Calculate the scalar product $\vec{v} \cdot \vec{F}$. What is the angle between $\vec{v}$ and $\vec{F}$?

27.9. A group of particles is traveling in a magnetic field of unknown magnitude and direction. You observe that a proton moving at 1.50 km/s in the $+x$-direction experiences a force of 2.25×10^{-16} N in the $+y$-direction, and an electron moving at 4.75 km/s in the $-z$-direction experiences a force of 8.50×10^{-16} N. (a) What are the magnitude and direction of the magnetic field? (b) What are the magnitude and direction of the magnetic force on an electron moving in the $-y$-direction at 3.2 km/s?

Section 27.3 Magnetic Field Lines and Magnetic Flux

27.10. The magnetic flux through one face of a cube is $+0.120$ Wb. (a) What must the total magnetic flux through the other five faces of the cube be? (b) Why didn't you need to know the dimensions of the cube in order to answer part (a)? (c) Suppose the magnetic flux is due to a permanent magnet like that shown in Fig. 27.11. In a sketch, show where the cube in part (a) might be located relative to the magnet.

27.11. A circular area with a radius of 6.50 cm lies in the xy-plane. What is the magnitude of the magnetic flux through this circle due to a uniform magnetic field $B = 0.230$ T (a) in the $+z$-direction; (b) at an angle of 53.1° from the $+z$-direction; (c) in the $+y$-direction?

27.12. The magnetic field $\vec{B}$ in a certain region is 0.128 T, and its direction is that of the $+z$-axis in Fig. 27.45. (a) What is the magnetic flux across the surface *abcd* in the figure? (b) What is the magnetic flux across the surface *befc*? (c) What is the magnetic flux across the surface *aefd*? (d) What is the net flux through all five surfaces that enclose the shaded volume?

27.13. An open plastic soda bottle with an opening diameter of 2.5 cm is placed on a table. A uniform 1.75-T magnetic field directed upward and oriented 25° from vertical encompasses the bottle. What is the total magnetic flux through the plastic of the soda bottle?

Figure **27.45** Exercise 27.12.

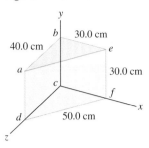

Section 27.4 Motion of Charged Particles in a Magnetic Field

27.14. A particle with charge 6.40×10^{-19} C travels in a circular orbit with radius 4.68 mm due to the force exerted on it by a magnetic field with magnitude 1.65 T and perpendicular to the orbit. (a) What is the magnitude of the linear momentum $\vec{p}$ of the particle? (b) What is the magnitude of the angular momentum $\vec{L}$ of the particle?

27.15. An electron at point A in Fig. 27.46 has a speed v_0 of 1.41×10^6 m/s. Find (a) the magnitude and direction of the magnetic field that will cause the electron to follow the semicircular path from A to B, and (b) the time required for the electron to move from A to B.

Figure **27.46** Exercise 27.15.

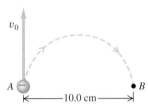

27.16. Repeat Exercise 27.15 for the case in which the particle is a proton rather than an electron.

27.17. A 150-g ball containing 4.00×10^8 excess electrons is dropped into a 125-m vertical shaft. At the bottom of the shaft, the ball suddenly enters a uniform horizontal magnetic field that has magnitude 0.250 T and direction from east to west. If air resistance is negligibly small, find the magnitude and direction of the force that this magnetic field exerts on the ball just as it enters the field.

27.18. An alpha particle (a He nucleus, containing two protons and two neutrons and having a mass of 6.64×10^{-27} kg) traveling horizontally at 35.6 km/s enters a uniform, vertical, 1.10-T magnetic field. (a) What is the diameter of the path followed by this alpha particle? (b) What effect does the magnetic field have on the speed of the particle? (c) What are the magnitude and direction of the acceleration of the alpha particle while it is in the magnetic field? (d) Explain why the speed of the particle does not change even though an unbalanced external force acts on it.

27.19. Fusion Reactor. If two deuterium nuclei (charge $+e$, mass 3.34×10^{-27} kg) get close enough together, the attraction of the strong nuclear force will fuse them to make an isotope of helium, releasing vast amounts of energy. The range of this force is about 10^{-15} m. This is the principle behind the fusion reactor. The deuterium nuclei are moving much too fast to be contained by physical walls, so they are confined magnetically. (a) How fast would two nuclei have to move so that in a head-on collision they would get close enough to fuse? (Treat the nuclei as point charges, and assume that a separation of 1.0×10^{-15} is required for fusion.) (b) What strength magnetic field is needed to make deuterium nuclei with this speed travel in a circle of diameter 2.50 m?

27.20. (a) An ^{16}O nucleus (charge $+8e$) moving horizontally from west to east with a speed of 500 km/s experiences a magnetic force of 0.00320 nN vertically downward. Find the magnitude and direc-

tion of the weakest magnetic field required to produce this force. Explain how this same force could be caused by a larger magnetic field. (b) An electron moves in a uniform, horizontal, 2.10-T magnetic field that is toward the west. What must the magnitude and direction of the minimum velocity of the electron be so that the magnetic force on it will be 4.60 pN, vertically upward? Explain how the velocity could be greater than this minimum value and the force still have this same magnitude and direction.

27.21. A deuteron (the nucleus of an isotope of hydrogen) has a mass of 3.34×10^{-27} kg and a charge of $+e$. The deuteron travels in a circular path with a radius of 6.96 mm in a magnetic field with magnitude 2.50 T. (a) Find the speed of the deuteron. (b) Find the time required for it to make half a revolution. (c) Through what potential difference would the deuteron have to be accelerated to acquire this speed?

27.22. In an experiment with cosmic rays, a vertical beam of particles that have charge of magnitude $3e$ and mass 12 times the proton mass enters a uniform horizontal magnetic field of 0.250 T and is bent in a semicircle of diameter 95.0 cm, as shown in Fig. 27.47. (a) Find the speed of the particles and the sign of their charge. (b) Is it reasonable to ignore the gravity force on the particles? (c) How does the speed of the particles as they enter the field compare to their speed as they exit the field?

Figure **27.47** Exercise 27.22.

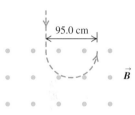

27.23. A physicist wishes to produce electromagnetic waves of frequency 3.0 THz (1 THz $= 1$ terahertz $= 10^{12}$ Hz) using a magnetron (see Example 27.3). (a) What magnetic field would be required? Compare this field with the strongest constant magnetic fields yet produced on earth, about 45 T. (b) Would there be any advantage to using protons instead of electrons in the magnetron? Why or why not?

27.24. A beam of protons traveling at 1.20 km/s enters a uniform magnetic field, traveling perpendicular to the field. The beam exits the magnetic field, leaving the field in a direction perpendicular to its original direction (Fig. 27.48). The beam travels a distance of 1.18 cm *while in the field*. What is the magnitude of the magnetic field?

Figure **27.48** Exercise 27.24.

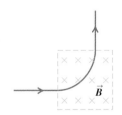

27.25. An electron in the beam of a TV picture tube is accelerated by a potential difference of 2.00 kV. Then it passes through a region of transverse magnetic field, where it moves in a circular arc with radius 0.180 m. What is the magnitude of the field?

27.26. A singly charged ion of ^{7}Li (an isotope of lithium) has a mass of 1.16×10^{-26} kg. It is accelerated through a potential difference of 220 V and then enters a magnetic field with magnitude 0.723 T perpendicular to the path of the ion. What is the radius of the ion's path in the magnetic field?

27.27. A proton ($q = 1.60 \times 10^{-19}$ C, $m = 1.67 \times 10^{-27}$ kg) moves in a uniform magnetic field $\vec{B} = (0.500\text{ T})\hat{\imath}$. At $t = 0$ the proton has velocity components $v_x = 1.50 \times 10^5$ m/s, $v_y = 0$, and $v_z = 2.00 \times 10^5$ m/s (see Example 27.4). (a) What are the magnitude and direction of the magnetic force acting on the proton? In addition to the magnetic field there is a uniform electric field in the $+x$-direction, $\vec{E} = (+2.00 \times 10^4 \text{ V/m})\hat{\imath}$. (b) Will the proton have a component of acceleration in the direction of the electric field?

(c) Describe the path of the proton. Does the electric field affect the radius of the helix? Explain. (d) At $t = T/2$, where T is the period of the circular motion of the proton, what is the x-component of the displacement of the proton from its position at $t = 0$?

Section 27.5 Applications of Motion of Charged Particles

27.28. (a) What is the speed of a beam of electrons when the simultaneous influence of an electric field of 1.56×10^4 V/m and a magnetic field of 4.62×10^{-3} T, with both fields normal to the beam and to each other, produces no deflection of the electrons? (b) In a diagram, show the relative orientation of the vectors $\vec{v}$, $\vec{E}$, and $\vec{B}$. (c) When the electric field is removed, what is the radius of the electron orbit? What is the period of the orbit?

27.29. A 150-V battery is connected across two parallel metal plates of area 28.5 cm^2 and separation 8.20 mm. A beam of alpha particles (charge $+2e$, mass 6.64×10^{-27} kg) is accelerated from rest through a potential difference of 1.75 kV and enters the region between the plates perpendicular to the electric field. What magnitude and direction of magnetic field are needed so that the alpha particles emerge undeflected from between the plates?

27.30. Crossed $\vec{E}$ and $\vec{B}$ Fields. A particle with initial velocity $\vec{v}_0 = (5.85 \times 10^3 \text{ m/s})\hat{\jmath}$ enters a region of uniform electric and magnetic fields. The magnetic field in the region is $\vec{B} = -(1.35 \text{ T})\hat{k}$. Calculate the magnitude and direction of the electric field in the region if the particle is to pass through undeflected, for a particle of charge (a) $+0.640$ nC and (b) -0.320 nC. You can ignore the weight of the particle.

27.31. Determining the Mass of an Isotope. The electric field between the plates of the velocity selector in a Bainbridge mass spectrometer (see Fig. 27.22) is 1.12×10^5 V/m, and the magnetic field in both regions is 0.540 T. A stream of singly charged selenium ions moves in a circular path with a radius of 31.0 cm in the magnetic field. Determine the mass of one selenium ion and the mass number of this selenium isotope. (The mass number is equal to the mass of the isotope in atomic mass units, rounded to the nearest integer. One atomic mass unit $= 1$ u $= 1.66 \times 10^{-27}$ kg.)

27.32. In the Bainbridge mass spectrometer (see Fig. 27.24), the magnetic-field magnitude in the velocity selector is 0.650 T, and ions having a speed of 1.82×10^6 m/s pass through undeflected. (a) What is the electric-field magnitude in the velocity selector? (b) If the separation of the plates is 5.20 mm, what is the potential difference between plates P and P'?

Section 27.6 Magnetic Force on a Current-Carrying Conductor

27.33. A straight 2.00-m, 150-g wire carries a current in a region where the earth's magnetic field is horizontal with a magnitude of 0.55 gauss. (a) What is the minimum value of the current in this wire so that its weight is completely supported by the magnetic force due to earth's field, assuming that no other forces except gravity act on it? Does it seem likely that such a wire could support this size of current? (b) Show how the wire would have to be oriented relative to the earth's magnetic field to be supported in this way.

27.34. An electromagnet produces a magnetic field of 0.550 T in a cylindrical region of radius 2.50 cm between its poles. A straight wire carrying a current of 10.8 A passes through the center of this region and is perpendicular to both the axis of the cylindrical region and the magnetic field. What magnitude of force is exerted on the wire?

27.35. A long wire carrying 4.50 A of current makes two 90° bends, as shown in Fig. 27.49. The bent part of the wire passes

Figure **27.49** Exercise 27.35.

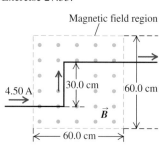

Magnetic field region

4.50 A · 30.0 cm · 60.0 cm · $\vec{B}$ · 60.0 cm

through a uniform 0.240-T magnetic field directed as shown in the figure and confined to a limited region of space. Find the magnitude and direction of the force that the magnetic field exerts on the wire.

27.36. A straight, vertical wire carries a current of 1.20 A downward in a region between the poles of a large superconducting electromagnet, where the magnetic field has magnitude $B = 0.588$ T and is horizontal. What are the magnitude and direction of the magnetic force on a 1.00-cm section of the wire that is in this uniform magnetic field, if the magnetic field direction is (a) east; (b) south; (c) 30.0° south of west?

27.37. A horizontal rod 0.200 m long is mounted on a balance and carries a current. At the location of the rod a uniform horizontal magnetic field has magnitude 0.067 T and direction perpendicular to the rod. The magnetic force on the rod is measured by the balance and is found to be 0.13 N. What is the current?

27.38. In Fig. 27.50, a wire carrying current into the plane of the figure is between the north and south poles of two bar magnets. What is the direction of the force exerted by the magnets on the wire?

Figure **27.50** Exercise 27.38.

27.39. A thin, 50.0-cm-long metal bar with mass 750 g rests on, but is not attached to, two metallic supports in a uniform 0.450-T magnetic field, as shown in Fig. 27.51. A battery and a 25.0-Ω resistor in series are connected to the supports. (a) What is the highest voltage the battery can have without breaking the circuit at the supports? (b) The battery voltage has the maximum value calculated in part (a). If the resistor suddenly gets partially short-circuited, decreasing its resistance to 2.0 Ω, find the initial acceleration of the bar.

Figure **27.51** Exercise 27.39.

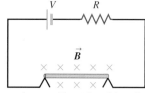

27.40. Magnetic Balance. The circuit shown in Fig. 27.52 is used to make a magnetic balance to weigh objects. The mass m to be measured is hung from the center of the bar that is in a uniform magnetic field of 1.50 T, directed into the plane of the figure. The battery voltage can be adjusted to vary the current in the circuit. The horizontal bar is 60.0 cm long and is made of extremely light-weight material. It is connected to the battery by thin vertical wires that can support no appreciable tension; all the weight of the suspended mass m is supported by the magnetic force on the bar. A resistor with

Figure **27.52** Exercise 27.40.

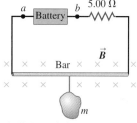

$R = 5.00 \, \Omega$ is in series with the bar; the resistance of the rest of the circuit is much less than this. (a) Which point, a or b, should be the positive terminal of the battery? (b) If the maximum terminal voltage of the battery is 175 V, what is the greatest mass m that this instrument can measure?

27.41. Consider the conductor and current in Example 27.8, but now let the magnetic field be parallel to the x-axis. (a) What are the magnitude and direction of the total magnetic force on the conductor? (b) In Example 27.8, the total force is the same as if we replaced the semicircle with a straight segment along the x-axis. Is that still true when the magnetic field is in this different direction? Can you explain why, or why not?

Section 27.7 Force and Torque on a Current Loop

27.42. The plane of a 5.0 cm $\times$ 8.0 cm rectangular loop of wire is parallel to a 0.19-T magnetic field. The loop carries a current of 6.2 A. (a) What torque acts on the loop? (b) What is the magnetic moment of the loop? (c) What is the maximum torque that can be obtained with the same total length of wire carrying the same current in this magnetic field?

27.43. Magnetic Moment of the Hydrogen Atom. In the Bohr model of the hydrogen atom (see Section 38.5), in the lowest energy state the electron orbits the proton at a speed of 2.2×10^6 m/s in a circular orbit of radius 5.3×10^{-11} m. (a) What is the orbital period of the electron? (b) If the orbiting electron is considered to be a current loop, what is the current I? (c) What is the magnetic moment of the atom due to the motion of the electron?

27.44. A rectangular coil of wire, 22.0 cm by 35.0 cm and carrying a current of 1.40 A, is oriented with the plane of its loop perpendicular to a uniform 1.50-T magnetic field, as shown in Fig. 27.53. (a) Calculate the net force and torque that the magnetic field exerts on the coil. (b) The coil is rotated through a 30.0° angle about the axis shown, with the left side coming out of the plane of the figure and the right side going into the plane. Calculate the net force and torque that the magnetic field now exerts on the coil. (*Hint:* In order to help visualize this three-dimensional problem, make a careful drawing of the coil as viewed along the rotation axis.)

Figure **27.53** Exercise 27.44.

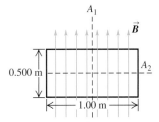

27.45. A uniform rectangular coil of total mass 210 g and dimensions 0.500 m $\times$ 1.00 m is oriented perpendicular to a uniform 3.00-T magnetic field (Fig. 27.54). A current of 2.00 A is suddenly started in the coil. (a) About which axis (A_1 or A_2) will the coil begin to rotate? Why? (b) Find the initial angular acceleration of the coil just after the current is started.

Figure **27.54** Exercise 27.45.

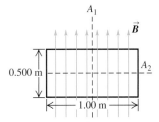

27.46. A circular coil with area A and N turns is free to rotate about a diameter that coincides with the x-axis. Current I is circu-

lating in the coil. There is a uniform magnetic field $\vec{B}$ in the positive y-direction. Calculate the magnitude and direction of the torque $\vec{\tau}$ and the value of the potential energy U, as given in Eq. (27.27), when the coil is oriented as shown in parts (a) through (d) of Fig. 27.55.

Figure **27.55** Exercise 27.46.

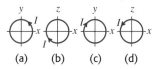

(a) (b) (c) (d)

27.47. A coil with magnetic moment $1.45 \, A \cdot m^2$ is oriented initially with its magnetic moment antiparallel to a uniform 0.835-T magnetic field. What is the change in potential energy of the coil when it is rotated 180° so that its magnetic moment is parallel to the field?

*Section 27.8 The Direct-Current Motor

*27.48. A dc motor with its rotor and field coils connected in series has an internal resistance of 3.2 Ω. When the motor is running at full load on a 120-V line, the emf in the rotor is 105 V. (a) What is the current drawn by the motor from the line? (b) What is the power delivered to the motor? (c) What is the mechanical power developed by the motor?

*27.49. In a shunt-wound dc motor with the field coils and rotor connected in parallel (Fig. 27.56), the resistance R_f of the field coils is 106 Ω, and the resistance R_r of the rotor is 5.9 Ω. When a potential difference of 120 V is applied to the brushes and the motor is running at full speed delivering mechanical power, the current supplied to it is 4.82 A. (a) What is the current in the field coils? (b) What is the current in the rotor? (c) What is the induced emf developed by the motor? (d) How much mechanical power is developed by this motor?

Figure **27.56** Exercises 27.49 and 27.50.

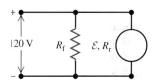

*27.50. A shunt-wound dc motor with the field coils and rotor connected in parallel (Fig. 27.56) operates from a 120-V dc power line. The resistance of the field windings, R_f, is 218 Ω. The resistance of the rotor, R_r, is 5.9 Ω. When the motor is running, the rotor develops an emf $\mathcal{E}$. The motor draws a current of 4.82 A from the line. Friction losses amount to 45.0 W. Compute (a) the field current; (b) the rotor current; (c) the emf $\mathcal{E}$; (d) the rate of development of thermal energy in the field windings; (e) the rate of development of thermal energy in the rotor; (f) the power input to the motor; (g) the efficiency of the motor.

*Section 27.9 The Hall Effect

*27.51. Figure 27.57 shows a portion of a silver ribbon with $z_1 = 11.8$ mm and $y_1 = 0.23$ mm, carrying a current of 120 A in the $+x$-direction. The ribbon lies in a uniform magnetic field, in the y-direction, with magnitude 0.95 T. Apply the simplified model of the Hall

Figure **27.57** Exercises 27.51 and 27.52.

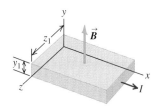

effect presented in Section 27.9. If there are 5.85×10^{28} free electrons per cubic meter, find (a) the magnitude of the drift velocity of the electrons in the x-direction; (b) the magnitude and direction of the electric field in the z-direction due to the Hall effect; (c) the Hall emf.

*27.52. Let Fig. 27.57 represent a strip of an unknown metal of the same dimensions as those of the silver ribbon in Exercise 27.51. When the magnetic field is 2.29 T and the current is 78.0 A, the Hall emf is found to be 131 μV. What does the simplified model of the Hall effect presented in Section 27.9 give for the density of free electrons in the unknown metal?

Problems

27.53. When a particle of charge $q > 0$ moves with a velocity of $\vec{v}_1$ at 45.0° from the $+x$-axis in the xy-plane, a uniform magnetic field exerts a force $\vec{F}_1$ along the $-z$-axis (Fig. 27.58). When the same particle moves with a velocity $\vec{v}_2$ with the same magnitude as $\vec{v}_1$ but along the $+z$-axis, a force $\vec{F}_2$ of magnitude F_2 is exerted on it along the $+x$-axis. (a) What are the magnitude (in terms of q, v_1, and F_2) and direction of the magnetic field? (b) What is the magnitude of $\vec{F}_1$ in terms of F_2?

Figure **27.58** Problem 27.53.

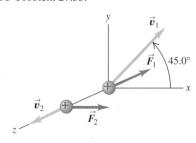

27.54. A particle with charge 9.45×10^{-8} C is moving in a region where there is a uniform magnetic field of 0.450 T in the $+x$-direction. At a particular instant of time the velocity of the particle has components $v_x = -1.68 \times 10^4$ m/s, $v_y = -3.11 \times 10^4$ m/s, and $v_z = 5.85 \times 10^4$ m/s. What are the components of the force on the particle at this time?

27.55. You wish to hit a target from several meters away with a charged coin having a mass of 5.0 g and a charge of $+2500$ μC. The coin is given an initial velocity of 12.8 m/s, and a downward, uniform electric field with field strength 27.5 N/C exists throughout the region. If you aim directly at the target and fire the coin horizontally, what magnitude and direction of uniform magnetic field are needed in the region for the coin to hit the target?

27.56. A cyclotron is to accelerate protons to an energy of 5.4 MeV. The superconducting electromagnet of the cyclotron produces a 3.5-T magnetic field perpendicular to the proton orbits. (a) When the protons have achieved a kinetic energy of 2.7 MeV, what is the radius of their circular orbit and what is their angular speed? (b) Repeat part (a) when the protons have achieved their final kinetic energy of 5.4 MeV.

27.57. The magnetic poles of a small cyclotron produce a magnetic field with magnitude 0.85 T. The poles have a radius of 0.40 m, which is the maximum radius of the orbits of the accelerated particles. (a) What is the maximum energy to which protons ($q = 1.60 \times 10^{-19}$ C, $m = 1.67 \times 10^{-27}$ kg) can be accelerated by this cyclotron? Give your answer in electron volts and in joules. (b) What is the time for one revolution of a proton orbiting at this

maximum radius? (c) What would the magnetic-field magnitude have to be for the maximum energy to which a proton can be accelerated to be twice that calculated in part (a)? (d) For $B = 0.85$ T, what is the maximum energy to which alpha particles ($q = 3.20 \times 10^{-19}$ C, $m = 6.65 \times 10^{-27}$ kg) can be accelerated by this cyclotron? How does this compare to the maximum energy for protons?

27.58. The force on a charged particle moving in a magnetic field can be computed as the vector sum of the forces due to each separate component of the magnetic field. As an example, a particle with charge q is moving with speed v in the $-y$-direction. It is moving in a uniform magnetic field $\vec{B} = B_x\hat{i} + B_y\hat{j} + B_z\hat{k}$. (a) What are the components of the force $\vec{F}$ exerted on the particle by the magnetic field? (b) If $q > 0$, what must the signs of the components of $\vec{B}$ be if the components of $\vec{F}$ are all nonnegative? (c) If $q < 0$ and $B_x = B_y = B_z > 0$, find the direction of $\vec{F}$ and find the magnitude of $\vec{F}$ in terms of $|q|$, v, and B_x.

27.59. A uniform, 458-g metal bar 75.0 cm long carries a current I in a uniform, horizontal, 1.55-T magnetic field as shown in Fig. 27.59. The bar is hinged at b but rests unattached at a. What is the largest current that can flow from a to b without breaking the electrical contact at a?

Figure **27.59** Problem 27.59.

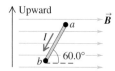

27.60. In the electron gun of a TV picture tube the electrons (charge $-e$, mass m) are accelerated by a voltage V. After leaving the electron gun, the electron beam travels a distance D to the screen; in this region there is a transverse magnetic field of magnitude B and no electric field. (a) Sketch the path of the electron beam in the tube. (b) Show that the approximate deflection of the beam due to this magnetic field is

$$d = \frac{BD^2}{2}\sqrt{\frac{e}{2mV}}$$

(*Hint:* Place the origin at the center of the electron beam's arc and compare an undeflected beam's path to the deflected beam's path.) (c) Evaluate this expression for $V = 750$ V, $D = 50$ cm, and $B = 5.0 \times 10^{-5}$ T (comparable to the earth's field). Is this deflection significant?

27.61. A particle with negative charge q and mass $m = 2.58 \times 10^{-15}$ kg is traveling through a region containing a uniform magnetic field $\vec{B} = -(0.120\ \text{T})\hat{k}$. At a particular instant of time the velocity of the particle is $\vec{v} = (1.05 \times 10^6\ \text{m/s})(-3\hat{i} + 4\hat{j} + 12\hat{k})$ and the force $\vec{F}$ on the particle has a magnitude of 1.25 N. (a) Determine the charge q. (b) Determine the acceleration $\vec{a}$ of the particle. (c) Explain why the path of the particle is a helix, and determine the radius of curvature R of the circular component of the helical path. (d) Determine the cyclotron frequency of the particle. (e) Although helical motion is not periodic in the full sense of the word, the x- and y-coordinates do vary in a periodic way. If the coordinates of the particle at $t = 0$ are $(x, y, z) = (R, 0, 0)$, determine its coordinates at a time $t = 2T$, where T is the period of the motion in the xy-plane.

27.62. A long, straight wire containing a semicircular region of radius 0.95 m is placed in a uniform magnetic field of magnitude 2.20 T as shown in Fig. 27.60. What is the net magnetic force acting on the wire when it carries a current of 3.40 A?

Figure **27.60** Problem 27.62.

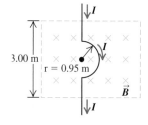

27.63. A magnetic field exerts a torque τ on a round current-carrying loop of wire. What will be the torque on this loop (in terms of τ) if its diameter is tripled?

27.64. A particle of charge $q > 0$ is moving at speed v in the $+z$-direction through a region of uniform magnetic field $\vec{B}$. The magnetic force on the particle is $\vec{F} = F_0(3\hat{i} + 4\hat{j})$, where F_0 is a positive constant. (a) Determine the components B_x, B_y, and B_z, or at least as many of the three components as is possible from the information given. (b) If it is given in addition that the magnetic field has magnitude $6F_0/qv$, determine as much as you can about the remaining components of $\vec{B}$.

27.65. Suppose the electric field between the plates P and P' in Fig. 27.24 is 1.88×10^4 V/m and the magnetic field in both regions is 0.701 T. If the source contains the three isotopes of krypton, ^{82}Kr, ^{84}Kr, and ^{86}Kr, and the ions are singly charged, find the distance between the lines formed by the three isotopes on the photographic plate. Assume the atomic masses of the isotopes (in atomic mass units) are equal to their mass numbers, 82, 84, and 86. (One atomic mass unit = 1 u = 1.66×10^{-27} kg.)

27.66. Mass Spectrograph. A mass spectrograph is used to measure the masses of ions, or to separate ions of different masses (see Section 27.5). In one design for such an instrument, ions with mass m and charge q are accelerated through a potential difference V. They then enter a uniform magnetic field that is perpendicular to their velocity, and they are deflected in a semicircular path of radius R. A detector measures where the ions complete the semicircle and from this it is easy to calculate R. (a) Derive the equation for calculating the mass of the ion from measurements of B, V, R, and q. (b) What potential difference V is needed so that singly ionized ^{12}C atoms will have $R = 50.0$ cm in a 0.150-T magnetic field? (c) Suppose the beam consists of a mixture of ^{12}C and ^{14}C ions. If V and B have the same values as in part (b), calculate the separation of these two isotopes at the detector. Do you think that this beam separation is sufficient for the two ions to be distinguished? (Make the assumption described in Problem 27.65 for the masses of the ions.)

27.67. A straight piece of conducting wire with mass M and length L is placed on a frictionless incline tilted at an angle θ from the horizontal (Fig. 27.61). There is a uniform, vertical magnetic field $\vec{B}$ at all points (produced by an arrangement of magnets not shown in the figure). To keep the wire from sliding down the incline, a voltage source is attached to the ends of the wire. When just the right amount of current flows through the wire, the wire remains at rest. Determine the magnitude and direction of the current in the wire that will cause the wire to remain at rest. Copy the figure and draw the direction of the current on your copy. In addition, show in a free-body diagram all the forces that act on the wire.

Figure **27.61** Problem 27.67.

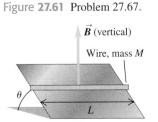

$\vec{B}$ (vertical)

Wire, mass M

θ

L

27.68. A 3.00-N metal bar, 1.50 m long and having a resistance of 10.0 Ω, rests horizontally on conducting wires connecting it to the circuit shown in Fig. 27.62. The bar is in a uniform, horizontal, 1.60-T magnetic field and is not attached to the wires in the circuit. What is the acceleration of the bar just after the switch S is closed?

Figure **27.62** Problem 27.68.

25.0 Ω S $\vec{B}$

120.0 V   10.0 Ω

27.69. Two positive ions having the same charge q but different masses m_1 and m_2 are accelerated horizontally from rest through a potential difference V. They then enter a region where there is a uniform magnetic field $\vec{B}$ normal to the plane of the trajectory. (a) Show that if the beam entered the magnetic field along the x-axis, the value of the y-coordinate for each ion at any time t is approximately

$$y = Bx^2 \left(\frac{q}{8mV}\right)^{1/2}$$

provided y remains much smaller than x. (b) Can this arrangement be used for isotope separation? Why or why not?

27.70. A plastic circular loop of radius R and a positive charge q is distributed uniformly around the circumference of the loop. The loop is then rotated around its central axis, perpendicular to the plane of the loop, with angular speed ω. If the loop is in a region where there is a uniform magnetic field $\vec{B}$ directed parallel to the plane of the loop, calculate the magnitude of the magnetic torque on the loop.

27.71. Determining Diet. One method for determining the amount of corn in early Native American diets is the *stable isotope ratio analysis* (SIRA) technique. As corn photosynthesizes, it concentrates the isotope carbon-13, whereas most other plants concentrate carbon-12. Overreliance on corn consumption can then be correlated with certain diseases, because corn lacks the essential amino acid lysine. Archaeologists use a mass spectrometer to separate the ^{12}C and ^{13}C isotopes in samples of human remains. Suppose you use a velocity selector to obtain singly ionized (missing one electron) atoms of speed 8.50 km/s, and you want to bend them within a uniform magnetic field in a semicircle of diameter 25.0 cm for the ^{12}C. The measured masses of these isotopes are 1.99×10^{-26} kg (^{12}C) and 2.16×10^{-26} kg (^{13}C). (a) What strength of magnetic field is required? (b) What is the diameter of the ^{13}C semicircle? (c) What is the separation of the ^{12}C and ^{13}C ions at the detector at the end of the semicircle? Is this distance large enough to be easily observed?

27.72. An Electromagnetic Rail Gun. A conducting bar with mass m and length L slides over horizontal rails that are connected to a voltage source. The voltage source maintains a constant current I in the rails and bar, and a constant, uniform, vertical magnetic field $\vec{B}$ fills the region between the rails (Fig. 27.63). (a) Find the magnitude and direction of the net force on the conducting bar. Ignore friction, air resistance, and electrical resistance. (b) If the bar has mass m, find the distance d that the bar must move along the rails from rest to attain speed v. (c) It has been suggested that rail guns based on this principle could accelerate payloads into earth orbit or beyond. Find the distance the bar must travel along the rails if it is to reach the escape speed for the earth (11.2 km/s). Let $B = 0.50$ T, $I = 2.0 \times 10^3$ A, $m = 25$ kg, and $L = 50$ cm. For simplicity assume the net force on the object is equal to the magnetic force, as in parts (a) and (b), even though gravity plays an important role in an actual launch in space.

Figure **27.63** Problem 27.72.

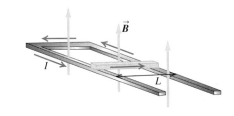

$\vec{B}$

I L

27.73. A long wire carrying a 6.00-A current reverses direction by means of two right-angle bends, as shown in Fig. 27.64. The part of the wire where the bend occurs is in a magnetic field of 0.666 T confined to the circular region of diameter 75 cm, as shown. Find the magnitude and direction of the net force that the magnetic field exerts on this wire.

Figure **27.64** Problem 27.73.

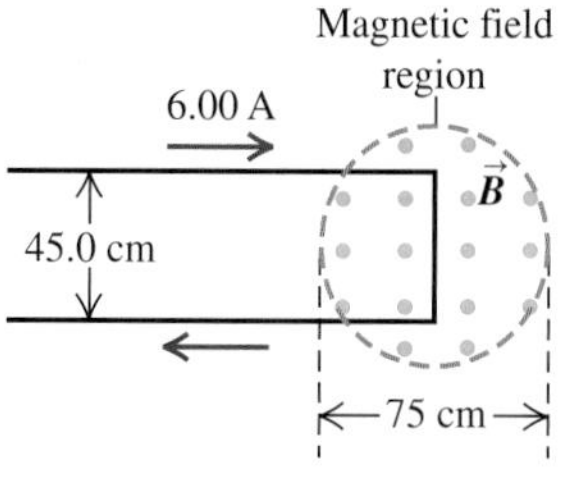

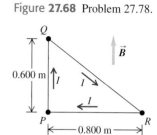

27.74. A wire 25.0 cm long lies along the z-axis and carries a current of 9.00 A in the $+z$-direction. The magnetic field is uniform and has components $B_x = -0.242$ T, $B_y = -0.985$ T, and $B_z = -0.336$ T. (a) Find the components of the magnetic force on the wire. (b) What is the magnitude of the net magnetic force on the wire?

27.75. The rectangular loop of wire shown in Fig. 27.65 has a mass of 0.15 g per centimeter of length and is pivoted about side ab on a frictionless axis. The current in the wire is 8.2 A in the direction shown. Find the magnitude and direction of the magnetic field parallel to the y-axis that will cause the loop to swing up until its plane makes an angle of 30.0° with the yz-plane.

Figure **27.65** Problem 27.75.

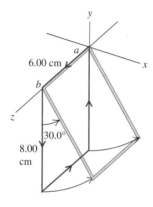

27.76. The rectangular loop shown in Fig. 27.66 is pivoted about the y-axis and carries a current of 15.0 A in the direction indicated. (a) If the loop is in a uniform magnetic field with magnitude 0.48 T in the $+x$-direction, find the magnitude and direction of the torque required to hold the loop in the position shown. (b) Repeat part (a) for the case in which the field is in the $-z$-direction. (c) For each of the above magnetic fields, what torque would be required if the loop were pivoted about an axis through its center, parallel to the y-axis?

Figure **27.66** Problem 27.76.

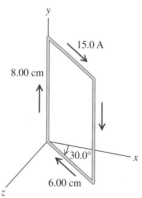

27.77. A thin, uniform rod with negligible mass and length 0.200 m is attached to the floor by a frictionless hinge at point P (Fig. 27.67). A horizontal spring with force constant $k = 4.80$ N/m connects the other end of the rod to a vertical wall. The rod is in a uniform magnetic field $B = 0.340$ T directed into the plane of the figure. There is current $I = 6.50$ A in the rod, in the direction shown. (a) Calculate the torque due to the magnetic force on the rod, for an axis at P. Is it correct to take the total magnetic force to act at the center of gravity of the rod when calculating the torque? Explain. (b) When the rod is in equilibrium

Figure **27.67**
Problem 27.77.

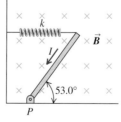

and makes an angle of 53.0° with the floor, is the spring stretched or compressed? (c) How much energy is stored in the spring when the rod is in equilibrium?

27.78. The triangular loop of wire shown in Fig. 27.68 carries a current $I = 5.00$ A in the direction shown. The loop is in a uniform magnetic field that has magnitude $B = 3.00$ T and the same direction as the current in side PQ of the loop. (a) Find the force exerted by the magnetic field on each side of the triangle. If the force is not zero, specify its direction. (b) What is the net force on the loop? (c) The loop is pivoted about an axis that lies along side PR. Use the forces calculated in part (a) to calculate the torque on each side of the loop (see Problem 27.77). (d) What is the magnitude of the net torque on the loop? Calculate the net torque from the torques calculated in part (c) and also from Eq. (27.28). Do these two results agree? (e) Is the net torque directed to rotate point Q into the plane of the figure or out of the plane of the figure?

Figure **27.68** Problem 27.78.

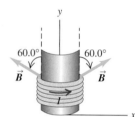

27.79. A Voice Coil. It was shown in Section 27.7 that the net force on a current loop in a *uniform* magnetic field is zero. The magnetic force on the voice coil of a loudspeaker (see Fig. 27.28) is nonzero because the magnetic field at the coil is not uniform. A voice coil in a loudspeaker has 50 turns of wire and a diameter of 1.56 cm, and the current in the coil is 0.950 A. Assume that the magnetic field at each point of the coil has a constant magnitude of 0.220 T and is directed at an angle of 60.0° outward from the normal to the plane of the coil (Fig. 27.69). Let the axis of the coil be in the y-direction. The current in the coil is in the direction shown (counterclockwise as viewed from a point above the coil on the y-axis). Calculate the magnitude and direction of the net magnetic force on the coil.

Figure **27.69**
Problem 27.79.

27.80. Paleoclimate. Climatologists can determine the past temperature of the earth by comparing the ratio of the isotope oxygen-18 to the isotope oxygen-16 in air trapped in ancient ice sheets, such as those in Greenland. In one method for separating these isotopes, a sample containing both of them is first singly ionized (one electron is removed) and then accelerated from rest through a potential difference V. This beam then enters a magnetic field B at right angles to the field and is bent into a quarter-circle. A particle detector at the end of the path measures the amount of each isotope, (a) Show that the separation Δr of the two isotopes at the detector is given by

$$\Delta r = \frac{\sqrt{2eV}}{eB}\left(\sqrt{m_{18}} - \sqrt{m_{16}}\right)$$

where m_{16} and m_{18} are the masses of the two oxygen isotopes, (b) The measured masses of the two isotopes are 2.66×10^{-26} kg (^{16}O) and 2.99×10^{-26} kg (^{18}O). If the magnetic field is 0.050 T, what must be the accelerating potential V so that these two isotopes will be separated by 4.00 cm at the detector?

27.81. Force on a Current Loop in a Nonuniform Magnetic Field. It was shown in Section 27.7 that the net force on a current loop in a *uniform* magnetic field is zero. But what if $\vec{B}$ is *not* uniform? Figure 27.70 shows a square loop of wire that lies in the *xy*-plane. The loop has corners at $(0, 0)$, $(0, L)$, $(L, 0)$, and (L, L) and carries a constant current I in the clockwise direction. The magnetic field has no *x*-component but has both *y*- and *z*-components: $\vec{B} = (B_0 z/L)\hat{j} + (B_0 y/L)\hat{k}$, where B_0 is a positive constant. (a) Sketch the magnetic field lines in the *yz*-plane. (b) Find the magnitude and direction of the magnetic force exerted on each of the sides of the loop by integrating Eq. (27.20). (c) Find the magnitude and direction of the net magnetic force on the loop.

Figure **27.70** Problems 27.81 and 27.82.

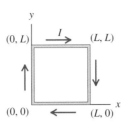

27.82. Torque on a Current Loop in a Nonuniform Magnetic Field. In Section 27.7 the expression for the torque on a current loop was derived assuming that the magnetic field $\vec{B}$ was uniform. But what if $\vec{B}$ is *not* uniform? Figure 27.70 shows a square loop of wire that lies in the *xy*-plane. The loop has corners at $(0, 0)$, $(0, L)$, $(L, 0)$, and (L, L) and carries a constant current I in the clockwise direction. The magnetic field has no *z*-component but has both *x*- and *y*-components: $\vec{B} = (B_0 y/L)\hat{i} + (B_0 x/L)\hat{j}$, where B_0 is a positive constant. (a) Sketch the magnetic field lines in the *xy*-plane. (b) Find the magnitude and direction of the magnetic force exerted on each of the sides of the loop by integrating Eq. (27.20). (c) If the loop is free to rotate about the *x*-axis, find the magnitude and direction of the magnetic torque on the loop. (d) Repeat part (c) for the case in which the loop is free to rotate about the *y*-axis. (e) Is Eq. (27.26), $\vec{\tau} = \vec{\mu} \times \vec{B}$, an appropriate description of the torque on this loop? Why or why not?

27.83. An insulated wire with mass $m = 5.40 \times 10^{-5}$ kg is bent into the shape of an inverted U such that the horizontal part has a length $l = 15.0$ cm. The bent ends of the wire are partially immersed in two pools of mercury, with 2.5 cm of each end below the mercury's surface. The entire structure is in a region containing a uniform 0.00650-T magnetic field directed into the page (Fig. 27.71). An electrical connection from the mercury pools is made through the ends of the wires. The mercury pools are connected to a 1.50-V battery and a switch S. When switch S is closed, the wire jumps 35.0 cm into the air, measured from its initial position. (a) Determine the speed v of the wire as it leaves the mercury. (b) Assuming that the current I through the wire was constant from the time the switch was closed until the wire left the mercury, determine I. (c) Ignoring the resistance of the mercury and the circuit wires, determine the resistance of the moving wire.

Figure **27.71** Problem 27.83.

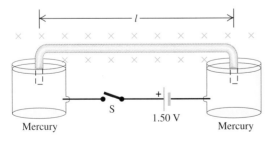

Mercury   S   1.50 V   Mercury

27.84. Derivation of Eq. (27.26) for a Circular Current Loop. A wire ring lies in the *xy*-plane with its center at the origin. The ring carries a counterclockwise current I (Fig. 27.72). A uniform magnetic field $\vec{B}$ is in the $+x$-direction, $\vec{B} = B_x \hat{i}$ (The result is easily extended to $\vec{B}$ in an arbitrary direction.) (a) In Fig. 27.72, show that the element $d\vec{l} = R\, d\theta(-\sin\theta\hat{i} + \cos\theta\hat{j})$, and find $d\vec{F} = I\, d\vec{l} \times \vec{B}$. (b) Integrate $d\vec{F}$ around the loop to show that the net force is zero. (c) From part (a), find $d\vec{\tau} = \vec{r} \times d\vec{F}$, where $\vec{r} = R(\cos\theta\hat{i} + \sin\theta\hat{j})$ is the vector from the center of the loop to the element $d\vec{l}$. (Note that $d\vec{l}$ is perpendicular to $\vec{r}$.) (d) Integrate $d\vec{\tau}$ over the loop to find the total torque $\vec{\tau}$ on the loop. Show that the result can be written as $\vec{\tau} = \vec{\mu} \times \vec{B}$, where $\mu = IA$. (*Note:* $\int\cos^2 x\, dx = \frac{1}{2}x + \frac{1}{4}\sin 2x$, $\int\sin^2 x\, dx = \frac{1}{2}x - \frac{1}{4}\sin 2x$, and $\int\sin x\cos x\, dx = \frac{1}{2}\sin^2 x$.)

Figure **27.72** Problem 27.84.

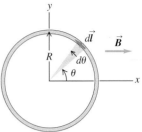

27.85. A circular loop of wire with area A lies in the *xy*-plane. As viewed along the *z*-axis looking in the $-z$-direction toward the origin, a current I is circulating clockwise around the loop. The torque produced by an external magnetic field $\vec{B}$ is given by $\vec{\tau} = D(4\hat{i} - 3\hat{j})$, where D is a positive constant, and for this orientation of the loop the magnetic potential energy $U = -\vec{\mu} \cdot \vec{B}$ is negative. The magnitude of the magnetic field is $B_0 = 13D/IA$. (a) Determine the vector magnetic moment of the current loop. (b) Determine the components B_x, B_y, and B_z of $\vec{B}$.

27.86. Quark Model of the Neutron. The neutron is a particle with zero charge. Nonetheless, it has a nonzero magnetic moment with *z*-component 9.66×10^{-27} A $\cdot$ m^2. This can be explained by the internal structure of the neutron. A substantial body of evidence indicates that a neutron is composed of three fundamental particles called *quarks*: an "up" (u) quark, of charge $+2e/3$, and two "down" (d) quarks, each of charge $-e/3$. The combination of the three quarks produces a net charge of $2e/3 - e/3 - e/3 = 0$. If the quarks are in motion, they can produce a nonzero magnetic moment. As a very simple model, suppose the u quark moves in a counterclockwise circular path and the d quarks move in a clockwise circular path, all of radius r and all with the same speed v (Fig. 27.73). (a) Determine the current due to the circulation of the u quark. (b) Determine the magnitude of the magnetic moment due to the circulating u quark. (c) Determine the magnitude of the magnetic moment of the three-quark system. (Be careful to use the correct magnetic moment directions.) (d) With what speed v must the quarks move if this model is to reproduce the magnetic moment of the neutron? Use $r = 1.20 \times 10^{-15}$ m (the radius of the neutron) for the radius of the orbits.

Figure **27.73** Problem 27.86.

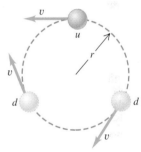

27.87. Using Gauss's Law for Magnetism. In a certain region of space, the magnetic field $\vec{B}$ is not uniform. The magnetic field has both a *z*-component and a component that points radially away from or toward the *z*-axis. The *z*-component is given by $B_z(z) = \beta z$, where β is a positive constant. The radial component B_r depends only on r, the radial distance from the *z*-axis. (a) Use Gauss's law for magnetism, Eq. (27.8), to find the radial component B_r as a function of r. (*Hint:* Try a cylindrical Gaussian surface of radius r concentric with the *z*-axis, with one end at $z = 0$ and the other at $z = L$.) (b) Sketch the magnetic field lines.

27.88. A circular ring with area 4.45 cm^2 is carrying a current of 12.5 A. The ring is free to rotate about a diameter. The ring, initially at rest, is immersed in a region of uniform magnetic field given by $\vec{B} = (1.15 \times 10^{-2}\,\text{T})(12\hat{i} + 3\hat{j} - 4\hat{k})$. The ring is positioned initially such that its magnetic moment is given by $\vec{\mu}_i = \mu(-0.800\hat{i} + 0.600\hat{j})$, where μ is the (positive) magnitude of the magnetic moment. The ring is released and turns through an angle of 90.0°, at which point its magnetic moment is given by $\vec{\mu}_f = -\mu\hat{k}$. (a) Determine the decrease in potential energy. (b) If the moment of inertia of the ring about a diameter is $8.50 \times 10^{-7}\,\text{kg}\cdot\text{m}^2$, determine the angular speed of the ring as it passes through the second position.

Challenge Problems

27.89. A particle with charge 2.15 μC and mass 3.20×10^{-11} kg is initially traveling in the $+y$-direction with a speed $v_0 = 1.45 \times 10^5$ m/s. It then enters a region containing a uniform magnetic field that is directed into, and perpendicular to, the page in Fig. 27.74. The magnitude of the field is 0.420 T. The region extends a distance of 25.0 cm along the initial direction of travel; 75.0 cm from the point of entry into the magnetic field region is a wall. The length of the field-free region is thus 50.0 cm. When the charged particle enters the magnetic field, it follows a curved path whose radius of curvature is R. It then leaves the magnetic field after a time t_1, having been deflected a distance Δx_1. The particle then travels in the field-free region and strikes the wall after undergoing a total deflection Δx. (a) Determine the radius R of the curved part of the path. (b) Determine t_1, the time the particle spends in the magnetic field. (c) Determine Δx_1, the horizontal deflection at the point of exit from the field. (d) Determine Δx, the total horizontal deflection.

Figure **27.74** Challenge Problem 27.89.

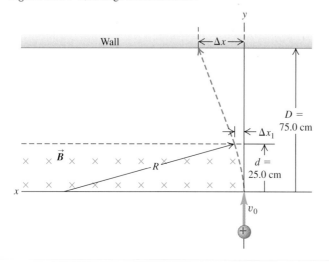

27.90.   The   Electromagnetic Pump. Magnetic forces acting on conducting fluids provide a convenient means of pumping these fluids. For example, this method can be used to pump blood without the damage to the cells that can be caused by a mechanical pump. A horizontal tube with rectangular cross section (height h, width w) is placed at right angles to a uniform magnetic field with magnitude B so that a length l is in the field (Fig. 27.75). The tube is filled with a conducting liquid, and an electric current of density J is maintained in the third mutually perpendicular direction. (a) Show that the difference of pressure between a point in the liquid on a vertical plane through ab and a point in the liquid on another vertical plane through cd, under conditions in which the liquid is prevented from flowing, is $\Delta p = JlB$. (b) What current density is needed to provide a pressure difference of 1.00 atm between these two points if $B = 2.20$ T and $l = 35.0$ mm?

27.91. A Cycloidal Path. A particle with mass m and positive charge q starts from rest at the origin shown in Fig. 27.76. There is a uniform electric field $\vec{E}$ in the $+y$-direction and a uniform magnetic field $\vec{B}$ directed out of the page. It is shown in more advanced books that the path is a *cycloid* whose radius of curvature at the top points is twice the y-coordinate at that level. (a) Explain why the path has this general shape and why it is repetitive. (b) Prove that the speed at any point is equal to $\sqrt{2qEy/m}$. (*Hint:* Use energy conservation.) (c) Applying Newton's second law at the top point and taking as given that the radius of curvature here equals $2y$, prove that the speed at this point is $2E/B$.

Figure **27.75** Challenge Problem 27.90.

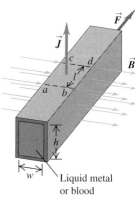

Liquid metal or blood

Figure **27.76** Challenge Problem 27.91.

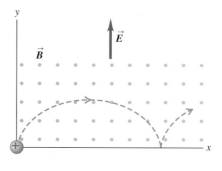

SOURCES OF MAGNETIC FIELD

? The immense cylinder in this photograph is actually a current-carrying coil, or solenoid, that generates a uniform magnetic field in its interior as part of an experiment at CERN, the European Laboratory for Particle Physics. If two such solenoids were joined end to end, how much stronger would the magnetic field become?

LEARNING GOALS

By studying this chapter, you will learn:

- The nature of the magnetic field produced by a single moving charged particle.

- How to describe the magnetic field produced by an element of a current-carrying conductor.

- How to calculate the magnetic field produced by a long, straight, current-carrying wire.

- Why wires carrying current in the same direction attract, while wires carrying opposing currents repel.

- How to calculate the magnetic field produced by a current-carrying wire bent into a circle.

- What Ampere's law is, and what it tells us about magnetic fields.

- How to use Ampere's law to calculate the magnetic field of symmetric current distributions.

In Chapter 27 we studied the forces exerted on moving charges and on current-carrying conductors in a magnetic field. We didn't worry about how the magnetic field got there; we simply took its existence as a given fact. But how are magnetic fields *created?* We know that both permanent magnets and electric currents in electromagnets create magnetic fields. In this chapter we will study these sources of magnetic field in detail.

We've learned that a charge creates an electric field and that an electric field exerts a force on a charge. But a *magnetic* field exerts a force only on a *moving* charge. Is it also true that a charge *creates* a magnetic field only when the charge is moving? In a word, yes.

Our analysis will begin with the magnetic field created by a single moving point charge. We can use this analysis to determine the field created by a small segment of a current-carrying conductor. Once we can do that, we can in principle find the magnetic field produced by *any* shape of conductor.

Then we will introduce Ampere's law, which plays a role in magnetism analogous to the role of Gauss's law in electrostatics. Ampere's law lets us exploit symmetry properties in relating magnetic fields to their sources.

Moving charged particles within atoms respond to magnetic fields and can also act as sources of magnetic field. We'll use these ideas to understand how certain magnetic materials can be used to intensify magnetic fields as well as why some materials such as iron act as permanent magnets.

28.1 Magnetic Field of a Moving Charge

Let's start with the basics, the magnetic field of a single point charge q moving with a constant velocity $\vec{v}$. In practical applications, such as the solenoid shown in the photo that opens this chapter, magnetic fields are produced by tremendous numbers of charged particles moving together in a current. But once we understand how to calculate the magnetic field due to a single point charge, it's a small leap to calculate the field due to a current-carrying wire or collection of wires.

28.1 (a) Magnetic-field vectors due to a moving positive point charge q. At each point, $\vec{B}$ is perpendicular to the plane of $\vec{r}$ and $\vec{v}$, and its magnitude is proportional to the sine of the angle between them. (b) Magnetic field lines in a plane containing a moving positive charge.

(a) Perspective view

Right-hand rule for the magnetic field due to a positive charge moving at constant velocity: Point the thumb of your right hand in the direction of the velocity. Your fingers now curl around the charge in the direction of the magnetic field lines. (If the charge is negative, the field lines are in the opposite direction.)

For these field points, $\vec{r}$ and $\vec{v}$ both lie in the beige plane, and $\vec{B}$ is perpendicular to this plane.

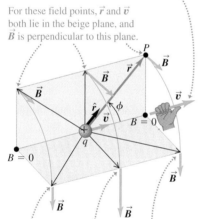

For these field points, $\vec{r}$ and $\vec{v}$ both lie in the gold plane, and $\vec{B}$ is perpendicular to this plane.

(b) View from behind the charge

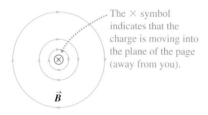

The $\times$ symbol indicates that the charge is moving into the plane of the page (away from you).

As we did for electric fields, we call the location of the moving charge at a given instant the **source point** and the point P where we want to find the field the **field point.** In Section 21.4 we found that at a field point a distance r from a point charge q, the magnitude of the *electric* field $\vec{E}$ caused by the charge is proportional to the charge magnitude $|q|$ and to $1/r^2$, and the direction of $\vec{E}$ (for positive q) is along the line from source point to field point. The corresponding relationship for the *magnetic* field $\vec{B}$ of a point charge q moving with constant velocity has some similarities and some interesting differences.

Experiments show that the magnitude of $\vec{B}$ is also proportional to $|q|$ and to $1/r^2$. But the *direction* of $\vec{B}$ is *not* along the line from source point to field point. Instead, $\vec{B}$ is perpendicular to the plane containing this line and the particle's velocity vector $\vec{v}$, as shown in Fig. 28.1. Furthermore, the field *magnitude* B is also proportional to the particle's speed v and to the sine of the angle ϕ. Thus the magnetic field magnitude at point P is given by

$$B = \frac{\mu_0}{4\pi} \frac{|q| v \sin\phi}{r^2} \tag{28.1}$$

where $\mu_0/4\pi$ is a proportionality constant (μ_0 is read as "mu-nought" or "mu-sub-zero"). The reason for writing the constant in this particular way will emerge shortly. We did something similar with Coulomb's law in Section 21.3.

Moving Charge: Vector Magnetic Field

We can incorporate both the magnitude and direction of $\vec{B}$ into a single vector equation using the vector product. To avoid having to say "the direction from the source q to the field point P" over and over, we introduce a *unit* vector $\hat{r}$ ("r-hat") that points from the source point to the field point. (We used $\hat{r}$ for the same purpose in Section 21.4.) This unit vector is equal to the vector $\vec{r}$ from the source to the field point divided by its magnitude: $\hat{r} = \vec{r}/r$. Then the $\vec{B}$ field of a moving point charge is

$$\vec{B} = \frac{\mu_0}{4\pi} \frac{q\vec{v} \times \hat{r}}{r^2} \quad \begin{array}{l} \text{(magnetic field of a point charge} \\ \text{with constant velocity)} \end{array} \tag{28.2}$$

Figure 28.1 shows the relationship of $\hat{r}$ to P and also shows the magnetic field $\vec{B}$ at several points in the vicinity of the charge. At all points along a line through the charge parallel to the velocity $\vec{v}$, the field is zero because $\sin\phi = 0$ at all such points. At any distance r from q, $\vec{B}$ has its greatest magnitude at points lying in the plane perpendicular to $\vec{v}$ because at all such points, $\phi = 90°$ and $\sin\phi = 1$. If the charge q is negative, the directions of $\vec{B}$ are opposite to those shown in Fig. 28.1.

Moving Charge: Magnetic Field Lines

A point charge in motion also produces an *electric* field, with field lines that radiate outward from a positive charge. The *magnetic* field lines are completely different. The above discussion shows that for a point charge moving with velocity $\vec{v}$, the magnetic field lines are *circles* centered on the line of $\vec{v}$ and lying in planes perpendicular to this line. The field-line directions for a positive charge are given by the following *right-hand rule,* one of several that we will encounter in this chapter for determining the direction of the magnetic field caused by different sources. Grasp the velocity vector $\vec{v}$ with your right hand so that your right thumb points in the direction of $\vec{v}$; your fingers then curl around the line of $\vec{v}$ in the same sense as the magnetic field lines, assuming q is positive. Figure 28.1a shows parts of a few field lines; Fig. 28.1b shows some field lines in a plane through q, perpendicular to $\vec{v}$, as seen by looking in the direction of $\vec{v}$. If the point charge is negative, the directions of the field and field lines are the opposite of those shown in Fig. 28.1.

Equations (28.1) and (28.2) describe the $\vec{B}$ field of a point charge moving with *constant* velocity. If the charge *accelerates*, the field can be much more complicated. We won't need these more complicated results for our purposes. (The moving charged particles that make up a current in a wire accelerate at points where the wire bends and the direction of $\vec{v}$ changes. But because the magnitude v_d of the drift velocity in a conductor is typically very small, the acceleration v_d^2/r is also very small, and the effects of acceleration can be ignored.)

As we discussed in Section 27.2, the unit of B is one tesla (1 T):

$$1\,\text{T} = 1\,\text{N} \cdot \text{s}/\text{C} \cdot \text{m} = 1\,\text{N}/\text{A} \cdot \text{m}$$

Using this with Eq. (28.1) or (28.2), we find that the units of the constant μ_0 are

$$1\,\text{N} \cdot \text{s}^2/\text{C}^2 = 1\,\text{N}/\text{A}^2 = 1\,\text{Wb}/\text{A} \cdot \text{m} = 1\,\text{T} \cdot \text{m}/\text{A}$$

In SI units the numerical value of μ_0 is exactly $4\pi \times 10^{-7}$. Thus

$$\mu_0 = 4\pi \times 10^{-7}\,\text{N} \cdot \text{s}^2/\text{C}^2 = 4\pi \times 10^{-7}\,\text{Wb}/\text{A} \cdot \text{m}$$
$$= 4\pi \times 10^{-7}\,\text{T} \cdot \text{m}/\text{A} \tag{28.3}$$

It may seem incredible that μ_0 has *exactly* this numerical value! In fact this is a *defined* value that arises from the definition of the ampere, as we'll discuss in Section 28.4.

We mentioned in Section 21.3 that the constant $1/4\pi\epsilon_0$ in Coulomb's law is related to the speed of light c:

$$k = \frac{1}{4\pi\epsilon_0} = (10^{-7}\,\text{N} \cdot \text{s}^2/\text{C}^2)c^2$$

When we study electromagnetic waves in Chapter 32, we will find that their speed of propagation in vacuum, which is equal to the speed of light c, is given by

$$c^2 = \frac{1}{\epsilon_0\mu_0} \tag{28.4}$$

If we solve the equation $k = 1/4\pi\epsilon_0$ for ϵ_0, substitute the resulting expression into Eq. (28.4), and solve for μ_0, we indeed get the value of μ_0 stated above. This discussion is a little premature, but it may give you a hint that electric and magnetic fields are intimately related to the nature of light.

Example 28.1   **Forces between two moving protons**

Two protons move parallel to the x-axis in opposite directions (Fig. 28.2) at the same speed v (small compared to the speed of light c). At the instant shown, find the electric and magnetic forces on the upper proton and determine the ratio of their magnitudes.

SOLUTION

IDENTIFY: The electric force is given by Coulomb's law. To find the magnetic force, we must first find the magnetic field that the lower proton produces at the position of the upper proton.

SET UP: We use Eq. (21.2) for Coulomb's law. Equation (28.2) gives us the magnetic field due to the lower proton, and the magnetic force law, Eq. (27.2), gives us the resulting magnetic force on the upper proton.

EXECUTE: From Coulomb's law, the magnitude of the electric force on the upper proton is

$$F_E = \frac{1}{4\pi\epsilon_0}\frac{q^2}{r^2}$$

28.2 Electric and magnetic forces between two moving protons.

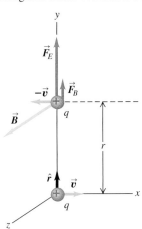

Continued

The forces are repulsive, and the force on the upper proton is vertically upward (in the $+y$-direction).

From the right-hand rule for the cross product $\vec{v} \times \hat{r}$ in Eq. (28.2), the $\vec{B}$-field due to the lower proton at the position of the upper proton is in the $+z$-direction (see Fig. 28.2). From Eq. (28.2), the magnitude of $\vec{B}$ is

$$B = \frac{\mu_0}{4\pi} \frac{qv}{r^2}$$

since $\phi = 90°$. Alternatively, from Eq. (28.2),

$$\vec{B} = \frac{\mu_0}{4\pi} \frac{q(v\hat{\imath}) \times \hat{\jmath}}{r^2} = \frac{\mu_0}{4\pi} \frac{qv}{r^2}\hat{k}$$

The velocity of the upper proton is $-\vec{v}$ and the magnetic force on it is $\vec{F} = q(-\vec{v}) \times \vec{B}$. Combining this with the expressions for $\vec{B}$, we find

$$F_B = \frac{\mu_0}{4\pi} \frac{q^2v^2}{r^2} \quad \text{or}$$

$$\vec{F}_B = q(-\vec{v}) \times \vec{B} = q(-v\hat{\imath}) \times \frac{\mu_0}{4\pi} \frac{qv}{r^2}\hat{k} = \frac{\mu_0}{4\pi} \frac{q^2v^2}{r^2}\hat{\jmath}$$

The magnetic interaction in this situation is also repulsive. The ratio of the magnitudes of the two forces is

$$\frac{F_B}{F_E} = \frac{\mu_0 q^2 v^2 / 4\pi r^2}{q^2 / 4\pi\epsilon_0 r^2} = \frac{\mu_0 v^2}{1/\epsilon_0} = \epsilon_0 \mu_0 v^2$$

Using the relationship $\epsilon_0\mu_0 = 1/c^2$, Eq. (28.4), we can express our result very simply as

$$\frac{F_B}{F_E} = \frac{v^2}{c^2}$$

When v is small in comparison to c, the speed of light, the magnetic force is much smaller than the electric force.

EVALUATE: Note that it is essential to use the same frame of reference in this entire calculation. We have described the velocities and the fields as they appear to an observer who is stationary in the coordinate system of Fig. 28.2. In a coordinate system that moves with one of the charges, one of the velocities would be zero, so there would be *no* magnetic force. The explanation of this apparent paradox provided one of the paths that led to the special theory of relativity.

Test Your Understanding of Section 28.1   (a) If two protons are traveling parallel to each other in the *same* direction and at the same speed, is the magnetic force between them (i) attractive or (ii) repulsive? (b) Is the net force between them (i) attractive, (ii) repulsive, or (iii) zero? (Assume that the protons' speed is much slower than the speed of light.)

28.2 Magnetic Field of a Current Element

Just as for the electric field, there is a **principle of superposition of magnetic fields:**

> **The total magnetic field caused by several moving charges is the vector sum of the fields caused by the individual charges.**

We can use this principle with the results of Section 28.1 to find the magnetic field produced by a current in a conductor.

We begin by calculating the magnetic field caused by a short segment $d\vec{l}$ of a current-carrying conductor, as shown in Fig. 28.3a. The volume of the segment is $A\,dl$, where A is the cross-sectional area of the conductor. If there are n moving charged particles per unit volume, each of charge q, the total moving charge dQ in the segment is

$$dQ = nqA\,dl$$

The moving charges in this segment are equivalent to a single charge dQ, traveling with a velocity equal to the *drift* velocity $\vec{v}_d$. (Magnetic fields due to the *random* motions of the charges will, on average, cancel out at every point.) From Eq. (28.1) the magnitude of the resulting field $d\vec{B}$ at any field point P is

$$dB = \frac{\mu_0}{4\pi} \frac{|dQ|v_d \sin\phi}{r^2} = \frac{\mu_0}{4\pi} \frac{n|q|v_d A\,dl \sin\phi}{r^2}$$

But from Eq. (25.2), $n|q|v_d A$ equals the current I in the element. So

$$dB = \frac{\mu_0}{4\pi} \frac{I\,dl \sin\phi}{r^2} \tag{28.5}$$

Current Element: Vector Magnectic Field

In vector form, using the unit vector $\hat{r}$ as in Section 28.1, we have

$$d\vec{B} = \frac{\mu_0}{4\pi} \frac{I\,d\vec{l} \times \hat{r}}{r^2} \qquad \text{(magnetic field of a current element)} \qquad (28.6)$$

where $d\vec{l}$ is a vector with length dl, in the same direction as the current in the conductor.

Equations (28.5) and (28.6) are called the **law of Biot and Savart** (pronounced "Bee-oh" and "Suh-var"). We can use this law to find the total magnetic field $\vec{B}$ at any point in space due to the current in a complete circuit. To do this, we integrate Eq. (28.6) over all segments $d\vec{l}$ that carry current; symbolically,

$$\vec{B} = \frac{\mu_0}{4\pi} \int \frac{I\,d\vec{l} \times \hat{r}}{r^2} \qquad (28.7)$$

In the following sections we will carry out this vector integration for several examples.

Current Element: Magnetic Field Lines

As Fig. 28.3 shows, the field vectors $d\vec{B}$ and the magnetic field lines of a current element are exactly like those set up by a positive charge dQ moving in the direction of the drift velocity $\vec{v}_{\mathrm{d}}$. The field lines are circles in planes perpendicular to $d\vec{l}$ and centered on the line of $d\vec{l}$. Their directions are given by the same right-hand rule that we introduced for point charges in Section 28.1.

We can't verify Eq. (28.5) or (28.6) directly because we can never experiment with an isolated segment of a current-carrying circuit. What we measure experimentally is the *total* $\vec{B}$ for a complete circuit. But we can still verify these equations indirectly by calculating $\vec{B}$ for various current configurations using Eq. (28.7) and comparing the results with experimental measurements.

If matter is present in the space around a current-carrying conductor, the field at a field point P in its vicinity will have an additional contribution resulting from the *magnetization* of the material. We'll return to this point in Section 28.8. However, unless the material is iron or some other ferromagnetic material, the additional field is small and is usually negligible. Additional complications arise if time-varying electric or magnetic fields are present or if the material is a superconductor; we'll return to these topics later.

28.3 (a) Magnetic-field vectors due to a current element $d\vec{l}$. (b) Magnetic field lines in a plane containing the current element $d\vec{l}$. Compare this figure to Fig. 28.1 for the field of a moving point charge.

(a) Perspective view

Right-hand rule for the magnetic field due to a current element: Point the thumb of your right hand in the direction of the current. Your fingers now curl around the current element in the direction of the magnetic field lines.

For these field points, $\vec{r}$ and $d\vec{l}$ both lie in the beige plane, and $d\vec{B}$ is perpendicular to this plane.

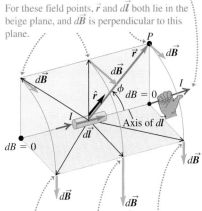

For these field points, $\vec{r}$ and $d\vec{l}$ both lie in the gold plane, and $d\vec{B}$ is perpendicular to this plane.

(b) View along the axis of the current element

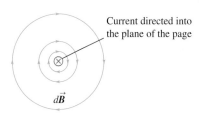

Current directed into the plane of the page

Problem-Solving Strategy 28.1 | **Magnetic-Field Calculations**

IDENTIFY *the relevant concepts:* The law of Biot and Savart allows you to calculate the magnetic field due to a current-carrying wire of any shape. The idea is to calculate the field due to a representative current element in the wire and then combine the contributions from all such elements to find the total field.

SET UP *the problem* using the following steps:
1. Make a diagram showing a representative current element and the point P at which the field is to be determined (the field point).
2. Draw the current element $d\vec{l}$, being careful that it points in the direction of the current.
3. Draw the unit vector $\hat{r}$. Note that it is always directed *from* the current element (the source point) to the field point P.
4. Identify the target variables. Usually they will be the magnitude and direction of the magnetic field $\vec{B}$.

EXECUTE *the solution* as follows:
1. Use Eq. (28.5) or (28.6) to express the magnetic field $d\vec{B}$ at P from the representative current element.
2. Add up all the $d\vec{B}$'s to find the total field at point P. In some situations the $d\vec{B}$'s at point P have the same direction for all the current elements; then the magnitude of the total $\vec{B}$ field is the sum of the magnitudes of the $d\vec{B}$'s. But often the $d\vec{B}$'s have different directions for different current elements. Then you have to set up a coordinate system and represent each $d\vec{B}$ in terms of its components. The integral for the total $\vec{B}$ is then expressed in terms of an integral for each component.
3. Sometimes you can use the symmetry of the situation to prove that one component of $\vec{B}$ must vanish. Always be alert for ways to use symmetry to simplify the problem.

Continued

4. Look for ways to use the principle of superposition of magnetic fields. Later in this chapter we'll determine the fields produced by certain simple conductor shapes; if you encounter a conductor of a complex shape that can be represented as a combination of these simple shapes, you can use superposition to find the field of the complex shape. Examples include a rectangular loop and a semicircle with straight line segments on both sides.

EVALUATE *your answer:* Often your answer will be a mathematical expression for $\vec{B}$ as a function of the position of the field point. Check the answer by examining its behavior in as many limits as you can.

Example 28.2 | **Magnetic field of a current segment**

A copper wire carries a steady current of 125 A to an electroplating tank. Find the magnetic field caused by a 1.0-cm segment of this wire at a point 1.2 m away from it, if the point is (a) point P_1, straight out to the side of the segment, and (b) point P_2, on a line at 30° to the segment, as shown in Fig. 28.4.

SOLUTION

IDENTIFY: Although Eqs. (28.5) and (28.6) are strictly to be used with infinitesimal current elements only, we may use them here since the segment's 1.0-cm length is much smaller than the 1.2-m distance to the field point.

SET UP: The current element is shown in red in Fig. 28.4 and points in the $-x$-direction (the direction of the current). The unit vector $\hat{r}$ for each field point is directed from the current element toward that point: $\hat{r}$ is in the $+y$-direction for point P_1 and at an angle of 30° above the $-x$-direction for point P_2.

EXECUTE: (a) From the right-hand rule, the direction of $\vec{B}$ at P_1 is *into* the xy-plane of Fig. 28.4. Or, using unit vectors, we note that $d\vec{l} = dl(-\hat{i})$. At point P_1, $\hat{r} = \hat{j}$, so in Eq. (28.6),

$$d\vec{l} \times \hat{r} = dl(-\hat{i}) \times \hat{j} = dl(-\hat{k})$$

The negative z-direction is *into* the plane.

To find the magnitude of $\vec{B}$, we use Eq. (28.5). At point P_1, the angle between $d\vec{l}$ and $\hat{r}$ is 90°, so

$$B = \frac{\mu_0}{4\pi} \frac{I \, dl \sin\phi}{r^2}$$

$$= (10^{-7} \, \text{T} \cdot \text{m/A}) \frac{(125 \, \text{A})(1.0 \times 10^{-2} \, \text{m})(\sin 90°)}{(1.2 \, \text{m})^2}$$

$$= 8.7 \times 10^{-8} \, \text{T}$$

28.4 Finding the magnetic field at two points due to a 1.0-cm segment of current-carrying wire (not shown to scale).

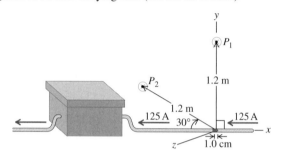

(b) At point P_2 the direction of $\vec{B}$ is again into the xy-plane of the figure. The angle between $d\vec{l}$ and $\hat{r}$ is 30°, and

$$B = (10^{-7} \, \text{T} \cdot \text{m/A}) \frac{(125 \, \text{A})(1.0 \times 10^{-2} \, \text{m})(\sin 30°)}{(1.2 \, \text{m})^2}$$

$$= 4.3 \times 10^{-8} \, \text{T}$$

EVALUATE: You can check our results for the direction of $\vec{B}$ by comparing them with Fig. 28.3. The xy-plane in Fig. 28.4 corresponds to the beige plane in Fig. 28.3. However, in the present example the direction of the current and hence of $d\vec{l}$ is the reverse of the direction shown in Fig. 28.3, so the direction of the magnetic field is reversed as well. Hence the field at points in the xy-plane in Fig. 28.4 must point *into*, not out of, that plane. This is just what we concluded above.

Note that these magnetic-field magnitudes are very small; for comparison the magnetic field of the earth is of the order of 10^{-4} T. Note also that the values are not the *total* fields at points P_1 and P_2, but only the contributions from the short segment of conductor described.

Test Your Understanding of Section 28.2 An infinitesimal current element located at the origin $(x = y = z = 0)$ carries current I in the positive y-direction. Rank the following locations in order of the strength of the magnetic field that the current element produces at that location, from largest to smallest value. (i) $x = L$, $y = 0$, $z = 0$; (ii) $x = 0$, $y = L$, $z = 0$; (iii) $x = 0$, $y = 0$, $z = L$; (iv) $x = L/\sqrt{2}$, $y = L/\sqrt{2}$, $z = 0$.

28.3 Magnetic Field of a Straight Current-Carrying Conductor

An important application of the law of Biot and Savart is finding the magnetic field produced by a straight current-carrying conductor. This result is useful because straight conducting wires are found in essentially all electric and electronic devices. Fig. 28.5 shows such a conductor with length $2a$ carrying a current I. We will find $\vec{B}$ at a point a distance x from the conductor on its perpendicular bisector.

We first use the law of Biot and Savart, Eq. (28.5), to find the field $d\vec{B}$ caused by the element of conductor of length $dl = dy$ shown in Fig. 28.5. From the figure, $r = \sqrt{x^2 + y^2}$ and $\sin\phi = \sin(\pi - \phi) = x/\sqrt{x^2 + y^2}$. The right-hand rule for the vector product $d\vec{l} \times \hat{r}$ shows that the *direction* of $d\vec{B}$ is into the plane of the figure, perpendicular to the plane; furthermore, the directions of the $d\vec{B}$'s from *all* elements of the conductor are the same. Thus in integrating Eq. (28.7), we can just add the *magnitudes* of the $d\vec{B}$'s, a significant simplification.

Putting the pieces together, we find that the magnitude of the total $\vec{B}$ field is

$$B = \frac{\mu_0 I}{4\pi} \int_{-a}^{a} \frac{x\, dy}{(x^2 + y^2)^{3/2}}$$

We can integrate this by trigonometric substitution or by using an integral table. The final result is

$$B = \frac{\mu_0 I}{4\pi} \frac{2a}{x\sqrt{x^2 + a^2}} \qquad (28.8)$$

When the length $2a$ of the conductor is very great in comparison to its distance x from point P, we can consider it to be infinitely long. When a is much larger than x, $\sqrt{x^2 + a^2}$ is approximately equal to a; hence in the limit $a \rightarrow \infty$, Eq. (28.8) becomes

$$B = \frac{\mu_0 I}{2\pi x}$$

The physical situation has axial symmetry about the y-axis. Hence $\vec{B}$ must have the same *magnitude* at all points on a circle centered on the conductor and lying in a plane perpendicular to it, and the *direction* of $\vec{B}$ must be everywhere tangent to such a circle. Thus, at all points on a circle of radius r around the conductor, the magnitude B is

$$B = \frac{\mu_0 I}{2\pi r} \qquad \text{(near a long, straight, current-carrying conductor)} \quad (28.9)$$

Part of the magnetic field around a long, straight, current-carrying conductor is shown in Fig. 28.6.

The geometry of this problem is similar to that of Example 21.11 (Section 21.5), in which we solved the problem of the *electric* field caused by an infinite line of charge. The same integral appears in both problems, and the field magnitudes in both problems are proportional to $1/r$. But the lines of $\vec{B}$ in the magnetic problem have completely different shapes than the lines of $\vec{E}$ in the analogous electrical problem. Electric field lines radiate outward from a positive line charge distribution (inward for negative charges). By contrast, magnetic field lines *encircle* the current that acts as their source. Electric field lines due to charges begin and end at those charges, but magnetic field lines always form closed loops and *never* have end points, irrespective of the shape of the current-carrying conductor that sets up the field. As we discussed in Section 27.3, this is a consequence of Gauss's law for magnetism, which states that the total magnetic flux through *any* closed surface is always zero:

$$\oint \vec{B} \cdot d\vec{A} = 0 \qquad \text{(magnetic flux through any closed surface)} \quad (28.10)$$

This implies that there are no isolated magnetic charges or magnetic monopoles. Any magnetic field line that enters a closed surface must also emerge from that surface.

28.5 Magnetic field produced by a straight current-carrying conductor of length $2a$.

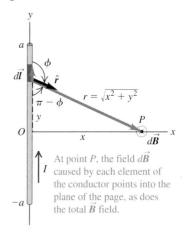

At point P, the field $d\vec{B}$ caused by each element of the conductor points into the plane of the page, as does the total $\vec{B}$ field.

28.6 Magnetic field around a long, straight, current-carrying conductor. The field lines are circles, with directions determined by the right-hand rule.

Right-hand rule for the magnetic field around a current-carrying wire: Point the thumb of your right hand in the direction of the current. Your fingers now curl around the wire in the direction of the magnetic field lines.

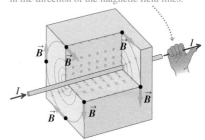

Example 28.3 | **Magnetic field of a single wire**

A long, straight conductor carries a current of 1.0 A. At what distance from the axis of the conductor is the magnetic field caused by the current equal in magnitude to the earth's magnetic field in Pittsburgh (about 0.5×10^{-4} T)?

SOLUTION

IDENTIFY: The straight conductor is described as being long, which means that its length is much greater than the distance from the conductor at which we measure the field. Hence we can use the ideas of this section.

SET UP: The geometry is the same as that in Fig. 28.6, so we use Eq. (28.8). All of the quantities in this equation are known except the target variable, the distance r.

EXECUTE: We solve Eq. (28.8) for r and insert the appropriate numbers:

$$r = \frac{\mu_0 I}{2\pi B}$$
$$= \frac{(4\pi \times 10^{-7}\ \text{T} \cdot \text{m/A})(1.0\ \text{A})}{(2\pi)(0.5 \times 10^{-4}\ \text{T})} = 4 \times 10^{-3}\ \text{m} = 4\ \text{mm}$$

EVALUATE: Currents of an ampere or so are typical of those found in the wiring of home appliances. This example shows that the magnetic fields produced by these appliances are very weak even at points very close to the wire. At greater distances the field becomes even weaker; for example, at five times the distance ($r = 20\ \text{mm} = 2\ \text{cm} = 2 \times 10^{-2}\ \text{m}$) the field is one-fifth as great ($B = 0.1 \times 10^{-4}\ \text{T}$).

Example 28.4 | **Magnetic field of two wires**

Fig. 28.7a is an end-on view of two long, straight, parallel wires perpendicular to the xy-plane, each carrying a current I but in opposite directions. (a) Find the magnitude and direction of $\vec{B}$ at points P_1, P_2, and P_3. (b) Find the magnitude and direction of $\vec{B}$ at any point on the x-axis to the right of wire 2 in terms of the x-coordinate of the point.

SOLUTION

IDENTIFY: We can find the magnetic fields $\vec{B}_1$ and $\vec{B}_2$ due to each wire using the ideas of this section. The principle of superposition of magnetic fields says that the total magnetic field $\vec{B}$ is the vector sum of $\vec{B}_1$ and $\vec{B}_2$.

SET UP: We use Eq. (28.9) to find the magnitude of the fields $\vec{B}_1$ (due to wire 1) and $\vec{B}_2$ (due to wire 2) at any point. We find the directions of these fields using the right-hand rule. The total magnetic field at the point in question is $\vec{B}_\text{total} = \vec{B}_1 + \vec{B}_2$.

EXECUTE: (a) Point P_1 is closer to wire 1 (distance $2d$) than to wire 2 (distance $4d$), so at this point the field magnitude B_1 is greater than the magnitude B_2:

$$B_1 = \frac{\mu_0 I}{2\pi(2d)} = \frac{\mu_0 I}{4\pi d} \qquad B_2 = \frac{\mu_0 I}{2\pi(4d)} = \frac{\mu_0 I}{8\pi d}$$

The right-hand rule shows that $\vec{B}_1$ is in the negative y-direction and $\vec{B}_2$ is in the positive y-direction. Since B_1 is the larger magnitude, the total field $\vec{B}_\text{total} = \vec{B}_1 + \vec{B}_2$ is in the negative y-direction, with magnitude

$$B_\text{total} = B_1 - B_2 = \frac{\mu_0 I}{4\pi d} - \frac{\mu_0 I}{8\pi d} = \frac{\mu_0 I}{8\pi d} \qquad \text{(point } P_1\text{)}$$

At point P_2, a distance d from both wires, $\vec{B}_1$ and $\vec{B}_2$ are both in the positive y-direction, and both have the same magnitude:

$$B_1 = B_2 = \frac{\mu_0 I}{2\pi d}$$

so $\vec{B}_\text{total}$ is also in the positive y-direction and has magnitude

$$B_\text{total} = B_1 + B_2 = \frac{\mu_0 I}{\pi d} \qquad \text{(point } P_2\text{)}$$

Finally, at point P_3 the right-hand rule shows that $\vec{B}_1$ is in the positive y-direction and $\vec{B}_2$ is in the negative y-direction. This point is farther from wire 1 (distance $3d$) than from wire 2 (distance d), so B_1 is less than B_2:

$$B_1 = \frac{\mu_0 I}{2\pi(3d)} = \frac{\mu_0 I}{6\pi d} \qquad B_2 = \frac{\mu_0 I}{2\pi d}$$

28.7 (a) Two long, straight conductors carrying equal currents in opposite directions. The conductors are seen end-on. (b) Map of the magnetic field produced by the two conductors. The field lines are closest together between the conductors, where the field is strongest.

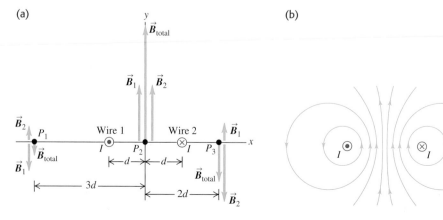

The total field is in the negative y-direction, the same as $\vec{B}_2$, and has magnitude

$$B_{\text{total}} = B_2 - B_1 = \frac{\mu_0 I}{2\pi d} - \frac{\mu_0 I}{6\pi d} = \frac{\mu_0 I}{3\pi d} \qquad \text{(point } P_3\text{)}$$

You should be able to use the right-hand rule to verify for yourself the directions of $\vec{B}_1$ and $\vec{B}_2$ for each point.

The fields $\vec{B}_1$, $\vec{B}_2$, and $\vec{B}_{\text{total}}$ at each of the three points are shown in Fig. 28.7a. The same technique can be used to find $\vec{B}_{\text{total}}$ at any point; for points off the x-axis, caution must be taken in vector addition, since $\vec{B}_1$ and $\vec{B}_2$ need no longer be simply parallel or antiparallel (see Problem 28.60). Figure 28.7b shows some of the magnetic field lines due to this combination of wires.

(b) At any point to the right of wire 2 (that is, for $x > d$), $\vec{B}_1$ and $\vec{B}_2$ are in the same directions as at P_3. As x increases, both $\vec{B}_1$ and $\vec{B}_2$ decrease in magnitude, so $\vec{B}_{\text{total}}$ must decrease as well. The magnitudes of the fields due to each wire are

$$B_1 = \frac{\mu_0 I}{2\pi(x + d)} \qquad \text{and} \qquad B_2 = \frac{\mu_0 I}{2\pi(x - d)}$$

At any field point to the right of wire 2, wire 2 is closer than wire 1, and so $B_2 > B_1$. Hence $\vec{B}_{\text{total}}$ is in the negative y-direction, the same as $\vec{B}_2$, and has magnitude

$$B_{\text{total}} = B_2 - B_1 = \frac{\mu_0 I}{2\pi(x - d)} - \frac{\mu_0 I}{2\pi(x + d)} = \frac{\mu_0 I d}{\pi(x^2 - d^2)}$$

where we combined the two terms using a common denominator.

EVALUATE: At points very far from the wires, so that x is much larger than d, the d^2 term in the denominator can be neglected, and

$$B_{\text{total}} = \frac{\mu_0 I d}{\pi x^2}$$

The magnetic-field magnitude for a single wire decreases with distance in proportion to $1/x$, as shown by Eq. (28.9); for two wires carrying opposite currents, $\vec{B}_1$ and $\vec{B}_2$ partially cancel each other, and so the magnitude of $\vec{B}_{\text{total}}$ decreases more rapidly, in proportion to $1/x^2$. This effect is used in communication systems such as telephone or computer networks. The wiring is arranged so that a conductor carrying a signal in one direction and the conductor carrying the return signal are side by side, as in Fig. 28.7a, or twisted around each other (Fig. 28.8). As a result, the magnetic field caused *outside* the conductors by these signals is greatly reduced and is less likely to exert unwanted forces on other information-carrying currents.

28.8 Computer cables, or cables for audio-video equipment, create little or no magnetic field. This is because within each cable, closely spaced wires carry current in both directions along the length of the cable. The magnetic fields from these opposing currents cancel each other.

Test Your Understanding of Section 28.3 The figure at right shows a circuit that lies on a horizontal table. A compass is placed on top of the circuit as shown. A battery is to be connected to the circuit so that when the switch is closed, the compass needle deflects counterclockwise. In which orientation, A or B, should the battery be placed in the circuit?

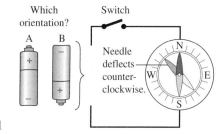

28.4 Force Between Parallel Conductors

In Example 28.4 (Section 28.3) we showed how to use the principle of superposition of magnetic fields to find the total field due to two long current-carrying conductors. Another important aspect of this configuration is the *interaction force* between the conductors. This force plays a role in many practical situations in which current-carrying wires are close to each other, and it also has fundamental significance in connection with the definition of the ampere. Figure 28.9 shows segments of two long, straight, parallel conductors separated by a distance r and carrying currents I and I' in the same direction. Each conductor lies in the magnetic field set up by the other, so each experiences a force. The diagram shows some of the field lines set up by the current in the lower conductor.

From Eq. (28.9) the lower conductor produces a $\vec{B}$ field that, at the position of the upper conductor, has magnitude

$$B = \frac{\mu_0 I}{2\pi r}$$

From Eq. (27.19) the force that this field exerts on a length L of the upper conductor is $\vec{F} = I'\vec{L} \times \vec{B}$, where the vector $\vec{L}$ is in the direction of the current I' and

28.9 Parallel conductors carrying currents in the same direction attract each other. The diagrams show how the magnetic field $\vec{B}$ caused by the current in the lower conductor exerts a force $\vec{F}$ on the upper conductor.

The magnetic field of the lower wire exerts an attractive force on the upper wire. By the same token, the upper wire attracts the lower one.

If the wires had currents in *opposite* directions, they would *repel* each other.

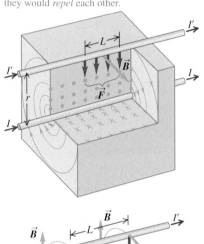

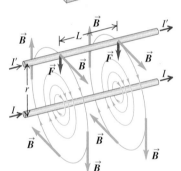

has magnitude L. Since $\vec{B}$ is perpendicular to the length of the conductor and hence to $\vec{L}$, the magnitude of this force is

$$F = I'LB = \frac{\mu_0 II'L}{2\pi r}$$

and the force *per unit length* F/L is

$$\frac{F}{L} = \frac{\mu_0 II'}{2\pi r} \qquad \text{(two long, parallel, current-carrying conductors)} \quad (28.11)$$

Applying the right-hand rule to $\vec{F} = I'\vec{L} \times \vec{B}$ shows that the force on the upper conductor is directed *downward*.

The current in the upper conductor also sets up a field at the position of the lower one. Two successive applications of the right-hand rule for vector products (one to find the direction of the $\vec{B}$ field due to the upper conductor, as in Section 28.2, and one to find the direction of the force that this field exerts on the lower conductor, as in Section 27.6) show that the force on the lower conductor is *upward*. Thus *two parallel conductors carrying current in the same direction attract each other.* If the direction of either current is reversed, the forces also reverse. *Parallel conductors carrying currents in opposite directions repel each other.*

Magnetic Forces and Defining the Ampere

The attraction or repulsion between two straight, parallel, current-carrying conductors is the basis of the official SI definition of the **ampere:**

> *One ampere* is that unvarying current that, if present in each of two parallel conductors of infinite length and one meter apart in empty space, causes each conductor to experience a force of exactly 2×10^{-7} newtons per meter of length.

From Eq. (28.11) you can see that this definition of the ampere is what leads us to choose the value of $4\pi \times 10^{-7}\ \text{T} \cdot \text{m/A}$ for μ_0. It also forms the basis of the SI definition of the coulomb, which is the amount of charge transferred in one second by a current of one ampere.

This is an *operational definition;* it gives us an actual experimental procedure for measuring current and defining a unit of current. In principle we could use this definition to calibrate an ammeter, using only a meter stick and a spring balance. For high-precision standardization of the ampere, coils of wire are used instead of straight wires, and their separation is only a few centimeters. Even more precise measurements of the standardized ampere are possible using a version of the Hall effect (see Section 27.9).

Mutual forces of attraction exist not only between *wires* carrying currents in the same direction, but also between the longitudinal elements of a single current-carrying conductor. If the conductor is a liquid or an ionized gas (a plasma), these forces result in a constriction of the conductor, as if its surface were acted on by an inward pressure. The constriction of the conductor is called the *pinch effect.* The high temperature produced by the pinch effect in a plasma has been used in one technique to bring about nuclear fusion.

Example 28.5   Forces between parallel wires

Two straight, parallel, superconducting wires 4.5 mm apart carry equal currents of 15,000 A in opposite directions. Should we worry about the mechanical strength of these wires?

SOLUTION

IDENTIFY: Whether or not we need to worry about the wires' mechanical strength depends on how much magnetic force each wire exerts on the other.

28.10 Our sketch for this problem.

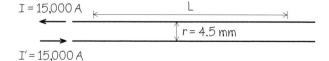

SET UP: Figure 28.10 shows the situation. Our target variable is the magnetic force per unit length of wire, which we find using Eq. (28.11).

EXECUTE: Because the currents are in opposite directions, the two conductors repel each other. From Eq. (28.11) the force per unit length is

$$\frac{F}{L} = \frac{\mu_0 II'}{2\pi r} = \frac{(4\pi \times 10^{-7}\ \text{T}\cdot\text{m/A})(15{,}000\ \text{A})^2}{(2\pi)(4.5 \times 10^{-3}\ \text{m})}$$

$$= 1.0 \times 10^4\ \text{N/m}$$

EVALUATE: This is a large force, more than one ton per meter, so the mechanical strengths of the conductors and insulating materials are certainly a significant consideration. Currents and separations of this magnitude are used in superconducting electromagnets in particle accelerators, and mechanical stress analysis is a crucial part of the design process.

Test Your Understanding of Section 28.4 A solenoid is a wire wound into a helical coil. The figure at right shows a solenoid that carries a current I. (a) Is the  *magnetic* force that one turn of the coil exerts on an adjacent turn (i) attractive, (ii) repulsive, or (iii) zero? (b) Is the *electric* force that one turn of the coil exerts on an adjacent turn (i) attractive, (ii) repulsive, or (iii) zero? (c) Is the *magnetic* force between opposite sides of the same turn of the coil (i) attractive, (ii) repulsive, or (iii) zero? (d) Is the *electric* force between opposite sides of the same turn of the coil (i) attractive, (ii) repulsive, or (iii) zero?

28.5 Magnetic Field of a Circular Current Loop

If you look inside a doorbell, a transformer, an electric motor, or an electromagnet (Fig. 28.11), you will find coils of wire with a large number of turns, spaced so closely that each turn is very nearly a planar circular loop. A current in such a coil is used to establish a magnetic field. So it is worthwhile to derive an expression for the magnetic field produced by a single circular conducting loop carrying a current or by N closely spaced circular loops forming a coil. In Section 27.7 we considered the force and torque on such a current loop placed in an external magnetic field produced by other currents; we are now about to find the magnetic field produced by the loop itself.

Figure 28.12 shows a circular conductor with radius a that carries a current I. The current is led into and out of the loop through two long, straight wires side by side; the currents in these straight wires are in opposite directions, and their magnetic fields very nearly cancel each other (see Example 28.4 in Section 28.3).

We can use the law of Biot and Savart, Eq. (28.5) or (28.6), to find the magnetic field at a point P on the axis of the loop, at a distance x from the center. As the figure shows, $d\vec{l}$ and $\hat{r}$ are perpendicular, and the direction of the field $d\vec{B}$ caused by this particular element $d\vec{l}$ lies in the xy-plane. Since $r^2 = x^2 + a^2$, the magnitude dB of the field due to element $d\vec{l}$ is

$$dB = \frac{\mu_0 I}{4\pi} \frac{dl}{(x^2 + a^2)} \tag{28.12}$$

The components of the vector $d\vec{B}$ are

$$dB_x = dB\cos\theta = \frac{\mu_0 I}{4\pi} \frac{dl}{(x^2 + a^2)} \frac{a}{(x^2 + a^2)^{1/2}} \tag{28.13}$$

$$dB_y = dB\sin\theta = \frac{\mu_0 I}{4\pi} \frac{dl}{(x^2 + a^2)} \frac{x}{(x^2 + a^2)^{1/2}} \tag{28.14}$$

The situation has rotational symmetry about the x-axis, so there cannot be a component of the total field $\vec{B}$ perpendicular to this axis. For every element $d\vec{l}$ there is a corresponding element on the opposite side of the loop, with opposite direction. These two elements give equal contributions to the x-component of $d\vec{B}$, given by Eq. (28.13), but *opposite* components perpendicular to the

28.11 This electromagnet contains a current-carrying coil with numerous turns of wire. The resulting magnetic field can pick up large quantities of steel bars and other iron-bearing items.

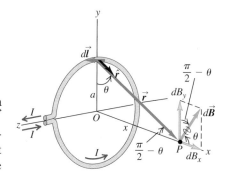

28.12 Magnetic field on the axis of a circular loop. The current in the segment $d\vec{l}$ causes the field $d\vec{B}$, which lies in the xy-plane. The currents in other $d\vec{l}$'s cause $d\vec{B}$'s with different components perpendicular to the x-axis; these components add to zero. The x-components of the $d\vec{B}$'s combine to give the total $\vec{B}$ field at point P.

x-axis. Thus all the perpendicular components cancel and only the *x*-components survive.

To obtain the *x*-component of the total field $\vec{B}$, we integrate Eq. (28.13), including all the $d\vec{l}$'s around the loop. Everything in this expression except dl is constant and can be taken outside the integral, and we have

$$B_x = \int \frac{\mu_0 I}{4\pi} \frac{a\,dl}{(x^2 + a^2)^{3/2}} = \frac{\mu_0 I a}{4\pi(x^2 + a^2)^{3/2}} \int dl$$

The integral of dl is just the circumference of the circle, $\int dl = 2\pi a$, and we finally get

$$B_x = \frac{\mu_0 I a^2}{2(x^2 + a^2)^{3/2}} \qquad \text{(on the axis of a circular loop)} \qquad (28.15)$$

The *direction* of the magnetic field on the axis of a current-carrying loop is given by a right-hand rule. If you curl the fingers of your right hand around the loop in the direction of the current, your right thumb points in the direction of the field (Fig. 28.13).

28.13 The right-hand rule for the direction of the magnetic field produced on the axis of a current-carrying coil.

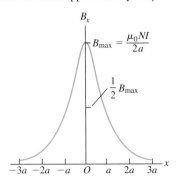

The right-hand rule for the magnetic field produced by a current in a loop:

When the fingers of your right hand curl in the direction of *I*, your right thumb points in the direction of $\vec{B}$.

Magnetic Field on the Axis of a Coil

Now suppose that instead of the single loop in Fig. 28.12 we have a coil consisting of *N* loops, all with the same radius. The loops are closely spaced so that the plane of each loop is essentially the same distance *x* from the field point *P*. Each loop contributes equally to the field, and the total field is *N* times the field of a single loop:

$$B_x = \frac{\mu_0 N I a^2}{2(x^2 + a^2)^{3/2}} \qquad \text{(on the axis of } N \text{ circular loops)} \qquad (28.16)$$

The factor *N* in Eq. (28.16) is the reason coils of wire, not single loops, are used to produce strong magnetic fields; for a desired field strength, using a single loop might require a current *I* so great as to exceed the rating of the loop's wire.

Figure 28.14 shows a graph of B_x as a function of *x*. The maximum value of the field is at $x = 0$, the center of the loop or coil:

28.14 Graph of the magnetic field along the axis of a circular coil with *N* turns. When *x* is much larger than *a*, the field magnitude decreases approximately as $1/x^3$.

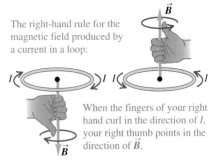

$$B_x = \frac{\mu_0 N I}{2a} \qquad \text{(at the center of } N \text{ circular loops)} \qquad (28.17)$$

As we go out along the axis, the field decreases in magnitude.

In Section 27.7 we defined the *magnetic dipole moment* μ (or *magnetic moment*) of a current-carrying loop to be equal to IA, where A is the cross-sectional area of the loop. If there are *N* loops, the total magnetic moment is NIA. The circular loop in Fig. 28.12 has area $A = \pi a^2$, so the magnetic moment of a single loop is $\mu = I\pi a^2$; for *N* loops, $\mu = NI\pi a^2$. Substituting these results into Eqs. (28.15) and (28.16), we find that both of these expressions can be written as

$$B_x = \frac{\mu_0 \mu}{2\pi(x^2 + a^2)^{3/2}} \qquad \begin{array}{l}\text{(on the axis of any number} \\ \text{of circular loops)}\end{array} \qquad (28.18)$$

We described a magnetic dipole in Section 27.7 in terms of its response to a magnetic field produced by currents outside the dipole. But a magnetic dipole is also a *source* of magnetic field; Eq. (28.18) describes the magnetic field *produced* by a magnetic dipole for points along the dipole axis. This field is directly proportional to the magnetic dipole moment μ. Note that the field along the *x*-axis is in the same direction as the vector magnetic moment $\vec{\mu}$; this is true on both the positive and negative x-axis.

CAUTION **Magnetic field of a coil** Equations (28.15), (28.16), and (28.18) are valid only on the *axis* of a loop or coil. Don't attempt to apply these equations at other points! ▍

Figure 28.15 shows some of the magnetic field lines surrounding a circular current loop (magnetic dipole) in planes through the axis. The directions of the field lines are given by the same right-hand rule as for a long, straight conductor. Grab the conductor with your right hand, with your thumb in the direction of the current; your fingers curl around in the same direction as the field lines. The field lines for the circular current loop are closed curves that encircle the conductor; they are *not* circles, however.

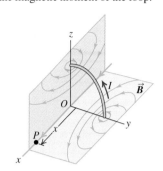

28.15 Magnetic field lines produced by the current in a circular loop. At points on the axis the $\vec{B}$ field has the same direction as the magnetic moment of the loop.

Example 28.6 Magnetic field of a coil

A coil consisting of 100 circular loops with radius 0.60 m carries a current of 5.0 A. (a) Find the magnetic field at a point along the axis of the coil, 0.80 m from the center. (b) Along the axis, at what distance from the center of the coil is the field magnitude $\frac{1}{8}$ as great as it is at the center?

SOLUTION

IDENTIFY: This problem asks about the magnetic field along the axis of a current-carrying coil, so we can use the ideas of this section.

SET UP: We want the field on the axis of the coil, not necessarily at its center, so we use Eq. (28.16). We are given $N = 100$, $I = 5.0$ A, and $a = 0.60$ m. In part (a) our target variable is the magnetic field at a given value of the coordinate x. In part (b) the target variable is the value of x at which the field has $\frac{1}{8}$ of the magnitude that it has at $x = 0$.

EXECUTE: (a) Using $x = 0.80$ m, from Eq. (28.16) we have

$$B_x = \frac{(4\pi \times 10^{-7} \,\text{T} \cdot \text{m/A})(100)(5.0 \,\text{A})(0.60 \,\text{m})^2}{2[(0.80 \,\text{m})^2 + (0.60 \,\text{m})^2]^{3/2}}$$

$$= 1.1 \times 10^{-4} \,\text{T}$$

(b) Considering Eq. (28.16), we want to find a value of x such that

$$\frac{1}{(x^2 + a^2)^{3/2}} = \frac{1}{8} \frac{1}{(0^2 + a^2)^{3/2}}$$

To solve this for x, we take the reciprocal of the whole thing and then take the $2/3$ power of both sides; the result is

$$x = \pm\sqrt{3}\,a = \pm 1.04 \,\text{m}$$

At a distance of about 1.7 radii from the center, the field has dropped off to $\frac{1}{8}$ its value at the center.

EVALUATE: We can check our answer in part (a) by first finding the magnetic moment and then substituting the result into Eq. (28.18):

$$\mu = NI\pi a^2 = (100)(5.0 \,\text{A})\pi(0.60 \,\text{m})^2 = 5.7 \times 10^2 \,\text{A} \cdot \text{m}^2$$

$$B_x = \frac{(4\pi \times 10^{-7} \,\text{T} \cdot \text{m/A})(5.7 \times 10^2 \,\text{A} \cdot \text{m}^2)}{2\pi[(0.80 \,\text{m})^2 + (0.60 \,\text{m})^2]^{3/2}} = 1.1 \times 10^{-4} \,\text{T}$$

The magnetic moment μ is relatively large, yet this is a rather small field, comparable in magnitude to the earth's magnetic field. This example may give you some idea of the difficulty of producing a field of 1 T or more.

Test Your Understanding of Section 28.5 Figure 28.12 shows the magnetic field $d\vec{B}$ produced at point P by a segment $d\vec{l}$ that lies on the positive y-axis (at the top of the loop). This field has components $dB_x > 0$, $dB_y > 0$, $dB_z = 0$. (a) What are the signs of the components of the field $d\vec{B}$ produced at P by a segment $d\vec{l}$ on the negative y-axis (at the bottom of the loop)? (i) $dB_x > 0$, $dB_y > 0$, $dB_z = 0$; (ii) $dB_x > 0$, $dB_y < 0$, $dB_z = 0$; (iii) $dB_x < 0$, $dB_y > 0$, $dB_z = 0$; (iv) $dB_x < 0$, $dB_y < 0$, $dB_z = 0$; (v) none of these. (b) What are the signs of the components of the field $d\vec{B}$ produced at P by a segment $d\vec{l}$ on the negative z-axis (at the right-hand side of the loop)? (i) $dB_x > 0$, $dB_y > 0$, $dB_z = 0$; (ii) $dB_x > 0$, $dB_y < 0$, $dB_z = 0$; (iii) $dB_x < 0$, $dB_y > 0$, $dB_z = 0$; (iv) $dB_x < 0$, $dB_y < 0$, $dB_z = 0$; (v) none of these.

28.6 Ampere's Law

So far our calculations of the magnetic field due to a current have involved finding the infinitesimal field $d\vec{B}$ due to a current element and then summing all the $d\vec{B}$'s to find the total field. This approach is directly analogous to our *electric-field* calculations in Chapter 21.

28.16 Three integration paths for the line integral of $\vec{B}$ in the vicinity of a long, straight conductor carrying current I *out* of the plane of the page (as indicated by the circle with a dot). The conductor is seen end-on.

(a) Integration path is a circle centered on the conductor; integration goes around the circle counterclockwise.

Result: $\oint \vec{B} \cdot d\vec{l} = \mu_0 I$

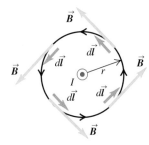

(b) Same integration path as in (a), but integration goes around the circle clockwise.

Result: $\oint \vec{B} \cdot d\vec{l} = -\mu_0 I$

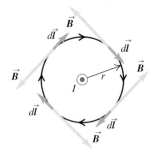

(c) An integration path that does not enclose the conductor.

Result: $\oint \vec{B} \cdot d\vec{l} = 0$

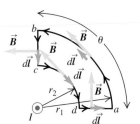

For the electric-field problem we found that in situations with a highly symmetric charge distribution, it was often easier to use Gauss's law to find $\vec{E}$. There is likewise a law that allows us to more easily find the *magnetic* fields caused by highly symmetric *current* distributions. But the law that allows us to do this, called *Ampere's law,* is rather different in character from Gauss's law.

Gauss's law for electric fields involves the flux of $\vec{E}$ through a closed surface; it states that this flux is equal to the total charge enclosed within the surface, divided by the constant ϵ_0. Thus this law relates electric fields and charge distributions. By contrast, Gauss's law for *magnetic* fields, Eq. (28.10), is *not* a relationship between magnetic fields and current distributions; it states that the flux of $\vec{B}$ through *any* closed surface is always zero, whether or not there are currents within the surface. So Gauss's law for $\vec{B}$ can't be used to determine the magnetic field produced by a particular current distribution.

Ampere's law is formulated not in terms of magnetic flux, but rather in terms of the *line integral* of $\vec{B}$ around a closed path, denoted by

$$\oint \vec{B} \cdot d\vec{l}$$

We used line integrals to define work in Chapter 6 and to calculate electric potential in Chapter 23. To evaluate this integral, we divide the path into infinitesimal segments $d\vec{l}$, calculate the scalar product of $\vec{B} \cdot d\vec{l}$ for each segment, and sum these products. In general, $\vec{B}$ varies from point to point, and we must use the value of $\vec{B}$ at the location of each $d\vec{l}$. An alternative notation is $\oint B_\parallel \, dl$, where $B_\parallel$ is the component of $\vec{B}$ parallel to $d\vec{l}$ at each point. The circle on the integral sign indicates that this integral is always computed for a *closed* path, one whose beginning and end points are the same.

Ampere's Law for a Long, Straight Conductor

To introduce the basic idea of Ampere's law, let's consider again the magnetic field caused by a long, straight conductor carrying a current I. We found in Section 28.3 that the field at a distance r from the conductor has magnitude

$$B = \frac{\mu_0 I}{2\pi r}$$

and that the magnetic field lines are circles centered on the conductor. Let's take the line integral of $\vec{B}$ around one such circle with radius r, as in Figure 28.16a. At every point on the circle, $\vec{B}$ and $d\vec{l}$ are parallel, and so $\vec{B} \cdot d\vec{l} = B \, dl$; since r is constant around the circle, B is constant as well. Alternatively, we can say that $B_\parallel$ is constant and equal to B at every point on the circle. Hence we can take B outside of the integral. The remaining integral $\oint dl$ is just the circumference of the circle, so

$$\oint \vec{B} \cdot d\vec{l} = \oint B_\parallel \, dl = B \oint dl = \frac{\mu_0 I}{2\pi r}(2\pi r) = \mu_0 I$$

The line integral is thus independent of the radius of the circle and is equal to μ_0 multiplied by the current passing through the area bounded by the circle.

In Fig. 28.16b the situation is the same, but the integration path now goes around the circle in the opposite direction. Now $\vec{B}$ and $d\vec{l}$ are antiparallel, so $\vec{B} \cdot d\vec{l} = -B \, dl$ and the line integral equals $-\mu_0 I$. We get the same result if the integration path is the same as in Fig. 28.16a, but the direction of the current is reversed. Thus the line integral $\oint \vec{B} \cdot d\vec{l}$ equals μ_0 multiplied by the current passing through the area bounded by the integration path, with a positive or negative sign depending on the direction of the current relative to the direction of integration.

There's a simple rule for the sign of the current; you won't be surprised to learn that it uses your right hand. Curl the fingers of your right hand around the integration path so that they curl in the direction of integration (that is, the direction that you use to evaluate $\oint \vec{B} \cdot d\vec{l}$). Then your right thumb indicates the positive current direction. Currents that pass through the integration path in this direction are positive; those in the opposite direction are negative. Using this rule, you should be able to convince yourself that the current is positive in Fig. 28.16a and negative in Fig. 28.16b. Here's another way to say the same thing: Looking at the surface bounded by the integration path, integrate counterclockwise around the path as in Fig. 28.16a. Currents moving toward you through the surface are positive, and those going away from you are negative.

An integration path that does *not* enclose the conductor is used in Fig. 28.16c. Along the circular arc ab of radius r_1, $\vec{B}$ and $d\vec{l}$ are parallel, and $B_\parallel = B_1 = \mu_0 I/2\pi r_1$; along the circular arc cd of radius r_2, $\vec{B}$ and $d\vec{l}$ are antiparallel and $B_\parallel = -B_2 = -\mu_0 I/2\pi r_2$. The $\vec{B}$ field is perpendicular to $d\vec{l}$ at each point on the straight sections bc and da, so $B_\parallel = 0$ and these sections contribute zero to the line integral. The total line integral is then

$$\oint \vec{B} \cdot d\vec{l} = \oint B_\parallel \, dl = B_1 \int_a^b dl + (0) \int_b^c dl + (-B_2) \int_c^d dl + (0) \int_d^a dl$$

$$= \frac{\mu_0 I}{2\pi r_1} (r_1 \theta) + 0 - \frac{\mu_0 I}{2\pi r_2} (r_2 \theta) + 0 = 0$$

The magnitude of $\vec{B}$ is greater on arc cd than on arc ab, but the arc length is less, so the contributions from the two arcs exactly cancel. Even though there is a magnetic field everywhere along the integration path, the line integral $\oint \vec{B} \cdot d\vec{l}$ is zero if there is no current passing through the area bounded by the path.

We can also derive these results for more general integration paths, such as the one in Figure 28.17. At the position of the line element $d\vec{l}$, the angle between $d\vec{l}$ and $\vec{B}$ is ϕ, and

$$\vec{B} \cdot d\vec{l} = B \, dl \cos\phi$$

From the figure, $dl \cos\phi = r \, d\theta$, where $d\theta$ is the angle subtended by $d\vec{l}$ at the position of the conductor and r is the distance of $d\vec{l}$ from the conductor. Thus

$$\oint \vec{B} \cdot d\vec{l} = \oint \frac{\mu_0 I}{2\pi r} (r \, d\theta) = \frac{\mu_0 I}{2\pi} \oint d\theta$$

But $\oint d\theta$ is just equal to 2π, the total angle swept out by the radial line from the conductor to $d\vec{l}$ during a complete trip around the path. So we get

$$\oint \vec{B} \cdot d\vec{l} = \mu_0 I \qquad (28.19)$$

This result doesn't depend on the shape of the path or on the position of the wire inside it. If the current in the wire is opposite to that shown, the integral has the opposite sign. But if the path doesn't enclose the wire (Fig. 28.17b), then the net change in θ during the trip around the integration path is zero; $\oint d\theta$ is zero instead of 2π and the line integral is zero.

Ampere's Law: General Statement

Equation (28.19) is almost, but not quite, the general statement of Ampere's law. To generalize it even further, suppose *several* long, straight conductors pass through the surface bounded by the integration path. The total magnetic field $\vec{B}$ at any point on the path is the vector sum of the fields produced by the individual conductors. Thus the line integral of the total $\vec{B}$ equals μ_0 times the *algebraic sum* of the currents. In calculating this sum, we use the sign rule for currents described above. If the integration path does not enclose a particular wire, the

28.17 (a) A more general integration path for the line integral of $\vec{B}$ around a long, straight conductor carrying current I *out* of the plane of the page. The conductor is seen end-on. (b) A more general integration path that does not enclose the conductor.

(a)

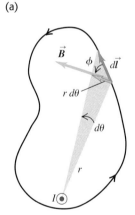

(b)

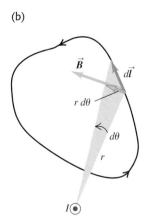

28.18 Ampere's law.

Perspective view

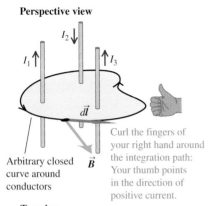

Arbitrary closed
curve around
conductors

Curl the fingers of
your right hand around
the integration path:
Your thumb points
in the direction of
positive current.

Top view

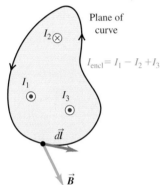

Plane of
curve

$I_{encl} = I_1 - I_2 + I_3$

Ampere's law: If we calculate the line integral
of the magnetic field around a closed curve, the
result equals μ_0 times the total enclosed current:
$\oint \vec{B} \cdot d\vec{l} = \mu_0 I_{encl}$

28.19 Two long, straight conductors carrying equal currents in opposite directions.
The conductors are seen end-on, and the
integration path is counterclockwise. The
line integral $\oint \vec{B} \cdot d\vec{l}$ gets zero contribution
from the upper and lower segments, a positive contribution from the left segment,
and a negative contribution from the right
segment; the net integral is zero.

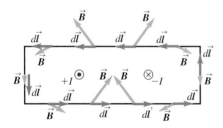

line integral of the $\vec{B}$ field of that wire is zero, because the angle θ for that wire
sweeps through a net change of zero rather than 2π during the integration. Any
conductors present that are not enclosed by a particular path may still contribute
to the value of $\vec{B}$ at every point, but the *line integrals* of their fields around the
path are zero.

Thus we can replace I in Eq. (28.19) with I_{encl}, the algebraic sum of the currents *enclosed* or *linked* by the integration path, with the sum evaluated by using
the sign rule just described (Fig. 28.18). Our statement of **Ampere's law** is then

$$\oint \vec{B} \cdot d\vec{l} = \mu_0 I_{encl} \qquad \text{(Ampere's law)} \qquad (28.20)$$

While we have derived Ampere's law only for the special case of the field of several long, straight, parallel conductors, Eq. (28.20) is in fact valid for conductors
and paths of *any* shape. The general derivation is no different in principle from
what we have presented, but the geometry is more complicated.

If $\oint \vec{B} \cdot d\vec{l} = 0$, it *does not* necessarily mean that $\vec{B} = 0$ everywhere along the
path, only that the total current through an area bounded by the path is zero. In
Figs. 28.16c and 28.17b, the integration paths enclose no current at all; in
Fig. 28.19 there are positive and negative currents of equal magnitude through
the area enclosed by the path. In both cases, $I_{encl} = 0$ and the line integral is zero.

CAUTION **Line integrals of electric and magnetic fields** In Chapter 23 we saw
that the line integral of the electrostatic field $\vec{E}$ around any closed path is equal to zero;
this is a statement that the electrostatic force $\vec{F} = q\vec{E}$ on a point charge q is conservative,
so this force does zero work on a charge that moves around a closed path that returns to
the starting point. You might think that the value of the line integral $\oint \vec{B} \cdot d\vec{l}$ is similarly
related to the question of whether the *magnetic* force is conservative. This isn't the case at
all. Remember that the magnetic force $\vec{F} = q\vec{v} \times \vec{B}$ on a moving charged particle is
always *perpendicular* to $\vec{B}$, so $\oint \vec{B} \cdot d\vec{l}$ is *not* related to the work done by the magnetic
force; as stated in Ampere's law, this integral is related only to the total current through a
surface bounded by the integration path. In fact, the magnetic force on a moving charged
particle is *not* conservative. A conservative force depends only on the position of the body
on which the force is exerted, but the magnetic force on a moving charged particle also
depends on the *velocity* of the particle. ∎

In the form we have stated it, Ampere's law turns out to be valid only if the
currents are steady and if no magnetic materials or time-varying electric fields
are present. In Chapter 29 we will see how to generalize Ampere's law for time-
varying fields.

Test Your Understanding of Section 28.6 The figure below shows magnetic
field lines through the center of a permanent magnet. The magnet is not connected to a
source of emf. One of the field lines is colored red. What can you conclude about the currents inside the permanent magnet within the region enclosed by this field line? (i) There
are no currents inside the magnet; (ii) there are currents directed out of the plane of the
page; (iii) there are currents directed into the plane of the page; (iv) not enough information given to decide.

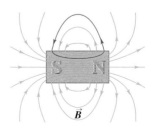

28.7 Applications of Ampere's Law

Ampere's law is useful when we can exploit the symmetry of a situation to evaluate the line integral of $\vec{B}$. Several examples are given below. Problem-Solving Strategy 28.2 is directly analogous to Problem Solving Strategy 22.1 (Section 22.4) for applications of Gauss's law; we suggest you review that strategy now and compare the two methods.

Problem-Solving Strategy 28.2 **Ampere's Law**

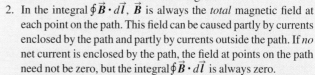

IDENTIFY *the relevant concepts:* Like Gauss's law for electricity, Ampere's law is always true but is most useful in situations where the magnetic field pattern is highly symmetrical. In such situations you can use Ampere's law to find a relationship between the magnetic field as a function of position and the current that generates the field.

SET UP *the problem* using the following steps:

1. Select the integration path you will use with Ampere's law. If you want to determine the magnetic field at a certain point, then the path must pass through that point. The integration path doesn't have to be any actual physical boundary. Usually it is a purely geometric curve; it may be in empty space, embedded in a solid body, or some of each. The integration path has to have enough *symmetry* to make evaluation of the integral possible. If the problem itself has cylindrical symmetry, the integration path will usually be a circle coaxial with the cylinder axis.

2. Determine the target variable(s). Usually this will be the magnitude of the $\vec{B}$ field as a function of position.

EXECUTE *the solution* as follows:

1. Carry out the integral $\oint \vec{B} \cdot d\vec{l}$ along your chosen integration path. If $\vec{B}$ is tangent to all or some portion of the integration path and has the same magnitude B at every point, then its line integral equals B multiplied by the length of that portion of the path. If $\vec{B}$ is perpendicular to some portion of the path, that portion makes no contribution to the integral.

2. In the integral $\oint \vec{B} \cdot d\vec{l}$, $\vec{B}$ is always the *total* magnetic field at each point on the path. This field can be caused partly by currents enclosed by the path and partly by currents outside the path. If *no* net current is enclosed by the path, the field at points on the path need not be zero, but the integral $\oint \vec{B} \cdot d\vec{l}$ is always zero.

3. Determine the current I_{encl} enclosed by the integration path. The sign of this current is given by a right-hand rule. Curl the fingers of your right hand so that they follow the integration path in the direction that you carry out the integration. Your right thumb then points in the direction of positive current. If $\vec{B}$ is tangent to the integration at all points along the path and I_{encl} is positive, then the direction of $\vec{B}$ is the same as the direction of the integration path; if instead I_{encl} is negative, $\vec{B}$ is in the direction opposite to that of the integration.

4. Use Ampere's law $\oint \vec{B} \cdot d\vec{l} = \mu_0 I$ to solve for the target variable.

EVALUATE *your answer:* If your result is an expression for the field magnitude as a function of position, you can check it by examining how the expression behaves in different limits.

Example 28.7 **Field of a long, straight, current-carrying conductor**

In Section 28.6 we derived Ampere's law using Eq. (28.9) for the field of a long, straight, current-carrying conductor. Reverse this process, and use Ampere's law to find the magnitude *and* direction of $\vec{B}$ for this situation.

SOLUTION

IDENTIFY: This situation has cylindrical symmetry, so we can use Ampere's law to find the magnetic field at all points a distance r from the conductor

SET UP: We take as our integration path a circle with radius r centered on the conductor and in a plane perpendicular to it, as in Fig. 28.16a (Section 28.6). At each point, $\vec{B}$ is tangent to this circle.

EXECUTE: With our choice of integration path, Ampere's law [Eq. (28.20)] becomes

$$\oint \vec{B} \cdot d\vec{l} = \oint B_{\parallel} \, dl = B(2\pi r) = \mu_0 I$$

Equation (28.9), $B = \mu_0 I / 2\pi r$, follows immediately.

Ampere's law determines the direction of $\vec{B}$ as well as its magnitude. Since we go around the integration path in the counterclockwise direction, the positive direction for current is out of the plane of Fig. 28.16a; this is the same as the actual current direction in the figure, so I is positive and the integral $\oint \vec{B} \cdot d\vec{l}$ is also positive. Since the $d\vec{l}$'s run counterclockwise, the direction of $\vec{B}$ must be counterclockwise as well, as shown in Fig. 28.16a.

EVALUATE: Our results are consistent with those in Section 28.6, as they must be.

Example 28.8 Field inside a long cylindrical conductor

A cylindrical conductor with radius R carries a current I. (Fig. 28.20). The current is uniformly distributed over the cross-sectional area of the conductor. Find the magnetic field as a function of the distance r from the conductor axis for points both inside $(r < R)$ and outside $(r > R)$ the conductor.

SOLUTION

IDENTIFY: Once again we have a current distribution with cylindrical symmetry. As for a long, straight, skinny current-carrying conductor, the magnetic field lines must be circles concentric with the conductor axis.

SET UP: To find the magnetic field *inside* the conductor, we take as our integration path a circle with radius $r < R$ as shown in Fig. 28.20. *Outside* the conductor, we again use a circle but with a radius $r > R$. In either case, the integration path takes advantage of the circular symmetry of the magnetic field pattern.

EXECUTE: Inside the conductor, $\vec{B}$ has the same magnitude at every point on the circular integration path and is tangent to the path. Thus the magnitude of the line integral is simply $B(2\pi r)$. If we use the right-hand rule for determining the sign of the current, the current through the brown area enclosed by the path is positive; hence $\vec{B}$ points in the same direction as the integration path, as shown. To find the current I_{encl} enclosed by the path, note that the current density (current per unit area) is $J = I/\pi R^2$, so $I_{encl} = J(\pi r^2) = Ir^2/R^2$. Finally, Ampere's law gives

$$B(2\pi r) = \mu_0 \frac{Ir^2}{R^2}$$

$$B = \frac{\mu_0 I}{2\pi} \frac{r}{R^2} \quad \text{(inside the conductor, } r < R) \quad (28.21)$$

For the circular integration path outside the conductor $(r > R)$, the same symmetry arguments apply and the magnitude of $\oint \vec{B} \cdot d\vec{l}$ is again $B(2\pi r)$. The right-hand rule gives the direction of $\vec{B}$ as shown in Fig. 28.20. For this path, $I_{encl} = I$, the total current in the conductor. Applying Ampere's law gives the same equation as in Example 28.7, with the same result for B:

$$B = \frac{\mu_0 I}{2\pi r} \quad \text{(outside the conductor, } r > R) \quad (28.22)$$

Outside the conductor, the magnetic field is the same as that of a long, straight conductor carrying current I, independent of the

28.20 To find the magnetic field at radius $r < R$, we apply Ampere's law to the circle enclosing the red area. The current through the red area is $(r^2/R^2)I$. To find the magnetic field at radius $r > R$, we apply Ampere's law to the circle enclosing the entire conductor.

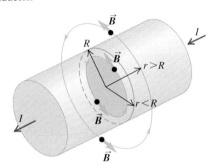

radius R over which the current is distributed. Indeed, the magnetic field outside *any* cylindrically symmetric current distribution is the same as if the entire current were concentrated along the axis of the distribution. This is analogous to the results of Examples 22.5 and 22.9 (Section 22.4), in which we found that the *electric* field outside a spherically symmetric *charged* body is the same as though the entire charge were concentrated at the center.

EVALUATE: Note that at the surface of the conductor $(r = R)$, Eq. (28.21) for $r < R$ and Eq. (28.22) for $r > R$ agree (as they must). Figure 28.21 shows a graph of B as a function of r, both inside and outside the conductor.

28.21 Magnitude of the magnetic field inside and outside a long, straight cylindrical conductor with radius R carrying a current I.

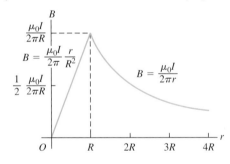

Example 28.9 Field of a solenoid

A solenoid consists of a helical winding of wire on a cylinder, usually circular in cross section. There can be hundreds or thousands of closely spaced turns, each of which can be regarded as a circular loop. There may be several layers of windings. For simplicity, Fig. 28.22 shows a solenoid with only a few turns. All turns carry the same current I, and the total $\vec{B}$ field at every point is the vector sum of the fields caused by the individual turns. The figure shows field lines in the xy- and xz-planes. We draw a set of field lines that are uniformly spaced at the center of the solenoid. Exact calculations show that for a long, closely wound solenoid, half of these field lines emerge from the ends and half "leak out" through the windings between the center and the end.

The field lines near the center of the solenoid are approximately parallel, indicating a nearly uniform $\vec{B}$; outside the solenoid, the

28.22 Magnetic field lines produced by the current in a solenoid. For clarity, only a few turns are shown.

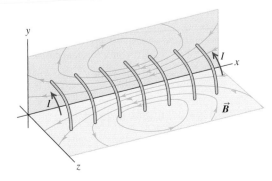

field lines are spread apart, and the magnetic field is weak. If the solenoid is long in comparison with its cross-sectional diameter and the coils are tightly wound, the *internal* field near the midpoint of the solenoid's length is very nearly uniform over the cross section and parallel to the axis, and the *external* field near the midpoint is very small.

Use Ampere's law to find the field at or near the center of such a long solenoid. The solenoid has n turns of wire per unit length and carries a current I.

SOLUTION

IDENTIFY: This is a highly symmetrical situation, with a uniform $\vec{B}$ field inside the solenoid and zero field outside. Hence we can use Ampere's law to find the field inside by using an appropriate choice of integration path.

SET UP: Fig. 28.23 shows the situation and our integration path, rectangle *abcd*. Side *ab*, with length L, is parallel to the axis of the solenoid. Sides *bc* and *da* are taken to be very long so that side *cd* is far from the solenoid; then the field at side *cd* is negligibly small.

EXECUTE: By symmetry, the $\vec{B}$ field along side *ab* is parallel to this side and is constant. In carrying out the Ampere's-law integration, we go along side *ab* in the same direction as $\vec{B}$. So for this side, $B_\parallel = +B$ and

$$\int_a^b \vec{B} \cdot d\vec{l} = BL$$

Along sides *bc* and *da*, $B_\parallel = 0$ because $\vec{B}$ is perpendicular to these sides; along side *cd*, $B_\parallel = 0$ because $\vec{B} = 0$. The integral $\oint \vec{B} \cdot d\vec{l}$ around the entire closed path therefore reduces to BL.

28.23 Our sketch for this problem.

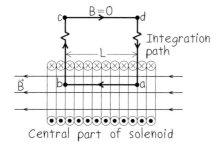

Central part of solenoid

The number of turns in length L is nL. Each of these turns passes once through the rectangle *abcd* and carries a current I, where I is the current in the windings. The total current enclosed by the rectangle is then $I_{encl} = nLI$. From Ampere's law, since the integral $\oint \vec{B} \cdot d\vec{l}$ is positive, I_{encl} must be positive as well; hence the current passing through the surface bounded by the integration path must be in the direction shown in Fig. 28.23. Ampere's law then gives the magnitude B:

$$BL = \mu_0 nLI$$
$$B = \mu_0 nI \qquad \text{(solenoid)} \qquad (28.23)$$

Side *ab* need not lie on the axis of the solenoid, so this calculation also proves that the field is uniform over the entire cross section at the center of the solenoid's length.

EVALUATE: Note that the *direction* of $\vec{B}$ inside the solenoid is in the same direction as the solenoid's vector magnetic moment $\vec{\mu}$. This is the same result that we found in Section 28.5 for a single current-carrying loop.

For points along the axis, the field is strongest at the center of the solenoid and drops off near the ends. For a solenoid that is very long in comparison to its diameter, the field at each end is exactly half as strong as the field at the center. For a short, fat solenoid the relationship is more complicated. Fig. 28.24 shows a graph of B as a function of x for points on the axis of a short solenoid.

28.24 Magnitude of the magnetic field at points along the axis of a solenoid with length $4a$, equal to four times its radius a. The field magnitude at each end is about half its value at the center. (Compare with Fig. 28.14 for the field of N circular loops.)

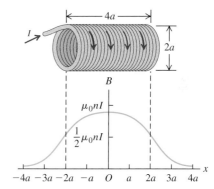

Example 28.10   **Field of a toroidal solenoid**

Figure 28.25a shows a doughnut-shaped **toroidal solenoid,** also called a *toroid,* wound with N turns of wire carrying a current I. In a practical version the turns would be more closely spaced than they are in the figure. Find the magnetic field at all points.

SOLUTION

IDENTIFY: The flow of current around the toroid's circumference produces a magnetic field component perpendicular to the plane of the figure, just as for the current loop discussed in Section 28.5. But if the coils are very tightly wound, we can consider them as circular loops that carry current between the inner and outer radii of the toroidal solenoid; the flow of current around the toroid's circumference is then negligible, and the perpendicular component of $\vec{B}$ is likewise negligible. In this idealized approximation the circular symmetry of the situation tells us that the

magnetic field lines must be circles concentric with the axis of the toroid.

SET UP: To take advantage of this symmetry in finding the field, we choose circular integration paths for use with Ampere's law. Three such paths are shown as black lines in Fig. 28.25b.

EXECUTE: First consider integration path 1 in Fig. 28.25b. If the toroidal solenoid produces any field at all in this region, it must be *tangent* to the path at all points, and $\oint \vec{B} \cdot d\vec{l}$ will equal the product of B and the circumference $l = 2\pi r$ of the path. But the total current enclosed by the path is zero, so from Ampere's law the field $\vec{B}$ must be zero everywhere on this path.

Similarly, if the toroidal solenoid produces any field along path 3, it must also be tangent to the path at all points. Each turn of the winding passes *twice* through the area bounded by this path,

Continued

28.25 (a) A toroidal solenoid. For clarity, only a few turns of the winding are shown. (b) Integration paths (black circles) used to compute the magnetic field $\vec{B}$ set up by the current (shown as dots and crosses).

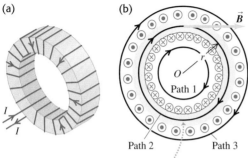

(a)   (b)

$\vec{B}$

Path 1

Path 2   Path 3

The magnetic field is confined almost entirely to the space enclosed by the windings (in blue).

carrying equal currents in opposite directions. The *net* current I_{encl} enclosed within this area is therefore zero, and hence $\vec{B} = 0$ at all points of the path. Conclusion: *The field of an idealized toroidal solenoid is confined completely to the space enclosed by the windings.* We can think of such an idealized toroidal solenoid as a tightly wound solenoid that has been bent into a circle.

Finally, we consider path 2, a circle with radius r. Again by symmetry we expect the $\vec{B}$ field to be tangent to the path, and $\oint \vec{B} \cdot d\vec{l}$ equals $2\pi rB$. Each turn of the winding passes *once* through the area bounded by path 2. The total current enclosed by the path is $I_{encl} = NI$, where N is the total number of turns in the winding; I_{encl} is

positive for the clockwise direction of integration in Fig. 28.25b, so $\vec{B}$ is in the direction shown. Then, from Ampere's law,

$$2\pi rB = \mu_0 NI$$

$$B = \frac{\mu_0 NI}{2\pi r} \qquad \text{(toroidal solenoid)} \qquad (28.24)$$

EVALUATE: The magnetic field is *not* uniform over a cross section of the core, because the radius r is larger at the outer side of the section than at the inner side. However, if the radial thickness of the core is small in comparison to r, the field varies only slightly across a section. In that case, considering that $2\pi r$ is the circumferential length of the toroid and that $N/2\pi r$ is the number of turns per unit length n, the field may be written as

$$B = \mu_0 nI$$

just as it is at the center of a long, *straight* solenoid.

In a real toroidal solenoid the turns are not precisely circular loops but rather segments of a bent helix. As a result, the field outside is not strictly zero. To estimate its magnitude, we imagine Fig. 28.25a as being roughly equivalent, for points outside the torus, to a circular loop with a single turn and radius r. Then we can use Eq. (28.17) to show that the field at the *center* of the torus is smaller than the field inside by approximately a factor of N/π.

The equations we have derived for the field in a closely wound straight or toroidal solenoid are strictly correct only for windings in *vacuum*. For most practical purposes, however, they can be used for windings in air or on a core of any nonmagnetic, nonsuperconducting material. In the next section we will show how they are modified if the core is a magnetic material.

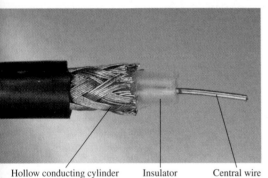

Hollow conducting cylinder   Insulator   Central wire

Test Your Understanding of Section 28.7 Consider a conducting wire that runs along the central axis of a hollow conducting cylinder. Such an arrangement, called a *coaxial cable,* has many applications in telecommunications. (The cable that connects a television set to a local cable provider is an example of a coaxial cable.) In such a cable a current I runs in one direction along the hollow conducting cylinder and is spread uniformly over the cylinder's cross-sectional area. An equal current runs in the opposite direction along the central wire. How does the magnitude B of the magnetic field outside such a cable depend on the distance r from the central axis of the cable? (i) B is proportional to $1/r$; (ii) B is proportional to $1/r^2$; (iii) B is zero at all points outside the cable.

*28.8 Magnetic Materials

In discussing how currents cause magnetic fields, we have assumed that the conductors are surrounded by vacuum. But the coils in transformers, motors, generators, and electromagnets nearly always have iron cores to increase the magnetic field and confine it to desired regions. Permanent magnets, magnetic recording tapes, and computer disks depend directly on the magnetic properties of materials; when you store information on a computer disk, you are actually setting up an array of microscopic permanent magnets on the disk. So it is worthwhile to examine some aspects of the magnetic properties of materials. After describing the atomic origins of magnetic properties, we will discuss three broad classes of magnetic behavior that occur in materials; these are called *paramagnetism, diamagnetism,* and *ferromagnetism.*

The Bohr Magneton

As we discussed briefly in Section 27.7, the atoms that make up all matter contain moving electrons, and these electrons form microscopic current loops that produce magnetic fields of their own. In many materials these currents are randomly oriented and cause no net magnetic field. But in some materials an external field (a field produced by currents outside the material) can cause these loops to become oriented preferentially with the field, so their magnetic fields *add* to the external field. We then say that the material is *magnetized.*

Let's look at how these microscopic currents come about. Figure 28.26 shows a primitive model of an electron in an atom. We picture the electron (mass m, charge $-e$) as moving in a circular orbit with radius r and speed v. This moving charge is equivalent to a current loop. In Section 27.7 we found that a current loop with area A and current I has a magnetic dipole moment μ given by $\mu = IA$; for the orbiting electron the area of the loop is $A = \pi r^2$. To find the current associated with the electron, we note that the orbital period T (the time for the electron to make one complete orbit) is the orbit circumference divided by the electron speed: $T = 2\pi r/v$. The equivalent current I is the total charge passing any point on the orbit per unit time, which is just the magnitude e of the electron charge divided by the orbital period T:

$$I = \frac{e}{T} = \frac{ev}{2\pi r}$$

The magnetic moment $\mu = IA$ is then

$$\mu = \frac{ev}{2\pi r}(\pi r^2) = \frac{evr}{2} \tag{28.25}$$

It is useful to express μ in terms of the *angular momentum L* of the electron. For a particle moving in a circular path, the magnitude of angular momentum equals the magnitude of momentum mv multiplied by the radius r, that is, $L = mvr$ (see Section 10.5). Comparing this with Eq. (28.25), we can write

$$\mu = \frac{e}{2m}L \tag{28.26}$$

Equation (28.26) is useful in this discussion because atomic angular momentum is *quantized;* its component in a particular direction is always an integer multiple of $h/2\pi$, where h is a fundamental physical constant called *Planck's constant.* (We will discuss the quantization of angular momentum in more detail in Chapter 41.) The numerical value of h is

$$h = 6.626 \times 10^{-34}\ \text{J} \cdot \text{s}$$

The quantity $h/2\pi$ thus represents a fundamental unit of angular momentum in atomic systems, just as e is a fundamental unit of charge. Associated with the quantization of $\vec{L}$ is a fundamental uncertainty in the *direction* of $\vec{L}$ and therefore of $\vec{\mu}$. In the following discussion, when we speak of the magnitude of a magnetic moment, a more precise statement would be "maximum component in a given direction." Thus, to say that a magnetic moment $\vec{\mu}$ is aligned with a magnetic field $\vec{B}$ really means that $\vec{\mu}$ has its maximum possible component in the direction of $\vec{B}$; such components are always quantized.

Equation (28.26) shows that associated with the fundamental unit of angular momentum is a corresponding fundamental unit of magnetic moment. If $L = h/2\pi$, then

$$\mu = \frac{e}{2m}\left(\frac{h}{2\pi}\right) = \frac{eh}{4\pi m} \tag{28.27}$$

This quantity is called the **Bohr magneton,** denoted by μ_B. Its numerical value is

$$\mu_B = 9.274 \times 10^{-24}\ \text{A} \cdot \text{m}^2 = 9.274 \times 10^{-24}\ \text{J/T}$$

You should verify that these two sets of units are consistent. The second set is useful when we compute the potential energy $U = -\vec{\mu} \cdot \vec{B}$ for a magnetic moment in a magnetic field.

Electrons also have an intrinsic angular momentum, called *spin,* that is not related to orbital motion but that can be pictured in a classical model as spinning

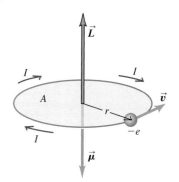

28.26 An electron moving with speed v in a circular orbit of radius r has an angular momentum $\vec{L}$ and an oppositely directed orbital magnetic dipole moment $\vec{\mu}$. It also has a spin angular momentum and an oppositely directed spin magnetic dipole moment.

on an axis. This angular momentum also has an associated magnetic moment, and its magnitude turns out to be almost exactly one Bohr magneton. (Effects having to do with quantization of the electromagnetic field cause the spin magnetic moment to be about $1.001\,\mu_B$.)

Paramagnetism

In an atom, most of the various orbital and spin magnetic moments of the electrons add up to zero. However, in some cases the atom has a net magnetic moment that is of the order of μ_B. When such a material is placed in a magnetic field, the field exerts a torque on each magnetic moment, as given by Eq. (27.26): $\vec{\tau} = \vec{\mu} \times \vec{B}$. These torques tend to align the magnetic moments with the field, the position of minimum potential energy, as we discussed in Section 27.7. In this position, the directions of the current loops are such as to *add* to the externally applied magnetic field.

We saw in Section 28.5 that the $\vec{B}$ field produced by a current loop is proportional to the loop's magnetic dipole moment. In the same way, the additional $\vec{B}$ field produced by microscopic electron current loops is proportional to the total magnetic moment $\vec{\mu}_{total}$ per unit volume V in the material. We call this vector quantity the **magnetization** of the material, denoted by $\vec{M}$:

$$\vec{M} = \frac{\vec{\mu}_{total}}{V} \tag{28.28}$$

The additional magnetic field due to magnetization of the material turns out to be equal simply to $\mu_0\vec{M}$, where μ_0 is the same constant that appears in the law of Biot and Savart and Ampere's law. When such a material completely surrounds a current-carrying conductor, the total magnetic field $\vec{B}$ in the material is

$$\vec{B} = \vec{B}_0 + \mu_0\vec{M} \tag{28.29}$$

where $\vec{B}_0$ is the field caused by the current in the conductor.

To check that the units in Eq. (28.29) are consistent, note that magnetization $\vec{M}$ is magnetic moment per unit volume. The units of magnetic moment are current times area $(A \cdot m^2)$, so the units of magnetization are $(A \cdot m^2)/m^3 = A/m$. From Section 28.1, the units of the constant μ_0 are $T \cdot m/A$. So the units of $\mu_0\vec{M}$ are the same as the units of $\vec{B}$: $(T \cdot m/A)(A/m) = T$.

A material showing the behavior just described is said to be **paramagnetic.** The result is that the magnetic field at any point in such a material is greater by a dimensionless factor K_m, called the **relative permeability** of the material, than it would be if the material were replaced by vacuum. The value of K_m is different for different materials; for common paramagnetic solids and liquids at room temperature, K_m typically ranges from 1.00001 to 1.003.

All of the equations in this chapter that relate magnetic fields to their sources can be adapted to the situation in which the current-carrying conductor is embedded in a paramagnetic material. All that need be done is to replace μ_0 by $K_m\mu_0$. This product is usually denoted as μ and is called the **permeability** of the material:

$$\mu = K_m\mu_0 \tag{28.30}$$

CAUTION **Two meanings of the symbol μ** Equation (28.30) involves some really dangerous notation because we have also used μ for magnetic dipole moment. It's customary to use μ for both quantities, but beware: From now on, every time you see a μ, make sure you know whether it is permeability or magnetic moment. You can usually tell from the context.

The amount by which the relative permeability differs from unity is called the **magnetic susceptibility,** denoted by χ_m:

$$\chi_m = K_m - 1 \tag{28.31}$$

Both K_m and χ_m are dimensionless quantities. Values of magnetic susceptibility for several materials are given in Table 28.1. For example, for aluminum, $\chi_m = 2.2 \times 10^{-5}$ and $K_m = 1.000022$. The first group of materials in the table are paramagnetic; we'll discuss the second group of materials, which are called *diamagnetic,* very shortly.

The tendency of atomic magnetic moments to align themselves parallel to the magnetic field (where the potential energy is minimum) is opposed by random thermal motion, which tends to randomize their orientations. For this reason, paramagnetic susceptibility always decreases with increasing temperature. In many cases it is inversely proportional to the absolute temperature T, and the magnetization M can be expressed as

$$M = C\frac{B}{T} \qquad (28.32)$$

This relationship is called *Curie's law,* after its discoverer, Pierre Curie (1859–1906). The quantity C is a constant, different for different materials, called the *Curie constant.*

As we described in Section 27.7, a body with atomic magnetic dipoles is attracted to the poles of a magnet. In most paramagnetic substances this attraction is very weak due to thermal randomization of the atomic magnetic moments. That's why a magnet can't be used to pick up objects made of aluminum (a paramagnetic substance). But at very low temperatures the thermal effects are reduced, the magnetization increases in accordance with Curie's law, and the attractive forces are greater.

Table 28.1 Magnetic Susceptibilities of Paramagnetic and Diamagnetic Materials at $T = 20°C$

Material	$\chi_m = K_m - 1 \ (\times 10^{-5})$
Paramagnetic	
Iron ammonium alum	66
Uranium	40
Platinum	26
Aluminum	2.2
Sodium	0.72
Oxygen gas	0.19
Diamagnetic	
Bismuth	−16.6
Mercury	−2.9
Silver	−2.6
Carbon (diamond)	−2.1
Lead	−1.8
Sodium chloride	−1.4
Copper	−1.0

Example 28.11 **Magnetic dipoles in a paramagnetic material**

Nitric oxide (NO) is a paramagnetic compound. Its molecules have a magnetic moment with a maximum component in any direction of about one Bohr magneton each. In a magnetic field with magnitude $B = 1.5$ T, compare the interaction energy of the magnetic moments with the field to the average translational kinetic energy of the molecules at a temperature of 300 K.

SOLUTION

IDENTIFY: This problem involves both the energy of a magnetic moment in a magnetic field (Chapter 27) and the average translational kinetic energy due to temperature (Chapter 18).

SET UP: In Section 27.7 we derived the equation $U = -\vec{\mu} \cdot \vec{B}$ for the interaction energy of a magnetic moment $\vec{\mu}$ with a $\vec{B}$ field. From Section 18.3 the average translational kinetic energy of a molecule at temperature T is $K = \frac{3}{2}kT$, where k is the Boltzmann constant.

EXECUTE: We can write the interaction energy as $U = -(\mu\cos\phi)B$, where $\mu\cos\phi$ is the component of the magnetic moment $\vec{\mu}$ in the direction of the $\vec{B}$ field. In our case the maximum value of the component $\mu\cos\phi$ is about μ_B, so

$$|U|_{max} \approx \mu_B B = (9.27 \times 10^{-24} \text{ J/T})(1.5 \text{ T})$$
$$= 1.4 \times 10^{-23} \text{ J} = 8.7 \times 10^{-5} \text{ eV}$$

The average translational kinetic energy K is

$$K = \frac{3}{2}kT = \frac{3}{2}(1.38 \times 10^{-23} \text{ J/K})(300 \text{ K})$$
$$= 6.2 \times 10^{-21} \text{ J} = 0.039 \text{ eV}$$

EVALUATE: At a temperature of 300 K the magnetic interaction energy is much *smaller* than the random kinetic energy, so we expect only a slight degree of alignment. This is why paramagnetic susceptibilities at ordinary temperature are usually very small.

Diamagnetism

In some materials the total magnetic moment of all the atomic current loops is zero when no magnetic field is present. But even these materials have magnetic effects because an external field alters electron motions within the atoms, causing additional current loops and induced magnetic dipoles comparable to the induced *electric* dipoles we studied in Section 28.5. In this case the additional field caused by these current loops is always *opposite* in direction to that of the external field. (This behavior is explained by Faraday's law of induction, which we will study in Chapter 29. An induced current always tends to cancel the field change that caused it.)

28.27 In this drawing adapted from a magnified photo, the arrows show the directions of magnetization in the domains of a single crystal of nickel. Domains that are magnetized in the direction of an applied magnetic field grow larger.

(a) No field

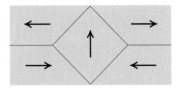

(b) Weak field

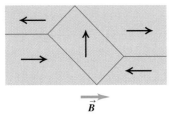

$\vec{B}$

(c) Stronger field

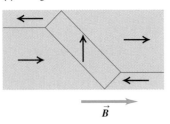

$\vec{B}$

28.28 A magnetization curve for a ferromagnetic material. The magnetization M approaches its saturation value M_{sat} as the magnetic field B_0 (caused by external currents) becomes large.

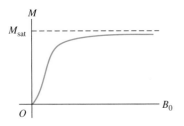

Such materials are said to be **diamagnetic.** They always have negative susceptibility, as shown in Table 28.1, and relative permeability K_m slightly *less* than unity, typically of the order of 0.99990 to 0.99999 for solids and liquids. Diamagnetic susceptibilities are very nearly temperature independent.

Ferromagnetism

There is a third class of materials, called **ferromagnetic** materials, that includes iron, nickel, cobalt, and many alloys containing these elements. In these materials, strong interactions between atomic magnetic moments cause them to line up parallel to each other in regions called **magnetic domains,** even when no external field is present. Figure 28.27 shows an example of magnetic domain structure. Within each domain, nearly all of the atomic magnetic moments are parallel.

When there is no externally applied field, the domain magnetizations are randomly oriented. But when a field $\vec{B}_0$ (caused by external currents) is present, the domains tend to orient themselves parallel to the field. The domain boundaries also shift; the domains that are magnetized in the field direction grow, and those that are magnetized in other directions shrink. Because the total magnetic moment of a domain may be many thousands of Bohr magnetons, the torques that tend to align the domains with an external field are much stronger than occur with paramagnetic materials. The relative permeability K_m is *much* larger than unity, typically of the order of 1,000 to 100,000. As a result, an object made of a ferromagnetic material such as iron is strongly magnetized by the field from a permanent magnet and is attracted to the magnet (see Fig. 27.38). A paramagnetic material such as aluminum is also attracted to a permanent magnet, but K_m for paramagnetic materials is so much smaller for such a material than for ferromagnetic materials that the attraction is very weak. Thus a magnet can pick up iron nails, but not aluminum cans.

As the external field is increased, a point is eventually reached at which nearly *all* the magnetic moments in the ferromagnetic material are aligned parallel to the external field. This condition is called *saturation magnetization;* after it is reached, further increase in the external field causes no increase in magnetization or in the additional field caused by the magnetization.

Figure 28.28 shows a "magnetization curve," a graph of magnetization M as a function of external magnetic field B_0, for soft iron. An alternative description of this behavior is that K_m is not constant but decreases as B_0 increases. (Paramagnetic materials also show saturation at sufficiently strong fields. But the magnetic fields required are so large that departures from a linear relationship between M and B_0 in these materials can be observed only at very low temperatures, 1 K or so.)

For many ferromagnetic materials the relationship of magnetization to external magnetic field is different when the external field is increasing from when it is decreasing. Figure 28.29a shows this relationship for such a material. When the material is magnetized to saturation and then the external field is reduced to zero, some magnetization remains. This behavior is characteristic of permanent magnets, which retain most of their saturation magnetization when the magnetizing field is removed. To reduce the magnetization to zero requires a magnetic field in the reverse direction.

This behavior is called **hysteresis,** and the curves in Fig. 28.29 are called *hysteresis loops.* Magnetizing and demagnetizing a material that has hysteresis involve the dissipation of energy, and the temperature of the material increases during such a process.

Ferromagnetic materials are widely used in electromagnets, transformer cores, and motors and generators, in which it is desirable to have as large a magnetic field as possible for a given current. Because hysteresis dissipates energy, materials that are used in these applications should usually have as narrow a hysteresis loop as possible. Soft iron is often used; it has high permeability without appreciable hysteresis. For permanent magnets a broad hysteresis loop is usually desirable, with large zero-field magnetization and large reverse field needed to demagnetize. Many kinds of steel and many alloys, such as Alnico, are commonly used for permanent magnets. The remaining magnetic field in such a material, after it has been magnetized to near saturation, is typically of the order of 1 T, corresponding to a remaining magnetization $M = B/\mu_0$ of about 800,000 A/m.

28.29 Hysteresis loops. The materials of both **(a)** and **(b)** remain strongly magnetized when B_0 is reduced to zero. Since **(a)** is also hard to demagnetize, it would be good for permanent magnets. Since **(b)** magnetizes and demagnetizes more easily, it could be used as a computer memory material. The material of **(c)** would be useful for transformers and other alternating-current devices where zero hysteresis would be optimal.

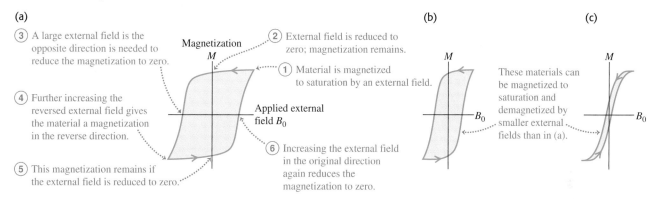

(a)

3 A large external field is the opposite direction is needed to reduce the magnetization to zero.

Magnetization M

2 External field is reduced to zero; magnetization remains.

1 Material is magnetized to saturation by an external field.

4 Further increasing the reversed external field gives the material a magnetization in the reverse direction.

Applied external field B_0

5 This magnetization remains if the external field is reduced to zero.

6 Increasing the external field in the original direction again reduces the magnetization to zero.

(b)

M

B_0

These materials can be magnetized to saturation and demagnetized by smaller external fields than in (a).

(c)

M

B_0

Example 28.12   A ferromagnetic material

A permanent magnet is made of a ferromagnetic material with a magnetization M of about 8×10^5 A/m. The magnet is in the shape of a cube of side 2 cm. (a) Find the magnetic dipole moment of the magnet. (b) Estimate the magnetic field due to the magnet at a point 10 cm from the magnet along its axis.

SOLUTION

IDENTIFY: This problem uses the relationship between magnetization and magnetic dipole moment, as well as the idea that a magnetic dipole produces a magnetic field.

SET UP: We find the magnetic dipole moment from the magnetization, which equals magnetic moment per unit volume. To estimate the magnetic field, we approximate the magnet as a current loop with the same magnetic moment and use the results of Section 28.5.

EXECUTE: (a) The total magnetic moment is the magnetization multiplied by the volume:

$$\mu_{total} = MV = (8 \times 10^5 \text{ A/m})(2 \times 10^{-2} \text{ m})^3 = 6 \text{ A} \cdot \text{m}^2$$

(b) We found in Section 28.5 that the magnetic field on the axis of a current loop with magnetic moment μ_{total} is given by Eq. (28.18),

$$B = \frac{\mu_0 \mu_{total}}{2\pi(x^2 + a^2)^{3/2}}$$

where x is the distance from the loop and a is its radius. We can use this same expression here, except that a refers to the size of the permanent magnet. Strictly speaking, there are complications because our magnet does not have the same geometry as a circular current loop. But because $x = 10$ cm is fairly large in comparison to the 2-cm size of the magnet, the term a^2 is negligible in comparison to x^2 and can be ignored. So

$$B \approx \frac{\mu_0 \mu_{total}}{2\pi x^3} = \frac{(4\pi \times 10^{-7} \text{ T} \cdot \text{m/A})(6 \text{ A} \cdot \text{m}^2)}{2\pi(0.1 \text{ m})^3}$$
$$= 1 \times 10^{-3} \text{ T} = 10 \text{ G}$$

which is about ten times stronger than the magnetic field of the earth. Such a magnet can easily deflect a compass needle.

EVALUATE: Note that we used μ_0, not the permeability μ of the magnetic material, in calculating B. The reason is that we are calculating B at a point *outside* the magnetic material. You would substitute permeability μ for μ_0 only if you were calculating B *inside* a material with relative permeability K_m, for which $\mu = K_m\mu_0$.

Test Your Understanding of Section 28.8   Which of the following materials are attracted to a magnet? (i) sodium; (ii) bismuth; (iii) lead; (iv) uranium.

Magnetic field of a moving charge: The magnetic field $\vec{B}$ created by a charge q moving with velocity $\vec{v}$ depends on the distance r from the source point (the location of q) to the field point (where $\vec{B}$ is measured). The $\vec{B}$ field is perpendicular to $\vec{v}$ and to $\hat{r}$, the unit vector directed from the source point to the field point. The principle of superposition of magnetic fields states that the total $\vec{B}$ field produced by several moving charges is the vector sum of the fields produced by the individual charges. (See Example 28.1.)

$$\vec{B} = \frac{\mu_0}{4\pi}\frac{q\vec{v} \times \hat{r}}{r^2} \qquad (28.2)$$

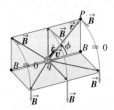

Magnetic field of a current-carrying conductor: The law of Biot and Savart gives the magnetic field $d\vec{B}$ created by an element $d\vec{l}$ of a conductor carrying current I. The field $d\vec{B}$ is perpendicular to both $d\vec{l}$ and $\hat{r}$, the unit vector from the element to the field point. The $\vec{B}$ field created by a finite current-carrying conductor is the integral of $d\vec{B}$ over the length of the conductor. (See Example 28.2.)

$$d\vec{B} = \frac{\mu_0}{4\pi}\frac{I\,d\vec{l} \times \hat{r}}{r^2} \qquad (28.6)$$

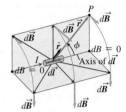

Magnetic field of a long, straight, current-carrying conductor: The magnetic field $\vec{B}$ at a distance r from a long, straight conductor carrying a current I has a magnitude that is inversely proportional to r. The magnetic field lines are circles coaxial with the wire, with directions given by the right-hand rule. (See Examples 28.3 and 28.4.)

$$B = \frac{\mu_0 I}{2\pi r} \qquad (28.9)$$

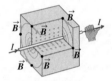

Magnetic force between current-carrying conductors: Two long, parallel, current-carrying conductors attract if the currents are in the same direction and repel if the currents are in opposite directions. The magnetic force per unit length between the conductors depends on their currents I and I' and their separation r. The definition of the ampere is based on this relationship. (See Example 28.5.)

$$\frac{F}{L} = \frac{\mu_0 II'}{2\pi r} \qquad (28.11)$$

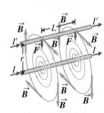

Magnetic field of a current loop: The law of Biot and Savart allows us to calculate the magnetic field produced along the axis of a circular conducting loop of radius a carrying current I. The field depends on the distance x along the axis from the center of the loop to the field point. If there are N loops, the field is multiplied by N. At the center of the loop, $x = 0$. (See Example 28.6.)

$$B_x = \frac{\mu_0 I a^2}{2(x^2 + a^2)^{3/2}} \qquad (28.15)$$
(circular loop)

$$B_x = \frac{\mu_0 NI}{2a} \qquad (28.17)$$
(center of N circular loops)

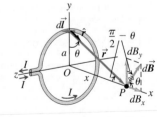

Ampere's law: Ampere's law states that the line integral of $\vec{B}$ around any closed path equals μ_0 times the net current through the area enclosed by the path. The positive sense of current is determined by a right-hand rule. (See Examples 28.7–28.10.)

$$\oint \vec{B} \cdot d\vec{l} = \mu_0 I_{\text{encl}} \qquad (28.20)$$

Magnetic fields due to current distributions: The table lists magnetic fields caused by several current distributions. In each case the conductor is carrying current I.

Current Distribution	Point in Magnetic Field	Magnetic-Field Magnitude
Long, straight conductor	Distance r from conductor	$B = \dfrac{\mu_0 I}{2\pi r}$
Circular loop of radius a	On axis of loop	$B = \dfrac{\mu_0 I a^2}{2(x^2 + a^2)^{3/2}}$
	At center of loop	$B = \dfrac{\mu_0 I}{2a}$ (for N loops, multiply these expressions by N)
Long cylindrical conductor of radius R	Inside conductor, $r < R$	$B = \dfrac{\mu_0 I}{2\pi}\dfrac{r}{R^2}$
	Outside conductor, $r > R$	$B = \dfrac{\mu_0 I}{2\pi r}$
Long, closely wound solenoid with n turns per unit length, near its midpoint	Inside solenoid, near center	$B = \mu_0 n I$
	Outside solenoid	$B \approx 0$
Tightly wound toroidal solenoid (toroid) with N turns	Within the space enclosed by the windings, distance r from symmetry axis	$B = \dfrac{\mu_0 N I}{2\pi r}$
	Outside the space enclosed by the windings	$B \approx 0$

---

*Magnetic materials: When magnetic materials are present, the magnetization of the material causes an additional contribution to $\vec{B}$. For paramagnetic and diamagnetic materials, μ_0 is replaced in magnetic-field expressions by $\mu = K_m\mu_0$, where μ is the permeability of the material and K_m is its relative permeability. The magnetic susceptibility χ_m is defined as $\chi_m = K_m - 1$. Magnetic susceptibilities for paramagnetic materials are small positive quantities; those for diamagnetic materials are small negative quantities. For ferromagnetic materials, K_m is much larger than unity and is not constant. Some ferromagnetic materials are permanent magnets, retaining their magnetization even after the external magnetic field is removed. (See Examples 28.11 and 28.12.)

Key Terms

source point, *958*
field point, *958*
principle of superposition of magnetic fields, *960*
law of Biot and Savart, *961*
ampere, *966*

Ampere's law, *972*
toroidal solenoid, *975*
Bohr magneton, *977*
magnetization, *978*
paramagnetic, *978*
relative permeability, *978*

permeability, *978*
magnetic susceptibility, *978*
diamagnetic, *980*
ferromagnetic, *980*
magnetic domain, *980*
hysteresis, *980*

Answer to Chapter Opening Question ?

There would be *no* change in the magnetic field strength. From Example 28.9 (Section 28.7), the field inside a solenoid has magnitude $B = \mu_0 n I$, where n is the number of turns of wire per unit length. Joining two solenoids end to end doubles both the number of turns and the length, so the number of turns per unit length is unchanged.

Answers to Test Your Understanding Questions

28.1 Answer: (a) (i), (b) (ii)   The situation is the same as shown in Fig. 28.2 except that the upper proton has velocity $\vec{v}$ rather than $-\vec{v}$. The magnetic field due to the lower proton is the same as shown in Fig. 28.2, but the direction of the magnetic force $\vec{F} = q\vec{v} \times \vec{B}$ on the upper proton is reversed. Hence the magnetic force is attractive. Since the speed v is small compared to c, the

magnetic force is much smaller in magnitude than the repulsive electric force and the net force is still repulsive.

28.2 Answer: (i) and (iii) (tie), (iv), (ii)   From Eq. (28.5), the magnitude of the field dB due to a current element of length dl carrying current I is $dB = (\mu/4\pi)(I\,dl\sin\phi/r^2)$. In this expression r is the distance from the element to the field point, and ϕ is the angle between the direction of the current and a vector from the current element to the field point. All four points are the same distance $r = L$ from the current element, so the value of dB is proportional to the value of $\sin\phi$. For the four points the angle is (i) $\phi = 90°$, (ii) $\phi = 0$, (iii) $\phi = 90°$, and (iv) $\phi = 45°$, so the values of $\sin\phi$ are (i) 1, (ii) 0, (iii) 1, and (iv) $1/\sqrt{2}$.

28.3 Answer: A   This orientation will cause current to flow clockwise around the circuit. Hence current will flow south through the wire that lies under the compass. From the right-hand rule for the magnetic field produced by a long, straight, current-carrying conductor, this will produce a magnetic field that points to the left at the position of the compass (which lies atop the wire). The combination of the northward magnetic field of the earth and the westward field produced by the current gives a net magnetic field to the northwest, so the compass needle will swing counterclockwise to align with this field.

28.4 Answers: (a) (i), (b) (iii), (c) (ii), (d) (iii) Current flows in the same direction in adjacent turns of the coil, so the magnetic forces between these turns are attractive. Current flows in opposite directions on opposite sides of the same turn, so the magnetic forces between these sides are repulsive. Thus the magnetic forces on the solenoid turns squeeze them together in the direction along its axis but push them apart radially. The *electric* forces are zero because the wire is electrically neutral, with as much positive charge as there is negative charge.

28.5 Answers: (a) (ii), (b) (v) The vector $d\vec{B}$ is in the direction of $d\vec{l} \times \vec{r}$. For a segment on the negative y-axis, $d\vec{l} = -\hat{k}\,dl$ points in the negative z-direction and $\vec{r} = x\hat{i} + a\hat{j}$. Hence $d\vec{l} \times \vec{r} = (a\,dl)\hat{i} - (x\,dl)\hat{j}$, which has a positive x-component, a negative y-component and zero z-component. For a segment on the negative z-axis, $d\vec{l} = \hat{j}\,dl$ points in the positive y-direction and $\vec{r} = x\hat{i} + a\hat{k}$. Hence $d\vec{l} \times \vec{r} = (a\,dl)\hat{i} - (x\,dl)\hat{k}$, which has a positive x-component, zero y-component, and a negative z-component.

28.6 Answer: (ii) Imagine carrying out the integral $\oint \vec{B} \cdot d\vec{l}$ along an integration path that goes clockwise around the red magnetic field line. At each point along the path the magnetic field $\vec{B}$ and the infinitesimal segment $d\vec{l}$ are both tangent to the path, so $\vec{B} \cdot d\vec{l}$ is positive at each point and the integral $\oint \vec{B} \cdot d\vec{l}$ is likewise positive. It follows from Ampere's law $\oint \vec{B} \cdot d\vec{l} = \mu_0 I_{\text{encl}}$ and the right-hand rule that the integration path encloses a current directed out of the plane of the page. There are no currents in the empty space outside the magnet, so there must be currents inside the magnet (see Section 28.8).

28.7 Answer: (iii) By symmetry, any $\vec{B}$ field outside the cable must circulate around the cable, with circular field lines like those surrounding the solid cylindrical conductor in Fig. 28.20. Choose an integration path like the one shown in Fig. 28.20 with radius $r > R$, so that the path completely encloses the cable. As in Example 28.8, the integral $\oint \vec{B} \cdot d\vec{l}$ for this path has magnitude $B(2\pi r)$. From Ampere's law this is equal to $\mu_0 I_{\text{encl}}$. The net enclosed current I_{encl} is zero because it includes two currents of equal magnitude but opposite direction: one in the central wire and one in the hollow cylinder. Hence $B(2\pi r) = 0$, and so $B = 0$ for any value of r outside the cable. (The field is nonzero *inside* the cable; see Exercise 28.37.)

28.8 Answer: (i), (iv) Sodium and uranium are paramagnetic materials and hence are attracted to a magnet, while bismuth and lead are diamagnetic materials that are repelled by a magnet. (See Table 28.1.)

PROBLEMS

For instructor-assigned homework, go to **www.masteringphysics.com**

Discussion Questions

Q28.1. A topic of current interest in physics research is the search (thus far unsuccessful) for an isolated magnetic pole, or magnetic *monopole*. If such an entity were found, how could it be recognized? What would its properties be?

Q28.2. Streams of charged particles emitted from the sun during periods of solar activity create a disturbance in the earth's magnetic field. How does this happen?

Q28.3. The text discussed the magnetic field of an infinitely long, straight conductor carrying a current. Of course, there is no such thing as an infinitely long *anything*. How do you decide whether a particular wire is long enough to be considered infinite?

Q28.4. Two parallel conductors carrying current in the same direction attract each other. If they are permitted to move toward each other, the forces of attraction do work. From where does the energy come? Does this contradict the assertion in Chapter 27 that magnetic forces on moving charges do no work? Explain.

Q28.5. Pairs of conductors carrying current into or out of the power-supply components of electronic equipment are sometimes twisted together to reduce magnetic-field effects. Why does this help?

Q28.6. Suppose you have three long, parallel wires arranged so that in cross section they are at the corners of an equilateral triangle. Is there any way to arrange the currents so that all three wires attract each other? So that all three wires repel each other? Explain.

Q28.7. In deriving the force on one of the long, current-carrying conductors in Section 28.4, why did we use the magnetic field due to only one of the conductors? That is, why didn't we use the *total* magnetic field due to *both* conductors?

Q28.8. Two concentric, coplanar, circular loops of wire of different diameter carry currents in the same direction. Describe the nature of the force exerted on the inner loop by the outer loop and on the outer loop by the inner loop.

Q28.9. A current was sent through a helical coil spring. The spring contracted, as though it had been compressed. Why?

Q28.10. What are the relative advantages and disadvantages of Ampere's law and the law of Biot and Savart for practical calculations of magnetic fields?

Q28.11. Magnetic field lines never have a beginning or an end. Use this to explain why it is reasonable for the field of a toroidal solenoid to be confined entirely to its interior, while a straight solenoid *must* have some field outside.

Q28.12. If the magnitude of the magnetic field a distance R from a very long, straight, current-carrying wire is B, at what distance from the wire will the field have magnitude $3B$?

Q28.13. Two very long, parallel wires carry equal currents in opposite directions. (a) Is there any place that their magnetic fields completely cancel? If so, where? If not, why not? (b) How would the answer to part (a) change if the currents were in the same direction?

Q28.14. In the circuit shown in Figure 28.30, when switch S is suddenly closed, the wire L is pulled toward the lower wire carrying current I. Which (a or b) is the positive terminal of the battery? How do you know?

Figure 28.30
Question Q28.14.

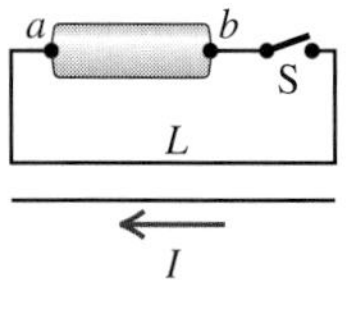

Q28.15. A metal ring carries a current that causes a magnetic field B_0 at the center of the ring and a field B at point P a distance x

from the center along the axis of the ring. If the radius of the ring is doubled, find the magnetic field at the center. Will the field at point *P* change by the same factor? Why?

*Q28.16. Why should the permeability of a paramagnetic material be expected to decrease with increasing temperature?

*Q28.17. If a magnet is suspended over a container of liquid air, it attracts droplets to its poles. The droplets contain only liquid oxygen; even though nitrogen is the primary constituent of air, it is not attracted to the magnet. Explain what this tells you about the magnetic susceptibilities of oxygen and nitrogen, and explain why a magnet in ordinary, room-temperature air doesn't attract molecules of oxygen *gas* to its poles.

*Q28.18. What features of atomic structure determine whether an element is diamagnetic or paramagnetic? Explain.

*Q28.19. The magnetic susceptibility of paramagnetic materials is quite strongly temperature dependent, but that of diamagnetic materials is nearly independent of temperature Why the difference?

*Q28.20. A cylinder of iron is placed so that it is free to rotate around its axis. Initially the cylinder is at rest, and a magnetic field is applied to the cylinder so that it is magnetized in a direction parallel to its axis. If the direction of the *external* field is suddenly reversed, the direction of magnetization will also reverse and the cylinder will begin rotating around its axis. (This is called the *Einstein-de Haas effect.*) Explain why the cylinder begins to rotate.

*Q28.21. The discussion of magnetic forces on current loops in Section 27.7 commented that no net force is exerted on a complete loop in a uniform magnetic field, only a torque. Yet magnetized materials that contain atomic current loops certainly *do* experience net forces in magnetic fields. How is this discrepancy resolved?

*Q28.22. Show that the units $A \cdot m^2$ and J/T for the Bohr magneton are equivalent.

Exercises

Section 26.1 Magnetic Field of a Moving Charge

28.1. A $+6.00\text{-}\mu C$ point charge is moving at a constant 8.00×10^6 m/s in the $+y$-direction, relative to a reference frame. At the instant when the point charge is at the origin of this reference frame, what is the magnetic-field vector $\vec{B}$ it produces at the following points: (a) $x = 0.500$ m, $y = 0$, $z = 0$; (b) $x = 0$, $y = -0.500$ m, $z = 0$; (c) $x = 0$, $y = 0$, $z = +0.500$ m; (d) $x = 0$, $y = -0.500$ m, $z = +0.500$ m?

28.2. Fields Within the Atom. In the Bohr model of the hydrogen atom, the electron moves in a circular orbit of radius 5.3×10^{-11} m with a speed of 2.2×10^6 m/s. If we are viewing the atom in such a way that the electron's orbit is in the plane of the paper with the electron moving clockwise, find the magnitude and direction of the electric and magnetic fields that the electron produces at the location of the nucleus (treated as a point).

28.3. An electron moves at $0.100c$ as shown in Fig. 28.31. Find the magnitude and direction of the magnetic field this electon produces at the following points, each $2.00\ \mu$m from the electron: (a) points *A* and *B*; (b) point *C*; (c) point *D*.

28.4. An alpha particle (charge $+2e$) and an electron move in opposite directions from the same point, each with the speed of 2.50×10^5 m/s (Fig. 28.32). Find the magnitude and direction of the total magnetic field these charges produce at point *P*, which is 1.75 nm from each of them.

Figure **28.31** Exercise 28.3.

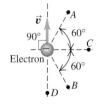

Figure **28.32** Exercise 28.4.

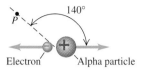

28.5. A $-4.80\text{-}\mu C$ charge is moving at a constant speed of 6.80×10^5 m/s in the $+x$-direction relative to a reference frame. At the instant when the point charge is at the origin, what is the magnetic-field vector it produces at the following points: (a) $x = 0.500$ m, $y = 0$, $z = 0$; (b) $x = 0$, $y = 0.500$ m, $z = 0$; (c) $x = 0.500$ m, $y = 0.500$ m, $z = 0$; (d) $x = 0$, $y = 0$, $z = 0.500$ m?

28.6. Positive point charges $q = +8.00\ \mu C$ and $q' = +3.00\ \mu C$ are moving relative to an observer at point *P*, as shown in Fig. 28.33. The distance *d* is 0.120 m, $v = 4.50 \times 10^6$ m/s, and $v' = 9.00 \times 10^6$ m/s. (a) When the two charges are at the locations shown in the figure, what are the magnitude and direction of the net magnetic field they produce at point *P*? (b) What are the magnitude and direction of the electric and magnetic forces that each charge exerts on the other, and what is the ratio of the magnitude of the electric force to the magnitude of the magnetic force? (c) If the direction of $\vec{v}'$ is reversed, so both charges are moving in the same direction, what are the magnitude and direction of the magnetic forces that the two charges exert on each other?

Figure **28.33** Exercises 28.6 and 28.7.

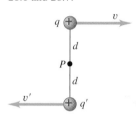

28.7. Figure 28.33 shows two point charges, q and q', moving relative to an observer at point *P*. Suppose that the lower charge is actually *negative*, with $q' = -q$. (a) Find the magnetic field (magnitude and direction) produced by the two charges at point *P* if (i) $v' = v/2$; (ii) $v' = v$; (iii) $v' = 2v$. (b) Find the direction of the magnetic force that q exerts on q', and find the direction of the magnetic force that q' exerts on q. (c) If $v = v' = 3.00 \times 10^5$ m/s, what is the ratio of the magnitude of the magnetic force acting on each charge to that of the Coulomb force acting on each charge?

28.8. An electron and a proton are each moving at 845 km/s in perpendicular paths as shown in Fig. 28.34. At the instant when they are at the positions shown in the figure, find the magnitude and direction of (a) the total magnetic field they produce at the origin; (b) the magnetic field the electron produces at the location of the proton; (c) the total electrical force and the total magnetic force that the electron exerts on the proton.

Figure **28.34** Exercise 28.8.

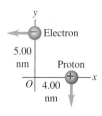

Section 28.2 Magnetic Field of a Current Element

28.9. A straight wire caries a 10.0-A current (Fig. 28.35). *ABCD* is a rectangle with point *D* in the middle of a 1.10-mm segment of the wire and point *C* in the wire. Find the magnitude and direction of the magnetic field due to this segment at (a) point *A*; (b) point *B*; (c) point *C*.

Figure **28.35** Exercise 28.9.

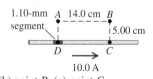

28.10. A long, straight wire, carrying a current of 200 A, runs through a cubical wooden box, entering and leaving through holes in the centers of opposite faces (Fig. 28.36). The length of each side of the box is 20.0 cm. Consider an element dl of the wire 0.100 cm long at the center of the box. Compute the magnitude dB of the magnetic field produced by this element at the points a, b, c, d, and e in Fig. 28.36. Points a, c, and d are at the centers of the faces of the cube; point b is at the midpoint of one edge; and point e is at a corner. Copy the figure and show the directions and relative magnitudes of the field vectors. (*Note:* Assume that the length dl is small in comparison to the distances from the current element to the points where the magnetic field is to be calculated.)

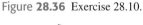
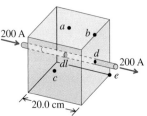

Figure **28.36** Exercise 28.10.

28.11. A long, straight wire lies along the z-axis and carries a 4.00-A current in the $+z$-direction. Find the magnetic field (magnitude and direction) produced at the following points by a 0.500-mm segment of the wire centered at the origin: (a) $x = 2.00$ m, $y = 0$, $z = 0$; (b) $x = 0$, $y = 2.00$ m, $z = 0$; (c) $x = 2.00$ m, $y = 2.00$ m, $z = 0$; (d) $x = 0$, $y = 0$, $z = 2.00$ m.

28.12. Two parallel wires are 5.00 cm apart and carry currents in opposite directions, as shown in Fig. 28.37. Find the magnitude and direction of the magnetic field at point P due to two 1.50-mm segments of wire that are opposite each other and each 8.00 cm from P.

Figure **28.37** Exercise 28.12.

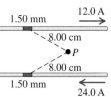

28.13. A wire carrying a 28.0-A current bends through a right angle. Consider two 2.00-mm segments of wire, each 3.00 cm from the bend (Fig. 28.38). Find the magnitude and direction of the magnetic field these two segments produce at point P, which is midway between them.

Figure **28.38** Exercise 28.13.

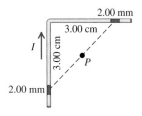

28.14. A square wire loop 10.0 cm on each side carries a clockwise current of 15.0 A. Find the magnitude and direction of the magnetic field at its center due to the four 1.20-mm wire segments at the midpoint of each side.

Section 28.3 Magnetic Field of a Straight Current-Carrying Conductor

28.15. The Magnetic Field from a Lightning Bolt. Lightning bolts can carry currents up to approximately 20 kA. We can model such a current as the equivalent of a very long, straight wire. (a) If you were unfortunate enough to be 5.0 m away from such a lightning bolt, how large a magnetic field would you expe-

rience? (b) How does this field compare to one you would experience by being 5.0 cm from a long, straight household current of 10 A?

28.16. A very long, straight horizontal wire carries a current such that 3.50×10^{18} electrons per second pass any given point going from west to east. What are the magnitude and direction of the magnetic field this wire produces at a point 4.00 cm directly above it?

28.17. (a) How large a current would a very long, straight wire have to carry so that the magnetic field 2.00 cm from the wire is equal to 1.00 G (comparable to the earth's northward-pointing magnetic field)? (b) If the wire is horizontal with the current running from east to west, at what locations would the magnetic field of the wire point in the same direction as the horizontal component of the earth's magnetic field? (c) Repeat part (b) except the wire is vertical with the current going upward.

28.18. Two long, straight wires, one above the other, are seperated by a distance $2a$ and are parallel to the x-axis. Let the $+y$-axis be in the plane of the wires in the direction from the lower wire to the upper wire. Each wire carries current I in the $+x$-direction. What are the magnitude and direction of the net magnetic field of the two wires at a point in the plane of the wires (a) midway between them; (b) at a distance a above the upper wire; (c) at a distance a below the lower wire?

28.19. A long, straight wire lies along the y-axis and carries a current $I = 8.00$ A in the $-y$-direction (Fig. 28.39). In addition to the magnetic field due to the current in the wire, a uniform magnetic field $\vec{B}_0$ with magnitude 1.50×10^{-6} T is in the $+x$-direction What is the total field (magnitude and direction) at the following points in the xz-plane: (a) $x = 0$, $z = 1.00$ m; (b) $x = 1.00$ m, $z = 0$; (c) $x = 0$, $z = -0.25$ m?

Figure **28.39** Exercise 28.19.

28.20. Effect of Transmission Lines. Two hikers are reading a compass under an overhead transmission line that is 5.50 m above the ground and carries a current of 800 A in a horizontal direction from north to south. (a) Find the magnitude and direction of the magnetic field at a point on the ground directly under the conductor. (b) One hiker suggests they walk on another 50 m to avoid inaccurate compass readings caused by the current. Considering that the magnitude of the earth's field is of the order of 0.5×10^{-4} T, is the current really a problem?

28.21. Two long, straight, parallel wires, 10.0 cm apart, carry equal 4.00-A currents in the same direction, as shown in Fig. 28.40. Find the magnitude and direction of the magnetic field at (a) point P_1, midway between the wires; (b) point P_2, 25.0 cm to the right of P_1; (c) point P_3, 20.0 cm directly above P_1.

Figure **28.40** Exercise 28.21.

28.22. Two long, parallel transmission lines, 40.0 cm apart, carry 25.0-A and 75.0-A currents. Find all locations where the net magnetic field of the two wires is zero if these currents are in (a) the same direction and (b) the opposite direction.

28.23. Four, long, parallel power lines each carry 100-A currents. A cross-sectional diagram of these lines is a square, 20.0 cm on each side. For each of the three cases shown in Fig. 28.41, calculate the magnetic field at the center of the square.

Figure **28.41** Exercise 28.23.

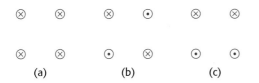

(a)   (b)   (c)

28.24. Four very long, current-carrying wires in the same plane intersect to form a square 40.0 cm on each side, as shown in Fig. 28.42. Find the magnitude and direction of the current I so that the magnetic field at the center of the square is zero.

Figure **28.42**
Exercise 28.24.

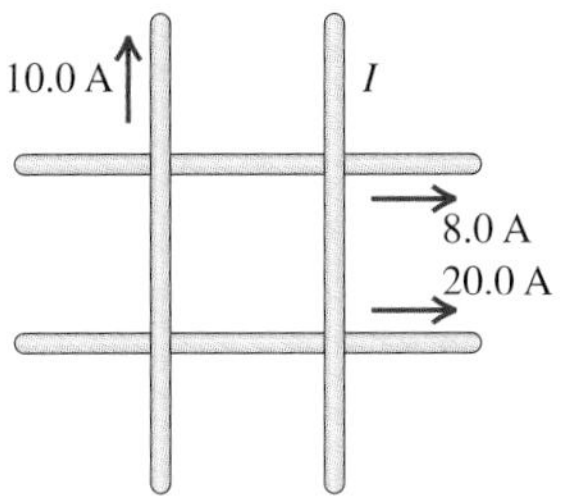

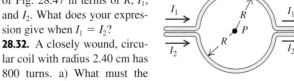

Section 28.4 Force Between Parallel Conductors

28.25. Two long, parallel wires are separated by a distance of 0.400 m (Fig. 28.43). The currents I_1 and I_2 have the directions shown. (a) Calculate the magnitude of the force exerted by each wire on a 1.20-m length of the other. Is the force attractive or repulsive? (b) Each current is doubled, so that I_1 becomes 10.0 A and I_2 becomes 4.00 A. Now what is the magnitude of the force that each wire exerts on a 1.20-m length of the other?

Figure **28.43** Exercise 28.25.

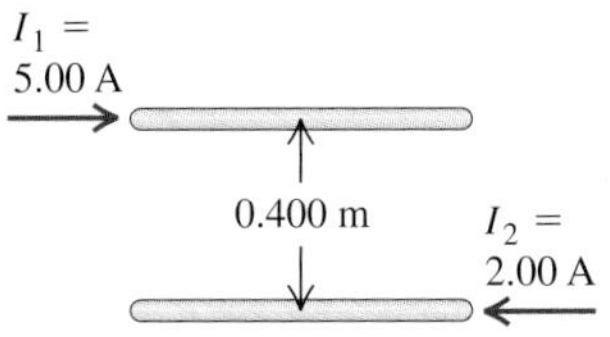

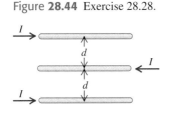

28.26. Two long, parallel wires are separated by a distance of 2.50 cm. The force per unit length that each wire exerts on the other is 4.00×10^{-5} N/m, and the wires repel each other. The current in one wire is 0.600 A. (a) What is the current in the second wire? (b) Are the two currents in the same direction or in opposite directions?

28.27. Lamp Cord Wires. The wires in a household lamp cord are typically 3.0 mm apart center to center and carry equal currents in opposite directions. If the cord carries current to a 100-W light bulb connected across a 120-V potential difference, what force per meter does each wire of the cord exert on the other? Is the force attractive or repulsive? Is this force large enough so it should be considered in the design of lamp cord? (Model the lamp cord as a very long straight wire.)

28.28. Three parallel wires each carry current I in the directions shown in Fig. 28.44. If the separation between adjacent wires is d, calculate the magnitude and direction of the net magnetic force per unit length on each wire.

Figure **28.44** Exercise 28.28.

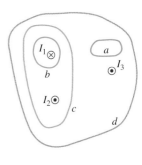

28.29. A long, horizontal wire AB rests on the surface of a table and carries a current I. Horizontal wire CD is vertically above wire AB and is free to slide up and down on the two vertical metal guides C and D (Fig. 28.45). Wire CD is connected through the sliding contacts to another wire that also carries a current I, opposite in direction to the current in wire AB. The mass per unit length of the wire CD is λ. To what equilibrium height h will the wire CD rise, assuming that the magnetic force on it is due entirely to the current in the wire AB?

Figure **28.45** Exercise 28.29.

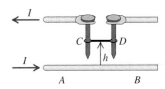

Section 28.5 Magnetic Field of a Circular Current Loop

28.30. Calculate the magnitude and direction of the magnetic field at point P due to the current in the semicircular section of wire shown in Fig. 28.46. (*Hint:* Does the current in the long, straight section of the wire produce any field at P?)

Figure **28.46** Exercise 28.30.

28.31. Calculate the magnitude of the magnetic field at point P of Fig. 28.47 in terms of R, I_1, and I_2. What does your expression give when $I_1 = I_2$?

28.32. A closely wound, circular coil with radius 2.40 cm has 800 turns. a) What must the current in the coil be if the magnetic field at the center of the coil is 0.0580 T? b) At what distance x from the center of the coil, on the axis of the coil, is the magnetic field half its value at the center?

Figure **28.47** Exercise 28.31.

28.33. A closely wound, circular coil with a diameter of 4.00 cm has 600 turns and carries a current of 0.500 A. What is the magnitude of the magnetic field (a) at the center of the coil and (b) at a point on the axis of the coil 8.00 cm from its center?

28.34. A closely wound coil has a radius of 6.00 cm and carries a current of 2.50 A. How many turns must it have if, at a point on the coil axis 6.00 cm from the center of the coil, the magnetic field is 6.39×10^{-4} T?

Section 28.6 Ampere's Law

28.35. A closed curve encircles several conductors. The line integral $\oint \vec{B} \cdot d\vec{l}$ around this curve is 3.83×10^{-4} T · m. (a) What is the net current in the conductors? (b) If you were to integrate around the curve in the opposite direction, what would be the value of the line integral? Explain.

28.36. Figure 28.48 shows, in cross section, several conductors that carry currents through the plane of the figure. The currents have the magnitudes $I_1 = 4.0$ A, $I_2 = 6.0$ A, and $I_3 = 2.0$ A, and the directions shown. Four paths, labeled a through d, are shown. What is the line integral $\oint \vec{B} \cdot d\vec{l}$ for each path? Each integral involves going around the path in the counterclockwise direction. Explain your answers.

Figure **28.48**
Exercise 28.36.

Section 28.7 Applications of Ampere's Law

28.37. Coaxial Cable. A solid conductor with radius a is supported by insulating disks on the axis of a conducting tube with inner radius b and outer radius c (Fig. 28.49). The central conductor and tube carry equal currents I in opposite directions. The currents are distributed uniformly over the cross sections of each conductor. Derive an expression for the magnitude of the magnetic field (a) at points outside the central, solid conductor but inside the tube $(a < r < b)$ and (b) at points outside the tube $(r > c)$.

Figure **28.49**
Exercise 28.37.

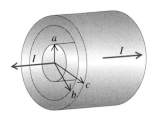

28.38. Repeat Exercise 28.37 for the case in which the current in the central, solid conductor is I_1, the current in the tube is I_2, and these currents are in the same direction rather than in opposite directions.

28.39. A long, straight, cylindrical wire of radius R carries a current uniformly distributed over its cross section. At what location is the magnetic field produced by this current equal to half of its largest value? Consider points inside and outside the wire.

28.40. A 15.0-cm-long solenoid with radius 2.50 cm is closely wound with 600 turns of wire. The current in the windings is 8.00 A. Compute the magnetic field at a point near the center of the solenoid.

28.41. A solenoid is designed to produce a magnetic field of 0.0270 T at its center. It has radius 1.40 cm and length 40.0 cm, and the wire can carry a maximum current of 12.0 A. (a) What minimum number of turns per unit length must the solenoid have? (b) What total length of wire is required?

28.42. As a new electrical technician, you are designing a large solenoid to produce a uniform 0.150 T magnetic field near the center of the solenoid. You have enough wire for 4000 circular turns. This solenoid must be 1.40 m long and 20.0 cm in diameter. What current will you need to produce the necessary field?

28.43. A magnetic field of 37.2 T has been achieved at the MIT Francis Bitter National Magnetic Laboratory. Find the current needed to achieve such a field (a) 2.00 cm from a long, straight wire; (b) at the center of a circular coil of radius 42.0 cm that has 100 turns; (c) near the center of a solenoid with radius 2.40 cm, length 32.0 cm, and 40,000 turns.

28.44. A toroidal solenoid (see Example 28.10) has inner radius $r_1 = 15.0$ cm and outer radius $r_2 = 18.0$ cm. The solenoid has 250 turns and carries a current of 8.50 A. What is the magnitude of the magnetic field at the following distances from the center of the torus: (a) 12.0 cm; (b) 16.0 cm; (c) 20.0 cm?

28.45. A wooden ring whose mean diameter is 14.0 cm is wound with a closely spaced toroidal winding of 600 turns. Compute the magnitude of the magnetic field at the center of the cross section of the windings when the current in the windings is 0.650 A.

*Section 28.8 Magnetic Materials

*28.46. A toroidal solenoid with 400 turns of wire and a mean radius of 6.0 cm carries a current of 0.25 A. The relative permeability of the core is 80. (a) What is the magnetic field in the core? (b) What part of the magnetic field is due to atomic currents?

*28.47. A toroidal solenoid with 500 turns is wound on a ring with a mean radius of 2.90 cm. Find the current in the winding that is required to set up a magnetic field of 0.350 T in the ring (a) if the ring is made of annealed iron $(K_m = 1400)$ and (b) if the ring is made of silicon steel $(K_m = 5200)$.

*28.48. The current in the windings of a toroidal solenoid is 2.400 A. There are 500 turns, and the mean radius is 25.00 cm. The toroidal solenoid is filled with a magnetic material. The magnetic field inside the windings is found to be 1.940 T. Calculate (a) the relative permeability and (b) the magnetic susceptibility of the material that fills the toroid.

*28.49. A long solenoid with 60 turns of wire per centimeter carries a current of 0.15 A. The wire that makes up the solenoid is wrapped around a solid core of silicon steel $(K_m = 5200)$. (The wire of the solenoid is jacketed with an insulator so that none of the current flows into the core.) (a) For a point inside the core, find the magnitudes of (i) the magnetic field $\vec{B}_0$ due to the solenoid current; (ii) the magnetization $\vec{M}$; (iii) the total magnetic field $\vec{B}$. (b) In a sketch of the solenoid and core, show the directions of the vectors $\vec{B}$, $\vec{B}_0$, and $\vec{M}$ inside the core.

*28.50. Curie's Law. Experimental measurements of the magnetic susceptibility of iron ammonium alum are given in the table. Graph values of $1/\chi_m$ against Kelvin temperature. Does the material obey Curie's law? If so, what is the Curie constant?

T (°C)	χ_m
−258.15	129×10^{-4}
−173	19.4×10^{-4}
−73	9.7×10^{-4}
27	6.5×10^{-4}

Problems

28.51. A pair of point charges, $q = +8.00\ \mu C$ and $q' = -5.00\ \mu C$, are moving as shown in Fig 28.50 with speeds $v = 9.00 \times 10^4$ m/s and $v' = 6.50 \times 10^4$ m/s. When the charges are at the locations shown in the figure, what are the magnitude and direction of (a) the magnetic field produced at the origin and (b) the magnetic force that q' exerts on q?

Figure **28.50**
Problem 28.51.

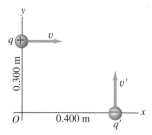

28.52. A long, straight wire carries a current of 2.50 A. An electron is traveling in the vicinity of the wire. At the instant when the electron is 4.50 cm from the wire and traveling with a speed of 6.00×10^4 m/s directly toward the wire, what are the magnitude and direction (relative to the direction of the current) of the force that the magnetic field of the current exerts on the electron?

28.53. A long, straight wire carries a 25.0-A current. An electron is fired parallel to this wire with a velocity of 250 km/s in the same direction as the current, 2.00 cm from the wire. (a) Find the magnitude and direction of the electron's initial acceleration. (b) What should be the magnitude and direction of a uniform electric field that will allow the electron to continue to travel parallel to the wire? (c) Is it necessary to include the effects of gravity? Justify your answer.

28.54. In Fig. 28.51 the battery branch of the circuit is very far from the two horizontal segments containing two resistors. These horizontal segments are separated by 5.00 cm, and they are much longer than 5.00 cm. A proton (charge $+e$) is fired at 650 km/s from a point midway between the upper two horizontal segments of the circuit. The initial velocity of the proton is in the plane of the

Figure **28.51** Problem 28.54.

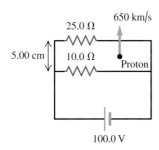

circuit and is directed toward the upper wire. Find the magnitude and direction of the initial magnetic force on the proton.

28.55. Two identical circular, wire loops 40.0 cm in diameter each carry a current of 1.50 A in the same direction. These loops are parallel to each other and are 25.0 cm apart. Line ab is normal to the plane of the loops and passes through their centers. A proton is fired at 2400 km/s perpendicular to line ab from a point midway between the centers of the loops. Find the magnitude and direction of the magnetic force these loops exert on the proton just after it is fired.

28.56. Two very long, straight wires carry currents as shown in Fig. 28.52. For each case, find all locations where the net magnetic field is zero.

Figure **28.52** Problem 28.56.

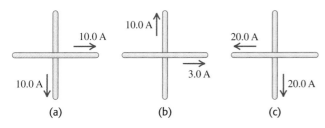

(a)   (b)   (c)

28.57. A negative point charge $q = -7.20$ mC is moving in a reference frame. When the point charge is at the origin, the magnetic field it produces at the point $x = 25.0$ cm, $y = 0$, $z = 0$ is $\vec{B} = (6.00 \ \mu\text{T})\hat{j}$, and its speed is 800 km/s. (a) What are the x-, y-, and z-components of the velocity $\vec{v}_0$ of the charge? (b) At this same instant, what is the magnitude of the magnetic field that the charge produces at the point $x = 0$, $y = 25.0$ cm, $z = 0$?

28.58. A neophyte magnet designer tells you that he can produce a magnetic field $\vec{B}$ in vacuum that points everywhere in the x-direction and that increases in magnitude with increasing x. That is, $\vec{B} = B_0(x/a)\hat{i}$, where B_0 and a are constants with units of teslas and meters, respectively. Use Gauss's law for magnetic fields to show that this claim is *impossible*. (*Hint:* Use a Gaussian surface in the shape of a rectangular box, with edges parallel to the x-, y-, and z-axes.)

28.59. Two long, straight, parallel wires are 1.00 m apart (Fig. 28.53). The wire on the left carries a current I_1 of 6.00 A into the plane of the paper. (a) What must the magnitude and direction of the current I_2 be for the net field at point P to be zero? (b) Then what are the magnitude and direction of the net field at Q? (c) Then what is the magnitude of the net field at S?

Figure **28.53**
Problem 28.59.

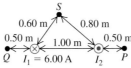

28.60. Figure 28.54 shows an end view of two long, parallel wires perpendicular to the xy-plane, each carrying a current I but in opposite directions. (a) Copy the diagram, and draw vectors to show the $\vec{B}$ field of each wire and the net $\vec{B}$ field at point P. (b) Derive the expression for the magnitude of $\vec{B}$ at any point on the x-axis in terms of the x-coordinate of the point. What is the direction of $\vec{B}$? (c) Graph the magnitude of $\vec{B}$ at points on the x-axis. (d) At what value of x is the magnitude of $\vec{B}$ a maximum? (e) What is the magnitude of $\vec{B}$ when $x \gg a$?

28.61. Refer to the situation in Problem 28.60. Suppose that a third long, straight wire, parallel to the other two, passes through point P (see Fig. 28.54) and that each wire carries a current $I = 6.00$ A. Let $a = 40.0$ cm and $x = 60.0$ cm. Find the magnitude and direction of the force per unit length on the third wire, (a) if the current in it is directed into the plane of the figure, and (b) if the current in it is directed out of the plane of the figure.

28.62. A pair of long, rigid metal rods, each of length L, lie parallel to each other on a perfectly smooth table. Their ends are connected by identical, very light conducting springs of force constant k (Fig. 28.55) and negligible unstretched length. If a current I runs through this circuit, the springs will stretch. At what separation will the rods remain at rest? Assume that k is large enough so that the separation of the rods will be much less than L.

28.63. Two long, parallel wires hang by 4.00-cm-long cords from a common axis (Fig. 28.56). The wires have a mass per unit length of 0.0125 kg/m and carry the same current in opposite directions. What is the current in each wire if the cords hang at an angle of 6.00° with the vertical?

Figure **28.54** Problems
28.60 and 28.61.

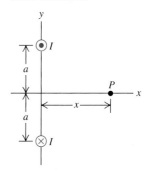

Figure **28.55**
Problem 28.62.

Figure **28.56** Problem 28.63.

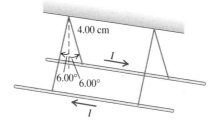

28.64. The long, straight wire AB shown in Fig. 28.57 carries a current of 14.0 A. The rectangular loop whose long edges are parallel to the wire carries a current of 5.00 A. Find the magnitude and direction of the net force exerted on the loop by the magnetic field of the wire.

Figure **28.57** Problem 28.64.

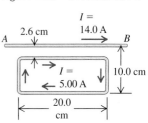

28.65. A circular wire loop of radius a has N turns and carries a current I. A second loop with N' turns of radius a' carries current I' and is located on the axis of the first loop, a distance x from the center of the first loop. The second loop is tipped so that its axis is at an angle θ from the axis of the first loop. The distance x is large compared to both a and a'. (a) Find the magnitude of the torque exerted on the second loop by the first loop. (b) Find the potential energy for the second loop due to this interaction. (c) What simplifications result from having x much larger than a? From having x much larger than a'?

28.66. The wire semicircles shown in Fig. 28.58 have radii a and b. Calculate the net magnetic field (magnitude and direction) that the current in the wires produces at point P.

Figure **28.58** Problem 28.66.

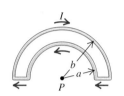

28.67. Helmholtz Coils. Fig. 28.59 is a sectional view of two circular coils with radius a, each wound with N turns of wire carrying a current I, circulating in the same direction in both coils. The coils are separated by a distance a equal to their radii. In this configuration the coils are called Helmholtz coils; they produce a very uniform magnetic field in the region between them. (a) Derive the expression for the magnitude B of the magnetic field at a point on the axis a distance x to the right of point P, which is midway between the coils. (b) Graph B versus x for $x = 0$ to $x = a/2$. Compare this graph to one for the magnetic field due to the right-hand coil alone. (c) From part (a), obtain an expression for the magnitude of the magnetic field at point P. (d) Calculate the magnitude of the magnetic field at P if $N = 300$ turns, $I = 6.00$ A, and $a = 8.00$ cm. (e) Calculate dB/dx and d^2B/dx^2 at P ($x = 0$). Discuss how your results show that the field is very uniform in the vicinity of P.

Figure **28.59** Problem 28.67.

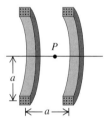

28.68. A circular wire of diameter D lies on a horizontal table and carries a current I. In Fig. 28.60 point A marks the center of the circle and point C is on its rim. (a) Find the magnitude and direction of the magnetic field at point A. (b) The wire is now unwrapped so it is straight, centered on point C, and perpendicular to the line AC, but the same current is maintained in it. Now find the magnetic field at point A. (c) Which field is greater: the one in part (a) or in part (b)? By what factor? Why is this result physically reasonable?

Figure **28.60** Problem 28.68.

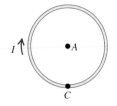

28.69. The wire in Fig. 28.61 carries current I in the direction shown. The wire consists of a very long, straight section, a quarter-circle with radius R, and another long, straight section. What are the magnitude and direction of the net magnetic field at the center of curvature of the quarter-circle section (point P)?

Figure **28.61** Problem 28.69.

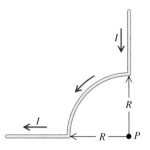

28.70. The wire shown in Fig. 28.62 is infinitely long and carries a current I. Calculate the magnitude and direction of the magnetic field that this current produces at point P.

Figure **28.62** Problem 28.70.

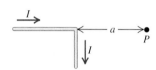

28.71. A long, straight wire with a circular cross section of radius R carries a current I. Assume that the current density is not constant across the cross section of the wire, but rather varies as $J = \alpha r$, where α is a constant. (a) By the requirement that J integrated over the cross section of the wire gives the total current I, calculate the constant α in terms of I and R. (b) Use Ampere's law to calculate the magnetic field $B(r)$ for (i) $r \le R$ and (ii) $r \ge R$. Express your answers in terms of I.

28.72. (a) For the coaxial cable of Exercise 28.37, derive an expression for the magnitude of the magnetic field at points inside the central solid conductor $(r < a)$. Compare your result when $r = a$ to the results of part (a) of Exercise 28.37 at that same point. (b) For this coaxial cable derive an expression for the field within the tube $(b < r < c)$. Compare your result when $r = b$ to part (a) of Exercise 28.37 at that same point. Compare your result when $r = c$ to part (b) of Exercise 28.37 at that same point.

28.73. The electric field of an infinite line of positive charge is directed radially outward from the wire and can be calculated using Gauss's law for the electric field (see Example 22.6 in Section 22.4). Use Gauss's law for magnetism to show that the *magnetic* field of a straight, infinitely long, current-carrying *conductor* cannot have a radial component.

28.74. A conductor is made in the form of a hollow cylinder with inner and outer radii a and b, respectively. It carries a current I uniformly distributed over its cross section. Derive expressions for the magnitude of the magnetic field in the regions (a) $r < a$; (b) $a < r < b$; (c) $r > b$.

28.75. Knowing Magnetic Fields Inside and Out. You are given a hollow copper cylinder with inner radius a and outer radius $3a$. The cylinder's length is $200a$ and its electrical resistance to current flowing down its length is R. To test its suitability for use in a circuit, you connect the ends of the cylinder to a voltage source, causing a current I to flow down the length of the cylinder. The current is spread uniformly over the cylinder's cross section. You are interested in knowing the strength of the magnetic field that the current produces within the solid part of the cylinder, at a radius $2a$ from the cylinder axis. But since it's not easy to insert a magnetic-field probe into the solid metal, you decide instead to measure the field at a point outside the cylinder where the field should be as strong as at radius $2a$. At what distance from the axis of the cylinder should you place the probe?

28.76. A circular loop has radius R and carries current I_2 in a clockwise direction (Fig. 28.63). The center of the loop is a distance D above a long, straight wire. What are the magnitude and direction of the current I_1 in the wire if the magnetic field at the center of the loop is zero?

Figure **28.63** Problem 28.76.

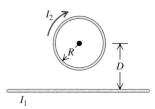

28.77. A long, straight, solid cylinder, oriented with its axis in the z-direction, carries a current whose current density is $\vec{J}$. The current density, although symmetrical about the cylinder axis, is not constant but varies according to the relationship

$$\vec{J} = \frac{2I_0}{\pi a^2}\left[1 - \left(\frac{r}{a}\right)^2\right]\hat{k} \quad \text{for } r \leq a$$
$$= 0 \quad \text{for } r \geq a$$

where a is the radius of the cylinder, r is the radial distance from the cylinder axis, and I_0 is a constant having units of amperes. (a) Show that I_0 is the total current passing through the entire cross section of the wire. (b) Using Ampere's law, derive an expression for the magnitude of the magnetic field $\vec{B}$ in the region $r \geq a$. (c) Obtain an expression for the current I contained in a circular cross section of radius $r \leq a$ and centered at the cylinder axis. (d) Using Ampere's law, derive an expression for the magnitude of the magnetic field $\vec{B}$ in the region $r \leq a$. How do your results in parts (b) and (d) compare for $r = a$?

28.78. A long, straight, solid cylinder, oriented with its axis in the z-direction, carries a current whose current density is $\vec{J}$. The current density, although symmetrical about the cylinder axis, is not constant and varies according to the relationship

$$\vec{J} = \left(\frac{b}{r}\right)e^{(r-a)/\delta}\hat{k} \quad \text{for } r \leq a$$
$$= 0 \quad \text{for } r \geq a$$

where the radius of the cylinder is $a = 5.00$ cm, r is the radial distance from the cylinder axis, b is a constant equal to 600 A/m, and δ is a constant equal to 2.50 cm. (a) Let I_0 be the total current passing through the entire cross section of the wire. Obtain an expression for I_0 in terms of b, δ, and a. Evaluate your expression to obtain a numerical value for I_0. (b) Using Ampere's law, derive an expression for the magnetic field $\vec{B}$ in the region $r \geq a$. Express your answer in terms of I_0 rather than b. (c) Obtain an expression for the current I contained in a circular cross section of radius $r \leq a$ and centered at the cylinder axis. Express your answer in terms of I_0 rather than b. (d) Using Ampere's law, derive an expression for the magnetic field $\vec{B}$ in the region $r \leq a$. (e) Evaluate the magnitude of the magnetic field at $r = \delta$, $r = a$, and $r = 2a$.

28.79. Integrate B_x as given in Eq. (28.15) from $-\infty$ to $+\infty$; that is, calculate $\int_{-\infty}^{+\infty} B_x\, dx$. Explain the significance of your result.

28.80. In a region of space where there are no conduction or displacement currents, it is impossible to have a uniform magnetic field that abruptly drops to zero. To prove this statement, use the method of contradiction: Assume that such a case *is* possible, and then show that your assumption contradicts a law of nature. (a) In the bottom half of a piece of paper, draw evenly spaced, horizontal lines representing a uniform magnetic field to your right. Use dashed lines to draw a rectangle *abcda* with horizontal side *ab* in the magnetic field region and horizontal side *cd* in the top half of your paper where $B = 0$. (b) Show that integration around your rectangle contradicts Ampere's law.

28.81. An Infinite Current Sheet. Long, straight conductors with square cross sections and each carrying current I are laid side by side to form an infinite current sheet (Fig. 28.64). The conductors lie in the xy-plane, are parallel to the y-axis, and carry current in the $+y$-direction There are n conductors per unit length measured along the x-axis. (a) What are the magnitude and direction of the magnetic field a distance a below the current sheet? (b) What are the magnitude and direction of the magnetic field a distance a above the current sheet?

Figure **28.64** Problem 28.81.

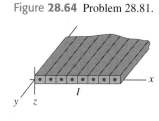

28.82. Long, straight conductors with square cross section, each carrying current I, are laid side by side to form an infinite current sheet with current directed out of the plane of the page (Fig. 28.65). A second infinite current sheet is a distance d below the first and is parallel to it. The second sheet carries current into the plane of the page. Each sheet has n conductors per unit length. (Refer to Problem 28.81.) Calculate the magnitude and direction of the net magnetic field at (a) point P (above the upper sheet); (b) point R (midway between the two sheets); (c) point S (below the lower sheet).

Figure **28.65** Problem 28.82.

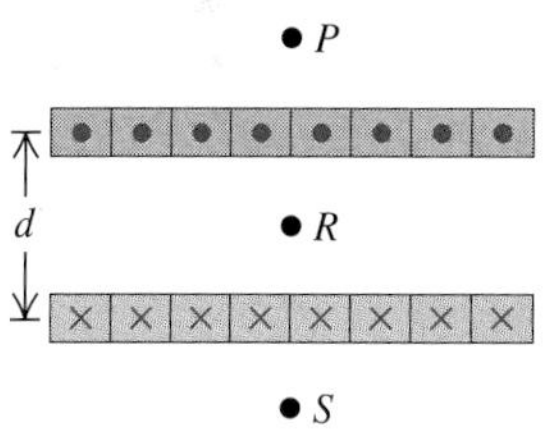

28.83. A piece of iron has magnetization $M = 6.50 \times 10^4$ A/m. Find the average magnetic dipole moment *per atom* in this piece of iron. Express your answer both in A·m² and in Bohr magnetons. The density of iron is given in Table 14.1, and the atomic mass of iron (in grams per mole) is given in Appendix D. The chemical symbol for iron is Fe.

28.84. (a) In Section 27.7 we discussed how a magnetic dipole, such as a current loop or a magnetized object, can be attracted or repelled by a permanent magnet. Use this to explain why *either* pole of a magnet *attracts* both paramagnetic materials and (initially unmagnetized) ferromagnetic materials, but *repels* diamagnetic materials. (b) The force that a magnet exerts on an object is directly proportional to the object's magnetic moment. A particular magnet is just strong enough to pick up a cube of annealed iron $(K_m = 1400)$ 2.00 cm on a side so that the iron sticks to one of the magnet's poles; that is, the magnet exerts an upward force on the iron cube equal to the cube's weight. If you tried to use this magnet to pick up a 2.00-cm cube of aluminum instead, what would be the upward force on the cube? How does this compare to the weight of the cube? Could the magnet pick up the cube? (*Hint:* You will need to use information from Tables 14.1 and 28.1.) (c) If you tried to use the magnet to pick up a 2.00-cm cube of silver, what would be the magnitude and direction of the force on the cube? How does this magnitude compare to the weight of the cube? Would the effects of the magnetic force be noticeable?

Challenge Problems

28.85. Two long, straight conducting wires with linear mass density λ are suspended from cords so that they are each horizontal, parallel to each other, and a distance d apart. The back ends of the wires are connected to each other by a slack, low-resistance connecting wire. A charged capacitor (capacitance C) is now added to the system; the positive plate of the capacitor (initial charge $+Q_0$) is connected to the front end of one of the wires, and the negative plate of the capacitor (initial charge $-Q_0$) is connected to the front end of the other wire (Fig. 28.66). Both of these connections are also made by slack, low-resistance wires. When the connection is made, the wires are pushed aside by the repulsive force between the wires, and each wire has an initial horizontal velocity of magnitude v_0. Assume that the time constant for the capacitor to discharge is negligible compared to the time it takes for any appreciable displacement in the position of the wires to occur. (a) Show that the initial speed v_0 of either wire is given by

$$v_0 = \frac{\mu_0 Q_0^2}{4\pi\lambda RCd}$$

where R is the total resistance of the circuit. (b) To what height h will each wire rise as a result of the circuit connection?

Figure 28.66 Challenge Problem 28.85.

28.86. A wide, long, insulating belt has a uniform positive charge per unit area σ on its upper surface. Rollers at each end move the belt to the right at a constant speed v. Calculate the magnitude and direction of the magnetic field produced by the moving belt at a point just above its surface. (*Hint:* At points near the surface and far from its edges or ends, the moving belt can be considered to be an infinite current sheet like that in Problem 28.81.)

28.87. A Charged Dielectric Disk. A thin disk of dielectric material with radius a has a total charge $+Q$ distributed uniformly over its surface. It rotates n times per second about an axis perpendicular to the surface of the disk and passing through its center. Find the magnetic field at the center of the disk. (*Hint:* Divide the disk into concentric rings of infinitesimal width.)

28.88. A wire in the shape of a semicircle with radius a is oriented in the yz-plane with its center of curvature at the origin (Fig. 28.67). If the current in the wire is I, calculate the magnetic-field components produced at point P, a distance x out along the x-axis. (*Note:* Do not forget the contribution from the straight wire at the bottom of the semicircle that runs from $z = -a$ to $z = +a$. You may use the fact that the fields of the two antiparallel currents at $z > a$ cancel, but you must explain *why* they cancel.)

Figure 28.67 Challenge Problem 28.88.

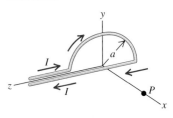

ELECTROMAGNETIC INDUCTION

? When a credit card is "swiped" through a card reader, the information coded in a magnetic pattern on the back of the card is transmitted to the cardholder's bank. Why is it necessary to swipe the card rather than holding it motionless in the card reader's slot?

LEARNING GOALS

By studying this chapter, you will learn:

- The experimental evidence that a changing magnetic field induces an emf.

- How Faraday's law relates the induced emf in a loop to the change in magnetic flux through the loop.

- How to determine the direction of an induced emf.

- How to calculate the emf induced in a conductor moving through a magnetic field.

- How a changing magnetic flux generates an electric field that is very different from that produced by an arrangement of charges.

- The four fundamental equations that completely describe both electricity and magnetism.

Almost every modern device or machine, from a computer to a washing machine to a power drill, has electric circuits at its heart. We learned in Chapter 25 that an electromotive force (emf) is required for a current to flow in a circuit; in Chapter 25 and 26 we almost always took the source of emf to be a battery. But for the vast majority of electric devices that are used in industry and in the home (including any device that you plug into a wall socket), the source of emf is *not* a battery but an electrical generating station. Such a station produces electric energy by converting other forms of energy: gravitational potential energy at a hydroelectric plant, chemical energy in a coal- or oil-fired plant, nuclear energy at a nuclear plant. But how is this energy conversion done? In other words, what is the physics behind the production of almost all of our electric energy needs?

The answer is a phenomenon known as *electromagnetic induction:* If the magnetic flux through a circuit changes, an emf and a current are induced in the circuit. In a power-generating station, magnets move relative to coils of wire to produce a changing magnetic flux in the coils and hence an emf. Other key components of electric power systems, such as transformers, also depend on magnetically induced emfs. Indeed, thanks to its key role in electric power generation, electromagnetic induction is one of the foundations of our technological society.

The central principle of electromagnetic induction, and the keystone of this chapter, is *Faraday's law.* This law relates induced emf to changing magnetic flux in any loop, including a closed circuit. We also discuss Lenz's law, which helps us to predict the directions of induced emfs and currents. This chapter provides the principles we need to understand electrical energy-conversion devices such as motors, generators, and transformers.

Electromagnetic induction tells us that a time-varying magnetic field can act as a source of electric field. We will also see how a time-varying *electric* field can act as a source of *magnetic* field. These remarkable results form part of a neat package of formulas, called *Maxwell's equations,* that describe the behavior of electric and magnetic fields in *any* situation. Maxwell's equations pave the way toward an understanding of electromagnetic waves, the topic of Chapter 32.

29.1 Induction Experiments

Act|v
Phys|cs
ONLINE

13.9 Electomagnetic Induction

During the 1830s, several pioneering experiments with magnetically induced emf were carried out in England by Michael Faraday and in the United States by Joseph Henry (1797–1878), later the first director of the Smithsonian Institution. Figure 29.1 shows several examples. In Figure 29.1a, a coil of wire is connected to a galvanometer. When the nearby magnet is stationary, the meter shows no current. This isn't surprising; there is no source of emf in the circuit. But when we *move* the magnet either toward or away from the coil, the meter shows current in the circuit, but *only* while the magnet is moving (Fig. 29.1b). If we keep the magnet stationary and move the coil, we again detect a current during the motion. We call this an **induced current,** and the corresponding emf required to cause this current is called an **induced emf.**

In Fig. 29.1c we replace the magnet with a second coil connected to a battery. When the second coil is stationary, there is no current in the first coil. However, when we move the second coil toward or away from the first or move the first toward or away from the second, there is current in the first coil, but again *only* while one coil is moving relative to the other.

Finally, using the two-coil setup in Fig. 29.1d, we keep both coils stationary and vary the current in the second coil, either by opening and closing the switch or by changing the resistance of the second coil with the switch closed (perhaps by changing the second coil's temperature). We find that as we open or close the switch, there is a momentary current pulse in the first circuit. When we vary the resistance (and thus the current) in the second coil, there is an induced current in the first circuit, but only while the current in the second circuit is changing.

To explore further the common elements in these observations, let's consider a more detailed series of experiments with the situation shown in Figure 29.2. We connect a coil of wire to a galvanometer, then place the coil between the

29.1 Demonstrating the phenomenon of induced current.

(a) A stationary magnet does NOT induce a current in a coil.

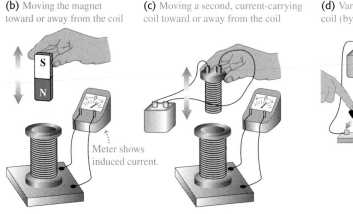

All these actions DO induce a current in the coil. What do they have in common?*

(b) Moving the magnet toward or away from the coil

(c) Moving a second, current-carrying coil toward or away from the coil

(d) Varying the current in the second coil (by closing or opening a switch)

Meter shows zero current.

Meter shows induced current.

*They cause the magnetic field through the coil to *change.*

poles of an electromagnet whose magnetic field we can vary. Here's what we observe:

1. When there is no current in the electromagnet, so that $\vec{B} = 0$, the galvanometer shows no current.
2. When the electromagnet is turned on, there is a momentary current through the meter as $\vec{B}$ increases.
3. When $\vec{B}$ levels off at a steady value, the current drops to zero, no matter how large $\vec{B}$ is.
4. With the coil in a horizontal plane, we squeeze it so as to decrease the cross-sectional area of the coil. The meter detects current only *during* the deformation, not before or after. When we increase the area to return the coil to its original shape, there is current in the opposite direction, but only while the area of the coil is changing.
5. If we rotate the coil a few degrees about a horizontal axis, the meter detects current during the rotation, in the same direction as when we decreased the area. When we rotate the coil back, there is a current in the opposite direction during this rotation.
6. If we jerk the coil out of the magnetic field, there is a current during the motion, in the same direction as when we decreased the area.
7. If we decrease the number of turns in the coil by unwinding one or more turns, there is a current during the unwinding, in the same direction as when we decreased the area. If we wind more turns onto the coil, there is a current in the opposite direction during the winding.
8. When the magnet is turned off, there is a momentary current in the direction opposite to the current when it was turned on.
9. The faster we carry out any of these changes, the greater the current.
10. If all these experiments are repeated with a coil that has the same shape but different material and different resistance, the current in each case is inversely proportional to the total circuit resistance. This shows that the induced emfs that are causing the current do not depend on the material of the coil but only on its shape and the magnetic field.

The common element in all these experiments is changing *magnetic flux* Φ_B through the coil connected to the galvanometer. In each case the flux changes either because the magnetic field changes with time or because the coil is moving through a nonuniform magnetic field. Check back through the list to verify this statement. Faraday's law of induction, the subject of the next section, states that in all of these situations the induced emf is proportional to the *rate of change* of magnetic flux Φ_B through the coil. The *direction* of the induced emf depends on whether the flux is increasing or decreasing. If the flux is constant, there is no induced emf.

Induced emfs are not mere laboratory curiosities but have a tremendous number of practical applications. If you are reading these words indoors, you are making use of induced emfs right now! At the power plant that supplies your neighborhood, an electric generator produces an emf by varying the magnetic flux through coils of wire. (In the next section we'll see in detail how this is done.) This emf supplies the voltage between the terminals of the wall sockets in your home, and this voltage supplies the power to your reading lamp. Indeed, any appliance that you plug into a wall socket makes use of induced emfs.

Magnetically induced emfs, just like the emfs discussed in Section 25.4, are always the result of the action of *nonelectrostatic* forces. When these forces are the result of additional electric fields induced by changing magnetic fields, we have to distinguish carefully between electric fields produced by charges (according to Coulomb's law) and those produced by changing magnetic fields. We'll denote these by $\vec{E}_c$ (where c stands for Coulomb or conservative) and $\vec{E}_n$ (where n stands for non-Coulomb or nonconservative), respectively. We'll return to this distinction later in this chapter and the next.

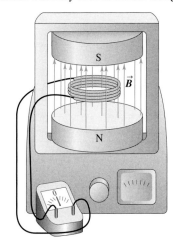

29.2 A coil in a magnetic field. When the $\vec{B}$ field is constant and the shape, location, and orientation of the coil do not change, no current is induced in the coil. A current is induced when any of these factors change.

29.3 Calculating the magnetic flux through an area element.

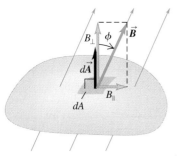

Magnetic flux through element of area $d\vec{A}$:
$$d\Phi_B = \vec{B} \cdot d\vec{A} = B_\perp \, dA = B \, dA \cos\phi$$

29.2 Faraday's Law

The common element in all induction effects is changing magnetic flux through a circuit. Before stating the simple physical law that summarizes all of the kinds of experiments described in Section 29.1, let's first review the concept of magnetic flux Φ_B (which we introduced in Section 27.3). For an infinitesimal-area element $d\vec{A}$ in a magnetic field $\vec{B}$ (Figure 29.3), the magnetic flux $d\Phi_B$ through the area is

$$d\Phi_B = \vec{B} \cdot d\vec{A} = B_\perp \, dA = B \, dA \cos\phi$$

where $B_\perp$ is the component of $\vec{B}$ perpendicular to the surface of the area element and ϕ is the angle between $\vec{B}$ and $d\vec{A}$. (As in Chapter 27, be careful to distinguish between two quantities named "phi," ϕ and Φ_B.) The total magnetic flux Φ_B through a finite area is the integral of this expression over the area:

$$\Phi_B = \int \vec{B} \cdot d\vec{A} = \int B \, dA \cos\phi \qquad (29.1)$$

If $\vec{B}$ is uniform over a flat area $\vec{A}$, then

$$\Phi_B = \vec{B} \cdot \vec{A} = BA \cos\phi \qquad (29.2)$$

Figure 29.4 reviews the rules for using Eq. (29.2).

CAUTION **Choosing the direction of $d\vec{A}$ or $\vec{A}$** In Eqs. (29.1) and (29.2) we have to be careful to define the direction of the vector area $d\vec{A}$ or $\vec{A}$ unambiguously. There are always two directions perpendicular to any given area, and the sign of the magnetic flux through the area depends on which one we choose to be positive. For example, in Fig. 29.3 we chose $d\vec{A}$ to point upward so ϕ is less than 90° and $\vec{B} \cdot d\vec{A}$ is positive. We could have chosen instead to have $d\vec{A}$ point downward, in which case ϕ would have been greater than 90° and $\vec{B} \cdot d\vec{A}$ would have been negative. Either choice is equally good, but once we make a choice we must stick with it. ▮

Faraday's law of induction states:

The induced emf in a closed loop equals the negative of the time rate of change of magnetic flux through the loop.

In symbols, Faraday's law is

$$\mathcal{E} = -\frac{d\Phi_B}{dt} \qquad (\text{Faraday's law of induction}) \qquad (29.3)$$

29.4 Calculating the flux of a uniform magnetic field through a flat area. (Compare to Fig. 22.6, which shows the rules for calculating the flux of a uniform *electric* field.)

Surface is face-on to magnetic field:
• $\vec{B}$ and $\vec{A}$ are parallel (the angle between $\vec{B}$ and $\vec{A}$ is $\phi = 0$).
• The magnetic flux $\Phi_B = \vec{B} \cdot \vec{A} = BA$.

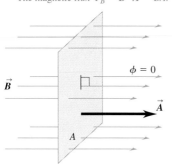

Surface is tilted from a face-on orientation by an angle ϕ:
• The angle between $\vec{B}$ and $\vec{A}$ is ϕ.
• The magnetic flux $\Phi_B = \vec{B} \cdot \vec{A} = BA \cos\phi$.

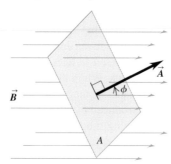

Surface is edge-on to magnetic field:
• $\vec{B}$ and $\vec{A}$ are perpendicular (the angle between $\vec{B}$ and $\vec{A}$ is $\phi = 90°$).
• The magnetic flux $\Phi_B = \vec{B} \cdot \vec{A} = BA \cos 90° = 0$.

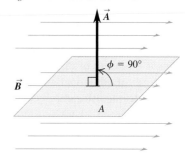

To understand the negative sign, we have to introduce a sign convention for the induced emf $\mathcal{E}$. But first let's look at a simple example of this law in action.

Example 29.1 Emf and current induced in a loop

The magnetic field between the poles of the electromagnet in Figure 29.5 is uniform at any time, but its magnitude is increasing at the rate of 0.020 T/s. The area of the conducting loop in the field is 120 cm², and the total circuit resistance, including the meter, is 5.0 Ω. (a) Find the induced emf and the induced current in the circuit. (b) If the loop is replaced by one made of an insulator, what effect does this have on the induced emf and induced current?

SOLUTION

IDENTIFY: The magnetic flux through the loop changes as the magnetic field changes. Hence there will be an induced emf in the loop, and we can find its value (one of our target variables) using Faraday's law. We can determine the current produced in the loop by this emf (our other target variable) using the same techniques as in Chapter 25.

SET UP: We calculate the magnetic flux using Eq. (29.2) and then use Faraday's law given by Eq. (29.3) to determine the resulting induced emf $\mathcal{E}$. Then we calculate the induced current produced by this emf using the relationship $\mathcal{E} = IR$, where R is the total resistance of the circuit that includes the loop.

29.5 A stationary conducting loop in an increasing magnetic field.

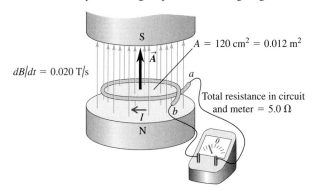

$dB/dt = 0.020\ \text{T/s}$

$A = 120\ \text{cm}^2 = 0.012\ \text{m}^2$

Total resistance in circuit and meter = 5.0 Ω

EXECUTE: (a) The vector area of the loop is perpendicular to the plane of the loop; we choose it to be vertically upward. Then the vectors $\vec{A}$ and $\vec{B}$ are parallel. Since $\vec{B}$ is uniform, the magnetic flux through the loop is $\Phi_B = \vec{B} \cdot \vec{A} = BA\cos 0 = BA$. The area $A = 0.012\ \text{m}^2$ is constant, so the rate of change of magnetic flux is

$$\frac{d\Phi_B}{dt} = \frac{d(BA)}{dt} = \frac{dB}{dt}A = (0.020\ \text{T/s})(0.012\ \text{m}^2)$$
$$= 2.4 \times 10^{-4}\ \text{V} = 0.24\ \text{mV}$$

This, apart from a sign that we haven't discussed yet, is the induced emf $\mathcal{E}$. The corresponding induced current is

$$I = \frac{\mathcal{E}}{R} = \frac{2.4 \times 10^{-4}\ \text{V}}{5.0\ \Omega} = 4.8 \times 10^{-5}\ \text{A} = 0.048\ \text{mA}$$

(b) By changing to a loop made of insulator, we've made the resistance of the loop very high. Faraday's law, Eq. (29.3), does not involve the resistance of the circuit in any way, so the induced *emf* does not change. But the *current* will be smaller, as given by the equation $I = \mathcal{E}/R$. If the loop is made of a perfect insulator with infinite resistance, the induced current is zero even though an emf is present. This situation is analogous to an isolated battery whose terminals aren't connected to anything: There is an emf present, but no current flows.

EVALUATE: It's worthwhile to verify unit consistency in this calculation. There are many ways to do this; one is to note that because of the magnetic force relationship $\vec{F} = q\vec{v} \times \vec{B}$, the units of magnetic field are the units of force divided by the units of (charge times velocity): $1\ \text{T} = (1\ \text{N})/(1\ \text{C} \cdot \text{m/s})$. The units of magnetic flux can then be expressed as $(1\ \text{T})(1\ \text{m}^2) = 1\ \text{N} \cdot \text{s} \cdot \text{m/C}$, and the rate of change of magnetic flux as $1\ \text{N} \cdot \text{m/C} = 1\ \text{J/C} = 1\ \text{V}$. Thus the unit of $d\Phi_B/dt$ is the volt, as required by Eq. (29.3). Also recall that the unit of magnetic flux is the weber (Wb): $1\ \text{T} \cdot \text{m}^2 = 1\ \text{Wb}$, so $1\ \text{V} = 1\ \text{Wb/s}$.

Direction of Induced EMF

We can find the direction of an induced emf or current by using Eq. (29.3) together with some simple sign rules. Here's the procedure:

1. Define a positive direction for the vector area $\vec{A}$.
2. From the directions of $\vec{A}$ and the magnetic field $\vec{B}$, determine the sign of the magnetic flux Φ_B and its rate of change $d\Phi_B/dt$. Figure 29.6 shows several examples.
3. Determine the sign of the induced emf or current. If the flux is increasing, so $d\Phi_B/dt$ is positive, then the induced emf or current is negative; if the flux is decreasing, $d\Phi_B/dt$ is negative and the induced emf or current is positive.

29.6 The magnetic flux is becoming (a) more positive, (b) less positive, (c) more negative, and (d) less negative. Therefore Φ_B is increasing in (a) and (d) and decreasing in (b) and (c). In (a) and (d) the emfs are negative (they are opposite to the direction of the curled fingers of your right hand when your right thumb points along $\vec{A}$). In (b) and (c) the emfs are positive (in the same direction as the curled fingers).

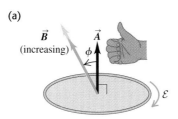

(a)

• Flux is positive ($\Phi_B > 0$) ...
• ... and becoming more positive ($d\Phi_B/dt > 0$).
• Induced emf is negative ($\mathcal{E} < 0$).

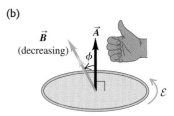

(b)

• Flux is positive ($\Phi_B > 0$) ...
• ... and becoming less positive ($d\Phi_B/dt < 0$).
• Induced emf is positive ($\mathcal{E} > 0$).

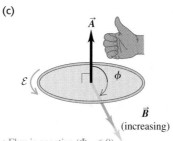

(c)

• Flux is negative ($\Phi_B < 0$) ...
• ... and becoming more negative ($d\Phi_B/dt < 0$).
• Induced emf is positive ($\mathcal{E} > 0$).

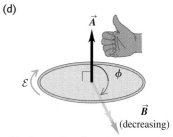

(d)

• Flux is negative ($\Phi_B < 0$) ...
• ... and becoming less negative ($d\Phi_B/dt > 0$).
• Induced emf is negative ($\mathcal{E} < 0$).

4. Finally, determine the direction of the induced emf or current using your right hand. Curl the fingers of your right hand around the $\vec{A}$ vector, with your right thumb in the direction of $\vec{A}$. If the induced emf or current in the circuit is *positive*, it is in the same direction as your curled fingers; if the induced emf or current is *negative*, it is in the opposite direction.

In Example 29.1, in which $\vec{A}$ is upward, a positive $\mathcal{E}$ would be directed counterclockwise around the loop, as seen from above. Both $\vec{A}$ and $\vec{B}$ are upward in this example, so Φ_B is positive; the magnitude B is increasing, so $d\Phi_B/dt$ is positive. Hence by Eq. (29.3), $\mathcal{E}$ in Example 29.1 is *negative*. Its actual direction is thus *clockwise* around the loop, as seen from above.

If the loop in Fig. 29.5 is a conductor, an induced current results from this emf; this current is also clockwise, as Fig. 29.5 shows. This induced current produces an additional magnetic field through the loop, and the right-hand rule described in Section 28.6 shows that this field is *opposite* in direction to the increasing field produced by the electromagnet. This is an example of a general rule called *Lenz's law,* which says that any induction effect tends to oppose the change that caused it; in this case the change is the increase in the flux of the electromagnet's field through the loop. (We'll study this law in detail in the next section.)

You should check out the signs of the induced emfs and currents for the list of experiments in Section 29.1. For example, when the loop in Fig. 29.2 is in a constant field and we tilt it or squeeze it to *decrease* the flux through it, the induced emf and current are counterclockwise, as seen from above.

CAUTION **Induced emfs are caused by changes in flux** Since magnetic flux plays a central role in Faraday's law, it's tempting to think that *flux* is the cause of induced emf and that an induced emf will appear in a circuit whenever there is a magnetic field in the region bordered by the circuit. But Eq. (29.3) shows that only a *change* in flux through a circuit, not flux itself, can induce an emf in a circuit. If the flux through a circuit has a constant value, whether positive, negative, or zero, there is no induced emf. ∎

If we have a coil with N identical turns, and if the flux varies at the same rate through each turn, the *total* rate of change through all the turns is N times as large as for a single turn. If Φ_B is the flux through each turn, the total emf in a coil with N turns is

$$\mathcal{E} = -N\frac{d\Phi_B}{dt} \qquad (29.4)$$

As we discussed in this chapter's introduction, induced emfs play an essential role in the generation of electric power for commercial use. Several of the following examples explore different methods of producing emfs by the motion of a conductor relative to a magnetic field, giving rise to a changing flux through a circuit.

Problem-Solving Strategy 29.1   **Faraday's Law**

IDENTIFY: *the relevant concepts:*   Faraday's law applies when there is a changing magnetic flux. To use the law, make sure you can identify an area through which there is a flux of magnetic field. This will usually be the area enclosed by a loop, usually made of a conducting material (though not always—see part (b) of Example 29.1). As always, identify the target variable(s).

SET UP *the problem* using the following steps:
1. Faraday's law relates the induced emf to the rate of change of magnetic flux. To calculate this rate of change, you first have to understand what is making the flux change. Is the conductor moving? Is it changing orientation? Is the magnetic field changing? Remember that it's not the flux itself that counts, but its *rate of change*.
2. Choose a direction for the area vector $\vec{A}$ or $d\vec{A}$. The direction must always be perpendicular to the plane of the area. Note that you always have two choices of direction. For instance, if the plane of the area is horizontal, $\vec{A}$ could point straight up or straight down. It's like choosing which direction is the positive

one in a problem involving motion in a straight line; it doesn't matter which direction you choose, just so you use it consistently throughout the problem.

EXECUTE *the solution* as follows:
1. Calculate the magnetic flux using Eq. (29.2) if $\vec{B}$ is uniform over the area of the loop or Eq. (29.1) if it isn't uniform, being mindful of the direction you chose for the area vector.
2. Calculate the induced emf using Eq. (29.3) or (29.4). If your conductor has N turns in a coil, don't forget to multiply by N. Remember the sign rule for the positive direction of emf and use it consistently.
3. If the circuit resistance is known, you can calculate the magnitude of the induced current I using $\mathcal{E} = IR$.

EVALUATE *your answer:*   Check your results for the proper units, and double-check that you have properly implemented the sign rules for calculating magnetic flux and induced emf.

Example 29.2   **Magnitude and direction of an induced emf**

A coil of wire containing 500 circular loops with radius 4.00 cm is placed between the poles of a large electromagnet, where the magnetic field is uniform and at an angle of 60° with the plane of the coil. The field decreases at a rate of 0.200 T/s. What are the magnitude and direction of the induced emf?

SOLUTION

IDENTIFY: Our target variable is the emf induced by a varying magnetic flux through the coil. The flux varies because the magnetic field decreases in amplitude.

SET UP: We choose the area vector $\vec{A}$ to be in the direction shown in Figure 29.7. With this choice, the geometry is very similar to Fig. 29.6b. That figure will help us determine the direction of the induced emf.

EXECUTE: The magnetic field is uniform over the loop, so we can calculate the flux using Eq. (29.2): $\Phi_B = BA\cos\phi$, where $\phi = 30°$. In this expression, the only quantity that changes with time is the magnitude B of the field.

CAUTION   **Remember how ϕ is defined** You may have been tempted to say that $\phi = 60°$ in this problem. If so, remember that ϕ is the angle between $\vec{A}$ and $\vec{B}$, *not* the angle between $\vec{B}$ and the plane of the loop. ▮

29.7 Our sketch for this problem.

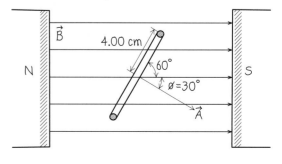

Continued

The rate of change of the flux is $d\Phi_B/dt = (dB/dt)A\cos\phi$. In our problem, $dB/dt = -0.200$ T/s and $A = \pi(0.0400$ m$)^2 = 0.00503$ m^2, so

$$\frac{d\Phi_B}{dt} = \frac{dB}{dt}A\cos 30°$$

$$= (-0.200 \text{ T/s})(0.00503 \text{ m}^2)(0.866)$$

$$= -8.71 \times 10^{-4} \text{ T} \cdot \text{m}^2/\text{s} = -8.71 \times 10^{-4} \text{ Wb/s}$$

From Eq. (29.4), the induced emf in the coil of $N = 500$ turns is

$$\mathcal{E} = -N\frac{d\Phi_B}{dt}$$

$$= -(500)(-8.71 \times 10^{-4} \text{ Wb/s}) = 0.435 \text{ V}$$

Note that the answer is positive. This means that when you point your right thumb in the direction of the area vector $\vec{A}$ (30° above the magnetic field $\vec{B}$), the positive direction for $\mathcal{E}$ is in the direction of the curled fingers of your right hand. Hence the emf in this example is in this same direction (compare Fig. 29.6b). If you were viewing the coil from the left side in Fig. 29.7a and looking in the direction of $\vec{A}$, the emf would be clockwise.

EVALUATE: If the ends of the wire are connected together, the direction of current in the coil is in the same direction as the emf— that is, clockwise as seen from the left side of the coil. A clockwise current gives added magnetic flux through the coil in the same direction as the flux from the electromagnet, and therefore tends to oppose the decrease in total flux. We'll see more examples of this in Section 29.3.

Conceptual Example 29.3 | The search coil

One practical way to measure magnetic field strength uses a small, closely wound coil with N turns called a *search coil*. The coil, of area A, is initially held so that its area vector $\vec{A}$ is aligned with a magnetic field with magnitude B. The coil is then either quickly rotated a quarter-turn about a diameter or quickly pulled out of the field. Explain how this device can be used to measure the value of B.

SOLUTION

Initially, the flux through the coil is $\Phi_B = NBA$; when the coil is rotated or pulled from the field, the flux decreases rapidly from NBA to zero. While the flux is decreasing, there is a momentary induced emf, and a momentary induced current occurs in an external circuit connected to the coil. The rate of change of flux through the coil is proportional to the current, or rate of flow of charge, so it is easy to show that the *total* flux change is proportional to the total charge that flows around the circuit. We can build an instrument that measures this total charge, and from this we can compute B. We leave the details as a problem (see Exercise 29.3). Strictly speaking, this method gives only the *average* field over the area of the coil. But if the area is small, this average field is very nearly equal to the field at the center of the coil.

Example 29.4 | Generator I: A simple alternator

Figure 29.8a shows a simple version of an *alternator*, a device that generates an emf. A rectangular loop is made to rotate with constant angular speed ω about the axis shown. The magnetic field $\vec{B}$ is uniform and constant. At time $t = 0$, $\phi = 0$. Determine the induced emf.

SOLUTION

IDENTIFY: Again the emf (our target variable) is produced by a varying magnetic flux. In this situation, however, the magnetic field $\vec{B}$ is constant; the flux changes because the direction of $\vec{A}$ changes as the loop rotates.

29.8 (a) Schematic diagram of an alternator. A conducting loop rotates in a magnetic field, producing an emf. Connections from each end of the loop to the external circuit are made by means of that end's slip ring. The system is shown at the time when the angle $\phi = \omega t = 90°$. (b) Graph of the flux through the loop and the resulting emf at terminals ab, along with corresponding positions of the loop during one complete rotation.

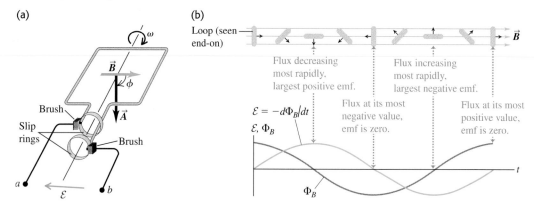

SET UP: Figure 29.8a shows the direction of the area vector $\vec{A}$. Note that as the loop rotates, the angle ϕ between $\vec{A}$ and $\vec{B}$ increases at a constant rate.

EXECUTE: Again the magnetic field is uniform over the loop, so the magnetic flux is easy to calculate. The rate of change of the angle ϕ is equal to ω, the angular speed of the loop, so we can write $\phi = \omega t$. Hence

$$\Phi_B = BA\cos\phi = BA\cos\omega t$$

The derivative of $\cos\omega t$ is $(d/dt)\cos\omega t = -\omega\sin\omega t$. Hence, by Faraday's law [Eq. (29.3)] the induced emf is

$$\mathcal{E} = -\frac{d\Phi_B}{dt} = \omega BA\sin\omega t$$

EVALUATE: The induced emf $\mathcal{E}$ varies sinusoidally with time (Fig. 29.8b). When the plane of the loop is perpendicular to $\vec{B}$ ($\phi = 0$ or $180°$), Φ_B reaches its maximum and minimum values. At these times, its instantaneous rate of change is zero and $\mathcal{E}$ is zero. Also, $\mathcal{E}$ is greatest in absolute value when the plane of the loop is parallel to $\vec{B}$ ($\phi = 90°$ or $270°$) and Φ_B is changing most rapidly. Finally, we note that the induced emf does not depend on the *shape* of the loop, but only on its area. Because $\mathcal{E}$ is directly proportional to ω and B, some tachometers use the emf in a rotating coil to measure rotational speed. Other devices use an emf of this kind to measure magnetic field.

We can use the alternator as a source of emf in an external circuit by use of two *slip rings,* which rotate with the loop, as shown in Fig. 29.8a. The rings slide against stationary contacts called *brushes,* which are connected to the output terminals a and b. Since the emf varies sinusoidally, the current that results in the circuit is an *alternating* current that also varies sinusoidally in magnitude

and direction. An alternator is also called an *alternating-current* (ac) *generator* for this reason. The amplitude of the emf can be increased by increasing the rotation speed, the field magnitude, or the loop area or by using N loops instead of one, as in Eq. (29.4).

Alternators are used in automobiles to generate the currents in the ignition, the lights, and the entertainment system. The arrangement is a little different than in this example; rather than having a rotating loop in a magnetic field, the loop stays fixed and an electromagnet rotates. (The rotation is provided by a mechanical connection between the alternator and the engine.) But the result is the same; the flux through the loop varies sinusoidally, producing a sinusoidally varying emf. Larger alternators of this same type are used in electric power plants (Figure 29.9).

29.9 A commercial alternator uses many loops of wire wound around a barrel-like structure called an armature. The armature and wire remain stationary while electromagnets rotate on a shaft (not shown) through the center of the armature. The resulting induced emf is far larger than would be possible with a single loop of wire.

Example 29.5   Generator II: A DC generator and back emf in a motor

The alternator in Example 29.4 produces a sinusoidally varying emf and hence an alternating current. We can use a similar scheme to make a *direct-current* (dc) *generator* that produces an emf that always has the same sign. A prototype dc generator is shown in Fig. 29.10a. The arrangement of split rings is called a *commutator;* it reverses the connections to the external circuit at angular positions where the emf reverses. The resulting emf is shown in Fig. 29.10b. Commercial dc generators have a large number of coils and commutator segments; this arrangement smooths out

the bumps in the emf, so the terminal voltage is not only one-directional but also practically constant. This brush-and-commutator arrangement is the same as that in the direct-current motor we discussed in Section 27.8. The motor's *back emf* is just the emf induced by the changing magnetic flux through its rotating coil. Consider a motor with a square coil 10.0 cm on a side, with 500 turns of wire. If the magnetic field has magnitude 0.200 T, at what rotation speed is the *average* back emf of the motor equal to 112 V?

29.10 (a) Schematic diagram of a dc generator, using a split-ring commutator. The ring halves are attached to the loop and rotate with it. (b) Graph of the resulting induced emf at terminals ab. Compare to Fig. 29.8b.

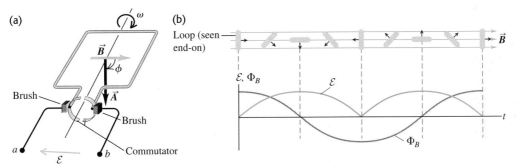

Continued

SOLUTION

IDENTIFY: As far as the rotating loop is concerned, the situation is the same as in Example 29.4 except that we now have N turns of wire. Without the commutator, the emf would alternate between positive and negative values and have an average value of zero (Fig. 29.8b). But with the commutator added, the emf is never negative and its average value is positive (Fig. 29.10b). Using our result from Example 29.4, we'll determine an expression for this average value and solve that expression for the rotational speed ω (our target variable).

SET UP: The setup is the same as in Example 29.4.

EXECUTE: Comparing Figs. 29.8b and 29.10b shows that the back emf of the motor is just the absolute value of the emf found for an alternator in Example 29.4, multiplied by the number of turns N in the coil as in Eq. (29.4):

$$|\mathcal{E}| = N\omega BA |\sin \omega t|$$

To find the *average* back emf, we replace $|\sin \omega t|$ by its average value. The average value of the sine function is found by integrating $\sin \omega t$ over half a cycle, from $t = 0$ to $t = T/2 = \pi/\omega$, and then dividing by the elapsed time π/ω. During this half cycle, the sine function is positive, so $|\sin \omega t| = \sin \omega t$, and we find

$$(|\sin \omega t|)_{av} = \frac{\displaystyle\int_0^{\pi/\omega} \sin \omega t \, dt}{\pi/\omega} = \frac{2}{\pi}$$

or about 0.64. The average back emf is then

$$\mathcal{E}_{av} = \frac{2N\omega BA}{\pi}$$

The back emf is proportional to the rotation speed ω, as was stated without proof in Section 27.8. Solving for ω, we obtain

$$\omega = \frac{\pi \mathcal{E}_{av}}{2NBA}$$

$$= \frac{\pi (112 \text{ V})}{2 (500)(0.200 \text{ T})(0.100 \text{ m})^2} = 176 \text{ rad/s}$$

We used the relationships $1 \text{ V} = 1 \text{ Wb/s} = 1 \text{ T} \cdot \text{m}^2/\text{s}$ from Example 29.1. We were able to add "radians" to the units of the answer because it is a dimensionless quantity, as we discussed in Chapter 9. The rotation speed can also be written as

$$\omega = 176 \text{ rad/s} \frac{1 \text{ rev}}{2\pi \text{ rad}} \frac{60 \text{ s}}{1 \text{ min}} = 1680 \text{ rev/min}$$

EVALUATE: The average back emf is directly proportional to ω. Hence the slower the rotation speed, the less the back emf and the greater the possibility of burning out the motor, as we described in Example 27.11 (Section 27.8).

While we have used a very simple model of a generator in this and the preceding example, the same principles apply to the operation of commercial generators.

Example 29.6   Generator III: The slidewire generator

Figure 29.11 shows a U-shaped conductor in a uniform magnetic field $\vec{B}$ perpendicular to the plane of the figure, directed *into* the page. We lay a metal rod with length L across the two arms of the conductor, forming a circuit, and move the rod to the right with constant velocity $\vec{v}$. This induces an emf and a current, which is why this device is called a *slidewire generator*. Find the magnitude and direction of the resulting induced emf.

29.11 A slidewire generator. The magnetic field $\vec{B}$ and the vector area $\vec{A}$ are both directed into the figure. The increase in magnetic flux (caused by an increase in area) induces the emf and current.

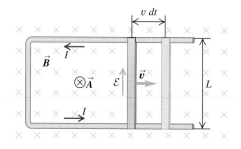

SOLUTION

IDENTIFY: The magnetic flux changes because the area of the loop—bounded on the right by the moving rod—is increasing. Our target variable is the emf $\mathcal{E}$ induced in this expanding loop.

SET UP: The magnetic field is uniform over the area of the loop, so we can again calculate the magnetic flux using $\Phi_B = BA \cos \phi$. We choose the area vector $\vec{A}$ to point straight into the plane of the picture, in the same direction as $\vec{B}$. With this choice a positive emf will be one that is directed clockwise around the loop. (You can check this with the right-hand rule. Using your right hand, point your thumb into the page and curl your fingers as in Fig. 29.6.)

EXECUTE: Since $\vec{B}$ and $\vec{A}$ point in the same direction, the angle $\phi = 0$ and $\Phi_B = BA$. The magnetic field magnitude B is constant, so the induced emf is

$$\mathcal{E} = -\frac{d\Phi_B}{dt} = -B\frac{dA}{dt}$$

To calculate dA/dt, note that in a time dt the sliding rod moves a distance $v \, dt$ (Fig. 29.11) and the loop area increases by an amount $dA = Lv \, dt$. Hence the induced emf is

$$\mathcal{E} = -B\frac{Lv \, dt}{dt} = -BLv$$

The minus sign tells us that the emf is directed *counterclockwise* around the loop. The induced current is also counterclockwise, as shown in the figure.

EVALUATE: Note that the emf is constant if the velocity $\vec{v}$ of the rod is constant. In this case the slidewire generator acts as a *direct-current* generator. It's not a very practical device because the rod eventually moves beyond the U-shaped conductor and loses contact, after which the current stops.

Example 29.7   **Work and power in the slidewire generator**

In the slidewire generator of Example 29.6, energy is dissipated in the circuit owing to its resistance. Let the resistance of the circuit (made up of the moving slidewire and the U-shaped conductor that connects the ends of the slidewire) at a given point in the slidewire's motion be R. Show that the rate at which energy is dissipated in the circuit is exactly equal to the rate at which work must be done to move the rod through the magnetic field.

SOLUTION

IDENTIFY: Our target variables are the *rates* at which energy is dissipated and at which work is done. This means that we'll be working with the concept of power (recall Section 6.4). Energy is dissipated in the circuit because there is resistance; to describe this we'll need the ideas of Section 25.5. It takes work to move the rod because there is an induced current flowing through it. The magnetic field exerts a force on this current-carrying rod, and whoever is pushing the rod has to do work against this force.

SET UP: We found the induced emf $\mathcal{E}$ in this circuit in Example 29.6. The current I in the circuit equals the absolute value of $\mathcal{E}$ divided by the resistance R, and the rate at which energy is dissipated in the rod is $P_{\text{dissipated}} = I^2 R$. The magnetic force on the rod is $\vec{F} = I\vec{L} \times \vec{B}$; the vector $\vec{L}$ points along the rod in the direction of the current. Figure 29.12 shows that this force is opposite to the velocity of the rod, and so to maintain the motion a force of equal magnitude must be applied in the direction of the rod's motion (that is, in the direction of $\vec{v}$). The rate of doing work is equal to

29.12 The magnetic force $\vec{F} = I\vec{L} \times \vec{B}$ that acts on the rod due to the induced current is to the left, opposite to $\vec{v}$.

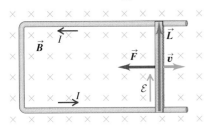

the product of the applied force and the speed of the rod: $P_{\text{applied}} = Fv$.

EXECUTE: First we'll calculate $P_{\text{dissipated}}$. From Example 29.6, $\mathcal{E} = -BLv$. Hence the current in the rod is

$$I = \frac{|\mathcal{E}|}{R} = \frac{BLv}{R}$$

and the rate of energy dissipation is

$$P_{\text{dissipated}} = I^2 R = \left(\frac{BLv}{R}\right)^2 R = \frac{B^2 L^2 v^2}{R}$$

To calculate P_{applied}, we first calculate the magnitude of $\vec{F} = I\vec{L} \times \vec{B}$. Since $\vec{L}$ and $\vec{B}$ are perpendicular, this magnitude is

$$F = ILB = \frac{BLv}{R}LB = \frac{B^2 L^2 v}{R}$$

Hence the rate at which work is done by this applied force is

$$P_{\text{applied}} = Fv = \frac{B^2 L^2 v^2}{R}$$

EVALUATE: The rate at which work is done is just equal to the rate at which energy is dissipated in the resistance.

CAUTION **You can't violate energy conservation** You might think that reversing the direction of $\vec{B}$ or of $\vec{v}$ might make it possible to have the magnetic force $\vec{F} = I\vec{L} \times \vec{B}$ be in the *same* direction as $\vec{v}$. This would be a pretty neat trick. Once the rod was moving, the changing magnetic flux would induce an emf and a current, and the magnetic force on the rod would make it move even faster, increasing the emf and current; this would go on until the rod was moving at tremendous speed and producing electric power at a prodigious rate. If this seems too good to be true, not to mention a violation of energy conservation, that's because it is. Reversing $\vec{B}$ also reverses the sign of the induced emf and current and hence the direction of $\vec{L}$, so the magnetic force still opposes the motion of the rod; a similar result holds true if we reverse $\vec{v}$. This behavior is part of Lenz's law, to be discussed in Section 29.3.

Generators As Energy Converters

Example 29.7 shows that the slidewire generator doesn't produce electric energy out of nowhere; the energy is supplied by whatever body exerts the force that keeps the rod moving. All that the generator does is to *convert* that energy into a different form. The equality between the rate at which *mechanical* energy is supplied to a generator and the rate at which *electric* energy is generated holds for all types of generators. This is true in particular for the alternator described in Example 29.4. (We are neglecting the effects of friction in the bearings of an alternator or between the rod and the U-shaped conductor of a slidewire generator. If these are included, the conservation of energy demands that the energy lost to friction is not available for conversion to electric energy. In real generators the friction is kept to a minimum to keep the energy-conversion process as efficient as possible.)

In Chapter 27 we stated that the magnetic force on moving charges can never do work. But you might think that the magnetic force $\vec{F} = I\vec{L} \times \vec{B}$ in Example 29.7 *is* doing (negative) work on the current-carrying rod as it moves, contradicting our earlier statement. In fact, the work done by the magnetic force is actually zero. The moving charges that make up the current in the rod in Fig. 29.12 have a vertical component of velocity, causing a horizontal component of force on these charges. As a result, there is a horizontal displacement of charge within the rod, the left side acquiring a net positive charge and the right side a net negative charge. The result is a horizontal component of electric field, perpendicular to the length of the rod (analogous to the Hall effect, described in Section 27.9). It is this field, in the direction of motion of the rod, that does work on the mobile charges in the rod and hence indirectly on the atoms making up the rod.

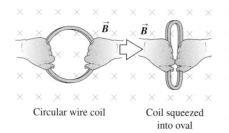

Circular wire coil   Coil squeezed into oval

Test Your Understanding of Section 29.2   The figure at left shows a wire coil being squeezed in a uniform magnetic field. (a) While the coil is being squeezed, is the induced emf in the coil (i) clockwise, (ii) counterclockwise, or (iii) zero? (b) Once the coil has reached its final squeezed shape, is the induced emf in the coil (i) clockwise, (ii) counterclockwise, or (iii) zero?

29.3 Lenz's Law

Lenz's law is a convenient alternative method for determining the direction of an induced current or emf. Lenz's law is not an independent principle; it can be derived from Faraday's law. It always gives the same results as the sign rules we introduced in connection with Faraday's law, but it is often easier to use. Lenz's law also helps us gain intuitive understanding of various induction effects and of the role of energy conservation. H. F. E. Lenz (1804–1865) was a Russian scientist who duplicated independently many of the discoveries of Faraday and Henry. **Lenz's law** states:

> **The direction of any magnetic induction effect is such as to oppose the cause of the effect.**

The "cause" may be changing flux through a stationary circuit due to a varying magnetic field, changing flux due to motion of the conductors that make up the circuit, or any combination. If the flux in a stationary circuit changes, as in Examples 29.1 and 29.2, the induced current sets up a magnetic field of its own. Within the area bounded by the circuit, this field is *opposite* to the original field if the original field is *increasing* but is in the *same* direction as the original field if the latter is *decreasing*. That is, the induced current opposes the *change in flux* through the circuit (*not* the flux itself).

If the flux change is due to motion of the conductors, as in Examples 29.3 through 29.7, the direction of the induced current in the moving conductor is such that the direction of the magnetic-field force on the conductor is opposite in direction to its motion. Thus the motion of the conductor, which caused the induced current, is opposed. We saw this explicitly for the slidewire generator in Example 29.7. In all these cases the induced current tries to preserve the *status quo* by opposing motion or a change of flux.

Lenz's law is also directly related to energy conservation. If the induced current in Example 29.7 were in the direction opposite to that given by Lenz's law, the magnetic force on the rod would accelerate it to ever-increasing speed with no external energy source, even though electric energy is being dissipated in the circuit. This would be a clear violation of energy conservation and doesn't happen in nature.

Conceptual Example 29.8   **The slidewire generator, revisited**

In Fig. 29.11, the induced current in the loop causes an additional magnetic field in the area bounded by the loop. The direction of the induced current is counterclockwise. From the discussion of Section 28.2, we see that the direction of the additional magnetic field caused by this current is *out of* the plane of the figure. Its direction is opposite that of the original magnetic field, so it tends to cancel the effect of that field. This is consistent with the prediction of Lenz's law.

Finding the direction of induced current

In Fig. 29.13 there is a uniform magnetic field $\vec{B}$ through the coil. The magnitude of the field is increasing, and the resulting induced emf causes an induced current. Use Lenz's law to determine the direction of the induced current.

SOLUTION

This situation is the same as in Example 29.1 (Section 29.2). By Lenz's law the induced current must produce a magnetic field $\vec{B}_{induced}$ inside the coil that is downward, opposing the change in flux. Using the right-hand rule we described in Section 28.5 for the direction of the magnetic field produced by a circular loop, $\vec{B}_{induced}$ will be in the desired direction if the induced current flows as shown in Fig. 29.13.

Figure 29.14 shows several applications of Lenz's law to the similar situation of a magnet moving near a conducting loop. In each of the four cases shown, the induced current produces a mag-

29.13 The induced current due to the change in $\vec{B}$ is clockwise, as seen from above the loop. The added field $\vec{B}_{induced}$ that it causes is downward, opposing the change in the upward field $\vec{B}$.

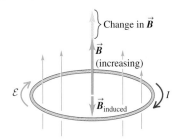

netic field of its own, in a direction that opposes the change in flux through the loop due to the magnet's motion.

29.14 Directions of induced currents as a bar magnet moves along the axis of a conducting loop. If the bar magnet is stationary, there is no induced current.

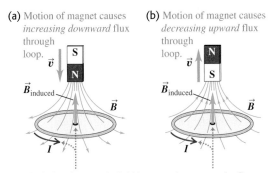

(a) Motion of magnet causes *increasing downward* flux through loop.

(b) Motion of magnet causes *decreasing upward* flux through loop.

The induced magnetic field is *upward* to oppose the flux change. To produce this induced field, the induced current must be *counterclockwise* as seen from above the loop.

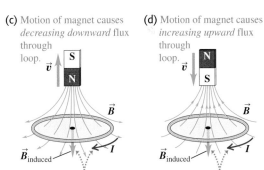

(c) Motion of magnet causes *decreasing downward* flux through loop.

(d) Motion of magnet causes *increasing upward* flux through loop.

The induced magnetic field is *downward* to oppose the flux change. To produce this induced field, the induced current must be *clockwise* as seen from above the loop.

Lenz's Law and the Response to Flux Changes

Since an induced current always opposes any change in magnetic flux through a circuit, how is it possible for the flux to change at all? The answer is that Lenz's law gives only the *direction* of an induced current; the *magnitude* of the current depends on the resistance of the circuit. The greater the circuit resistance, the less the induced current that appears to oppose any change in flux and the easier it is for a flux change to take effect. If the loop in Fig. 29.14 were made out of wood (an insulator), there would be almost no induced current in response to changes in the flux through the loop.

Conversely, the less the circuit resistance, the greater the induced current and the more difficult it is to change the flux through the circuit. If the loop in Fig. 29.14 is a good conductor, an induced current flows as long as the magnet moves relative to the loop. Once the magnet and loop are no longer in relative motion, the induced current very quickly decreases to zero because of the nonzero resistance in the loop.

The extreme case occurs when the resistance of the circuit is *zero*. Then the induced current in Fig. 29.14 will continue to flow even after the induced emf has disappeared—that is, even after the magnet has stopped moving relative to the loop. Thanks to this *persistent current*, it turns out that the flux through the loop is exactly the same as it was before the magnet started to move, so the flux through a loop of zero resistance *never* changes. Exotic materials called *superconductors* do indeed have zero resistance; we discuss these further in Section 29.8.

29.4 Motional Electromotive Force

29.15 A conducting rod moving in a uniform magnetic field. (a) The rod, the velocity, and the field are mutually perpendicular. (b) Direction of induced current in the circuit.

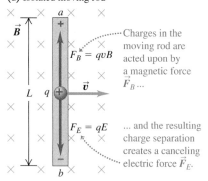

(a) Isolated moving rod

Charges in the moving rod are acted upon by a magnetic force $\vec{F}_B$...

... and the resulting charge separation creates a canceling electric force $\vec{F}_E$.

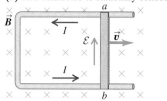

(b) Rod connected to stationary conductor

The motional emf $\mathcal{E}$ in the moving rod creates an electric field in the stationary conductor.

We've seen several situations in which a conductor moves in a magnetic field, as in the generators discussed in Examples 29.4 through 29.7. We can gain additional insight into the origin of the induced emf in these situations by considering the magnetic forces on mobile charges in the conductor. Figure 29.15a shows the same moving rod that we discussed in Example 29.6, separated for the moment from the U-shaped conductor. The magnetic field $\vec{B}$ is uniform and directed into the page, and we move the rod to the right at a constant velocity $\vec{v}$. A charged particle q in the rod then experiences a magnetic force $\vec{F} = q\vec{v} \times \vec{B}$ with magnitude $F = |q|vB$. We'll assume in the following discussion that q is positive; in that case the direction of this force is upward along the rod, from b toward a.

This magnetic force causes the free charges in the rod to move, creating an excess of positive charge at the upper end a and negative charge at the lower end b. This in turn creates an electric field $\vec{E}$ within the rod, in the direction from a toward b (opposite to the magnetic force). Charge continues to accumulate at the ends of the rod until $\vec{E}$ becomes large enough for the downward electric force (with magnitude qE) to cancel exactly the *upward* magnetic force (with magnitude qvB). Then $qE = qvB$ and the charges are in equilibrium.

The magnitude of the potential difference $V_{ab} = V_a - V_b$ is equal to the electric field magnitude E multiplied by the length L of the rod. From the above discussion, $E = vB$, so

$$V_{ab} = EL = vBL \qquad (29.5)$$

with point a at higher potential than point b.

Now suppose the moving rod slides along a stationary U-shaped conductor, forming a complete circuit (Fig. 29.15b). No *magnetic* force acts on the charges in the stationary U-shaped conductor, but the charge that was near points a and b redistributes itself along the stationary conductor, creating an *electric* field within it. This field establishes a current in the direction shown. The moving rod has become a source of electromotive force; within it, charge moves from lower to higher potential, and in the remainder of the circuit, charge moves from higher to lower potential. We call this emf a **motional electromotive force,** denoted by $\mathcal{E}$. From the above discussion, the magnitude of this emf is

$$\mathcal{E} = vBL \qquad \text{(motional emf; length and velocity perpendicular to uniform } \vec{B}) \qquad (29.6)$$

corresponding to a force per unit charge of magnitude vB acting for a distance L along the moving rod. If the total circuit resistance of the U-shaped conductor and the sliding rod is R, the induced current I in the circuit is given by $vBL = IR$. This is the same result we obtained in Section 29.2 using Faraday's law, and indeed motional emf is a particular case of Faraday's law, one of the several examples described in Section 29.2.

The emf associated with the moving rod in Fig. 29.15 is analogous to that of a battery with its positive terminal at a and its negative terminal at b, although the origins of the two emfs are quite different. In each case a nonelectrostatic force acts on the charges in the device, in the direction from b to a, and the emf is the work per unit charge done by this force when a charge moves from b to a in the device. When the device is connected to an external circuit, the direction of cur-

Act|v
ONLINE
Phys|cs

13.10 Motional EMF

rent is from *b* to *a* in the device and from *a* to *b* in the external circuit. While we have discussed motional emf in terms of a closed circuit like that in Fig. 29.15b, a motional emf is also present in the isolated moving rod in Fig. 29.15a, in the same way that a battery has an emf even when it's not part of a circuit.

The direction of the induced emf in Fig. 29.15 can be deduced by using Lenz's law, even if (as in Fig. 29.15a) the conductor does not form a complete circuit. In this case we can mentally complete the circuit between the ends of the conductor and use Lenz's law to determine the direction of the current. From this we can deduce the polarity of the ends of the open-circuit conductor. The direction from the − end to the + end within the conductor is the direction the current would have if the circuit were complete.

You should verify that if we express v in meters per second, B in teslas, and L in meters, then $\mathcal{E}$ is in volts. (Recall that $1 \text{ V} = 1 \text{ J/C}$.)

Motional emf: General Form

We can generalize the concept of motional emf for a conductor with *any* shape, moving in any magnetic field, uniform or not (assuming that the magnetic field at each point does not vary with time). For an element $d\vec{l}$ of conductor, the contribution $d\mathcal{E}$ to the emf is the magnitude dl multiplied by the component of $\vec{v} \times \vec{B}$ (the magnetic force per unit charge) parallel to $d\vec{l}$; that is,

$$d\mathcal{E} = (\vec{v} \times \vec{B}) \cdot d\vec{l}$$

For any closed conducting loop, the total emf is

$$\mathcal{E} = \oint (\vec{v} \times \vec{B}) \cdot d\vec{l} \qquad \text{(motional emf: closed conducting loop)} \quad \text{(29.7)}$$

This expression looks very different from our original statement of Faraday's law, Eq. (29.3), which stated that $\mathcal{E} = -d\Phi_B/dt$. In fact, though, the two statements are equivalent. It can be shown that the rate of change of magnetic flux through a moving conducting loop is always given by the negative of the expression in Eq. (29.7). Thus this equation gives us an alternative formulation of Faraday's law. This alternative is often more convenient than the original one in problems with *moving* conductors. But when we have *stationary* conductors in changing magnetic fields, Eq. (29.7) *cannot* be used; in this case, $\mathcal{E} = -d\Phi_B/dt$ is the only correct way to express Faraday's law.

Example 29.10 Calculating motional emf

Suppose the moving rod in Fig. 29.15b is 0.10 m long, the velocity v is 2.5 m/s, the total resistance of the loop is 0.030 Ω, and B is 0.60 T. Find $\mathcal{E}$, the induced current, and the force acting on the rod.

SOLUTION

IDENTIFY: The first target variable is the *motional* emf $\mathcal{E}$ due to the rod's motion. We'll find the current from the values of $\mathcal{E}$ and the resistance R. The force on the rod is actually a magnetic force exerted by $\vec{B}$ on the current in the rod.

SET UP: We'll use the motional emf expression developed in this section, the familiar relationship $\mathcal{E} = IR$, and the formula $\vec{F} = I\vec{L} \times \vec{B}$ for the magnetic force on a current-carrying rod of length $L = 0.10$ m.

EXECUTE: From Eq. (29.6) the emf is

$$\mathcal{E} = vBL = (2.5 \text{ m/s})(0.60 \text{ T})(0.10 \text{ m}) = 0.15 \text{ V}$$

The resulting induced current in the loop is

$$I = \frac{\mathcal{E}}{R} = \frac{0.15 \text{ V}}{0.030 \ \Omega} = 5.0 \text{ A}$$

The magnetic force on the rod carrying this current is directed *opposite* to the rod's motion. You can see this by applying the right-hand rule for vector products to the formula $\vec{F} = I\vec{L} \times \vec{B}$. The vector $\vec{L}$ points from *b* to *a* in Fig. 29.15, in the same direction as the induced current in the rod. Since $\vec{L}$ and $\vec{B}$ are perpendicular, this force has magnitude

$$F = ILB = (5.0 \text{ A})(0.10 \text{ m})(0.60 \text{ T}) = 0.30 \text{ N}$$

EVALUATE: We can check our answer for the direction of $\vec{F}$ by using Lenz's law. If we take the area vector $\vec{A}$ to point into the plane of the loop, the magnetic flux is positive and increasing as the rod moves to the right and increases the area of the loop. Lenz's law tells us that a force appears to oppose this increase in flux. Hence the force on the rod is to the left, opposite its motion.

Example 29.11 The Faraday disk dynamo

A conducting disk with radius R, shown in Fig. 29.16, lies in the xy-plane and rotates with constant angular velocity ω about the z-axis. The disk is in a uniform, constant $\vec{B}$ field parallel to the z-axis. Find the induced emf between the center and the rim of the disk.

SOLUTION

IDENTIFY: A motional emf is present because the conducting disk moves relative to the $\vec{B}$ field. The complication is that different parts of the disk move at different speeds v, depending on their distance from the rotation axis. We'll address this by considering small segments of the disk and adding (actually integrating) their contributions to determine our target variable, the emf between the center and the rim.

SET UP: Consider the small segment of the disk labeled by its velocity vector $\vec{v}$. The magnetic force per unit charge on this segment is $\vec{v} \times \vec{B}$, which points radially outward from the center of the disk. Hence the induced emf tends to make a current flow radially outward, which tells us that the moving conducting path to think about here is a straight line from the center to the rim. We can find the emf from each small disk segment along this line using the expression $d\mathcal{E} = (\vec{v} \times \vec{B}) \cdot d\vec{l}$ and then integrate to find the total emf.

CAUTION **Speed in a rotating disk** You might be tempted to use Eq. (29.5) and simply multiply vB times the length of the moving conducting path, which is just the radius R. That wouldn't be right, because v has different values at different points along the path. ▮

EXECUTE: Let's consider the motional emf $d\mathcal{E}$ due to a small radial segment at a distance r from the rotation axis. The associated length vector $d\vec{l}$ (of length dr) points radially outward, in the same direction as $\vec{v} \times \vec{B}$. The vectors $\vec{v}$ and $\vec{B}$ are perpendicular, and the magnitude of $\vec{v}$ is $v = \omega r$. Hence the total emf between center and rim is the sum of all such contributions:

$$\mathcal{E} = \int_0^R \omega B r \, dr = \frac{1}{2} \omega B R^2$$

EVALUATE: We can use this device as a source of emf in a circuit by completing the circuit through stationary brushes (b in the figure) that contact the disk and its conducting shaft as shown. The emf in such a disk was studied by Faraday; the device is called *a Faraday disk dynamo* or a *homopolar generator.* Unlike the alternator in Example 29.4, the Faraday disk dynamo is a direct-current generator; it produces an emf that is constant in time. Can you use Lenz's law to show that, for the direction of rotation in Fig. 29.16, the current in the external circuit must be in the direction shown?

29.16 A conducting disk with radius R rotating at an angular speed ω in a magnetic field $\vec{B}$. The emf is induced along radial lines of the disk and is applied to an external circuit through the two sliding contacts labeled b.

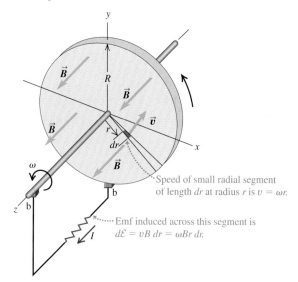

Speed of small radial segment of length dr at radius r is $v = \omega r$.

Emf induced across this segment is $d\mathcal{E} = vB \, dr = \omega Br \, dr$.

Test Your Understanding of Section 29.4 The earth's magnetic field points toward (magnetic) north. For simplicity, assume that the field has no vertical component (as is the case near the earth's equator). (a) If you hold a metal rod in your hand and walk toward the east, how should you orient the rod to get the maximum motional emf between its ends? (i) east-west; (ii) north-south; (iii) up-down; (iv) you get the same motional emf with all of these orientations. (b) How should you hold it to get *zero* emf as you walk toward the east? (i) east-west; (ii) north-south; (iii) up-down; (iv) none of these. (c) In which direction should you travel so that the motional emf across the rod is zero no matter how the rod is oriented? (i) west; (ii) north; (iii) south; (iv) straight up; (v) straight down.

29.5 Induced Electric Fields

When a conductor moves in a magnetic field, we can understand the induced emf on the basis of magnetic forces on charges in the conductor, as described in Section 29.4. But an induced emf also occurs when there is a changing flux through a stationary conductor. What is it that pushes the charges around the circuit in this type of situation?

As an example, let's consider the situation shown in Fig. 29.17. A long, thin solenoid with cross-sectional area A and n turns per unit length is encircled at its center by a circular conducting loop. The galvanometer G measures the current in the loop. A current I in the winding of the solenoid sets up a magnetic field $\vec{B}$ along the solenoid axis, as shown, with magnitude B as calculated in Example 28.9 (Section 28.7): $B = \mu_0 nI$, where n is the number of turns per unit length. If we neglect the small field outside the solenoid and take the area vector $\vec{A}$ to point in the same direction as $\vec{B}$, then the magnetic flux Φ_B through the loop is

$$\Phi_B = BA = \mu_0 nIA$$

When the solenoid current I changes with time, the magnetic flux Φ_B also changes, and according to Faraday's law the induced emf in the loop is given by

$$\mathcal{E} = -\frac{d\Phi_B}{dt} = -\mu_0 nA\frac{dI}{dt} \tag{29.8}$$

If the total resistance of the loop is R, the induced current in the loop, which we may call I', is $I' = \mathcal{E}/R$.

But what *force* makes the charges move around the loop? It can't be a magnetic force because the conductor isn't moving in a magnetic field and in fact isn't even *in* a magnetic field. We are forced to conclude that there has to be an **induced electric field** in the conductor *caused by the changing magnetic flux.* This may be a little jarring; we are accustomed to thinking about electric field as being caused by electric charges, and now we are saying that a changing magnetic field somehow acts as a source of electric field. Furthermore, it's a strange sort of electric field. When a charge q goes once around the loop, the total work done on it by the electric field must be equal to q times the emf $\mathcal{E}$. That is, the electric field in the loop *is not conservative,* as we used the term in Chapter 23, because the line integral of $\vec{E}$ around a closed path is not zero. Indeed, this line integral, representing the work done by the induced $\vec{E}$ field per unit charge, is equal to the induced emf $\mathcal{E}$:

$$\oint \vec{E} \cdot d\vec{l} = \mathcal{E} \tag{29.9}$$

From Faraday's law the emf $\mathcal{E}$ is also the negative of the rate of change of magnetic flux through the loop. Thus for this case we can restate Faraday's law as

$$\oint \vec{E} \cdot d\vec{l} = -\frac{d\Phi_B}{dt} \quad \text{(stationary integration path)} \tag{29.10}$$

Note that Faraday's law is always true in the form $\mathcal{E} = -d\Phi_B/dt$; the form given in Eq. (29.10) is valid *only* if the path around which we integrate is *stationary.*

As an example of a situation to which Eq. (29.10) can be applied, consider the stationary circular loop in Fig. 29.17b, which we take to have radius r. Because of cylindrical symmetry, the electric field $\vec{E}$ has the same magnitude at every point on the circle and is tangent to it at each point. (Symmetry would also permit the field to be *radial,* but then Gauss's law would require the presence of a net charge inside the circle, and there is none.) The line integral in Eq. (29.10) becomes simply the magnitude E times the circumference $2\pi r$ of the loop, $\oint \vec{E} \cdot d\vec{l} = 2\pi rE$, and Eq. (29.10) gives

$$E = \frac{1}{2\pi r}\left|\frac{d\Phi_B}{dt}\right| \tag{29.11}$$

The directions of $\vec{E}$ at points on the loop are shown in Fig. 29.17b. We know that $\vec{E}$ has to have the direction shown when $\vec{B}$ in the solenoid is increasing, because

29.17 (a) The windings of a long solenoid carry a current I that is increasing at a rate dI/dt. The magnetic flux in the solenoid is increasing at a rate $d\Phi_B/dt$, and this changing flux passes through a wire loop. An emf $\mathcal{E} = -d\Phi_B/dt$ is induced in the loop, inducing a current I' that is measured by the galvanometer G. (b) Cross-sectional view.

(a)

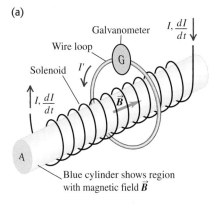

(b)

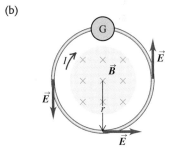

$\oint \vec{E} \cdot d\vec{l}$ has to be negative when $d\Phi_B/dt$ is positive. The same approach can be used to find the induced electric field *inside* the solenoid when the solenoid $\vec{B}$ field is changing; we leave the details to you (see Exercise 29.29).

Nonelectrostatic Electric Fields

Now let's summarize what we've learned. Faraday's law, Eq. (29.3), is valid for two rather different situations. In one, an emf is induced by magnetic forces on charges when a conductor moves through a magnetic field. In the other, a time-varying magnetic field induces an electric field in a stationary conductor and hence induces an emf; in fact, the $\vec{E}$ field is induced even when no conductor is present. This $\vec{E}$ field differs from an electro*static* field in an important way. It is *nonconservative;* the line integral $\oint \vec{E} \cdot d\vec{l}$ around a closed path is not zero, and when a charge moves around a closed path, the field does a nonzero amount of work on it. It follows that for such a field the concept of *potential* has no meaning. We call such a field a **nonelectrostatic field.** In contrast, an electro*static* field is *always* conservative, as we discussed in Section 23.1, and always has an associated potential function. Despite this difference, the fundamental effect of *any* electric field is to exert a force $\vec{F} = q\vec{E}$ on a charge q. This relationship is valid whether $\vec{E}$ is a conservative field produced by a charge distribution or a nonconservative field caused by changing magnetic flux.

So a changing magnetic field acts as a source of electric field of a sort that we *cannot* produce with any static charge distribution. This may seem strange, but it's the way nature behaves. What's more, we'll see in Section 29.7 that a changing *electric* field acts as a source of *magnetic* field. We'll explore this symmetry between the two fields in greater detail in our study of electromagnetic waves in Chapter 32.

If any doubt remains in your mind about the reality of magnetically induced electric fields, consider a few of the many practical applications (Fig. 29.18). In the playback head of a tape deck, currents are induced in a stationary coil as the variously magnetized regions of the tape move past it. Computer disk drives operate on the same principle. Pickups in electric guitars use currents induced in stationary pickup coils by the vibration of nearby ferromagnetic strings. Alternators in most cars use rotating magnets to induce currents in stationary coils. The list goes on and on; whether we realize it or not, magnetically induced electric fields play an important role in everyday life.

29.18 Applications of induced electric fields. **(a)** Data are stored on a computer hard disk in a pattern of magnetized areas on the surface of the disk. To read these data, a coil on a movable arm is placed next to the spinning disk. The coil experiences a changing magnetic flux, inducing a current whose characteristics depend on the pattern coded on the disk. **(b)** This hybrid automobile has both a gasoline engine and an electric motor. As the car comes to a halt, the spinning wheels run the motor backward so that it acts as a generator. The resulting induced current is used to recharge the car's batteries. **(c)** The rotating crankshaft of a piston-engine airplane spins a magnet, inducing an emf in an adjacent coil and generating the spark that ignites fuel in the engine cylinders. This keeps the engine running even if the airplane's other electrical systems fail.

Example 29.12 Induced electric fields

Suppose the long solenoid in Fig. 29.17a is wound with 500 turns per meter and the current in its windings is increasing at the rate of 100 A/s. The cross-sectional area of the solenoid is $4.0 \text{ cm}^2 = 4.0 \times 10^{-4} \text{ m}^2$. (a) Find the magnitude of the induced emf in the wire loop outside the solenoid. (b) Find the magnitude of the induced electric field within the loop if its radius is 2.0 cm.

SOLUTION

IDENTIFY: As in Fig. 29.17b, the increasing magnetic field inside the solenoid causes a change in the magnetic flux through the wire loop and hence induces an electric field $\vec{E}$ around the loop. Our target variables are the induced emf $\mathcal{E}$ and the magnitude of $\vec{E}$.

SET UP: We use Eq. (29.8) to determine the emf. Determining the field magnitude E is simplified because the loop and the solenoid share the same central axis. Hence, by symmetry, the electric field is tangent to the loop and has the same magnitude all the way around its circumference. This makes it easy to find E from the emf $\mathcal{E}$ using Eq. (29.9).

EXECUTE: (a) From Eq. (29.8), the induced emf is

$$\mathcal{E} = -\frac{d\Phi_B}{dt} = -\mu_0 n A \frac{dI}{dt}$$
$$= -(4\pi \times 10^{-7} \text{ Wb/A} \cdot \text{m})(500 \text{ turns/m})$$
$$\times (4.0 \times 10^{-4} \text{ m}^2)(100 \text{ A/s})$$
$$= -25 \times 10^{-6} \text{ Wb/s} = -25 \times 10^{-6} \text{ V} = -25 \,\mu\text{V}$$

(b) By symmetry the line integral $\oint \vec{E} \cdot d\vec{l}$ has absolute value $2\pi r E$ (disregarding the direction in which we integrate around the loop). This is equal to the absolute value of the emf, so

$$E = \frac{|\mathcal{E}|}{2\pi r} = \frac{25 \times 10^{-6} \text{ V}}{2\pi (2.0 \times 10^{-2} \text{ m})} = 2.0 \times 10^{-4} \text{ V/m}$$

EVALUATE: In Fig. 29.17b the magnetic flux *into* the plane of the figure is increasing. According to the right-hand rule for induced emf (illustrated in Fig. 29.6), a positive emf would be clockwise around the loop; the negative sign of $\mathcal{E}$ shows that the emf is in the counterclockwise direction. Can you also show this using Lenz's law?

Test Your Understanding of Section 29.5   If you wiggle a magnet back and forth in your hand, are you generating an electric field? If so, is this electric field conservative?

*29.6 Eddy Currents

In the examples of induction effects that we have studied, the induced currents have been confined to well-defined paths in conductors and other components forming a circuit. However, many pieces of electrical equipment contain masses of metal moving in magnetic fields or located in changing magnetic fields. In situations like these we can have induced currents that circulate throughout the volume of a material. Because their flow patterns resemble swirling eddies in a river, we call these **eddy currents.**

As an example, consider a metallic disk rotating in a magnetic field perpendicular to the plane of the disk but confined to a limited portion of the disk's area, as shown in Fig. 29.19a. Sector *Ob* is moving across the field and has an emf induced in it. Sectors *Oa* and *Oc* are not in the field, but they provide return conducting paths for charges displaced along *Ob* to return from *b* to *O*. The result is a circulation of eddy currents in the disk, somewhat as sketched in Fig. 29.19b.

We can use Lenz's law to decide on the direction of the induced current in the neighborhood of sector *Ob*. This current must experience a magnetic force $\vec{F} = I\vec{L} \times \vec{B}$ that *opposes* the rotation of the disk, and so this force must be to the right in Fig. 29.19b. Since $\vec{B}$ is directed into the plane of the disk, the current and hence $\vec{L}$ have downward components. The return currents lie outside the field, so they do not experience magnetic forces. The interaction between the eddy currents

29.19 Eddy currents induced in a rotating metal disk.

(a) Metal disk rotating through a magnetic field

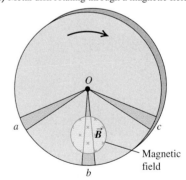

(b) Resulting eddy currents and braking force

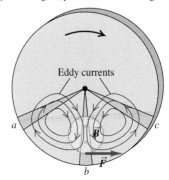

29.20 (a) A metal detector at an airport security checkpoint generates an alternating magnetic field $\vec{B}_0$. This induces eddy currents in a conducting object carried through the detector. The eddy currents in turn produce an alternating magnetic field $\vec{B}'$, and this field induces a current in the detector's receiver coil. (b) Portable metal detectors work on the same principle.

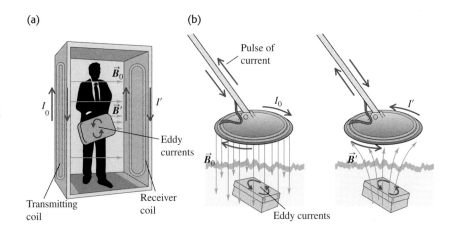

(a)   (b)

29.21 As Jupiter's moon Io moves around its orbit, the planet's powerful magnetic field induces eddy currents within Io. The lower closeup image shows two simultaneous volcanic eruptions on Io, triggered in part by eddy current heating.

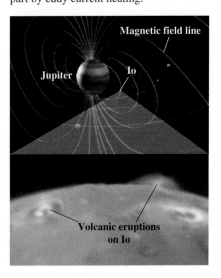

and the field causes a braking action on the disk. Such effects can be used to stop the rotation of a circular saw quickly when the power is turned off. Some sensitive balances use this effect to damp out vibrations. Eddy current braking is used on some electrically powered rapid-transit vehicles. Electromagnets mounted in the cars induce eddy currents in the rails; the resulting magnetic fields cause braking forces on the electromagnets and thus on the cars.

Eddy currents have many other practical uses. The shiny metal disk in the electric power company's meter outside your house rotates as a result of eddy currents. These currents are induced in the disk by magnetic fields caused by sinusoidally varying currents in a coil. In induction furnaces, eddy currents are used to heat materials in completely sealed containers for processes in which it is essential to avoid the slightest contamination of the materials. The metal detectors used at airport security checkpoints (Fig. 29.20a) operate by detecting eddy currents induced in metallic objects. Similar devices (Fig. 29.20b) are used to find buried treasure such as bottlecaps and lost pennies.

A particularly dramatic example of eddy currents in action is Jupiter's moon Io, which is slightly larger than the earth's moon (Fig. 29.21a). Io moves rapidly through Jupiter's intense magnetic field, and this sets up strong eddy currents within Io's interior. These currents dissipate energy at a rate of 10^{12} W, equivalent to setting off a one-kiloton nuclear weapon inside Io every four seconds! This dissipated energy helps to keep Io's interior hot and so helps to cause volcanic eruptions on its surface, like those in Fig. 29.21b. (Gravitational effects from Jupiter cause even more heating.)

Eddy currents also have undesirable effects. In an alternating-current transformer, coils wrapped around an iron core carry a sinusoidally varying current. The resulting eddy currents in the core waste energy through I^2R heating and themselves set up an unwanted opposing emf in the coils. To minimize these effects, the core is designed so that the paths for eddy currents are as narrow as possible. We'll describe how this is done when we discuss transformers in detail in Section 31.6.

Test Your Understanding of Section 29.6 Suppose that the magnetic field in Fig. 29.19 were directed out of the plane of the figure and the disk were rotating counterclockwise. Compared to the directions of the force $\vec{F}$ and the eddy currents shown in Fig. 29.19b, what would the new directions be? (i) The force $\vec{F}$ and the eddy currents would both be in the same direction; (ii) the force $\vec{F}$ would be in the same direction, but the eddy currents would be in the opposite direction; (iii) the force $\vec{F}$ would be in the opposite direction, but the eddy currents would be in the same direction; (iv) the force $\vec{F}$ and the eddy currents would be in the opposite directions.

29.7 Displacement Current and Maxwell's Equations

We have seen that a varying magnetic field gives rise to an induced electric field. In one of the more remarkable examples of the symmetry of nature, it turns out that a varying *electric* field gives rise to a *magnetic* field. This effect is of tremendous importance, for it turns out to explain the existence of radio waves, gamma rays, and visible light, as well as all other forms of electromagnetic waves.

Generalizing Ampere's Law

To see the origin of the relationship between varying electric fields and magnetic fields, let's return to Ampere's law as given in Section 28.6, Eq. (28.20):

$$\oint \vec{B} \cdot d\vec{l} = \mu_0 I_{\text{encl}}$$

The problem with Ampere's law in this form is that it is *incomplete*. To see why, let's consider the process of charging a capacitor (Fig. 29.22). Conducting wires lead current i_C into one plate and out of the other; the charge Q increases, and the electric field $\vec{E}$ between the plates increases. The notation i_C indicates *conduction* current to distinguish it from another kind of current we are about to encounter, called *displacement* current i_D. We use lowercase i's and v's to denote instantaneous values of currents and potential differences, respectively, that may vary with time.

Let's apply Ampere's law to the circular path shown. The integral $\oint \vec{B} \cdot d\vec{l}$ around this path equals $\mu_0 I_{\text{encl}}$. For the plane circular area bounded by the circle, I_{encl} is just the current i_C in the left conductor. But the surface that bulges out to the right is bounded by the same circle, and the current through that surface is zero. So $\oint \vec{B} \cdot d\vec{l}$ is equal to $\mu_0 i_C$, and at the same time it is equal to zero! This is a clear contradiction.

But something else is happening on the bulged-out surface. As the capacitor charges, the electric field $\vec{E}$ and the electric *flux* Φ_E through the surface are increasing. We can determine their rates of change in terms of the charge and current. The instantaneous charge is $q = Cv$, where C is the capacitance and v is the instantaneous potential difference. For a parallel-plate capacitor, $C = \epsilon_0 A/d$, where A is the plate area and d is the spacing. The potential difference v between plates is $v = Ed$, where E is the electric field magnitude between plates. (We neglect fringing and assume that $\vec{E}$ is uniform in the region between the plates.) If this region is filled with a material with permittivity ϵ, we replace ϵ_0 by ϵ everywhere; we'll use ϵ in the following discussion.

Substituting these expressions for C and v into $q = Cv$, we can express the capacitor charge q as

$$q = Cv = \frac{\epsilon A}{d}(Ed) = \epsilon EA = \epsilon \Phi_E \tag{29.12}$$

where $\Phi_E = EA$ is the electric flux through the surface.

As the capacitor charges, the rate of change of q is the conduction current, $i_C = dq/dt$. Taking the derivative of Eq. (29.12) with respect to time, we get

$$i_C = \frac{dq}{dt} = \epsilon \frac{d\Phi_E}{dt} \tag{29.13}$$

Now, stretching our imagination a little, we invent a fictitious **displacement current** i_D in the region between the plates, defined as

$$i_D = \epsilon \frac{d\Phi_E}{dt} \quad \text{(displacement current)} \tag{29.14}$$

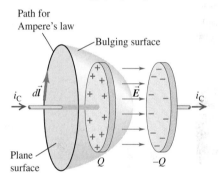

29.22 Parallel-plate capacitor being charged. The conduction current through the plane surface is i_C, but there is no conduction current through the surface that bulges out to pass between the plates. The two surfaces have a common boundary, so this difference in I_{encl} leads to an apparent contradiction in applying Ampere's law.

That is, we imagine that the changing flux through the curved surface in Fig. 29.22 is somehow equivalent, in Ampere's law, to a conduction current through that surface. We include this fictitious current, along with the real conduction current i_C, in Ampere's law:

$$\oint \vec{B} \cdot d\vec{l} = \mu_0 (i_C + i_D)_{\text{encl}} \qquad \text{(generalized Ampere's law)} \qquad (29.15)$$

Ampere's law in this form is obeyed no matter which surface we use in Fig. 29.22. For the flat surface, i_D is zero; for the curved surface, i_C is zero; and i_C for the flat surface equals i_D for the curved surface. Equation (29.15) remains valid in a magnetic material, provided that the magnetization is proportional to the external field and we replace μ_0 by μ.

The fictitious current i_D was invented in 1865 by the Scottish physicist James Clerk Maxwell (1831–1879), who called it displacement current. There is a corresponding *displacement current density* $j_D = i_D/A$; using $\Phi_E = EA$ and dividing Eq. (29.14) by A, we find

$$j_D = \epsilon \frac{dE}{dt} \qquad (29.16)$$

We have pulled the concept out of thin air, as Maxwell did, but we see that it enables us to save Ampere's law in situations such as that in Fig. 29.22.

Another benefit of displacement current is that it lets us generalize Kirchhoff's junction rule, discussed in Section 26.2. Considering the left plate of the capacitor plate, we have conduction current into it but none out of it. But when we include the displacement current, we have conduction current coming in one side and an equal displacement current coming out the other side. With this generalized meaning of the term "current," we can speak of current going *through* the capacitor.

The Reality of Displacement Current

You might well ask at this point whether displacement current has any real physical significance or whether it is just a ruse to satisfy Ampere's law and Kirchhoff's junction rule. Here's a fundamental experiment that helps to answer that question. We take a plane circular area between the capacitor plates, as shown in Fig. 29.23. If displacement current really plays the role in Ampere's law that we have claimed, then there ought to be a magnetic field in the region between the plates while the capacitor is charging. We can use our generalized Ampere's law, including displacement current, to predict what this field should be.

To be specific, let's picture round capacitor plates with radius R. To find the magnetic field at a point in the region between the plates at a distance r from the axis, we apply Ampere's law to a circle of radius r passing through the point, with $r < R$. This circle passes through points a and b in Fig. 29.23. The total current enclosed by the circle is j_D times its area, or $(i_D/\pi R^2)(\pi r^2)$. The integral $\oint \vec{B} \cdot d\vec{l}$ in Ampere's law is just B times the circumference $2\pi r$ of the circle, and because $i_D = i_C$ for the charging capacitor, Ampere's law becomes

$$\oint \vec{B} \cdot d\vec{l} = 2\pi r B = \mu_0 \frac{r^2}{R^2} i_C \qquad \text{or}$$

$$B = \frac{\mu_0}{2\pi} \frac{r}{R^2} i_C \qquad (29.17)$$

This result predicts that in the region between the plates $\vec{B}$ is zero at the axis and increases linearly with distance from the axis. A similar calculation shows that *outside* the region between the plates (that is, for $r > R$), $\vec{B}$ is the same as though the wire were continuous and the plates not present at all.

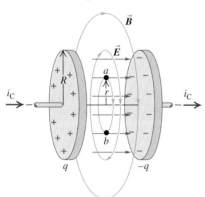

29.23 A capacitor being charged by a current i_C has a displacement current equal to i_C between the plates, with displacement-current density $j_D = \epsilon \, dE/dt$. This can be regarded as the source of the magnetic field between the plates.

When we *measure* the magnetic field in this region, we find that it really is there and that it behaves just as Eq. (29.17) predicts. This confirms directly the role of displacement current as a source of magnetic field. It is now established beyond reasonable doubt that displacement current, far from being just an artifice, is a fundamental fact of nature. Maxwell's discovery was the bold step of an extraordinary genius.

Maxwell's Equations of Electromagnetism

We are now in a position to wrap up in a single package *all* of the relationships between electric and magnetic fields and their sources. This package consists of four equations, called **Maxwell's equations.** Maxwell did not discover all of these equations single-handedly (though he did develop the concept of displacement current). But he did put them together and recognized their significance, particularly in predicting the existence of electromagnetic waves.

For now we'll state Maxwell's equations in their simplest form, for the case in which we have charges and currents in otherwise empty space. In Chapter 32 we'll discuss how to modify these equations if a dielectric or a magnetic material is present.

Two of Maxwell's equations involve an integral of $\vec{E}$ or $\vec{B}$ over a closed surface. The first is simply Gauss's law for electric fields, Eq. (22.8), which states that the surface integral of $E_\perp$ over any closed surface equals $1/\epsilon_0$ times the total charge Q_{encl} enclosed within the surface:

$$\oint \vec{E} \cdot d\vec{A} = \frac{Q_{\text{encl}}}{\epsilon_0} \qquad \text{(Gauss's law for } \vec{E}\text{)} \qquad (29.18)$$

The second is the analogous relationship for *magnetic* fields, Eq. (27.8), which states that the surface integral of $B_\perp$ over any closed surface is always zero:

$$\oint \vec{B} \cdot d\vec{A} = 0 \qquad \text{(Gauss's law for } \vec{B}\text{)} \qquad (29.19)$$

This statement means, among other things, that there are no magnetic monopoles (single magnetic charges) to act as sources of magnetic field.

The third equation is Ampere's law including displacement current. This states that both conduction current i_C and displacement current $\epsilon_0 d\Phi_E/dt$, where Φ_E is electric flux, act as sources of magnetic field:

$$\oint \vec{B} \cdot d\vec{l} = \mu_0 \left(i_C + \epsilon_0 \frac{d\Phi_E}{dt} \right)_{\text{encl}} \qquad \text{(Ampere's law)} \qquad (29.20)$$

The fourth and final equation is Faraday's law. It states that a changing magnetic field or magnetic flux induces an electric field:

$$\oint \vec{E} \cdot d\vec{l} = -\frac{d\Phi_B}{dt} \qquad \text{(Faraday's law)} \qquad (29.21)$$

If there is a changing magnetic flux, the line integral in Eq. (29.21) is not zero, which shows that the $\vec{E}$ field produced by a changing magnetic flux is not conservative. Recall that this line integral must be carried out over a *stationary* closed path.

It's worthwhile to look more carefully at the electric field $\vec{E}$ and its role in Maxwell's equations. In general, the total $\vec{E}$ field at a point in space can be the superposition of an electrostatic field $\vec{E}_c$ caused by a distribution of charges at rest and a magnetically induced, nonelectrostatic field $\vec{E}_n$. (The subscript c stands for Coulomb or conservative; the subscript n stands for non-Coulomb, nonelectrostatic, or nonconservative.) That is,

$$\vec{E} = \vec{E}_c + \vec{E}_n$$

The electrostatic part $\vec{E}_c$ is *always* conservative, so $\oint \vec{E}_c \cdot d\vec{l} = 0$. This conservative part of the field does not contribute to the integral in Faraday's law, so we can take $\vec{E}$ in Eq. (29.21) to be the total electric field $\vec{E}$, including both the part $\vec{E}_c$ due to charges and the magnetically induced part $\vec{E}_n$. Similarly, the nonconservative part $\vec{E}_n$ of the $\vec{E}$ field does not contribute to the integral in Gauss's law, because this part of the field is not caused by static charges. Hence $\oint \vec{E}_n \cdot d\vec{A}$ is always zero. We conclude that in all the Maxwell equations, $\vec{E}$ is the total electric field; these equations don't distinguish between conservative and nonconservative fields.

Symmetry in Maxwell's Equations

There is a remarkable symmetry in Maxwell's four equations. In empty space where there is no charge, the first two equations (Eqs. (29.18) and (29.19)) are identical in form, one containing $\vec{E}$ and the other containing $\vec{B}$. When we compare the second two equations, Eq. (29.20) says that a changing electric flux creates a magnetic field, and Eq. (29.21) says that a changing magnetic flux creates an electric field. In empty space, where there is no conduction current, $i_C = 0$ and the two equations have the same form, apart from a numerical constant and a negative sign, with the roles of $\vec{E}$ and $\vec{B}$ exchanged in the two equations.

We can rewrite Eqs. (29.20) and (29.21) in a different but equivalent form by introducing the definitions of electric and magnetic flux, $\Phi_E = \int \vec{E} \cdot d\vec{A}$ and $\Phi_B = \int \vec{B} \cdot d\vec{A}$, respectively. In empty space, where there is no charge or conduction current, $i_C = 0$ and $Q_{encl} = 0$, and we have

$$\oint \vec{B} \cdot d\vec{l} = \epsilon_0 \mu_0 \frac{d}{dt} \int \vec{E} \cdot d\vec{A} \tag{29.22}$$

$$\oint \vec{E} \cdot d\vec{l} = -\frac{d}{dt} \int \vec{B} \cdot d\vec{A} \tag{29.23}$$

Again we notice the symmetry between the roles of $\vec{E}$ and $\vec{B}$ in these expressions.

The most remarkable feature of these equations is that a time-varying field of *either* kind induces a field of the other kind in neighboring regions of space. Maxwell recognized that these relationships predict the existence of electromagnetic disturbances consisting of time-varying electric and magnetic fields that travel or *propagate* from one region of space to another, even if no matter is present in the intervening space. Such disturbances, called *electromagnetic waves,* provide the physical basis for light, radio and television waves, infrared, ultraviolet, x rays, and the rest of the electromagnetic spectrum. We will return to this vitally important topic in Chapter 32.

Although it may not be obvious, *all* the basic relationships between fields and their sources are contained in Maxwell's equations. We can derive Coulomb's law from Gauss's law, we can derive the law of Biot and Savart from Ampere's law, and so on. When we add the equation that defines the $\vec{E}$ and $\vec{B}$ fields in terms of the forces that they exert on a charge q, namely,

$$\vec{F} = q(\vec{E} + \vec{v} \times \vec{B}) \tag{29.24}$$

we have *all* the fundamental relationships of electromagnetism!

Finally, we note that Maxwell's equations would have even greater symmetry between the $\vec{E}$ and $\vec{B}$ fields if single magnetic charges (magnetic monopoles) existed. The right side of Eq. (29.19) would contain the total *magnetic* charge enclosed by the surface, and the right side of Eq. (29.21) would include a magnetic monopole current term. Perhaps you can begin to see why some physicists wish that magnetic monopoles existed; they would help to perfect the mathematical poetry of Maxwell's equations.

The discovery that electromagnetism can be wrapped up so neatly and elegantly is a very satisfying one. In conciseness and generality, Maxwell's equations are in the same league with Newton's laws of motion and the laws of thermodynamics. Indeed, a major goal of science is learning how to express very broad and general relationships in a concise and compact form. Maxwell's synthesis of electromagnetism stands as a towering intellectual achievement, comparable to the Newtonian synthesis we described at the end of Section 12.5 and to the development of relativity and quantum mechanics in the 20th century.

Test Your Understanding of Section 29.7 (a) Which of Maxwell's equations explains how a credit card reader works? (b) Which one describes how a wire carrying a steady current generates a magnetic field?

*29.8 Superconductivity

The most familiar property of a superconductor is the sudden disappearance of all electrical resistance when the material is cooled below a temperature called the *critical temperature,* denoted by T_c. We discussed this behavior and the circumstances of its discovery in Section 25.2. But superconductivity is far more than just the absence of measurable resistance. Superconductors also have extraordinary *magnetic* properties. We'll explore some of these properties in this section.

The first hint of unusual magnetic properties was the discovery that for any superconducting material the critical temperature T_c changes when the material is placed in an externally produced magnetic field $\vec{B}_0$. Figure 29.24 shows this dependence for mercury, the first element in which superconductivity was observed. As the external field magnitude B_0 increases, the superconducting transition occurs at lower and lower temperature. When B_0 is greater than 0.0412 T, *no* superconducting transition occurs. The minimum magnitude of magnetic field that is needed to eliminate superconductivity at a temperature below T_c is called the *critical field,* denoted by B_c.

The Meissner Effect

Another aspect of the magnetic behavior of superconductors appears if we place a homogeneous sphere of a superconducting material in a uniform applied magnetic field $\vec{B}_0$ at a temperature T greater than T_c. The material is then in the normal phase, not the superconducting phase. The field is as shown in Figure 29.25a. Now we lower the temperature until the superconducting transition occurs. (We assume that the magnitude of $\vec{B}_0$ is not large enough to prevent the phase transition.) What happens to the field?

Measurements of the field outside the sphere show that the field lines become distorted as in Fig. 29.25b. There is no longer any field inside the material, except possibly in a very thin surface layer a hundred or so atoms thick. If a coil is wrapped around the sphere, the emf induced in the coil shows that during the superconducting transition the magnetic flux through the coil decreases from its initial value to zero; this is consistent with the absence of field inside the material. Finally, if the field is now turned off while the material is still in its superconducting phase, no emf is induced in the coil, and measurements show no field outside the sphere (Fig. 29.25c).

We conclude that during a superconducting transition in the presence of the field $\vec{B}_0$, all of the magnetic flux is expelled from the bulk of the sphere, and the

29.24 Phase diagram for pure mercury, showing the critical magnetic field B_c and its dependence on temperature. Superconductivity is impossible above the critical temperature T_c. The curves for other superconducting materials are similar but with different numerical values.

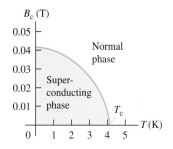

29.25 A superconducting material (a) above the critical temperature and (b), (c) below the critical temperature.

(a) Superconducting material in an external magnetic field $\vec{B}_0$ at $T > T_c$.

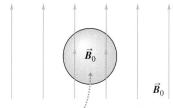

The field inside the material is very nearly equal to $\vec{B}_0$.

(b) The temperature is lowered to $T < T_c$, so the material becomes superconducting.

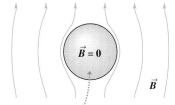

Magnetic flux is expelled from the material, and the field inside it is zero (Meissner effect).

(c) When the external field is turned off at $T < T_c$, the field is zero everywhere.

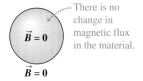

There is no change in magnetic flux in the material.

magnetic flux Φ_B through the coil becomes zero. This expulsion of magnetic flux is called the *Meissner effect.* As shown in Fig. 29.25b, this expulsion crowds the magnetic field lines closer together to the side of the sphere, increasing $\vec{B}$ there.

Superconductor Levitation and Other Applications

The diamagnetic nature of a superconductor has some interesting *mechanical* consequences. A paramagnetic or ferromagnetic material is attracted by a permanent magnet because the magnetic dipoles in the material align with the nonuniform magnetic field of the permanent magnet. (We discussed this in Section 27.7.) For a diamagnetic material the magnetization is in the opposite sense, and a diamagnetic material is *repelled* by a permanent magnet. By Newton's third law the magnet is also repelled by the diamagnetic material. Figure 29.26 shows the repulsion between a specimen of a high-temperature superconductor and a magnet; the magnet is supported ("levitated") by this repulsive magnetic force.

The behavior we have described is characteristic of what are called *type-I superconductors.* There is another class of superconducting materials called *type-II superconductors.* When such a material in the superconducting phase is placed in a magnetic field, the bulk of the material remains superconducting, but thin filaments of material, running parallel to the field, may return to the normal phase. Currents circulate around the boundaries of these filaments, and there *is* magnetic flux inside them. Type-II superconductors are used for electromagnets because they usually have much larger values of B_c than do type-I materials, permitting much larger magnetic fields without destroying the superconducting state. Type-II superconductors have *two* critical magnetic fields: the first, B_{c1}, is the field at which magnetic flux begins to enter the material, forming the filaments just described, and the second, B_{c2}, is the field at which the material becomes normal.

Many important and exciting applications of superconductors are under development. Superconducting electromagnets have been used in research laboratories for several years. Their advantages compared to conventional electromagnets include greater efficiency, compactness, and greater field magnitudes. Once a current is established in the coil of a superconducting electromagnet, no additional power input is required because there is no resistive energy loss. The coils can also be made more compact because there is no need to provide channels for the circulation of cooling fluids. Superconducting magnets routinely attain steady fields of the order of 10 T, much larger than the maximum fields that are available with ordinary electromagnets.

Superconductors are attractive for long-distance electric power transmission and for energy-conversion devices, including generators, motors, and transformers. Very sensitive measurements of magnetic fields can be made with superconducting quantum interference devices (SQUIDs), which can detect changes in magnetic flux of less than 10^{-14} Wb; these devices have applications in medicine, geology, and other fields. The number of potential uses for superconductors has increased greatly since the discovery in 1987 of high-temperature superconductors. These materials have critical temperatures that are above the temperature of liquid nitrogen (about 77 K) and so are comparatively easy to attain. Development of practical applications of superconductor science promises to be an exciting chapter in contemporary technology.

29.26 A superconductor (the black slab) exerts a repulsive force on a magnet (the metallic cylinder), supporting the magnet in midair.

Faraday's law: Faraday's law states that the induced emf in a closed loop equals the negative of the time rate of change of magnetic flux through the loop. This relationship is valid whether the flux change is caused by a changing magnetic field, motion of the loop, or both. (See Examples 29.1–29.7.)

$$\mathcal{E} = -\frac{d\Phi_B}{dt} \tag{29.3}$$

The magnet's motion causes a *changing* magnetic field through the coil, inducing a current in the coil.

Lenz's law: Lenz's law states that an induced current or emf always tends to oppose or cancel out the change that caused it. Lenz's law can be derived from Faraday's law and is often easier to use. (See Examples 29.8 and 29.9.)

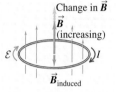

Motional emf: If a conductor moves in a magnetic field, a motional emf is induced. (See Examples 29.10 and 29.11.)

$$\mathcal{E} = vBL \tag{29.6}$$

(conductor with length L moves in uniform $\vec{B}$ field, $\vec{L}$ and $\vec{v}$ both perpendicular to $\vec{B}$ and to each other)

$$\mathcal{E} = \oint (\vec{v} \times \vec{B}) \cdot d\vec{l} \tag{29.7}$$

(all or part of a closed loop moves in a $\vec{B}$ field)

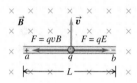

Induced electric fields: When an emf is induced by a changing magnetic flux through a stationary conductor, there is an induced electric field $\vec{E}$ of nonelectrostatic origin. This field is nonconservative and cannot be associated with a potential. (See Example 29.12.)

$$\oint \vec{E} \cdot d\vec{l} = -\frac{d\Phi_B}{dt} \tag{29.10}$$

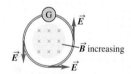

Displacement current and Maxwell's equations: A time-varying electric field generates a displacement current i_D, which acts as a source of magnetic field in exactly the same way as conduction current. The relationships between electric and magnetic fields and their sources can be stated compactly in four equations, called Maxwell's equations. Together they form a complete basis for the relationship of $\vec{E}$ and $\vec{B}$ fields to their sources.

$$i_D = \epsilon \frac{d\Phi_E}{dt} \tag{29.14}$$

(displacement current)

$$\oint \vec{E} \cdot d\vec{A} = \frac{Q_{encl}}{\epsilon_0} \tag{29.18}$$

(Gauss's law for $\vec{E}$ fields)

$$\oint \vec{B} \cdot d\vec{A} = 0 \tag{29.19}$$

(Gauss's law for $\vec{B}$ fields)

$$\oint \vec{B} \cdot d\vec{l} = \mu_0 \left(i_C + \epsilon_0 \frac{d\Phi_E}{dt} \right)_{encl} \tag{29.20}$$

(Ampere's law including displacement current)

$$\oint \vec{E} \cdot d\vec{l} = -\frac{d\Phi_B}{dt} \tag{29.21}$$

(Faraday's law)

Key Terms

Answer to Chapter Opening Question

?

As the magnetic stripe moves through the card reader, the coded pattern of magnetization in the stripe causes a varying magnetic flux and hence an induced current in the reader's circuits. If the card does not move, there is no induced emf or current and none of the credit card's information is read.

Answers to Test Your Understanding Questions

29.2 Answers: (a) (i), (b) (iii) (a) Initially there is magnetic flux into the plane of the page, which we call positive. While the loop is being squeezed, the flux is becoming less positive $(d\Phi_B/dt < 0)$ and so the induced emf is positive as in Fig. 29.6b $(\mathcal{E} = -d\Phi_B/dt > 0)$. If you point the thumb of your right hand into the page, your fingers curl clockwise, so this is the direction of positive induced emf. (b) Since the coil's shape is no longer changing, the magnetic flux is not changing and there is no induced emf.

29.3 Answers: (a) (i), (b) (iii) In (a), as in the original situation, the magnet and loop are approaching each other and the downward flux through the loop is increasing. Hence the induced emf and induced current are the same. In (b), since the magnet and loop are moving together, the flux through the loop is not changing and no emf is induced.

29.4 Answers: (a) (iii); (b) (i) or (ii); (c) (ii) or (iii) You will get the maximum motional emf if you hold the rod vertically, so that its length is perpendicular to both the magnetic field and the direction of motion. With this orientation, $\vec{L}$ is parallel to $\vec{v} \times \vec{B}$. If you hold the rod in any horizontal orientation, $\vec{L}$ will be perpendicular to $\vec{v} \times \vec{B}$ and no emf will be induced. If you walk due north or south, $\vec{v} \times \vec{B} = 0$ and no emf will be induced for any orientation of the rod.

29.5 Answers: yes, no The magnetic field at a fixed position changes as you move the magnet. Such induced electric fields are *not* conservative.

29.6 Answer: (iii) By Lenz's law, the force must oppose the motion of the disk through the magnetic field. Since the disk material is now moving to the right through the field region, the force $\vec{F}$ is to the left—that is, in the opposite direction to that shown in Fig. 29.19b. To produce a leftward magnetic force $\vec{F} = I\vec{L} \times \vec{B}$ on currents moving through a magnetic field $\vec{B}$ directed out of the plane of the figure, the eddy currents must be moving downward in the figure—that is, in the same direction shown in Fig. 29.19b.

29.7 Answers: (a) Faraday's law, (b) Ampere's law A credit card reader works by inducing currents in the reader's coils as the card's magnetized stripe is swiped (see the answer to the chapter opening question). Ampere's law describes how currents of all kinds (both conduction currents and displacement currents) give rise to magnetic fields.

PROBLEMS

For instructor-assigned homework, go to **www.masteringphysics.com**

Discussion Questions

Q29.1. A sheet of copper is placed between the poles of an electromagnet with the magnetic field perpendicular to the sheet. When the sheet is pulled out, a considerable force is required, and the force required increases with speed. Explain.

Q29.2. In Fig. 29.8, if the angular speed ω of the loop is doubled, then the frequency with which the induced current changes direction doubles, and the maximum emf also doubles. Why? Does the torque required to turn the loop change? Explain.

Q29.3. Two circular loops lie side by side in the same plane. One is connected to a source that supplies an increasing current; the other is a simple closed ring. Is the induced current in the ring in the same direction as the current in the loop connected to the source, or opposite? What if the current in the first loop is decreasing? Explain.

Q29.4. A farmer claimed that the high-voltage transmission lines running parallel to his fence induced dangerously high voltages on the fence. Is this within the realm of possibility? Explain. (The lines carry alternating current that changes direction 120 times each second.)

Q29.5. A long, straight conductor passes through the center of a metal ring, perpendicular to its plane. If the current in the conductor increases, is a current induced in the ring? Explain.

Q29.6. A student asserted that if a permanent magnet is dropped down a vertical copper pipe, it eventually reaches a terminal velocity even if there is no air resistance. Why should this be? Or should it?

Q29.7. An airplane is in level flight over Antarctica, where the magnetic field of the earth is mostly directed upward away from the ground. As viewed by a passenger facing toward the front of the plane, is the left or the right wingtip at higher potential? Does your answer depend on the direction the plane is flying?

Q29.8. Consider the situation in Exercise 29.19. In part (a), find the direction of the force that the large circuit exerts on the small one. Explain how this result is consistent with Lenz's law.

Q29.9. A metal rectangle is close to a long, straight, current-carrying wire, with two of its sides parallel to the wire. If the current in the long wire is decreasing, is the rectangle repelled by or attracted to the wire? Explain why this result is consistent with Lenz's law.

Q29.10. A square conducting loop is in a region of uniform, constant magnetic field. Can the loop be rotated about an axis along one side and no emf be induced in the loop? Discuss, in terms of the orientation of the rotation axis relative to the magnetic-field direction.

Q29.11. Example 29.7 discusses the external force that must be applied to the slidewire to move it at constant speed. If there were a break in the left-hand end of the U-shaped conductor, how much force would be needed to move the slidewire at constant speed? As in the example, you can ignore friction.

Q29.12. In the situation shown in Fig. 29.16, would it be appropriate to ask how much *energy* an electron gains during a complete trip around the wire loop with current I'? Would it be appropriate to ask what *potential difference* the electron moves through during such a complete trip? Explain your answers.

Q29.13. A metal ring is oriented with the plane of its area perpendicular to a spatially uniform magnetic field that increases at a steady rate. If the radius of the ring is doubled, by what factor do (a) the emf induced in the ring and (b) the electric field induced in the ring change?

Q29.14. For Eq. (29.6), show that if v is in meters per second, B in teslas, and L in meters, then the units of the right-hand side of the equation are joules per coulomb or volts (the correct SI units for $\mathcal{E}$).

Q29.15. Can one have a displacement current as well as a conduction current within a conductor? Explain.

Q29.16. Your physics study partner asks you to consider a parallel-plate capacitor that has a dielectric completely filling the volume between the plates. He then claims that Eqs. (29.13) and (29.14) show that the conduction current in the dielectric equals the displacement current in the dielectric. Do you agree? Explain.

Q29.17. Match the mathematical statements of Maxwell's equations as given in Section 29.7 to these verbal statements. (a) Closed electric field lines are evidently produced only by changing magnetic flux. (b) Closed magnetic field lines are produced both by the motion of electric charge and by changing electric flux. (c) Electric field lines can start on positive charges and end on negative charges. (d) Evidently there are no magnetic monopoles on which to start and end magnetic field lines.

Q29.18. If magnetic monopoles existed, the right-hand side of Eq. (29.21) would include a term proportional to the current of magnetic monopoles. Suppose a steady monopole current is moving in a long straight wire. Sketch the *electric* field lines that such a current would produce.

Q29.19. If magnetic monopoles existed, the right-hand side of Eq. (29.19) would be proportional to the total enclosed *magnetic* charge. Suppose an infinite line of magnetic monopoles were on the x-axis. Sketch the magnetic field lines that this line of monopoles would produce.

Exercises

Section 29.2 Faraday's Law

29.1. A flat, rectangular coil consisting of 50 turns measures 25.0 cm by 30.0 cm. It is in a uniform, 1.20-T, magnetic field, with the plane of the coil parallel to the field. In 0.222 s, it is rotated so that the plane of the coil is perpendicular to the field. (a) What is the change in the magnetic flux through the coil due to this rotation? (b) Find the magnitude of the average emf induced in the coil during this rotation.

29.2. In a physics laboratory experiment, a coil with 200 turns enclosing an area of 12 cm^2 is rotated in 0.040 s from a position where its plane is perpendicular to the earth's magnetic field to a position where its plane is parallel to the field. The earth's magnetic field at the lab location is 6.0×10^{-5} T. (a) What is the total magnetic flux through the coil before it is rotated? After it is rotated? b) What is the average emf induced in the coil?

29.3. Search Coils and Credit Cards. (a) Derive the equation relating the total charge Q that flows through a search coil (Conceptual Example 29.3) to the magnetic-field magnitude B. The search

coil has N turns, each with area A, and the flux through the coil is decreased from its initial maximum value to zero in a time Δt. The resistance of the coil is R, and the total charge is $Q = I\Delta t$, where I is the average current induced by the change in flux. (b) In a credit card reader, the magnetic strip on the back of a credit card is rapidly "swiped" past a coil within the reader. Explain, using the same ideas that underlie the operation of a search coil, how the reader can decode the information stored in the pattern of magnetization on the strip. (c) Is it necessary that the credit card be "swiped" through the reader at exactly the right speed? Why or why not?

29.4. A closely wound search coil (Exercise 29.3) has an area of 3.20 cm^2, 120 turns, and a resistance of 60.0 Ω. It is connected to a charge-measuring instrument whose resistance is 45.0 Ω. When the coil is rotated quickly from a position parallel to a uniform magnetic field to a position perpendicular to the field, the instrument indicates a charge of 3.56×10^{-5} C. What is the magnitude of the field?

29.5. A circular loop of wire with a radius of 12.0 cm and oriented in the horizontal xy-plane is located in a region of uniform magnetic field. A field of 1.5 T is directed along the positive z-direction, which is upward. (a) If the loop is removed from the field region in a time interval of 2.0 ms, find the average emf that will be induced in the wire loop during the extraction process. (b) If the coil is viewed looking down on it from above, is the induced current in the loop clockwise or counterclockwise?

29.6. A coil 4.00 cm in radius, containing 500 turns, is placed in a uniform magnetic field that varies with time according to $B = (0.0120 \text{ T/s})t + (3.00 \times 10^{-5} \text{ T/s}^4)t^4$. The coil is connected to a 600-Ω resistor, and its plane is perpendicular to the magnetic field. You can ignore the resistance of the coil. (a) Find the magnitude of the induced emf in the coil as a function of time. (b) What is the current in the resistor at time $t = 5.00$ s?

29.7. The current in the long, straight wire AB shown in Fig. 29.27 is upward and is increasing steadily at a rate di/dt. (a) At an instant when the current is i, what are the magnitude and direction of the field $\vec{B}$ at a distance r to the right of the wire? (b) What is the flux $d\Phi_B$ through the narrow, shaded strip? (c) What is the total flux through the loop? (d) What is the induced emf in the loop? (e) Evaluate the numerical value of the induced emf if $a = 12.0$ cm, $b = 36.0$ cm, $L = 24.0$ cm, and $di/dt = 9.60$ A/s.

Figure **29.27** Exercise 29.7.

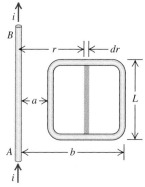

29.8. A flat, circular, steel loop of radius 75 cm is at rest in a uniform magnetic field, as shown in an edge-on view in Fig. 29.28. The field is changing with time, according to $B(t) = (1.4 \text{ T})e^{-(0.057 \text{ s}^{-1})t}$. (a) Find the emf induced in the loop as a function of time. (b) When is the induced emf equal to $\frac{1}{10}$ of its initial value? (c) Find the direction of the current induced in the loop, as viewed from above the loop.

Figure **29.28** Exercise 29.8.

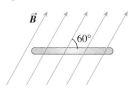

29.9. Shrinking Loop. A circular loop of flexible iron wire has an initial circumference of 165.0 cm, but its circumference is decreasing at a constant rate of 12.0 cm/s due to a tangential pull on the wire. The loop is in a constant, uniform magnetic field oriented perpendicular to the plane of the loop and with magnitude 0.500 T. (a) Find the emf induced in the loop at the instant when 9.0 s have passed. (b) Find the direction of the induced current in the loop as viewed looking along the direction of the magnetic field.

29.10. A rectangle measuring 30.0 cm by 40.0 cm is located inside a region of a spatially uniform magnetic field of 1.25 T, with the field perpendicular to the plane of the coil (Fig. 29.29). The coil is pulled out at a steady rate of 2.00 cm/s traveling perpendicular to the field lines. The region of the field ends abruptly as shown. Find the emf induced in this coil when it is (a) all inside the field; (b) partly inside the field; (c) all outside the field.

Figure **29.29** Exercise 29.10.

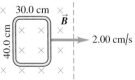

29.11. In a region of space, a magnetic field points in the $+x$-direction (toward the right). Its magnitude varies with position according to the formula $B_x = B_0 + bx$, where B_0 and b are positive constants, for $x \geq 0$. A flat coil of area A moves with uniform speed v from right to left with the plane of its area always perpendicular to this field. (a) What is the emf induced in this coil while it is to the right of the origin? (b) As viewed from the origin, what is the direction (clockwise or counterclockwise) of the current induced in the coil? (c) If instead the coil moved from left to right, what would be the answers to parts (a) and (b)?

29.12. Back emf. A motor with a brush-and-commutator arrangement, as described in Example 29.5, has a circular coil with radius 2.5 cm and 150 turns of wire. The magnetic field has magnitude 0.060 T, and the coil rotates at 440 rev/min. (a) What is the maximum emf induced in the coil? (b) What is the average back emf?

29.13. The armature of a small generator consists of a flat, square coil with 120 turns and sides with a length of 1.60 cm. The coil rotates in a magnetic field of 0.0750 T. What is the angular speed of the coil if the maximum emf produced is 24.0 mV?

29.14. A flat, rectangular coil of dimensions l and w is pulled with uniform speed v through a uniform magnetic field B with the plane of its area perpendicular to the field (Fig. 29.30). (a) Find the emf induced in this coil. (b) If the speed and magnetic field are both tripled, what is the induced emf?

Figure **29.30** Exercise 29.14.

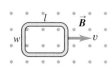

Figure **29.31** Exercise 29.15 and 29.30.

Section 29.3 Lenz's Law

29.15. A circular loop of wire is in a region of spatially uniform magnetic field, as shown in Fig. 29.31. The magnetic field is directed into the plane of the figure. Determine the direction (clockwise or counterclockwise) of the induced current in the loop when (a) B is increasing; (b) B is decreasing; (c) B is constant with value B_0. Explain your reasoning.

29.16. The current in Fig. 29.32 obeys the equation $I(t) = I_0 e^{-bt}$, where $b > 0$. Find the direction (clockwise or counterclockwise) of the current induced in the round coil for $t > 0$.

29.17. Using Lenz's law, determine the direction of the current in resistor ab of

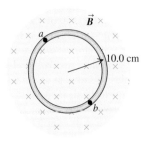

Figure **29.32** Exercise 29.16.

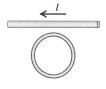

Fig. 29.33 when (a) switch S is opened after having been closed for several minutes; (b) coil B is brought closer to coil A with the switch closed; (c) the resistance of R is decreased while the switch remains closed.

Figure **29.33** Exercise 29.17.

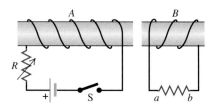

29.18. A cardboard tube is wrapped with two windings of insulated wire wound in opposite directions, as shown in Fig. 29.34. Terminals a and b of winding A may be connected to a battery through a reversing switch. State whether the induced current in the resistor R is from left to right or from right to left in the following circumstances: (a) the current in winding A is from a to b and is increasing; (b) the current in winding A is from b to a and is decreasing; (c) the current in winding A is from b to a and is increasing.

Figure **29.34** Exercise 29.18.

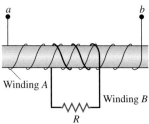

29.19. A small, circular ring is inside a larger loop that is connected to a battery and a switch, as shown in Fig. 29.35. Use Lenz's law to find the direction of the current induced in the small ring (a) just after switch S is closed; (b) after S has been closed a long time; (c) just after S has been reopened after being closed a long time.

Figure **29.35** Exercise 29.19.

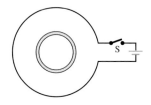

29.20. A 1.50-m-long metal bar is pulled to the right at a steady 5.0 m/s perpendicular to a uniform, 0.750-T magnetic field. The bar rides on parallel metal rails connected through a 25.0-Ω resistor, as shown in Fig. 29.36, so the apparatus makes a complete circuit. You can ignore the resistance of the bar and the rails. (a) Calculate the magnitude of the emf induced in the circuit. (b) Find the direction of the current induced in the circuit (i) using the magnetic force on the charges in the moving bar; (ii) using Faraday's law; (iii) using Lenz's law. (c) Calculate the current through the resistor.

Figure **29.36** Exercise 29.20 and Problem 29.64.

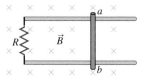

Section 29.4 Motional Electromotive Force

29.21. In Fig. 29.37 a conducting rod of length $L = 30.0$ cm moves in a magnetic field $\vec{B}$ of magnitude 0.450 T directed into the plane of the figure. The rod moves with speed $v = 5.00$ m/s in the direction shown. (a) what is the potential difference between the ends of the rod? (b) Which point, *a* to *b*, is at higher potential? (c) When the charges in the rod are in equilibrium, what are the magnitude and direction of the electric field within the rod? (d) When the charges in the rod are in equilibrium, which point, *a* or *b*, has an excess of positive charge? (e) What is the potential difference across the rod if it moves (i) parallel to *ab* and (ii) directly out of the page?

Figure 29.37 Exercise 29.21.

29.22. For the situation in Exercise 29.20, find (a) the motional emf in the bar and (b) the current through the resistor.

29.23. Are Motional emfs a Practical Source of Electricity? How fast (in m/s and mph) would a 5.00-cm copper bar have to move at right angles to a 0.650-T magnetic field to generate 1.50 V (the same as a AA battery) across its ends? Does this seem like a practical way to generate electricity?

29.24. Motional emfs in Transportation.   Airplanes and trains move through the earth's magnetic field at rather high speeds, so it is reasonable to wonder whether this field can have a substantial effect on them. We shall use a typical value of 0.50 G for the earth's field (a) The French TGV train and the Japanese "bullet train" reach speeds of up to 180 mph moving on tracks about 1.5 m apart. At top speed moving perpendicular to the earth's magnetic field, what potential difference is induced across the tracks as the wheels roll? Does this seem large enough to produce noticeable effects? (b) The Boeing 747-400 aircraft has a wingspan of 64.4 m and a cruising speed of 565 mph. If there is no wind blowing (so that this is also their speed relative to the ground), what is the maximum potential difference that could be induced between the opposite tips of the wings? Does this seem large enough to cause problems with the plane?

29.25. The conducting rod *ab* shown in Fig. 29.38 makes contact with metal rails *ca* and *db*. The apparatus is in a uniform magnetic field of 0.800 T, perpendicular to the plane of the figure (a) Find the magnitude of the emf induced in the rod when it is moving toward the right with a speed 7.50 m/s. (b) In what direction does the current flow in the rod? (c) If the resistance of the circuit *abdc* is 1.50 Ω (assumed to be constant), find the force (magnitude and direction) required to keep the rod moving to the right with a constant speed of 7.50 m/s. You can ignore friction. (d) Compare the rate at which mechanical work is done by the force (Fv) with the rate at which thermal energy is developed in the circuit ($I^2 R$).

Figure 29.38 Exercise 29.25.

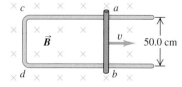

29.26. A square loop of wire with side length *L* and resistance *R* is moved at constant speed *v* across a uniform magnetic field confined to a square region whose sides are twice the length of those of the square loop (Fig. 29.39). (a) Graph the external force *F* needed to move the loop at constant speed as a function of the coordinate *x* from *x* = −2*L* to *x* = +2*L*. (The coordinate *x* is measured from the center of the magnetic-field region to the center of the loop. It is negative when the center of the loop is to the left

Figure 29.39 Exercise 29.26.

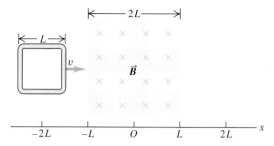

of the center of the magnetic-field region. Take positive force to be to the right.) (b) Graph the induced current in the loop as a function of *x*. Take counterclockwise currents to be positive.

29.27. A 1.41-m bar moves through a uniform, 1.20-T magnetic field with a speed of 2.50 m/s (Fig. 29.40). In each case, find the emf induced between the ends of this bar and identify which, if any, end (*a* or *b*) is at the higher potential. The bar moves in the direction of (a) the +*x*-axis; (b) the −*y*-axis; (c) the +*z*-axis. (d) How should this bar move so that the emf across its ends has the greatest possible value with *b* at a higher potential than *a*, and what is this maximum emf?

Figure 29.40 Exercise 29.27.

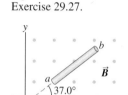

Section 29.5 Induced Electric Fields

29.28. A long, thin solenoid has 900 turns per meter and radius 2.50 cm. The current in the solenoid is increasing at a uniform rate of 60.0 A/s. What is the magnitude of the induced electric field at a point near the center of the solenoid and (a) 0.500 cm from the axis of the solenoid; (b) 1.00 cm from the axis of the solenoid?

29.29. The magnetic field within a long, straight solenoid with a circular cross section and radius *R* is increasing at a rate of dB/dt. (a) What is the rate of change of flux through a circle with radius r_1 inside the solenoid, normal to the axis of the solenoid, and with center on the solenoid axis? (b) Find the magnitude of the induced electric field inside the solenoid, at a distance r_1 from its axis. Show the direction of this field in a diagram. (c) What is the magnitude of the induced electric field *outside* the solenoid, at a distance r_2 from the axis? (d) Graph the magnitude of the induced electric field as a function of the distance *r* from the axis from *r* = 0 to *r* = 2*R*. (e) What is the magnitude of the induced emf in a circular turn of radius *R*/2 that has its center on the solenoid axis? (f) What is the magnitude of the induced emf if the radius in part (e) is *R*? (g) What is the induced emf if the radius in part (e) is 2*R*?

29.30. The magnetic field $\vec{B}$ at all points within the colored circle shown in Fig. 29.31 has an initial magnitude of 0.750 T. (The circle could represent approximately the space inside a long, thin solenoid.) The magnetic field is directed into the plane of the diagram and is decreasing at the rate of −0.0350 T/s. (a) What is the shape of the field lines of the induced electric field shown in Fig. 29.31, within the colored circle? (b) What are the magnitude and direction of this field at any point on the circular conducting ring with radius 0.100 m? (c) What is the current in the ring if its resistance is 4.00 Ω? (d) What is the emf between points *a* and *b* on the ring? (e) If the ring is cut at some point and the ends are separated slightly, what will be the emf between the ends?

29.31. A long, thin solenoid has 400 turns per meter and radius 1.10 cm. The current in the solenoid is increasing at a uniform rate *di/dt*. The induced electric field at a point near the center of the solenoid and 3.50 cm from its axis is 8.00×10^{-6} V/m. Calculate *di/dt*.

29.32. A metal ring 4.50 cm in diameter is placed between the north and south poles of large magnets with the plane of its area perpendicular to the magnetic field. These magnets produce an initial uniform field of 1.12 T between them but are gradually pulled apart, causing this field to remain uniform but decrease steadily at 0.250 T/s. (a) What is the magnitude of the electric field induced in the ring? (b) In which direction (clockwise or counterclockwise) does the current flow as viewed by someone on the south pole of the magnet?

29.33. A long, straight solenoid with a cross-sectional area of 8.00 cm^2 is wound with 90 turns of wire per centimeter, and the windings carry a current of 0.350 A. A second winding of 12 turns encircles the solenoid at its center. The current in the solenoid is turned off such that the magnetic field of the solenoid becomes zero in 0.0400 s. What is the average induced emf in the second winding?

Section 29.7 Displacement Current and Maxwell's Equations

29.34. A dielectric of permittivity 3.5×10^{-11} F/m completely fills the volume between two capacitor plates. For $t > 0$ the electric flux through the dielectric is $(8.0 \times 10^3 \text{ V} \cdot \text{m/s}^3)t^3$. The dielectric is ideal and nonmagnetic; the conduction current in the dielectric is zero. At what time does the displacement current in the dielectric equal 21 μA?

29.35. The electric flux through a certain area of a dielectric is $(8.76 \times 10^3 \text{ V} \cdot \text{m/s}^4)t^4$. The displacement current through that area is 12.9 pA at time $t = 26.1$ ms. Calculate the dielectric constant for the dielectric.

29.36. A parallel-plate, air-filled capacitor is being charged as in Fig. 29.23. The circular plates have radius 4.00 cm, and at a particular instant the conduction current in the wires is 0.280 A. (a) What is the displacement current density j_D in the air space between the plates? (b) What is the rate at which the electric field between the plates is changing? (c) What is the induced magnetic field between the plates at a distance of 2.00 cm from the axis? (d) At 1.00 cm from the axis?

29.37. Displacement Current in a Dielectric. Suppose that the parallel plates in Fig. 29.23 have an area of 3.00 cm^2 and are separated by a 2.50-mm-thick sheet of dielectric that completely fills the volume between the plates. The dielectric has dielectric constant 4.70. (You can ignore fringing effects.) At a certain instant, the potential difference between the plates is 120 V and the conduction current i_C equals 6.00 mA. At this instant, what are (a) the charge q on each plate; (b) the rate of change of charge on the plates; (c) the displacement current in the dielectric?

29.38. In Fig. 29.23 the capacitor plates have area 5.00 cm^2 and separation 2.00 mm. The plates are in vacuum. The charging current i_C has a *constant* value of 1.80 mA. At $t = 0$ the charge on the plates is zero. (a) Calculate the charge on the plates, the electric field between the plates, and the potential difference between the plates when $t = 0.500$ μs. (b) Calculate dE/dt, the time rate of change of the electric field between the plates. Does dE/dt vary in time? (c) Calculate the displacement current density j_D between the plates, and from this the total displacement current i_D. How do i_C and i_D compare?

29.39. Displacement Current in a Wire. A long, straight, copper wire with a circular cross-sectional area of 2.1 mm^2 carries a current of 16 A. The resistivity of the material is 2.0×10^{-8} $\Omega \cdot$ m.

(a) What is the uniform electric field in the material? (b) If the current is changing at the rate of 4000 A/s, at what rate is the electric field in the material changing? (c) What is the displacement current density in the material in part (b)? (*Hint:* Since K for copper is very close to 1, use $\epsilon = \epsilon_0$.) (d) If the current is changing as in part (b), what is the magnitude of the magnetic field 6.0 cm from the center of the wire? Note that both the conduction current and the displacement current should be included in the calculation of B. Is the contribution from the displacement current significant?

*Section 29.8 Superconductivity

*29.40. A long, straight wire made of a type-I superconductor carries a constant current I along its length. Show that the current cannot be uniformly spread over the wire's cross section but instead must all be at the surface.

*29.41. A type-II superconductor in an external field between B_{c1} and B_{c2} has regions that contain magnetic flux and have resistance, and also has superconducting regions. What is the resistance of a long, thin cylinder of such material?

*29.42. At temperatures near absolute zero, B_c approaches 0.142 T for vanadium, a type-I superconductor. The normal phase of vanadium has a magnetic susceptibility close to zero. Consider a long, thin vanadium cylinder with its axis parallel to an external magnetic field $\vec{B}_0$ in the $+x$-direction. At points far from the ends of the cylinder, by symmetry, all the magnetic vectors are parallel to the x-axis. At temperatures near absolute zero, what are the resultant magnetic field $\vec{B}$ and the magnetization $\vec{M}$ inside and outside the cylinder (far from the ends) for (a) $\vec{B}_0 = (0.130 \text{ T})\hat{i}$ and (b) $\vec{B}_0 = (0.260 \text{ T})\hat{i}$?

*29.43. The compound SiV_3 is a type-II superconductor. At temperatures near absolute zero the two critical fields are $B_{c1} = 55.0$ mT and $B_{c2} = 15.0$ T. The normal phase of SiV_3 has a magnetic susceptibility close to zero. A long, thin SiV_3 cylinder has its axis parallel to an external magnetic field $\vec{B}_0$ in the $+x$-direction. At points far from the ends of the cylinder, by symmetry, all the magnetic vectors are parallel to the x-axis. At a temperature near absolute zero the external magnetic field is slowly increased from zero. What are the resultant magnetic field $\vec{B}$ and the magnetization $\vec{M}$ inside the cylinder at points far from its ends (a) just before the magnetic flux begins to penetrate the material, and (b) just after the material becomes completely normal?

Problems

29.44. A Changing Magnetic Field. You are testing a new data-acquisition system. This system allows you to record a graph of the current in a circuit as a function of time. As part of the test, you are using a circuit made up of a 4.00-cm-radius, 500-turn coil of copper wire connected in series to a 600-Ω resistor. Copper has resistivity 1.72×10^{-8} $\Omega \cdot$ m, and the wire used for the coil has diameter 0.0300 mm. You place the coil on a table that is tilted 30.0° from the horizontal and that lies between the poles of an electromagnet. The electromagnet generates a vertically upward magnetic field that is zero for $t < 0$, equal to $(0.120 \text{ T}) \times (1 - \cos \pi t)$ for $0 \le t \le 1.00$ s, and equal to 0.240 T for $t > 1.00$ s. (a) Draw the graph that should be produced by your data-acquisition system. (This is a full-featured system, so the graph will include labels and numerical values on its axes.) (b) If you were looking vertically downward at the coil, would the current be flowing clockwise or counterclockwise?

29.45. In the circuit shown in Fig. 29.41 the capacitor has capacitance $C = 20\ \mu\text{F}$ and is initially charged to 100 V with the polarity shown. The resistor R_0 has resistance $10\ \Omega$. At time $t = 0$ the switch is closed. The small circuit is not connected in any way to the large one. The wire of the small circuit has a resistance of $1.0\ \Omega/\text{m}$ and contains 25 loops. The large circuit is a rectangle 2.0 m by 4.0 m, while the small one has dimensions $a = 10.0$ cm and $b = 20.0$ cm. The distance c is 5.0 cm. (The figure is not drawn to scale.) Both circuits are held stationary. Assume that only the wire nearest the small circuit produces an appreciable magnetic field through it. (a) Find the current in the large circuit 200 μs after S is closed. (b) Find the current in the small circuit 200 μs after S is closed. (*Hint:* See Problem 29.7.) (c) Find the direction of the current in the small circuit. (d) Justify why we can ignore the magnetic field from all the wires of the large circuit except for the wire closest to the small circuit.

Figure **29.41** Problem 29.45.

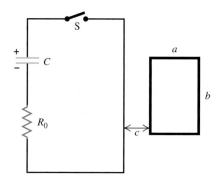

29.46. A flat coil is oriented with the plane of its area at right angles to a spatially uniform magnetic field. The magnitude of this field varies with time according to the graph in Fig. 29.42. Sketch a qualitative (but accurate!) graph of the emf induced in the coil as a function of time. Be sure to identify the times t_1, t_2, and t_3 on your graph.

Figure **29.42** Problem 29.46.

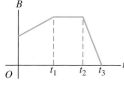

29.47. A circular wire loop of radius a and resistance R initially has a magnetic flux through it due to an external magnetic field. The external field then decreases to zero. A current is induced in the loop while the external field is changing; however, this current does not stop at the instant that the external field stops changing. The reason is that the current itself generates a magnetic field, which gives rise to a flux through the loop. If the current changes, the flux through the loop changes as well, and an induced emf appears in the loop to oppose the change. (a) The magnetic field at the center of the loop of radius a produced by a current i in the loop is given by $B = \mu_0 i/2a$. If we use the crude approximation that the field has this same value at all points within the loop, what is the flux of this field through the loop? (b) By using Faraday's law, Eq. (29.3), and the relationship $\mathcal{E} = iR$, show that after the external field has stopped changing, the current in the loop obeys the differential equation

$$\frac{di}{dt} = -\left(\frac{2R}{\pi\mu_0 a}\right)i$$

(c) If the current has the value i_0 at $t = 0$, the instant that the external field stops changing, solve the equation in part (b) to find i as a

function of time for $t > 0$. (*Hint:* In Section 26.4 we encountered a similar differential equation, Eq. (26.15), for the quantity q. This equation for i may be solved in the same way.) (d) If the loop has radius $a = 50$ cm and resistance $R = 0.10\ \Omega$, how long after the external field stops changing will the current be equal to $0.010i_0$ (that is, $\frac{1}{100}$ of its initial value)? (e) In solving the examples in this chapter, we ignored the effects described in this problem. Explain why this is a good approximation.

29.48. A coil is stationary in a spatially uniform, external, time-varying magnetic field. The emf induced in this coil as a function of time is shown if Fig. 29.43. Sketch a clear qualitative graph of the external magnetic field as a function of time, given that it started from zero. Include the points t_1, t_2, t_3, and t_4 on your graph.

Figure **29.43**
Problem 29.48.

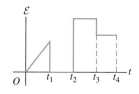

29.49. In Fig. 29.44 the loop is being pulled to the right at constant speed v. A constant current I flows in the long wire, in the direction shown. (a) Calculate the magnitude of the net emf $\mathcal{E}$ induced in the loop. Do this two ways: (i) by using Faraday's law of induction (*Hint:* See Problem 29.7) and (ii) by looking at the emf induced in each segment of the loop due to its motion. (b) Find the direction (clockwise or counterclockwise) of the current induced in the loop. Do this two ways: (i) using Lenz's law and (ii) using the magnetic force on charges in the loop. (c) Check your answer for the emf in part (a) in the following special cases to see whether it is physically reasonable: (i) The loop is stationary; (ii) the loop is very thin, so $a \rightarrow 0$; (iii) the loop gets very far from the wire.

Figure **29.44** Problem 29.49.

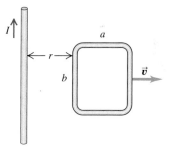

29.50. Suppose the loop in Fig. 29.45 is (a) rotated about the y-axis; (b) rotated about the x-axis; (c) rotated about an edge parallel to the z-axis. What is the maximum induced emf in each case if $A = 600\ \text{cm}^2$, $\omega = 35.0\ \text{rad/s}$, and $B = 0.450$ T?

Figure **29.45** Problem 29.50.

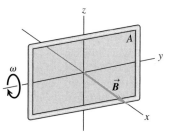

29.51. As a new electrical engineer for the local power company, you are assigned the project of designing a generator of sinusoidal ac voltage with a maximum voltage of 120 V. Besides plenty of wire, you have two strong magnets that can produce a constant uniform magnetic field of 1.5 T over a square area of 10.0 cm on a side when they are 12.0 cm apart. The basic design should consist of a square coil turning in the uniform magnetic field. To have an acceptable coil resistance, the coil can have at most 400 loops. What is the minimum rotation rate (in rpm) of the coil so it will produce the required voltage?

29.52. Make a Generator? You are shipwrecked on a deserted tropical island. You have some electrical devices that you could operate using a generator but you have no magnets. The earth's magnetic field at your location is horizontal and has magnitude 8.0×10^{-5} T, and you decide to try to use this field for a generator by rotating a large circular coil of wire at a high rate. You need to produce a peak emf of 9.0 V and estimate that you can rotate the coil at 30 rpm by turning a crank handle. You also decide that to have an acceptable coil resistance, the maximum number of turns the coil can have is 2000. (a) What area must the coil have? (b) If the coil is circular, what is the maximum translational speed of a point on the coil as it rotates? Do you think this device is feasible? Explain.

29.53. A flexible circular loop 6.50 cm in diameter lies in a magnetic field with magnitude 0.950 T, directed into the plane of the page as shown in Fig. 29.46. The loop is pulled at the points indicated by the arrows, forming a loop of zero area in 0.250 s. (a) Find the average induced emf in the circuit. (b) What is the direction of the current in R: from a to b or from b to a? Explain your reasoning.

Figure **29.46** Problem 29.53.

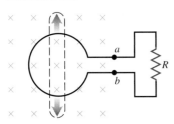

29.54. A Circuit Within a Circuit. Fig. 29.47 shows a small circuit within a larger one, both lying on the surface of a table. The switch is closed at $t = 0$ with the capacitor initially uncharged. Assume that the small circuit has no appreciable effect on the larger one. (a) What is the direction (a to b or to a) of the current in the resistor r (i) the instant after the switch is closed and (ii) one time constant after the switch is closed? (b) Sketch a graph of the current in the small circuit as a function of time, calling clockwise positive.

Figure **29.47** Problem 29.54.

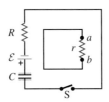

29.55. Terminal Speed. A conducting rod with length L, mass m, and resistance R moves without friction on metal rails as shown in Fig. 29.11. A uniform magnetic field $\vec{B}$ is directed into the plane of the figure. The rod starts from rest and is acted on by a constant force $\vec{F}$ directed to the right. The rails are infinitely long and have negligible resistance. (a) Graph the speed of the rod as a function of time. (b) Find an expression for the terminal speed (the speed when the acceleration of the rod is zero).

29.56. Terminal Speed. A bar of length $L = 0.8$ m is free to slide without friction on horizontal rails, as shown in Fig. 29.48. There is a uniform magnetic field $B = 1.5$ T directed into the plane

of the figure. At one end of the rails there is a battery with emf $\mathcal{E} = 12$ V and a switch. The bar has mass 0.90 kg and resistance 5.0 Ω, and all other resistance in the circuit can be ignored. The switch is closed at time $t = 0$. (a) Sketch the speed of the bar as a function of time. (b) Just after the switch is closed, what is the acceleration of the bar? (c) What is the acceleration of the bar when its speed is 2.0 m/s? (d) What is the terminal speed of the bar?

Figure **29.48** Problem 29.56.

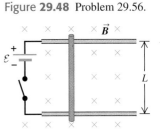

29.57. Antenna emf. A satellite, orbiting the earth at the equator at an altitude of 400 km, has an antenna that can be modeled as a 2.0-m-long rod. The antenna is oriented perpendicular to the earth's surface. At the equator, the earth's magnetic field is essentially horizontal and has a value of 8.0×10^{-5} T; ignore any changes in B with altitude. Assuming the orbit is circular, determine the induced emf between the tips of the antenna.

29.58. emf in a Bullet. At the equator, the earth's magnetic field is approximately horizontal, is directed toward the north, and has a value of 8×10^{-5} T. (a) Estimate the emf induced between the top and bottom of a bullet shot horizontally at a target on the equator if the bullet is shot toward the east. Assume the bullet has a length of 1 cm and a diameter of 0.4 cm and is traveling at 300 m/s. Which is at higher potential: the top or bottom of the bullet? (b) What is the emf if the bullet travels south? (c) What is the emf induced between the front and back of the bullet for any horizontal velocity?

29.59. A very long, cylindrical wire of radius R carries a current I_0 uniformly distributed across the cross section of the wire. Calculate the magnetic flux through a rectangle that has one side of length W running down the center of the wire and another side of length R, as shown in Fig. 29.49 (see Problem 29.7).

Figure **29.49** Problem 29.59.

29.60. A circular conducting ring with radius $r_0 = 0.0420$ m lies in the xy-plane in a region of uniform magnetic field $\vec{B} = B_0[1 - 3(t/t_0)^2 + 2(t/t_0)^3]\hat{k}$. In this expression, $t_0 = 0.0100$ s and is constant, t is time, $\hat{k}$ is the unit vector in the $+z$-direction, and $B_0 = 0.0800$ T and is constant. At points a and b (Fig. 29.50) there is a small gap in the ring with wires leading to an external circuit of resistance $R = 12.0$ Ω. There is no magnetic field at the location of the external circuit. (a) Derive an expression, as a function of time, for the total magnetic flux Φ_B through the ring. (b) Determine the emf induced in the ring at time $t = 5.00 \times 10^{-3}$ s. What is the polarity of the emf? (c) Because of the internal resistance of the ring, the current through R at the time given in part (b) is only 3.00 mA. Determine the internal resist-

Figure **29.50** Problem 29.60.

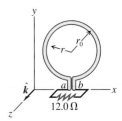

ance of the ring. (d) Determine the emf in the ring at a time $t = 1.21 \times 10^{-2}$ s. What is the polarity of the emf? (e) Determine the time at which the current through R reverses its direction.

29.61. The long, straight wire shown in Fig. 29.51a carries constant current I. A metal bar with length L is moving at constant velocity $\vec{v}$, as shown in the figure. Point a is a distance d from the wire. (a) Calculate the emf induced in the bar. (b) Which point, a or b, is at higher potential? (c) If the bar is replaced by a rectangular wire loop of resistance R (Fig. 29.51b), what is the magnitude of the current induced in the loop?

Figure **29.51** Problem 29.61.

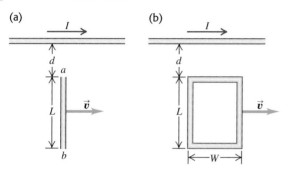

29.62. The cube shown in Fig. 29.52, 50.0 cm on a side, is in a uniform magnetic field of 0.120 T, directed along the positive y-axis. Wires A, C, and D move in the directions indicated, each with a speed of 0.350 m/s. (Wire A moves parallel to the xy-plane, C moves at an angle of 45.0° below the xy-plane, and D moves parallel to the xz-plane.) What is the potential difference between the ends of each wire?

Figure **29.52** Problem 29.62.

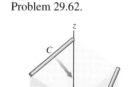

29.63. A slender rod, 0.240 m long, rotates with an angular speed of 8.80 rad/s about an axis through one end and perpendicular to the rod. The plane of rotation of the rod is perpendicular to a uniform magnetic field with a magnitude of 0.650 T. (a) What is the induced emf in the rod? (b) What is the potential difference between its ends? (c) Suppose instead the rod rotates at 8.80 rad/s about an axis through its center and perpendicular to the rod. In this case, what is the potential difference between the ends of the rod? Between the center of the rod and one end?

29.64. A Magnetic Exercise Machine. You have designed a new type of exercise machine with an extremely simple mechanism (Fig. 29.36). A vertical bar of silver (chosen for its low resistivity and because it makes the machine look cool) with length $L = 3.0$ m is free to move left or right without friction on silver rails. The entire apparatus is placed in a horizontal, uniform magnetic field of strength 0.25 T. When you push the bar to the left or right, the bar's motion sets up a current in the circuit that includes the bar. The resistance of the bar and the rails can be neglected. The magnetic field exerts a force on the current-carrying bar, and this force opposes the bar's motion. The health benefit is from the exercise that you do in working against this force. (a) Your design goal is that the person doing the exercise is to do work at the rate of 25 watts when moving the bar at a steady 2.0 m/s. What should be the resistance R? (b) You decide you want to be able to vary the power required from the person, to adapt

the machine to the person's strength and fitness. If the power is to be increased to 50 W by altering R while leaving the other design parameters constant, should R be increased or decreased? Calculate the value of R for 50 W. (c) When you start to construct a prototype machine, you find it is difficult to produce a 0.25-T magnetic field over such a large area. If you decrease the length of the bar to 0.20 m while leaving B, v, and R the same as in part (a), what will be the power required of the person?

29.65. A rectangular loop with width L and a slide wire with mass m are as shown in Fig. 29.53. A uniform magnetic field $\vec{B}$ is directed perpendicular to the plane of the loop into the plane of the figure. The slide wire is given an initial speed of v_0 and then released. There is no friction between the slide wire and the loop, and the resistance of the loop is negligible in comparison to the resistance R of the slide wire. (a) Obtain an expression for F, the magnitude of the force exerted on the wire while it is moving at speed v. (b) Show that the distance x that the wire moves before coming to rest is $x = mv_0R/a^2B^2$.

Figure **29.53** Problem 29.65.

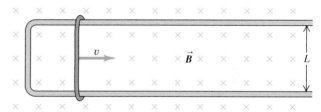

29.66. A 25.0-cm-long metal rod lies in the xy-plane and makes an angle of 36.9° with the positive x-axis and an angle of 53.1° with the positive y-axis. The rod is moving in the $+x$-direction with a speed of 4.20 m/s. The rod is in a uniform magnetic field $\vec{B} = (0.120 \text{ T})\hat{i} - (0.220 \text{ T})\hat{j} - (0.0900 \text{ T})\hat{k}$. (a) What is the magnitude of the emf induced in the rod? (b) Indicate in a sketch which end of the rod is at higher potential.

29.67. The magnetic field $\vec{B}$, at all points within a circular region of radius R, is uniform in space and directed into the plane of the page as shown in Fig. 29.54. (The region could be a cross section inside the windings of a long, straight solenoid.) If the magnetic field is increasing at a rate dB/dt, what are the magnitude and direction of the force on a stationary positive point charge q located at points a, b, and c? (Point a is a distance r above the center of the region, point b is a distance r to the right of the center, and point c is at the center of the region.)

Figure **29.54** Problem 29.67.

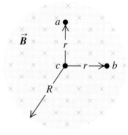

29.68. An airplane propeller of total length L rotates around its center with angular speed ω in a magnetic field that is perpendicular to the plane of rotation. Modeling the propeller as a thin, uniform bar, find the potential difference between (a) the center and either end of the propeller and (b) the two ends. (c) If the field is the earth's field of 0.50 G and the propeller turns at 220 rpm and is 2.0 m long, what is the potential difference between the middle and either end? It this large enough to be concerned about?

29.69. It is impossible to have a uniform electric field that abruptly drops to zero in a region of space in which the magnetic field is constant and in which there are no electric charges. To prove this statement, use the method of contradiction: Assume that such a case is possible and then show that your assumption contradicts a law of nature. (a) In the bottom half of a piece of paper, draw evenly spaced horizontal lines representing a uniform electric field to your right. Use dashed lines to draw a rectangle *abcda* with horizontal side *ab* in the electric-field region and horizontal side *cd* in the top half of your paper where $E = 0$. (b) Show that integration around your rectangle contradicts Faraday's law, Eq. (29.21).

29.70. Falling Square Loop. A vertically oriented, square loop of copper wire falls from a region where the field $\vec{B}$ is horizontal, uniform, and perpendicular to the plane of the loop, into a region where the field is zero. The loop is released from rest and initially is entirely within the magnetic-field region. Let the side length of the loop be *s* and let the diameter of the wire be *d*. The resistivity of copper is ρ_R and the density of copper is ρ_m. If the loop reaches its terminal speed while its upper segment is still in the magnetic-field region, find an expression for the terminal speed.

29.71. In a region of space where there are no conduction or displacement currents, it is impossible to have a uniform magnetic field that abruptly drops to zero. To prove this statement, use the method of contradiction: Assume that such a case *is* possible, and then show that your assumption contradicts a law of nature. (a) In the bottom half of a piece of paper, draw evenly spaced horizontal lines representing a uniform magnetic field to your right. Use dashed lines to draw a rectangle *abcda* with horizontal side *ab* in the magnetic-field region and horizontal side *cd* in the top half of your paper where $B = 0$. (b) Show that integration around your rectangle contradicts Ampere's law, Eq. (29.15).

29.72. A capacitor has two parallel plates with area *A* separated by a distance *d*. The space between plates is filled with a material having dielectric constant *K*. The material is not a perfect insulator but has resistivity ρ. The capacitor is initially charged with charge of magnitude Q_0 on each plate that gradually discharges by conduction through the dielectric. (a) Calculate the conduction current density $j_C(t)$ in the dielectric. (b) Show that at any instant the displacement current density in the dielectric is equal in magnitude to the conduction current density but opposite in direction, so the *total* current density is zero at every instant.

29.73. A rod of pure silicon (resistivity $\rho = 2300 \ \Omega \cdot m$) is carrying a current. The electric field varies sinusoidally with time according to $E = E_0 \sin \omega t$, where $E_0 = 0.450 \ V/m$, $\omega = 2\pi f$, and the frequency $f = 120$ Hz. (a) Find the magnitude of the maximum conduction current density in the wire. (b) Assuming $\epsilon = \epsilon_0$, find the maximum displacement current density in the wire, and compare with the result of part (a). (c) At what frequency *f* would the maximum conduction and displacement densities become equal if $\epsilon = \epsilon_0$ (which is not actually the case)? (d) At the frequency determined in part (c), what is the relative *phase* of the conduction and displacement currents?

Challenge Problems

29.74. A square, conducting, wire loop of side *L*, total mass *m*, and total resistance *R* initially lies in the horizontal *xy*-plane, with corners at $(x, y, z) = (0, 0, 0)$, $(0, L, 0)$, $(L, 0, 0)$, and $(L, L, 0)$. There is a uniform, upward magnetic field $\vec{B} = B\hat{k}$ in the space within and around the loop. The side of the loop that extends from $(0, 0, 0)$ to $(L, 0, 0)$ is held in place on the *x*-axis; the rest of the loop is free to pivot around this axis. When the loop is released, it begins to rotate due to the gravitational torque. (a) Find the *net* torque (magnitude and direction) that acts on the loop when it has rotated through an angle ϕ from its original orientation and is

rotating downward at an angular speed ω. (b) Find the angular acceleration of the loop at the instant described in part (a). (c) Compared to the case with zero magnetic field, does it take the loop a longer or shorter time to rotate through 90°? Explain. (d) Is mechanical energy conserved as the loop rotates downward? Explain.

29.75. A square conducting loop, 20.0 cm on a side, is placed in the same magnetic field as shown in Exercise 29.30. (See Fig. 29.55; the center of the square loop is at the center of the magnetic-field region.) (a) Copy Fig. 29.55, and draw vectors to show the directions and relative magnitudes of the induced electric field $\vec{E}$ at points *a*, *b*, and *c*. (b) Prove that the component of $\vec{E}$ along the loop has the same value at every point of the loop and is equal to that of the ring shown in Fig. 29.31 (see Exercise 29.30). (c) What current is induced in the loop if its resistance is 1.90 Ω? (d) What is the potential difference between points *a* and *b*?

Figure **29.55** Challenge Problem 29.75.

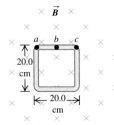

29.76. A uniform, square, conducting loop, 20.0 cm on a side, is placed in the same magnetic field as shown in Exercise 29.30, with side *ac* along a diameter and with point *b* at the center of the field (Fig. 29.56). (a) Copy Fig. 29.56, and draw vectors to show the direction and relative magnitude of the induced electric field $\vec{E}$ at the lettered points. (b) What is the induced emf in side *ac*? (c) What is the induced emf in the loop? (d) What is the current in the loop if its resistance is 1.90 Ω? (e) What is the potential difference between points *a* and *c*? Which is at higher potential?

Figure **29.56** Challenge Problem 29.76.

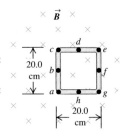

29.77. A metal bar with length *L*, mass *m*, and resistance *R* is placed on frictionless metal rails that are inclined at an angle ϕ above the horizontal. The rails have negligible resistance. A uniform magnetic field of magnitude *B* is directed downward as shown in Fig. 29.57. The bar is released from rest and slides down the rails. (a) Is the direction of the current induced in the bar from *a* to *b* or from *b* to *a*? (b) What is the terminal speed of the bar? (c) What is the induced current in the bar when the terminal speed has been reached? (d) After the terminal speed has been reached, at what rate is electrical energy being converted to thermal energy in the resistance of the bar? (e) After the terminal speed has been reached, at what rate is work being done on the bar by gravity? Compare your answer to that in part (d).

Figure **29.57** Challenge Problem 29.77.

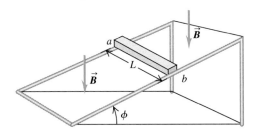

29.78. Consider a uniform metal disk rotating through a perpendicular magnetic field $\vec{B}$, as shown in Fig. 29.19a. The disk has mass m, radius R, and thickness t, is made of a material with resistivity ρ, and is rotating clockwise in Fig. 29.19a with angular speed ω. The magnetic field is directed into the plane of the disk. Suppose that the region to which the magnetic field is confined is not circular, as shown in Fig. 29.19a, but is a small square with sides of length L $(L \ll R)$ centered a distance d from the point O (the center of the disk). The sides of this square are horizontal and vertical in Fig. 29.19a. (a) Show that the current induced within the square is approximately equal to $I = \omega dBLt/\rho$. In which direction does this current flow? (*Hint:* Assume that the resistance to the current is confined to the region of the square. The current also encounters resistance as it flows outside the region to which the magnetic field is confined, as shown in Fig. 29.19b; however, this resistance is relatively small, since the current can flow through such a wide area. Recall Eq. (25.10) for resistance, given in Section 25.3.) (b) Show that the induced current gives rise to a torque of approximate magnitude $\tau = \omega d^2B^2L^2t/\rho$ that opposes the rotation of the disk (that is, a counterclockwise torque). (c) What would be the magnitudes and directions of the induced current and torque if the direction of $\vec{B}$ were still into the plane of the disk but the disk rotated counterclockwise? What if the direction of $\vec{B}$ were out of the plane and the disk rotated counterclockwise?

INDUCTANCE

LEARNING GOALS

By studying this chapter, you will learn:

- How a time-varying current in one coil can induce an emf in a second, unconnecetd coil.

- How to relate the induced emf in a circuit to the rate of change of current in the same circuit.

- How to calculate the energy stored in a magnetic field.

- How to analyze circuits that include both a resistor and an inductor (coil).

- Why electrical oscillations occur in circuits that include both an inductor and a capacitor.

- Why oscillations decay in circuits with an inductor, a resistor, and a capacitor.

?Many traffic lights change when a car rolls up to the intersection. How does the light sense the presence of the car?

Take a length of copper wire and wrap it around a pencil to form a coil. If you put this coil in a circuit, does it behave any differently than a straight piece of wire? Remarkably, the answer is yes. In an ordinary gasoline-powered car, a coil of this kind makes it possible for the 12-volt car battery to provide thousands of volts to the spark plugs, which in turn makes it possible for the plugs to fire and make the engine run. Other coils of this type are used to keep fluorescent light fixtures shining. Larger coils placed under city streets are used to control the operation of traffic signals. All of these applications, and many others, involve the *induction* effects that we studied in Chapter 29.

A changing current in a coil induces an emf in an adjacent coil. The coupling between the coils is described by their *mutual inductance*. A changing current in a coil also induces an emf in that same coil. Such a coil is called an *inductor,* and the relationship of current to emf is described by the *inductance* (also called *self-inductance*) of the coil. If a coil is initially carrying a current, energy is released when the current decreases; this principle is used in automotive ignition systems. We'll find that this released energy was stored in the magnetic field caused by the current that was initially in the coil, and we'll look at some of the practical applications of magnetic-field energy.

We'll also take a first look at what happens when an inductor is part of a circuit. In Chapter 31 we'll go on to study how inductors behave in alternating-current circuits; in that chapter we'll learn why inductors play an essential role in modern electronics, including communication systems, power supplies, and many other devices.

30.1 Mutual Inductance

In Section 28.4 we considered the magnetic interaction between two wires carrying *steady* currents; the current in one wire causes a magnetic field, which exerts a force on the current in the second wire. But an additional interaction arises between two circuits when there is a *changing* current in one of the circuits. Consider two neighboring coils of wire, as in Fig. 30.1. A current flowing in coil 1 produces a magnetic field $\vec{B}$ and hence a magnetic flux through coil 2. If the current in coil 1 changes, the flux through coil 2 changes as well; according to Faraday's law, this induces an emf in coil 2. In this way, a change in the current in one circuit can induce a current in a second circuit.

Let's analyze the situation shown in Fig. 30.1 in more detail. We will use lowercase letters to represent quantities that vary with time; for example, a time-varying current is i, often with a subscript to identify the circuit. In Fig. 30.1 a current i_1 in coil 1 sets up a magnetic field (as indicated by the blue lines), and some of these field lines pass through coil 2. We denote the magnetic flux through *each* turn of coil 2, caused by the current i_1 in coil 1, as Φ_{B2}. (If the flux is different through different turns of the coil, then Φ_{B2} denotes the *average* flux.) The magnetic field is proportional to i_1, so Φ_{B2} is also proportional to i_1. When i_1 changes, Φ_{B2} changes; this changing flux induces an emf $\mathcal{E}_2$ in coil 2, given by

$$\mathcal{E}_2 = -N_2 \frac{d\Phi_{B2}}{dt} \tag{30.1}$$

We could represent the proportionality of Φ_{B2} and i_1 in the form $\Phi_{B2} = (\text{constant})i_1$, but instead it is more convenient to include the number of turns N_2 in the relationship. Introducing a proportionality constant M_{21}, called the **mutual inductance** of the two coils, we write

$$N_2\Phi_{B2} = M_{21}i_1 \tag{30.2}$$

where Φ_{B2} is the flux through a *single* turn of coil 2. From this,

$$N_2 \frac{d\Phi_{B2}}{dt} = M_{21}\frac{di_1}{dt}$$

and we can rewrite Eq. (30.1) as

$$\mathcal{E}_2 = -M_{21}\frac{di_1}{dt} \tag{30.3}$$

That is, a change in the current i_1 in coil 1 induces an emf in coil 2 that is directly proportional to the rate of change of i_1 (Fig. 30.2).

We may also write the definition of mutual inductance, Eq. (30.2), as

$$M_{21} = \frac{N_2\Phi_{B2}}{i_1}$$

If the coils are in vacuum, the flux Φ_{B2} through each turn of coil 2 is directly proportional to the current i_1. Then the mutual inductance M_{21} is a constant that depends only on the geometry of the two coils (the size, shape, number of turns, and orientation of each coil and the separation between the coils). If a magnetic material is present, M_{21} also depends on the magnetic properties of the material. If the material has nonlinear magnetic properties, that is, if the relative permeability K_m (defined in Section 28.8) is not constant and magnetization is not proportional to magnetic field, then Φ_{B2} is no longer directly proportional to i_1. In that case the mutual inductance also depends on the value of i_1. In this discussion we will assume that any magnetic material present has constant K_m so that flux *is* directly proportional to current and M_{21} depends on geometry only.

We can repeat our discussion for the opposite case in which a changing current i_2 in coil 2 causes a changing flux Φ_{B1} and an emf $\mathcal{E}_1$ in coil 1. We might expect that the corresponding constant M_{12} would be different from M_{21} because in general the two coils are not identical and the flux through them is not the same. It turns out, however, that M_{12} is *always* equal to M_{21}, even when the two coils are not symmetric. We call this common value simply the mutual inductance,

30.1 A current i_1 in coil 1 gives rise to a magnetic flux through coil 2.

Mutual inductance: If the current in coil 1 is changing, the changing flux through coil 2 induces an emf in coil 2.

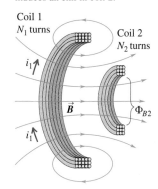

30.2 This electric toothbrush makes use of mutual inductance. The base contains a coil that is supplied with alternating current from a wall socket. This varying current induces an emf in a coil within the toothbrush itself, which is used to recharge the toothbrush battery.

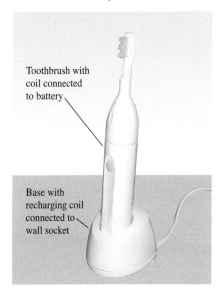

Toothbrush with coil connected to battery

Base with recharging coil connected to wall socket

denoted by the symbol M without subscripts; it characterizes completely the induced-emf interaction of two coils. Then we can write

$$\mathcal{E}_2 = -M\frac{di_1}{dt} \quad \text{and} \quad \mathcal{E}_1 = -M\frac{di_2}{dt} \qquad \text{(mutually induced emfs)} \quad (30.4)$$

where the mutual inductance M is

$$M = \frac{N_2\Phi_{B2}}{i_1} = \frac{N_1\Phi_{B1}}{i_2} \qquad \text{(mutual inductance)} \qquad (30.5)$$

The negative signs in Eq. (30.4) are a reflection of Lenz's law. The first equation says that a change in current in coil 1 causes a change in flux through coil 2, inducing an emf in coil 2 that opposes the flux change; in the second equation the roles of the two coils are interchanged.

CAUTION **Only a time-varying current induces an emf** Note that only a *time-varying* current in a coil can induce an emf and hence a current in a second coil. Equations (30.4) show that the induced emf in each coil is directly proportional to the *rate of change* of the current in the other coil, not to the value of the current. A steady current in one coil, no matter how strong, cannot induce a current in a neighboring coil. ∎

The SI unit of mutual inductance is called the **henry** (1 H), in honor of the American physicist Joseph Henry (1797–1878), one of the discoverers of electromagnetic induction. From Eq. (30.5), one henry is equal to *one weber per ampere.* Other equivalent units, obtained by using Eq. (30.4), are *one volt-second per ampere, one ohm-second,* or *one joule per ampere squared:*

$$1\,\text{H} = 1\,\text{Wb}/\text{A} = 1\,\text{V}\cdot\text{s}/\text{A} = 1\,\Omega\cdot\text{s} = 1\,\text{J}/\text{A}^2$$

Just as the farad is a rather large unit of capacitance (see Section 24.1), the henry is a rather large unit of mutual inductance. As Example 30.1 shows, typical values of mutual inductance can be in the millihenry (mH) or microhenry (μH) range.

Drawbacks and Uses of Mutual Inductance

Mutual inductance can be a nuisance in electric circuits, since variations in current in one circuit can induce unwanted emfs in other nearby circuits. To minimize these effects, multiple-circuit systems must be designed so that M is as small as possible; for example, two coils would be placed far apart or with their planes perpendicular.

Happily, mutual inductance also has many useful applications. A *transformer,* used in alternating-current circuits to raise or lower voltages, is fundamentally no different from the two coils shown in Fig. 30.1. A time-varying alternating current in one coil of the transformer produces an alternating emf in the other coil; the value of M, which depends on the geometry of the coils, determines the amplitude of the induced emf in the second coil and hence the amplitude of the output voltage. (We'll describe transformers in more detail in Chapter 31 after we've discussed alternating current in greater depth.)

Example 30.1 **Calculating mutual inductance**

In one form of Tesla coil (a high-voltage generator that you may have seen in a science museum), a long solenoid with length l and cross-sectional area A is closely wound with N_1 turns of wire. A coil with N_2 turns surrounds it at its center (Fig. 30.3). Find the mutual inductance.

SOLUTION

IDENTIFY: Mutual inductance occurs in this situation because a current in one of the coils sets up a magnetic field that causes a flux through the other coil.

30.3 A long solenoid with cross-sectional area A and N_1 turns (shown in black) is surrounded at its center by a coil with N_2 turns (shown in blue).

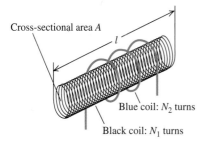

Cross-sectional area A

l

Blue coil: N_2 turns

Black coil: N_1 turns

SET UP: We use Eq. (30.5) to determine the mutual inductance M. According to that equation, we need to know either (a) the flux Φ_{B2} through each turn of the outer coil due to a current i_1 in the solenoid or (b) the flux Φ_{B1} through each turn of the solenoid due to a current i_2 in the outer coil. We choose option (a) since from Example 28.9 (Section 28.7) we have a simple expression for the field at the center of a long current-carrying solenoid, given by Eq. (28.23). Note that we are not given a value for the current i_1 in the solenoid. This omission is not cause for alarm, however: The value of the mutual inductance doesn't depend on the value of the current, so the quantity i_1 should cancel out when we calculate M.

EXECUTE: From Example 28.9, a long solenoid carrying current i_1 produces a magnetic field $\vec{B}_1$ that points along the axis of the solenoid. The field magnitude B_1 is proportional to i_1 and to n_1, the number of turns per unit length:

$$B_1 = \mu_0 n_1 i_1 = \frac{\mu_0 N_1 i_1}{l}$$

The flux through a cross section of the solenoid equals $B_1 A$. Since a very long solenoid produces no magnetic field outside of its coil, this is also equal to the flux Φ_{B2} through each turn of the outer, surrounding coil, no matter what the cross-sectional area of the outer coil. From Eq. (30.5) the mutual inductance M is

$$M = \frac{N_2 \Phi_{B2}}{i_1} = \frac{N_2 B_1 A}{i_1} = \frac{N_2}{i_1} \frac{\mu_0 N_1 i_1}{l} A = \frac{\mu_0 A N_1 N_2}{l}$$

EVALUATE: The mutual inductance of any two coils is always proportional to the product $N_1 N_2$ of their numbers of turns. Notice that the mutual inductance M depends only on the geometry of the two coils, not on the current.

Here's a numerical example to give you an idea of magnitudes. Suppose $l = 0.50$ m, $A = 10$ cm^2 = 1.0×10^{-3} m^2, $N_1 = 1000$ turns, and $N_2 = 10$ turns. Then

$$M = \frac{(4\pi \times 10^{-7} \text{ Wb/A} \cdot \text{m})(1.0 \times 10^{-3} \text{ m}^2)(1000)(10)}{0.50 \text{ m}}$$

$$= 25 \times 10^{-6} \text{ Wb/A} = 25 \times 10^{-6} \text{ H} = 25 \ \mu\text{H}$$

Example 30.2   Emf due to mutual inductance

In Example 30.1, suppose the current i_2 in the outer, surrounding coil is given by $i_2 = (2.0 \times 10^6 \text{ A/s})t$ (currents in wires can indeed increase this rapidly for brief periods). (a) At time $t = 3.0 \ \mu\text{s}$, what average magnetic flux through each turn of the solenoid is caused by the current in the outer, surrounding coil? (b) What is the induced emf in the solenoid?

SOLUTION

IDENTIFY: In Example 30.1 we found the mutual inductance by relating the current in the solenoid to the flux produced in the outer coil. In this example we are given the current in the outer coil and want to find the resulting flux in the solenoid. The key point is that the mutual inductance is the *same* in either case.

SET UP: Given the value of the mutual inductance $M = 25 \ \mu\text{H}$ from Example 30.1, we use Eq. (30.5) to determine the flux Φ_{B1} through each turn of the solenoid caused by a given current i_2 in the outer coil. We then use Eq. (30.4) to determine the emf induced in the solenoid by the time variation of the outer coil's current.

EXECUTE: (a) At time $t = 3.0 \ \mu\text{s} = 3.0 \times 10^{-6}$ s, the current in the outer coil (coil 2) is $i_2 = (2.0 \times 10^6 \text{ A/s})(3.0 \times 10^{-6} \text{ s}) =$

6.0 A. To find the average flux through each turn of the solenoid (coil 1), we solve Eq. (30.5) for Φ_{B1}:

$$\Phi_{B1} = \frac{Mi_2}{N_1} = \frac{(25 \times 10^{-6} \text{ H})(6.0 \text{ A})}{1000} = 1.5 \times 10^{-7} \text{ Wb}$$

Note that this is an *average* value; the flux can vary considerably between the center and the ends of the solenoid.

(b) The induced emf $\mathcal{E}_1$ is given by Eq. (30.4):

$$\mathcal{E}_1 = -M \frac{di_2}{dt} = -(25 \times 10^{-6} \text{ H}) \frac{d}{dt}[(2.0 \times 10^6 \text{ A/s})t]$$

$$= -(25 \times 10^{-6} \text{ H})(2.0 \times 10^6 \text{ A/s}) = -50 \text{ V}$$

EVALUATE: This is a substantial induced emf in response to a very rapid rate of change of current. In an operating Tesla coil, there is a high-frequency alternating current rather than a continuously increasing current as in this example; both di_2/dt and $\mathcal{E}_1$ alternate as well, with amplitudes that can be thousands of times larger than in this example.

Test Your Understanding of Section 30.1   Consider the Tesla coil described in Example 30.1. If you make the solenoid out of twice as much wire, so that it has twice as many turns and is twice as long, how much larger is the mutual inductance? (i) M is four times greater; (ii) M is twice as great; (iii) M is unchanged; (iv) M is $\frac{1}{2}$ as great; (v) M is $\frac{1}{4}$ as great.

(MP)

30.2 Self-Inductance and Inductors

In our discussion of mutual inductance we considered two separate, independent circuits: A current in one circuit creates a magnetic field and this field gives rise to a flux through the second circuit. If the current in the first circuit changes, the flux through the second circuit changes and an emf is induced in the second circuit.

An important related effect occurs even if we consider only a *single* isolated circuit. When a current is present in a circuit, it sets up a magnetic field that causes a magnetic flux through the *same* circuit; this flux changes when the current changes. Thus any circuit that carries a varying current has an emf induced in it by the variation in *its own* magnetic field. Such an emf is called a **self-induced emf.** By Lenz's law, a self-induced emf always opposes the change in the current that caused the emf and so tends to make it more difficult for variations in current to occur. For this reason, self-induced emfs can be of great importance whenever there is a varying current.

Self-induced emfs can occur in *any* circuit, since there is always some magnetic flux through the closed loop of a current-carrying circuit. But the effect is greatly enhanced if the circuit includes a coil with N turns of wire (Fig. 30.4). As a result of the current i, there is an average magnetic flux Φ_B through each turn of the coil. In analogy to Eq. (30.5) we define the **self-inductance L** of the circuit as

$$L = \frac{N\Phi_B}{i} \qquad \text{(self-inductance)} \tag{30.6}$$

30.4 The current i in the circuit causes a magnetic field $\vec{B}$ in the coil and hence a flux through the coil.

Self-inductance: If the current i in the coil is changing, the changing flux through the coil induces an emf in the coil.

When there is no danger of confusion with mutual inductance, the self-inductance is called simply the **inductance.** Comparing Eqs. (30.5) and (30.6), we see that the units of self-inductance are the same as those of mutual inductance; the SI unit of self-inductance is one henry.

If the current i in the circuit changes, so does the flux Φ_B; from rearranging Eq. (30.6) and taking the derivative with respect to time, the rates of change are related by

$$N\frac{d\Phi_B}{dt} = L\frac{di}{dt}$$

From Faraday's law for a coil with N turns, Eq. (29.4), the self-induced emf is $\mathcal{E} = -N\,d\Phi_B/dt$, so it follows that

$$\mathcal{E} = -L\frac{di}{dt} \qquad \text{(self-induced emf)} \tag{30.7}$$

The minus sign in Eq. (30.7) is a reflection of Lenz's law; it says that the self-induced emf in a circuit opposes any change in the current in that circuit. (Later in this section we'll explore in greater depth the significance of this minus sign.)

Equation (30.7) also states that the self-inductance of a circuit is the magnitude of the self-induced emf per unit rate of change of current. This relationship makes it possible to measure an unknown self-inductance in a relatively simple way: Change the current in the circuit at a known rate di/dt, measure the induced emf, and take the ratio to determine L.

Inductors As Circuit Elements

A circuit device that is designed to have a particular inductance is called an **inductor,** or a *choke.* The usual circuit symbol for an inductor is

Like resistors and capacitors, inductors are among the indispensable circuit elements of modern electronics. Their purpose is to oppose any variations in the current through the circuit. An inductor in a direct-current circuit helps to maintain a steady current despite any fluctuations in the applied emf; in an alternating-current circuit, an inductor tends to suppress variations of the current that are more rapid than desired. In this chapter and the next we will explore the behavior and applications of inductors in circuits in more detail.

To understand the behavior of circuits containing inductors, we need to develop a general principle analogous to Kirchhoff's loop rule (discussed in Section 26.2). To apply that rule, we go around a conducting loop, measuring potential differences across successive circuit elements as we go. The algebraic sum of these differences around any closed loop must be zero because the electric field produced by charges distributed around the circuit is *conservative.* In Section 29.7 we denoted such a conservative field as $\vec{E}_\mathrm{c}$.

When an inductor is included in the circuit, the situation changes. The magnetically induced electric field within the coils of the inductor is *not* conservative; as in Section 29.7, we'll denote it by $\vec{E}_\mathrm{n}$. We need to think very carefully about the roles of the various fields. Let's assume we are dealing with an inductor whose coils have negligible resistance. Then a negligibly small electric field is required to make charge move through the coils, so the *total* electric field $\vec{E}_\mathrm{c} + \vec{E}_\mathrm{n}$ within the coils must be zero, even though neither field is individually zero. Because $\vec{E}_\mathrm{c}$ is nonzero, we know there have to be accumulations of charge on the terminals of the inductor and the surfaces of its conductors, to produce this field.

Consider the circuit shown in Fig. 30.5; the box contains some combination of batteries and variable resistors that enables us to control the current i in the circuit. According to Faraday's law, Eq. (29.10), the line integral of $\vec{E}_\mathrm{n}$ around the circuit is the negative of the rate of change of flux through the circuit, which in turn is given by Eq. (30.7). Combining these two relationships, we get

$$\oint \vec{E}_\mathrm{n} \cdot d\vec{l} = -L\frac{di}{dt}$$

where we integrate clockwise around the loop (the direction of the assumed current). But $\vec{E}_\mathrm{n}$ is different from zero only within the inductor. Therefore the integral of $\vec{E}_\mathrm{n}$ around the whole loop can be replaced by its integral only from a to b through the inductor; that is,

$$\int_a^b \vec{E}_\mathrm{n} \cdot d\vec{l} = -L\frac{di}{dt}$$

Next, because $\vec{E}_\mathrm{c} + \vec{E}_\mathrm{n} = 0$ at each point within the inductor coils, we can rewrite this as

$$\int_a^b \vec{E}_\mathrm{c} \cdot d\vec{l} = L\frac{di}{dt}$$

But this integral is just the potential V_{ab} of point a with respect to point b, so we finally obtain

$$V_{ab} = V_a - V_b = L\frac{di}{dt} \tag{30.8}$$

We conclude that there is a genuine potential difference between the terminals of the inductor, associated with conservative, electrostatic forces, despite the fact that the electric field associated with the magnetic induction effect is nonconservative. Thus we are justified in using Kirchhoff's loop rule to analyze circuits that include inductors. Equation (30.8) gives the potential difference across an inductor in a circuit.

30.5 A circuit containing a source of emf and an inductor. The source is variable, so the current i and its rate of change di/dt can be varied.

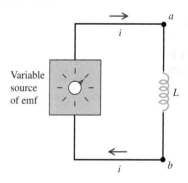

30.6 (a) The potential difference across a resistor depends on the current. (b), (c), (d) The potential difference across an inductor depends on the rate of change of the current.

(a) Resistor with current i flowing from a to b: potential drops from a to b.

$V_{ab} = iR > 0$

(b) Inductor with *constant* current i flowing from a to b: no potential difference.

i constant: $di/dt = 0$

$$V_{ab} = L\frac{di}{dt} = 0$$

$\mathcal{E} = 0$

(c) Inductor with *increasing* current i flowing from a to b: potential drops from a to b.

i increasing: $di/dt > 0$

$$V_{ab} = L\frac{di}{dt} > 0$$

$\mathcal{E}$

(d) Inductor with *decreasing* current i flowing from a to b: potential increases from a to b.

i decreasing: $di/dt < 0$

$$V_{ab} = L\frac{di}{dt} < 0$$

$\mathcal{E}$

30.7 These fluorescent light tubes are wired in series with an inductor, or ballast, that helps to sustain the current flowing through the tubes.

CAUTION **Self-induced emf opposes changes in current** Note that the self-induced emf does not oppose the current i itself; rather, it opposes any *change* (di/dt) in the current. Thus the circuit behavior of an inductor is quite different from that of a resistor. Figure 30.6 compares the behaviors of a resistor and an inductor and summarizes the sign relationships. ∎

Applications of Inductors

Because an inductor opposes changes in current, it plays an important role in fluorescent light fixtures (Fig. 30.7). In such fixtures, current flows from the wiring into the gas that fills the tube, ionizing the gas and causing it to glow. However, an ionized gas or *plasma* is a highly nonohmic conductor: The greater the current, the more highly ionized the plasma becomes and the lower its resistance. If a sufficiently large voltage is applied to the plasma, the current can grow so much that it damages the circuitry outside the fluorescent tube. To prevent this problem, an inductor or *magnetic ballast* is put in series with the fluorescent tube to keep the current from growing out of bounds.

The ballast also makes it possible for the fluorescent tube to work with the alternating voltage provided by household wiring. This voltage oscillates sinusoidally with a frequency of 60 Hz, so that it goes momentarily to zero 120 times per second. If there were no ballast, the plasma in the fluorescent tube would rapidly deionize when the voltage went to zero and the tube would shut off. With a ballast present, a self-induced emf sustains the current and keeps the tube lit. Magnetic ballasts are also used for this purpose in streetlights (which obtain their light from a glowing vapor of mercury or sodium atoms) and in neon lights. (In compact fluorescent lamps, the magnetic ballast is replaced by a more complicated scheme for regulating current. This scheme utilizes transistors, discussed in Chapter 42.)

The self-inductance of a circuit depends on its size, shape, and number of turns. For N turns close together, it is always proportional to N^2. It also depends on the magnetic properties of the material enclosed by the circuit. In the following examples we will assume that the circuit encloses only vacuum (or air, which from the standpoint of magnetism is essentially vacuum). If, however, the flux is concentrated in a region containing a magnetic material with permeability μ, then in the expression for B we must replace μ_0 (the permeability of vacuum) by $\mu = K_m\mu_0$, as discussed in Section 28.8. If the material is diamagnetic or paramagnetic, this replacement makes very little difference, since K_m is very close to 1. If the material is *ferromagnetic,* however, the difference is of crucial importance. A solenoid wound on a soft iron core having $K_m = 5000$ can have an inductance approximately 5000 times as great as that of the same solenoid with an air core. Ferromagnetic-core inductors are very widely used in a variety of electronic and electric-power applications.

An added complication is that with ferromagnetic materials the magnetization is in general not a linear function of magnetizing current, especially as saturation is approached. As a result, the inductance is not constant but can depend on current in a fairly complicated way. In our discussion we will ignore this complication and assume always that the inductance is constant. This is a reasonable assumption even for a ferromagnetic material if the magnetization remains well below the saturation level.

Because automobiles contain steel, a ferromagnetic material, driving an automobile over a coil causes an appreciable increase in the coil's inductance. **?** This effect is used in traffic light sensors, which use a large, current-carrying coil embedded under the road surface near an intersection. The circuitry connected to the coil detects the inductance change as a car drives over. When a preprogrammed number of cars have passed over the coil, the light changes to green to allow the cars through the intersection.

Example 30.3 Calculating self-inductance

A toroidal solenoid with cross-sectional area A and mean radius r is closely wound with N turns of wire (Fig. 30.8). The toroid is wound on a nonmagnetic core. Determine its self-inductance L. Assume that B is uniform across a cross section (that is, neglect the variation of B with distance from the toroid axis).

SOLUTION

IDENTIFY: Our target variable is the self-inductance L of the toroidal solenoid.

SET UP: We can determine L in one of two ways: either with Eq. (30.6), which requires knowing the flux Φ_B through each turn and the current i in the coil, or from Eq. (30.7), which requires knowing the self-induced emf $\mathcal{E}$ due to a given rate of change of

30.8 Determining the self-inductance of a closely wound toroidal solenoid. For clarity, only a few turns of the winding are shown. Part of the toroid has been cut away to show the cross-sectional area A and radius r.

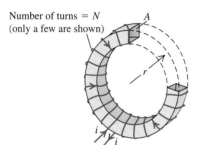

Number of turns = N
(only a few are shown)

current di/dt. We are not given any information about the emf, so we must use the first approach. We use the results of Example 28.10 (Section 28.7), in which we found the magnetic field in the interior of a toroidal solenoid.

EXECUTE: From Eq. (30.6), the self-inductance is $L = N\Phi_B/i$. From Example 28.10, the field magnitude at a distance r from the toroid axis is $B = \mu_0 Ni/2\pi r$. If we assume that the field has this magnitude over the entire cross-sectional area A, then the magnetic flux through the cross section is

$$\Phi_B = BA = \frac{\mu_0 NiA}{2\pi r}$$

The flux Φ_B is the same through each turn, and the self-inductance L is

$$L = \frac{N\Phi_B}{i} = \frac{\mu_0 N^2 A}{2\pi r} \qquad \text{(self-inductance of a toroidal solenoid)}$$

EVALUATE: Suppose $N = 200$ turns, $A = 5.0 \text{ cm}^2 = 5.0 \times 10^{-4} \text{ m}^2$, and $r = 0.10$ m; then

$$L = \frac{(4\pi \times 10^{-7} \text{ Wb/A} \cdot \text{m})(200)^2(5.0 \times 10^{-4} \text{ m}^2)}{2\pi(0.10 \text{ m})}$$
$$= 40 \times 10^{-6} \text{ H} = 40 \ \mu\text{H}$$

Later in this chapter we will use the expression $L = \mu_0 N^2 A/2\pi r$ for the inductance of a toroidal solenoid to help develop an expression for the energy stored in a magnetic field.

Example 30.4 Calculating self-induced emf

If the current in the toroidal solenoid in Example 30.3 increases uniformly from 0 to 6.0 A in 3.0 μs, find the magnitude and direction of the self-induced emf.

SOLUTION

IDENTIFY: We are given L, the self-inductance, and di/dt, the rate of change of the current. Our target variable is the self-induced emf.

SET UP: We calculate the emf using Eq. (30.7).

EXECUTE: The rate of change of the solenoid current is $di/dt = (6.0 \text{ A})/(3.0 \times 10^{-6} \text{ s}) = 2.0 \times 10^6 \text{ A/s}$. From Eq. (30.7), the magnitude of the induced emf is

$$|\mathcal{E}| = L\left|\frac{di}{dt}\right| = (40 \times 10^{-6} \text{ H})(2.0 \times 10^6 \text{ A/s}) = 80 \text{ V}$$

The current is increasing, so according to Lenz's law the direction of the emf is opposite to that of the current. This corresponds to the situation in Fig. 30.6c; the emf is in the direction from b to a, like a battery with a as the $+$ terminal and b the $-$ terminal, tending to oppose the current increase from the external circuit.

EVALUATE: This example shows that even a small inductance L can give rise to a substantial induced emf if the current changes rapidly.

Test Your Understanding of Section 30.2 Rank the following inductors in order of the potential difference V_{ab}, from most positive to most negative. In each case the inductor has zero resistance and the current flows from point a through the inductor to point b. (i) The current through a 2.0-μH inductor increases from 1.0 A to 2.0 A in 0.50 s; (ii) the current through a 4.0-μH inductor decreases from 3.0 A to 0 in 2.0 s; (iii) the current through a 1.0-μH inductor remains constant at 4.0 A; (iv) the current through a 1.0-μH inductor increases from 0 to 4.0 A in 0.25 s.

30.3 Magnetic-Field Energy

Establishing a current in an inductor requires an input of energy, and an inductor carrying a current has energy stored in it. Let's see how this comes about. In Fig. 30.5, an increasing current i in the inductor causes an emf $\mathcal{E}$ between its terminals, and a corresponding potential difference V_{ab} between the terminals of the source, with point a at higher potential than point b. Thus the source must be adding energy to the inductor, and the instantaneous power P (rate of transfer of energy into the inductor) is $P = V_{ab}i$.

Energy Stored in an Inductor

We can calculate the total energy input U needed to establish a final current I in an inductor with inductance L if the initial current is zero. We assume that the inductor has zero resistance, so no energy is dissipated within the inductor. Let the current at some instant be i and let its rate of change be di/dt; the current is increasing, so $di/dt > 0$. The voltage between the terminals a and b of the inductor at this instant is $V_{ab} = L\,di/dt$, and the rate P at which energy is being delivered to the inductor (equal to the instantaneous power supplied by the external source) is

$$P = V_{ab}i = Li\frac{di}{dt}$$

The energy dU supplied to the inductor during an infinitesimal time interval dt is $dU = P\,dt$, so

$$dU = Li\,di$$

The total energy U supplied while the current increases from zero to a final value I is

$$U = L\int_0^I i\,di = \frac{1}{2}LI^2 \qquad \text{(energy stored in an inductor)} \qquad (30.9)$$

After the current has reached its final steady value I, $di/dt = 0$ and no more energy is input to the inductor. When there is no current, the stored energy U is zero; when the current is I, the energy is $\frac{1}{2}LI^2$.

When the current decreases from I to zero, the inductor acts as a source that supplies a total amount of energy $\frac{1}{2}LI^2$ to the external circuit. If we interrupt the circuit suddenly by opening a switch or yanking a plug from a wall socket, the current decreases very rapidly, the induced emf is very large, and the energy may be dissipated in an arc across the switch contacts. This large emf is the electrical analog of the large force exerted by a car running into a brick wall and stopping very suddenly.

30.9 A resistor is a device in which energy is irrecoverably dissipated. By contrast, energy stored in a current-carrying inductor can be recovered when the current decreases to zero.

Resistor with current i: energy is *dissipated*.

Inductor with current i: energy is *stored*.

CAUTION   Energy, resistors, and inductors It's important not to confuse the behavior of resistors and inductors where energy is concerned (Fig. 30.9). Energy flows into a resistor whenever a current passes through it, whether the current is steady or varying; this energy is dissipated in the form of heat. By contrast, energy flows into an ideal, zero-resistance inductor only when the current in the inductor *increases*. This energy is not dissipated; it is stored in the inductor and released when the current *decreases*. When a steady current flows through an inductor, there is no energy flow in or out. ∎

Magnetic Energy Density

The energy in an inductor is actually stored in the magnetic field within the coil, just as the energy of a capacitor is stored in the electric field between its plates. We can develop relationships for magnetic-field energy analogous to those we obtained for electric-field energy in Section 24.3 [Eqs. (24.9) and (24.11)]. We will concentrate on one simple case, the ideal toroidal solenoid. This system has the advantage that its magnetic field is confined completely to a finite region of space within its core. As in Example 30.3, we assume that the cross-sectional area A is small enough that we can pretend that the magnetic field is uniform over the area. The volume V enclosed by the toroidal solenoid is approximately equal to the circumference $2\pi r$ multiplied by the area A: $V = 2\pi rA$. From Example 30.3, the self-inductance of the toroidal solenoid with vacuum within its coils is

$$L = \frac{\mu_0 N^2 A}{2\pi r}$$

From Eq. (30.9), the energy U stored in the toroidal solenoid when the current is I is

$$U = \frac{1}{2}LI^2 = \frac{1}{2}\frac{\mu_0 N^2 A}{2\pi r}I^2$$

The magnetic field and therefore this energy are localized in the volume $V = 2\pi rA$ enclosed by the windings. The energy *per unit volume,* or *magnetic energy density,* is $u = U/V$:

$$u = \frac{U}{2\pi rA} = \frac{1}{2}\mu_0\frac{N^2 I^2}{(2\pi r)^2}$$

We can express this in terms of the magnitude B of the magnetic field inside the toroidal solenoid. From Eq. (28.24) in Example 28.10 (Section 28.7), this is

$$B = \frac{\mu_0 NI}{2\pi r}$$

and so

$$\frac{N^2 I^2}{(2\pi r)^2} = \frac{B^2}{\mu_0^2}$$

When we substitute this into the above equation for u, we finally find the expression for **magnetic energy density** in vacuum:

$$u = \frac{B^2}{2\mu_0} \qquad \text{(magnetic energy density in vacuum)} \qquad (30.10)$$

This is the magnetic analog of the energy per unit volume in an *electric* field in vacuum, $u = \frac{1}{2}\epsilon_0 E^2$, which we derived in Section 24.3.

When the material inside the toroid is not vacuum but a material with (constant) magnetic permeability $\mu = K_m\mu_0$, we replace μ_0 by μ in Eq. (30.10). The energy per unit volume in the magnetic field is then

$$u = \frac{B^2}{2\mu} \qquad \text{(magnetic energy density in a material)} \qquad (30.11)$$

Although we have derived Eq. (30.11) only for one special situation, it turns out to be the correct expression for the energy per unit volume associated with *any* magnetic-field configuration in a material with constant permeability. For vacuum, Eq. (30.11) reduces to Eq. (30.10). We will use the expressions for electric-field and magnetic-field energy in Chapter 32 when we study the energy associated with electromagnetic waves.

30.10 The energy required to fire an automobile spark plug is derived from magnetic-field energy stored in the ignition coil.

Magnetic-field energy plays an important role in the ignition systems of gasoline-powered automobiles. A primary coil of about 250 turns is connected to the car's battery and produces a strong magnetic field. This coil is surrounded by a secondary coil with some 25,000 turns of very fine wire. When it is time for a spark plug to fire (see Fig. 20.5 in Section 20.3), the current to the primary coil is interrupted, the magnetic field quickly drops to zero, and an emf of tens of thousands of volts is induced in the secondary coil. The energy stored in the magnetic field thus goes into a powerful pulse of current that travels through the secondary coil to the spark plug, generating the spark that ignites the fuel–air mixture in the engine's cylinders (Fig. 30.10).

Example 30.5 Storing energy in an inductor

The electric-power industry would like to find efficient ways to store surplus energy generated during low-demand hours to help meet customer requirements during high-demand hours. Perhaps a large inductor can be used. What inductance would be needed to store $1.00 \text{ kW} \cdot \text{h}$ of energy in a coil carrying a 200-A current?

SOLUTION

IDENTIFY: We are given the required amount of stored energy U and the current I. Our target variable is the self-inductance L.

SET UP: We solve for L using Eq. (30.9)

EXECUTE: We have $I = 200$ A and $U = 1.00 \text{ kW} \cdot \text{h} = (1.00 \times 10^3 \text{ W})(3600 \text{ s}) = 3.60 \times 10^6$ J. Solving Eq. (30.9) for L, we find

$$L = \frac{2U}{I^2} = \frac{2(3.60 \times 10^6 \text{ J})}{(200 \text{ A})^2} = 180 \text{ H}$$

This is more than a *million* times greater than the self-inductance of the toroidal solenoid of Example 30.3 (Section 30.2).

EVALUATE: Conventional wires that are to carry 200 A would have to be of large diameter to keep the resistance low and avoid unacceptable energy losses due to I^2R heating. As a result, a 180-H inductor using conventional wire would be very large (room-size). A superconducting inductor could be much smaller, since the resistance of a superconductor is zero and much thinner wires could be used; one drawback is that the wires would have to be kept at low temperature to remain superconducting, and energy would have to be used to maintain this low temperature. As a result, this scheme is impractical with present technology.

Example 30.6 Magnetic energy density

In a proton accelerator used in elementary particle physics experiments, the trajectories of protons are controlled by bending magnets that produce a magnetic field of 6.6 T. What is the energy density in this field in the vacuum between the poles of such a magnet?

SOLUTION

IDENTIFY: Our target variable is the magnetic energy density u. we are given the magnitude B of the magnetic field.

SET UP: In a vacuum, $\mu = \mu_0$ and the energy density is given by Eq. (30.10).

EXECUTE: The energy density in the magnetic field is

$$u = \frac{B^2}{2\mu_0} = \frac{(6.6 \text{ T})^2}{2(4\pi \times 10^{-7} \text{ T} \cdot \text{m/A})} = 1.73 \times 10^7 \text{ J/m}^3$$

EVALUATE: As an interesting comparison, the heat of combustion of natural gas, expressed on an energy per unit volume basis, is about $3.8 \times 10^7 \text{ J/m}^3$.

Test Your Understanding of Section 30.3 The current in a solenoid is reversed in direction while keeping the same magnitude. (a) Does this change the magnetic field within the solenoid? (b) Does this change the magnetic energy density in the solenoid?

30.4 The *R-L* Circuit

Let's look at some examples of the circuit behavior of an inductor. One thing is clear already; an inductor in a circuit makes it difficult for rapid changes in current to occur, thanks to the effects of self-induced emf. Equation (30.7) shows that the greater the rate of change of current di/dt, the greater the self-induced emf and the greater the potential difference between the inductor terminals. This equation, together with Kirchhoff's rules (see Section 26.2), gives us the principles we need to analyze circuits containing inductors.

Act|v
ONLINE
Phys|cs

14.1   The *RL* Circuit

Problem-Solving Strategy 30.1 | **Inductors in Circuits**

IDENTIFY *the relevant concepts:*   An inductor is just another circuit element, like a source of emf, a resistor, or a capacitor. One key difference is that when an inductor is included in a circuit, all the voltages, currents, and capacitor charges are in general functions of time, not constants as they have been in most of our previous circuit analysis. But Kirchhoff's rules, which we studied in Section 26.2, are still valid. When the voltages and currents vary with time, Kirchhoff's rules hold at each instant of time.

SET UP *the problem* using the following steps:
1. Follow the same procedure described in Problem-Solving Strategy 26.2 in Section 26.2. (Now would be an excellent time to review that strategy.) Draw a large circuit diagram and label all quantities, known and unknown. Apply the junction rule immediately at any junction.
2. Determine which quantities are the target variables.

EXECUTE *the solution* as follows:
1. As in Problem-Solving Strategy 26.2, apply Kirchhoff's loop rule to each loop in the circuit.

2. As in all circuit analysis, getting the correct sign for each potential difference is essential. (You should review the rules given in Problem-Solving Strategy 26.2.) To get the correct sign for the potential difference between the terminals of an inductor, remember Lenz's law and the sign rule described in Section 30.2 in conjunction with Eq. (30.7) and Fig. 30.6. In Kirchhoff's loop rule, when we go through an inductor in the *same* direction as the assumed current, we encounter a voltage *drop* equal to $L\,di/dt$, so the corresponding term in the loop equation is $-L\,di/dt$. When we go through an inductor in the *opposite* direction from the assumed current, the potential difference is reversed and the term to use in the loop equation is $+L\,di/dt$.
3. As always, solve for the target variables.

EVALUATE *your answer:*   Check whether your answer is consistent with the way that inductors behave. If the current through an inductor is changing, your result should indicate that the potential difference across the inductor opposes the change. If not, you probably used an incorrect sign somewhere in your calculation.

Current Growth in an *R-L* Circuit

We can learn several basic things about inductor behavior by analyzing the circuit of Fig. 30.11. A circuit that includes both a resistor and an inductor, and possibly a source of emf, is called an ***R-L* circuit.** The inductor helps to prevent rapid changes in current, which can be useful if a steady current is required but the external source has a fluctuating emf. The resistor R may be a separate circuit element, or it may be the resistance of the inductor windings; every real-life inductor has some resistance unless it is made of superconducting wire. By closing switch S_1, we can connect the *R-L* combination to a source with constant emf $\mathcal{E}$. (We assume that the source has zero internal resistance, so the terminal voltage equals the emf.)

Suppose both switches are open to begin with, and then at some initial time $t = 0$ we close switch S_1. The current cannot change suddenly from zero to some final value, since di/dt and the induced emf in the inductor would both be infinite. Instead, the current begins to grow at a rate that depends only on the value of L in the circuit.

Let i be the current at some time t after switch S_1 is closed, and let di/dt be its rate of change at that time. The potential difference v_{ab} across the resistor at that time is

$$v_{ab} = iR$$

and the potential difference v_{bc} across the inductor is

$$v_{bc} = L\frac{di}{dt}$$

30.11 An *R-L* circuit.

Closing switch S_1 connects the *R-L* combination in series with a source of emf $\mathcal{E}$.

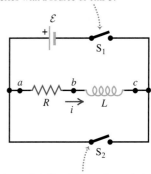

Closing switch S_2 while opening switch S_1 disconnnects the combination from the source.

Note that if the current is in the direction shown in Fig. 30.11 and is increasing, then both v_{ab} and v_{bc} are positive; a is at a higher potential than b, which in turn is at a higher potential than c. (Compare to Figs. 30.6a and c.) We apply Kirchhoff's loop rule, starting at the negative terminal and proceeding counterclockwise around the loop:

$$\mathcal{E} - ir - L\frac{di}{dt} = 0 \tag{30.12}$$

Solving this for di/dt, we find that the rate of increase of current is

$$\frac{di}{dt} = \frac{\mathcal{E} - iR}{L} = \frac{\mathcal{E}}{L} - \frac{R}{L}i \tag{30.13}$$

At the instant that switch S_1 is first closed, $i = 0$ and the potential drop across R is zero. The initial rate of change of current is

$$\left(\frac{di}{dt}\right)_{\text{initial}} = \frac{\mathcal{E}}{L}$$

As we would expect, the greater the inductance L, the more slowly the current increases.

As the current increases, the term $(R/L)i$ in Eq. (30.13) also increases, and the *rate* of increase of current given by Eq. (30.13) becomes smaller and smaller. This means that the current is approaching a final, steady-state value I. When the current reaches this value, its rate of increase is zero. Then Eq. (30.13) becomes

$$\left(\frac{di}{dt}\right)_{\text{final}} = 0 = \frac{\mathcal{E}}{L} - \frac{R}{L}I \quad \text{and}$$

$$I = \frac{\mathcal{E}}{R}$$

The *final* current I does not depend on the inductance L; it is the same as it would be if the resistance R alone were connected to the source with emf $\mathcal{E}$.

Figure 30.12 shows the behavior of the current as a function of time. To derive the equation for this curve (that is, an expression for current as a function of time), we proceed just as we did for the charging capacitor in Section 26.4. First we rearrange Eq. (30.13) to the form

$$\frac{di}{i - (\mathcal{E}/R)} = -\frac{R}{L}dt$$

This separates the variables, with i on the left side and t on the right. Then we integrate both sides, renaming the integration variables i' and t' so that we can use i and t as the upper limits. (The lower limit for each integral is zero, corresponding to zero current at the initial time $t = 0$.) We get

$$\int_0^i \frac{di'}{i' - (\mathcal{E}/R)} = -\int_0^t \frac{R}{L}dt'$$

$$\ln\left(\frac{i - (\mathcal{E}/R)}{-\mathcal{E}/R}\right) = -\frac{R}{L}t$$

Now we take exponentials of both sides and solve for i. We leave the details for you to work out; the final result is

$$i = \frac{\mathcal{E}}{R}\left(1 - e^{-(R/L)t}\right) \quad \text{(current in an } R\text{-}L \text{ circuit with emf)} \tag{30.14}$$

This is the equation of the curve in Fig. 30.12. Taking the derivative of Eq. (30.14), we find

$$\frac{di}{dt} = \frac{\mathcal{E}}{L}e^{-(R/L)t} \tag{30.15}$$

30.12 Graph of i versus t for growth of current in an R-L circuit with an emf in series. The final current is $I = \mathcal{E}/R$; after one time constant τ, the current is $1 - 1/e$ of this value.

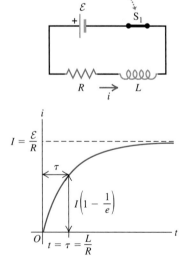

Switch S_1 is closed at $t = 0$.

At time $t = 0$, $i = 0$ and $di/dt = \mathcal{E}/L$. As $t \to \infty$, $i \to \mathcal{E}/R$ and $di/dt \to 0$, as we predicted.

As Fig. 30.12 shows, the instantaneous current i first rises rapidly, then increases more slowly and approaches the final value $I = \mathcal{E}/R$ asymptotically. At a time equal to L/R the current has risen to $(1 - 1/e)$, or about 63%, of its final value. The quantity L/R is therefore a measure of how quickly the current builds toward its final value; this quantity is called the **time constant** for the circuit, denoted by τ:

$$\tau = \frac{L}{R} \qquad \text{(time constant for an } R\text{-}L \text{ circuit)} \qquad (30.16)$$

In a time equal to 2τ, the current reaches 86% of its final value; in 5τ, 99.3%; and in 10τ, 99.995%. (Compare the discussion in Section 26.4 of charging a capacitor of capacitance C that was in series with a resistor of resistance R; the time constant for that situation was the product RC.)

The graphs of i versus t have the same general shape for all values of L. For a given value of R, the time constant τ is greater for greater values of L. When L is small, the current rises rapidly to its final value; when L is large, it rises more slowly. For example, if $R = 100\ \Omega$ and $L = 10\ H$,

$$\tau = \frac{L}{R} = \frac{10\ \text{H}}{100\ \Omega} = 0.10\ \text{s}$$

and the current increases to about 63% of its final value in 0.10 s. (Recall that $1\ \text{H} = 1\ \Omega \cdot \text{s}$.) But if $L = 0.010\ \text{H}$, $\tau = 1.0 \times 10^{-4}\ \text{s} = 0.10\ \text{ms}$, and the rise is much more rapid.

Energy considerations offer us additional insight into the behavior of an R-L circuit. The instantaneous rate at which the source delivers energy to the circuit is $P = \mathcal{E}i$. The instantaneous rate at which energy is dissipated in the resistor is i^2R, and the rate at which energy is stored in the inductor is $iv_{bc} = Li\ di/dt$ [or, equivalently, $(d/dt)(\frac{1}{2}Li^2) = Li\ di/dt$]. When we multiply Eq. (30.12) by i and rearrange, we find

$$\mathcal{E}i = i^2R + Li\frac{di}{dt} \qquad (30.17)$$

Of the power $\mathcal{E}i$ supplied by the source, part (i^2R) is dissipated in the resistor and part $(Li\ di/dt)$ goes to store energy in the inductor. This discussion is completely analogous to our power analysis for a charging capacitor, given at the end of Section 26.4.

Example 30.7   Analyzing an *R-L* circuit

A sensitive electronic device of resistance 175 Ω is to be connected to a source of emf by a switch. The device is designed to operate with a current of 36 mA, but to avoid damage to the device, the current can rise to no more than 4.9 mA in the first 58 μs after the switch is closed. To protect the device, it is connected in series with an inductor as in Fig. 30.11; the switch in question is S_1. (a) What emf must the source have? Assume negligible internal resistance. (b) What inductance is required? (c) What is the time constant?

SOLUTION

IDENTIFY: This problem concerns current growth in an R-L circuit, so we can use the ideas of this section.

SET UP: Figure 30.12 shows that the final current is $I = \mathcal{E}/R$. Since the resistance is given, the emf is determined by the require-

ment that the final current is to be 36 mA. The other requirement is that the current be no more than $i = 4.9$ mA at $t = 58\ \mu$s; to satisfy this, we use Eq. (30.14) for the current as a function of time and solve for the inductance, which is the only unknown quantity. Equation (30.16) then tells us the time constant.

EXECUTE: (a) Using $I = 36$ mA $= 0.036$ A and $R = 175\ \Omega$ in the expression $I = \mathcal{E}/R$ for the final current and solving for the emf, we find

$$\mathcal{E} = IR = (0.036\ \text{A})(175\ \Omega) = 6.3\ \text{V}$$

(b) To find the required inductance, we solve Eq. (30.14) for L. First we multiply through by $(-R/\mathcal{E})$ and then add 1 to both sides to obtain

$$1 - \frac{iR}{\mathcal{E}} = e^{-(R/L)t}$$

Continued

Then we take natural logs of both sides, solve for L, and insert the numbers:

$$L = \frac{-Rt}{\ln(1 - iR/\mathcal{E})}$$

$$= \frac{-(175\ \Omega)(58 \times 10^{-6}\ \text{s})}{\ln[1 - (4.9 \times 10^{-3}\ \text{A})(175\ \Omega)/(6.3\ \text{V})]} = 69\ \text{mH}$$

(c) From Eq. (30.16),

$$\tau = \frac{L}{R} = \frac{69 \times 10^{-3}\ \text{H}}{175\ \Omega} = 3.9 \times 10^{-4}\ \text{s} = 390\ \mu\text{s}$$

EVALUATE: We note that 58 μs is much less than the time constant. In 58 μs the current builds up only from zero to 4.9 mA, a small fraction of its final value of 36 mA; after 390 μs the current equals $(1 - 1/e)$ of its final value, or about $(0.63)(36\ \text{mA}) = 23\ \text{mA}$.

Current Decay in an R-L Circuit

30.13 Graph of i versus t for decay of current in an R-L circuit. After one time constant τ, the current is $1/e$ of its initial value.

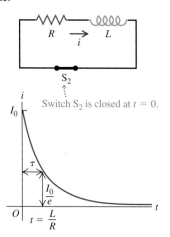

Switch S_2 is closed at $t = 0$.

Now suppose switch S_1 in the circuit of Fig. 30.11 has been closed for a while and the current has reached the value I_0. Resetting our stopwatch to redefine the initial time, we close switch S_2 at time $t = 0$, bypassing the battery. (At the same time we should open S_1 to save the battery from ruin.) The current through R and L does not instantaneously go to zero but decays smoothly, as shown in Fig. 30.13. The Kirchhoff's-rule loop equation is obtained from Eq. (30.12) by simply omitting the $\mathcal{E}$ term. We challenge you to retrace the steps in the above analysis and show that the current i varies with time according to

$$i = I_0 e^{-(R/L)t} \tag{30.18}$$

where I_0 is the initial current at time $t = 0$. The time constant, $\tau = L/R$, is the time for current to decrease to $1/e$, or about 37%, of its original value. In time 2τ it has dropped to 13.5%, in time 5τ to 0.67%, and in 10τ to 0.0045%.

The energy that is needed to maintain the current during this decay is provided by the energy stored in the magnetic field of the inductor. The detailed energy analysis is simpler this time. In place of Eq. (30.17) we have

$$0 = i^2 R + Li\frac{di}{dt} \tag{30.19}$$

In this case, $Li\ di/dt$ is negative; Eq. (30.19) shows that the energy stored in the inductor *decreases* at a rate equal to the rate of dissipation of energy $i^2 R$ in the resistor.

This entire discussion should look familiar; the situation is very similar to that of a charging and discharging capacitor, analyzed in Section 26.4. It would be a good idea to compare that section with our discussion of the R-L circuit.

Example 30.8 **Energy in an R-L circuit**

When the current in an R-L circuit is decaying, what fraction of the original energy stored in the inductor has been dissipated after 2.3 time constants?

SOLUTION

IDENTIFY: This problem concerns current decay in an R-L circuit as well as the relationship between the current in an inductor and the amount of stored energy.

SET UP: The current i at any time t for this situation is given by Eq. (30.18). The stored energy associated with this current is given by Eq. (30.9), $U = \frac{1}{2}Li^2$.

EXECUTE: From Eq. (30.18), the current i at any time t is

$$i = I_0 e^{-(R/L)t}$$

The energy U in the inductor at *any* time is obtained by substituting this expression into $U = \frac{1}{2}Li^2$. We obtain

$$U = \frac{1}{2}LI_0^2 e^{-2(R/L)t} = U_0 e^{-2(R/L)t}$$

where $U_0 = \frac{1}{2}LI_0^2$ is the energy at the initial time $t = 0$. When $t = 2.3\tau = 2.3L/R$, we have

$$U = U_0 e^{-2(2.3)} = U_0 e^{-4.6} = 0.010\ U_0$$

That is, only 0.010 or 1.0% of the energy initially stored in the inductor remains, so 99.0% has been dissipated in the resistor.

EVALUATE: To get a sense of what this result means, consider the *R-L* circuit we analyzed in Example 30.7, for which the time constant is 390 μs. With $L = 69$ mH $= 0.069$ H and an initial current $I_0 = 36$ mA $= 0.036$ A, the amount of energy in the inductor initially is $U_0 = \frac{1}{2}LI_0^2 = \frac{1}{2}(0.069$ H$)(0.036$ A$)^2 = 4.5 \times 10^{-5}$ J. Of this, 99.0% or 4.4×10^{-5} J is dissipated in $2.3(390 \mu s) =$

9.0×10^{-4} s $= 0.90$ ms. In other words, this circuit can be powered off almost completely in 0.90 ms, and can be powered on in the same amount of time. The minimum time for a complete on-off cycle is therefore 1.8 ms. For many purposes, such as in fast switching networks for telecommunication, an even shorter cycle time is required. In such cases a smaller time constant $\tau = L/R$ is needed.

Test Your Understanding of Section 30.4 (a) In Fig. 30.11, what are the algebraic signs of the potential differences v_{ab} and v_{bc} when switch S_1 is closed and switch S_2 is open? (i) $v_{ab} > 0$, $v_{bc} > 0$; (ii) $v_{ab} > 0$, $v_{bc} < 0$; (iii) $v_{ab} < 0$, $v_{bc} > 0$; (iv) $v_{ab} < 0$, $v_{bc} < 0$. (b) What are the signs of v_{ab} and v_{bc} when S_1 is open, S_2 is closed, and current is flowing in the direction shown? (i) $v_{ab} > 0$, $v_{bc} > 0$; (ii) $v_{ab} > 0$, $v_{bc} < 0$; (iii) $v_{ab} < 0$, $v_{bc} > 0$; (iv) $v_{ab} < 0$, $v_{bc} < 0$.

30.5 The *L-C* Circuit

A circuit containing an inductor and a capacitor shows an entirely new mode of behavior, characterized by *oscillating* current and charge. This is in sharp contrast to the *exponential* approach to a steady-state situation that we have seen with both *R-C* and *R-L* circuits. In the **L-C circuit** in Fig. 30.14a we charge the

Activ Physics ONLINE

14.2 AC Circuits: The *RLC* Oscillator (Questions 1–6)

30.14 In an oscillating *L-C* circuit, the charge on the capacitor and the current through the inductor both vary sinusoidally with time. Energy is transferred between magnetic energy in the inductor (U_B) and electric energy in the capacitor (U_E). As in simple harmonic motion, the total energy E remains constant. (Compare Fig. 13.14 in Section 13.3.)

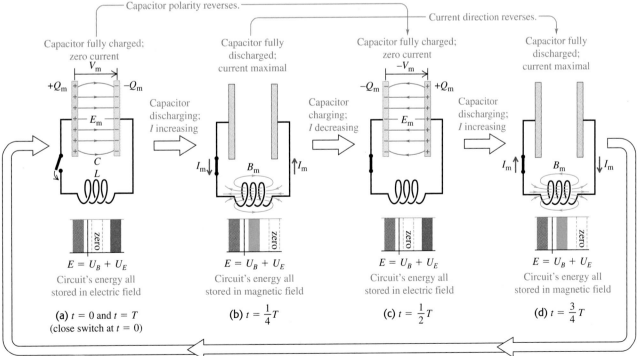

Capacitor polarity reverses. ———
Current direction reverses. ———

Capacitor fully charged; zero current
V_m
$+Q_m$ $-Q_m$
E_m
C
L

Capacitor discharging; *I* increasing

Capacitor fully discharged; current maximal
I_m B_m I_m

Capacitor charging; *I* decreasing

Capacitor fully charged; zero current
$-V_m$
$-Q_m$ $+Q_m$
E_m

Capacitor discharging; *I* increasing

Capacitor fully discharged; current maximal
I_m B_m I_m

zero

$E = U_B + U_E$
Circuit's energy all stored in electric field

zero

$E = U_B + U_E$
Circuit's energy all stored in magnetic field

zero

$E = U_B + U_E$
Circuit's energy all stored in electric field

zero

$E = U_B + U_E$
Circuit's energy all stored in magnetic field

(a) $t = 0$ and $t = T$
(close switch at $t = 0$)

(b) $t = \frac{1}{4}T$

(c) $t = \frac{1}{2}T$

(d) $t = \frac{3}{4}T$

Capacitor charging; *I* decreasing

capacitor to a potential difference V_m and initial charge $Q = CV_m$ on its left-hand plate and then close the switch. What happens?

The capacitor begins to discharge through the inductor. Because of the induced emf in the inductor, the current cannot change instantaneously; it starts at zero and eventually builds up to a maximum value I_m. During this buildup the capacitor is discharging. At each instant the capacitor potential equals the induced emf, so as the capacitor discharges, the *rate of change* of current decreases. When the capacitor potential becomes zero, the induced emf is also zero, and the current has leveled off at its maximum value I_m. Figure 30.14b shows this situation; the capacitor has completely discharged. The potential difference between its terminals (and those of the inductor) has decreased to zero, and the current has reached its maximum value I_m.

During the discharge of the capacitor, the increasing current in the inductor has established a magnetic field in the space around it, and the energy that was initially stored in the capacitor's electric field is now stored in the inductor's magnetic field.

Although the capacitor is completely discharged in Fig. 30.14b, the current persists (it cannot change instantaneously), and the capacitor begins to charge with polarity opposite to that in the initial state. As the current decreases, the magnetic field also decreases, inducing an emf in the inductor in the *same* direction as the current; this slows down the decrease of the current. Eventually, the current and the magnetic field reach zero, and the capacitor has been charged in the sense *opposite* to its initial polarity (Fig. 30.14c), with potential difference $-V_m$ and charge $-Q$ on its left-hand plate.

The process now repeats in the reverse direction; a little later, the capacitor has again discharged, and there is a current in the inductor in the opposite direction (Fig. 30.14d). Still later, the capacitor charge returns to its original value (Fig. 30.14a), and the whole process repeats. If there are no energy losses, the charges on the capacitor continue to oscillate back and forth indefinitely. This process is called an **electrical oscillation.**

From an energy standpoint the oscillations of an electrical circuit transfer energy from the capacitor's electric field to the inductor's magnetic field and back. The *total* energy associated with the circuit is constant. This is analogous to the transfer of energy in an oscillating mechanical system from potential energy to kinetic energy and back, with constant total energy. As we will see, this analogy goes much further.

Electrical Oscillations in an *L-C* Circuit

To study the flow of charge in detail, we proceed just as we did for the *R-L* circuit. Figure 30.15 shows our definitions of q and i.

30.15 Applying Kirchhoff's loop rule to the *L-C* circuit. The direction of travel around the loop in the loop equation is shown. Just after the circuit is completed and the capacitor first begins to discharge, as in Fig. 30.14a, the current is negative (opposite to the direction shown).

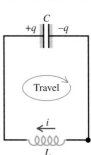

CAUTION **Positive current in an *L-C* circuit** After examining Fig. 30.14, the positive direction for current in Fig. 30.15 may seem backward to you. In fact we've chosen this direction to simplify the relationship between current and capacitor charge. We define the current at each instant to be $i = dq/dt$, the rate of change of the charge on the left-hand capacitor plate. Hence if the capacitor is initially charged and begins to discharge as in Figs. 30.14a and 30.14b, then $dq/dt < 0$ and the initial current i is negative; the direction of the current is then opposite to the (positive) direction shown in Fig. 30.15. ▮

We apply Kirchhoff's loop rule to the circuit in Fig. 30.15. Starting at the lower-right corner of the circuit and adding voltages as we go clockwise around the loop, we obtain

$$-L\frac{di}{dt} - \frac{q}{C} = 0$$

Since $i = dq/dt$, it follows that $di/dt = d^2q/dt^2$. We substitute this expression into the above equation and divide by $-L$ to obtain

$$\frac{d^2q}{dt^2} + \frac{1}{LC}q = 0 \qquad (L\text{-}C \text{ circuit}) \qquad (30.20)$$

Equation (30.20) has exactly the same form as the equation we derived for simple harmonic motion in Section 13.2, Eq. (13.4). That equation is $d^2x/dt^2 = -(k/m)x$, or

$$\frac{d^2x}{dt^2} + \frac{k}{m}x = 0$$

(You should review Section 13.2 before going on with this discussion.) In the *L-C* circuit the capacitor charge q plays the role of the displacement x, and the current $i = dq/dt$ is analogous to the particle's velocity $v_x = dx/dt$. The inductance L is analogous to the mass m, and the reciprocal of the capacitance, $1/C$, is analogous to the force constant k.

Pursuing this analogy, we recall that the angular frequency $\omega = 2\pi f$ of the harmonic oscillator is equal to $(k/m)^{1/2}$, and the position is given as a function of time by Eq. (13.13),

$$x = A\cos(\omega t + \phi)$$

where the amplitude A and the phase angle ϕ depend on the initial conditions. In the analogous electrical situation the capacitor charge q is given by

$$q = Q\cos(\omega t + \phi) \qquad (30.21)$$

and the angular frequency ω of oscillation is given by

$$\omega = \sqrt{\frac{1}{LC}} \qquad \begin{array}{l}\text{(angular frequency of oscillation}\\\text{in an }L\text{-}C\text{ circuit)}\end{array} \qquad (30.22)$$

You should verify that Eq. (30.21) satisfies the loop equation, Eq. (30.20), when ω has the value given by Eq. (30.22). In doing this, you will find that the instantaneous current $i = dq/dt$ is given by

$$i = -\omega Q\sin(\omega t + \phi) \qquad (30.23)$$

Thus the charge and current in an *L-C* circuit oscillate sinusoidally with time, with an angular frequency determined by the values of L and C. The ordinary frequency f, the number of cycles per second, is equal to $\omega/2\pi$ as always. The constants Q and ϕ in Eqs. (30.21) and (30.23) are determined by the initial conditions. If at time $t = 0$ the left-hand capacitor plate in Fig. 30.15 has its maximum charge Q and the current i is zero, then $\phi = 0$. If $q = 0$ at time $t = 0$, then $\phi = \pm\pi/2$ rad.

Energy in an *L-C* Circuit

We can also analyze the *L-C* circuit using an energy approach. The analogy to simple harmonic motion is equally useful here. In the mechanical problem a body with mass m is attached to a spring with force constant k. Suppose we displace the body a distance A from its equilibrium position and release it from rest at time $t = 0$. The kinetic energy of the system at any later time is $\frac{1}{2}mv_x^2$, and its elastic potential energy is $\frac{1}{2}kx^2$. Because the system is conservative, the sum of these energies equals the initial energy of the system, $\frac{1}{2}kA^2$. We find the velocity v_x at any position x just as we did in Section 13.3, Eq. (13.22):

$$v_x = \pm\sqrt{\frac{k}{m}}\sqrt{A^2 - x^2} \qquad (30.24)$$

The *L-C* circuit is also a conservative system. Again let Q be the maximum capacitor charge. The magnetic-field energy $\frac{1}{2}Li^2$ in the inductor at any time corresponds to the kinetic energy $\frac{1}{2}mv^2$ of the oscillating body, and the electric-field energy $q^2/2C$ in the capacitor corresponds to the elastic potential energy $\frac{1}{2}kx^2$ of the spring. The sum of these energies equals the total energy $Q^2/2C$ of the system:

$$\frac{1}{2}Li^2 + \frac{q^2}{2C} = \frac{Q^2}{2C} \tag{30.25}$$

The total energy in the *L-C* circuit is *constant;* it oscillates between the magnetic and the electric forms, just as the constant total mechanical energy in simple harmonic motion is constant and oscillates between the kinetic and potential forms.

Solving Eq. (30.25) for i, we find that when the charge on the capacitor is q, the current i is

$$i = \pm\sqrt{\frac{1}{LC}}\sqrt{Q^2 - q^2} \tag{30.26}$$

You can verify this equation by substituting q from Eq. (30.21) and i from Eq. (30.23). Comparing Eqs. (30.24) and (30.26), we see that current $i = dq/dt$ and charge q are related in the same way as are velocity $v_x = dx/dt$ and position x in the mechanical problem.

The analogies between simple harmonic motion and *L-C* circuit oscillations are summarized in Table 30.1. The striking parallel shown there between mechanical and electrical oscillations is one of many such examples in physics. This parallel is so close that we can solve complicated mechanical and acoustical problems by setting up analogous electrical circuits and measuring the currents and voltages that correspond to the mechanical and acoustical quantities to be determined. This is the basic principle of many analog computers. This analogy can be extended to *damped* oscillations, which we consider in the next section. In Chapter 31 we will extend the analogy further to include *forced* electrical oscillations, which occur in all alternating-current circuits.

Table 30.1 Oscillation of a Mass-Spring System Compared with Electrical Oscillation in an *L-C* Circuit

Mass-Spring System

Kinetic energy $= \frac{1}{2}mv_x^2$

Potential energy $= \frac{1}{2}kx^2$

$\frac{1}{2}mv_x^2 + \frac{1}{2}kx^2 = \frac{1}{2}kA^2$

$v_x = \pm\sqrt{k/m}\sqrt{A^2 - x^2}$

$v_x = dx/dt$

$\omega = \sqrt{\dfrac{k}{m}}$

$x = A\cos(\omega t + \phi)$

Inductor-Capacitor Circuit

Magnetic energy $= \frac{1}{2}Li^2$

Electric energy $= q^2/2C$

$\frac{1}{2}Li^2 + q^2/2C = Q^2/2C$

$i = \pm\sqrt{1/LC}\sqrt{Q^2 - q^2}$

$i = dq/dt$

$\omega = \sqrt{\dfrac{1}{LC}}$

$q = Q\cos(\omega t + \phi)$

Example 30.9 **An oscillating circuit**

A 300-V dc power supply is used to charge a 25-μF capacitor. After the capacitor is fully charged, it is disconnected from the power supply and connected across a 10-mH inductor. The resistance in the circuit is negligible. (a) Find the frequency and period of oscillation of the circuit. (b) Find the capacitor charge and the circuit current 1.2 ms after the inductor and capacitor are connected.

SOLUTION

IDENTIFY: Our target variables are the frequency f and period T, as well as the values of charge q and current i at a given time t.

SET UP: We are given the capacitance C and the inductance L, from which we can calculate the frequency and period using Eq. (30.22). We find the charge and current using Eqs. (30.21) and (30.23). Initially the capacitor is fully charged and the current is zero, as in Fig. 30.14a, so the phase angle is $\phi = 0$ [see the discussion that follows Eq. (30.23)].

EXECUTE: (a) The natural *angular* frequency is

$$\omega = \sqrt{\frac{1}{LC}} = \sqrt{\frac{1}{(10 \times 10^{-3}\,\text{H})(25 \times 10^{-6}\,\text{F})}}$$
$$= 2.0 \times 10^3\,\text{rad/s}$$

The frequency f is $1/2\pi$ times this:

$$f = \frac{\omega}{2\pi} = \frac{2.0 \times 10^3\,\text{rad/s}}{2\pi\,\text{rad/cycle}} = 320\,\text{Hz}$$

The period is the reciprocal of the frequency:

$$T = \frac{1}{f} = \frac{1}{320\,\text{Hz}} = 3.1 \times 10^{-3}\,\text{s} = 3.1\,\text{ms}$$

(b) Since the period of the oscillation is $T = 3.1$ ms, $t = 1.2$ ms equals $0.38T$; this corresponds to a situation intermediate between

Fig. 30.14b $(t = T/4)$ and Fig. 30.14c $(t = T/2)$. Comparing those figures to Fig. 30.15, we expect the capacitor charge q to be negative (that is, there will be negative charge on the left-hand plate of the capacitor) and the current i to be negative as well (that is, current will be traveling in a counterclockwise direction).

To find the value of q, we use Eq. (30.21). The charge is maximum at $t = 0$, so $\phi = 0$ and $Q = C\mathcal{E} = (25 \times 10^{-6}\,\text{F})(300\,\text{V}) = 7.5 \times 10^{-3}\,\text{C}$. The charge q at any time is

$$q = (7.5 \times 10^{-3}\,\text{C})\cos\omega t$$

At time $t = 1.2 \times 10^{-3}$ s,

$$\omega t = (2.0 \times 10^3\,\text{rad/s})(1.2 \times 10^{-3}\,\text{s}) = 2.4\,\text{rad}$$
$$q = (7.5 \times 10^{-3}\,\text{C})\cos(2.4\,\text{rad}) = -5.5 \times 10^{-3}\,\text{C}$$

The current i at any time is

$$i = -\omega Q\sin\omega t$$

At time $t = 1.2 \times 10^{-3}$ s,

$$i = -(2.0 \times 10^3\,\text{rad/s})(7.5 \times 10^{-3}\,\text{C})\sin(2.4\,\text{rad}) = -10\,\text{A}$$

EVALUATE: Note that the signs of q and i are both negative, as we predicted.

Example 30.10 Energy in an oscillating circuit

Consider again the *L-C* circuit of Example 30.9. 9 (a) Find the magnetic energy and electric energy at $t = 0$. (b) Find the magnetic energy and electric energy at $t = 1.2$ ms.

SOLUTION

IDENTIFY: This problem asks for the magnetic energy (stored in the inductor) and the electric energy (stored in the capacitor) at two different times during the oscillation of the *L-C* circuit.

SET UP: From Example 30.9 we know the values of the capacitor charge q and circuit current i for both of the times of interest. We use them to calculate the magnetic energy stored in the inductor, given by $U_B = \frac{1}{2}Li^2$, and the electric energy stored in the capacitor, given by $U_E = q^2/2C$.

EXECUTE: (a) At $t = 0$ there is no current and $q = Q$. Hence there is no magnetic energy, and all the energy in the circuit is in the form of electric energy in the capacitor:

$$U_B = \frac{1}{2}Li^2 = 0 \qquad U_E = \frac{Q^2}{2C} = \frac{(7.5 \times 10^{-3}\,\text{C})^2}{2(25 \times 10^{-6}\,\text{F})} = 1.1\,\text{J}$$

(b) As we mentioned in Example 30.9, $t = 1.2$ ms corresponds to a situation intermediate between Fig. 30.14b $(t = T/4)$ and Fig. 30.14c $(t = T/2)$. So we expect the energy to be part magnetic and part electric at this time. From Example 30.9, $i = -10$ A and $q = -5.5 \times 10^{-3}$ C, so

$$U_B = \frac{1}{2}Li^2 = \frac{1}{2}(10 \times 10^{-3}\,\text{H})(-10\,\text{A})^2 = 0.5\,\text{J}$$

$$U_E = \frac{q^2}{2C} = \frac{(-5.5 \times 10^{-3}\,\text{C})^2}{2(25 \times 10^{-6}\,\text{F})} = 0.6\,\text{J}$$

EVALUATE: The magnetic and electric energies are the same at $t = 3T/8 = 0.375T$, exactly halfway between the situations in Figs. 30.14b and 30.14c. The time we are considering here is slightly later and U_B is slightly less than U_E, as we would expect. We emphasize that at *all* times, the *total* energy $E = U_B + U_E$ has the same value, 1.1 J. An *L-C* circuit without resistance is a conservative system; no energy is dissipated.

Test Your Understanding of Section 30.5 One way to think about the energy stored in an *L-C* circuit is to say that the circuit elements do positive or negative work on the charges that move back and forth through the circuit. (a) Between stages (a) and (b) in Fig. 30.14, does the capacitor do positive work or negative work on the charges? (b) What kind of force (electric or magnetic) does the capacitor exert on the charges to do this work? (c) During this process, does the inductor do positive or negative work on the charges? (d) What kind of force (electric or magnetic) does the inductor exert on the charges?

30.6 The *L-R-C* Series Circuit

In our discussion of the *L-C* circuit we assumed that there was no *resistance* in the circuit. This is an idealization, of course; every real inductor has resistance in its windings, and there may also be resistance in the connecting wires. Because of resistance, the electromagnetic energy in the circuit is dissipated and converted to other forms, such as internal energy of the circuit materials. Resistance in an electric circuit is analogous to friction in a mechanical system.

Suppose an inductor with inductance L and a resistor of resistance R are connected in series across the terminals of a charged capacitor, forming an **L-R-C series circuit.** As before, the capacitor starts to discharge as soon as the circuit

Actjv
Physjcs
ONLINE

14.2 AC Circuits: The *RLC* Oscillator (Questions 7–10)

30.16 Graphs of capacitor charge as a function of time in an *L-R-C* series circuit with initial charge *Q*.

(a) Underdamped circuit (small resistance *R*)

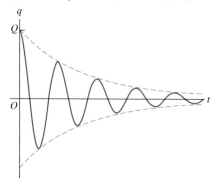

(b) Critically damped circuit (larger resistance *R*)

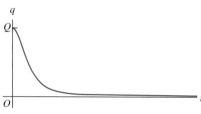

(c) Overdamped circuit (very large resistance *R*)

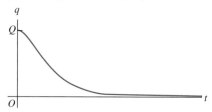

30.17 An *L-R-C* series circuit.

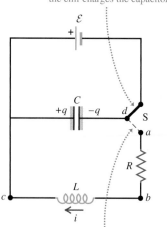

When switch S is in this position, the emf charges the capacitor.

When switch S is moved to this position, the capacitor discharges through the resistor and inductor.

is completed. But because of i^2R losses in the resistor, the magnetic-field energy acquired by the inductor when the capacitor is completely discharged is *less* than the original electric-field energy of the capacitor. In the same way, the energy of the capacitor when the magnetic field has decreased to zero is still smaller, and so on.

If the resistance *R* is relatively small, the circuit still oscillates, but with **damped harmonic motion** (Fig. 30.16a), and we say that the circuit is **underdamped.** If we increase *R*, the oscillations die out more rapidly. When *R* reaches a certain value, the circuit no longer oscillates; it is **critically damped** (Fig. 30.16b). For still larger values of *R*, the circuit is **overdamped** (Fig. 30.16c), and the capacitor charge approaches zero even more slowly. We used these same terms to describe the behavior of the analogous mechanical system, the damped harmonic oscillator, in Section 13.7.

Analyzing an *L-R-C* Circuit

To analyze *L-R-C* circuit behavior in detail, we consider the circuit shown in Fig. 30.17. It is like the *L-C* circuit of Fig. 30.15 except for the added resistor *R*; we also show the source that charges the capacitor initially. The labeling of the positive senses of *q* and *i* are the same as for the *L-C* circuit.

First we close the switch in the upward position, connecting the capacitor to a source of emf $\mathcal{E}$ for a long enough time to ensure that the capacitor acquires its final charge $Q = C\mathcal{E}$ and any initial oscillations have died out. Then at time $t = 0$ we flip the switch to the downward position, removing the source from the circuit and placing the capacitor in series with the resistor and inductor. Note that the initial current is negative, opposite in direction to the direction of *i* shown in the figure.

To find how *q* and *i* vary with time, we apply Kirchhoff's loop rule. Starting at point *a* and going around the loop in the direction *abcda*, we obtain the equation

$$-iR - L\frac{di}{dt} - \frac{q}{C} = 0$$

Replacing *i* with dq/dt and rearranging, we get

$$\frac{d^2q}{dt^2} + \frac{R}{L}\frac{dq}{dt} + \frac{1}{LC}q = 0 \tag{30.27}$$

Note that when $R = 0$, this reduces to Eq. (30.20) for an *L-C* circuit.

There are general methods for obtaining solutions of Eq. (30.27). The form of the solution is different for the underdamped (small *R*) and overdamped (large *R*) cases. When R^2 is less than $4L/C$, the solution has the form

$$q = Ae^{-(R/2L)t}\cos\left(\sqrt{\frac{1}{LC} - \frac{R^2}{4L^2}}\,t + \phi\right) \tag{30.28}$$

where *A* and ϕ are constants. We invite you to take the first and second derivatives of this function and show by direct substitution that it does satisfy Eq. (30.27).

This solution corresponds to the *underdamped* behavior shown in Fig. 30.16a; the function represents a sinusoidal oscillation with an exponentially decaying amplitude. (Note that the exponential factor $e^{-(R/2L)t}$ is *not* the same as the factor $e^{-(R/L)t}$ that we encountered in describing the *R-L* circuit in Section 30.4.) When $R = 0$, Eq. (30.28) reduces to Eq. (30.21) for the oscillations in an *L-C* circuit. If *R* is not zero, the angular frequency of the oscillation is *less* than $1/(LC)^{1/2}$

because of the term containing R. The angular frequency ω' of the damped oscillations is given by

$$\omega' = \sqrt{\frac{1}{LC} - \frac{R^2}{4L^2}} \qquad \text{(underdamped } L\text{-}R\text{-}C \text{ series circuit)} \qquad (30.29)$$

When $R = 0$, this reduces to Eq. (30.22), $\omega = (1/LC)^{1/2}$. As R increases, ω' becomes smaller and smaller. When $R^2 = 4L/C$, the quantity under the radical becomes zero; the system no longer oscillates, and the case of *critical damping* (Fig. 30.16b) has been reached. For still larger values of R the system behaves as in Fig. 30.16c. In this case the circuit is *overdamped,* and q is given as a function of time by the sum of two decreasing exponential functions.

In the *underdamped* case the phase constant ϕ in the cosine function of Eq. (30.28) provides for the possibility of both an initial charge and an initial current at time $t = 0$, analogous to an underdamped harmonic oscillator given both an initial displacement and an initial velocity (see Exercise 30.38).

We emphasize once more that the behavior of the *L-R-C* series circuit is completely analogous to that of the damped harmonic oscillator studied in Section 13.7. We invite you to verify, for example, that if you start with Eq. (13.41) and substitute q for x, L for m, $1/C$ for k, and R for the damping constant b, the result is Eq. (30.27). Similarly, the cross-over point between underdamping and overdamping occurs at $b^2 = 4km$ for the mechanical system and at $R^2 = 4L/C$ for the electrical one. Can you find still other aspects of this analogy?

The practical applications of the *L-R-C* series circuit emerge when we include a sinusoidally varying source of emf in the circuit. This is analogous to the *forced oscillations* that we discussed in Section 13.7, and there are analogous *resonance* effects. Such a circuit is called an *alternating-current (ac) circuit;* the analysis of ac circuits is the principal topic of the next chapter.

Example 30.11 **An underdamped *L-R-C* series circuit**

What resistance R is required (in terms of L and C) to give an *L-R-C* circuit a frequency that is one-half the undamped frequency?

SOLUTION

IDENTIFY: This problem concerns an underdamped *L-R-C* series circuit (Fig. 30.16a): we want the resistance to be great enough to reduce the oscillation frequency to one-half of the undamped value, but not so great that the oscillator become criticaly damped (Fig. 30.1b) or overdamped (Fig. 30.16c).

SET UP: The angular frequency of an underdamped *L-R-C* series circuit is given by Eq. (30.29); the angular frequency of an undamped *L-C* circuit is given by Eq. (30.22). We use these to solve for the target variable R.

EXECUTE: We want ω' given by Eq. (30.29) to be equal to one-half of ω given by Eq. (30.22):

$$\sqrt{\frac{1}{LC} - \frac{R^2}{4L^2}} = \frac{1}{2}\sqrt{\frac{1}{LC}}$$

When we square both sides and solve for R, we get

$$R = \sqrt{\frac{3L}{C}}$$

For example, adding 35 Ω to the circuit of Example 30.9 would reduce the frequency from 320 Hz to 160 Hz.

EVALUATE: The circuit becomes critically damped with no oscillations when $R = \sqrt{4L/C}$. Our result for R is smaller than that, as it should be; we want the circuit to be underdamped.

Test Your Understanding of Section 30.6 An *L-R-C* series circuit includes a 2.0-Ω resistor. At $t = 0$ the capacitor charge is 2.0 μC. for which of the following values of the inductance and capacitance will the charge on the capacitor *not* oscillate? (i) $L = 3.0\ \mu$H, $C = 6.0\ \mu$F; (ii) $L = 6.0\ \mu$H, $C = 3.0\ \mu$F; (iii) $L = 3.0\ \mu$H, $C = 3.0\ \mu$F.

Mutual inductance When a changing current i_1 in one circuit causes a changing magnetic flux in a second circuit, an emf $\mathcal{E}_2$ is induced in the second circuit. Likewise, a changing current i_2 in the second circuit induces an emf $\mathcal{E}_1$ in the first circuit. The mutual inductance M depends on the geometry of the two coils and the material between them. If the circuits are coils of wire with N_1 and N_2 turns, M can be expressed in terms of the average flux Φ_{B2} through each turn of coil 2 that is caused by the current i_1 in coil 1, or in terms of the average flux Φ_{B1} through each turn of coil 1 that is caused by the current i_2 in coil 2. The SI unit of mutual inductance is the henry, abbreviated H. (See Examples 30.1 and 30.2.)

$$\mathcal{E}_2 = -M\frac{di_1}{dt} \quad \text{and} \quad \mathcal{E}_1 = -M\frac{di_2}{dt} \quad (30.4)$$

$$M = \frac{N_2\Phi_{B2}}{i_1} = \frac{N_1\Phi_{B1}}{i_2} \quad (30.5)$$

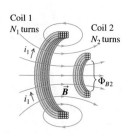

Self-inductance A changing current i in any circuit causes a self-induced emf $\mathcal{E}$. The inductance (or self-inductance) L depends on the geometry of the circuit and the material surrounding it. The inductance of a coil of N turns is related to the average flux Φ_B through each turn caused by the current i in the coil. An inductor is a circuit device, usually including a coil of wire, intended to have a substantial inductance. (See Examples 30.3 and 30.4.)

$$\mathcal{E} = -L\frac{di}{dt} \quad (30.7)$$

$$L = \frac{N\Phi_B}{i} \quad (30.6)$$

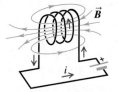

Magnetic-field energy An inductor with inductance L carrying current I has energy U associated with the inductor's magnetic field. The magnetic energy density u (energy per unit volume) is proportional to the square of the magnetic field magnitude. (See Examples 30.5 and 30.6.)

$$U = \frac{1}{2}LI^2 \quad (30.9)$$

$$u = \frac{B^2}{2\mu_0} \quad \text{(in vacuum)} \quad (30.10)$$

$$u = \frac{B^2}{2\mu} \quad (30.11)$$
(in a material with magnetic permeability μ)

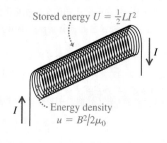

R-L circuits In a circuit containing a resistor R, an inductor L, and a source of emf, the growth and decay of current are exponential. The time constant τ is the time required for the current to approach within a fraction $1/e$ of its final value. (See Examples 30.7 and 30.8.)

$$\tau = \frac{L}{R} \quad (30.16)$$

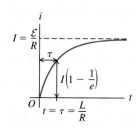

L-C circuits: A circuit that contains inductance L and capacitance C undergoes electrical oscillations with an angular frequency ω that depends on L and C. Such a circuit is analogous to a mechanical harmonic oscillator, with inductance L analogous to mass m, the reciprocal of capacitance $1/C$ to force constant k, charge q to displacement x, and current i to velocity v_x. (See Examples 30.9 and 30.10.)

$$\omega = \sqrt{\frac{1}{LC}} \quad (30.22)$$

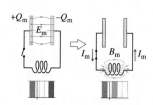

L-R-C series circuits: A circuit that contains inductance, resistance, and capacitance undergoes damped oscillations for sufficiently small resistance. The frequency ω' of damped oscillations depends on the values of L, R, and C. As R increases, the damping increases; if R is greater than a certain value, the behavior becomes overdamped and no longer oscillates. The cross-over between underdamping and overdamping occurs when $R^2 = 4L/C$; when this condition is satisfied, the oscillations are critically damped. (See Example 30.11.)

$$\omega' = \sqrt{\frac{1}{LC} - \frac{R^2}{4L^2}}$$ (30.29)

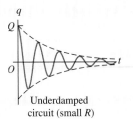

Underdamped circuit (small R)

Key Terms

mutual inductance, *1031*
henry, *1032*
self-induced emf, *1034*
inductance (self-inductance), *1034*
inductor, *1034*

magnetic energy density, *1040*
R-L circuit, *1041*
time constant, *1043*
L-C circuit, *1045*
electrical oscillation, *1046*

L-R-C series circuit, *1050*
damped harmonic motion, *1050*
underdamped, *1050*
critically damped, *1050*
overdamped, *1050*

Answer to Chapter Opening Question ?

As explained in Section 30.2, traffic light sensors work by measuring the change in inductance of a coil embedded under the road surface when a car drives over it.

Answers to Test Your Understanding Questions

30.1 Answer: (iii) Doubling both the length of the solenoid (l) and the number of turns of wire in the solenoid (N_1) would have *no* effect on the mutual inductance M. Example 30.1 shows that M depends on the ratio of these quantities, which would remain unchanged. This is because the magnetic field produced by the solenoid depends on the number of turns *per unit length,* and the proposed change has no effect on this quantity.

30.2 Answer: (iv), (i), (iii), (ii) From Eq. (30.8), the potential difference across the inductor is $V_{ab} = L\,di/dt$. For the four cases we find (i) $V_{ab} = (2.0\,\mu\text{H})(2.0\,\text{A} - 1.0\,\text{A})/(0.50\,\text{s}) = 4.0\,\mu\text{V}$; (ii) $V_{ab} = (4.0\,\mu\text{H})(0 - 3.0\,\text{A})/(2.0\,\text{s}) = -6.0\,\mu\text{V}$; (iii) $V_{ab} = 0$ because the rate of change of current is zero; and (iv) $V_{ab} = (1.0\,\mu\text{H})(4.0\,\text{A} - 0)/(0.25\,\text{s}) = 16\,\mu\text{V}$.

30.3 Answers: (a) yes, (b) no Reversing the direction of the current has no effect on the magnetic field magnitude, but it causes the direction of the magnetic field to reverse. It has no effect on the magnetic-field energy density, which is proportional to the square of the *magnitude* of the magnetic field.

30.4 Answers: (a) (i), (b) (ii) Recall that v_{ab} is the potential at a minus the potential at b, and similarly for v_{bc}. For either arrangement of the switches, current flows through the resistor from a to b. The upstream end of the resistor is always at the higher potential, so v_{ab} is positive. With S_1 closed and S_2 open, the current through the inductor flows from b to c and is increasing. The self-induced emf opposes this increase and is therefore directed from c toward b, which means that b is at the higher potential. Hence v_{bc} is positive. With S_1 open and S_2 closed, the inductor current again flows from b to c but is now decreasing. The self-induced emf is directed from b to c in an effort to sustain the decaying current, so c is at the higher potential and v_{bc} is negative.

30.5 Answers: (a) positive, (b) electric, (c) negative, (d) electric The capacitor loses energy between stages (a) and (b), so it does positive work on the charges. It does this by exerting an electric force that pushes current away from the positively charged left-hand capacitor plate and toward the negatively charged right-hand plate. At the same time, the inductor gains energy and does negative work on the moving charges. Although the inductor stores magnetic energy, the force that the inductor exerts is *electric*. This force comes about from the inductor's self-induced emf (see Section 30.2).

30.6 Answers: (i), (iii) There are no oscillations if $R^2 \geq 4L/C$. In each case $R^2 = (2.0\,\Omega)^2 = 4.0\,\Omega^2$. In case (i) $4L/C = 4(3.0\,\mu\text{H})/(6.0\,\mu\text{F}) = 2.0\,\Omega^2$, so there are no oscillations (the system is overdamped); in case (ii) $4L/C = 4(6.0\,\mu\text{H})/(3.0\,\mu\text{F}) = 8.0\,\Omega^2$, so there are oscillations (the system is underdamped); and in case (iii) $4L/C = 4(3.0\,\mu\text{H})/(3.0\,\mu\text{F}) = 4.0\,\Omega^2$, so there are no oscillations (the system is critically damped).

PROBLEMS

For instructor-assigned homework, go to **www.masteringphysics.com**

Discussion Questions

Q30.1. In an electric trolley or bus system, the vehicle's motor draws current from an overhead wire by means of a long arm with an attachment at the end that slides along the overhead wire. A brilliant electric spark is often seen when the attachment crosses a junction in the wires where contact is momentarily lost. Explain this phenomenon.

Q30.2. A transformer consists basically of two coils in close proximity but not in electrical contact. A current in one coil magnetically induces an emf in the second coil, with properties that can be controlled by adjusting the geometry of the two coils. Such a device will work only with alternating current, however, and not with direct current. Explain.

Q30.3. In Fig. 30.1, if coil 2 is turned 90° so that its axis is vertical, does the mutual inductance increase or decrease? Explain.

Q30.4. The tightly wound toroidal solenoid is one of the few configurations for which it is easy to calculate self-inductance. What features of the toroidal solenoid give it this simplicity?

Q30.5. Two identical, closely wound, circular coils, each having self-inductance L, are placed next to each other, so that they are coaxial and almost touching. If they are connected in series, what is the self-inductance of the combination? What if they are connected in parallel? Can they be connected so that the total inductance is zero? Explain.

Q30.6. Two closely wound circular coils have the same number of turns, but one has twice the radius of the other. How are the self-inductances of the two coils related? Explain your reasoning.

Q30.7. You are to make a resistor by winding a wire around a cylindrical form. To make the inductance as small as possible, it is proposed that you wind half the wire in one direction and the other half in the opposite direction. Would this achieve the desired result? Why or why not?

Q30.8. For the same magnetic field strength B, is the energy density greater in vacuum or in a magnetic material? Explain. Does Eq. (30.11) imply that for a long solenoid in which the current is I the energy stored is proportional to $1/\mu$? And does this mean that for the same current less energy is stored when the solenoid is filled with a ferromagnetic material rather than with air? Explain.

Q30.9. In Section 30.5 Kirchhoff's loop rule is applied to an L-C circuit where the capacitor is initially fully charged and the equation $-L\,di/dt - q/C = 0$ is derived. But as the capacitor starts to discharge, the current increases from zero. The equation says $L\,di/dt = -q/C$, so it says $L\,di/dt$ is negative. Explain how $L\,di/dt$ can be negative when the current is increasing.

Q30.10. In Section 30.5 the relationship $i = dq/dt$ is used in deriving Eq. (30.20). But a flow of current corresponds to a decrease in the charge on the capacitor. Explain, therefore, why this is the correct equation to use in the derivation, rather than $i = -dq/dt$.

Q30.11. In the R-L circuit shown in Fig. 30.11, when switch S_1 is closed, the potential v_{ab} changes suddenly and discontinuously, but the current does not. Explain why the voltage can change suddenly but the current can't.

Q30.12. In the R-L circuit shown in Fig. 30.11, is the current in the resistor always the same as the current in the inductor? How do you know?

Q30.13. Suppose there is a steady current in an inductor. If you attempt to reduce the current to zero instantaneously by quickly opening a switch, an arc can appear at the switch contacts. Why? Is it physically possible to stop the current instantaneously? Explain.

Q30.14. In an R-L-C circuit, what criteria could be used to decide whether the system is overdamped or underdamped? For example, could we compare the maximum energy stored during one cycle to the energy dissipated during one cycle? Explain.

Exercises

Section 30.1 Mutual Inductance

30.1. Two coils have mutual inductance $M = 3.25 \times 10^{-4}$ H. The current i_1 in the first coil increases at a uniform rate of 830 A/s. (a) What is the magnitude of the induced emf in the second coil? Is it constant? (b) Suppose that the current described is in the second coil rather than the first. What is the magnitude of the induced emf in the first coil?

30.2. Two coils are wound around the same cylindrical form, like the coils in Example 30.1. When the current in the first coil is decreasing at a rate of -0.242 A/s, the induced emf in the second coil has magnitude 1.65×10^{-3} V. (a) What is the mutual inductance of the pair of coils? (b) If the second coil has 25 turns, what is the flux through each turn when the current in the first coil equals 1.20 A? (c) If the current in the second coil increases at a rate of 0.360 A/s, what is the magnitude of the induced emf in the first coil?

30.3. From Eq. (30.5) $1\,\text{H} = 1\,\text{Wb/A}$, and from Eq. (30.4) $1\,\text{H} = 1\,\Omega \cdot \text{s}$. Show that these two definitions are equivalent.

30.4. A solenoidal coil with 25 turns of wire is wound tightly around another coil with 300 turns (see Example 30.1). The inner solenoid is 25.0 cm long and has a diameter of 2.00 cm. At a certain time, the current in the inner solenoid is 0.120 A and is increasing at a rate of 1.75×10^3 A/s. For this time, calculate; (a) the average magnetic flux through each turn of the inner solenoid; (b) the mutual inductance of the two solenoids; (c) the emf induced in the outer solenoid by the changing current in the inner solenoid.

30.5. Two toroidal solenoids are wound around the same form so that the magnetic field of one passes through the turns of the other. Solenoid 1 has 700 turns, and solenoid 2 has 400 turns. When the current in solenoid 1 is 6.52 A, the average flux through each turn of solenoid 2 is 0.0320 Wb. (a) What is the mutual inductance of the pair of solenoids? (b) When the current in solenoid 2 is 2.54 A, what is the average flux through each turn of solenoid 1?

Section 30.2 Self-Inductance and Inductors

30.6. A toroidal solenoid has 500 turns, cross-sectional area 6.25 cm², and mean radius 4.00 cm. (a) Calcualte the coil's self-inductance. (b) If the current decreases uniformly from 5.00 A to 2.00 A in 3.00 ms, calculate the self-induced emf in the coil. (c) The current is directed from terminal a of the coil to terminal b. Is the direction of the induced emf from a to b or from b to a?

30.7. At the instant when the current in an inductor is increasing at a rate of 0.0640 A/s, the magnitude of the self-induced emf is 0.0160 V. (a) What is the inductance of the inductor? (b) If the inductor is a solenoid with 400 turns, what is the average magnetic flux through each turn when the current is 0.720 A?

30.8. When the current in a toroidal solenoid is changing at a rate of 0.0260 A/s, the magnitude of the induced emf is 12.6 mV. When the current equals 1.40 A, the average flux through each turn of the solenoid is 0.00285 Wb. How many turns does the solenoid have?

30.9. The inductor in Fig. 30.18 has inductance 0.260 H and carries a current in the direction shown that is decreasing at a uniform rate, $di/dt = -0.0180$ A/s. (a) Find the self-induced emf. (b) Which end of the inductor, a or b, is at a higher potential?

Figure 30.18
Exercises 30.9 and 30.10.

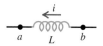

30.10. The inductor shown in Fig. 30.18 has inductance 0.260 H and carries a current in the direction shown. The current is changing at a constant rate. (a) The potential between points a and b is $V_{ab} = 1.04$ V, with point a at higher potential. Is the current increasing or decreasing? b) If the current at $t = 0$ is 12.0 A, what is the current at $t = 2.00$ s?

30.11. Inductance of a Solenoid. A long, straight solenoid has N turns, uniform cross-sectional area A, and length l. Show that the inductance of this solenoid is given by the equation $L = \mu_0 A N^2/l$. Assume that the magnetic field is uniform inside the solenoid and zero outside. (Your answer is approximate because B is actually smaller at the ends than at the center. For this reason, your answer is actually an upper limit on the inductance.)

Section 30.3 Magnetic-Field Energy

30.12. An inductor used in a dc power supply has an inductance of 12.0 H and a resistance of 180 Ω. It carries a current of 0.300 A. (a) What is the energy stored in the magnetic field? (b) At what rate is thermal energy developed in the inductor? (c) Does your answer to part (b) mean that the magnetic-field energy is decreasing with time? Explain.

30.13. An air-filled toroidal solenoid has a mean radius of 15.0 cm and a cross-sectional area of 5.00 cm^2. When the current is 12.0 A, the energy stored is 0.390 J. How many turns does the winding have?

30.14. An air-filled toroidal solenoid has 300 turns of wire, a mean radius of 12.0 cm, and a cross-sectional area of 4.00 cm^2. If the current is 5.00 A, calculate: (a) the magnetic field in the solenoid; (b) the self-inductance of the solenoid; (c) the energy stored in the magnetic field; (d) the energy density in the magnetic field. (e) Check your answer for part (d) by dividing your answer to part (c) by the volume of the solenoid.

30.15. A solenoid 25.0 cm long and with a cross-sectional area of 0.500 cm^2 contains 400 turns of wire and carries a current of 80.0 A. Calculate: (a) the magnetic field in the solenoid; (b) the energy density in the magnetic field if the solenoid is filled with air; (c) the total energy contained in the coil's magnetic field (assume the field is uniform); (d) the inductance of the solenoid.

30.16. It has been proposed to use large inductors as energy storage devices. (a) How much electrical energy is converted to light and thermal energy by a 200-W light bulb in one day? (b) If the amount of energy calculated in part (a) is stored in an inductor in which the current is 80.0 A, what is the inductance?

30.17. Starting from Eq. (30.9), derive in detail Eq. (30.11) for the energy density in a toroidal solenoid filled with a magnetic material.

30.18. It is proposed to store $1.00 \text{ kW} \cdot \text{h} = 3.60 \times 10^6$ J of electrical energy in a uniform magnetic field with magnitude 0.600 T. (a) What volume (in vacuum) must the magnetic field occupy to store this amount of energy? (b) If instead this amount of energy is to be stored in a volume (in vacuum) equivalent to a cube 40.0 cm on a side, what magnetic field is required?

Section 30.4 The R-L Circuit

30.19. An inductor with an inductance of 2.50 H and a resistance of 8.00 Ω is connected to the terminals of a battery with an emf of 6.00 V and negligible internal resistance. Find (a) the initial rate of increase of current in the circuit; (b) the rate of increase of current at the instant when the current is 0.500 A; (c) the current 0.250 s after the circuit is closed; (d) the final steady-state current.

30.20. A 15.0-Ω resistor and a coil are connected in series with a 6.30-V battery with negligible internal resistance and a closed switch. (a) At 2.00 ms after the switch is opened the current has decayed to 0.210 A. Calculate the inductance of the coil. (b) Calculate the time constant of the circuit. (c) How long after the switch is closed will the current reach 1.00% of its original value?

30.21. A 35.0-V battery with negligible internal resistance, a 50.0-Ω resistor, and a 1.25-mH inductor with negligible resistance are all connected in series with an open switch. The switch is suddenly closed. (a) How long after closing the switch will the current through the inductor reach one-half of its maximum value? (b) How long after closing the switch will the energy stored in the inductor reach one-half of its maximum value?

30.22. In Fig. 30.11, switch S_1 is closed while switch S_2 is kept open. The inductance is $L = 0.115$ H, and the resistance is $R = 120 \Omega$. (a) When the current has reached its final value, the energy stored in the inductor is 0.260 J. What is the emf $\mathcal{E}$ of the battery? (b) After the current has reached its final value, S_1 is

opened and S_2 is closed. How much time does it take for the energy stored in the inductor to decrease to 0.130 J, half the original value?

30.23. Show that L/R has units of time.

30.24. Write an equation corresponding to Eq. (30.13) for the current shown in Fig. 30.11 just after switch S_2 is closed and switch S_1 is opened, if the initial current is I_0. Use integration methods to verify Eq. (30.18).

30.25. In Fig. 30.11, suppose that $\mathcal{E} = 60.0$ V, $R = 240 \Omega$, and $L = 0.160$ H. With switch S_2 open, switch S_1 is left closed until a constant current is established. Then S_2 is closed and S_1 opened, taking the battery out of the circuit. (a) What is the initial current in the resistor, just after S_2 is closed and S_1 is opened? (b) What is the current in the resistor at $t = 4.00 \times 10^{-4}$ s? (c) What is the potential difference between points b and c at $t = 4.00 \times 10^{-4}$ s? Which point is at a higher potential? (d) How long does it take the current to decrease to half its initial value?

30.26. In Fig. 30.11, suppose that $\mathcal{E} = 60.0$ V, $R = 240 \Omega$, and $L = 0.160$ H. Initially there is no current in the circuit. Switch S_2 is left open, and switch S_1 is closed. (a) Just after S_1 is closed, what are the potential differences v_{ab} and v_{bc}? (b) A long time (many time constants) after S_1 is closed, what are v_{ab} and v_{bc}? (c) What are v_{ab} and v_{bc} at an intermediate time when $i = 0.150$ A?

30.27. Refer to Exercise 30.19. (a) What is the power input to the inductor from the battery as a function of time if the circuit is completed at $t = 0$? (b) What is the rate of dissipation of energy in the resistance of the inductor as a function of time? (c) What is the rate at which the energy of the magnetic field in the inductor is increasing, as a function of time? (d) Compare the results of parts (a), (b), and (c).

Section 30.5 The L-C Circuit

30.28. A 20.0-μF capacitor is charged by a 150.0-V power supply, then disconnected from the power and connected in series with a 0.280-mH inductor. Calculate: (a) the oscillation frequency of the circuit; (b) the energy stored in the capacitor at time $t = 0$ ms (the moment of connection with the inductor); (c) the energy stored in the inductor at $t = 1.30$ ms.

30.29. A 7.50-nF capacitor is charged up to 12.0 V, then disconnected from the power supply and connected in series through a coil. The period of oscillation of the circuit is then measured to be 8.60×10^{-5} s. Calculate: (a) the inductance of the coil; (b) the maximum charge on the capacitor; (c) the total energy of the circuit; (d) the maximum current in the circuit.

30.30. A 18.0-μF capacitor is placed across a 22.5-V battery for several seconds and is then connected across a 12.0-mH inductor that has no appreciable resistance. (a) After the capacitor and inductor are connected together, find the maximum current in the circuit. When the current is a maximum, what is the charge on the capacitor? (b) How long after the capacitor and inductor are connected together does it take for the capacitor to be completely discharged for the first time? For the second time? (c) Sketch graphs of the charge on the capacitor plates and the current through the inductor as functions of time.

30.31. L-C Oscillations. A capacitor with capacitance 6.00×10^{-5} F is charged by connecting it to a 12.0-V battery. The capacitor is disconnected from the battery and connected across an inductor with $L = 1.50$ H. (a) What are the angular frequency ω of the electrical oscillations and the period of these oscillations (the time for one oscillation)? (b) What is the initial charge on the capacitor? (c) How much energy is initially stored in the capacitor? (d) What is the charge on the capacitor 0.0230 s after the connection to the inductor is made? Interpret the sign of your answer.

(e) At the time given in part (d), what is the current in the inductor? Interpret the sign of your answer. (f) At the time given in part (d), how much electrical energy is stored in the capacitor and how much is stored in the inductor?

30.32. A Radio Tuning Circuit. The minimum capacitance of a variable capacitor in a radio is 4.18 pF. (a) What is the inductance of a coil connected to this capacitor if the oscillation frequency of the L-C circuit is 1600×10^3 Hz, corresponding to one end of the AM radio broadcast band, when the capacitor is set to its minimum capacitance? (b) The frequency at the other end of the broadcast band is 540×10^3 Hz. What is the maximum capacitance of the capacitor if the oscillation frequency is adjustable over the range of the broadcast band?

30.33. An L-C circuit containing an 80.0-mH inductor and a 1.25-nF capacitor oscillates with a maximum current of 0.750 A. Calculate: (a) the maximum charge on the capacitor and (b) the oscillation frequency of the circuit. (c) Assuming the capacitor had its maximum charge at time $t = 0$, calculate the energy stored in the inductor after 2.50 ms of oscillation.

30.34. In an L-C circuit, $L = 85.0$ mH and $C = 3.20$ μF. During the oscillations the maximum current in the inductor is 0.850 mA. (a) What is the maximum charge on the capacitor? (b) What is the magnitude of the charge on the capacitor at an instant when the current in the inductor has magnitude 0.500 mA?

30.35. (a) Using Eqs. (30.21) and (30.23) for an L-C circuit, write expressions for the energy stored in the capacitor as a function of time and for the energy stored in the inductor as a function of time. (b) Using Eq. (30.22) and the trigonometric identity $\sin^2 x + \cos^2 x = 1$, show that the total energy in the L-C circuit is constant and equal to $Q^2/2C$.

30.36. Show that the differential equation of Eq. (30.20) is satisfied by the function $q = Q\cos(\omega t + \phi)$, with ω given by $1/\sqrt{LC}$.

30.37. Show that $\sqrt{LC}$ has units of time.

Section 30.6 The L-R-C Series Circuit

30.38. For the circuit of Fig. 30.17, let $C = 15.0$ nF, $L = 22$ mH, and $R = 75.0$ Ω (a) Calculate the oscillation frequency of the circuit once the capacitor has been charged and the switch has been connected to point a (b) How long will it take for the amplitude of the oscillation to decay to 10.0% of its original value? (c) What value of R would result in a critically damped circuit?

30.39. (a) In Eq. (13.41), substitute q for x, L for m, $1/C$ for k, and R for the damping constant b. Show that the result is Eq. (30.27). (b) Make these same substitutions in Eq. (13.43) and show that Eq. (30.29) results. (c) Make these same substitutions in Eq. (13.42) and show that Eq. (30.28) results.

30.40. (a) Take first and second derivatives with respect to time of q given in Eq. (30.28), and show that it is a solution of Eq. (30.27). (b) At $t = 0$ the switch shown in Fig. 30.17 is thrown so that it connects points d and a; at this time, $q = Q$ and $i = dq/dt = 0$. Show that the constants ϕ and A in Eq. (30.28) are given by

$$\tan\phi = -\frac{R}{2L\sqrt{(1/LC) - (R^2/4L^2)}} \quad \text{and} \quad A = \frac{Q}{\cos\phi}$$

30.41. An L-R-C circuit has $L = 0.450$ H, $C = 2.50 \times 10^{-5}$ F, and resistance R. (a) What is the angular frequency of the circuit when $R = 0$? (b) What value must R have to give a 5.0% decrease in angular frequency compared to the value calculated in part (a)?

30.42. Show that the quantity $\sqrt{L/C}$ has units of resistance (ohms).

Problems

30.43. One solenoid is centered inside another. The outer one has a length of 50.0 cm and contains 6750 coils, while the coaxial inner solenoid is 3.0 cm long and 0.120 cm in diameter and contains 15 coils. The current in the outer solenoid is changing at 37.5 A/s. (a) what is the mutual inductance of these solenoids? (b) Find the emf induced in the innner solenoid.

30.44. A coil has 400 turns and self-inductance 3.50 mH. The current in the coil varies with time according to $i = (680$ mA$)\cos(\pi t/0.0250$ s$)$. (a) What is the maximum emf induced in the coil? (b) What is the maximum average flux through each turn of the coil? (c) At $t = 0.0180$ s, what is the magnitude of the induced emf?

30.45. A Differentiating Circuit. The current in a resistanceless inductor is caused to vary with time as shown in the graph of Fig. 30.19. (a) Sketch the pattern that would be observed on the screen of an oscilloscope connected to the terminals of the inductor. (The oscilloscope spot sweeps horizontally across the screen at a constant speed, and its vertical deflection is proportional to the potential difference between the inductor terminals.) (b) Explain why a circuit with an inductor can be described as a "differentiating circuit."

Figure **30.19** Problem 30.45

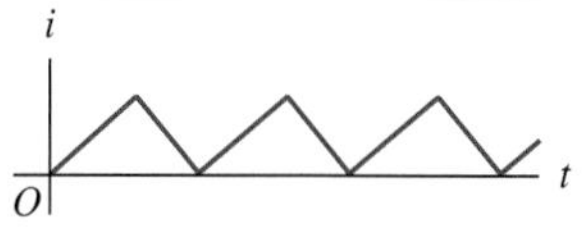

30.46. A 0.250-H inductor carries a time-varying current given by the expression $i = (124$ mA$)\cos[(240\pi/s) t]$. (a) Find an expression for the induced emf as a function of time. Graph the current and induced emf as functions of time for $t = 0$ to $t = \frac{1}{60}$ s. (b) What is the maximum emf? What is the current when the induced emf is a maximum? (c) What is the maximum current? What is the induced emf when the current is a maximum?

30.47. Inductors in Series and Parallel. You are given two inductors, one of self-inductance L_1 and the other of self-inductance L_2. (a) You connect the two inductors in series and arrange them so that their mutual inductance is negligible. Show that the equivalent inductance of the combination is $L_{eq} = L_1 + L_2$. (b) You now connect the two inductors in parallel, again arranging them so that their mutual inductance is negligible. Show that the equivalent inductance of the combination is $L_{eq} = (1/L_1 + 1/L_2)^{-1}$. (Hint: For either a series or a parallel combination, the potential difference across the combination is $L_{eq}(di/dt)$, where i is the current through the combination. For a parallel combination, i is the sum of the currents through the two inductors.)

30.48. A Coaxial Cable. A small solid conductor with radius a is supported by insulating, nonmagnetic disks on the axis of a thin-walled tube with inner radius b. The inner and outer conductors carry equal currents i in opposite directions. (a) Use Ampere's law to find the magnetic field at any point in the volume between the conductors. (b) Write the expression for the flux $d\Phi_B$ through a narrow strip of length l parallel to the axis, of width dr, at a distance r from the axis of the cable and lying in a plane containing the axis. (c) Integrate your expression from part (b) over the volume between the two conductors to find the total flux produced by a current i in the central conductor. (d) Show that the inductance of a length l of the cable is

$$L = l\frac{\mu_0}{2\pi}\ln\left(\frac{b}{a}\right)$$

(e) Use Eq. (30.9) to calculate the energy stored in the magnetic field for a length l of the cable.

30.49. Consider the coaxial cable of Problem 30.48. The conductors carry equal currents i in opposite directions. (a) Use Ampere's law to find the magnetic field at any point in the volume between the conductors. (b) Use the energy density for a magnetic field, Eq. (30.10), to calculate the energy stored in a thin, cylindrical shell between the two conductors. Let the cylindrical shell have inner radius r, outer radius $r + dr$, and length l. (c) integrate your result in part (b) over the volume between the two conductors to find the total energy stored in the magnetic field for a length l of the cable. (d) Use your result in part (c) and Eq. (30.9) to calculate the inductance L of a length l of the cable. Compare your result to L calculated in part (d) of Problem 30.48.

30.50. A toroidal solenoid has a mean radius r and a cross-sectional area A and is wound uniformly with N_1 turns. A second toroidal solenoid with N_2 turns is wound uniformly around the first. The two coils are wound in the same direction. (a) Derive an expression for the inductance L_1 when only the first coil is used and an expression for L_2 when only the second coil is used. (b) Show that $M^2 = L_1 L_2$.

30.51. (a) What would have to be the self-inductance of a solenoid for it to store 10.0 J of energy when a 1.50-A current runs throught it? (b) If this solenoid's cross-sectional diameter is 4.00 cm, and if you could wrap its coils to a density of 10 coils/mm, how long would the solenoid be? (See Exercise 30.11.) Is this a realistic length for ordinary laboratory use?

30.52. An inductor is connected to the terminals of a battery that has an emf of 12.0 V and negligible internal resistance. The current is 4.86 mA at 0.725 ms after the connection is completed. After a long time the current is 6.45 mA. What are (a) the resistance R of the inductor and (b) the inductance L of the inductor?

30.53. Continuation of Exercises 30.19 and 30.27. (a) How much energy is stored in the magnetic field of the inductor one time constant after the battery has been connected? Compute this both by integrating the expression in Exercise 30.27(c) and by using Eq. (30.9), and compare the results. (b) Integrate the expression obtained in Exercise 30.27(a) to find the *total* energy supplied by the battery during the time interval considered in part (a). (c) Integrate the expression obtained in Exercise 30.27(b) to find the *total* energy dissipated in the resistance of the inductor during the same time period. (d) Compare the results obtained in parts (a), (b), and (c).

30.54. Continuation of Exercise 30.25. (a) What is the total energy initially stored in the inductor? (b) At $t = 4.00 \times 10^{-4}$ s, at what rate is the energy stored in the inductor decreasing? (c) At $t = 4.00 \times 10^{-4}$ s, at what rate is electrical energy being converted into thermal energy in the resistor? (d) Obtain an expression for the rate at which electrical energy is being converted into thermal energy in the resistor as a function of time. Integrate this expression from $t = 0$ to $t = \infty$ to obtain the total electrical energy dissipated in the resistor. Compare your result to that of part (a).

30.55. The equation preceding Eq. (30.27) may be converted into an energy relationship. Multiply both sides of this equation by $-i = -dq/dt$. The first term then becomes $i^2 R$. Show that the second term can be written as $d(\frac{1}{2}Li^2)/dt$, and that the third term can be written as $d(q^2/2C)/dt$. What does the resulting equation say about energy conservation in the circuit?

30.56. A 5.00-μF capacitor is initially charged to a potential of 16.0 V. It is then connected in series with a 3.75-mH inductor. (a) What is the total energy stored in this circuit? (b) What is the maximum current in the inductor? What is the charge on the capacitor plates at the instant the current in the inductor is maximal?

30.57. An Electromagnetic Car Alarm. Your latest invention is a car alarm that produces sound at a particularly annoying frequency of 3500 Hz. To do this, the car-alarm circuitry must produce an alternating electric current of the same frequency. That's why your design includes an inductor and a capacitor in series. The maximum voltage across the capacitor is to be 12.0 V (the same voltage as the car battery). To produce a sufficiently loud sound, the capacitor must store 0.0160 J of energy. What values of capacitance and inductance should you choose for your car-alarm circuit?

30.58. An *L-C* circuit consists of a 60.0-mH inductor and a 250-μF capacitor. The initial charge on the capacitor is 6.00 μC, and the initial current in the inductor is zero. (a) What is the maximum voltage across the capacitor? (b) What is the maximum current in the inductor? (c) What is the maximum energy stored in the inductor? (d) When the current in the inductor has half its maximum value, what is the charge on the capacitor and what is the energy stored in the inductor?

30.59. Solar Magnetic Energy. Magnetic fields within a sunspot can be as strong as 0.4 T. (By comparison, the earth's magnetic field is about $1/10{,}000$ as strong.) Sunspots can be as large as 25,000 km in radius. The material in a sunspot has a density of about 3×10^{-4} kg/m^3. Assume μ for the sunspot material is μ_0. If 100% of the magnetic-field energy stored in a sunspot could be used to eject the sunspot's material away from the sun's surface, at what speed would that material be ejected? Compare to the sun's escape speed, which is about 6×10^5 m/s. (*Hint:* Calcualte the kinetic energy the magnetic field could supply to 1 m^3 of sunspot material.)

30.60. While studying a coil of unknown inductance and internal resistance, you connect it in series with a 25.0-V battery and a 150-Ω resistor. You then place an oscilloscope across one of these circuit elements and use the oscilloscope to measure the voltage across the circuit element as a function of time. The result is shown in Fig. 30.20. (a) Across which circuit element (coil or resistor) is the oscilloscope connected? How do you know this? (b) Find the inductance and the internal resistance of the coil. (c) Carefully make a quantitative sketch showing the voltage versus time you would observe if you put the oscilloscope across the other circuit element (resistor or coil).

Figure **30.20** Problem 30.60.

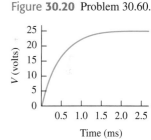

30.61. In the lab, you are trying to find the inductance and internal resistance of a solenoid. You place it in series with a battery of negligible internal resistance, a 10.0-Ω resistor, and a switch. You then put an oscilloscope across one of these circuit elements to measure the voltage across that circuit element as a function of time. You close the switch, and the oscilloscope shows voltage versus time as shown in Fig. 30.21. (a) Across which circuit element (solenoid or resistor) is the oscilloscope connected? How do you know this? (b) Why doesn't the graph approach zero as $t \rightarrow \infty$? (c) What is the emf of the battery? (d) Find the maximum current in the circuit. (e) What are the internal resistance and self-inductance of the solenoid?

Figure **30.21** Problem 30.61.

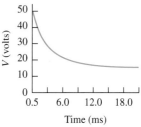

30.62. In the circuit shown in Fig. 30.22, find the reading in each ammeter and voltmeter (a) just after switch S is closed and (b) after S has been closed a very long time.

Figure **30.22** Problem 30.62.

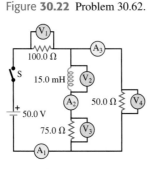

30.63. In the circuit shown in Fig. 30.23, switch S is closed at time $t = 0$ with no charge initially on the capacitor. (a) Find the reading of each ammeter and each voltmeter just after S is closed. (b) Find the reading of each meter after a long time has elapsed. (c) Find the maximum charge on the capacitor. (d) Draw a qualitative graph of the reading of voltmeter V_2 as a function of time.

Figure **30.23** Problem 30.63.

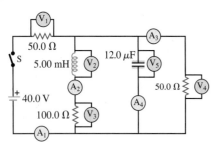

30.64. In the circuit shown in Fig. 30.24 the battery and the inductor have no appreciable internal resistance and there is no current in the circuit. After the switch is closed, find the readings of the ammeter (A) and voltmeters $(V_1$ and $V_2)$ (a) the instant after the switch is closed and (b) after the switch has been closed for a very long time. (c) Which answers in parts (a) and (b) would change if the inductance were 24.0 mH instead?

Figure **30.24** Problem 30.64.

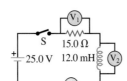

30.65. In the circuit shown in Fig. 30.25, switch S is closed at time $t = 0$. (a) Find the reading of each meter just after S is closed. (b) What does each meter read long after S is closed?

Figure **30.25** Problem 30.65.

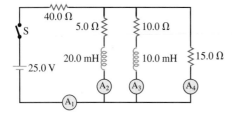

30.66. In the circuit shown in Fig. 30.26, switch S has been closed for a long enough time so that the current reads a steady 3.50 A. Suddenly, switch S_2 is closed and S_1 is opened at the same instant. (a) What is the maximum charge that the capacitor will receive? (b) What is the current in the inductor at this time?

Figure **30.26** Problem 30.66.

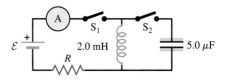
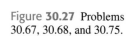

30.67. In the circuit shown in Fig. 30.27, $\mathcal{E} = 60.0$ V, $R_1 = 40.0\ \Omega$, $R_2 = 25.0\ \Omega$, and $L = 0.300$ H. Switch S is closed at $t = 0$. Just after the switch is closed, (a) what is the potential difference v_{ab} across the resistor R_1; (b) which point, a or b, is at a higher potential; (c) what is the potential difference v_{cd} across the inductor L; (d) which point, c or d, is at a higher potential? The switch is left closed a long time and then opened. Just after the switch is opened, (e) what is the potential difference v_{ab} across the resistor R_1; (f) which point, a or b, is at a higher potential; (g) what is the potential difference v_{cd} across the inductor L; (h) which point, c or d, is at a higher potential?

Figure **30.27** Problems 30.67, 30.68, and 30.75.

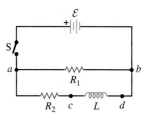

30.68. In the circuit shown in Fig. 30.27, $\mathcal{E} = 60.0$ V, $R_1 = 40.0\ \Omega$, $R_2 = 25.0\ \Omega$, and $L = 0.300$ H. (a) Switch S is closed. At some time t afterward the current in the inductor is increasing at a rate of $di/dt = 50.0$ A/s. At this instant, what are the current i_1 through R_1 and the current i_2 through R_2? (*Hint:* Analyze two separate loops: one containing $\mathcal{E}$ and R_1 and the other containing $\mathcal{E}$, R_2, and L.) (b) After the switch has been closed a long time, it is opened again. Just after it is opened, what is the current through R_1?

30.69. Consider the circuit shown in Fig. 30.28. Let $\mathcal{E} = 36.0$ V, $R_0 = 50.0\ \Omega$, $R = 150\ \Omega$, and $L = 4.00$ H. (a) Switch S_1 is closed and switch S_2 is left open. Just after S_1 is closed, what are the current i_0 through R_0 and the potential differences v_{ac} and v_{cb}? (b) After S_1 has been closed a long time $(S_2$ is still open) so that the current has reached its final, steady value, what are i_0, v_{ac}, and v_{cb}? (c) Find the expressions for i_0, v_{ac}, and v_{cb} as functions of the time t since S_1 was closed. Your results should agree with part (a) when $t = 0$ and with part (b) when $t \rightarrow \infty$. Graph i_0, v_{ac}, and v_{cb} versus time.

Figure **30.28** Problems 30.69 and 30.70.

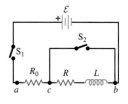

30.70. After the current in the circuit of Fig. 30.28 has reached its final, steady value with switch S_1 closed and S_2 open, switch S_2 is closed, thus short-circuiting the inductor. (Switch S_1 remains closed. See Problem 30.69 for numerical values of the circuit elements.) (a) Just after S_2 is closed, what are v_{ac} and v_{cb}, and what are the currents through R_0, R, and S_2? (b) A long time after S_2 is closed, what are v_{ac} and v_{cb}, and what are the currents through R_0, R, and S_2? (c) Derive expressions for the currents through R_0, R, and S_2 as functions of the time t that has elapsed since S_2 was closed. Your results should agree with part (a) when $t = 0$ and with part (b) when $t \rightarrow \infty$. Graph these three currents versus time.

30.71. In the circuit shown in Fig. 30.29, the switch has been open for a long time and is suddenly closed. Neither the battery nor the inductors have any appreciable resistance. Review the results of Problem 30.47. (a) What do the ammeter and voltmeter read just after S is closed? (b) What do the ammeter and the voltmeter read after S has been closed a very long time? (c) What do the ammeter and the voltmeter read 0.115 ms after S is closed?

30.72. In the circuit shown in Fig. 30.30, neither the battery nor the inductors have any appreciable resistance, the capacitors are initially uncharged, and the switch S has been in position 1 for a very long time. Review the results of Problem 30.47. (a) What is the current in the circuit? (b) The switch is now suddenly flipped to position 2. Find the maximum charge that each capacitor will receive, and how much time after the switch is flipped it will take them to acquire this charge.

30.73. We have ignored the variation of the magnetic field across the cross section of a toroidal solenoid. Let's now examine the validity of that approximation. A certain toroidal solenoid has a rectangular cross section (Fig. 30.31). It has N uniformly spaced turns, with air inside. The magnetic field at a point inside the toroid is given by the equation derived in Example 28.11 (Section 28.7). *Do not* assume the field is uniform over the cross section. (a) Show that the magnetic flux through a cross section of the toroid is

$$\Phi_B = \frac{\mu_0 N i h}{2\pi} \ln\left(\frac{b}{a}\right)$$

(b) Show that the inductance of the toroidal solenoid is given by

$$L = \frac{\mu_0 N^2 h}{2\pi} \ln\left(\frac{b}{a}\right)$$

(c) The fraction b/a may be written as

$$\frac{b}{a} = \frac{a + b - a}{a} = 1 + \frac{b - a}{a}$$

Use the power series expansion $\ln(1 + z) = z + z^2/2 + \cdots$, valid for $|z| < 1$, to show that when $b - a$ is much less than a, the inductance is approximately equal to

$$L = \frac{\mu_0 N^2 h (b - a)}{2\pi a}$$

Compare this result with the result given in Example 30.3 (Section 30.2).

30.74. In Fig. 30.32 the switch is closed, with the capacitor having the polarity shown. Find the direction (clockwise or counter-clockwise) of the current induced in the rectangular wire loop A.

30.75. Demonstrating Inductance. A common demonstration of induc-

Figure **30.29** Problem 30.71.

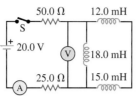

Figure **30.30** Problem 30.72.

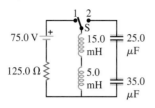

Figure **30.31** Problem 30.73.

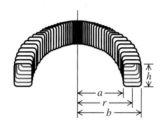

Figure **30.32** Problem 30.74.

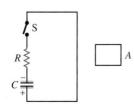

tance employs a circuit such as the one shown in Fig. 30.27. Switch S is closed, and the light bulb (represented by resistance R_1) just barely glows. After a period of time, switch S is opened, and the bulb lights up brightly for a short period of time. To understand this effect, think of an inductor as a device that imparts an "inertia" to the current, preventing a discontinuous change in the current through it. (a) Derive, as explicit functions of time, expressions for i_1 (the current through the light bulb) and i_2 (the current through the inductor) after switch S is closed. (b) After a long period of time, the currents i_1 and i_2 reach their steady-state values. Obtain expressions for these steady-state currents. (c) Switch S is now opened. Obtain an expression for the current through the inductor and light bulb as an explicit function of time. (d) You have been asked to design a demonstration apparatus using the circuit shown in Fig. 30.27 with a 22.0-H inductor and a 40.0-W light bulb. You are to connect a resistor in series with the inductor, and R_2 represents the sum of that resistance plus the internal resistance of the inductor. When switch S is opened, a transient current is to be set up that starts at 0.600 A and is not to fall below 0.150 A until after 0.0800 s. For simplicity, assume that the resistance of the light bulb is constant and equals the resistance the bulb must have to dissipate 40.0 W at 120 V. Determine R_2 and $\mathcal{E}$ for the given design considerations. (e) With the numerical values determined in part (d), what is the current through the light bulb just before the switch is opened? Does this result confirm the qualitative description of what is observed in the demonstration?

Challenge Problems

30.76. Consider the circuit shown in Fig. 30.33. The circuit elements are as follows: $\mathcal{E} = 32.0$ V, $L = 0.640$ H, $C = 2.00$ μF, and $R = 400$ Ω. At time $t = 0$, switch S is closed. The current through the inductor is i_1, the current through the capacitor branch is i_2, and the charge on the capacitor is q_2. (a) Using Kirchhoff's rules, verify the circuit equations

Figure **30.33** Challenge Problem 30.76.

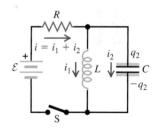

$$R(i_1 + i_2) + L\left(\frac{di_1}{dt}\right) = \mathcal{E}$$

$$R(i_2 + i_2) + \frac{q_2}{C} = \mathcal{E}$$

(b) What are the initial values of i_1, i_2, and q_2? (c) Show by direct substitution that the following solutions for i_1 and q_2 satisfy the circuit equations from part (a). Also, show that they satisfy the initial conditions

$$i_1 = \left(\frac{\mathcal{E}}{R}\right)[1 - e^{-\beta t}(2\omega RC)^{-1}\sin(\omega t) + \cos(\omega t)]$$

$$q_2 = \left(\frac{\mathcal{E}}{\omega R}\right)e^{-\beta t}\sin(\omega t)$$

where $\beta = (2RC)^{-1}$ and $\omega = [(LC)^{-1} - (2RC)^{-2}]^{1/2}$. (d) Determine the time t_1 at which i_2 first becomes zero.

30.77. A Volume Gauge. A tank containing a liquid has turns of wire wrapped around it, causing it to act like an inductor. The liquid content of the tank can be measured by using its inductance to determine the height of the liquid in the tank. The inductance of the tank changes from a value of L_0 corresponding to a relative permeability of 1 when the tank is empty to a value of L_f corresponding to a relative permeability of K_m (the relative permeability of the liquid) when the tank is full. The appropriate electronic circuitry can determine the inductance to five significant figures and thus the effective relative permeability of the combined air and liquid within the rectangular cavity of the tank. The four sides of the tank each have width W and height D (Fig. 30.34). The height of the liquid in the tank is d. You can ignore any fringing effects and assume that the relative permeability of the material of which the tank is made can be ignored. (a) Derive an expression for d as a function of L, the inductance corresponding to a certain fluid height, L_0, L_f, and D. (b) What is the inductance (to five significant figures) for a tank $\frac{1}{4}$ full, $\frac{1}{2}$ full, $\frac{3}{4}$ full, and completely full if the tank contains liquid oxygen? Take $L_0 = 0.63000$ H. The magnetic susceptibility of liquid oxygen is $\chi_m = 1.52 \times 10^{-3}$. (c) Repeat part (b) for mercury. The magnetic susceptibility of mercury is given in Table 28.1. (d) For which material is this volume gauge more practical?

30.78. Two coils are wrapped around each other as shown in Fig. 30.3. The current travels in the same sense around each coil. One coil has self-inductance L_1, and the other coil has self-inductance L_2. The mutual inductance of the two coils is M. (a) Show that if the two coils are connected in series, the equivalent inductance of the combination is $L_{eq} = L_1 + L_2 + 2M$.

Figure **30.34** Challenge Problem 30.77.

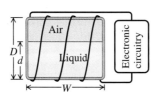

(b) Show that if the two coils are connected in parallel, the equivalent inductance of the combination is

$$L_{eq} = \frac{L_1 L_2 - M^2}{L_1 + L_2 - 2M}$$

(*Hint:* See the hint for Problem 30.47.)

30.79. Consider the circuit shown in Fig. 30.35. Switch S is closed at time $t = 0$, causing a current i_1 through the inductive branch and a current i_2 through the capacitive branch. The initial charge on the capacitor is zero, and the charge at time t is q_2. (a) Derive expressions for i_1, i_2, and q_2 as functions of time. Express your answers in terms of $\mathcal{E}$, L, C, R_1, R_2, and t. For the remainder of the problem let the circuit elements have the following values: $\mathcal{E} = 48$ V, $L = 8.0$ H, $C = 20\ \mu$F, $R_1 = 25\ \Omega$, and $R_2 = 5000\ \Omega$. (b) What is the initial current through the inductive branch? What is the initial current through the capacitive branch? (c) What are the currents through the inductive and capacitive branches a long time after the switch has been closed? How long is a "long time"? Explain. (d) At what time t_1 (accurate to two significant figures) will the currents i_1 and i_2 be equal? (*Hint:* You might consider using series expansions for the exponentials.) (e) For the conditions given in part (d), determine i_1. (f) The total current through the battery is $i = i_1 + i_2$. At what time t_2 (accurate to two significant figures) will i equal one-half of its final value? (*Hint:* The numerical work is greatly simplified if one makes suitable approximations. A sketch of i_1 and i_2 versus t may help you decide what approximations are valid.)

Figure **30.35** Challenge Problem 30.79.

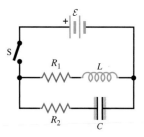

ALTERNATING CURRENT

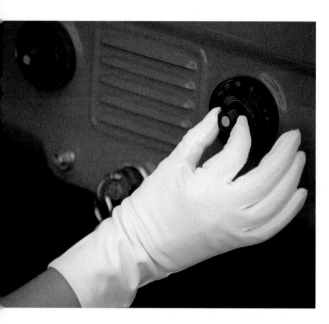

? Waves from a broadcasting station produce an alternating current in the circuits of a radio (like the one in this classic car). If a radio is tuned to a station at a frequency of 1000 kHz, does it also detect the transmissions from a station broadcasting at 600 kHz?

LEARNING GOALS

By studying this chapter, you will learn:

- How phasors make it easy to describe sinusoidally varying quantities.

- How to use reactance to describe the voltage across a circuit element that carries an alternating current.

- How to analyze an *L-R-C* series circuit with a sinusoidal emf.

- What determines the amount of power flowing into or out of an alternating-current circuit.

- How an *L-R-C* series circuit responds to sinusoidal emfs of different frequencies.

- Why transformers are useful, and how they work.

D uring the 1880s in the United States there was a heated and acrimonious debate between two inventors over the best method of electric-power distribution. Thomas Edison favored direct current (dc)—that is, steady current that does not vary with time. George Westinghouse favored **alternating current (ac),** with sinusoidally varying voltages and currents. He argued that transformers (which we will study in this chapter) can be used to step the voltage up and down with ac but not with dc; low voltages are safer for consumer use, but high voltages and correspondingly low currents are best for long-distance power transmission to minimize i^2R losses in the cables.

Eventually, Westinghouse prevailed, and most present-day household and industrial power-distribution systems operate with alternating current. Any appliance that you plug into a wall outlet uses ac, and many battery-powered devices such as radios and cordless telephones make use of the dc supplied by the battery to create or amplify alternating currents. Circuits in modern communication equipment, including pagers and television, also make extensive use of ac.

In this chapter we will learn how resistors, inductors, and capacitors behave in circuits with sinusoidally varying voltages and currents. Many of the principles that we found useful in Chapters 25, 28, and 30 are applicable, along with several new concepts related to the circuit behavior of inductors and capacitors. A key concept in this discussion is *resonance,* which we studied in Chapter 13 for mechanical systems.

31.1 Phasors and Alternating Currents

To supply an alternating current to a circuit, a source of alternating emf or voltage is required. An example of such a source is a coil of wire rotating with constant angular velocity in a magnetic field, which we discussed in Example 29.4 (Section 29.2). This develops a sinusoidal alternating emf and is the prototype of the commercial alternating-current generator or *alternator* (see Fig. 29.8).

We use the term **ac source** for any device that supplies a sinusoidally varying voltage (potential difference) v or current i. The usual circuit-diagram symbol for an ac source is

A sinusoidal voltage might be described by a function such as

$$v = V\cos\omega t \qquad (31.1)$$

In this expression, v (lowercase) is the *instantaneous* potential difference; V (uppercase) is the maximum potential difference, which we call the **voltage amplitude;** and ω is the *angular frequency,* equal to 2π times the frequency f (Fig. 31.1).

In the United States and Canada, commercial electric-power distribution systems always use a frequency of $f = 60$ Hz, corresponding to $\omega = (2\pi \text{ rad})(60 \text{ s}^{-1}) = 377$ rad/s; in much of the rest of the world, $f = 50$ Hz ($\omega = 314$ rad/s) is used. Similarly, a sinusoidal current might be described as

$$i = I\cos\omega t \qquad (31.2)$$

where i (lowercase) is the instantaneous current and I (uppercase) is the maximum current or **current amplitude.**

Phasor Diagrams

To represent sinusoidally varying voltages and currents, we will use rotating vector diagrams similar to those we used in the study of simple harmonic motion in Section 13.2 (see Figs. 13.5b and 13.6). In these diagrams the instantaneous value of a quantity that varies sinusoidally with time is represented by the *projection* onto a horizontal axis of a vector with a length equal to the amplitude of the quantity. The vector rotates counterclockwise with constant angular speed ω. These rotating vectors are called **phasors,** and diagrams containing them are called **phasor diagrams.** Figure 31.2 shows a phasor diagram for the sinusoidal current described by Eq. (31.2). The projection of the phasor onto the horizontal axis at time t is $I\cos\omega t$; this is why we chose to use the cosine function rather than the sine in Eq. (31.2).

> **CAUTION** **Just what is a phasor?** A phasor is not a real physical quantity with a direction in space, such as velocity, momentum, or electric field. Rather, it is a *geometric* entity that helps us to describe and analyze physical quantities that vary sinusoidally with time. In Section 13.2 we used a single phasor to represent the position of a point mass undergoing simple harmonic motion. In this chapter we will use phasors to *add* sinusoidal voltages and currents. Combining sinusoidal quantities with phase differences then becomes a matter of vector addition. We will find a similar use for phasors in Chapters 35 and 36 in our study of interference effects with light. ▮

Rectified Alternating Current

How do we measure a sinusoidally varying current? In Section 26.3 we used a d'Arsonval galvanometer to measure steady currents. But if we pass a *sinusoidal* current through a d'Arsonval meter, the torque on the moving coil varies sinusoidally, with one direction half the time and the opposite direction the other half. The needle may wiggle a little if the frequency is low enough, but its average deflection is zero. Hence a d'Arsonval meter by itself isn't very useful for measuring alternating currents.

31.1 The voltage across a sinusoidal ac source.

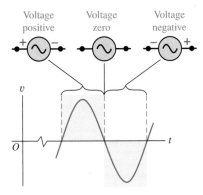

31.2 A phasor diagram.

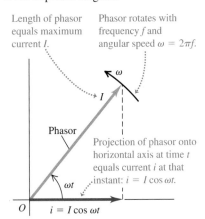

To get a measurable one-way current through the meter, we can use *diodes*, which we described in Section 25.3. A diode (or rectifier) is a device that conducts better in one direction than in the other; an ideal diode has zero resistance for one direction of current and infinite resistance for the other. One possible arrangement is shown in Fig. 31.3a. The current through the galvanometer G is always upward, regardless of the direction of the current from the ac source (i.e., which part of the cycle the source is in). The current through G is as shown by the graph in Fig. 31.2b. It pulsates but always has the same direction, and the average meter deflection is *not* zero. This arrangement of diodes is called a *full-wave rectifier circuit.*

The **rectified average current** I_{rav} is defined so that during any whole number of cycles, the total charge that flows is the same as though the current were constant with a value equal to I_{rav}. The notation I_{rav} and the name *rectified average current* emphasize that this is *not* the average of the original sinusoidal current. In Fig. 31.3b the total charge that flows in time t corresponds to the area under the curve of i versus t (recall that $i = dq/dt$, so q is the integral of t); this area must equal the rectangular area with height I_{rav}. We see that I_{rav} is less than the maximum current I; the two are related by

$$I_{rav} = \frac{2}{\pi}I = 0.637I \qquad \begin{array}{l}\text{(rectified average value} \\ \text{of a sinusoidal current)}\end{array} \qquad (31.3)$$

(The factor of $2/\pi$ is the average value of $|\cos\omega t|$ or of $|\sin\omega t|$; see Example 29.5 in Section 29.2.) The galvanometer deflection is proportional to I_{rav}. The galvanometer scale can be calibrated to read I, I_{rav}, or, most commonly, I_{rms} (discussed below).

Root-Mean-Square (rms) Values

A more useful way to describe a quantity that can be either positive or negative is the *root-mean-square (rms) value*. We used rms values in Section 18.3 in connection with the speeds of molecules in a gas. We *square* the instantaneous current i, take the *average* (mean) value of i^2, and finally take the *square root* of that average. This procedure defines the **root-mean-square current,** denoted as I_{rms} (Fig. 31.4). Even when i is negative, i^2 is always positive, so I_{rms} is never zero (unless i is zero at every instant).

Here's how we obtain I_{rms} for a sinusoidal current, like that shown in Fig. 31.4. If the instantaneous current is given by $i = I\cos\omega t$, then

$$i^2 = I^2\cos^2\omega t$$

Using a double-angle formula from trigonometry,

$$\cos^2 A = \frac{1}{2}(1 + \cos 2A)$$

we find

$$i^2 = I^2\frac{1}{2}(1 + \cos 2\omega t) = \frac{1}{2}I^2 + \frac{1}{2}I^2\cos 2\omega t$$

The average of $\cos 2\omega t$ is zero because it is positive half the time and negative half the time. Thus the average of i^2 is simply $I^2/2$. The square root of this is I_{rms}:

$$I_{rms} = \frac{I}{\sqrt{2}} \qquad \text{(root-mean-square value of a sinusoidal current)} \qquad (31.4)$$

31.3 (a) A full-wave rectifier circuit. (b) Graph of the resulting current through the galvanometer G.

(a) A full-wave rectifier circuit

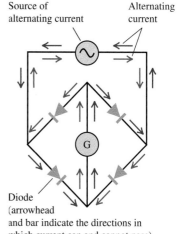

Diode
(arrowhead
and bar indicate the directions in
which current can and cannot pass)

(b) Graph of the full-wave rectified current and its average value, the rectified average current I_{rav}

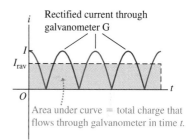

Area under curve = total charge that flows through galvanometer in time t.

31.4 Calculating the root-mean-square (rms) value of an alternating current.

Meaning of the rms value of a sinusoidal quantity (here, ac current with $I = 3$ A):

① Graph current i versus time.

② *Square* the instantaneous current i.

③ Take the *average* (mean) value of i^2.

④ Take the *square root* of that average.

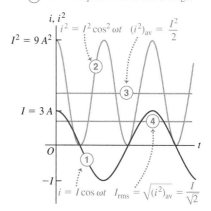

31.5 This wall socket delivers a root-mean-square voltage of 120 V. Sixty times per second, the instantaneous voltage across its terminals varies from $(\sqrt{2})(120 \text{ V}) = 170 \text{ V}$ to -170 V and back again.

In the same way, the root-mean-square value of a sinusoidal voltage with amplitude (maximum value) V is

$$V_{rms} = \frac{V}{\sqrt{2}} \qquad \text{(root-mean-square value of a sinusoidal voltage)} \quad (31.5)$$

We can convert a rectifying ammeter into a voltmeter by adding a series resistor, just as for the dc case discussed in Section 26.3. Meters used for ac voltage and current measurements are nearly always calibrated to read rms values, not maximum or rectified average. Voltages and currents in power distribution systems are always described in terms of their rms values. The usual household power supply, "120-volt ac," has an rms voltage of 120 V (Fig. 31.5). The voltage amplitude is

$$V = \sqrt{2} V_{rms} = \sqrt{2}(120 \text{ V}) = 170 \text{ V}$$

Example 31.1 Current in a personal computer

The plate on the back of a personal computer says that it draws 2.7 A from a 120-V, 60-Hz line. For this computer, what are (a) the average current, (b) the average of the square of the current, and (c) the current amplitude?

SOLUTION

IDENTIFY: This example is about alternating current.

SET UP: In parts (b) and (c) we use the idea that the root-mean-square current, given by Eq. (31.4), is the *square root* of the *mean* (average) of the *square* of the current.

EXECUTE: (a) The average of *any* sinusoidal alternating current, over any whole number of cycles, is zero.

(b) The current given is the rms value: $I_{rms} = 2.7$ A. The target variable $(i^2)_{av}$ is the *mean* of the *square* of the current. The rms current is the square root of this target variable, so

$$I_{rms} = \sqrt{(i^2)_{av}} \quad \text{or} \quad (i^2)_{av} = (I_{rms})^2 = (2.7 \text{ A})^2 = 7.3 \text{ A}^2$$

(c) From Eq. (31.4) the current amplitude I is

$$I = \sqrt{2} I_{rms} = \sqrt{2}(2.7 \text{ A}) = 3.8 \text{ A}$$

Figure 31.6 shows our graphs of i and i^2.

EVALUATE: Why would we be interested in the average of the square of the current? Recall that the rate at which energy is dissipated in a resistor R equals $i^2 R$. This rate varies if the current is alternating, so it is best described by its average value $(i^2)_{av} R = I_{rms}^2 R$. We make use of this idea in Section 31.4.

31.6 Our graphs of the current i and the square of the current i^2 versus time t.

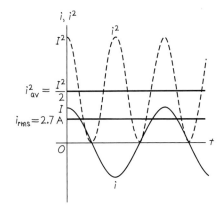

Test Your Understanding of Section 31.1 The figure at left shows four different current phasors with the same angular frequency ω. At the time shown, which phasor corresponds to (a) a positive current that is becoming more positive; (b) a positive current that is decreasing toward zero; (c) a negative current that is becoming more negative; (d) a negative current that is decreasing in magnitude toward zero?

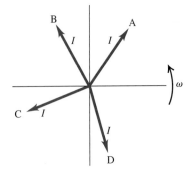

31.2 Resistance and Reactance

In this section we will derive voltage–current relationships for individual circuit elements carrying a sinusoidal current. We'll consider resistors, inductors, and capacitors.

Resistor in an ac Circuit

First let's consider a resistor with resistance R through which there is a sinusoidal current given by Eq. (31.2): $i = I\cos\omega t$. The positive direction of current is counterclockwise around the circuit, as in Fig. 31.7a. The current amplitude (maximum current) is I. From Ohm's law the instantaneous potential v_R of point a with respect to point b (that is, the instantaneous voltage across the resistor) is

$$v_R = iR = (IR)\cos\omega t \qquad (31.6)$$

The maximum voltage V_R, the *voltage amplitude,* is the coefficient of the cosine function:

$$V_R = IR \quad \text{(amplitude of voltage across a resistor, ac circuit)} \qquad (31.7)$$

Hence we can also write

$$v_R = V_R\cos\omega t \qquad (31.8)$$

The current i and voltage v_R are both proportional to $\cos\omega t$, so the current is *in phase* with the voltage. Equation (31.7) shows that the current and voltage amplitudes are related in the same way as in a dc circuit.

Figure 31.7b shows graphs of i and v_R as functions of time. The vertical scales for current and voltage are different, so the relative heights of the two curves are not significant. The corresponding phasor diagram is given in Fig. 31.7c. Because i and v_R are *in phase* and have the same frequency, the current and voltage phasors rotate together; they are parallel at each instant. Their projections on the horizontal axis represent the instantaneous current and voltage, respectively.

Inductor in an ac Circuit

Next, we replace the resistor in Fig. 31.7 with a pure inductor with self-inductance L and zero resistance (Fig. 31.8a). Again we assume that the current is $i = I\cos\omega t$, with the positive direction of current taken as counterclockwise around the circuit.

Although there is no resistance, there is a potential difference v_L between the inductor terminals a and b because the current varies with time, giving rise to a self-induced emf. The induced emf in the direction of i is given by Eq. (30.7), $\mathcal{E} = -L\, di/dt$; however, the voltage v_L is *not* simply equal to $\mathcal{E}$. To see why, notice that if the current in the inductor is in the positive (counterclockwise) direction from a to b and is increasing, then di/dt is positive and the induced emf is directed to the left to oppose the increase in current; hence point a is at higher potential than is point b. Thus the potential of point a with respect to point b is positive and is given by $v_L = +L\, di/dt$, the *negative* of the induced emf. (You should convince

31.7 Resistance R connected across an ac source.

(a) Circuit with ac source and resistor

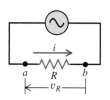

(b) Graphs of current and voltage versus time

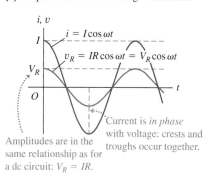

Amplitudes are in the same relationship as for a dc circuit: $V_R = IR$.

Current is *in phase* with voltage: crests and troughs occur together.

(c) Phasor diagram

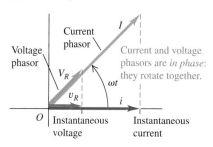

Current and voltage phasors are *in phase:* they rotate together.

31.8 Inductance L connected across an ac source.

(a) Circuit with ac source and inductor

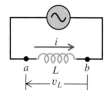

(b) Graphs of current and voltage versus time

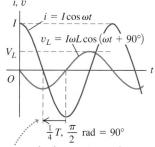

$\frac{1}{4}T$, $\frac{\pi}{2}$ rad $= 90°$

Voltage curve *leads* current curve by a quarter-cycle (corresponding to $\phi = \pi/2$ rad $= 90°$).

(c) Phasor diagram

Voltage phasor *leads* current phasor by $\phi = \pi/2$ rad $= 90°$.

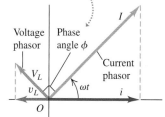

Act|v
Phys|cs
ONLINE

14.3   AC Circuits: The Driven Oscillator
        (Questions 1–5)

yourself that this expression gives the correct sign of v_L in *all* cases, including i counterclockwise and decreasing, i clockwise and increasing, and i clockwise and decreasing; you should also review Section 30.2.) So we have

$$v_L = L\frac{di}{dt} = L\frac{d}{dt}(I\cos\omega t) = -I\omega L\sin\omega t \qquad (31.9)$$

The voltage v_L across the inductor at any instant is proportional to the *rate of change* of the current. The points of maximum voltage on the graph correspond to maximum steepness of the current curve, and the points of zero voltage are the points where the current curve instantaneously levels off at its maximum and minimum values (Fig. 31.8b). The voltage and current are "out of step" or *out of phase* by a quarter-cycle. Since the voltage peaks occur a quarter-cycle earlier than the current peaks, we say that the voltage *leads* the current by 90°. The phasor diagram in Fig. 31.8c also shows this relationship; the voltage phasor is ahead of the current phasor by 90°.

We can also obtain this phase relationship by rewriting Eq. (31.9) using the identity $\cos(A + 90°) = -\sin A$:

$$v_L = I\omega L\cos(\omega t + 90°) \qquad (31.10)$$

This result shows that the voltage can be viewed as a cosine function with a "head start" of 90° relative to the current.

As we have done in Eq. (31.10), we will usually describe the phase of the *voltage* relative to the *current,* not the reverse. Thus if the current i in a circuit is

$$i = I\cos\omega t$$

and the voltage v of one point with respect to another is

$$v = V\cos(\omega t + \phi)$$

we call ϕ the **phase angle;** it gives the phase of the *voltage* relative to the *current.* For a pure resistor, $\phi = 0$, and for a pure inductor, $\phi = 90°$.

From Eq. (31.9) or (31.10) the amplitude V_L of the inductor voltage is

$$V_L = I\omega L \qquad (31.11)$$

We define the **inductive reactance** X_L of an inductor as

$$X_L = \omega L \qquad \text{(inductive reactance)} \qquad (31.12)$$

Using X_L, we can write Eq. (31.11) in a form similar to Eq. (31.7) for a resistor $(V_R = IR)$:

$$V_L = IX_L \qquad \text{(amplitude of voltage across an inductor, ac circuit)} \qquad (31.13)$$

Because X_L is the ratio of a voltage and a current, its SI unit is the ohm, the same as for resistance.

CAUTION **Inductor voltage and current are not in phase** Keep in mind that Eq. (31.13) is a relationship between the *amplitudes* of the oscillating voltage and current for the inductor in Fig. 31.8a. It does *not* say that the voltage at any instant is equal to the current at that instant multiplied by X_L. As Fig. 31.8b shows, the voltage and current are 90° out of phase. Voltage and current are in phase only for resistors, as in Eq. (31.6). ▮

The Meaning of Inductive Reactance

The inductive reactance X_L is really a description of the self-induced emf that opposes any change in the current through the inductor. From Eq. (31.13), for a given current amplitude I the voltage $v_L = +L\,di/dt$ across the inductor and the self-induced emf $\mathcal{E} = -L\,di/dt$ both have an amplitude V_L that is directly proportional to X_L. According to Eq. (31.12), the inductive reactance and self-induced emf increase with more rapid variation in current (that is, increasing angular frequency ω) and increasing inductance L.

If an oscillating voltage of a given amplitude V_L is applied across the inductor terminals, the resulting current will have a smaller amplitude I for larger values of X_L. Since X_L is proportional to frequency, a high-frequency voltage applied to the inductor gives only a small current, while a lower-frequency voltage of the same amplitude gives rise to a larger current. Inductors are used in some circuit applications, such as power supplies and radio-interference filters, to block high frequencies while permitting lower frequencies or dc to pass through. A circuit device that uses an inductor for this purpose is called a *low-pass filter* (see Problem 31.50).

Example 31.2 An inductor in an ac circuit

Suppose you want the current amplitude in a pure inductor in a radio receiver to be 250 μA when the voltage amplitude is 3.60 V at a frequency of 1.60 MHz (corresponding to the upper end of the AM broadcast band). (a) What inductive reactance is needed? What inductance? (b) If the voltage amplitude is kept constant, what will be the current amplitude through this inductor at 16.0 MHz? At 160 kHz?

SOLUTION

IDENTIFY: We are not told about any other elements of the circuit of which the inductor is part. Nor should we care about those other elements, since from the perspective of this example, all they do is provide the inductor with an oscillating voltage. Hence all of those other circuit elements are lumped into the ac source shown in Fig. 31.8a.

SET UP: We are given the current amplitude I and the voltage amplitude V. Our target variables in part (a) are the inductive reactance X_L at 1.60 MHz and the inductance L, which we find using Eqs. (31.13) and (31.12). Once we know L, we use these same two equations to find the inductive reactance and current amplitude at any other frequency.

EXECUTE: (a) From Eq. (31.13),

$$X_L = \frac{V_L}{I} = \frac{3.60\ \text{V}}{250 \times 10^{-6}\ \text{A}} = 1.44 \times 10^4\ \Omega = 14.4\ \text{k}\Omega$$

From Eq. (31.12), with $\omega = 2\pi f$, we find

$$L = \frac{X_L}{2\pi f} = \frac{1.44 \times 10^4\ \Omega}{2\pi(1.60 \times 10^6\ \text{Hz})} = 1.43 \times 10^{-3}\ \text{H} = 1.43\ \text{mH}$$

(b) Combining Eqs. (31.12) and (31.13), we find that the current amplitude is $I = V_L/X_L = V_L/\omega L = V_L/2\pi f L$. Thus the current amplitude is inversely proportional to the frequency f. Since $I = 250\ \mu$A at $f = 1.60$ MHz, the current amplitude at 16.0 MHz (ten times the original frequency) will be one-tenth as great, or 25.0 μA; at 160 kHz = 0.160 MHz (one-tenth of the original frequency) the current amplitude is ten times as great, or 2500 μA = 2.50 mA.

EVALUATE: In general, the lower the frequency of an oscillating voltage applied across an inductor, the greater the amplitude of the oscillating current that results.

Capacitor in an ac Circuit

Finally, we connect a capacitor with capacitance C to the source, as in Fig. 31.9a, producing a current $i = I\cos\omega t$ through the capacitor. Again, the positive direction of current is counterclockwise around the circuit.

CAUTION **Alternating current through a capacitor** You may object that charge can't really move through the capacitor because its two plates are insulated from each other. True enough, but as the capacitor charges and discharges, there is at each instant a current i into one plate, an equal current out of the other plate, and an equal *displacement* current between the plates just as though the charge were being conducted through the capacitor. (You may want to review the discussion of displacement current in Section 29.7.) Thus we often speak about alternating current *through* a capacitor. ▮

To find the instantaneous voltage v_C across the capacitor—that is, the potential of point a with respect to point b—we first let q denote the charge on the left-hand plate of the capacitor in Fig. 31.9a (so $-q$ is the charge on the right-hand plate). The current i is related to q by $i = dq/dt$; with this definition, positive current corresponds to an increasing charge on the left-hand capacitor plate. Then

$$i = \frac{dq}{dt} = I\cos\omega t$$

Integrating this, we get

$$q = \frac{I}{\omega}\sin\omega t \qquad (31.14)$$

31.9 Capacitor C connected across an ac source.

(a) Circuit with ac source and capacitor

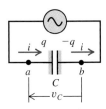

(b) Graphs of current and voltage versus time

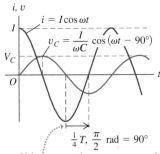

Voltage curve *lags* current curve by a quarter-cycle (corresponding to $\phi = \pi/2$ rad $= 90°$).

(c) Phasor diagram

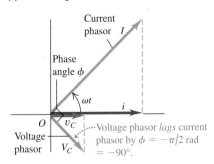

Also, from Eq. (24.1) the charge q equals the voltage v_C multiplied by the capacitance, $q = Cv_C$. Using this in Eq. (31.14), we find

$$v_C = \frac{I}{\omega C} \sin \omega t \tag{31.15}$$

The instantaneous current i is equal to the rate of change dq/dt of the capacitor charge q; since $q = Cv_C$, i is also proportional to the rate of change of voltage. (Compare to an inductor, for which the situation is reversed and v_L is proportional to the rate of change of i.) Figure 31.9b shows v_C and i as functions of t. Because $i = dq/dt = C\,dv_C/dt$, the current has its greatest magnitude when the v_C curve is rising or falling most steeply and is zero when the v_C curve instantaneously levels off at its maximum and minimum values.

The capacitor voltage and current are out of phase by a quarter-cycle. The peaks of voltage occur a quarter-cycle *after* the corresponding current peaks, and we say that the voltage *lags* the current by 90°. The phasor diagram in Fig. 31.9c shows this relationship; the voltage phasor is behind the current phasor by a quarter-cycle, or 90°.

We can also derive this phase difference by rewriting Eq. (31.15), using the identity $\cos(A - 90°) = \sin A$:

$$v_C = \frac{I}{\omega C} \cos(\omega t - 90°) \tag{31.16}$$

This corresponds to a phase angle $\phi = -90°$. This cosine function has a "late start" of 90° compared with the current $i = I\cos \omega t$.

Equations (31.15) and (31.16) show that the *maximum* voltage V_C (the voltage amplitude) is

$$V_C = \frac{I}{\omega C} \tag{31.17}$$

To put this expression in a form similar to Eq. (31.7) for a resistor, $V_R = IR$, we define a quantity X_C, called the **capacitive reactance** of the capacitor, as

$$X_C = \frac{1}{\omega C} \quad \text{(capacitive reactance)} \tag{31.18}$$

Then

$$V_C = IX_C \quad \text{(amplitude of voltage across a capacitor, ac circuit)} \tag{31.19}$$

The SI unit of X_C is the ohm, the same as for resistance and inductive reactance, because X_C is the ratio of a voltage and a current.

CAUTION **Capacitor voltage and current are not in phase** Remember that Eq. (31.19) for a capacitor, like Eq. (31.13) for an inductor, is *not* a statement about the instantaneous values of voltage and current. The instantaneous values are actually 90° out of phase, as Fig. 31.9b shows. Rather, Eq. (31.19) relates the *amplitudes* of the voltage and current. ▮

The Meaning of Capacitive Reactance

The capacitive reactance of a capacitor is inversely proportional both to the capacitance C and to the angular frequency ω; the greater the capacitance and the higher the frequency, the *smaller* the capacitive reactance X_C. Capacitors tend to pass high-frequency current and to block low-frequency currents and dc, just the opposite of inductors. A device that preferentially passes signals of high frequency is called a *high-pass filter* (see Problem 31.49).

| Example 31.3 | **A resistor and a capacitor in an ac circuit** |

A 200-Ω resistor is connected in series with a 5.0-μF capacitor. The voltage across the resistor is $v_R = (1.20 \text{ V}) \cos(2500 \text{ rad/s})t$. (a) Derive an expression for the circuit current. (b) Determine the capacitive reactance of the capacitor. (c) Derive an expression for the voltage across the capacitor.

SOLUTION

IDENTIFY: Since this is a series circuit, the current is the same through the capacitor as through the resistor. Our target variables are the current i, capacitive reactance X_C, and capacitor voltage v_C.

SET UP: Figure 31.10 shows the circuit. We find the current through the resistor, and hence through the circuit as a whole, using Eq. (31.6). We use Eq. (31.18) to find the capacitive reactance X_C, Eq. (31.19) to find the voltage amplitude, and Eq. (31.16) to write an expression for the instantaneous voltage across the capacitor.

EXECUTE: (a) Using $v_R = iR$, we find that the current i in the resistor and through the circuit as a whole is

$$i = \frac{v_R}{R} = \frac{(1.20 \text{ V}) \cos(2500 \text{ rad/s})t}{200 \text{ Ω}}$$

$$= (6.0 \times 10^{-3} \text{ A}) \cos(2500 \text{ rad/s})t$$

(b) From Eq. (31.18), the capacitive reactance at $\omega = 2500 \text{ rad/s}$ is

$$X_C = \frac{1}{\omega C} = \frac{1}{(2500 \text{ rad/s})(5.0 \times 10^{-6} \text{ F})} = 80 \text{ Ω}$$

31.10 Our sketch for this problem.

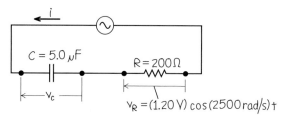

(c) From Eq. (31.19), the amplitude V_C of the voltage across the capacitor is

$$V_C = IX_C = (6.0 \times 10^{-3} \text{ A})(80 \text{ Ω}) = 0.48 \text{ V}$$

The 80-Ω reactance of the capacitor is 40% of the resistor's 200-Ω resistance, so the value of V_C is 40% of V_R. The instantaneous capacitor voltage v_C is given by Eq. (31.16):

$$v_C = V_C \cos(\omega t - 90°)$$

$$= (0.48 \text{ V}) \cos[(2500 \text{ rad/s})t - \pi/2 \text{ rad}]$$

EVALUATE: Although the *current* through the capacitor is the same as through the resistor, the *voltages* across these two devices are different in both amplitude and phase. Note that in the expression for v_C we converted the 90° to $\pi/2$ rad so that all the angular quantities have the same units. In ac circuit analysis, phase angles are often given in degrees, so be careful to convert to radians when necessary.

Comparing ac Circuit Elements

Table 31.1 summarizes the relationships of voltage and current amplitudes for the three circuit elements we have discussed. Note again that *instantaneous* voltage and current are proportional in a resistor, where there is zero phase difference between v_R and i (see Fig. 31.7b). The instantaneous voltage and current are *not* proportional in an inductor or capacitor, because there is a 90° phase difference in both cases (see Figs. 31.8b and 31.9b).

Figure 31.11 shows how the resistance of a resistor and the reactances of an inductor and a capacitor vary with angular frequency ω. Resistance R is independent of frequency, while the reactances X_L and X_C are not. If $\omega = 0$, corresponding to a dc circuit, there is *no* current through a capacitor because $X_C \to \infty$, and there is no inductive effect because $X_L = 0$. In the limit $\omega \to \infty$, X_L also approaches infinity, and the current through an inductor becomes vanishingly small; recall that the self-induced emf opposes rapid changes in current. In this same limit, X_C and the voltage across a capacitor both approach zero; the current changes direction so rapidly that no charge can build up on either plate.

Figure 31.12 shows an application of the above discussion to a loudspeaker system. Low-frequency sounds are produced by the *woofer*, which is a speaker

31.11 Graphs of R, X_L, and X_C as functions of angular frequency ω.

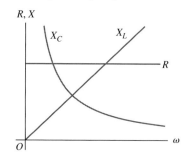

Table 31.1 Circuit Elements with Alternating Current

Circuit Element	Amplitude Relationship	Circuit Quantity	Phase of v
Resistor	$V_R = IR$	R	In phase with i
Inductor	$V_L = IX_L$	$X_L = \omega L$	Leads i by 90°
Capacitor	$V_C = IX_C$	$X_C = 1/\omega C$	Lags i by 90°

31.12 (a) The two speakers in this loud speaker system are connected in parallel to the amplifier. (b) Graphs of current amplitude in the tweeter and woofer as functions of frequency for a given amplifier voltage amplitude.

(a) A crossover network in a loudspeaker system

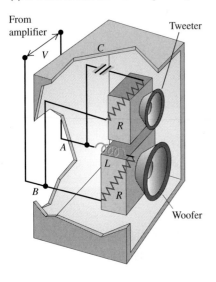

From amplifier

Tweeter

V

C

R

A

L

B

R

Woofer

(b) Graphs of rms current as functions of frequency for a given amplifier voltage

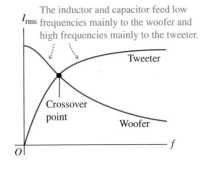

I_{rms} The inductor and capacitor feed low frequencies mainly to the woofer and high frequencies mainly to the tweeter.

Tweeter

Crossover point

Woofer

O

f

with large diameter; the *tweeter,* a speaker with smaller diameter, produces high-frequency sounds. In order to route signals of different frequency to the appropriate speaker, the woofer and tweeter are connected in parallel across the amplifier output. The capacitor in the tweeter branch blocks the low-frequency components of sound but passes the higher frequencies; the inductor in the woofer branch does the opposite.

Test Your Understanding of Section 31.2 An oscillating voltage of fixed amplitude is applied across a circuit element. If the frequency of this voltage is increased, will the amplitude of the current through the element (i) increase, (ii) decrease, or (iii) remain the same if it is (a) a resistor, (b) an inductor, or (c) a capacitor?

31.3 The *L-R-C* Series Circuit

Many ac circuits used in practical electronic systems involve resistance, inductive reactance, and capacitive reactance. A simple example is a series circuit containing a resistor, an inductor, a capacitor, and an ac source, as shown in Fig. 31.13a. (In Section 30.6 we considered the behavior of the current in an *L-R-C* series circuit *without* a source.)

To analyze this and similar circuits, we will use a phasor diagram that includes the voltage and current phasors for each of the components. In this circuit, because of Kirchhoff's loop rule, the instantaneous *total* voltage v_{ad} across all three components is equal to the source voltage at that instant. We will show that the phasor representing this total voltage is the *vector sum* of the phasors for the individual voltages. Complete phasor diagrams for this circuit are shown in Figs. 31.13b and 31.13c. These may appear complex, but we'll explain them one step at a time.

Let's assume that the source supplies a current i given by $i = I\cos\omega t$. Because the circuit elements are connected in series, the current at any instant is the same at every point in the circuit. Thus a *single phasor I*, with length proportional to the current amplitude, represents the current in *all* circuit elements.

As in Section 31.2, we use the symbols v_R, v_L, and v_C for the instantaneous voltages across R, L, and C, and the symbols V_R, V_L, and V_C for the maximum voltages. We denote the instantaneous and maximum *source* voltages by v and V. Then, in Fig. 31.13a, $v = v_{ad}$, $v_R = v_{ab}$, $v_L = v_{bc}$, and $v_C = v_{cd}$.

We have shown that the potential difference between the terminals of a resistor is *in phase* with the current in the resistor and that its maximum value V_R is given by Eq. (31.7):

$$V_R = IR$$

31.13 An *L-R-C* series circuit with an ac source.

(a) Series *R-L-C* circuit

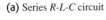
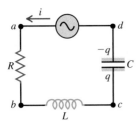

a

d

i

R

-q

C

q

b

c

L

(b) Phasor diagram for the case $X_L > X_C$

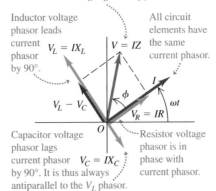

Source voltage phasor is the vector sum of the V_R, V_L, and V_C phasors.

Inductor voltage phasor leads current phasor by 90°.

$V_L = IX_L$

$V = IZ$

All circuit elements have the same current phasor.

ϕ

ωt

I

$V_L - V_C$

$V_R = IR$

O

Capacitor voltage phasor lags current phasor by 90°. It is thus always antiparallel to the V_L phasor.

$V_C = IX_C$

Resistor voltage phasor is in phase with current phasor.

(c) Phasor diagram for the case $X_L < X_C$

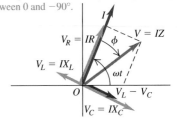

If $X_L < X_C$, the source voltage phasor lags the current phasor, $X < 0$, and ϕ is a negative angle between 0 and −90°.

I

$V_R = IR$

ϕ

$V = IZ$

$V_L = IX_L$

ωt

O

$V_L - V_C$

$V_C = IX_C$

Act|v
Phys|cs
ONLINE

14.3 AC Circuits: The Driven Oscillator
(Questions 6, 7, and 10)

The phasor V_R in Fig. 31.13b, in phase with the current phasor I, represents the voltage across the resistor. Its projection onto the horizontal axis at any instant gives the instantaneous potential difference v_R.

The voltage across an inductor *leads* the current by 90°. Its voltage amplitude is given by Eq. (31.13):

$$V_L = IX_L$$

The phasor V_L in Fig. 31.13b represents the voltage across the inductor, and its projection onto the horizontal axis at any instant equals v_L.

The voltage across a capacitor *lags* the current by 90°. Its voltage amplitude is given by Eq. (31.19):

$$V_C = IX_C$$

The phasor V_C in Fig. 31.13b represents the voltage across the capacitor, and its projection onto the horizontal axis at any instant equals v_C.

The instantaneous potential difference v between terminals a and d is equal at every instant to the (algebraic) sum of the potential differences v_R, v_L, and v_C. That is, it equals the sum of the *projections* of the phasors V_R, V_L, and V_C. But the sum of the projections of these phasors is equal to the *projection* of their *vector sum*. So the vector sum V must be the phasor that represents the source voltage v and the instantaneous total voltage v_{ad} across the series of elements.

To form this vector sum, we first subtract the phasor V_C from the phasor V_L. (These two phasors always lie along the same line, with opposite directions.) This gives the phasor $V_L - V_C$. This is always at right angles to the phasor V_R, so from the Pythagorean theorem the magnitude of the phasor V is

$$V = \sqrt{V_R^2 + (V_L - V_C)^2} = \sqrt{(IR)^2 + (IX_L - IX_C)^2} \quad \text{or}$$
$$V = I\sqrt{R^2 + (X_L - X_C)^2} \tag{31.20}$$

We define the **impedance** Z of an ac circuit as the ratio of the voltage amplitude across the circuit to the current amplitude in the circuit. From Eq. (31.20) the impedance of the *L-R-C* series circuit is

$$Z = \sqrt{R^2 + (X_L - X_C)^2} \tag{31.21}$$

so we can rewrite Eq. (31.20) as

$$V = IZ \quad \text{(amplitude of voltage across an ac circuit)} \tag{31.22}$$

While Eq. (31.21) is valid only for an *L-R-C* series circuit, we can use Eq. (31.22) to define the impedance of *any* network of resistors, inductors, and capacitors as the ratio of the amplitude of the voltage across the network to the current amplitude. The SI unit of impedance is the ohm.

The Meaning of Impedance and Phase Angle

Equation (31.22) has a form similar to $V = IR$, with impedance Z in an ac circuit playing the role of resistance R in a dc circuit. Just as direct current tends to follow the path of least resistance, so alternating current tends to follow the path of lowest impedance (Fig. 31.14). Note, however, that impedance is actually a function of R, L, and C, as well as of the angular frequency ω. We can see this by substituting Eq. (31.12) for X_L and Eq. (31.18) for X_C into Eq. (31.21), giving the following complete expression for Z for a series circuit:

$$Z = \sqrt{R^2 + (X_L - X_C)^2}$$
$$= \sqrt{R^2 + [\omega L - (1/\omega C)]^2} \tag{31.23}$$
(impedance of an *L-R-C* series circuit)

31.14 This gas-filled glass sphere has an alternating voltage between its surface and the electrode at its center. The glowing streamers show the resulting alternating current that passes through the gas. When you touch the outside of the sphere, your fingertips and the inner surface of the sphere act as the plates of a capacitor, and the sphere and your body together form an *L-R-C* series circuit. The current (which is low enough to be harmless) is drawn to your fingers because the path through your body has a low impedance.

Hence for a given amplitude V of the source voltage applied to the circuit, the amplitude $I = V/Z$ of the resulting current will be different at different frequencies. We'll explore this frequency dependence in detail in Section 31.5.

In the phasor diagram shown in Fig. 31.13b, the angle ϕ between the voltage and current phasors is the phase angle of the source voltage v with respect to the current i; that is, it is the angle by which the source voltage leads the current. From the diagram,

$$\tan\phi = \frac{V_L - V_C}{V_R} = \frac{I(X_L - X_C)}{IR} = \frac{X_L - X_C}{R}$$

$$\tan\phi = \frac{\omega L - 1/\omega C}{R} \qquad \text{(phase angle of an } L\text{-}R\text{-}C \text{ series circuit)} \quad (31.24)$$

If the current is $i = I\cos\omega t$, then the source voltage v is

$$v = V\cos(\omega t + \phi) \qquad (31.25)$$

Figure 31.13b shows the behavior of a circuit in which $X_L > X_C$. Figure 31.13c shows the behavior when $X_L < X_C$; the voltage phasor V lies on the opposite side of the current phasor I and the voltage *lags* the current. In this case, $X_L - X_C$ is *negative,* $\tan\phi$ is negative, and ϕ is a negative angle between 0 and $-90°$. Since X_L and X_C depend on frequency, the phase angle ϕ depends on frequency as well. We'll examine the consequences of this in Section 31.5.

All of the expressions that we've developed for an L-R-C series circuit are still valid if one of the circuit elements is missing. If the resistor is missing, we set $R = 0$; if the inductor is missing, we set $L = 0$. But if the capacitor is missing, we set $C = \infty$, corresponding to the absence of any potential difference $(v_C = q/C = 0)$ or any capacitive reactance $(X_C = 1/\omega C = 0)$.

In this entire discussion we have described magnitudes of voltages and currents in terms of their *maximum* values, the voltage and current *amplitudes.* But we remarked at the end of Section 31.1 that these quantities are usually described in terms of rms values, not amplitudes. For any sinusoidally varying quantity the rms value is always $1/\sqrt{2}$ times the amplitude. All the relationships between voltage and current that we have derived in this and the preceding sections are still valid if we use rms quantities throughout instead of amplitudes. For example, if we divide Eq. (31.22) by $\sqrt{2}$, we get

$$\frac{V}{\sqrt{2}} = \frac{I}{\sqrt{2}}Z$$

which we can rewrite as

$$V_{\text{rms}} = I_{\text{rms}}Z \qquad (31.26)$$

We can translate Eqs. (31.7), (31.13), and (31.19) in exactly the same way.

We have considered only ac circuits in which an inductor, a resistor, and a capacitor are in series. You can do a similar analysis for a *parallel L-R-C* circuit; see Problem 31.54.

Finally, we remark that in this section we have been describing the *steady-state* condition of a circuit, the state that exists after the circuit has been connected to the source for a long time. When the source is first connected, there may be additional voltages and currents, called *transients,* whose nature depends on the time in the cycle when the circuit is initially completed. A detailed analysis of transients is beyond our scope. They always die out after a sufficiently long time, and they do not affect the steady-state behavior of the circuit. But they can cause dangerous and damaging surges in power lines, which is why delicate electronic systems such as computers are often provided with power-line surge protectors.

Problem-Solving Strategy 31.1 **Alternating-Current Circuits**

IDENTIFY *the relevant concepts:*   All of the concepts that we used to analyze direct-current circuits also apply to alternating-current circuits. However, we must be careful to distinguish between the amplitudes of alternating currents and voltages and their instantaneous values. We must also keep in mind the distinctions between resistance (for resistors), reactance (for inductors or capacitors), and impedance (for composite circuits).

SET UP *the problem* using the following steps:
1. Draw a diagram of the circuit and label all known and unknown quantities.
2. Determine the target variables.

EXECUTE *the solution* as follows:
1. Use the relationships derived in Sections 31.2 and 31.3 to solve for the target variables, using the following hints.
2. In ac circuit problems it is nearly always easiest to work with angular frequency ω. If you are given the ordinary frequency f, expressed in Hz, convert it using the relationship $\omega = 2\pi f$.
3. Keep in mind a few basic facts about phase relationships. For a resistor, voltage and current are always *in phase,* and the two corresponding phasors in a phasor diagram always have the same direction. For an inductor, the voltage always *leads* the current by 90° (i.e., $\phi = +90°$), and the voltage phasor is always turned 90° counterclockwise from the current phasor. For a capacitor, the voltage always *lags* the current by 90° (i.e., $\phi = -90°$), and the voltage phasor is always turned 90° clockwise from the current phasor.

4. Remember that with ac circuits, all voltages and currents are sinusoidal functions of time instead of being constant, but Kirchhoff's rules hold nonetheless at each instant. Thus, in a series circuit, the instantaneous current is the same in all circuit elements; in a parallel circuit, the instantaneous potential difference is the same across all circuit elements.
5. Inductive reactance, capacitive reactance, and impedance are analogous to resistance; each represents the ratio of voltage amplitude V to current amplitude I in a circuit element or combination of elements. Keep in mind, however, that phase relationships play an essential role. The effects of resistance and reactance have to be combined by *vector* addition of the corresponding voltage phasors, as in Figs. 31.13b and 31.13c. When you have several circuit elements in series, for example, you can't just *add* all the numerical values of resistance and reactance to get the impedance; that would ignore the phase relationships.

EVALUATE *your answer:*   When working with a series *L-R-C* circuit, you can check your results by comparing the values of the inductive reactance X_L and the capacitive reactance X_C. If $X_L > X_C$, then the voltage amplitude across the inductor is greater than that across the capacitor and the phase angle ϕ is positive (between 0 and 90°). If $X_L < X_C$, then the voltage amplitude across the inductor is less than that across the capacitor and the phase angle ϕ is negative (between 0 and −90°).

Example 31.4 **An *L-R-C* series circuit I**

In the series circuit of Fig. 31.13a, suppose $R = 300 \ \Omega$, $L = 60 \ \text{mH}$, $C = 0.50 \ \mu\text{F}$, $V = 50 \ \text{V}$, and $\omega = 10{,}000 \ \text{rad/s}$. Find the reactances X_L and X_C, the impedance Z, the current amplitude I, the phase angle ϕ, and the voltage amplitude across each circuit element.

SOLUTION

IDENTIFY: This problem uses the ideas developed in Section 31.2 and this section about the behavior of circuit elements in an ac circuit.

SET UP: We use Eqs. (31.12) and (31.18) to determine the reactances and Eq. (31.23) to find the impedance. We then use Eq. (31.22) to find the current amplitude and Eq. (31.24) to calculate the phase angle. Given this information, the relationships in Table 31.1 tell us the voltage amplitudes.

EXECUTE: The inductive and capacitive reactances are

$$X_L = \omega L = (10{,}000 \ \text{rad/s})(60 \ \text{mH}) = 600 \ \Omega$$

$$X_C = \frac{1}{\omega C} = \frac{1}{(10{,}000 \ \text{rad/s})(0.50 \times 10^{-6} \ \text{F})} = 200 \ \Omega$$

The impedance Z of the circuit is

$$Z = \sqrt{R^2 + (X_L - X_C)^2} = \sqrt{(300 \ \Omega)^2 + (600 \ \Omega - 200 \ \Omega)^2}$$
$$= 500 \ \Omega$$

With source voltage amplitude $V = 50 \ \text{V}$ the current amplitude is

$$I = \frac{V}{Z} = \frac{50 \ \text{V}}{500 \ \Omega} = 0.10 \ \text{A}$$

The phase angle ϕ is

$$\phi = \arctan\frac{X_L - X_C}{R} = \arctan\frac{400 \ \Omega}{300 \ \Omega} = 53°$$

From Table 31.1, the voltage amplitudes V_R, V_L, and V_C across the resistor, inductor, and capacitor, respectively, are

$$V_R = IR = (0.10 \ \text{A})(300 \ \Omega) = 30 \ \text{V}$$
$$V_L = IX_L = (0.10 \ \text{A})(600 \ \Omega) = 60 \ \text{V}$$
$$V_C = IX_C = (0.10 \ \text{A})(200 \ \Omega) = 20 \ \text{V}$$

EVALUATE: Note that $X_L > X_C$ and hence the voltage amplitude across the inductor is greater than across the capacitor and ϕ is negative. The value $\phi = -53°$ means that the voltage *leads* the current by 53°; this is like the situation shown in Fig. 31.13b.

Note that the source voltage amplitude $V = 50 \ \text{V}$ is *not* equal to the sum of the voltage amplitudes across the separate circuit elements. (That is, $50 \ \text{V} \neq 30 \ \text{V} + 60 \ \text{V} + 20 \ \text{V}$.) Make sure you understand why not!

Example 31.5 | An *L-R-C* series circuit II

For the *L-R-C* series circuit described in Example 31.4, describe the time dependence of the instantaneous current and each instantaneous voltage.

SOLUTION

IDENTIFY: In Example 31.4 we found the *amplitudes* of the current and voltages. Now our task is to find expressions for the *instantaneous values* of the current and voltages. As we learned in Section 31.2, the voltage across a resistor is in phase with the current but the voltages across an inductor or capacitor are not. We also learned in this section that ϕ is the phase angle between the source voltage and the current.

SET UP: If we describe the current using Eq. (31.2), the voltages are given by Eq. (31.8) for the resistor, Eq. (31.10) for the inductor, Eq. (31.16) for the capacitor, and Eq. (31.25) for the source.

EXECUTE: The current and all of the voltages oscillate with the same angular frequency, $\omega = 10{,}000$ rad/s, and hence with the same period, $2\pi/\omega = 2\pi/(10{,}000 \text{ rad/s}) = 6.3 \times 10^{-4}$ s $= 0.63$ ms. Using Eq. (31.2), the current is

$$i = I\cos\omega t = (0.10 \text{ A})\cos(10{,}000 \text{ rad/s})t$$

This choice simply means that we choose $t = 0$ to be an instant when the current is maximum. The resistor voltage is *in phase* with the current, so

$$v_R = V_R\cos\omega t = (30 \text{ V})\cos(10{,}000 \text{ rad/s})t$$

The inductor voltage *leads* the current by 90°, so

$$v_L = V_L\cos(\omega t + 90°) = -V_L\sin\omega t$$
$$= -(60 \text{ V})\sin(10{,}000 \text{ rad/s})t$$

The capacitor voltage *lags* the current by 90°, so

$$v_C = V_C\cos(\omega t - 90°) = V_C\sin\omega t$$
$$= (20 \text{ V})\sin(10{,}000 \text{ rad/s})t$$

31.15 Graphs of the source voltage v, resistor voltage v_R, inductor voltage v_L, and capacitor voltage v_C as functions of time for the situation of Example 31.4. The current, which is not shown, is in phase with the resistor voltage.

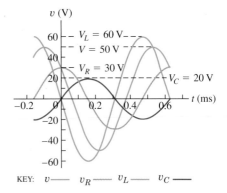

KEY: v —— v_R ——— v_L —— v_C ——

Finally, the source voltage (equal to the voltage across the entire combination of resistor, inductor, and capacitor) *leads* the current by $\phi = 53°$, so

$$v = V\cos(\omega t + \phi)$$
$$= (50 \text{ V})\cos\left[(10{,}000 \text{ rad/s})t + \left(\frac{2\pi \text{ rad}}{360°}\right)(53°)\right]$$
$$= (50 \text{ V})\cos[(10{,}000 \text{ rad/s})t + 0.93 \text{ rad}]$$

EVALUATE: Figure 31.15 graphs the various voltages versus time. The inductor voltage has a larger amplitude than the capacitor voltage because $X_L > X_C$. While the source voltage amplitude V is not equal to the sum of the individual voltage amplitudes V_R, V_L, and V_C, the *instantaneous* source voltage v is always equal to the sum of the instantaneous voltages v_R, v_L, and v_C. You should verify this by measuring the values of the voltages shown in the graph at different values of the time t.

Test Your Understanding of Section 31.3 Rank the following ac circuits in order of their current amplitude, from highest to lowest value. (i) the circuit in Example 31.4; (ii) the circuit in Example 31.4 with the capacitor and inductor both removed; (iii) the circuit in Example 31.4 with the resistor and capacitor both removed; (iv) the circuit in Example 31.4 with the resistor and inductor both removed.

31.4 Power in Alternating-Current Circuits

Alternating currents play a central role in systems for distributing, converting, and using electrical energy, so it's important to look at power relationships in ac circuits. For an ac circuit with instantaneous current i and current amplitude I, we'll consider an element of that circuit across which the instantaneous potential difference is v with voltage amplitude V. The instantaneous power p delivered to this circuit element is

$$p = vi$$

Let's first see what this means for individual circuit elements. We'll assume in each case that $i = I\cos\omega t$.

Power in a Resistor

Suppose first that the circuit element is a *pure resistor R*, as in Fig. 31.7a; then $v = v_R$ and i are *in phase*. We obtain the graph representing p by multiplying the heights of the graphs of v and i in Fig. 31.7b at each instant. This graph is shown by the black curve in Fig. 31.16a. The product vi is always positive because v and i are always either both positive or both negative. Hence energy is supplied *to* the resistor at every instant for both directions of i, although the power is not constant.

The power curve for a pure resistor is symmetrical about a value equal to one-half its maximum value VI, so the *average power* P_{av} is

$$P_{av} = \frac{1}{2}VI \qquad \text{(for a pure resistor)} \qquad (31.27)$$

An equivalent expression is

$$P_{av} = \frac{V}{\sqrt{2}}\frac{I}{\sqrt{2}} = V_{rms}I_{rms} \qquad \text{(for a pure resistor)} \qquad (31.28)$$

Also, $V_{rms} = I_{rms}R$, so we can express P_{av} by any of the equivalent forms

$$P_{av} = I_{rms}^2 R = \frac{V_{rms}^2}{R} = V_{rms}I_{rms} \qquad \text{(for a pure resistor)} \qquad (31.29)$$

Note that the expressions in Eq. (31.29) have the same form as the corresponding relationships for a dc circuit, Eq. (25.18). Also note that they are valid only for pure resistors, not for more complicated combinations of circuit elements.

Power in an Inductor

Next we connect the source to a pure inductor L, as in Fig. 31.8a. The voltage $v = v_L$ leads the current i by 90°. When we multiply the curves of v and i, the product vi is *negative* during the half of the cycle when v and i have *opposite* signs. The power curve, shown in Fig. 31.16b, is symmetrical about the horizontal axis; it is positive half the time and negative the other half, and the average power is zero. When p is positive, energy is being supplied to set up the magnetic field in the inductor; when p is negative, the field is collapsing and the inductor is returning energy to the source. The net energy transfer over one cycle is zero.

31.16 Graphs of current, voltage, and power as functions of time for **(a)** a pure resistor, **(b)** a pure inductor, **(c)** a pure capacitor, and **(d)** an arbitrary ac circuit that can have resistance, inductance, and capacitance.

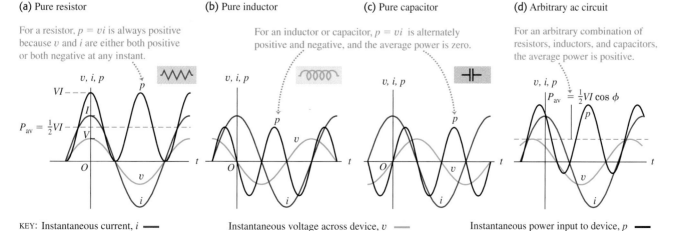

Power in a Capacitor

Finally, we connect the source to a pure capacitor C, as in Fig. 31.9a. The voltage $v = v_C$ lags the current i by 90°. Figure 31.16c shows the power curve; the average power is again zero. Energy is supplied to charge the capacitor and is returned to the source when the capacitor discharges. The net energy transfer over one cycle is again zero.

Power in a General ac Circuit

In *any* ac circuit, with any combination of resistors, capacitors, and inductors, the voltage v across the entire circuit has some phase angle ϕ with respect to the current i. Then the instantaneous power p is given by

$$p = vi = \left[V\cos(\omega t + \phi)\right]\left[I\cos\omega t\right] \qquad (31.30)$$

The instantaneous power curve has the form shown in Fig. 31.16d. The area between the positive loops and the horizontal axis is greater than the area between the negative loops and the horizontal axis, and the average power is positive.

We can derive from Eq. (31.30) an expression for the *average* power P_{av} by using the identity for the cosine of the sum of two angles:

$$p = \left[V(\cos\omega t\cos\phi - \sin\omega t\sin\phi)\right]\left[I\cos\omega t\right]$$
$$= VI\cos\phi\cos^2\omega t - VI\sin\phi\cos\omega t\sin\omega t$$

From the discussion in Section 31.1 that led to Eq. (31.4), we see that the average value of $\cos^2\omega t$ (over one cycle) is $\frac{1}{2}$. The average value of $\cos\omega t\sin\omega t$ is zero because this product is equal to $\frac{1}{2}\sin 2\omega t$, whose average over a cycle is zero. So the average power P_{av} is

$$P_{av} = \frac{1}{2}VI\cos\phi = V_{rms}I_{rms}\cos\phi \qquad \begin{array}{l}\text{(average power into a}\\\text{general ac circuit)}\end{array} \qquad (31.31)$$

31.17 Using phasors to calculate the average power for an arbitrary ac circuit.

Average power $= \frac{1}{2}I(V\cos\phi)$, where $V\cos\phi$ is the component of V in phase with I.

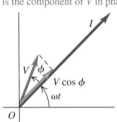

When v and i are in phase, so $\phi = 0$, the average power equals $\frac{1}{2}VI = V_{rms}I_{rms}$; when v and i are 90° out of phase, the average power is zero. In the general case, when v has a phase angle ϕ with respect to i, the average power equals $\frac{1}{2}I$ multiplied by $V\cos\phi$, the component of the voltage phasor that is *in phase* with the current phasor. Figure 31.17 shows the general relationship of the current and voltage phasors. For the *L-R-C* series circuit, Figs. 31.13b and 31.13c show that $V\cos\phi$ equals the voltage amplitude V_R for the resistor; hence Eq. (31.31) is the average power dissipated in the resistor. On average there is no energy flow into or out of the inductor or capacitor, so none of P_{av} goes into either of these circuit elements.

The factor $\cos\phi$ is called the **power factor** of the circuit. For a pure resistance, $\phi = 0$, $\cos\phi = 1$, and $P_{av} = V_{rms}I_{rms}$. For a pure inductor or capacitor, $\phi = \pm 90°$, $\cos\phi = 0$, and $P_{av} = 0$. For an *L-R-C* series circuit the power factor is equal to R/Z; we leave the proof of this statement to you (see Exercise 31.27).

A low power factor (large angle ϕ of lag or lead) is usually undesirable in power circuits. The reason is that for a given potential difference, a large current is needed to supply a given amount of power. This results in large i^2R losses in the transmission lines. Your electric power company may charge a higher rate to a client with a low power factor. Many types of ac machinery draw a *lagging* current; that is, the current drawn by the machinery lags the applied voltage. Hence the voltage leads the current, so $\phi > 0$ and $\cos\phi < 1$. The power factor can be corrected toward the ideal value of 1 by connecting a capacitor in parallel with the load. The current drawn by the capacitor *leads* the voltage (that is, the voltage across the capacitor lags the current), which compensates for the lagging current in the other branch of the circuit. The capacitor itself absorbs no net power from the line.

Example 31.6   **Power in a hair dryer**

An electric hair dryer is rated at 1500 W at 120 V. The rated power of this hair dryer, or of any other ac device, is the *average* power drawn by the device, and the rated voltage is the *rms* voltage. Calculate (a) the resistance, (b) the rms current, and (c) the maximum instantaneous power. Assume that the hair dryer is a pure resistor. (The hair dryer's heating element acts as a resistor.)

SOLUTION

IDENTIFY: We assume that the hair dryer is a pure resistor. We are given the average power $P_{av} = 1500$ W and the rms voltage $V_{rms} = 120$ V. Our target variables are the resistance R, the rms current I_{rms}, and the maximum value of the instantaneous power p.

SET UP: We solve Eq. (31.29) to determine the resistance R. We find the rms current from V_{rms} and P_{av} using Eq. (31.28), and we find the maximum instantaneous power from Eq. (31.30).

EXECUTE: (a) From Eq. (31.29), the resistance is

$$R = \frac{V_{rms}^{2}}{P_{av}} = \frac{(120 \text{ V})^{2}}{1500 \text{ W}} = 9.6 \text{ }\Omega$$

(b) From Eq. (31.28),

$$I_{rms} = \frac{P_{av}}{V_{rms}} = \frac{1500 \text{ W}}{120 \text{ V}} = 12.5 \text{ A}$$

(c) For a pure resistor, the voltage and current are in phase and the phase angle ϕ is zero. Hence from Eq. (31.30), the instantaneous power is $p = VI\cos^{2}\omega t$ and the maximum instantaneous power is $p_{max} = VI$. From Eq. (31.27), this is twice the average power P_{av}, so

$$p_{max} = VI = 2P_{av} = 2(1500 \text{ W}) = 3000 \text{ W}$$

EVALUATE: We can confirm our result in part (b) by using Eq. (31.7): $I_{rms} = V_{rms}/R = (120 \text{ V})/(9.6 \text{ }\Omega) = 12.5$ A. Note that some manufacturers of stereo amplifiers state power outputs in terms of the peak value rather than the lower average value, to mislead the unwary consumer.

Example 31.7   **Power in an *L-R-C* series circuit**

For the *L-R-C* series circuit of Example 31.4, (a) calculate the power factor; and (b) calculate the average power delivered to the entire circuit and to each circuit element.

SOLUTION

IDENTIFY: We can use all of the results found in Example 31.4.

SET UP: The power factor is simply the cosine of the phase angle ϕ, and Eq. (31.31) allows us to find the average power delivered in terms of ϕ and the amplitudes of voltage and current.

EXECUTE: (a) The power factor is $\cos\phi = \cos 53° = 0.60$.

(b) From Eq. (31.31) the average power delivered to the circuit is

$$P_{av} = \frac{1}{2}VI\cos\phi = \frac{1}{2}(50 \text{ V})(0.10 \text{ A})(0.60) = 1.5 \text{ W}$$

EVALUATE: While P_{av} is the average power delivered to the *L-R-C* combination, all of this power is dissipated in the resistor. The average power delivered to a pure inductor or pure capacitor is always zero (see Figs. 31.16b and 31.16c).

Test Your Understanding of Section 31.4   Figure 31.16d shows that during part of a cycle of oscillation, the instantaneous power delivered to the circuit is negative. This means that energy is being extracted from the circuit. (a) Where is the energy extracted from? (i) the resistor; (ii) the inductor; (iii) the capacitor; (iv) the ac source; (v) more than one of these. (b) Where does the energy go? (i) the resistor; (ii) the inductor; (iii) the capacitor; (iv) the ac source; (v) more than one of these.

31.5 Resonance in Alternating-Current Circuits

Much of the practical importance of *L-R-C* series circuits arises from the way in which such circuits respond to sources of different angular frequency ω. For example, one type of tuning circuit used in radio receivers is simply an *L-R-C* series circuit. A radio signal of any given frequency produces a current of the same frequency in the receiver circuit, but the amplitude of the current is *greatest* if the signal frequency equals the particular frequency to which the receiver circuit is "tuned." This effect is called *resonance*. The circuit is designed so that signals at other than the tuned frequency produce currents that are too small to make an audible sound come out of the radio's speakers.

Activ
Physics
ONLINE

14.3 AC Circuits: The Driven Oscillator
(Questions 8, 9, and 11)

31.18 How variations in the angular frequency of an ac circuit affect (a) reactances, resistance, and impedance, and (b) impedance, current amplitude, and phase angle.

(a) Reactance, resistance, and impedance as functions of angular frequency

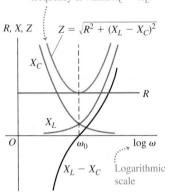

Impedance Z is least at the angular frequency at which $X_C = X_L$.

$Z = \sqrt{R^2 + (X_L - X_C)^2}$

(b) Impedance, current, and phase angle as functions of angular frequency

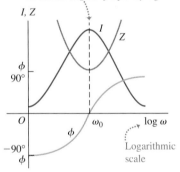

Current peaks at the angular frequency at which impedance is least. This is the *resonance angular frequency* ω_0.

To see how an *L-R-C* series circuit can be used in this way, suppose we connect an ac source with constant voltage amplitude V but adjustable angular frequency ω across an *L-R-C* series circuit. The current that appears in the circuit has the same angular frequency as the source and a current amplitude $I = V/Z$, where Z is the impedance of the *L-R-C* series circuit. This impedance depends on the frequency, as Eq. (31.23) shows. Figure 31.18a shows graphs of R, X_L, X_C, and Z as functions of ω. We have used a logarithmic angular frequency scale so that we can cover a wide range of frequencies. As the frequency increases, X_L increases and X_C decreases; hence there is always one frequency at which X_L and X_C are equal and $X_L - X_C$ is zero. At this frequency the impedance $Z = \sqrt{R^2 + (X_L - X_C)^2}$ has its *smallest* value, equal simply to the resistance R.

Circuit Behavior at Resonance

As we vary the angular frequency ω of the source, the current amplitude $I = V/Z$ varies as shown in Fig. 31.18b; the *maximum* value of I occurs at the frequency at which the impedance Z is *minimum*. This peaking of the current amplitude at a certain frequency is called **resonance.** The angular frequency ω_0 at which the resonance peak occurs is called the **resonance angular frequency.** This is the angular frequency at which the inductive and capacitive reactances are equal, so at resonance,

$$X_L = X_C \qquad \omega_0 L = \frac{1}{\omega_0 C} \qquad \omega_0 = \frac{1}{\sqrt{LC}} \qquad \begin{array}{l}\text{(}L\text{-}R\text{-}C \text{ series circuit}\\ \text{at resonance)}\end{array} \qquad (31.32)$$

Note that this is equal to the natural angular frequency of oscillation of an *L-C* circuit, which we derived in Section 30.5, Eq. (30.22). The **resonance frequency** f_0 is $\omega_0/2\pi$. This is the frequency at which the greatest current appears in the circuit for a given source voltage amplitude; in other words, f_0 is the frequency to which the circuit is "tuned."

It's instructive to look at what happens to the *voltages* in an *L-R-C* series circuit at resonance. The current at any instant is the same in L and C. The voltage across an inductor always *leads* the current by 90°, or $\frac{1}{4}$ cycle, and the voltage across a capacitor always *lags* the current by 90°. Therefore the instantaneous voltages across L and C always differ in phase by 180°, or $\frac{1}{2}$ cycle; they have opposite signs at each instant. At the resonance frequency, and *only* at the resonance frequency, $X_L = X_C$ and the voltage amplitudes $V_L = IX_L$ and $V_C = IX_C$ are *equal;* then the instantaneous voltages across L and C add to zero at each instant, and the *total* voltage v_{bd} across the *L-C* combination in Fig. 31.13a is exactly zero. The voltage across the resistor is then equal to the source voltage. So at the resonance frequency the circuit behaves as if the inductor and capacitor weren't there at all!

The *phase* of the voltage relative to the current is given by Eq. (31.24). At frequencies below resonance, X_C is greater than X_L; the capacitive reactance dominates, the voltage *lags* the current, and the phase angle ϕ is between zero and $-90°$. Above resonance, the inductive reactance dominates; the voltage *leads* the current, and the phase angle is between zero and $+90°$. This variation of ϕ with angular frequency is shown in Fig. 31.18b.

Tailoring an ac Circuit

If we can vary the inductance L or the capacitance C of a circuit, we can also vary the resonance frequency. This is exactly how a radio or television receiving set is "tuned" to receive a particular station. In the early days of radio this was accomplished by use of capacitors with movable metal plates whose overlap could be varied to change C. (This is what is being done with the radio tuning knob shown in the photograph that opens this chapter.) A more modern approach is to vary L by using a coil with a ferrite core that slides in or out.

In a series L-R-C circuit the impedance reaches its minimum value and the current its maximum value at the resonance frequency. The middle curve in Fig. 31.19 is a graph of current as a function of frequency for such a circuit, with source voltage amplitude $V = 100$ V, $L = 2.0$ H, $C = 0.50 \mu$F, and $R = 500 \Omega$. This curve is called a *response curve* or a *resonance curve*. The resonance angular frequency is $\omega_0 = (LC)^{-1/2} = 1000$ rad/s. As we expect, the curve has a peak at this angular frequency.

The resonance frequency is determined by L and C; what happens when we change R? Figure 31.19 also shows graphs of I as a function of ω for $R = 200 \Omega$ and for $R = 2000 \Omega$. The curves are similar for frequencies far away from resonance, where the impedance is dominated by X_L or X_C. But near resonance, where X_L and X_C nearly cancel each other, the curve is higher and more sharply peaked for small values of R and broader and flatter for large values of R. At resonance, $Z = R$ and $I = V/R$, so the maximum height of the curve is inversely proportional to R.

The shape of the response curve is important in the design of radio and television receiving circuits. The sharply peaked curve is what makes it possible to discriminate between two stations broadcasting on adjacent frequency bands. But if the peak is *too* sharp, some of the information in the received signal is lost, such as the high-frequency sounds in music. The shape of the resonance curve is also related to the overdamped and underdamped oscillations that we described in Section 30.6. A sharply peaked resonance curve corresponds to a small value of R and a lightly damped oscillating system; a broad, flat curve goes with a large value of R and a heavily damped system.

In this section we have discussed resonance in an L-R-C *series* circuit. Resonance can also occur in an ac circuit in which the inductor, resistor, and capacitor are connected in *parallel*. We leave the details to you (see Problem 31.55).

Resonance phenomena occur not just in ac circuits, but in all areas of physics. We discussed examples of resonance in *mechanical* systems in Sections 13.8 and 16.5. The amplitude of a mechanical oscillation peaks when the driving-force frequency is close to a natural frequency of the system; this is analogous to the peaking of the current in an L-R-C series circuit. We suggest that you review the sections on mechanical resonance now, looking for the analogies. Other important examples of resonance occur in atomic and nuclear physics and in the study of fundamental particles (high-energy physics).

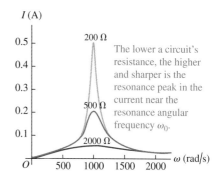

31.19 Graph of current amplitude I as a function of angular frequency ω for an L-R-C series circuit with $V = 100$ V, $L = 2.0$ H, $C = 0.50 \mu$F, and three different values of the resistance R.

Example 31.8 Tuning a radio

The series circuit in Fig. 31.20 is similar to arrangements that are sometimes used in radio tuning circuits. This circuit is connected to the terminals of an ac source with a constant rms terminal voltage of 1.0 V and a variable frequency. Find (a) the resonance frequency; (b) the inductive reactance, the capacitive reactance, and the impedance at the resonance frequency; (c) the rms current at resonance; and (d) the rms voltage across each circuit element at resonance.

SOLUTION

IDENTIFY: The circuit in Fig. 31.20 is a series L-R-C circuit, but with meters added to measure the rms current and voltages (which are our target variables).

SET UP: Equation (31.32) includes the formula for the resonance angular frequency ω_0, from which we find the resonance frequency f_0. We find the remaining target variables using the results of Sections 31.2 and 31.3.

31.20 A radio tuning circuit at resonance. The circles denote rms current and voltages.

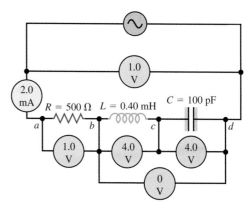

Continued

EXECUTE: (a) The resonance angular frequency is

$$\omega_0 = \frac{1}{\sqrt{LC}} = \frac{1}{\sqrt{(0.40 \times 10^{-3}\,\text{H})(100 \times 10^{-12}\,\text{F})}}$$
$$= 5.0 \times 10^6\,\text{rad/s}$$

The corresponding frequency $f_0 = \omega_0/2\pi$ is

$$f_0 = 8.0 \times 10^5\,\text{Hz} = 800\,\text{kHz}$$

This corresponds to the lower part of the AM radio band.

(b) At this frequency,

$$X_L = \omega L = (5.0 \times 10^6\,\text{rad/s})(0.40 \times 10^{-3}\,\text{H}) = 2000\,\Omega$$

$$X_C = \frac{1}{\omega C} = \frac{1}{(5.0 \times 10^6\,\text{rad/s})(100 \times 10^{-12}\,\text{F})} = 2000\,\Omega$$

Since $X_L = X_C$ and $X_L - X_C = 0$, Eq. (31.23) shows that the impedance Z at resonance is equal to the resistance: $Z = R = 500\,\Omega$.

(c) From Eq. (31.26) the rms current at resonance is

$$I_{\text{rms}} = \frac{V_{\text{rms}}}{Z} = \frac{V_{\text{rms}}}{R} = \frac{1.0\,\text{V}}{500\,\Omega} = 0.0020\,\text{A} = 2.0\,\text{mA}$$

(d) The rms potential difference across the resistor is

$$V_{R\text{-rms}} = I_{\text{rms}}R = (0.0020\,\text{A})(500\,\Omega) = 1.0\,\text{V}$$

The rms potential differences across the inductor and capacitor are, respectively:

$$V_{L\text{-rms}} = I_{\text{rms}}X_L = (0.0020\,\text{A})(2000\,\Omega) = 4.0\,\text{V}$$
$$V_{C\text{-rms}} = I_{\text{rms}}X_C = (0.0020\,\text{A})(2000\,\Omega) = 4.0\,\text{V}$$

EVALUATE: The potential differences across the inductor and the capacitor have equal rms values and amplitudes, but are 180° out of phase and so add to zero at each instant. Note also that at resonance, $V_{R\text{-rms}}$ is equal to the source voltage V_{rms}, while in this example, $V_{L\text{-rms}}$ and $V_{C\text{-rms}}$ are both considerably *larger* than V_{rms}.

Test Your Understanding of Section 31.5   How does the resonance frequency of an *L-R-C* series circuit change if the plates of the capacitor are brought closer together? (i) It increases; (ii) it decreases; (iii) it is unaffected.

31.6 Transformers

One of the great advantages of ac over dc for electric-power distribution is that it is much easier to step voltage levels up and down with ac than with dc. For long-distance power transmission it is desirable to use as high a voltage and as small a current as possible; this reduces i^2R losses in the transmission lines, and smaller wires can be used, saving on material costs. Present-day transmission lines routinely operate at rms voltages of the order of 500 kV. On the other hand, safety considerations and insulation requirements dictate relatively low voltages in generating equipment and in household and industrial power distribution. The standard voltage for household wiring is 120 V in the United States and Canada and 240 V in many other countries. The necessary voltage conversion is accomplished by the use of **transformers.**

How Transformers Work

31.21 Schematic diagram of an idealized step-up transformer. The primary is connected to an ac source; the secondary is connected to a device with resistance R.

The induced emf *per turn* is the same in both coils, so we adjust the ratio of terminal voltages by adjusting the ratio of turns:

$$\frac{V_2}{V_1} = \frac{N_2}{N_1}$$

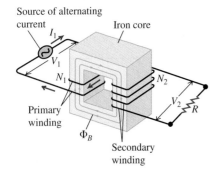

Source of alternating current

Iron core

I_1

V_1

N_1

N_2

V_2

R

Primary winding

Φ_B

Secondary winding

Figure 31.21 shows an idealized transformer. The key components of the transformer are two coils or *windings,* electrically insulated from each other but wound on the same core. The core is typically made of a material, such as iron, with a very large relative permeability K_m. This keeps the magnetic field lines due to a current in one winding almost completely within the core. Hence almost all of these field lines pass through the other winding, maximizing the *mutual inductance* of the two windings (see Section 30.1). The winding to which power is supplied is called the **primary;** the winding from which power is delivered is called the **secondary.** The circuit symbol for a transformer with an iron core, such as those used in power distribution systems, is

Here's how a transformer works. The ac source causes an alternating current in the primary, which sets up an alternating flux in the core; this induces an emf in each winding, in accordance with Faraday's law. The induced emf in the secondary gives rise to an alternating current in the secondary, and this delivers energy to the device to which the secondary is connected. All currents and emfs have the same frequency as the ac source.

Let's see how the voltage across the secondary can be made larger or smaller in amplitude than the voltage across the primary. We neglect the resistance of the windings and assume that all the magnetic field lines are confined to the iron core, so at any instant the magnetic flux Φ_B is the same in each turn of the primary and secondary windings. The primary winding has N_1 turns and the secondary winding has N_2 turns. When the magnetic flux changes because of changing currents in the two coils, the resulting induced emfs are

$$\mathcal{E}_1 = -N_1\frac{d\Phi_B}{dt} \quad \text{and} \quad \mathcal{E}_2 = -N_2\frac{d\Phi_B}{dt} \tag{31.33}$$

The flux *per turn* Φ_B is the same in both the primary and the secondary, so Eqs. (31.33) show that the induced emf *per turn* is the same in each. The ratio of the secondary emf $\mathcal{E}_2$ to the primary emf $\mathcal{E}_1$ is therefore equal at any instant to the ratio of secondary to primary turns:

$$\frac{\mathcal{E}_2}{\mathcal{E}_1} = \frac{N_2}{N_1} \tag{31.34}$$

Since $\mathcal{E}_1$ and $\mathcal{E}_2$ both oscillate with the same frequency as the ac source, Eq. (31.34) also gives the ratio of the amplitudes or of the rms values of the induced emfs. If the windings have zero resistance, the induced emfs $\mathcal{E}_1$ and $\mathcal{E}_2$ are equal to the terminal voltages across the primary and the secondary, respectively; hence

$$\frac{V_2}{V_1} = \frac{N_2}{N_1} \quad \begin{array}{l}\text{(terminal voltages of transformer}\\ \text{primary and secondary)}\end{array} \tag{31.35}$$

where V_1 and V_2 are either the amplitudes or the rms values of the terminal voltages. By choosing the appropriate turns ratio N_2/N_1, we may obtain any desired secondary voltage from a given primary voltage. If $N_2 > N_1$, as in Fig. 31.21, then $V_2 > V_1$ and we have a *step-up* transformer; if $N_2 < N_1$, then $V_2 < V_1$ and we have a *step-down* transformer. At a power generating station, step-up transformers are used; the primary is connected to the power source and the secondary is connected to the transmission lines, giving the desired high voltage for transmission. Near the consumer, step-down transformers lower the voltage to a value suitable for use in home or industry (Fig. 31.22).

Even the relatively low voltage provided by a household wall socket is too high for many electronic devices, so a further step-down transformer is necessary. This is the role of an "ac adapter" (also called a "power cube" or "power adapter"), such as those used to recharge a mobile phone or laptop computer from line voltage. Such adapters contain a step-down transformer that converts line voltage to a lower value, typically 3 to 12 volts, as well as diodes to convert alternating current to the direct current that small electronic devices require (Fig. 31.23).

Energy Considerations for Transformers

If the secondary circuit is completed by a resistance R, then the amplitude or rms value of the current in the secondary circuit is $I_2 = V_2/R$. From energy considerations, the power delivered to the primary equals that taken out of the secondary (since there is no resistance in the windings), so

$$V_1 I_1 = V_2 I_2 \quad \text{(currents in transformer primary and secondary)} \tag{31.36}$$

31.22 The cylindrical can near the top of this power pole is a step-down transformer. It converts the high-voltage ac in the power lines to low-voltage (120 V) ac, which is then distributed to the surrounding homes and businesses.

31.23 An ac adapter like this one converts household ac into low-voltage dc for use in electronic devices. It contains a step-down transformer to lower the voltage and diodes to rectify the output current (see Fig. 31.3).

We can combine Eqs. (31.35) and (31.36) and the relationship $I_2 = V_2/R$ to eliminate V_2 and I_2; we obtain

$$\frac{V_1}{I_1} = \frac{R}{(N_2/N_1)^2} \tag{31.37}$$

This shows that when the secondary circuit is completed through a resistance R, the result is the same as if the *source* had been connected directly to a resistance equal to R divided by the square of the turns ratio, $(N_2/N_1)^2$. In other words, the transformer "transforms" not only voltages and currents, but resistances as well. More generally, we can regard a transformer as "transforming" the *impedance* of the network to which the secondary circuit is completed.

Equation (31.37) has many practical consequences. The power supplied by a source to a resistor depends on the resistances of both the resistor and the source. It can be shown that the power transfer is greatest when the two resistances are *equal*. The same principle applies in both dc and ac circuits. When a high-impedance ac source must be connected to a low-impedance circuit, such as an audio amplifier connected to a loudspeaker, the source impedance can be *matched* to that of the circuit by use of a transformer with an appropriate turns ratio N_2/N_1.

Real transformers always have some energy losses. (That's why an ac adapter like the one shown in Fig. 31.23 feels warm to the touch after it's been in use for a while; the transformer is heated by the dissipated energy.) The windings have some resistance, leading to i^2R losses. There are also energy losses through hysteresis in the core (see Section 28.8). Hysteresis losses are minimized by the use of soft iron with a narrow hysteresis loop.

Another important mechanism for energy loss in a transformer core involves eddy currents (see Section 29.6). Consider a section AA through an iron transformer core (Fig. 31.24a). Since iron is a conductor, any such section can be pictured as several conducting circuits, one within the other (Fig. 31.24b). The flux through each of these circuits is continually changing, so eddy currents circulate in the entire volume of the core, with lines of flow that form planes perpendicular to the flux. These eddy currents are very undesirable; they waste energy through i^2R heating and themselves set up an opposing flux.

The effects of eddy currents can be minimized by the use of a *laminated* core, that is, one built up of thin sheets or laminae. The large electrical surface resistance of each lamina, due either to a natural coating of oxide or to an insulating varnish, effectively confines the eddy currents to individual laminae (Fig. 31.24c). The possible eddy-current paths are narrower, the induced emf in each path is smaller, and the eddy currents are greatly reduced. The alternating magnetic field exerts forces on the current-carrying laminae that cause them to vibrate back and forth; this vibration causes the characteristic "hum" of an operating transformer. You can hear this same "hum" from the magnetic ballast of a fluorescent light fixture (see Section 30.2).

Thanks to the use of soft iron cores and lamination, transformer efficiencies are usually well over 90%; in large installations they may reach 99%.

31.24 (a) Primary and secondary windings in a transformer. (b) Eddy currents in the iron core, shown in the cross section at AA. (c) Using a laminated core reduces the eddy currents.

(a) Schematic transformer

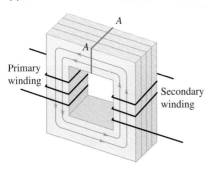

(b) Large eddy currents in solid core

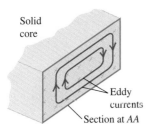

(c) Smaller eddy currents in laminated core

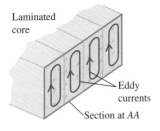

Example 31.9 **"Wake up and smell the (transformer)!"**

A friend brings back from Europe a device that she claims to be the world's greatest coffeemaker. Unfortunately, it was designed to operate from a 240-V line to obtain the 960 W of power that it needs. (a) What can she do to operate it at 120 V? (b) What current will the coffeemaker draw from the 120-V line? (c) What is the resistance of the coffeemaker? (The voltages are rms values.)

SOLUTION

IDENTIFY: Our friend needs a step-up transformer to convert the 120-V ac available in the home to the 240-V ac that the cof-

feemaker requires. This problem is about the properties of this transformer.

SET UP: We use Eq. (31.35) to determine the transformer turns ratio N_2/N_1, the relationship $P_{av} = V_{rms}I_{rms}$ for a resistor to find the current draw, and Eq. (31.37) to calculate the resistance.

EXECUTE: (a) To get $V_2 = 240$ V from $V_1 = 120$ V, the required turns ratio is $N_2/N_1 = V_2/V_1 = (240\text{ V})/(120\text{ V}) = 2$. That is, the secondary coil (connected to the coffeemaker) should have twice as many turns as the primary coil (connected to the 120-V line).

(b) The rms current I_1 in the 120-V primary is found by using $P_{av} = V_1I_1$, where P_{av} is the average power drawn by the coffee-maker and hence the power supplied by the 120-V line. (We're assuming that there are no energy losses in the transformer.) Hence $I_1 = P_{av}/V_1 = (960 \text{ W})/(120 \text{ V}) = 8.0 \text{ A}$. The secondary current is then $I_2 = P_{av}/V_2 = (960 \text{ W})/(240 \text{ V}) = 4.0 \text{ A}$.

(c) We have $V_1 = 120 \text{ V}$, $I_1 = 8.0 \text{ A}$, and $N_2/N_1 = 2$, so

$$\frac{V_1}{I_1} = \frac{120 \text{ V}}{8.0 \text{ A}} = 15 \text{ }\Omega$$

From Eq. (31.37),

$$R = 2^2(15 \text{ }\Omega) = 60 \text{ }\Omega$$

EVALUATE: As a check, $V_2/R = (240 \text{ V})/(60 \text{ }\omega) = 4.0 \text{ A} = I_2$, the same value obtained previously. you can also check this result for r by using the expression $P_{av} = V_2^2/R$ for the power drawn by the coffeemaker.

Test Your Understanding of Section 31.6 Each of the following four transformers has 1000 turns in its primary coil. Rank the transformers from largest to smallest number of turns in the secondary coil. (i) converts 120-V ac into 6.0-V ac; (ii) converts 120-V ac into 240-V ac; (iii) converts 240-V ac into 6.0-V ac; (iv) converts 240-V ac into 120-V ac.

Phasors and alternating current: An alternator or ac source produces an emf that varies sinusoidally with time. A sinusoidal voltage or current can be represented by a phasor, a vector that rotates counterclockwise with constant angular velocity ω equal to the angular frequency of the sinusoidal quantity. Its projection on the horizontal axis at any instant represents the instantaneous value of the quantity.

For a sinusoidal current, the rectified average and rms (root-mean-square) currents are proportional to the current amplitude I. Similarly, the rms value of a sinusoidal voltage is proportional to the voltage amplitude V. (See Example 31.1.)

$$I_{rav} = \frac{2}{\pi} I = 0.637 I \qquad (31.3)$$

$$I_{rms} = \frac{I}{\sqrt{2}} \qquad (31.4)$$

$$V_{rms} = \frac{V}{\sqrt{2}} \qquad (31.5)$$

Voltage, current, and phase angle: In general, the instantaneous voltage between two points in an ac circuit is not in phase with the instantaneous current passing through those points. The quantity ϕ is called the phase angle of the voltage relative to the current.

$$i = I\cos\omega t$$
$$v = V\cos(\omega t + \phi) \qquad (31.2)$$

Resistance and reactance: The voltage across a resistor R is in phase with the current. The voltage across an inductor L leads the current by $90°$ ($\phi = +90°$), while the voltage across a capacitor C lags the current by $90°$ ($\phi = -90°$). The voltage amplitude across each type of device is proportional to the current amplitude I. An inductor has inductive reactance $X_L = \omega L$, and a capacitor has capacitive reactance $X_C = 1/\omega C$. (See Examples 31.2 and 31.3.)

$$V_R = IR \qquad (31.7)$$

$$V_L = IX_L \qquad (31.13)$$

$$V_C = IX_C \qquad (31.19)$$

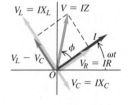

Impedance and the *L-R-C* series circuit: In a general ac circuit, the voltage and current amplitudes are related by the circuit impedance Z. In an L-R-C series circuit, the values of L, R, C, and the angular frequency ω determine the impedance and the phase angle ϕ of the voltage relative to the current. (See Examples 31.4 and 31.5.)

$$V = IZ \qquad (31.22)$$

$$Z = \sqrt{R^2 + (X_L - X_C)^2}$$
$$= \sqrt{R^2 + [\omega L - (1/\omega C)]^2} \qquad (31.23)$$

$$\tan\phi = \frac{\omega L - 1/\omega C}{R} \qquad (31.24)$$

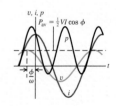

Power in ac circuits: The average power input P_{av} to an ac circuit depends on the voltage and current amplitudes (or, equivalently, their rms values) and the phase angle ϕ of the voltage relative to the current. The quantity $\cos\phi$ is called the power factor. (See Examples 31.6 and 31.7.)

$$P_{av} = \frac{1}{2} VI\cos\phi$$
$$= V_{rms} I_{rms} \cos\phi \qquad (31.31)$$

Resonance in ac circuits: In an L-R-C series circuit, the current becomes maximum and the impedance becomes minimum at an angular frequency called the resonance angular frequency. This phenomenon is called resonance. At resonance the voltage and current are in phase, and the impedance Z is equal to the resistance R. (See Example 31.8.)

$$\omega_0 = \frac{1}{\sqrt{LC}} \qquad (31.32)$$

Transformers: A transformer is used to transform the voltage and current levels in an ac circuit. In an ideal transformer with no energy losses, if the primary winding has N_1 turns and the secondary winding has N_2 turns, the amplitudes (or rms values) of the two voltages are related by Eq. (31.35). The amplitudes (or rms values) of the primary and secondary voltages and currents are related by Eq. (31.36). (See Example 31.9.)

$$\frac{V_2}{V_1} = \frac{N_2}{N_1} \quad (31.35)$$

$$V_1 I_1 = V_2 I_2 \quad (31.36)$$

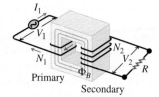

Key Terms

alternating current (ac), *1061*
ac source, *1062*
voltage amplitude, *1062*
current amplitude, *1062*
phasor, *1062*
phasor diagram, *1062*
rectified average current, *1063*

root-mean-square (rms) current, *1063*
phase angle, *1066*
inductive reactance, *1066*
capacitive reactance, *1068*
impedance, *1071*
power factor, *1076*
resonance, *1078*

resonance angular frequency, *1078*
resonance frequency, *1078*
transformer, *1080*
primary, *1080*
secondary, *1080*

Answer to Chapter Opening Question ?

Yes. In fact, the radio simultaneously detects transmissions at *all* frequencies. However, a radio is an *L-R-C* series circuit, and at any given time it is tuned to have a resonance at just one frequency. Hence the response of the radio to that frequency is much greater than its response to any other frequency, which is why you hear only one broadcasting station through the radio's speaker. (You can sometimes hear a second station if its frequency is sufficiently close to the tuned frequency.)

Answers to Test Your Understanding Questions

31.1 Answers: (a) D; (b) A; (c) B; (d) C For each phasor, the actual current is represented by the projection of that phasor onto the horizontal axis. The phasors all rotate counterclockwise around the origin with angular speed ω, so at the instant shown the projection of phasor A is positive but trending toward zero; the projection of phasor B is negative and becoming more negative; the projection of phasor C is negative but trending toward zero; and the projection of phasor D is positive and becoming more positive.

31.2 Answers: (a) (iii); (b) (ii); (c) (i) For a resistor, $V_R = IR$, so $I = V_R/R$. The voltage amplitude V_R and resistance R do not change with frequency, so the current amplitude I remains constant. For an inductor, $V_L = IX_L = I\omega L$, so $I = V_L/\omega L$. The voltage amplitude V_L and inductance L are constant, so the current amplitude I decreases as the frequency increases. For a capacitor, $V_C = IX_C = I/\omega C$, so $I = V_C\omega C$. The voltage amplitude V_C and capacitance C are constant, so the current amplitude I increases as the frequency increases.

31.3 Answer: (iv), (ii), (i), (iii) For the circuit in Example 31.4, $I = V/Z = (50\text{ V})/(500\ \Omega) = 0.10$ A. If the capacitor and inductor are removed so that only the ac source and resistor remain, the circuit is like that shown in Fig. 31.7a; then $I = V/R = (50\text{ V})/(300\ \Omega) = 0.17$ A. If the resistor and capacitor are removed so that only the ac source and inductor remain, the circuit is like that shown in Fig. 31.8a; then $I = V/X_L = (50\text{ V})/(600\ \Omega) = 0.083$ A. Finally, if the resistor and inductor are removed so that only the ac source and capacitor remain, the circuit is like that shown in Fig. 31.9a; then $I = V/X_C = (50\text{ V})/(200\ \Omega) = 0.25$ A.

31.4 Answers: (a) (v); (b) (iv) The energy cannot be extracted from the resistor, since energy is dissipated in a resistor and cannot be recovered. Instead, the energy must be extracted from either the inductor (which stores magnetic-field energy) or the capacitor (which stores electric-field energy). Positive power means that energy is being transferred from the ac source to the circuit, so *negative* power implies that energy is being transferred back into the source.

31.5 Answer: (ii) The capacitance C increases if the plate spacing is decreased (see Section 24.1). Hence the resonance frequency $f_0 = \omega_0/2\pi = 1/2\pi\sqrt{LC}$ decreases.

31.6 Answer: (ii), (iv), (i), (iii) From Eq. (31.35) the turns ratio is $N_2/N_1 = V_2/V_1$, so the number of turns in the secondary is $N_2 = N_1V_2/V_1$. Hence for the four cases we have (i) $N_2 = (1000)(6.0\text{ V})/(120\text{ V}) = 50$ turns; (ii) $N_2 = (1000)(240\text{ V})/(120\text{ V}) = 2000$ turns; (iii) $N_2 = (1000)(6.0\text{ V})/(240\text{ V}) = 25$ turns; and (iv) $N_2 = (1000)(120\text{ V})/(240\text{ V}) = 500$ turns. Note that (i), (iii), and (iv) are step-down transformers with fewer turns in the secondary than in the primary, while (ii) is a step-up transformer with more turns in the secondary than in the primary.

PROBLEMS

For instructor-assigned homework, go to **www.masteringphysics.com**

Discussion Questions

Q31.1. Household electric power in most of western Europe is supplied at 240 V, rather than the 120 V that is standard in the United States and Canada. What are the advantages and disadvantages of each system?

Q31.2. The current in an ac power line changes direction 120 times per second, and its average value is zero. Explain how it is possible for power to be transmitted in such a system.

Q31.3. In an ac circuit, why is the average power for an inductor and a capacitor zero, but not for a resistor?

Q31.4. Equation (31.14) was derived by using the relationship $i = dq/dt$ between the current and the charge on the capacitor. In Fig. 31.9a the positive counterclockwise current increases the charge on the capacitor. When the charge on the left plate is positive but decreasing in time, is $i = dq/dt$ still correct or should it be $i = -dq/dt$? Is $i = dq/dt$ still correct when the right-hand plate has positive charge that is increasing or decreasing in magnitude? Explain.

Q31.5. Fluorescent lights often use an inductor, called a ballast, to limit the current through the tubes. Why is it better to use an inductor rather than a resistor for this purpose?

Q31.6. Equation (31.9) says that $v_{ab} = L \, di/dt$ (see Fig. 31.8a). Using Faraday's law, explain why point a is at higher potential than point b when i is in the direction shown in Fig. 31.8a and is increasing in magnitude. When i is counterclockwise and decreasing in magnitude, is $v_{ab} = L \, di/dt$ still correct, or should it be $v_{ab} = -L \, di/dt$? Is $v_{ab} = L \, di/dt$ still correct when i is clockwise and increasing or decreasing in magnitude? Explain.

Q31.7. Is it possible for the power factor of an L-R-C series ac circuit to be zero? Justify your answer on *physical* grounds.

Q31.8. In a series L-R-C circuit, can the instantaneous voltage across the capacitor exceed the source voltage at that same instant? Can this be true for the instantaneous voltage across the inductor? Across the resistor? Explain.

Q31.9. In a series L-R-C circuit, what are the phase angle ϕ and power factor $\cos\phi$ when the resistance is much smaller than the inductive or capacitive reactance and the circuit is operated far from resonance? Explain.

Q31.10. When a series L-R-C circuit is connected across a 120-V ac line, the voltage rating of the capacitor may be exceeded even if it is rated at 200 or 400 V. How can this be?

Q31.11. In Example 31.6 (Section 31.4), a hair dryer was treated as a pure resistor. But because there are coils in the heating element and in the motor that drives the blower fan, a hair dryer also has inductance. Qualitatively, does including an inductance increase or decrease the values of R, I_{rms}, and P?

Q31.12. A light bulb and a parallel-plate capacitor with air between the plates are connected in series to an ac source. What happens to the brightness of the bulb when a dielectric is inserted between the plates of the capacitor? Explain.

Q31.13. A coil of wire wrapped on a hollow tube and a light bulb are connected in series to an ac source. What happens to the brightness of the bulb when an iron rod is inserted in the tube?

Q31.14. A circuit consists of a light bulb, a capacitor, and an inductor connected in series to an ac source. What happens to the brightness of the bulb when the inductor is removed? When the inductor is left in the circuit but the capacitor is removed? Explain.

Q31.15. A circuit consists of a light bulb, a capacitor, and an inductor connected in series to an ac source. Is it possible for both the capacitor and the inductor to be removed and the brightness of the bulb to remain the same? Explain.

Q31.16. Can a transformer be used with dc? Explain. What happens if a transformer designed for 120-V ac is connected to a 120-V dc line?

Q31.17. An ideal transformer has N_1 windings in the primary and N_2 windings in its secondary. If you double only the number of secondary windings, by what factor does (a) the voltage amplitude

in the secondary change, and (b) the effective resistance of the secondary circuit change?

Q31.18. Some electrical appliances operate equally well on ac or dc, and others work only on ac or only on dc. Give examples of each, and explain the differences.

Exercises

Section 31.1 Phasors and Alternating Currents

31.1. The plate on the back of a certain computer scanner says that the unit draws 0.34 A of current from a 120-V, 60-Hz line. Find (a) the root-mean-square current, (b) the current amplitude, (c) the average current; (d) the average square of the current.

31.2. A sinusoidal current $i = I\cos\omega t$ has an rms value $I_{rms} = 2.10$ A. (a) What is the current amplitude? (b) The current is passed through a full-wave rectifier circuit. What is the rectified average current? (c) Which is larger: I_{rms} or I_{rav}? Explain, using graphs of i^2 and of the rectified current.

31.3. The voltage across the terminals of an ac power supply varies with time according to Eq. (31.1). The voltage amplitude is $V = 45.0$ V. What are (a) the root-mean-square potential difference V_{rms}? and (b) the average potential difference V_{av} between the two terminals of the power supply?

Section 31.2 Resistance and Reactance

31.4. A 2.20-μF capacitor is connected across an ac source whose voltage amplitude is kept constant at 60.0 V but whose frequency can be varied. Find the current amplitude when the angular frequency is (a) 100 rad/s; (b) 1000 rad/s; (c) 10,000 rad/s. (d) Show the results of parts (a) through (c) in a plot of log I versus log ω.

31.5. A 5.00-H inductor with negligible resistance is connected across the ac source of Exercise 31.4. Find the current amplitude when the angular frequency is (a) 100 rad/s; (b) 1000 rad/s; (c) 10,000 rad/s. (d) Show the results of parts (a) through (c) in a plot of log I versus log ω.

31.6. A capacitance C and an inductance L are operated at the same angular frequency. (a) At what angular frequency will they have the same reactance? (b) If $L = 5.00$ mH and $C = 3.50 \, \mu$F, what is the numerical value of the angular frequency in part (a), and what is the reactance of each element?

31.7. In each circuit described next, an ac voltage source producing a current $i = I\cos\omega t$ is connected to an additional circuit element. (a) The ac source is connected across a resistor R. Sketch graphs of the current in the circuit and the potential difference across the resistor as functions of time, covering two cycles of oscillation. Put both graphs on the *same* set of axes so you can compare them. (b) Do the same as in part (a), except suppose the resistor is replaced by an inductor L. Sketch the same graphs as in part (a), but this time across the inductor instead of the resistor. (c) Do the same as in part (a), except suppose the resistor is replaced by a capacitor C. Sketch the same graphs as in part (a), except now across the capacitor instead of the resistor. (d) Sketch phasor diagrams for each of the preceding cases.

31.8. (a) Compute the reactance of a 0.450-H inductor at frequencies of 60.0 Hz and 600 Hz. (b) Compute the reactance of a 2.50-μF capacitor at the same frequencies. (c) At what frequency is the reactance of a 0.450-H inductor equal to that of a 2.50-μF capacitor?

31.9. (a) What is the reactance of a 3.00-H inductor at a frequency of 80.0 Hz? (b) What is the inductance of an inductor whose reactance is 120 Ω at 80.0 Hz? (c) What is the reactance of a 4.00-μF capacitor at a frequency of 80.0 Hz? (d) What is the capacitance of a capacitor whose reactance is 120 Ω at 80.0 Hz?

31.10. A Radio Inductor. You want the current amplitude through a 0.450-mH inductor (part of the circuitry for a radio receiver) to be 2.60 mA when a sinusoidal voltage with amplitude 12.0 V is applied across the inductor. What frequency is required?

31.11. Kitchen Capacitance. The wiring for a refrigerator contains a starter capacitor. A voltage of amplitude 170 V and frequency 60.0 Hz applied across the capacitor is to produce a current amplitude of 0.850 A through the capacitor. What capacitance C is required?

31.12. A 250-Ω resistor is connected in series with a 4.80-μF capacitor. The voltage across the capacitor is $v_C = (7.60\ \text{V})\sin[(120\ \text{rad/s})t]$. (a) Determine the capacitive reactance of the capacitor. (b) Derive an expression for the voltage v_R across the resistor.

31.13. A 150-Ω resistor is connected in series with a 0.250-H inductor. The voltage across the resistor is $v_R = (3.80\ \text{V})\cos[(720\ \text{rad/s})t]$. (a) Derive an expression for the circuit current. (b) Determine the inductive reactance of the inductor. (c) Derive an expression for the voltage v_L across the inductor.

Section 31.3 The *L-R-C* Series Circuit

31.14. You have a 200-Ω resistor, a 0.400-H inductor, and a 6.00-μF capacitor. Suppose you take the resistor and inductor and make a series circuit with a voltage source that has voltage amplitude 30.0 V and an angular frequency of 250 rad/s. (a) What is the impedance of the circuit? (b) What is the current amplitude? (c) What are the voltage amplitudes across the resistor and across the inductor? (d) What is the phase angle ϕ of the source voltage with respect to the current? Does the source voltage lag or lead the current? (e) Construct the phasor diagram.

31.15. (a) For the *R-L* circuit of Exercise 31.14, graph v, v_R, and v_L versus t for $t = 0$ to $t = 50.0$ ms. The current is given by $i = I\cos\omega t$, so $v = V\cos(\omega t + \phi)$. (b) What are v, v_R, and v_L at $t = 20.0$ ms? Compare $v_R + v_L$ to v at this instant. (c) Repeat part (b) for $t = 40.0$ ms.

31.16. Repeat Exercise 31.14 with the circuit consisting of only the capacitor and the inductor in series. For part (c), calculate the voltage amplitudes across the capacitor and across the inductor.

31.17. Repeat Exercise 31.14 with the circuit consisting of only the resistor and the capacitor in series. For part (c), calculate the voltage amplitudes across the resistor and across the capacitor.

31.18. (a) For the *R-C* circuit of Exercise 31.17, graph v, v_R, and v_C versus t for $t = 0$ to $t = 50.0$ ms. The current is given by $i = I\cos\omega t$, so $v = V\cos(\omega t + \phi)$. (b) What are v, v_R, and v_C at $t = 20.0$ ms? Compare $v_R + v_C$ to v at this instant. (c) Repeat part (b) for $t = 40.0$ ms.

31.19. The resistor, inductor, capacitor, and voltage source described in Exercise 31.14 are connected to form an *L-R-C* series circuit. (a) What is the impedance of the circuit? (b) What is the current amplitude? (c) What is the phase angle of the source voltage with respect to the current? Does the source voltage lag or lead the current? (d) What are the voltage amplitudes across the resistor, inductor, and capacitor? (e) Explain how it is possible for the voltage amplitude across the capacitor to be greater than the voltage amplitude across the source.

31.20. (a) For the *L-R-C* circuit of Exercise 31.19, graph v, v_R, v_L, and v_C versus t for $t = 0$ to $t = 50.0$ ms. The current is given by $i = I\cos\omega t$, so $v = V\cos(\omega t + \phi)$. (b) What are v, v_R, v_L, and v_C at $t = 20.0$ ms? Compare $v_R + v_L + v_C$ to v at this instant. (c) Repeat part (b) for $t = 40.0$ ms.

31.21. Analyzing an *L-R-C* Circuit. You have a 200-Ω resistor, a 0.400-H inductor, a 5.00-μF capacitor, and a variable-frequency ac source with an amplitude of 3.00 V. You connect all four elements together to form a series circuit. (a) At what frequency will the current in the circuit be greatest? What will be the current amplitude at this frequency? (b) What will be the current amplitude at an angular frequency of 400 rad/s? At this frequency, will the source voltage lead or lag the current?

31.22. An *L-R-C* series circuit is constructed using a 175-Ω resistor, a 12.5-μF capacitor, and an 8.00-mH inductor, all connected across an ac source having a variable frequency and a voltage amplitude of 25.0 V. (a) At what angular frequency will the impedance be smallest, and what is the impedance at this frequency? (b) At the angular frequency in part (a), what is the maximum current through the inductor? (c) At the angular frequency in part (a), find the potential difference across the ac source, the resistor, the capacitor, and the inductor at the instant that the current is equal to one-half its greatest positive value. (d) In part (c), how are the potential differences across the resistor, inductor, and capacitor related to the potential difference across the ac source?

31.23. In an *L-R-C* series circuit, the rms voltage across the resistor is 30.0 V, across the capacitor it is 90.0 V, and across the inductor it is 50.0 V. What is the rms voltage of the source?

31.24. Define the reactance X of an *L-R-C* circuit to be $X = X_L - X_C$. (a) Show that $X = 0$ when the angular frequency ω of the current is equal to the resonance angular frequency ω_0. (b) What is the sign of X when $\omega > \omega_0$? (c) What is the sign of X when $\omega < \omega_0$? (d) Graph X versus ω.

Section 31.4 Power in Alternating-Current Circuits

31.25. The power of a certain CD player operating at 120 V rms is 20.0 W. Assuming that the CD player behaves like a pure resistance, find (a) the maximum instantaneous power; (b) the rms current; (c) the resistance of this player.

31.26. In a series *L-R-C* circuit, the components have the following values: $L = 20.0$ mH, $C = 140$ nF, and $R = 350$ Ω. The generator has an rms voltage of 120 V and a frequency of 1.25 kHz. Determine (a) the power supplied by the generator; and (b) the power dissipated in the resistor.

31.27. (a) Show that for an *L-R-C* series circuit the power factor is equal to R/Z. (*Hint:* Use the phasor diagram; see Fig. 31.13b.) (b) Show that for any ac circuit, not just one containing pure resistance only, the average power delivered by the voltage source is given by $P_{\text{av}} = I_{\text{rms}}^2 R$.

31.28. An *L-R-C* series circuit is connected to a 120-Hz ac source that has $V_{\text{rms}} = 80.0$ V. The circuit has a resistance of 75.0 Ω and an impedance at this frequency of 105 Ω. What average power is delivered to the circuit by the source?

31.29. An *L-R-C* series circuit with $L = 0.120$ H, $R = 240$ Ω, and $C = 7.30\ \mu$F carries an rms current of 0.450 A with a frequency of 400 Hz. (a) What are the phase angle and power factor for this circuit? (b) What is the impedance of the circuit? (c) What is the rms voltage of the source? (d) What average power is delivered by the source? (e) What is the average rate at which electrical energy is converted to thermal energy in the resistor? (f) What is the average rate at which electrical energy is dissipated (converted to other forms) in the capacitor? (g) In the inductor?

31.30. A series ac circuit contains a 250-Ω resistor, a 15-mH inductor, a 3.5-μF capacitor, and an ac power source of voltage amplitude 45 V operating at an angular frequency of 360 rad/s, (a) What is the power factor of this circuit? (b) Find the average power delivered to the entire circuit. (c) What is the average power delivered to the resistor, to the capacitor, and to the inductor?

Section 31.5 Resonance in Alternating-Current Circuits

31.31. In an L-R-C series circuit, $R = 300\ \Omega$, $L = 0.400\ H$, and $C = 6.00 \times 10^{-8}\ F$. When the ac source operates at the resonance frequency of the circuit, the current amplitude is 0.500 A. (a) What is the voltage amplitude of the source? (b) What is the amplitude of the voltage across the resistor, across the inductor, and across the capacitor? (c) What is the average power supplied by the source?

31.32. An L-R-C series circuit consists of a source with voltage amplitude 120 V and angular frequency 50.0 rad/s, a resistor with $R = 400\ \Omega$ an inductor with $L = 9.00\ H$, and a capacitor with capacitance C. (a) For what value of C will the current amplitude in the circuit be a maximum? (b) When C has the value calculated in part (a), what is the amplitude of the voltage across the inductor?

31.33. In an L-R-C series circuit, $R = 150\ \Omega$, $L = 0.750\ H$, and $C = 0.0180\ \mu F$. The source has voltage amplitude $V = 150\ V$ and a frequency equal to the resonance frequency of the circuit. (a) What is the power factor? (b) What is the average power delivered by the source? (c) The capacitor is replaced by one with $C = 0.0360\ \mu F$ and the source frequency is adjusted to the new resonance value. Then what is the average power delivered by the source?

31.34. In an L-R-C series circuit, $R = 400\ \Omega$, $L = 0.350\ H$, and $C = 0.0120\ \mu F$. (a) What is the resonance angular frequency of the circuit? (b) The capacitor can withstand a peak voltage of 550 V. If the voltage source operates at the resonance frequency, what maximum voltage amplitude can it have if the maximum capacitor voltage is not exceeded?

31.35. A series circuit consists of an ac source of variable frequency, a 115-Ω resistor, a 1.25-μF capacitor, and a 4.50-mH inductor. Find the impedance of this circuit when the angular frequency of the ac source is adjusted to (a) the resonance angular frequency; (b) twice the resonance angular frequency; (c) half the resonance angular frequency.

31.36. In an L-R-C series circuit, $L = 0.280\ H$ and $C = 4.00\ \mu F$. The voltage amplitude of the source is 120 V. (a) What is the resonance angular frequency of the circuit? (b) When the source operates at the resonance angular frequency, the current amplitude in the circuit is 1.70 A. What is the resistance R of the resistor? (c) At the resonance angular frequency, what are the peak voltages across the inductor, the capacitor, and the resistor?

Section 31.6 Transformers

31.37. A Step-Down Transformer.   A transformer connected to a 120-V (rms) ac line is to supply 12.0 V (rms) to a portable electronic device. The load resistance in the secondary is 5.00 Ω. (a) What should the ratio of primary to secondary turns of the transformer be? (b) What rms current must the secondary supply? (c) What average power is delivered to the load? (d) What resistance connected directly across the 120-V line would draw the same power as the transformer? Show that this is equal to 5.00 Ω times the square of the ratio of primary to secondary turns.

31.38. A Step-Up Transformer.   A transformer connected to a 120-V (rms) ac line is to supply 13,000 V (rms) for a neon sign. To reduce shock hazard, a fuse is to be inserted in the primary circuit; the fuse is to blow when the rms current in the secondary circuit exceeds 8.50 mA. (a) What is the ratio of secondary to primary turns of the transformer? (b) What power must be supplied to the

transformer when the rms secondary current is 8.50 mA? (c) What current rating should the fuse in the primary circuit have?

31.39. Off to Europe!   You plan to take your hair blower to Europe, where the electrical outlets put out 240 V instead of the 120 V seen in the United States. The blower puts out 1600 W at 120 V. (a) What could you do to operate your blower via the 240-V line in Europe? (b) What current will your blower draw from a European outlet? (c) What resistance will your blower appear to have when operated at 240 V?

Problems

31.40. Figure 31.12a shows the crossover network in a loudspeaker system. One branch consists of a capacitor C and a resistor R in series (the tweeter). This branch is in parallel with a second branch (the woofer) that consists of an inductor L and a resistor R in series. The same source voltage with angular frequency ω is applied across each parallel branch. (a) What is the impedance of the tweeter branch? (b) What is the impedance of the woofer branch? (c) Explain why the currents in the two branches are equal when the impedances of the branches are equal. (d) Derive an expression for the frequency f that corresponds to the crossover point in Fig. 31.12b.

31.41. A coil has a resistance of 48.0 Ω. At a frequency of 80.0 Hz the voltage across the coil leads the current in it by 52.3°. Determine the inductance of the coil.

31.42. Five infinite-impedance voltmeters, calibrated to read rms values, are connected as shown in Fig 31.25. Let $R = 200\ \Omega$, $L = 0.400\ H$, $C = 6.00\ \mu F$, and $V = 30.0\ V$. What is the reading of each voltmeter if (a) $\omega = 200\ rad/s$; and (b) $\omega = 1000\ rad/s$?

Figure **31.25** Problem 31.42.

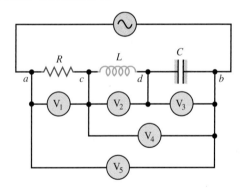

31.43. A sinusoidal current is given by $i = I\cos\omega t$. The full-wave rectified current is shown in Fig. 31.3b. (a) Let t_1 and t_2 be the two smallest positive times at which the rectified current is zero. Express t_1 and t_2 in terms of ω. (b) Find the area under the rectified i versus t curve between t_1 and t_2 by computing the integral $\int_{t_1}^{t_2} i\ dt$. Since $dq = i\ dt$, this area equals the charge that flows during the t_1 to t_2 time interval. (c) Set the result in part (b) equal to $I_{rav}(t_2 - t_1)$ and calculate I_{rav} in terms of the current amplitude I. Compare your answer to Eq. (31.3).

31.44. A large electromagnetic coil is connected to a 120-Hz ac source. The coil has resistance 400 Ω, and at this source frequency the coil has inductive reactance 250 Ω. (a) What is the inductance of the coil? (b) What must the rms voltage of the source be if the coil is to consume an average electrical power of 800 W?

31.45. A series circuit has an impedance of 60.0 Ω and a power factor of 0.720 at 50.0 Hz. The source voltage lags the current. (a) What circuit element, an inductor or a capacitor, should be placed in series with the circuit to raise its power factor? (b) What size element will raise the power factor to unity?

31.46. A circuit consists of a resistor and a capacitor in series with an ac source that supplies an rms voltage of 240 V. At the frequency of the source the reactance of the capacitor is 50.0 Ω. The rms current in the circuit is 3.00 A. What is the average power supplied by the source?

31.47. An *L-R-C* series circuit consists of a 50.0-Ω resistor, a 10.0-μF capacitor, a 3.50-mH inductor, and an ac voltage source of voltage amplitude 60.0 V operating at 1250 Hz. (a) Find the current amplitude and the voltage amplitudes across the inductor, the resistor, and the capacitor. Why can the voltage amplitudes add up to *more* than 60.0 V? (b) If the frequency is now doubled, but nothing else is changed, which of the quantities in part (a) will change? Find the new values for those that do change.

31.48. At a frequency ω_1 the reactance of a certain capacitor equals that of a certain inductor. (a) If the frequency is changed to $\omega_2 = 2\omega_1$, what is the ratio of the reactance of the inductor to that of the capacitor? Which reactance is larger? (b) If the frequency is changed to $\omega_3 = \omega_1/3$, what is the ratio of the reactance of the inductor to that of the capacitor? Which reactance is larger? (c) If the capacitor and inductor are placed in series with a resistor of resistance R to form a series *L-R-C* circuit, what will be the resonance angular frequency of the circuit?

31.49. A High-Pass Filter. One application of *L-R-C* series circuits is to high-pass or low-pass filters, which filter out either the low- or high-frequency components of a signal. A high-pass filter is shown in Fig. 31.26, where the output voltage is taken across the *L-R* combination. (The *L-R* combination represents an inductive coil that also has resistance due to the large length of wire in the coil.) Derive an expression for V_{out}/V_s, the ratio of the output and source voltage amplitudes, as a function of the angular frequency ω of the source. Show that when ω is small, this ratio is proportional to ω and thus is small, and show that the ratio approaches unity in the limit of large frequency.

Figure **31.26** Problem 31.49.

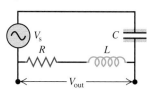

31.50. A Low-Pass Filter. Figure 31.27 shows a low-pass filter (see Problem 31.49); the output voltage is taken across the capacitor in an *L-R-C* series circuit. Derive an expression for V_{out}/V_s, the ratio of the output and source voltage amplitudes, as a function of the angular frequency ω of the source. Show that when ω is large, this ratio is proportional to ω^{-2} and thus is very small, and show that the ratio approaches unity in the limit of small frequency.

Figure **31.27** Problem 31.50.

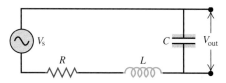

31.51. An *L-R-C* series circuit is connected to an ac source of constant voltage amplitude V and variable angular frequency ω. (a) Show that the current amplitude, as a function of ω, is

$$I = \frac{V}{\sqrt{R^2 + (\omega L - 1/\omega C)^2}}$$

(b) Show that the average power dissipated in the resistor is

$$P = \frac{V^2 R/2}{R^2 + (\omega L - 1/\omega C)^2}$$

(c) Show that I and P are *both* maximum when $\omega = 1/\sqrt{LC}$; that is, when the source frequency equals the resonance frequency of the circuit. (d) Graph P as a function of ω for $V = 100$ V, $R = 200$ Ω, $L = 2.0$ H, and $C = 0.50$ μF. Compare to the light purple curve in Fig. 31.19. Discuss the behavior of I and P in the limits $\omega = 0$ and $\omega \to \infty$.

31.52. An *L-R-C* series circuit is connected to an ac source of constant voltage amplitude V and variable angular frequency ω. Using the results of Problem 31.51, find an expression for (a) the amplitude V_L of the voltage across the inductor as a function of ω; and (b) the amplitude V_C of the voltage across the capacitor as a function of ω. (c) Graph V_L and V_C as functions of ω for $V = 100$ V, $R = 200$ Ω, $L = 2.0$ H, and $C = 0.50$ μF. (d) Discuss the behavior of V_L and V_C in the limits $\omega = 0$ and $\omega \to \infty$. For what value of ω is $V_L = V_C$? What is the significance of this value of ω?

31.53. An *L-R-C* series circuit is connected to an ac source of constant voltage amplitude V and variable angular frequency ω. (a) Show that the time-averaged energy stored in the inductor is $U_B = \frac{1}{4}LI^2$ and the time-averaged energy stored in the capacitor is $U_E = \frac{1}{4}CV^2$. (b) Use the results of Problems 31.51 and 31.52 to find expressions for U_B and U_E as functions of ω. (c) Graph U_B and U_E as functions of ω for $V = 100$ V, $R = 200$ Ω, $L = 2.0$ H, and $C = 0.50$ μF. (d) Discuss the behavior of U_B and U_E in the limits $\omega = 0$ and $\omega \to \infty$. For what value of ω is $U_B = U_E$? What is the significance of this value of ω?

31.54. The L-R-C Parallel Circuit. A resistor, inductor, and capacitor are connected in parallel to an ac source with voltage amplitude V and angular frequency ω. Let the source voltage be given by $v = V\cos\omega t$. (a) Show that the instantaneous voltages v_R, v_L, and v_C at any instant are each equal to v and that $i = i_R + i_L + i_C$, where i is the current through the source and i_R, i_L, and i_C are the currents through the resistor, the inductor, and the capacitor, respectively. (b) What are the phases of i_R, i_L, and i_C with respect to v? Use current phasors to represent i, i_R, i_L, and i_C. In a phasor diagram, show the phases of these four currents with respect to v. (c) Use the phasor diagram of part (b) to show that the current amplitude I for the current i through the source is given by $I = \sqrt{I_R^2 + (I_C - I_L)^2}$. (d) Show that the result of part (c) can be written as $I = V/Z$, with $1/Z = \sqrt{1/R^2 + (\omega C - 1/\omega L)^2}$.

31.55. Parallel Resonance. The impedance of an *L-R-C* parallel circuit was derived in Problem 31.54. (a) Show that at the resonance angular frequency $\omega_0 = 1/\sqrt{LC}$, $I_C = I_L$, and I is a *minimum*. (b) Since I is a minimum at resonance, is it correct to say that the power delivered to the resistor is also a minimum at $\omega = \omega_0$? Explain. (c) At resonance, what is the phase angle of the source current with respect to the source voltage? How does this compare to the phase angle for an *L-R-C* series circuit at resonance? (d) Draw the circuit diagram for an *L-R-C* parallel circuit. Arrange the circuit elements in your diagram so that the resistor is closest to the ac source. Justify the following statement: When the angular frequency of the source is $\omega = \omega_0$, there is *no* current flowing between (i) the part of the circuit that includes the source and the resistor and (ii) the part that includes the inductor and capacitor, so you could cut the wires connecting these two parts of the circuit without affecting the currents. (e) Is the statement in part (d) still valid if we consider that any real inductor or capacitor also has some resistance of its own? Explain.

31.56. A 400-Ω resistor and a 6.00-μF capacitor are connected in parallel to an ac generator that supplies an rms voltage of 220 V at an angular frequency of 360 rad/s. Use the results of Problem 31.54. Note that since there is no inductor in the circuit, the $1/\omega L$ term is not present in the expression for Z. Find (a) the current amplitude in the resistor; (b) the current amplitude in the capacitor; (c) the phase angle of the source current with respect to the source voltage; (d) the amplitude of the current through the generator. (e) Does the source current lag or lead the source voltage?

31.57. An L-R-C parallel circuit is connected to an ac source of constant voltage amplitude V and variable angular frequency ω. (a) Using the results of Problem 31.54, find expressions for the amplitudes I_R, I_L, and I_C of the currents through the resistor, inductor, and capacitor as functions of ω. (b) Graph I_R, I_L, and I_C as functions of ω for $V = 100$ V, $R = 200\ \Omega$, $L = 2.0$ H, and $C = 0.50\ \mu$F. (c) Discuss the behavior of I_L and I_C in the limits $\omega = 0$ and $\omega \to \infty$. Explain why I_L and I_C behave as they do in these limits. (d) Calculate the resonance frequency (in Hz) of the circuit, and sketch the phasor diagram at the resonance frequency. (e) At the resonance frequency, what is the current amplitude through the source? (f) At the resonance frequency, what is the current amplitude through the resistor, through the inductor, and through the capacitor?

31.58. An L-R-C series circuit consists of a 2.50-μF capacitor, a 5.00-mH inductor, and a 75.0-Ω resistor connected across an ac source of voltage amplitude 15.0 V having variable frequency. (a) Under what circumstances is the average power delivered to the circuit equal to $\frac{1}{2}V_{rms}I_{rms}$? (b) Under the conditions of part (a), what is the average power delivered to each circuit element and what is the maximum current through the capacitor?

31.59. In an L-R-C series circuit the magnitude of the phase angle is 54.0°, with the source voltage lagging the current. The reactance of the capacitor is 350 Ω, and the resistor resistance is 180 Ω. The average power delivered by the source is 140 W. Find (a) the reactance of the inductor; (b) the rms current; (c) the rms voltage of the source.

31.60. An L-R-C series circuit has $R = 500\ \Omega$, $L = 2.00$ H, $C = 0.500\ \mu$F, and $V = 100$ V. (a) For $\omega = 800$ rad/s, calculate V_R, V_L, V_C, and ϕ. Using a single set of axes, graph v, v_R, v_L, and v_C as functions of time. Include two cycles of v on your graph. (b) Repeat part (a) for $\omega = 1000$ rad/s. (c) Repeat part (a) for $\omega = 1250$ rad/s.

31.61. In an L-R-C series circuit, the source has a voltage amplitude of 120 V, $R = 80.0\ \Omega$, and the reactance of the capacitor is 480 Ω. The voltage amplitude across the capacitor is 360 V. (a) What is the current amplitude in the circuit? (b) What is the impedance? (c) What two values can the reactance of the inductor have? (d) For which of the two values found in part (c) is the angular frequency less than the resonance angular frequency? Explain.

31.62. A series circuit consists of a 1.50-mH inductor, a 125-Ω resistor, and a 25.0-nF capacitor connected across an ac source having an rms voltage of 35.0 V and variable frequency. (a) At what angular frequency will the current amplitude be equal to $\frac{1}{3}$ of its maximum possible value? (b) At the frequency in part (a) what are the current amplitude and the voltage amplitude across each of the circuit elements (including the ac source)?

31.63. The current in a certain circuit varies with time as shown in Fig. 31.28. Find the average current and the rms current in terms of I_0.

Figure **31.28** Problem 31.63.

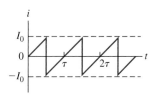

31.64. The Resonance Width. Consider an L-R-C series circuit with a 1.80-H inductor, a 0.900-μF capacitor, and a 300-Ω resistor. The source has terminal rms voltage $V_{rms} = 60.0$ V and variable angular frequency ω. (a) What is the resonance angular frequency ω_0 of the circuit? (b) What is the rms current through the circuit at resonance, I_{rms-0}? (c) For what two values of the angular frequency, ω_1 and ω_2, is the rms current half the resonance value? (d) The quantity $|\omega_1 - \omega_2|$ defines the *resonance width*. Calculate I_{rms-0} and the resonance width for $R = 300\ \Omega$, 30.0 Ω, and 3.00 Ω. Describe how your results compare to the discussion in Section 31.5.

31.65. An inductor, a capacitor, and a resistor are all connected in series across an ac source. If the resistance, inductance, and capacitance are all doubled, by what factor does each of the following quantities change? Indicate whether they increase or decrease: (a) the resonance angular frequency; (b) the inductive reactance; (c) the capacitive reactance. (d) Does the impedance double?

31.66. A transformer consists of 275 primary windings and 834 secondary windings. If the potential difference across the primary coil is 25.0 V, (a) what is the voltage across the secondary coil, and (b) what is the effective load resistance of the secondary coil if it is connected across a 125-Ω resistor?

31.67. You want to double the resonance angular frequency of a series R-L-C circuit by changing only the *pertinent* circuit elements all by the same factor. (a) Which ones should you change? (b) By what factor should you change them?

31.68. A resistance R, capacitance C, and inductance L are connected in series to a voltage source with amplitude V and variable angular frequency ω. If $\omega = \omega_0$, the resonance angular frequency, find (a) the maximum current in the resistor; (b) the maximum voltage across the capacitor; (c) the maximum voltage across the inductor; (d) the maximum energy stored in the capacitor; (e) the maximum energy stored in the inductor. Give your answers in terms of R, C, L, and V.

31.69. Repeat Problem 31.68 for the case $\omega = \omega_0/2$.

31.70. Repeat Problem 31.68 for the case $\omega = 2\omega_0$.

31.71. Finding an Unknown Inductance. Your boss gives you an inductor and asks you to measure its inductance. You have available a resistor, an ac voltmeter of high impedance, a capacitor, and an ac source. Explain how you might use these to determine the inductance, and cite any other piece of equipment you may need. Be sure to explain clearly how to use the equipment and what you need to measure to find the unknown inductance.

31.72. An L-R-C series circuit draws 220 W from a 120-V (rms), 50.0-Hz ac line. The power factor is 0.560, and the source voltage leads the current. (a) What is the net resistance R of the circuit? (b) Find the capacitance of the series capacitor that will result in a power factor of unity when it is added to the original circuit. (c) What power will then be drawn from the supply line?

31.73. In an L-R-C series circuit the current is given by $i = I\cos\omega t$. The voltage amplitudes for the resistor, inductor, and capacitor are V_R, V_L, and V_C. (a) Show that the instantaneous power into the resistor is $p_R = V_R I \cos^2 \omega t = \frac{1}{2} V_R I (1 + \cos 2\omega t)$. What does this expression give for the average power into the resistor? (b) Show that the instantaneous power into the inductor is $p_L = -V_L I \sin \omega t \cos \omega t = -\frac{1}{2} V_L I \sin 2\omega t$. What does this expression give for the average power into the inductor? (c) Show that the instantaneous power into the capacitor is $p_C = V_C I \sin \omega t \cos \omega t = \frac{1}{2} V_C I \sin 2\omega t$. What does this expression give for the average power into the capacitor? (d) The instantaneous power delivered by the source is shown in Section 31.4 to be $p = VI \cos \omega t (\cos \phi \cos \omega t - \sin \phi \sin \omega t)$. Show that $p_R + p_L + p_C$ equals p at each instant of time.

Challenge Problems

31.74. (a) At what angular frequency is the voltage amplitude across the *resistor* in an *L-R-C* series circuit at maximum value? (b) At what angular frequency is the voltage amplitude across the *inductor* at maximum value? (c) At what angular frequency is the voltage amplitude across the *capacitor* at maximum value? (You may want to refer to the results of Problem 31.52.)

31.75. Complex Numbers in a Circuit. The voltage across a circuit element in an ac circuit is not necessarily in phase with the current through that circuit element. Therefore the voltage amplitudes across the circuit elements in a branch in an ac circuit do not add algebraically. A method that is commonly employed to simplify the analysis of an ac circuit driven by a sinusoidal source is to represent the impedance Z as a *complex* number. The resistance R is taken to be the real part of the impedance, and the reactance $X = X_L - X_C$ is taken to be the imaginary part. Thus, for a branch containing a resistor, inductor, and capacitor in series, the complex impedance is $Z_{\text{cpx}} = R + iX$, where $i^2 = -1$. If the voltage amplitude across the branch is V_{cpx}, we define a *complex* current amplitude by $I_{\text{cpx}} = V_{\text{cpx}}/Z_{\text{cpx}}$. The *actual* current amplitude is the absolute value of the complex current amplitude, that is, $I = (I_{\text{cpx}}^* I_{\text{cpx}})^{1/2}$. The phase angle ϕ of the current with respect to

the source voltage is given by $\tan \phi = \text{Im}(I_{\text{cpx}})/\text{Re}(I_{\text{cpx}})$. The voltage amplitudes $V_{R\text{-cpx}}$, $V_{L\text{-cpx}}$, and $V_{C\text{-cpx}}$ across the resistance, inductance, and capacitance, respectively, are found by multiplying I_{cpx} by R, iX_L, or $-iX_C$, respectively. From the complex representation for the voltage amplitudes, the voltage across a branch is just the algebraic sum of the voltages across each circuit element; $V_{\text{cpx}} = V_{R\text{-cpx}} + V_{L\text{-cpx}} + V_{C\text{-cpx}}$. The actual value of any current amplitude or voltage amplitude is the absolute value of the corresponding complex quantity. Consider the series *L-R-C* circuit shown in Fig. 31.29. The values of the circuit elements, the source voltage amplitude, and the source angular frequency are as shown. Use the phasor diagram techniques presented in Section 31.1 to solve for (a) the current amplitude; and (b) the phase angle ϕ of the current with respect to the source voltage. (Note that this angle is the negative of the phase angle defined in Fig. 31.13.) Now analyze the same circuit using the complex-number approach. (c) Determine the complex impedance of the circuit, Z_{cpx}. Take the absolute value to obtain Z, the actual impedance of the circuit. (d) Take the voltage amplitude of the source, V_{cpx}, to be real, and find the complex current amplitude I_{cpx}. Find the actual current amplitude by taking the absolute value of I_{cpx}. (e) Find the phase angle ϕ of the current with respect to the source voltage by using the real and imaginary parts of I_{cpx}, as explained above. (f) Find the complex representations of the voltages across the resistance, the inductance, and the capacitance. (g) Adding the answers found in part (f), verify that the sum of these complex numbers is real and equal to 200 V, the voltage of the source.

Figure **31.29** Challenge Problem 31.75.

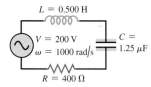

32

ELECTROMAGNETIC WAVES

LEARNING GOALS

By studying this chapter, you will learn:

• Why there are both electric and magnetic fields in a light wave.

• How the speed of light is related to the fundamental constants of electricity and magnetism.

• How to describe the propagation of a sinusoidal electromagnetic wave.

• What determines the amount of power carried by an electromagnetic wave.

• How to describe standing electromagnetic waves.

? Metal objects reflect not only visible light but also radio waves. What aspect of metals makes them so reflective?

What is light? This question has been asked by humans for centuries, but there was no answer until electricity and magnetism were unified into the single discipline of *electromagnetism,* as described by Maxwell's equations. These equations show that a time-varying magnetic field acts as a source of electric field and that a time-varying electric field acts as a source of magnetic field. These $\vec{E}$ and $\vec{B}$ fields can sustain each other, forming an *electromagnetic wave* that propagates through space. Visible light emitted by the glowing filament of a light bulb is one example of an electromagnetic wave; other kinds of electromagnetic waves are produced by sources such as TV and radio stations, microwave oscillators for ovens and radar, x-ray machines, and radioactive nuclei.

In this chapter we'll use Maxwell's equations as the theoretical basis for understanding electromagnetic waves. We'll find that these waves carry both energy and momentum. In sinusoidal electromagnetic waves, the $\vec{E}$ and $\vec{B}$ fields are sinusoidal functions of time and position, with a definite frequency and wavelength. The various types of electromagnetic waves—visible light, radio, x rays, and others—differ only in their frequency and wavelength. Our study of optics in the following chapters will be based in part on the electromagnetic nature of light.

Unlike waves on a string or sound waves in a fluid, electromagnetic waves do not require a material medium; the light that you see coming from the stars at night has traveled without difficulty across tens or hundreds of light-years of (nearly) empty space. Nonetheless, electromagnetic waves and mechanical waves have much in common and are described in much the same language. Before reading further in this chapter, you should review the properties of mechanical waves as discussed in Chapters 15 and 16.

32.1 Maxwell's Equations and Electromagnetic Waves

In the last several chapters we studied various aspects of electric and magnetic fields. We learned that when the fields don't vary with time, such as an electric field produced by charges at rest or the magnetic field of a steady current, we can analyze the electric and magnetic fields independently without considering interactions between them. But when the fields vary with time, they are no longer independent. Faraday's law (see Section 29.2) tells us that a time-varying magnetic field acts as a source of electric field, as shown by induced emfs in inductors and transformers. Ampere's law, including the displacement current discovered by Maxwell (see Section 29.7), shows that a time-varying electric field acts as a source of magnetic field. This mutual interaction between the two fields is summarized in Maxwell's equations, presented in Section 29.7.

Thus, when *either* an electric or a magnetic field is changing with time, a field of the other kind is induced in adjacent regions of space. We are led (as Maxwell was) to consider the possibility of an electromagnetic disturbance, consisting of time-varying electric and magnetic fields, that can propagate through space from one region to another, even when there is no matter in the intervening region. Such a disturbance, if it exists, will have the properties of a *wave*, and an appropriate term is **electromagnetic wave.**

Such waves do exist; radio and television transmission, light, x rays, and many other kinds of radiation are examples of electromagnetic waves. Our goal in this chapter is to see how such waves are explained by the principles of electromagnetism that we have studied thus far and to examine the properties of these waves.

Electricity, Magnetism, and Light

As often happens in the development of science, the theoretical understanding of electromagnetic waves evolved along a considerably more devious path than the one just outlined. In the early days of electromagnetic theory (the early 19th century), two different units of electric charge were used: one for electrostatics and the other for magnetic phenomena involving currents. In the system of units used at that time, these two units of charge had different physical dimensions. Their *ratio* had units of velocity, and measurements showed that the ratio had a numerical value that was precisely equal to the speed of light, 3.00×10^8 m/s. At the time, physicists regarded this as an extraordinary coincidence and had no idea how to explain it.

In searching to understand this result, Maxwell (Fig. 32.1) proved in 1865 that an electromagnetic disturbance should propagate in free space with a speed equal to that of light and hence that light waves were likely to be electromagnetic in nature. At the same time, he discovered that the basic principles of electromagnetism can be expressed in terms of the four equations that we now call **Maxwell's equations,** which we discussed in Section 29.7. These four equations are (1) Gauss's law for electric fields; (2) Gauss's law for magnetic fields, showing the absence of magnetic monopoles; (3) Ampere's law, including displacement current; and (4) Faraday's law:

$$\oint \vec{E} \cdot d\vec{A} = \frac{Q_{encl}}{\epsilon_0} \qquad \text{(Gauss's law)} \tag{29.18}$$

$$\oint \vec{B} \cdot d\vec{A} = 0 \qquad \text{(Gauss's law for magnetism)} \tag{29.19}$$

$$\oint \vec{B} \cdot d\vec{l} = \mu_0 \left(i_C + \epsilon_0 \frac{d\Phi_E}{dt} \right)_{encl} \qquad \text{(Ampere's law)} \tag{29.20}$$

$$\oint \vec{E} \cdot d\vec{l} = -\frac{d\Phi_B}{dt} \qquad \text{(Faraday's law)} \tag{29.21}$$

32.1 James Clerk Maxwell (1831–1879) was the first person to truly understand the fundamental nature of light. He also made major contributions to thermodynamics, optics, astronomy, and color photography. Albert Einstein described Maxwell's accomplishments as "the most profound and the most fruitful that physics has experienced since the time of Newton."

32.2 (a) Every mobile phone, wireless modem, or radio transmitter emits signals in the form of electromagnetic waves that are made by accelerating charges. (b) Power lines carry a strong alternating current, which means that a substantial amount of charge is accelerating back and forth and generating electromagnetic waves. These waves can produce a buzzing sound from your car radio when you drive near the lines.

These equations apply to electric and magnetic fields *in vacuum.* If a material is present, the permittivity ϵ_0 and permeability μ_0 of free space are replaced by the permittivity ϵ and permeability μ of the material. If the values of ϵ and μ are different at different points in the regions of integration, then ϵ and μ have to be transferred to the left sides of Eqs. (29.18) and (29.20), respectively, and placed inside the integrals. The ϵ in Eq. (29.20) also has to be included in the integral that gives $d\Phi_E/dt$.

According to Maxwell's equations, a point charge at rest produces a static $\vec{E}$ field but no $\vec{B}$ field; a point charge moving with a constant velocity (see Section 28.1) produces both $\vec{E}$ and $\vec{B}$ fields. Maxwell's equations can also be used to show that in order for a point charge to produce electromagnetic waves, the charge must *accelerate.* In fact, it's a general result of Maxwell's equations that *every* accelerated charge radiates electromagnetic energy (Fig. 32.2).

Generating Electromagnetic Radiation

One way in which a point charge can be made to emit electromagnetic waves is by making it oscillate in simple harmonic motion, so that it has an acceleration at almost every instant (the exception is when the charge is passing through its equilibrium position). Figure 32.3 shows some of the electric field lines produced by such an oscillating point charge. Field lines are *not* material objects, but you may nonetheless find it helpful to think of them as behaving somewhat like strings that extend from the point charge off to infinity. Oscillating the charge up and down makes waves that propagate outward from the charge along these "strings." Note that the charge does not emit waves equally in all directions; the waves are strongest at 90° to the axis of motion of the charge, while there are *no* waves along this axis. This is just what the "string" picture would lead you to conclude. There is also a *magnetic* disturbance that spreads outward from the charge; this is not shown in Fig. 32.3. Because the electric and magnetic disturbances spread or radiate away from the source, the name **electromagnetic radiation** is used interchangeably with the phrase "electromagnetic waves."

Electromagnetic waves with macroscopic wavelengths were first produced in the laboratory in 1887 by the German physicist Heinrich Hertz. As a source of waves, he used charges oscillating in *L-C* circuits of the sort discussed in Section 30.5; he detected the resulting electromagnetic waves with other circuits tuned to the same frequency. Hertz also produced electromagnetic *standing waves* and measured the distance between adjacent nodes (one half-wavelength) to determine the wavelength. Knowing the resonant frequency of his circuits, he then found the speed of the waves from the wavelength–frequency relationship $v = \lambda f$. He established that their speed was the same as that of light; this verified Maxwell's theoretical prediction directly. The SI unit of frequency is named in honor of Hertz: One hertz (1 Hz) equals one cycle per second.

32.3 Electric field lines of a point charge oscillating in simple harmonic motion, seen at five instants during an oscillation period T. The charge's trajectory is in the plane of the drawings. At $t = 0$ the point charge is at its maximum upward displacement. The arrow shows one "kink" in the lines of $\vec{E}$ as it propagates outward from the point charge. The magnetic field (not shown) comprises circles that lie in planes perpendicular to these figures and concentric with the axis of oscillation.

(a) $t = 0$

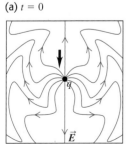

$\vec{E}$

(b) $t = T/4$

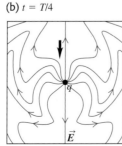

$\vec{E}$

(c) $t = T/2$

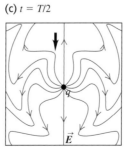

$\vec{E}$

(d) $t = 3T/4$

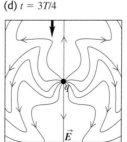

$\vec{E}$

(e) $t = T$

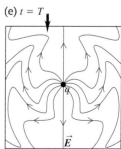

$\vec{E}$

The modern value of the speed of light, which we denote by the symbol c, is 299,792,458 m/s. (Recall from Section 1.3 that this value is the basis of our standard of length: one meter is defined to be the distance that light travels in 1/299,792,458 second.) For our purposes, $c = 3.00 \times 10^8$ m/s is sufficiently accurate.

The possible use of electromagnetic waves for long-distance communication does not seem to have occurred to Hertz. It remained to Marconi and others to make radio communication a familiar household experience. In a radio *transmitter,* electric charges are made to oscillate along the length of the conducting antenna, producing oscillating field disturbances like those shown in Fig. 32.3. Since many charges oscillate together in the antenna, the disturbances are much stronger than those of a single oscillating charge and can be detected at a much greater distance. In a radio *receiver* the antenna is also a conductor; the fields of the wave emanating from a distant transmitter exert forces on free charges within the receiver antenna, producing an oscillating current that is detected and amplified by the receiver circuitry.

For the remainder of this chapter our concern will be with electromagnetic waves themselves, not with the rather complex problem of how they are produced.

The Electromagnetic Spectrum

Electromagnetic waves cover an extremely broad spectrum of wavelength and frequency. This **electromagnetic spectrum** encompasses radio and TV transmission, visible light, infrared and ultraviolet radiation, x rays, and gamma rays. Electromagnetic waves have been detected with frequencies from at least 1 to 10^{24} Hz; the most commonly encountered portion of the spectrum is shown in Fig. 32.4, which gives approximate wavelength and frequency ranges for the various segments. Despite vast differences in their uses and means of production, these are all electromagnetic waves with the same propagation speed (in vacuum) $c = 299,792,458$ m/s. Electromagnetic waves may differ in frequency f and wavelength λ, but the relationship $c = \lambda f$ in vacuum holds for each.

We can detect only a very small segment of this spectrum directly through our sense of sight. We call this range **visible light.** Its wavelengths range from about 400 to 700 nm (400 to 700×10^{-9} m), with corresponding frequencies from about 750 to 430 THz (7.5 to 4.3×10^{14} Hz). Different parts of the visible spectrum evoke in humans the sensations of different colors. Wavelengths for colors in the visible spectrum are given (very approximately) in Table 32.1.

Ordinary white light includes all visible wavelengths. However, by using special sources or filters, we can select a narrow band of wavelengths within a range of a few nm. Such light is approximately *monochromatic* (single-color) light. Absolutely monochromatic light with only a single wavelength is an unattainable

Table 32.1 Wavelengths of Visible Light

400 to 440 nm	Violet
440 to 480 nm	Blue
480 to 560 nm	Green
560 to 590 nm	Yellow
590 to 630 nm	Orange
630 to 700 nm	Red

32.4 The electromagnetic spectrum. The frequencies and wavelengths found in nature extend over such a wide range that we have to use a logarithmic scale to show all important bands. The boundaries between bands are somewhat arbitrary.

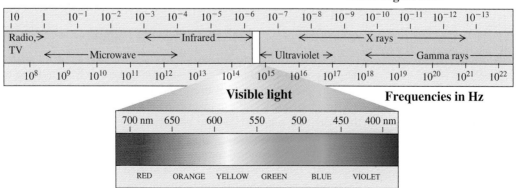

idealization. When we use the expression "monochromatic light with $\lambda = 550$ nm" with reference to a laboratory experiment, we really mean a small band of wavelengths *around* 550 nm. Light from a *laser* is much more nearly monochromatic than is light obtainable in any other way.

Invisible forms of electromagnetic radiation are no less important than visible light. Our system of global communication, for example, depends on radio waves: AM radio uses waves with frequencies from 5.4×10^5 Hz to 1.6×10^6 Hz, while FM radio broadcasts are at frequencies from 8.8×10^7 Hz to 1.08×10^8 Hz. (Television broadcasts use frequencies that bracket the FM band.) Microwaves are also used for communication (for example, by cellular phones and wireless networks) and for weather radar (at frequencies near 3×10^9 Hz). Many cameras have a device that emits a beam of infrared radiation; by analyzing the properties of the infrared radiation reflected from the subject, the camera determines the distance to the subject and automatically adjusts the focus. Ultraviolet radiation has shorter wavelengths than visible light; as we will learn in Chapter 36, this property allows it to be focused into very narrow beams for high-precision applications such as LASIK eye surgery. X rays are able to penetrate through flesh, which makes them invaluable in dentistry and medicine. The shortest-wavelength electromagnetic radiation, gamma rays, is produced in nature by radioactive materials (see Chapter 43). Gamma rays, which are very energetic, are used in medicine to destroy cancer cells.

Test Your Understanding of Section 32.1 (a) Is it possible to have a purely electric wave propagate through empty space—that is, a wave made up of an electric field but no magnetic field? (b) What about a purely magnetic wave, with a magnetic field but no electric field?

32.2 Plane Electromagnetic Waves and the Speed of Light

We are now ready to develop the basic ideas of electromagnetic waves and their relationship to the principles of electromagnetism. Our procedure will be to postulate a simple field configuration that has wavelike behavior. We'll assume an electric field $\vec{E}$ that has only a *y*-component and a magnetic field $\vec{B}$ with only a *z*-component, and we'll assume that both fields move together in the $+x$-direction with a speed c that is initially unknown. (As we go along, it will become clear why we choose $\vec{E}$ and $\vec{B}$ to be perpendicular to the direction of propagation as well as to each other.) Then we will test whether these fields are physically possible by asking whether they are consistent with Maxwell's equations, particularly Ampere's law and Faraday's law. We'll find that the answer is yes, provided that c has a particular value. We'll also show that the *wave equation,* which we encountered during our study of mechanical waves in Chapter 15, can be derived from Maxwell's equations.

A Simple Plane Electromagnetic Wave

Using an *xyz*-coordinate system (Fig. 32.5), we imagine that all space is divided into two regions by a plane perpendicular to the *x*-axis (parallel to the *yz*-plane). At every point to the left of this plane there are a uniform electric field $\vec{E}$ in the $+y$-direction and a uniform magnetic field $\vec{B}$ in the $+z$-direction, as shown. Furthermore, we suppose that the boundary plane, which we call the *wave front,* moves to the right in the $+x$-direction with a constant speed c, the value of which we'll leave undetermined for now. Thus the $\vec{E}$ and $\vec{B}$ fields travel to the right into previously field-free regions with a definite speed. The situation, in short, describes a rudimentary electromagnetic wave. A wave such as this, in which at

32.5 An electromagnetic wave front. The plane representing the wave front moves to the right (in the positive *x*-direction) with speed *c*.

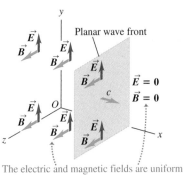

The electric and magnetic fields are uniform behind the advancing wave front and zero in front of it.

any instant the fields are uniform over any plane perpendicular to the direction of propagation, is called a **plane wave.** In the case shown in Fig. 32.5, the fields are zero for planes to the right of the wave front and have the same values on all planes to the left of the wave front; later we will consider more complex plane waves.

We won't concern ourselves with the problem of actually *producing* such a field configuration. Instead, we simply ask whether it is consistent with the laws of electromagnetism—that is, with Maxwell's equations. We'll consider each of these four equations in turn.

Let us first verify that our wave satisfies Maxwell's first and second equations—that is, Gauss's laws for electric and magnetic fields. To do this, we take as our Gaussian surface a rectangular box with sides parallel to the xy, xz, and yz coordinate planes (Fig. 32.6). The box encloses no electric charge. You can show that the total electric flux and magnetic flux through the box are both zero, even if part of the box is in the region where $E = B = 0$. This would *not* be the case if $\vec{E}$ or $\vec{B}$ had an x-component, parallel to the direction of propagation. We leave the proof as a problem (see Problem 32.42). Thus to satisfy Maxwell's first and second equations, the electric and magnetic fields must be perpendicular to the direction of propagation; that is, the wave must be **transverse.**

The next of Maxwell's equations to be considered is Faraday's law:

$$\oint \vec{E} \cdot d\vec{l} = -\frac{d\Phi_B}{dt} \qquad (32.1)$$

To test whether our wave satisfies Faraday's law, we apply this law to a rectangle *efgh* that is parallel to the xy-plane (Fig. 32.7a). As shown in Fig. 32.7b, a cross section in the xy-plane, this rectangle has height a and width Δx. At the time shown, the wave front has progressed partway through the rectangle, and $\vec{E}$ is zero along the side *ef*. In applying Faraday's law we take the vector area $d\vec{A}$ of rectangle *efgh* to be in the $+z$-direction. With this choice the right-hand rule requires that we integrate $\vec{E} \cdot d\vec{l}$ *counterclockwise* around the rectangle. At every point on side *ef*, $\vec{E}$ is zero. At every point on sides *fg* and *he*, $\vec{E}$ is either zero or perpendicular to $d\vec{l}$. Only side *gh* contributes to the integral. On this side, $\vec{E}$ and $d\vec{l}$ are opposite, and we obtain

$$\oint \vec{E} \cdot d\vec{l} = -Ea \qquad (32.2)$$

Hence, the left-hand side of Eq. (32.1) is nonzero.

To satisfy Faraday's law, Eq. (32.1), there must be a component of $\vec{B}$ in the z-direction (perpendicular to $\vec{E}$) so that there can be a nonzero magnetic flux Φ_B through the rectangle *efgh* and a nonzero derivative $d\Phi_B/dt$. Indeed, in our wave, $\vec{B}$ has *only* a z-component. We have assumed that this component is in the *positive* z-direction; let's see whether this assumption is consistent with Faraday's law. During a time interval dt the wave front moves a distance $c\,dt$ to the right in Fig. 32.7b, sweeping out an area $ac\,dt$ of the rectangle *efgh*. During this interval the magnetic flux Φ_B through the rectangle *efgh* increases by $d\Phi_B = B(ac\,dt)$, so the rate of change of magnetic flux is

$$\frac{d\Phi_B}{dt} = Bac \qquad (32.3)$$

Now we substitute Eqs. (32.2) and (32.3) into Faraday's law, Eq. (32.1); we get

$$-Ea = -Bac$$

$$E = cB \qquad \text{(electromagnetic wave in vacuum)} \qquad (32.4)$$

This shows that our wave is consistent with Faraday's law only if the wave speed c and the magnitudes of the perpendicular vectors $\vec{E}$ and $\vec{B}$ are related as in

32.6 Gaussian surface for a plane electromagnetic wave.

The electric field is the same on the top and bottom sides of the Gaussian surface, so the total electric flux through the surface is zero.

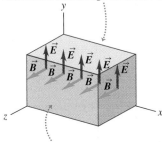

The magnetic field is the same on the left and right sides of the Gaussian surface, so the total magnetic flux through the surface is zero.

32.7 (a) Applying Faraday's law to a plane wave. (b) In a time dt, the magnetic flux through the rectangle in the xy-plane increases by an amount $d\Phi_B$. This increase equals the flux through the shaded rectangle with area $ac\,dt$; that is, $d\Phi_B = Bac\,dt$. Thus $d\Phi_B/dt = Bac$.

(a) In time dt, the wave front moves a distance $c\,dt$ in the $+x$-direction.

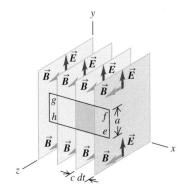

(b) Side view of situation in **(a)**

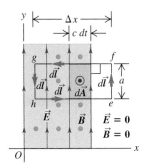

Eq. (32.4). Note that if we had assumed that $\vec{B}$ was in the *negative z*-direction, there would have been an additional minus sign in Eq. (32.4); since E, c, and B are all positive magnitudes, no solution would then have been possible. Furthermore, any component of $\vec{B}$ in the *y*-direction (parallel to $\vec{E}$) would not contribute to the changing magnetic flux Φ_B through the rectangle *efgh* (which is parallel to the *xy*-plane) and so would not be part of the wave.

Finally, we carry out a similar calculation using Ampere's law, the remaining member of Maxwell's equations. There is no conduction current $(i_C = 0)$, so Ampere's law is

$$\oint \vec{B} \cdot d\vec{l} = \mu_0 \epsilon_0 \frac{d\Phi_E}{dt} \tag{32.5}$$

32.8 (a) Applying Ampere's law to a plane wave. (Compare to Fig. 32.7a.) (b) In a time dt, the electric flux through the rectangle in the *xz*-plane increases by an amount $d\Phi_E$. This increase equals the flux through the shaded rectangle with area $ac\,dt$; that is, $d\Phi_E = Eac\,dt$. Thus $d\Phi_E/dt = Eac$.

(a) In time dt, the wave front moves a distance $c\,dt$ in the $+x$-direction.

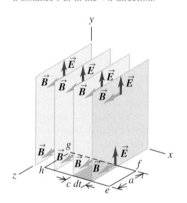

(b) Top view of situation in (a)

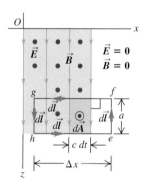

To check whether our wave is consistent with Ampere's law, we move our rectangle so that it lies in the *xz*-plane, as shown in Fig. 32.8, and we again look at the situation at a time when the wave front has traveled partway through the rectangle. We take the vector area $d\vec{A}$ in the $+y$-direction, and so the right-hand rule requires that we integrate $\vec{B} \cdot d\vec{l}$ counterclockwise around the rectangle. The $\vec{B}$ field is zero at every point along side *ef*, and at each point on sides *fg* and *he* it is either zero or perpendicular to $d\vec{l}$. Only side *gh*, where $\vec{B}$ and $d\vec{l}$ are parallel, contributes to the integral, and we find

$$\oint \vec{B} \cdot d\vec{l} = Ba \tag{32.6}$$

Hence, the left-hand side of Ampere's law, Eq. (32.5), is nonzero; the right-hand side must be nonzero as well. Thus $\vec{E}$ must have a *y*-component (perpendicular to $\vec{B}$) so that the electric flux Φ_E through the rectangle and the time derivative $d\Phi_E/dt$ can be nonzero. We come to the same conclusion that we inferred from Faraday's law: In an electromagnetic wave, $\vec{E}$ and $\vec{B}$ must be mutually perpendicular.

In a time interval dt the electric flux Φ_E through the rectangle increases by $d\Phi_E = E(ac\,dt)$. Since we chose $d\vec{A}$ to be in the $+y$-direction, this flux change is positive; the rate of change of electric field is

$$\frac{d\Phi_E}{dt} = Eac \tag{32.7}$$

Substituting Eqs. (32.6) and (32.7) into Ampere's law, Eq. (32.5), we find

$$Ba = \epsilon_0 \mu_0 Eac$$

$$B = \epsilon_0 \mu_0 cE \quad \text{(electromagnetic wave in vacuum)} \tag{32.8}$$

Thus our assumed wave obeys Ampere's law only if B, c, and E are related as in Eq. (32.8).

Our electromagnetic wave must obey *both* Ampere's law and Faraday's law, so Eqs. (32.4) and (32.8) must both be satisfied. This can happen only if $\epsilon_0 \mu_0 c = 1/c$, or

$$c = \frac{1}{\sqrt{\epsilon_0 \mu_0}} \quad \text{(speed of electromagnetic waves in vacuum)} \tag{32.9}$$

Inserting the numerical values of these quantities, we find

$$c = \frac{1}{\sqrt{(8.85 \times 10^{-12} \text{ C}^2/\text{N} \cdot \text{m}^2)(4\pi \times 10^{-7} \text{ N}/\text{A}^2)}}$$
$$= 3.00 \times 10^8 \text{ m/s}$$

Our assumed wave is consistent with all of Maxwell's equations, provided that the wave front moves with the speed given above, which you should recognize as the speed of light! Note that the *exact* value of c is defined to be 299,792,458 m/s; the modern value of ϵ_0 is defined to agree with this when used in Eq. (32.9) (see Section 21.3).

Key Properties of Electromagnetic Waves

We chose a simple wave for our study in order to avoid mathematical complications, but this special case illustrates several important features of *all* electromagnetic waves:

1. The wave is *transverse;* both $\vec{E}$ and $\vec{B}$ are perpendicular to the direction of propagation of the wave. The electric and magnetic fields are also perpendicular to each other. The direction of propagation is the direction of the vector product $\vec{E} \times \vec{B}$ (Fig. 32.9).
2. There is a definite ratio between the magnitudes of $\vec{E}$ and $\vec{B}$: $E = cB$.
3. The wave travels in vacuum with a definite and unchanging speed.
4. Unlike mechanical waves, which need the oscillating particles of a medium such as water or air to transmit a wave, electromagnetic waves require no medium. What's "waving" in an electromagnetic wave are the electric and magnetic fields.

We can generalize this discussion to a more realistic situation. Suppose we have several wave fronts in the form of parallel planes perpendicular to the x-axis, all of which are moving to the right with speed c. Suppose that the $\vec{E}$ and $\vec{B}$ fields are the same at all points within a single region between two planes, but that the fields differ from region to region. The overall wave is a plane wave, but one in which the fields vary in steps along the x-axis. Such a wave could be constructed by superposing several of the simple step waves we have just discussed (shown in Fig. 32.5). This is possible because the $\vec{E}$ and $\vec{B}$ fields obey the superposition principle in waves just as in static situations: When two waves are superposed, the total $\vec{E}$ field at each point is the vector sum of the $\vec{E}$ fields of the individual waves, and similarly for the total $\vec{B}$ field.

We can extend the above development to show that a wave with fields that vary in steps is also consistent with Ampere's and Faraday's laws, provided that the wave fronts all move with the speed c given by Eq. (32.9). In the limit that we make the individual steps infinitesimally small, we have a wave in which the $\vec{E}$ and $\vec{B}$ fields at any instant vary *continuously* along the x-axis. The entire field pattern moves to the right with speed c. In Section 32.3 we will consider waves in which $\vec{E}$ and $\vec{B}$ are *sinusoidal* functions of x and t. Because at each point the magnitudes of $\vec{E}$ and $\vec{B}$ are related by $E = cB$, the periodic variations of the two fields in any periodic traveling wave must be *in phase*.

Electromagnetic waves have the property of **polarization.** In the above discussion the choice of the y-direction for $\vec{E}$ was arbitrary. We could just as well have specified the z-axis for $\vec{E}$; then $\vec{B}$ would have been in the $-y$-direction. A wave in which $\vec{E}$ is always parallel to a certain axis is said to be **linearly polarized** along that axis. More generally, *any* wave traveling in the x-direction can be represented as a superposition of waves linearly polarized in the y- and z-directions. We will study polarization in greater detail, with special emphasis on polarization of light, in Chapter 33.

*Derivation of the Electromagnetic Wave Equation

Here is an alternative derivation of Eq. (32.9) for the speed of electromagnetic waves. It is more mathematical than our other treatment, but it includes a derivation of the wave equation for electromagnetic waves. This part of the section can be omitted without loss of continuity in the chapter.

32.9 A right-hand rule for electromagnetic waves relates the directions of $\vec{E}$, $\vec{B}$, and the direction of propagation.

Right-hand rule for an electromagnetic wave:

① Point the thumb of your right hand in the wave's direction of propagation.

② Imagine rotating the $\vec{E}$ field vector 90° in the sense your fingers curl.

That is the direction of the $\vec{B}$ field.

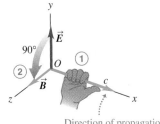

Direction of propagation
= direction of $\vec{E} \times \vec{B}$.

32.10 Faraday's law applied to a rectangle with height a and width Δx parallel to the xy-plane.

(a)

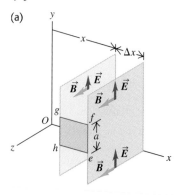

(b) Side view of the situation in (a)

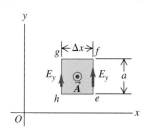

32.11 Ampere's law applied to a rectangle with height a and width Δx parallel to the xz-plane.

(a)

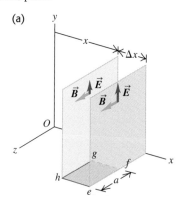

(b) Top view of the situation in (a)

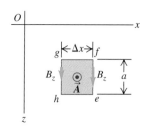

During our discussion of mechanical waves in Section 15.3, we showed that a function $y(x, t)$ that represents the displacement of any point in a mechanical wave traveling along the x-axis must satisfy a differential equation, Eq. (15.12):

$$\frac{\partial^2 y(x, t)}{\partial x^2} = \frac{1}{v^2} \frac{\partial^2 y(x, t)}{\partial t^2} \tag{32.10}$$

This equation is called the **wave equation,** and v is the speed of propagation of the wave.

To derive the corresponding equation for an electromagnetic wave, we again consider a plane wave. That is, we assume that at each instant, E_y and B_z are uniform over any plane perpendicular to the x-axis, the direction of propagation. But now we let E_y and B_z vary continuously as we go along the x-axis; then each is a function of x and t. We consider the values of E_y and B_z on two planes perpendicular to the x-axis, one at x and one at $x + \Delta x$.

Following the same procedure as previously, we apply Faraday's law to a rectangle lying parallel to the xy-plane, as in Fig. 32.10. This figure is similar to Fig. 32.7. Let the left end gh of the rectangle be at position x, and let the right end ef be at position $(x + \Delta x)$. At time t, the values of E_y on these two sides are $E_y(x, t)$ and $E_y(x + \Delta x, t)$, respectively. When we apply Faraday's law to this rectangle, we find that instead of $\oint \vec{E} \cdot d\vec{l} = -Ea$ as before, we have

$$\oint \vec{E} \cdot d\vec{l} = -E_y(x, t)a + E_y(x + \Delta x, t)a$$
$$= a[E_y(x + \Delta x, t) - E_y(x, t)] \tag{32.11}$$

To find the magnetic flux Φ_B through this rectangle, we assume that Δx is small enough that B_z is nearly uniform over the rectangle. In that case, $\Phi_B = B_z(x, t)A = B_z(x, t)a\,\Delta x$, and

$$\frac{d\Phi_B}{dt} = \frac{\partial B_z(x, t)}{\partial t} a\,\Delta x$$

We use partial-derivative notation because B_z is a function of both x and t. When we substitute this expression and Eq. (32.11) into Faraday's law, Eq. (32.1), we get

$$a[E_y(x + \Delta x, t) - E_y(x, t)] = -\frac{\partial B_z}{\partial t} a\,\Delta x$$
$$\frac{E_y(x + \Delta x, t) - E_y(x, t)}{\Delta x} = -\frac{\partial B_z}{\partial t}$$

Finally, imagine shrinking the rectangle down to a sliver so that Δx approaches zero. When we take the limit of this equation as $\Delta x \to 0$, we get

$$\frac{\partial E_y(x, t)}{\partial x} = -\frac{\partial B_z(x, t)}{\partial t} \tag{32.12}$$

This equation shows that if there is a time-varying component B_z of magnetic field, there must also be a component E_y of electric field that varies with x, and conversely. We put this relationship on the shelf for now; we'll return to it soon.

Next we apply Ampere's law to the rectangle shown in Fig. 32.11. The line integral $\oint \vec{B} \cdot d\vec{l}$ becomes

$$\oint \vec{B} \cdot d\vec{l} = -B_z(x + \Delta x, t)a + B_z(x, t)a \tag{32.13}$$

Again assuming that the rectangle is narrow, we approximate the electric flux Φ_E through it as $\Phi_E = E_y(x, t)A = E_y(x, t)a\,\Delta x$. The rate of change of Φ_E, which we need for Ampere's law, is then

$$\frac{d\Phi_E}{dt} = \frac{\partial E_y(x, t)}{\partial t} a\,\Delta x$$

Now we substitute this expression and Eq. (32.13) into Ampere's law, Eq. (32.5):

$$-B_z(x + \Delta x, t)a + B_z(x, t)a = \epsilon_0\mu_0\frac{\partial E_y(x, t)}{\partial t}a\,\Delta x$$

Again we divide both sides by $a\,\Delta x$ and take the limit as $\Delta x \to 0$. We find

$$-\frac{\partial B_z(x, t)}{\partial x} = \epsilon_0\mu_0\frac{\partial E_y(x, t)}{\partial t} \tag{32.14}$$

Now comes the final step. We take the partial derivatives with respect to x of both sides of Eq. (32.12), and we take the partial derivatives with respect to t of both sides of Eq. (32.14). The results are

$$-\frac{\partial^2 E_y(x, t)}{\partial x^2} = \frac{\partial^2 B_z(x, t)}{\partial x \partial t}$$

$$-\frac{\partial^2 B_z(x, t)}{\partial x \partial t} = \epsilon_0\mu_0\frac{\partial^2 E_y(x, t)}{\partial t^2}$$

Combining these two equations to eliminate B_z, we finally find

$$\frac{\partial^2 E_y(x, t)}{\partial x^2} = \epsilon_0\mu_0\frac{\partial^2 E_y(x, t)}{\partial t^2} \quad \begin{array}{l}\text{(electromagnetic wave}\\ \text{equation in vacuum)}\end{array} \tag{32.15}$$

This expression has the same form as the general wave equation, Eq. (32.10). Because the electric field E_y must satisfy this equation, it behaves as a wave with a pattern that travels through space with a definite speed. Furthermore, comparison of Eqs. (32.15) and (32.10) shows that the wave speed v is given by

$$\frac{1}{v^2} = \epsilon_0\mu_0 \quad \text{or} \quad v = \frac{1}{\sqrt{\epsilon_0\mu_0}}$$

This agrees with Eq. (32.9) for the speed c of electromagnetic waves.

We can show that B_z also must satisfy the same wave equation as E_y, Eq. (32.15). To prove this, we take the partial derivative of Eq. (32.12) with respect to t and the partial derivative of Eq. (32.14) with respect to x and combine the results. We leave this derivation as a problem (see Problem 32.37).

Test Your Understanding of Section 32.2 For each of the following electromagnetic waves, state the direction of the magnetic field. (a) The wave is propagating in the positive z-direction, and $\vec{E}$ is in the positive x-direction; (b) the wave is propagating in the positive y-direction, and $\vec{E}$ is in the negative z-direction; (c) the wave is propagating in the negative x-direction, and $\vec{E}$ is in the positive z-direction.

32.3 Sinusoidal Electromagnetic Waves

Sinusoidal electromagnetic waves are directly analogous to sinusoidal transverse mechanical waves on a stretched string, which we studied in Section 15.3. In a sinusoidal electromagnetic wave, $\vec{E}$ and $\vec{B}$ at any point in space are sinusoidal functions of time, and at any instant of time the *spatial* variation of the fields is also sinusoidal.

Some sinusoidal electromagnetic waves are *plane waves;* they share with the waves described in Section 32.2 the property that at any instant the fields are uniform over any plane perpendicular to the direction of propagation. The entire pattern travels in the direction of propagation with speed c. The directions of $\vec{E}$ and $\vec{B}$ are perpendicular to the direction of propagation (and to each other), so the wave is *transverse.* Electromagnetic waves produced by an oscillating point charge, shown in Fig. 32.3, are an example of sinusoidal waves that are *not* plane

10.1 Properties of Mechanical Waves

32.12 Waves passing through a small area at a sufficiently great distance from a source can be treated as plane waves.

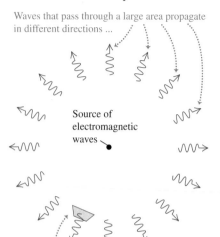

Waves that pass through a large area propagate in different directions ...

Source of electromagnetic waves

... but waves that pass through a small area all propagate in nearly the same direction, so we can treat them as plane waves.

waves. But if we restrict our observations to a relatively small region of space at a sufficiently great distance from the source, even these waves are well approximated by plane waves (Fig. 32.12). In the same way, the curved surface of the (nearly) spherical earth appears flat to us because of our small size relative to the earth's radius. In this section we'll restrict our discussion to plane waves.

The frequency f, the wavelength λ, and the speed of propagation c of any periodic wave are related by the usual wavelength–frequency relationship $c = \lambda f$. If the frequency f is the power-line frequency of 60 Hz, the wavelength is

$$\lambda = \frac{c}{f} = \frac{3 \times 10^8 \text{ m/s}}{60 \text{ Hz}} = 5 \times 10^6 \text{ m} = 5000 \text{ km}$$

which is of the order of the earth's radius! For a wave with this frequency, even a distance of many kilometers includes only a small fraction of a wavelength. But if the frequency is 10^8 Hz (100 MHz), typical of commercial FM radio broadcasts, the wavelength is

$$\lambda = \frac{3 \times 10^8 \text{ m/s}}{10^8 \text{ Hz}} = 3 \text{ m}$$

and a moderate distance can include many complete waves.

Fields of a Sinusoidal Wave

Figure 32.13 shows a linearly polarized sinusoidal electromagnetic wave traveling in the $+x$-direction. The $\vec{E}$ and $\vec{B}$ vectors are shown for only a few points on the positive x-axis. Note that the electric and magnetic fields oscillate in phase: $\vec{E}$ is maximum where $\vec{B}$ is maximum and $\vec{E}$ is zero where $\vec{B}$ is zero. Note also that where $\vec{E}$ is in the $+y$-direction, $\vec{B}$ is in the $+z$-direction; where $\vec{E}$ is in the $-y$-direction, $\vec{B}$ is in the $-z$-direction. At all points the vector product $\vec{E} \times \vec{B}$ is in the direction in which the wave is propagating (the $+x$-direction). We mentioned this in Section 32.2 in the list of characteristics of electromagnetic waves.

32.13 Representation of the electric and magnetic fields as functions of x for a linearly polarized sinusoidal plane electromagnetic wave. One wavelength of the wave is shown at time $t = 0$. The fields are shown only for points along the x-axis.

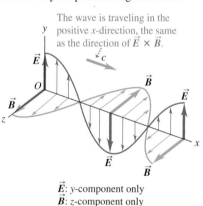

The wave is traveling in the positive x-direction, the same as the direction of $\vec{E} \times \vec{B}$.

$\vec{E}$: y-component only
$\vec{B}$: z-component only

CAUTION **In a plane wave, $\vec{E}$ and $\vec{B}$ are everywhere** Figure 32.13 may give you the erroneous impression that the electric and magnetic fields exist only along the x-axis. In fact, in a sinusoidal plane wave there are electric and magnetic fields at *all* points in space. Imagine a plane perpendicular to the x-axis (that is, parallel to the yz-plane) at a particular point, at a particular time; the fields have the same values at all points in that plane. The values are different on different planes.

We can describe electromagnetic waves by means of *wave functions,* just as we did in Section 15.3 for waves on a string. One form of the wave function for a transverse wave traveling in the $+x$-direction along a stretched string is Eq. (15.7):

$$y(x, t) = A\cos(kx - \omega t)$$

where $y(x, t)$ is the transverse displacement from its equilibrium position at time t of a point with coordinate x on the string. The quantity A is the maximum displacement, or *amplitude,* of the wave; ω is its *angular frequency,* equal to 2π times the frequency f; and k is the *wave number,* equal to $2\pi/\lambda$, where λ is the wavelength.

Let $E_y(x, t)$ and $B_z(x, t)$ represent the instantaneous values of the y-component of $\vec{E}$ and the z-component of $\vec{B}$, respectively, in Fig. 32.13, and let E_{max} and B_{max} represent the maximum values, or *amplitudes,* of these fields. The wave functions for the wave are then

$$E_y(x, t) = E_{max}\cos(kx - \omega t) \qquad B_z(x, t) = B_{max}\cos(kx - \omega t) \quad (32.16)$$

(sinusoidal electromagnetic plane wave, propagating in $+x$-direction)

We can also write the wave functions in vector form:

$$\vec{E}(x, t) = \hat{j}E_{max}\cos(kx - \omega t)$$
$$\vec{B}(x, t) = \hat{k}B_{max}\cos(kx - \omega t)$$

(32.17)

CAUTION **The symbol k has two meanings** Note the two different k's: the unit vector $\hat{k}$ in the z-direction and the wave number k. Don't get these confused!

The sine curves in Fig. 32.13 represent instantaneous values of the electric and magnetic fields as functions of x at time $t = 0$—that is, $\vec{E}(x, t = 0)$ and $\vec{B}(x, t = 0)$. As time goes by, the wave travels to the right with speed c. Equations (32.16) and (32.17) show that at any point the sinusoidal oscillations of $\vec{E}$ and $\vec{B}$ are *in phase*. From Eq. (32.4) the amplitudes must be related by

$$E_{max} = cB_{max} \qquad \text{(electromagnetic wave in vacuum)} \qquad (32.18)$$

These amplitude and phase relationships are also required for $E(x, t)$ and $B(x, t)$ to satisfy Eqs. (32.12) and (32.14), which came from Faraday's law and Ampere's law, respectively. Can you verify this statement? (See Problem 32.36.)

Figure 32.14 shows the electric and magnetic fields of a wave traveling in the *negative* x-direction. At points where $\vec{E}$ is in the positive y-direction, $\vec{B}$ is in the *negative* z-direction; where $\vec{E}$ is in the negative y-direction, $\vec{B}$ is in the *positive* z-direction. The wave functions for this wave are

$$E_y(x, t) = E_{max}\cos(kx + \omega t) \quad B_z(x, t) = -B_{max}\cos(kx + \omega t) \quad (32.19)$$

(sinusoidal electromagnetic plane wave, propagating in $-x$-direction)

As with the wave traveling in the $+x$-direction, at any point the sinusoidal oscillations of the $\vec{E}$ and $\vec{B}$ fields are *in phase,* and the vector product $\vec{E} \times \vec{B}$ points in the direction of propagation.

The sinusoidal waves shown in Figs. 32.13 and 32.14 are both linearly polarized in the y-direction; the $\vec{E}$ field is always parallel to the y-axis. Example 32.1 concerns a wave that is linearly polarized in the z-direction.

32.14 Representation of one wavelength of a linearly polarized sinusoidal plane electromagnetic wave traveling in the negative x-direction at $t = 0$. The fields are shown only for points along the x-axis. (Compare with Fig. 32.13.)

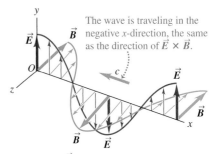

The wave is traveling in the negative x-direction, the same as the direction of $\vec{E} \times \vec{B}$.

$\vec{E}$: y-component only
$\vec{B}$: z-component only

Problem-Solving Strategy 32.1 **Electromagnetic Waves**

IDENTIFY *the relevant concepts:* Many of the same ideas that apply to mechanical waves (discussed in Chapters 15 and 16) also apply to electromagnetic waves. The new feature is that the wave is described by two quantities, electric field $\vec{E}$ and magnetic field $\vec{B}$, instead of by a single quantity, such as the displacement of a string.

SET UP *the problem* using the following steps:
1. Draw a diagram showing the direction of wave propagation and the directions of $\vec{E}$ and $\vec{B}$.
2. Determine the target variables.

EXECUTE *the solution* as follows:
1. For problems involving electromagnetic waves, the best approach is to concentrate on basic relationships, such as the relationship of $\vec{E}$ to $\vec{B}$ (both magnitude and direction), how the wave speed is determined, the transverse nature of the waves, and so on. Keep these relationships in mind when working through the mathematical details.
2. For sinusoidal electromagnetic waves, you need to use the language developed for sinusoidal mechanical waves in Chap-

ters 15 and 16. Don't hesitate to go back and review that material, including the problem-solving strategies suggested in those chapters.
3. Keep in mind the basic relationships for periodic waves: $v = \lambda f$ and $\omega = vk$. For electromagnetic waves in vacuum, $v = c$. Be careful to distinguish between ordinary frequency f, usually expressed in hertz, and angular frequency $\omega = 2\pi f$, expressed in rad/s. Also remember that the wave number is $k = 2\pi/\lambda$.

EVALUATE *your answer:* Check that your result is reasonable. For electromagnetic waves in vacuum, the magnitude of the magnetic field in teslas is much smaller (by a factor of 3.00×10^8) than the magnitude of the electric field in volts per meter. If your answer suggests otherwise, you probably made an error using the relationship $E = cB$. (We'll see later in this section that the relationship between E and B is different for electromagnetic waves in a material medium.)

Example 32.1   **Fields of a laser beam**

A carbon dioxide laser emits a sinusoidal electromagnetic wave that travels in vacuum in the negative x-direction. The wavelength is 10.6 μm and the $\vec{E}$ field is parallel to the z-axis, with maximum magnitude of 1.5 MV/m. Write vector equations for $\vec{E}$ and $\vec{B}$ as functions of time and position.

SOLUTION

IDENTIFY: This problem concerns a sinusoidal electromagnetic wave of the sort we have described in this section.

SET UP: Equations (32.19) describe a wave traveling in the negative x-direction with $\vec{E}$ along the y-axis—that is, a wave that is linearly polarized along the y-axis. By contrast, the wave in this example is linearly polarized along the z-axis. At points where $\vec{E}$ is in the positive z-direction, $\vec{B}$ must be in the positive y-direction for the vector product $\vec{E} \times \vec{B}$ to be in the negative x-direction (the direction of propagation). Figure 32.15 shows a wave that satisfies these requirements.

EXECUTE: A possible pair of wave functions that describe the wave shown in Fig. 32.15 are

$$\vec{E}(x, t) = \hat{k} E_{max} \cos(kx + \omega t)$$
$$\vec{B}(x, t) = \hat{\jmath} B_{max} \cos(kx + \omega t)$$

32.15 Our sketch for this problem.

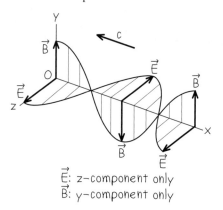

$\vec{E}$: z–component only
$\vec{B}$: y–component only

The plus sign in the arguments of the cosine functions indicates that the wave is propagating in the negative x-direction, as it should. Faraday's law requires that $E_{max} = cB_{max}$ [Eq. (32.18)], so

$$B_{max} = \frac{E_{max}}{c} = \frac{1.5 \times 10^6 \text{ V/m}}{3.0 \times 10^8 \text{ m/s}} = 5.0 \times 10^{-3} \text{ T}$$

To check unit consistency, note that 1 V = 1 Wb/s and 1 Wb/m^2 = 1 T.

We have $\lambda = 10.6 \times 10^{-6}$ m, so the wave number and angular frequency are

$$k = \frac{2\pi}{\lambda} = \frac{2\pi \text{ rad}}{10.6 \times 10^{-6} \text{ m}} = 5.93 \times 10^5 \text{ rad/m}$$

$$\omega = ck = (3.00 \times 10^8 \text{ m/s})(5.93 \times 10^5 \text{ rad/m})$$
$$= 1.78 \times 10^{14} \text{ rad/s}$$

Substituting these values into the above wave functions, we get

$$\vec{E}(x, t) = \hat{k}(1.5 \times 10^6 \text{ V/m}) \cos[(5.93 \times 10^5 \text{ rad/m})x + (1.78 \times 10^{14} \text{ rad/s})t]$$

$$\vec{B}(x, t) = \hat{\jmath}(5.0 \times 10^{-3} \text{ T}) \cos[(5.93 \times 10^5 \text{ rad/m})x + (1.78 \times 10^{14} \text{ rad/s})t]$$

With these equations we can find the fields in the laser beam at any particular position and time by substituting specific values of x and t.

EVALUATE: As we expect, the magnitude B_{max} in teslas is much smaller than the magnitude E_{max} in volts per meter. To check the directions of $\vec{E}$ and $\vec{B}$, note that $\vec{E} \times \vec{B}$ is in the direction of $\hat{k} \times \hat{\jmath} = -\hat{\imath}$. This is as it should be for a wave that propagates in the negative x-direction.

Our expressions for $\vec{E}(x, t)$ and $\vec{B}(x, t)$ are not the only possible solutions. We could always add a phase ϕ to the arguments of the cosine function, so that $kx + \omega t$ would become $kx + \omega t + \phi$. To determine the value of ϕ we would need to know $\vec{E}$ and $\vec{B}$ either as functions of x at a given time t or as functions of t at a given coordinate x. However, the statement of the problem doesn't include this information.

Electromagnetic Waves in Matter

So far, our discussion of electromagnetic waves has been restricted to waves in *vacuum*. But electromagnetic waves can also travel in *matter;* think of light traveling through air, water, or glass. In this subsection we extend our analysis to electromagnetic waves in nonconducting materials—that is, *dielectrics*.

In a dielectric the wave speed is not the same as in vacuum, and we denote it by v instead of c. Faraday's law is unaltered, but in Eq. (32.4), derived from Faraday's law, the speed c is replaced by v. In Ampere's law the displacement current is given not by $\epsilon_0 \, d\Phi_E/dt$, where Φ_E is the flux of $\vec{E}$ through a surface, but by $\epsilon \, d\Phi_E/dt = K\epsilon_0 \, d\Phi_E/dt$, where K is the dielectric constant and ϵ is the permittivity of the dielectric. (We introduced these quantities in Section 24.4.) Also, the constant μ_0 in Ampere's law must be replaced by $\mu = K_m \mu_0$, where K_m is the relative permeability of the dielectric and μ is its permeability (see Section 28.8). Hence Eqs. (32.4) and (32.8) are replaced by

$$E = vB \quad \text{and} \quad B = \epsilon \mu v E \quad (32.20)$$

Following the same procedure as for waves in vacuum, we find that the wave speed v is

$$v = \frac{1}{\sqrt{\epsilon\mu}} = \frac{1}{\sqrt{KK_m}}\frac{1}{\sqrt{\epsilon_0\mu_0}} = \frac{c}{\sqrt{KK_m}}\qquad \begin{array}{l}\text{(speed of electromagnetic}\\ \text{waves in a dielectric)}\end{array}\quad (32.21)$$

For most dielectrics the relative permeability K_m is very nearly equal to unity (except for insulating ferromagnetic materials). When $K_m \cong 1$,

$$v = \frac{1}{\sqrt{K}}\frac{1}{\sqrt{\epsilon_0\mu_0}} = \frac{c}{\sqrt{K}}$$

Because K is always greater than unity, the speed v of electromagnetic waves in a dielectric is always *less* than the speed c in vacuum by a factor of $1/\sqrt{K}$ (Fig. 32.16). The ratio of the speed c in vacuum to the speed v in a material is known in optics as the **index of refraction** n of the material. When $K_m \cong 1$,

$$\frac{c}{v} = n = \sqrt{KK_m} \cong \sqrt{K} \qquad (32.22)$$

Usually, we can't use the values of K in Table 24.1 in this equation because those values are measured using *constant* electric fields. When the fields oscillate rapidly, there is usually not time for the re-orientating of electric dipoles that occurs with steady fields. Values of K with rapidly varying fields are usually much *smaller* than the values in the table. For example, K for water is 80.4 for steady fields but only about 1.8 in the frequency range of visible light. Thus the dielectric "constant" K is actually a function of frequency, called the *dielectric function* in more advanced treatments.

32.16 The dielectric constant K of water is about 1.8 for visible light, so the speed of visible light in water is slower than in vacuum by a factor of $1/\sqrt{K} = 1/\sqrt{1.8} = 0.75$.

Example 32.2 Electromagnetic waves in different materials

(a) While visiting a jewelry store one evening, you hold a diamond up to the light of a street lamp. The heated sodium vapor in the street lamp emits yellow light with a frequency of 5.09×10^{14} Hz. Find the wavelength in vacuum, the speed of wave propagation in diamond, and the wavelength in diamond. At this frequency, diamond has the properties $K = 5.84$ and $K_m = 1.00$. (b) A radio wave with a frequency of 90.0 MHz (in the FM radio broadcast band) passes from vacuum into an insulating ferrite (a ferromagnetic material used in computer cables to suppress radio interference). Find the wavelength in vacuum, the speed of wave propagation in the ferrite, and the wavelength in the ferrite. At this frequency, the ferrite has the properties $K = 10.0$ and $K_m = 1000$.

SOLUTION

IDENTIFY: We use the relationship among wave speed, wavelength, and frequency. We also use the relationship among the speed of electromagnetic waves in a medium and the values of dielectric constant K and relative permeability K_m for the medium.

SET UP: In each case we find the wavelength in vacuum using $c = \lambda f$. The wave speed v is given by Eq. (32.21). Once we know the value of v, we use $v = \lambda f$ to find the wavelength in the material in question.

EXECUTE: (a) The wavelength in vacuum of the sodium light is

$$\lambda_{vacuum} = \frac{c}{f} = \frac{3.00 \times 10^8 \text{ m/s}}{5.09 \times 10^{14} \text{ Hz}} = 5.89 \times 10^{-7} \text{ m} = 589 \text{ nm}$$

The wave speed in diamond is

$$v_{diamond} = \frac{c}{\sqrt{KK_m}} = \frac{3.00 \times 10^8 \text{ m/s}}{\sqrt{(5.84)(1.00)}} = 1.24 \times 10^8 \text{ m/s}$$

This is about two-fifths of the speed in vacuum. The wavelength is proportional to the wave speed and so is reduced by the same factor:

$$\lambda_{diamond} = \frac{v_{diamond}}{f} = \frac{1.24 \times 10^8 \text{ m/s}}{5.09 \times 10^{14} \text{ Hz}}$$
$$= 2.44 \times 10^{-7} \text{ m} = 244 \text{ nm}$$

(b) Following the same steps as in part (a), we find that the wavelength in vacuum of the radio wave is

$$\lambda_{vacuum} = \frac{c}{f} = \frac{3.00 \times 10^8 \text{ m/s}}{90.0 \times 10^6 \text{ Hz}} = 3.33 \text{ m}$$

The wave speed in the ferrite is

$$v_{ferrite} = \frac{c}{\sqrt{KK_m}} = \frac{3.00 \times 10^8 \text{ m/s}}{\sqrt{(10.0)(1000)}} = 3.00 \times 10^6 \text{ m/s}$$

Continued

This is only 1% of the speed of light in a vacuum, so the wavelength is likewise 1% as large as the wavelength in vacuum:

$$\lambda_{ferrite} = \frac{v_{ferrite}}{f} = \frac{3.00 \times 10^9 \text{ m/s}}{90.0 \times 10^6 \text{ Hz}} = 3.33 \times 10^{-2} \text{ m} = 3.33 \text{ cm}$$

EVALUATE: The speed of light in transparent materials like diamond is typically between c and $0.2c$. As our results in part (b) show, the speed of electromagnetic waves in dense materials like ferrite can be *far* slower than in vacuum.

Test Your Understanding of Section 32.3 The first of Eqs. (32.17) gives the electric field for a plane wave as measured at points along the x-axis. For this plane wave, how does the electric field at points *off* the x-axis differ from the expression in Eqs. (32.17)? (i) The amplitude is different; (ii) the phase is different; (iii) both the amplitude and phase are different; (iv) none of these.

32.4 Energy and Momentum in Electromagnetic Waves

It is a familiar fact that energy is associated with electromagnetic waves; think of the energy in the sun's radiation. Practical applications of electromagnetic waves, such as microwave ovens, radio transmitters, and lasers for eye surgery, all make use of the energy that these waves carry. To understand how to utilize this energy, it's helpful to derive detailed relationships for the energy in an electromagnetic wave.

We begin with the expressions derived in Sections 24.3 and 30.3 for the **energy densities** in electric and magnetic fields; we suggest you review those derivations now. Equations (24.11) and (30.10) show that in a region of empty space where $\vec{E}$ and $\vec{B}$ fields are present, the total energy density u is given by

$$u = \frac{1}{2}\epsilon_0 E^2 + \frac{1}{2\mu_0}B^2 \qquad (32.23)$$

where ϵ_0 and μ_0 are, respectively, the permittivity and permeability of free space. For electromagnetic waves in vacuum, the magnitudes E and B are related by

$$B = \frac{E}{c} = \sqrt{\epsilon_0\mu_0}\,E \qquad (32.24)$$

Combining Eqs. (32.23) and (32.24), we can also express the energy density u in a simple electromagnetic wave in vacuum as

$$u = \frac{1}{2}\epsilon_0 E^2 + \frac{1}{2\mu_0}(\sqrt{\epsilon_0\mu_0}\,E)^2 = \epsilon_0 E^2 \qquad (32.25)$$

This shows that in vacuum, the energy density associated with the $\vec{E}$ field in our simple wave is equal to the energy density of the $\vec{B}$ field. In general, the electric-field magnitude E is a function of position and time, as for the sinusoidal wave described by Eqs. (32.16); thus the energy density u of an electromagnetic wave, given by Eq. (32.25), also depends in general on position and time.

Electromagnetic Energy Flow and the Poynting Vector

Electromagnetic waves such as those we have described are *traveling* waves that transport energy from one region to another. For instance, in the wave described in Section 32.2 the $\vec{E}$ and $\vec{B}$ fields advance with time into regions where originally no fields were present and carry the energy density u with them as they advance. We can describe this energy transfer in terms of energy transferred *per unit time per unit cross-sectional area,* or *power per unit area,* for an area perpendicular to the direction of wave travel.

To see how the energy flow is related to the fields, consider a stationary plane, perpendicular to the x-axis, that coincides with the wave front at a certain time. In a time dt after this, the wave front moves a distance $dx = c\,dt$ to the right of the plane. Considering an area A on this stationary plane (Fig. 32.17), we note that the energy in the space to the right of this area must have passed through the area to reach the new location. The volume dV of the relevant region is the base area A times the length $c\,dt$, and the energy dU in this region is the energy density u times this volume:

$$dU = u\,dV = (\epsilon_0 E^2)(Ac\,dt)$$

This energy passes through the area A in time dt. The energy flow per unit time per unit area, which we will call S, is

$$S = \frac{1}{A}\frac{dU}{dt} = \epsilon_0 c E^2 \qquad \text{(in vacuum)} \qquad (32.26)$$

Using Eqs. (32.15) and (32.25), we can derive the alternative forms

$$S = \frac{\epsilon_0}{\sqrt{\epsilon_0\mu_0}}E^2 = \sqrt{\frac{\epsilon_0}{\mu_0}}E^2 = \frac{EB}{\mu_0} \qquad \text{(in vacuum)} \qquad (32.27)$$

The derivation of Eq. (32.27) from Eq. (32.26) is left as a problem (see Exercise 32.29). The units of S are energy per unit time per unit area, or power per unit area. The SI unit of S is $1\ \text{J/s}\cdot\text{m}^2$ or $1\ \text{W/m}^2$.

We can define a *vector* quantity that describes both the magnitude and direction of the energy flow rate:

$$\vec{S} = \frac{1}{\mu_0}\vec{E} \times \vec{B} \qquad \text{(Poynting vector in vacuum)} \qquad (32.28)$$

The vector $\vec{S}$ is called the **Poynting vector**; it was introduced by the British physicist John Poynting (1852–1914). Its direction is in the direction of propagation of the wave (Fig. 32.18). Since $\vec{E}$ and $\vec{B}$ are perpendicular, the magnitude of $\vec{S}$ is $S = EB/\mu_0$; from Eqs. (32.26) and (32.27) this is the energy flow per unit area and per unit time through a cross-sectional area perpendicular to the propagation direction. The total energy flow per unit time (power, P) out of any closed surface is the integral of $\vec{S}$ over the surface:

$$P = \oint \vec{S} \cdot d\vec{A}$$

For the sinusoidal waves studied in Section 32.3, as well as for other more complex waves, the electric and magnetic fields at any point vary with time, so the Poynting vector at any point is also a function of time. Because the frequencies of typical electromagnetic waves are very high, the time variation of the Poynting vector is so rapid that it's most appropriate to look at its *average* value. The magnitude of the average value of $\vec{S}$ at a point is called the **intensity** of the radiation at that point. The SI unit of intensity is the same as for S, $1\ \text{W/m}^2$ (watt per square meter).

Let's work out the intensity of the sinusoidal wave described by Eqs. (32.17). We first substitute $\vec{E}$ and $\vec{B}$ into Eq. (32.28):

$$\vec{S}(x, t) = \frac{1}{\mu_0}\vec{E}(x, t) \times \vec{B}(x, t)$$

$$= \frac{1}{\mu_0}[\hat{\jmath}E_{\max}\cos(kx - \omega t)] \times [\hat{k}B_{\max}\cos(kx - \omega t)]$$

32.17 A wave front at a time dt after it passes through the stationary plane with area A.

At time dt, the volume between the stationary plane and the wave front contains an amount of electromagnetic energy $dU = uAc\,dt$.

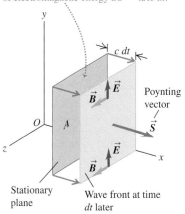

32.18 These rooftop solar panels are tilted to be face-on to the sun—that is, face-on to the Poynting vector of electromagnetic waves from the sun, so that the panels can absorb the maximum amount of wave energy.

The vector product of the unit vectors is $\hat{\jmath} \times \hat{k} = \hat{\imath}$ and $\cos^2(kx - \omega t)$ is never negative, so $\vec{S}(x, t)$ always points in the positive x-direction (the direction of wave propagation). The x-component of the Poynting vector is

$$S_x(x, t) = \frac{E_{max}B_{max}}{\mu_0}\cos^2(kx - \omega t) = \frac{E_{max}B_{max}}{2\mu_0}[1 + \cos 2(kx - \omega t)]$$

The time average value of $\cos 2(kx - \omega t)$ is zero because at any point, it is positive during one half-cycle and negative during the other half. So the average value of the Poynting vector over a full cycle is $\vec{S}_{av} = \hat{\imath}S_{av}$, where

$$S_{av} = \frac{E_{max}B_{max}}{2\mu_0}$$

That is, the magnitude of the average value of $\vec{S}$ for a sinusoidal wave (the intensity I of the wave) is $\frac{1}{2}$ the maximum value. By using the relationships $E_{max} = B_{max}c$ and $\epsilon_0\mu_0 = 1/c^2$, we can express the intensity in several equivalent forms:

$$
\begin{aligned}
I = S_{av} &= \frac{E_{max}B_{max}}{2\mu_0} = \frac{E_{max}^2}{2\mu_0 c} \\
&= \frac{1}{2}\sqrt{\frac{\epsilon_0}{\mu_0}}E_{max}^2 = \frac{1}{2}\epsilon_0 c E_{max}^2
\end{aligned}
\qquad
\begin{array}{l}\text{(intensity of a sinusoidal} \\ \text{wave in vacuum)}\end{array}
\qquad (32.29)
$$

We invite you to verify that these expressions are all equivalent.

For a wave traveling in the $-x$-direction, represented by Eqs. (32.19), the Poynting vector is in the $-x$-direction at every point, but its magnitude is the same as for a wave traveling in the $+x$-direction. Verifying these statements is left to you (see Exercise 32.24).

CAUTION **Poynting vector vs. intensity** At any point x, the magnitude of the Poynting vector varies with time. Hence, the *instantaneous* rate at which electromagnetic energy in a sinusoidal plane wave arrives at a surface is not constant. This may seem to contradict everyday experience; the light from the sun, a light bulb, or the laser in a grocery-store scanner appears steady and unvarying in strength. In fact the Poynting vector from these sources *does* vary in time, but the variation isn't noticeable because the oscillation frequency is so high (around 5×10^{14} Hz for visible light). All that you sense is the *average* rate at which energy reaches your eye, which is why we commonly use intensity (the average value of S) to describe the strength of electromagnetic radiation. ∎

Throughout this discussion we have considered only electromagnetic waves propagating in vacuum. If the waves are traveling in a dielectric medium, however, the expressions for energy density [Eq. (32.23)], the Poynting vector [Eq. (32.28)], and the intensity of a sinusoidal wave [Eq. (32.29)] must be modified. It turns out that the required modifications are quite simple: Just replace ϵ_0 with the permittivity ϵ of the dielectric, replace μ_0 with the permeability μ of the dielectric, and replace c with the speed v of electromagnetic waves in the dielectric. Remarkably, the energy densities in the $\vec{E}$ and $\vec{B}$ fields are equal even in a dielectric.

Example 32.3 **Energy in a nonsinusoidal wave**

For the nonsinusoidal wave described in Section 32.2, suppose that $E = 100$ V/m $= 100$ N/C. Find the value of B, the energy density, and the rate of energy flow per unit area S.

SOLUTION

IDENTIFY: In the wave described in Section 32.2, the electric and magnetic fields are uniform behind the wave front. Hence the target variables B, u, and S must also be uniform behind the wave front.

SET UP: Given the value of the magnitude E, we calculate the magnitude B using Eq. (32.4), the energy density u using Eq. 32.25), and the rate of energy flow per unit area S using Eq. (32.27). (Note that we cannot use Eq. (32.29), which applies to sinusoidal waves only.)

EXECUTE: From Eq. (32.4),

$$B = \frac{E}{c} = \frac{100 \text{ V/m}}{3.00 \times 10^8 \text{ m/s}} = 3.33 \times 10^{-7} \text{ T}$$

From Eq. (32.25),

$$u = \epsilon_0 E^2 = (8.85 \times 10^{-12} \text{ C}^2/\text{N} \cdot \text{m}^2)(100 \text{ N/C})^2$$
$$= 8.85 \times 10^{-8} \text{ N/m}^2 = 8.85 \times 10^{-8} \text{ J/m}^3$$

The magnitude of the Poynting vector is

$$S = \frac{EB}{\mu_0} = \frac{(100 \text{ V/m})(3.33 \times 10^{-7} \text{ T})}{4\pi \times 10^{-7} \text{ T} \cdot \text{m/A}}$$
$$= 26.5 \text{ V} \cdot \text{A/m}^2 = 26.5 \text{ W/m}^2$$

EVALUATE: We can check our result for S by using an alternative formula from Eq. (32.26):

$$S = \epsilon_0 c E^2$$
$$= (8.85 \times 10^{-12} \text{ C}^2/\text{N} \cdot \text{m}^2)(3.00 \times 10^8 \text{ m/s})(100 \text{ N/C})^2$$
$$= 26.5 \text{ W/m}^2$$

Since $\vec{E}$ and $\vec{B}$ have the same values at all points behind the wave front, the energy density u and Poynting vector magnitude S likewise have the same value everywhere behind the wave front. In front of the wave front, $\vec{E} = 0$ and $\vec{B} = 0$ and so $u = 0$ and $S = 0$; where there are no fields, there is no field energy.

Example 32.4 Energy in a sinusoidal wave

A radio station on the surface of the earth radiates a sinusoidal wave with an average total power of 50 kW (Fig. 32.19). Assuming that the transmitter radiates equally in all directions above the ground (which is unlikely in real situations), find the amplitudes E_{max} and B_{max} detected by a satellite at a distance of 100 km from the antenna.

SOLUTION

IDENTIFY: This is a sinusoidal wave, so we use the idea that the intensity is equal to the magnitude of the average value of the Poynting vector. We are not given the value of the intensity, but we *are* given the average total power of the transmitter. We use the idea that the intensity is the same as the average power per unit area.

SET UP: Figure 32.19 shows a hemisphere of radius 100 km centered on the transmitter. We divide the average power of the transmitter by the surface area of this hemisphere to find the intensity I at

32.19 A radio station radiates waves into the hemisphere shown.

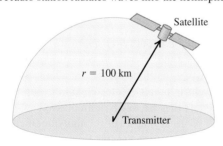

this distance from the transmitter. We then use Eq. (32.29) to find the electric-field magnitude and Eq. (32.4) to find the magnetic-field magnitude.

EXECUTE: The surface area of a hemisphere of radius $r = 100 \text{ km} = 1.00 \times 10^5 \text{ m}$ is

$$A = 2\pi R^2 = 2\pi(1.00 \times 10^5 \text{ m})^2 = 6.28 \times 10^{10} \text{ m}^2$$

All the radiated power passes through this surface, so the average power per unit area (that is, the intensity) is

$$I = \frac{P}{A} = \frac{P}{2\pi R^2} = \frac{5.00 \times 10^4 \text{ W}}{6.28 \times 10^{10} \text{ m}^2} = 7.96 \times 10^{-7} \text{ W/m}^2$$

From Eqs. (32.29), $I = S_{av} = E_{max}^2/2\mu_0 c$, so

$$E_{max} = \sqrt{2\mu_0 c S_{av}}$$
$$= \sqrt{2(4\pi \times 10^{-7} \text{ T} \cdot \text{m/A})(3.00 \times 10^8 \text{ m/s})(7.96 \times 10^{-7} \text{ W/m}^2)}$$
$$= 2.45 \times 10^{-2} \text{ V/m}$$

From Eq. (32.4),

$$B_{max} = \frac{E_{max}}{c} = 8.17 \times 10^{-11} \text{ T}$$

EVALUATE: Note that the magnitude of E_{max} is comparable to fields commonly seen in the laboratory, but B_{max} is extremely small in comparison to $\vec{B}$ fields we saw in previous chapters. For this reason, most detectors of electromagnetic radiation respond to the effect of the electric field, not the magnetic field. Loop radio antennas are an exception.

Electromagnetic Momentum Flow and Radiation Pressure

By using the observation that energy is required to establish electric and magnetic fields, we have shown that electromagnetic waves transport energy. It can also be shown that electromagnetic waves carry *momentum p*, with a corresponding momentum density (momentum *dp* per volume *dV*) of magnitude

$$\frac{dp}{dV} = \frac{EB}{\mu_0 c^2} = \frac{S}{c^2} \tag{32.30}$$

This momentum is a property of the field; it is not associated with the mass of a moving particle in the usual sense.

There is also a corresponding momentum flow rate. The volume *dV* occupied by an electromagnetic wave (speed *c*) that passes through an area *A* in time *dt* is

$dV = Ac\,dt$. When we substitute this into Eq. (32.30) and rearrange, we find that the momentum flow rate per unit area is

$$\frac{1}{A}\frac{dp}{dt} = \frac{S}{c} = \frac{EB}{\mu_0 c} \qquad \text{(flow rate of electromagnetic momentum)} \quad (32.31)$$

This is the momentum transferred per unit surface area per unit time. We obtain the *average* rate of momentum transfer per unit area by replacing S in Eq. (32.31) by $S_{\text{av}} = I$.

This momentum is responsible for the phenomenon of **radiation pressure.** When an electromagnetic wave is completely absorbed by a surface, the wave's momentum is also transferred to the surface. For simplicity we'll consider a surface perpendicular to the propagation direction. Using the ideas developed in Section 8.1, we see that the rate dp/dt at which momentum is transferred to the absorbing surface equals the *force* on the surface. The average force per unit area due to the wave, or *radiation pressure* p_{rad}, is the average value of dp/dt divided by the absorbing area A. (We use the subscript "rad" to distinguish pressure from momentum, for which the symbol p is also used.) From Eq. (32.31) the radiation pressure is

$$p_{\text{rad}} = \frac{S_{\text{av}}}{c} = \frac{I}{c} \qquad \text{(radiation pressure, wave totally absorbed)} \quad (32.32)$$

If the wave is totally reflected, the momentum change is twice as great, and the pressure is

$$p_{\text{rad}} = \frac{2S_{\text{av}}}{c} = \frac{2I}{c} \qquad \text{(radiation pressure, wave totally reflected)} \quad (32.33)$$

For example, the value of I (or S_{av}) for direct sunlight, before it passes through the earth's atmosphere, is approximately $1.4\ \text{kW/m}^2$. From Eq. (32.32) the corresponding average pressure on a completely absorbing surface is

$$p_{\text{rad}} = \frac{I}{c} = \frac{1.4 \times 10^3\ \text{W/m}^2}{3.0 \times 10^8\ \text{m/s}} = 4.7 \times 10^{-6}\ \text{Pa}$$

From Eq. (32.33) the average pressure on a totally *reflecting* surface is twice this: $2I/c$ or $9.4 \times 10^{-6}\ \text{Pa}$. These are very small pressures, of the order of 10^{-10} atm, but they can be measured with sensitive instruments.

The radiation pressure of sunlight is much greater *inside* the sun than at the earth (see Problem 32.43). Inside stars that are much more massive and luminous than the sun, radiation pressure is so great that it substantially augments the gas pressure within the star and so helps to prevent the star from collapsing under its own gravity. In some cases the radiation pressure of stars can have dramatic effects on the material surrounding the stars (Fig. 32.20).

32.20 At the center of this interstellar gas cloud is a group of intensely luminous stars that exert tremendous radiation pressure on their surroundings. Aided by a "wind" of particles emanating from the stars, over the past million years the radiation pressure has carved out a bubble within the cloud 70 light-years across.

Example 32.5   Power and pressure from sunlight

An earth-orbiting satellite has solar-energy–collecting panels with a total area of 4.0 m² (Fig. 32.21). If the sun's radiation is perpendicular to the panels and is completely absorbed, find the average solar power absorbed and the average force associated with radiation pressure.

SOLUTION

IDENTIFY: This problem uses the relationships among intensity, power, radiation pressure, and force.

SET UP: In the above discussion we calculated the intensity I (power per unit area) of sunlight as well as the radiation pressure p_{rad} (force per unit area) of sunlight on an absorbing surface. (We calculated these values for points above the atmosphere, which is where the satellite orbits.) Multiplying each value by the area of the solar panels gives the average power absorbed and the net radiation force on the panels.

EXECUTE: The intensity I (power per unit area) is $1.4 \times 10^3 \text{ W/m}^2$. Although the light from the sun is not a simple sinusoidal wave, we can still use the relationship that the average power P is the intensity I times the area A:

$$P = IA = (1.4 \times 10^3 \text{ W/m}^2)(4.0 \text{ m}^2)$$
$$= 5.6 \times 10^3 \text{ W} = 5.6 \text{ kW}$$

The radiation pressure of sunlight on an absorbing surface is $p_{rad} = 4.7 \times 10^{-6} \text{ Pa} = 4.7 \times 10^{-6} \text{ N/m}^2$. The total force F is the pressure p_{rad} times the area A:

$$F = p_{rad}A = (4.7 \times 10^{-6} \text{ N/m}^2)(4.0 \text{ m}^2) = 1.9 \times 10^{-5} \text{ N}$$

EVALUATE: The absorbed power is quite substantial. Part of it can be used to power the equipment aboard the satellite; the rest goes into heating the panels, either directly or due to inefficiencies in the photocells contained in the panels.

32.21 Solar panels on a satellite.

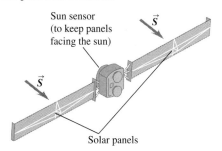

The total radiation force is comparable to the weight (on earth) of a single grain of salt. Over time, however, this small force can have a noticeable effect on the orbit of a satellite like that in Fig. 32.21, and so radiation pressure must be taken into account.

Test Your Understanding of Section 32.4   Figure 32.13 shows one wavelength of a sinusoidal electromagnetic wave at time $t = 0$. For which of the following four values of x is (a) the energy density a maximum; (b) the energy density a minimum; (c) the magnitude of the instantaneous (not average) Poynting vector a maximum; (d) the magnitude of the instantaneous (not average) Poynting vector a minimum? (i) $x = 0$; (ii) $x = \lambda/4$; (iii) $x = \lambda/2$; (iv) $x = 3\lambda/4$.

32.5 Standing Electromagnetic Waves

Electromagnetic waves can be *reflected;* the surface of a conductor (like a polished sheet of metal) or of a dielectric (such as a sheet of glass) can serve as a reflector. The superposition principle holds for electromagnetic waves just as for electric and magnetic fields. The superposition of an incident wave and a reflected wave forms a **standing wave.** The situation is analogous to standing waves on a stretched string, discussed in Section 15.7; you should review that discussion.

Suppose a sheet of a perfect conductor (zero resistivity) is placed in the yz-plane of Fig. 32.22 and a linearly polarized electromagnetic wave, traveling in the negative x-direction, strikes it. As we discussed in Section 23.4, $\vec{E}$ cannot have a component parallel to the surface of a perfect conductor. Therefore in the present situation, $\vec{E}$ must be zero everywhere in the yz-plane. The electric field of the *incident* electromagnetic wave is *not* zero at all times in the yz-plane. But this incident wave induces oscillating currents on the surface of the conductor, and these currents give rise to an additional electric field. The *net* electric field, which is the vector sum of this field and the incident $\vec{E}$, is zero everywhere inside and on the surface of the conductor.

The currents induced on the surface of the conductor also produce a *reflected* wave that travels out from the plane in the $+x$-direction. Suppose the incident wave is described by the wave functions of Eqs. (32.19) (a sinusoidal wave traveling in the $-x$-direction) and the reflected wave by the negative of Eqs. (32.16) (a sinusoidal wave traveling in the $+x$-direction). We take the *negative* of the wave given by Eqs. (32.16) so that the incident and reflected electric fields cancel at $x = 0$ (the plane of the conductor, where the total electric field must be zero). The superposition principle states that the total $\vec{E}$ field at any point is the vector sum of the $\vec{E}$ fields of the incident and reflected waves, and similarly for the $\vec{B}$ field. Therefore the wave functions for the superposition of the two waves are

$$E_y(x, t) = E_{max}[\cos(kx + \omega t) - \cos(kx - \omega t)]$$
$$B_z(x, t) = B_{max}[-\cos(kx + \omega t) - \cos(kx - \omega t)]$$

32.22 Representation of the electric and magnetic fields of a linearly polarized electromagnetic standing wave when $\omega t = 3\pi/4$ rad. In any plane perpendicular to the x-axis, E is maximum (an antinode) where B is zero (a node), and vice versa. As time elapses, the pattern does *not* move along the x-axis; instead, at every point the $\vec{E}$ and $\vec{B}$ vectors simply oscillate.

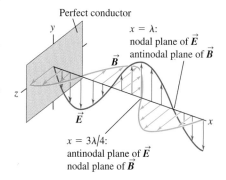

We can expand and simplify these expressions, using the identities

$$\cos(A \pm B) = \cos A \cos B \mp \sin A \sin B$$

The results are

$$E_y(x, t) = -2E_{\text{max}} \sin kx \sin \omega t \tag{32.34}$$

$$B_z(x, t) = -2B_{\text{max}} \cos kx \cos \omega t \tag{32.35}$$

Equation (32.34) is analogous to Eq. (15.28) for a stretched string. We see that at $x = 0$ the electric field $E_y(x = 0, t)$ is *always* zero; this is required by the nature of the ideal conductor, which plays the same role as a fixed point at the end of a string. Furthermore, $E_y(x, t)$ is zero at *all* times at points in those planes perpendicular to the x-axis for which $\sin kx = 0$; that is, $kx = 0$, π, 2π, ... Since $k = 2\pi/\lambda$, the positions of these planes are

$$x = 0, \frac{\lambda}{2}, \lambda, \frac{3\lambda}{2}, \ldots \qquad \text{(nodal planes of } \vec{E}) \tag{32.36}$$

These planes are called the **nodal planes** of the $\vec{E}$ field; they are the equivalent of the nodes, or nodal points, of a standing wave on a string. Midway between any two adjacent nodal planes is a plane on which $\sin kx = \pm 1$; on each such plane, the magnitude of $E(x, t)$ equals the maximum possible value of $2E_{\text{max}}$ twice per oscillation cycle. These are the **antinodal planes** of $\vec{E}$, corresponding to the antinodes of waves on a string.

The total magnetic field is zero at all times at points in planes on which $\cos kx = 0$. This occurs where

$$x = \frac{\lambda}{4}, \frac{3\lambda}{4}, \frac{5\lambda}{4}, \ldots \qquad \text{(nodal planes of } \vec{B}) \tag{32.37}$$

These are the nodal planes of the $\vec{B}$ field; there is an antinodal plane of $\vec{B}$ midway between any two adjacent nodal planes.

Figure 32.22 shows a standing-wave pattern at one instant of time. The magnetic field is *not* zero at the conducting surface $(x = 0)$, and there is no reason it should be. The surface currents that must be present to make $\vec{E}$ exactly zero at the surface cause magnetic fields at the surface. The nodal planes of each field are separated by one half-wavelength. The nodal planes of one field are mid-way between those of the other; hence the nodes of $\vec{E}$ coincide with antinodes of $\vec{B}$, and conversely. Compare this situation to the distinction between pressure nodes and displacement nodes in Section 16.4.

The total electric field is a *sine* function of t, and the total magnetic field is a *cosine* function of t. The sinusoidal variations of the two fields are therefore 90° out of phase at each point. At times when $\sin \omega t = 0$, the electric field is zero *everywhere*, and the magnetic field is maximum. When $\cos \omega t = 0$, the magnetic field is zero everywhere, and the electric field is maximum. This is in contrast to a wave traveling in one direction, as described by Eqs. (32.16) or (32.19) separately, in which the sinusoidal variations of $\vec{E}$ and $\vec{B}$ at any particular point are *in phase*. It is interesting to check that Eqs. (32.34) and (32.35) satisfy the wave equation, Eq. (32.15). They also satisfy Eqs. (32.12) and (32.14) (the equivalents of Faraday's and Ampere's laws); we leave the proofs of these statements to you (see Exercise 32.34).

Standing Waves in a Cavity

Pursuing the stretched-string analogy, we may now insert a second conducting plane, parallel to the first and a distance L from it, along the $+x$-axis. The cavity between the two planes is analogous to a stretched string held at the points $x = 0$ and $x = L$. Both conducting planes must be nodal planes for $\vec{E}$; a standing wave can exist only when the second plane is placed at one of the positions where $E(x, t) = 0$. That is, for a standing wave to exist, L must be an integer multiple of $\lambda/2$. The wavelengths that satisfy this condition are

$$\lambda_n = \frac{2L}{n} \qquad (n = 1, 2, 3, \ldots) \qquad (32.38)$$

The corresponding frequencies are

$$f_n = \frac{c}{\lambda_n} = n\frac{c}{2L} \qquad (n = 1, 2, 3, \ldots) \qquad (32.39)$$

Thus there is a set of *normal modes,* each with a characteristic frequency, wave shape, and node pattern (Fig. 32.23). By measuring the node positions, we can measure the wavelength. If the frequency is known, the wave speed can be determined. This technique was first used by Hertz in the 1880s in his pioneering investigations of electromagnetic waves.

A laser has two mirrors; a standing wave is set up in the cavity between the mirrors. One of the mirrors has a small, partially transmitting aperture that allows waves to escape from this end of the laser.

Conducting surfaces are not the only reflectors of electromagnetic waves. Reflections also occur at an interface between two insulating materials with different dielectric or magnetic properties. The mechanical analog is a junction of two strings with equal tension but different linear mass density. In general, a wave incident on such a boundary surface is partly transmitted into the second material and partly reflected back into the first. For example, light is transmitted through a glass window, but its surfaces also reflect light.

32.23 A typical microwave oven sets up a standing electromagnetic wave with $\lambda = 12.2$ cm, a wavelength that is strongly absorbed by the water in food. Because the wave has nodes spaced $\lambda/2 = 6.1$ cm apart, the food must be rotated while cooking. Otherwise, the portion that lies at a node—where the electric-field amplitude is zero—will remain cold.

Example 32.6   Intensity in a standing wave

Calculate the intensity of the standing wave discussed in this section.

SOLUTION

IDENTIFY: The intensity I of the wave is the average value S_{av} of the magnitude of the Poynting vector.

SET UP: We first find the instantaneous value of the Poynting vector and then average it over a whole number of cycles of the wave to determine I.

EXECUTE: Using the wave functions of Eqs. (32.34) and (32.35) in the expression for the Poynting vector $\vec{S}$, Eq. (32.28), we find

$$\vec{S}(x, t) = \frac{1}{\mu_0}\vec{E}(x, t) \times \vec{B}(x, t)$$

$$= \frac{1}{\mu_0}[-2\hat{\jmath}E_{max}\sin kx\cos\omega t] \times [-2\hat{k}B_{max}\cos kx\sin\omega t]$$

$$= \hat{\imath}\frac{E_{max}B_{max}}{\mu_0}(2\sin kx\cos kx)(2\sin\omega t\cos\omega t)$$

$$= \hat{\imath}S_x(x, t)$$

Using the identity $\sin 2A = 2\sin A\cos A$, we can rewrite $S_x(x, t)$ as

$$S_x(x, t) = \frac{E_{max}B_{max}\sin 2kx\sin 2\omega t}{\mu_0}$$

The average value of a sine function over any whole number of cycles is zero. Thus *the time average of $\vec{S}$ at any point is zero;* $I = S_{av} = 0$.

EVALUATE: This is just what we should expect. We formed our standing wave by superposing two waves with the same frequency and amplitude, traveling in opposite directions. All the energy transferred by one wave is completely cancelled by an equal amount transferred in the opposite direction by the other wave. When we use waves to transmit power, it is important to avoid reflections that give rise to standing waves.

Example 32.7   Standing waves in a cavity

Electromagnetic standing waves are set up in a cavity with two parallel, highly conducting walls separated by 1.50 cm. (a) Calculate the longest wavelength and lowest frequency of electromagnetic standing waves between the walls. (b) For this longest-wavelength standing wave, where in the cavity does $\vec{E}$ have maximum magnitude? Where is $\vec{E}$ zero? Where does $\vec{B}$ have maximum magnitude? Where is $\vec{B}$ zero?

SOLUTION

IDENTIFY: This problem uses the idea that only certain electromagnetic normal modes are possible for electromagnetic waves in a cavity, just as only certain normal modes are possible for standing waves on a string.

SET UP: The longest possible wavelength and lowest possible frequency correspond to the $n = 1$ mode in Eqs. (32.38) and (32.39). We use these equations to determine the values of λ and f. Equations (32.36) and (32.37) then tell us the locations of the nodal planes of $\vec{E}$ and $\vec{B}$; the antinodal planes of each field are midway between adjacent nodal planes.

EXECUTE: (a) From Eq. (32.38), the $n = 1$ wavelength is

$$\lambda_1 = 2L = 2(1.50 \text{ cm}) = 3.00 \text{ cm}$$

The corresponding frequency is given by Eq. (32.38) with $n = 1$:

$$f_1 = \frac{c}{2L} = \frac{3.00 \times 10^8 \text{ m/s}}{2(1.50 \times 10^{-2} \text{ m})} = 1.00 \times 10^{10} \text{ Hz} = 10 \text{ GHz}$$

(b) With $n = 1$ there is a single half-wavelength between the walls. The electric field has nodal planes ($\vec{E} = 0$) at the walls and an antinodal plane (where the maximum magnitude of $\vec{E}$ occurs) midway between them. The magnetic field has *antinodal* planes at the walls and a nodal plane midway between them.

EVALUATE: One application of standing waves of this kind is to produce an oscillating $\vec{E}$ field of definite frequency, which in turn is used to probe the behavior of a small sample of material placed inside the cavity. To subject the sample to the strongest possible field, the sample should be placed near the center of the cavity, at the antinode of $\vec{E}$.

Test Your Understanding of Section 32.5   In the standing wave described in Example 32.7, is there any point in the cavity where the energy density is zero at all times? If so, where? If not, why not?

Maxwell's equations and electromagnetic waves: Maxwell's equations predict the existence of electromagnetic waves that propagate in vacuum at the speed of light c. The electromagnetic spectrum covers frequencies from at least 1 to 10^{24} Hz and a correspondingly broad range of wavelengths. Visible light, with wavelengths from 400 to 700 nm, is only a very small part of this spectrum. In a plane wave, $\vec{E}$ and $\vec{B}$ are uniform over any plane perpendicular to the propagation direction. Faraday's law and Ampere's law both give relationships between the magnitudes of $\vec{E}$ and $\vec{B}$; requiring both of these relationships to be satisfied gives an expression for c in terms of ϵ_0 and μ_0. Electromagnetic waves are transverse; the $\vec{E}$ and $\vec{B}$ fields are perpendicular to the direction of propagation and to each other. The direction of propagation is the direction of $\vec{E} \times \vec{B}$.

$$E = cB \qquad (32.4)$$

$$B = \epsilon_0 \mu_0 cE \qquad (32.8)$$

$$c = \frac{1}{\sqrt{\epsilon_0 \mu_0}} \qquad (32.9)$$

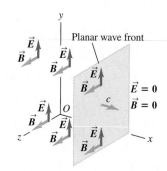

Sinusoidal electromagnetic waves: Equations (32.17) and (32.18) describe a sinusoidal plane electromagnetic wave traveling in vacuum in the $+x$-direction. (See Example 32.1.)

$$\vec{E}(x, t) = \hat{j}E_{max}\cos(kx - \omega t)$$
$$\vec{B}(x, t) = \hat{k}B_{max}\cos(kx - \omega t) \qquad (32.17)$$

$$E_{max} = cB_{max} \qquad (32.18)$$

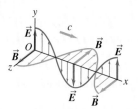

Electromagnetic waves in matter: When an electromagnetic wave travels through a dielectric, the wave speed v is less than the speed of light in vacuum c. (See Example 32.2.)

$$v = \frac{1}{\sqrt{\epsilon\mu}} = \frac{1}{\sqrt{KK_m}}\frac{1}{\sqrt{\epsilon_0\mu_0}}$$
$$= \frac{c}{\sqrt{KK_m}} \qquad (32.21)$$

Energy and momentum in electromagnetic waves: The energy flow rate (power per unit area) in an electromagnetic wave in a vacuum is given by the Poynting vector $\vec{S}$. The magnitude of the time-averaged value of the Poynting vector is called the intensity I of the wave. Electromagnetic waves also carry momentum. When an electromagnetic wave strikes a surface, it exerts a radiation pressure p_{rad}. If the surface is perpendicular to the wave propagation direction and is totally absorbing, $p_{rad} = I/c$; if the surface is a perfect reflector, $p_{rad} = 2I/c$. (See Examples 32.3–32.5.)

$$\vec{S} = \frac{1}{\mu_0}\vec{E} \times \vec{B} \qquad (32.28)$$

$$I = S_{av} = \frac{E_{max}B_{max}}{2\mu_0} = \frac{E_{max}^2}{2\mu_0 c}$$
$$= \frac{1}{2}\sqrt{\frac{\epsilon_0}{\mu_0}}E_{max}^2$$
$$= \frac{1}{2}\epsilon_0 c E_{max}^2 \qquad (32.29)$$

$$\frac{1}{A}\frac{dp}{dt} = \frac{S}{c} = \frac{EB}{\mu_0 c} \qquad (32.31)$$
(flow rate of electromagnetic momentum)

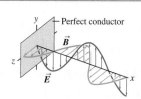

Standing electromagnetic waves: If a perfect reflecting surface is placed at $x = 0$, the incident and reflected waves form a standing wave. Nodal planes for $\vec{E}$ occur at $kx = 0, \pi, 2\pi, \ldots$, and nodal planes for $\vec{B}$ at $kx = \pi/2, 3\pi/2, 5\pi/2, \ldots$. At each point, the sinusoidal variations of $\vec{E}$ and $\vec{B}$ with time are 90° out of phase. (See Examples 32.6 and 32.7.)

Key Terms

electromagnetic wave, *1093*
Maxwell's equations, *1093*
electromagnetic radiation, *1094*
electromagnetic spectrum, *1095*
visible light, *1095*
plane wave, *1097*

transverse wave, *1097*
polarization, *1099*
linearly polarized, *1099*
wave equation, *1100*
index of refraction, *1105*
energy density, *1106*

Poynting vector, *1107*
intensity, *1107*
radiation pressure, *1110*
standing wave, *1111*
nodal plane, *1112*
antinodal plane, *1112*

Answer to Chapter Opening Question ?

Metals are reflective because they are good conductors of electricity. When an electromagnetic wave strikes a conductor, the electric field of the wave sets up currents on the conductor surface that generate a reflected wave. For a perfect conductor, this reflected wave is just as intense as the incident wave. Tarnished metals are less shiny because their surface is oxidized and less conductive; polishing the metal removes the oxide and exposes the conducting metal.

Answers to Test Your Understanding Questions

32.1 Answers: (a) no, (b) no A purely electric wave would have a varying electric field. Such a field necessarily generates a magnetic field through Ampere's law, Eq. (29.20), so a purely electric wave is impossible. In the same way, a purely magnetic wave is impossible: The varying magnetic field in such a wave would automatically give rise to an electric field through Faraday's law, Eq. (29.21).

32.2 Answers: (a) positive y-direction, (b) negative x-direction, (c) positive y-direction You can verify these answers by using the right-hand rule to show that $\vec{E} \times \vec{B}$ in each case is in the direction of propagation, or by using the rule shown in Fig. 32.9.

32.3 Answer: (iv) In an ideal electromagnetic plane wave, at any instant the fields are the same anywhere in a plane perpendicular to the direction of propagation. The plane wave described by Eqs. (32.17) is propagating in the x-direction, so the fields depend on the coordinate x and time t but do *not* depend on the coordinates y and z.

32.4 Answers: (a) (i) and (iii), (b) (ii) and (iv), (c) (i) and (iii), (d) (ii) and (iv) Both the energy density u and the Poynting vector magnitude S are maximum where the $\vec{E}$ and $\vec{B}$ fields have their maximum magnitudes. (The direction of the fields doesn't matter.) From Fig. 32.13, this occurs at $x = 0$ and $x = \lambda/2$. Both u and S have a minimum value of zero; that occurs where $\vec{E}$ and $\vec{B}$ are both zero. From Fig. 32.13, this occurs at $x = \lambda/4$ and $x = 3\lambda/4$.

32.5 Answer: no There are places where $\vec{E} = 0$ at all times (at the walls) and the electric energy density $\frac{1}{2}\epsilon_0 E^2$ is always zero. There are also places where $\vec{B} = 0$ at all times (on the plane midway between the walls) and the magnetic energy density $B^2/2\mu_0$ is always zero. However, there are *no* locations where both $\vec{E}$ and $\vec{B}$ are always zero. Hence the energy density at any point in the standing wave is always nonzero.

PROBLEMS

For instructor-assigned homework, go to **www.masteringphysics.com**

Discussion Questions

Q32.1. By measuring the electric and magnetic fields at a point in space where there is an electromagnetic wave, can you determine the direction from which the wave came? Explain.

Q32.2. According to Ampere's law, is it possible to have both a conduction current and a displacement current at the same time? Is it possible for the effects of the two kinds of current to cancel each other exactly so that *no* magnetic field is produced? Explain.

Q32.3. Give several examples of electromagnetic waves that are encountered in everyday life. How are they all alike? How do they differ?

Q32.4. Sometimes neon signs located near a powerful radio station are seen to glow faintly at night, even though they are not turned on. What is happening?

Q32.5. Is polarization a property of all electromagnetic waves, or is it unique to visible light? Can sound waves be polarized? What fundamental distinction in wave properties is involved? Explain.

Q32.6. Suppose that a positive point charge q is initially at rest on the x-axis, in the path of the electromagnetic plane wave described in Section 32.2. Will the charge move after the wave front reaches it? If not, why not? If the charge does move, describe its motion qualitatively. (Remember that $\vec{E}$ and $\vec{B}$ have the same value at all points behind the wave front.)

Q32.7. The light beam from a searchlight may have an electric-field magnitude of 1000 V/m, corresponding to a potential difference of 1500 V between the head and feet of a 1.5-m-tall person on whom the light shines. Does this cause the person to feel a strong electric shock? Why or why not?

Q32.8. For a certain sinusoidal wave of intensity I, the amplitude of the magnetic field is B. What would be the amplitude (in terms of B) in a similar wave of twice the intensity?

Q32.9. The magnetic-field amplitude of the electromagnetic wave from the laser described in Example 32.1 (Section 32.3) is about 100 times greater than the earth's magnetic field. If you illuminate a compass with the light from this laser, would you expect the compass to deflect? Why or why not?

Q32.10. Most automobiles have vertical antennas for receiving radio broadcasts. Explain what this tells you about the direction of polarization of $\vec{E}$ in the radio waves used in broadcasting.

Q32.11. If a light beam carries momentum, should a person holding a flashlight feel a recoil analogous to the recoil of a rifle when it is fired? Why is this recoil not actually observed?

Q32.12. A light source radiates a sinusoidal electromagnetic wave uniformly in all directions. This wave exerts an average pressure p on a perfectly reflecting surface a distance R away from it. What average pressure (in terms of p) would this wave exert on a perfectly absorbing surface that was twice as far from the source?

Q32.13. Does an electromagnetic *standing* wave have energy? Does it have momentum? Are your answers to these questions the same as for a *traveling* wave? Why or why not?

Q32.14. When driving on the upper level of the Bay Bridge, westbound from Oakland to San Francisco, you can easily pick up a number of radio stations on your car radio. But when driving eastbound on the lower level of the bridge, which has steel girders on either side to support the upper level, the radio reception is much worse. Why is there a difference?

Exercises

Section 32.2 Plane Electromagnetic Waves and the Speed of Light

32.1. (a) How much time does it take light to travel from the moon to the earth, a distance of 384,000 km? (b) Light from the star Sirius takes 8.61 years to reach the earth. What is the distance from earth to Sirius in kilometers?

32.2. TV Ghosting. In a TV picture, ghost images are formed when the signal from the transmitter travels to the receiver both directly and indirectly after reflection from a building or other large metallic mass. In a 25-inch set, the ghost is about 1.0 cm to the right of the principal image if the reflected signal arrives 0.60 μs after the principal signal. In this case, what is the difference in path lengths for the two signals?

32.3. For an electromagnetic wave propagating in air, determine the frequency of a wave with a wavelength of (a) 5.0 km; (b) 5.0 m; (c) 5.0 μm; (d) 5.0 nm.

32.4. Ultraviolet Radiation. There are two categories of ultraviolet light. Ultraviolet A (UVA) has a wavelength ranging from 320 nm to 400 nm. It is not so harmful to the skin and is necessary for the production of vitamin D. UVB, with a wavelength between 280 nm and 320 nm, is much more dangerous because it causes skin cancer. (a) Find the frequency ranges of UVA and UVB. (b) What are the ranges of the wave numbers for UVA and UVB?

Section 32.3 Sinusoidal Electromagnetic Waves

32.5. A sinusoidal electromagnetic wave having a magnetic field of amplitude 1.25 μT and a wavelength of 432 nm is traveling in the +x-direction through empty space. (a) What is the frequency of this wave? (b) What is the amplitude of the associated electric field? (c) Write the equations for the electric and magnetic fields as functions of x and t in the form of Eqs. (32.17).

32.6. An electromagnetic wave of wavelength 435 nm is traveling in vacuum in the −z-direction The electric field has amplitude 2.70×10^{-3} V/m and is parallel to the x-axis. What are (a) the frequency and (b) the magnetic-field amplitude? (c) Write the vector equations for $\vec{E}(z, t)$ and $\vec{B}(z, t)$.

32.7. A sinusoidal electromagnetic wave of frequency 6.10×10^{14} Hz travels in vacuum in the +z-direction. The $\vec{B}$-field is parallel to the y-axis and has amplitude 5.80×10^{-4} T. Write the vector equations for $\vec{E}(z, t)$ and $\vec{B}(z, t)$.

32.8. The electric field of a sinusoidal electromagnetic wave obeys the equation $E = -(375 \text{ V/m}) \sin[(5.97 \times 10^{15} \text{ rad/s})t + (1.99 \times 10^{7} \text{ rad/m})x]$. (a) What are the amplitudes of the electric and magnetic fields of this wave? (b) What are the frequency, wavelength, and period of the wave? Is this light visible to humans? (c) What is the speed of the wave?

32.9. An electromagnetic wave has an electric field given by $\vec{E}(y, t) = -(3.10 \times 10^5 \text{ V/m})\hat{k} \sin[ky - (12.65 \times 10^{12} \text{ rad/s})t]$. (a) In which direction is the wave traveling? (b) What is the wavelength of the wave? (c) Write the vector equation for $\vec{B}(y, t)$.

32.10. An electromagnetic wave has a magnetic field given by $\vec{B}(x, t) = (8.25 \times 10^{-9} \text{ T})\hat{j} \sin[(1.38 \times 10^{4} \text{ rad/m})x + \omega t]$. (a) In which direction is the wave traveling? (b) What is the frequency f of the wave? (c) Write the vector equation for $\vec{E}(x, t)$.

32.11. Radio station WCCO in Minneapolis broadcasts at a frequency of 830 kHz. At a point some distance from the transmitter, the magnetic-field amplitude of the electromagnetic wave from WCCO is 4.82×10^{-11} T. Calculate (a) the wavelength; (b) the wave number; (c) the angular frequency; (d) the electric-field amplitude.

32.12. The electric-field amplitude near a certain radio transmitter is 3.85×10^{-3} V/m What is the amplitude of $\vec{B}$? How does this compare in magnitude with the earth's field?

32.13. An electromagnetic wave with frequency 5.70×10^{14} Hz propagates with a speed of 2.17×10^8 m/s in a certain piece of glass. Find (a) the wavelength of the wave in the glass; (b) the wavelength of a wave of the same frequency propagating in air; (c) the index of refraction n of the glass for an electromagnetic wave with this frequency; (d) the dielectric constant for glass at this frequency, assuming that the relative permeability is unity.

32.14. An electromagnetic wave with frequency 65.0 Hz travels in an insulating magnetic material that has dielectric constant 3.64 and relative permeability 5.18 at this frequency. The electric field has amplitude 7.20×10^{-3} V/m. (a) What is the speed of propagation of the wave? (b) What is the wavelength of the wave? (c) What is the amplitude of the magnetic field? (d) What is the intensity of the wave?

Section 32.4 Energy and Momentum in Electromagnetic Waves

32.15. Fields from a Light Bulb. We can reasonably model a 75-W incandescent light-bulb as a sphere 6.0 cm in diameter. Typically, only about 5% of the energy goes to visible light; the rest goes largely to nonvisible infrared radiation. (a) What is the visible-light intensity (in W/m²) at the surface of the bulb? (b) What are the amplitudes of the electric and magnetic fields at this surface, for a sinusoidal wave with this intensity?

32.16. Consider each of the following electric and magnetic-field orientations. In each case, what is the direction of propagation of the wave? (a) $\vec{E} = E\hat{i}, \vec{B} = -B\hat{j}$; (b) $\vec{E} = E\hat{j}, \vec{B} = B\hat{i}$; (c) $\vec{E} = -E\hat{k}, \vec{B} = -B\hat{i}$; (d) $\vec{E} = E\hat{i}, \vec{B} = -B\hat{k}$.

32.17. A sinusoidal electromagnetic wave is propagating in a vacuum in the +z-direction. If at a particular instant and at a certain point in space the electric field is in the +x-direction and has magnitude 4.00 V/m, what are the magnitude and direction of the magnetic field of the wave at this same point in space and instant in time?

32.18. A sinusoidal electromagnetic wave from a radio station passes perpendicularly through an open window that has area 0.500 m². At the window, the electric field of the wave has rms value 0.0200 V/m. How much energy does this wave carry through the window during a 30.0-s commercial?

32.19. Testing a Space Radio Transmitter. You are a NASA mission specialist on your first flight aboard the space shuttle. Thanks to your extensive training in physics, you have been assigned to evaluate the performance of a new radio transmitter on board the International Space Station (ISS). Perched on the shuttle's movable arm, you aim a sensitive detector at the ISS, which is 2.5 km away. You find that the electric-field amplitude of the radio waves coming from the ISS transmitter is 0.090 V/m and that the frequency of the waves is 244 MHz. Find the following: (a) the intensity of the radio wave at your location; (b) the magnetic-field amplitude of the wave at your location; (c) the total power output of the ISS radio transmitter. (d) What assumptions, if any, did you make in your calculations?

32.20. The intensity of a cylindrical laser beam is 0.800 W/m^2. The cross-sectional area of the beam is $3.0 \times 10^{-4} \text{ m}^2$ and the intensity is uniform across the cross section of the beam. (a) What is the average power output of the laser? (b) What is the rms value of the electric field in the beam?

32.21. A space probe 2.0×10^{10} m from a star measures the total intensity of electromagnetic radiation from the star to be $5.0 \times 10^3 \text{ W/m}^2$. If the star radiates uniformly in all directions, what is its total average power output?

32.22. A sinusoidal electromagnetic wave emitted by a cellular phone has a wavelength of 35.4 cm and an electric-field amplitude of $5.40 \times 10^{-2} \text{ V/m}$ at a distance of 250 m from the antenna. Calculate (a) the frequency of the wave; (b) the magnetic-field amplitude; (c) the intensity of the wave.

32.23. A monochromatic light source with power output 60.0 W radiates light of wavelength 700 nm uniformly in all directions. Calculate E_{max} and B_{max} for the 700-nm light at a distance of 5.00 m from the source.

32.24. For the electromagnetic wave represented by Eq. (32.19), show that the Poynting vector (a) is in the same direction as the propagation of the wave and (b) has average magnitude given by Eqs. (32.29).

32.25. An intense light source radiates uniformly in all directions. At a distance of 5.0 m from the source, the radiation pressure on a perfectly absorbing surface is 9.0×10^{-6} Pa. What is the total average power output of the source?

32.26. Television Broadcasting. Public television station KQED in San Francisco broadcasts a sinusoidal radio signal at a power of 316 kW. Assume that the wave spreads out uniformly into a hemisphere above the ground. At a home 5.00 km away from the antenna, (a) what average pressure does this wave exert on a totally reflecting surface, (b) what are the amplitudes of the electric and magnetic fields of the wave, and (c) what is the average density of the energy this wave carries? (d) For the energy density in part (c), what percentage is due to the electric field and what percentage is due to the magnetic field?

32.27. If the intensity of direct sunlight at a point on the earth's surface is 0.78 kW/m^2, find (a) the average momentum density (momentum per unit volume) in the sunlight and (b) the average momentum flow rate in the sunlight.

32.28. In the 25-ft Space Simulator facility at NASA's Jet Propulsion Laboratory, a bank of overhead arc lamps can produce light of intensity 2500 W/m^2 at the floor of the facility. (This simulates the intensity of sunlight near the planet Venus.) Find the average radiation pressure (in pascals and in atmospheres) on (a) a totally absorbing section of the floor and (b) a totally reflecting section of the floor. (c) Find the average momentum density (momentum per unit volume) in the light at the floor.

32.29. Verify that all the expressions in Eqs. (32.27) are equivalent to Eq. (32.26).

Section 32.5 Standing Electromagnetic Waves

32.30. An electromagnetic standing wave in air of frequency 750 MHz is set up between two conducting planes 80.0 cm apart. At which positions between the planes could a point charge be placed at rest so that it would *remain* at rest? Explain.

32.31. A standing electromagnetic wave in a certain material has frequency 2.20×10^{10} Hz. The nodal planes of $\vec{B}$ are 3.55 mm apart. Find (a) the wavelength of the wave in this material; (b) the

distance between adjacent nodal planes of the $\vec{E}$ field; (c) the speed of propagation of the wave.

32.32. An electromagnetic standing wave in air has frequency 75.0 MHz. (a) What is the distance between nodal planes of the $\vec{E}$ field? (b) What is the distance between a nodal plane of $\vec{E}$ and the closest nodal plane of $\vec{B}$?

32.33. An electromagnetic standing wave in a certain material has frequency 1.20×10^{10} Hz and speed of propagation $2.10 \times 10^8 \text{ m/s}$. (a) What is the distance between a nodal plane of $\vec{B}$ and the closest antinodal plane of $\vec{B}$? (b) What is the distance between an antinodal plane of $\vec{E}$ and the closest antinodal plane of $\vec{B}$? (c) What is the distance between a nodal plane of $\vec{E}$ and the closest nodal plane of $\vec{B}$?

32.34. Show that the electric and magnetic fields for standing waves given by Eqs. (32.34) and (32.35) (a) satisfy the wave equation, Eq. (32.15), and (b) satisfy Eqs. (32.12) and (32.14).

32.35. Microwave Oven. The microwaves in a certain microwave oven have a wavelength of 12.2 cm. (a) How wide must this oven be so that it will contain five antinodal planes of the electric field along its width in the standing wave pattern? (b) What is the frequency of these microwaves? (c) Suppose a manufacturing error occurred and the oven was made 5.0 cm longer than specified in part (a). In this case, what would have to be the frequency of the microwaves for there still to be five antinodal planes of the electric field along the width of the oven?

Problems

32.36. Consider a sinusoidal electromagnetic wave with fields $\vec{E} = E_{max} \hat{j} \sin(kx - \omega t)$ and $\vec{B} = B_{max} \hat{k} \sin(kx - \omega t + \phi)$, with $-\pi \leq \phi \leq \pi$. Show that if $\vec{E}$ and $\vec{B}$ are to satisfy Eqs. (32.12) and (32.14), then $E_{max} = cB_{max}$ and $\phi = 0$. (The result $\phi = 0$ means the $\vec{E}$ and $\vec{B}$ fields oscillate in phase.)

32.37. Show that the *magnetic* field $B_z(x, t)$ in a plane electromagnetic wave propagating in the $+x$-direction must satisfy Eq. (32.15). (*Hint:* Take the partial derivative of Eq. (32.12) with respect to t and the partial derivative of Eq. (32.14) with respect to x. Then combine the results.)

32.38. For a sinusoidal electromagnetic wave in vacuum, such as that described by Eq. (32.16), show that the *average* energy density in the electric field is the same as that in the magnetic field.

32.39. A satellite 575 km above the earth's surface transmits sinusoidal electromagnetic waves of frequency 92.4 MHz uniformly in all directions, with a power of 25.0 kW. (a) What is the intensity of these waves as they reach a receiver at the surface of the earth directly below the satellite? (b) What are the amplitudes of the electric and magnetic fields at the receiver? (c) If the receiver has a totally absorbing panel measuring 15.0 cm by 40.0 cm oriented with its plane perpendicular to the direction the waves travel, what average force do these waves exert on the panel? Is this force large enough to cause significant effects?

32.40. A plane sinusoidal electromagnetic wave in air has a wavelength of 3.84 cm and an $\vec{E}$-field amplitude of 1.35 V/m. (a) What is the frequency? (b) What is the $\vec{B}$-field amplitude? (c) What is the intensity? (d) What average force does this radiation exert on a totally absorbing surface with area 0.240 m^2 perpendicular to the direction of propagation?

32.41. A small helium-neon laser emits red visible light with a power of 3.20 mW in a beam that has a diameter of 2.50 mm. (a) What are the amplitudes of the electric and magnetic fields of the light? (b) What are the average energy densities associated with the electric field and with the magnetic field? (c) What is the total energy contained in a 1.00-m length of the beam?

32.42. Consider a plane electromagnetic wave such as that shown in Fig. 32.5, but in which $\vec{E}$ and $\vec{B}$ also have components in the x-direction (along the direction of wave propagation). Use Gauss's law for electric and magnetic fields to show that the components E_x and B_x must both be equal to zero so that the fields $\vec{E}$ and $\vec{B}$ are both transverse. (*Hint:* Use a Gaussian surface like that shown in Fig. 32.6. Of the two faces parallel to the yz-plane, choose one to be to the left of the wave front and the other to be to the right of the wave front.)

32.43. The sun emits energy in the form of electromagnetic waves at a rate of 3.9×10^{26} W. This energy is produced by nuclear reactions deep in the sun's interior. (a) Find the intensity of electromagnetic radiation and the radiation pressure on an absorbing object at the surface of the sun (radius $r = R = 6.96 \times 10^5$ km) and at $r = R/2$, in the sun's interior. Ignore any scattering of the waves as they move radially outward from the center of the sun. Compare to the values given in Section 32.4 for sunlight just before it enters the earth's atmosphere. (b) The gas pressure at the sun's surface is about 1.0×10^4 Pa; at $r = R/2$, the gas pressure is calculated from solar models to be about 4.7×10^{13} Pa Comparing with your results in part (a), would you expect that radiation pressure is an important factor in determining the structure of the sun? Why or why not?

32.44. It has been proposed to place solar-power-collecting satellites in earth orbit. The power they collect would be beamed down to the earth as microwave radiation. For a microwave beam with a cross-sectional area of 36.0 m^2 and a total power of 2.80 kW at the earth's surface, what is the amplitude of the electric field of the beam at the earth's surface?

32.45. Two square reflectors, each 1.50 cm on a side and of mass 4.00 g, are located at opposite ends of a thin, extremely light, 1.00-m rod that can rotate without friction and in a vacuum about an axle perpendicular to it through its center (Fig. 32.24). These reflectors are small enough to be treated as point masses in moment-of-inertia calculations. Both reflectors are illuminated on one face by a sinusoidal light wave having an electric field of amplitude 1.25 N/C that falls uniformly on both surfaces and always strikes them perpendicular to the plane of their surfaces. One reflector is covered with a perfectly absorbing coating, and the other is covered with a perfectly reflecting coating. What is the angular acceleration of this device?

Figure **32.24** Problem 32.45.

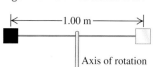

32.46. The plane of a flat surface is perpendicular to the propagation direction of an electromagnetic wave of intensity I. The surface absorbs a fraction w of the incident intensity, where $0 \leq w \leq 1$, and reflects the rest. (a) Show that the radiation pressure on the surface equals $(2 - w)I/c$. (b) Show that this expression gives the correct results for a surface that is (i) totally absorbing and (ii) totally reflective. (c) For an incident intensity of 1.40 kW/m^2, what is the radiation pressure for 90% absorption? For 90% reflection?

32.47. A cylindrical conductor with a circular cross section has a radius a and a resistivity ρ and carries a constant current I. (a) What are the magnitude and direction of the electric-field vector $\vec{E}$ at a point just inside the wire at a distance a from the axis? (b) What are the magnitude and direction of the magnetic-field vector $\vec{B}$ at the same point? (c) What are the magnitude and direction of the Poynting vector $\vec{S}$ at the same point? (The direction of $\vec{S}$ is the direction in which electromagnetic energy flows into or out of the conductor.) (d) Use the result in part (c) to find the rate of flow of energy into the volume occupied by a length l of the conductor.

(*Hint:* Integrate $\vec{S}$ over the surface of this volume.) Compare your result to the rate of generation of thermal energy in the same volume. Discuss why the energy dissipated in a current-carrying conductor, due to its resistance, can be thought of as entering through the cylindrical sides of the conductor.

32.48. A source of sinusoidal electromagnetic waves radiates uniformly in all directions. At 10.0 m from this source, the amplitude of the electric field is measured to be 1.50 N/C. What is the electric-field amplitude at a distance of 20.0 cm from the source?

32.49. A circular loop of wire can be used as a radio antenna. If a 18.0-cm-diameter antenna is located 2.50 km from a 95.0-MHz source with a total power of 55.0 kW, what is the maximum emf induced in the loop? (Assume that the plane of the antenna loop is perpendicular to the direction of the radiation's magnetic field and that the source radiates uniformly in all directions.)

32.50. In a certain experiment, a radio transmitter emits sinusoidal electromagnetic waves of frequency 110.0 MHz in opposite directions inside a narrow cavity with reflectors at both ends, causing a standing wave pattern to occur. (a) How far apart are the nodal planes of the magnetic field? (b) If the standing wave pattern is determined to be in its eighth harmonic, how long is the cavity?

32.51. Flashlight to the Rescue.   You are the sole crew member of the interplanetary spaceship *T:1339 Vorga*, which makes regular cargo runs between the earth and the mining colonies in the asteroid belt. You are working outside the ship one day while at a distance of 2.0 AU from the sun. [1 AU (astronomical unit) is the average distance from the earth to the sun, 149,600,000 km.] Unfortunately, you lose contact with the ship's hull and begin to drift away into space. You use your spacesuit's rockets to try to push yourself back toward the ship, but they run out of fuel and stop working before you can return to the ship. You find yourself in an awkward position, floating 16.0 m from the spaceship with zero velocity relative to it. Fortunately, you are carrying a 200-W flashlight. You turn on the flashlight and use its beam as a "light rocket" to push yourself back toward the ship. (a) If you, your spacesuit, and the flashlight have a combined mass of 150 kg, how long will it take you to get back to the ship? (b) Is there another way you could use the flashlight to accomplish the same job of returning you to the ship?

32.52. The 19th-century inventor Nikola Tesla proposed to transmit electric power via sinusoidal electromagnetic waves. Suppose power is to be transmitted in a beam of cross-sectional area 100 m^2. What electric- and magnetic-field amplitudes are required to transmit an amount of power comparable to that handled by modern transmission lines (that carry voltages and currents of the order of 500 kV and 1000 A)?

32.53. Global Positioning System (GPS).   The GPS network consists of 24 satellites, each of which makes two orbits around the earth per day. Each satellite transmits a 50.0-W (or even less) sinusoidal electromagnetic signal at two frequencies, one of which is 1575.42 MHz. Assume that a satellite transmits half of its power at each frequency and that the waves travel uniformly in a downward hemisphere. (a) What average intensity does a GPS receiver on the ground, directly below the satellite, receive? (*Hint:* First use Newton's laws to find the altitude of the satellite.) (b) What are the amplitudes of the electric and magnetic fields at the GPS receiver in part (a), and how long does it take the signal to reach the receiver? (c) If the receiver is a square panel 1.50 cm on a side that absorbs all of the beam, what average pressure does the signal exert on it? (d) What wavelength must the receiver be tuned to?

32.54. NASA is giving serious consideration to the concept of *solar sailing*. A solar sailcraft uses a large, low-mass sail and the energy and momentum of sunlight for propulsion. (a) Should the sail be absorbing or reflective? Why? (b) The total power output of the sun is 3.9×10^{26} W. How large a sail is necessary to propel a 10,000-kg spacecraft against the gravitational force of the sun? Express your result in square kilometers. (c) Explain why your answer to part (b) is independent of the distance from the sun.

32.55. Interplanetary space contains many small particles referred to as *interplanetary dust*. Radiation pressure from the sun sets a lower limit on the size of such dust particles. To see the origin of this limit, consider a spherical dust particle of radius R and mass density ρ. (a) Write an expression for the gravitational force exerted on this particle by the sun (mass M) when the particle is a distance r from the sun. (b) Let L represent the luminosity of the sun, equal to the rate at which it emits energy in electromagnetic radiation. Find the force exerted on the (totally absorbing) particle due to solar radiation pressure, remembering that the intensity of the sun's radiation also depends on the distance r. The relevant area is the cross-sectional area of the particle, *not* the total surface area of the particle. As part of your answer, explain why this is so. (c) The mass density of a typical interplanetary dust particle is about 3000 kg/m^3. Find the particle radius R such that the gravitational and radiation forces acting on the particle are equal in magnitude. The luminosity of the sun is 3.9×10^{26} W. Does your answer depend on the distance of the particle from the sun? Why or why not? (d) Explain why dust particles with a radius less than that found in part (c) are unlikely to be found in the solar system. [*Hint:* Construct the ratio of the two force expressions found in parts (a) and (b).]

Challenge Problems

32.56. The Classical Hydrogen Atom. The electron in a hydrogen atom can be considered to be in a circular orbit with a radius of 0.0529 nm and a kinetic energy of 13.6 eV. If the electron behaved classically, how much energy would it radiate per second (see Challenge Problem 32.57)? What does this tell you about the use of classical physics in describing the atom?

32.57. Electromagnetic radiation is emitted by accelerating charges. The rate at which energy is emitted from an accelerating charge that has charge q and acceleration a is given by

$$\frac{dE}{dt} = \frac{q^2 a^2}{6\pi\epsilon_0 c^3}$$

where c is the speed of light. (a) Verify that this equation is dimensionally correct. (b) If a proton with a kinetic energy of 6.0 MeV is traveling in a particle accelerator in a circular orbit of radius 0.750 m, what fraction of its energy does it radiate per second? (c) Consider an electron orbiting with the same speed and radius. What fraction of its energy does it radiate per second?

32.58. Electromagnetic waves propagate much differently in *conductors* than they do in dielectrics or in vacuum. If the resistivity of the conductor is sufficiently low (that is, if it is a sufficiently good conductor), the oscillating electric field of the wave gives rise to an oscillating conduction current that is much larger than the displacement current. In this case, the wave equation for an electric field $\vec{E}(x, t) = E_y(x, t)\hat{\jmath}$ propagating in the $+x$-direction within a conductor is

$$\frac{\partial^2 E_y(x, t)}{\partial x^2} = \frac{\mu}{\rho} \frac{\partial E_y(x, t)}{\partial t}$$

where μ is the permeability of the conductor and ρ is its resistivity. (a) A solution to this wave equation is

$$E_y(x, t) = E_{max} e^{-k_C x} \sin(k_C x - \omega t)$$

where $k_C = \sqrt{\omega\mu/2\rho}$. Verify this by substituting $E_y(x, t)$ into the above wave equation. (b) The exponential term shows that the electric field decreases in amplitude as it propagates. Explain why this happens. (*Hint:* The field does work to move charges within the conductor. The current of these moving charges causes $i^2 R$ heating within the conductor, raising its temperature. Where does the energy to do this come from?). (c) Show that the electric-field amplitude decreases by a factor of $1/e$ in a distance $1/k_C = \sqrt{2\rho/\omega\mu}$, and calculate this distance for a radio wave with frequency $f = 1.0$ MHz in copper (resistivity 1.72×10^{-8} $\Omega \cdot$ m; permeability $\mu = \mu_0$). Since this distance is so short, electromagnetic waves of this frequency can hardly propagate at all into copper. Instead, they are reflected at the surface of the metal. This is why radio waves cannot penetrate through copper or other metals, and why radio reception is poor inside a metal structure.

THE NATURE AND PROPAGATION OF LIGHT

33

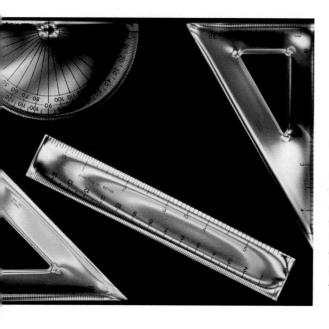

? These drafting tools are made of clear plastic, but a rainbow of colors appears when they are placed between two special filters called polarizers. How does this cause the colors?

LEARNING GOALS

By studying this chapter, you will learn:

- What light rays are, and how they are related to wave fronts.

- The laws that govern the reflection and refraction of light.

- The circumstances under which light is totally reflected at an interface.

- How to make polarized light out of ordinary light.

- How Huygens's principle helps us analyze reflection and refraction.

Blue lakes, ochre deserts, green forests, and multicolored rainbows can be enjoyed by anyone who has eyes with which to see them. But by studying the branch of physics called **optics,** which deals with the behavior of light and other electromagnetic waves, we can reach a deeper appreciation of the visible world. A knowledge of the properties of light allows us to understand the blue color of the sky and the design of optical devices such as telescopes, microscopes, cameras, eyeglasses, and the human eye. The same basic principles of optics also lie at the heart of modern developments such as the laser, optical fibers, holograms, optical computers, and new techniques in medical imaging.

The importance of optics to physics, and to science and engineering in general, is so great that we will devote the next four chapters to its study. In this chapter we begin with a study of the laws of reflection and refraction and the concepts of dispersion, polarization, and scattering of light. Along the way we compare the various possible descriptions of light in terms of particles, rays, or waves, and we introduce Huygens's principle, an important link that connects the ray and wave viewpoints. In Chapter 34 we'll use the ray description of light to understand how mirrors and lenses work, and we'll see how mirrors and lenses are used in optical instruments such as cameras, microscopes, and telescopes. We'll explore the wave characteristics of light further in Chapters 35 and 36.

33.1 The Nature of Light

Until the time of Isaac Newton (1642–1727), most scientists thought that light consisted of streams of particles (called *corpuscles*) emitted by light sources. Galileo and others tried (unsuccessfully) to measure the speed of light. Around

1665, evidence of *wave* properties of light began to be discovered. By the early 19th century, evidence that light is a wave had grown very persuasive.

In 1873, James Clerk Maxwell predicted the existence of electromagnetic waves and calculated their speed of propagation, as we learned in Chapter 32. This development, along with the experimental work of Heinrich Hertz starting in 1887, showed conclusively that light is indeed an electromagnetic wave.

The Two Personalities of Light

The wave picture of light is not the whole story, however. Several effects associated with emission and absorption of light reveal a particle aspect, in that the energy carried by light waves is packaged in discrete bundles called *photons* or *quanta*. These apparently contradictory wave and particle properties have been reconciled since 1930 with the development of quantum electrodynamics, a comprehensive theory that includes *both* wave and particle properties. The *propagation* of light is best described by a wave model, but understanding emission and absorption requires a particle approach.

33.1 An electric heating element emits primarily infrared radiation. But if its temperature is high enough, it also emits a discernible amount of visible light.

The fundamental sources of all electromagnetic radiation are electric charges in accelerated motion. All bodies emit electromagnetic radiation as a result of thermal motion of their molecules; this radiation, called *thermal radiation,* is a mixture of different wavelengths. At sufficiently high temperatures, all matter emits enough visible light to be self-luminous; a very hot body appears "red-hot" (Fig. 33.1) or "white-hot." Thus hot matter in any form is a light source. Familiar examples are a candle flame, hot coals in a campfire, the coils in an electric room heater, and an incandescent lamp filament (which usually operates at a temperature of about 3000°C).

Light is also produced during electrical discharges through ionized gases. The bluish light of mercury-arc lamps, the orange-yellow of sodium-vapor lamps, and the various colors of "neon" signs are familiar. A variation of the mercury-arc lamp is the *fluorescent* lamp (see Fig. 30.7). This light source uses a material called a *phosphor* to convert the ultraviolet radiation from a mercury arc into visible light. This conversion makes fluorescent lamps more efficient than incandescent lamps in transforming electrical energy into light.

A light source that has attained prominence in the last forty years is the *laser.* In most light sources, light is emitted independently by different atoms within the source; in a laser, by contrast, atoms are induced to emit light in a cooperative, coherent fashion. The result is a very narrow beam of radiation that can be enormously intense and that is much more nearly *monochromatic,* or single-frequency, than light from any other source. Lasers are used by physicians for microsurgery, in CD players and computers to scan the information encoded on a compact disc or CD-ROM, in industry to cut through steel and to fuse high-melting-point materials, and in many other applications (Fig. 33.2).

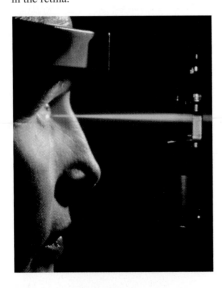

33.2 Ophthalmic surgeons use lasers for repairing detached retinas and for cauterizing blood vessels in retinopathy. Pulses of blue-green light from an argon laser are ideal for this purpose, since they pass harmlessly through the transparent part of the eye but are absorbed by red pigments in the retina.

No matter what its source, electromagnetic radiation travels in vacuum at the same speed. As we saw in Sections 1.3 and 32.1, the speed of light in vacuum is defined to be

$$c = 2.99792458 \times 10^8 \text{ m/s}$$

or 3.00×10^8 m/s to three significant figures. The duration of one second is defined by the cesium clock (see Section 1.3), so one meter is defined to be the distance that light travels in $1/299{,}792{,}458$ s.

Waves, Wave Fronts, and Rays

We often use the concept of a **wave front** to describe wave propagation. We introduced this concept in Section 32.2 to describe the leading edge of a wave. More generally, we define a wave front as *the locus of all adjacent points at which the phase of vibration of a physical quantity associated with the wave is the same.* That is, at any instant, all points on a wave front are at the same part of the cycle of their variation.

When we drop a pebble into a calm pool, the expanding circles formed by the wave crests, as well as the circles formed by the wave troughs between them, are wave fronts. Similarly, when sound waves spread out in still air from a pointlike source, or when electromagnetic radiation spreads out from a pointlike emitter, any spherical surface that is concentric with the source is a wave front, as shown in Fig. 33.3. In diagrams of wave motion we usually draw only parts of a few wave fronts, often choosing consecutive wave fronts that have the same phase and thus are one wavelength apart, such as crests of water waves. Similarly, a diagram for sound waves might show only the "pressure crests," the surfaces over which the pressure is maximum, and a diagram for electromagnetic waves might show only the "crests" on which the electric or magnetic field is maximum.

We will often use diagrams that show the shapes of the wave fronts or their cross sections in some reference plane. For example, when electromagnetic waves are radiated by a small light source, we can represent the wave fronts as spherical surfaces concentric with the source or, as in Fig. 33.4a, by the circular intersections of these surfaces with the plane of the diagram. Far away from the source, where the radii of the spheres have become very large, a section of a spherical surface can be considered as a plane, and we have a *plane* wave like those discussed in Sections 32.2 and 32.3 (Fig, 33.4b).

To describe the directions in which light propagates, it's often convenient to represent a light wave by **rays** rather than by wave fronts. Rays were used to describe light long before its wave nature was firmly established. In a particle theory of light, rays are the paths of the particles. From the wave viewpoint *a ray is an imaginary line along the direction of travel of the wave.* In Fig. 33.4a the rays are the radii of the spherical wave fronts, and in Fig. 33.4b they are straight lines perpendicular to the wave fronts. When waves travel in a homogeneous isotropic material (a material with the same properties in all regions and in all directions), the rays are always straight lines normal to the wave fronts. At a boundary surface between two materials, such as the surface of a glass plate in air, the wave speed and the direction of a ray may change, but the ray segments in the air and in the glass are straight lines.

The next several chapters will give you many opportunities to see the interplay of the ray, wave, and particle descriptions of light. The branch of optics for which the ray description is adequate is called **geometric optics;** the branch dealing specifically with wave behavior is called **physical optics.** This chapter and the following one are concerned mostly with geometric optics. In Chapters 35 and 36 we will study wave phenomena and physical optics.

Test Your Understanding of Section 33.1   Some crystals are *not* isotropic: Light travels through the crystal at a higher speed in some directions than in others. In a crystal in which light travels at the same speed in the *x*- and *z*-directions but at a faster speed in the *y*-direction, what would be the shape of the wave fronts produced by a light source at the origin? (i) spherical, like those shown in Fig. 33.3; (ii) ellipsoidal, flattened along the *y*-axis; (iii) ellipsoidal, stretched out along the *y*-axis. ▮

(MP)

33.2 **Reflection and Refraction**

In this section we'll use the *ray* model of light to explore two of the most important aspects of light propagation: **reflection** and **refraction.** When a light wave strikes a smooth interface separating two transparent materials (such as air and glass or water and glass), the wave is in general partly *reflected* and partly *refracted* (transmitted) into the second material, as shown in Fig. 33.5a. For example, when you look into a restaurant window from the street, you see a reflection of the street scene, but a person inside the restaurant can look out through the window at the same scene as light reaches him by refraction.

33.3 Spherical wave fronts of sound spread out uniformly in all directions from a point source in a motionless medium, such as still air, that has the same properties in all regions and in all directions. Electromagnetic waves in vacuum also spread out as shown here.

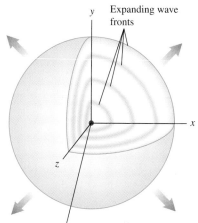

Point sound source producing spherical sound waves (alternating compressions and rarefactions of air)

33.4 Wave fronts (blue) and rays (purple).

(a)

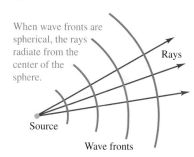

When wave fronts are spherical, the rays radiate from the center of the sphere.

Rays

Source

Wave fronts

(b)

When wave fronts are planar, the rays are perpendicular to the wave fronts and parallel to each other.

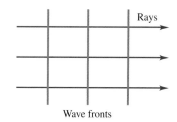

Rays

Wave fronts

Activ Physics
ONLINE

15.1   Reflection and Refraction
15.3   Refraction Applications

33.5 (a) A plane wave is in part reflected and in part refracted at the boundary between two media (in this case, air and glass). The light that reaches the inside of the coffee shop is refracted twice, once entering the glass and once exiting the glass. (b), (c) How light behaves at the interface between the air outside the coffee shop (material a) and the glass (material b). For the case shown here, material b has a larger index of refraction that material a $(n_b > n_a)$ and the angle θ_b is smaller than θ_a.

(a) Plane waves reflected and refracted from a window

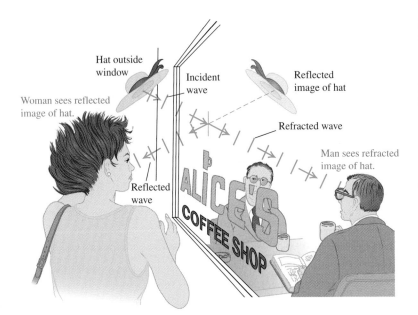

(b) The waves in the outside air and glass represented by rays

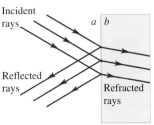

(c) The representation simplified to show just one set of rays

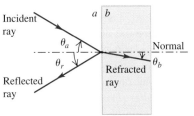

The segments of plane waves shown in Fig. 33.5a can be represented by bundles of rays forming *beams* of light (Fig. 33.5b). For simplicity we often draw only one ray in each beam (Fig. 33.5c). Representing these waves in terms of rays is the basis of geometric optics. We begin our study with the behavior of an individual ray.

We describe the directions of the incident, reflected, and refracted (transmitted) rays at a smooth interface between two optical materials in terms of the angles they make with the *normal* (perpendicular) to the surface at the point of incidence, as shown in Fig. 33.5c. If the interface is rough, both the transmitted light and the reflected light are scattered in various directions, and there is no single angle of transmission or reflection. Reflection at a definite angle from a very smooth surface is called **specular reflection** (from the Latin word for "mirror"); scattered reflection from a rough surface is called **diffuse reflection.** This distinction is shown in Fig. 33.6. Both kinds of reflection can occur with either transparent materials or *opaque* materials that do not transmit light. The vast majority of objects in your environment (including clothing, plants, other people, and this book) are visible to you because they reflect light in a diffuse manner from their surfaces. Our primary concern, however, will be with specular reflection from a very smooth surface such as highly polished glass, plastic, or metal. Unless stated otherwise, when referring to "reflection" we will always mean *specular* reflection.

The **index of refraction** of an optical material (also called the **refractive index**), denoted by n, plays a central role in geometric optics. It is the ratio of the speed of light c in vacuum to the speed v in the material:

$$n = \frac{c}{v} \quad \text{(index of refraction)} \tag{33.1}$$

Light always travels *more slowly* in a material than in vacuum, so the value of n in anything other than vacuum is always greater than unity. For vacuum, $n = 1$.

33.6 Two types of reflection.

(a) Specular reflection

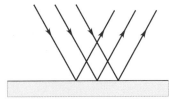

(b) Diffuse reflection

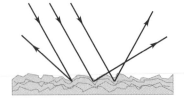

Since n is a ratio of two speeds, it is a pure number without units. (The relationship of the value of n to the electric and magnetic properties of a material is described in Section 32.3.)

CAUTION **Wave speed and index of refraction** Keep in mind that the wave speed v is *inversely* proportional to the index of refraction n. The greater the index of refraction in a material, the *slower* the wave speed in that material. Failure to remember this point can lead to serious confusion! ▮

The Laws of Reflection and Refraction

Experimental studies of the directions of the incident, reflected, and refracted rays at a smooth interface between two optical materials lead to the following conclusions (Fig. 33.7):

1. **The incident, reflected, and refracted rays and the normal to the surface all lie in the same plane.** The plane of the three rays is perpendicular to the plane of the boundary surface between the two materials. We always draw ray diagrams so that the incident, reflected, and refracted rays are in the plane of the diagram.
2. **The angle of reflection θ_r is equal to the angle of incidence θ_a for all wavelengths and for any pair of materials.** That is, in Fig. 33.5c,

$$\theta_r = \theta_a \quad \text{(law of reflection)} \tag{33.2}$$

This relationship, together with the observation that the incident and reflected rays and the normal all lie in the same plane, is called the **law of reflection.**

3. For monochromatic light and for a given pair of materials, a and b, on opposite sides of the interface, **the ratio of the sines of the angles θ_a and θ_b, where both angles are measured from the normal to the surface, is equal to the inverse ratio of the two indexes of refraction:**

$$\frac{\sin \theta_a}{\sin \theta_b} = \frac{n_b}{n_a} \tag{33.3}$$

or

$$n_a \sin \theta_a = n_b \sin \theta_b \quad \text{(law of refraction)} \tag{33.4}$$

This experimental result, together with the observation that the incident and refracted rays and the normal all lie in the same plane, is called the **law of refraction** or **Snell's law,** after the Dutch scientist Willebrord Snell (1591–1626). There is some doubt that Snell actually discovered it. The discovery that $n = c/v$ came much later.

While these results were first observed experimentally, they can be derived theoretically from a wave description of light. We do this in Section 33.7.

Equations (33.3) and (33.4) show that when a ray passes from one material (a) into another material (b) having a larger index of refraction $(n_b > n_a)$ and hence a slower wave speed, the angle θ_b with the normal is *smaller* in the second material than the angle θ_a in the first; hence the ray is bent *toward* the normal (Fig. 33.8a). When the second material has a *smaller* index of refraction than the first material $(n_b < n_a)$ and hence a faster wave speed, the ray is bent *away from* the normal (Fig. 33.8b).

No matter what the materials on either side of the interface, in the case of *normal* incidence the transmitted ray is not bent at all (Fig. 33.8c). In this case $\theta_a = 0$ and $\sin \theta_a = 0$, so from Eq. (33.4) θ_b is also equal to zero, so the transmitted ray is

33.7 The laws of reflection and refraction.

1. The incident, reflected, and refracted rays and the normal to the surface all lie in the same plane.

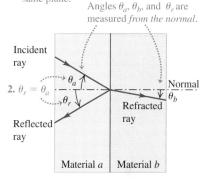

Angles θ_a, θ_b, and θ_r are measured *from the normal*.

2. $\theta_r = \theta_a$

3. When a monochromatic light ray crosses the interface between two given materials a and b, the angles θ_a and θ_b are related to the indexes of refraction of a and b by

$$\frac{\sin \theta_a}{\sin \theta_b} = \frac{n_b}{n_a}.$$

33.8 Refraction and reflection in three cases. (a) Material b has a larger index of refraction than material a. (b) Material b has a smaller index of refraction than material a. (c) The incident light ray is normal to the interface between the materials.

(a) A ray entering a material of *larger* index of refraction bends *toward* the normal.

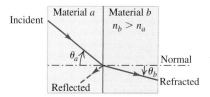

(b) A ray entering a material of *smaller* index of refraction bends *away from* the normal.

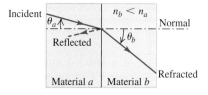

(c) A ray oriented along the normal does not bend, regardless of the materials.

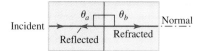

33.9 (a) This ruler is actually straight, but it appears to bend at the surface of the water. (b) Light rays from any submerged object bend away from the normal when they emerge into the air. As seen by an observer above the surface of the water, the object appears to be much closer to the surface than it actually is.

(a) A straight ruler half-immersed in water

(b) Why the ruler appears bent

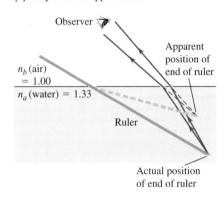

also normal to the interface. Equation (33.2) shows that θ_r, too, is equal to zero, so the reflected ray travels back along the same path as the incident ray.

The law of refraction explains why a partially submerged ruler or drinking straw appears bent; light rays coming from below the surface change in direction at the air–water interface, so the rays appear to be coming from a position above their actual point of origin (Fig. 33.9). A similar effect explains the appearance of the setting sun (Fig. 33.10).

An important special case is refraction that occurs at an interface between vacuum, for which the index of refraction is unity by definition, and a material. When a ray passes from vacuum into a material (b), so that $n_a = 1$ and $n_b > 1$, the ray is always bent *toward* the normal. When a ray passes from a material into vacuum, so that $n_a > 1$ and $n_b = 1$, the ray is always bent *away from* the normal.

The laws of reflection and refraction apply regardless of which side of the interface the incident ray comes from. If a ray of light approaches the interface in

33.10 (a) The index of refraction of air is slightly greater than 1, so light rays from the setting sun bend downward when they enter our atmosphere. (The effect is exaggerated in this figure.) (b) Stronger refraction occurs for light coming from the lower limb of the sun (the part that appears closest to the horizon), which passes through denser air in the lower atmosphere. As a result, the setting sun appears flattened vertically. (See Problem 33.55.)

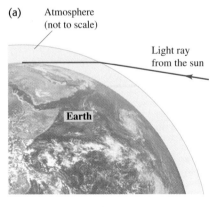

Fig. 33.8a or 33.8b from the right rather than from the left, there are again reflected and refracted rays; these two rays, the incident ray, and the normal to the surface again lie in the same plane. Furthermore, the path of a refracted ray is *reversible;* it follows the same path when going from *b* to *a* as when going from *a* to *b*. [You can verify this using Eq. (33.4).] Since reflected and incident rays make the same angle with the normal, the path of a reflected ray is also reversible. That's why when you see someone's eyes in a mirror, they can also see you.

The *intensities* of the reflected and refracted rays depend on the angle of incidence, the two indexes of refraction, and the polarization (that is, the direction of the electric-field vector) of the incident ray. The fraction reflected is smallest at normal incidence ($\theta_a = 0°$), where it is about 4% for an air–glass interface. This fraction increases with increasing angle of incidence to 100% at grazing incidence, when $\theta_a = 90°$.

It's possible to use Maxwell's equations to predict the amplitude, intensity, phase, and polarization states of the reflected and refracted waves. Such an analysis is beyond our scope, however.

The index of refraction depends not only on the substance but also on the wavelength of the light. The dependence on wavelength is called *dispersion;* we will consider it in Section 33.4. Indexes of refraction for several solids and liquids are given in Table 33.1 for a particular wavelength of yellow light.

The index of refraction of air at standard temperature and pressure is about 1.0003, and we will usually take it to be exactly unity. The index of refraction of a gas increases as its density increases. Most glasses used in optical instruments have indexes of refraction between about 1.5 and 2.0. A few substances have larger indexes; one example is diamond, with 2.417.

Table 33.1 Index of Refraction for Yellow Sodium Light $\lambda_0 = 589$ nm

Substance	Index of Refraction, n
Solids	
Ice (H_2O)	1.309
Fluorite (CaF_2)	1.434
Polystyrene	1.49
Rock salt (NaCl)	1.544
Quartz (SiO_2)	1.544
Zircon ($ZrO_2 \cdot SiO_2$)	1.923
Diamond (C)	2.417
Fabulite ($SrTiO_3$)	2.409
Rutile (TiO_2)	2.62
Glasses (typical values)	
Crown	1.52
Light flint	1.58
Medium flint	1.62
Dense flint	1.66
Lanthanum flint	1.80
Liquids at 20°C	
Methanol (CH_3OH)	1.329
Water (H_2O)	1.333
Ethanol (C_2H_5OH)	1.36
Carbon tetrachloride (CCl_4)	1.460
Turpentine	1.472
Glycerine	1.473
Benzene	1.501
Carbon disulfide (CS_2)	1.628

Index of Refraction and the Wave Aspects of Light

We have discussed how the direction of a light ray changes when it passes from one material to another material with a different index of refraction. It's also important to see what happens to the *wave* characteristics of the light when this happens.

First, the frequency f of the wave does not change when passing from one material to another. That is, the number of wave cycles arriving per unit time must equal the number leaving per unit time; this is a statement that the boundary surface cannot create or destroy waves.

Second, the wavelength λ of the wave *is* different in general in different materials. This is because in any material, $v = \lambda f$; since f is the same in any material as in vacuum and v is always less than the wave speed c in vacuum, λ is also correspondingly reduced. Thus the wavelength λ of light in a material is *less than* the wavelength λ_0 of the same light in vacuum. From the above discussion, $f = c/\lambda_0 = v/\lambda$. Combining this with Eq. (33.1), $n = c/v$, we find

$$\lambda = \frac{\lambda_0}{n} \qquad \text{(wavelength of light in a material)} \qquad (33.5)$$

When a wave passes from one material into a second material with larger index of refraction, so that $n_b > n_a$, the wave speed decreases. The wavelength $\lambda_b = \lambda_0/n_b$ in the second material is then shorter than the wavelength $\lambda_a = \lambda_0/n_a$ in the first material. If instead the second material has a smaller index of refraction than the first material, so that $n_b < n_a$, then the wave speed increases. Then the wavelength λ_b in the second material is longer than the wavelength λ_a in the first material. This makes intuitive sense; the waves get "squeezed" (the wavelength gets shorter) if the wave speed decreases and get "stretched" (the wavelength gets longer) if the wave speed increases.

Problem-Solving Strategy 33.1   Reflection and Refraction

IDENTIFY *the relevant concepts:* You need to use the ideas of this section, called *geometric optics,* whenever light encounters a boundary between two different materials. In general, part of the light is reflected back into the first material and part is refracted into the second material. These ideas apply to electromagnetic radiation of all frequencies and wavelengths, not just visible light.

SET UP *the problem* using the following steps:
1. In geometric optics problems involving rays and angles, *always* start by drawing a large, neat diagram. Label all known angles and indexes of refraction.
2. Determine the target variables.

EXECUTE *the solution* as follows:
1. Apply the laws of reflection, Eq. (33.2), and refraction, Eq. (33.4). Remember to always measure the angles of incidence, reflection, and refraction from the *normal* to the surface where the reflection and refraction occur, *never* from the surface itself.

2. You will often have to use some simple geometry or trigonometry in working out angular relationships. The sum of the interior angles in a triangle is 180°, an angle and its complement differ by 180°, and so on. Ask yourself, "What information am I given?", "What do I need to know in order to find this angle?", or "What other angles or other quantities can I compute using the information given in the problem?"
3. Remember that the frequency of the light does not change when it moves from one material to another, but the wavelength changes in accordance with Eq. (33.5).

EVALUATE *your answer:* In problems that involve refraction, check that the direction of refraction makes sense. If the second material has a higher index of refraction than the first material, the refracted ray bends toward the normal and the refracted angle is smaller than the incident angle. If the first material has the higher index of refraction, the refracted ray bends away from the normal and the refracted angle is larger than the incident angle. Do your results agree with these rules?

Example 33.1   Reflection and refraction

In Fig. 33.11, material *a* is water and material *b* is a glass with index of refraction 1.52. If the incident ray makes an angle of 60° with the normal, find the directions of the reflected and refracted rays.

SOLUTION

IDENTIFY: This is a problem in geometric optics. We are given the incident angle and the index of refraction of each material, and we need to find the reflected and refracted angles.

33.11 Reflection and refraction of light passing from water to glass.

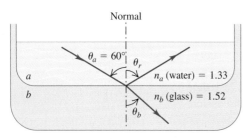

SET UP: Figure 33.11 shows the rays and angles for this situation. The target variables are the reflected angle θ_r and the refracted angle θ_b. Since n_b is greater than n_a, the refracted angle must be smaller than the incident angle θ_a; this is shown in the figure.

EXECUTE: According to Eq. (33.2), the angle the reflected ray makes with the normal is the same as that of the incident ray, so $\theta_r = \theta_a = 60.0°$.

To find the direction of the refracted ray, we use Snell's law, Eq.(33.4), with $n_a = 1.33$, $n_b = 1.52$, and $\theta_a = 60.0°$. We find

$$n_a \sin\theta_a = n_b \sin\theta_b$$

$$\sin\theta_b = \frac{n_a}{n_b}\sin\theta_a = \frac{1.33}{1.52}\sin 60.0° = 0.758$$

$$\theta_b = 49.3°$$

EVALUATE: The second material has a larger refractive index than the first, just like the situation shown in Fig. 33.8a. Hence, the refracted ray is bent toward the normal as the wave slows down upon entering the second material, and $\theta_b < \theta_a$.

Example 33.2   Index of refraction in the eye

The wavelength of the red light from a helium-neon laser is 633 nm in air but 474 nm in the aqueous humor inside your eyeball. Calculate the index of refraction of the aqueous humor and the speed and frequency of the light in this substance.

SOLUTION

IDENTIFY: The key ideas here are the relationship between index of refraction n and wave speed v and the relationship between index of refraction and wavelength λ.

SET UP: We use the definition of index of refraction given by Eq. (33.1), $n = c/v$, as well as Eq. (33.5), $\lambda = \lambda_0/n$. It will also be

helpful to use the relationship $v = \lambda f$ among wave speed, wavelength, and frequency.

EXECUTE: The index of refraction of air is very close to unity, so we assume that the wavelengths in air and vacuum are the same. Then the wavelength λ in the material is given by Eq. (33.5) with $\lambda_0 = 633$ nm:

$$\lambda = \frac{\lambda_0}{n} \qquad n = \frac{\lambda_0}{\lambda} = \frac{633 \text{ nm}}{474 \text{ nm}} = 1.34$$

This is about the same index of refraction as for water. Then $n = c/v$ gives

$$v = \frac{c}{n} = \frac{3.00 \times 10^8 \text{ m/s}}{1.34} = 2.25 \times 10^8 \text{ m/s}$$

Finally, from $v = \lambda f$,

$$f = \frac{v}{\lambda} = \frac{2.25 \times 10^8 \text{ m/s}}{474 \times 10^{-9} \text{ m}} = 4.74 \times 10^{14} \text{ Hz}$$

EVALUATE: Note that while the speed and wavelength have different values in air and in the aqueous humor, the *frequency* in air, f_0, is the same as the frequency f in the aqueous humor:

$$f_0 = \frac{c}{\lambda_0} = \frac{3.00 \times 10^8 \text{ m/s}}{633 \times 10^{-9} \text{ m}} = 4.74 \times 10^{14} \text{ Hz}$$

This illustrates the general rule that when a light wave passes from one material into another, the wave frequency is unchanged.

Example 33.3   A twice-reflected ray

Two mirrors are perpendicular to each other. A ray traveling in a plane perpendicular to both mirrors is reflected from one mirror, then the other, as shown in Fig. 33.12. What is the ray's final direction relative to its original direction?

SOLUTION

IDENTIFY: This problem involves only the law of reflection.

SET UP: There are two reflections in this situation, so we must apply the law of reflection twice.

EXECUTE: For mirror 1 the angle of incidence is θ_1, and this equals the angle of reflection. The sum of interior angles in the triangle shown in the figure is $180°$, so we see that the angles of incidence and reflection for mirror 2 are both $90° - \theta_1$. The total change in direction of the ray after both reflections is therefore $2(90° - \theta_1) + 2\theta_1 = 180°$. That is, the ray's final direction is opposite to its original direction.

EVALUATE: An alternative viewpoint is that specular reflection reverses the sign of the component of light velocity perpendicular to the surface but leaves the other components unchanged. We invite you to verify this in detail. You should also be able to use this result to show that when a ray of light is successively reflected by three mirrors forming a corner of a cube (a "corner reflector"), its final direction is again opposite to its original direction. This principle is widely used in tail-light lenses and bicycle reflectors to

33.12 A ray moving in the *xy*-plane. The first reflection changes the sign of the *y*-component of its velocity, and the second reflection changes the sign of the *x*-component. For a different ray with a *z*-component of velocity, a third mirror (perpendicular to the two shown) could be used to change the sign of that component.

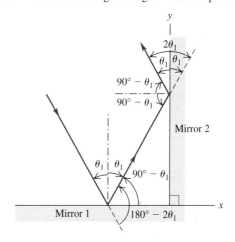

improve their night-time visibility. Apollo astronauts placed arrays of corner reflectors on the moon. By use of laser beams reflected from these arrays, the earth–moon distance has been measured to within 0.15 m.

Test Your Understanding of Section 33.2   You are standing on the shore of a lake. You spot a tasty fish swimming some distance below the lake surface. (a) If you want to spear the fish, should you aim the spear (i) above, (ii) below, or (iii) directly at the apparent position of the fish? (b) If instead you use a high-power laser to simultaneously kill and cook the fish, should you aim the laser (i) above, (ii) below, or (iii) directly at the apparent position of the fish?

33.3 Total Internal Reflection

We have described how light is partially reflected and partially transmitted at an interface between two materials with different indexes of refraction. Under certain circumstances, however, *all* of the light can be reflected back from the interface, with none of it being transmitted, even though the second material is transparent. Figure 33.13a shows how this can occur. Several rays are shown radiating from a point source in material a with index of refraction n_a. The rays strike the surface of a second material b with index n_b, where $n_a > n_b$. (For

Activ
ONLINE
Physics

15.2   Total Internal Reflection

33.13 (a) Total internal reflection. The angle of incidence for which the angle of refraction is 90° is called the critical angle: this is the case for ray 3. The reflected portions of rays 1, 2, and 3 are omitted for clarity. (b) Rays of laser light enter the water in the fishbowl from above; they are reflected at the bottom by mirrors tilted at slightly different angles. One ray undergoes total internal reflection at the air–water interface.

(a) Total internal reflection

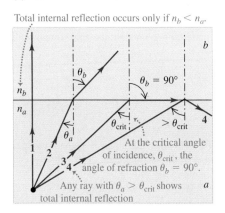

(b) Total internal reflection demonstrated with a laser, mirrors, and water in a fishbowl

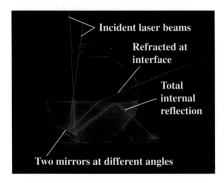

instance, materials a and b could be water and air, respectively.) From Snell's law of refraction,

$$\sin\theta_b = \frac{n_a}{n_b}\sin\theta_a$$

Because n_a/n_b is greater than unity, $\sin\theta_b$ is larger than $\sin\theta_a$; the ray is bent *away from* the normal. Thus there must be some value of θ_a *less than* 90° for which Snell's law gives $\sin\theta_b = 1$ and $\theta_b = 90°$. This is shown by ray 3 in the diagram, which emerges just grazing the surface at an angle of refraction of 90°. Compare the diagram in Fig. 33.13a to the photograph of light rays in Fig. 33.13b.

The angle of incidence for which the refracted ray emerges tangent to the surface is called the **critical angle,** denoted by θ_{crit}. (A more detailed analysis using Maxwell's equations shows that as the incident angle approaches the critical angle, the transmitted intensity approaches zero.) If the angle of incidence is *larger* than the critical angle, the sine of the angle of refraction, as computed by Snell's law, would have to be greater than unity, which is impossible. Beyond the critical angle, the ray *cannot* pass into the upper material; it is trapped in the lower material and is completely reflected at the boundary surface. This situation, called **total internal reflection,** occurs only when a ray is incident on the interface with a second material whose index of refraction is *smaller* than that of the material in which the ray is traveling.

We can find the critical angle for two given materials by setting $\theta_b = 90°\,(\sin\theta_b = 1)$ in Snell's law. We then have

$$\sin\theta_{\text{crit}} = \frac{n_b}{n_a} \qquad \text{(critical angle for total internal reflection)} \qquad (33.6)$$

Total internal reflection will occur if the angle of incidence θ_a is larger than or equal to θ_{crit}.

Applications of Total Internal Reflection

Total internal reflection finds numerous uses in optical technology. As an example, consider glass with index of refraction $n = 1.52$. If light propagating within this glass encounters a glass–air interface, the critical angle is

$$\sin\theta_{\text{crit}} = \frac{1}{1.52} = 0.658 \qquad \theta_{\text{crit}} = 41.1°$$

(a) Total internal reflection in a Porro prism

If the incident beam is oriented as shown, total internal reflection occurs on the 45° faces (because, for a glass–air interface, $\theta_{crit} = 41.1°$).

(b) Binoculars use Porro prisms to reflect the light to each eyepiece.

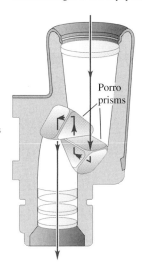

Porro prisms

33.14 **(a)** Total internal reflection in a Porro prism. **(b)** A combination of two Porro prisms in binoculars.

The light will be *totally reflected* if it strikes the glass–air surface at an angle of 41.1° or larger. Because the critical angle is slightly smaller than 45°, it is possible to use a prism with angles of 45°−45°−90° as a totally reflecting surface. As reflectors, totally reflecting prisms have some advantages over metallic surfaces such as ordinary coated-glass mirrors. While no metallic surface reflects 100% of the light incident on it, light can be *totally* reflected by a prism. The reflecting properties of a prism have the additional advantages of being permanent and unaffected by tarnishing.

A 45°−45°−90° prism, used as in Fig. 33.14a, is called a *Porro* prism. Light enters and leaves at right angles to the hypotenuse and is totally reflected at each of the shorter faces. The total change of direction of the rays is 180°. Binoculars often use combinations of two Porro prisms, as in Fig. 33.14b.

When a beam of light enters at one end of a transparent rod (Fig. 33.15), the light can be totally reflected internally if the index of refraction of the rod is greater than that of the surrounding material. The light is "trapped" within the rod even if the rod is curved, provided that the curvature is not too great. Such a rod is sometimes called a *light pipe*. A bundle of fine glass or plastic fibers behaves in the same way and has the advantage of being flexible. A bundle may consist of thousands of individual fibers, each of the order of 0.002 to 0.01 mm in diameter. If the fibers are assembled in the bundle so that the relative positions of the ends are the same (or mirror images) at both ends, the bundle can transmit an image, as shown in Fig. 33.16.

Fiber-optic devices have found a wide range of medical applications in instruments called *endoscopes,* which can be inserted directly into the bronchial tubes, the bladder, the colon, and so on, for direct visual examination. A bundle of fibers can be enclosed in a hypodermic needle for study of tissues and blood vessels far beneath the skin.

Fiber optics also have applications in communication systems, in which they are used to transmit a modulated laser beam. The rate at which information can be transmitted by a wave (light, radio, or whatever) is proportional to the frequency. To see qualitatively why this is so, consider modulating (modifying) the wave by chopping off some of the wave crests. Suppose each crest represents a binary digit, with a chopped-off crest representing a zero and an unmodified crest representing a one. The number of binary digits we can transmit per unit time is thus proportional to the frequency of the wave. Infrared and visible-light waves have much higher frequency than do radio waves, so a modulated laser beam can transmit an enormous amount of information through a single fiber-optic cable.

33.15 A transparent rod with refractive index greater than that of the surrounding material.

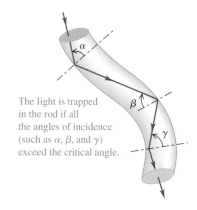

The light is trapped in the rod if all the angles of incidence (such as α, β, and γ) exceed the critical angle.

33.16 Image transmission by a bundle of optical fibers.

33.17 To maximize their brilliance, diamonds are cut so that there is total internal reflection on their back surfaces.

Another advantage of optical fibers is that they can be made thinner than conventional copper wire, so more fibers can be bundled together in a cable of a given diameter. Hence more distinct signals (for instance, different phone lines) can be sent over the same cable. Because fiber-optic cables are electrical insulators, they are immune to electrical interference from lightning and other sources, and they don't allow unwanted currents between source and receiver. For these and other reasons, fiber-optic cables are playing an increasingly important role in long-distance telephone, television, and Internet communication.

Total internal reflection also plays an important role in the design of jewelry. The brilliance of diamond is due in large measure to its very high index of refraction ($n = 2.417$) and correspondingly small critical angle. Light entering a cut diamond is totally internally reflected from facets on its back surface, and then emerges from its front surface (Fig. 33.17). "Imitation diamond" gems, such as cubic zirconia, are made from less expensive crystalline materials with comparable indexes of refraction.

Conceptual Example 33.4   A leaky periscope

A periscope for a submarine uses two totally reflecting $45°-45°-90°$ prisms with total internal reflection on the sides adjacent to the $45°$ angles. It springs a leak, and the bottom prism is covered with water. Explain why the periscope no longer works.

SOLUTION

The critical angle for water ($n_b = 1.33$) on glass ($n_a = 1.52$) is

$$\theta_{crit} = \arcsin\frac{1.33}{1.52} = 61.0°$$

The $45°$ angle of incidence for a totally reflecting prism is *smaller than* the $61°$ critical angle, so total internal reflection does not occur at the glass–water boundary. Most of the light is transmitted into the water, and very little is reflected back into the prism.

Test Your Understanding of Section 33.3   In which of the following situations is there total internal reflection? (i) Light propagating in water ($n = 1.33$) strikes a water–air interface at an incident angle of $70°$; (ii) light propagating in glass ($n = 1.52$) strikes a glass–water interface at an incident angle of $70°$; (iii) light propagating in water strikes a water–glass interface at an incident angle of $70°$.

33.18 Variation of index of refraction n with wavelength for different transparent materials. The horizontal axis shows the wavelength λ_0 of the light *in vacuum;* the wavelength in the material is equal to $\lambda = \lambda_0/n$.

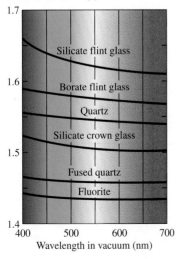

Index of refraction (n)

Silicate flint glass

Borate flint glass

Quartz

Silicate crown glass

Fused quartz

Fluorite

Wavelength in vacuum (nm)

*33.4 Dispersion

Ordinary white light is a superposition of waves with wavelengths extending throughout the visible spectrum. The speed of light *in vacuum* is the same for all wavelengths, but the speed in a material substance is different for different wavelengths. Therefore the index of refraction of a material depends on wavelength. The dependence of wave speed and index of refraction on wavelength is called **dispersion.**

Figure 33.18 shows the variation of index of refraction n with wavelength for a few common optical materials. Note that the horizontal axis of this figure is the wavelength of the light *in vacuum,* λ_0; the wavelength in the material is given by Eq. (33.5), $\lambda = \lambda_0/n$. In most materials the value of n *decreases* with increasing wavelength and decreasing frequency, and thus n *increases* with decreasing wavelength and increasing frequency. In such a material, light of longer wavelength has greater speed than light of shorter wavelength.

Figure 33.19 shows a ray of white light incident on a prism. The deviation (change of direction) produced by the prism increases with increasing index of refraction and frequency and decreasing wavelength. Violet light is deviated most, and red is deviated least; other colors are in intermediate positions. When it comes out of the prism, the light is spread out into a fan-shaped beam, as shown.

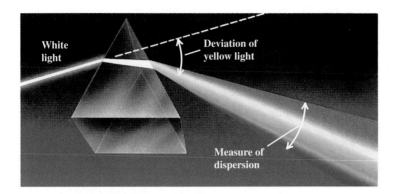

33.19 Dispersion of light by a prism. The band of colors is called a spectrum.

The light is said to be *dispersed* into a spectrum. The amount of dispersion depends on the *difference* between the refractive indexes for violet light and for red light. From Fig. 33.18 we can see that for a substance such as fluorite, the difference between the indexes for red and violet is small, and the dispersion will also be small. A better choice of material for a prism whose purpose is to produce a spectrum would be silicate flint glass, for which there is a larger difference in the value of *n* between red and violet.

As we mentioned in Section 33.3, the brilliance of diamond is due in part to its unusually large refractive index; another important factor is its large dispersion, which causes white light entering a diamond to emerge as a multicolored spectrum. Crystals of rutile and of strontium titanate, which can be produced synthetically, have about eight times the dispersion of diamond.

Rainbows

When you experience the beauty of a rainbow, as in Fig. 33.20a, you are seeing the combined effects of dispersion, refraction, and reflection. Sunlight comes from behind you, enters a water droplet, is (partially) reflected from the back surface of the droplet, and is refracted again upon exiting the droplet (Fig. 33.20b). A light ray that enters the middle of the raindrop is reflected straight back. All other rays exit the raindrop within an angle Δ of that middle ray, with many rays "piling up" at the angle Δ. What you see is a disk of light of angular radius Δ centered on the down-sun point (the point in the sky opposite the sun); due to the "piling up" of light rays, the disk is brightest around its rim, which we see as a rainbow (Fig. 33.20c). Because no light reaches your eye from angles larger than Δ, the sky looks dark outside the rainbow (see Fig. 33.20a). The value of the angle Δ depends on the index of refraction of the water that makes up the raindrops, which in turn depends on the wavelength (Fig. 33.20d). The bright disk of red light is slightly larger than that for orange light, which in turn is slightly larger than that for yellow light, and so on. As a result, you see the rainbow as a band of colors.

In many cases you can see a second, larger rainbow. It is the result of dispersion, refraction, and *two* reflections from the back surface of the droplet (Fig. 33.20e). Each time a light ray hits the back surface, part of the light is refracted out of the drop (not shown in Fig. 33.20); after two such hits, relatively little light is left inside the drop, which is why the secondary rainbow is noticeably fainter than the primary rainbow. Just as a mirror held up to a book reverses the printed letters, so the second reflection reverses the sequence of colors in the secondary rainbow. You can see this effect in Fig 33.20a.

33.5 Polarization

Polarization is a characteristic of all transverse waves. This chapter is about light, but to introduce some basic polarization concepts, let's go back to the transverse waves on a string that we studied in Chapter 15. For a string that in

16.9   Physical Optics: Polarization

33.20 How rainbows form.

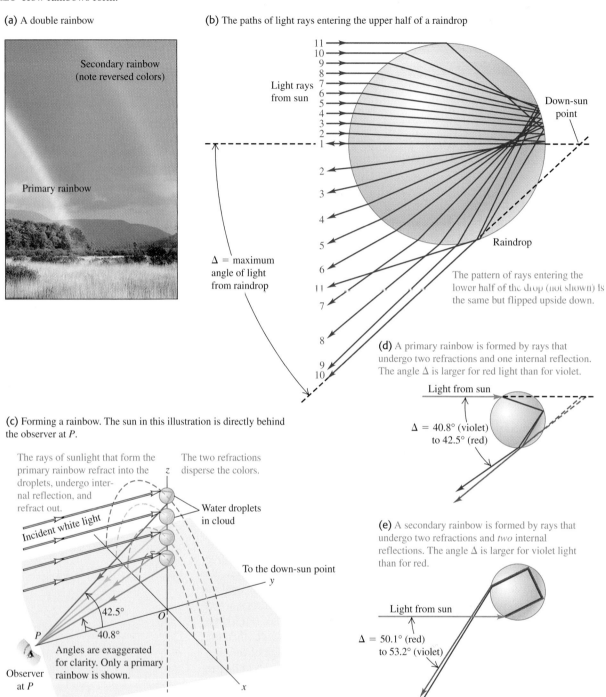

(a) A double rainbow

(b) The paths of light rays entering the upper half of a raindrop

Light rays from sun

Down-sun point

Δ = maximum angle of light from raindrop

Raindrop

The pattern of rays entering the lower half of the drop (not shown) is the same but flipped upside down.

(c) Forming a rainbow. The sun in this illustration is directly behind the observer at P.

The rays of sunlight that form the primary rainbow refract into the droplets, undergo internal reflection, and refract out.

The two refractions disperse the colors.

Incident white light

Water droplets in cloud

To the down-sun point

42.5°

40.8°

Angles are exaggerated for clarity. Only a primary rainbow is shown.

Observer at P

(d) A primary rainbow is formed by rays that undergo two refractions and one internal reflection. The angle Δ is larger for red light than for violet.

Light from sun

$\Delta = 40.8°$ (violet) to $42.5°$ (red)

(e) A secondary rainbow is formed by rays that undergo two refractions and *two* internal reflections. The angle Δ is larger for violet light than for red.

Light from sun

$\Delta = 50.1°$ (red) to $53.2°$ (violet)

equilibrium lies along the x-axis, the displacements may be along the y-direction, as in Fig. 33.21a. In this case the string always lies in the xy-plane. But the displacements might instead be along the z-axis, as in Fig. 33.21b; then the string always lies in the xz-plane.

When a wave has only y-displacements, we say that it is **linearly polarized** in the y-direction; a wave with only z-displacements is linearly polarized in the z-direction. For mechanical waves we can build a **polarizing filter**, or **polarizer**, that permits only waves with a certain polarization direction to pass. In Fig. 33.21c the string can slide vertically in the slot without friction, but no hori-

33.21 (a), (b) Polarized waves on a string. (c) Making a polarized wave on a string from an unpolarized one using a polarizing filter.

(a) Transverse wave linearly polarized in the y-direction

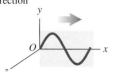

(b) Transverse wave linearly polarized in the z-direction

(c) The slot functions as a polarizing filter, passing only components polarized in the y-direction.

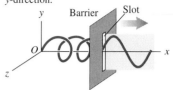

zontal motion is possible. This filter passes waves that are polarized in the y-direction but blocks those that are polarized in the z-direction.

This same language can be applied to electromagnetic waves, which also have polarization. As we learned in Chapter 32, an electromagnetic wave is a *transverse* wave; the fluctuating electric and magnetic fields are perpendicular to each other and to the direction of propagation. We always define the direction of polarization of an electromagnetic wave to be the direction of the *electric*-field vector $\vec{E}$, not the magnetic field, because many common electromagnetic-wave detectors respond to the electric forces on electrons in materials, not the magnetic forces. Thus the electromagnetic wave described by Eq. (32.17),

$$\vec{E}(x, t) = \hat{j}E_{max}\cos(kx - \omega t)$$
$$\vec{B}(x, t) = \hat{k}B_{max}\cos(kx - \omega t)$$

is said to be polarized in the y-direction because the electric field has only a y-component.

CAUTION **The meaning of "polarization"** It's unfortunate that the same word "polarization" that is used to describe the direction of $\vec{E}$ in an electromagnetic wave is also used to describe the shifting of electric charge within a body, such as in response to a nearby charged body; we described this latter kind of polarization in Section 21.2 (see Fig. 21.7). You should remember that while these two concepts have the same name, they do not describe the same phenomenon. ∎

Polarizing Filters

Waves emitted by a radio transmitter are usually linearly polarized. The vertical antennas that are used for radio broadcasting emit waves that, in a horizontal plane around the antenna, are polarized in the vertical direction (parallel to the antenna) (Fig. 33.22a). Rooftop TV antennas have horizontal elements in the United States and vertical elements in Great Britain because the transmitted waves have different polarizations.

33.22 (a) Electrons in the red and white broadcast antenna oscillate vertically, producing vertically polarized electromagnetic waves that propagate away from the antenna in the horizontal direction. (The small gray antennas are for relaying cellular phone signals.) (b) No matter how this light bulb is oriented, the random motion of electrons in the filament produces unpolarized light waves.

(a)

(b)

The situation is different for visible light. Light from ordinary sources, such as incandescent light bulbs and fluorescent light fixtures, is *not* polarized (Fig. 33.22b). The "antennas" that radiate light waves are the molecules that make up the sources. The waves emitted by any one molecule may be linearly polarized, like those from a radio antenna. But any actual light source contains a tremendous number of molecules with random orientations, so the emitted light is a random mixture of waves linearly polarized in all possible transverse directions. Such light is called **unpolarized light** or **natural light.** To create polarized light from unpolarized natural light requires a filter that is analogous to the slot for mechanical waves in Fig. 33.21c.

Polarizing filters for electromagnetic waves have different details of construction, depending on the wavelength. For microwaves with a wavelength of a few centimeters, a good polarizer is an array of closely spaced, parallel conducting wires that are insulated from each other. (Think of a barbecue grill with the outer metal ring replaced by an insulating one.) Electrons are free to move along the length of the conducting wires and will do so in response to a wave whose $\vec{E}$ field is parallel to the wires. The resulting currents in the wires dissipate energy by I^2R heating; the dissipated energy comes from the wave, so whatever wave passes through the grid is greatly reduced in amplitude. Waves with $\vec{E}$ oriented perpendicular to the wires pass through almost unaffected, since electrons cannot move through the air between the wires. Hence a wave that passes through such a filter will be predominantly polarized in the direction perpendicular to the wires.

The most common polarizing filter for visible light is a material known by the trade name Polaroid, widely used for sunglasses and polarizing filters for camera lenses. Developed originally by the American scientist Edwin H. Land, this material incorporates substances that have **dichroism,** a selective absorption in which one of the polarized components is absorbed much more strongly than the other (Fig. 33.23). A Polaroid filter transmits 80% or more of the intensity of a wave that is polarized parallel to a certain axis in the material, called the **polarizing axis,** but only 1% or less for waves that are polarized perpendicular to this axis. In one type of Polaroid filter, long-chain molecules within the filter are oriented with their axis perpendicular to the polarizing axis; these molecules preferentially absorb light that is polarized along their length, much like the conducting wires in a polarizing filter for microwaves.

Using Polarizing Filters

An *ideal* polarizing filter (polarizer) passes 100% of the incident light that is polarized in the direction of the filter's polarizing axis but completely blocks all light that is polarized perpendicular to this axis. Such a device is an unattainable idealization, but the concept is useful in clarifying the basic ideas. In the following discussion we will assume that all polarizing filters are ideal. In Fig. 33.24 unpolarized light is incident on a flat polarizing filter. The polarizing axis is represented by the blue line. The $\vec{E}$ vector of the incident wave can be represented in terms of components parallel and perpendicular to the polarizer axis; only the component of $\vec{E}$ parallel to the polarizing axis is transmitted. Hence the light emerging from the polarizer is linearly polarized parallel to the polarizing axis.

When unpolarized light is incident on an ideal polarizer as in Fig. 33.24, the intensity of the transmitted light is *exactly half* that of the incident unpolarized light, no matter how the polarizing axis is oriented. Here's why: We can resolve the $\vec{E}$ field of the incident wave into a component parallel to the polarizing axis and a component perpendicular to it. Because the incident light is a random mixture of all states of polarization, these two components are, on average, equal. The ideal polarizer transmits only the component that is parallel to the polarizing axis, so half the incident intensity is transmitted.

33.23 A Polaroid filter is illuminated by unpolarized natural light (shown by $\vec{E}$ vectors that point in all directions perpendicular to the direction of propagation). The transmitted light is linearly polarized along the polarizing axis (shown by $\vec{E}$ vectors along the polarization direction only).

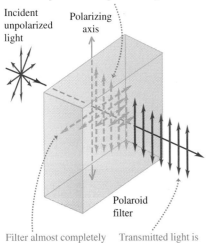

Filter only partially absorbs vertically polarized component of light.

Incident unpolarized light

Polarizing axis

Filter almost completely absorbs horizontally polarized component of light.

Polaroid filter

Transmitted light is linearly polarized in the vertical direction.

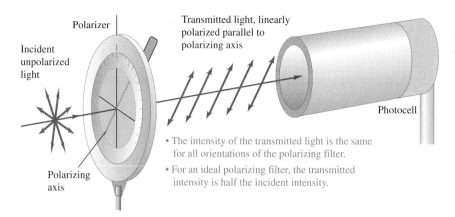

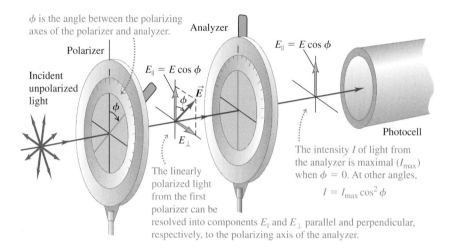

33.24 Unpolarized natural light is incident on the polarizing filter. The photocell measures the intensity of the transmitted linearly polarized light.

Polarizer

Incident unpolarized light

Transmitted light, linearly polarized parallel to polarizing axis

Photocell

• The intensity of the transmitted light is the same for all orientations of the polarizing filter.
• For an ideal polarizing filter, the transmitted intensity is half the incident intensity.

Polarizing axis

ϕ is the angle between the polarizing axes of the polarizer and analyzer.

Polarizer

Analyzer

Incident unpolarized light

$E_{\parallel} = E \cos \phi$

$\vec{E}$

ϕ

$E_{\perp}$

$E_{\parallel} = E \cos \phi$

Photocell

The linearly polarized light from the first polarizer can be resolved into components $E_{\parallel}$ and $E_{\perp}$ parallel and perpendicular, respectively, to the polarizing axis of the analyzer.

The intensity I of light from the analyzer is maximal (I_{max}) when $\phi = 0$. At other angles,

$$I = I_{max} \cos^2 \phi$$

33.25 An ideal analyzer transmits only the electric field component parallel to its transmission direction (that is, its polarizing axis).

What happens when the linearly polarized light emerging from a polarizer passes through a second polarizer, as in Fig. 33.25? Consider the general case in which the polarizing axis of the second polarizer, or *analyzer*, makes an angle ϕ with the polarizing axis of the first polarizer. We can resolve the linearly polarized light that is transmitted by the first polarizer into two components, as shown in Fig. 33.25, one parallel and the other perpendicular to the axis of the analyzer. Only the parallel component, with amplitude $E\cos\phi$, is transmitted by the analyzer. The transmitted intensity is greatest when $\phi = 0$, and it is zero when polarizer and analyzer are *crossed* so that $\phi = 90°$ (Fig. 33.26). To determine the direction of polarization of the light transmitted by the first polarizer, rotate the analyzer until the photocell in Fig. 33.25 measures zero intensity; the polarization axis of the first polarizer is then perpendicular to that of the analyzer.

33.26 These photos show the view through Polaroid sunglasses whose polarizing axes are (left) aligned ($\phi = 0$) and (right) perpendicular ($\phi = 90°$). The transmitted intensity is greatest when the axes are aligned; it is zero when the axes are perpendicular.

To find the transmitted intensity at intermediate values of the angle ϕ, we recall from our energy discussion in Section 32.4 that the intensity of an electromagnetic wave is proportional to the *square* of the amplitude of the wave [see Eq.(32.29)]. The ratio of transmitted to incident *amplitude* is $\cos\phi$, so the ratio of transmitted to incident *intensity* is $\cos^2\phi$. Thus the intensity of the light transmitted through the analyzer is

$$I = I_{max}\cos^2\phi \qquad \text{(Malus's law, polarized light passing through an analyzer)} \qquad (33.7)$$

where I_{max} is the maximum intensity of light transmitted (at $\phi = 0$) and I is the amount transmitted at angle ϕ. This relationship, discovered experimentally by Etienne Louis Malus in 1809, is called **Malus's law.** Malus's law applies *only* if the incident light passing through the analyzer is already linearly polarized.

Problem-Solving Strategy 33.2   **Linear Polarization**

IDENTIFY *the relevant concepts:*   Remember that in all electromagnetic waves, including light waves, the direction of the $\vec{E}$ field is the direction of polarization and is perpendicular to the propagation direction. When working with polarizers, you are really dealing with components of $\vec{E}$ parallel and perpendicular to the polarizing axis. Everything you know about components of vectors is applicable here.

SET UP *the problem* using the following steps:
1. Just as for problems in geometric optics, you should *always* start by drawing a large, neat diagram. Label all known angles, including the angles of any and all polarizing axes.
2. Determine the target variables.

EXECUTE *the solution* as follows:
1. Remember that a polarizer lets pass only electric-field components parallel to its polarizing axis.
2. If the incident light is linearly polarized and has amplitude E and intensity I_{max}, the light that passes through an ideal polar-

izer has amplitude $E\cos\phi$ and intensity $I_{max}\cos^2\phi$, where ϕ is the angle between the incident polarization direction and the filter's polarizing axis.

3. Unpolarized light is a random mixture of all possible polarization states, so on the average it has equal components in any two perpendicular directions. When passed through an ideal polarizer, unpolarized light becomes linearly polarized light with half the incident intensity. Partially linearly polarized light is a superposition of linearly polarized and unpolarized light.
4. The intensity (average power per unit area) of a wave is proportional to the *square* of its amplitude. If you find that two waves differ in amplitude by a certain factor, their intensities differ by the square of that factor.

EVALUATE *your answer:*   Check your answer for any obvious errors. If your results say that light emerging from a polarizer has greater intensity than the incident light, something's wrong: a polarizer can't add energy to a light wave.

Example 33.5   **Two polarizers in combination**

In Fig. 33.25 the incident unpolarized light has intensity I_0. Find the intensities transmitted by the first and second polarizers if the angle between the axes of the two filters is 30°.

SOLUTION

IDENTIFY: This problem involves a polarizer (a polarizing filter on which unpolarized light shines, producing polarized light) and an analyzer (a second polarizing filter on which the polarized light shines).

SET UP: The diagram has already been drawn for us in Fig. 33.25. We are given the intensity I_0 of the incident natural light and the angle $\phi = 30°$ between the polarizing axes. Our target variables are the intensities of the light emerging from the first polarizer and of the light emerging from the second polarizer.

EXECUTE: As we explained above, the intensity of the linearly polarized light transmitted by the first filter is $I_0/2$. According to Eq. (33.7) with $\phi = 30°$, the second filter reduces the intensity by a factor of $\cos^2 30° = \frac{3}{4}$. Thus the intensity transmitted by the second polarizer is

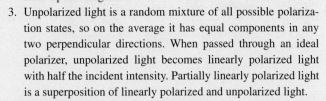

$$\left(\frac{I_0}{2}\right)\left(\frac{3}{4}\right) = \frac{3}{8}I_0$$

EVALUATE: Note that the intensity decreases after each passage through a polarizer. The only situation in which the transmitted intensity does *not* decrease is if the polarizer is ideal (so it absorbs none of the light that passes through it) and if the incident light is linearly polarized along the polarizing axis, so $\phi = 0$.

33.27 When light is incident on a reflecting surface at the polarizing angle, the reflected light is linearly polarized.

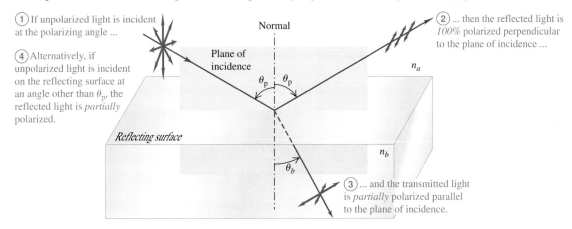

① If unpolarized light is incident at the polarizing angle ...

④ Alternatively, if unpolarized light is incident on the reflecting surface at an angle other than θ_p, the reflected light is *partially* polarized.

Normal

Plane of incidence

θ_p θ_p

n_a

② ... then the reflected light is *100%* polarized perpendicular to the plane of incidence ...

Reflecting surface

n_b

θ_b

③ ... and the transmitted light is *partially* polarized parallel to the plane of incidence.

Polarization by Reflection

Unpolarized light can be polarized, either partially or totally, by *reflection*. In Fig. 33.27, unpolarized natural light is incident on a reflecting surface between two transparent optical materials; the plane containing the incident and reflected rays and the normal to the surface is called the **plane of incidence.** For most angles of incidence, waves for which the electric-field vector $\vec{E}$ is perpendicular to the plane of incidence (that is, parallel to the reflecting surface) are reflected more strongly than those for which $\vec{E}$ lies in this plane. In this case the reflected light is *partially polarized* in the direction perpendicular to the plane of incidence.

But at one particular angle of incidence, called the **polarizing angle** θ_p, the light for which $\vec{E}$ lies in the plane of incidence is *not reflected at all* but is completely refracted. At this same angle of incidence the light for which $\vec{E}$ is perpendicular to the plane of incidence is partially reflected and partially refracted. The *reflected* light is therefore *completely* polarized perpendicular to the plane of incidence, as shown in Fig. 33.27. The *refracted* (transmitted) light is *partially* polarized parallel to this plane; the refracted light is a mixture of the component parallel to the plane of incidence, all of which is refracted, and the remainder of the perpendicular component.

In 1812 the British scientist Sir David Brewster discovered that when the angle of incidence is equal to the polarizing angle θ_p, the reflected ray and the refracted ray are perpendicular to each other (Fig. 33.28). In this case the angle of refraction θ_b becomes the complement of θ_p, so $\theta_b = 90° - \theta_p$. From the law of refraction,

$$n_a \sin\theta_p = n_b \sin\theta_b$$

so we find

$$n_a \sin\theta_p = n_b \sin(90° - \theta_p) = n_b \cos\theta_p$$

$$\tan\theta_p = \frac{n_b}{n_a} \qquad \text{(Brewster's law for the polarizing angle)} \qquad (33.8)$$

This relationship is known as **Brewster's law.** Although discovered experimentally, it can also be *derived* from a wave model using Maxwell's equations.

Polarization by reflection is the reason polarizing filters are widely used in sunglasses (Fig. 33.26). When sunlight is reflected from a horizontal surface, the plane of incidence is vertical, and the reflected light contains a preponderance of

33.28 The significance of the polarizing angle. The open circles represent a component of $\vec{E}$ that is perpendicular to the plane of the figure (the plane of incidence) and parallel to the surface between the two materials.

Note: This is a side view of the situation shown in Fig. 33.27.

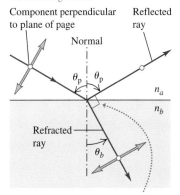

Component perpendicular to plane of page

Reflected ray

Normal

θ_p θ_p

n_a

n_b

Refracted ray

θ_b

When light strikes a surface at the polarizing angle, the reflected and refracted rays are perpendicular to each other and

$$\tan\theta_p = \frac{n_b}{n_a}$$

light that is polarized in the horizontal direction. When the reflection occurs at a smooth asphalt road surface or the surface of a lake, it causes unwanted glare. Vision can be improved by eliminating this glare. The manufacturer makes the polarizing axis of the lens material vertical, so very little of the horizontally polarized light reflected from the road is transmitted to the eyes. The glasses also reduce the overall intensity of the transmitted light to somewhat less than 50% of the intensity of the unpolarized incident light.

Example 33.6   Reflection from a swimming pool's surface

Sunlight reflects off the smooth surface of an unoccupied swimming pool. (a) At what angle of reflection is the light completely polarized? (b) What is the corresponding angle of refraction for the light that is transmitted (refracted) into the water? (c) At night an underwater floodlight is turned on in the pool. Repeat parts (a) and (b) for rays from the floodlight that strike the smooth surface from below.

SOLUTION

IDENTIFY: This problem involves polarization by reflection at an air–water interface in parts (a) and (b) and at a water–air interface in part (c).

SET UP: Figure 33.29 shows our sketches of the light rays for the situation during the day [parts (a) and (b)] and at night [part (c)]. In

part (a) we're looking for the polarizing angle for light that is first in air, then in water; we find this with Brewster's law, Eq. (33.8). In part (b) we want the angle of the refracted light for this situation. In part (c) we again want the polarizing angle, but for light that is first in water, then in air. Again we use Eq. (33.8) to determine this angle.

EXECUTE: (a) The top part of Fig. 33.29 shows the situation during the day. Since the light moves from air toward water, we have $n_a = 1.00$ (air) and $n_b = 1.33$ (water). From Eq. (33.8),

$$\theta_p = \arctan\frac{n_b}{n_a} = \arctan\frac{1.33}{1.00} = 53.1°$$

(b) The incident light is at the polarizing angle, so the reflected and refracted rays are perpendicular; hence

$$\theta_p + \theta_b = 90°$$
$$\theta_b = 90° - 53.1° = 36.9°$$

(c) The situation at night is shown in the bottom part of Fig. 33.29. Now the light is *first* in the water, then in the air, so $n_a = 1.33$ and $n_b = 1.00$. Again using Eq. (33.8), we have

$$\theta_p = \arctan\frac{1.00}{1.33} = 36.9°$$
$$\theta_b = 90° - 36.9° = 53.1°$$

EVALUATE: We can check our answer in part (b) using Snell's law, $n_a\sin\theta_a = n_b\sin\theta_b$, or

$$\sin\theta_b = \frac{n_a\sin\theta_p}{n_b} = \frac{1.00\sin 53.1°}{1.33} = 0.600$$
$$\theta_b = 36.9°$$

Note that the two polarizing angles found in parts (a) and (c) add to 90°. This is *not* an accident; can you see why?

33.29 Our sketches for this problem.

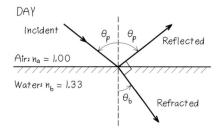

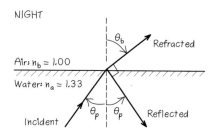

Circular and Elliptical Polarization

Light and other electromagnetic radiation can also have *circular* or *elliptical* polarization. To introduce these concepts, let's return once more to mechanical waves on a stretched string. In Fig. 33.21, suppose the two linearly polarized waves in parts (a) and (b) are in phase and have equal amplitude. When they are superposed, each point in the string has simultaneous *y*- and *z*-displacements of equal magnitude. A little thought shows that the resultant wave lies in a plane oriented at 45° to the *y*- and *z*-axes (i.e., in a plane making a 45° angle with the *xy*- and *xz*-planes). The amplitude of the resultant wave is larger by a factor of $\sqrt{2}$ than that of either component wave, and the resultant wave is linearly polarized.

But now suppose the two equal-amplitude waves differ in phase by a quarter-cycle. Then the resultant motion of each point corresponds to a superposition of two simple harmonic motions at right angles, with a quarter-cycle phase difference. The *y*-displacement at a point is greatest at times when the *z*-displacement is zero, and vice versa. The motion of the string as a whole then no longer takes place in a single plane. It can be shown that each point on the rope moves in a *circle* in a plane parallel to the *yz*-plane. Successive points on the rope have successive phase differences, and the overall motion of the string has the appearance of a rotating helix. This is shown to the left of the polarizing filter in Fig. 33.21c. This particular superposition of two linearly polarized waves is called **circular polarization.** By convention, the wave is said to be *right circularly polarized* when the sense of motion of a particle of the string, to an observer looking *backward* along the direction of propagation, is *clockwise;* the wave is said to be *left circularly polarized* if the sense of motion is the reverse.

Figure 33.30 shows the analogous situation for an electromagnetic wave. Two sinusoidal waves of equal amplitude, polarized in the *y*- and *z*-directions and with a quarter-cycle phase difference, are superposed. The result is a wave in which the $\vec{E}$ vector at each point has a constant magnitude but *rotates* around the direction of propagation. The wave in Fig. 33.30 is propagating toward you and the $\vec{E}$ vector appears to be rotating clockwise, so it is called a *right circularly polarized* electromagnetic wave. If instead the $\vec{E}$ vector of a wave coming toward you appears to be rotating counterclockwise, it is called a *left circularly polarized* electromagnetic wave.

If the phase difference between the two component waves is something other than a quarter-cycle, or if the two component waves have different amplitudes, then each point on the string traces out not a circle but an *ellipse*. The resulting wave is said to be **elliptically polarized.**

For electromagnetic waves with radio frequencies, circular or elliptical polarization can be produced by using two antennas at right angles, fed from the same transmitter but with a phase-shifting network that introduces the appropriate phase difference. For light, the phase shift can be introduced by use of a material that exhibits *birefringence*—that is, has different indexes of refraction for different directions of polarization. A common example is calcite $(CaCO_3)$. When a

33.30 Circular polarization of an electromagnetic wave moving toward you parallel to the *x*-axis. The *y*-component of $\vec{E}$ lags the *z*-component by a quarter-cycle. This phase difference results in right circular polarization.

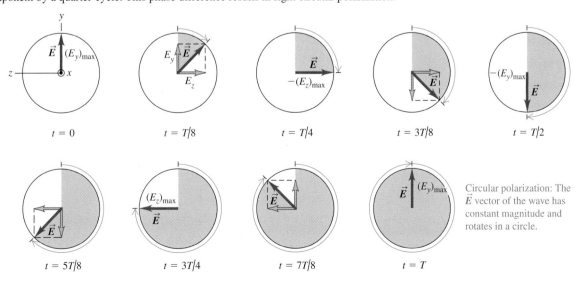

Circular polarization: The $\vec{E}$ vector of the wave has constant magnitude and rotates in a circle.

calcite crystal is oriented appropriately in a beam of unpolarized light, its refractive index (for a wavelength in vacuum of 589 nm) is 1.658 for one direction of polarization and 1.486 for the perpendicular direction. When two waves with equal amplitude and with perpendicular directions of polarization enter such a material, they travel with different speeds. If they are in phase when they enter the material, then in general they are no longer in phase when they emerge. If the crystal is just thick enough to introduce a quarter-cycle phase difference, then the crystal converts linearly polarized light to circularly polarized light. Such a crystal is called a *quarter-wave plate.* Such a plate also converts circularly polarized light to linearly polarized light. Can you prove this? (See Problem 33.43.)

Photoelasticity

Some optical materials that are not normally birefringent become so when they are subjected to mechanical stress. This is the basis of the science of *photoelasticity.* Stresses in girders, boiler plates, gear teeth, and cathedral pillars can be analyzed by constructing a transparent model of the object, usually of a plastic material, subjecting it to stress, and examining it between a polarizer and an analyzer in the crossed position. Very complicated stress distributions can be studied by these optical methods.

Figure 33.31 is a photograph of a photoelastic model under stress. The polarized light that enters the model can be thought of as having a component along each of the two directions of the birefringent plastic. Since these two components travel through the plastic at different speeds, the light that emerges from the other side of the model can have a different overall direction of polarization. Hence some of this transmitted light will be able to pass through the analyzer even though its polarization axis is at a 90° angle to the polarizer's axis, and the stressed areas in the plastic will appear as bright spots. The amount of birefringence is different for different wavelengths and hence different colors of light; the color that appears at each location in Fig. 33.31 is that for which the transmitted light is most nearly polarized along the analyzer's polarization axis.

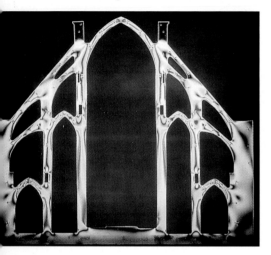

33.31 Photoelastic stress analysis of a model of a cross section of a Gothic cathedral. The masonry construction that was used for this kind of building had great strength in compression but very little in tension (see Section 11.4). Inadequate buttressing and high winds sometimes caused tensile stresses in normally compressed structural elements, leading to some spectacular collapses.

Test Your Understanding of Section 33.5 You are taking a photograph of a sunlit high-rise office building. In order to minimize the reflections from the building's windows, you place a polarizing filter on the camera lens. How should you orient the filter? (i) with the polarizing axis vertical; (ii) with the polarizing axis horizontal; (iii) either orientation will minimize the reflections just as well; (iv) neither orientation will have any effect.

*33.6 Scattering of Light

The sky is blue. Sunsets are red. Skylight is partially polarized; that's why the sky looks darker from some angles than from others when it is viewed through Polaroid sunglasses. As we will see, a single phenomenon is responsible for all of these effects.

When you look at the daytime sky, the light that you see is sunlight that has been absorbed and then re-radiated in a variety of directions. This process is called **scattering.** (If the earth had no atmosphere, the sky would appear as black in the daytime as it does at night, just as it does to an astronaut in space or on the moon; you would see the sun's light only if you looked directly at it, and the stars would be visible in the daytime.) Figure 33.32 shows some of the details of the scattering process. Sunlight, which is unpolarized, comes from the left along the x-axis and passes over an observer looking vertically upward along the y-axis. (We are viewing the situation from the side.) Consider the molecules of the earth's atmosphere located at point O. The electric field in the beam of sunlight sets the electric charges in these molecules into vibration.

33.32 When the sunbathing observer on the left looks up, he sees blue, polarized sunlight that has been scattered by air molecules. The observer on the right sees reddened, unpolarized light when he looks at the sun.

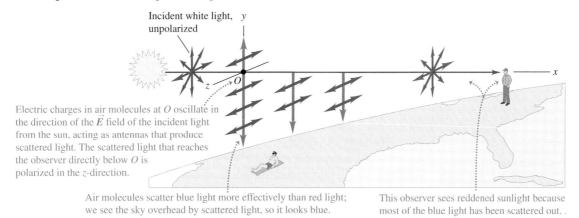

Incident white light, unpolarized

Electric charges in air molecules at O oscillate in the direction of the $\vec{E}$ field of the incident light from the sun, acting as antennas that produce scattered light. The scattered light that reaches the observer directly below O is polarized in the z-direction.

Air molecules scatter blue light more effectively than red light; we see the sky overhead by scattered light, so it looks blue.

This observer sees reddened sunlight because most of the blue light has been scattered out.

Since light is a transverse wave, the direction of the electric field in any component of the sunlight lies in the yz-plane, and the motion of the charges takes place in this plane. There is no field, and hence no motion of charges, in the direction of the x-axis.

An incident light wave sets the electric charges in the molecules at point O vibrating along the line of $\vec{E}$. We can resolve this vibration into two components, one along the y-axis and the other along the z-axis. Each component in the incident light produces the equivalent of two molecular "antennas," oscillating with the same frequency as the incident light and lying along the y- and z-axes.

We mentioned in Chapter 32 that an oscillating charge, like those in an antenna, does not radiate in the direction of its oscillation. (See Fig. 32.3 in Section 32.1.) Thus the "antenna" along the y-axis does not send any light to the observer directly below it, although it does emit light in other directions. Therefore the only light reaching this observer comes from the other molecular "antenna," corresponding to the oscillation of charge along the z-axis. This light is linearly polarized, with its electric field along the z-axis (parallel to the "antenna"). The red vectors on the y-axis below point O in Fig. 33.32 show the direction of polarization of the light reaching the observer.

As the original beam of sunlight passes though the atmosphere, its intensity decreases as its energy goes into the scattered light. Detailed analysis of the scattering process shows that the intensity of the light scattered from air molecules increases in proportion to the fourth power of the frequency (inversely to the fourth power of the wavelength). Thus the intensity ratio for the two ends of the visible spectrum is $(700 \text{ nm}/400 \text{ nm})^4 = 9.4$. Roughly speaking, scattered light contains nine times as much blue light as red, and that's why the sky is blue.

Clouds contain a high concentration of water droplets or ice crystals, which also scatter light. Because of this high concentration, light passing through the cloud has many more opportunities for scattering than does light passing through a clear sky. Thus light of *all* wavelengths is eventually scattered out of the cloud, so the cloud looks white (Fig. 33.33). Milk looks white for the same reason; the scattering is due to fat globules in the milk. If you dilute milk by mixing it with enough water, the concentration of fat globules will be so low that only blue light will be substantially scattered; the dilute solution will look blue, not white. (Non-fat milk, which also has a very low concentration of globules, looks somewhat bluish for this same reason.)

Near sunset, when sunlight has to travel a long distance through the earth's atmosphere, a substantial fraction of the blue light is removed by scattering. White light minus blue light looks yellow or red. This explains the yellow or red hue that we so often see from the setting sun (and that is seen by the observer at the far right of Fig. 33.32).

33.33 Clouds are white because they efficiently scatter sunlight of all wavelengths.

Because skylight is partially polarized, polarizers are useful in photography. The sky in a photograph can be darkened by orienting the polarizer axis to be perpendicular to the predominant direction of polarization of the scattered light. The most strongly polarized light comes from parts of the sky that are 90° away from the sun—for example, from directly overhead when the sun is on the horizon at sunrise or sunset.

33.7 Huygens's Principle

The laws of reflection and refraction of light rays that we introduced in Section 33.2 were discovered experimentally long before the wave nature of light was firmly established. However, we can *derive* these laws from wave considerations and show that they are consistent with the wave nature of light. The same kind of analysis that we use here will be of central importance in Chapters 35 and 36 in our discussion of physical optics.

We begin with a principle called **Huygens's principle.** This principle, stated originally by the Dutch scientist Christiaan Huygens in 1678, is a geometrical method for finding, from the known shape of a wave front at some instant, the shape of the wave front at some later time. Huygens assumed that **every point of a wave front may be considered the source of secondary wavelets that spread out in all directions with a speed equal to the speed of propagation of the wave.** The new wave front at a later time is then found by constructing a surface *tangent* to the secondary wavelets or, as it is called, the *envelope* of the wavelets. All the results that we obtain from Huygens's principle can also be obtained from Maxwell's equations. Thus it is not an independent principle, but it is often very convenient for calculations with wave phenomena.

Huygens's principle is shown in Fig. 33.34. The original wave front AA' is traveling outward from a source, as indicated by the arrows. We want to find the shape of the wave front after a time interval t. Let v be the speed of propagation of the wave; then in time t it travels a distance vt. We construct several circles (traces of spherical wavelets) with radius $r = vt$, centered at points along AA'. The trace of the envelope of these wavelets, which is the new wave front, is the curve BB'. We are assuming that the speed v is the same at all points and in all directions.

33.34 Applying Huygens's principle to wave front AA' to construct a new wave front BB'.

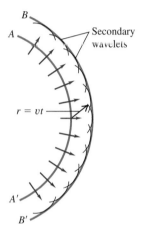

33.35 Using Huygens's principle to derive the law of reflection.

(a) Successive positions of a plane wave AA' as it is reflected from a plane surface

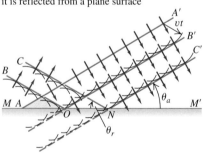

Reflection and Huygens's Principle

To derive the law of reflection from Huygens's principle, we consider a plane wave approaching a plane reflecting surface. In Fig. 33.35a the lines AA', OB', and NC' represent successive positions of a wave front approaching the surface MM'. Point A on the wave front AA' has just arrived at the reflecting surface. We can use Huygens's principle to find the position of the wave front after a time interval t. With points on AA' as centers, we draw several secondary wavelets with radius vt. The wavelets that originate near the upper end of AA' spread out unhindered, and their envelope gives the portion OB' of the new wave front. If the reflecting surface were not there, the wavelets originating near the lower end of AA' would similarly reach the positions shown by the broken circular arcs. Instead, these wavelets strike the reflecting surface.

The effect of the reflecting surface is to *change the direction* of travel of those wavelets that strike it, so the part of a wavelet that would have penetrated the surface actually lies to the left of it, as shown by the full lines. The first such wavelet is centered at point A; the envelope of all such reflected wavelets is the portion OB of the wave front. The trace of the entire wave front at this instant is the bent line BOB'. A similar construction gives the line CNC' for the wave front after another interval t.

(b) Magnified portion of **(a)**

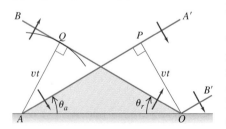

From plane geometry the angle θ_a between the incident *wave front* and the *surface* is the same as that between the incident *ray* and the *normal* to the surface and is therefore the angle of incidence. Similarly, θ_r is the angle of reflection. To find the relationship between these angles, we consider Fig. 33.35b. From O we draw $OP = vt$, perpendicular to AA'. Now OB, by construction, is tangent to a circle of radius vt with center at A. If we draw AQ from A to the point of tangency, the triangles APO and OQA are congruent because they are right triangles with the side AO in common and with $AQ = OP = vt$. The angle θ_a therefore equals the angle θ_r, and we have the law of reflection.

Refraction and Huygens's Principle

We can derive the law of *refraction* by a similar procedure. In Fig. 33.36a we consider a wave front, represented by line AA', for which point A has just arrived at the boundary surface SS' between two transparent materials a and b, with indexes of refraction n_a and n_b and wave speeds v_a and v_b. (The *reflected* waves are not shown in the figure; they proceed as in Fig. 33.35.) We can apply Huygens's principle to find the position of the refracted wave fronts after a time t.

With points on AA' as centers, we draw several secondary wavelets. Those originating near the upper end of AA' travel with speed v_a and, after a time interval t, are spherical surfaces of radius $v_a t$. The wavelet originating at point A, however, is traveling in the second material b with speed v_b and at time t is a spherical surface of radius $v_b t$. The envelope of the wavelets from the original wave front is the plane whose trace is the bent line BOB'. A similar construction leads to the trace CPC' after a second interval t.

The angles θ_a and θ_b between the surface and the incident and refracted wave fronts are the angle of incidence and the angle of refraction, respectively. To find the relationship between these angles, refer to Fig. 33.36b. We draw $OQ = v_a t$, perpendicular to AQ, and we draw $AB = v_b t$, perpendicular to BO. From the right triangle AOQ,

$$\sin\theta_a = \frac{v_a t}{AO}$$

and from the right triangle AOB,

$$\sin\theta_b = \frac{v_b t}{AO}$$

Combining these, we find

$$\frac{\sin\theta_a}{\sin\theta_b} = \frac{v_a}{v_b} \qquad (33.9)$$

We have defined the index of refraction n of a material as the ratio of the speed of light c in vacuum to its speed v in the material: $n_a = c/v_a$ and $n_b = c/v_b$. Thus

$$\frac{n_b}{n_a} = \frac{c/v_b}{c/v_a} = \frac{v_a}{v_b}$$

and we can rewrite Eq. (33.9) as

$$\frac{\sin\theta_a}{\sin\theta_b} = \frac{n_b}{n_a} \qquad \text{or}$$

$$n_a \sin\theta_a = n_b \sin\theta_b$$

which we recognize as Snell's law, Eq. (33.4). So we have derived Snell's law from a wave theory. Alternatively, we may choose to regard Snell's law as an experimental result that defines the index of refraction of a material; in that case

33.36 Using Huygens's principle to derive the law of refraction. The case $v_b < v_a \ (n_b > n_a)$ is shown.

(a) Successive positions of a plane wave AA' as it is refracted by a plane surface

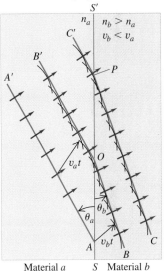

(b) Magnified portion of **(a)**

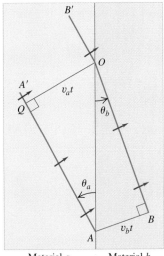

33.37 How mirages are formed.

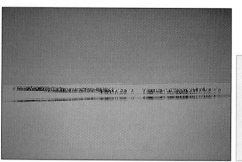

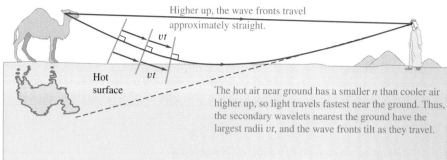

Higher up, the wave fronts travel approximately straight.

vt

Hot surface

vt

The hot air near ground has a smaller n than cooler air higher up, so light travels fastest near the ground. Thus, the secondary wavelets nearest the ground have the largest radii vt, and the wave fronts tilt as they travel.

this analysis helps to confirm the relationship $v = c/n$ for the speed of light in a material.

Mirages offer an interesting example of Huygens's principle in action. When the surface of pavement or desert sand is heated intensely by the sun, a hot, less dense, smaller-n layer of air forms near the surface. The speed of light is slightly greater in the hotter air near the ground, the Huygens wavelets have slightly larger radii, the wave fronts tilt slightly, and rays that were headed toward the surface with a large angle of incidence (near 90°) can be bent up as shown in Fig. 33.37. Light farther from the ground is bent less and travels nearly in a straight line. The observer sees the object in its natural position, with an inverted image below it, as though seen in a horizontal reflecting surface. Even when the turbulence of the heated air prevents a clear inverted image from being formed, the mind of the thirsty traveler can interpret the apparent reflecting surface as a sheet of water.

It is important to keep in mind that Maxwell's equations are the fundamental relationships for electromagnetic wave propagation. But it is a remarkable fact that Huygens's principle anticipated Maxwell's analysis by two centuries. Maxwell provided the theoretical underpinning for Huygens's principle. Every point in an electromagnetic wave, with its time-varying electric and magnetic fields, acts as a source of the continuing wave, as predicted by Ampere's and Faraday's laws.

Test Your Understanding of Section 33.7 Sound travels faster in warm air than in cold air. Imagine a weather front that runs north-south, with warm air to the west of the front and cold air to the east. A sound wave traveling in a northeast direction in the warm air encounters this front. How will the direction of this sound wave change when it passes into the cold air? (i) The wave direction will deflect toward the north; (ii) the wave direction will deflect toward the east; (iii) the wave direction will be unchanged.

Light and its properties: Light is an electromagnetic wave. When emitted or absorbed, it also shows particle properties. It is emitted by accelerated electric charges. The speed of light is a fundamental physical constant.

$$n = \frac{c}{v} \qquad (33.1)$$

$$\lambda = \frac{\lambda_0}{n} \qquad (33.5)$$

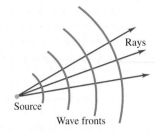

A wave front is a surface of constant phase; wave fronts move with a speed equal to the propagation speed of the wave. A ray is a line along the direction of propagation, perpendicular to the wave fronts. Representation of light by rays is the basis of geometric optics.

When light is transmitted from one material to another, the frequency of the light is unchanged, but the wavelength and wave speed can change. The index of refraction n of a material is the ratio of the speed of light in vacuum c to the speed v in the material. If λ_0 is the wavelength in vacuum, the same wave has a shorter wavelength λ in a medium with index of refraction n. (See Example 33.2.)

The variation of index of refraction n with wavelength λ is called dispersion. Usually n decreases with increasing λ.

Reflection and refraction: At a smooth interface between two optical materials, the incident, reflected, and refracted rays and the normal to the interface all lie in a single plane called the plane of incidence. The law of reflection states that the angles of incidence and reflection are equal. The law of refraction relates the angles of incidence and refraction to the indexes of refraction of the materials. Angles of incidence, reflection, and refraction are always measured from the normal to the surface. (See Examples 33.1 and 33.3.)

$$\theta_r = \theta_a \qquad (33.2)$$
(law of reflection)

$$n_a \sin\theta_a = n_b \sin\theta_b \qquad (33.4)$$
(law of refraction)

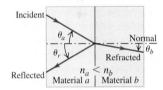

Total internal reflection: When a ray travels in a material of greater index of refraction n_a toward a material of smaller index n_b, total internal reflection occurs at the interface when the angle of incidence exceeds a critical angle θ_{crit}. (See Example 33.4.)

$$\sin\theta_{crit} = \frac{n_b}{n_a} \qquad (33.6)$$

Polarization of light: The direction of polarization of a linearly polarized electromagnetic wave is the direction of the $\vec{E}$ field. A polarizing filter passes waves that are linearly polarized along its polarizing axis and blocks waves polarized perpendicularly to that axis. When polarized light of intensity I_{max} is incident on a polarizing filter used as an analyzer, the intensity I of the light transmitted through the analyzer depends on the angle ϕ between the polarization direction of the incident light and the polarizing axis of the analyzer. (See Example 33.5.) When two linearly polarized waves with a phase difference are superposed, the result is circularly or elliptically polarized light. In this case the $\vec{E}$ vector is not confined to a plane containing the direction of propagation, but rather describes circles or ellipses in planes perpendicular to the propagation direction.

Light is scattered by air molecules. The scattered light is partially polarized.

$$I = I_{max}\cos^2\phi \qquad (33.7)$$
(Malus's law)

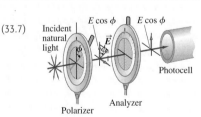

Polarization by reflection: When unpolarized light strikes an interface between two materials, Brewster's law states that the reflected light is completely polarized perpendicular to the plane of incidence (parallel to the interface) if the angle of incidence equals the polarizing angle θ_p. (See Example 33.6.)

$$\tan\theta_p = \frac{n_b}{n_a} \quad (33.8)$$
(Brewster's law)

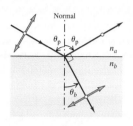
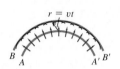

Huygens's principle: Huygens's principle states that if the position of a wave front at one instant is known, then the position of the front at a later time can be constructed by imagining the front as a source of secondary wavelets. Huygens's principle can be used to derive the laws of reflection and refraction.

$r = vt$

Key Terms

optics, *1121*
wave front, *1122*
ray, *1123*
geometric optics, *1123*
physical optics, *1123*
reflection, *1123*
refraction, *1123*
specular reflection, *1124*
diffuse reflection, *1124*
index of refraction (refractive index), *1124*

law of reflection, *1125*
law of refraction (Snell's law), *1125*
critical angle, *1130*
total internal reflection, *1130*
dispersion, *1132*
linear polarization, *1134*
polarizing filter (polarizer), *1134*
unpolarized light (natural light), *1135*
dichroism, *1136*
polarizing axis, *1136*

Malus's law, *1138*
plane of incidence, *1139*
polarizing angle, *1139*
Brewster's law, *1139*
circular polarization, *1141*
elliptical polarization, *1141*
scattering, *1142*
Huygens's principle, *1144*

Answer to Chapter Opening Question ?

This is the same effect as shown in Fig. 33.31. The drafting tools are placed between two polarizing filters whose polarizing axes are perpendicular. In places where the clear plastic is under stress, the plastic becomes birefringent; that is, light travels through it at a speed that depends on its polarization. The result is that the light that emerges from the plastic has a different polarization than the light that enters. A spot on the plastic appears bright if the emerging light has the same polarization as the second polarizing filter. The amount of birefringence depends on the wavelength of the light as well as the amount of stress on the plastic, so different colors are seen at different locations on the plastic.

you use a laser beam, you should aim *at* the apparent position of the fish: The beam of laser light takes the same path from you to the fish as ordinary light takes from the fish to you (though in the opposite direction).

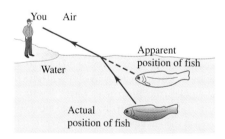

Answers to Test Your Understanding Questions

33.1 Answer: (iii) The waves go farther in the y-direction in a given amount of time than in the other directions, so the wave fronts are elongated in the y-direction.
33.2 Answers: (a) (ii), (b) (iii) As shown in the figure, light rays coming from the fish bend away from the normal when they pass from the water $(n = 1.33)$ into the air $(n = 1.00)$. As a result, the fish appears to be higher in the water than it actually is. Hence you should aim a spear *below* the apparent position of the fish. If

33.3 Answers: (i), (ii) Total internal reflection can occur only if two conditions are met: n_b must be less than n_a, and the critical angle θ_{crit} (where $\sin\theta_{\text{crit}} = n_b/n_a$) must be smaller than the angle of incidence θ_a. In the first two cases both conditions are met: The critical angles are (i) $\theta_{\text{crit}} = \sin^{-1}(1/1.33) = 48.8°$ and (ii) $\theta_{\text{crit}} = \sin^{-1}(1.33/1.52) = 61.0°$, both of which are smaller than $\theta_a = 70°$. In the third case $n_b = 1.52$ is greater than $n_a = 1.33$, so total internal reflection cannot occur for any incident angle.

33.5 Answer: (ii) The sunlight reflected from the windows of the high-rise building is partially polarized in the vertical direction, since each window lies in a vertical plane. The Polaroid filter in front of the lens is oriented with its polarizing axis perpendicular to the dominant direction of polarization of the reflected light.

33.7 Answer: (ii) Huygens's principle applies to waves of all kinds, including sound waves. Hence this situation is exactly like that shown in Fig. 33.36, with material *a* representing the warm air, material *b* representing the cold air in which the waves travel more slowly, and the interface between the materials representing the weather front. North is toward the top of the figure and east is toward the right, so Fig. 33.36 shows that the rays (which indicate the direction of propagation) deflect toward the east.

PROBLEMS

For instructor-assigned homework, go to **www.masteringphysics.com**

Discussion Questions

Q33.1. Light requires about 8 minutes to travel from the sun to the earth. Is it delayed appreciably by the earth's atmosphere? Explain.

Q33.2. Sunlight or starlight passing through the earth's atmosphere is always bent toward the vertical. Why? Does this mean that a star is not really where it appears to be? Explain.

Q33.3. A beam of light goes from one material into another. On *physical* grounds, explain *why* the wavelength changes but the frequency and period do not.

Q33.4. A student claimed that, because of atmospheric refraction (see Discussion Question Q33.2), the sun can be seen after it has set and that the day is therefore longer than it would be if the earth had no atmosphere. First, what does she mean by saying that the sun can be seen after it has set? Second, comment on the validity of her conclusion.

Q33.5. When hot air rises from a radiator or heating duct, objects behind it appear to shimmer or waver. What causes this?

Q33.6. Devise straightforward experiments to measure the speed of light in a given glass using (a) Snell's law; (b) total internal reflection; (c) Brewster's law.

Q33.7. Sometimes when looking at a window, you see two reflected images slightly displaced from each other. What causes this?

Q33.8. If you look up from underneath toward the surface of the water in your aquarium, you may see an upside-down reflection of your pet fish in the surface of the water. Explain how this can happen.

Q33.9. A ray of light in air strikes a glass surface. Is there a range of angles for which total reflection occurs? Explain.

Q33.10. When light is incident on an interface between two materials, the angle of the refracted ray depends on the wavelength, but the angle of the reflected ray does not. Why should this be?

Q33.11. A salesperson at a bargain counter claims that a certain pair of sunglasses has Polaroid filters; you suspect that the glasses are just tinted plastic. How could you find out for sure?

Q33.12. Does it make sense to talk about the polarization of a *longitudinal* wave, such as a sound wave? Why or why not?

Q33.13. How can you determine the direction of the polarizing axis of a single polarizer?

Q33.14. It has been proposed that automobile windshields and headlights should have polarizing filters to reduce the glare of oncoming lights during night driving. Would this work? How should the polarizing axes be arranged? What advantages would this scheme have? What disadvantages?

Q33.15. When a sheet of plastic food wrap is placed between two crossed polarizers, no light is transmitted. When the sheet is stretched in one direction, some light passes through the crossed polarizers. What is happening?

Q33.16. If you sit on the beach and look at the ocean through Polaroid sunglasses, the glasses help to reduce the glare from sunlight reflecting off the water. But if you lie on your side on the beach, there is little reduction in the glare. Explain why there is a difference.

Q33.17. When unpolarized light is incident on two crossed polarizers, no light is transmitted. A student asserted that if a third polarizer is inserted between the other two, some transmission will occur. Does this make sense? How can adding a third filter *increase* transmission?

Q33.18. For the old "rabbit-ear" style TV antennas, it's possible to alter the quality of reception considerably simply by changing the orientation of the antenna. Why?

Q33.19. In Fig. 33.32, since the light that is scattered out of the incident beam is polarized, why is the transmitted beam not also partially polarized?

Q33.20. You are sunbathing in the late afternoon when the sun is relatively low in the western sky. You are lying flat on your back, looking straight up through Polaroid sunglasses. To minimize the amount of sky light reaching your eyes, how should you lie: with your feet pointing north, east, south, west, or in some other direction? Explain your reasoning.

Q33.21. Light scattered from blue sky is strongly polarized because of the nature of the scattering process described in Section 33.6. But light scattered from white clouds is usually *not* polarized. Why not?

Q33.22. Atmospheric haze is due to water droplets or smoke particles ("smog"). Such haze reduces visibility by scattering light, so that the light from distant objects becomes randomized and images become indistinct. Explain why visibility through haze can be improved by wearing red-tinted sunglasses, which filter out blue light.

Q33.23. The explanation given in Section 33.6 for the color of the setting sun should apply equally well to the *rising* sun, since sunlight travels the same distance through the atmosphere to reach your eyes at either sunrise or sunset. Typically, however, sunsets are redder than sunrises. Why? (*Hint:* Particles of all kinds in the atmosphere contribute to scattering.)

Q33.24. Huygens's principle also applies to sound waves. During the day, the temperature of the atmosphere decreases with increasing altitude above the ground. But at night, when the ground cools, there is a layer of air just above the surface in which the temperature *increases* with altitude. Use this to explain why sound waves from distant sources can be heard more clearly at night than in the daytime. (*Hint:* The speed of sound increases with increasing temperature. Use the ideas displayed in Fig. 33.37 for light.)

Q33.25. Can water waves be reflected and refracted? Give examples. Does Huygens's principle apply to water waves? Explain.

Exercises

Section 33.2 Reflection and Refraction

33.1. Two plane mirrors intersect at right angles. A laser beam strikes the first of them at a point 11.5 cm from their point of intersection, as shown in Fig. 33.38 For what angle of incidence at the first mirror will this ray strike the midpoint of the second mirror (which is 28.0 cm long) after reflecting from the first mirror?

Figure **33.38** Exercise 33.1.

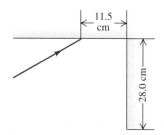

33.2. Three plane mirrors intersect at right angles. A beam of laser light strikes the first of them at an angle θ with respect to the normal (Fig. 33.39). (a) Show that when this ray is reflected off of the other two mirrors and crosses the original ray, the angle α between these two rays will be $\alpha = 180° - 2\theta$. (b) For what angle θ will the two rays be perpendicular when they cross?

Figure **33.39** Exercise 33.2

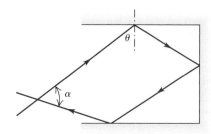

33.3. A beam of light has a wavelength of 650 nm in vacuum. (a) What is the speed of this light in a liquid whose index of refraction at this wavelength is 1.47? (b) What is the wavelength of these waves in the liquid?

33.4. Light with a frequency of 5.80×10^{14} Hz travels in a block of glass that has an index of refraction of 1.52. What is the wavelength of the light (a) in vacuum and (b) in the glass?

33.5. A light beam travels at 1.94×10^8 m/s in quartz. The wavelength of the light in quartz is 355 nm. (a) What is the index of refraction of quartz at this wavelength? (b) If this same light travels through air, what is its wavelength there?

33.6. Light of a certain frequency has a wavelength of 438 nm in water. What is the wavelength of this light in benzene?

33.7. A parallel beam of light in air makes an angle of 47.5° with the surface of a glass plate having a refractive index of 1.66. (a) What is the angle between the reflected part of the beam and the surface of the glass? (b) What is the angle between the refracted beam and the surface of the glass?

33.8. Using a fast-pulsed laser and electronic timing circuitry, you find that light travels 2.50 m within a plastic rod in 11.5 ns. What is the refractive index of the plastic?

33.9. Light traveling in air is incident on the surface of a block of plastic at an angle of 62.7° to the normal and is bent so that it makes a 48.1° angle with the normal in the plastic. Find the speed of light in the plastic.

33.10. (a) A tank containing methanol has walls 2.50 cm thick made of glass of refractive index 1.550. Light from the outside air strikes the glass at a 41.3° angle with the normal to the glass. Find the angle the light makes with the normal in the methanol. (b) The tank is emptied and refilled with an unknown liquid. If light incident at the same angle as in part (a) enters the liquid in the tank at an angle of 20.2° from the normal, what is the refractive index of the unknown liquid?

33.11. (a) Light passes through three parallel slabs of different thicknesses and refractive indexes. The light is incident in the first slab and finally refracts into the third slab. Show that the middle slab has no effect on the final direction of the light. That is, show that the direction of the light in the third slab is the same as if the light had passed directly from the first slab into the third slab. (b) Generalize this result to a stack of N slabs. What determines the final direction of the light in the last slab?

33.12. A horizontal, parallel-sided plate of glass having a refractive index of 1.52 is in contact with the surface of water in a tank. A ray coming from above in air makes an angle of incidence of 35.0° with the normal to the top surface of the glass. (a) What angle does the ray refracted into the water make with the normal to the surface? (b) What is the dependence of this angle on the refractive index of the glass?

33.13. In a material having an index of refraction n, a light ray has frequency f, wavelength λ, and speed v. What are the frequency, wavelength, and speed of this light (a) in vacuum and (b) in a material having refractive index n'? In each case, express your answers in terms of *only* f, λ, v, n, and n'.

33.14. Prove that a ray of light reflected from a plane mirror rotates through an angle of 2θ when the mirror rotates through an angle θ about an axis perpendicular to the plane of incidence.

33.15. A ray of light is incident on a plane surface separating two sheets of glass with refractive indexes 1.70 and 1.58. The angle of incidence is 62.0°, and the ray originates in the glass with $n = 1.70$. Compute the angle of refraction.

33.16. In Example 33.1 the water–glass interface is horizontal. If instead this interface were tilted 15.0° above the horizontal, with the right side higher than the left side, what would be the angle from the vertical of the ray in the glass? (The ray in the water still makes an angle of 60.0° with the vertical.)

Section 33.3 Total Internal Reflection

33.17. Light Pipe. Light enters a solid pipe made of plastic having an index of refraction of 1.60. The light travels parallel to the upper part of the pipe (Fig. 33.40). You want to cut the face AB so that all the light will reflect back into the pipe after it first strikes that face. (a) What is the largest that θ can be if the pipe is in air? (b) If the pipe is immersed in water of refractive index 1.33, what is the largest that θ can be?

Figure **33.40** Exercise 33.17

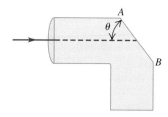

33.18. A beam of light is traveling inside a solid glass cube having index of refraction 1.53. It strikes the surface of the cube from the inside. (a) If the cube is in air, at what minimum angle with the normal inside the glass will this light *not* enter the air at this surface? (b) What would be the minimum angle in part (a) if the cube were immersed in water?

33.19. The critical angle for total internal reflection at a liquid–air interface is 42.5°. (a) If a ray of light traveling in the liquid has an angle of incidence at the interface of 35.0°, what angle does the refracted ray in the air make with the normal? (b) If a ray of light traveling in air has an angle of incidence at the interface of 35.0°, what angle does the refracted ray in the liquid make with the normal?

33.20. At the very end of Wagner's series of operas *Ring of the Nibelung*, Brünnhilde takes the golden ring from the finger of the dead Siegfried and throws it into the Rhine, where it sinks to the bottom of the river. Assuming that the ring is small enough compared to the depth of the river to be treated as a point and that the Rhine is 10.0 m deep where the ring goes in, what is the area of the largest circle at the surface of the water over which light from the ring could escape from the water?

33.21. A ray of light is traveling in a glass cube that is totally immersed in water. You find that if the ray is incident on the glass–water interface at an angle to the normal larger than 48.7°, no light is refracted into the water. What is the refractive index of the glass?

33.22. Light is incident along the normal on face *AB* of a glass prism of refractive index 1.52, as shown in Fig. 33.41. Find the largest value the angle α can have without any light refracted out of the prism at face *AC* if (a) the prism is immersed in air and (b) the prism is immersed in water.

Figure **33.41** Exercise 33.22.

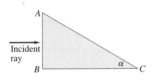

33.23. A ray of light in diamond (index of refraction 2.42) is incident on an interface with air. What is the *largest* angle the ray can make with the normal and not be totally reflected back into the diamond?

Section 33.4 Dispersion

33.24. A beam of light strikes a sheet of glass at an angle of 57.0° with the normal in air. You observe that red light makes an angle of 38.1° with the normal in the glass, while violet light makes a 36.7° angle. (a) What are the indexes of refraction of this glass for these colors of light? (b) What are the speeds of red and violet light in the glass?

Section 33.5 Polarization

33.25. A beam of unpolarized light of intensity I_0 passes through a series of ideal polarizing filters with their polarizing directions turned to various angles as shown in Fig. 33.42. (a) What is the light intensity (in terms of I_0) at points *A*, *B*, and *C*? (b) If we remove the middle filter, what will be the light intensity at point *C*?

Figure **33.42** Exercise 33.25.

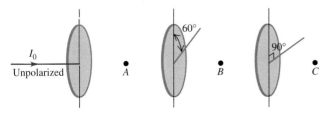

33.26. Light traveling in water strikes a glass plate at an angle of incidence of 53.0°; part of the beam is reflected and part is refracted. If the reflected and refracted portions make an angle of 90.0° with each other, what is the index of refraction of the glass?

33.27. A parallel beam of unpolarized light in air is incident at an angle of 54.5° (with respect to the normal) on a plane glass surface. The reflected beam is completely linearly polarized. (a) What is the refractive index of the glass? (b) What is the angle of refraction of the transmitted beam?

33.28. Light of original intensity I_0 passes through two ideal polarizing filters having their polarizing axes oriented as shown in Fig. 33.43. You want to adjust the angle ϕ so that the intensity at point *P* is equal to $I_0/10$. (a) If the original light is unpolarized, what should ϕ be? (b) If the original light is linearly polarized in the same direction as the polarizing axis of the first polarizer the light reaches, what should ϕ be?

Figure **33.43** Exercise 33.28.

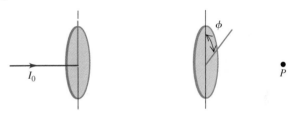

33.29. A beam of polarized light passes through a polarizing filter. When the angle between the polarizing axis of the filter and the direction of polarization of the light is θ, the intensity of the emerging beam is *I*. If you now want the intensity to be $I/2$, what should be the angle (in terms of θ) between the polarizing angle of the filter and the original direction of polarization of the light?

33.30. The refractive index of a certain glass is 1.66. For what incident angle is light reflected from the surface of this glass completely polarized if the glass is immersed in (a) air and (b) water?

33.31. Unpolarized light of intensity $20.0 \ \text{W/cm}^2$ is incident on two polarizing filters. The axis of the first filter is at an angle of 25.0° counterclockwise from the vertical (viewed in the direction the light is traveling), and the axis of the second filter is at 62.0° counterclockwise from the vertical. What is the intensity of the light after it has passed through the second polarizer?

33.32. A polarizer and an analyzer are oriented so that the maximum amount of light is transmitted. To what fraction of its maximum value is the intensity of the transmitted light reduced when the analyzer is rotated through (a) 22.5°; (b) 45.0°; (c) 67.5°?

33.33. Three Polarizing Filters. Three polarizing filters are stacked with the polarizing axes of the second and third at 45.0° and 90.0°, respectively, with that of the first. (a) If unpolarized light of intensity I_0 is incident on the stack, find the intensity and state of polarization of light emerging from each filter. (b) If the second filter is removed, what is the intensity of the light emerging from each remaining filter?

33.34. Three polarizing filters are stacked, with the polarizing axis of the second and third filters at 23.0° and 62.0°, respectively, to that of the first. If unpolarized light is incident on the stack, the light has intensity $75.0 \ \text{W/cm}^2$ after it passes through the stack. If the incident intensity is kept constant, what is the intensity of the light after it has passed through the stack if the second polarizer is removed?

*Section 33.6 Scattering of Light

33.35. A beam of white light passes through a uniform thickness of air. If the intensity of the scattered light in the middle of the green part of the visible spectrum is I, find the intensity (in terms of I) of scattered light in the middle of (a) the red part of the spectrum and (b) the violet part of the spectrum. Consult Table 32.1.

Section 33.7 Huygens's Principle

33.36. Bending Around Corners. Traveling particles do not bend around corners, but waves do. To see why, suppose that a plane wave front strikes the edge of a sharp object traveling perpendicular to the surface (Fig. 33.44). Use Huygens's principle to show that this wave will bend around the upper edge of the object. (*Note:* This effect, called *diffraction*, can easily be seen for water waves, but it also occurs for light, as you will see in Chapters 35 and 36. However due to the very short wavelength of visible light, it is not so apparent in daily life.)

Figure **33.44**
Exercise 33.36.

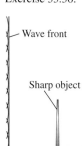

Problems

33.37. The Corner Reflector. An inside corner of a cube is lined with mirrors to make a corner reflector (see Example 33.3 in Section 33.2). A ray of light is reflected successively from each of three mutually perpendicular mirrors; show that its final direction is always exactly opposite to its initial direction.

33.38. A light beam is directed parallel to the axis of a hollow cylindrical tube. When the tube contains only air, it takes the light 8.72 ns to travel the length of the tube, but when the tube is filled with a transparent jelly, it takes the light 2.04 ns longer to travel its length. What is the refractive index of this jelly?

33.39. Light traveling in a material of refractive index n_1 is incident at angle θ_1 with respect to the normal at the interface with a slab of material that has parallel faces and refractive index n_2. After the light passes through this material, it is refracted into a material with refractive index n_3 and in this third material it makes an angle of θ_3 with the normal. (a) Find θ_3 in terms of θ_1 and the refractive indexes of the materials. (b) The ray in the third material is now reversed, so that it is incident on the n_3-to-n_2 interface with the angle θ_3 found in part (a). Show that when the light refracts into the material with refractive index n_1, the angle it makes with the normal is angle θ_1. This shows that the refracted ray is reversible. (c) Are reflected rays also reversible? Explain.

33.40. In a physics lab, light with wavelength 490 nm travels in air from a laser to a photocell in 17.0 ns. When a slab of glass 0.840 m thick is placed in the light beam, with the beam incident along the normal to the parallel faces of the slab, it takes the light 21.2 ns to travel from the laser to the photocell. What is the wavelength of the light in the glass?

33.41. A ray of light is incident in air on a block of a transparent solid whose index of refraction is n. If $n = 1.38$, what is the *largest* angle of incidence θ_a for which total internal reflection will occur at the vertical face (point A shown in Fig. 33.45)?

Figure **33.45**
Problem 33.41.

33.42. A light ray in air strikes the right-angle prism shown in Fig. 33.46. This ray consists of two different wavelengths. When it emerges at face AB, it has been split into two different rays that diverge from each other by 8.50°. Find the index of refraction of the prism for each of the two wavelengths.

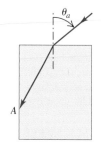

Figure **33.46** Problem 33.42.

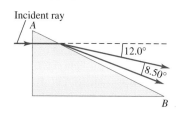

33.43. A quarter-wave plate converts linearly polarized light to circularly polarized light. Prove that a quarter-wave plate also converts circularly polarized light to linearly polarized light.

33.44. A glass plate 2.50 mm thick, with an index of refraction of 1.40, is placed between a point source of light with wavelength 540 nm (in vacuum) and a screen. The distance from source to screen is 1.80 cm. How many wavelengths are there between the source and the screen?

33.45. Old photographic plates were made of glass with a light-sensitive emulsion on the front surface. This emulsion was somewhat transparent. When a bright point source is focused on the front of the plate, the developed photograph will show a halo around the image of the spot. If the glass plate is 3.10 mm thick and the halos have an inner radius of 5.34 mm, what is the index of refraction of the glass? (*Hint:* Light from the spot on the front surface is scattered in all directions by the emulsion. Some of it is then totally reflected at the back surface of the plate and returns to the front surface.)

33.46. After a long day of driving you take a late-night swim in a motel swimming pool. When you go to your room, you realize that you have lost your room key in the pool. You borrow a powerful flashlight and walk around the pool, shining the light into it. The light shines on the key, which is lying on the bottom of the pool, when the flashlight is held 1.2 m above the water surface and is directed at the surface a horizontal distance of 1.5 m from the edge (Fig. 33.47). If the water here is 4.0 m deep, how far is the key from the edge of the pool?

Figure **33.47** Problem 33.46.

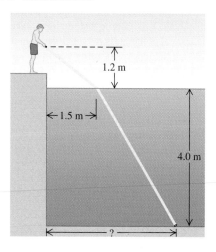

33.47. You sight along the rim of a glass with vertical sides so that the top rim is lined up with the opposite edge of the bottom (Fig. 33.48a). The glass is a thin-walled, hollow cylinder 16.0 cm high with a top and bottom of the glass diameter of 8.0 cm. While you keep your eye in the same position, a friend fills the glass with a transparent liquid, and you then see a dime that is lying at the center of the bottom of the glass (Fig. 33.48b). What is the index of refraction of the liquid?

Figure **33.48** Problem 33.47.

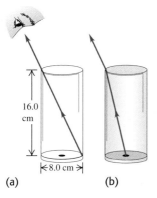

(a)   (b)

33.48. A beaker with a mirrored bottom is filled with a liquid whose index of refraction is 1.63. A light beam strikes the top surface of the liquid at an angle of 42.5° from the normal. At what angle from the normal will the beam exit from the liquid after traveling down through the liquid, reflecting from the mirrored bottom, and returning to the surface?

33.49. A thin layer of ice $(n = 1.309)$ floats on the surface of water $(n = 1.333)$ in a bucket. A ray of light from the bottom of the bucket travels upward through the water. (a) What is the largest angle with respect to the normal that the ray can make at the ice–water interface and still pass out into the air above the ice? (b) What is this angle after the ice melts?

33.50. A 45°−45°−90° prism is immersed in water. A ray of light is incident normally on one of its shorter faces. What is the minimum index of refraction that the prism must have if this ray is to be totally reflected within the glass at the long face of the prism?

33.51. The prism shown in Fig. 33.49 has a refractive index of 1.66, and the angles A are 25.0°. Two light rays m and n are parallel as they enter the prism. What is the angle between them after they emerge?

Figure **33.49** Problem 33.51.

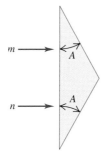

33.52. Light is incident normally on the short face of a 30°−60°−90° prism (Fig. 33.50). A drop of liquid is placed on the hypotenuse of the prism. If the index of the prism is 1.62, find the maximum index that the liquid may have if the light is to be totally reflected.

Figure **33.50** Problem 33.52.

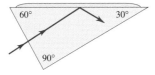

33.53. A horizontal cylindrical tank 2.20 m in diameter is half full of water. The space above the water is filled with a pressurized gas of unknown refractive index. A small laser can move along the curved bottom of the water and aims a light beam toward the center of the water surface (Fig. 33.51). You observe that when the laser has moved a distance $S = 1.09$ m or more (measured along the curved surface) from the lowest point in the water, no light enters the gas. (a) What is the index of refraction of the gas? (b) How long does it take the light beam to travel from the laser to the rim of the tank when (i) $S > 1.09$ m and (ii) $S < 1.09$ m?

Figure **33.51** Problem 33.53.

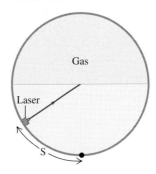

33.54. A large cube of glass has a metal reflector on one face and water on an adjoining face (Fig. 33.52). A light beam strikes the reflector, as shown. You observe that as you gradually increase the angle of the light beam, if $\theta \geq 59.2°$ no light enters the water. What is the speed of light in this glass?

Figure **33.52** Problem 33.54.

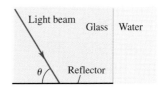

33.55. When the sun is either rising or setting and appears to be just on the horizon, it is in fact *below* the horizon. The explanation for this seeming paradox is that light from the sun bends slightly when entering the earth's atmosphere, as shown in Fig. 33.53. Since our perception is based on the idea that light travels in straight lines, we perceive the light to be coming from an apparent position that is an angle δ above the sun's true position. (a) Make the simplifying assumptions that the atmosphere has uniform density, and hence uniform index of refraction n, and extends to a height h above the earth's surface, at which point it abruptly stops. Show that the angle δ is given by

$$\delta = \arcsin\left(\frac{nR}{R + h}\right) - \arcsin\left(\frac{R}{R + h}\right)$$

where $R = 6378$ km is the radius of the earth. (b) Calculate δ using $n = 1.0003$ and $h = 20$ km. How does this compare to the

Figure **33.53** Problem 33.55.

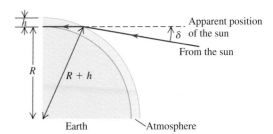

angular radius of the sun, which is about one quarter of a degree? (In actuality a light ray from the sun bends gradually, not abruptly, since the density and refractive index of the atmosphere change gradually with altitude.)

33.56. Fermat's Principle of Least Time. A ray of light traveling with speed c leaves point 1 shown in Fig. 33.54 and is reflected to point 2. The ray strikes the reflecting surface a horizontal distance x from point 1. (a) Show that the time t required for the light to travel from 1 to 2 is

$$t = \frac{\sqrt{y_1^2 + x^2} + \sqrt{y_2^2 + (l - x)^2}}{c}$$

(b) Take the derivative of t with respect to x. Set the derivative equal to zero to show that this time reaches its *minimum* value when $\theta_1 = \theta_2$, which is the law of reflection and corresponds to the actual path taken by the light. This is an example of Fermat's *principle of least time*, which states that among all possible paths between two points, the one actually taken by a ray of light is that for which the time of travel is a *minimum*. (In fact, there are some cases in which the time is a maximum rather than a minimum.)

Figure **33.54** Problem 33.56.

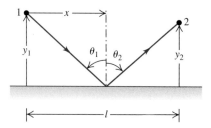

33.57. A ray of light goes from point A in a medium in which the speed of light is v_1 to point B in a medium in which the speed is v_2 (Fig. 33.55). The ray strikes the interface a horizontal distance x to the right of point A. (a) Show that the time required for the light to go from A to B is

$$t = \frac{\sqrt{h_1^2 + x^2}}{v_1} + \frac{\sqrt{h_2^2 + (l - x)^2}}{v_2}$$

(b) Take the derivative of t with respect to x. Set this derivative equal to zero to show that this time reaches its *minimum* value when $n_1 \sin\theta_1 = n_2 \sin\theta_2$. This is Snell's law, and corresponds to the actual path taken by the light. This is another example of Fermat's principle of least time (see Problem 33.56).

Figure **33.55** Problem 33.57.

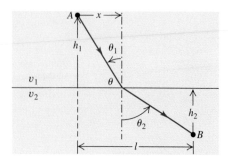

33.58. Light is incident in air at an angle θ_a (Fig. 33.56) on the upper surface of a transparent plate, the surfaces of the plate being plane and parallel to each other. (a) Prove that $\theta_a = \theta'_a$. (b) Show that this is true for any number of different parallel plates. (c) Prove that the lateral displacement d of the emergent beam is given by the relationship

$$d = t\frac{\sin(\theta_a - \theta'_b)}{\cos\theta'_b}$$

where t is the thickness of the plate. (d) A ray of light is incident at an angle of 66.0° on one surface of a glass plate 2.40 cm thick with an index of refraction 1.80. The medium on either side of the plate is air. Find the lateral displacement between the incident and emergent rays.

Figure **33.56** Problem 33.58.

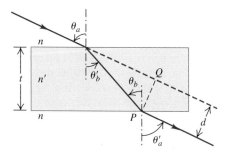

33.59. Light traveling downward is incident on a horizontal film of thickness t, as shown in Fig. 33.57. The incident ray splits into two rays, A and B. Ray A reflects from the top of the film. Ray B reflects from the bottom of the film and then refracts back into the material that is above the film. If the film has parallel faces, show that rays A and B end up parallel to each other.

Figure **33.57** Problem 33.59.

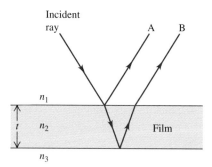

33.60. A thin beam of white light is directed at a flat sheet of silicate flint glass at an angle of 20.0° to the surface of the sheet. Due to dispersion in the glass, the beam is spread out as shown in a spectrum in Fig. 33.58. The refractive index of silicate flint glass versus wavelength is graphed in Fig. 33.18. (a) The rays a and b shown in Fig. 33.58 correspond to the extremes of the visible spectrum. Which corresponds to red and which to violet? Explain your reasoning. (b) For what thickness d of the glass sheet will the spectrum be 1.0 mm wide, as shown (see Problem 33.58)?

Figure **33.58** Problem 33.60.

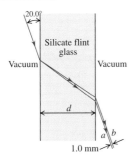

33.61. Angle of Deviation. The incident angle θ_a shown in Fig. 33.59 is chosen so that the light passes symmetrically through the prism, which has refractive index n and apex angle A. (a) Show that the angle of deviation δ (the angle between the initial and final directions of the ray) is given by

$$\sin\frac{A+\delta}{2} = n\sin\frac{A}{2}$$

(When the light passes through symmetrically, as shown, the angle of deviation is a minimum.) (b) Use the result of part (a) to find the angle of deviation for a ray of light passing symmetrically through a prism having three equal angles $(A = 60.0°)$ and $n = 1.52$. (c) A certain glass has a refractive index of 1.61 for red light (700 nm) and 1.66 for violet light (400 nm). If both colors pass through symmetrically, as described in part (a), and if $A = 60.0°$, find the difference between the angles of deviation for the two colors.

Figure **33.59** Problem 33.61.

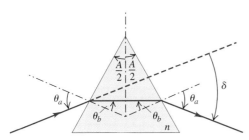

33.62. A beam of unpolarized sunlight strikes the vertical plastic wall of a water tank at an unknown angle. Some of the light reflects from the wall and enters the water (Fig. 33.60). The refractive index of the plastic wall is 1.61. If the light that has been reflected from the wall into the water is observed to be completely polarized, what angle does this beam make with the normal inside the water?

Figure **33.60** Problem 33.62.

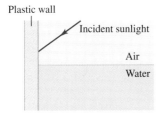

33.63. A beam of light traveling horizontally is made of an unpolarized component with intensity I_0 and a polarized component

with intensity I_p. The plane of polarization of the polarized component is oriented at an angle of θ with respect to the vertical. The data in the table give the intensity measured through a polarizer with an orientation of ϕ with respect to the vertical. (a) What is the orientation of the polarized component? (That is, what is the angle θ?) (b) What are the values of I_0 and I_p?

$\phi(°)$	$I_{total}(\text{W/m}^2)$	$\phi(°)$	$I_{total}(\text{W/m}^2)$
0	18.4	100	8.6
10	21.4	110	6.3
20	23.7	120	5.2
30	24.8	130	5.2
40	24.8	140	6.3
50	23.7	150	8.6
60	21.4	160	11.6
70	18.4	170	15.0
80	15.0	180	18.4
90	11.6		

33.64. A certain birefringent material has indexes of refraction n_1 and n_2 for the two perpendicular components of linearly polarized light passing through it. The corresponding wavelengths are $\lambda_1 = \lambda_0/n_1$ and λ_0/n_2, where λ_0 is the wavelength in vacuum. (a) If the crystal is to function as a quarter-wave plate, the number of wavelengths of each component within the material must differ by $\frac{1}{4}$. Show that the minimum thickness for a quarter-wave plate is

$$d = \frac{\lambda_0}{4(n_1 - n_2)}$$

(b) Find the minimum thickness of a quarter-wave plate made of siderite $(\text{FeO}\cdot\text{CO}_2)$ if the indexes of refraction are $n_1 = 1.875$ and $n_2 = 1.635$ and the wavelength in vacuum is $\lambda_0 = 589$ nm.

Challenge Problems

33.65. Consider two vibrations of equal amplitude and frequency but differing in phase, one along the x-axis,

$$x = a\sin(\omega t - \alpha)$$

and the other along the y-axis,

$$y = a\sin(\omega t - \beta)$$

These can be written as follows:

$$\frac{x}{a} = \sin\omega t\cos\alpha - \cos\omega t\sin\alpha \qquad (1)$$

$$\frac{y}{a} = \sin\omega t\cos\beta - \cos\omega t\sin\beta \qquad (2)$$

(a) Multiply Eq. (1) by $\sin\beta$ and Eq. (2) by $\sin\alpha$, and then subtract the resulting equations. (b) Multiply Eq. (1) by $\cos\beta$ and Eq. (2) by $\cos\alpha$, and then subtract the resulting equations. (c) Square and add the results of parts (a) and (b). (d) Derive the equation $x^2 + y^2 - 2xy\cos\delta = a^2\sin^2\delta$, where $\delta = \alpha - \beta$. (e) Use the above result to justify each of the diagrams in Fig. 33.61 (next page). In the figure, the angle given is the phase difference between two simple harmonic motions of the same frequency and amplitude, one horizontal (along the x-axis) and the other vertical (along the y-axis). The figure thus shows the resultant motion from the superposition of the two perpendicular harmonic motions.

Figure **33.61** Challenge Problem 33.65.

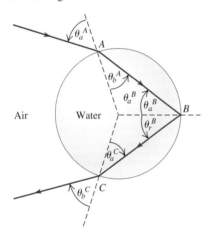

0	$\dfrac{\pi}{4}$	$\dfrac{\pi}{2}$	$\dfrac{3\pi}{4}$	π	$\dfrac{5\pi}{4}$	$\dfrac{3\pi}{2}$	$\dfrac{7\pi}{4}$	2π

33.66. A rainbow is produced by the reflection of sunlight by spherical drops of water in the air. Figure 33.62 shows a ray that refracts into a drop at point A, is reflected from the back surface of the drop at point B, and refracts back into the air at point C. The angles of incidence and refraction, θ_a and θ_b, are shown at points A and C, and the angles of incidence and reflection, θ_a and θ_r, are shown at point B. (a) Show that $\theta_a^B = \theta_b^A$, $\theta_a^C = \theta_b^A$, and $\theta_b^C = \theta_a^A$. (b) Show that the angle in radians between the ray before it enters the drop at A and after it exits at C (the total angular deflection of the ray) is $\Delta = 2\theta_a^A - 4\theta_b^A + \pi$. (*Hint:* Find the angular deflec-

Figure **33.62** Challenge Problem 33.66.

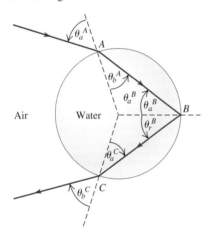

tions that occur at A, B, and C, and add them to get Δ.) (c) Use Snell's law to write Δ in terms of θ_a^A and n, the refractive index of the water in the drop. (d) A rainbow will form when the angular deflection Δ is *stationary* in the incident angle θ_a^A—that is, when $d\Delta/d\theta_a^A = 0$. If this condition is satisfied, all the rays with incident angles close to θ_a^A will be sent back in the same direction, producing a bright zone in the sky. Let θ_1 be the value of θ_a^A for which this occurs. Show that $\cos^2\theta_1 = \frac{1}{3}(n^2 - 1)$. (*Hint:* You may find the derivative formula $d(\arcsin u(x))/dx = (1 - u^2)^{-1/2} (du/dx)$ helpful.) (e) The index of refraction in water is 1.342 for violet light and 1.330 for red light. Use the results of parts (c) and (d) to find θ_1 and Δ for violet and red light. Do your results agree with the angles shown in Fig. 33.20d? When you view the rainbow, which color, red or violet, is higher above the horizon?

33.67. A *secondary rainbow* is formed when the incident light undergoes two internal reflections in a spherical drop of water as shown in Fig. 33.20e. (See Challenge Problem 33.66.) (a) In terms of the incident angle θ_a^A and the refractive index n of the drop, what is the angular deflection Δ of the ray? That is, what is the angle between the ray before it enters the drop and after it exits? (b) What is the incident angle θ_2 for which the derivative of Δ with respect to the incident angle θ_a^A is zero? (c) The indexes of refraction for red and violet light in water are given in part (e) of Challenge Problem 33.66. Use the results of parts (a) and (b) to find θ_2 and Δ for violet and red light. Do your results agree with the angles shown in Fig. 33.20e? When you view a secondary rainbow, is red or violet higher above the horizon? Explain.

GEOMETRIC OPTICS

34

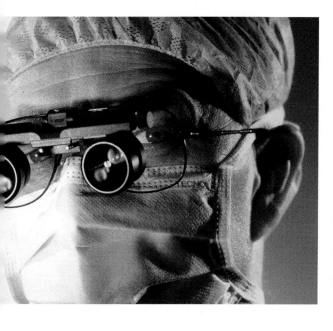

? How do magnifying lenses work? At what distance from the object being examined do they provide the sharpest view?

LEARNING GOALS

By studying this chapter, you will learn:

- How a plane mirror forms an image.

- Why concave and convex mirrors form different kinds of image.

- How images can be formed by a curved interface between two transparent materials.

- What aspects of a lens determine the type of image that it produces.

- What determines the field of view of a camera lens.

- What causes various defects in human vision, and how they can be corrected.

- The principle of the simple magnifier.

- How microscopes and telescopes work.

Your reflection in the bathroom mirror, the view of the moon through a telescope, the patterns seen in a kaleidoscope—all of these are examples of *images.* In each case the object that you're looking at appears to be in a different place than its actual position: Your reflection is on the other side of the mirror, the moon appears to be much closer when seen through a telescope, and objects seen in a kaleidoscope seem to be in many places at the same time. In each case, light rays that come from a point on an object are deflected by reflection or refraction (or a combination of the two), so they converge toward or appear to diverge from a point called an *image point.* Our goal in this chapter is to see how this is done and to explore the different kinds of images that can be made with simple optical devices.

To understand images and image formation, all we need are the ray model of light, the laws of reflection and refraction, and some simple geometry and trigonometry. The key role played by geometry in our analysis is the reason for the name *geometric optics* that is given to the study of how light rays form images. We'll begin our analysis with one of the simplest image-forming optical devices, a plane mirror. We'll go on to study how images are formed by curved mirrors, by refracting surfaces, and by thin lenses. Our results will lay the foundation for understanding many familiar optical instruments, including camera lenses, magnifiers, the human eye, microscopes, and telescopes.

34.1 Reflection and Refraction at a Plane Surface

Before discussing what is meant by an image, we first need the concept of **object** as it is used in optics. By an *object* we mean anything from which light rays radiate. This light could be emitted by the object itself if it is *self-luminous,* like the glowing filament of a light bulb. Alternatively, the light could be emitted by

Act|v Physics
ONLINE

15.4 Geometric Optics: Plane Mirrors

34.1 Light rays radiate from a point object P in all directions.

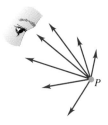

34.2 Light rays from the object at point P are reflected from a plane mirror. The reflected rays entering the eye look as though they had come from image point P'.

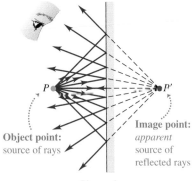

Object point: source of rays

Image point: *apparent* source of reflected rays

Plane mirror

34.3 Light rays from the object at point P are refracted at the plane interface. The refracted rays entering the eye look as though they had come from image point P'.

When $n_a > n_b$, P' is closer to the surface than P; for $n_a < n_b$, the reverse is true.

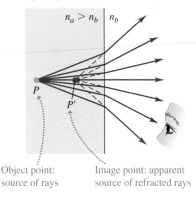

$n_a > n_b$ | n_b

Object point: source of rays

Image point: apparent source of refracted rays

another source (such as a lamp or the sun) and then reflected from the object; an example is the light you see coming from the pages of this book. Figure 34.1 shows light rays radiating in all directions from an object at a point P. For an observer to see this object directly, there must be no obstruction between the object and the observer's eyes. Note that light rays from the object reach the observer's left and right eyes at different angles; these differences are processed by the observer's brain to infer the *distance* from the observer to the object.

The object in Fig. 34.1 is a **point object** that has no physical extent. Real objects with length, width, and height are called **extended objects.** To start with, we'll consider only an idealized point object, since we can always think of an extended object as being made up of a very large number of point objects.

Suppose some of the rays from the object strike a smooth, plane reflecting surface (Fig. 34.2). This could be the surface of a material with a different index of refraction, which reflects part of the incident light, or a polished metal surface that reflects almost 100% of the light that strikes it. We will always draw the reflecting surface as a black line with a shaded area behind it, as in Fig. 34.2. Bathroom mirrors have a thin sheet of glass that lies in front of and protects the reflecting surface; we'll ignore the effects of this thin sheet.

According to the law of reflection, all rays striking the surface are reflected at an angle from the normal equal to the angle of incidence. Since the surface is plane, the normal is in the same direction at all points on the surface, and we have *specular* reflection. After the rays are reflected, their directions are the same as though they had come from point P'. We call point P an *object point* and point P' the corresponding *image point,* and we say that the reflecting surface forms an **image** of point P. An observer who can see only the rays reflected from the surface, and who doesn't know that he's seeing a reflection, *thinks* that the rays originate from the image point P'. The image point is therefore a convenient way to describe the directions of the various reflected rays, just as the object point P describes the directions of the rays arriving at the surface *before* reflection.

If the surface in Fig. 34.2 were *not* smooth, the reflection would be *diffuse,* and rays reflected from different parts of the surface would go in uncorrelated directions (see Fig. 33.6b). In this case there would not be a definite image point P' from which all reflected rays seem to emanate. You can't see your reflection in the surface of a tarnished piece of metal because its surface is rough; polishing the metal smoothes the surface so that specular reflection occurs and a reflected image becomes visible.

An image is also formed by a plane *refracting* surface, as shown in Fig. 34.3. Rays coming from point P are refracted at the interface between two optical materials. When the angles of incidence are small, the final directions of the rays after refraction are the same as though they had come from point P', as shown, and again we call P' an *image point.* In Section 33.2 we described how this effect makes underwater objects appear closer to the surface than they really are (see Fig. 33.9).

In both Figs. 34.2 and 34.3 the rays do not actually pass through the image point P'. Indeed, if the mirror in Fig. 34.2 is opaque, there is no light at all on its right side. If the outgoing rays don't actually pass through the image point, we call the image a **virtual image.** Later we will see cases in which the outgoing rays really *do* pass through an image point, and we will call the resulting image a **real image.** The images that are formed on a projection screen, on the photographic film in a camera, and on the retina of your eye are real images.

Image Formation by a Plane Mirror

Let's concentrate for now on images produced by *reflection;* we'll return to refraction later in the chapter. To find the precise location of the virtual image P' that a plane mirror forms of an object at P, we use the construction shown in Fig. 34.4. The figure shows two rays diverging from an object point P at a distance s to the left of a plane mirror. We call s the **object distance.** The ray PV is incident normally on the mirror (that is, it is perpendicular to the mirror surface), and it returns along its original path.

The ray PB makes an angle θ with PV. It strikes the mirror at an angle of incidence θ and is reflected at an equal angle with the normal. When we extend the two reflected rays backward, they intersect at point P', at a distance s' behind the mirror. We call s' the **image distance.** The line between P and P' is perpendicular to the mirror. The two triangles PVB and $P'VB$ are congruent, so P and P' are at equal distances from the mirror, and s and s' have equal magnitudes. The image point P' is located exactly opposite the object point P as far *behind* the mirror as the object point is from the front of the mirror.

We can repeat the construction of Fig. 34.4 for each ray diverging from P. The directions of *all* the outgoing reflected rays are the same as though they had originated at point P', confirming that P' is the *image* of P. No matter where the observer is located, she will always see the image at the point P'.

Sign Rules

Before we go further, let's introduce some general sign rules. These may seem unnecessarily complicated for the simple case of an image formed by a plane mirror, but we want to state the rules in a form that will be applicable to *all* the situations we will encounter later. These will include image formation by a plane or spherical reflecting or refracting surface, or by a pair of refracting surfaces forming a lens. Here are the rules:

1. **Sign rule for the object distance:** When the object is on the same side of the reflecting or refracting surface as the incoming light, the object distance s is positive; otherwise, it is negative.
2. **Sign rule for the image distance:** When the image is on the same side of the reflecting or refracting surface as the outgoing light, the image distance s' is positive; otherwise, it is negative.
3. **Sign rule for the radius of curvature of a spherical surface:** When the center of curvature C is on the same side as the outgoing light, the radius of curvature is positive; otherwise, it is negative.

Figure 34.5 illustrates rules 1 and 2 for two different situations. For a mirror the incoming and outgoing sides are always the same; for example, in Figs. 34.2, 34.4, and 34.5a they are both the left side. For the refracting surfaces in Figs. 34.3 and 34.5b the incoming and outgoing sides are on the left and right sides, respectively, of the interface between the two materials. (Note that other textbooks may use different rules.)

In Figs. 34.4 and 34.5a the object distance s is *positive* because the object point P is on the incoming side (the left side) of the reflecting surface. The image distance s' is *negative* because the image point P' is *not* on the outgoing side (the left side) of the surface. The object and image distances s and s' are related simply by

$$s = -s' \qquad \text{(plane mirror)} \qquad (34.1)$$

For a plane reflecting or refracting surface, the radius of curvature is infinite and not a particularly interesting or useful quantity; in these cases we really don't need sign rule 3. But this rule will be of great importance when we study image formation by *curved* reflecting and refracting surfaces later in the chapter.

Image of an Extended Object: Plane Mirror

Next we consider an *extended* object with finite size. For simplicity we often consider an object that has only one dimension, like a slender arrow, oriented parallel to the reflecting surface; an example is the arrow PQ in Fig. 34.6. The distance from the head to the tail of an arrow oriented in this way is called its *height;* in Fig. 34.6 the height is y. The image formed by such an extended object is an

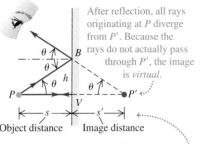

34.4 Construction for determining the location of the image formed by a plane mirror. The image point P' is as far behind the mirror as the object point P is in front of it.

After reflection, all rays originating at P diverge from P'. Because the rays do not actually pass through P', the image is *virtual.*

Triangles PVB and $P'VB$ are congruent, so $|s| = |s'|$.

34.5 For both of these situations, the object distance s is positive (rule 1) and the image distance s' is negative (rule 2).

(a) Plane mirror

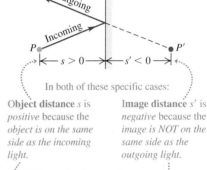

In both of these specific cases:

Object distance s is *positive* because the object is on the same side as the incoming light.

Image distance s' is *negative* because the image is NOT on the same side as the outgoing light.

(b) Plane refracting interface

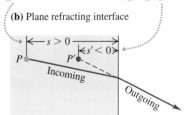

34.6 Construction for determining the height of an image formed by reflection at a plane reflecting surface.

For a plane mirror, PQV and $P'Q'V$ are congruent, so $y = y'$ and the object and image are the same size (the lateral magnification is 1).

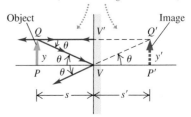

extended image; to each point on the object, there corresponds a point on the image. Two of the rays from Q are shown; *all* the rays from Q appear to diverge from its image point Q' after reflection. The image of the arrow is the line $P'Q'$, with height y'. Other points of the object PQ have image points between P' and Q'. The triangles PQV and $P'Q'V$ are congruent, so the object PQ and image $P'Q'$ have the same size and orientation, and $y = y'$.

The ratio of image height to object height, y'/y, in *any* image-forming situation is called the **lateral magnification** m; that is,

$$m = \frac{y'}{y} \qquad \text{(lateral magnification)} \qquad (34.2)$$

Thus for a plane mirror the lateral magnification m is unity. When you look at yourself in a plane mirror, your image is the same size as the real you.

In Fig. 34.6 the image arrow points in the *same* direction as the object arrow; we say that the image is **erect.** In this case, y and y' have the same sign, and the lateral magnification m is positive. The image formed by a plane mirror is always erect, so y and y' have both the same magnitude and the same sign; from Eq. (34.2) the lateral magnification of a plane mirror is always $m = +1$. Later we will encounter situations in which the image is **inverted;** that is, the image arrow points in the direction *opposite* to that of the object arrow. For an inverted image, y and y' have *opposite* signs, and the lateral magnification m is *negative*.

The object in Fig. 34.6 has only one dimension. Figure 34.7 shows a *three-dimensional* object and its three-dimensional virtual image formed by a plane mirror. The object and image are related in the same way as a left hand and a right hand.

CAUTION **Reflections in a plane mirror** At this point, you may be asking, "Why does a plane mirror reverse images left and right but not top and bottom?" This question is quite misleading! As Fig. 34.7 shows, the up-down image $P'Q'$ and the left-right image $P'S'$ are parallel to their objects and are not reversed at all. Only the front-back image $P'R'$ is reversed relative to PR. Hence it's most correct to say that a plane mirror reverses *back to front.* To verify this object-image relationship, point your thumbs along PR and $P'R'$, your forefingers along PQ and $P'Q'$, and your middle fingers along PS and $P'S'$. When an object and its image are related in this way, the image is said to be **reversed;** this means that *only* the front-back dimension is reversed.

The reversed image of a three-dimensional object formed by a plane mirror is the same *size* as the object in all its dimensions. When the transverse dimensions of object and image are in the same direction, the image is erect. Thus a plane mirror always forms an erect but reversed image. Figure 34.8 illustrates this point.

An important property of all images formed by reflecting or refracting surfaces is that an *image* formed by one surface or optical device can serve as the *object* for a second surface or device. Figure 34.9 shows a simple example. Mirror 1 forms an image P_1' of the object point P, and mirror 2 forms another image P_2', each in the way we have just discussed. But in addition, the image P_1' formed by mirror 1 serves an object for mirror 2, which then forms an image of this object at point P_3' as shown. Similarly, mirror 1 uses the image P_2' formed by mirror 2 as an object and forms an image of it. We leave it to you to show that this image point is also at P_3'. The idea that an image formed by one device can act as the object for a second device is of great importance in geometric optics. We will use it later in this chapter to locate the image formed by two successive curved-surface refractions in a lens. This idea will help us to understand image formation by combinations of lenses, as in a microscope or a refracting telescope.

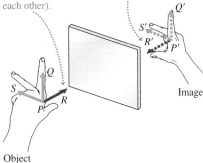

34.7 The image formed by a plane mirror is virtual, erect, and reversed. It is the same size as the object.

An image made by a plane mirror is reversed back to front: the image thumb $P'R'$ and object thumb PR point in opposite directions (toward each other).

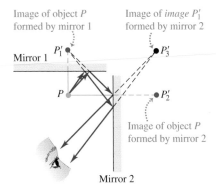

34.8 The image formed by a plane mirror is reversed; the image of a right hand is a left hand, and so on. (The hand is resting on a horizontal mirror.) Are images of the letters H and A reversed?

34.9 Images P_1' and P_2' are formed by a single reflection of each ray from the object at P. Image P_3', located by treating either of the other images as an object, is formed by a double reflection of each ray.

Test Your Understanding of Section 34.1 If you walk directly toward a plane mirror at a speed v, at what speed does your image approach you? (i) slower than v; (ii) v; (iii) faster than v but slower than $2v$; (iv) $2v$; (v) faster than $2v$.

34.2 Reflection at a Spherical Surface

A plane mirror produces an image that is the same size as the object. But there are many applications for mirrors in which the image and object must be of different sizes. A magnifying mirror used when applying makeup gives an image that is *larger* than the object, and surveillance mirrors (used in stores to help spot shoplifters) give an image that is *smaller* than the object. There are also applications of mirrors in which a *real* image is desired, so light rays do indeed pass through the image point P'. A plane mirror by itself cannot perform any of these tasks. Instead, *curved* mirrors are used.

Image of a Point Object: Spherical Mirror

We'll consider the special (and easily analyzed) case of image formation by a *spherical* mirror. Figure 34.10a shows a spherical mirror with radius of curvature R, with its concave side facing the incident light. The **center of curvature** of the surface (the center of the sphere of which the surface is a part) is at C, and the **vertex** of the mirror (the center of the mirror surface) is at V. The line CV is called the **optic axis**. Point P is an object point that lies on the optic axis; for the moment, we assume that the distance from P to V is greater than R.

Ray PV, passing through C, strikes the mirror normally and is reflected back on itself. Ray PB, at an angle α with the axis, strikes the mirror at B, where the angles of incidence and reflection are θ. The reflected ray intersects the axis at point P'. We will show shortly that *all* rays from P intersect the axis at the *same* point P', as in Fig. 34.10b, provided that the angle α is small. Point P' is therefore the *image* of object point P. Unlike the reflected rays in Fig. 34.1, the reflected rays in Fig. 34.10b actually do intersect at point P', then diverge from P' as if they had originated at this point. Thus P' is a *real* image.

To see the usefulness of having a real image, suppose that the mirror is in a darkened room in which the only source of light is a self-luminous object at P. If you place a small piece of photographic film at P', all the rays of light coming from point P that reflect off the mirror will strike the same point P' on the film; when developed, the film will show a single bright spot, representing a sharply focused image of the object at point P. This principle is at the heart of most astronomical telescopes, which use large concave mirrors to make photographs of celestial objects. With a *plane* mirror like that in Fig. 34.2, placing a piece of film at the image point P' would be a waste of time; the light rays never actually pass through the image point, and the image can't be recorded on film. Real images are *essential* for photography.

Let's now find the location of the real image point P' in Fig. 34.10a and prove the assertion that all rays from P intersect at P' (provided that their angle with the optic axis is small). The object distance, measured from the vertex V, is s; the image distance, also measured from V, is s'. The signs of s, s', and the radius of curvature R are determined by the sign rules given in Section 34.1. The object point P is on the same side as the incident light, so according to sign rule 1, s is positive. The image point P' is on the same side as the reflected light, so according to sign rule 2, the image distance s' is also positive. The center of curvature C is on the same side as the reflected light, so according to sign rule 3, R, too, is positive; R is always positive when reflection occurs at the *concave* side of a surface Fig. 34.11).

34.10 (a) A concave spherical mirror forms a real image of a point object P on the mirror's optic axis. (b) The eye sees some of the outgoing rays and perceives them as having come from P'.

(a) Construction for finding the position P' of an image formed by a concave spherical mirror

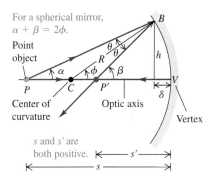

(b) The paraxial approximation, which holds for rays with small α

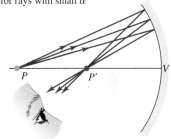

All rays from P that have a small angle α pass through P', forming a real image.

34.11 The sign rule for the radius of a spherical mirror.

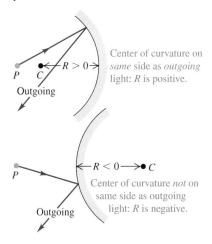

We now use the following theorem from plane geometry: An exterior angle of a triangle equals the sum of the two opposite interior angles. Applying this theorem to triangles PBC and $P'BC$ in Fig. 34.10a, we have

$$\phi = \alpha + \theta \qquad \beta = \phi + \theta$$

Eliminating θ between these equations gives

$$\alpha + \beta = 2\phi \qquad (34.3)$$

We may now compute the image distance s'. Let h represent the height of point B above the optic axis, and let δ represent the short distance from V to the foot of this vertical line. We now write expressions for the tangents of α, β, and ϕ, remembering that s, s', and R are all positive quantities:

$$\tan\alpha = \frac{h}{s - \delta} \qquad \tan\beta = \frac{h}{s' - \delta} \qquad \tan\phi = \frac{h}{R - \delta}$$

These trigonometric equations cannot be solved as simply as the corresponding algebraic equations for a plane mirror. However, *if the angle α is small,* the angles β and ϕ are also small. The tangent of an angle that is much less than one radian is nearly equal to the angle itself (measured in radians), so we can replace $\tan \alpha$ by α, and so on, in the equations above. Also, if α is small, we can neglect the distance δ compared with s', s, and R. So for small angles we have the following approximate relationships:

$$\alpha = \frac{h}{s} \qquad \beta = \frac{h}{s'} \qquad \phi = \frac{h}{R}$$

Substituting these into Eq. (34.3) and dividing by h, we obtain a general relationship among s, s', and R:

$$\frac{1}{s} + \frac{1}{s'} = \frac{2}{R} \qquad \left(\text{object–image relationship, spherical mirror}\right) \quad (34.4)$$

This equation does not contain the angle α. Hence *all* rays from P that make sufficiently small angles with the axis intersect at P' after they are reflected; this verifies our earlier assertion. Such rays, nearly parallel to the axis and close to it, are called **paraxial rays.** (The term **paraxial approximation** is often used for the approximations we have just described.) Since all such reflected light rays converge on the image point, a concave mirror is also called a *converging mirror.*

Be sure you understand that Eq. (34.4), as well as many similar relationships that we will derive later in this chapter and the next, is only *approximately* correct. It results from a calculation containing approximations, and it is valid only for paraxial rays. If we increase the angle α that a ray makes with the optic axis, the point P' where the ray intersects the optic axis moves somewhat closer to the vertex than for a paraxial ray. As a result, a spherical mirror, unlike a plane mirror, does not form a precise point image of a point object; the image is "smeared out." This property of a spherical mirror is called **spherical aberration.** When the primary mirror of the Hubble Space Telescope (Fig. 34.12a) was manufactured, tiny errors were made in its shape that led to an unacceptable amount of spherical aberration (Fig. 34.12b). The performance of the telescope improved dramatically after the installation of corrective optics (Fig. 34.12c).

If the radius of curvature becomes infinite $(R = \infty)$, the mirror becomes *plane,* and Eq. (34.4) reduces to Eq. (34.1) for a plane reflecting surface.

Focal Point and Focal Length

When the object point P is very far from the spherical mirror $(s = \infty)$, the incoming rays are parallel. (The star shown in Fig. 34.12c is an example of such a distant object.) From Eq. (34.4) the image distance s' in this case is given by

$$\frac{1}{\infty} + \frac{1}{s'} = \frac{2}{R} \qquad s' = \frac{R}{2}$$

34.12 (a), (b) Soon after the Hubble Space Telescope (HST) was placed in orbit in 1990, it was discovered that the concave primary mirror (also called the *objective mirror*) was too shallow by about $1/50$ the width of a human hair, leading to spherical aberration of the star's image. (c) After corrective optics were installed in 1993, the effects of spherical aberration were almost completely eliminated.

(a) The 2.4-m-diameter primary mirror of the Hubble Space Telescope

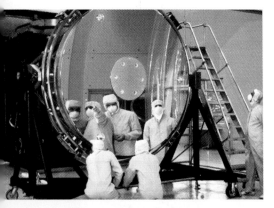

(b) A star seen with the original mirror

(c) The same star with corrective optics

The situation is shown in Fig. 34.13a. The beam of incident parallel rays converges, after reflection from the mirror, to a point F at a distance $R/2$ from the vertex of the mirror. The point F at which the incident parallel rays converge is called the **focal point;** we say that these rays are brought to a focus. The distance from the vertex to the focal point, denoted by f, is called the **focal length.** We see that f is related to the radius of curvature R by

$$f = \frac{R}{2} \qquad \text{(focal length of a spherical mirror)} \qquad (34.5)$$

The opposite situation is shown in Fig. 34.13b. Now the *object* is placed at the focal point F, so the object distance is $s = f = R/2$. The image distance s' is again given by Eq. (34.4):

$$\frac{2}{R} + \frac{1}{s'} = \frac{2}{R} \qquad \frac{1}{s'} = 0 \qquad s' = \infty$$

With the object at the focal point, the reflected rays in Fig. 34.13b are parallel to the optic axis; they meet only at a point infinitely far from the mirror, so the image is at infinity.

Thus the focal point F of a spherical mirror has the properties that (1) any incoming ray parallel to the optic axis is reflected through the focal point and (2) any incoming ray that passes through the focal point is reflected parallel to the optic axis. For spherical mirrors these statements are true only for paraxial rays. For parabolic mirrors these statements are *exactly* true; this is why parabolic mirrors are preferred for astronomical telescopes. Spherical or parabolic mirrors are used in flashlights and headlights to form the light from the bulb into a parallel beam. Some solar-power plants use an array of plane mirrors to simulate an approximately spherical concave mirror; light from the sun is collected by the mirrors and directed to the focal point, where a steam boiler is placed. (The concepts of focal point and focal length also apply to lenses, as we'll see in Section 34.4.)

We will usually express the relationship between object and image distances for a mirror, Eq. (34.4), in terms of the focal length f:

$$\frac{1}{s} + \frac{1}{s'} = \frac{1}{f} \qquad \text{(object–image relationship, spherical mirror)} \qquad (34.6)$$

Image of an Extended Object: Spherical Mirror

Now suppose we have an object with *finite* size, represented by the arrow PQ in Fig. 34.14, perpendicular to the optic axis CV. The image of P formed by paraxial rays is at P'. The object distance for point Q is very nearly equal to that for point P, so the image $P'Q'$ is nearly straight and perpendicular to the axis. Note that the object and image arrows have different sizes, y and y', respectively, and that they have opposite orientation. In Eq. (34.2) we defined the *lateral magnification m* as the ratio of image size y' to object size y:

$$m = \frac{y'}{y}$$

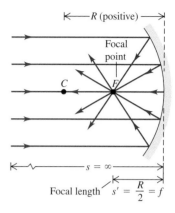

34.13 The focal point and focal length of a concave mirror.

(a) All parallel rays incident on a spherical mirror reflect through the focal point.

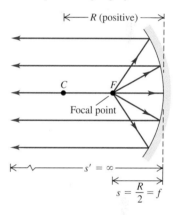

(b) Rays diverging from the focal point reflect to form parallel outgoing rays.

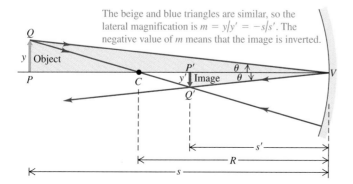

The beige and blue triangles are similar, so the lateral magnification is $m = y/y' = -s/s'$. The negative value of m means that the image is inverted.

34.14 Construction for determining the position, orientation, and height of an image formed by a concave spherical mirror.

Because triangles *PVQ* and *P'VQ'* in Fig. 34.14 are *similar,* we also have the relationship $y/s = -y'/s'$. The negative sign is needed because object and image are on opposite sides of the optic axis; if *y* is positive, *y'* is negative. Therefore

$$m = \frac{y'}{y} = -\frac{s'}{s} \qquad \text{(lateral magnification, spherical mirror)} \qquad (34.7)$$

If *m* is positive, the image is erect in comparison to the object; if *m* is negative, the image is *inverted* relative to the object, as in Fig. 34.14. For a *plane* mirror, $s = -s'$, so $y' = y$ and $m = +1$; since *m* is positive, the image is erect, and since $|m| = 1$, the image is the same size as the object.

CAUTION **Lateral magnification can be less than 1** Although the ratio of image size to object size is called the *lateral magnification,* the image formed by a mirror or lens may be larger than, smaller than, or the same size as the object. If it is smaller, then the lateral magnification is less than unity in absolute value: $|m| < 1$. The image formed by an astronomical telescope mirror or a camera lens is usually *much* smaller than the object. For example, the image of the bright star shown in Fig. 34.12c is just a few millimeters across, while the star itself is hundreds of thousands of kilometers in diameter. ▇

In our discussion of concave mirrors we have so far considered only objects that lie *outside* or at the focal point, so that the object distance *s* is greater than or equal to the (positive) focal length *f*. In this case the image point is on the same side of the mirror as the outgoing rays, and the image is real and inverted. If an object is placed *inside* the focal point of a concave mirror, so that $s < f$, the resulting image is *virtual* (that is, the image point is on the opposite side of the mirror from the object), *erect,* and *larger* than the object. Mirrors used when applying makeup (referred to at the beginning of this section) are concave mirrors; in use, the distance from the face to the mirror is less than the focal length, and an enlarged, erect image is seen. You can prove these statements about concave mirrors by applying Eqs. (34.6) and (34.7) (see Exercise 34.11). We'll also be able to verify these results later in this section, after we've learned some graphical methods for relating the positions and sizes of the object and the image.

Example 34.1 **Image formation by a concave mirror I**

A concave mirror forms an image, on a wall 3.00 m from the mirror, of the filament of a headlight lamp 10.0 cm in front of the mirror. (a) What are the radius of curvature and focal length of the mirror? (b) What is the height of the image if the height of the object is 5.00 mm?

SOLUTION

IDENTIFY: This problem uses the ideas developed in this section. Our target variables are the radius of curvature *R*, focal length *f*, and image height *y'*.

SET UP: Figure 34.15 shows the situation. We are given the distances from the mirror to the object (s) and from the mirror to the image (s'). We use the object–image relationship given by Eq. (34.6) to determine the focal length *f*, and then find the radius of curvature *R* using Eq. (34.5). Equation (34.7) lets us calculate the image height *y'* from the distances *s* and *s'* and the object height *y*.

EXECUTE: (a) Both the object and the image are on the concave side of the mirror (the reflective side), so both object distance and

34.15 Our sketch for this problem.

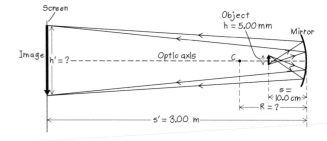

image distance are positive; we have $s = 10.0$ cm and $s' = 300$ cm. From Eq. (34.4),

$$\frac{1}{10.0 \text{ cm}} + \frac{1}{300 \text{ cm}} = \frac{2}{R}$$

$$R = \frac{2}{0.100 \text{ cm}^{-1} + 3.33 \times 10^{-3} \text{ cm}^{-1}} = 19.4 \text{ cm}$$

The focal length of the mirror is $f = R/2 = 9.7$ cm.

(b) From Eq. (34.7) the lateral magnification is

$$m = \frac{y'}{y} = -\frac{s'}{s} = -\frac{300 \text{ cm}}{10.0 \text{ cm}} = -30.0$$

Because m is negative, the image is inverted. The height of the image is 30.0 times the height of the object, or $(30.0)(5.00 \text{ mm}) = 150$ mm.

EVALUATE: Note that the object is placed just outside the focal point ($s = 10.0$ cm compared to $f = 9.7$ cm). This is very similar to what is done in automobile headlights. With the filament close to the focal point, the concave mirror produces a beam of nearly parallel rays.

Conceptual Example 34.2 | **Image formation by a concave mirror II**

In Example 34.1, suppose that the left half of the mirror's reflecting surface is covered with nonreflective soot. What effect will this have on the image of the filament?

SOLUTION

It would be natural to guess that the image would now show only half of the filament. But in fact the image will still show the *entire* filament. The explanation can be seen by examining Fig. 34.10b. Light rays coming from any object point P are reflected from *all* parts of the mirror and converge on the corresponding image point P'. If part of the mirror surface is made nonreflective or is removed altogether, the light rays from the remaining reflective surface still form an image of every part of the object.

The only effect of reducing the reflecting area is that the image becomes dimmer because less light energy reaches the image point. In our example the reflective area of the mirror is reduced by one-half, and the image will be one-half as bright. *Increasing* the reflective area makes the image brighter. To make reasonably bright images of distant stars, astronomical telescopes use mirrors that are up to several meters in diameter. Figure 34.12a shows an example.

Convex Mirrors

In Fig. 34.16a the *convex* side of a spherical mirror faces the incident light. The center of curvature is on the side opposite to the outgoing rays; according to sign rule 3 in Section 34.1, R is negative (see Fig. 34.11). Ray PB is reflected, with the angles of incidence and reflection both equal to θ. The reflected ray, projected backward, intersects the axis at P'. As with a concave mirror, *all* rays from P that are reflected by the mirror diverge from the same point P', provided that the angle α is small. Therefore P' is the image of P. The object distance s is positive, the image distance s' is negative, and the radius of curvature R is *negative* for a *convex* mirror.

Figure 34.16b shows two rays diverging from the head of the arrow PQ and the virtual image $P'Q'$ of this arrow. The same procedure that we used for a concave mirror can be used to show that for a convex mirror,

$$\frac{1}{s} + \frac{1}{s'} = \frac{2}{R}$$

and the lateral magnification is

$$m = \frac{y'}{y} = -\frac{s'}{s}$$

34.16 Image formation by a convex mirror.

(a) Construction for finding the position of an image formed by a convex mirror

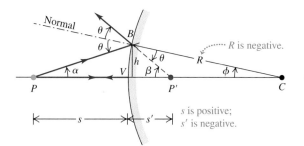

(b) Construction for finding the magnification of an image formed by a convex mirror

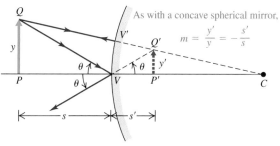

34.17 The focal point and focal length of a convex mirror.

(a) Paraxial rays incident on a convex spherical mirror diverge from a virtual focal point.

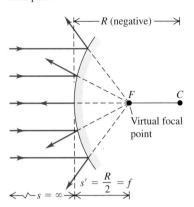

(b) Rays aimed at the virtual focal point are parallel to the axis after reflection.

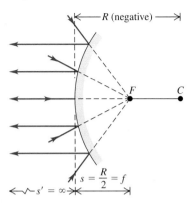

These expressions are exactly the same as Eqs. (34.4) and (34.7) for a concave mirror. Thus when we use our sign rules consistently, Eqs. (34.4) and (34.7) are valid for both concave and convex mirrors.

When R is negative (convex mirror), incoming rays that are parallel to the optic axis are not reflected through the focal point F. Instead, they diverge as though they had come from the point F at a distance f *behind* the mirror, as shown in Fig. 34.17a. In this case, f is the focal length, and F is called a *virtual focal point*. The corresponding image distance s' is negative, so both f and R are negative, and Eq. (34.5), $f = R/2$, holds for convex as well as concave mirrors. In Fig. 34.17b the incoming rays are converging as though they would meet at the virtual focal point F, and they are reflected parallel to the optic axis.

In summary, Eqs. (34.4) through (34.7), the basic relationships for image formation by a spherical mirror, are valid for both concave and convex mirrors, provided that we use the sign rules consistently.

Example 34.3 Santa's image problem

Santa checks himself for soot, using his reflection in a shiny silvered Christmas tree ornament 0.750 m away (Fig. 34.18a). The diameter of the ornament is 7.20 cm. Standard reference works state that he is a "right jolly old elf," so we estimate his height to be 1.6 m. Where and how tall is the image of Santa formed by the ornament? Is it erect or inverted?

SOLUTION

IDENTIFY: Santa is the object, and the surface of the ornament closest to Santa acts as a convex mirror. The relationships among object distance, image distance, focal length, and magnification are the same as for concave mirrors, provided we use the sign rules consistently.

34.18 (a) The ornament forms a virtual, reduced, erect image of Santa. (b) Our sketch of two of the rays forming the image.

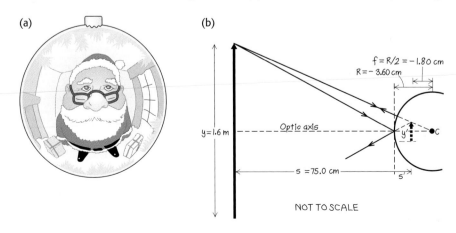

NOT TO SCALE

SET UP: Figure 34.18b shows the situation. Since the mirror is convex, its radius of curvature and focal length are negative. The object distance is $s = 0.750 \text{ m} = 75.0 \text{ cm}$ and Santa's height is $y = 1.6 \text{ m}$. We use Eq. (34.6) to determine the image distance s', and then use Eq. (34.7) to find the lateral magnification m and hence the image height y'. The sign of m tells us whether the image is erect or inverted.

EXECUTE: The radius of the convex mirror (half the diameter) is $R = -(7.20 \text{ cm})/2 = -3.60 \text{ cm}$, and the focal length is $f = R/2 = -1.80 \text{ cm}$. From Eq. (34.6),

$$\frac{1}{s'} = \frac{1}{f} - \frac{1}{s} = \frac{1}{-1.80 \text{ cm}} - \frac{1}{75.0 \text{ cm}}$$

$$s' = -1.76 \text{ cm}$$

Because s' is negative, the image is behind the mirror—that is, on the side opposite to the outgoing light (Fig. 34.18b)—and it is vir-

tual. The image is about halfway between the front surface of the ornament and its center.

The lateral magnification m is given by Eq. (34.7):

$$m = \frac{y'}{y} = -\frac{s'}{s} = -\frac{-1.76 \text{ cm}}{75.0 \text{ cm}} = 0.0234$$

Because m is positive, the image is erect. It is only about 0.0234 as tall as Santa himself:

$$y' = my = (0.0234)(1.6 \text{ m}) = 3.8 \times 10^{-2} \text{ m} = 3.8 \text{ cm}$$

EVALUATE: When the object distance s is positive, a convex mirror *always* forms an erect, virtual, reduced, reversed image. For this reason, convex mirrors are used for shoplifting surveillance in stores, at blind intersections, and as "wide-angle" rear-view mirrors for cars and trucks (including those that bear the legend "Objects in mirror are closer than they appear").

Graphical Methods for Mirrors

In Examples 34.1 and 34.3, we used Eqs. (34.6) and (34.7) to find the position and size of the image formed by a mirror. We can also determine the properties of the image by a simple *graphical* method. This method consists of finding the point of intersection of a few particular rays that diverge from a point of the object (such as point Q in Fig. 34.19) and are reflected by the mirror. Then (neglecting aberrations) *all* rays from this object point that strike the mirror will intersect at the same point. For this construction we always choose an object point that is *not* on the optic axis. Four rays that we can usually draw easily are shown in Fig. 34.19. These are called **principal rays.**

1. *A ray parallel to the axis,* after reflection, passes through the focal point F of a concave mirror or appears to come from the (virtual) focal point of a convex mirror.
2. *A ray through (or proceeding toward) the focal point F* is reflected parallel to the axis.
3. *A ray along the radius* through or away from the center of curvature C intersects the surface normally and is reflected back along its original path.
4. *A ray to the vertex V* is reflected forming equal angles with the optic axis.

34.19 The graphical method of locating an image formed by spherical mirror. The colors of the rays are for identification only; they do not refer to specific colors of light.

(a) Principal rays for concave mirror

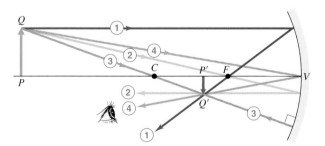

(b) Principal rays for convex mirror

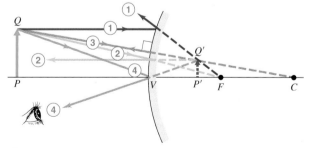

① Ray parallel to axis reflects through focal point.
② Ray through focal point reflects parallel to axis.
③ Ray through center of curvature intersects the surface normally and reflects along its original path.
④ Ray to vertex reflects symmetrically around optic axis.

① Reflected parallel ray appears to come from focal point.
② Ray toward focal point reflects parallel to axis.
③ As with concave mirror: Ray radial to center of curvature intersects the surface normally and reflects along its original path.
④ As with concave mirror: Ray to vertex reflects symmetrically around optic axis.

Once we have found the position of the image point by means of the intersection of any two of these principal rays $(1, 2, 3, 4)$, we can draw the path of any other ray from the object point to the same image point.

CAUTION **Principal rays are not the only rays** Although we've emphasized the principal rays, in fact *any* ray from the object that strikes the mirror will pass through the image point (for a real image) or appear to originate from the image point (for a virtual image). Usually, you only need to draw the principal rays, because these are all you need to locate the image. ▮

Problem-Solving Strategy 34.1   Image Formation by Mirrors

IDENTIFY *the relevant concepts:*   There are two different and complementary ways to solve problems involving image formation by mirrors. One approach uses equations, while the other involves drawing a principal-ray diagram. A successful problem solution uses *both* approaches.

SET UP *the problem:*   Determine the target variables. The three key quantities are the focal length, object distance, and image distance; typically you'll be given two of these and will have to determine the third.

EXECUTE *the solution* as follows:

1. The principal-ray diagram is to geometric optics what the free-body diagram is to mechanics. In any problem involving image formation by a mirror, *always* draw a principal-ray diagram first if you have enough information. (The same advice should be followed when dealing with lenses in the following sections.)

2. It is usually best to orient your diagrams consistently with the incoming rays traveling from left to right. Don't draw a lot of other rays at random; stick with the principal rays, the ones you know something about. Use a ruler and measure distances carefully! A freehand sketch will *not* give good results.

3. If your principal rays don't converge at a real image point, you may have to extend them straight backward to locate a virtual image point, as in Fig. 34.19b. We recommend drawing the extensions with broken lines. Another useful aid is to color-code the different principal rays, as is done in Fig. 34.19.

4. Check your results using Eq. (34.6), $1/s + 1/s' = 1/f$, and the lateral magnification equation, Eq. (34.7). The results you find using this equation must be consistent with your principal-ray diagram; if not, double check both your calculations and your diagram.

5. Pay careful attention to signs on object and image distances, radii of curvature, and object and image heights. A negative sign on any of these quantities *always* has significance. Use the equations and the sign rules carefully and consistently, and they will tell you the truth! Note that the *same* sign rules (given in Section 34.1) work for all four cases in this chapter: reflection and refraction from plane and spherical surfaces.

EVALUATE *your answer:*   You've already checked your results by using both diagrams and equations. But it always helps to take a look back and ask yourself, "Do these results make sense?"

Example 34.4   Concave mirror, different object distances

A concave mirror has a radius of curvature with absolute value 20 cm. Find graphically the image of an object in the form of an arrow perpendicular to the axis of the mirror at each of the following object distances: (a) 30 cm, (b) 20 cm, (c) 10 cm, and (d) 5 cm. Check the construction by *computing* the size and lateral magnification of each image.

SOLUTION

IDENTIFY: This problem asks us to use *both* graphical methods and calculations to find the image made by a mirror. This is a good practice to follow in all problems that involve image formation.

SET UP: We are given the radius of curvature $R = 20$ cm (positive since the mirror is concave) and hence the focal length $f = R/2 = 10$ cm. In each case we are told the object distance s and are asked to find the image distance s' and the lateral magnification $m = -s'/s$.

EXECUTE: Figure 34.20 shows the principal-ray diagrams for the four cases. Study each of these diagrams carefully, comparing each numbered ray with the description above. Several points are worth

noting. First, in (b) the object and image distances are equal. Ray 3 cannot be drawn in this case because a ray from Q through the center of curvature C does not strike the mirror. Ray 2 cannot be drawn in (c) because a ray from Q toward F also does not strike the mirror. In this case the outgoing rays are parallel, corresponding to an infinite image distance. In (d) the outgoing rays have no real intersection point; they must be extended backward to find the point from which they appear to diverge—that is, from the *virtual image point Q'*. The case shown in (d) illustrates the general observation that an object placed inside the focal point of a concave mirror produces a virtual image.

Measurements of the figures, with appropriate scaling, give the following approximate image distances: (a) 15 cm; (b) 20 cm; (c) ∞ or −∞ (because the outgoing rays are parallel and do not converge at any finite distance); (d) −10 cm. To *compute* these distances, we use Eq. (34.6) with $f = 10$ cm:

(a) $\dfrac{1}{30 \text{ cm}} + \dfrac{1}{s'} = \dfrac{1}{10 \text{ cm}}$ $s' = 15$ cm

(b) $\dfrac{1}{20 \text{ cm}} + \dfrac{1}{s'} = \dfrac{1}{10 \text{ cm}}$ $s' = 20$ cm

(c) $\dfrac{1}{10\text{ cm}} + \dfrac{1}{s'} = \dfrac{1}{10\text{ cm}}$ $\qquad s' = \infty \;(\text{or} -\infty)$

(d) $\dfrac{1}{5\text{ cm}} + \dfrac{1}{s'} = \dfrac{1}{10\text{ cm}}$ $\qquad s' = -10\text{ cm}$

In (a) and (b) the image is real; in (d) it is virtual. In (c) the image is formed at infinity.

The lateral magnifications measured from the figures are approximately (a) $-\frac{1}{2}$; (b) -1; (c) ∞ or $-\infty$ (because the image distance is infinite); (d) $+2$. *Computing* the magnifications from Eq. (34.7), we find:

(a) $m = -\dfrac{15\text{ cm}}{30\text{ cm}} = -\dfrac{1}{2}$

(b) $m = -\dfrac{20\text{ cm}}{20\text{ cm}} = -1$

(c) $m = -\dfrac{\infty\text{ cm}}{10\text{ cm}} = -\infty \;(\text{or} +\infty)$

(d) $m = -\dfrac{-10\text{ cm}}{5\text{ cm}} = +2$

In (a) and (b) the image is inverted; in (d) it is erect.

EVALUATE: Notice the trend as the object is moved closer to the mirror. When the object is far from the mirror, as in Fig. 34.20a, the image is smaller than the object, inverted, and real. As the object distance decreases, the image moves farther from the mirror and increases in size (Fig. 34.20b). When the object is at the focal point, the image is at infinity (Fig. 34.20c). If the object is moved inside the focal point, the image becomes larger than the object, erect, and virtual (Fig. 34.20d). You can test these conclusions by looking at objects reflected in the concave bowl of a metal spoon.

34.20 Using principal-ray diagrams to locate the image $P'Q'$ made by a concave mirror.

(a) Construction for $s = 30$ cm

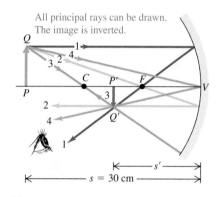

All principal rays can be drawn. The image is inverted.

(b) Construction for $s = 20$ cm

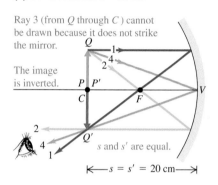

Ray 3 (from Q through C) cannot be drawn because it does not strike the mirror.

The image is inverted.

s and s' are equal.

(c) Construction for $s = 10$ cm

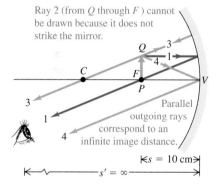

Ray 2 (from Q through F) cannot be drawn because it does not strike the mirror.

Parallel outgoing rays correspond to an infinite image distance.

(d) Construction for $s = 5$ cm

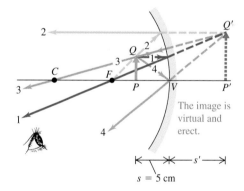

The image is virtual and erect.

Test Your Understanding of Section 34.2 A cosmetics mirror is designed so that your reflection appears right-side up and enlarged. (a) Is the mirror concave or convex? (b) To see an enlarged image, what should be the distance from the mirror (of focal length f) to your face? (i) $|f|$; (ii) less than $|f|$; (iii) greater than $|f|$.

34.3 Refraction at a Spherical Surface

As we mentioned in Section 34.1, images can be formed by refraction as well as by reflection. To begin with, let's consider refraction at a spherical surface—that is, at a spherical interface between two optical materials with different indexes of refraction. This analysis is directly applicable to some real optical systems, such as the human eye. It also provides a stepping-stone for the analysis of lenses, which usually have *two* spherical (or nearly spherical) surfaces.

Image of a Point Object: Spherical Refracting Surface

In Fig. 34.21 a spherical surface with radius R forms an interface between two materials with different indexes of refraction n_a and n_b. The surface forms an image P' of an object point P; we want to find how the object and image distances (s and s') are related. We will use the same sign rules that we used for spherical mirrors. The center of curvature C is on the outgoing side of the surface, so R is positive. Ray PV strikes the vertex V and is perpendicular to the surface (that is, to the plane that is tangent to the surface at the point of incidence V). It passes into the second material without deviation. Ray PB, making an angle α with the axis, is incident at an angle θ_a with the normal and is refracted at an angle θ_b. These rays intersect at P', a distance s' to the right of the vertex. The figure is drawn for the case $n_a < n_b$. The object and image distances are both positive.

We are going to prove that if the angle α is small, *all* rays from P intersect at the same point P', so P' is the *real image* of P. We use much the same approach as we did for spherical mirrors in Section 34.2. We again use the theorem that an exterior angle of a triangle equals the sum of the two opposite interior angles; applying this to the triangles PBC and $P'BC$ gives

$$\theta_a = \alpha + \phi \qquad \phi = \beta + \theta_b \qquad (34.8)$$

From the law of refraction,

$$n_a \sin \theta_a = n_b \sin \theta_b$$

Also, the tangents of α, β, and ϕ are

$$\tan \alpha = \frac{h}{s + \delta} \qquad \tan \beta = \frac{h}{s' - \delta} \qquad \tan \phi = \frac{h}{R - \delta} \qquad (34.9)$$

For paraxial rays, θ_a and θ_b are both small in comparison to a radian, and we may approximate both the sine and tangent of either of these angles by the angle itself (measured in radians). The law of refraction then gives

$$n_a \theta_a = n_b \theta_b$$

Combining this with the first of Eqs. (34.8), we obtain

$$\theta_b = \frac{n_a}{n_b} (\alpha + \phi)$$

When we substitute this into the second of Eqs. (34.8), we get

$$n_a \alpha + n_b \beta = (n_b - n_a) \phi \qquad (34.10)$$

Now we use the approximations $\tan \alpha = \alpha$, and so on, in Eqs. (34.9) and also neglect the small distance δ; those equations then become

$$\alpha = \frac{h}{s} \qquad \beta = \frac{h}{s'} \qquad \phi = \frac{h}{R}$$

34.21 Construction for finding the position of the image point P' of a point object P formed by refraction at a spherical surface. The materials to the left and right of the interface have refractive indexes n_a and n_b, respectively. In the case shown here, $n_a < n_b$.

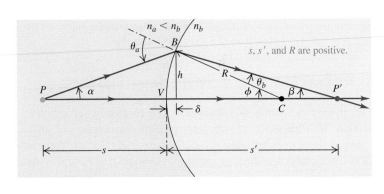

Finally, we substitute these into Eq. (34.10) and divide out the common factor h. We obtain

$$\frac{n_a}{s} + \frac{n_b}{s'} = \frac{n_b - n_a}{R} \qquad \text{(object–image relationship, spherical refracting surface)} \qquad (34.11)$$

This equation does not contain the angle α, so the image distance is the same for *all* paraxial rays emanating from P; this proves our assertion that P' is the image of P.

To obtain the lateral magnification m for this situation, we use the construction in Fig. 34.22. We draw two rays from point Q, one through the center of curvature C and the other incident at the vertex V. From the triangles PQV and $P'Q'V$,

$$\tan \theta_a = \frac{y}{s} \qquad \tan \theta_b = \frac{-y'}{s'}$$

and from the law of refraction,

$$n_a \sin \theta_a = n_b \sin \theta_b$$

For small angles,

$$\tan \theta_a = \sin \theta_a \qquad \tan \theta_b = \sin \theta_b$$

so finally

$$\frac{n_a y}{s} = -\frac{n_b y'}{s'} \qquad \text{or}$$

$$m = \frac{y'}{y} = -\frac{n_a s'}{n_b s} \qquad \text{(lateral magnification, spherical refracting surface)} \qquad (34.12)$$

Equations (34.11) and (34.12) can be applied to both convex and concave refracting surfaces, provided that you use the sign rules consistently. It doesn't matter whether n_b is greater or less than n_a. To verify these statements, you should construct diagrams like Figs. 34.21 and 34.22 for the following three cases: (i) $R > 0$ and $n_a > n_b$, (ii) $R < 0$ and $n_a < n_b$, and (iii) $R < 0$ and $n_a > n_b$. Then in each case, use your diagram to again derive Eqs. (34.11) and (34.12).

Here's a final note on the sign rule for the radius of curvature R of a surface. For the convex reflecting surface in Fig. 34.16, we considered R negative, but the convex *refracting* surface in Fig. 34.21 has a *positive* value of R. This may seem inconsistent, but it isn't. The rule is that R is positive if the center of curvature C is on the outgoing side of the surface and negative if C is on the other side. For the convex reflecting surface in Fig. 34.16, R is negative because point C is to the right of the surface but outgoing rays are to the left. For the convex refracting surface in Fig. 34.21, R is positive because both C and the outgoing rays are to the right of the surface.

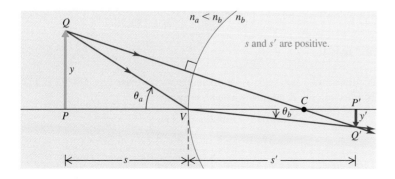

34.22 Construction for determining the height of an image formed by refraction at a spherical surface. In the case shown here, $n_a < n_b$.

34.23 Light rays refract as they pass through the curved surfaces of these water droplets.

Refraction at a curved surface is one reason gardeners avoid watering plants at midday. As sunlight enters a water drop resting on a leaf (Fig. 34.23), the light rays are refracted toward each other as in Figs. 34.21 and 34.22. The sunlight that strikes the leaf is therefore more concentrated and able to cause damage.

An important special case of a spherical refracting surface is a *plane* surface between two optical materials. This corresponds to setting $R = \infty$ in Eq. (34.11). In this case,

$$\frac{n_a}{s} + \frac{n_b}{s'} = 0 \qquad \text{(plane refracting surface)} \qquad (34.13)$$

To find the lateral magnification m for this case, we combine this equation with the general relationship, Eq. (34.12), obtaining the simple result

$$m = 1$$

That is, the image formed by a *plane* refracting surface always has the same lateral size as the object, and it is always erect.

An example of image formation by a plane refracting surface is the appearance of a partly submerged drinking straw or canoe paddle. When viewed from some angles, the object appears to have a sharp bend at the water surface because the submerged part appears to be only about three-quarters of its actual distance below the surface. (We commented on the appearance of a submerged object in Section 33.2; see Fig. 33.9.)

Example 34.5   Image formation by refraction I

A cylindrical glass rod in air (Fig. 34.24) has index of refraction 1.52. One end is ground to a hemispherical surface with radius $R = 2.00$ cm. (a) Find the image distance of a small object on the axis of the rod, 8.00 cm to the left of the vertex. (b) Find the lateral magnification.

SOLUTION

IDENTIFY: This problem uses the ideas of refraction at a curved surface. Our target variables are the image distance s' and the lateral magnification m.

SET UP: Here material a is air $(n_a = 1.00)$ and material b is the glass of which the rod is made $(n_b = 1.52)$. We are given $s =$

34.24 The glass rod in air forms a real image.

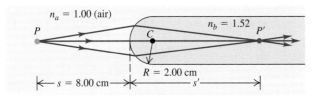

8.00 cm; the radius of the spherical surface is positive $(R = +2.00$ cm$)$ because the center of curvature is on the outgoing side of the surface. We use Eq. (34.11) to determine the image distance and Eq. (34.12) to find the lateral magnification.

EXECUTE: (a) From Eq. (34.11),

$$\frac{1.00}{8.00 \text{ cm}} + \frac{1.52}{s'} = \frac{1.52 - 1.00}{+2.00 \text{ cm}}$$
$$s' = +11.3 \text{ cm}$$

(b) From Eq. (34.12),

$$m = -\frac{n_a s'}{n_b s} = -\frac{(1.00)(11.3 \text{ cm})}{(1.52)(8.00 \text{ cm})} = -0.929$$

EVALUATE: Because the image distance s' is positive, the image is formed 11.3 cm to the *right* of the vertex (on the outgoing side), as shown in Fig. 34.24. The value of m tells us that the image is somewhat smaller than the object, and it is inverted. If the object is an arrow 1.000 mm high, pointing upward, the image is an arrow 0.929 mm high, pointing downward.

Example 34.6   Image formation by refraction II

The glass rod in Example 34.5 is immersed in water (index of refraction $n = 1.33$), as shown in Fig. 34.25. The other quantities have the same values as before. Find the image distance and lateral magnification.

SOLUTION

IDENTIFY: The situation is the same as in Example 34.5 except that now $n_a = 1.33$.

SET UP: As in Example 34.5, we use Eqs. (34.11) and (34.12) to determine s' and m, respectively.

EXECUTE: From Eq. (34.11),

$$\frac{1.33}{8.00 \text{ cm}} + \frac{1.52}{s'} = \frac{1.52 - 1.33}{+2.00 \text{ cm}}$$
$$s' = -21.3 \text{ cm}$$

34.25 When immersed in water, the glass rod forms a virtual image.

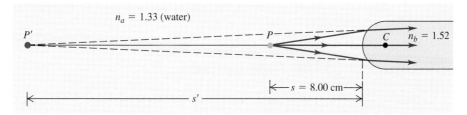

The lateral magnification in this case is

$$m = -\frac{(1.33)(-21.3 \text{ cm})}{(1.52)(8.00 \text{ cm})} = +2.33$$

EVALUATE: The negative value of s' means that after the rays are refracted by the surface, they are not converging but *appear* to diverge from a point 21.3 cm to the *left* of the vertex. We saw a similar case in the reflection of light from a convex mirror; we call the point a *virtual image*. In this example the surface forms a virtual image 21.3 cm to the left of the vertex. The vertical image is erect (because m is positive) and 2.33 times as large as the object.

Example 34.7 **Apparent depth of a swimming pool**

Swimming pool owners know that the pool always looks shallower than it really is and that it is important to identify the deep parts conspicuously so that people who can't swim won't jump into water that's over their heads. If a nonswimmer looks straight down into water that is actually 2.00 m (about 6 ft, 7 in.) deep, how deep does it appear to be?

SOLUTION

IDENTIFY: The surface of the water acts as a plane refracting surface.

SET UP: Figure 34.26 shows the situation. To determine the apparent depth of the pool, we imagine that there is an arrow PQ painted on the bottom of the pool. The refracting surface of the pool forms a virtual image $P'Q'$ of this arrow. We use Eq. (34.13) to find the depth of this arrow; it tells us the apparent depth of the pool.

EXECUTE: The object distance is the actual depth of the pool, $s = 2.00$ m. Material a is the water ($n_a = 1.33$) and material b is air ($n_b = 1.00$). The position of the image is given by Eq. (34.13):

$$\frac{n_a}{s} + \frac{n_b}{s'} = \frac{1.33}{2.00 \text{ m}} + \frac{1.00}{s'} = 0$$

$$s' = -1.50 \text{ m}$$

The image distance is negative. From the sign rules in Section 34.1, this means that the image is virtual and on the incoming side of the refracting surface—that is, on the same side as the object. The apparent depth is 1.50 m (about 4 ft, 11 in.), or only three-quarters of the actual depth. A 6-ft nonswimmer who didn't allow for this effect would be in trouble.

EVALUATE: Recall that the lateral magnification for a plane refracting surface is $m = 1$. Hence the image $P'Q'$ of the arrow is the same *horizontal length* as the actual arrow PQ. Only its depth is different. You can see this effect in Fig. 34.27.

34.26 Arrow $P'Q'$ is the virtual image of the underwater arrow PQ. The angles of the ray with the vertical are exaggerated for clarity.

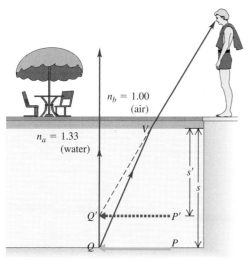

34.27 The submerged portion of this straw appears to be at a shallower depth (closer to the surface) than it actually is.

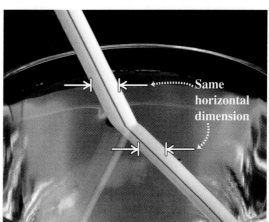

Test Your Understanding of Section 34.3   The water droplets in Fig. 34.23 have radius of curvature R and index of refraction $n = 1.33$. Can they form an image of the sun on the leaf?

34.4 Thin Lenses

The most familiar and widely used optical device (after the plane mirror) is the *lens*. A lens is an optical system with two refracting surfaces. The simplest lens has two *spherical* surfaces close enough together that we can neglect the distance between them (the thickness of the lens); we call this a **thin lens.** If you wear eyeglasses or contact lenses while reading, you are viewing these words through a pair of thin lenses. We can analyze thin lenses in detail using the results of Section 34.3 for refraction by a single spherical surface. However, we postpone this analysis until later in the section so that we can first discuss the properties of thin lenses.

Properties of a Lens

A lens of the shape shown in Fig. 34.28 has the property that when a beam of rays parallel to the axis passes through the lens, the rays converge to a point F_2 (Fig. 34.28a) and form a real image at that point. Such a lens is called a **converging lens.** Similarly, rays passing through point F_1 emerge from the lens as a beam of parallel rays (Fig. 34.28b). The points F_1 and F_2 are called the first and second *focal points,* and the distance f (measured from the center of the lens) is called the *focal length.* Note the similarities between the two focal points of a converging lens and the single focal point of a concave mirror (Fig. 34.13). As for a concave mirror, the focal length of a converging lens is defined to be a *positive* quantity, and such a lens is also called a *positive lens.*

The central horizontal line in Fig. 34.28 is called the *optic axis,* as with spherical mirrors. The centers of curvature of the two spherical surfaces lie on and define the optic axis. The two focal lengths in Fig. 34.28, both labeled f, *are always equal* for a thin lens, even when the two sides have different curvatures. We will derive this somewhat surprising result later in the section, when we derive the relationship of f to the index of refraction of the lens and the radii of curvature of its surfaces.

Image of an Extended Object: Converging Lens

Like a concave mirror, a converging lens can form an image of an extended object. Figure 34.29 shows how to find the position and lateral magnification of an image made by a thin converging lens. Using the same notation and sign rules as before, we let s and s' be the object and image distances, respectively, and let y and y' be the object and image heights. Ray QA, parallel to the optic axis before refraction, passes through the second focal point F_2 after refraction. Ray QOQ' passes undeflected straight through the center of the lens because at the center the two surfaces are parallel and (we have assumed) very close together.

34.28 F_1 and F_2 are the first and second focal points of a converging thin lens. The numerical value of f is positive.

(a)

Optic axis (passes through centers of curvature of both lens surfaces)

Second focal point: the point to which incoming parallel rays converge

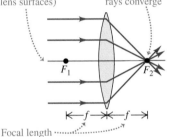

Focal length
• Measured from lens center
• Always the same on both sides of the lens
• Positive for a converging thin lens

(b)

First focal point: Rays diverging from this point emerge from the lens parallel to the axis.

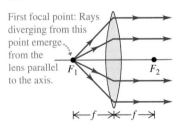

34.29 Construction used to find image position for a thin lens. To emphasize that the lens is assumed to be very thin, the ray QAQ' is shown as bent at the midplane of the lens rather than at the two surfaces and ray QOQ' is shown as a straight line.

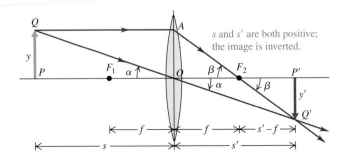

s and s' are both positive; the image is inverted.

There is refraction where the ray enters and leaves the material but no net change in direction.

The two angles labeled α in Fig. 34.29 are equal. Therefore the two right triangles PQO and $P'Q'O$ are *similar,* and ratios of corresponding sides are equal. Thus

$$\frac{y}{s} = -\frac{y'}{s'} \quad \text{or} \quad \frac{y'}{y} = -\frac{s'}{s} \tag{34.14}$$

(The reason for the negative sign is that the image is below the optic axis and y' is negative.) Also, the two angles labeled β are equal, and the two right triangles OAF_2 and $P'Q'F_2$ are similar, so

$$\frac{y}{f} = -\frac{y'}{s' - f} \quad \text{or}$$

$$\frac{y'}{y} = -\frac{s' - f}{f} \tag{34.15}$$

We now equate Eqs. (34.14) and (34.15), divide by s', and rearrange to obtain

$$\frac{1}{s} + \frac{1}{s'} = \frac{1}{f} \quad \text{(object–image relationship, thin lens)} \tag{34.16}$$

This analysis also gives the lateral magnification $m = y'/y$ for the lens; from Eq. (34.14),

$$m = -\frac{s'}{s} \quad \text{(lateral magnification, thin lens)} \tag{34.17}$$

The negative sign tells us that when s and s' are both positive, as in Fig. 34.29, the image is *inverted,* and y and y' have opposite signs.

Equations (34.16) and (34.17) are the basic equations for thin lenses. They are *exactly* the same as the corresponding equations for spherical mirrors, Eqs. (34.6) and (34.7). As we will see, the same sign rules that we used for spherical mirrors are also applicable to lenses. In particular, consider a lens with a positive focal length (a converging lens). When an object is outside the first focal point F_1 of this lens (that is, when $s > f$), the image distance s' is positive (that is, the image is on the same side as the outgoing rays); this image is real and inverted, as in Fig. 34.29. An object placed inside the first focal point of a converging lens, so that $s < f$, produces an image with a negative value of s'; this image is located on the same side of the lens as the object and is virtual, erect, and larger than the object. You can verify these statements algebraically using Eqs. (34.16) and (34.17); we'll also verify them in the next section, using graphical methods analogous to those introduced for mirrors in Section 34.2.

Figure 34.30 shows how a lens forms a three-dimensional image of a three-dimensional object. Point R is nearer the lens than point P. From Eq. (34.16),

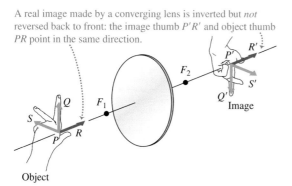

A real image made by a converging lens is inverted but *not* reversed back to front: the image thumb $P'R'$ and object thumb PR point in the same direction.

34.30 The image $S'P'Q'R'$ of a three-dimensional object $SPQR$ is not reversed by a lens.

34.31 F_2 and F_1 are the second and first focal points of a diverging thin lens, respectively. The numerical value of f is negative.

(a)

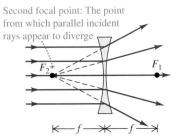

Second focal point: The point from which parallel incident rays appear to diverge

F_2 F_1

For a diverging thin lens, f is negative.

(b)

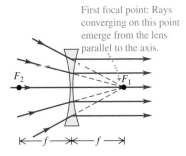

First focal point: Rays converging on this point emerge from the lens parallel to the axis.

F_2 F_1

34.32 Various types of lenses.

(a)   **Converging lenses**

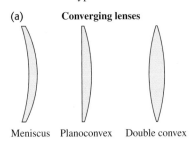

Meniscus   Planoconvex   Double convex

(b)   **Diverging lenses**

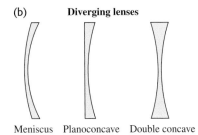

Meniscus   Planoconcave   Double concave

image point R' is farther from the lens than is image point P', and the image $P'R'$ points in the same direction as the object PR. Arrows $P'S'$ and $P'Q'$ are reversed relative to PS and PQ.

Let's compare Fig. 34.30 with Fig. 34.7, which shows the image formed by a plane *mirror*. We note that the image formed by the lens is inverted, but it is *not* reversed front to back along the optic axis. That is, if the object is a left hand, its image is also a left hand. You can verify this by pointing your left thumb along PR, your left forefinger along PQ, and your left middle finger along PS. Then rotate your hand 180°, using your thumb as an axis; this brings the fingers into coincidence with $P'Q'$ and $P'S'$. In other words, an *inverted* image is equivalent to an image that has been rotated by 180° about the lens axis.

Diverging Lenses

So far we have been discussing *converging* lenses. Figure 34.31 shows a **diverging lens;** the beam of parallel rays incident on this lens *diverges* after refraction. The focal length of a diverging lens is a negative quantity, and the lens is also called a *negative lens*. The focal points of a negative lens are reversed, relative to those of a positive lens. The second focal point, F_2, of a negative lens is the point from which rays that are originally parallel to the axis *appear to diverge* after refraction, as in Fig. 34.31a. Incident rays converging toward the first focal point F_1, as in Fig. 34.31b, emerge from the lens parallel to its axis. Comparing with Section 34.2, you can see that a diverging lens has the same relationship to a converging lens as a convex mirror has to a concave mirror.

Equations (34.16) and (34.17) apply to *both* positive and negative lenses. Figure 34.32 shows various types of lenses, both converging and diverging. Here's an important observation: *Any lens that is thicker at its center than at its edges is a converging lens with positive f; and any lens that is thicker at its edges than at its center is a diverging lens with negative f* (provided that the lens has a greater index of refraction than the surrounding material). We can prove this using the *lensmaker's equation,* which it is our next task to derive.

The Lensmaker's Equation

We'll now derive Eq. (34.16) in more detail and at the same time derive the *lensmaker's equation,* which is a relationship among the focal length f, the index of refraction n of the lens, and the radii of curvature R_1 and R_2 of the lens surfaces. We use the principle that an image formed by one reflecting or refracting surface can serve as the object for a second reflecting or refracting surface.

We begin with the somewhat more general problem of two spherical interfaces separating three materials with indexes of refraction n_a, n_b, and n_c, as shown in Fig. 34.33. The object and image distances for the first surface are s_1 and s_1', and those for the second surface are s_2 and s_2'. We assume that the lens is thin, so that the distance t between the two surfaces is small in comparison with the object and

34.33 The image formed by the first surface of a lens serves as the object for the second surface. The distances s_1' and s_2 are taken to be equal; this is a good approximation if the lens thickness t is small.

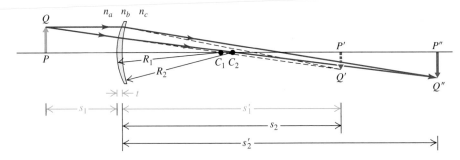

image distances and can therefore be neglected. This is usually the case with eyeglass lenses (Fig. 34.34). Then s_2 and s_1' have the same magnitude but opposite sign. For example, if the first image is on the outgoing side of the first surface, s_1' is positive. But when viewed as an object for the second surface, the first image is *not* on the incoming side of that surface. So we can say that $s_2 = -s_1'$.

We need to use the single-surface equation, Eq. (34.11), twice, once for each surface. The two resulting equations are

$$\frac{n_a}{s_1} + \frac{n_b}{s_1'} = \frac{n_b - n_a}{R_1}$$

$$\frac{n_b}{s_2} + \frac{n_c}{s_2'} = \frac{n_c - n_b}{R_2}$$

Ordinarily, the first and third materials are air or vacuum, so we set $n_a = n_c = 1$. The second index n_b is that of the lens, which we can call simply n. Substituting these values and the relationship $s_2 = -s_1'$, we get

$$\frac{1}{s_1} + \frac{n}{s_1'} = \frac{n - 1}{R_1}$$

$$-\frac{n}{s_1'} + \frac{1}{s_2'} = \frac{1 - n}{R_2}$$

To get a relationship between the initial object position s_1 and the final image position s_2', we add these two equations. This eliminates the term n/s_1', and we obtain

$$\frac{1}{s_1} + \frac{1}{s_2'} = (n - 1)\left(\frac{1}{R_1} - \frac{1}{R_2}\right)$$

Finally, thinking of the lens as a single unit, we call the object distance simply s instead of s_1, and we call the final image distance s' instead of s_2'. Making these substitutions, we have

$$\frac{1}{s} + \frac{1}{s'} = (n - 1)\left(\frac{1}{R_1} - \frac{1}{R_2}\right) \qquad (34.18)$$

Now we compare this with the other thin-lens equation, Eq. (34.16). We see that the object and image distances s and s' appear in exactly the same places in both equations and that the focal length f is given by

$$\frac{1}{f} = (n - 1)\left(\frac{1}{R_1} - \frac{1}{R_2}\right) \qquad \text{(lensmaker's equation for a thin lens)} \qquad (34.19)$$

This is the **lensmaker's equation.** In the process of rederiving the relationship between object distance, image distance, and focal length for a thin lens, we have also derived an expression for the focal length f of a lens in terms of its index of refraction n and the radii of curvature R_1 and R_2 of its surfaces. This can be used to show that all the lenses in Fig. 34.32a are converging lenses with positive focal lengths and that all the lenses in Fig. 34.32b are diverging lenses with negative focal lengths (see Exercise 34.30).

We use all our sign rules from Section 34.1 with Eqs. (34.18) and (34.19). For example, in Fig. 34.35, s, s', and R_1 are positive, but R_2 is negative.

It is not hard to generalize Eq. (34.19) to the situation in which the lens is immersed in a material with an index of refraction greater than unity. We invite you to work out the lensmaker's equation for this more general situation.

We stress that the paraxial approximation is indeed an approximation! Rays that are at sufficiently large angles to the optic axis of a spherical lens will not be brought to the same focus as paraxial rays; this is the same problem of spherical

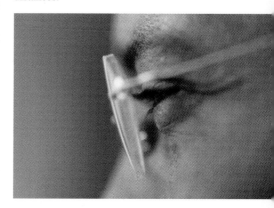

34.34 These eyeglass lenses satisfy the thin-lens approximation: Their thickness is small compared to the object and image distances.

34.35 A converging thin lens with a positive focal length f.

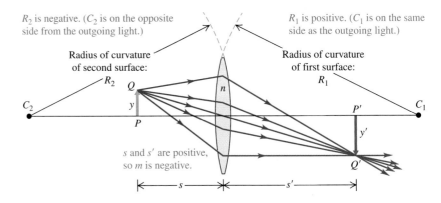

R_2 is negative. (C_2 is on the opposite side from the outgoing light.)

R_1 is positive. (C_1 is on the same side as the outgoing light.)

Radius of curvature of second surface: R_2

Radius of curvature of first surface: R_1

s and s' are positive, so m is negative.

aberration that plagues spherical *mirrors* (see Section 34.2). To avoid this and other limitations of thin spherical lenses, lenses of more complicated shape are used in precision optical instruments.

Example 34.8 Determining the focal length of a lens

(a) Suppose the absolute values of the radii of curvature of the lens surfaces in Fig. 34.35 are both equal to 10 cm and the index of refraction is $n = 1.52$. What is the focal length f of the lens? (b) Suppose the lens in Fig. 34.31 also has $n = 1.52$, and the absolute values of the radii of curvature of its lens surfaces are also both equal to 10 cm. What is the focal length of this lens?

SOLUTION

IDENTIFY: We are asked to find the focal length of (a) a lens that is convex on both sides (Fig. 34.35) and (b) a lens that is concave on both sides (Fig. 34.31).

SET UP: We use the lensmaker's equation, Eq. (34.19), to determine the focal length in each situation. We take account of whether the surfaces are convex or concave by paying careful attention to the signs of the radii of curvature R_1 and R_2.

EXECUTE: (a) Figure 34.35 shows that the center of curvature of the first surface (C_1) is on the outgoing side of the lens, while the center of curvature of the second surface (C_2) is on the *incoming*

side. Hence R_1 is positive but R_2 is negative. $R_1 = +10$ cm, $R_2 = -10$ cm. From Eq. (34.19),

$$\frac{1}{f} = (1.52 - 1)\left(\frac{1}{+10 \text{ cm}} - \frac{1}{-10 \text{ cm}}\right)$$

$$f = 9.6 \text{ cm}$$

(b) For a double-concave lens the center of curvature of the first surface is on the *incoming* side, while the center of curvature of the second surface is on the outgoing side. Hence R_1 is negative and R_2 is positive: $R_1 = -10$ cm, $R_2 = +10$ cm. Again using Eq. (34.19),

$$\frac{1}{f} = (1.52 - 1)\left(\frac{1}{-10 \text{ cm}} - \frac{1}{+10 \text{ cm}}\right)$$

$$f = -9.6 \text{ cm}$$

EVALUATE: In part (a) the focal length is positive, so this is a converging lens; this makes sense, since the lens is thicker at its center than at its edges. In part (b) the focal length is *negative*, so this is a *diverging* lens; this also makes sense, since the lens is thicker at its edges than at its center.

Graphical Methods for Lenses

We can determine the position and size of an image formed by a thin lens by using a graphical method very similar to the one we used in Section 34.2 for spherical mirrors. Again we draw a few special rays called *principal rays* that diverge from a point of the object that is *not* on the optic axis. The intersection of these rays, after they pass through the lens, determines the position and size of the image. In using this graphical method, we will consider the entire deviation of a ray as occurring at the midplane of the lens, as shown in Fig. 34.36. This is consistent with the assumption that the distance between the lens surfaces is negligible.

The three principal rays whose paths are usually easy to trace for lenses are shown in Fig. 34.36:

1. *A ray parallel to the axis* emerges from the lens in a direction that passes through the second focal point F_2 of a converging lens, or appears to come from the second focal point of a diverging lens.
2. *A ray through the center of the lens* is not appreciably deviated; at the center of the lens the two surfaces are parallel, so this ray emerges at essentially the same angle at which it enters and along essentially the same line.

34.36 The graphical method of locating an image formed by a thin lens. The colors of the rays are for identification only; they do not refer to specific colors of light. (Compare Fig. 34.19 for spherical mirrors.)

(a) Converging lens

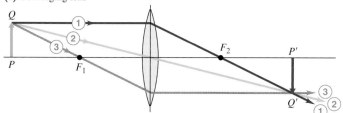

① Parallel incident ray refracts to pass through second focal point F_2.
② Ray through center of lens does not deviate appreciably.
③ Ray through the first focal point F_1 emerges parallel to the axis.

(b) Diverging lens

① Parallel incident ray appears after refraction to have come from the second focal point F_2.
② Ray through center of lens does not deviate appreciably.
③ Ray aimed at the first focal point F_1 emerges parallel to the axis.

3. *A ray through (or proceeding toward) the first focal point F_1 emerges parallel to the axis.*

When the image is real, the position of the image point is determined by the intersection of any two rays 1, 2, and 3 (Fig. 34.36a). When the image is virtual, we extend the diverging outgoing rays backward to their intersection point to find the image point (Fig. 34.36b).

CAUTION **Principal rays are not the only rays** Keep in mind that *any* ray from the object that strikes the lens will pass through the image point (for a real image) or appear to originate from the image point (for a virtual image). (We made a similar comment about image formation by mirrors in Section 34.2.) We've emphasized the principal rays because they're the only ones you need to draw to locate the image. ∎

Figure 34.37 shows principal-ray diagrams for a converging lens for several object distances. We suggest you study each of these diagrams very carefully, comparing each numbered ray with the above description.

34.37 Formation of images by a thin converging lens for various object distances. The principal rays are numbered. (Compare Fig. 34.20 for a concave spherical mirror.)

(a) Object O is outside focal point; image I is real.

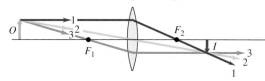

(b) Object O is closer to focal point; image I is real and farther away.

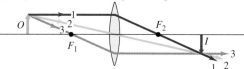

(c) Object O is even closer to focal point; image I is real and even farther away.

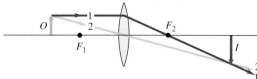

(d) Object O is at focal point; image I is at infinity.

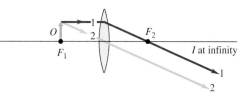

(e) Object O is inside focal point; image I is virtual and larger than object.

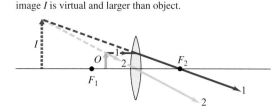

(f) A virtual object O (light rays are *converging* on lens)

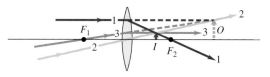

Parts (a), (b), and (c) of Fig. 34.37 help explain what happens in focusing a camera. For a photograph to be in sharp focus, the film must be at the position of the real image made by the camera's lens. The image distance increases as the object is brought closer, so the film is moved farther behind the lens (i.e., the lens is moved farther in front of the film). In Fig. 34.37d the object is at the focal point; ray 3 can't be drawn because it doesn't pass through the lens. In Fig. 34.37e the object distance is less than the focal length. The outgoing rays are divergent, and the image is *virtual;* its position is located by extending the outgoing rays backward, so the image distance s' is negative. Note also that the image is erect and larger than the object. (We'll see the usefulness of this in Section 34.6.) Figure 34.37f corresponds to a *virtual object.* The incoming rays do not diverge from a real object, but are *converging* as though they would meet at the tip of the virtual object O on the right side; the object distance s is negative in this case. The image is real and is located between the lens and the second focal point. This situation can arise if the rays that strike the lens in Fig. 34.37f emerge from another converging lens (not shown) to the left of the figure.

Problem-Solving Strategy 34.2 Image Formation by Thin Lenses

IDENTIFY *the relevant concepts:* Problem-Solving Strategy 34.1 (Section 34.2) for mirrors is equally applicable here, and you should review it now. As for mirrors, you should solve problems involving image formation by lenses using *both* equations and a principal-ray diagram.

SET UP *the problem:* As always, determine the target variables.

EXECUTE *the solution* as follows:
1. Always begin with a principal-ray diagram if you have enough information. Orient your diagrams consistently so that light travels from left to right. Don't just sketch these diagrams; draw the rays with a ruler and measure the distances carefully.
2. Draw the principal rays so they bend at the midplane of the lens, as shown in Fig. 34.36. For a lens there are only three principal rays, compared to four for a mirror. Be sure to draw *all three* whenever possible. The intersection of any two determines the image, but if the third doesn't pass through the same intersection point, you know you have made a mistake. Redundancy can be useful in spotting errors.

3. If the outgoing principal rays don't converge at a real image point, the image is virtual. Then you have to extend the outgoing rays backward to find the virtual image point, which lies on the *incoming* side of the lens.
4. The same sign rules we have used for mirrors and single refracting surfaces (see Section 34.1) are also applicable for thin lenses. Be extremely careful to get your signs right and to interpret the signs of results correctly.
5. Use Eqs. (34.16) and (34.17) to confirm by calculation your graphical results for the image position and size. This gives an extremely useful consistency check.
6. The *image* from one lens or mirror may serve as the *object* for another. In that case, be careful in finding the object and image *distances* for this intermediate image; be sure you include the distance between the two elements (lenses and/or mirrors) correctly.

EVALUATE *your answer:* Cast a critical eye on your diagrams and calculations to make certain that your results are consistent.

Example 34.9 Image location and magnification with a converging lens

A converging lens has a focal length of 20 cm. Find graphically the image location for an object at each of the following distances from the lens: (a) 50 cm; (b) 20 cm; (c) 15 cm; (d) −40 cm. Determine the magnification in each case. Check your results by calculating the image position and lateral magnification from Eqs. (34.16) and (34.17), respectively.

SOLUTION

IDENTIFY: This problem illustrates the usefulness of both graphical and computational methods for problems with thin lenses, just as for problems with curved mirrors.

SET UP: In each case we are given the focal length $f = 20$ cm and the value of the object distance s. Our target variables are the image distance s' and the lateral magnification $m = -s'/s$.

EXECUTE: The appropriate principal-ray diagrams are shown in (a) Fig. 34.37a, (b) Fig. 34.37d, (c) Fig. 34.37e, and (d) Fig. 34.37f. The approximate image distances, from measurements of these diagrams, are 35 cm, $-\infty$, -40 cm, and 15 cm, and the approximate magnifications are $-\frac{2}{3}$, $+\infty$, and $+3$, and $+\frac{1}{3}$, respectively.

Calculating the image positions from Eq. (34.16), we find

(a) $\dfrac{1}{50\text{ cm}} + \dfrac{1}{s'} = \dfrac{1}{20\text{ cm}}$ $s' = 33.3$ cm

(b) $\dfrac{1}{20\text{ cm}} + \dfrac{1}{s'} = \dfrac{1}{20\text{ cm}}$ $s' = \pm\infty$

(c) $\dfrac{1}{15\text{ cm}} + \dfrac{1}{s'} = \dfrac{1}{20\text{ cm}}$ $s' = -60$ cm

(d) $\dfrac{1}{-40\text{ cm}} + \dfrac{1}{s'} = \dfrac{1}{20\text{ cm}}$ $s' = 13.3$ cm

The graphical results are fairly close to these except for part (c); the accuracy of the diagram in Fig. 34.37e is limited because the rays extended backward have nearly the same direction.

From Eq. (34.17) the lateral magnifications are

(a) $m = -\dfrac{33.3\ \text{cm}}{50\ \text{cm}} = -\dfrac{2}{3}$

(b) $m = -\dfrac{\pm\infty\ \text{cm}}{20\ \text{cm}} = \pm\infty$

(c) $m = -\dfrac{-60\ \text{cm}}{15\ \text{cm}} = +4$

(d) $m = -\dfrac{13.3\ \text{cm}}{-40\ \text{cm}} = +\dfrac{1}{3}$

EVALUATE: Note that s' is positive in parts (a) and (d) but negative in part (c). This makes sense: The image is real in parts (a) and (d) but virtual in part (c). The light rays that emerge from the lens in part (b) are parallel and never converge, so the image can be regarded as being at either $+\infty$ or $-\infty$.

The values of magnification tell us that the image is inverted in part (a) and erect in parts (c) and (d), in accordance with the principal-ray diagrams. The infinite value of magnification in part (b) is another way of saying that the image is formed infinitely far away.

Example 34.10   Image formation by a diverging lens

You are given a thin diverging lens. You find that a beam of parallel rays spreads out after passing through the lens, as though all the rays came from a point 20.0 cm from the center of the lens. You want to use this lens to form an erect virtual image that is $\frac{1}{3}$ the height of the object. (a) Where should the object be placed? (b) Draw a principal-ray diagram.

SOLUTION

IDENTIFY: The observation with parallel rays shows that the focal length is $f = -20$ cm. We want the lateral magnification to be $m = +\frac{1}{3}$ (positive because the image is to be erect).

SET UP: We use the given information to determine the ratio s'/s from Eq. (34.17) and then determine the object distance s with Eq. (34.16).

EXECUTE: (a) From Eq. (34.17), $m = +\frac{1}{3} = -s'/s$, so $s' = -s/3$. If we insert this result into Eq. (34.16), we find

$$\frac{1}{s} + \frac{1}{-s/3} = \frac{1}{-20.0\ \text{cm}}$$

$$s = 40.0\ \text{cm}$$

$$s' = -\frac{s}{3} = -\frac{40.0\ \text{cm}}{3} = -13.3\ \text{cm}$$

The image distance is negative, so the object and image are on the same side of the lens.

(b) Figure 34.38 is a principal-ray diagram for this problem, with the rays numbered in the same way as in Fig. 34.36b.

EVALUATE: A diverging lens is often mounted in the front door of a home. It provides the occupant of the home with an erect, reduced image of anyone standing outside the door. The occupant can see the outside person's entire height and decide whether to let him or her in.

34.38 Principal-ray diagram for an image formed by a thin diverging lens.

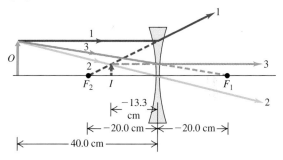

Example 34.11   An image of an image

An object 8.0 cm high is placed 12.0 cm to the left of a converging lens of focal length 8.0 cm. A second converging lens of focal length 6.0 cm is placed 36.0 cm to the right of the first lens. Both lenses have the same optic axis. Find the position, size, and orientation of the image produced by the two lenses in combination. (Combinations of converging lenses are used in telescopes and microscopes, to be discussed in Section 34.7.)

SOLUTION

IDENTIFY: The situation is shown in Fig. 34.39. The object O lies outside the first focal point F_1 of the first lens, so this lens produces a real image I. The light rays that strike the second lens diverge from this real image just as if I was a material object. Hence the

image made by the *first* lens acts as an *object* for the *second* lens. Our goal is to determine the properties of the final image made by the second lens.

SET UP: We use both graphical and computational methods to determine the properties of the final image.

EXECUTE: In Fig. 34.39 (next page) we have drawn principal rays 1, 2, and 3 from the head of the object arrow O to find the position of the first image I and principal rays $1'$, $2'$, and $3'$ from the head of the first image to find the position of the second image I' made by the second lens (even though rays $2'$ and $3'$ don't actually exist in this case). Note that the image is inverted *twice*, once by each lens, so the second image I' has the same orientation as the original object.

Continued

To *calculate* the position and size of the second image I', we must first find the position and size of the first image I. Applying Eq. (34.16), $1/s + 1/s' = 1/f$, to the first lens gives

$$\frac{1}{12.0 \text{ cm}} + \frac{1}{s_1'} = \frac{1}{8.0 \text{ cm}} \qquad s_1' = +24.0 \text{ cm}$$

The first image I is 24.0 cm to the right of the first lens. The lateral magnification is $m_1 = -(24.0 \text{ cm})/(12.0 \text{ cm}) = -2.00$, so the height of the first image is $(-2.0)(8.0 \text{ cm}) = -16.0 \text{ cm}$.

The first image is 36.0 cm − 24.0 cm = 12.0 cm to the left of the second lens, so the object distance for the second lens is +12.0 cm. Using Eq. (34.16) for the second lens gives the position of the second and final image:

$$\frac{1}{12.0 \text{ cm}} + \frac{1}{s_2'} = \frac{1}{6.0 \text{ cm}} \qquad s_2' = +12.0 \text{ cm}$$

The final image is 12.0 cm to the right of the second lens and 48.0 cm to the right of the first lens. The magnification produced by the second converging lens is $m_2 = -(12.0 \text{ cm})/(12.0 \text{ cm}) = -1.0$.

EVALUATE: The value of m_2 means that the final image is just as large as the first image but has the opposite orientation. This is also shown in the principal-ray diagram.

34.39 Principal-ray diagram for a combination of two converging lenses. The first lens makes a real image of the object. This real image acts as an object for the second lens.

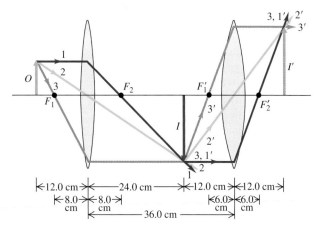

Test Your Understanding of Section 34.4 A diverging lens and an object are positioned as shown in the figure at left. Which of the rays A, B, C, and D could emanate from point Q at the top of the object?

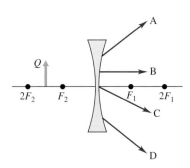

34.5 Cameras

The concept of *image,* which is so central to understanding simple mirror and lens systems, plays an equally important role in the analysis of optical instruments (also called *optical devices*). Among the most common optical devices are cameras, which make an image of an object and record it either electronically or on film.

The basic elements of a **camera** are a light-tight box ("camera" is a Latin word meaning "a room or enclosure"), a converging lens, a shutter to open the lens for a prescribed length of time, and a light-sensitive recording medium (Fig. 34.40). In a digital camera this is an electronic detector called a charge-coupled device (CCD) array; in an older camera, this is photographic film. The lens forms an inverted real image on the recording medium of the object being photographed. High-quality camera lenses have several elements, permitting partial correction of various *aberrations,* including the dependence of

34.40 Key elements of a digital camera.

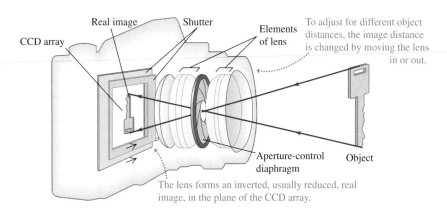

34.41 (a), (b), (c) Three photographs taken with the same camera from the same position in the Boston Public Garden using lenses with focal lengths $f = 28$ mm, 105 mm, and 300 mm. Increasing the focal length increases the image size proportionately. (d) The larger the value of f, the smaller the angle of view. The angles shown here are for a camera with image area 24 mm $\times$ 36 mm (corresponding to 35-mm film) and refer to the angle of view along the diagonal dimension of the film.

(a) $f = 28$ mm

(b) $f = 105$ mm

(c) $f = 300$ mm

(d) The angles of view for the photos in **(a)–(c)**

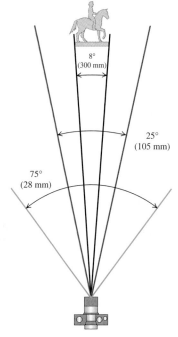

index of refraction on wavelength and the limitations imposed by the paraxial approximation.

When the camera is in proper *focus,* the position of the recording medium coincides with the position of the real image formed by the lens. The resulting photograph will then be as sharp as possible. With a converging lens, the image distance increases as the object distance decreases (see Figs. 34.41a, 34.41b, and 34.41c, and the discussion in Section 34.4). Hence in "focusing" the camera, we move the lens closer to the film for a distant object and farther from the film for a nearby object.

Camera Lenses: Focal Length

The choice of the focal length f for a camera lens depends on the film size and the desired angle of view. Figure 34.41 shows three photographs taken on 35-mm film with the same camera at the same position, but with lenses of different focal lengths. A lens of long focal length, called a *telephoto* lens, gives a small angle of view and a large image of a distant object (such as the statue in Fig. 34.41c); a lens of short focal length gives a small image and a wide angle of view (as in Fig. 34.41a) and is called a *wide-angle* lens. To understand this behavior, recall that the focal length is the distance from the lens to the image when the object is infinitely far away. In general, for *any* object distance, using a lens of longer focal length gives a greater image distance. This also increases the height of the image; as was discussed in Section 34.4, the ratio of the image height y' to the object height y (the *lateral magnification*) is equal in absolute value to the ratio of image distance s' to the object distance s [Eq. (34.17)]:

$$m = \frac{y'}{y} = -\frac{s'}{s}$$

With a lens of short focal length, the ratio s'/s is small, and a distant object gives only a small image. When a lens with a long focal length is used, the image of this same object may entirely cover the area of the film. Hence the longer the focal length, the narrower the angle of view (Fig. 34.41d).

Camera Lenses: f-Number

For the film to record the image properly, the total light energy per unit area reaching the film (the "exposure") must fall within certain limits. This is controlled by the *shutter* and the *lens aperture.* The shutter controls the time interval during which light enters the lens. This is usually adjustable in steps corresponding to factors of about 2, often from 1 s to $\frac{1}{1000}$ s.

The intensity of light reaching the film is proportional to the area viewed by the camera lens and to the effective area of the lens. The size of the area that the lens "sees" is proportional to the square of the angle of view of the lens, and so is roughly proportional to $1/f^2$. The effective area of the lens is controlled by means of an adjustable lens aperture, or *diaphragm,* a nearly circular hole with variable diameter D; hence the effective area is proportional to D^2. Putting these factors together, we see that the intensity of light reaching the film with a particular lens is proportional to D^2/f^2. The light-gathering capability of a lens is commonly expressed by photographers in terms of the ratio f/D, called the **f-number** of the lens:

$$f\text{-number} = \frac{\text{Focal length}}{\text{Aperture diameter}} = \frac{f}{D} \qquad (34.20)$$

For example, a lens with a focal length $f = 50$ mm and an aperture diameter $D = 25$ mm is said to have an f-number of 2, or "an aperture of $f/2$." The light intensity reaching the film is *inversely* proportional to the square of the f-number.

For a lens with a variable-diameter aperture, increasing the diameter by a factor of $\sqrt{2}$ changes the f-number by $1/\sqrt{2}$ and increases the intensity at the film by a factor of 2. Adjustable apertures usually have scales labeled with successive numbers (often called *f-stops*) related by factors of $\sqrt{2}$, such as

$$f/2 \quad f/2.8 \quad f/4 \quad f/5.6 \quad f/8 \quad f/11 \quad f/16$$

and so on. The larger numbers represent smaller apertures and exposures, and each step corresponds to a factor of 2 in intensity (Fig. 34.42). The actual *exposure* (total amount of light reaching the film) is proportional to both the aperture area and the time of exposure. Thus $f/4$ and $\frac{1}{500}$ s, $f/5.6$ and $\frac{1}{250}$ s, and $f/8$ and $\frac{1}{125}$ s all correspond to the same exposure.

Zoom Lenses and Projectors

Many photographers use a *zoom lens,* which is not a single lens but a complex collection of several lens elements that give a continuously variable focal length, often over a range as great as 10 to 1. Figures 34.43a and 34.43b show a simple system with variable focal length, and Fig. 34.43c shows a typical zoom lens for a single-lens reflex camera. Zoom lenses give a range of image sizes of a given object. It is an enormously complex problem in optical design to keep the image in focus and maintain a constant f-number while the focal length changes. When you vary the focal length of a typical zoom lens, two groups of elements move within the lens and a diaphragm opens and closes.

A *projector* for viewing slides, digital images, or motion pictures operates very much like a camera in reverse. In a movie projector, a lamp shines on the

34.42 A camera lens with an adjustable diaphragm.

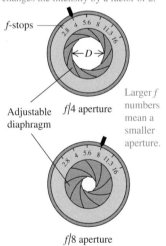

Changing the diameter by a factor of $\sqrt{2}$ changes the intensity by a factor of 2.

f-stops

←D→

Adjustable diaphragm $f/4$ aperture

Larger f numbers mean a smaller aperture.

$f/8$ aperture

34.43 A simple zoom lens uses a converging lens and a diverging lens in tandem. **(a)** When the two lenses are close together, the combination behaves like a single lens of long focal length. **(b)** If the two lenses are moved farther apart, the combination behaves like a short-focal-length lens. **(c)** A typical zoom lens for a single-lens reflex camera, containing twelve elements arranged in four groups.

(a) Zoom lens set for long focal length

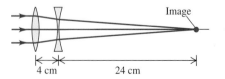

Image

4 cm   24 cm

(b) Zoom lens set for short focal length

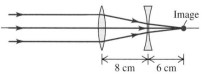

Image

8 cm   6 cm

(c) A practical zoom lens

film, which acts as an object for the projection lens. The lens forms a real, enlarged, inverted image of the film on the projection screen. Because the image is inverted, the film goes through the projector upside down so that the image on the screen appears right-side up.

Example 34.12   **Photographic exposures**

A common telephoto lens for a 35-mm camera has a focal length of 200 mm and a range of f-stops from $f/5.6$ to $f/45$. (a) What is the corresponding range of aperture diameters? (b) What is the corresponding range of intensity of the image on the film?

SOLUTION

IDENTIFY: Part (a) of this problem uses the relationship among focal length, aperture diameter, and f-number for a lens. Part (b) uses the relationship between intensity and aperture diameter.

SET UP: We use Eq. (34.20) to relate the diameter D (the target variable) to the f-number and the focal length $f = 200$ mm. The intensity of the light reaching the film is proportional to D^2/f^2; since f is the same in each case, we conclude that the intensity in this case is proportional to D^2, the square of the aperture diameter.

EXECUTE: (a) From Eq. (34.20) the range of diameters is from

$$D = \frac{f}{f\text{-number}} = \frac{200 \text{ mm}}{5.6} = 36 \text{ mm}$$

to

$$D = \frac{200 \text{ mm}}{45} = 4.4 \text{ mm}$$

(b) Because the intensity is proportional to the square of the diameter, the ratio of the intensity at $f/5.6$ to the intensity at $f/45$ is

$$\left(\frac{36 \text{ mm}}{4.4 \text{ mm}}\right)^2 = \left(\frac{45}{5.6}\right)^2 = 65 \qquad (\text{about } 2^6)$$

EVALUATE: If the correct exposure time at $f/5.6$ is $\frac{1}{1000}$ s, then at $f/45$ it is $(65)\left(\frac{1}{1000} \text{ s}\right) = \frac{1}{15}$ s to compensate for the lower intensity. This illustrates a general rule: The smaller the aperture and the larger the f-number, the longer the required exposure time. Nevertheless, many photographers prefer to use small apertures so that only the central part of the lens is used to make the image. This minimizes aberrations that occur near the edges of the lens and gives the sharpest possible images.

Test Your Understanding of Section 34.5   When used with 35-mm film (image area 24 mm × 36 mm), a lens with $f = 50$ mm gives a 45° angle of view and is called a "normal lens." When used with a CCD array that measures 5 mm × 5 mm, this same lens is (i) a wide-angle lens; (ii) a normal lens; (iii) a telephoto lens.

34.6 The Eye

The optical behavior of the eye is similar to that of a camera. The essential parts of the human eye, considered as an optical system, are shown in Fig. 34.44a. The eye is nearly spherical and about 2.5 cm in diameter. The front portion is somewhat more sharply curved and is covered by a tough, transparent membrane called the

34.44 (a) The eye. (b) There are two types of light-sensitive cells on the retina. The rods are more sensitive to light than the cones, but only the cones are sensitive to differences in color. A typical human eye contains about 1.3×10^8 rods and about 7×10^6 cones.

(a) Diagram of the eye

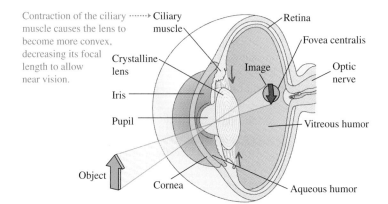

(b) Scanning electron micrograph showing retinal rods and cones in different colors

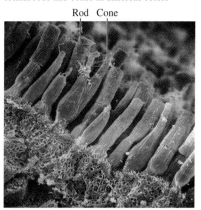

Table 34.1 Receding of Near Point with Age

Age (years)	Near Point (cm)
10	7
20	10
30	14
40	22
50	40
60	200

34.45 Refractive errors for **(a)** a normal eye, **(b)** a myopic (nearsighted) eye, and **(c)** a hyperopic (farsighted) eye viewing a very distant object. The dashed blue curve indicates the required position of the retina.

(a) Normal eye

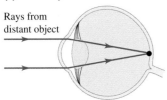

(b) Myopic (nearsighted) eye

Eye too long or cornea too sharply curved . . .   . . . rays focus in front of the retina.

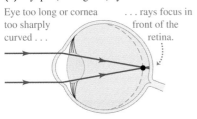

(c) Hyperopic (farsighted) eye

Eye too short or cornea not curved enough . . .   . . . rays focus behind the retina.

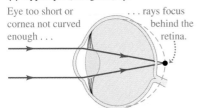

cornea. The region behind the cornea contains a liquid called the *aqueous humor.* Next comes the *crystalline lens,* a capsule containing a fibrous jelly, hard at the center and progressively softer at the outer portions. The crystalline lens is held in place by ligaments that attach it to the ciliary muscle, which encircles it. Behind the lens, the eye is filled with a thin watery jelly called the *vitreous humor.* The indexes of refraction of both the aqueous humor and the vitreous humor are about 1.336, nearly equal to that of water. The crystalline lens, while not homogeneous, has an average index of 1.437. This is not very different from the indexes of the aqueous and vitreous humors. As a result, most of the refraction of light entering the eye occurs at the outer surface of the cornea.

Refraction at the cornea and the surfaces of the lens produces a *real image* of the object being viewed. This image is formed on the light-sensitive *retina,* lining the rear inner surface of the eye. The retina plays the same role as the film in a camera. The *rods* and *cones* in the retina act like an array of miniature photocells (Fig. 34.44b); they sense the image and transmit it via the *optic nerve* to the brain. Vision is most acute in a small central region called the *fovea centralis,* about 0.25 mm in diameter.

In front of the lens is the *iris.* It contains an aperture with variable diameter called the *pupil,* which opens and closes to adapt to changing light intensity. The receptors of the retina also have intensity adaptation mechanisms.

For an object to be seen sharply, the image must be formed exactly at the location of the retina. The eye adjusts to different object distances s by changing the focal length f of its lens; the lens-to-retina distance, corresponding to s', does not change. (Contrast this with focusing a camera, in which the focal length is fixed and the lens-to-film distance is changed.) For the normal eye, an object at infinity is sharply focused when the ciliary muscle is relaxed. To permit sharp imaging on the retina of closer objects, the tension in the ciliary muscle surrounding the lens increases, the ciliary muscle contracts, the lens bulges, and the radii of curvature of its surfaces decrease; this decreases the focal length. This process is called *accommodation.*

The extremes of the range over which distinct vision is possible are known as the *far point* and the *near point* of the eye. The far point of a normal eye is at infinity. The position of the near point depends on the amount by which the ciliary muscle can increase the curvature of the crystalline lens. The range of accommodation gradually diminishes with age because the crystalline lens grows throughout a person's life (it is about 50% larger at age 60 than at age 20) and the ciliary muscles are less able to distort a larger lens. For this reason, the near point gradually recedes as one grows older. This recession of the near point is called *presbyopia.* Table 34.1 shows the approximate position of the near point for an average person at various ages. For example, an average person 50 years of age cannot focus on an object that is closer than about 40 cm.

Defects of Vision

Several common defects of vision result from incorrect distance relationships in the eye. A normal eye forms an image on the retina of an object at infinity when the eye is relaxed (Fig. 34.45a). In the *myopic* (nearsighted) eye, the eyeball is too long from front to back in comparison with the radius of curvature of the cornea (or the cornea is too sharply curved), and rays from an object at infinity are focused in front of the retina (Fig. 34.45b). The most distant object for which an image can be formed on the retina is then nearer than infinity. In the *hyperopic* (farsighted) eye, the eyeball is too short or the cornea is not curved enough, and the image of an infinitely distant object is behind the retina (Fig. 34.45c). The myopic eye produces *too much* convergence in a parallel bundle of rays for an image to be formed on the retina; the hyperopic eye, *not enough* convergence.

All of these defects can be corrected by the use of corrective lenses (eyeglasses or contact lenses). The near point of either a presbyopic or a hyperopic

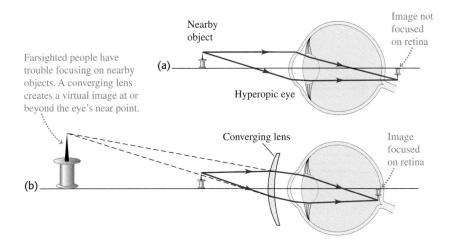

Farsighted people have trouble focusing on nearby objects. A converging lens creates a virtual image at or beyond the eye's near point.

34.46 (a) An uncorrected hyperopic (farsighted) eye. (b) A positive (converging) lens gives the extra convergence needed for a hyperopic eye to focus the image on the retina.

34.47 (a) An uncorrected myopic (nearsighted) eye. (b) A negative (diverging) lens spreads the rays farther apart to compensate for the excessive convergence of the myopic eye.

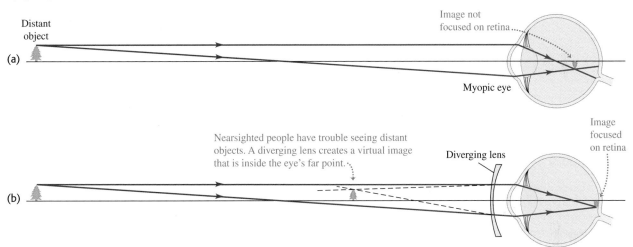

Nearsighted people have trouble seeing distant objects. A diverging lens creates a virtual image that is inside the eye's far point.

eye is *farther* from the eye than normal. To see clearly an object at normal reading distance (often assumed to be 25 cm), we need a lens that forms a virtual image of the object at or beyond the near point. This can be accomplished by a converging (positive) lens, as shown in Fig. 34.46. In effect the lens moves the object farther away from the eye to a point where a sharp retinal image can be formed. Similarly, correcting the myopic eye involves using a diverging (negative) lens to move the image closer to the eye than the actual object, as shown in Fig. 34.47.

Astigmatism is a different type of defect in which the surface of the cornea is not spherical but rather more sharply curved in one plane than in another. As a result, horizontal lines may be imaged in a different plane from vertical lines (Fig. 34.48a). Astigmatism may make it impossible, for example, to focus clearly on the horizontal and vertical bars of a window at the same time.

Astigmatism can be corrected by use of a lens with a *cylindrical* surface. For example, suppose the curvature of the cornea in a horizontal plane is correct to focus rays from infinity on the retina but the curvature in the vertical plane is too great to form a sharp retinal image. When a cylindrical lens with its axis horizontal is placed before the eye, the rays in a horizontal plane are unaffected, but the additional divergence of the rays in a vertical plane causes these to be sharply imaged on the retina (Fig. 34.48b).

Lenses for vision correction are usually described in terms of the **power,** defined as the reciprocal of the focal length expressed in meters. The unit of power is the **diopter.** Thus a lens with $f = 0.50$ m has a power of 2.0 diopters,

34.48 One type of astigmatism and how it is corrected.

(a) Vertical lines are imaged in front of the retina.

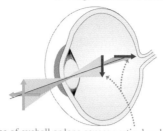

Shape of eyeball or lens causes vertical and horizontal elements to focus at different distances.

(b) A cylindrical lens corrects for astigmatism.

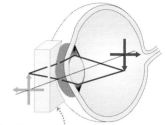

This cylindrical lens is curved in the vertical, but not the horizontal, direction; it changes the focal length of vertical elements.

$f = -0.25$ m corresponds to -4.0 diopters, and so on. The numbers on a prescription for glasses are usually powers expressed in diopters. When the correction involves both astigmatism and myopia or hyperopia, there are three numbers: one for the spherical power, one for the cylindrical power, and an angle to describe the orientation of the cylinder axis.

An alternative approach for correcting many defects of vision is to reshape the cornea. This is often done using a procedure called *laser-assisted in situ keratomileusis,* or LASIK. An incision is made into the cornea and a flap of outer corneal tissue is folded back. A pulsed ultraviolet laser with a beam only 50 μm wide (about $\frac{1}{200}$ the width of a human hair) is then used to vaporize away microscopic areas of the underlying tissue. The flap is then folded back into position, where it conforms to the new shape "carved" by the laser.

Example 34.13 Correcting for farsightedness

The near point of a certain hyperopic eye is 100 cm in front of the eye. To see clearly an object that is 25 cm in front of the eye, what contact lens is required?

SOLUTION

IDENTIFY: We want the lens to form a virtual image of the object at the near point of the eye, 100 cm from it. That is, when $s = 25$ cm, we want s' to be 100 cm.

SET UP: Figure 34.49 shows the situation. We determine the required focal length of the contact lens using the object-image relationship for a thin lens, Eq. (34.16).

EXECUTE: From Eq. (34.16),

$$\frac{1}{f} = \frac{1}{s} + \frac{1}{s'} = \frac{1}{+25 \text{ cm}} + \frac{1}{-100 \text{ cm}}$$

$$f = +33 \text{ cm}$$

We need a converging lens with focal length $f = 33$ cm. The corresponding power is $1/(0.33 \text{ m})$, or $+3.0$ diopters.

EVALUATE: In this example we used a contact lens to correct hyperopia. Had we used eyeglasses, we would have had to account for the separation between the eye and the eyeglass lens, and a somewhat different power would have been required (see Example 34.14).

34.49 Using a contact lens to correct for farsightedness.

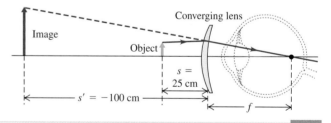

Example 34.14 Correcting for nearsightedness

The far point of a certain myopic eye is 50 cm in front of the eye. To see clearly an object at infinity, what eyeglass lens is required? Assume that the lens is worn 2 cm in front of the eye.

SOLUTION

IDENTIFY: The far point of a myopic eye is nearer than infinity. To see clearly objects beyond the far point, we need a lens that

forms a virtual image of such objects no farther from the eye than the far point.

SET UP: Figure 34.50 shows the situation. Assume that the virtual image of the object at infinity is formed at the far point, 50 cm in front of the eye and 48 cm in front of the eyeglass lens. Then when

$s = \infty$, we want s' to be -48 cm. As in Example 34.13, we use the values of s and s' to calculate the required focal length.

EXECUTE: From Eq. (34.16),

$$\frac{1}{f} = \frac{1}{s} + \frac{1}{s'} = \frac{1}{\infty} + \frac{1}{-48 \text{ cm}}$$

$$f = -48 \text{ cm}$$

We need a *diverging* lens with focal length -48 cm $= -0.48$ m. The power is -2.1 diopter.

EVALUATE: If a *contact* lens were used instead, we would need $f = -50$ cm and a power of -2.0 diopters. Can you see why?

34.50 Using a contact lens to correct for nearsightedness.

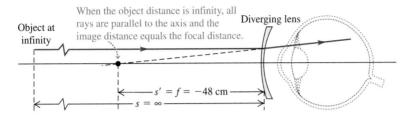

When the object distance is infinity, all rays are parallel to the axis and the image distance equals the focal distance.

Object at infinity

Diverging lens

$s' = f = -48$ cm

$s = \infty$

Test Your Understanding of Section 34.6 A certain eyeglass lens is thin at its center, even thinner at its top and bottom edges, and relatively thick at its left and right edges. What defects of vision is this lens intended to correct? (i) hyperopia for objects oriented both vertically and horizontally; (ii) myopia for objects oriented both vertically and horizontally; (iii) hyperopia for objects oriented vertically and myopia for objects oriented horizontally; (iv) hyperopia for objects oriented horizontally and myopia for objects oriented vertically.

34.7 The Magnifier

The apparent size of an object is determined by the size of its image on the retina. If the eye is unaided, this size depends on the *angle* θ subtended by the object at the eye, called its **angular size** (Fig. 34.51a).

To look closely at a small object, such as an insect or a crystal, you bring it close to your eye, making the subtended angle and the retinal image as large as possible. But your eye cannot focus sharply on objects that are closer than the near point, so the angular size of an object is greatest (that is, it subtends the largest possible viewing angle) when it is placed at the near point. In the following discussion we will assume an average viewer for whom the near point is 25 cm from the eye.

34.51 (a) The angular size θ is largest when the object is at the near point. (b) The magnifier gives a virtual image at infinity. This virtual image appears to the eye to be a real object subtending a larger angle θ' at the eye.

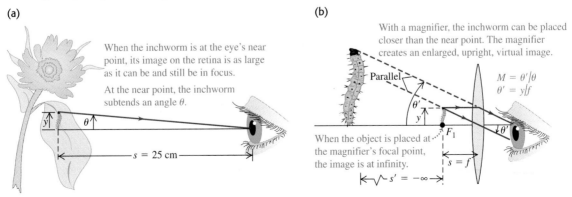

(a)

When the inchworm is at the eye's near point, its image on the retina is as large as it can be and still be in focus.

At the near point, the inchworm subtends an angle θ.

$s = 25$ cm

(b)

With a magnifier, the inchworm can be placed closer than the near point. The magnifier creates an enlarged, upright, virtual image.

Parallel

$M = \theta'/\theta$
$\theta' = y/f$

When the object is placed at the magnifier's focal point, the image is at infinity.

F_1

$s = f$

$s' = -\infty$

A converging lens can be used to form a virtual image that is larger and farther from the eye than the object itself, as shown in Fig. 34.51b. Then the object can be moved closer to the eye, and the angular size of the image may be substantially larger than the angular size of the object at 25 cm without the lens. A lens used in this way is called a **magnifier,** otherwise known as a *magnifying glass* or a *simple magnifier.* The virtual image is most comfortable to view when it is placed at infinity, so that the ciliary muscle of the eye is relaxed; this means that the object is placed at the focal point F_1 of the magnifier. In the following discussion we assume that this is done.

In Fig. 34.51a the object is at the near point, where it subtends an angle θ at the eye. In Fig. 34.51b a magnifier in front of the eye forms an image at infinity, and the angle subtended at the magnifier is θ'. The usefulness of the magnifier is given by the ratio of the angle θ' (with the magnifier) to the angle θ (without the magnifier). This ratio is called the **angular magnification M:**

$$M = \frac{\theta'}{\theta} \qquad \text{(angular magnification)} \tag{34.21}$$

> **CAUTION** **Angular magnification vs. lateral magnification** Don't confuse the *angular* magnification M with the *lateral* magnification m. Angular magnification is the ratio of the *angular* size of an image to the angular size of the corresponding object; lateral magnification refers to the ratio of the *height* of an image to the height of the corresponding object. For the situation shown in Fig. 34.51b, the angular magnification is about $3\times$, since the inchworm subtends an angle about three times larger than that in Fig. 34.51a; hence the inchworm will look about three times larger to the eye. The *lateral* magnification $m = -s'/s$ in Fig. 34.51b is *infinite* because the virtual image is at infinity, but that doesn't mean that the inchworm looks infinitely large through the magnifier! (That's why we didn't attempt to draw an infinitely large inchworm in Fig. 34.51b.) When dealing with a magnifier, M is useful but m is not. ▪

To find the value of M, we first assume that the angles are small enough that each angle (in radians) is equal to its sine and its tangent. Using Fig. 34.451a and drawing the ray in Fig. 34.51b that passes undeviated through the center of the lens, we find that θ and θ' (in radians) are

$$\theta = \frac{y}{25 \text{ cm}} \qquad \theta' = \frac{y}{f}$$

Combining these expressions with Eq. (34.21), we find

$$M = \frac{\theta'}{\theta} = \frac{y/f}{y/25 \text{ cm}} = \frac{25 \text{ cm}}{f} \qquad \begin{array}{l} \text{(angular magnification} \\ \text{for a simple magnifier)} \end{array} \tag{34.22}$$

It may seem that we can make the angular magnification as large as we like by decreasing the focal length f. In fact, the aberrations of a simple double-convex lens set a limit to M of about $3\times$ to $4\times$. If these aberrations are corrected, the angular magnification may be made as great as $20\times$. When greater magnification than this is needed, we usually use a compound microscope, discussed in the next section.

Test Your Understanding of Section 34.7   You are examining a gem using a magnifier. If you change to a different magnifier with twice the focal length of the first one, (i) you will have to hold the object at twice the distance and the angular magnification will be twice as great; (ii) you will have to hold the object at twice the distance and the angular magnification will be $\frac{1}{2}$ as great; (iii) you will have to hold the object at $\frac{1}{2}$ the distance and the angular magnification will be twice as great; (iv) you will have to hold the object at $\frac{1}{2}$ the distance and the angular magnification will be $\frac{1}{2}$ as great.

34.8 Microscopes and Telescopes

Cameras, eyeglasses, and magnifiers use a single lens to form an image. Two important optical devices that use *two* lenses are the microscope and the telescope. In each device a primary lens, or *objective,* forms a real image, and a second lens, or *eyepiece,* is used as a magnifier to make an enlarged, virtual image.

Microscopes

When we need greater magnification than we can get with a simple magnifier, the instrument that we usually use is the **microscope,** sometimes called a *compound microscope.* The essential elements of a microscope are shown in Fig. 34.52a. To analyze this system, we use the principle that an image formed by one optical element such as a lens or mirror can serve as the object for a second element. We used this principle in Section 34.4 when we derived the thin-lens equation by repeated application of the single-surface refraction equation; we used this principle again in Example 34.11 (Section 34.4), in which the image formed by a lens was used as the object of a second lens.

The object O to be viewed is placed just beyond the first focal point F_1 of the **objective,** a converging lens that forms a real and enlarged image I (Fig. 34.52b). In a properly designed instrument this image lies just inside the first focal point F_1' of a second converging lens called the **eyepiece** or *ocular.* (The reason the image should lie just *inside* F_1' is left for you to discover; see Problem 34.108.) The eyepiece acts as a simple magnifier, as discussed in Section 34.7, and forms a final virtual image I' of I. The position of I' may be anywhere between the near

34.52 (a) Elements of a microscope. (b) The object O is placed just outside the first focal point of the objective (the distance s_1 has been exaggerated for clarity). (c) This microscope image shows single-celled organisms about 2×10^{-4} m (0.2 mm) across. Typical light microscopes can resolve features as small as 2×10^{-7} m, comparable to the wavelength of light.

(a) Elements of a microscope

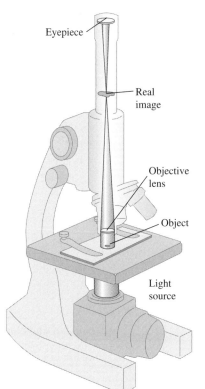

Eyepiece

Real image

Objective lens

Object

Light source

(b) Microscope optics

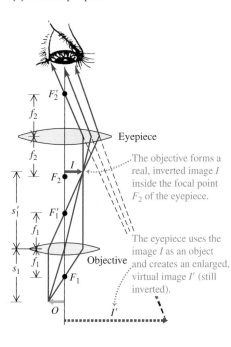

F_2'

f_2

Eyepiece

f_2

I

F_2

s_1'

F_1'

f_1

f_1 Objective

s_1

F_1

O I'

The objective forms a real, inverted image I inside the focal point F_2 of the eyepiece.

The eyepiece uses the image I as an object and creates an enlarged, virtual image I' (still inverted).

(c) Single-celled freshwater algae (*Micrasterias denticulata*)

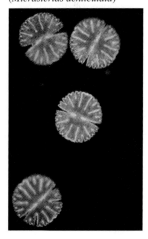

and far points of the eye. Both the objective and the eyepiece of an actual microscope are highly corrected compound lenses with several optical elements, but for simplicity we show them here as simple thin lenses.

As for a simple magnifier, what matters when viewing through a microscope is the *angular* magnification M. The overall angular magnification of the compound microscope is the product of two factors. The first factor is the *lateral* magnification m_1 of the objective, which determines the linear size of the real image I; the second factor is the *angular* magnification M_2 of the eyepiece, which relates the angular size of the virtual image seen through the eyepiece to the angular size that the real image I would have if you viewed it *without* the eyepiece. The first of these factors is given by

$$m_1 = -\frac{s_1'}{s_1} \tag{34.23}$$

where s_1 and s_1' are the object and image distances, respectively, for the objective lens. Ordinarily, the object is very close to the focal point, and the resulting image distance s_1' is very great in comparison to the focal length f_1 of the objective lens. Thus s_1 is approximately equal to f_1, and we can write $m_1 = -s_1'/f_1$.

The real image I is close to the focal point F_1' of the eyepiece, so to find the eyepiece angular magnification, we can use Eq. (34.22): $M_2 = (25\text{ cm})/f_2$, where f_2 is the focal length of the eyepiece (considered as a simple lens). The overall angular magnification M of the compound microscope (apart from a negative sign, which is customarily ignored) is the product of the two magnifications:

$$M = m_1 M_2 = \frac{(25\text{ cm})s_1'}{f_1 f_2} \quad \text{(angular magnification for a microscope)} \tag{34.24}$$

where s_1', f_1, and f_2 are measured in centimeters. The final image is inverted with respect to the object. Microscope manufacturers usually specify the values of m_1 and M_2 for microscope components rather than the focal lengths of the objective and eyepiece.

Equation (34.24) shows that the angular magnification of a microscope can be increased by using an objective of shorter focal length f_1, thereby increasing m_1 and the size of the real image I. Most optical microscopes have a rotating "turret" with three or more objectives of different focal lengths so that the same object can be viewed at different magnifications. The eyepiece should also have a short focal length f_2 to help to maximize the value of M.

To take a photograph using a microscope (called a *photomicrograph* or *micrograph*), the eyepiece is removed and a camera placed so that the real image I falls on the camera's CCD array or film. Figure 34.52c shows such a photograph. In this case what matters is the *lateral* magnification of the microscope as given by Eq. (34.23).

Telescopes

The optical system of a **telescope** is similar to that of a compound microscope. In both instruments the image formed by an objective is viewed through an eyepiece. The key difference is that the telescope is used to view large objects at large distances and the microscope is used to view small objects close at hand. Another difference is that many telescopes use a curved mirror, not a lens, as an objective.

Figure 34.53 shows an *astronomical telescope*. Because this telescope uses a lens as an objective, it is called a *refracting telescope* or *refractor*. The objective lens forms a real, reduced image I of the object. This image is the object for the eyepiece lens, which forms an enlarged, virtual image of I. Objects that are viewed with a telescope are usually so far away from the instrument that the first

34.53 Optical system of an astronomical refracting telescope.

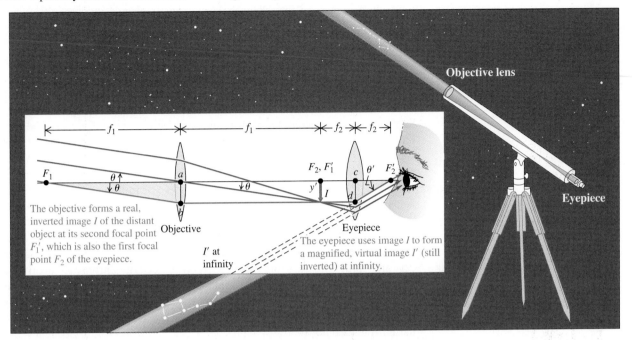

image I is formed very nearly at the second focal point of the objective lens. If the final image I' formed by the eyepiece is at infinity (for most comfortable viewing by a normal eye), the first image must also be at the first focal point of the eyepiece. The distance between objective and eyepiece, which is the length of the telescope, is therefore the *sum* of the focal lengths of objective and eyepiece, $f_1 + f_2$.

The angular magnification M of a telescope is defined as the ratio of the angle subtended at the eye by the final image I' to the angle subtended at the (unaided) eye by the object. We can express this ratio in terms of the focal lengths of objective and eyepiece. In Fig. 34.53 the ray passing through F_1, the first focal point of the objective, and through F'_2, the second focal point of the eyepiece, is shown in red. The object (not shown) subtends an angle θ at the objective and would subtend essentially the same angle at the unaided eye. Also, since the observer's eye is placed just to the right of the focal point F'_2, the angle subtended at the eye by the final image is very nearly equal to the angle θ'. Because bd is parallel to the optic axis, the distances ab and cd are equal to each other and also to the height y' of the real image I. Because the angles θ and θ' are small, they may be approximated by their tangents. From the right triangles F_1ab and F'_2cd,

$$\theta = \frac{-y'}{f_1} \qquad \theta' = \frac{y'}{f_2}$$

and the angular magnification M is

$$M = \frac{\theta'}{\theta} = -\frac{y'/f_2}{y'/f_1} = -\frac{f_1}{f_2} \qquad \text{(angular magnification for a telescope)} \qquad (34.25)$$

The angular magnification M of a telescope is equal to the ratio of the focal length of the objective to that of the eyepiece. The negative sign shows that the final image is inverted. Equation (34.25) shows that to achieve good angular magnification, a *telescope* should have a *long* objective focal length f_1. By contrast, Eq. (34.24) shows that a *microscope* should have a *short* objective focal length. However, a telescope objective with a long focal length should also have a large diameter D so that the f-number f_1/D will not be too large; as described in

Section 34.5, a large *f*-number means a dim, low-intensity image. Telescopes typically do not have interchangeable objectives; instead, the magnification is varied by using different eyepieces with different focal lengths f_2. Just as for a microscope, smaller values of f_2 give larger angular magnifications.

An inverted image is no particular disadvantage for astronomical observations. When we use a telescope or binoculars—essentially a pair of telescopes mounted side by side—to view objects on the earth, though, we want the image to be right-side up. In prism binoculars, this is accomplished by reflecting the light several times along the path from the objective to the eyepiece. The combined effect of the reflections is to flip the image both horizontally and vertically. Binoculars are usually described by two numbers separated by a multiplication sign, such as 7×50. The first number is the angular magnification *M*, and the second is the diameter of the objective lenses (in millimeters). The diameter helps to determine the light-gathering capacity of the objective lenses and thus the brightness of the image.

In the *reflecting telescope* (Fig. 34.54a) the objective lens is replaced by a concave mirror. In large telescopes this scheme has many advantages, both theoretical and practical. Mirrors are inherently free of chromatic aberrations (dependence of focal length on wavelength), and spherical aberrations (associated with the paraxial approximation) are easier to correct than with a lens. The reflecting surface is sometimes parabolic rather than spherical. The material of the mirror need not be transparent, and it can be made more rigid than a lens, which has to be supported only at its edges.

The largest reflecting telescopes in the world, the Keck telescopes atop Mauna Kea in Hawaii, each have an objective mirror of overall diameter 10 m made up of 36 separate hexagonal reflecting elements.

34.54 (a), (b), (c) Three designs for reflecting telescopes. (d) This photo shows the interior of the Gemini North telescope, which uses the design shown in (c). The objective mirror is 8 meters in diameter.

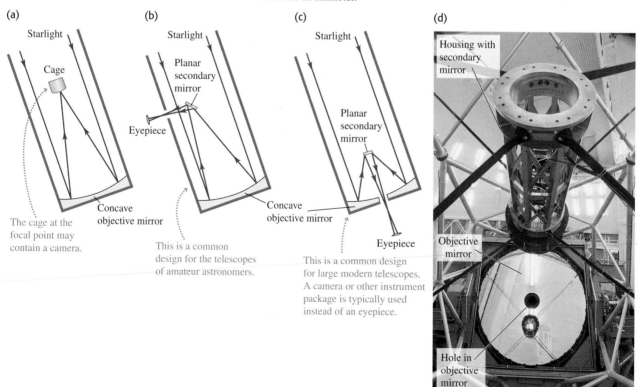

(a)
Starlight

Cage

Concave objective mirror

The cage at the focal point may contain a camera.

(b)
Starlight

Planar secondary mirror

Eyepiece

Concave objective mirror

This is a common design for the telescopes of amateur astronomers.

(c)
Starlight

Planar secondary mirror

Concave objective mirror

Eyepiece

This is a common design for large modern telescopes. A camera or other instrument package is typically used instead of an eyepiece.

(d)
Housing with secondary mirror

Objective mirror

Hole in objective mirror

One challenge in designing reflecting telescopes is that the image is formed in front of the objective mirror, in a region traversed by incoming rays. Isaac Newton devised one solution to this problem. A flat secondary mirror oriented at 45° to the optic axis causes the image to be formed in a hole on the side of the telescope, where it can be magnified with an eyepiece (Fig. 34.54b). Another solution uses a secondary mirror that causes the focused light to pass through a hole in the objective mirror (Fig. 34.54c). Large research telescopes, as well as many amateur telescopes, use this design (Fig. 34.54d).

Like a microscope, when a telescope is used for photography the eyepiece is removed and a CCD array or photographic film is placed at the position of the real image formed by the objective. (Some long-focal-length "lenses" for photography are actually reflecting telescopes used in this way.) Most telescopes used for astronomical research are never used with an eyepiece.

Test Your Understanding of Section 34.8   Which gives a lateral magnification of greater absolute value: (i) the objective lens in a microscope (Fig. 34.52); (ii) the objective lens in a refracting telescope (Fig. 34.53); or (iii) not enough information is given to decide?

Reflection or refraction at a plane surface: When rays diverge from an object point P and are reflected or refracted, the directions of the outgoing rays are the same as though they had diverged from a point P' called the image point. If they actually converge at P' and diverge again beyond it, P' is a real image of P; if they only appear to have diverged from P', it is a virtual image. Images can be either erect or inverted.

Plane mirror

Lateral magnification: The lateral magnification m in any reflecting or refracting situation is defined as the ratio of image height y' to object height y. When m is positive, the image is erect; when m is negative, the image is inverted.

$$m = \frac{y'}{y} \qquad (34.2)$$

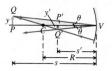

Focal point and focal length: The focal point of a mirror is the point where parallel rays converge after reflection from a concave mirror, or the point from which they appear to diverge after reflection from a convex mirror. Rays diverging from the focal point of a concave mirror are parallel after reflection; rays converging toward the focal point of a convex mirror are parallel after reflection. The distance from the focal point to the vertex is called the focal length, denoted as f. The focal points of a lens are defined similarly.

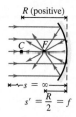

R (positive)

$$s = \infty$$
$$s' = \frac{R}{2} = f$$

Relating object and image distances: The formulas for object distance s and image distance s' for plane and spherical mirrors and single refracting surfaces are summarized in the table. The equation for a plane surface can be obtained from the corresponding equation for a spherical surface by setting $R = \infty$. (See Examples 34.1–34.7.)

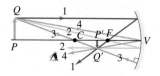

	Plane Mirror	Spherical Mirror	Plane Refracting Surface	Spherical Refracting Surface
Object and image distances	$\frac{1}{s} + \frac{1}{s'} = 0$	$\frac{1}{s} + \frac{1}{s'} = \frac{2}{R} = \frac{1}{f}$	$\frac{n_a}{s} + \frac{n_b}{s'} = 0$	$\frac{n_a}{s} + \frac{n_b}{s'} = \frac{n_b - n_a}{R}$
Lateral magnification	$m = -\frac{s'}{s} = 1$	$m = -\frac{s'}{s}$	$m = -\frac{n_a s'}{n_b s} = 1$	$m = -\frac{n_a s'}{n_b s}$

Object-image relationships derived in this chapter are valid only for rays close to and nearly parallel to the optic axis; these are called paraxial rays. Nonparaxial rays do not converge precisely to an image point. This effect is called spherical aberration.

Thin lenses: The object-image relationships, given by Eq. (34.16), is the same for a thin lens as for a spherical mirror. Equation (34.19), the lensmaker's equation, relates the focal length of a lens to its index of refraction and the radii of curvature of its surfaces. (See Examples 34.8–34.11.)

$$\frac{1}{s} + \frac{1}{s'} = \frac{1}{f} \qquad (34.16)$$

$$\frac{1}{f} = (n - 1)\left(\frac{1}{R_1} - \frac{1}{R_2}\right) \qquad (34.19)$$

Sign rules: The following sign rules are used with all plane and spherical reflecting and refracting surfaces.

- $s > 0$ when the object is on the incoming side of the surface (a real object); $s < 0$ otherwise.
- $s' > 0$ when the image is on the outgoing side of the surface (a real image); $s' < 0$ otherwise.
- $R > 0$ when the center of curvature is on the outgoing side of the surface; $R < 0$ otherwise.
- $m > 0$ when the image is erect; $m < 0$ when inverted.

Cameras: A camera forms a real, inverted, reduced image of the object being photographed on a light-sensitive surface. The amount of light striking this surface is controlled by the shutter speed and the aperture. The intensity of this light is inversely proportional to the square of the *f*-number of the lens. (See Example 34.12.)

$$f\text{-number} = \frac{\text{Focal length}}{\text{Aperture diameter}} \qquad (34.20)$$
$$= \frac{f}{D}$$

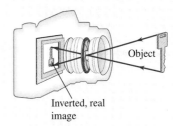

Inverted, real image

The eye: In the eye, refraction at the surface of the cornea forms a real image on the retina. Adjustment for various object distances is made by squeezing the lens, thereby making it bulge and decreasing its focal length. A nearsighted eye is too long for its lens; a farsighted eye is too short. The power of a corrective lens, in diopters, is the reciprocal of the focal length in meters. (See Examples 34.13 and 34.14.)

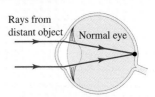

The simple magnifier: The simple magnifier creates a virtual image whose angular size θ' is larger than the angular size θ of the object itself at a distance of 25 cm, the nominal closest distance for comfortable viewing. The angular magnification M of a simple magnifier is the ratio of the angular size of the virtual image to that of the object at this distance.

$$M = \frac{\theta'}{\theta} = \frac{25\text{ cm}}{f} \qquad (34.22)$$

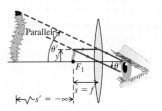

Microscopes and telescopes: In a compound microscope, the objective lens forms a first image in the barrel of the instrument, and the eyepiece forms a final virtual image, often at infinity, of the first image. The telescope operates on the same principle, but the object is far away. In a reflecting telescope, the objective lens is replaced by a concave mirror, which eliminates chromatic aberrations.

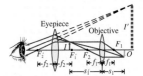

Key Terms

Answer to Chapter Opening Question ?

A magnifying lens (simple magnifier) produces a virtual image with a large angular size that is infinitely far away, so you can see it in sharp focus with your eyes relaxed. (A surgeon doing microsurgery would not appreciate having to strain his eyes while working.) The object should be at the focal point of the lens, so the object and lens are separated by one focal length.

Answers to Test Your Understanding Questions

34.1 Answer: (iv) When you are a distance s from the mirror, your image is a distance s on the other side of the mirror and the distance from you to your image is $2s$. As you move toward the mirror, the distance $2s$ changes at twice the rate of the distance s, so your image moves toward you at speed $2v$.

34.2 Answers: (a) concave, (b) (ii) A convex mirror always produces an erect image, but that image is smaller than the object (see

Fig. 34.16b). Hence a concave mirror must be used. The image will be erect and enlarged only if the distance from the object (your face) to the mirror is less than the focal length of the mirror, as in Fig. 34.20d.

34.3 Answer: no The sun is very far away, so the object distance is essentially infinite: $s = \infty$ and $1/s = 0$. Material a is air ($n_a = 1.00$) and material b is water ($n_b = 1.33$), so the image position s' is given by

$$\frac{n_a}{s} + \frac{n_b}{s'} = \frac{n_b - n_a}{R} \quad \text{or} \quad 0 + \frac{1.33}{s'} = \frac{1.33 - 1.00}{R}$$

$$s' = \frac{1.33}{0.33}R = 4.0R$$

The image would be formed 4.0 drop radii from the front surface of the drop. But since each drop is only a part of a complete sphere, the distance from the front to the back of the drop is less than $2R$. Thus the rays of sunlight never reach the image point, and the drops do not form an image of the sun on the leaf. While the rays are not focused to a point, they are nonetheless concentrated and can cause damage to the leaf.

34.4 Answers: A and C When rays A and D are extended backward, they pass through focal point F_2; thus, before they passed through the lens, they were parallel to the optic axis. The figures

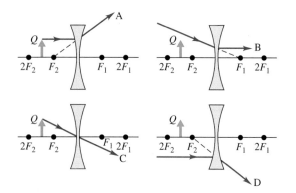

show that ray A emanated from point Q, but ray D did not. Ray B is parallel to the optic axis, so before it passed through the lens, it was directed toward focal point F_1. Hence it cannot have come from point Q. Ray C passes through the center of the lens and hence is not deflected by its passage; tracing the ray backward shows that it emanates from point Q.

34.5 Answer: (iii) The smaller image area of the CCD array means that the angle of view is decreased for a given focal length. Individual objects make images of the same size in either case; when a smaller light-sensitive area is used, fewer images fit into the area and the field of view is narrower.

34.6 Answer: (iii) This lens is designed to correct for a type of astigmatism. Along the vertical axis, the lens is configured as a converging lens; along the horizontal axis, the lens is configured as a diverging lens. Hence the eye is hyperopic (see Fig. 34.46) for objects that are oriented vertically but myopic for objects that are oriented horizontally (see Fig. 34.47). Without correction, the eye focuses vertical objects behind the retina but horizontal objects in front of the retina.

34.7 Answer: (ii) The object must be held at the focal point, which is twice as far away if the focal length f is twice as great. Equation (24.22) shows that the angular magnification M is inversely proportional to f, so doubling the focal length makes M $\frac{1}{2}$ as great. To improve the magnification, you should use a magnifier with a *shorter* focal length.

34.8 Answer: (i) The objective lens of a microscope is designed to make enlarged images of small objects, so the absolute value of its lateral magnification m is greater than 1. By contrast, the objective lens of a refracting telescope is designed to make *reduced* images. For example, the moon is thousands of kilometers in diameter, but its image may fit on a CCD array a few centimeters across. Thus $|m|$ is much less than 1 for a refracting telescope. (In both cases m is negative because the objective makes an inverted image, which is why the question asks about the absolute value of m.)

PROBLEMS

For instructor-assigned homework, go to **www.masteringphysics.com**

Discussion Questions

Q34.1. A spherical mirror is cut in half horizontally. Will an image be formed by the bottom half of the mirror? If so, where will the image be formed?

Q34.2. For the situation shown in Fig. 34.3, is the image distance s' positive or negative? Is the image real or virtual? Explain your answers.

Q34.3. The laws of optics also apply to electromagnetic waves invisible to the eye. A satellite TV dish is used to detect radio waves coming from orbiting satellites. Why is a curved reflecting surface (a "dish") used? The dish is always concave, never convex; why? The actual radio receiver is placed on an arm and suspended in front of the dish. How far in front of the dish should it be placed?

Q34.4. Explain why the focal length of a *plane* mirror is infinite, and explain what it means for the focal point to be at infinity.

Q34.5. If a spherical mirror is immersed in water, does its focal length change? Explain.

Q34.6. For what range of object positions does a concave spherical mirror form a real image? What about a convex spherical mirror?

Q34.7. When a room has mirrors on two opposite walls, an infinite series of reflections can be seen. Discuss this phenomenon in terms of images. Why do the distant images appear fainter?

Q34.8. For a spherical mirror, if $s = f$, then $s' = \infty$, and the lateral magnification m is infinite. Does this make sense? If so, what does it mean?

Q34.9. You may have noticed a small convex mirror next to your bank's ATM. Why is this mirror convex, as opposed to flat or concave? What considerations determine its radius of curvature?

Q34.10. A student claims that she can start a fire on a sunny day using just the sun's rays and a concave mirror. How is this done? Is the concept of image relevant? Can she do the same thing with a convex mirror? Explain.

Q34.11. A person looks at his reflection in the concave side of a shiny spoon. Is it right side up or inverted? Does it matter how far his face is from the spoon? What if he looks in the convex side? (Try this yourself!)

Q34.12. In Example 34.4 (Section 34.2), there appears to be an ambiguity for the case $s = 10$ cm as to whether s' is $+\infty$ or $-\infty$ and whether the image is erect or inverted. How is this resolved? Or is it?

Q34.13. Suppose that in the situation of Example 34.7 of Section 34.3 (see Fig. 34.26) a vertical arrow 2.00 m tall is painted on the side of the pool beneath the water line. According to the calculations in the example, this arrow would appear to the person shown in Fig. 34.26 to be 1.50 m long. But the discussion following Eq. (34.13) states that the magnification for a plane refracting surface is $m = 1$, which suggests that the arrow would appear to the person to be 2.00 m long. How can you resolve this apparent contradiction?

Q34.14. The bottom of the passenger side mirror on your car notes, "Objects in mirror are closer than they appear." Is this true? Why?

Q34.15. How could you very quickly make an approximate measurement of the focal length of a converging lens? Could the same method be applied if you wished to use a diverging lens? Explain.

Q34.16. The focal length of a simple lens depends on the color (wavelength) of light passing through it. Why? Is it possible for a lens to have a positive focal length for some colors and negative for others? Explain.

Q34.17. When a converging lens is immersed in water, does its focal length increase or decrease in comparison with the value in air? Explain.

Q34.18. A spherical air bubble in water can function as a lens. Is it a converging or diverging lens? How is its focal length related to its radius?

Q34.19. Can an image formed by one reflecting or refracting surface serve as an object for a second reflection or refraction? Does it matter whether the first image is real or virtual? Explain.

Q34.20. If a piece of photographic film is placed at the location of a real image, the film will record the image. Can this be done with a virtual image? How might one record a virtual image?

Q34.21. According to the discussion in Section 34.2, light rays are reversible. Are the formulas in the table in this chapter's Summary still valid if object and image are interchanged? What does reversibility imply with respect to the *forms* of the various formulas?

Q34.22. You've entered a survival contest that will include building a crude telescope. You are given a large box of lenses. Which two lenses do you pick? How do you quickly identify them?

Q34.23. You can't see clearly underwater with the naked eye, but you *can* if you wear a face mask or goggles (with air between your eyes and the mask or goggles). Why is there a difference? Could you instead wear eyeglasses (with water between your eyes and the eyeglasses) in order to see underwater? If so, should the lenses be converging or diverging? Explain.

Q34.24. You take a lens and mask it so that light can pass through only the bottom half of the lens. How does the image formed by the masked lens compare to the image formed before masking?

Exercises

Section 34.1 Reflection and Refraction at a Plane Surface

34.1. A candle 4.85 cm tall is 39.2 cm to the left of a plane mirror. Where is the image formed by the mirror, and what is the height of this image?

34.2. The image of a tree just covers the length of a plane mirror 4.00 cm tall when the mirror is held 35.0 cm from the eye. The tree is 28.0 m from the mirror. What is its height?

34.3. As shown in Fig. 34.9, mirror 1 uses the image P_2' formed by mirror 2 as an object and forms an image of it. Show that this image is at point P_3' in the figure.

Section 34.2 Reflection at a Spherical Surface

34.4. A concave mirror has a radius of curvature of 34.0 cm. (a) What is its focal length? (b) If the mirror is immersed in water (refractive index 1.33), what is its focal length?

34.5. An object 0.600 cm tall is placed 16.5 cm to the left of the vertex of a concave spherical mirror having a radius of curvature of 22.0 cm. (a) Draw a principal-ray diagram showing the formation of the image. (b) Determine the position, size, orientation, and nature (real or virtual) of the image.

34.6. Repeat Exercise 34.5 for the case in which the mirror is convex.

34.7. The diameter of Mars is 6794 km, and its minimum distance from the earth is 5.58×10^7 km. When Mars is at this distance, find the diameter of the image of Mars formed by a spherical, concave, telescope mirror with a focal length of 1.75 m.

34.8. An object is 24.0 cm from the center of a silvered spherical glass Christmas tree ornament 6.00 cm in diameter. What are the position and magnification of its image?

34.9. A coin is placed next to the convex side of a thin spherical glass shell having a radius of curvature of 18.0 cm. An image of the 1.5-cm-tall coin is formed 6.00 cm behind the glass shell. Where is the coin located? Determine the size, orientation, and nature (real or virtual) of the image.

34.10. You hold a spherical salad bowl 90 cm in front of your face with the bottom of the bowl facing you. The salad bowl is made of polished metal with a 35-cm radius of curvature. (a) Where is the image of your 2.0-cm-tall nose located? (b) What are the image's size, orientation, and nature (real or virtual)?

34.11. (a) Show that Eq. (34.6) can be written as $s' = sf/(s - f)$ and hence that the lateral magnification, given by Eq. (34.7), can be expressed as $m = f/(f - s)$. (b) Use these formulas for s' and m to graph s' as a function of s for the case $f > 0$ (a concave mirror). (c) For what values of s is s' positive, so that the image is real? (d) For what values of s is s' negative, so that the image is virtual? (e) Where is the image if the object is just inside the focal point (s slightly less than f)? (f) Where is the image if the object is at infinity? (g) Where is the image if the object is next to the mirror ($s = 0$)? (h) Graph m as a function of s for the case of a concave mirror. (i) For which values of s is the image erect and larger than the object? (j) For what values of s is the image inverted? (k) For which values of s is the image smaller than the object? (l) What happens to the size of the image when the object is placed at the focal point?

34.12. Using the formulas for s' and m obtained in part (a) of Exercise 34.11, graph s' as a function of s, and graph m as a function of s, for the case $f < 0$ (a convex mirror), so that $f = -|f|$. (a) For which values of s is s' positive? (b) For what values of s is s' negative? (c) Where is the image if the object is at infinity? (d) Where is the image if the object is next to the mirror ($s = 0$)? For which values of s is the image (e) erect; (f) inverted; (g) larger than the object; (h) smaller than the object?

34.13. Dental Mirror. A dentist uses a curved mirror to view teeth on the upper side of the mouth. Suppose she wants an erect image with a magnification of 2.00 when the mirror is 1.25 cm from a tooth. (Treat this problem as though the object and image lie along a straight line.) (a) What kind of mirror (concave or convex) is needed? Use a ray diagram to decide, without performing any calculations. (b) What must be the focal length and radius of curvature of this mirror? (c) Draw a principal-ray diagram to check your answer in part (b).

34.14. A spherical, concave, shaving mirror has a radius of curvature of 32.0 cm. (a) What is the magnification of a person's face when it is 12.0 cm to the left of the vertex of the mirror? (b) Where is the image? Is the image real or virtual? (c) Draw a principal-ray diagram showing the formation of the image.

Section 34.3 Refraction at a Spherical Surface

34.15. A speck of dirt is embedded 3.50 cm below the surface of a sheet of ice $(n = 1.309)$. What is its apparent depth when viewed at normal incidence?

34.16. A tank whose bottom is a mirror is filled with water to a depth of 20.0 cm. A small fish floats motionless 7.0 cm under the surface of the water. (a) What is the apparent depth of the fish when viewed at normal incidence? (b) What is the apparent depth of the image of the fish when viewed at normal incidence?

34.17. A Spherical Fish Bowl. A small tropical fish is at the center of a water-filled, spherical fish bowl 28.0 cm in diameter. (a) Find the apparent position and magnification of the fish to an observer outside the bowl. The effect of the thin walls of the bowl may be ignored. (b) A friend advised the owner of the bowl to keep it out of direct sunlight to avoid blinding the fish, which might swim into the focal point of the parallel rays from the sun. Is the focal point actually within the bowl?

34.18. The left end of a long glass rod 6.00 cm in diameter has a convex hemispherical surface 3.00 cm in radius. The refractive index of the glass is 1.60. Determine the position of the image if an object is placed in air on the axis of the rod at the following distances to the left of the vertex of the curved end: (a) infinitely far, (b) 12.0 cm; (c) 2.00 cm.

34.19. The glass rod of Exercise 34.18 is immersed in oil $(n = 1.45)$. An object placed to the left of the rod on the rod's axis is to be imaged 1.20 m inside the rod. How far from the left end of the rod must the object be located to form the image?

34.20. The left end of a long glass rod 8.00 cm in diameter, with an index of refraction 1.60, is ground and polished to a convex hemispherical surface with a radius of 4.00 cm. An object in the form of an arrow 1.50 mm tall, at right angles to the axis of the rod, is located on the axis 24.0 cm to the left of the vertex of the convex surface. Find the position and height of the image of the arrow formed by paraxial rays incident on the convex surface. Is the image erect or inverted?

34.21. Repeat Exercise 34.20 for the case in which the end of the rod is ground to a *concave* hemispherical surface with radius 4.00 cm.

34.22. The glass rod of Exercise 34.21 is immersed in a liquid. An object 14.0 cm from the vertex of the left end of the rod and on its axis is imaged at a point 9.00 cm from the vertex inside the liquid. What is the index of refraction of the liquid?

Section 34.4 Thin Lenses

34.23. An insect 3.75 mm tall is placed 22.5 cm to the left of a thin planoconvex lens. The left surface of this lens is flat, the right surface has a radius of curvature of magnitude 13.0 cm, and the index of refraction of the lens material is 1.70. (a) Calculate the location and size of the image this lens forms of the insect. Is it real or virtual? Erect or inverted? (b) Repeat part (a) if the lens is reversed.

34.24. A lens forms an image of an object. The object is 16.0 cm from the lens. The image is 12.0 cm from the lens on the same side as the object. (a) What is the focal length of the lens? Is the lens converging or diverging? (b) If the object is 8.50 mm tall, how tall is the image? Is it erect or inverted? (c) Draw a principal-ray diagram.

34.25. A converging meniscus lens (see Fig. 34.32a) with a refractive index of 1.52 has spherical surfaces whose radii are 7.00 cm and 4.00 cm. What is the position of the image if an object is placed 24.0 cm to the left of the lens? What is the magnification?

34.26. A converging lens with a focal length of 90.0 cm forms an image of a 3.20-cm-tall real object that is to the left of the lens. The image is 4.50 cm tall and inverted. Where are the object and image located in relation to the lens? Is the image real or virtual?

34.27. A converging lens forms an image of an 8.00-mm-tall real object. The image is 12.0 cm to the left of the lens, 3.40 cm tall, and erect. What is the focal length of the lens? Where is the object located?

34.28. A photographic slide is to the left of a lens. The lens projects an image of the slide onto a wall 6.00 m to the right of the slide. The image is 80.0 times the size of the slide. (a) How far is the slide from the lens? (b) Is the image erect or inverted? (c) What is the focal length of the lens? (d) Is the lens converging or diverging?

34.29. A double-convex thin lens has surfaces with equal radii of curvature of magnitude 2.50 cm. Looking through this lens, you observe that it forms an image of a very distant tree at a distance of 1.87 cm from the lens. What is the index of refraction of the lens?

34.30. Six lenses in air are shown in Fig. 34.32. Each lens is made of a material with index of refraction $n > 1$. Considering each lens individually, imagine that light enters the lens from the left. Show that the three lenses shown in Fig. 34.32a have *positive* focal lengths and hence are *converging* lenses. In addition, show that the three lenses in Fig. 34.32b have *negative* focal lengths and hence are *diverging* lenses.

34.31. Exercises 34.11 and 34.12 deal with spherical mirrors. (a) Show that the equations for s' and m derived in part (a) of Exercise 34.11 also apply to a thin lens. (b) A concave mirror is used in Exercise 34.11. Repeat these exercises for a converging lens. Are there any differences in the results when the mirror is replaced by a lens? Explain. (c) A convex mirror is used in Exercise 34.12. Repeat these exercises for a diverging lens. Are there any differences in the results when the mirror is replaced by a lens? Explain.

34.32. A converging lens with a focal length of 12.0 cm forms a virtual image 8.00 mm tall, 17.0 cm to the right of the lens. Determine the position and size of the object. Is the image erect or inverted? Are the object and image on the same side or opposite sides of the lens? Draw a principal-ray diagram for this situation.

34.33. Repeat Exercise 34.32 for the case in which the lens is diverging, with a focal length of −48.0 cm.

34.34. An object is 16.0 cm to the left of a lens. The lens forms an image 36.0 cm to the right of the lens. (a) What is the focal length of the lens? Is the lens converging or diverging? (b) If the object is 8.00 mm tall, how tall is the image? Is it erect or inverted? (c) Draw a principal-ray diagram.

Section 34.5 Cameras

34.35. A camera lens has a focal length of 200 mm. How far from the lens should the subject for the photo be if the lens is 20.4 cm from the film?

34.36. When a camera is focused, the lens is moved away from or toward the film. If you take a picture of your friend, who is standing 3.90 m from the lens, using a camera with a lens with a 85-mm focal length, how far from the film is the lens? Will the whole image of your friend, who is 175 cm tall, fit on film that is 24 × 36 mm?

34.37. Figure 34.41 shows photographs of the same scene taken with the same camera with lenses of different focal length. If the object is 200 m from the lens, what is the magnitude of the lateral magnification for a lens of focal length (a) 28 mm; (b) 105 mm; (c) 300 mm?

34.38. A photographer takes a photograph of a Boeing 747 airliner (length 70.7 m) when it is flying directly overhead at an altitude of 9.50 km. The lens has a focal length of 5.00 m. How long is the image of the airliner on the film?

34.39. Choosing a Camera Lens. The picture size on ordinary 35-mm camera film is 24 mm × 36 mm. Focal lengths of lenses available for 35-mm cameras typically include 28, 35, 50 (the "normal" lens), 85, 100, 135, 200, and 300 mm, among others. Which of these lenses should be used to photograph the following objects, assuming that the object is to fill most of the picture area? (a) a building 240 m tall and 160 m wide at a distance of 600 m, and (b) a mobile home 9.6 m in length at a distance of 40.0 m.

34.40. Zoom Lens. Consider the simple model of the zoom lens shown in Fig. 34.43a. The converging lens has focal length $f_1 = 12$ cm, and the diverging lens has focal length $f_2 = -12$ cm. The lenses are separated by 4 cm as shown in Fig. 34.43a. (a) For a distant object, where is the image of the converging lens? (b) The image of the converging lens serves as the object for the diverging lens. What is the object distance for the diverging lens? (c) Where is the final image? Compare your answer to Fig. 34.43a. (d) Repeat parts (a), (b), and (c) for the situation shown in Fig. 34.43b, in which the lenses are separated by 8 cm.

34.41. A camera lens has a focal length of 180.0 mm and an aperture diameter of 16.36 mm. (a) What is the f-number of the lens? (b) If the correct exposure of a certain scene is $\frac{1}{30}$ s at $f/11$, what is the correct exposure at $f/2.8$?

34.42. Recall that the intensity of light reaching film in a camera is proportional to the effective area of the lens. Camera A has a lens with an aperture diameter of 8.00 mm. It photographs an object using the correct exposure time of $\frac{1}{30}$ s. What exposure time should be used with camera B in photographing the same object with the same film if this camera has a lens with an aperture diameter of 23.1 mm?

34.43. Photography. A 35-mm camera has a standard lens with focal length 50 mm and can focus on objects between 45 cm and infinity. (a) Is the lens for such a camera a concave or a convex lens? (b) The camera is focused by rotating the lens, which moves it on the camera body and changes its distance from the film. In what range of distances between the lens and the film plane must the lens move to focus properly over the 45 cm to infinity range?

34.44. You wish to project the image of a slide on a screen 9.00 m from the lens of a slide projector. (a) If the slide is placed 15.0 cm from the lens, what focal length lens is required? (b) If the dimensions of the picture on a 35-mm color slide are 24 mm × 36 mm, what is the minimum size of the projector screen required to accommodate the image?

Section 34.6 The Eye

34.45. (a) Where is the near point of an eye for which a contact lens with a power of +2.75 diopters is prescribed? (b) Where is the far point of an eye for which a contact lens with a power of −1.30 diopters is prescribed for distant vision?

34.46. Curvature of the Cornea. In a simplified model of the human eye, the aqueous and vitreous humors and the lens all have a refractive index of 1.40, and all the refraction occurs at the

cornea, whose vertex is 2.60 cm from the retina. What should be the radius of curvature of the cornea such that the image of an object 40.0 cm from the cornea's vertex is focused on the retina?

34.47. Corrective Lenses. Determine the power of the corrective contact lenses required by (a) a hyperopic eye whose near point is at 60.0 cm and (b) a myopic eye whose far point is at 60.0 cm.

Section 34.7 The Magnifier

34.48. A thin lens with a focal length of 6.00 cm is used as a simple magnifier. (a) What angular magnification is obtainable with the lens if the object is at the focal point? (b) When an object is examined through the lens, how close can it be brought to the lens? Assume that the image viewed by the eye is at the near point, 25.0 cm from the eye, and that the lens is very close to the eye.

34.49. The focal length of a simple magnifier is 8.00 cm. Assume the magnifier is a thin lens placed very close to the eye. (a) How far in front of the magnifier should an object be placed if the image is formed at the observer's near point, 25.0 cm in front of her eye? (b) If the object is 1.00 mm high, what is the height of its image formed by the magnifier?

34.50. You want to view an insect 2.00 mm in length through a magnifier. If the insect is to be at the focal point of the magnifier, what focal length will give the image of the insect an angular size of 0.025 radian?

34.51. You are examining an ant with a magnifying lens that has focal length 5.00 cm. If the image of the ant appears 25.0 cm from the lens, how far is the ant from the lens? On which side of the lens is the image located?

Section 34.8 Microscopes and Telescopes

34.52. Resolution of a Microscope. The image formed by a microscope objective with a focal length of 5.00 mm is 160 mm from its second focal point. The eyepiece has a focal length of 26.0 mm. (a) What is the angular magnification of the microscope? (b) The unaided eye can distinguish two points at its near point as separate if they are about 0.10 mm apart. What is the minimum separation between two points that can be observed (or resolved) through this microscope?

34.53. The focal length of the eyepiece of a certain microscope is 18.0 mm. The focal length of the objective is 8.00 mm. The distance between objective and eyepiece is 19.7 cm. The final image formed by the eyepiece is at infinity. Treat all lenses as thin. (a) What is the distance from the objective to the object being viewed? (b) What is the magnitude of the linear magnification produced by the objective? (c) What is the overall angular magnification of the microscope?

34.54. A certain microscope is provided with objectives that have focal lengths of 16 mm, 4 mm, and 1.9 mm and with eyepieces that have angular magnifications of 5× and 10×. Each objective forms an image 120 mm beyond its second focal point. Determine (a) the largest overall angular magnification obtainable and (b) the least overall angular magnification obtainable.

34.55. The Yerkes refracting telescope of the University of Chicago has an objective 1.02 m in diameter with an f-number of 19.0. (This is the largest-diameter refracting telescope in the world.) What is its focal length?

34.56. The eyepiece of a refracting telescope (see Fig. 34.53) has a focal length of 9.00 cm. The distance between objective and eyepiece is 1.80 m, and the final image is at infinity. What is the angular magnification of the telescope?

34.57. A telescope is constructed from two lenses with focal lengths of 95.0 cm and 15.0 cm, the 95.0-cm lens being used as the objective. Both the object being viewed and the final image are at infinity. (a) Find the angular magnification for the telescope. (b) Find the height of the image formed by the objective of a building 60.0 m tall, 3.00 km away. (c) What is the angular size of the final image as viewed by an eye very close to the eyepiece?

34.58. Saturn is viewed through the Lick Observatory refracting telescope (objective focal length 18 m). If the diameter of the image of Saturn produced by the objective is 1.7 mm, what angle does Saturn subtend from when viewed from earth?

34.59. A reflecting telescope (Fig. 34.55a) is to be made by using a spherical mirror with a radius of curvature of 1.30 m and an eyepiece with a focal length of 1.10 cm. The final image is at infinity. (a) What should the distance between the eyepiece and the mirror vertex be if the object is taken to be at infinity? (b) What will the angular magnification be?

Figure **34.55** Exercises 34.59 and 34.60 and Problem 34.112.

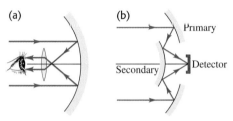

34.60. A Cassegrain telescope is a reflecting telescope that uses two mirrors, the secondary mirror focusing the image through a hole in the primary mirror (similar to that shown in Fig. 34.55b). You wish to focus the image of a distant galaxy onto the detector shown in the figure. If the primary mirror has a focal length of 2.5 m, the secondary mirror has a focal length of -1.5 m and the distance from the vertex of the primary mirror to the detector is 15 cm. What should be the distance between the vertices of the two mirrors?

Problems

34.61. If you run away from a plane mirror at 2.40 m/s, at what speed does your image move away from you?

34.62. An object is placed between two plane mirrors arranged at right angles to each other at a distance d_1 from the surface of one mirror and a distance d_2 from the other. (a) How many images are formed? Show the location of the images in a diagram. (b) Draw the paths of rays from the object to the eye of an observer.

34.63. What is the size of the smallest vertical plane mirror in which a woman of height h can see her full-length image?

34.64. A light bulb is 4.00 m from a wall. You are to use a concave mirror to project an image of the bulb on the wall, with the image 2.25 times the size of the object. How far should the mirror be from the wall? What should its radius of curvature be?

34.65. A concave mirror is to form an image of the filament of a headlight lamp on a screen 8.00 m from the mirror. The filament is 6.00 mm tall, and the image is to be 36.0 cm tall. (a) How far in front of the vertex of the mirror should the filament be placed? (b) What should be the radius of curvature of the mirror?

34.66. Rear-View Mirror. A mirror on the passenger side of your car is convex and has a radius of curvature with magnitude 18.0 cm. (a) Another car is seen in this side mirror and is 13.0 m behind the mirror. If this car is 1.5 m tall, what is the height of the image? (b) The mirror has a warning attached that objects viewed in it are closer than they appear. Why is this so?

34.67. Suppose the lamp filament shown in Example 34.1 (Section 34.2) is moved to a position 8.0 cm in front of the mirror. (a) Where is the image located now? Is it real or virtual? (b) What is the height of the image? Is it erect or inverted? (c) In Example 34.1, the filament is 10.0 cm in front of the mirror, and an image of the filament is formed on a wall 3.00 m from the mirror. If the filament is 8.0 cm from the mirror, can a wall be placed so that an image is formed on it? If so, where should the wall be placed? If not, why not?

34.68. Where must you place an object in front of a concave mirror with radius R so that the image is erect and $2\frac{1}{2}$ times the size of the object? Where is the image?

34.69. Virtual Object. If the light incident from the left onto a convex mirror does not diverge from an object point but instead converges toward a point at a (negative) distance s to the right of the mirror, this point is called a *virtual object*. (a) For a convex mirror having a radius of curvature of 24.0 cm, for what range of virtual-object positions is a real image formed? (b) What is the orientation of this real image? (c) Draw a principal-ray diagram showing the formation of such an image.

34.70. A layer of benzene $(n = 1.50)$ 2.60 cm deep floats on water $(n = 1.33)$ that is 6.50 cm deep. What is the apparent distance from the upper benzene surface to the bottom of the water layer when it is viewed at normal incidence?

34.71. Sketch the various possible thin lenses that can be obtained by combining two surfaces whose radii of curvature are 4.00 cm and 8.00 cm in absolute magnitude. Which are converging and which are diverging? Find the focal length of each if the surfaces are made of glass with index of refraction 1.60.

34.72. Figure 34.56 shows a small plant near a thin lens. The ray shown is one of the principal rays for the lens. Each square is 2.0 cm along the horizontal direction, but the vertical direction is not to the same scale. Use information from the diagram to answer the following questions: (a) Using only the ray shown, decide what type of lens (converging or diverging) this is. (b) What is the focal length of the lens? (c) Locate the image by drawing the other two principal rays. (d) Calculate where the image should be, and compare this result with the graphical solution in part (c).

Figure **34.56** Problem 34.72.

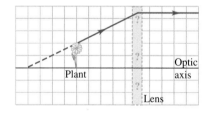

34.73. You are in your car driving on a highway at 25 m/s when you glance in the passenger side mirror (a convex mirror with radius of curvature 150 cm) and notice a truck approaching. If the image of the truck is approaching the vertex of the mirror at a speed of 1.5 m/s when the truck is 2.0 m away, what is the speed of the truck relative to the highway?

34.74. A microscope is focused on the upper surface of a glass plate. A second plate is then placed over the first. To focus on the bottom surface of the second plate, the microscope must be raised 0.780 mm. To focus on the upper surface, it must be raised another 2.50 mm. Find the index of refraction of the second plate.

34.75. Three-Dimensional Image. The *longitudinal* magnification is defined as $m' = ds'/ds$. It relates the longitudinal dimension of a small object to the longitudinal dimension of its image. (a) Show that for a spherical mirror, $m' = -m^2$. What is the significance of the fact that m' is *always* negative? (b) A wire frame in the form of a small cube 1.00 mm on a side is placed with its center on the axis of a concave mirror with radius of curvature 150.0 cm. The sides of the cube are all either parallel or perpendicular to the axis. The cube face toward the mirror is 200.0 cm to the left of the mirror vertex. Find (i) the location of the image of this face and of the opposite face of the cube; (ii) the lateral and longitudinal magnifications; (iii) the shape and dimensions of each of the six faces of the image.

34.76. Refer to Problem 34.75. Show that the longitudinal magnification m' for refraction at a spherical surface is given by

$$m' = -\frac{n_b}{n_a}m^2$$

34.77. Pinhole Camera. A pinhole camera is just a rectangular box with a tiny hole in one face. The film is on the face opposite this hole, and that is where the image is formed. The camera forms an image *without* a lens. (a) Make a clear ray diagram to show how a pinhole camera can form an image on the film without using a lens. (*Hint:* Put an object outside the hole, and then draw rays passing through the hole to the opposite side of the box.) (b) A certain pinhole camera is a box that is 25 cm square and 20.0 cm deep, with the hole in the middle of one of the 25 cm × 25 cm faces. If this camera is used to photograph a fierce chicken that is 18 cm high and 1.5 m in front of the camera, how large is the image of this bird on the film? What is the magnification of this camera?

34.78. A Glass Rod. Both ends of a glass rod with index of refraction 1.60 are ground and polished to convex hemispherical surfaces. The radius of curvature at the left end is 6.00 cm, and the radius of curvature at the right end is 12.0 cm. The length of the rod between vertices is 40.0 cm. The object for the surface at the left end is an arrow that lies 23.0 cm to the left of the vertex of this surface. The arrow is 1.50 mm tall and at right angles to the axis. (a) What constitutes the object for the surface at the right end of the rod? (b) What is the object distance for this surface? (c) Is the object for this surface real or virtual? (*Hint:* See Problem 34.69.) (d) What is the position of the final image? (e) Is the final image real or virtual? Is it erect or inverted with respect to the original object? (f) What is the height of the final image?

34.79. The rod in Problem 34.78 is shortened to a distance of 25.0 cm between its vertices; the curvatures of its ends remain the same. As in Problem 34.78, the object for the surface at the left end is an arrow that lies 23.0 cm to the left of the vertex of this surface. The arrow is 1.50 mm tall and at right angles to the axis. (a) What is the object distance for the surface at the right end of the rod? (b) Is the object for this surface real or virtual? (c) What is the position of the final image? (d) Is the final image real or virtual? Is it erect or inverted with respect to the original object? (e) What is the height of the final image?

34.80. Figure 34.57 shows an object and its image formed by a thin lens. (a) What is the focal length of the lens, and what type of lens (converging or diverging) is it? (b) What is the height of the image? Is it real or virtual?

Figure **34.57** Problem 34.80

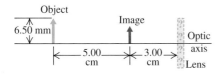

34.81. Figure 34.58 shows an object and its image formed by a thin lens. (a) What is the focal length of the lens, and what type of lens

(converging or diverging) is it? (b) What is the height of the image? Is it real or virtual?

Figure **34.58** Problem 34.81

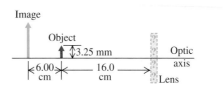

34.82. A transparent rod 30.0 cm long is cut flat at one end and rounded to a hemispherical surface of radius 10.0 cm at the other end. A small object is embedded within the rod along its axis and halfway between its ends, 15.0 cm from the flat end and 15.0 cm from the vertex of the curved end. When viewed from the flat end of the rod, the apparent depth of the object is 9.50 cm from the flat end. What is its apparent depth when viewed from the curved end?

34.83. A solid glass hemisphere of radius 12.0 cm and index of refraction $n = 1.50$ is placed with its flat face downward on a table. A parallel beam of light with a circular cross section 3.80 mm in diameter travels straight down and enters the hemisphere at the center of its curved surface. (a) What is the diameter of the circle of light formed on the table? (b) How does your result depend on the radius of the hemisphere?

34.84. A thick-walled wine goblet sitting on a table can be considered to be a hollow glass sphere with an outer radius of 4.00 cm and an inner radius of 3.40 cm. The index of refraction of the goblet glass is 1.50. (a) A beam of parallel light rays enters the side of the empty goblet along a horizontal radius. Where, if anywhere, will an image be formed? (b) The goblet is filled with white wine ($n = 1.37$). Where is the image formed?

34.85. Focus of the Eye. The cornea of the eye has a radius of curvature of approximately 0.50 cm, and the aqueous humor behind it has an index of refraction of 1.35. The thickness of the cornea itself is small enough that we shall neglect it. The depth of a typical human eye is around 25 mm. (a) What would have to be the radius of curvature of the cornea so that it alone would focus the image of a distant mountain on the retina, which is at the back of the eye opposite the cornea? (b) If the cornea focused the mountain correctly on the retina as described in part (a), would it also focus the text from a computer screen on the retina if that screen were 25 cm in front of the eye? If not, where would it focus that text: in front of or behind the retina? (c) Given that the cornea has a radius of curvature of about 5.0 mm, where does it actually focus the mountain? Is this in front of or behind the retina? Does this help you see why the eye needs help from a lens to complete the task of focusing?

34.86. A transparent rod 50.0 cm long and with a refractive index of 1.60 is cut flat at the right end and rounded to a hemispherical surface with a 15.0-cm radius at the left end. An object is placed on the axis of the rod 12.0 cm to the left of the vertex of the hemispherical end. (a) What is the position of the final image? (b) What is its magnification?

34.87. What should be the index of refraction of a transparent sphere in order for paraxial rays from an infinitely distant object to be brought to a focus at the vertex of the surface opposite the point of incidence?

34.88. A glass rod with a refractive index of 1.55 is ground and polished at both ends to hemispherical surfaces with radii of 6.00 cm. When an object is placed on the axis of the rod, 25.0 cm to the left of the left-hand end, the final image is formed 65.0 cm to the right of the right-hand end. What is the length of the rod measured between the vertices of the two hemispherical surfaces?

34.89. Two thin lenses with focal lengths of magnitude 15.0 cm, the first diverging and the second converging, are placed 12.00 cm apart. An object 4.00 mm tall is placed 5.00 cm to the left of the first (diverging) lens. (a) Where is the image formed by the first lens located? (b) How far from the object is the final image formed? (c) Is the final image real or virtual? (d) What is the height of the final image? Is the final image erect or inverted?

34.90. The radii of curvature of the surfaces of a thin converging meniscus lens are $R_1 = +12.0$ cm and $R_2 = +28.0$ cm. The index of refraction is 1.60. (a) Compute the position and size of the image of an object in the form of an arrow 5.00 mm tall, perpendicular to the lens axis, 45.0 cm to the left of the lens. (b) A second converging lens with the same focal length is placed 3.15 m to the right of the first. Find the position and size of the final image. Is the final image erect or inverted with respect to the original object? (c) Repeat part (b) except with the second lens 45.0 cm to the right of the first.

34.91. An object to the left of a lens is imaged by the lens on a screen 30.0 cm to the right of the lens. When the lens is moved 4.00 cm to the right, the screen must be moved 4.00 cm to the left to refocus the image. Determine the focal length of the lens.

34.92. For refraction at a spherical surface, the first focal length f is defined as the value of s corresponding to $s' = \infty$, as shown in Fig. 34.59a. The second focal length f' is defined as the value of s' when $s = \infty$, as shown in Fig. 34.59b. (a) Prove that $n_a/n_b = f/f'$. (b) Prove that the general relationship between object and image distance is

$$\frac{f}{s} + \frac{f'}{s'} = 1$$

Figure **34.59** Problem 34.92.

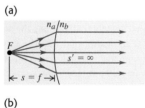
(a)

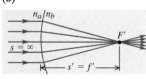
(b)

34.93. A convex mirror and a concave mirror are placed on the same optic axis, separated by a distance $L = 0.600$ m. The radius of curvature of each mirror has a magnitude of 0.360 m. A light source is located a distance x from the concave mirror, as shown in Fig. 34.60. (a) What distance x will result in the rays from the source returning to the source after reflecting first from the convex mirror and then from the concave mirror? (b) Repeat part (a), but now let the rays reflect first from the concave mirror and then from the convex one.

Figure **34.60** Problem 34.93.

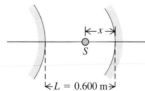

$$\leftarrow L = 0.600 \text{ m} \rightarrow$$

34.94. As shown in Fig. 34.61 the candle is at the center of curvature of the concave mirror, whose focal length is 10.0 cm. The converging lens has a focal length of 32.0 cm and is 85.0 cm to the right of the candle. The candle is viewed looking through the lens

from the right. The lens forms two images of the candle. The first is formed by light passing directly through the lens. The second image is formed from the light that goes from the candle to the mirror, is reflected, and then passes through the lens. (a) For each of these two images, draw a principal-ray diagram that locates the image. (b) For each image, answer the following questions: (i) Where is the image? (ii) Is the image real or virtual? (iii) Is the image erect or inverted with respect to the original object?

Figure **34.61** Problem 34.94.

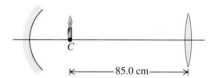

34.95. One end of a long glass rod is ground to a convex hemispherical shape. This glass has an index of refraction of 1.55. When a small leaf is placed 20.0 cm in front of the center of the hemisphere along the optic axis, an image is formed inside the glass 9.12 cm from the spherical surface. Where would the image be formed if the glass were now immersed in water (refractive index 1.33) but nothing else were changed?

34.96. Two Lenses in Contact. (a) Prove that when two thin lenses with focal lengths f_1 and f_2 are placed *in contact*, the focal length f of the combination is given by the relationship

$$\frac{1}{f} = \frac{1}{f_1} + \frac{1}{f_2}$$

(b) A converging meniscus lens (see Fig. 34.32a) has an index of refraction of 1.55 and radii of curvature for its surfaces of 4.50 cm and 9.00 cm. The concave surface is placed upward and filled with carbon tetrachloride (CCl_4), which has $n = 1.46$. What is the focal length of the CCl_4–glass combination?

34.97. Rays from a lens are converging toward a point image P located to the right of the lens. What thickness t of glass with index of refraction 1.60 must be interposed between the lens and P for the image to be formed at P', located 0.30 cm to the right of P? The locations of the piece of glass and of points P and P' are shown in Fig. 34.62.

Figure **34.62** Problem 34.97.

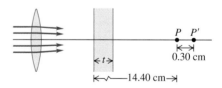

34.98. A Lens in a Liquid. A lens obeys Snell's law, bending light rays at each surface an amount determined by the index of refraction of the lens and the index of the medium in which the lens is located. (a) Equation (34.19) assumes that the lens is surrounded by air. Consider instead a thin lens immersed in a liquid with refractive index n_{liq}. Prove that the focal length f' is then given by Eq. (34.19) with n replaced by n/n_{liq}. (b) A thin lens with index n has focal length f in vacuum. Use the result of part (a) to show that when this lens is immersed in a liquid of index n_{liq}, it will have a new focal length given by

$$f' = \left[\frac{n_{\text{liq}}(n-1)}{n - n_{\text{liq}}}\right] f$$

34.99. When an object is placed at the proper distance to the left of a converging lens, the image is focused on a screen 30.0 cm to the right of the lens. A diverging lens is now placed 15.0 cm to the right of the converging lens, and it is found that the screen must be moved 19.2 cm farther to the right to obtain a sharp image. What is the focal length of the diverging lens?

34.100. A convex spherical mirror with a focal length of magnitude 24.0 cm is placed 20.0 cm to the left of a plane mirror. An object 0.250 cm tall is placed midway between the surface of the plane mirror and the vertex of the spherical mirror. The spherical mirror forms multiple images of the object. Where are the two images of the object formed by the spherical mirror that are closest to the spherical mirror, and how tall is each image?

34.101. A glass plate 3.50 cm thick, with an index of refraction of 1.55 and plane parallel faces, is held with its faces horizontal and its lower face 6.00 cm above a printed page. Find the position of the image of the page formed by rays making a small angle with the normal to the plate.

34.102. A symmetric, double-convex, thin lens made of glass with index of refraction 1.52 has a focal length in air of 40.0 cm. The lens is sealed into an opening in the left-hand end of a tank filled with water. At the right-hand end of the tank, opposite the lens, is a plane mirror 90.0 cm from the lens. The index of refraction of the water is $\frac{4}{3}$. (a) Find the position of the image formed by the lens–water–mirror system of a small object outside the tank on the lens axis and 70.0 cm to the left of the lens. (b) Is the image real or virtual? (c) Is it erect or inverted? (d) If the object has a height of 4.00 mm, what is the height of the image?

34.103. You have a camera with a 35.0-mm focal length lens and 36.0-mm-wide film. You wish to take a picture of a 12.0-m-long sailboat but find that the image of the boat fills only $\frac{1}{4}$ of the width of the film. (a) How far are you from the boat? (b) How much closer must the boat be to you for its image to fill the width of the film?

34.104. An object is placed 18.0 cm from a screen. (a) At what two points between object and screen may a converging lens with a 3.00-cm focal length be placed to obtain an image on the screen? (b) What is the magnification of the image for each position of the lens?

34.105. Three thin lenses, each with a focal length of 40.0 cm, are aligned on a common axis; adjacent lenses are separated by 52.0 cm. Find the position of the image of a small object on the axis, 80.0 cm to the left of the first lens.

34.106. A camera with a 90-mm-focal-length lens is focused on an object 1.30 m from the lens. To refocus on an object 6.50 m from the lens, by how much must the distance between the lens and the film be changed? To refocus on the more distant object, is the lens moved toward or away from the film?

34.107. The derivation of the expression for angular magnification, Eq. (34.22), assumed a near point of 25 cm. In fact, the near point changes with age as shown in Table 34.1. In order to achieve an angular magnification of 2.0×, what focal length should be used by a person of (a) age 10; (b) age 30; (c) age 60? (d) If the lens that gives $M = 2.0$ for a 10-year-old is used by a 60-year-old, what angular magnification will the older viewer obtain? (e) Does your answer in part (d) mean that older viewers are able to see more highly magnified images than younger viewers? Explain.

34.108. Angular Magnification. In deriving Eq. (34.22) for the angular magnification of a magnifier, we assumed that the object is placed at the focal point of the magnifier so that the virtual image is formed at infinity. Suppose instead that the object is placed so that the virtual image appears at an average viewer's near point of 25 cm, the closest point at which the viewer can bring an object into focus. (a) Where should the object be placed to achieve this? Give your answer in terms of the magnifier focal length f. (b) What angle θ' will an object of height y subtend at the position found in part (a)? (c) Find the angular magnification M with the object at the position found in part (a). The angle θ is the same as in Fig. 34.51a, since it refers to viewing the object *without* the magnifier. (d) For a convex lens with $f = +10.0$ cm, what is the value of M with the object at the position found in part (a)? How many times greater is M in this case than in the case where the image is formed at infinity? (e) In the description of a compound microscope in Section 34.8, it is stated that in a properly designed instrument, the real image formed by the objective lies *just inside* the first focal point F_1' of the eyepiece. What advantages are gained by having the image formed by the objective be just inside F_1', as opposed to precisely at F_1'? What happens if the image formed by the objective is *just outside* F_1'?

34.109. In one form of cataract surgery the person's natural lens, which has become cloudy, is replaced by an artificial lens. The refracting properties of the replacement lens can be chosen so that the person's eye focuses on distant objects. But there is no accommodation, and glasses or contact lenses are needed for close vision. What is the power, in diopters, of the corrective contact lenses that will enable a person who has had such surgery to focus on the page of a book at a distance of 24 cm?

34.110. A Nearsighted Eye. A certain very nearsighted person cannot focus on anything farther than 36.0 cm from the eye. Consider the simplified model of the eye described in Exercise 34.46. If the radius of curvature of the cornea is 0.75 cm when the eye is focusing on an object 36.0 cm from the cornea vertex and the indexes of refraction are as described in Exercise 34.46, what is the distance from the cornea vertex to the retina? What does this tell you about the shape of the nearsighted eye?

34.111. Focal Length of a Zoom Lens. Figure 34.63 shows a simple version of a zoom lens. The converging lens has focal length f_1, and the diverging lens has focal length $f_2 = -|f_2|$. The two lenses are separated by a variable distance d that is always less than f_1. Also, the magnitude of the focal length of the diverging lens satisfies the inequality $|f_2| > (f_1 - d)$. To determine the effective focal length of the combination lens, consider a bundle of parallel rays of radius r_0 entering the converging lens. (a) Show that the radius of the ray bundle decreases to $r_0' = r_0(f_1 - d)/f_1$ at the point that it enters the diverging lens. (b) Show that the final image I' is formed a distance $s_2' = |f_2|(f_1 - d)/(|f_2| - f_1 + d)$ to the right of the diverging lens. (c) If the rays that emerge from the diverging lens and reach the final image point are extended backward to the left of the diverging lens, they will eventually expand to the original radius r_0 at some point Q. The distance from the final image I' to the point Q is the *effective focal length* f of the lens combination; if the combination were replaced by a single lens of focal length f placed at Q, parallel rays would still be

Figure **34.63** Problem 34.111.

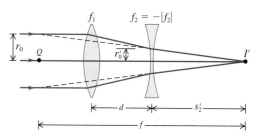

brought to a focus at I'. Show that the effective focal length is given by $f = f_1|f_2|/(|f_2| - f_1 + d)$. (d) If $f_1 = 12.0$ cm, $f_2 = -18.0$ cm, and the separation d is adjustable between 0 and 4.0 cm, find the maximum and minimum focal lengths of the combination. What value of d gives $f = 30.0$ cm?

34.112. A certain reflecting telescope, constructed as shown in Fig. 34.55a, has a spherical mirror with a radius of curvature of 96.0 cm and an eyepiece with a focal length of 1.20 cm. If the angular magnification has a magnitude of 36 and the object is at infinity, find the position of the eyepiece and the position and nature (real or virtual) of the final image. (*Note:* $|M|$ is *not* equal to $|f_1/f_2|$, so the image formed by the eyepiece is *not* at infinity.)

34.113. A microscope with an objective of focal length 8.00 mm and an eyepiece of focal length 7.50 cm is used to project an image on a screen 2.00 m from the eyepiece. Let the image distance of the objective be 18.0 cm. (a) What is the lateral magnification of the image? (b) What is the distance between the objective and the eyepiece?

34.114. The Galilean Telescope. Figure 34.64 is a diagram of a *Galilean telescope,* or *opera glass,* with both the object and its final image at infinity. The image I serves as a virtual object for the eyepiece. The final image is virtual and erect. (a) Prove that the angular magnification is $M = -f_1/f_2$. (b) A Galilean telescope is to be constructed with the same objective lens as in Exercise 34.57. What focal length should the eyepiece have if this telescope is to have the same magnitude of angular magnification as the one in Exercise 34.57? (c) Compare the lengths of the telescopes.

Figure **34.64** Problem 34.114.

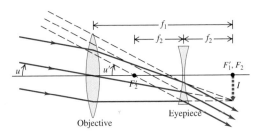

Challenge Problems

34.115. An Object at an Angle. A 16.0-cm-long pencil is placed at a 45.0° angle, with its center 15.0 cm above the optic axis and 45.0 cm from a lens with a 20.0-cm focal length as shown in Fig. 34.65. (Note that the figure is not drawn to scale.) Assume that

Figure **34.65** Challenge Problem 34.115.

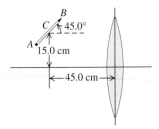

the diameter of the lens is large enough for the paraxial approximation to be valid. (a) Where is the image of the pencil? (Give the location of the images of the points A, B, and C on the object, which are located at the eraser, point, and center of the pencil, respectively.) (b) What is the length of the image (that is, the distance between the images of points A and B)? (c) Show the orientation of the image in a sketch.

34.116. *Spherical aberration* is a blurring of the image formed by a spherical mirror. It occurs because parallel rays striking the mirror far from the optic axis are focused at a different point than are rays near the axis. This problem is usually minimized by using only the center of a spherical mirror. (a) Show that for a spherical concave mirror, the focus moves toward the mirror as the parallel rays move toward the outer edge of the mirror. (*Hint:* Derive an analytic expression for the distance from the vertex to the focus of the ray for a particular parallel ray. This expression should be in terms of (i) the radius of curvature R of the mirror and (ii) the angle θ between the incident ray and a line connecting the center of curvature of the mirror with the point where the ray strikes the mirror.) (b) What value of θ produces a 2% change in the location of the focus, compared to the location for θ very close to zero?

34.117. (a) For a lens with focal length f, find the smallest distance possible between the object and its real image. (b) Graph the distance between the object and the real image as a function of the distance of the object from the lens. Does your graph agree with the result you found in part (a)?

34.118. Two mirrors are placed together as shown in Fig. 34.66. (a) Show that a point source in front of these mirrors and its two images lie on a circle. (b) Find the center of the circle. (c) In a diagram, show where an observer should stand so as to be able to see both images.

Figure **34.66** Challenge Problem 34.118.

34.119. People with normal vision cannot focus their eyes underwater if they aren't wearing a face mask or goggles and there is water in contact with their eyes (see Discussion Question Q34.23). (a) Why not? (b) With the simplified model of the eye described in Exercise 34.46, what corrective lens (specified by focal length as measured in air) would be needed to enable a person underwater to focus an infinitely distant object? (Be careful—the focal length of a lens underwater is *not* the same as in air! See Problem 34.98. Assume that the corrective lens has a refractive index of 1.62 and that the lens is used in eyeglasses, not goggles, so there is water on both sides of the lens. Assume that the eyeglasses are 2.00 cm in front of the eye.)

INTERFERENCE

35

? Soapy water is colorless, but when blown into bubbles it shows vibrant colors. How does the thickness of the bubble walls determine the particular colors that appear?

LEARNING GOALS

By studying this chapter, you will learn:

- What happens when two waves combine, or interfere, in space.

- How to understand the interference pattern formed by the interference of two coherent light waves.

- How to calculate the intensity at various points in an interference pattern.

- How interference occurs when light reflects from the two surfaces of a thin film.

- How interference makes it possible to measure extremely small distances.

An ugly black oil spot on the pavement can become a thing of beauty after a rain, when the oil reflects a rainbow of colors. Multicolored reflections can also be seen from the surfaces of soap bubbles and compact discs. These familiar sights give us a hint that there are aspects of light that we haven't yet explored.

In our discussion of lenses, mirrors, and optical instruments we used the model of *geometric optics,* in which we represent light as *rays,* straight lines that are bent at a reflecting or refracting surface. But many aspects of the behavior of light *can't* be understood on the basis of rays. We have already learned that light is fundamentally a *wave,* and in some situations we have to consider its wave properties explicitly. If two or more light waves of the same frequency overlap at a point, the total effect depends on the *phases* of the waves as well as their amplitudes. The resulting patterns of light are a result of the *wave* nature of light and cannot be understood on the basis of rays. Optical effects that depend on the wave nature of light are grouped under the heading **physical optics.**

In this chapter we'll look at *interference* phenomena that occur when two waves combine. The colors seen in oil films and soap bubbles are a result of interference between light reflected from the front and back surfaces of a thin film of oil or soap solution. Effects that occur when *many* sources of waves are present are called *diffraction* phenomena; we'll study these in Chapter 36. In that chapter we'll see that diffraction effects occur whenever a wave passes through an aperture or around an obstacle. They are important in practical applications of physical optics such as diffraction gratings, x-ray diffraction, and holography.

While our primary concern is with light, interference and diffraction can occur with waves of *any* kind. As we go along, we'll point out applications to other types of waves such as sound and water waves.

35.1 Interference and Coherent Sources

As we discussed in Chapter 15, the term **interference** refers to any situation in which two or more waves overlap in space. When this occurs, the total wave at any point at any instant of time is governed by the **principle of superposition,** which we introduced in Section 15.6 in the context of waves on a string. This principle also applies to electromagnetic waves and is the most important principle in all of physical optics, so make sure you understand it well. The principle of superposition states:

When two or more waves overlap, the resultant displacement at any point and at any instant is found by adding the instantaneous displacements that would be produced at the point by the individual waves if each were present alone.

(In some special physical situations, such as electromagnetic waves propagating in a crystal, this principle may not apply. A discussion of these is beyond our scope.)

We use the term "displacement" in a general sense. With waves on the surface of a liquid, we mean the actual displacement of the surface above or below its normal level. With sound waves, the term refers to the excess or deficiency of pressure. For electromagnetic waves, we usually mean a specific component of electric or magnetic field.

Interference in Two or Three Dimensions

We have already discussed one important case of interference, in which two identical waves propagating in opposite directions combine to produce a *standing wave.* We saw this in Chapters 15 and 16 for transverse waves on a string and for longitudinal waves in a fluid filling a pipe; we described the same phenomenon for electromagnetic waves in Section 32.5. In all of these cases the waves propagated along only a single axis: along a string, along the length of a fluid-filled pipe, or along the propagation direction of an electromagnetic plane wave. But light waves can (and do) travel in *two* or *three* dimensions, as can any kind of wave that propagates in a two- or three-dimensional medium. In this section we'll see what happens when we combine waves that spread out in two or three dimensions from a pair of identical wave sources.

Interference effects are most easily seen when we combine *sinusoidal* waves with a single frequency f and wavelength λ. Figure 35.1 shows a "snapshot" or "freeze-frame" of a *single* source S_1 of sinusoidal waves and some of the wave fronts produced by this source. The figure shows only the wave fronts corresponding to wave *crests,* so the spacing between successive wave fronts is one wavelength. The material surrounding S_1 is uniform, so the wave speed is the same in all directions, and there is no refraction (and hence no bending of the wave fronts). If the waves are two-dimensional, like waves on the surface of a liquid, the circles in Fig. 35.1 represent circular wave fronts; if the waves propagate in three dimensions, the circles represent spherical wave fronts spreading away from S_1.

In optics, sinusoidal waves are characteristic of **monochromatic light** (light of a single color). While it's fairly easy to make water waves or sound waves of a single frequency, common sources of light *do not* emit monochromatic (single-frequency) light. For example, incandescent light bulbs and flames emit a continuous distribution of wavelengths. However, there are several ways to produce *approximately* monochromatic light. For example, some filters block all but a very narrow range of wavelengths. By far the most nearly monochromatic source that is available at present is the *laser.* An example is the helium–neon laser, which emits red light at 632.8 nm with a wavelength range of the order of ± 0.000001 nm, or about one part in 10^9. As we analyze interference and diffrac-

35.1 A "snapshot" of sinusoidal waves of frequency f and wavelength λ spreading out from source S_1 in all directions.

Wave fronts: crests of the wave (frequency f) separated by one wavelength λ

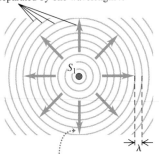

The wave fronts move outward from source S_1 at the wave speed $v = f\lambda$.

tion effects in this chapter and the next, we will assume that we are working with monochromatic waves (unless we explicitly state otherwise).

Constructive and Destructive Interference

Two identical sources of monochromatic waves, S_1 and S_2, are shown in Fig. 35.2a. The two sources produce waves of the same amplitude and the same wavelength λ. In addition, the two sources are permanently *in phase;* they vibrate in unison. They might be two synchronized agitators in a ripple tank, two loud-speakers driven by the same amplifier, two radio antennas powered by the same transmitter, or two small holes or slits in an opaque screen, illuminated by the same monochromatic light source. We will see that if there were not a constant phase relationship between the two sources, the phenomena we are about to dis-cuss would not occur. Two monochromatic sources of the same frequency and with any definite, constant phase relationship (not necessarily in phase) are said to be **coherent.** We also use the term *coherent waves* (or, for light waves, *coherent light*) to refer to the waves emitted by two such sources.

If the waves emitted by the two coherent sources are *transverse,* like electro-magnetic waves, then we will also assume that the wave disturbances produced by both sources have the same *polarization* (that is, they lie along the same line). For example, the sources S_1 and S_2 in Fig. 35.2a could be two radio antennas in the form of long rods oriented parallel to the z-axis (perpendicular to the plane of the figure); at any point in the xy-plane the waves produced by both antennas have $\vec{E}$ fields with only a z-component. Then we need only a single scalar func-tion to describe each wave; this makes the analysis much easier.

We position the two sources of equal amplitude, equal wavelength, and (if the waves are transverse) the same polarization along the y-axis in Fig. 35.2a, equi-distant from the origin. Consider a point a on the x-axis. From symmetry the two distances from S_1 to a and from S_2 to a are *equal;* waves from the two sources thus require equal times to travel to a. Hence waves that leave S_1 and S_2 in phase arrive at a in phase. The two waves add, and the total amplitude at a is *twice* the amplitude of each individual wave. This is true for *any* point on the x-axis.

Similarly, the distance from S_2 to point b is exactly two wavelengths *greater* than the distance from S_1 to b. A wave crest from S_1 arrives at b exactly two cycles earlier than a crest emitted at the same time from S_2, and again the two waves arrive in phase. As at point a, the total amplitude is the sum of the ampli-tudes of the waves from S_1 and S_2.

In general, when waves from two or more sources arrive at a point *in phase,* the amplitude of the resultant wave is the *sum* of the amplitudes of the individual waves; the individual waves reinforce each other. This is called **constructive interference** (Fig. 35.2b). Let the distance from S_1 to any point P be r_1, and let the distance from S_2 to P be r_2. For constructive interference to occur at P, the path difference $r_2 - r_1$ for the two sources must be an integral multiple of the wavelength λ:

$$r_2 - r_1 = m\lambda \qquad (m = 0, \pm 1, \pm 2, \pm 3, \dots)$$

(constructive interference, sources in phase) (35.1)

In Fig. 35.2a, points a and b satisfy Eq. (35.1) with $m = 0$ and $m = +2$, respectively.

Something different occurs at point c in Fig. 35.2a. At this point, the path dif-ference $r_2 - r_1 = -2.50\lambda$, which is a *half-integral* number of wavelengths. Waves from the two sources arrive at point c exactly a half-cycle out of phase. A crest of one wave arrives at the same time as a crest in the opposite direction (a "trough") of the other wave (Fig. 35.2c). The resultant amplitude is the *difference* between the two individual amplitudes. If the individual amplitudes are equal, then the total amplitude is *zero!* This cancellation or partial cancellation of the

35.2 (a) A "snapshot" of sinusoidal waves spreading out from two coherent sources S_1 and S_2. Constructive interference occurs at point a (equidistant from the two sources) and (b) at point b. (c) Destructive interference occurs at point c.

(a) Two coherent wave sources separated by a distance 4λ

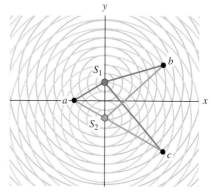

(b) Conditions for constructive interference: Waves interfere constructively if their path lengths differ by an integral number of wavelengths: $r_2 - r_1 = m\lambda$.

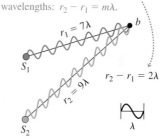

(c) Conditions for destructive interference: Waves interfere destructively if their path lengths differ by a half-integral number of wavelengths: $r_2 - r_1 = (m + \frac{1}{2})\lambda$.

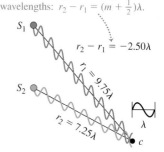

individual waves is called **destructive interference.** The condition for destructive interference in the situation shown in Fig. 35.2a is

$$r_2 - r_1 = \left(m + \frac{1}{2}\right)\lambda \quad (m = 0, \pm 1, \pm 2, \pm 3, \dots)$$

(destructive interference, sources in phase) (35.2)

The path difference at point c in Fig. 35.2a satisfies Eq. (35.2) with $m = -3$.

Figure 35.3 shows the same situation as in Fig. 35.2a, but with red curves that denote all points on which *constructive* interference occurs. On each curve, the path difference $r_2 - r_1$ is equal to an integer m times the wavelength, as in Eq. (35.1). These curves are called **antinodal curves.** They are directly analogous to *antinodes* in the standing-wave patterns described in Chapters 15 and 16 and Section 32.5. In a standing wave formed by interference between waves propagating in opposite directions, the antinodes are points at which the amplitude is maximum; likewise, the wave amplitude in the situation of Fig. 35.3 is maximum along the antinodal curves. Not shown in Fig. 35.3 are the **nodal curves,** which are the curves denoting points on which *destructive* interference occurs in accordance with Eq. (35.2); these are analogous to the *nodes* in a standing-wave pattern. A nodal curve lies between each two adjacent antinodal curves in Fig. 35.3; one such curve, corresponding to $r_2 - r_1 = -2.50\lambda$, passes through point c.

In some cases, such as two loudspeakers or two radio-transmitter antennas, the interference pattern is three-dimensional. Think of rotating the color curves of Fig. 35.3 around the y-axis; then maximum constructive interference occurs at all points on the resulting surfaces of revolution.

CAUTION **Interference patterns are not standing waves** The interference patterns in Figs. 35.2a and 35.3 are *not* standing waves, though they have some similarities to the standing-wave patterns described in Chapters 15 and 16 and Section 32.5. In a standing wave, the interference is between two waves propagating in opposite directions; a stationary pattern of antinodes and nodes appears, and there is *no* net energy flow in either direction (the energy in the wave is left "standing"). In the situations shown in Figs. 35.2a and 35.3, there is likewise a stationary pattern of antinodal and nodal curves, but there is a net flow of energy *outward* from the two sources. From the energy standpoint, all that interference does is to "channel" the energy flow so that it is greatest along the antinodal curves and least along the nodal curves.

For Eqs. (35.1) and (35.2) to hold, the two sources must have the same wavelength and must *always* be in phase. These conditions are rather easy to satisfy for sound waves (see Example 16.15 in Section 16.6). But with *light* waves there is no practical way to achieve a constant phase relationship (coherence) with two independent sources. This is because of the way light is emitted. In ordinary light sources, atoms gain excess energy by thermal agitation or by impact with accelerated electrons. An atom that is "excited" in such a way begins to radiate energy and continues until it has lost all the energy it can, typically in a time of the order of 10^{-8} s. The many atoms in a source ordinarily radiate in an unsynchronized and random phase relationship, and the light that is emitted from *two* such sources has no definite phase relationship.

However, the light from a single source can be split so that parts of it emerge from two or more regions of space, forming two or more *secondary sources.* Then any random phase change in the source affects these secondary sources equally and does not change their *relative* phase.

The distinguishing feature of light from a *laser* is that the emission of light from many atoms is synchronized in frequency and phase. As a result, the random phase changes mentioned above occur much less frequently. Definite phase relationships are preserved over correspondingly much greater lengths in the beam, and laser light is much more coherent than ordinary light.

35.3 The same as Fig. 35.2a, but with red antinodal curves (curves of maximum amplitude) superimposed. All points on each curve satisfy Eq. (35.1) with the value of m shown. The nodal curves (not shown) lie between each adjacent pair of antinodal curves.

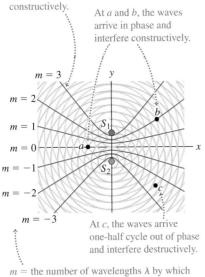

Antinodal curves (red) mark positions where the waves from S_1 and S_2 interfere constructively.

At a and b, the waves arrive in phase and interfere constructively.

At c, the waves arrive one-half cycle out of phase and interfere destructively.

m = the number of wavelengths λ by which the path lengths from S_1 and S_2 differ.

Test Your Understanding of Section 35.1   Consider a point in Fig. 35.3 on the positive *y*-axis above S_1. Does this point lie on (i) an antinodal curve; (ii) a nodal curve; or (iii) neither? *(Hint: The distance between S_1 and S_2 is 4λ.)*

35.2 Two-Source Interference of Light

The interference pattern produced by two coherent sources of *water* waves of the same wavelength can be readily seen in a ripple tank with a shallow layer of water (Fig. 35.4). This pattern is not directly visible when the interference is between *light* waves, since light traveling in a uniform medium cannot be seen. (A shaft of afternoon sunlight in a room is made visible by scattering from airborne dust particles.)

One of the earliest quantitative experiments to reveal the interference of light from two sources was performed in 1800 by the English scientist Thomas Young. We will refer back to this experiment several times in this and later chapters, so it's important to understand it in detail. Young's apparatus is shown in perspective in Fig. 35.5a. A light source (not shown) emits monochromatic light; however, this light is not suitable for use in an interference experiment because emissions from different parts of an ordinary source are not synchronized. To remedy this, the light is directed at a screen with a narrow slit S_0, 1 μm or so wide. The light emerging from the slit originated from only a small region of the light source; thus slit S_0 behaves more nearly like the idealized source shown in Fig. 35.1. (In modern versions of the experiment, a laser is used as a source of coherent light, and the slit S_0 isn't needed.) The light from slit S_0 falls on a screen with two other narrow slits S_1 and S_2, each 1 μm or so wide and a few tens or hundreds of micrometers apart. Cylindrical wave fronts spread out from slit S_0 and reach slits S_1 and S_2 *in phase* because they travel equal distances from S_0. The waves *emerging* from slits S_1 and S_2 are therefore also always in phase, so S_1 and S_2 are *coherent* sources. The interference of waves from S_1 and S_2 produces a pattern in space like that to the right of the sources in Figs. 35.2a and 35.3.

35.4 The concepts of constructive interference and destructive interference apply to these water waves as well as to light waves and sound waves.

(a) Interference of light waves passing through two slits

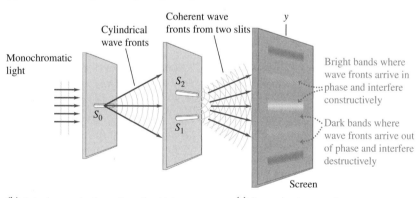

35.5 (a) Young's experiment to show interference of light passing through two slits. A pattern of bright and dark areas appears on the screen (see Fig. 35.6).
(b) Geometrical analysis of Young's experiment. For the case shown, $r_2 > r_1$ and both *y* and θ are positive. If point *P* is on the other side of the screen's center, $r_2 < r_1$ and both *y* and θ are negative.
(c) Approximate geometry when the distance *R* to the screen is much greater than the distance *d* between the slits.

(b) Actual geometry (seen from the side)

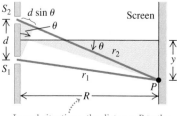

In real situations, the distance *R* to the screen is usually very much greater than the distance *d* between the slits ...

(c) Approximate geometry

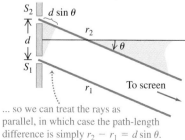

... so we can treat the rays as parallel, in which case the path-length difference is simply $r_2 - r_1 = d \sin \theta$.

Act|v
Phys|cs

16.1 Two-Source Interference:
Introduction

16.1 Two-Source Interference:
Qualitative Questions

16.1 Two-Source Interference:
Problems

To visualize the interference pattern, a screen is placed so that the light from S_1 and S_2 falls on it (Fig. 35.5b). The screen will be most brightly illuminated at points P, where the light waves from the slits interfere constructively, and will be darkest at points where the interference is destructive.

To simplify the analysis of Young's experiment, we assume that the distance R from the slits to the screen is so large in comparison to the distance d between the slits that the lines from S_1 and S_2 to P are very nearly parallel, as in Fig. 35.5c. This is usually the case for experiments with light; the slit separation is typically a few millimeters, while the screen may be a meter or more away. The difference in path length is then given by

$$r_2 - r_1 = d\sin\theta \qquad (35.3)$$

where θ is the angle between a line from slits to screen (shown in blue in Fig. 35.5c) and the normal to the plane of the slits (shown as a thin black line).

Constructive and Destructive Two-Slit Interference

We found in Section 35.1 that constructive interference (reinforcement) occurs at points where the path difference is an integral number of wavelengths, $m\lambda$, where $m = 0, \pm 1, \pm 2, \pm 3, \ldots$. So the bright regions on the screen in Fig. 35.5 occur at angles θ for which

$$d\sin\theta = m\lambda \qquad (m = 0, \pm 1, \pm 2, \ldots) \qquad \begin{array}{l}\text{(constructive inter-}\\\text{ference, two slits)}\end{array} \quad (35.4)$$

Similarly, destructive interference (cancellation) occurs, forming dark regions on the screen, at points for which the path difference is a half-integral number of wavelengths, $\left(m + \frac{1}{2}\right)\lambda$:

$$d\sin\theta = \left(m + \frac{1}{2}\right)\lambda \qquad (m = 0, \pm 1, \pm 2, \ldots) \qquad \begin{array}{l}\text{(destructive inter-}\\\text{ference, two slits)}\end{array} \quad (35.5)$$

35.6 Photograph of interference fringes produced on a screen in Young's double-slit experiment.

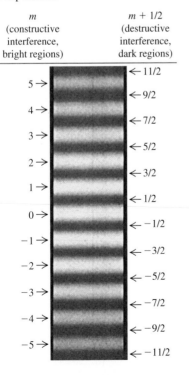

Thus the pattern on the screen of Figs. 35.5a and 35.5b is a succession of bright and dark bands, or **interference fringes,** parallel to the slits S_1 and S_2. A photograph of such a pattern is shown in Fig. 35.6. The center of the pattern is a bright band corresponding to $m = 0$ in Eq. (35.4); this point on the screen is equidistant from the two slits.

We can derive an expression for the positions of the centers of the bright bands on the screen. In Fig. 35.5b, y is measured from the center of the pattern, corresponding to the distance from the center of Fig. 35.6. Let y_m be the distance from the center of the pattern $(\theta = 0)$ to the center of the mth bright band. Let θ_m be the corresponding value of θ; then

$$y_m = R\tan\theta_m$$

In experiments such as this, the distances y_m are often much smaller than the distance R from the slits to the screen. Hence θ_m is very small, $\tan\theta_m$ is very nearly equal to $\sin\theta_m$, and

$$y_m = R\sin\theta_m$$

Combining this with Eq. (35.4), we find that *for small angles only,*

$$y_m = R\frac{m\lambda}{d} \qquad \text{(constructive interference in Young's experiment)} \quad (35.6)$$

We can measure R and d, as well as the positions y_m of the bright fringes, so this experiment provides a direct measurement of the wavelength λ. Young's experiment was in fact the first direct measurement of wavelengths of light.

CAUTION **Equation (35.6) is for small angles only** While Eqs. (35.4) and (35.5) are valid at any angle, Eq. (35.6) is valid only for *small* angles. It can be used *only* if the distance R from slits to screen is much greater than the slit separation d and if R is much greater than the distance y_m from the center of the interference pattern to the mth bright fringe. ▮

The distance between adjacent bright bands in the pattern is *inversely* proportional to the distance d between the slits. The closer together the slits are, the more the pattern spreads out. When the slits are far apart, the bands in the pattern are closer together.

While we have described the experiment that Young performed with visible light, the results given in Eqs. (35.4) and (35.5) are valid for *any* type of wave, provided that the resultant wave from two coherent sources is detected at a point that is far away in comparison to the separation d.

Example 35.1 **Two-slit interference**

In a two-slit interference experiment, the slits are 0.200 mm apart, and the screen is at a distance of 1.00 m. The third bright fringe (not counting the central bright fringe straight ahead from the slits) is found to be displaced 9.49 mm from the central fringe (Fig. 35.7). Find the wavelength of the light used.

SOLUTION

IDENTIFY: This problem asks us to determine the wavelength λ from the dimensions $d = 0.200$ mm (slit separation), $R = 1.00$ m (distance from slits to screen), and $y_m = 9.49$ mm (distance of the third bright fringe from the center of the pattern).

SET UP: The third bright fringe corresponds to $m = 3$ in Eqs. (35.4) and (35.6), as well as to the bright fringe labeled $m = 3$ in Fig. 35.6. To determine the value of the target variable λ, we may use Eq. (35.6) since $R = 1.00$ m is much greater than $d = 0.200$ mm or $y_3 = 9.49$ mm.

EXECUTE: Solving Eq. (35.6) for λ, we find

$$\lambda = \frac{y_m d}{mR} = \frac{(9.49 \times 10^{-3}\text{ m})(0.200 \times 10^{-3}\text{ m})}{(3)(1.00\text{ m})}$$

$$= 633 \times 10^{-9}\text{ m} = 633\text{ nm}$$

35.7 Using a two-slit interference experiment to measure the wavelength of light.

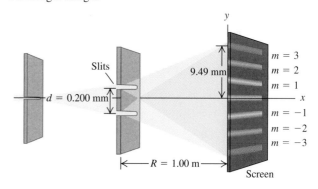

EVALUATE: This bright fringe could also correspond to $m = -3$; can you show that this gives the same result for λ?

Example 35.2 **Broadcast pattern of a radio station**

A radio station operating at a frequency of 1500 kHz = 1.5×10^6 Hz (near the top end of the AM broadcast band) has two identical vertical dipole antennas spaced 400 m apart, oscillating in phase. At distances much greater than 400 m, in what directions is the intensity greatest in the resulting radiation pattern? (This is not just a hypothetical problem. It is often desirable to beam most of the radiated energy from a radio transmitter in particular directions rather than uniformly in all directions. Pairs or rows of antennas are often used to produce the desired radiation pattern.)

SOLUTION

IDENTIFY: The two antennas, shown in Fig. 35.8, correspond to sources S_1 and S_2 in Fig. 35.5. Hence we can apply the ideas of two-slit interference to this problem.

35.8 Two radio antennas broadcasting in phase. The purple arrows indicate the directions of maximum intensity. The waves that are emitted toward the lower half of the figure are not shown.

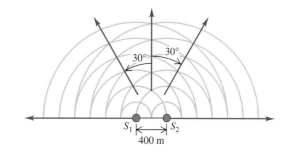

Continued

SET UP: Since the resultant wave is detected at distances much greater than $d = 400$ m, we may use Eq. (35.4) to give the directions of the intensity *maxima,* the values of θ for which the path difference is zero or a whole number of wavelengths.

EXECUTE: The wavelength is $\lambda = c/f = 200$ m. From Eq. (35.4) with $m = 0, \pm 1$, and ± 2, the intensity maxima are given by

$$\sin\theta = \frac{m\lambda}{d} = \frac{m(200 \text{ m})}{400 \text{ m}} = \frac{m}{2} \qquad \theta = 0, \pm 30°, \pm 90°$$

In this example, values of m greater than 2 or less than -2 give values of $\sin\theta$ greater than 1 or less than -1, which is impossible. There is *no* direction for which the path difference is three or more wavelengths. Thus values of m of ± 3 and beyond have no physical meaning in this example.

EVALUATE: We can check our result by calculating the angles for *minimum* intensity (destructive interference). There should be one intensity minimum between each pair of intensity maxima, just as in the interference pattern shown in Fig. 35.6. The angles of the intensity minima are given by Eq. (35.5) with $m = -2, -1, 0$, and 1:

$$\sin\theta = \frac{(m + \frac{1}{2})\lambda}{d} = \frac{m + \frac{1}{2}}{2} \qquad \theta = \pm 14.5°, \pm 48.6°$$

(Other values of m have no physical significance in this example.) Note that these angles are intermediate between the angles for intensity maxima, as they should be. Note also that since the angles are not small, the angles for the minima are *not* exactly halfway between the angles for the maxima.

Test Your Understanding of Section 35.2 You shine a tunable laser (whose wavelength can be adjusted by turning a knob) on a pair of closely spaced slits. The light emerging from the two slits produces an interference pattern on a screen like that shown in Fig. 35.6. If you adjust the wavelength so that the laser light changes from red to blue, how will the spacing between bright fringes change? (i) The spacing increases; (ii) the spacing decreases; (iii) the spacing is unchanged; (iv) not enough information is given to decide.

35.3 Intensity in Interference Patterns

In Section 35.2 we found the positions of maximum and minimum intensity in a two-source interference pattern. Let's now see how to find the intensity at *any* point in the pattern. To do this, we have to combine the two sinusoidally varying fields (from the two sources) at a point P in the radiation pattern, taking proper account of the phase difference of the two waves at point P, which results from the path difference. The intensity is then proportional to the square of the resultant electric-field amplitude, as we learned in Chapter 32.

To calculate the intensity, we will assume that the two sinusoidal functions (corresponding to waves from the two sources) have equal amplitude E and that the $\vec{E}$ fields lie along the same line (have the same polarization). This assumes that the sources are identical and neglects the slight amplitude difference caused by the unequal path lengths (the amplitude decreases with increasing distance from the source). From Eq. (32.29), each source by itself would give an intensity $\frac{1}{2}\epsilon_0 cE^2$ at point P. If the two sources are in phase, then the waves that arrive at P differ in phase by an amount proportional to the difference in their path lengths, $(r_2 - r_1)$. If the phase angle between these arriving waves is ϕ, then we can use the following expressions for the two electric fields superposed at P:

$$E_1(t) = E\cos(\omega t + \phi)$$
$$E_2(t) = E\cos\omega t$$

Here is our program. The superposition of the two fields at P is a sinusoidal function with some amplitude E_P that depends on E and the phase difference ϕ. First we'll work on finding the amplitude E_P if E and ϕ are known. Then we'll find the intensity I of the resultant wave, which is proportional to E_P^2. Finally, we'll relate the phase difference ϕ to the path difference, which is determined by the geometry of the situation.

Amplitude in Two-Source Interference

To add the two sinusoidal functions with a phase difference, we use the same *phasor* representation that we used for simple harmonic motion (Section 13.2) and for voltages and currents in ac circuits (Section 31.1). We suggest that you review these sections so that phasors are fresh in your mind. Each sinusoidal function is represented by a rotating vector (phasor) whose projection on the horizontal axis at any instant represents the instantaneous value of the sinusoidal function.

In Fig. 35.9, E_1 is the horizontal component of the phasor representing the wave from source S_1, and E_2 is the horizontal component of the phasor for the wave from S_2. As shown in the diagram, both phasors have the same magnitude E, but E_1 is *ahead* of E_2 in phase by an angle ϕ. Both phasors rotate counterclockwise with constant angular speed ω, and the sum of the projections on the horizontal axis at any time gives the instantaneous value of the total E field at point P. Thus the amplitude E_P of the resultant sinusoidal wave at P is the magnitude of the dark red phasor in the diagram (labeled E_P); this is the *vector sum* of the other two phasors. To find E_P, we use the law of cosines and the trigonometric identity $\cos(\pi - \phi) = -\cos\phi$:

$$E_P^2 = E^2 + E^2 - 2E^2\cos(\pi - \phi)$$
$$= E^2 + E^2 + 2E^2\cos\phi$$

Then, using the identity $1 + \cos\phi = 2\cos^2(\phi/2)$, we obtain

$$E_P^2 = 2E^2(1 + \cos\phi) = 4E^2\cos^2\left(\frac{\phi}{2}\right)$$

$$E_P = 2E\left|\cos\frac{\phi}{2}\right| \qquad \text{(amplitude in two-source interference)} \qquad (35.7)$$

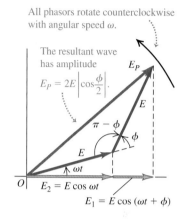

35.9 Phasor diagram for the superposition at a point P of two waves of equal amplitude E with a phase difference ϕ.

You can also obtain this result algebraically without using phasors (see Problem 35.48).

When the two waves are in phase, $\phi = 0$ and $E_P = 2E$. When they are exactly a half-cycle out of phase, $\phi = \pi$ rad $= 180°$, $\cos(\phi/2) = \cos(\pi/2) = 0$, and $E_P = 0$. Thus the superposition of two sinusoidal waves with the same frequency and amplitude but with a phase difference yields a sinusoidal wave with the same frequency and an amplitude between zero and twice the individual amplitudes, depending on the phase difference.

Intensity in Two-Source Interference

To obtain the intensity I at point P, we recall from Section 32.4 that I is equal to the average magnitude of the Poynting vector, S_{av}. For a sinusoidal wave with electric-field amplitude E_P, this is given by Eq. (32.29) with E_{max} replaced by E_P. Thus we can express the intensity in any of the following equivalent forms:

$$I = S_{av} = \frac{E_P^2}{2\mu_0 c} = \frac{1}{2}\sqrt{\frac{\epsilon_0}{\mu_0}}E_P^2 = \frac{1}{2}\epsilon_0 c E_P^2 \qquad (35.8)$$

The essential content of these expressions is that I is proportional to E_P^2. When we substitute Eq. (35.7) into the last expression in Eq. (35.8), we get

$$I = \frac{1}{2}\epsilon_0 c E_P^2 = 2\epsilon_0 c E^2\cos^2\frac{\phi}{2} \qquad (35.9)$$

In particular, the *maximum* intensity I_0, which occurs at points where the phase difference is zero $(\phi = 0)$, is

$$I_0 = 2\epsilon_0 c E^2$$

Note that the maximum intensity I_0 is *four times* (not twice) as great as the intensity $\frac{1}{2}\epsilon_0 c E^2$ from each individual source.

Substituting the expression for I_0 into Eq. (35.9), we can express the intensity I at any point very simply in terms of the maximum intensity I_0:

$$I = I_0\cos^2\frac{\phi}{2} \qquad \text{(intensity in two-source interference)} \qquad (35.10)$$

For some phase angles ϕ the intensity is I_0, four times as great as for an individual wave source, but for other phase angles the intensity is zero. If we average Eq. (35.10) over all possible phase differences, the result is $I_0/2 = \epsilon_0 c E^2$ (the average of $\cos^2(\phi/2)$ is $\frac{1}{2}$). This is just twice the intensity from each individual source, as we should expect. The total energy output from the two sources isn't changed by the interference effects, but the energy is redistributed (as we mentioned in Section 35.1).

Phase Difference and Path Difference

Our next task is to find how the phase difference ϕ between the two fields at point P is related to the geometry of the situation. We know that ϕ is proportional to the difference in path length from the two sources to point P. When the path difference is one wavelength, the phase difference is one cycle, and $\phi = 2\pi$ rad $= 360°$. When the path difference is $\lambda/2$, $\phi = \pi$ rad $= 180°$, and so on. That is, the ratio of the phase difference ϕ to 2π is equal to the ratio of the path difference $r_2 - r_1$ to λ:

$$\frac{\phi}{2\pi} = \frac{r_2 - r_1}{\lambda}$$

Thus a path difference $(r_2 - r_1)$ causes a phase difference given by

$$\phi = \frac{2\pi}{\lambda}(r_2 - r_1) = k(r_2 - r_1) \qquad \begin{array}{l}\text{(phase difference related}\\\text{to path difference)}\end{array} \qquad (35.11)$$

where $k = 2\pi/\lambda$ is the *wave number* introduced in Section 15.3.

If the material in the space between the sources and P is anything other than vacuum, we must use the wavelength *in the material* in Eq. (35.11). If the material has index of refraction n, then

$$\lambda = \frac{\lambda_0}{n} \qquad \text{and} \qquad k = nk_0 \qquad (35.12)$$

where λ_0 and k_0 are the wavelength and the wave number, respectively, in vacuum.

Finally, if the point P is far away from the sources in comparison to their separation d, the path difference is given by Eq. (35.3):

$$r_2 - r_1 = d\sin\theta$$

Combining this with Eq. (35.11), we find

$$\phi = k(r_2 - r_1) = kd\sin\theta = \frac{2\pi d}{\lambda}\sin\theta \qquad (35.13)$$

When we substitute this into Eq. (35.10), we find

$$I = I_0\cos^2\left(\frac{1}{2}kd\sin\theta\right) = I_0\cos^2\left(\frac{\pi d}{\lambda}\sin\theta\right) \qquad \begin{array}{l}\text{(intensity far from}\\\text{two sources)}\end{array} \qquad (35.14)$$

The directions of *maximum* intensity occur when the cosine has the values ±1—that is, when

$$\frac{\pi d}{\lambda}\sin\theta = m\pi \qquad (m = 0, \pm1, \pm2, \dots)$$

35.10 Intensity distribution in the interference pattern from two identical slits.

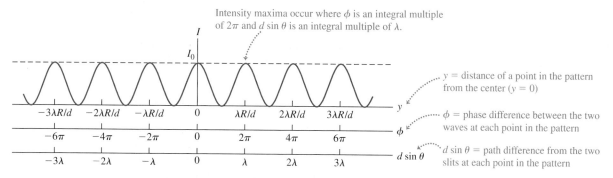

Intensity maxima occur where ϕ is an integral multiple of 2π and $d\sin\theta$ is an integral multiple of λ.

y = distance of a point in the pattern from the center ($y = 0$)

ϕ = phase difference between the two waves at each point in the pattern

$d\sin\theta$ = path difference from the two slits at each point in the pattern

or

$$d\sin\theta = m\lambda$$

in agreement with Eq. (35.4). We leave it to you to show that Eq. (35.5) for the zero-intensity directions can also be derived from Eq. (35.14) (see Exercise 35.24).

As we noted in Section 35.2, in experiments with light we visualize the interference pattern due to two slits by using a screen placed at a distance R from the slits. We can describe positions on the screen with the coordinate y; the positions of the bright fringes are given by Eq. (35.6), where ordinarily $y \ll R$. In that case, $\sin\theta$ is approximately equal to y/R, and we obtain the following expressions for the intensity at *any* point on the screen as a function of y:

$$I = I_0\cos^2\left(\frac{kdy}{2R}\right) = I_0\cos^2\left(\frac{\pi dy}{\lambda R}\right) \qquad \text{(intensity in two-slit interference)} \quad (35.15)$$

Figure 35.10 shows a graph of Eq. (35.15); we can compare this with the photographically recorded pattern of Fig. 35.6. The peaks in Fig. 35.10 all have the same intensity, while those in Fig. 35.6 fade off as we go away from the center. We'll explore the reasons for this variation in peak intensity in Chapter 36.

Example 35.3 **A directional transmitting antenna array**

Suppose the two identical radio antennas in Fig. 35.8 are moved to be only 10.0 m apart and the frequency of the radiated waves is increased to $f = 60.0$ MHz. The intensity at a distance of 700 m in the $+x$-direction (corresponding to $\theta = 0$ in Fig. 35.5) is $I_0 = 0.020$ W/m^2. (a) What is the intensity in the direction $\theta = 4.0°$? (b) In what direction near $\theta = 0$ is the intensity $I_0/2$? (c) In what directions is the intensity zero?

SOLUTION

IDENTIFY: This problem involves the intensity distribution as a function of *direction*—that is, as a function of angle. (In other problems we are concerned with the intensity as a function of *position* on a screen, as in the interference pattern shown in Fig. 35.6.)

SET UP: Because the 700-m distance from the antennas to the point where the intensity is measured is much greater than the distance between the antennas $(d = 10.0$ m$)$, the amplitudes of the waves from the two antennas are very nearly equal. Hence we can use Eq. (35.14) to relate intensity I and angle θ.

EXECUTE: To use Eq. (35.14), we must first find the wavelength λ using the relationship $c = \lambda f$:

$$\lambda = \frac{c}{f} = \frac{3.00 \times 10^8 \text{ m/s}}{60.0 \times 10^6 \text{ s}^{-1}} = 5.00 \text{ m}$$

The spacing $d = 10.0$ m between the antennas is just twice the wavelength. Equation (35.14) then becomes

$$I = I_0\cos^2\left(\frac{\pi d}{\lambda}\sin\theta\right)$$

$$= (0.020 \text{ W/m}^2)\cos^2\left[\frac{\pi(10.0 \text{ m})}{5.00 \text{ m}}\sin\theta\right]$$

$$= (0.020 \text{ W/m}^2)\cos^2[(2.00\pi \text{ rad})\sin\theta]$$

(a) When $\theta = 4.0°$,

$$I = (0.020 \text{ W/m}^2)\cos^2[(2.00\pi \text{ rad})\sin 4.0°]$$

$$= 0.016 \text{ W/m}^2$$

Continued

This is about 82% of the intensity at $\theta = 0$.

(b) The intensity I equals $I_0/2$ when the cosine in Eq. (35.14) has the value $\pm 1/\sqrt{2}$. This occurs when $2.00\pi \sin\theta = \pm\pi/4$ rad, so that $\sin\theta = \pm(1/8.00) = \pm 0.125$ and $\theta = \pm 7.2°$.

(c) The intensity is zero when $\cos[(2.00\pi \text{ rad})\sin\theta] = 0$. This occurs when $2.00\pi \sin\theta = \pm\pi/2, \pm 3\pi/2, \pm 5\pi/2, \ldots$, or $\sin\theta = \pm 0.250, \pm 0.750, \pm 1.25, \ldots$. Values of $\sin\theta$ greater than 1 have no meaning, and we find

$$\theta = \pm 14.5°, \pm 48.6°$$

EVALUATE: The condition in part (b) that $I = I_0/2$, so that $(2.00\pi \text{ rad})\sin\theta = \pm\pi/4$ rad, is also satisfied when $\sin\theta = \pm 0.375, \pm 0.625$, or ± 0.875 so that $\theta = \pm 22.0°, \pm 38.7°$, or $\pm 61.0°$. (Can you verify this?) It would be incorrect to include these angles in the solution, however, because the problem asked for the angle *near* $\theta = 0$ at which $I = I_0/2$. These additional values of θ aren't the ones we're looking for.

Test Your Understanding of Section 35.3   A two-slit interference experiment uses coherent light of wavelength 5.00×10^{-7} m. Rank the following points in the interference pattern according to the intensity at each point, from highest to lowest. (i) a point that is closer to one slit than the other by 4.00×10^{-7} m; (ii) a point where the light waves received from the two slits are out of phase by 4.00 rad; (iii) a point that is closer to one slit than the other by 7.50×10^{-7} m; (iv) a point where the light waves received by the two slits are out of phase by 2.00 rad.

35.4 Interference in Thin Films

You often see bright bands of color when light reflects from a thin layer of oil floating on water or from a soap bubble (see the photograph that opens this chapter). These are the results of interference. Light waves are reflected from the front and back surfaces of such thin films, and constructive interference between the two reflected waves (with different path lengths) occurs in different places for different wavelengths. Figure 35.11a shows the situation. Light shining on the upper surface of a thin film with thickness t is partly reflected at the upper surface (path abc). Light *transmitted* through the upper surface is partly reflected at the lower surface (path $abdef$). The two reflected waves come together at point P on the retina of the eye. Depending on the phase relationship, they may interfere constructively or destructively. Different colors have different wavelengths, so the interference may be constructive for some colors and destructive for others. That's why we see colored rings or fringes in Fig. 35.11b (which shows a thin film of oil floating on water) and in the photograph that opens this chapter (which shows thin films of soap solution that make up the bubble walls). The complex shapes of the colored rings in each photograph result from variations in the thickness of the film.

Thin-Film Interference and Phase Shifts During Reflection

Let's look at a simplified situation in which *monochromatic* light reflects from two nearly parallel surfaces at nearly normal incidence. Figure 35.12 shows two plates of glass separated by a thin wedge, or film, of air. We want to consider interference between the two light waves reflected from the surfaces adjacent to the air wedge, as shown. (Reflections also occur at the top surface of the upper plate and the bottom surface of the lower plate; to keep our discussion simple, we won't include these.) The situation is the same as in Fig. 35.11a except that the film (wedge) thickness is not uniform. The path difference between the two waves is just twice the thickness t of the air wedge at each point. At points where $2t$ is an integer number of wavelengths, we expect to see constructive interference and a bright area; where it is a half-integer number of wavelengths, we expect to see destructive interference and a dark area. Along the line where the plates are in contact, there is practically *no* path difference, and we expect a bright area.

When we carry out the experiment, the bright and dark fringes appear, but they are interchanged! Along the line where the plates are in contact, we find a

35.11 (a) A diagram and (b) a photograph showing interference of light reflected from a thin film.

(a) Interference between rays reflected from the two surfaces of a thin film

Light reflected from the upper and lower surfaces of the film comes together in the eye at P and undergoes interference.

Some colors interfere constructively and others destructively, creating the color bands we see.

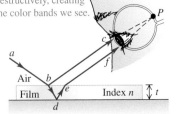

(b) The rainbow fringes of an oil slick on water

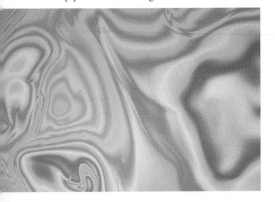

dark fringe, not a bright one. This suggests that one or the other of the reflected waves has undergone a half-cycle phase shift during its reflection. In that case the two waves that are reflected at the line of contact are a half-cycle out of phase even though they have the same path length.

In fact, this phase shift can be predicted from Maxwell's equations and the electromagnetic nature of light. The details of the derivation are beyond our scope, but here is the result. Suppose a light wave with electric-field amplitude E_i is traveling in an optical material with index of refraction n_a. It strikes, at normal incidence, an interface with another optical material with index n_b. The amplitude E_r of the wave reflected from the interface is proportional to the amplitude E_i of the incident wave and is given by

$$E_r = \frac{n_a - n_b}{n_a + n_b} E_i \qquad \text{(normal incidence)} \qquad (35.16)$$

This result shows that the incident and reflected amplitudes have the same sign when n_a is larger than n_b and opposite sign when n_b is larger than n_a. We can distinguish three cases, as shown in Fig. 35.13:

Figure 35.13a: When $n_a > n_b$, light travels more slowly in the first material than in the second. In this case, E_r and E_i have the same sign, and the phase shift of the reflected wave relative to the incident wave is zero. This is analogous to reflection of a transverse mechanical wave on a heavy rope at a point where it is tied to a lighter rope or a ring that can move vertically without friction.
Figure 35.13b: When $n_a = n_b$, the amplitude E_r of the reflected wave is zero. The incident light wave can't "see" the interface, and there is *no* reflected wave.
Figure 35.13c: When $n_a < n_b$, light travels more slowly in the second material than in the first. In this case, E_r and E_i have opposite signs, and the phase shift of the reflected wave relative to the incident wave is π rad (180° or a half-cycle). This is analogous to reflection (with inversion) of a transverse mechanical wave on a light rope at a point where it is tied to a heavier rope or a rigid support.

Let's compare with the situation of Fig. 35.12. For the wave reflected from the upper surface of the air wedge, n_a (glass) is greater than n_b, so this wave has zero phase shift. For the wave reflected from the lower surface, n_a (air) is less than n_b (glass), so this wave has a half-cycle phase shift. Waves that are reflected from the line of contact have no path difference to give additional phase shifts, and they interfere destructively; this is what we observe. You can use the above

35.12 Interference between light waves reflected from the two sides of an air wedge separating two glass plates. The angles and the thickness of the air wedge have been exaggerated for clarity; in the text we assume that the light strikes the upper plate at normal incidence and that the distances h and t are much less than l.

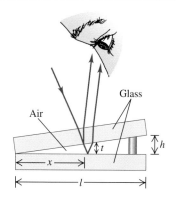

35.13 Upper figures: electromagnetic waves striking an interface between optical materials at normal incidence (shown as a small angle for clarity). Lower figures: mechanical wave pulses on ropes.

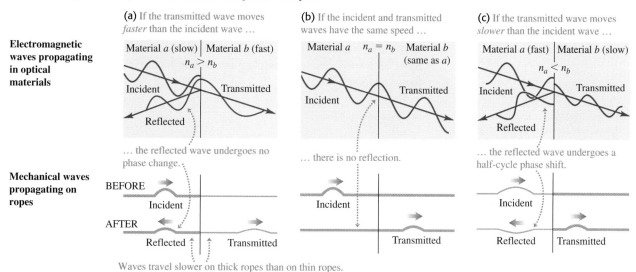

principle to show that for normal incidence, the wave reflected at point b in Fig. 35.11a is shifted by a half-cycle, while the wave reflected at d is not (if there is air below the film).

We can summarize this discussion mathematically. If the film has thickness t, the light is at normal incidence and has wavelength λ in the film; if neither or both of the reflected waves from the two surfaces have a half-cycle reflection phase shift, the conditions for constructive and destructive interference are

$$2t = m\lambda \qquad (m = 0, 1, 2, \dots)$$

(constructive reflection from thin film, no relative phase shift)   (35.17a)

$$2t = \left(m + \frac{1}{2}\right)\lambda \qquad (m = 0, 1, 2, \dots)$$

(destructive reflection from thin film, no relative phase shift)   (35.17b)

If *one* of the two waves has a half-cycle reflection phase shift, the conditions for constructive and destructive interference are reversed:

$$2t = \left(m + \frac{1}{2}\right)\lambda \qquad (m = 0, 1, 2, \dots)$$

(constructive reflection from thin film, half-cycle relative phase shift)   (35.18a)

$$2t = m\lambda \qquad (m = 0, 1, 2, \dots)$$

(destructive reflection from thin film, half-cycle relative phase shift)   (35.18b)

Thin and Thick Films

You may wonder why we have emphasized *thin* films in our discussion. We have done so because of a principle we introduced in Section 35.1: In order for two waves to cause a steady interference pattern, the waves must be *coherent,* with a definite and constant phase relationship. However, the sun and light bulbs emit light in a stream of short bursts, each of which is only a few micrometers long (1 micrometer $= 1\ \mu m = 10^{-6}\ m$). If light reflects from the two surfaces of a thin film, the two reflected waves are part of the same burst (Fig. 35.14a). Hence these waves are coherent and interference occurs as we have described. If the film is too thick, however, the two reflected waves will belong to different bursts (Fig. 35.14b). There is no definite phase relationship between different light bursts, so the two waves are incoherent and there is no fixed interference pattern. That's why you see interference colors in light reflected from an oil slick a few micrometers thick (Fig. 35.11b), but you do *not* see such colors in the light reflected from a pane of window glass with a thickness of a few millimeters (a thousand times greater).

35.14 (a) Light reflecting from a thin film produces a steady interference pattern, but (b) light reflecting from a thick film does not.

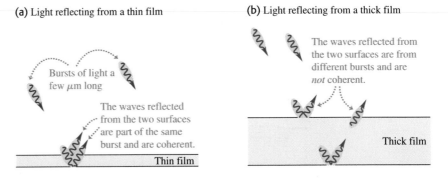

(a) Light reflecting from a thin film

Bursts of light a few μm long

The waves reflected from the two surfaces are part of the same burst and are coherent.

Thin film

(b) Light reflecting from a thick film

The waves reflected from the two surfaces are from different bursts and are *not* coherent.

Thick film

| Problem-Solving Strategy 35.1 | **Interference in Thin Films** |

IDENTIFY *the relevant concepts:* Problems with thin films involve interference of two waves, one reflected from the film's front surface and one reflected from the back surface. Typically you will be asked to relate the wavelength, the index of refraction of the film, and the dimensions of the film.

SET UP *the problem* using the following steps:
1. Make a drawing showing the geometry of the thin film. Your drawing should also depict the materials that adjoin the film; their properties determine whether one or both of the reflected waves have a half-cycle phase shift.
2. Determine the target variable.

EXECUTE *the solution* as follows:
1. Apply the rule for phase changes to each reflected wave. There is a half-cycle phase shift when $n_b > n_a$, and none when $n_b < n_a$.

2. If neither reflected wave undergoes a phase shift, or if both reflected waves do, you can apply Eqs. (35.17). If only one of the reflected waves undergoes a phase shift, you must use Eqs. (35.18).
3. Solve the resulting interference equation for the target variable. If the film consists of anything other than vacuum, be sure to use the wavelength of light *in the film* in your calculations. If the film is anything except vacuum, this is smaller than the wavelength in vacuum by a factor of n. (For air, $n = 1.000$ to four-figure precision.)
4. If you are asked about the wave that is transmitted through the film, keep in mind that *minimum* intensity in the *reflected* wave corresponds to *maximum transmitted* intensity, and vice versa.

EVALUATE *your answer:* You can interpret your results by examining what would happen if the wavelength were changed or if the film had a different thickness.

| Example 35.4 | **Thin-film interference I** |

Suppose the two glass plates in Fig. 35.12 are two microscope slides 10.0 cm long. At one end they are in contact; at the other end they are separated by a piece of paper 0.0200 mm thick. What is the spacing of the interference fringes seen by reflection? Is the fringe at the line of contact bright or dark? Assume monochromatic light with a wavelength in air of $\lambda = \lambda_0 = 500$ nm.

SOLUTION

IDENTIFY: We'll consider only interference between the light reflected from the upper and lower surfaces of the air wedge between the slides. The glass plate is a millimeter or so thick, so we can ignore interference between the light reflected from the upper and lower surfaces of this plate (see Fig. 35.14b).

SET UP: Figure 35.15 depicts the situation. Light travels more slowly in the glass of the microscope slides than it does in air. Hence the wave reflected from the upper surface of the air wedge has no phase shift (see Fig. 35.13a), while the wave reflected from the lower surface has a half-cycle phase shift (see Fig. 35.13c).

35.15 Our sketch for this problem.

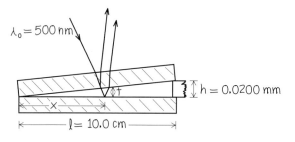

EXECUTE: Since only one of the reflected waves undergoes a phase shift, the condition for *destructive* interference (a dark fringe) is Eq. (35.18b):

$$2t = m\lambda_0 \qquad (m = 0, 1, 2, \ldots)$$

From similar triangles in Fig. 35.15 the thickness t of the air wedge at each point is proportional to the distance x from the line of contact:

$$\frac{t}{x} = \frac{h}{l}$$

Combining this with Eq. (35.18b), we find

$$\frac{2xh}{l} = m\lambda_0$$

$$x = m\frac{l\lambda_0}{2h} = m\frac{(0.100\text{ m})(500 \times 10^{-9}\text{ m})}{(2)(0.0200 \times 10^{-3}\text{ m})} = m(1.25\text{ mm})$$

Successive dark fringes, corresponding to successive integer values of m, are spaced 1.25 mm apart. Substituting $m = 0$ into this equation gives $x = 0$, corresponding to the line of contact between the two slides (at the left-hand side of Fig. 35.15). Hence there is a dark fringe at the line of contact.

EVALUATE: Our result shows that the fringe spacing is proportional to the wavelength of the light used; the fringes would be farther apart with red light (larger λ_0) than with blue light (smaller λ_0). If we use white light, the reflected light at any point is a mixture of wavelengths for which constructive interference occurs; the wavelengths that interfere destructively are weak or absent in the reflected light. (This same effect explains the colors seen when an oil film on water is illuminated by white light, as in Fig. 35.11b).

Example 35.5 Thin-film interference II

In Example 35.4, suppose the glass plates have $n = 1.52$ and the space between plates contains water $(n = 1.33)$ instead of air. What happens now?

SOLUTION

IDENTIFY: The index of refraction of the water film is still less than that of the glass on either side of the film, so the phase shifts are the same as in Example 35.4. The only difference is that the wavelength in water is different than in air.

SET UP: Once again we use Eq. (35.18b) to find the positions of the dark fringes. The wavelengths λ in water is related to the wavelength λ_0 in air (essentially vacuum) by Eq. (33.5), $\lambda = \lambda_0/n$.

EXECUTE: In the film of water $(n = 1.33)$, the wavelength is

$$\lambda = \frac{\lambda_0}{n} = \frac{500 \text{ nm}}{1.33} = 376 \text{ nm}$$

When we replace λ_0 by λ in the expression from Example 35.4 for the position x of the mth dark fringe, we find that the fringe spacing is reduced by the same factor of 1.33 and is equal to 0.940 mm. Note that there is still a dark fringe at the line of contact.

EVALUATE: Can you see that to return to the same fringe spacing as in Example 35.4, the dimension h in Fig. 35.15 would have to be reduced to $(0.0200 \text{ mm})/1.33 = 0.0150 \text{ mm}$? This shows that what matters in thin-film interference is the *ratio* between the wavelength and the thickness of the film. [You can see this by considering Eqs. (35.17a) and (35.17b).]

Example 35.6 Thin-film interference III

Suppose the upper of the two plates in Example 35.4 is a plastic material with $n = 1.40$, the wedge is filled with a silicone grease having $n = 1.50$, and the bottom plate is a dense flint glass with $n = 1.60$. What happens now?

SOLUTION

IDENTIFY: The geometry is still as shown in Fig. 35.15, but now half-cycle phase shifts occur at *both* surfaces of the wedge of grease (see Fig. 35.13c).

SET UP: Figure 35.16 shows the situation. Since there is a half-cycle phase shift at both surfaces, there is no *relative* phase shift and we must use Eq. (35.17b) to find the positions of the dark fringes.

EXECUTE: The value of λ to use in Eq. (35.17b) is the wavelength in the silicone grease: $\lambda = \lambda_0/n = (500 \text{ nm})/1.50 = 333 \text{ nm}$. You can readily show that the fringe spacing is 0.833 mm. Note that the two reflected waves from the line of contact are in phase (they both undergo the same phase shift), so the line of contact is at a *bright* fringe.

35.16 Our sketch for this problem.

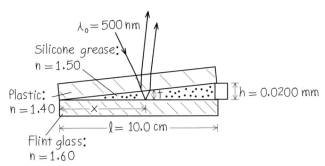

EVALUATE: What would happen if you carefully removed the upper microscope slide so that the grease wedge retained its shape? There would still be half-cycle phase changes at the upper and lower surfaces of the wedge, so the pattern of fringes would be the same as with the upper slide present.

Newton's Rings

Figure 35.17a shows the convex surface of a lens in contact with a plane glass plate. A thin film of air is formed between the two surfaces. When you view the setup with monochromatic light, you see circular interference fringes (Fig. 35.17b). These were studied by Newton and are called **Newton's rings.**

We can use interference fringes to compare the surfaces of two optical parts by placing the two in contact and observing the interference fringes. Figure 35.18 is a photograph made during the grinding of a telescope objective lens. The lower, larger-diameter, thicker disk is the correctly shaped master, and the smaller, upper disk is the lens under test. The "contour lines" are Newton's interference fringes; each one indicates an additional distance between the specimen and the master of one half-wavelength. At 10 lines from the center spot the distance between the two surfaces is five wavelengths, or about 0.003 mm. This

(a) A convex lens in contact with a glass plane

(b) Newton's rings: circular interference fringes

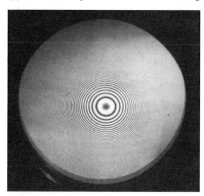

35.17 (a) Air film between a convex lens and a plane surface. The thickness of the film t increases from zero as we move out from the center, giving (b) a series of alternating dark and bright rings for monochromatic light.

isn't very good; high-quality lenses are routinely ground with a precision of less than one wavelength. The surface of the primary mirror of the Hubble Space Telescope was ground to a precision of better than $\frac{1}{50}$ wavelength. Unfortunately, it was ground to incorrect specifications, creating one of the most precise errors in the history of optical technology (see Section 34.2).

Nonreflective and Reflective Coatings

Nonreflective coatings for lens surfaces make use of thin-film interference. A thin layer or film of hard transparent material with an index of refraction smaller than that of the glass is deposited on the lens surface, as in Fig. 35.19. Light is reflected from both surfaces of the layer. In both reflections the light is reflected from a medium of greater index than that in which it is traveling, so the same phase change occurs in both reflections. If the film thickness is a quarter (one-fourth) of the wavelength *in the film* (assuming normal incidence), the total path difference is a half-wavelength. Light reflected from the first surface is then a half-cycle out of phase with light reflected from the second, and there is destructive interference.

The thickness of the nonreflective coating can be a quarter-wavelength for only one particular wavelength. This is usually chosen in the central yellow-green portion of the spectrum ($\lambda = 550$ nm), where the eye is most sensitive. Then there is somewhat more reflection at both longer (red) and shorter (blue) wavelengths, and the reflected light has a purple hue. The overall reflection from a lens or prism surface can be reduced in this way from 4–5% to less than 1%. This treatment is particularly important in eliminating stray reflected light in highly corrected photographic lenses with many individual pieces of glass and many air-glass surfaces. It also increases the net amount of light that is *transmitted* through the lens, since light that is not reflected will be transmitted. The same principle is used to minimize reflection from silicon photovoltaic solar cells ($n = 3.5$) by use of a thin surface layer of silicon monoxide ($\text{SiO}, n = 1.45$); this helps to increase the amount of light that actually reaches the solar cells.

If a quarter-wavelength thickness of a material with an index of refraction *greater* than that of glass is deposited on glass, then the reflectivity is *increased,* and the deposited material is called a **reflective coating.** In this case there is a half-cycle phase shift at the air–film interface but none at the film–glass interface, and reflections from the two sides of the film interfere constructively. For example, a coating with refractive index 2.5 causes 38% of the incident energy to be reflected, compared with 4% or so with no coating. By use of multiple-layer coatings, it is possible to achieve nearly 100% transmission or reflection for particular wavelengths. Some practical applications of these coatings are for color separation in color television cameras and for infrared "heat reflectors" in motion-picture projectors, solar cells, and astronauts' visors. Reflective coatings occur in nature on the scales of herring and other silvery fish; this gives these fish their characteristic shiny appearance (see Problem 35.56).

35.18 The surface of a telescope objective lens under inspection during manufacture.

35.19 A nonreflective coating has an index of refraction intermediate between those of glass and air.

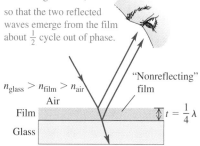

Example 35.7   A nonreflective coating

A commonly used lens coating material is magnesium fluoride, MgF_2, with $n = 1.38$. What thickness should a nonreflective coating have for 550-nm light if it is applied to glass with $n = 1.52$?

SOLUTION

IDENTIFY: This coating is of the sort depicted in Fig. 35.19.

SET UP: The thickness must be one-quarter of the wavelength in the coating.

EXECUTE: The wavelength of yellow-green light in air is $\lambda_0 = 550$ nm, so its wavelength in the MgF_2 coating is

$$\lambda = \frac{\lambda_0}{n} = \frac{550 \text{ nm}}{1.38} = 400 \text{ nm}$$

To be a nonreflective film, the coating should have a thickness of one-quarter λ, or 100 nm. This is a very thin film, no more than a few hundred molecules thick.

EVALUATE: Note that such a coating becomes *reflective* if its thickness is equal to one-*half* of a wavelength; then light reflected from the lower surface of the coating travels one wavelength farther than light reflected from the upper surface, so the two waves are in phase and interfere constructively. This occurs for light with a wavelength in MgF_2 of 200 nm and a wavelength in air of $(200 \text{ nm})(1.38) = 276$ nm. This is an ultraviolet wavelength (see Section 32.1), so designers of optical lenses with nonreflective coatings need not worry about enhanced reflection of this kind.

Test Your Understanding of Section 35.4   A thin layer of benzene $(n = 1.501)$ lies on top of a sheet of fluorite $(n = 1.434)$. It is illuminated from above with light whose wavelength in benzene is 400 nm. Which of the following possible thicknesses of the benzene layer will maximize the brightness of the reflected light? (i) 100 nm; (ii) 200 nm; (iii) 300 nm; (iv) 400 nm.

35.5 The Michelson Interferometer

An important experimental device that uses interference is the **Michelson interferometer.** In the late 19th century, it helped to provide one of the key experimental underpinnings of the theory of relativity. More recently, Michelson interferometers have been used to make precise measurements of wavelengths and of very small distances, such as the minute changes in thickness of an axon when a nerve impulse propagates along its length. Like the Young two-slit experiment, a Michelson interferometer takes monochromatic light from a single source and divides it into two waves that follow different paths. In Young's experiment, this is done by sending part of the light through one slit and part through another; in a Michelson interferometer a device called a *beam splitter* is used. Interference occurs in both experiments when the two light waves are recombined.

How a Michelson Interferometer Works

The principal components of a Michelson interferometer are shown schematically in Fig. 35.20. A ray of light from a monochromatic source A strikes the beam splitter C, which is a glass plate with a thin coating of silver on its right side. Part of the light (ray 1) passes through the silvered surface and the compensator plate D and is reflected from mirror M_1. It then returns through D and is reflected from the silvered surface of C to the observer. The remainder of the light (ray 2) is reflected from the silvered surface at point P to the mirror M_2 and back through C to the observer's eye. The purpose of the compensator plate D is to ensure that rays 1 and 2 pass through the same thickness of glass; plate D is cut from the same piece of glass as plate C, so their thicknesses are identical to within a fraction of a wavelength.

The whole apparatus in Fig. 35.20 is mounted on a very rigid frame, and the position of mirror M_2 can be adjusted with a fine, very accurate micrometer screw. If the distances L_1 and L_2 are exactly equal and the mirrors M_1 and M_2 are exactly at right angles, the virtual image of M_1 formed by reflection at the silvered

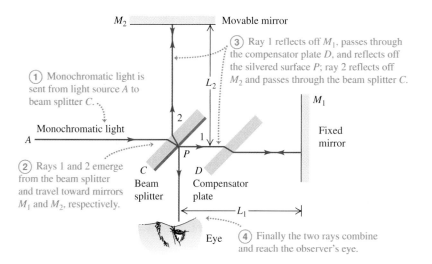

surface of plate C coincides with mirror M_2. If L_1 and L_2 are *not* exactly equal, the image of M_1 is displaced slightly from M_2; and if the mirrors are not exactly perpendicular, the image of M_1 makes a slight angle with M_2. Then the mirror M_2 and the virtual image of M_1 play the same roles as the two surfaces of a wedge-shaped thin film (see Section 35.4), and light reflected from these surfaces forms the same sort of interference fringes.

Suppose the angle between mirror M_2 and the virtual image of M_1 is just large enough that five or six vertical fringes are present in the field of view. If we now move the mirror M_2 slowly either backward or forward a distance $\lambda/2$, the difference in path length between rays 1 and 2 changes by λ, and each fringe moves to the left or right a distance equal to the fringe spacing. If we observe the fringe positions through a telescope with a crosshair eyepiece and m fringes cross the crosshairs when we move the mirror a distance y, then

$$y = m\frac{\lambda}{2} \qquad \text{or} \qquad \lambda = \frac{2y}{m} \qquad\qquad (35.19)$$

If m is several thousand, the distance y is large enough that it can be measured with good accuracy, and we can obtain an accurate value for the wavelength λ. Alternatively, if the wavelength is known, a distance y can be measured by simply counting fringes when M_2 is moved by this distance. In this way, distances that are comparable to a wavelength of light can be measured with relative ease.

The Michelson-Morley Experiment

The original application of the Michelson interferometer was to the historic **Michelson-Morley experiment.** Before the electromagnetic theory of light and Einstein's special theory of relativity became established, most physicists believed that the propagation of light waves occurred in a medium called the **ether,** which was believed to permeate all space. In 1887 the American scientists Albert Michelson and Edward Morley used the Michelson interferometer in an attempt to detect the motion of the earth through the ether. Suppose the interferometer in Fig. 35.20 is moving from left to right relative to the ether. According to the ether theory, this would lead to changes in the speed of light in the portions of the path shown as horizontal lines in the figure. There would be fringe shifts relative to the positions that the fringes would have if the instrument were at rest in the ether. Then when the entire instrument was rotated 90°, the other portions of the paths would be similarly affected, giving a fringe shift in the opposite direction.

Michelson and Morley expected that the motion of the earth through the ether would cause a fringe shift of about four-tenths of a fringe when the instrument was rotated. The shift that was actually observed was less than a hundredth of a fringe and, within the limits of experimental uncertainty, appeared to be exactly zero. Despite its orbital motion around the sun, the earth appeared to be *at rest* relative to the ether. This negative result baffled physicists until Einstein developed the special theory of relativity in 1905. Einstein postulated that the speed of a light wave in vacuum has the same magnitude c relative to *all* inertial reference frames, no matter what their velocity may be relative to each other. The presumed ether then plays no role, and the concept of an ether has been abandoned.

The theory of relativity is a well-established cornerstone of modern physics, and we will study it in detail in Chapter 37. In retrospect, the Michelson-Morley experiment gives strong experimental support to the special theory of relativity, and it is often called the most significant "negative-result" experiment ever performed.

Test Your Understanding of Section 35.5   You are observing the pattern of fringes in a Michelson interferometer like that shown in Fig. 35.20. If you change the index of refraction (but not the thickness) of the compensator plate, will the pattern change?

Interference and coherent sources: Monochromatic light is light with a single frequency. Coherence is a definite, unchanging phase relationship between two waves. The overlap of waves from two coherent sources of monochromatic light forms an interference pattern. The principle of superposition states that the total wave disturbance at any point is the sum of the disturbances from the separate waves.

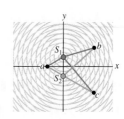

Two-source interference of light: When two sources are in phase, constructive interference occurs at points where the difference in path length from the two sources is zero or an integer number of wavelengths; destructive interference occurs at points where the path difference is a half-integer number of wavelengths. If two sources separated by a distance d are both very far from a point P, and the line from the sources to P makes an angle θ with the line perpendicular to the line of the sources, then the condition for constructive interference at P is Eq. (35.4). The condition for destructive interference is Eq. (35.5). When θ is very small, the position y_m of the mth bright fringe on a screen located a distance R from the sources is given by Eq. (35.6). (See Examples 35.1 and 35.2.)

$$d\sin\theta = m\lambda \quad (m = 0, \pm 1, \pm 2, \ldots)$$
(constructive interference)   (35.4)

$$d\sin\theta = \left(m + \frac{1}{2}\right)\lambda$$
(35.5)
$$(m = 0, \pm 1, \pm 2, \ldots)$$
(destructive interference)

$$y_m = R\frac{m\lambda}{d}$$
(35.6)
(bright fringes)

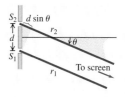

Intensity in interference patterns: When two sinusoidal waves with equal amplitude E and phase difference ϕ are superimposed, the resultant amplitude E_P and intensity I are given by Eqs. (35.7) and (35.10), respectively. If the two sources emit in phase, the phase difference ϕ at a point P (located a distance r_1 from source 1 and a distance r_2 from source 2) is directly proportional to the difference in path length $r_2 - r_1$. (See Example 35.3.)

$$E_P = 2E\left|\cos\frac{\phi}{2}\right|$$
(35.7)

$$I = I_0\cos^2\frac{\phi}{2}$$
(35.10)

$$\phi = \frac{2\pi}{\lambda}(r_2 - r_1) = k(r_2 - r_1) \quad (35.11)$$

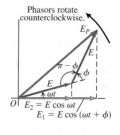

Interference in thin films: When light is reflected from both sides of a thin film of thickness t and no phase shift occurs at either surface, constructive interference between the reflected waves occurs when $2t$ is equal to an integral number of wavelengths. If a half-cycle phase shift occurs at one surface, this is the condition for destructive interference. A half-cycle phase shift occurs during reflection whenever the index of refraction in the second material is greater than that in the first. (See Examples 35.4–35.7.)

$$2t = m\lambda \quad (m = 0, 1, 2, \ldots)$$
(constructive reflection from thin film, no relative phase shift)   (35.17a)

$$2t = \left(m + \frac{1}{2}\right)\lambda \quad (m = 0, 1, 2, \ldots)$$
(destructive reflection from thin film, no relative phase shift)   (35.17b)

$$2t = \left(m + \frac{1}{2}\right)\lambda \quad (m = 0, 1, 2, \ldots)$$
(constructive reflection from thin film, half-cycle relative phase shift)   (35.18a)

$$2t = m\lambda \quad (m = 0, 1, 2, \ldots)$$
(destructive reflection from thin film, half-cycle relative phase shift)   (35.18b)

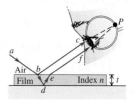

Michelson interferometer: The Michelson interferometer uses a monochromatic light source and can be used for high-precision measurements of wavelengths. Its original purpose was to detect motion of the earth relative to a hypothetical ether, the supposed medium for electromagnetic waves. The ether has never been detected, and the concept has been abandoned; the speed of light is the same relative to all observers. This is part of the foundation of the special theory of relativity.

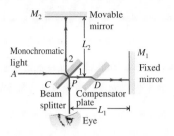

Key Terms

physical optics, *1207*
interference, *1208*
principle of superposition, *1208*
monochromatic light, *1208*
coherent, *1209*
constructive interference, *1209*

destructive interference, *1210*
antinodal curves, *1210*
nodal curves, *1210*
interference fringes, *1212*
Newton's rings, *1222*
nonreflective coating, *1223*

reflective coating, *1223*
Michelson interferometer, *1224*
Michelson-Morley experiment, *1225*
ether, *1225*

Answer to Chapter Opening Question ?

The colors appear due to constructive interference between light waves reflected from the outer and inner surfaces of the soap bubble. The thickness of the bubble walls at each point determines the wavelength of light for which the most constructive interference occurs and hence the color that appears the brightest at that point (see Example 35.4 in Section 35.4).

Answers to Test Your Understanding Questions

35.1 Answer: (i)   At any point P on the positive y-axis above S_1, the distance r_2 from S_2 to P is greater than the distance r_1 from S_1 to P by 4λ. This corresponds to $m = 4$ in Eq. (35.1), the equation for constructive interference. Hence all such points make up an antinodal curve.

35.2 Answer: (ii)   Blue light has a shorter wavelength than red light (see Section 32.1). Equation (35.6) tells us that the distance y_m from the center of the pattern to the mth bright fringe is proportional to the wavelength λ. Hence all of the fringes will move toward the center of the pattern as the wavelength decreases, and the spacing between fringes will decrease.

35.3 Answer: (i), (iv), (ii), (iii)   In cases (i) and (iii) we are given the wavelength λ and path difference $d\sin\theta$. Hence we use

Eq. (35.14), $I = I_0\cos^2[(\pi d\sin\theta)/\lambda]$. In parts (ii) and (iii) we are given the phase difference ϕ and we use Eq. (35.10), $I = I_0\cos^2(\phi/2)$. We find:
(i) $I = I_0\cos^2[\pi(4.00 \times 10^{-7}\,\text{m})/(5.00 \times 10^{-7}\,\text{m})] = I_0\cos^2(0.800\pi\,\text{rad}) = 0.655I_0$;
(ii) $I = I_0\cos^2[(4.00\,\text{rad})/2] = I_0\cos^2(2.00\,\text{rad}) = 0.173I_0$;
(iii) $I = I_0\cos^2[\pi(7.50 \times 10^{-7}\,\text{m})/(5.00 \times 10^{-7}\,\text{m})] = I_0\cos^2(1.50\pi\,\text{rad}) = 0$;
(iv) $I = I_0\cos^2[(2.00\,\text{rad})/2] = I_0\cos^2(1.00\,\text{rad}) = 0.292I_0$.

35.4 Answers: (i) and (iii)   Benzene has a larger index of refraction than air, so light that reflects off the upper surface of the benzene undergoes a half-cycle phase shift. Fluorite has a *smaller* index of refraction than benzene, so light that reflects off the benzene–fluorite interface does not undergo a phase shift. Hence the equation for constructive reflection is Eq. (35.18a), $2t = (m + \frac{1}{2})\lambda$, which we can rewrite as $t = (m + \frac{1}{2})\lambda/2 = (m + \frac{1}{2})(400\,\text{mm})/2 = 100\,\text{nm}, 300\,\text{nm}, 500\,\text{nm}, \ldots$.

35.5 Answer: yes   Changing the index of refraction changes the wavelength of the light inside the compensator plate, and so changes the nuimber of wavelengths within the thickness of the plate. Hence this has the same effect as changing the distance L_1 from the beam splitter to mirror M_1, which would change the interference pattern.

PROBLEMS

For instructor-assigned homework, go to **www.masteringphysics.com**

Discussion Questions

Q35.1. A two-slit interference experiment is set up, and the fringes are displayed on a screen. Then the whole apparatus is immersed in the nearest swimming pool. How does the fringe pattern change?

Q35.2. Could an experiment similar to Young's two-slit experiment be performed with sound? How might this be carried out? Does it matter that sound waves are longitudinal and electromagnetic waves are transverse? Explain.

Q35.3. Monochromatic coherent light passing through two thin slits is viewed on a distant screen. Are the bright fringes equally spaced on the screen? If so, why? If not, which ones are closest to being equally spaced?

Q35.4. In a two-slit interference pattern on a distant screen, are the bright fringes midway between the dark fringes? Is this ever a good approximation?

Q35.5. Would the headlights of a distant car form a two-source interference pattern? If so, how might it be observed? If not, why not?

Q35.6. The two sources S_1 and S_2 shown in Fig. 35.3 emit waves of the same wavelength λ and are in phase with each other. Suppose S_1 is a weaker source, so that the waves emitted by S_1 have half the amplitude of the waves emitted by S_2. How would this affect the positions of the antinodal lines and nodal lines? Would there be total reinforcement at points on the antinodal curves? Would there be total cancellation at points on the nodal curves? Explain your answers.

Q35.7. Could the Young two-slit interference experiment be performed with gamma rays? If not, why not? If so, discuss differences in the experimental design compared to the experiment with visible light.

Q35.8. Coherent red light illuminates two narrow slits that are 25 cm apart. Will a two-slit interference pattern be observed when the light from the slits falls on a screen? Explain.

Q35.9. Coherent light with wavelength λ falls on two narrow slits separated by a distance d. If d is less than some minimum value, no dark fringes are observed. Explain. In terms of λ, what is this minimum value of d?

Q35.10. A fellow student, who values memorizing equations above understanding them, combines Eqs. (35.4) and (35.13) to "prove" that ϕ can *only* equal $2\pi m$. How would you explain to this student that ϕ can have values other than $2\pi m$?

Q35.11. If the monochromatic light shown in Fig. 35.5a were replaced by white light, would a two-slit interference pattern be seen on the screen? Explain.

Q35.12. In using the superposition principle to calculate intensities in interference patterns, could you add the intensities of the waves instead of their amplitudes? Explain.

Q35.13. A glass windowpane with a thin film of water on it reflects less than when it is perfectly dry. Why?

Q35.14. A *very* thin soap film $(n = 1.33)$, whose thickness is much less than a wavelength of visible light, looks black; it appears to reflect no light at all. Why? By contrast, an equally thin layer of soapy water $(n = 1.33)$ on glass $(n = 1.50)$ appears quite shiny. Why is there a difference?

Q35.15. Interference can occur in thin films. Why is it important that the films be *thin?* Why don't you get these effects with a relatively *thick* film? Where should you put the dividing line between "thin" and "thick"? Explain your reasoning.

Q35.16. If we shine white light on an air wedge like that shown in Fig. 35.12, the colors that are weak in the light *reflected* from any point along the wedge are strong in the light *transmitted* through the wedge. Explain why this should be so.

Q35.17. Monochromatic light is directed at normal incidence on a thin film. There is destructive interference for the reflected light, so the intensity of the reflected light is very low. What happened to the energy of the incident light?

Q35.18. When a thin oil film spreads out on a puddle of water, the thinnest part of the film looks dark in the resulting interference pattern. What does this tell you about the relative magnitudes of the refractive indexes of oil and water?

Exercises

Section 35.1 Interference and Coherent Sources

35.1. Two coherent sources A and B of radio waves are 5.00 m apart. Each source emits waves with wavelength 6.00 m. Consider points along the line between the two sources. At what distances, if any, from A is the interference (a) constructive and (b) destructive?

35.2. Radio Interference. Two radio antennas A and B radiate in phase. Antenna B is 120 m to the right of antenna A. Consider point Q along the extension of the line connecting the antennas, a horizontal distance of 40 m to the right of antenna B. The frequency, and hence the wavelength, of the emitted waves can be varied. (a) What is the longest wavelength for which there will be destructive interference at point Q? (b) What is the longest wavelength for which there will be constructive interference at point Q?

35.3. A radio transmitting station operating at a frequency of 120 MHz has two identical antennas that radiate in phase. Antenna B is 9.00 m to the right of antenna A. Consider point P between the antennas and along the line connecting them, a horizontal distance x to the right of antenna A. For what values of x will constructive interference occur at point P?

35.4. Two light sources can be adjusted to emit monochromatic light of any visible wavelength. The two sources are coherent, 2.04 μm apart, and in line with an observer, so that one source is 2.04 μm farther from the observer than the other. (a) For what visible wavelengths (400 to 700 nm) will the observer see the brightest light, owing to constructive interference? (b) How would your answers to part (a) be affected if the two sources were not in line with the observer, but were still arranged so that one source is 2.04 μm farther away from the observer than the other? (c) For what visible wavelengths will there be *destructive* interference at the location of the observer?

35.5. Two speakers, emitting identical sound waves of wavelength 2.0 m in phase with each other, and an observer are located as shown in Fig. 35.21. (a) At the observer's location, what is the path difference for waves from the two speakers? (b) Will the sound waves interfere constructively or destructively at the observer's location—or something in between constructive and destructive? (c) Suppose the observer now increases her distance from the speakers to 17.0 m, staying directly in front of the same speaker as initially. Answer the questions of parts (a) and (b) for this new situation.

Figure 35.21
Exercise 35.5

35.6. Figure 35.3 shows the wave pattern produced by two identical, coherent sources emitting waves with wavelength λ and separated by a distance $d = 4\lambda$. (a) Explain why the positive y-axis above S_1 constitutes an antinodal curve with $m = +4$ and why the negative y-axis below S_2 constitutes an antinodal curve with $m = -4$. (b) Draw the wave pattern produced when the separation between the sources is reduced to 3λ. In your drawing, sketch all antinodal curves—that is, the curves on which $r_2 - r_1 = m\lambda$. Label each curve by its value of m. (c) In general, what determines the maximum (most positive) and minimum (most negative) values of the integer m that labels the antinodal lines? (d) Suppose the separation between the sources is increased to $7\frac{1}{2}\lambda$. How many antinodal curves will there be? To what values of m do they correspond? Explain your reasoning. (You should not have to make a drawing to answer these questions.)

35.7. Consider Fig. 35.3, which could represent interference between water waves in a ripple tank. Pick at least three points on the antinodal curve labeled "$m = 3$," and make measurements from the figure to show that Eq. (35.1) is indeed satisfied. Explain what measurements you made and how you measured the wavelength λ.

Section 35.2 Two-Source Interference of Light

35.8. Young's experiment is performed with light from excited helium atoms $(\lambda = 502$ nm$)$. Fringes are measured carefully on a screen 1.20 m away from the double slit, and the center of the 20th fringe (not counting the central bright fringe) is found to be 10.6 mm from the center of the central bright fringe. What is the separation of the two slits?

35.9. Two slits spaced 0.450 mm apart are placed 75.0 cm from a screen. What is the distance between the second and third dark lines of the interference pattern on the screen when the slits are illuminated with coherent light with a wavelength of 500 nm?

35.10. Coherent light with wavelength 450 nm falls on a double slit. On a screen 1.80 m away, the distance between dark fringes is 4.20 mm. What is the separation of the slits?

35.11. Coherent light from a sodium-vapor lamp is passed through a filter that blocks everything except light of a single wavelength. It then falls on two slits separated by 0.460 mm. In the resulting interference pattern on a screen 2.20 m away, adjacent bright fringes are separated by 2.82 mm. What is the wavelength?

35.12. Coherent light with wavelength 400 nm passes through two very narrow slits that are separated by 0.200 mm and the interference pattern is observed on a screen 4.00 m from the slits. (a) What is the width (in mm) of the central interference maximum? (b) What is the width of the first-order bright fringe?

35.13. Two very narrow slits are spaced 1.80 μm apart and are placed 35.0 cm from a screen. What is the distance between the first and second dark lines of the interference pattern when the slits are illuminated with coherent light with $\lambda = 550$ nm? (*Hint:* The angle θ in Eq. (35.5) is *not* small.)

35.14. Coherent light that contains two wavelengths, 660 nm (red) and 470 nm (blue), passes through two narrow slits separated by 0.300 mm, and the interference pattern is observed on a screen 5.00 m from the slits. What is the distance on the screen between the first-order bright fringes for the two wavelengths?

35.15. Coherent light with wavelength 600 nm passes through two very narrow slits and the interference pattern is observed on a screen 3.00 m from the slits. The first-order bright fringe is at 4.84 mm from the center of the central bright fringe. For what wavelength of light will the first-order dark fringe be observed at this same point on the screen?

35.16. Coherent light of frequency 6.32×10^{14} Hz passes through two thin slits and falls on a screen 85.0 cm away. You observe that the third bright fringe occurs at ± 3.11 cm on either side of the central bright fringe. (a) How far apart are the two slits? (b) At what distance from the central bright fringe will the third dark fringe occur?

35.17. Two thin parallel slits that are 0.0116 mm apart are illuminated by a laser beam of wavelength 585 nm. (a) On a very large distant screen, what is the *total* number of bright fringes (those indicating complete constructive interference), including the central fringe and those on both sides of it? Solve this problem without calculating all the angles! (*Hint:* What is the largest that $\sin\theta$ can be? What does this tell you is the largest value of m?) (b) At what angle, relative to the original direction of the beam, will the fringe that is most distant from the central bright fringe occur?

35.18. An FM radio station has a frequency of 107.9 MHz and uses two identical antennas mounted at the same elevation, 12.0 m apart. The antennas radiate in phase. The resulting radiation pattern has a maximum intensity along a horizontal line perpendicular to the line joining the antennas and midway between them. Assume that the intensity is observed at distances from the antennas that are much greater than 12.0 m. (a) At which other angles (measured from the line of maximum intensity) is the intensity maximum? (b) At which angles is it zero?

Section 35.3 Intensity in Interference Patterns

35.19. In a two-slit interference pattern, the intensity at the peak of the central maximum is I_0. (a) At a point in the pattern where the phase difference between the waves from the two slits is 60.0°, what is the intensity? (b) What is the path difference for 480-nm light from the two slits at a point where the phase angle is 60.0°?

35.20. Coherent sources A and B emit electromagnetic waves with wavelength 2.00 cm. Point P is 4.86 m from A and 5.24 m from B. What is the phase difference at P between these two waves?

35.21. Coherent light with wavelength 500 nm passes through narrow slits separated by 0.340 mm. At a distance from the slits large compared to their separation, what is the phase difference (in radians) in the light from the two slits at an angle of 23.0° from the centerline?

35.22. GPS Transmission. The GPS (Global Positioning System) satellites are approximately 5.18 m across and transmit two low-power signals, one of which is at 1575.42 MHz (in the UHF band). In a series of laboratory tests on the satellite, you put two 1575.42-MHz UHF transmitters at opposite ends of the satellite. These broadcast in phase uniformly in all directions. You measure the intensity at points on a circle that is several hundred meters in radius and centered on the satellite. You measure angles on this circle relative to a point that lies along the centerline of the satellite (that is, the perpendicular bisector of a line which extends from one transmitter to the other). At this point on the circle, the measured intensity is 2.00 W/m². (a) At how many other angles in the range $0° < \theta < 90°$ is the intensity also 2.00 W/m²? (b) Find the four smallest angles in the range $0° < \theta < 90°$ for which the intensity is 2.00 W/m². (c) What is the intensity at a point on the circle at an angle of 4.65° from the centerline?

35.23. Two slits spaced 0.260 mm apart are placed 0.700 m from a screen and illuminated by coherent light with a wavelength of 660 nm. The intensity at the center of the central maximum ($\theta = 0°$) is I_0. (a) What is the distance on the screen from the center of the central maximum to the first minimum? (b) What is the distance on the screen from the center of the central maximum to the point where the intensity has fallen to $I_0/2$?

35.24. Show that Eq. (35.14) gives zero-intensity directions that agree with Eq. (35.5).

35.25. Points A and B are 56.0 m apart along an east-west line. At each of these points, a radio transmitter is emitting a 12.5-MHz signal horizontally. These transmitters are in phase with other and emit their beams uniformly in a horizontal plane. A receiver is taken 0.500 km north of the AB line and initially placed at point C, directly opposite the midpoint of AB. The receiver can be moved only along an east-west direction but, due to its limited sensitivity, it must always remain within a range so that the intensity of the signal it receives from the transmitter is no less than $\frac{1}{4}$ of its maximum value. How far from point C (along an east-west line) can the receiver be moved and always be able to pick up the signal?

35.26. Consider two antennas separated by 9.00 m that radiate in phase at 120 MHz, as described in Exercise 35.3. A receiver placed 150 m from both antennas measures an intensity I_0. The receiver is moved so that it is 1.8 m closer to one antenna than to the other. (a) What is the phase difference ϕ between the two radio waves produced by this path difference? (b) In terms of I_0, what is the intensity measured by the receiver at its new position?

Section 35.4 Interference in Thin Films

35.27. What is the thinnest film of a coating with $n = 1.42$ on glass ($n = 1.52$) for which destructive interference of the red component (650 nm) of an incident white light beam in air can take place by reflection?

35.28. Nonglare Glass. When viewing a piece of art that is behind glass, one often is affected by the light that is reflected off the front of the glass (called *glare*), which can make it difficult to see the art clearly. One solution is to coat the outer surface of the glass with a film to cancel part of the glare. (a) If the glass has a refractive index of 1.62 and you use TiO_2, which has an index of refraction of 2.62, as the coating, what is the minimum film thickness that will cancel light of wavelength 505 nm? (b) If this coating is too thin to stand up to wear, what other thickness would also work? Find only the three thinnest ones.

35.29. Two rectangular pieces of plane glass are laid one upon the other on a table. A thin strip of paper is placed between them at one edge so that a very thin wedge of air is formed. The plates are illuminated at normal incidence by 546-nm light from a mercury-vapor lamp. Interference fringes are formed, with 15.0 fringes per centimeter. Find the angle of the wedge.

35.30. A plate of glass 9.00 cm long is placed in contact with a second plate and is held at a small angle with it by a metal strip 0.0800 mm thick placed under one end. The space between the plates is filled with air. The glass is illuminated from above with light having a wavelength in air of 656 nm. How many interference fringes are observed per centimeter in the reflected light?

35.31. A uniform film of TiO_2, 1036 nm thick and having index of refraction 2.62, is spread uniformly over the surface of crown glass of refractive index 1.52. Light of wavelength 520.0 nm falls at normal incidence onto the film from air. You want to increase the thickness of this film so that the reflected light cancels. (a) What is the *minimum* thickness of TiO_2 that you must *add* so the reflected light cancels as desired? (b) After you make the adjustment in part (a), what is the path difference between the light reflected off the top of the film and the light that cancels it after traveling through the film? Express your answer in (i) nanometers and (ii) wavelengths of the light in the TiO_2 film.

35.32. A plastic film with index of refraction 1.85 is put on the surface of a car window to increase the reflectivity and thus to keep the interior of the car cooler. The window glass has index of refraction 1.52. (a) What minimum thickness is required if light with wavelength 550 nm in air reflected from the two sides of the film is to interfere constructively? (b) It is found to be difficult to manufacture and install coatings as thin as calculated in part (a). What is the next greatest thickness for which there will also be constructive interference?

35.33. The walls of a soap bubble have about the same index of refraction as that of plain water, $n = 1.33$. There is air both inside and outside the bubble. (a) What wavelength (in air) of visible light is most strongly reflected from a point on a soap bubble where its wall is 290 nm thick? To what color does this correspond (see Fig. 32.4 and Table 32.1)? (b) Repeat part (a) for a wall thickness of 340 nm.

35.34. Light with wavelength 648 nm in air is incident perpendicularly from air on a film 8.76 μm thick and with refractive index 1.35. Part of the light is reflected from the first surface of the film, and part enters the film and is reflected back at the second surface, where the film is again in contact with air. (a) How many waves are contained along the path of this second part of the light in its round trip through the film? (b) What is the phase difference between these two parts of the light as they leave the film?

35.35. Compact Disc Player. A compact disc (CD) is read from the bottom by a semiconductor laser with wavelength 790 nm passing through a plastic substrate of refractive index 1.8. When the beam encounters a pit, part of the beam is reflected from the pit and part from the flat region between the pits, so these two beams interfere with each other (Fig. 35.22). What must the minimum pit depth be so that the part of the beam reflected from a pit cancels the part of the beam reflected from the flat region? (It is this cancellation that allows the player to recognize the beginning and end of a pit. For a fuller explanation of the physics behind CD technology, see the article "The Compact Disc Digital Audio System," by Thomas D. Rossing, in the December 1987 issue of *The Physics Teacher.*)

Figure **35.22** Exercise 35.35.

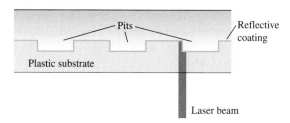

35.36. What is the thinnest soap film (excluding the case of zero thickness) that appears black when illuminated with light with wavelength 480 nm? The index of refraction of the film is 1.33, and there is air on both sides of the film.

Section 35.5 The Michelson Interferometer

35.37. How far must the mirror M_2 (see Fig. 35.20) of the Michelson interferometer be moved so that 1800 fringes of He-Ne laser light ($\lambda = 633$ nm) move across a line in the field of view?

35.38. Jan first uses a Michelson interferometer with the 606-nm light from a krypton-86 lamp. He displaces the movable mirror away from him, counting 818 fringes moving across a line in his field of view. Then Linda replaces the krypton lamp with filtered 502-nm light from a helium lamp and displaces the movable mirror toward her. She also counts 818 fringes, but they move across the line in her field of view opposite to the direction they moved for Jan. Assume that both Jan and Linda counted to 818 correctly. (a) What distance did each person move the mirror? (b) What is the resultant displacement of the mirror?

Problems

35.39. The radius of curvature of the convex surface of a planoconvex lens is 95.2 cm. The lens is placed convex side down on a perfectly flat glass plate that is illuminated from above with red light having a wavelength of 580 nm. Find the diameter of the second bright ring in the interference pattern.

35.40. Newton's rings can be seen when a planoconvex lens is placed on a flat glass surface (see Problem 35.39). For a particular lens with an index of refraction of $n = 1.50$ and a glass plate with an index of $n = 1.80$, the diameter of the third bright ring is 0.850 mm. If water ($n = 1.33$) now fills the space between the lens and the plate, what is the new diameter of this ring?

35.41. Suppose you illuminate two thin slits by monochromatic coherent light in air and find that they produce their first interference *minima* at $\pm 35.20°$ on either side of the central bright spot. You then immerse these slits in a transparent liquid and illuminate them with the same light. Now you find that the first minima occur at $\pm 19.46°$ instead. What is the index of refraction of this liquid?

35.42. A very thin sheet of brass contains two thin parallel slits. When a laser beam shines on these slits at normal incidence and room temperature $(20.0°C)$, the first interference dark fringes occur at $±32.5°$ from the original direction of the laser beam when viewed from some distance. If this sheet is now slowly heated up to 135°C, by how many degrees do these dark fringes change position? Do they move closer together or get farther apart? See Table 17.1 for pertinent information, and ignore any effects that might occur due to change in the thickness of the slits. (*Hint:* Since thermal expansion normally produces very small changes in length, you can use differentials to find the change in the angle.)

35.43. Two speakers, 2.50 m apart, are driven by the same audio oscillator so that each one produces a sound consisting of *two* distinct frequencies, 0.900 kHz and 1.20 kHz. The speed of sound in the room is 344 m/s. Find all the angles relative to the usual center line in front of (and far from) the speakers at which *both* frequencies interfere constructively.

35.44. Two radio antennas radiating in phase are located at points A and B, 200 m apart (Fig. 35.23). The radio waves have a frequency of 5.80 MHz. A radio receiver is moved out from point B along a line perpendicular to the line connecting A and B (line BC shown in Fig. 35.23). At what distances from B will there be *destructive* interference? (*Note:* The distance of the receiver from the sources is not large in comparison to the separation of the sources, so Eq. (35.5) does not apply.)

Figure **35.23** Problem 35.44.

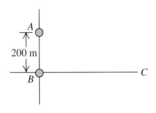

35.45. One round face of a 3.25-m, solid, cylindrical plastic pipe is covered with a thin black coating that completely blocks light. The opposite face is covered with a fluorescent coating that glows when it is struck by light. Two straight, thin, parallel scratches, 0.225 mm apart, are made in the center of the black face. When laser light of wavelength 632.8 nm shines through the slits perpendicular to the black face, you find that the central bright fringe on the opposite face is 5.82 mm wide, measured between the dark fringes that border it on either side. What is the index of refraction of the plastic?

35.46. A uniform thin film of material of refractive index 1.40 coats a glass plate of refractive index 1.55. This film has the proper thickness to cancel normally incident light of wavelength 525 nm that strikes the film surface from air, but it is somewhat greater than the minimum thickness to achieve this cancellation. As time goes by, the film wears away at a steady rate of 4.20 nm per year. What is the minimum number of years before the reflected light of this wavelength is now enhanced instead of cancelled?

35.47. (a) In Fig. 35.3, suppose source S_2 is *not* in phase with S_1, but instead is *out* of phase by $\frac{1}{2}$ cycle. In this situation, Eq. (35.1) is the condition for *destructive* interference, and Eq. (35.2) is the condition for *constructive* interference. Explain why this is so. (b) Suppose S_2 *leads* S_1 by a phase angle ϕ; that is, if the displacement of source S_1 is given by $x_1(t) = A\cos\omega t$, then the displacement of source S_2 is $x_2(t) = A\cos(\omega t + \phi)$. (In the situation of part (a), $\phi = \pi$.) Find expressions for the values of the path difference $r_2 - r_1$ that correspond to constructive interference and to destructive interference.

35.48. The electric fields received at point P from two identical, coherent wave sources are $E_1(t) = E\cos(\omega t + \phi)$ and $E_2(t) = E\cos\omega t$. (a) Use one of the trigonometric identities in Appendix B to show that the resultant wave is $E_P(t) = 2E\cos(\phi/2)\cos(\omega t + \phi/2)$. (b) Show that the amplitude of this resultant wave is given by Eq. (35.7). (c) Use the result of part (a)

to show that at an interference maximum, the amplitude of the resultant wave is in phase with the original waves $E_1(t)$ and $E_2(t)$. (d) Use the result of part (a) to show that near an interference minimum, the resultant wave is approximately $\frac{1}{4}$ cycle out of phase with either of the original waves. (e) Show that the *instantaneous* Poynting vector at point P has magnitude $S = 4\epsilon_0 cE^2\cos^2(\phi/2)\cos^2(\omega t + \phi/2)$ and that the *time-averaged* Poynting vector is given by Eq. (35.9).

35.49. Let the two sources S_1 and S_2 shown in Fig. 35.3 be located at $y = d$ and $y = -d$, respectively. (a) Rewrite Eq. (35.1) in terms of the x- and y-coordinates of a point P in Fig. 35.3 at which constructive interference occurs. (b) Your expression in part (a) is the equation for the antinodal curves shown in Fig. 35.3. Show that these curves are hyperbolas. (*Hint:* You may want to review the definition of a hyperbola in analytic geometry.) (c) Repeat part (a) for Eq. (35.2), which describes points at which *destructive* interference occurs, and show that the *nodal* curves (not shown in Fig. 35.3) are also hyperbolas.

35.50. Consider a two-slit interference experiment in which the two slits are of different widths. As measured on a distant screen, the amplitude of the wave from the first slit is E, while the amplitude of the wave from the second slit is $2E$. (a) Show that the intensity at any point in the interference pattern is

$$I = I_0\left(\frac{5}{9} + \frac{4}{9}\cos\phi\right)$$

where ϕ is the phase difference between the two waves as measured at a particular point on the screen and I_0 is the maximum intensity in the pattern. (b) Graph I versus ϕ (like Fig. 35.10). What is the minimum value of the intensity, and for which values of ϕ does it occur?

35.51. A thin uniform film of refractive index 1.750 is placed on a sheet of glass of refractive index 1.50. At room temperature $(20.0°C)$, this film is just thick enough for light with wavelength 582.4 nm reflected off the top of the film to be cancelled by light reflected from the top of the glass. After the glass is placed in an oven and slowly heated to 170°C, you find that the film cancels reflected light with wavelength 588.5 nm. What is the coefficient of linear expansion of the film? (Ignore any changes in the refractive index of the film due to the temperature change.)

35.52. Red light with wavelength 700 nm is passed through a two-slit apparatus. At the same time, monochromatic visible light with another wavelength passes through the same apparatus. As a result, most of the pattern that appears on the screen is a mixture of two colors; however, the center of the third bright fringe $(m = 3)$ of the red light appears pure red, with none of the other color. What are the possible wavelengths of the second type of visible light? Do you need to know the slit spacing to answer this question? Why or why not?

35.53. Consider a two-slit interference pattern, for which the intensity distribution is given by Eq. (35.14). Let θ_m be the angular position of the mth bright fringe, where the intensity is I_0. Assume that θ_m is small, so that $\sin\theta_m \cong \theta_m$. Let θ_m^+ and θ_m^- be the two angles on either side of θ_m for which $I = \frac{1}{2}I_0$. The quantity $\Delta\theta_m = |\theta_m^+ - \theta_m^-|$ is the half-width of the mth fringe. Calculate $\Delta\theta_m$. How does $\Delta\theta_m$ depend on m?

35.54. White light reflects at normal incidence from the top and bottom surfaces of a glass plate $(n = 1.52)$. There is air above and below the plate. Constructive interference is observed for light whose wavelength in air is 477.0 nm. What is the thickness of the plate if the next longer wavelength for which there is constructive interference is 540.6 nm?

35.55. A source S of monochromatic light and a detector D are both located in air a distance h above a horizontal plane sheet of glass, and are separated by a horizontal distance x. Waves reaching D directly from S interfere with waves that reflect off the glass. The distance x is small compared to h so that the reflection is at close to normal incidence. (a) Show that the condition for constructive interference is $\sqrt{x^2 + 4h^2} - x = (m + \frac{1}{2})\lambda$, and the condition for destructive interference is $\sqrt{x^2 + 4h^2} - x = m\lambda$. (*Hint:* Take into account the phase change on reflection.) (b) Let $h = 24$ cm and $x = 14$ cm. What is the longest wavelength for which there will be constructive interference?

35.56. Reflective Coatings and Herring.   Herring and related fish have a brilliant silvery appearance that camouflages them while they are swimming in a sunlit ocean. The silveriness is due to *platelets* attached to the surfaces of these fish. Each platelet is made up of several alternating layers of crystalline guanine ($n = 1.80$) and of cytoplasm ($n = 1.333$, the same as water), with a guanine layer on the outside in contact with the surrounding water (Fig. 35.24). In one typical platelet, the guanine layers are 74 nm thick and the cytoplasm layers are 100 nm thick. (a) For light striking the platelet surface at normal incidence, for which vacuum wavelengths of visible light will all of the reflections R_1, R_2, R_3, R_4, and R_5, shown in Fig. 35.24, be approximately in phase? If white light is shone on this platelet, what color will be most strongly reflected (see Fig. 32.4)? The surface of a herring has very many platelets side by side with layers of different thickness, so that *all* visible wavelengths are reflected. (b) Explain why such a "stack" of layers is more reflective than a single layer of guanine with cytoplasm underneath. (A stack of five guanine layers separated by cytoplasm layers reflects more than 80% of incident light at the wavelength for which it is "tuned.") (c) The color that is most strongly reflected from a platelet depends on the angle at which it is viewed. Explain why this should be so. (You can see these changes in color by examining a herring from different angles. Most of the platelets on these fish are oriented in the same way, so that they are vertical when the fish is swimming.)

Figure **35.24** Problem 35.56.

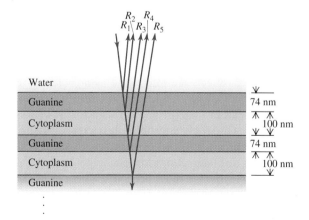

35.57. Two thin parallel slits are made in an opaque sheet of film. When a monochromatic beam of light is shone through them at normal incidence, the first bright fringes in the transmitted light occur in air at $\pm18.0°$ with the original direction of the light beam on a distant screen when the apparatus is in air. When the appara-

tus is immersed in a liquid, the same bright fringes now occur at $\pm12.6°$. Find the index of refraction of the liquid.

35.58. An oil tanker spills a large amount of oil ($n = 1.45$) into the sea ($n = 1.33$). (a) If you look down onto the oil spill from overhead, what predominant wavelength of light do you see at a point where the oil is 380 nm thick? What color is the light? (*Hint:* See Table 32.1.) (b) In the water under the slick, what visible wavelength (as measured in air) is predominant in the transmitted light at the same place in the slick as in part (a)?

35.59. In a Young's two-slit experiment a piece of glass with an index of refraction n and a thickness L is placed in front of the upper slit. (a) Describe qualitatively what happens to the interference pattern. (b) Derive an expression for the intensity I of the light at points on a screen as a function of n, L, and θ. Here θ is the usual angle measured from the center of the two slits. That is, determine the equation analogous to Eq. (35.14) but that also involves L and n for the glass plate. (c) From your result in part (b) derive an expression for the values of θ that locate the maxima in the interference pattern [that is, derive an equation analogous to Eq. (35.4)].

35.60. After a laser beam passes through two thin parallel slits, the first completely dark fringes occur at $\pm15.0°$ with the original direction of the beam, as viewed on a screen far from the slits. (a) What is the ratio of the distance between the slits to the wavelength of the light illuminating the slits? (b) What is the smallest angle, relative to the original direction of the laser beam, at which the intensity of the light is $\frac{1}{10}$ the maximum intensity on the screen?

Challenge Problems

35.61. The index of refraction of a glass rod is 1.48 at $T = 20.0°C$ and varies linearly with temperature, with a coefficient of $2.50 \times 10^{-5}/C°$. The coefficient of linear expansion of the glass is $5.00 \times 10^{-6}/C°$. At $20.0°C$ the length of the rod is 3.00 cm. A Michelson interferometer has this glass rod in one arm, and the rod is being heated so that its temperature increases at a rate of $5.00 \ C°/\text{min}$. The light source has wavelength $\lambda = 589$ nm, and the rod initially is at $T = 20.0°C$. How many fringes cross the field of view each minute?

35.62. Figure 35.25 shows an interferometer known as *Fresnel's biprism*. The magnitude of the prism angle A is extremely small. (a) If S_0 is a very narrow source slit, show that the separation of the two virtual coherent sources S_1 and S_2 is given by $d = 2aA(n - 1)$, where n is the index of refraction of the material of the prism. (b) Calculate the spacing of the fringes of green light with wavelength 500 nm on a screen 2.00 m from the biprism. Take $a = 0.200$ m, $A = 3.50$ mrad, and $n = 1.50$.

Figure **35.25** Challenge Problem 35.62.

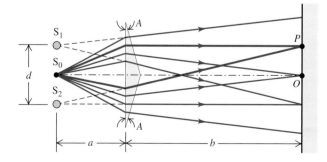

36

DIFFRACTION

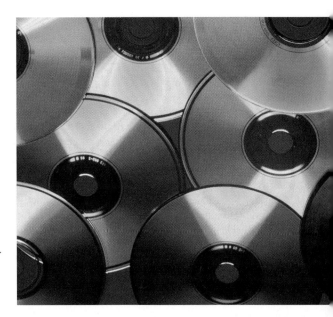

? The laser used to read a compact disc (CD) has a wavelength of 780 nm, while the laser used to read a DVD has a wavelength of 650 nm. How does this make it possible for a DVD to hold more information than a CD?

LEARNING GOALS

By studying this chapter, you will learn:

- What happens when coherent light shines on an object with an edge or aperture.

- How to understand the diffraction pattern formed when coherent light passes through a narrow slit.

- How to calculate the intensity at various points in a single-slit diffraction pattern.

- What happens when coherent light shines on an array of narrow, closely spaced slits.

- How scientists use diffraction gratings for precise measurements of wavelength.

- How x-ray diffraction reveals the arrangement of atoms in a crystal.

- How diffraction sets limits on the smallest details that can be seen with a telescope.

Everyone is used to the idea that sound bends around corners. If sound didn't behave this way, you couldn't hear a police siren that's out of sight around a corner or the speech of a person whose back is turned to you. What may surprise you (and certainly surprised many scientists of the early 19th century) is that *light* can bend around corners as well. When light from a point source falls on a straightedge and casts a shadow, the edge of the shadow is never perfectly sharp. Some light appears in the area that we expect to be in the shadow, and we find alternating bright and dark fringes in the illuminated area. In general, light emerging from apertures doesn't behave precisely according to the predictions of the straight-line ray model of geometric optics.

The reason for these effects is that light, like sound, has wave characteristics. In Chapter 35 we studied the interference patterns that can arise when two light waves are combined. In this chapter we'll investigate interference effects due to combining *many* light waves. Such effects are referred to as *diffraction*. We'll find that the behavior of waves after they pass through an aperture is an example of diffraction; each infinitesimal part of the aperture acts as a source of waves, and the resulting pattern of light and dark is a result of interference among the waves emanating from these sources.

Light emerging from arrays of apertures also forms patterns whose character depends on the color of the light and the size and spacing of the apertures. Examples of this effect include the colors of iridescent butterflies and the "rainbow" you see reflected from the surface of a compact disc. We'll explore similar effects with x rays that are used to study the atomic structure of solids and liquids. Finally, we'll look at the physics of a *hologram,* a special kind of interference pattern recorded on photographic film and reproduced. When properly illuminated, it forms a three-dimensional image of the original object.

36.1 Fresnel and Fraunhofer Diffraction

According to geometric optics, when an opaque object is placed between a point light source and a screen, as in Fig. 36.1, the shadow of the object forms a perfectly sharp line. No light at all strikes the screen at points within the shadow, and the area outside the shadow is illuminated nearly uniformly. But as we saw in Chapter 35, the *wave* nature of light causes effects that can't be understood with the simple model of geometric optics. An important class of such effects occurs when light strikes a barrier that has an aperture or an edge. The interference patterns formed in such a situation are grouped under the heading **diffraction.**

An example of diffraction is shown in Fig. 36.2. The photograph in Fig. 36.2a was made by placing a razor blade halfway between a pinhole, illuminated by monochromatic light, and a photographic film. The film recorded the shadow cast by the blade. Figure 36.2b is an enlargement of a region near the shadow of the right edge of the blade. The position of the *geometric* shadow line is indicated by arrows. The area outside the geometric shadow is bordered by alternating bright and dark bands. There is some light in the shadow region, although this is not very visible in the photograph. The first bright band in Fig. 36.2b, just to the right of the geometric shadow, is considerably brighter than in the region of uniform illumination to the extreme right. This simple experiment gives us some idea of the richness and complexity of what might seem to be a simple idea, the casting of a shadow by an opaque object.

We don't often observe diffraction patterns such as Fig. 36.2 in everyday life because most ordinary light sources are not monochromatic and are not point sources. If we use a white frosted light bulb instead of a point source in Fig. 36.1, each wavelength of the light from every point of the bulb forms its own diffraction pattern, but the patterns overlap to such an extent that we can't see any individual pattern.

Diffraction and Huygens's Principle

Diffraction patterns can be analyzed by use of Huygens's principle (see Section 33.7). Let's review that principle briefly. Every point of a wave front can be considered the source of secondary wavelets that spread out in all directions with a speed equal to the speed of propagation of the wave. The position of the wave front at any later time is the *envelope* of the secondary waves at that time. To find the resultant displacement at any point, we combine all the individual displacements

36.1 A point source of light illuminates a straightedge.

Geometric optics predicts that this situation should produce a sharp boundary between illumination and solid shadow.

DOESN'T HAPPEN

That's NOT what really happens!

Point source

Straightedge

Area of illumination

Geometric shadow

Screen

36.2 An example of diffraction.

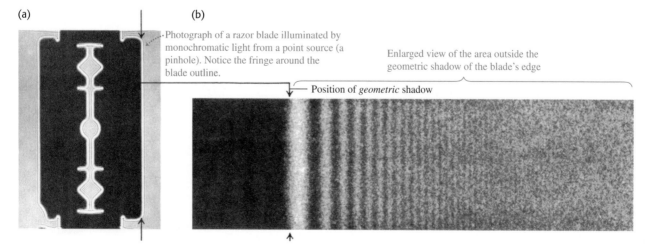

(a)

(b)

Photograph of a razor blade illuminated by monochromatic light from a point source (a pinhole). Notice the fringe around the blade outline.

Enlarged view of the area outside the geometric shadow of the blade's edge

Position of *geometric* shadow

produced by these secondary waves, using the superposition principle and taking into account their amplitudes and relative phases.

In Fig. 36.1, both the point source and the screen are relatively close to the obstacle forming the diffraction pattern. This situation is described as *near-field diffraction* or **Fresnel diffraction,** pronounced "Freh-nell" (after the French scientist Augustin Jean Fresnel, 1788–1827). If the source, obstacle, and screen are far enough away that all lines from the source to the obstacle can be considered parallel and all lines from the obstacle to a point in the pattern can be considered parallel, the phenomenon is called *far-field diffraction* or **Fraunhofer diffraction** (after the German physicist Joseph von Fraunhofer, 1787–1826). We will restrict the following discussion to Fraunhofer diffraction, which is usually simpler to analyze in detail than Fresnel diffraction.

Diffraction is sometimes described as "the bending of light around an obstacle." But the process that causes diffraction is present in the propagation of *every* wave. When part of the wave is cut off by some obstacle, we observe diffraction effects that result from interference of the remaining parts of the wave fronts. Optical instruments typically use only a limited portion of a wave; for example, a telescope uses only the part of a wave that is admitted by its objective lens or mirror. Thus diffraction plays a role in nearly all optical phenomena.

Finally, we emphasize that there is no fundamental distinction between *interference* and *diffraction*. In Chapter 35 we used the term *interference* for effects involving waves from a small number of sources, usually two. *Diffraction* usually involves a *continuous* distribution of Huygens's wavelets across the area of an aperture, or a very large number of sources or apertures. But both categories of phenomena are governed by the same basic physics of superposition and Huygens's principle.

Test Your Understanding of Section 36.1   Can *sound* waves undergo diffraction around an edge?

36.2 Diffraction from a Single Slit

In this section we'll discuss the diffraction pattern formed by plane-wave (parallel-ray) monochromatic light when it emerges from a long, narrow slit, as shown in Fig. 36.3. We call the narrow dimension the *width,* even though in this figure it is a vertical dimension.

According to geometric optics, the transmitted beam should have the same cross section as the slit, as in Fig. 36.3a. What is *actually* observed is the pattern shown in Fig. 36.3b. The beam spreads out vertically after passing through the

---

36.3 (a) The "shadow" of a horizontal slit as incorrectly predicted by geometric optics. (b) A horizontal slit actually produces a diffraction pattern. The slit width has been greatly exaggerated.

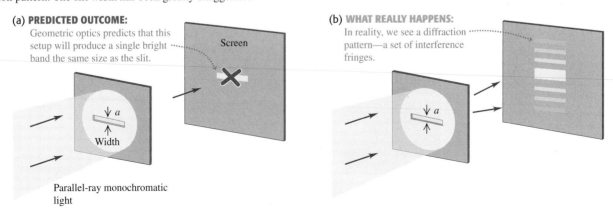

(a) **PREDICTED OUTCOME:**
Geometric optics predicts that this setup will produce a single bright band the same size as the slit.

Screen

a
Width

Parallel-ray monochromatic light

(b) **WHAT REALLY HAPPENS:**
In reality, we see a diffraction pattern—a set of interference fringes.

a

slit. The diffraction pattern consists of a central bright band, which may be much broader than the width of the slit, bordered by alternating dark and bright bands with rapidly decreasing intensity. About 85% of the power in the transmitted beam is in the central bright band, whose width is found to be *inversely* proportional to the width of the slit. In general, the smaller the width of the slit, the broader the entire diffraction pattern. (The *horizontal* spreading of the beam in Fig. 36.3b is negligible because the horizontal dimension of the slit is relatively large.) You can easily observe a similar diffraction pattern by looking at a point source, such as a distant street light, through a narrow slit formed between your two thumbs held in front of your eye; the retina of your eye corresponds to the screen.

Single-Slit Diffraction: Locating the Dark Fringes

Figure 36.4 shows a side view of the same setup; the long sides of the slit are perpendicular to the figure, and plane waves are incident on the slit from the left. According to Huygens's principle, each element of area of the slit opening can be considered as a source of secondary waves. In particular, imagine dividing the slit into several narrow strips of equal width, parallel to the long edges and perpendicular to the page. Two such strips are shown in Fig. 36.4a. Cylindrical secondary wavelets, shown in cross section, spread out from each strip.

In Fig. 36.4b a screen is placed to the right of the slit. We can calculate the resultant intensity at a point P on the screen by adding the contributions from the individual wavelets, taking proper account of their various phases and amplitudes. It's easiest to do this calculation if we assume that the screen is far enough away that all the rays from various parts of the slit to a particular point P on the screen are parallel, as in Fig. 36.4c. An equivalent situation is Fig. 36.4d, in which the rays to the lens are parallel and the lens forms a reduced image of the same pattern that would be formed on an infinitely distant screen without the lens. We might expect that the various light paths through the lens would introduce additional phase shifts, but in fact it can be shown that all the paths have *equal* phase shifts, so this is not a problem.

The situation of Fig. 36.4b is Fresnel diffraction; those in Figs. 36.4c and 36.4d, where the outgoing rays are considered parallel, are Fraunhofer diffraction. We can derive quite simply the most important characteristics of the Fraunhofer diffraction pattern from a single slit. First consider two narrow strips, one just below the top edge of the drawing of the slit and one at its center, shown in end view in Fig. 36.5. The difference in path length to point P is $(a/2)\sin\theta$, where a is the slit width and θ is the angle between the perpendicular to the slit and a line from the center of the slit to P. Suppose this path difference happens to be equal to $\lambda/2$; then light from these two strips arrives at point P with a half-cycle phase difference, and cancellation occurs.

36.4 Diffraction by a single rectangular slit. The long sides of the slit are perpendicular to the figure.

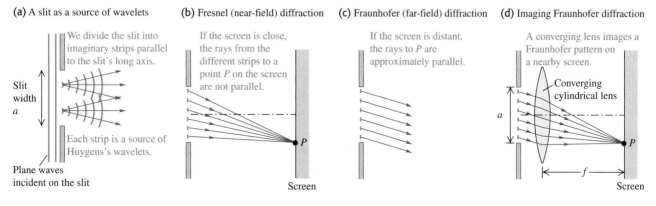

(a) A slit as a source of wavelets

We divide the slit into imaginary strips parallel to the slit's long axis.

Slit width a

Each strip is a source of Huygens's wavelets.

Plane waves incident on the slit

(b) Fresnel (near-field) diffraction

If the screen is close, the rays from the different strips to a point P on the screen are not parallel.

P

Screen

(c) Fraunhofer (far-field) diffraction

If the screen is distant, the rays to P are approximately parallel.

(d) Imaging Fraunhofer diffraction

A converging lens images a Fraunhofer pattern on a nearby screen.

Converging cylindrical lens

a

P

f

Screen

36.5 Side view of a horizontal slit. When the distance x to the screen is much greater than the slit width a, the rays from a distance $a/2$ apart may be considered parallel.

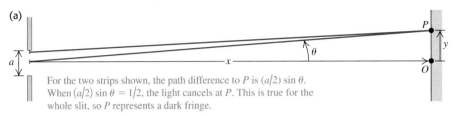

(a)

For the two strips shown, the path difference to P is $(a/2) \sin \theta$.
When $(a/2) \sin \theta = 1/2$, the light cancels at P. This is true for the whole slit, so P represents a dark fringe.

(b) Enlarged view of the top half of the slit

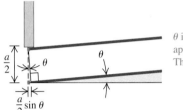

θ is usually very small, so we can use the approximations $\sin \theta = \theta$ and $\tan \theta = \theta$. Then the condition for a dark band is

$$y_m = x \frac{m\lambda}{a}$$

Similarly, light from two strips immediately *below* the two in the figure also arrives at P a half-cycle out of phase. In fact, the light from *every* strip in the top half of the slit cancels out the light from a corresponding strip in the bottom half. The result is complete cancellation at P for the combined light from the entire slit, giving a dark fringe in the interference pattern. That is, a dark fringe occurs whenever

$$\frac{a}{2}\sin\theta = \pm\frac{\lambda}{2} \quad \text{or} \quad \sin\theta = \pm\frac{\lambda}{a} \tag{36.1}$$

The plus-or-minus ($\pm$) sign in Eq. (36.1) says that there are symmetrical dark fringes above and below point O in Fig. 36.5a. The upper fringe ($\theta > 0$) occurs at a point P where light from the bottom half of the slit travels $\lambda/2$ farther to P than does light from the top half; the lower fringe ($\theta < 0$) occurs where light from the *top* half travels $\lambda/2$ farther than light from the *bottom* half.

We may also divide the screen into quarters, sixths, and so on, and use the above argument to show that a dark fringe occurs whenever $\sin\theta = \pm 2\lambda/a$, $\pm 3\lambda/a$, and so on. Thus the condition for a *dark* fringe is

$$\sin\theta = \frac{m\lambda}{a} \quad (m = \pm 1, \pm 2, \pm 3, \dots) \qquad \text{(dark fringes in single-slit diffraction)} \tag{36.2}$$

For example, if the slit width is equal to ten wavelengths ($a = 10\lambda$), dark fringes occur at $\sin\theta = \pm\frac{1}{10}, \pm\frac{2}{10}, \pm\frac{3}{10}, \dots$. Between the dark fringes are bright fringes. We also note that $\sin\theta = 0$ corresponds to a *bright* band; in this case, light from the entire slit arrives at P in phase. Thus it would be wrong to put $m = 0$ in Eq. (36.2). The central bright fringe is wider than the other bright fringes, as Fig. 36.3 shows. In the small-angle approximation that we will use below, it is exactly *twice* as wide.

With light, the wavelength λ is of the order of 500 nm = 5×10^{-7} m. This is often much smaller than the slit width a; a typical slit width is 10^{-2} cm = 10^{-4} m. Therefore the values of θ in Eq. (36.2) are often so small that the approximation $\sin\theta \approx \theta$ (where θ is in radians) is a very good one. In that case we can rewrite this equation as

$$\theta = \frac{m\lambda}{a} \quad (m = \pm 1, \pm 2, \pm 3, \dots) \qquad \text{(for small angles } \theta)$$

where θ is in *radians*. Also, if the distance from slit to screen is x, as in Fig. 36.5a, and the vertical distance of the mth dark band from the center of the pattern is y_m, then $\tan\theta = y_m/x$. For small θ we may also approximate $\tan\theta$ by θ (in radians), and we then find

$$y_m = x\frac{m\lambda}{a} \quad (\text{for } y_m \ll x) \tag{36.3}$$

Figure 36.6 is a photograph of a single-slit diffraction pattern with the $m = \pm1, \pm2$, and ±3 minima labeled.

CAUTION **Single-slit diffraction vs. two-slit interference** Equation (36.3) has the same form as the equation for the two-slit pattern, Eq. (35.6), except that in Eq. (36.3) we use x rather than R for the distance to the screen. But Eq. (36.3) gives the positions of the *dark* fringes in a *single-slit* pattern rather than the *bright* fringes in a *double-slit* pattern. Also, $m = 0$ in Eq. (36.2) is *not* a dark fringe. Be careful! ▮

36.6 Photograph of the Fraunhofer diffraction pattern of a single horizontal slit.

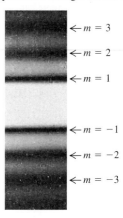

$\leftarrow m = 3$
$\leftarrow m = 2$
$\leftarrow m = 1$

$\leftarrow m = -1$
$\leftarrow m = -2$
$\leftarrow m = -3$

Example 36.1 **Single-slit diffraction**

You pass 633-nm laser light through a narrow slit and observe the diffraction pattern on a screen 6.0 m away. You find that the distance on the screen between the centers of the first minima outside the central bright fringe is 32 mm (Fig. 36.7). How wide is the slit?

SOLUTION

IDENTIFY: This problem involves the relationship between the dark fringes in a single-slit diffraction pattern and the width of the slit (our target variable).

36.7 A single-slit diffraction experiment.

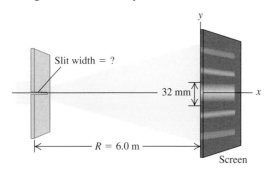

Slit width = ?

32 mm

$R = 6.0$ m

Screen

SET UP: The distances between points on the screen are much smaller than the distance from the slit to the screen, so the angle θ shown in Fig. 36.5a is very small. Hence we can use the approximate relationship of Eq. (36.3) to solve for the slit width a (the target variable).

EXECUTE: The first minimum corresponds to $m = 1$ in Eq. (36.3). The distance y_1 from the central maximum to the first minimum on either side is half the distance between the two first minima, so $y_1 = (32 \text{ mm})/2$. Substituting these values and solving for a, we find

$$a = \frac{x\lambda}{y_1} = \frac{(6.0 \text{ m})(633 \times 10^{-9} \text{ m})}{(32 \times 10^{-3} \text{ m})/2}$$
$$= 2.4 \times 10^{-4} \text{ m} = 0.24 \text{ mm}$$

EVALUATE: The angle θ is small only if the wavelength is small compared to the slit width. Since $\lambda = 633 \text{ nm} = 6.33 \times 10^{-7}$ m and we have found $a = 0.24 \text{ mm} = 2.4 \times 10^{-4}$ m, our result is consistent with this: The wavelength is $(6.33 \times 10^{-7} \text{ m})/(2.4 \times 10^{-4} \text{ m}) = 0.0026$ as large as the slit width. Can you show that the distance between the *second* minima on the two sides is $2(32 \text{ mm}) = 64$ mm, and so on?

Test Your Understanding of Section 36.2 Rank the following single-slit diffraction experiments in order of the size of the angle from the center of the diffraction pattern to the first dark fringe, from largest to smallest (i) wavelength 400 nm, slit width 0.20 mm; (ii) wavelength 600 nm, slit width 0.20 mm; (iii) wavelength 400 nm, slit width 0.30 mm; (iv) wavelength 600 nm, slit width 0.30 mm.

(MP)

36.3 Intensity in the Single-Slit Pattern

We can derive an expression for the intensity distribution for the single-slit diffraction pattern by the same phasor-addition method that we used in Section 35.3 to obtain Eqs. (35.10) and (35.14) for the two-slit interference pattern. We again imagine a plane wave front at the slit subdivided into a large number of strips. We superpose the contributions of the Huygens wavelets from all the strips at a point P on a distant screen at an angle θ from the normal to the slit plane

36.8 Using phasor diagrams to find the amplitude of the $\vec{E}$ field in single-slit diffraction. Each phasor represents the $\vec{E}$ field from a single strip within the slit.

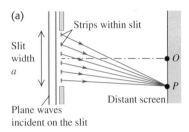

(a)
Slit width a
Strips within slit
O
P
Distant screen
Plane waves incident on the slit

(b) At the center of the diffraction pattern (point O), the phasors from all strips within the slit are in phase.

E_0

(c) Phasor diagram at a point slightly off the center of the pattern; β = total phase difference between the first and last phasors.

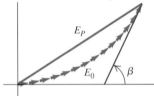

E_P
E_0
β

(d) As in (c), but in the limit that the slit is subdivided into infinitely many strips

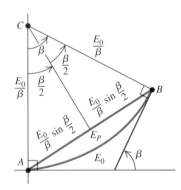

C
β
$\frac{E_0}{\beta}$
$\frac{\beta}{2}$
$\frac{E_0}{\beta}$
$\frac{\beta}{2}$
$E_0 \sin\frac{\beta}{2}$
B
$E_0 \sin\frac{\beta}{2}$
E_P
A
E_0
β

(Fig. 36.8a). To do this, we use a phasor to represent the sinusoidally varying $\vec{E}$ field from each individual strip. The magnitude of the vector sum of the phasors at each point P is the amplitude E_P of the total $\vec{E}$ field at that point. The intensity at P is proportional to E_P^2.

At the point O shown in Figure 36.8a, corresponding to the center of the pattern where $\theta = 0$, there are negligible path differences for $x \gg a$; the phasors are all essentially *in phase* (that is, have the same direction). In Fig. 36.8b we draw the phasors at time $t = 0$ and denote the resultant amplitude at O by E_0. In this illustration we have divided the slit into 14 strips.

Now consider wavelets arriving from different strips at point P in Fig. 36.8a, at an angle θ from point O. Because of the differences in path length, there are now phase differences between wavelets coming from adjacent strips; the corresponding phasor diagram is shown in Fig. 36.8c. The vector sum of the phasors is now part of the perimeter of a many-sided polygon, and E_P, the amplitude of the resultant electric field at P, is the *chord*. The angle β is the total phase difference between the wave from the top strip of Fig. 36.8a and the wave from the bottom strip; that is, β is the phase of the wave received at P from the top strip with respect to the wave received at P from the bottom strip.

We may imagine dividing the slit into narrower and narrower strips. In the limit that there is an infinite number of infinitesimally narrow strips, the curved trail of phasors becomes an *arc of a circle* (Fig. 36.8d), with arc length equal to the length E_0 in Fig. 36.8b. The center C of this arc is found by constructing perpendiculars at A and B. From the relationship among arc length, radius, and angle, the radius of the arc is E_0/β; the amplitude E_P of the resultant electric field at P is equal to the chord AB, which is $2(E_0/\beta)\sin(\beta/2)$. (Note that β *must* be in radians!) We then have

$$E_P = E_0 \frac{\sin(\beta/2)}{\beta/2} \qquad \text{(amplitude in single-slit diffraction)} \qquad (36.4)$$

The intensity at each point on the screen is proportional to the square of the amplitude given by Eq. (36.4). If I_0 is the intensity in the straight-ahead direction where $\theta = 0$ and $\beta = 0$, then the intensity I at any point is

$$I = I_0 \left[\frac{\sin(\beta/2)}{\beta/2}\right]^2 \qquad \text{(intensity in single-slit diffraction)} \qquad (36.5)$$

We can express the phase difference β in terms of geometric quantities, as we did for the two-slit pattern. From Eq. (35.11) the phase difference is $2\pi/\lambda$ times the path difference. Figure 36.5 shows that the path difference between the ray from the top of the slit and the ray from the middle of the slit is $(a/2)\sin\theta$. The path difference between the rays from the top of the slit and the bottom of the slit is twice this, so

$$\beta = \frac{2\pi}{\lambda}a\sin\theta \qquad (36.6)$$

and Eq. (36.5) becomes

$$I = I_0 \left\{\frac{\sin[\pi a(\sin\theta)/\lambda]}{\pi a(\sin\theta)/\lambda}\right\}^2 \qquad \text{(intensity in single-slit diffraction)} \qquad (36.7)$$

This equation expresses the intensity directly in terms of the angle θ. In many calculations it is easier first to calculate the phase angle β, using Eq. (36.6), and then to use Eq. (36.5).

Equation (36.7) is plotted in Fig. 36.9a. Note that the central intensity peak is much larger than any of the others. This means that most of the power in the wave remains within an angle θ from the perpendicular to the slit, where $\sin\theta = \lambda/a$ (the first diffraction minimum). You can see this easily in Fig. 36.9b, which is a photograph of water waves undergoing single-slit diffraction. Note also that the peak intensities in Fig. 36.9a decrease rapidly as we go away from the center of the pattern. (Compare Fig. 36.6, which shows a single-slit diffraction pattern for light.)

The dark fringes in the pattern are the places where $I = 0$. These occur at points for which the numerator of Eq. (36.5) is zero so that β is a multiple of 2π. From Eq. (36.6) this corresponds to

$$\frac{a\sin\theta}{\lambda} = m \qquad (m = \pm1, \pm2, \dots)$$

$$\sin\theta = \frac{m\lambda}{a} \qquad (m = \pm1, \pm2, \dots) \tag{36.8}$$

This agrees with our previous result, Eq. (36.2). Note again that $\beta = 0$ (corresponding to $\theta = 0$) is *not* a minimum. Equation (36.5) is indeterminate at $\beta = 0$, but we can evaluate the limit as $\beta \to 0$ using L'Hôpital's rule. We find that at $\beta = 0$, $I = I_0$, as we should expect.

Intensity Maxima in the Single-Slit Pattern

We can also use Eq. (36.5) to calculate the positions of the peaks, or *intensity maxima,* and the intensities at these peaks. This is not quite as simple as it may appear. We might expect the peaks to occur where the sine function reaches the value ±1—namely, where $\beta = \pm\pi, \pm3\pi, \pm5\pi$, or in general,

$$\beta \approx \pm(2m + 1)\pi \qquad (m = 0, 1, 2, \dots) \tag{36.9}$$

This is *approximately* correct, but because of the factor $(\beta/2)^2$ in the denominator of Eq. (36.5), the maxima don't occur precisely at these points. When we take the derivative of Eq. (36.5) with respect to β and set it equal to zero to try to find the maxima and minima, we get a transcendental equation that has to be solved numerically. In fact there is *no* maximum near $\beta = \pm\pi$. The first maxima on either side of the central maximum, near $\beta = \pm3\pi$, actually occur at $\pm2.860\pi$. The second side maxima, near $\beta = \pm5\pi$, are actually at $\pm4.918\pi$, and so on. The error in Eq. (36.9) vanishes in the limit of large m—that is, for intensity maxima far from the center of the pattern.

To find the intensities at the side maxima, we substitute these values of β back into Eq. (36.5). Using the approximate expression in Eq. (36.9), we get

$$I_m \approx \frac{I_0}{\left(m + \frac{1}{2}\right)^2 \pi^2} \tag{36.10}$$

where I_m is the intensity of the mth side maximum and I_0 is the intensity of the central maximum. Equation (36.10) gives the series of intensities

$$0.0450I_0 \qquad 0.0162I_0 \qquad 0.0083I_0$$

and so on. As we have pointed out, this equation is only approximately correct. The actual intensities of the side maxima turn out to be

$$0.0472I_0 \qquad 0.0165I_0 \qquad 0.0083I_0 \qquad \dots$$

Note that the intensities of the side maxima decrease very rapidly, as Fig. 36.9a also shows. Even the first side maxima have less than 5% of the intensity of the central maximum.

Width of the Single-Slit Pattern

For small angles the angular spread of the diffraction pattern is inversely proportional to the slit width a or, more precisely, to the ratio of a to the wavelength λ. Figure 36.10 shows graphs of intensity I as a function of the angle θ for three values of the ratio a/λ.

36.9 (a) Intensity versus angle in single-slit diffraction. The values of m label intensity minima given by Eq. (36.8). Most of the wave power goes into the central intensity peak (between the $m = 1$ and $m = -1$ intensity minima). (b) These water waves passing through a small aperture behave exactly like light waves in single-slit diffraction. Only the diffracted waves within the central intensity peak are visible; the waves at larger angles are too faint to see.

(a)
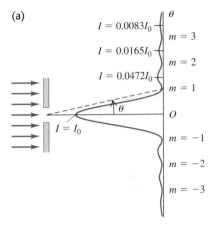

(b)
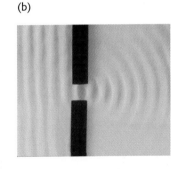

36.10 The single-slit diffraction pattern depends on the ratio of the slit width a to the wavelength λ.

(a) $a = \lambda$

If the slit width is equal to or narrower than the wavelength, only one broad maximum forms.

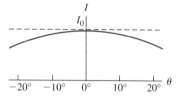

(b) $a = 5\lambda$

The wider the slit (or the shorter the wavelength), the narrower and sharper is the central peak.

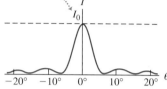

(c) $a = 8\lambda$

With light waves, the wavelength λ is often much smaller than the slit width a, and the values of θ in Eqs. (36.6) and (36.7) are so small that the approximation $\sin\theta = \theta$ is very good. With this approximation the position θ_1 of the first minimum beside the central maximum, corresponding to $\beta/2 = \pi$, is, from Eq. (36.7),

$$\theta_1 = \frac{\lambda}{a} \tag{36.11}$$

This characterizes the width (angular spread) of the central maximum, and we see that it is *inversely* proportional to the slit width a. When the small-angle approximation is valid, the central maximum is exactly twice as wide as each side maximum. When a is of the order of a centimeter or more, θ_1 is so small that we can consider practically all the light to be concentrated at the geometrical focus. But when a is less than λ, the central maximum spreads over 180°, and the fringe pattern is not seen at all.

It's important to keep in mind that diffraction occurs for *all* kinds of waves, not just light. Sound waves undergo diffraction when they pass through a slit or aperture such as an ordinary doorway. The sound waves used in speech have wavelengths of about a meter or greater, and a typical doorway is less than 1 m wide; in this situation, a is less than λ, and the central intensity maximum extends over 180°. This is why the sounds coming through an open doorway can easily be heard by an eavesdropper hiding out of sight around the corner. In the same way, sound waves can bend around the head of an instructor who faces the blackboard while lecturing (Fig. 36.11). By contrast, there is essentially no diffraction of visible light through such a doorway because the width a is very much greater than the wavelength λ (of order 5×10^{-7} m). You can *hear* around corners because typical sound waves have relatively long wavelengths; you cannot *see* around corners because the wavelength of visible light is very short.

36.11 The sound waves used in speech have a long wavelength (about 1 m) and can easily bend around this instructor's head. By contrast, light waves have very short wavelengths and undergo very little diffraction. Hence you can't *see* around his head!

Example 36.2   **Single-slit diffraction: Intensity I**

(a) In a single-slit diffraction pattern, what is the intensity at a point where the total phase difference between wavelets from the top and bottom of the slit is 66 rad? (b) If this point is 7.0° away from the central maximum, how many wavelengths wide is the slit?

SOLUTION

IDENTIFY: This problem asks us to find the intensity at a point in a single-slit diffraction pattern where there is a specified phase difference between waves coming from the two edges of the slit (Fig. 36.8a). It also asks us to relate phase difference, slit width, wavelength, and the θ shown in Fig. 36.9a.

SET UP: The total phase difference between wavelets from the two edges of the slit is the quantity we called β in Fig. 36.8d. Given $\beta = 66$ rad, we use Eq. (36.5) to find the intensity I at the point in question, and we use Eq. (36.6) to find the slit width a in terms of the wavelength λ.

EXECUTE: (a) Since $\beta = 66$ rad, $\beta/2 = 33$ rad and Eq. (36.5) becomes

$$I = I_0\left[\frac{\sin(33\text{ rad})}{33\text{ rad}}\right]^2 = (9.2 \times 10^{-4})I_0$$

(b) We solve Eq. (36.6) for a:

$$a = \frac{\beta\lambda}{2\pi\sin\theta} = \frac{(66\text{ rad})\lambda}{(2\pi\text{ rad})\sin 7.0°} = 86\lambda$$

For example, for 550-nm light, the slit width a is $(86)(550\text{ nm}) = 4.7 \times 10^{-5}$ m $= 0.047$ mm, or roughly $\frac{1}{20}$ mm.

EVALUATE: To what point in the diffraction pattern does this value of β correspond? To find out, note that $\beta = 66$ rad $= 21\pi$. Com-paring to Eq. (36.9) shows that this is approximately equal to the value of β at the *tenth* side maximum, well beyond the range shown in Fig. 36.9a (which shows only the first three side max-ima). The intensity is very much less than the intensity I_0 at the central maximum. (The *actual* position of this maximum is at $\beta = 65.91$ rad $= 20.98\pi$, or approximately midway between the minima at $\beta = 20\pi$ and $\beta = 22\pi$.)

Example 36.3   Single-slit diffraction: Intensity II

In the experiment described in Example 36.1 (Section 36.2), what is the intensity at a point on the screen 3.0 mm from the center of the pattern? The intensity at the center of the pattern is I_0.

SOLUTION

IDENTIFY: This is similar to Example 36.2, except that we are not given the value of the phase difference β at the point in question.

SET UP: We use geometry to determine the angle θ for our point and then use Eq. (36.7) to calculate the intensity I (our target variable).

EXECUTE: Referring to Fig. 36.5a, we have $y = 3.0$ mm and $x = 6.0$ m, so $\tan\theta = y/x = (3.0 \times 10^{-3}\text{ m})/(6.0\text{ m}) = 5.0 \times$ 10^{-4}; since this is so small, the values of $\tan\theta$, $\sin\theta$, and θ (in radi-ans) are all nearly the same. Then, using Eq. (36.7), we have

$$\frac{\pi a\sin\theta}{\lambda} = \frac{\pi(2.4 \times 10^{-4}\text{ m})(5.0 \times 10^{-4})}{6.33 \times 10^{-7}\text{ m}} = 0.60$$

$$I = I_0\left(\frac{\sin 0.60}{0.60}\right)^2 = 0.89I_0$$

EVALUATE: Examining Fig. 36.9a shows that an intensity this large can occur only within the central intensity maximum. This checks out; from Example 36.1, the first intensity minimum ($m = 1$ in Fig. 36.9a) is $(32\text{ mm})/2 = 16$ mm from the center of the pattern, so the point in question here does, indeed, lie within the central maximum.

Test Your Understanding of Section 36.3   Coherent electromagnetic radi-ation is sent through a slit of width 0.0100 mm. For which of the following wave-lengths will there be *no* points in the diffraction pattern where the intensity is zero? (i) blue light of wavelength 500 nm; (ii) infrared light of wavelength 10.6 μm; (iii) microwaves of wavelength 1.00 mm; (iv) ultraviolet light of wavelength 50.0 nm.

36.4 Multiple Slits

In Sections 35.2 and 35.3 we analyzed interference from two point sources or from two very narrow slits; in this analysis we ignored effects due to the finite (that is, nonzero) slit width. In Sections 36.2 and 36.3 we considered the diffrac-tion effects that occur when light passes through a single slit of finite width. Additional interesting effects occur when we have two slits with finite width or when there are several very narrow slits.

Two Slits of Finite Width

Let's take another look at the two-slit pattern in the more realistic case in which the slits have finite width. If the slits are narrow in comparison to the wavelength, we can assume that light from each slit spreads out uniformly in all directions to the right of the slit. We used this assumption in Section 35.3 to calculate the inter-ference pattern described by Eq. (35.10) or (35.15), consisting of a series of equally spaced, equally intense maxima. However, when the slits have finite width, the peaks in the two-slit interference pattern are modulated by the single-slit diffraction pattern characteristic of the width of each slit.

36.12 Finding the intensity pattern for two slits of finite width.

(a) Single-slit diffraction pattern for a slit width a

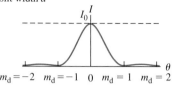

(b) Two-slit interference pattern for narrow slits whose separation d is four times the width of the slit in **(a)**

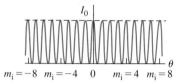

(c) Calculated intensity pattern for two slits of width a and separation $d = 4a$, including both interference and diffraction effects

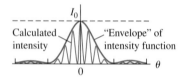

(d) Actual photograph of the pattern calculated in **(c)**

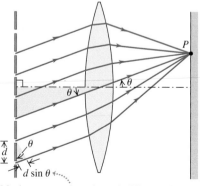

For $d = 4a$, every fourth interference maximum at the sides ($m_i = \pm 4, \pm 8, ...$) is missing.

36.13 Multiple-slit diffraction. Here a lens is used to give a Fraunhofer pattern on a nearby screen, as in Fig. 36.4d.

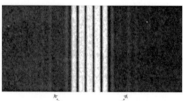

Maxima occur where the path difference for adjacent slits is a whole number of wavelengths: $d \sin\theta = m\lambda$.

Figure 36.12a shows the intensity in a single-slit diffraction pattern with slit width a. The *diffraction minima* are labeled by the integer $m_d = \pm 1, \pm 2, \dots$ ("d" for "diffraction"). Figure 36.12b shows the pattern formed by two very narrow slits with distance d between slits, where d is four times as great as the single-slit width a in Fig. 36.12a; that is, $d = 4a$. The *interference maxima* are labeled by the integer $m_i = 0, \pm 1, \pm 2, \dots$ ("i" for "interference"). We note that the spacing between adjacent minima in the single-slit pattern is four times as great as in the two-slit pattern. Now suppose we widen each of the narrow slits to the same width a as that of the single slit in Fig. 36.12a. Figure 36.12c shows the pattern from two slits with width a, separated by a distance (between centers) $d = 4a$. The effect of the finite width of the slits is to superimpose the two patterns—that is, to multiply the two intensities at each point. The two-slit peaks are in the same positions as before, but their intensities are modulated by the single-slit pattern, which acts as an "envelope" for the intensity function. The expression for the intensity shown in Fig. 36.12c is proportional to the product of the two-slit and single-slit expressions, Eqs. (35.10) and (36.5):

$$I = I_0 \cos^2\frac{\phi}{2}\left[\frac{\sin(\beta/2)}{\beta/2}\right]^2 \quad \text{(two slits of finite width)} \quad (36.12)$$

where, as before,

$$\phi = \frac{2\pi d}{\lambda}\sin\theta \qquad \beta = \frac{2\pi a}{\lambda}\sin\theta$$

Note that in Fig. 36.12c, every fourth interference maximum at the sides is *missing* because these interference maxima ($m_i = \pm 4, \pm 8, \dots$) coincide with diffraction minima ($m_d = \pm 1, \pm 2, \dots$). This can also be seen in Fig. 36.12d, which is a photograph of an actual pattern with $d = 4a$. You should be able to convince yourself that there will be "missing" maxima whenever d is an integer multiple of a.

Figures 36.12c and 36.12d show that as you move away from the central bright maximum of the two-slit pattern, the intensity of the maxima decreases. This is a result of the single-slit modulating pattern shown in Fig. 36.12a; mathematically, the decrease in intensity arises from the factor $(\beta/2)^2$ in the denominator of Eq. (36.12). This decrease in intensity can also be seen in Fig. 35.6 (Section 35.2). The narrower the slits, the broader the single-slit pattern (as in Fig. 36.10) and the slower the decrease in intensity from one interference maximum to the next.

Shall we call the pattern in Fig. 36.12d *interference* or *diffraction*? It's really both, since it results from superposition of waves coming from various parts of the two apertures. There is no truly fundamental distinction between interference and diffraction.

Several Slits

Next let's consider patterns produced by *several* very narrow slits. As we will see, systems of narrow slits are of tremendous practical importance in *spectroscopy,* the determination of the particular wavelengths of light coming from a source. Assume that each slit is narrow in comparison to the wavelength, so its diffraction pattern spreads out nearly uniformly. Figure 36.13 shows an array of eight narrow slits, with distance d between adjacent slits. Constructive interference occurs for rays at angle θ to the normal that arrive at point P with a path difference between adjacent slits equal to an integer number of wavelengths,

$$d\sin\theta = m\lambda \qquad (m = 0, \pm 1, \pm 2, \dots)$$

This means that reinforcement occurs when the phase difference ϕ at P for light from adjacent slits is an integer multiple of 2π. That is, the maxima in the pattern occur at the *same* positions as for *two* slits with the same spacing. To this extent the pattern resembles the two-slit pattern.

But what happens *between* the maxima? In the two-slit pattern, there is exactly one intensity minimum located midway between each pair of maxima, corresponding to angles for which the phase difference between waves from the two sources is π, 3π, 5π, and so on. In the eight-slit pattern these are also minima because the light from adjacent slits cancels out in pairs, corresponding to the phasor diagram in Fig. 36.14a. But these are not the only minima in the eight-slit pattern. For example, when the phase difference ϕ from adjacent sources is $\pi/4$, the phasor diagram is as shown in Fig. 36.14b; the total (resultant) phasor is zero, and the intensity is zero. When $\phi = \pi/2$, we get the phasor diagram of Fig. 36.14c, and again both the total phasor and the intensity are zero. More generally, the intensity with eight slits is zero whenever ϕ is an integer multiple of $\pi/4$, *except* when ϕ is a multiple of 2π. Thus there are seven minima for every maximum.

Detailed calculation shows that the eight-slit pattern is as shown in Fig. 36.15b. The large maxima, called *principal maxima,* are in the same positions as for the two-slit pattern of Fig. 36.15a but are much narrower. If the phase difference ϕ between adjacent slits is slightly different from a multiple of 2π, the waves from slits 1 and 2 will be only a little out of phase; however, the phase difference between slits 1 and 3 will be greater, that between slits 1 and 4 will be greater still, and so on. This leads to a partial cancellation for angles that are only slightly different from the angle for a maximum, giving the narrow maxima in Fig. 36.15b. The maxima are even narrower with 16 slits (Fig. 36.15c).

You should show that when there are N slits, there are $(N - 1)$ minima between each pair of principal maxima and a minimum occurs whenever ϕ is an integral multiple of $2\pi/N$ (except when ϕ is an integral multiple of 2π, which gives a principal maximum). There are small *secondary* intensity maxima between the minima; these become smaller in comparison to the principal maxima as N increases. The greater the value of N, the narrower the principal maxima become. From an energy standpoint the total power in the entire pattern is proportional to N. The height of each principal maximum is proportional to N^2, so from energy conservation the width of each principal maximum must be proportional to $1/N$. As we will see in the next section, the narrowness of the principal maxima in a multiple-slit pattern is of great practical importance in physics and astronomy.

36.14 Phasor diagrams for light passing through eight narrow slits. Intensity maxima occur when the phase difference $\phi = 0, 2\pi, 4\pi, \dots$. Between the maxima at $\phi = 0$ and $\phi = 2\pi$ are seven minima, corresponding to $\phi = \pi/4, \pi/2, 3\pi/4, \pi, 5\pi/4, 3\pi/2,$ and $7\pi/4$. Can you draw phasor diagrams for the other minima?

(a) Phasor diagram for $\phi = \pi$

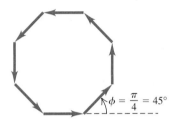

$\phi = \pi = 180°$

(b) Phasor diagram for $\phi = \dfrac{\pi}{4}$

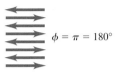

$\phi = \dfrac{\pi}{4} = 45°$

(c) Phasor diagram for $\phi = \dfrac{\pi}{2}$

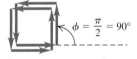

$\phi = \dfrac{\pi}{2} = 90°$

36.15 Interference patterns for N equally spaced, very narrow slits. **(a)** Two slits. **(b)** Eight slits. **(c)** Sixteen slits. The vertical scales are different for each graph; I_0 is the maximum intensity for a single slit, and the maximum intensity for N slits is $N^2 I_0$. The width of each peak is proportional to $1/N$.

(a) $N = 2$: two slits produce one minimum between adjacent maxima.

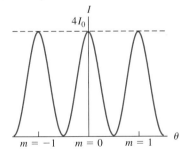

(b) $N = 8$: eight slits produce taller, narrower maxima in the same locations, separated by seven minima.

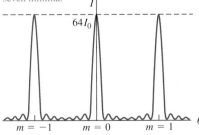

(c) $N = 16$: with 16 slits, the maxima are even taller and narrower, with more intervening minima.

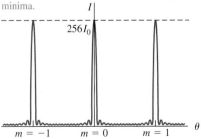

Test Your Understanding of Section 36.4 Suppose two slits, each of width a, are separated by a distance $d = 2.5a$. Are there any missing maxima in the interference pattern produced by these slits? If so, which are missing? If not, why not?

36.16 A portion of a transmission diffraction grating. The separation between the centers of adjacent slits is *d*.

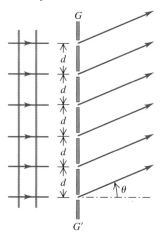

36.17 The millions of microscopic scales in the wings of the tropical butterfly *Morpho peleides* act as a reflection grating. When viewed at the right angle, these scales strongly reflect blue light. This may be a defense mechanism: The flashes of light from the flapping wings of a *Morpho* could momentarily dazzle predators such as lizards and birds.

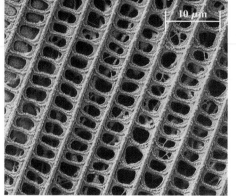

36.5 The Diffraction Grating

We have just seen that increasing the number of slits in an interference experiment (while keeping the spacing of adjacent slits constant) gives interference patterns in which the maxima are in the same positions, but progressively narrower, than with two slits. Because these maxima are so narrow, their angular position, and hence the wavelength, can be measured to very high precision. As we will see, this effect has many important applications.

An array of a large number of parallel slits, all with the same width *a* and spaced equal distances *d* between centers, is called a **diffraction grating.** The first one was constructed by Fraunhofer using fine wires. Gratings can be made by using a diamond point to scratch many equally spaced grooves on a glass or metal surface, or by photographic reduction of a pattern of black and white stripes on paper. For a grating, what we have been calling *slits* are often called *rulings* or *lines*.

In Fig. 36.16, *GG'* is a cross section of a *transmission grating;* the slits are perpendicular to the plane of the page, and an interference pattern is formed by the light that is transmitted through the slits. The diagram shows only six slits; an actual grating may contain several thousand. The spacing *d* between centers of adjacent slits is called the *grating spacing.* A plane monochromatic wave is incident normally on the grating from the left side. We assume far-field (Fraunhofer) conditions; that is, the pattern is formed on a screen that is far enough away that all rays emerging from the grating and going to a particular point on the screen can be considered to be parallel.

We found in Section 36.4 that the principal intensity maxima with multiple slits occur in the same directions as for the two-slit pattern. These are the directions for which the path difference for adjacent slits is an integer number of wavelengths. So the positions of the maxima are once again given by

$$d\sin\theta = m\lambda \qquad (m = 0, \pm1, \pm2, \pm3, \dots) \qquad \text{(intensity maxima,} \atop \text{multiple slits)} \qquad (36.13)$$

The intensity patterns for two, eight, and 16 slits displayed in Fig. 36.15 show the progressive increase in sharpness of the maxima as the number of slits increases.

When a grating containing hundreds or thousands of slits is illuminated by a beam of parallel rays of monochromatic light, the pattern is a series of very sharp lines at angles determined by Eq. (36.13). The $m = \pm1$ lines are called the *first-order lines,* the $m = \pm2$ lines the *second-order lines,* and so on. If the grating is illuminated by white light with a continuous distribution of wavelengths, each value of *m* corresponds to a continuous spectrum in the pattern. The angle for each wavelength is determined by Eq. (36.13); for a given value of *m*, long wavelengths (the red end of the spectrum) lie at larger angles (that is, are deviated more from the straight-ahead direction) than do the shorter wavelengths at the violet end of the spectrum.

As Eq. (36.13) shows, the sines of the deviation angles of the maxima are proportional to the ratio λ/d. For substantial deviation to occur, the grating spacing *d* should be of the same order of magnitude as the wavelength λ. Gratings for use with visible light (λ from 400 to 700 nm) usually have about 1000 slits per millimeter; the value of *d* is the *reciprocal* of the number of slits per unit length, so *d* is of the order of $\frac{1}{1000}$ mm = 1000 nm.

In a *reflection grating,* the array of equally spaced slits shown in Fig. 36.16 is replaced by an array of equally spaced ridges or grooves on a reflective screen. The reflected light has maximum intensity at angles where the phase difference between light waves reflected from adjacent ridges or grooves is an integral multiple of 2π. If light of wavelength λ is incident normally on a reflection grating with a spacing *d* between adjacent ridges or grooves, the *reflected* angles at which intensity maxima occur are given by Eq. (36.13). The iridescent colors of certain butterflies arise from microscopic ridges on the butterfly's wings that form a reflection grating (Fig 36.17). When the wings are viewed from different angles, corresponding to varying θ in Eq. (36.13), the wavelength and color that are predominantly reflected to the viewer's eye vary as well.

The rainbow-colored reflections that you see from the surface of a compact disc are a reflection-grating effect (Fig. 36.18). The "grooves" are tiny pits 0.1 μm deep in the surface of the disc, with a uniform radial spacing of $d = 1.60 \ \mu\text{m} = 1600 \ \text{nm}$. Information is coded on the CD by varying the *length* of the pits; the reflection-grating aspect of the disc is merely an aesthetic side benefit.

36.18 Microscopic pits on the surface of this compact disc act as a reflection grating, splitting white light into its component colors.

Example 36.4 **Width of a grating spectrum**

The wavelengths of the visible spectrum are approximately 400 nm (violet) to 700 nm (red). (a) Find the angular width of the first-order visible spectrum produced by a plane grating with 600 slits per millimeter when white light falls normally on the grating. (b) Do the first-order and second-order spectra overlap? What about the second-order and third-order spectra? Do your answers depend on the grating spacing?

SOLUTION

IDENTIFY: The first-, second-, and third-order spectra correspond to $m = 1$, 2, and 3 in Eq. (36.13). This problem asks us to look at the angles spanned by the visible spectrum in each of these orders.

SET UP: We use Eq. (36.13) with $m = 1$ to find the angular deviation θ for 400-nm violet light and 700-nm red light in the first-order spectrum. The difference between these is the angular width of the first-order spectrum, our target variable in part (a). Using the same technique for $m = 2$ and $m = 3$ tells us the maximum and minimum angular deviation for these orders.

EXECUTE: (a) The grating spacing d is

$$d = \frac{1}{600 \ \text{slits/mm}} = 1.67 \times 10^{-6} \ \text{m}$$

From Eq. (36.13), with $m = 1$, the angular deviation θ_v of the violet light (400 nm or 400×10^{-9} m) is

$$\sin\theta_\text{v} = \frac{400 \times 10^{-9} \ \text{m}}{1.67 \times 10^{-6} \ \text{m}} = 0.240$$

$$\theta_\text{v} = 13.9°$$

The angular deviation θ_r of the red light (700 nm) is

$$\sin\theta_\text{r} = \frac{700 \times 10^{-9} \ \text{m}}{1.67 \times 10^{-6} \ \text{m}} = 0.419$$

$$\theta_\text{r} = 24.8°$$

So the angular width of the first-order visible spectrum is

$$24.8° - 13.9° = 10.9°$$

(b) From Eq. (36.13), with a grating spacing of d the angular deviation $\theta_{\text{v}m}$ of the 400-nm violet light in the mth-order spectrum is given by

$$\sin\theta_{\text{v}m} = \frac{m(400 \times 10^{-9} \ \text{m})}{d}$$

$$= \frac{4.00 \times 10^{-7} \ \text{m}}{d} \quad (m = 1)$$

$$= \frac{8.00 \times 10^{-7} \ \text{m}}{d} \quad (m = 2)$$

$$= \frac{1.20 \times 10^{-6} \ \text{m}}{d} \quad (m = 3)$$

Similarly, the angular deviation $\theta_{\text{r}m}$ of the 700-nm red light in the mth-order spectrum is given by

$$\sin\theta_{\text{r}m} = \frac{m(700 \times 10^{-9} \ \text{m})}{d}$$

$$= \frac{7.00 \times 10^{-7} \ \text{m}}{d} \quad (m = 1)$$

$$= \frac{1.40 \times 10^{-6} \ \text{m}}{d} \quad (m = 2)$$

$$= \frac{2.10 \times 10^{-6} \ \text{m}}{d} \quad (m = 3)$$

The greater the value of $\sin\theta$, the greater the value of θ (for angles between zero and 90°). Hence our results show that for any value of the grating spacing d, the largest angle (at the red end) of the $m = 1$ spectrum is always less than the smallest angle (at the violet end) of the $m = 2$ spectrum, so the first and second orders *never* overlap. By contrast, the largest (red) angle of the $m = 2$ spectrum is always greater than the smallest (violet) angle of the $m = 3$ spectrum, so the second and third orders *always* overlap.

EVALUATE: The fundamental reason the first-order and second-order visible spectra don't overlap is that the human eye is sensitive to only a narrow range of wavelengths. Can you show that if the eye could detect wavelengths from 400 nm to 900 nm (in the near-infrared range), the first and second orders *would* overlap?

36.19 (a) A visible-light photograph of the sun. (b) Sunlight is dispersed into a spectrum by a diffraction grating. Specific wavelengths are absorbed as sunlight passes through the sun's atmosphere, leaving dark lines in the spectrum.

(a)

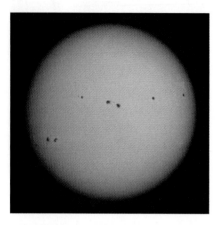

(b)

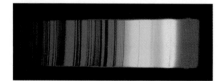

Grating Spectrographs

Diffraction gratings are widely used to measure the spectrum of light emitted by a source, a process called *spectroscopy* or *spectrometry*. Light incident on a grating of known spacing is dispersed into a spectrum. The angles of deviation of the maxima are then measured, and Eq. (36.13) is used to compute the wavelength. With a grating that has many slits, very sharp maxima are produced, and the angle of deviation (and hence the wavelength) can be measured very precisely.

An important application of this technique is to astronomy. As light generated within the sun passes through the sun's atmosphere, certain wavelengths are selectively absorbed. The result is that the spectrum of sunlight produced by a diffraction grating has dark *absorption lines* (Fig. 36.19). Experiments in the laboratory show that different types of atoms and ions absorb light at different wavelengths. By comparing these laboratory results with the wavelengths of absorption lines in the spectrum of sunlight, astronomers can deduce the chemical composition of the sun's atmosphere. The same technique is used to make chemical assays of galaxies that are millions of light-years away.

Figure 36.20 shows one design for a *grating spectrograph* used in astronomy. A transmission grating is used in the figure; in other setups, a reflection grating is used. In older designs a prism was used rather than a grating, and a spectrum was formed by dispersion (see Section 33.4) rather than diffraction. However, there is no simple relationship between wavelength and angle of deviation for a prism, prisms absorb some of the light that passes through them, and they are less effective for many nonvisible wavelengths that are important in astronomy. For these and other reasons, gratings are preferred in precision applications.

Resolution of a Grating Spectrograph

In spectroscopy it is often important to distinguish slightly differing wavelengths. The minimum wavelength difference $\Delta\lambda$ that can be distinguished by a spectrograph is described by the **chromatic resolving power** R, defined as

$$R = \frac{\lambda}{\Delta\lambda} \qquad \text{(chromatic resolving power)} \qquad (36.14)$$

36.20 A schematic diagram of a diffraction-grating spectrograph for use in astronomy. Note that the light does not strike the grating normal to its surface, so the intensity maxima are given by a somewhat different expression than Eq. (36.13). (See Problem 36.66).

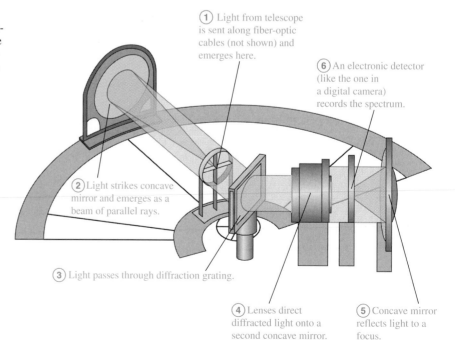

1 Light from telescope is sent along fiber-optic cables (not shown) and emerges here.

6 An electronic detector (like the one in a digital camera) records the spectrum.

2 Light strikes concave mirror and emerges as a beam of parallel rays.

3 Light passes through diffraction grating.

4 Lenses direct diffracted light onto a second concave mirror.

5 Concave mirror reflects light to a focus.

As an example, when sodium atoms are heated, they emit strongly at the yellow wavelengths 589.00 nm and 589.59 nm. A spectrograph that can barely distinguish these two lines in the spectrum of sodium light (called the *sodium doublet*) has a chromatic resolving power $R = (589.00 \text{ nm})/(0.59 \text{ nm}) = 1000$. (You can see these wavelengths when boiling water on a gas range. If the water boils over onto the flame, dissolved sodium from table salt emits a burst of yellow light.)

We can derive an expression for the resolving power of a diffraction grating used in a spectrograph. Two different wavelengths give diffraction maxima at slightly different angles. As a reasonable (though arbitrary) criterion, let's assume that we can distinguish them as two separate peaks if the maximum of one coincides with the first minimum of the other.

From our discussion in Section 36.4 the *m*th-order maximum occurs when the phase difference ϕ for adjacent slits is $\phi = 2\pi m$. The first minimum beside that maximum occurs when $\phi = 2\pi m + 2\pi/N$, where N is the number of slits. The phase difference is also given by $\phi = (2\pi d \sin\theta)/\lambda$, so the angular interval $d\theta$ corresponding to a small increment $d\phi$ in the phase shift can be obtained from the differential of this equation:

$$d\phi = \frac{2\pi d \cos\theta \, d\theta}{\lambda}$$

When $d\phi = 2\pi/N$, this corresponds to the angular interval $d\theta$ between a maximum and the first adjacent minimum. Thus $d\theta$ is given by

$$\frac{2\pi}{N} = \frac{2\pi d \cos\theta \, d\theta}{\lambda} \qquad \text{or} \qquad d\cos\theta \, d\theta = \frac{\lambda}{N}$$

CAUTION **Watch out for different uses of the symbol d** Don't confuse the spacing d with the differential "d" in the angular interval $d\theta$ or in the phase shift increment $d\phi$! ▮

Now we need to find the angular spacing $d\theta$ between maxima for two slightly different wavelengths. This is easy; we have $d\sin\theta = m\lambda$, so the differential of this equation gives

$$d\cos\theta \, d\theta = m \, d\lambda$$

According to our criterion, the limit or resolution is reached when these two angular spacings are equal. Equating the two expressions for the quantity $(d\cos\theta \, d\theta)$, we find

$$\frac{\lambda}{N} = m \, d\lambda \qquad \text{and} \qquad \frac{\lambda}{d\lambda} = Nm$$

If $\Delta\lambda$ is small, we can replace $d\lambda$ by $\Delta\lambda$, and the resolving power R is given simply by

$$R = \frac{\lambda}{\Delta\lambda} = Nm \qquad\qquad (36.15)$$

The greater the number of slits N, the better the resolution; also, the higher the order m of the diffraction-pattern maximum that we use, the better the resolution.

Test Your Understanding of Section 36.5 What minimum number of slits would be required in a grating to resolve the sodium doublet in the fourth order? (i) 250; (ii) 400; (iii) 1000; (iv) 4000.

36.6 X-Ray Diffraction

X rays were discovered by Wilhelm Röntgen (1845–1923) in 1895, and early experiments suggested that they were electromagnetic waves with wavelengths of the order of 10^{-10} m. At about the same time, the idea began to emerge that in a crystalline solid the atoms are arranged in a regular repeating pattern, with spacing between adjacent atoms also of the order of 10^{-10} m. Putting these two ideas together, Max von Laue (1879–1960) proposed in 1912 that a crystal might serve as a kind of three-dimensional diffraction grating for x rays. That is, a beam of x rays might be scattered (that is, absorbed and re-emitted) by the individual atoms in a crystal, and the scattered waves might interfere just like waves from a diffraction grating.

The first **x-ray diffraction** experiments were performed in 1912 by Friederich, Knipping, and von Laue, using the experimental setup sketched in Fig. 36.21a. The scattered x rays *did* form an interference pattern, which they recorded on photographic film. Figure 36.21b is a photograph of such a pattern. These experiments verified that x rays *are* waves, or at least have wavelike properties, and also that the atoms in a crystal *are* arranged in a regular pattern (Fig. 36.22). Since that time, x-ray diffraction has proved to be an invaluable research tool, both for measuring x-ray wavelengths and for studying the structure of crystals and complex molecules.

A Simple Model of X-Ray Diffraction

To better understand x-ray diffraction, we consider first a two-dimensional scattering situation, as shown in Fig. 36.23a, in which a plane wave is incident on a rectangular array of scattering centers. The situation might be a ripple tank with an array of small posts, 3-cm microwaves striking an array of small conducting spheres, or x rays incident on an array of atoms. In the case of electromagnetic waves, the wave induces an oscillating electric dipole moment in each scatterer. These dipoles act like little antennas, emitting scattered waves. The resulting interference pattern is the superposition of all these scattered waves. The situation is different from that with a diffraction grating, in which the waves from all the slits are emitted *in phase* (for a plane wave at normal incidence). Here the scattered waves are *not* all in phase because their distances from the *source* are different. To compute the interference pattern, we have to consider the *total* path differences for the scattered waves, including the distances from source to scatterer and from scatterer to observer.

As Fig. 36.23b shows, the path length from source to observer is the same for all the scatterers in a single row if the two angles θ_a and θ_r are equal. Scattered radia-

36.21 (a) An x-ray diffraction experiment. (b) Diffraction pattern (or *Laue pattern*) formed by directing a beam of x rays at a thin section of quartz crystal.

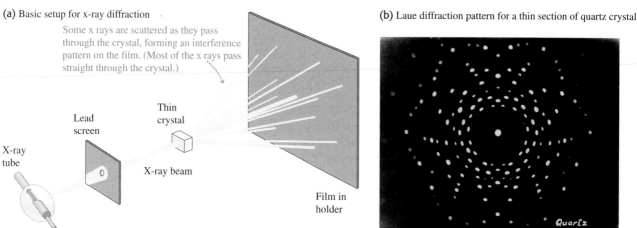

(a) Basic setup for x-ray diffraction

Some x rays are scattered as they pass through the crystal, forming an interference pattern on the film. (Most of the x rays pass straight through the crystal.)

X-ray tube

Lead screen

Thin crystal

X-ray beam

Film in holder

(b) Laue diffraction pattern for a thin section of quartz crystal

Quartz

tion from *adjacent* rows is *also* in phase if the path difference for adjacent rows is an integer number of wavelengths. Figure 36.23c shows that this path difference is $2d\sin\theta$, where θ is the common value of θ_a and θ_r. Therefore the conditions for radiation from the *entire array* to reach the observer in phase are (1) the angle of incidence must equal the angle of scattering and (2) the path difference for adjacent rows must equal $m\lambda$, where m is an integer. We can express the second condition as

$$2d\sin\theta = m\lambda \qquad (m = 1, 2, 3, \ldots)$$

(Bragg condition for constructive interference from an array) (36.16)

CAUTION **Scattering from an array** In Eq. (36.16) the angle θ is measured with respect to the *surface* of the crystal, rather than with respect to the *normal* to the plane of an array of slits or a grating. Also, note that the path difference in Eq. (36.16) is $2d\sin\theta$, not $d\sin\theta$ as in Eq. (36.13) for a diffraction grating. ∎

In directions for which Eq. (36.16) is satisfied, we see a strong maximum in the interference pattern. We can describe this interference in terms of *reflections* of the wave from the horizontal rows of scatterers in Fig. 36.23a. Strong reflection (constructive interference) occurs at angles such that the incident and scattered angles are equal and Eq. (36.16) is satisfied. Since $\sin\theta$ can never be greater than 1, Eq. (36.16) says that to have constructive interference the quantity $m\lambda$ must be less than $2d$ and so λ must be less than $2d/m$. For example, the value of d in an NaCl crystal (Fig. 36.22) is only 0.282 nm. Hence to have the mth-order maximum present in the diffraction pattern, λ must be less than $2(0.282\text{ nm})/m$; that is, $\lambda < 0.564$ nm for $m = 1$, $\lambda < 0.282$ nm for $m = 2$, $\lambda < 0.188$ nm for $m = 3$, and so on. These are all x-ray wavelengths (see Fig. 32.4), which is why x rays are used for studying crystal structure.

We can extend this discussion to a three-dimensional array by considering *planes* of scatterers instead of *rows*. Figure 36.24 shows two different sets of parallel planes that pass through all the scatterers. Waves from all the scatterers in a

36.22 Model of the arrangement of ions in a crystal of NaCl (table salt). The spacing of adjacent atoms is 0.282 nm. (The electron clouds of the atoms actually overlap slightly.)

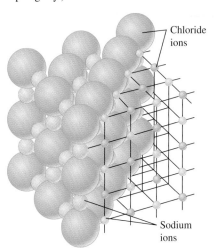

Chloride ions

Sodium ions

36.23 A two-dimensional model of scattering from a rectangular array. Note that the angles in (b) are measured from the *surface* of the array, not from its normal.

(a) Scattering of waves from a rectangular array

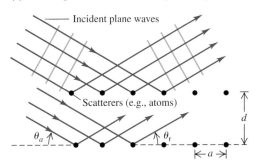

(b) Scattering from adjacent atoms in a row
Interference from adjacent atoms in a row is constructive when the path lengths $a\cos\theta_a$ and $a\cos\theta_r$ are equal, so that the angle of incidence θ_a equals the angle of reflection (scattering) θ_r.

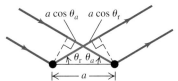

(c) Scattering from atoms in adjacent rows
Interference from atoms in adjacent rows is constructive when the path difference $2d\sin\theta$ is an integral number of wavelengths, as in Eq. (36.16).

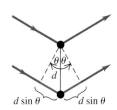

36.24 A cubic crystal and two different families of crystal planes. There are also three sets of planes parallel to the cube faces, with spacing a.

(a) Spacing of planes is $d = a/\sqrt{2}$.

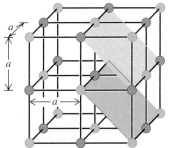

(b) Spacing of planes is $d = a/\sqrt{3}$.

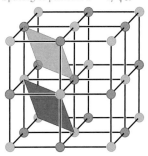

given plane interfere constructively if the angles of incidence and scattering are equal. There is also constructive interference between planes when Eq. (36.16) is satisfied, where d is now the distance between adjacent planes. Because there are many different sets of parallel planes, there are also many values of d and many sets of angles that give constructive interference for the whole crystal lattice. This phenomenon is called **Bragg reflection,** and Eq. (36.16) is called the **Bragg condition,** in honor of Sir William Bragg and his son Laurence Bragg, two pioneers in x-ray analysis.

CAUTION **Bragg *reflection* is really Bragg *interference*** While we are using the term *reflection,* remember that we are dealing with an *interference* effect. In fact, the reflections from various planes are closely analogous to interference effects in thin films (see Section 35.4). ▮

36.25 The British scientist Rosalind Franklin made this groundbreaking x-ray diffraction image of DNA in 1953. The dark bands arranged in a cross provided the first evidence of the helical structure of the DNA molecule.

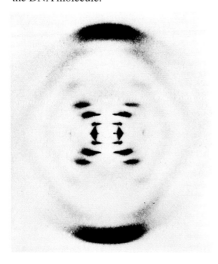

As Fig. 36.21b shows, in x-ray diffraction there is nearly complete cancellation in all but certain very specific directions in which constructive interference occurs and forms bright spots. Such a pattern is usually called an x-ray *diffraction* pattern, although *interference* pattern might be more appropriate.

We can determine the wavelength of x rays by examining the diffraction pattern for a crystal of known structure and known spacing between atoms, just as we determined wavelengths of visible light by measuring patterns from slits or gratings. (The spacing between atoms in simple crystals of known structure, such as sodium chloride, can be found from the density of the crystal and Avogadro's number.) Then, once we know the x-ray wavelength, we can use x-ray diffraction to explore the structure and determine the spacing between atoms in crystals with unknown structure.

X-ray diffraction is by far the most important experimental tool in the investigation of crystal structure of solids. X-ray diffraction also plays an important role in studies of the structures of liquids and of organic molecules. It has been one of the chief experimental techniques in working out the double-helix structure of DNA (Fig. 36.25) and subsequent advances in molecular genetics.

Example 36.5   X-ray diffraction

You direct a beam of x rays with wavelength 0.154 nm at certain planes of a silicon crystal. As you increase the angle of incidence from zero, you find the first strong interference maximum from these planes when the beam makes an angle of 34.5° with the planes. (a) How far apart are the planes? (b) Will you find other interference maxima from these planes at larger angles?

SOLUTION

IDENTIFY: This problem involves Bragg reflection of x rays from the planes of a crystal.

SET UP: In part (a) we use the Bragg condition, Eq. (36.16), to relate the wavelength λ and the angle θ for the $m = 1$ interference maximum (both of which are given) to the spacing d between planes (which is the target variable). Given the value of d, we use the Bragg condition again in part (b) to find the values of θ for interference maxima corresponding to other values of m.

EXECUTE: (a) We solve the Bragg equation, Eq. (36.16), for d and set $m = 1$:

$$d = \frac{m\lambda}{2\sin\theta} = \frac{(1)(0.154 \text{ nm})}{2\sin 34.5°} = 0.136 \text{ nm}$$

This is the distance between adjacent planes.

(b) To calculate other angles, we solve Eq. (36.16) for $\sin\theta$:

$$\sin\theta = \frac{m\lambda}{2d} = m\frac{0.154 \text{ nm}}{2(0.136 \text{ nm})} = m(0.566)$$

Values of m of 2 or greater give values of $\sin\theta$ greater than unity, which is impossible. Hence there are *no* other angles for interference maxima for this particular set of crystal planes.

EVALUATE: Our result in part (b) shows that there *would* be a second interference maximum if the quantity $\lambda/2d$ were equal to 0.500 or less. This would be the case if the wavelength of the x rays were less than $2d = 0.272$ nm. How short would the wavelength need to be to have *three* interference maxima?

Test Your Understanding of Section 36.6 You are doing an x-ray diffraction experiment with a crystal in which the atomic planes are 0.200 nm apart. You are using x rays of wavelength 0.100 nm. Will the fifth-order maximum be present in the diffraction pattern?

36.7 Circular Apertures and Resolving Power

We have studied in detail the diffraction patterns formed by long, thin slits or arrays of slits. But an aperture of *any* shape forms a diffraction pattern. The diffraction pattern formed by a *circular* aperture is of special interest because of its role in limiting how well an optical instrument can resolve fine details. In principle, we could compute the intensity at any point P in the diffraction pattern by dividing the area of the aperture into small elements, finding the resulting wave amplitude and phase at P, and then integrating over the aperture area to find the resultant amplitude and intensity at P. In practice, the integration cannot be carried out in terms of elementary functions. We will simply *describe* the pattern and quote a few relevant numbers.

The diffraction pattern formed by a circular aperture consists of a central bright spot surrounded by a series of bright and dark rings, as shown in Fig. 36.26. We can describe the pattern in terms of the angle θ, representing the angular radius of each ring. If the aperture diameter is D and the wavelength is λ, the angular radius θ_1 of the first *dark* ring is given by

$$\sin\theta_1 = 1.22\frac{\lambda}{D} \qquad \text{(diffraction by a circular aperture)} \qquad (36.17)$$

The angular radii of the next two dark rings are given by

$$\sin\theta_2 = 2.23\frac{\lambda}{D} \qquad \sin\theta_3 = 3.24\frac{\lambda}{D} \qquad (36.18)$$

Between these are bright rings with angular radii given by

$$\sin\theta = 1.63\frac{\lambda}{D}, \qquad 2.68\frac{\lambda}{D}, \qquad 3.70\frac{\lambda}{D} \qquad (36.19)$$

and so on. The central bright spot is called the **Airy disk,** in honor of Sir George Airy (1801–1892), Astronomer Royal of England, who first derived the expression for the intensity in the pattern. The angular radius of the Airy disk is that of the first dark ring, given by Eq. (36.17).

The intensities in the bright rings drop off very quickly with increasing angle. When D is much larger than the wavelength λ, the usual case for optical instruments, the peak intensity in the first ring is only 1.7% of the value at the center of the Airy disk, and the peak intensity of the second ring is only 0.4%. Most (85%) of the light energy falls within the Airy disk. Figure 36.27 shows a diffraction pattern from a circular aperture.

Act|v
Phys|cs
16.7   Circular Hole Diffraction
16.8   Resolving Power

36.26 Diffraction pattern formed by a circular aperture of diameter D. The pattern consists of a central bright spot and alternating dark and bright rings. The angular radius θ_1 of the first dark ring is shown. (This diagram is not drawn to scale.)

36.27 Photograph of the diffraction pattern formed by a circular aperture.

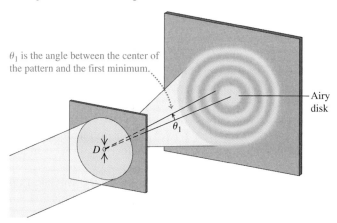

θ_1 is the angle between the center of the pattern and the first minimum.

Airy disk

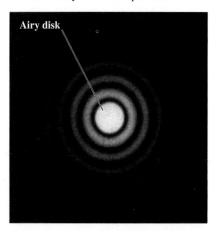

Airy disk

36.28 Diffraction patterns of four very small ("point") sources of light. The photographs were made with a circular aperture in front of the lens. (a) The aperture is so small that the patterns of sources 3 and 4 overlap and are barely resolved by Rayleigh's criterion. Increasing the size of the aperture decreases the size of the diffraction patterns, as shown in (b) and (c).

(a) Small aperture

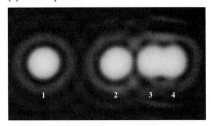

(b) Medium aperture

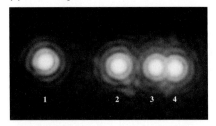

(c) Large aperture

Diffraction and Image Formation

Diffraction has far-reaching implications for image formation by lenses and mirrors. In our study of optical instruments in Chapter 34 we assumed that a lens with focal length f focuses a parallel beam (plane wave) to a *point* at a distance f from the lens. This assumption ignored diffraction effects. We now see that what we get is not a point but the diffraction pattern just described. If we have two point objects, their images are not two points but two diffraction patterns. When the objects are close together, their diffraction patterns overlap; if they are close enough, their patterns overlap almost completely and cannot be distinguished. The effect is shown in Fig. 36.28, which presents the patterns for four very small "point" sources of light. In Fig. 36.28a the image of the left-hand source is well separated from the others, but the images of the middle and right-hand sources have merged. In Fig. 36.28b, with a larger aperture diameter and hence smaller Airy disks, the middle and right-hand images are better resolved. In Fig. 36.28c, with a still larger aperture, they are well resolved.

A widely used criterion for resolution of two point objects, proposed by the English physicist Lord Rayleigh (1842–1919) and called **Rayleigh's criterion,** is that the objects are just barely resolved (that is, distinguishable) if the center of one diffraction pattern coincides with the first minimum of the other. In that case the angular separation of the image centers is given by Eq. (36.17). The angular separation of the *objects* is the same as that of the *images* made by a telescope, microscope, or other optical device. So two point objects are barely resolved, according to Rayleigh's criterion, when their angular separation is given by Eq. (36.17).

The minimum separation of two objects that can just be resolved by an optical instrument is called the **limit of resolution** of the instrument. The smaller the limit of resolution, the greater the *resolution,* or **resolving power,** of the instrument. Diffraction sets the ultimate limits on resolution of lenses. *Geometric* optics may make it seem that we can make images as large as we like. Eventually, though, we always reach a point at which the image becomes larger but does not gain in detail. The images in Fig. 36.28 would not become sharper with further enlargement.

CAUTION **Resolving power vs. chromatic resolving power** Be careful not to confuse the resolving power of an optical instrument with the *chromatic* resolving power of a grating (described in Section 36.5). Resolving power refers to the ability to distinguish the images of objects that appear close to each other, when looking either through an optical instrument or at a photograph made with the instrument. Chromatic resolving power describes how well different wavelengths can be distinguished in a spectrum formed by a diffraction grating. ▮

Rayleigh's criterion combined with Eq. (36.17) shows that resolution (resolving power) improves with larger diameter; it also improves with shorter wavelengths. Ultraviolet microscopes have higher resolution than visible-light microscopes. In electron microscopes the resolution is limited by the wavelengths associated with the electrons, which have wavelike aspects (to be discussed further in Chapter 39). These wavelengths can be made 100,000 times smaller than wavelengths of visible light, with a corresponding gain in resolution. Resolving power also explains the difference in storage capacity between compact discs (CDs) and digital video discs (DVDs). Information is stored in both of these in a series of tiny pits. In order not to lose information in the scanning process, the scanning optics must be able to resolve two adjacent pits so that they do not seem to blend into a single pit (see sources 3 and 4 in Fig. 36.28). The red laser used in a DVD player has a shorter wavelength (650 nm) and hence better resolving power than the infrared laser in a CD player (780 nm). Hence pits can be spaced closer together in a DVD than in a CD, and more information can be stored on a disc of the same size (4.7 gigabytes on a DVD versus 700 megabytes, or 0.7 gigabyte, on a CD). The latest disc storage technology uses a blue-violet laser of 405-nm wavelength; this makes it possible to use an even smaller pit spacing and hence store even more data (15 to 25 gigabytes) on a disc of the same size as a CD or DVD.

Diffraction is an important consideration for satellite "dishes," parabolic reflectors designed to receive satellite transmission. Satellite dishes have to be able to pick up transmissions from two satellites that are only a few degrees apart, transmitting at the same frequency; the need to resolve two such transmissions determines the minimum diameter of the dish. As higher frequencies are used, the needed diameter decreases. For example, when two satellites 5.0° apart broadcast 7.5-cm microwaves, the minimum dish diameter to resolve them (by Rayleigh's criterion) is about 1.0 m.

One reason for building very large telescopes is to increase the aperture diameter and thus minimize diffraction effects. The effective diameter of a telescope can be increased by using arrays of smaller telescopes. The Very Large Array (VLA) is a collection of 27 radio telescopes that can be spread out in a Y-shaped arrangement 36 km across (Fig. 36.29a). Hence the effective aperture diameter is 36 km, giving the VLA a limit of resolution of less than 3×10^{-7} rad. This is comparable, in the optical realm, to being able to read the bottom line of an eye chart 7 km away! Such an arrangement is called a *radio interferometer* because it makes use of the phase differences between the signals received in different telescopes. The same principle can also be used to improve the resolution of visible-light telescopes (Fig. 36.29b).

36.29 By simultaneously observing the same object with widely separated telescopes, astronomers can obtain far better resolving power than with a single telescope.

(a) Radio interferometry. The Very Large Array 80 km west of Socorro, New Mexico, consists of 27 radio dishes that can be moved on tracks; at their greatest separation, their resolution equals that of a single dish 36 km across.

(b) Optical interferometry. The four 8.2-m telescopes of the European Southern Observatory's Very Large Telescope in Cerro Paranal, Chile, can be combined optically in pairs. Functioning together, the outer two telescopes have the resolution of a single telescope 130 m across.

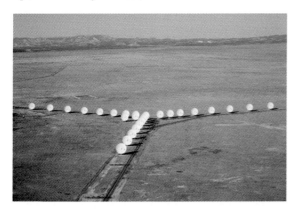

Example 36.6   **Resolving power of a camera lens**

A camera lens with focal length $f = 50$ mm and maximum aperture $f/2$ forms an image of an object 9.0 m away. (a) If the resolution is limited by diffraction, what is the minimum distance between two points on the object that are barely resolved, and what is the corresponding distance between image points? (b) How does the situation change if the lens is "stopped down" to $f/16$? Assume that $\lambda = 500$ nm in both cases.

SOLUTION

IDENTIFY: This example uses ideas from this section as well as Sections 34.4 (in which we discussed image formation by a lens) and 34.5 (in which the idea of f-number was introduced).

SET UP: From Eq. (34.20) the f-number of a lens is its focal length f divided by the aperture diameter D. We use the information provided to determine D and then use Eq. (36.17) to find the angular separation θ between two barely resolved points on the object. We then use the geometry of image formation by a lens (see Section 34.4) to determine the distance between those points and the distance between the corresponding image points.

EXECUTE: (a) The aperture diameter is $D = f/(f\text{-number}) = (50 \text{ mm})/2 = 25 \text{ mm} = 25 \times 10^{-3}$ m. From Eq. (36.17) the

Continued

angular separation θ of two object points that are barely resolved is given by

$$\theta \approx \sin\theta = 1.22\frac{\lambda}{D} = 1.22\frac{500 \times 10^{-9} \text{ m}}{25 \times 10^{-3} \text{ m}}$$

$$= 2.4 \times 10^{-5} \text{ rad}$$

Let y be the separation of the object points, and let y' be the separation of the corresponding image points. We know from our thin-lens analysis in Section 34.4 that, apart from sign, $y/s = y'/s'$. Thus the angular separations of the object points and the corresponding image points are both equal to θ. Because the object distance s is much greater than the focal length $f = 50$ mm, the image distance s' is approximately equal to f. Thus

$$\frac{y}{9.0 \text{ m}} = 2.4 \times 10^{-5} \qquad y = 2.2 \times 10^{-4} \text{ m} = 0.22 \text{ mm}$$

$$\frac{y'}{50 \text{ mm}} = 2.4 \times 10^{-5} \qquad y' = 1.2 \times 10^{-3} \text{ mm}$$

$$= 0.0012 \text{ mm} \approx \frac{1}{800} \text{ mm}$$

(b) The aperture diameter is now $(50 \text{ mm})/16$, or one-eighth as large as before. The angular separation between barely resolved points is eight times as great, and the values of y and y' are also eight times as great as before:

$$y = 1.8 \text{ mm} \qquad y' = 0.0096 \text{ mm} = \frac{1}{100} \text{ mm}$$

Only the best camera lenses can approach this resolving power.

EVALUATE: Many photographers use the smallest possible aperture for maximum sharpness, since lens aberrations cause light rays that are far from the optic axis to converge to a different image point than do rays near the axis. Photographers should be aware that, as this example shows, diffraction effects become more significant at small apertures. One cause of fuzzy images has to be balanced against another.

Test Your Understanding of Section 36.7 You have been asked to compare four different proposals for telescopes to be placed in orbit, above the blurring effects of the earth's atmosphere. Rank the proposed telescopes in order of their ability to resolve small details, from best to worst. (i) a radio telescope 100 m in diameter observing at a wavelength of 21 cm; (ii) an optical telescope 2.0 m in diameter observing at a wavelength of 500 nm; (iii) an ultraviolet telescope 1.0 m in diameter observing at a wavelength of 100 nm; (iv) an infrared telescope 2.0 m in diameter observing at a wavelength of 10 μm.

*36.8 Holography

Holography is a technique for recording and reproducing an image of an object through the use of interference effects. Unlike the two-dimensional images recorded by an ordinary photograph or television system, a holographic image is truly three-dimensional. Such an image can be viewed from different directions to reveal different sides and from various distances to reveal changing perspective. If you had never seen a hologram, you wouldn't believe it was possible!

Figure 36.30a shows the basic procedure for making a hologram. We illuminate the object to be holographed with monochromatic light, and we place a photographic film so that it is struck by scattered light from the object and also by direct light from the source. In practice, the light source must be a laser, for reasons we will discuss later. Interference between the direct and scattered light leads to the formation and recording of a complex interference pattern on the film.

To form the images, we simply project light through the developed film, as shown in Fig. 36.30b. Two images are formed: a virtual image on the side of the film nearer the source and a real image on the opposite side.

Holography and Interference Patterns

A complete analysis of holography is beyond our scope, but we can gain some insight into the process by looking at how a single point is holographed and imaged. Consider the interference pattern that is formed on a sheet of photographic negative film by the superposition of an incident plane wave and a spherical wave, as shown in Fig. 36.31a. The spherical wave originates at a point

36.30 (a) A hologram is the record on film of the interference pattern formed with light from the coherent source and light scattered from the object. (b) Images are formed when light is projected through the hologram. The observer sees the virtual image formed behind the hologram.

(a) Recording a hologram   (b) Viewing the hologram

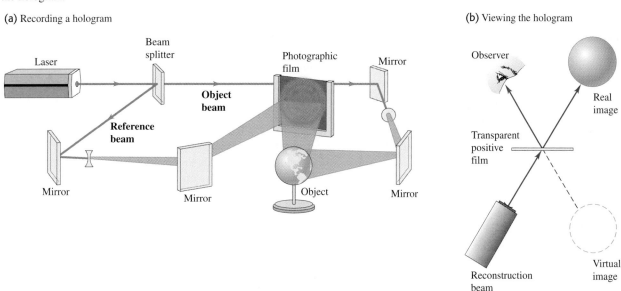

36.31 (a) Constructive interference of the plane and spherical waves occurs in the plane of the film at every point Q for which the distance b_m from P is greater than the distance b_0 from P to O by an integral number of wavelengths $m\lambda$. For the point Q shown, $m = 2$. (b) When a plane wave strikes a transparent positive print of the developed film, the diffracted wave consists of a wave converging to P' and then diverging again and a diverging wave that appears to originate at P. These waves form the real and virtual images, respectively.

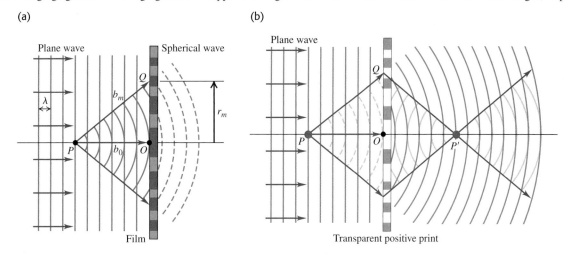

source P at a distance b_0 from the film; P may in fact be a small object that scatters part of the incident plane wave. We assume that the two waves are monochromatic and coherent and that the phase relationship is such that constructive interference occurs at point O on the diagram. Then constructive interference will *also* occur at any point Q on the film that is farther from P than O is by an integer number of wavelengths. That is, if $b_m - b_0 = m\lambda$, where m is an integer, then constructive interference occurs. The points where this condition is satisfied form circles on the film centered at O, with radii r_m given by

$$b_m - b_0 = \sqrt{b_0^2 + r_m^2} - b_0 = m\lambda \qquad (m = 1, 2, 3, \dots) \qquad (36.20)$$

Solving this for r_m^2, we find

$$r_m^2 = \lambda(2mb_0 + m^2\lambda)$$

36.32 Two views of the same hologram seen from different angles.

Ordinarily, b_0 is very much larger than λ, so we neglect the second term in parentheses and obtain

$$r_m = \sqrt{2m\lambda b_0} \qquad (m = 1, 2, 3, \dots) \qquad (36.21)$$

The interference pattern consists of a series of concentric bright circular fringes with radii given by Eq. (36.21). Between these bright fringes are dark fringes.

Now we develop the film and make a transparent positive print, so the bright-fringe areas have the greatest transparency on the film. Then we illuminate it with monochromatic plane-wave light of the same wavelength λ that we used initially. In Fig. 36.31b, consider a point P' at a distance b_0 along the axis from the film. The centers of successive bright fringes differ in their distances from P' by an integer number of wavelengths, and therefore a strong *maximum* in the diffracted wave occurs at P'. That is, light converges to P' and then diverges from it on the opposite side. Therefore P' is a *real image* of point P.

This is not the entire diffracted wave, however. The interference of the wavelets that spread out from all the transparent areas forms a second spherical wave that is diverging rather than converging. When this wave is traced back behind the film in Fig. 36.31b, it appears to be spreading out from point P. Thus the total diffracted wave from the hologram is a superposition of a spherical wave converging to form a real image at P' and a spherical wave that diverges as though it had come from the virtual image point P.

Because of the principle of superposition for waves, what is true for the imaging of a single point is also true for the imaging of any number of points. The film records the superposed interference pattern from the various points, and when light is projected through the film, the various image points are reproduced simultaneously. Thus the images of an extended object can be recorded and reproduced just as for a single point object. Figure 36.32 shows photographs of a holographic image from two different angles, showing the changing perspective in this three-dimensional image.

In making a hologram, we have to overcome two practical problems. First, the light used must be *coherent* over distances that are large in comparison to the dimensions of the object and its distance from the film. Ordinary light sources *do not* satisfy this requirement, for reasons that we discussed in Section 35.1. Therefore laser light is essential for making a hologram. (Ordinary white light can be used for *viewing* certain types of hologram, such as those used on credit cards.) Second, extreme mechanical stability is needed. If any relative motion of source, object, or film occurs during exposure, even by as much as a quarter of a wavelength, the interference pattern on the film is blurred enough to prevent satisfactory image formation. These obstacles are not insurmountable, however, and holography has become important in research, entertainment, and a wide variety of technological applications.

Fresnel and Fraunhofer diffraction: Diffraction occurs when light passes through an aperture or around an edge. When the source and the observer are so far away from the obstructing surface that the outgoing rays can be considered parallel, it is called Fraunhofer diffraction. When the source or the observer is relatively close to the obstructing surface, it is Fresnel diffraction.

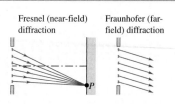

Fresnel (near-field) diffraction

Fraunhofer (far-field) diffraction

Single-slit diffraction: Monochromatic light sent through a narrow slit of width a produces a diffraction pattern on a distant screen. Equation (36.2) gives the condition for destructive interference (a dark fringe) at a point P in the pattern at angle θ. Equation (36.7) gives the intensity in the pattern as a function of θ. (See Examples 36.1–36.3.)

$$\sin\theta = \frac{m\lambda}{a} \quad (m = \pm1, \pm2, \ldots)$$

(36.2)

$$I = I_0\left\{\frac{\sin[\pi a(\sin\theta)/\lambda]}{\pi a(\sin\theta)/\lambda}\right\}^2$$

(36.7)

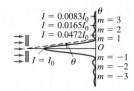

Diffraction gratings: A diffraction grating consists of a large number of thin parallel slits, spaced a distance d apart. The condition for maximum intensity in the interference pattern is the same as for the two-source pattern, but the maxima for the grating are very sharp and narrow. (See Example 36.4.)

$$d\sin\theta = m\lambda$$
$$(m = 0, \pm1, \pm2, \pm3, \ldots)$$

(36.13)

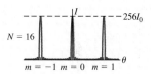

X-ray diffraction: A crystal serves as a three-dimensional diffraction grating for x rays with wavelengths of the same order of magnitude as the spacing between atoms in the crystal. For a set of crystal planes spaced a distance d apart, constructive interference occurs when the angles of incidence and scattering (measured from the crystal planes) are equal and when the Bragg condition [Eq. (36.16)] is satisfied. (See Example 36.5.)

$$2d\sin\theta = m\lambda \quad (m = 1, 2, 3, \ldots)$$

(36.16)

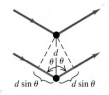

Circular apertures and resolving power: The diffraction pattern from a circular aperture of diameter D consists of a central bright spot, called the Airy disk, and a series of concentric dark and bright rings. Equation (36.17) gives the angular radius θ_1 of the first dark ring, equal to the angular size of the Airy disk. Diffraction sets the ultimate limit on resolution (image sharpness) of optical instruments. According to Rayleigh's criterion, two point objects are just barely resolved when their angular separation θ is given by Eq. (36.17). (See Example 36.6.)

$$\sin\theta_1 = 1.22\frac{\lambda}{D}$$

(36.17)

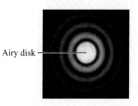

Airy disk

Key Terms

Answer to Chapter Opening Question   ?

The shorter wavelength of a DVD scanning laser gives it superior resolving power, so information can be more tightly packed onto a DVD than a CD. See Section 36.7 for details.

Answers to Test Your Understanding Questions

36.1 Answer: yes   When you hear the voice of someone standing around a corner, you are hearing sound waves that underwent diffraction. If there were no diffraction of sound, you could hear sounds only from objects that were in plain view.

36.2 Answers: (ii), (i) and (iv) (tie), (iii)   The angle θ of the first dark fringe is given by Eq. (36.2) with $m = 1$, or $\sin\theta = \lambda/a$. The larger the value of the ratio λ/a, the larger the value of $\sin\theta$ and hence the value of θ. The ratio λ/a in each case is (i) $(400\text{ nm})/(0.20\text{ mm}) = (4.0 \times 10^{-7}\text{ m})/(2.0 \times 10^{-4}\text{ m}) = 2.0 \times 10^{-3}$; (ii) $(600\text{ nm})/(0.20\text{ mm}) = (6.0 \times 10^{-7}\text{ m})/(2.0 \times 10^{-4}\text{ m}) = 3.0 \times 10^{-3}$; (iii) $(400\text{ nm})/(0.30\text{ mm}) = (4.0 \times 10^{-7}\text{ m})/(3.0 \times 10^{-4}\text{ m}) = 1.3 \times 10^{-3}$; (iv) $(600\text{ nm})/(0.30\text{ mm}) = (6.0 \times 10^{-7}\text{ m})/(3.0 \times 10^{-4}\text{ m}) = 2.0 \times 10^{-3}$.

36.3 Answers: (ii) and (iii)   If the slit width a is less than the wavelength λ, there are no points in the diffraction pattern at which the intensity is zero (see Fig. 36.10a). The slit width is $0.0100\text{ mm} = 1.00 \times 10^{-5}\text{ m}$, so this condition is satisfied for (ii) $(\lambda = 10.6\ \mu\text{m} = 10.6 \times 10^{-5}\text{ m})$ and (iii) $(\lambda = 1.00\text{ mm} = 1.00 \times 10^{-3}\text{ m})$ but not for (i) $(\lambda = 500\text{ nm} = 500 \times 10^{-7})$ or (iv) $(\lambda = 50.0\text{ nm} = 5.00 \times 10^{-8}\text{ m})$.

36.4 Answers: yes; $m_i = \pm 5, \pm 10, \ldots$ A "missing maximum" satisfies both $d\sin\theta = m_i\lambda$ (the condition for an interference maxi-

mum) and $a\sin\theta = m_d\lambda$ (the condition for a diffraction minimum). Substituting $d = 2.5a$, we can combine these two conditions into the relationship $m_i = 2.5m_d$. This is satisfied for $m_i = \pm 5$ and $m_d = \pm 2$ (the fifth interference maximum is missing because it coincides with the second diffraction minimum), $m_i = \pm 10$ and $m_d = \pm 4$ (the tenth interference maximum is missing because it coincides with the fourth diffraction minimum), and so on.

36.5 Answer: (i)   As described in the text, the resolving power needed is $R = Nm = 1000$. In the first order $(m = 1)$ we need $N = 1000$ slits, but in the fourth order $(m = 4)$ we need only $N = R/m = 1000/4 = 250$ slits. (These numbers are only approximate because of the arbitrary nature of our criterion for resolution and because real gratings always have slight imperfections in the shapes and spacings of the slits.)

36.6 Answer: no   The angular position of the mth maximum is given by Eq. (36.16), $2d\sin\theta = m\lambda$. With $d = 0.200\text{ nm}$, $\lambda = 0.100\text{ nm}$, and $m = 5$, this gives $\sin\theta = m\lambda/2d = (5)(0.100\text{ nm})/(2)(0.200\text{ nm}) = 1.25$. Since the sine function can never be greater than 1, this means that there is no solution to this equation and the $m = 5$ maximum does not appear.

36.7 Answer: (iii), (ii), (iv), (i)   Rayleigh's criterion combined with Eq. (36.17) shows that the smaller the value of the ratio λ/D, the better the resolving power of a telescope of diameter D. For the four telescopes, this ratio is equal to (i) $(21\text{ cm})/(100\text{ m}) = (0.21\text{ m})/(100\text{ m}) = 2.1 \times 10^{-3}$;   (ii) $(500\text{ nm})/(2.0\text{ m}) = (5.0 \times 10^{-7}\text{ m})/(2.0\text{ m}) = 2.5 \times 10^{-7}$;   (iii) $(100\text{ nm})/(1.0\text{ m}) = (1.0 \times 10^{-7}\text{ m})/(1.0\text{ m}) = 1.0 \times 10^{-7}$;   (iv) $(10\ \mu\text{m})/(2.0\text{ m}) = (1.0 \times 10^{-5}\text{ m})/(2.0\text{ m}) = 5.0 \times 10^{-6}$.

PROBLEMS

For instructor-assigned homework, go to **www.masteringphysics.com**

Discussion Questions

Q36.1. Why can we readily observe diffraction effects for sound waves and water waves, but not for light? Is this because light travels so much faster than these other waves? Explain.

Q36.2. What is the difference between Fresnel and Fraunhofer diffraction? Are they different *physical* processes? Explain.

Q36.3. You use a lens of diameter D and light of wavelength λ and frequency f to form an image of two closely spaced and distant objects. Which of the following will increase the resolving power? (a) Use a lens with a smaller diameter; (b) use light of higher frequency; (c) use light of longer wavelength. In each case justify your answer.

Q36.4. Light of wavelength λ and frequency f passes through a single slit of width a. The diffraction pattern is observed on a screen a distance x from the slit. Which of the following will *decrease* the width of the central maximum? (a) Decrease the slit

width; (b) decrease the frequency f of the light; (c) decrease the wavelength λ of the light; (d) decrease the distance x of the screen from the slit. In each case justify your answer.

Q36.5. In a diffraction experiment with waves of wavelength λ, there will be *no* intensity minima (that is, no dark fringes) if the slit width is small enough. What is the maximum slit width for which this occurs? Explain your answer.

Q36.6. The predominant sound waves used in human speech have wavelengths in the range from 1.0 to 3.0 meters. Using the ideas of diffraction, explain how it is possible to hear a person's voice even when he is facing away from you.

Q36.7. In single-slit diffraction, what is $\sin(\beta/2)$ when $\theta = 0$? In view of your answer, why is the single-slit intensity *not* equal to zero at the center?

Q36.8. A rainbow ordinarily shows a range of colors (see Section 33.4). But if the water droplets that form the rainbow are small enough, the rainbow will appear white. Explain why, using diffraction ideas. How small do you think the raindrops would have to be for this to occur?

Q36.9. Some loudspeaker horns for outdoor concerts (at which the entire audience is seated on the ground) are wider vertically than horizontally. Use diffraction ideas to explain why this is more efficient at spreading the sound uniformly over the audience than either a square speaker horn or a horn that is wider horizontally than vertically. Would this still be the case if the audience were seated at different elevations, as in an amphitheater? Why or why not?

Q36.10. Figure 31.12 (Section 31.2) shows a loudspeaker system. Low-frequency sounds are produced by the *woofer,* which is a speaker with large diameter; the *tweeter,* a speaker with smaller diameter, produces high-frequency sounds. Use diffraction ideas to explain why the tweeter is more effective for distributing high-frequency sounds uniformly over a room than is the woofer.

Q36.11. Information is stored on an audio compact disc, CD-ROM, or DVD disc in a series of pits on the disc. These pits are scanned by a laser beam. An important limitation on the amount of information that can be stored on such a disc is the width of the laser beam. Explain why this should be, and explain how using a shorter-wavelength laser allows more information to be stored on a disc of the same size.

Q36.12. With which color of light can the Hubble Space Telescope see finer detail in a distant astronomical object: red, blue, or ultraviolet? Explain your answer.

Q36.13. A typical telescope used by amateur astronomers has a mirror 20 cm in diameter. With such a telescope (and a filter to cut the intensity of sunlight to a safe level for viewing), fine details can be seen on the surface of the sun. Explain why a *radio* telescope would have to be *much* larger to "see" comparable details on the sun.

Q36.14. Could x-ray diffraction effects with crystals be observed by using visible light instead of x rays? Why or why not?

Q36.15. Why is a diffraction grating better than a two-slit setup for measuring wavelengths of light?

Q36.16. One sometimes sees rows of evenly spaced radio antenna towers. A student remarked that these act like diffraction gratings. What did she mean? Why would one want them to act like a diffraction grating?

Q36.17. If a hologram is made using 600-nm light and then viewed with 500-nm light, how will the images look compared to those observed when viewed with 600-nm light? Explain.

Q36.18. A hologram is made using 600-nm light and then viewed by using white light from an incandescent bulb. What will be seen? Explain.

Q36.19. Ordinary photographic film reverses black and white, in the sense that the most brightly illuminated areas become blackest upon development (hence the term *negative*). Suppose a hologram negative is viewed directly, without making a positive transparency. How will the resulting images differ from those obtained with the positive? Explain.

Exercises

Section 36.2 Diffraction from a Single Slit

36.1. Monochromatic light from a distant source is incident on a slit 0.750 mm wide. On a screen 2.00 m away, the distance from the central maximum of the diffraction pattern to the first minimum is measured to be 1.35 mm. Calculate the wavelength of the light.

36.2. Parallel rays of green mercury light with a wavelength of 546 nm pass through a slit covering a lens with a focal length of 60.0 cm. In the focal plane of the lens the distance from the central maximum to the first minimum is 10.2 mm. What is the width of the slit?

36.3. Light of wavelength 585 nm falls on a slit 0.0666 mm wide. (a) On a very large distant screen, how many *totally* dark fringes (indicating complete cancellation) will there be, including both sides of the central bright spot? Solve this problem *without* calculating all the angles! (*Hint:* What is the largest that $\sin\theta$ can be? What does this tell you is the largest that m can be?) (b) At what angle will the dark fringe that is most distant from the central bright fringe occur?

36.4. Light of wavelength 633 nm from a distant source is incident on a slit 0.750 mm wide, and the resulting diffraction pattern is observed on a screen 3.50 m away. What is the distance between the two dark fringes on either side of the central bright fringe?

36.5. Diffraction occurs for all types of waves, including sound waves. High-frequency sound from a distant source with wavelength 9.00 cm passes through a narrow slit 12.0 cm wide. A microphone is placed 40.0 cm directly in front of the center of the slit, corresponding to point *O* in Fig. 36.5a. The microphone is then moved in a direction perpendicular to the line from the center of the slit to point *O*. At what distances from *O* will the intensity detected by the microphone be zero?

36.6. Tsunami! On December 26, 2004, a violent magnitude-9.1 earthquake occurred off the coast of Sumatra. This quake triggered a huge tsunami (similar to a tidal wave) that killed more than 150,000 people. Scientists observing the wave on the open ocean measured the time between crests to be 1.0 h and the speed of the wave to be 800 km/h. Computer models of the evolution of this enormous wave showed that it bent around the continents and spread to all the oceans of the earth. When the wave reached the gaps between continents, it diffracted between them as through a slit. (a) What was the wavelength of this tsunami? (b) The distance between the southern tip of Africa and northern Antarctica is about 4500 km, while the distance between the southern end of Australia and Antarctica is about 3700 km. As an approximation, we can model this wave's behavior by using Fraunhofer diffraction. Find the smallest angle away from the central maximum for which the waves would cancel after going through each of these continental gaps.

36.7. A series of parallel linear water wave fronts are traveling directly toward the shore at 15.0 cm/s on an otherwise placid lake. A long concrete barrier that runs parallel to the shore at a distance of 3.20 m away has a hole in it. You count the wave crests and observe that 75.0 of them pass by each minute, and you also observe that no waves reach the shore at ±61.3 cm from the point directly opposite the hole, but waves do reach the shore everywhere within this distance. (a) How wide is the hole in the barrier? (b) At what other angles do you find no waves hitting the shore?

36.8. Monochromatic light of wavelength 580 nm passes through a single slit and the diffraction pattern is observed on a screen. Both the source and screen are far enough from the slit for Fraunhofer diffraction to apply. (a) If the first diffraction minima are at ±90.0°, so the central maximum completely fills the screen, what is the width of the slit? (b) For the width of the slit as calculated in part (a), what is the ratio of the intensity at $\theta = 45.0°$ to the intensity at $\theta = 0$?

36.9. Doorway Diffraction. Sound of frequency 1250 Hz leaves a room through a 1.00-m-wide doorway (see Exercise 36.5). At which angles relative to the centerline perpendicular to the doorway will someone outside the room hear no sound? Use 344 m/s for the speed of sound in air and assume that the source and listener are both far enough from the doorway for Fraunhofer diffraction to apply. You can ignore effects of reflections.

36.10. Light waves, for which the electric field is given by $E_y(x, t) = E_{max}\sin[(1.20 \times 10^7 \text{ m}^{-1})x - \omega t]$, pass through a slit and produce the first dark bands at $\pm 28.6°$ from the center of the diffraction pattern. (a) What is the frequency of this light? (b) How wide is the slit? (c) At which angles will other dark bands occur?

36.11. Parallel rays of light with wavelength 620 nm pass through a slit covering a lens with a focal length of 40.0 cm. The diffraction pattern is observed in the focal plane of the lens, and the distance from the center of the central maximum to the first minimum is 36.5 cm. What is the width of the slit? (*Note:* The angle that locates the first minimum is *not* small.)

36.12. Monochromatic electromagnetic radiation with wavelength λ from a distant source passes through a slit. The diffraction pattern is observed on a screen 2.50 m from the slit. If the width of the central maximum is 6.00 mm, what is the slit width a if the wavelength is (a) 500 nm (visible light); (b) 50.0 μm (infrared radiation); (c) 0.500 nm (x rays)?

36.13. Red light of wavelength 633 nm from a helium–neon laser passes through a slit 0.350 mm wide. The diffraction pattern is observed on a screen 3.00 m away. Define the width of a bright fringe as the distance between the minima on either side. (a) What is the width of the central bright fringe? (b) What is the width of the first bright fringe on either side of the central one?

Section 36.3 Intensity in the Single-Slit Pattern

36.14. Monochromatic light of wavelength $\lambda = 620$ nm from a distant source passes through a slit 0.450 mm wide. The diffraction pattern is observed on a screen 3.00 m from the slit. In terms of the intensity I_0 at the peak of the central maximum, what is the intensity of the light at the screen the following distances from the center of the central maximum: (a) 1.00 mm; (b) 3.00 mm; (c) 5.00 mm?

36.15. A slit 0.240 mm wide is illuminated by parallel light rays of wavelength 540 nm. The diffraction pattern is observed on a screen that is 3.00 m from the slit. The intensity at the center of the central maximum ($\theta = 0°$) is 6.00×10^{-6} W/m^2. (a) What is the distance on the screen from the center of the central maximum to the first minimum? (b) What is the intensity at a point on the screen midway between the center of the central maximum and the first minimum?

36.16. Laser light of wavelength 632.8 nm falls normally on a slit that is 0.0250 mm wide. The transmitted light is viewed on a distant screen where the intensity at the center of the central bright fringe is 8.50 W/m^2. (a) Find the maximum number of totally dark fringes on the screen, assuming the screen is large enough to show them all. (b) At what angle does the dark fringe that is most distant from the center occur? (c) What is the maximum intensity of the bright fringe that occurs immediately before the dark fringe in part (b)? Approximate the angle at which this fringe occurs by assuming it is midway between the angles to the dark fringes on either side of it.

36.17. A single-slit diffraction pattern is formed by monochromatic electromagnetic radiation from a distant source passing through a slit 0.105 mm wide. At the point in the pattern 3.25° from the center of the central maximum, the total phase difference between wavelets from the top and bottom of the slit is 56.0 rad. (a) What is the wavelength of the radiation? (b) What is the intensity at this point, if the intensity at the center of the central maximum is I_0?

36.18. Consider a single-slit diffraction experiment in which the amplitude of the wave at point O in Fig. 36.5a is E_0. For each of the following cases, draw a phasor diagram like that in Fig. 36.8c and determine *graphically* the amplitude of the wave at the point in question. (*Hint:* Use Eq. (36.6) to determine the value of β for each case.) Compute the intensity and compare to Eq. (36.5). (a) $\sin\theta = \lambda/2a$; (b) $\sin\theta = \lambda/a$; (c) $\sin\theta = 3\lambda/2a$.

36.19. Public Radio station KXPR-FM in Sacramento broadcasts at 88.9 MHz. The radio waves pass between two tall skyscrapers that are 15.0 m apart along their closest walls. (a) At what horizontal angles, relative to the original direction of the waves, will a distant antenna not receive any signal from this station? (b) If the maximum intensity is 3.50 W/m^2 at the antenna, what is the intensity at $\pm5.00°$ from the center of the central maximum at the distant antenna?

Section 36.4 Multiple Slits

36.20. Diffraction and Interference Combined. Consider the interference pattern produced by two parallel slits of width a and separation d, in which $d = 3a$. The slits are illuminated by normally incident light of wavelength λ. (a) First we ignore diffraction effects due to the slit width. At what angles θ from the central maximum will the next four maxima in the two-slit interference pattern occur? Your answer will be in terms of d and λ. (b) Now we include the effects of diffraction. If the intensity at $\theta = 0$ is I_0, what is the intensity at each of the angles in part (a)? (c) Which double-slit interference maxima are missing in the pattern? (d) Compare your results to those illustrated in Fig. 36.12c. In what ways is your result different?

36.21. Number of Fringes in a Diffraction Maximum. In Fig. 36.12c the central diffraction maximum contains exactly seven interference fringes, and in this case $d/a = 4$. (a) What must the ratio d/a be if the central maximum contains exactly five fringes? (b) In the case considered in part (a), how many fringes are contained within the first diffraction maximum on one side of the central maximum?

36.22. An interference pattern is produced by eight parallel and equally spaced, narrow slits. There is an interference minimum when the phase difference ϕ between light from adjacent slits is $\pi/4$. The phasor diagram is given in Fig. 36.14b. For which pairs of slits is there totally destructive interference?

36.23. An interference pattern is produced by light of wavelength 580 nm from a distant source incident on two identical parallel slits separated by a distance (between centers) of 0.530 mm. (a) If the slits are very narrow, what would be the angular positions of the first-order and second-order, two-slit, interference maxima? (b) Let the slits have width 0.320 mm. In terms of the intensity I_0 at the center of the central maximum, what is the intensity at each of the angular positions in part (a)?

36.24. Monochromatic light illuminates a pair of thin parallel slits at normal incidence, producing an interference pattern on a distant screen. The width of each slit is $\frac{1}{7}$ the center-to-center distance between the slits. (a) Which interference maxima are missing in the pattern on the screen? (b) Does the answer to part (a) depend on the wavelength of the light used? Does the location of the missing maxima depend on the wavelength?

36.25. An interference pattern is produced by four parallel and equally spaced, narrow slits. By drawing appropriate phasor diagrams, show that there is an interference minimum when the phase difference ϕ from adjacent slits is (a) $\pi/2$; (b) π; (c) $3\pi/2$. In each case, for which pairs of slits is there totally destructive interference?

36.26. A diffraction experiment involving two thin parallel slits yields the pattern of closely spaced bright and dark fringes shown in Fig. 36.33. Only the central portion of the pattern is shown in the figure. The bright spots are equally spaced at 1.53 mm center to center (except for the missing spots) on a screen 2.50 m from the slits. The light source was a He-Ne laser producing a wavelength of 632.8 nm. (a) How far apart are the two slits? (b) How wide is each one?

Figure **36.33** Exercise 36.26

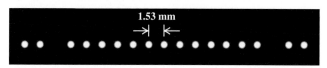

36.27. Laser light of wavelength 500.0 nm illuminates two identical slits, producing an interference pattern on a screen 90.0 cm from the slits. The bright bands are 1.00 cm apart, and the third bright bands on either side of the central maximum are missing in the pattern. Find the width and the separation of the two slits.

Section 36.5 The Diffraction Grating

36.28. Monochromatic light is at normal incidence on a plane transmission grating. The first-order maximum in the interference pattern is at an angle of 8.94°. What is the angular position of the fourth-order maximum?

36.29. If a diffraction grating produces its third-order bright band at an angle of 78.4° for light of wavelength 681 nm, find (a) the number of slits per centimeter for the grating and (b) the angular location of the first-order and second-order bright bands. (c) Will there be a fourth-order bright band? Explain.

36.30. If a diffraction grating produces a third-order bright spot for red light (of wavelength 700 nm) at 65.0° from the central maximum, at what angle will the second-order bright spot be for violet light (of wavelength 400 nm)?

36.31. Visible light passes through a diffraction grating that has 900 slits/cm, and the interference pattern is observed on a screen that is 2.50 m from the grating. (a) Is the angular position of the first-order spectrum small enough for $\sin\theta \approx \theta$ to be a good approximation? (b) In the first-order spectrum, the maxima for two different wavelengths are separated on the screen by 3.00 mm. What is the difference in these wavelengths?

36.32. The wavelength range of the visible spectrum is approximately 400–700 nm. White light falls at normal incidence on a diffraction grating that has 350 slits/mm. Find the angular width of the visible spectrum in (a) the first order and (b) the third order. (*Note:* An advantage of working in higher orders is the greater angular spread and better resolution. A disadvantage is the overlapping of different orders, as shown in Example 36.4.)

36.33. Measuring Wavelengths with a CD. A laser beam of wavelength $\lambda = 632.8$ nm shines at normal incidence on the reflective side of a compact disc. The tracks of tiny pits in which information is coded onto the CD are 1.60 μm apart. For what angles of reflection (measured from the normal) will the intensity of light be maximum?

36.34. (a) What is the wavelength of light that is deviated in the first order through an angle of 13.5° by a transmission grating having 5000 slits/cm? (b) What is the second-order deviation of this wavelength? Assume normal incidence.

36.35. Plane monochromatic waves with wavelength 520 nm are incident normally on a plane transmission grating having 350 slits/mm. Find the angles of deviation in the first, second, and third orders.

36.36. Identifying Isotopes by Spectra. Different isotopes of the same element emit light at slightly different wavelengths. A wavelength in the emission spectrum of a hydrogen atom is 656.45 nm; for deuterium, the corresponding wavelength is 656.27 nm. (a) What minimum number of slits is required to resolve these two wavelengths in second order? (b) If the grating has 500.00 slits/mm, find the angles and angular separation of these two wavelengths in the second order.

36.37. A typical laboratory diffraction grating has 5.00×10^3 lines/cm, and these lines are contained in a 3.50-cm width of grating. (a) What is the chromatic resolving power of such a grating in the first order? (b) Could this grating resolve the lines of the sodium doublet (see Section 36.5) in the first order? (c) While doing spectral analysis of a star, you are using this grating in the *second* order to resolve spectral lines that are very close to the 587.8002-nm spectral line of iron. (i) For wavelengths longer than the iron line, what is the shortest wavelength you could distinguish from the iron line? (ii) For wavelengths shorter than the iron line, what is the longest wavelength you could distinguish from the iron line? (iii) What is the range of wavelengths you could *not* distinguish from the iron line?

36.38. The light from an iron arc includes many different wavelengths. Two of these are at $\lambda = 587.9782$ nm and $\lambda = 587.8002$ nm. You wish to resolve these spectral lines in first order using a grating 1.20 cm in length. What minimum number of slits per centimeter must the grating have?

Section 36.6 X-Ray Diffraction

36.39. X rays of wavelength 0.0850 nm are scattered from the atoms of a crystal. The second-order maximum in the Bragg reflection occurs when the angle θ in Fig. 36.23 is 21.5°. What is the spacing between adjacent atomic planes in the crystal?

36.40. If the planes of a crystal are 3.50 Å (1 Å = 10^{-10} m = 1 Ångstrom unit) apart, (a) what wavelength of electromagnetic waves is needed so that the first strong interference maximum in the Bragg reflection occurs when the waves strike the planes at an angle of 15.0°, and in what part of the electromagnetic spectrum do these waves lie? (See Fig. 32.4.) (b) At what other angles will strong interference maxima occur?

Section 36.7 Circular Apertures and Resolving Power

36.41. Due to blurring caused by atmospheric distortion, the best resolution that can be obtained by a normal, earth-based, visible-light telescope is about 0.3 arcsecond (there are 60 arcminutes in a degree and 60 arcseconds in an arcminute). (a) Using Rayleigh's criterion, calculate the diameter of an earth-based telescope that gives this resolution with 550-nm light. (b) Increasing the telescope diameter beyond the value found in part (a) will increase the light-gathering power of the telescope, allowing more distant and dimmer astronomical objects to be studied, but it will not improve the resolution. In what ways are the Keck telescopes (each of 10-m diameter) atop Mauna Kea in Hawaii superior to the Hale Telescope (5-m diameter) on Palomar Mountain in California? In what ways are they *not* superior? Explain.

36.42. If you can read the bottom row of your doctor's eye chart, your eye has a resolving power of 1 arcminute, equal to $\frac{1}{60}$ degree. If this resolving power is diffraction limited, to what effective diameter of your eye's optical system does this correspond? Use Rayleigh's criterion and assume $\lambda = 550$ nm.

36.43. Two satellites at an altitude of 1200 km are separated by 28 km. If they broadcast 3.6-cm microwaves, what minimum receiving-dish diameter is needed to resolve (by Rayleigh's criterion) the two transmissions?

36.44. The Very Long Baseline Array can resolve (by Rayleigh's criterion) signals from sources separated by 1.0×10^{-8} rad. If the effective diameter of the receiver is 8000 km, what is the wavelength of these signals?

36.45. Monochromatic light with wavelength 620 nm passes through a circular aperture with diameter 7.4 μm. The resulting diffraction pattern is observed on a screen that is 4.5 m from the aperture. What is the diameter of the Airy disk on the screen?

36.46. Photography. A wildlife photographer uses a moderate telephoto lens of focal length 135 mm and maximum aperture $f/4.00$ to photograph a bear that is 11.5 m away. Assume the wavelength is 550 nm. (a) What is the width of the smallest feature on the bear that this lens can resolve if it is opened to its maximum aperture? (b) If, to gain depth of field, the photographer stops the lens down to $f/22.0$, what would be the width of the smallest resolvable feature on the bear?

36.47. Observing Jupiter. You are asked to design a space telescope for earth orbit. When Jupiter is 5.93×10^8 km away (its closest approach to the earth), the telescope is to resolve, by Rayleigh's criterion, features on Jupiter that are 250 km apart. What minimum-diameter mirror is required? Assume a wavelength of 500 nm.

36.48. A converging lens 7.20 cm in diameter has a focal length of 300 mm. If the resolution is diffraction limited, how far away can an object be if points on it 4.00 mm apart are to be resolved (according to Rayleigh's criterion)? Use $\lambda = 550$ nm.

36.49. Hubble Versus Arecibo. The Hubble Space Telescope has an aperture of 2.4 m and focuses visible light (400–700 nm). The Arecibo radio telescope in Puerto Rico is 305 m (1000 ft) in diameter (it is built in a mountain valley) and focuses radio waves of wavelength 75 cm. (a) Under optimal viewing conditions, what is the smallest crater that each of these telescopes could resolve on our moon? (b) If the Hubble Space Telescope were to be converted to surveillance use, what is the highest orbit above the surface of the earth it could have and still be able to resolve the license plate (not the letters, just the plate) of a car on the ground? Assume optimal viewing conditions, so that the resolution is diffraction limited.

36.50. Searching for Starspots. The Hale Telescope on Palomar Mountain in California has a mirror 200 in. (5.08 m) in diameter and it focuses visible light. Given that a large sunspot is about 10,000 mi in diameter, what is the most distant star on which this telescope could resolve a sunspot to see whether other stars have them? (Assume optimal viewing conditions, so that the resolution is diffraction limited.) Are there any stars this close to us, besides our sun?

36.51. Searching for Planets. The Keck Telescopes, on Mauna Kea, Hawaii have a 10.0-m-diameter mirror. Could these telescopes resolve Jupiter-sized planets about our nearest star, Alpha Centauri, which is 4.28 light-years away?

Problems

36.52. Suppose the entire apparatus (slit, screen, and space in between) in Exercise 36.4 is immersed in water $(n = 1.33)$. Then what is the distance between the two dark fringes?

36.53. Consider a single-slit diffraction pattern. The center of the central maximum, where the intensity is I_0, is located at $\theta = 0$. (a) Let θ_+ and θ_- be the two angles on either side of $\theta = 0$ for which $I = \frac{1}{2}I_0$. $\Delta\theta = |\theta_+ - \theta_-|$ is called the *full width at half maximum*, or *FWHM*, of the central diffraction maximum. Solve for $\Delta\theta$ when the ratio between slit width a and wavelength λ is (i) $a/\lambda = 2$; (ii) $a/\lambda = 5$; (iii) $a/\lambda = 10$. (*Hint:* Your equation for θ_+ or θ_- cannot be solved analytically. You must use trial and error or solve it graphically.) (b) The width of the central maximum can alternatively be defined as $2\theta_0$, where θ_0 is the angle that locates the minimum on one side of the central maximum. Calculate $2\theta_0$ for each case considered in part (a), and compare to $\Delta\theta$.

36.54. A loudspeaker having a diaphragm that vibrates at 1250 Hz is traveling at 80.0 m/s directly toward a pair of holes in a very large wall in a region for which the speed of sound is 344 m/s. You observe that the sound coming through the openings first cancels at $\pm 12.7°$ with respect to the original direction of the speaker when observed far from the wall. (a) How far apart are the two openings? (b) At what angles would the sound first cancel if the source stopped moving?

36.55. Measuring Refractive Index. A thin slit illuminated by light of frequency f produces its first dark band at $\pm 38.2°$ in air. When the entire apparatus (slit, screen, and space in between) is immersed in an unknown transparent liquid, the slit's first dark bands occur instead at $\pm 17.4°$. Find the refractive index of the liquid.

36.56. Grating Design. Your boss asks you to design a diffraction grating that will disperse the first-order visible spectrum through an angular range of $15.0°$ (see Example 36.4 in Section 36.5). (a) What must the number of slits per centimeter be for this grating? (b) At what angles will the first-order visible spectrum begin and end?

36.57. A slit 0.360 mm wide is illuminated by parallel rays of light that have a wavelength of 540 nm. The diffraction pattern is observed on a screen that is 1.20 m from the slit. The intensity at the center of the central maximum ($\theta = 0°$) is I_0. (a) What is the distance on the screen from the center of the central maximum to the first minimum? (b) What is the distance on the screen from the center of the central maximum to the point where the intensity has fallen to $I_0/2$? (See Problem 36.53, part (a), for a hint about how to solve for the phase angle β.)

36.58. The intensity of light in the Fraunhofer diffraction pattern of a single slit is

$$I = I_0 \left(\frac{\sin\gamma}{\gamma}\right)^2$$

where

$$\gamma = \frac{\pi a \sin\theta}{\lambda}$$

(a) Show that the equation for the values of γ at which I is a maximum is $\tan\gamma = \gamma$. (b) Determine the three smallest positive values of γ that are solutions of this equation. (*Hint:* You can use a trial-and-error procedure. Guess a value of γ and adjust your guess to bring $\tan\gamma$ closer to γ. A graphical solution of the equation is very helpful in locating the solutions approximately, to get good initial guesses.)

36.59. Angular Width of a Principal Maximum. Consider N evenly spaced, narrow slits. Use the small-angle approximation $\sin\theta = \theta$ (for θ in radians) to prove the following: For an intensity maximum that occurs at an angle θ, the intensity minima immediately adjacent to this maximum are at angles $\theta + \lambda/Nd$ and $\theta - \lambda/Nd$, so that the angular width of the principal maximum is $2\lambda/Nd$. This is proportional to $1/N$, as we concluded in Section 36.4 on the basis of energy conservation.

36.60. The Expanding Universe. A cosmologist who is studying the light from a galaxy has identified the spectrum of hydrogen but finds that the wavelengths are somewhat shifted from those found in the laboratory. In the lab, the H_α line has a wavelength of 656.3 nm. The cosmologist is using a transmission diffraction grating having 5758 lines/cm in the first order and finds that the first bright fringe for the H_α line occurs at $\pm 23.41°$ from the central spot. How fast is the galaxy moving? Express your answer in m/s and as a percentage of the speed of light. Is it moving toward us or away from us? (*Hint:* See Section 16.8.)

36.61. Phasor Diagram for Eight Slits. An interference pattern is produced by eight equally spaced, narrow slits. Figure 36.14 shows phasor diagrams for the cases in which the phase difference ϕ between light from adjacent slits is $\phi = \pi$, $\phi = \pi/4$, and $\phi = \pi/2$. Each of these cases gives an intensity minimum. The caption for Fig. 36.14 also claims that minima occur for $\phi = 3\pi/4$, $\phi = 5\pi/4$, $\phi = 3\pi/2$, and $\phi = 7\pi/4$. (a) Draw the phasor diagram for each of these four cases, and explain why each diagram proves that there is in fact a minimum. (*Note:* You may find it helpful to use a different colored pencil for each slit!) (b) For each of the four cases $\phi = 3\pi/4$, $\phi = 5\pi/4$, $\phi = 3\pi/2$, and $\phi = 7\pi/4$, for which pairs of slits is there totally destructive interference?

36.62. X-Ray Diffraction of Salt. X rays with a wavelength of 0.125 nm are scattered from a cubic array (of a sodium chloride crystal), for which the spacing of adjacent atoms is $a = 0.282$ nm. (a) If diffraction from planes parallel to a cube face is considered, at what angles θ of the incoming beam relative to the crystal planes will maxima be observed? (b) Repeat part (a) for diffraction produced by the planes shown in Fig. 36.24a, which are separated by $a/\sqrt{2}$.

36.63. At the end of Section 36.4, the following statements were made about an array of N slits. Explain, using phasor diagrams, why each statement is true. (a) A minimum occurs whenever ϕ is an integral multiple of $2\pi/N$, except when ϕ is an integral multiple of 2π (which gives a principal maximum). (b) There are $(N-1)$ minima between each pair of principal maxima.

36.64. In Eq. (36.12), consider the case in which $d = a$. In a sketch, show that in this case the two slits reduce to a single slit with width $2a$. Then show that Eq. (36.12) reduces to Eq. (36.5) with slit width $2a$.

36.65. What is the longest wavelength that can be observed in the third order for a transmission grating having 6500 slits/cm? Assume normal incidence.

36.66. (a) Figure 36.16 shows plane waves of light incident *normally* on a diffraction grating. If instead the light strikes the grating at an angle of incidence θ' (measured from the normal), show that the condition for an intensity maximum is *not* Eq. (36.13), but rather

$$d(\sin\theta + \sin\theta') = m\lambda \qquad (m = 0, \pm 1, \pm 2, \pm 3, \dots)$$

(b) For the grating described in Example (Section 36.5), with 600 slits/mm, find the angles of the maxima corresponding to $m = 0$, 1, and -1 with red light ($\lambda = 650$ nm) for the cases $\theta' = 0$ (normal incidence) and $\theta' = 20.0°$.

36.67. A diffraction grating has 650 slits/mm. What is the highest order that contains the entire visible spectrum? (The wavelength range of the visible spectrum is approximately 400–700 nm.)

36.68. *Quasars,* an abbreviation for *quasi-stellar radio sources,* are distant objects that look like stars through a telescope but that emit far more electromagnetic radiation than an entire normal galaxy of stars. An example is the bright object below and to the left of center in Fig. 36.34; the other elongated objects in this image are normal galaxies. The leading model for the structure of a quasar is a galaxy with a supermassive black hole at its center. In this model, the radiation is emitted by interstellar gas and dust within the galaxy as this material falls toward the black hole. The radiation is thought to emanate from a region just a few light-years in diameter. (The diffuse glow surrounding the bright quasar shown in Fig. 36.34 is thought to be this quasar's host galaxy.) To investigate this model of quasars and to study other exotic astronomical objects, the Russian Space Agency plans to place a radio telescope in an orbit that extends to 77,000 km from the earth. When the signals from this telescope are combined with signals from the ground-based telescopes of the VLBA, the resolution will be that of a single radio telescope 77,000 km in diameter. What is the size of the smallest detail that this arrangement could resolve in quasar 3C 405, which is 7.2×10^8 light-years from earth, using radio waves at a frequency of 1665 MHz? (*Hint:* Use Rayleigh's criterion.) Give your answer in light-years and in kilometers.

Figure 36.34 Problem 36.68

36.69. Phased-Array Radar. In one common type of radar installation, a rotating antenna sweeps a radio beam around the sky. But in a *phased-array* radar system, the antennas remain stationary and the beam is swept electronically. To see how this is done, consider an array of N antennas that are arranged along the horizontal x-axis at $x = 0, \pm d, \pm 2d, \dots, \pm (N-1)d/2$. (The number N is odd.) Each antenna emits radiation uniformly in all directions in the horizontal xy-plane. The antennas all emit radiation coherently, with the same amplitude E_0 and the same wavelength λ. The relative phase δ of the emission from adjacent antennas can be varied, however. If the antenna at $x = 0$ emits a signal that is given by $E_0\cos\omega t$, as measured at a point next to the antenna, the antenna at $x = d$ emits a signal given by $E_0\cos(\omega t + \delta)$, as measured at a point next to that antenna. The corresponding quantity for the antenna at $x = -d$ is $E_0\cos(\omega t - \delta)$; for the antennas at $x = \pm 2d$, it is $E_0\cos(\omega t \pm 2\delta)$; and so on. (a) If $\delta = 0$, the interference pattern at a distance from the antennas is large compared to d and has a principal maximum at $\theta = 0$ (that is, in the $+y$-direction, perpendicular to the line of the antennas). Show that if $d < \lambda$, this is the *only* principal interference maximum in the angular range $-90° < \theta < 90°$. Hence this principal maximum describes a beam emitted in the direction $\theta = 0$. As described in Section 36.4, if N is large, the beam will have a large intensity and be quite narrow. (b) If $\delta \neq 0$, show that the principal intensity maximum described in part (a) is located at

$$\theta = \arcsin\left(\frac{\delta\lambda}{2\pi d}\right)$$

where δ is measured in radians. Thus, by varying δ from positive to negative values and back again, which can easily be done electronically, the beam can be made to sweep back and forth around $\theta = 0$. (c) A weather radar unit to be installed on an airplane emits radio waves at 8800 MHz. The unit uses 15 antennas in an array 28.0 cm long (from the antenna at one end of the array to the antenna at the other end). What must the maximum and minimum values of δ be (that is, the most positive and most negative values) if the radar beam is to sweep $45°$ to the left or right of the airplane's direction of flight? Give your answer in radians.

36.70. Underwater Photography. An underwater camera has a lens of focal length 35.0 mm and a maximum aperture of $f/2.80$. The film it uses has an emulsion that is sensitive to light of frequency 6.00×10^{14} Hz. If the photographer takes a picture of an object 2.75 m in front of the camera with the lens wide open, what is the width of the smallest resolvable detail on the subject if the object is (a) a fish underwater with the camera in the water and (b) a person on the beach, with the camera out of the water?

36.71. An astronaut in orbit can just resolve two point sources on the earth that are 75.0 m apart. Assume that the resolution is diffraction limited, and use Rayleigh's criterion. What is the astronaut's altitude above the earth? Treat her eye as a circular aperture with a diameter of 4.00 mm (the diameter of her pupil), and take the wavelength of the light to be 500 nm.

36.72. Observing Planets Beyond Our Solar System. NASA is considering a project called *Planet Imager* that would give astronomers the ability to see details on planets orbiting other stars. Using the same principle as the Very Large Array (see Section 36.7), *Planet Imager* will use an array of infrared telescopes spread over thousands of kilometers of space. (Visible light would give even better resolution. Unfortunately, at visible wavelengths, stars are so bright that a planet would be lost in the glare. This is less of a problem at infrared wavelengths.) (a) If *Planet Imager* has an effective diameter of 6000 km and observes infrared radiation at a wavelength of 10 μm, what is the greatest distance at which it would be able to observe details as small as 250 km across (about the size of the greater Los Angeles area) on a planet? Give your answer in light-years (see Appendix E). (*Hint:* Use Rayleigh's criterion.) (b) For comparison, consider the resolution of a single infrared telescope in space that has a diameter of 1.0 m and that observes 10-μm radiation. What is the size of the smallest details that such a telescope could resolve at the distance of the nearest star to the sun, Proxima Centauri, which is 4.22 light-years distant? How does this compare to the diameter of the earth $(1.27 \times 10^4 \text{ km})$? To the average distance from the earth to the sun $(1.50 \times 10^8 \text{ km})$? Would a single telescope of this kind be able to detect the presence of a planet like the earth, in an orbit the size of the earth's orbit, around *any* other star? Explain. (c) Sup-

pose *Planet Imager* is used to observe a planet orbiting the star 70 Virginis, which is 59 light-years from our solar system. A planet (though not an earthlike one) has in fact been detected orbiting this star, not by imaging it directly but by observing the slight "wobble" of the star as both it and the planet orbit their common center of mass. What is the size of the smallest details that *Planet Imager* could hope to resolve on the planet of 70 Virginis? How does this compare to the diameter of the planet, assumed to be comparable to that of Jupiter $(1.38 \times 10^5 \text{ km})$? (Although the planet of 70 Virginis is thought to be at least 6.6 times more massive than Jupiter, its radius is probably not too different from that of Jupiter. The reason is that such large planets are thought to be composed primarily of gases, not rocky material, and hence can be greatly compressed by the mutual gravitational attraction of different parts of the planet.)

Challenge Problems

36.73. It is possible to calculate the intensity in the single-slit Fraunhofer diffraction pattern *without* using the phasor method of Section 36.3. Let y' represent the position of a point within the slit of width a in Fig. 36.5a, with $y' = 0$ at the center of the slit so that the slit extends from $y' = -a/2$ to $y' = a/2$. We imagine dividing the slit up into infinitesimal strips of width dy', each of which acts as a source of secondary wavelets. (a) The amplitude of the total wave at the point O on the distant screen in Fig. 36.5a is E_0. Explain why the amplitude of the wavelet from each infinitesimal strip within the slit is $E_0(dy'/a)$, so that the electric field of the wavelet a distance x from the infinitesimal strip is $dE = E_0(dy'/a)\sin(kx - \omega t)$. (b) Explain why the wavelet from each strip as detected at point P in Fig. 36.5a can be expressed as

$$dE = E_0\frac{dy'}{a}\sin[k(D - y'\sin\theta) - \omega t]$$

where D is the distance from the center of the slit to point P and $k = 2\pi/\lambda$. (c) By integrating the contributions dE from all parts of the slit, show that the total wave detected at point P is

$$E = E_0\sin(kD - \omega t)\frac{\sin[ka(\sin\theta)/2]}{ka(\sin\theta)/2}$$

$$= E_0\sin(kD - \omega t)\frac{\sin[\pi a(\sin\theta)/\lambda]}{\pi a(\sin\theta)/\lambda}$$

(The trigonometric identities in Appendix B will be useful.) Show that at $\theta = 0$, corresponding to point O in Fig. 36.5a, the wave is $E = E_0\sin(Kd - \omega t)$ and has amplitude E_0, as stated in part (a). (d) Use the result of part (c) to show that if the intensity at point O is I_0, then the intensity at a point P is given by Eq. (36.7).

36.74. Intensity Pattern of N Slits. (a) Consider an arrangement of N slits with a distance d between adjacent slits. The slits emit coherently and in phase at wavelength λ. Show that at a time t, the electric field at a distant point P is

$$\begin{aligned} E_P(t) &= E_0\cos(kR - \omega t) + E_0\cos(kR - \omega t + \phi) \\ &+ E_0\cos(kR - \omega t + 2\phi) + \cdots \\ &+ E_0\cos(kR - \omega t + (N - 1)\phi) \end{aligned}$$

where E_0 is the amplitude at P of the electric field due to an individual slit, $\phi = (2\pi d\sin\theta)/\lambda$, θ is the angle of the rays reaching P (as measured from the perpendicular bisector of the slit arrangement), and R is the distance from P to the most distant slit. In this problem, assume that R is much larger than d. (b) To carry out the sum in part (a), it is convenient to use the complex-number relationship

$$e^{iz} = \cos z + i \sin z$$

where $i = \sqrt{-1}$. In this expression, $\cos z$ is the *real part* of the complex number e^{iz}, and $\sin z$ is its *imaginary part*. Show that the electric field $E_P(t)$ is equal to the real part of the complex quantity

$$\sum_{n=0}^{N-1} E_0 e^{i(kR - \omega t + n\phi)}$$

(c) Using the properties of the exponential function that $e^A e^B = e^{(A+B)}$ and $(e^A)^n = e^{nA}$, show that the sum in part (b) can be written as

$$E_0 \left(\frac{e^{iN\phi} - 1}{e^{i\phi} - 1} \right) e^{i(kR - \omega t)} = E_0 \left(\frac{e^{iN\phi/2} - e^{-iN\phi/2}}{e^{i\phi/2} - e^{-i\phi/2}} \right) e^{i[kR - \omega t + (N-1)\phi/2]}$$

Then, using the relationship $e^{iz} = \cos z + i \sin z$, show that the (real) electric field at point P is

$$E_P(t) = \left[E_0 \frac{\sin(N\phi/2)}{\sin(\phi/2)} \right] \cos[kR - \omega t + (N-1)\phi/2]$$

The quantity in the first square brackets in this expression is the amplitude of the electric field at P. (d) Use the result for the electric-field amplitude in part (c) to show that the intensity at an angle θ is

$$I = I_0 \left[\frac{\sin(N\phi/2)}{\sin(\phi/2)} \right]^2$$

where I_0 is the maximum intensity for an individual slit. (e) Check the result in part (d) for the case $N = 2$. It will help to recall that $\sin 2A = 2 \sin A \cos A$. Explain why your result differs from Eq. (35.10), the expression for the intensity in two-source interference, by a factor of 4. (*Hint:* Is I_0 defined in the same way in both expressions?)

36.75. Intensity Pattern of N Slits, Continued. Part (d) of Challenge Problem 36.74 gives an expression for the intensity in the interference pattern of N identical slits. Use this result to verify the following statements. (a) The maximum intensity in the pattern is $N^2 I_0$. (b) The principal maximum at the center of the pattern extends from $\phi = -2\pi/N$ to $\phi = 2\pi/N$, so its width is inversely proportional to $1/N$. (c) A minimum occurs whenever ϕ is an integral multiple of $2\pi/N$, except when ϕ is an integral multiple of 2π (which gives a principal maximum). (d) There are $(N - 1)$ minima between each pair of principal maxima. (e) Halfway between two principal maxima, the intensity can be no greater than I_0; that is, it can be no greater than $1/N^2$ times the intensity at a principal maximum.

RELATIVITY

LEARNING GOALS

By studying this chapter, you will learn:

- The two postulates of Einstein's special theory of relativity, and what motivates these postulates.

- Why different observers can disagree about whether two events are simultaneous.

- How relativity predicts that moving clocks run slow, and experimental evidence that confirms this.

- How the length of an object changes due to the object's motion.

- How the velocity of an object depends on the frame of reference from which it is observed.

- How the theory of relativity modifies the relationship between velocity and momentum.

- How to solve problems involving work and kinetic energy for particles moving at relativistic speeds.

- Some of the key concepts of Einstein's general theory of relativity.

? At Brookhaven National Laboratory in New York, atomic nuclei are accelerated to 99.995% of the ultimate speed limit of the universe—the speed of light. Is there also an upper limit on the *kinetic energy* of a particle?

When the year 1905 began, Albert Einstein was an unknown 25-year-old clerk in the Swiss patent office. By the end of that amazing year he had published three papers of extraordinary importance. One was an analysis of Brownian motion; a second (for which he was awarded the Nobel Prize) was on the photoelectric effect. In the third, Einstein introduced his **special theory of relativity,** proposing drastic revisions in the Newtonian concepts of space and time.

The special theory of relativity has made wide-ranging changes in our understanding of nature, but Einstein based it on just two simple postulates. One states that the laws of physics are the same in all inertial frames of reference; the other states that the speed of light in vacuum is the same in all inertial frames. These innocent-sounding propositions have far-reaching implications. Here are three: (1) Events that are simultaneous for one observer may not be simultaneous for another. (2) When two observers moving relative to each other measure a time interval or a length, they may not get the same results. (3) For the conservation principles for momentum and energy to be valid in all inertial systems, Newton's second law and the equations for momentum and kinetic energy have to be revised.

Relativity has important consequences in *all* areas of physics, including electromagnetism, atomic and nuclear physics, and high-energy physics. Although many of the results derived in this chapter may run counter to your intuition, the theory is in solid agreement with experimental observations.

37.1 Invariance of Physical Laws

Let's take a look at the two postulates that make up the special theory of relativity. Both postulates describe what is seen by an observer in an *inertial frame of reference,* which we introduced in Section 4.2. The theory is "special" in the sense that it applies to observers in such special reference frames.

Einstein's First Postulate

Einstein's first postulate, called the **principle of relativity,** states: **The laws of physics are the same in every inertial frame of reference.** If the laws differed, that difference could distinguish one inertial frame from the others or make one frame somehow more "correct" than another. Here are two examples. Suppose you watch two children playing catch with a ball while the three of you are aboard a train moving with constant velocity. Your observations of the motion *of the ball,* no matter how carefully done, can't tell you how fast (or whether) the train is moving. This is because Newton's laws of motion are the same in every inertial frame.

Another example is the electromotive force (emf) induced in a coil of wire by a nearby moving permanent magnet. In the frame of reference in which the *coil* is stationary (Fig. 37.1a), the moving magnet causes a change of magnetic flux through the coil, and this induces an emf. In a different frame of reference in which the *magnet* is stationary (Fig. 37.1b), the motion of the coil through a magnetic field induces the emf. According to the principle of relativity, both of these frames of reference are equally valid. Hence the same emf must be induced in both situations shown in Fig. 37.1. As we saw in Chapter 29, this is indeed the case, so Faraday's law is consistent with the principle of relativity. Indeed, *all* of the laws of electromagnetism are the same in every inertial frame of reference.

Equally significant is the prediction of the speed of electromagnetic radiation, derived from Maxwell's equations (see Section 32.2). According to this analysis, light and all other electromagnetic waves travel in vacuum with a constant speed, now defined to equal exactly 299,792,458 m/s. (We often use the approximate value $c = 3.00 \times 10^8$ m/s, which is within one part in 1000 of the exact value.) As we will see, the speed of light in vacuum plays a central role in the theory of relativity.

Einstein's Second Postulate

During the 19th century, most physicists believed that light traveled through a hypothetical medium called the *ether,* just as sound waves travel through air. If so, the speed of light measured by observers would depend on their motion relative to the ether and would therefore be different in different directions. The Michelson-Morley experiment, described in Section 35.5, was an effort to detect motion of the earth relative to the ether. Einstein's conceptual leap was to recognize that if Maxwell's equations are valid in all inertial frames, then the speed of light in vacuum should also be the same in all frames and in all directions. In fact, Michelson and Morley detected *no* ether motion across the earth, and the ether concept has been discarded. Although Einstein may not have known about this negative result, it supported his bold hypothesis of the constancy of the speed of light in vacuum.

> **Einstein's second postulate states:** **The speed of light in vacuum is the same in all inertial frames of reference and is independent of the motion of the source.**

Let's think about what this means. Suppose two observers measure the speed of light in vacuum. One is at rest with respect to the light source, and the other is moving away from it. Both are in inertial frames of reference. According to the principle of relativity, the two observers must obtain the same result, despite the fact that one is moving with respect to the other.

If this seems too easy, consider the following situation. A spacecraft moving past the earth at 1000 m/s fires a missile straight ahead with a speed of 2000 m/s (relative to the spacecraft) (Fig. 37.2). What is the missile's speed relative to the earth? Simple, you say; this is an elementary problem in relative velocity (see Section 3.5). The correct answer, according to Newtonian mechanics, is 3000 m/s. But now suppose the spacecraft turns on a searchlight, pointing in the same direction in which the missile was fired. An observer on the spacecraft measures the

37.1 The same emf is induced in the coil whether (**a**) the magnet moves relative to the coil or (**b**) the coil moves relative to the magnet.

(a)

(b)

37.2 (a) Newtonian mechanics makes correct predictions about relatively slow-moving objects; (b) it makes incorrect predictions about the behavior of light.

(a)

A spaceship (S') moves with speed $v_{S'/S} = 1000$ m/s relative to an observer on earth (S).

A missile (M) is fired with speed $v_{M/S'} = 2000$ m/s relative to the spaceship.

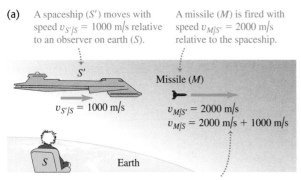

$v_{S'/S} = 1000$ m/s

Missile (M)

$v_{M/S'} = 2000$ m/s
$v_{M/S} = 2000$ m/s + 1000 m/s

S Earth

NEWTONIAN MECHANICS HOLDS: Newtonian mechanics tells us correctly that the missile moves with speed $v_{M/S} = 3000$ m/s relative to the observer on earth.

(b)

A light beam (L) is emitted from the spaceship at speed c.

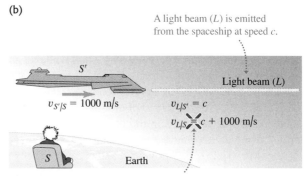

$v_{S'/S} = 1000$ m/s

Light beam (L)

$v_{L/S'} = c$
$v_{L/S} \ne c + 1000$ m/s

S Earth

NEWTONIAN MECHANICS FAILS: Newtonian mechanics tells us *incorrectly* that the light moves at a speed greater than c relative to the observer on earth ... which would contradict Einstein's second postulate.

speed of light emitted by the searchlight and obtains the value c. According to Einstein's second postulate, the motion of the light after it has left the source cannot depend on the motion of the source. So the observer on earth who measures the speed of this same light must also obtain the value c, *not* $c + 1000$ m/s. This result contradicts our elementary notion of relative velocities, and it may not appear to agree with common sense. But "common sense" is intuition based on everyday experience, and this does not usually include measurements of the speed of light.

The Ultimate Speed Limit

Einstein's second postulate immediately implies the following result:

It is impossible for an inertial observer to travel at c, the speed of light in vacuum.

We can prove this by showing that travel at c implies a logical contradiction. Suppose that the spacecraft S' in Fig. 37.2b is moving at the speed of light relative to an observer on the earth, so that $v_{S'/S} = c$. If the spacecraft turns on a headlight, the second postulate now asserts that the earth observer S measures the headlight beam to be also moving at c. Thus this observer measures that the headlight beam and the spacecraft move together and are always at the same point in space. But Einstein's second postulate also asserts that the headlight beam moves at a speed c relative to the spacecraft, so they *cannot* be at the same point in space. This contradictory result can be avoided only if it is impossible for an inertial observer, such as a passenger on the spacecraft, to move at c. As we go through our discussion of relativity, you may find yourself asking the question Einstein asked himself as a 16-year-old student, "What would I see if I were traveling at the speed of light?" Einstein realized only years later that his question's basic flaw was that he could *not* travel at c.

The Galilean Coordinate Transformation

Let's restate this argument symbolically, using two inertial frames of reference, labeled S for the observer on earth and S' for the moving spacecraft, as shown in Fig. 37.3. To keep things as simple as possible, we have omitted the z-axes. The x-axes of the two frames lie along the same line, but the origin O' of frame S' moves relative to the origin O of frame S with constant velocity u along the common x-x'-axis. We on earth set our clocks so that the two origins coincide at time $t = 0$, so their separation at a later time t is ut.

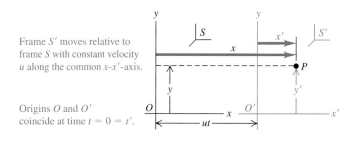

Frame S' moves relative to frame S with constant velocity u along the common x-x'-axis.

Origins O and O' coincide at time $t = 0 = t'$.

37.3 The position of particle P can be described by the coordinates x and y in frame of reference S or by x' and y' in frame S'.

CAUTION **Choose your inertial frame coordinates wisely** Many of the equations derived in this chapter are true *only* if you define your inertial reference frames as stated in the preceding paragraph. For instance, the positive x-direction must be the direction in which the origin O' moves relative to the origin O. In Fig. 37.3 this direction is to the right; if instead O' moves to the left relative to O, you must define the positive x-direction to be to the left. ▮

Now think about how we describe the motion of a particle P. This might be an exploratory vehicle launched from the spacecraft or a pulse of light from a laser. We can describe the *position* of this particle by using the earth coordinates (x, y, z) in S or the spacecraft coordinates (x', y', z') in S'. Figure 37.3 shows that these are simply related by

$$x = x' + ut \qquad y = y' \qquad z = z' \qquad \begin{matrix}\text{(Galilean coordinate} \\ \text{transformation)}\end{matrix} \qquad (37.1)$$

These equations, based on the familiar Newtonian notions of space and time, are called the **Galilean coordinate transformation.**

If particle P moves in the x-direction, its instantaneous velocity v_x as measured by an observer stationary in S is $v_x = dx/dt$. Its velocity v'_x as measured by an observer stationary in S' is $v'_x = dx'/dt$. We can derive a relationship between v_x and v'_x by taking the derivative with respect to t of the first of Eqs. (37.1):

$$\frac{dx}{dt} = \frac{dx'}{dt} + u$$

Now dx/dt is the velocity v_x measured in S, and dx'/dt is the velocity v'_x measured in S', so we get the *Galilean velocity transformation* for one-dimensional motion:

$$v_x = v'_x + u \qquad \text{(Galilean velocity transformation)} \qquad (37.2)$$

Although the notation differs, this result agrees with our discussion of relative velocities in Section 3.5.

Now here's the fundamental problem. Applied to the speed of light in vacuum, Eq. (37.2) says that $c = c' + u$. Einstein's second postulate, supported subsequently by a wealth of experimental evidence, says that $c = c'$. This is a genuine inconsistency, not an illusion, and it demands resolution. If we accept this postulate, we are forced to conclude that Eqs. (37.1) and (37.2) *cannot* be precisely correct, despite our convincing derivation. These equations have to be modified to bring them into harmony with this principle.

The resolution involves some very fundamental modifications in our kinematic concepts. The first idea to be changed is the seemingly obvious assumption that the observers in frames S and S' use the same *time scale,* formally stated as $t = t'$. Alas, we are about to show that this everyday assumption cannot be correct; the two observers *must* have different time scales. We must define the velocity v' in frame S' as $v' = dx'/dt'$, not as dx'/dt; the two quantities are not the same. The difficulty lies in the concept of *simultaneity,* which is our next topic. A careful analysis of simultaneity will help us develop the appropriate modifications of our notions about space and time.

37.2 Relativity of Simultaneity

37.4 An event has a definite position and time—for instance, on the pavement directly below the center of the Eiffel Tower at midnight on New Year's Eve.

Measuring times and time intervals involves the concept of **simultaneity.** In a given frame of reference, an **event** is an occurrence that has a definite position and time (Fig. 37.4). When you say that you awoke at seven o'clock, you mean that two events (your awakening and your clock showing 7:00) occurred *simultaneously.* The fundamental problem in measuring time intervals is this: In general, two events that are simultaneous in one frame of reference are *not* simultaneous in a second frame that is moving relative to the first, even if both are inertial frames.

A Thought Experiment in Simultaneity

This may seem to be contrary to common sense. To illustrate the point, here is a version of one of Einstein's *thought experiments*—mental experiments that follow concepts to their logical conclusions. Imagine a train moving with a speed comparable to c, with uniform velocity (Fig. 37.5). Two lightning bolts strike a passenger car, one near each end. Each bolt leaves a mark on the car and one on the ground at the instant the bolt hits. The points on the ground are labeled A and B in the figure, and the corresponding points on the car are A' and B'. Stanley is stationary on the ground at O, midway between A and B. Mavis is moving with the train at O' in the middle of the passenger car, midway between A' and B'. Both Stanley and Mavis see both light flashes emitted from the points where the lightning strikes.

Suppose the two wave fronts from the lightning strikes reach Stanley at O simultaneously. He knows that he is the same distance from B and A, so Stanley concludes that the two bolts struck B and A simultaneously. Mavis agrees that the two wave fronts reached Stanley at the same time, but she disagrees that the flashes were emitted simultaneously.

Stanley and Mavis agree that the two wave fronts do not reach Mavis at the same time. Mavis at O' is moving to the right with the train, so she runs into the wave front from B' *before* the wave front from A' catches up to her. However, because she is in the middle of the passenger car equidistant from A' and B', her observation is that both wave fronts took the same time to reach her because both moved the same distance at the same speed c. (Recall that the speed of each wave front with respect to *either* observer is c.) Thus she concludes that the lightning bolt at B' struck *before* the one at A'. Stanley at O measures the two events to be simultaneous, but Mavis at O' does not! *Whether or not two events at different x-axis locations are simultaneous depends on the state of motion of the observer.*

You may want to argue that in this example the lightning bolts really *are* simultaneous and that if Mavis at O' could communicate with the distant points without the time delay caused by the finite speed of light, she would realize this. But that would be erroneous; the finite speed of information transmission is not the real issue. If O' is midway between A' and B', then in her frame of reference the time for a signal to travel from A' to O' is the same as that from B' to O'. Two signals arrive simultaneously at O' only if they were emitted simultaneously at A' and B'. In this example they *do not* arrive simultaneously at O', and so Mavis must conclude that the events at A' and B' were *not* simultaneous.

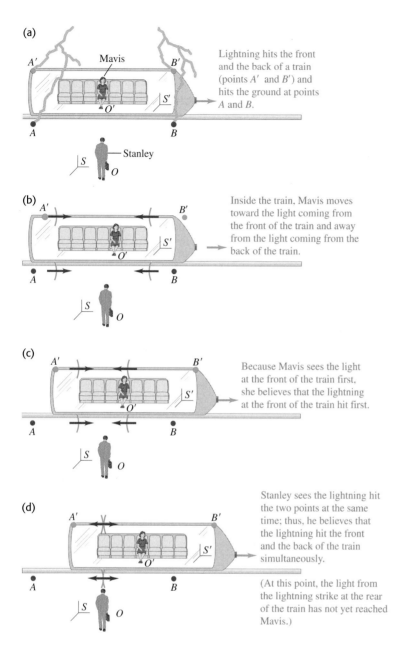

(a) Lightning hits the front and the back of a train (points A' and B') and hits the ground at points A and B.

(b) Inside the train, Mavis moves toward the light coming from the front of the train and away from the light coming from the back of the train.

(c) Because Mavis sees the light at the front of the train first, she believes that the lightning at the front of the train hit first.

(d) Stanley sees the lightning hit the two points at the same time; thus, he believes that the lightning hit the front and the back of the train simultaneously.

(At this point, the light from the lightning strike at the rear of the train has not yet reached Mavis.)

Furthermore, there is no basis for saying that Stanley is right and Mavis is wrong, or vice versa. According to the principle of relativity, no inertial frame of reference is more correct than any other in the formulation of physical laws. Each observer is correct *in his or her own frame of reference*. In other words, simultaneity is not an absolute concept. Whether two events are simultaneous depends on the frame of reference. As we mentioned at the beginning of this section, simultaneity plays an essential role in measuring time intervals. It follows that *the time interval between two events may be different in different frames of reference.* So our next task is to learn how to compare time intervals in different frames of reference.

Test Your Understanding of Section 37.2 Stanley, who works for the rail system shown in Fig. 37.5, has carefully synchronized the clocks at all of the rail stations. At the moment that Stanley measures all of the clocks striking noon, Mavis is on a high-speed passenger car traveling from Ogdenville toward North Haverbrook. According to Mavis, when the Ogdenville clock strikes noon, what time is it in North Haverbrook? (i) noon; (ii) before noon; (iii) after noon.

37.3 Relativity of Time Intervals

We can derive a quantitative relationship between time intervals in different coordinate systems. To do this, let's consider another thought experiment. As before, a frame of reference S' moves along the common x-x'-axis with constant speed u relative to a frame S. As discussed in Section 37.1, u must be less than the speed of light c. Mavis, who is riding along with frame S', measures the time interval between two events that occur at the *same* point in space. Event 1 is when a flash of light from a light source leaves O'. Event 2 is when the flash returns to O', having been reflected from a mirror a distance d away, as shown in Fig. 37.6a. We label the time interval Δt_0, using the subscript zero as a reminder that the apparatus is at rest, with zero velocity, in frame S'. The flash of light moves a total distance $2d$, so the time interval is

$$\Delta t_0 = \frac{2d}{c} \tag{37.3}$$

The round-trip time measured by Stanley in frame S is a different interval Δt; in his frame of reference the two events occur at *different* points in space. During the time Δt, the source moves relative to S a distance $u\,\Delta t$ (Fig. 37.6b). In S' the round-trip distance is $2d$ perpendicular to the relative velocity, but the round-trip distance in S is the longer distance $2l$, where

$$l = \sqrt{d^2 + \left(\frac{u\,\Delta t}{2}\right)^2}$$

In writing this expression, we have assumed that both observers measure the same distance d. We will justify this assumption in the next section. The speed of light is the same for both observers, so the round-trip time measured in S is

$$\Delta t = \frac{2l}{c} = \frac{2}{c}\sqrt{d^2 + \left(\frac{u\,\Delta t}{2}\right)^2} \tag{37.4}$$

We would like to have a relationship between Δt and Δt_0 that is independent of d. To get this, we solve Eq. (37.3) for d and substitute the result into Eq. (37.4), obtaining

$$\Delta t = \frac{2}{c}\sqrt{\left(\frac{c\,\Delta t_0}{2}\right)^2 + \left(\frac{u\,\Delta t}{2}\right)^2} \tag{37.5}$$

37.6 (a) Mavis, in frame of reference S', observes a light pulse emitted from a source at O' and reflected back along the same line. (b) How Stanley (in frame of reference S) and Mavis observe the same light pulse. The positions of O' at the times of departure and return of the pulse are shown.

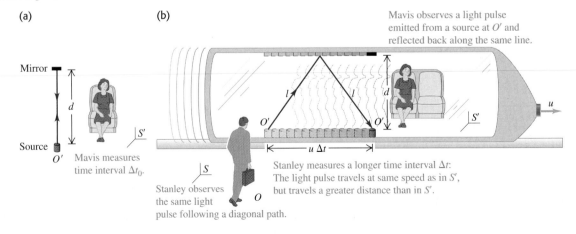

(a)

Mirror

d

Source

O' Mavis measures time interval Δt_0.

S'

(b)

Mavis observes a light pulse emitted from a source at O' and reflected back along the same line.

l l d

O' O'

u

S'

$\leftarrow u\,\Delta t \rightarrow$

S

Stanley observes the same light pulse following a diagonal path.

O

Stanley measures a longer time interval Δt: The light pulse travels at same speed as in S', but travels a greater distance than in S'.

Now we square this and solve for Δt; the result is

$$\Delta t = \frac{\Delta t_0}{\sqrt{1 - u^2/c^2}}$$

Since the quantity $\sqrt{1 - u^2/c^2}$ is less than 1, Δt is greater than Δt_0. Thus Stanley measures a *longer* round-trip time for the light pulse than does Mavis.

Time Dilation

We may generalize this important result. In a particular frame of reference, suppose that two events occur at the same point in space. The time interval between these events, as measured by an observer at rest in this same frame (which we call the *rest frame* of this observer), is Δt_0. Then an observer in a second frame moving with constant speed u relative to the rest frame will measure the time interval to be Δt, where

$$\Delta t = \frac{\Delta t_0}{\sqrt{1 - u^2/c^2}} \qquad \text{(time dilation)} \qquad (37.6)$$

We recall that no inertial observer can travel at $u = c$ and we note that $\sqrt{1 - u^2/c^2}$ is imaginary for $u > c$. Thus Eq. (37.6) gives sensible results only when $u < c$. The denominator of Eq. (37.7) is always smaller than 1, so Δt is always *larger* than Δt_0. Thus we call this effect **time dilation.**

Think of an old-fashioned pendulum clock that has one second between ticks, as measured by Mavis in the clock's rest frame; this is Δt_0. If the clock's rest frame is moving relative to Stanley, he measures a time between ticks Δt that is longer than one second. In brief, *observers measure any clock to run slow if it moves relative to them* (Fig. 37.7). Note that this conclusion is a direct result of the fact that the speed of light in vacuum is the same in both frames of reference.

The quantity $1/\sqrt{1 - u^2/c^2}$ in Eq. (37.6) appears so often in relativity that it is given its own symbol γ (the Greek letter gamma):

$$\gamma = \frac{1}{\sqrt{1 - u^2/c^2}} \qquad (37.7)$$

In terms of this symbol, we can express the time dilation formula, Eq. (37.6), as

$$\Delta t = \gamma \, \Delta t_0 \qquad \text{(time dilation)} \qquad (37.8)$$

As a further simplification, u/c is sometimes given the symbol β (the Greek letter beta); then $\gamma = 1/\sqrt{1 - \beta^2}$.

Figure 37.8 shows a graph of γ as a function of the relative speed u of two frames of reference. When u is very small compared to c, u^2/c^2 is much smaller than 1 and γ is very nearly *equal* to 1. In that limit, Eqs. (37.6) and (37.8) approach the Newtonian relationship $\Delta t = \Delta t_0$, corresponding to the same time interval in all frames of reference.

If the relative speed u is great enough that γ is appreciably greater than 1, the speed is said to be *relativistic;* if the difference between γ and 1 is negligibly small, the speed u is called *nonrelativistic*. Thus $u = 6.00 \times 10^7 \text{ m/s} = 0.200c$ (for which $\gamma = 1.02$) is a relativistic speed, but $u = 6.00 \times 10^4 \text{ m/s} = 0.000200c$ (for which $\gamma = 1.00000002$) is a nonrelativistic speed.

Proper Time

There is only one frame of reference in which a clock is at rest, and there are infinitely many in which it is moving. Therefore the time interval measured between two events (such as two ticks of the clock) that occur at the same point in a

37.7 This image shows an exploding star, called a *supernova*, within a distant galaxy. The brightness of a typical supernova decays at a certain rate. But supernovae that are moving away from us at a substantial fraction of the speed of light decay more slowly, in accordance with Eq. (37.6). The decaying supernova is a moving "clock" that runs slow.

37.8 The quantity $\gamma = 1/\sqrt{1 - u^2/c^2}$ as a function of the relative speed u of two frames of reference.

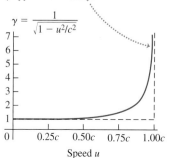

particular frame is a more fundamental quantity than the interval between events at different points. We use the term **proper time** to describe the time interval Δt_0 between two events that occur *at the same point.*

CAUTION   **Measuring time intervals** It is important to note that the time interval Δt in Eq. (37.6) involves events that occur at *different space points* in the frame of reference S. Note also that any differences between Δt and the proper time Δt_0 are *not* caused by differences in the times required for light to travel from those space points to an observer at rest in S. We assume that our observer is able to correct for differences in light transit times, just as an astronomer who's observing the sun understands that an event seen now on earth actually occurred 500 s ago on the sun's surface. Alternatively, we can use *two* observers, one stationary at the location of the first event and the other at the second, each with his or her own clock. We can synchronize these two clocks without difficulty, as long as they are at rest in the same frame of reference. For example, we could send a light pulse simultaneously to the two clocks from a point midway between them. When the pulses arrive, the observers set their clocks to a prearranged time. (But note that clocks that are synchronized in one frame of reference *are not* in general synchronized in any other frame.) ▪

37.9 A frame of reference pictured as a coordinate system with a grid of synchronized clocks.

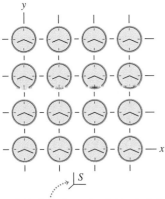

y

The grid is three dimensional; identical planes of clocks lie in front of and behind the page, connected by grid lines perpendicular to the page.

In thought experiments, it's often helpful to imagine many observers with synchronized clocks at rest at various points in a particular frame of reference. We can picture a frame of reference as a coordinate grid with lots of synchronized clocks distributed around it, as suggested by Fig. 37.9. Only when a clock is moving relative to a given frame of reference do we have to watch for ambiguities of synchronization or simultaneity.

Throughout this chapter we will frequently use phrases like "Stanley *observes* that Mavis passes the point $x = 5.00$ m, $y = 0$, $z = 0$ at time 2.00 s." This means that Stanley is using a grid of clocks in his frame of reference, like the grid shown in Fig. 37.9, to record the time of an event. We could restate the phrase as "When Mavis passes the point at $x = 5.00$ m, $y = 0$, $z = 0$, the clock at that location in Stanley's frame of reference reads 2.00 s." We will avoid using phrases like "Stanley *sees* that Mavis is a certain point at a certain time," because there is a time delay for light to travel to Stanley's eye from the position of an event.

Problem-Solving Strategy 37.1   **Time Dilation**   (MP)

IDENTIFY *the relevant concepts:*   The concept of time dilation is used whenever we compare the time intervals between events as measured by observers in different inertial frames of reference.

SET UP *the problem* using the following steps:
1. To describe a time interval, you must first decide what two events define the beginning and the end of the interval. You must also identify the two frames of reference in which the time interval is measured.
2. Determine what the target variable is.

EXECUTE *the solution* as follows:
1. In many problems involving time dilation, the time interval between events as measured in one frame of reference is the

proper time Δt_0. The proper time is the time interval between two events in a frame of reference in which the two events occur at the same point in space. The dilated time Δt is the longer time interval between the same two events as measured in a frame of reference that has a speed u relative to the first frame. The two events occur at different points as measured in the second frame. You will need to decide in which frame the time interval is Δt_0 and in which frame it is Δt.
2. Use Eq. (37.6) or (37.8) to relate Δt_0 and Δt, and then solve for the target variable.

EVALUATE *your answer:*   Note that Δt is never smaller than Δt_0, and u is never greater than c. If your results suggest otherwise, you need to rethink your calculation.

Example 37.1   **Time dilation at 0.990*c***

High-energy subatomic particles coming from space interact with atoms in the earth's upper atmosphere, producing unstable particles called *muons*. A muon decays with a mean lifetime of 2.20×10^{-6} s as measured in a frame of reference in which it is at rest. If a muon is moving at 0.990*c* (about 2.97×10^8 m/s) relative to the earth, what will you (an observer on earth) measure its mean lifetime to be?

SOLUTION

IDENTIFY: This problem concerns the muon's lifetime, which is the time interval between two events: the production of the muon and its subsequent decay. This lifetime is measured by two different observers: one who observes the muon at rest and another (you) who observes it moving at 0.990*c*.

SET UP: Let S be your frame of reference on earth, and let S' be the muon's frame of reference. The target variable is the interval between these events as measured in S.

EXECUTE: The time interval between the two events as measured in S', 2.20×10^{-6} s, is a *proper* time, since the two events occur at the same position relative to the muon. Hence $\Delta t_0 = 2.20 \times 10^{-6}$ s. The muon moves relative to the earth between the two events, so the two events occur at different positions as measured in S and the time interval in that frame is Δt (the target variable). From Eq. (37.6),

$$\Delta t = \frac{\Delta t_0}{\sqrt{1 - u^2/c^2}} = \frac{2.20 \times 10^{-6}\text{ s}}{\sqrt{1 - (0.990)^2}} = 15.6 \times 10^{-6}\text{ s}$$

EVALUATE: Our result predicts that the mean lifetime of the muon in the earth frame (Δt) is about seven times longer than in the muon's frame (Δt_0). This prediction has been verified experimentally; indeed, it was the first experimental confirmation of the time dilation formula, Eq. (37.6).

Example 37.2   Time dilation at jetliner speeds

An airplane flies from San Francisco to New York (about 4800 km, or 4.80×10^6 m) at a steady speed of 300 m/s (about 670 mi/h). How much time does the trip take, as measured by an observer on the ground? By an observer in the plane?

SOLUTION

IDENTIFY: Here we are interested in what our two observers measure for the time interval between the airplane departing from San Francisco and landing in New York.

SET UP: The target variables are the time intervals between these events as measured in the frame of reference of the ground S and in the frame of reference of the airplane S'.

EXECUTE: The two events occur at different positions (San Francisco and New York) as measured in S, so the time interval measured by ground observers corresponds to Δt in Eq. (37.6). To find it, we simply divide the distance by the speed:

$$\Delta t = \frac{4.80 \times 10^6\text{ m}}{300\text{ m/s}} = 1.60 \times 10^4\text{ s} \qquad (\text{about } 4\tfrac{1}{2}\text{ hours})$$

In the airplane's frame S', San Francisco and New York passing under the plane occur at the same point (the position of the plane). The time interval in the airplane is a proper time, corresponding to Δt_0 in Eq. (37.6). We have

$$\frac{u^2}{c^2} = \frac{(300\text{ m/s})^2}{(3.00 \times 10^8\text{ m/s})^2} = 1.00 \times 10^{-12}$$

From Eq. (37.6),

$$\Delta t_0 = (1.60 \times 10^4\text{ s}) \sqrt{1 - 1.00 \times 10^{-12}}$$

The radical can't be evaluated with adequate precision with an ordinary calculator. But we can approximate it using the binomial theorem (see Appendix B):

$$(1 - 1.00 \times 10^{-12})^{1/2} = 1 - \left(\frac{1}{2}\right)(1.00 \times 10^{-12}) + \cdots$$

The remaining terms are of the order of 10^{-24} or smaller and can be discarded. The approximate result for Δt_0 is

$$\Delta t_0 = (1.60 \times 10^4\text{ s})(1 - 0.50 \times 10^{-12})$$

The proper time Δt_0, measured in the airplane, is very slightly less (by less than one part in 10^{12}) than the time measured on the ground.

EVALUATE: We don't notice such effects in everyday life. But present-day atomic clocks (see Section 1.3) can attain a precision of about one part in 10^{13}. A cesium clock traveling a long distance in an airliner has been used to measure this effect and thereby verify Eq. (37.6) even at speeds much less than c.

Example 37.3   Just when is it proper?

Mavis boards a spaceship and then zips past Stanley on earth at a relative speed of $0.600c$. At the instant she passes, both start timers. (a) At the instant when Stanley measures that Mavis has traveled 9.00×10^7 m past him, what does Mavis's timer read? (b) At the instant when Mavis reads 0.400 s on her timer, what does Stanley read on his?

SOLUTION

IDENTIFY: This problem involves time dilation for two *different* sets of events: the starting and stopping of Mavis's timer, and the starting and stopping of Stanley's timer.

SET UP: Let S be Stanley's frame of reference, and let S' be Mavis's frame of reference. The two events of interest in part (a)

are when Mavis passes Stanley and when Stanley measures Mavis as having traveled a distance of 9.00×10^7 m; the target variables are the time intervals between these two events as measured in S and in S'. The two events in part (b) are when Mavis passes Stanley and when Mavis measures an elapsed time of 0.400 s; the target variable is the time interval between these two events as measured in S. As we will see, understanding this example hinges on understanding the difference between these two pairs of events.

EXECUTE: (a) The two events, Mavis passing the earth and Mavis reaching $x = 9.00 \times 10^7$ m as measured by Stanley, occur at different positions in Stanley's frame but at the same position in Mavis's frame. Hence the time interval in Stanley's frame S is Δt, while the time interval in Mavis's frame S' is the proper time Δt_0. As measured

Continued

by Stanley, Mavis moves at $0.600c = 0.600(3.00 \times 10^8 \text{ ms}) = 1.80 \times 10^8 \text{ m/s}$ and travels the 9.00×10^7 m in a time $\Delta t = (9.00 \times 10^7 \text{ m})/(1.80 \times 10^8 \text{ m/s}) = 0.500$ s. From Eq. (37.6), Mavis's timer reads an elapsed time of

$$\Delta t_0 = \Delta t \sqrt{1 - u^2/c^2} = 0.500 \text{ s} \sqrt{1 - (0.600)^2} = 0.400 \text{ s}$$

(b) It is tempting—but wrong—to answer that Stanley's timer reads 0.500 s. We are now considering a *different* pair of events, the starting and the reading of Stanley's timer, that both occur at the same point in Stanley's earth frame S. These two events occur at different positions in Mavis's frame S', so the time interval of 0.400 s that she measures between these events is equal to Δt.

(In her frame, Stanley passes her at time zero and is a distance behind her of $(1.80 \times 10^8 \text{ m/s})(0.400 \text{ s}) = 7.20 \times 10^7$ m at time 0.400 s.) The time on Stanley's timer is now the proper time:

$$\Delta t_0 = \Delta t \sqrt{1 - u^2/c^2} = 0.400 \text{ s} \sqrt{1 - (0.600)^2} = 0.320 \text{ s}$$

EVALUATE: If the difference between 0.500 s and 0.320 s still troubles you, consider the following: Stanley, taking proper account of the transit time of a signal from $x = 9.00 \times 10^7$ m, says that Mavis passed that point and his timer read 0.500 s at the same instant. But Mavis says that those two events occurred at different positions and were *not* simultaneous—she passed the point at the instant his timer read 0.320 s. This example shows the relativity of simultaneity.

The Twin Paradox

Equations (37.6) and (37.8) for time dilation suggest an apparent paradox called the **twin paradox.** Consider identical twin astronauts named Eartha and Astrid. Eartha remains on earth while her twin Astrid takes off on a high-speed trip through the galaxy. Because of time dilation, Eartha observes Astrid's heartbeat and all other life processes proceeding more slowly than her own. Thus to Eartha, Astrid ages more slowly; when Astrid returns to earth she is younger (has aged less) than Eartha.

Now here is the paradox: All inertial frames are equivalent. Can't Astrid make exactly the same arguments to conclude that Eartha is in fact the younger? Then each twin measures the other to be younger when they're back together, and that's a paradox.

To resolve the paradox, we recognize that the twins are *not* identical in all respects. While Eartha remains in an approximately inertial frame at all times, Astrid must *accelerate* with respect to that inertial frame during parts of her trip in order to leave, turn around, and return to earth. Eartha's reference frame is always approximately inertial; Astrid's is often far from inertial. Thus there is a real physical difference between the circumstances of the two twins. Careful analysis shows that Eartha is correct; when Astrid returns, she *is* younger than Eartha.

Test Your Understanding of Section 37.3 Samir (who is standing on the ground) starts his stopwatch at the instant that Maria flies past him in her spaceship at a speed of $0.600c$. At the same instant, Maria starts her stopwatch. (a) As measured in Samir's frame of reference, what is the reading on Maria's stopwatch at the instant that Samir's stopwatch reads 10.0 s? (i) 10.0 s; (ii) less than 10.0 s; (iii) more than 10.0 s. (b) As measured in Maria's frame of reference, what is the reading on Samir's stopwatch at the instant that Maria's stopwatch reads 10.0 s? (i) 10.0 s; (ii) less than 10.0 s; (iii) more than 10.0 s.

37.4 Relativity of Length

Not only does the time interval between two events depend on the observer's frame of reference, but the *distance* between two points may also depend on the observer's frame of reference. The concept of simultaneity is involved. Suppose you want to measure the length of a moving car. One way is to have two assistants make marks on the pavement at the positions of the front and rear bumpers. Then you measure the distance between the marks. But your assistants have to make their marks *at the same time*. If one marks the position of the front bumper at one time and the other marks the position of the rear bumper half a second later, you won't get the car's true length. Since we've learned that simultaneity isn't an absolute concept, we have to proceed with caution.

Act|v
Phys|cs
ONLINE

17.2 Relativity of Length

Lengths Parallel to the Relative Motion

To develop a relationship between lengths that are measured parallel to the direction of motion in various coordinate systems, we consider another thought experiment. We attach a light source to one end of a ruler and a mirror to the other end. The ruler is at rest in reference frame S', and its length in this frame is l_0 (Fig. 37.10a). Then the time Δt_0 required for a light pulse to make the round trip from source to mirror and back is

$$\Delta t_0 = \frac{2l_0}{c} \tag{37.9}$$

This is a proper time interval because departure and return occur at the same point in S'.

In reference frame S the ruler is moving to the right with speed u during this travel of the light pulse (Fig. 37.10b). The length of the ruler in S is l, and the time of travel from source to mirror, as measured in S, is Δt_1. During this interval the ruler, with source and mirror attached, moves a distance $u\,\Delta t_1$. The total length of path d from source to mirror is not l, but rather

$$d = l + u\,\Delta t_1 \tag{37.10}$$

The light pulse travels with speed c, so it is also true that

$$d = c\,\Delta t_1 \tag{37.11}$$

Combining Eqs. (37.10) and (37.11) to eliminate d, we find

$$c\,\Delta t_1 = l + u\,\Delta t_1 \quad \text{or}$$

$$\Delta t_1 = \frac{l}{c-u} \tag{37.12}$$

(Dividing the distance l by $c - u$ does *not* mean that light travels with speed $c - u$, but rather that the distance the pulse travels in S is greater than l.)

In the same way we can show that the time Δt_2 for the return trip from mirror to source is

$$\Delta t_2 = \frac{l}{c+u} \tag{37.13}$$

(a)

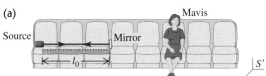

The ruler is stationary in Mavis's frame of reference S'. The light pulse travels a distance l_0 from the light source to the mirror.

37.10 (a) A ruler is at rest in Mavis's frame S'. A light pulse is emitted from a source at one end of the ruler, reflected by a mirror at the other end, and returned to the source position. (b) Motion of the light pulse as measured in Stanley's frame S.

(b)

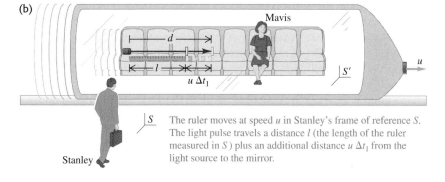

S The ruler moves at speed u in Stanley's frame of reference S. The light pulse travels a distance l (the length of the ruler measured in S) plus an additional distance $u\,\Delta t_1$ from the light source to the mirror.

The *total* time $\Delta t = \Delta t_1 + \Delta t_2$ for the round trip, as measured in S, is

$$\Delta t = \frac{l}{c - u} + \frac{l}{c + u} = \frac{2l}{c(1 - u^2/c^2)} \tag{37.14}$$

We also know that Δt and Δt_0 are related by Eq. (37.6) because Δt_0 is a proper time in S'. Thus EQ. (37.9) for the round-trip time in the rest frame S' of the ruler becomes

$$\Delta t \sqrt{1 - \frac{u^2}{c^2}} = \frac{2l_0}{c} \tag{37.15}$$

Finally, combining Eqs. (37.14) and (37.15) to eliminate Δt and simplifying, we obtain

$$l = l_0 \sqrt{1 - \frac{u^2}{c^2}} = \frac{l_0}{\gamma} \qquad \text{(length contraction)} \tag{37.16}$$

[We have used the quantity $\gamma = 1/\sqrt{1 - u^2/c^2}$ defined in Eq. (37.7).] Thus the length l measured in S, in which the ruler is moving, is *shorter* than the length l_0 measured in its rest frame S'.

CAUTION **Length contraction is real** This is *not* an optical illusion! The ruler really is shorter in reference frame S than it is in S'. ▮

A length measured in the frame in which the body is at rest (the rest frame of the body) is called a **proper length;** thus l_0 is a proper length in S', and the length measured in any other frame moving relative to S' is *less than* l_0. This effect is called **length contraction.**

When u is very small in comparison to c, γ approaches 1. Thus in the limit of small speeds we approach the Newtonian relationship $l = l_0$. This and the corresponding result for time dilation show that Eqs. (37.1), the Galilean coordinate transformation, are usually sufficiently accurate for relative speeds much smaller than c. If u is a reasonable fraction of c, however, the quantity $\sqrt{1 - u^2/c^2}$ can be appreciably less than 1. Then l can be substantially smaller than l_0, and the effects of length contraction can be substantial (Fig. 37.11).

Lengths Perpendicular to the Relative Motion

We have derived Eq. (37.16) for lengths measured in the direction *parallel* to the relative motion of the two frames of reference. Lengths that are measured *perpendicular* to the direction of motion are *not* contracted. To prove this, consider two identical meter sticks. One stick is at rest in frame S and lies along the positive y-axis with one end at O, the origin of S. The other is at rest in frame S' and lies along the positive y'-axis with one end at O', the origin of S'. Frame S' moves in the positive x-direction relative to frame S. Observers Stanley and Mavis, at rest in S and S' respectively, station themselves at the 50-cm mark of their sticks. At the instant the two origins coincide, the two sticks lie along the same line. At this instant, Mavis makes a mark on Stanley's stick at the point that coincides with her own 50-cm mark, and Stanley does the same to Mavis's stick.

Suppose for the sake of argument that Stanley observes Mavis's stick as longer than his own. Then the mark Stanley makes on her stick is *below* its center. In that case, Mavis will think Stanley's stick has become shorter, since half of its length coincides with *less* than half her stick's length. So Mavis observes moving sticks getting shorter and Stanley observes them getting longer. But this implies an asymmetry between the two frames that contradicts the basic postulate of relativity that tells us all inertial frames are equivalent. We conclude that consistency with the postulates of relativity requires that both observers measure the rulers as having the *same* length, even though to each observer one of them is stationary and the other is

37.11 The speed at which electrons traverse the 3-km beam line of the Stanford Linear Accelerator Center is slower than c by less than 1 cm/s. As measured in the reference frame of such an electron, the beam line (which extends from the top to the bottom of this photograph) is only about 15 cm long!

Beam line

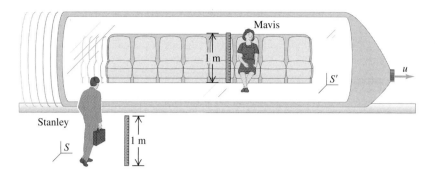

37.12 The meter sticks are perpendicular to the relative velocity. For any value of u, both Stanley and Mavis measure either meter stick to have a length of 1 meter.

moving (Fig. 37.12). So *there is no length contraction perpendicular to the direction of relative motion of the coordinate systems.* We used this result in our derivation of Eq. (37.6) in assuming that the distance d is the same in both frames of reference.

For example, suppose a moving rod of length l_0 makes an angle θ_0 with the direction of relative motion (the x-axis) as measured in its rest frame. Its length component in that frame parallel to the motion, $l_0 \cos\theta_0$, is contracted to $(l_0 \cos\theta_0)/\gamma$. However, its length component perpendicular to the motion, $l_0 \sin\theta_0$, remains the same.

Problem-Solving Strategy 37.2 | **Length Contraction**

IDENTIFY *the relevant concepts:*   The concept of length contraction is used whenever we compare the length of an object as measured by observers in different inertial frames of reference.

SET UP *the problem* using the following steps:
1. Decide what defines the length in question. If the problem statement describes an object such as a ruler, it is just the distance between the ends of the object. If, however, the problem is about a distance between two points with no object between them, it can help to envision a ruler or rod that extends from one point to the other.
2. Determine what the target variable is.

EXECUTE *the solution* as follows:
1. Determine the reference frame in which the object in question is at rest. In this frame, the length of the object is its proper

length l_0. In a second reference frame moving at speed u relative to the first frame, the object has contracted length l.
2. Keep in mind that length contraction occurs only for lengths parallel to the direction of relative motion of the two frames. Any length that is perpendicular to the relative motion is the same in both frames.
3. Use Eq. (37.16) to relate l and l_0, and then solve for the target variable.

EVALUATE *your answer:*   Check that your answers make sense: l is never larger than l_0, and u is never greater than c.

Example 37.4 | **How long is the spaceship?**

A spaceship flies past earth at a speed of $0.990c$. A crew member on board the spaceship measures its length, obtaining the value 400 m. What length do observers measure on earth?

SOLUTION

IDENTIFY: This problem asks us to relate the length of the spaceship—that is, the distance from its nose to its tail—as measured by observers in two different frames of reference: one on board the spaceship and the other on earth.

SET UP: The length in question is along the direction of relative motion (Fig. 37.13), so there will be length contraction as measured in one of the frames of reference. Our target variable is the length measured in the earth frame.

EXECUTE: The 400-m length of the spaceship is the *proper* length l_0 because it is measured in the frame in which the spaceship is

37.13 Measuring the length of a moving spaceship.

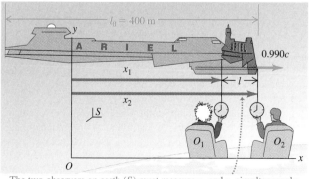

The two observers on earth (S) must measure x_2 and x_1 simultaneously to obtain the correct length $l = x_2 - x_1$ in their frame of reference.

Continued

at rest. We want to find the length l measured by observers on earth. From Eq. (37.16),

$$l = l_0 \sqrt{1 - \frac{u^2}{c^2}} = (400 \text{ m}) \sqrt{1 - (0.990)^2}$$

$$= 56.4 \text{ m}$$

EVALUATE: This answer makes sense: The spaceship is shorter in a frame in which it is in motion than in a frame in which it is at

rest. To measure the length l, two observers with synchronized clocks could measure the positions of the two ends of the spaceship simultaneously in the earth's reference frame, as shown in Fig. 37.13. (These two measurements will *not* appear simultaneous to an observer in the spaceship.)

Example 37.5 How far apart are the observers?

The two observers mentioned in Example 37.4 are 56.4 m apart on the earth. How far apart does the spaceship crew measure them to be?

SOLUTION

IDENTIFY: The two sets of observers are the same as in Example 37.4, but now the distance being measured is the separation between the two earth observers.

SET UP: The distance between the earth observers as measured on earth is a *proper* length, since the two observers are at rest in the earth frame. (Think of a length of pipe 56.4 m long that extends from O_1 to O_2 in Fig. 37.13. This pipe is at rest in the earth frame, so its length is a proper length.) The earth is moving relative to the spaceship at $0.990c$, so the spaceship crew will measure a distance shorter than 56.4 m between the two earth observers. The value that they measure is our target variable.

EXECUTE: With $l_0 = 56.4$ m and $u = 0.990c$, the length l that the crew members measure is

$$l = l_0 \sqrt{1 - \frac{u^2}{c^2}} = (56.4 \text{ m}) \sqrt{1 - (0.990)^2}$$

$$= 7.96 \text{ m}$$

EVALUATE: This answer does *not* say that the crew measures their spaceship to be both 400 m long and 7.96 m long. The observers on earth measure the spaceship to have a contracted length of 56.4 m because they are 56.4 m apart when they measure the positions of the ends at what they measure to be the same instant. (Viewed from the spaceship frame, the observers do not measure those positions simultaneously.) The crew then measures the 56.4 m proper length to be contracted to 7.96 m. The key point is that the measurements made in Example 37.4 (in which the earth observers measure the distance between the ends of the spaceship) are different from those made in this example (in which the spaceship crew measures the distance between the earth observers).

Conceptual Example 37.6 Moving with a muon

As was stated in Example 37.1, a muon has, on average, a proper lifetime of 2.20×10^{-6} s and a dilated lifetime of 15.6×10^{-6} s in a frame in which its speed is $0.990c$. Multiplying constant speed by time to find distance gives $0.990(3.00 \times 10^8 \text{ m/s}) \times (2.20 \times 10^{-6} \text{ s}) = 653$ m and $0.990(3.00 \times 10^8 \text{ m/s}) \times (15.6 \times 10^{-6} \text{ s}) = 4630$ m. Interpret these two distances.

SOLUTION

If an average muon moves at $0.990c$ past observers, they will measure it to be created at one point and then to decay 15.6×10^{-6} s later at another point 4630 m away. For example, this muon could be created level with the top of a mountain and then move straight down to decay at its base 4630 m below.

However, an observer moving with an average muon will say that it traveled only 653 m because it existed for only 2.20×10^{-6} s. To show that this answer is completely consistent,

consider the mountain. The 4630-m distance is its height, a proper length in the direction of motion. Relative to the observer traveling with this muon, the mountain moves up at $0.990c$ with the 4630-m length contracted to

$$l = l_0 \sqrt{1 - \frac{u^2}{c^2}} = (4630 \text{ m}) \sqrt{1 - (0.990)^2}$$

$$= 653 \text{ m}$$

Thus we see that length contraction is consistent with time dilation. The same is true for an electron moving at speed u in a linear accelerator (see Fig. 37.11). Compared to the values measured by a physicist standing alongside the accelerator, an observer riding along with the electron would measure the accelerator's length and the time to travel that length to both be shorter by a factor of $\sqrt{1 - u^2/c^2}$.

How an Object Moving Near c Would Appear

Let's think a little about the visual appearance of a moving three-dimensional body. If we could see the positions of all points of the body simultaneously, it would appear to shrink only in the direction of motion. But we *don't* see all the points simultaneously; light from points farther from us takes longer to reach us than does light from points near to us, so we see the farther points at the positions they had at earlier times.

Suppose we have a rectangular rod with its faces parallel to the coordinate planes. When we look end-on at the center of the closest face of such a rod at rest, we see only that face. (See the center rod in computer-generated Fig. 37.14a). But when that rod is moving past us toward the right at an appreciable fraction of the speed of light, we may also see its left side because of the earlier-time effect just described. That is, we can see some points that we couldn't see when the rod was at rest because the rod moves out of the way of the light rays from those points to us. Conversely, some light that can get to us when the rod is at rest is blocked by the moving rod. Because of all this, the rods in Figs. 37.14b and 37.14c appear rotated and distorted.

Test Your Understanding of Section 37.4   A miniature spaceship is flying past you, moving horizontally at a substantial fraction of the speed of light. At a certain instant, you observe that the nose and tail of the spaceship align exactly with the two ends of a meter stick that you hold in your hands. Rank the following distances in order from longest to shortest: (i) the proper length of the meter stick; (ii) the proper length of the spaceship; (iii) the length of the spaceship measured in your frame of reference; (iv) the length of the meter stick measured in the spaceship's frame of reference.

37.5 The Lorentz Transformations

In Section 37.1 we discussed the Galilean coordinate transformation equations, Eqs. (37.1). They relate the coordinates (x, y, z) of a point in frame of reference S to the coordinates (x', y', z') of the point in a second frame S'. The second frame moves with constant speed u relative to S in the positive direction along the common x-x'-axis. This transformation also assumes that the time scale is the same in the two frames of reference, as expressed by the additional relationship $t = t'$. This Galilean transformation, as we have seen, is valid only in the limit when u approaches zero. We are now ready to derive more general transformations that are consistent with the principle of relativity. The more general relationships are called the **Lorentz transformations.**

The Lorentz Coordinate Transformation

Our first question is this: When an event occurs at point (x, y, z) at time t, as observed in a frame of reference S, what are the coordinates (x', y', z') and time t' of the event as observed in a second frame S' moving relative to S with constant speed u in the $+x$-direction?

To derive the coordinate transformation, we refer to Fig. 37.15 (next page), which is the same as Fig. 37.3. As before, we assume that the origins coincide at the initial time $t = 0 = t'$. Then in S the distance from O to O' at time t is still ut. The coordinate x' is a *proper length* in S', so in S it is contracted by the factor $1/\gamma = \sqrt{1 - u^2/c^2}$, as in Eq. (37.16). Thus the distance x from O to P, as seen in S, is not simply $x = ut + x'$, as in the Galilean coordinate transformation, but

$$x = ut + x'\sqrt{1 - \frac{u^2}{c^2}} \qquad (37.17)$$

37.14 Computer simulation of the appearance of an array of 25 rods with square cross section. The center rod is viewed end-on. The simulation ignores color changes in the array caused by the Doppler effect (see Section 37.6).

(a) Array at rest

(b) Array moving to the right at 0.2c

(c) Array moving to the right at 0.9c

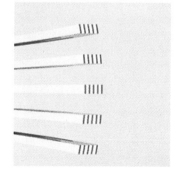

37.15 As measured in frame of reference S, x' is contracted to x'/γ, so $x = ut + x'/\gamma$ and $x' = \gamma(x - ut)$.

Frame S' moves relative to frame S with constant velocity u along the common x-x'-axis.

Origins O and O' coincide at time $t = 0 = t'$.

The Lorentz coordinate transformation relates the spacetime coordinates of an event as measured in the two frames: (x, y, z, t) in frame S and (x', y', z', t') in frame S'.

Solving this equation for x', we obtain

$$x' = \frac{x - ut}{\sqrt{1 - u^2/c^2}} \tag{37.18}$$

Equation (37.18) is part of the Lorentz coordinate transformation; another part is the equation giving t' in terms of x and t. To obtain this, we note that the principle of relativity requires that the *form* of the transformation from S to S' be identical to that from S' to S. The only difference is a change in the sign of the relative velocity component u. Thus from Eq. (37.17) it must be true that

$$x' = -ut' + x\sqrt{1 - \frac{u^2}{c^2}} \tag{37.19}$$

We now equate Eqs. (37.18) and (37.19) to eliminate x'. This gives us an equation for t' in terms of x and t. We leave the algebraic details for you to work out; the result is

$$t' = \frac{t - ux/c^2}{\sqrt{1 - u^2/c^2}} \tag{37.20}$$

As we discussed previously, lengths perpendicular to the direction of relative motion are not affected by the motion, so $y' = y$ and $z' = z$.

Collecting all these transformation equations, we have

$$
\begin{aligned}
x' &= \frac{x - ut}{\sqrt{1 - u^2/c^2}} = \gamma(x - ut) \\
y' &= y \\
z' &= z \\
t' &= \frac{t - ux/c^2}{\sqrt{1 - u^2/c^2}} = \gamma(t - ux/c^2)
\end{aligned}
\qquad
\begin{aligned}
&\text{(Lorentz coordinate} \\
&\text{transformation)}
\end{aligned}
\tag{37.21}
$$

These equations are the *Lorentz coordinate transformation,* the relativistic generalization of the Galilean coordinate transformation, Eqs. (37.1) and $t = t'$. For values of u that approach zero, the radicals in the denominators and γ approach 1, and the ux/c^2 term approaches zero. In this limit, Eqs. (37.21) become identical to Eqs. (37.1) along with $t = t'$. In general, though, both the coordinates and time of an event in one frame depend on its coordinates and time in another frame. *Space and time have become intertwined; we can no longer say that length and time have absolute meanings independent of the frame of reference.* For this reason, we refer to time and the three dimensions of space collectively as a four-dimensional entity called **spacetime,** and we call (x, y, z, t) together the **spacetime coordinates** of an event.

The Lorentz Velocity Transformation

We can use Eqs. (37.21) to derive the relativistic generalization of the Galilean velocity transformation, Eq. (37.2). We consider only one-dimensional motion along the x-axis and use the term "velocity" as being short for the "x-component of the velocity." Suppose that in a time dt a particle moves a distance dx, as measured in frame S. We obtain the corresponding distance dx' and time dt' in S' by taking differentials of Eqs. (37.21):

$$dx' = \gamma(dx - u\,dt)$$
$$dt' = \gamma(dt - u\,dx/c^2)$$

We divide the first equation by the second and then divide the numerator and denominator of the result by dt to obtain

$$\frac{dx'}{dt'} = \frac{\dfrac{dx}{dt} - u}{1 - \dfrac{u}{c^2}\dfrac{dx}{dt}}$$

Now dx/dt is the velocity v_x in S, and dx'/dt' is the velocity v_x' in S', so we finally obtain the relativistic generalization

$$v_x' = \frac{v_x - u}{1 - uv_x/c^2} \qquad \text{(Lorentz velocity transformation)} \qquad (37.22)$$

When u and v_x are much smaller than c, the denominator in Eq. (37.22) approaches 1, and we approach the nonrelativistic result $v_x' = v_x - u$. The opposite extreme is the case $v_x = c$; then we find

$$v_x' = \frac{c - u}{1 - uc/c^2} = \frac{c(1 - u/c)}{1 - u/c} = c$$

This says that anything moving with velocity $v_x = c$ measured in S also has velocity $v_x' = c$ measured in S', despite the relative motion of the two frames. So Eq. (37.22) is consistent with Einstein's postulate that the speed of light in vacuum is the same in all inertial frames of reference.

The principle of relativity tells us there is no fundamental distinction between the two frames S and S'. Thus the expression for v_x in terms of v_x' must have the same form as Eq. (37.22), with v_x changed to v_x', and vice versa, and the sign of u reversed. Carrying out these operations with Eq. (37.22), we find

$$v_x = \frac{v_x' + u}{1 + uv_x'/c^2} \qquad \text{(Lorentz velocity transformation)} \qquad (37.23)$$

This can also be obtained algebraically by solving Eq. (37.22) for v_x. Both Eqs. (37.22) and (37.23) are *Lorentz velocity transformations* for one-dimensional motion.

CAUTION **Use the correct reference frame coordinates** Keep in mind that the Lorentz transformation equations given by Eqs. (37.21), (37.22), and (37.23) assume that frame S' is moving in the positive x-direction with velocity u relative to frame S. You should always set up your coordinate system to follow this convention. ▮

When u is less than c, the Lorentz velocity transformations show us that a body moving with a speed less than c in one frame of reference always has a speed less than *c* in *every other* frame of reference. This is one reason for concluding that no material body may travel with a speed equal to or greater than that of light in vacuum, relative to *any* inertial frame of reference. The relativistic generalizations of energy and momentum, which we will explore later, give further support to this hypothesis.

Problem-Solving Strategy 37.3   Lorentz Transformations

IDENTIFY *the relevant concepts:*   The Lorentz *coordinate* transformation tells you how to relate the spacetime coordinates of an event in one inertial frame of reference to the spacetime coordinates of the same event in a second inertial frame. The Lorentz *velocity* transformation relates the velocity of an object in one inertial frame to its velocity in a second inertial frame.

SET UP *the problem* using the following steps:
1. Determine what the target variable is.
2. Define the two inertial frames *S* and *S'*. Remember that *S'* moves relative to *S* at a constant velocity *u* in the +*x*-direction.
3. If the coordinate transformation equations are needed, make a list of spacetime coordinates in the two frames, such as x_1, x_1', t_1, t_1', and so on. Label carefully which of these you know and which you don't.
4. In velocity-transformation problems, clearly identify the velocities *u* (the relative velocity of the two frames of reference), v_x (the velocity of the object relative to *S*), and v_x' (the velocity of the object relative to *S'*).

EXECUTE *the solution* as follows:
1. In a coordinate-transformation problem, use Eqs. (37.21) to solve for the spacetime coordinates of the event as measured in *S'* in terms of the corresponding values in *S*. (If you need to solve for the spacetime coordinates in *S* in terms of the corresponding values in *S'*, you can easily convert the expressions in Eqs. (37.21): Replace all of the primed quantities with unprimed ones, and vice versa, and replace *u* with −*u*.)
2. In a velocity-transformation problem, use either Eq. (37.22) or Eq. (37.23), as appropriate, to solve for the target variable.

EVALUATE *your answer:*   Don't be discouraged if some of your results don't seem to make sense or if they disagree with "common sense." It takes time to develop intuition about relativity; you'll gain it with experience. (One result that would definitely be in error is a speed greater than *c*.)

Example 37.7   Was it received before it was sent?

Winning an interstellar race, Mavis pilots her spaceship across a finish line in space at a speed of 0.600*c* relative to that line. A "hooray" message is sent from the back of her ship (event 2) at the instant (in her frame of reference) that the front of her ship crosses the line (event 1). She measures the length of her ship to be 300 m. Stanley is at the finish line and is at rest relative to it. When and where does he measure events 1 and 2 to occur?

SOLUTION

IDENTIFY: This example involves the Lorentz coordinate transformation.

SET UP: Our derivation of this transformation assumes that the origins of frames *S* and *S'* coincide at *t* = 0 = *t'*. Thus for simplicity we fix the origin of *S* at the finish line and the origin of *S'* at the front of the spaceship so that Stanley and Mavis measure event 1 to be at *x* = 0 = *x'* and *t* = 0 = *t'*.

Mavis in *S'* measures her spaceship to be 300 m long, so she has the "hooray" sent from 300 m behind her spaceship's front at the instant she measures the front to cross the finish line. That is, she measures event 2 at *x'* = −300 m and *t'* = 0.

Our target variables are the coordinate *x* and time *t* of event 2 that Stanley measures in *S*.

EXECUTE: To most easily solve for the target variables, we modify the first and last of Eqs. (37.21) to give *x* and *t* as functions of *x'* and *t'*. We do so by using the principle of relativity in the same way that we obtained Eq. (37.23) from Eq. (37.22). We remove the

primes from *x'* and *t'*, add primes to *x* and *t*, and replace each *u* with −*u*. The results are

$$x = \gamma(x' + ut') \quad \text{and} \quad t = \gamma(t' + ux'/c^2)$$

From Eq. (37.7), $\gamma = 1.25$ for $u = 0.600c = 1.80 \times 10^8$ m/s. We also substitute $x' = -300$ m, $t' = 0$, $c = 3.00 \times 10^8$ m/s, and $u = 1.80 \times 10^8$ m/s in the equations for *x* and *t* to find $x = -375$ m at $t = -7.50 \times 10^{-7}$ s = −0.750 μs for event 2.

EVALUATE: Mavis says that the events are simultaneous, but Stanley disagrees. In fact, he says that the "hooray" was sent *before* Mavis crossed the finish line. This does not mean that the effect preceded the cause. The fastest that Mavis can send a signal the length of her ship is 300 m/(3.00 × 10⁸ m/s) = 1.00 μs. She cannot send a signal from the front at the instant it crosses the finish line that would cause a "hooray" to be broadcast from the back at the same instant. She would have to send that signal from the front at least 1.00 μs before then, so she had to slightly anticipate her success.

Note that relativity *is* consistent. In his frame, Stanley measures Mavis's ship to be $l_0/\gamma = 300$ m/1.25 = 240 m long with its back at *x* = −375 m at *t* = −0.750 μs = −7.50 × 10⁻⁷ s when the "hooray" is sent. At that instant he thus measures the front of her 240-m-long ship to be a distance of (375 − 240) m = 135 m from the finish line. However, since (1.80 × 10⁸ m/s)(7.50 × 10⁻⁷ s) = 135 m, the front does cross the line at *t* = 0.

<table>
<tr><td>Example 37.8</td><td>**Relative velocities**</td></tr>
</table>

(a) A spaceship moving away from the earth with speed $0.900c$ fires a robot space probe in the same direction as its motion, with speed $0.700c$ relative to the spaceship. What is the probe's velocity relative to the earth? (b) A scoutship tries to catch up with the spaceship by traveling at $0.950c$ relative to the earth. What is the velocity of the scoutship relative to the spaceship?

SOLUTION

IDENTIFY: This example uses the Lorentz velocity transformation.

SET UP: Let the earth's frame of reference be S, and let the spaceship's frame of reference be S' (Fig. 37.16). The relative velocity of the two frames is $u = 0.700c$. The target variable in part (a) is

37.16 The spaceship, robot space probe, and scoutship.

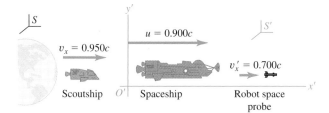

the velocity of the probe relative to S; the target variable in part (b) is the velocity of the scoutship relative to S'.

EXECUTE: (a) We are given the velocity of the probe relative to the spaceship, $v'_x = 0.700c$. We use Eq. (37.23) to determine its velocity v_x relative to the earth:

$$v_x = \frac{v'_x + u}{1 + uv'_x/c^2} = \frac{0.700c + 0.900c}{1 + (0.900c)(0.700c)/c^2} = 0.982c$$

(b) We are given the velocity of the scoutship relative to the earth, $v_x = 0.950c$. We use Eq. (37.22) to determine its velocity v'_x relative to the spaceship:

$$v'_x = \frac{v_x - u}{1 - uv_x/c^2} = \frac{0.950c - 0.900c}{1 - (0.900c)(0.950c)/c^2} = 0.345c$$

EVALUATE: It's instructive to compare our results to what we would have obtained had we used the Galilean velocity transformation formula, Eq. (37.2). In part (a) we would have found the probe's velocity relative to the earth to be $v_x = v'_x + u = 0.700c + 0.900c = 1.600c$. This value is greater than the speed of light and so must be incorrect. In part (b) we would have found the scoutship's velocity relative to the spaceship to be $v'_x = v_x - u = 0.950c - 0.900c = 0.050c$; the relativistically correct value, $v'_x = 0.345c$, is almost seven times greater than the incorrect Galilean value.

Test Your Understanding of Section 37.5 (a) In frame S events P_1 and P_2 occur at the same x-, y-, and z-coordinates, but event P_1 occurs before event P_2. In frame S', which event occurs first? (b) In frame S events P_3 and P_4 occur at the same time t and the same y- and z-coordinates, but event P_3 occurs at a less positive x-coordinate than event P_4. In frame S', which event occurs first?

*37.6 The Doppler Effect for Electromagnetic Waves

An additional important consequence of relativistic kinematics is the Doppler effect for electromagnetic waves. In our previous discussion of the Doppler effect (see Section 16.8) we quoted without proof the formula, Eq. (16.30), for the frequency shift that results from motion of a source of electromagnetic waves relative to an observer. We can now derive that result.

Here's a statement of the problem. A source of light is moving with constant speed u toward Stanley, who is stationary in an inertial frame (Fig. 37.17). As measured in its rest frame, the source emits light waves with frequency f_0 and period $T_0 = 1/f_0$. What is the frequency f of these waves as received by Stanley?

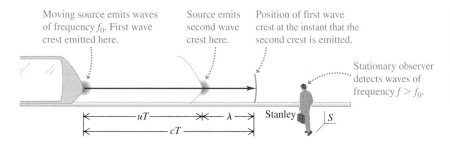

37.17 The Doppler effect for light. A light source moving at speed u relative to Stanley emits a wave crest, then travels a distance uT toward an observer and emits the next crest. In Stanley's reference frame S, the second crest is a distance λ behind the first crest.

Let T be the time interval between *emission* of successive wave crests as observed in Stanley's reference frame. Note that this is *not* the interval between the *arrival* of successive crests at his position, because the crests are emitted at different points in Stanley's frame. In measuring only the frequency f he receives, he does not take into account the difference in transit times for successive crests. Therefore the frequency he receives is *not* $1/T$. What is the equation for f?

During a time T the crests ahead of the source move a distance cT, and the source moves a shorter distance uT in the same direction. The distance λ between successive crests—that is, the wavelength—is thus $\lambda = (c - u)T$, as measured in Stanley's frame. The frequency that he measures is c/λ. Therefore

$$f = \frac{c}{(c - u)T} \tag{37.24}$$

So far we have followed a pattern similar to that for the Doppler effect for sound from a moving source (see Section 16.8). In that discussion our next step was to equate T to the time T_0 between emissions of successive wave crests by the source. However, due to time dilation it is *not* relativistically correct to equate T to T_0. The time T_0 is measured in the rest frame of the source, so it is a proper time. From Eq. (37.6), T_0 and T are related by

$$T = \frac{T_0}{\sqrt{1 - u^2/c^2}} = \frac{cT_0}{\sqrt{c^2 - u^2}}$$

or, since $T_0 = 1/f_0$,

$$\frac{1}{T} = \frac{\sqrt{c^2 - u^2}}{cT_0} = \frac{\sqrt{c^2 - u^2}}{c}f_0$$

Remember, $1/T$ is not equal to f. We must substitute this expression for $1/T$ into Eq. 37.24 to find f:

$$f = \frac{c}{c - u}\frac{\sqrt{c^2 - u^2}}{c}f_0$$

Using $c^2 - u^2 = (c - u)(c + u)$ gives

$$f = \sqrt{\frac{c + u}{c - u}}f_0 \qquad \begin{matrix}\text{(Doppler effect, electromagnetic} \\ \text{waves, source approaching observer)}\end{matrix} \tag{37.25}$$

37.18 This handheld radar gun emits a radio beam of frequency f_0, which in the frame of reference of an approaching car has a higher frequency f given by Eq. (37.25). The reflected beam also has frequency f in the car's frame, but has an even higher frequency f' in the police officer's frame. The radar gun calculates the car's speed by comparing the frequencies of the emitted beam and the doubly Doppler-shifted reflected beam. (Compare Example 16.19 in Section 16.8.)

This shows that when the source moves *toward* the observer, the observed frequency f is *greater* than the emitted frequency f_0. The difference $f - f_0 = \Delta f$ is called the Doppler frequency shift. When u/c is much smaller than 1, the fractional shift $\Delta f/f$ is also small and is approximately equal to u/c:

$$\frac{\Delta f}{f} = \frac{u}{c}$$

When the source moves *away from* the observer, we change the sign of u in Eq. 37.25 to get

$$f = \sqrt{\frac{c - u}{c + u}}f_0 \qquad \begin{matrix}\text{(Doppler effect, electromagnetic waves,} \\ \text{source moving away from observer)}\end{matrix} \tag{37.26}$$

This agrees with Eq. (16.30), which we quoted previously, with minor notation changes.

With light, unlike sound, there is no distinction between motion of source and motion of observer; only the *relative* velocity of the two is significant. The last four paragraphs of Section 16.8 discuss several practical applications of the Doppler effect with light and other electromagnetic radiation; we suggest you review those paragraphs now. Figure 37.18 shows one common application.

Example 37.9 **A jet from a black hole**

A number of galaxies have supermassive black holes at their centers (see Section 12.8). As material swirls around such a black hole, it is heated, becomes ionized, and generates strong magnetic fields. The resulting magnetic forces steer some of the material into high-speed jets that blast out of the galaxy and into intergalactic space (Figure 37.19). The blue light we observe from the jet in Fig. 37.19 has a frequency of 6.66×10^{14} Hz, but in the frame of reference of the jet material the light has a frequency of 5.55×10^{13} Hz (in the infrared region of the electro-

magnetic spectrum). At what speed is the jet material moving toward us?

SOLUTION

IDENTIFY: This problem involves the Doppler effect for electromagnetic waves.

SET UP: The frequency we observe is $f = 6.66 \times 10^{14}$ Hz, and the frequency in the frame of the source is $f_0 = 5.55 \times 10^{13}$ Hz. Since $f > f_0$, the source is approaching us and therefore we use Eq. (37.25) to find the target variable u.

EXECUTE: We need to solve Eq. (37.25) for u. That takes a little algebra; we'll leave it as an exercise for you to show that the result is

$$u = \frac{(f/f_0)^2 - 1}{(f/f_0) + 1} c$$

We have $f/f_0 = (6.66 \times 10^{14} \text{ Hz})/(5.55 \times 10^{13} \text{ Hz}) = 12.0$, so we find

$$u = \frac{(12.0)^2 - 1}{(12.0)^2 + 1} c = 0.986c$$

EVALUATE: Because the frequency shift is quite substantial, it would have been erroneous to use the approximate expression $\Delta f/f = u/c$. Had you tried to do so, you would have found $u = c \, \Delta f/f_0 = c(6.66 \times 10^{14} \text{ Hz} - 5.55 \times 10^{13} \text{ Hz})/(5.55 \times 10^{13} \text{ Hz}) = 11.0c$. This result cannot be correct because the jet material cannot travel faster than light.

37.19 This image shows a fast-moving jet 5000 light-years in length emanating from the center of the galaxy M87. The light from the jet is emitted by fast-moving electrons spiraling around magnetic field lines (see Fig. 27.16).

37.7 Relativistic Momentum

Newton's laws of motion have the same form in all inertial frames of reference. When we use transformations to change from one inertial frame to another, the laws should be *invariant* (unchanging). But we have just learned that the principle of relativity forces us to replace the Galilean transformations with the more general Lorentz transformations. As we will see, this requires corresponding generalizations in the laws of motion and the definitions of momentum and energy.

The principle of conservation of momentum states that *when two bodies interact, the total momentum is constant,* provided that the net external force acting on the bodies in an inertial reference frame is zero (for example, if they form an isolated system, interacting only with each other). If conservation of momentum is a valid physical law, it must be valid in *all* inertial frames of reference. Now, here's the problem: Suppose we look at a collision in one inertial coordinate system S and find that momentum is conserved. Then we use the Lorentz transformation to obtain the velocities in a second inertial system S'. We find that if we use the Newtonian definition of momentum $(\vec{p} = m\vec{v})$, momentum is *not* conserved in the second system! If we are convinced that the principle of relativity and the Lorentz transformation are correct, the only way to save momentum conservation is to generalize the *definition* of momentum.

We won't derive the correct relativistic generalization of momentum, but here is the result. Suppose we measure the mass of a particle to be m when it is at rest relative to us: We often call m the **rest mass.** We will use the term

37.20 Graph of the magnitude of the momentum of a particle of rest mass m as a function of speed v. Also shown is the Newtonian prediction, which gives correct results only at speeds much less than c.

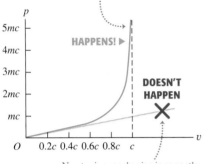

Relativistic momentum becomes infinite as v approaches c.

HAPPENS! ▶

DOESN'T HAPPEN ✗

Newtonian mechanics incorrectly predicts that momentum becomes infinite only if v becomes infinite.

material particle for a particle that has a nonzero rest mass. When such a particle has a velocity $\vec{v}$, its **relativistic momentum** $\vec{p}$ is

$$\vec{p} = \frac{m\vec{v}}{\sqrt{1 - v^2/c^2}} \qquad \text{(relativistic momentum)} \qquad (37.27)$$

When the particle's speed v is much less than c, this is approximately equal to the Newtonian expression $\vec{p} = m\vec{v}$, but in general the momentum is greater in magnitude than mv (Figure 37.20). In fact, as v approaches c, the momentum approaches infinity.

Relativity, Newton's Second Law, and Relativistic Mass

What about the relativistic generalization of Newton's second law? In Newtonian mechanics the most general form of the second law is

$$\vec{F} = \frac{d\vec{p}}{dt} \qquad (37.28)$$

That is, the net force $\vec{F}$ on a particle equals the time rate of change of its momentum. Experiments show that this result is still valid in relativistic mechanics, provided that we use the relativistic momentum given by Eq. 37.27. That is, the relativistically correct generalization of Newton's second law is

$$\vec{F} = \frac{d}{dt} \frac{m\vec{v}}{\sqrt{1 - v^2/c^2}} \qquad (37.29)$$

Because momentum is no longer directly proportional to velocity, the rate of change of momentum is no longer directly proportional to the acceleration. As a result, *constant force does not cause constant acceleration.* For example, when the net force and the velocity are both along the x-axis, Eq. 37.29 gives

$$F = \frac{m}{(1 - v^2/c^2)^{3/2}} a \qquad (\vec{F} \text{ and } \vec{v} \text{ along the same line}) \qquad (37.30)$$

where a is the acceleration, also along the x-axis. Solving Eq. 37.30 for the acceleration a gives

$$a = \frac{F}{m} \left(1 - \frac{v^2}{c^2}\right)^{3/2}$$

We see that as a particle's speed increases, the acceleration caused by a given force continuously *decreases.* As the speed approaches c, the acceleration approaches zero, no matter how great a force is applied. Thus it is impossible to accelerate a particle with nonzero rest mass to a speed equal to or greater than c. We again see that the speed of light in vacuum represents an ultimate speed limit.

Equation (37.27) for relativistic momentum is sometimes interpreted to mean that a rapidly moving particle undergoes an increase in mass. If the mass at zero velocity (the rest mass) is denoted by m, then the "relativistic mass" m_{rel} is given by

$$m_{rel} = \frac{m}{\sqrt{1 - v^2/c^2}}$$

Indeed, when we consider the motion of a system of particles (such as rapidly moving ideal-gas molecules in a stationary container), the total rest mass of the system is the sum of the relativistic masses of the particles, not the sum of their rest masses.

However, if blindly applied, the concept of relativistic mass has its pitfalls. As Eq. (37.29) shows, the relativistic generalization of Newton's second law is *not* $\vec{F} = m_{rel}\vec{a}$, and we will show in Section 37.8 that the relativistic kinetic energy of a particle is *not* $K = \frac{1}{2}m_{rel}v^2$. The use of relativistic mass has its supporters and detractors, some quite strong in their opinions. We will mostly deal with individual particles, so we will sidestep the controversy and use Eq. (37.27) as the generalized definition of momentum with m as a constant for each particle, independent of its state of motion.

We will use the abbreviation

$$\gamma = \frac{1}{\sqrt{1 - v^2/c^2}}$$

We used this abbreviation in Section 37.3 with v replaced by u, the relative speed of two coordinate systems. Here v is the speed of a particle in a particular coordinate system—that is, the speed of the particle's *rest frame* with respect to that system. In terms of γ, Eqs. (37.27) and (37.30) become

$$\vec{p} = \gamma m\vec{v} \qquad \text{(relativistic momentum)} \qquad (37.31)$$

$$F = \gamma^3 ma \qquad (\vec{F} \text{ and } \vec{v} \text{ along the same line}) \qquad (37.32)$$

In linear accelerators (used in medicine as well as nuclear and elementary-particle physics; see Fig. 37.11) the net force $\vec{F}$ and the velocity $\vec{v}$ of the accelerated particle are along the same straight line. But for much of the path in most *circular* accelerators the particle moves in uniform circular motion at constant speed v. Then the net force and velocity are perpendicular, so the force can do no work on the particle and the kinetic energy and speed remain constant. Thus the denominator in Eq. (37.29) is constant, and we obtain

$$F = \frac{m}{(1 - v^2/c^2)^{1/2}}a = \gamma ma \qquad (\vec{F} \text{ and } \vec{v} \text{ perpendicular}) \qquad (37.33)$$

Recall from Section 3.4 that if the particle moves in a circle, the net force and acceleration are directed inward along the radius r, and $a = v^2/r$.

What about the general case in which $\vec{F}$ and $\vec{v}$ are neither along the same line nor perpendicular? Then we can resolve the net force $\vec{F}$ at any instant into components parallel to and perpendicular to $\vec{v}$. The resulting acceleration will have corresponding components obtained from Eqs. (37.32) and (37.33). Because of the different γ^3 and γ factors, the acceleration components will not be proportional to the net force components. That is, *unless the net force on a relativistic particle is either along the same line as the particle's velocity or perpendicular to it, the net force and acceleration vectors are not parallel.*

Example 37.10   Relativistic dynamics of an electron

An electron (rest mass 9.11×10^{-31} kg, charge -1.60×10^{-19} C) is moving opposite to an electric field of magnitude $E = 5.00 \times 10^5$ N/C. All other forces are negligible in comparison to the electric field force. (a) Find the magnitudes of momentum and of acceleration at the instants when $v = 0.010c$, $0.90c$, and $0.99c$. (b) Find the corresponding accelerations if a net force of the same magnitude is perpendicular to the velocity.

SOLUTION

IDENTIFY: In addition to the expressions from this section for relativistic momentum and acceleration, we need the relationship between electric force and electric field from Chapter 21.

SET UP: In part (a) we use Eq. 37.31 to determine the magnitude of momentum and Eq. 37.32 to determine the magnitude of accel-

eration due to a force along the same line as the velocity. In part (b) the force is perpendicular to the velocity, so we use Eq. 37.33 to determine the magnitude of acceleration.

EXECUTE: (a) To find both the magnitude of momentum and the magnitude of acceleration, we need the values of $\gamma = \sqrt{1 - v^2/c^2}$ for each of the three speeds. We find $\gamma = 1.00$, 2.29, and 7.09. The values of the momentum magnitude p are

$p_1 = \gamma_1 m v_1$

$\quad = (1.00)(9.11 \times 10^{-31} \text{ kg})(0.010)(3.00 \times 10^8 \text{m/s})$

$\quad = 2.7 \times 10^{-24} \text{ kg} \cdot \text{m/s at } v_1 = 0.010c$

$p_2 = (2.29)(9.11 \times 10^{-31} \text{ kg})(0.90)(3.00 \times 10^8 \text{ m/s})$

$\quad = 5.6 \times 10^{-22} \text{ kg} \cdot \text{m/s at } v_2 = 0.90c$

Continued

$p_3 = (7.09)(9.11 \times 10^{-31} \text{ kg})(0.99)(3.00 \times 10^8 \text{ m/s})$

$\quad = 1.9 \times 10^{-21} \text{ kg} \cdot \text{m/s at } v_3 = 0.99c$

From Chapter 21, the magnitude of the force on the electron is

$F = |q|E = (1.60 \times 10^{-19} \text{ C})(5.00 \times 10^5 \text{ N/C})$

$\quad = 8.00 \times 10^{-14} \text{ N}$

From Eq. (37.32), $a = F/\gamma^3 m$. When $v = 0.010c$ and $\gamma = 1.00$,

$$a_1 = \frac{8.00 \times 10^{-14} \text{ N}}{(1.00)^3(9.11 \times 10^{-31} \text{ kg})} = 8.8 \times 10^{16} \text{ m/s}^2$$

The accelerations at the two higher speeds are smaller by factors of γ^3:

$$a_2 = 7.3 \times 10^{15} \text{ m/s}^2 \qquad a_3 = 2.5 \times 10^{14} \text{ m/s}^2$$

These last two accelerations are only 8.3% and 0.28%, respectively, of the values predicted by nonrelativistic mechanics.

(b) From Eq. (37.33), $a = F/\gamma m$ if $\vec{F}$ and $\vec{v}$ are perpendicular. When $v = 0.010c$ and $\gamma = 1.00$,

$$a_1 = \frac{8.00 \times 10^{-14} \text{ N}}{(1.00)(9.11 \times 10^{-31} \text{ kg})} = 8.8 \times 10^{16} \text{ m/s}^2$$

The accelerations at the two higher speeds are smaller by a factor of γ:

$$a_2 = 3.8 \times 10^{16} \text{ m/s}^2 \qquad a_3 = 1.2 \times 10^{16} \text{ m/s}^2$$

These accelerations are larger than the corresponding ones in part (a) by factors of γ^2.

EVALUATE: Our results in part (a) show that at higher speeds, the relativistic values of momentum differ more and more from the nonrelativistic values computed using $p = mv$. Note that the momentum at $0.99c$ is more than three times as great as at $0.90c$ because of the increase in the factor γ.

Our results also show that the acceleration drops off very quickly as v approaches c. At the Stanford Linear Accelerator Center, an essentially constant electric force is used to accelerate electrons to a speed only slightly less than c. If the acceleration were constant as predicted by Newtonian mechanics, this speed would be attained after the electrons had traveled a mere 1.5 cm. In fact, because of the decrease of acceleration with speed, a path length of 3 km is needed.

Test Your Understanding of Section 37.7   According to relativistic mechanics, when you double the speed of a particle, the magnitude of its momentum increases by (i) a factor of 2; (ii) a factor greater than 2; (iii) a factor between 1 and 2 that depends on the mass of the particle.

∎

37.8 Relativistic Work and Energy

When we developed the relationship between work and kinetic energy in Chapter 6, we used Newton's laws of motion. When we generalize these laws according to the principle of relativity, we need a corresponding generalization of the equation for kinetic energy.

Relativistic Kinetic Energy

We use the work–energy theorem, beginning with the definition of work. When the net force and displacement are in the same direction, the work done by that force is $W = \int F \, dx$. We substitute the expression for F from Eq. (37.30), the applicable relativistic version of Newton's second law. In moving a particle of rest mass m from point x_1 to point x_2,

$$W = \int_{x_1}^{x_2} F \, dx = \int_{x_1}^{x_2} \frac{ma \, dx}{(1 - v^2/c^2)^{3/2}} \tag{37.34}$$

To derive the generalized expression for kinetic energy K as a function of speed v, we would like to convert this to an integral on v. To do this, first remember that the kinetic energy of a particle equals the net work done on it in moving it from rest to the speed v: $K = W$. Thus we let the speeds be zero at point x_1 and v at point x_2. So as not to confuse the variable of integration with the final speed, we change v to v_x in Eq. 37.34. That is, v_x is the varying x-component of the velocity of the particle as the net force accelerates it from rest to a speed v. We also realize that dx and dv_x are the infinitesimal changes in x and v_x, respectively, in the time interval dt. Because $v_x = dx/dt$ and $a = dv_x/dt$, we can rewrite $a \, dx$ in Eq. (37.34) as

$$a \, dx = \frac{dv_x}{dt} dx = dx \frac{dv_x}{dt} = \frac{dx}{dt} dv_x = v_x dv_x$$

Making these substitutions gives us

$$K = W = \int_0^v \frac{mv_x dv_x}{(1 - v_x^2/c^2)^{3/2}} \qquad (37.35)$$

We can evaluate this integral by a simple change of variable; the final result is

$$K = \frac{mc^2}{\sqrt{1 - v^2/c^2}} - mc^2 = (\gamma - 1)mc^2 \qquad \begin{array}{l}\text{(relativistic kinetic} \\ \text{energy)}\end{array} \qquad (37.36)$$

As v approaches c, the kinetic energy approaches infinity. If Eq. 37.36 is correct, it must also approach the Newtonian expression $K = \frac{1}{2}mv^2$ when v is much smaller than c (Fig. 37.21). To verify this, we expand the radical, using the binomial theorem in the form

$$(1 + x)^n = 1 + nx + n(n - 1)x^2/2 + \cdots$$

In our case, $n = -\frac{1}{2}$ and $x = -v^2/c^2$, and we get

$$\gamma = \left(1 - \frac{v^2}{c^2}\right)^{-1/2} = 1 + \frac{1}{2}\frac{v^2}{c^2} + \frac{3}{8}\frac{v^4}{c^4} + \cdots$$

Combining this with $K = (\gamma - 1)mc^2$, we find

$$K = \left(1 + \frac{1}{2}\frac{v^2}{c^2} + \frac{3}{8}\frac{v^4}{c^4} + \cdots - 1\right)mc^2$$

$$= \frac{1}{2}mv^2 + \frac{3}{8}\frac{mv^4}{c^2} + \cdots \qquad (37.37)$$

When v is much smaller than c, all the terms in the series in Eq. (37.37) except the first are negligibly small, and we obtain the Newtonian expression $\frac{1}{2}mv^2$.

Rest Energy and $E = mc^2$

Equation (37.36) for the kinetic energy of a moving particle includes a term $mc^2/\sqrt{1 - v^2/c^2}$ that depends on the motion and a second energy term mc^2 that is independent of the motion. It seems that the kinetic energy of a particle is the difference between some **total energy** E and an energy mc^2 that it has even when it is at rest. Thus we can rewrite Eq. (37.36) as

$$E = K + mc^2 = \frac{mc^2}{\sqrt{1 - v^2/c^2}} = \gamma mc^2 \qquad \begin{array}{l}\text{(total energy of} \\ \text{a particle)}\end{array} \qquad (37.38)$$

For a particle at rest $(K = 0)$, we see that $E = mc^2$. The energy mc^2 associated with rest mass m rather than motion is called the **rest energy** of the particle.

There is in fact direct experimental evidence that rest energy really does exist. The simplest example is the decay of a neutral *pion*. This is an unstable subatomic particle of rest mass m_π; when it decays, it disappears and electromagnetic radiation appears. If a neutral pion has no kinetic energy before its decay, the total energy of the radiation after its decay is found to equal exactly $m_\pi c^2$. In many other fundamental particle transformations the sum of the rest masses of the particles changes. In every case there is a corresponding energy change, consistent with the assumption of a rest energy mc^2 associated with a rest mass m.

Historically, the principles of conservation of mass and of energy developed quite independently. The theory of relativity shows that they are actually two special cases of a single broader conservation principle, the *principle of*

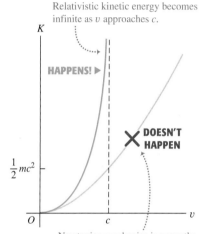

37.21 Graph of the kinetic energy of a particle of rest mass m as a function of speed v. Also shown is the Newtonian prediction, which gives correct results only at speeds much less than c.

Relativistic kinetic energy becomes infinite as v approaches c.

HAPPENS! ▶

DOESN'T HAPPEN

Newtonian mechanics incorrectly predicts that kinetic energy becomes infinite only if v becomes infinite.

conservation of mass and energy. In some physical phenomena, neither the sum of the rest masses of the particles nor the total energy other than rest energy is separately conserved, but there is a more general conservation principle: In an isolated system, when the sum of the rest masses changes, there is always a change in $1/c^2$ times the total energy other than the rest energy. This change is equal in magnitude but opposite in sign to the change in the sum of the rest masses.

This more general mass-energy conservation law is the fundamental principle involved in the generation of power through nuclear reactions. When a uranium nucleus undergoes fission in a nuclear reactor, the sum of the rest masses of the resulting fragments is *less than* the rest mass of the parent nucleus. An amount of energy is released that equals the mass decrease multiplied by c^2. Most of this energy can be used to produce steam to operate turbines for electric power generators (Fig. 37.22).

We can also relate the total energy E of a particle (kinetic energy plus rest energy) directly to its momentum by combining Eq. (37.27) for relativistic momentum and Eq. (37.38) for total energy to eliminate the particle's velocity. The simplest procedure is to rewrite these equations in the following forms:

$$\left(\frac{E}{mc^2}\right)^2 = \frac{1}{1-v^2/c^2} \quad \text{and} \quad \left(\frac{p}{mc}\right)^2 = \frac{v^2/c^2}{1-v^2/c^2}$$

Subtracting the second of these from the first and rearranging, we find

$$E^2 = (mc^2)^2 + (pc)^2 \qquad \begin{array}{l}\text{(total energy, rest energy,}\\ \text{and momentum)}\end{array} \qquad (37.39)$$

Again we see that for a particle at rest $(p = 0)$, $E = mc^2$.

Equation (37.39) also suggests that a particle may have energy and momentum even when it has no rest mass. In such a case, $m = 0$ and

$$E = pc \qquad \text{(zero rest mass)} \qquad (37.40)$$

In fact, zero rest mass particles do exist. Such particles always travel at the speed of light in vacuum. One example is the *photon*, the quantum of electromagnetic radiation (to be discussed in Chapter 38). Photons are emitted and absorbed during changes of state of an atomic or nuclear system when the energy and momentum of the system change.

37.22 Although the control room of a nuclear power plant is very complex, the physical principle whereby such a plant operates is a simple one: Part of the rest energy of atomic nuclei is converted to thermal energy, which in turn is used to produce steam to drive electric generators.

Example 37.11 **Energetic electrons**

(a) Find the rest energy of an electron $(m = 9.109 \times 10^{-31}\,\text{kg}$, $q = -e = -1.602 \times 10^{-19}\,\text{C})$ in joules and in electron volts. (b) Find the speed of an electron that has been accelerated by an electric field, from rest, through a potential increase of 20.0 kV (typical of TV picture tubes) or of 5.00 MV (a high-voltage x-ray machine).

SOLUTION

IDENTIFY: This problem uses the ideas of rest energy, relativistic kinetic energy, and (from Chapter 23) electric potential energy.

SET UP: We use the relationship $E = mc^2$ to find the rest energy and Eq. (37.38) to find the speed that gives the stated total energy.

EXECUTE: (a) The rest energy is

$$mc^2 = (9.109 \times 10^{-31}\,\text{kg})(2.998 \times 10^8\,\text{m/s})^2$$
$$= 8.187 \times 10^{-14}\,\text{J}$$

From the definition of the electron volt in Section 23.2, $1\,\text{eV} = 1.602 \times 10^{-19}\,\text{J}$. Using this, we find

$$mc^2 = (8.187 \times 10^{-14}\,\text{J})\frac{1\,\text{eV}}{1.602 \times 10^{-19}\,\text{J}}$$
$$= 5.11 \times 10^5\,\text{eV} = 0.511\,\text{MeV}$$

(b) In calculations such as this, it is often convenient to work with the quantity γ defined from the modified Eq. (37.7):

$$\gamma = \frac{1}{\sqrt{1-v^2/c^2}}$$

Solving this for v, we get

$$v = c\sqrt{1-(1/\gamma)^2}$$

The total energy E of the accelerated electron is the sum of its rest energy mc^2 and the kinetic energy eV_{ba} that it gains from the work done on it by the electric field in moving from point a to point b:

$$E = \gamma mc^2 = mc^2 + eV_{ba} \quad \text{or}$$

$$\gamma = 1 + \frac{eV_{ba}}{mc^2}$$

An electron accelerated through a potential increase of $V_{ba} = 20.0$ kV gains an amount of energy 20.0 keV, so for this electron we have

$$\gamma = 1 + \frac{20.0 \times 10^3 \text{ eV}}{0.511 \times 10^6 \text{ eV}} \quad \text{or}$$

$$= 1.039$$

and

$$v = c\sqrt{1 - (1/1.039)^2} = 0.272c$$

$$= 8.15 \times 10^7 \text{ m/s}$$

Repeating the calculation for $V_{ba} = 5.00$ MV, we find $eV_{ba}/mc^2 = 9.78$, $\gamma = 10.78$, and $v = 0.996c$.

EVALUATE: These results make sense: With $V_{ba} = 20.0$ kV, the added kinetic energy of 20.0 keV is less than 4% of the rest energy of 0.511 MeV, and the final speed is about one-fourth of the speed of light. With $V_{ba} = 5.00$ MV, the added kinetic energy of 5.00 MeV is much greater than the rest energy and the speed is close to c.

CAUTION **Three electron energies** The electron that accelerated from rest through a potential increase of 5.00 MV had a kinetic energy of 5.00 MeV. By convention we call such an electron a "5.00-MeV electron." A 5.00-MeV electron has a rest energy of 0.511 MeV (as do all electrons), a kinetic energy of 5.00 MeV, and a total energy of 5.51 MeV. Be careful not to confuse these different energies. ▮

Example 37.12 A relativistic collision

Two protons (each with $M = 1.67 \times 10^{-27}$ kg) are initially moving with equal speeds in opposite directions. They continue to exist after a head-on collision that also produces a neutral pion of mass $m = 2.40 \times 10^{-28}$ kg (Fig. 37.23). If the protons and the pion are at rest after the collision, find the initial speed of the protons. Energy is conserved in the collision.

SOLUTION

IDENTIFY: This problem uses the idea of relativistic total energy, which is conserved in the collision.

SET UP: We equate the (unknown) total energy of the two protons before the collision to the combined rest energies of the two protons and the pion after the collision. We then use Eq. (37.38) to solve for the speed of each proton.

EXECUTE: The total energy of each proton before the collision is γMc^2. By conservation of energy,

$$2(\gamma Mc^2) = 2(Mc^2) + mc^2$$

$$\gamma = 1 + \frac{m}{2M} = 1 + \frac{2.40 \times 10^{-28} \text{ kg}}{2(1.67 \times 10^{-27} \text{ kg})} = 1.072$$

so

$$v = c\sqrt{1 - (1/\gamma)^2} = 0.360c$$

37.23 In this collision the kinetic energy of two protons is transformed into the rest energy of a new particle, a pion.

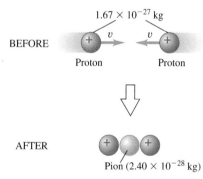

EVALUATE: The initial kinetic energy of each proton is $(\gamma - 1)Mc^2 = 0.072Mc^2$. The rest energy of a proton is 938 MeV, so the kinetic energy is $(0.072)(938 \text{ MeV}) = 67.5$ MeV. (These are "67.5-MeV protons.") You can verify that the rest energy of the pion is twice this, or 135 MeV. All the kinetic energy "lost" in this completely inelastic collision is transformed into the rest energy of the pion.

Test Your Understanding of Section 37.8   A proton is accelerated from rest by a constant force that always points in the direction of the particle's motion. Compared to the amount of kinetic energy that the proton gains during the first meter of its travel, how much kinetic energy does the proton gain during one meter of travel while it is moving at 99% of the speed of light? (i) the same amount; (ii) a greater amount; (iii) a smaller amount. ▮

37.9 Newtonian Mechanics and Relativity

The sweeping changes required by the principle of relativity go to the very roots of Newtonian mechanics, including the concepts of length and time, the equations of motion, and the conservation principles. Thus it may appear that we have destroyed the foundations on which Newtonian mechanics is built. In one sense this is true, yet the Newtonian formulation is still accurate whenever speeds are small in comparison with the speed of light in vacuum. In such cases, time dilation, length contraction, and the modifications of the laws of motion are so small that they are unobservable. In fact, every one of the principles of Newtonian mechanics survives as a special case of the more general relativistic formulation.

The laws of Newtonian mechanics are not *wrong;* they are *incomplete.* They are a limiting case of relativistic mechanics. They are *approximately* correct when all speeds are small in comparison to *c*, and they become exactly correct in the limit when all speeds approach zero. Thus relativity does not completely destroy the laws of Newtonian mechanics but *generalizes* them. Newton's laws rest on a very solid base of experimental evidence, and it would be very strange to advance a new theory that is inconsistent with this evidence. This is a common pattern in the development of physical theory. Whenever a new theory is in partial conflict with an older, established theory, the new must yield the same predictions as the old in areas in which the old theory is supported by experimental evidence. Every new physical theory must pass this test, called the **correspondence principle.**

The General Theory of Relativity

At this point we may ask whether the special theory of relativity gives the final word on mechanics or whether *further* generalizations are possible or necessary. For example, inertial frames have occupied a privileged position in our discussion. Can the principle of relativity be extended to noninertial frames as well?

Here's an example that illustrates some implications of this question. A student decides to go over Niagara Falls while enclosed in a large wooden box. During her free fall she can float through the air inside the box. She doesn't fall to the floor because both she and the box are in free fall with a downward acceleration of 9.8 m/s². But an alternative interpretation, from her point of view, is that she doesn't fall to the floor because her gravitational interaction with the earth has suddenly been turned off. As long as she remains in the box and it remains in free fall, she cannot tell whether she is indeed in free fall or whether the gravitational interaction has vanished.

A similar problem occurs in a space station in orbit around the earth. Objects in the space station *seem* to be weightless, but without looking outside the station there is no way to determine whether gravity has been turned off or whether the station and all its contents are accelerating toward the center of the earth. Figure 37.24 makes a similar point for a spaceship that is not in free fall but may be accelerating relative to an inertial frame or be at rest on the earth's surface.

These considerations form the basis of Einstein's **general theory of relativity.** If we cannot distinguish experimentally between a uniform gravitational field at a particular location and a uniformly accelerated reference frame, then there cannot be any real distinction between the two. Pursuing this concept, we may try to represent *any* gravitational field in terms of special characteristics of the coordinate system. This turns out to require even more sweeping revisions of our space-time concepts than did the special theory of relativity. In the general theory of relativity the geometric properties of space are affected by the presence of matter (Fig. 37.25).

The general theory of relativity has passed several experimental tests, including three proposed by Einstein. One test has to do with understanding the rotation of the axes of the planet Mercury's elliptical orbit, called the *precession of the perihelion.* (The perihelion is the point of closest approach to the sun.) A second test concerns the apparent bending of light rays from distant stars when they pass near the sun. The third test is the *gravitational red shift,* the increase in wave-

37.24 Without information from outside the spaceship, the astronaut cannot distinguish situation (b) from situation (c).

(a) An astronaut is about to drop her watch in a spaceship.

(b) In gravity-free space, the floor accelerates upward at $a = g$ and hits the watch.

$a = g$

(c) On the earth's surface, the watch accelerates downward at $a = g$ and hits the floor.

$a = 0$

Spaceship

g

37.25 A two-dimensional representation of curved space. We imagine the space (a plane) as being distorted as shown by a massive object (the sun). Light from a distant star (solid line) follows the distorted surface on its way to the earth. The dashed line shows the direction from which the light *appears* to be coming. The effect is greatly exaggerated; for the sun, the maximum deviation is only 0.00048°.

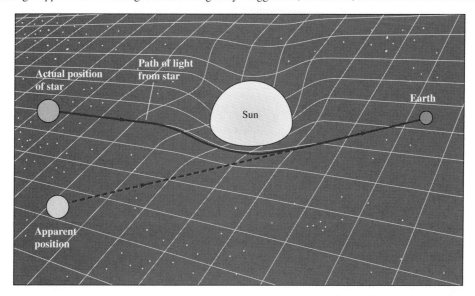

length of light proceeding outward from a massive source. Some details of the general theory are more difficult to test, but this theory has played a central role in investigations of the formation and evolution of stars, black holes, and studies of the evolution of the universe.

The general theory of relativity may seem to be an exotic bit of knowledge with little practical application. In fact, this theory plays an essential role in the global positioning system (GPS), which makes it possible to determine your position on the earth's surface to within a few meters using a handheld receiver (Fig. 37.26). The heart of the GPS system is a collection of more than two dozen satellites in very precise orbits. Each satellite emits carefully timed radio signals, and a GPS receiver simultaneously detects the signals from several satellites. The receiver then calculates the time delay between when each signal was emitted and when it was received, and uses this information to calculate the receiver's position. To ensure the proper timing of the signals, it's necessary to include corrections due to the special theory of relativity (because the satellites are moving relative to the receiver on earth) as well as the general theory (because the satellites are higher in the earth's gravitational field than the receiver). The corrections due to relativity are small—less than one part in 10^9—but are crucial to the superb precision of the GPS system.

37.26 A GPS receiver uses radio signals from the orbiting GPS satellites to determine its position. To account for the effects of relativity, the receiver must be tuned to a slightly higher frequency (10.23 MHz) than the frequency emitted by the satellites (10.22999999543 MHz).

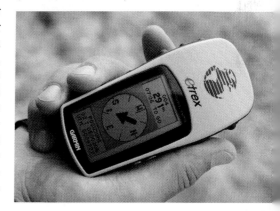

Invariance of physical laws, simultaneity: All of the fundamental laws of physics have the same form in all inertial frames of reference. The speed of light in vacuum is the same in all inertial frames and is independent of the motion of the source. Simultaneity is not an absolute concept; events that are simultaneous in one frame are not necessarily simultaneous in a second frame moving relative to the first.

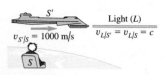

Time dilation: If two events occur at the same space point in a particular frame of reference, the time interval Δt_0 between the events as measured in that frame is called a proper time interval. If this frame moves with constant velocity u relative to a second frame, the time interval Δt between the events as observed in the second frame is longer than Δt_0. This effect is called time dilation. (Examples 37.1–37.3.)

$$\Delta t = \frac{\Delta t_0}{\sqrt{1 - u^2/c^2}} = \gamma \, \Delta t_0 \quad (37.6), (37.8)$$

$$\gamma = \frac{1}{\sqrt{1 - u^2/c^2}} \quad (37.7)$$

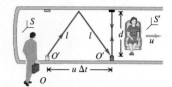

Length contraction: If two points are at rest in a particular frame of reference, the distance l_0 between the points as measured in that frame is called a proper length. If this frame moves with constant velocity u relative to a second frame and the distances are measured parallel to the motion, the distance l between the points as measured in the second frame is shorter than l_0. This effect is called length contraction. (See Examples 37.4–37.6.)

$$l = l_0\sqrt{1 - u^2/c^2} = \frac{l_0}{\gamma} \quad (37.16)$$

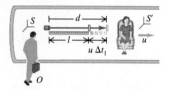

The Lorentz transformations: The Lorentz coordinate transformations relate the coordinates and time of an event in an inertial frame S to the coordinates and time of the same event as observed in a second inertial frame S' moving at velocity u relative to the first. For one-dimensional motion, a particle's velocities v_x in S and v_x' in S' are related by the Lorentz velocity transformation. (See Examples 37.7 and 37.8.)

$$x' = \frac{x - ut}{\sqrt{1 - u^2/c^2}} = \gamma(x - ut)$$

$$y' = y \qquad z' = z$$

$$t' = \frac{t - ux/c^2}{\sqrt{1 - u^2/c^2}} = \gamma(t - ux/c^2) \quad (37.21)$$

$$v_x' = \frac{v_x - u}{1 - uv_x/c^2} \quad (37.22)$$

$$v_x = \frac{v_x' + u}{1 + uv_x'/c^2} \quad (37.23)$$

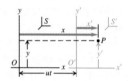

The Doppler effect for electromagnetic waves: The Doppler effect is the frequency shift in light from a source due to the relative motion of source and observer. For a source moving toward the observer with speed u, Eq. (37.25) gives the received frequency f in terms of the emitted frequency f_0. (See Example 37.9.)

$$f = \sqrt{\frac{c + u}{c - u}}\, f_0 \quad (37.25)$$

Moving source emits light of frequency f_0.

Stationary observer detects light of frequency $f > f_0$.

Relativistic momentum and energy: For a particle of rest mass m moving with velocity $\vec{v}$, the relativistic momentum $\vec{p}$ is given by Eq. (37.27) or (37.31) and the relativistic kinetic energy K is given by Eq. (37.36). The total energy E is the sum of the kinetic energy and the rest energy mc^2. The total energy can also be expressed in terms of the magnitude of momentum p and rest mass m. (See Examples 37.10–37.12.)

$$\vec{p} = \frac{m\vec{v}}{\sqrt{1 - v^2/c^2}} = \gamma m\vec{v} \quad (37.27), (37.31)$$

$$K = \frac{mc^2}{\sqrt{1 - v^2/c^2}} - mc^2 = (\gamma - 1)mc^2 \quad (37.36)$$

$$E = K + mc^2 = \frac{mc^2}{\sqrt{1 - v^2/c^2}} = \gamma mc^2 \quad (37.38)$$

$$E^2 = (mc^2)^2 + (pc)^2 \quad (37.39)$$

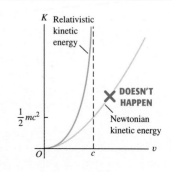

Newtonian mechanics and the special and general theories of relativity: The special theory of relativity is a generalization of Newtonian mechanics. All the principles of Newtonian mechanics are present as limiting cases when all the speeds are small compared to c. Further generalization to include noninertial frames of reference and their relationship to gravitational fields leads to the general theory of relativity.

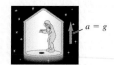

Key Terms

Answer to Chapter Opening Question **?**

No. While the speed of light c is the ultimate "speed limit" for any particle, there is *no* upper limit on a particle's kinetic energy (see Fig. 37.21). As the speed approaches c, a small increase in speed corresponds to a large increase in kinetic energy.

Answers to Test Your Understanding Questions

37.1 answers: (a) (i), (b) no You, too, will measure a spherical wave front that expands at the same speed c in all directions. This is a consequence of Einstein's second postulate. The wave front that you measure is *not* centered on the current position of the spaceship; rather, it is centered on the point P where the spaceship was located at the instant that it emitted the light pulse. For example, suppose the spaceship is moving at speed $c/2$. When your watch shows that a time t has elapsed since the pulse of light was emitted, your measurements will show that the wave front is a sphere of radius ct centered on P and that the spaceship is a distance $ct/2$ from P.

37.2 answer: (iii) In Mavis's frame of reference, the two events (the Ogdenville clock striking noon and the North Haverbrook clock striking noon) are not simultaneous. Figure 37.5 shows that the event toward the front of the rail car occurs first. Since the rail car is moving toward North Haverbrook, that clock struck noon before the one on Ogdenville. So, according to Mavis, it is after noon in North Haverbrook.

37.3 answers: (a) (ii), (b) (ii) The statement that moving clocks run slow refers to any clock that is moving relative to an observer. Maria and her stopwatch are moving relative to Samir, so Samir measures Maria's stopwatch to be running slow and to have ticked off fewer seconds than his own stopwatch. Samir and his stopwatch are moving relative to Maria, so she likewise measures Samir's stopwatch to be running slow. Each observer's measurement is correct for his or her own frame of reference. *Both* observers conclude that a moving stopwatch runs slow. This is consistent with the principle of relativity (see Section 37.1), which states that the laws of physics are the same in all inertial frames of reference.

37.4 answer: (ii), (i) and (iii) (tie), (iv) You measure the rest length of the stationary meter stick and the contracted length of the moving spaceship to both be 1 meter. The rest length of the spaceship is greater than the contracted length that you measure, and so

must be greater than 1 meter. A miniature observer on board the spaceship would measure a contracted length for the meter stick of less than 1 meter. Note that in your frame of reference the nose and tail of the spaceship can simultaneously align with the two ends of the meter stick, since in your frame of reference they have the same length of 1 meter. In the spaceship's frame these two alignments cannot happen simultaneously because the meter stick is shorter than the spaceship. Section 37.2 tells us that this shouldn't be a surprise; two events that are simultaneous to one observer may not be simultaneous to a second observer moving relative to the first one.

37.5 answers: (a) P_1, (b) P_4 (a) The last of Eqs. (37.21) tells us the times of the two events in S': $t_1' = \gamma(t_1 - ux_1/c^2)$ and $t_2' = \gamma(t_2 - ux_2/c^2)$. In frame S the two events occur at the same x-coordinate, so $x_1 = x_2$, and event P_1 occurs before event P_2, so $t_1 < t_2$. Hence you can see that $t_1' < t_2'$ and event P_1 happens before P_2 in frame S', too. This says that if event P_1 happens before P_2 in a frame of reference S where the two events occur at the same position, then P_1 happens before P_2 in any other frame moving relative to S. (b) In frame S the two events occur at different x-coordinates such that $x_3 < x_4$, and events P_3 and P_4 occur at the same time, so $t_3 = t_4$. Hence you can see that $t_3' = \gamma(t_3 - ux_3/c^2)$ is greater than $t_4' = \gamma(t_4 - ux_4/c^2)$, so event P_4 happens before P_3 in frame S'. This says that even though the two events are simultaneous in frame S, they need not be simultaneous in a frame moving relative to S.

37.7 answer: (ii) Equation (37.27) tells us that the magnitude of momentum of a particle with mass m and speed v is $p = mv/\sqrt{1 - v^2/c^2}$. If v increases by a factor of 2, the numerator mv increases by a factor of 2 *and* the denominator $\sqrt{1 - v^2/c^2}$ decreases. Hence p increases by a factor greater than 2. (Note that in order to double the speed, the initial speed must be less than $c/2$. That's because the speed of light is the ultimate speed limit.)

37.8 answer: (i) As the proton moves a distance s, the constant force of magnitude F does work $W = Fs$ and increases the kinetic energy by an amount $\Delta K = W = Fs$. This is true no matter what the speed of the proton before moving this distance. Thus the constant force increases the proton's kinetic energy by the same amount during the first meter of travel as during any subsequent meter of travel. (It's true that as the proton approaches the ultimate speed limit of c, the increase in the proton's *speed* is less and less with each subsequent meter of travel. That's not what the question is asking, however.)

PROBLEMS

For instructor-assigned homework, go to **www.masteringphysics.com** (MP)

Discussion Questions

Q37.1. You are standing on a train platform watching a high-speed train pass by. A light inside one of the train cars is turned on and then a little later it is turned off. (a) Who can measure the proper time interval for the duration of the light: you or a passenger on the train? (b) Who can measure the proper length of the train car, you or a passenger on the train? (c) Who can measure the proper length of a sign attached to a post on the train platform, you or a passenger on the train? In each case explain your answer.

Q37.2. If simultaneity is not an absolute concept, does that mean that we must discard the concept of causality? If event A is to *cause* event B, A must occur first. Is it possible that in some frames, A appears to be the cause of B, and in others, B appears to be the cause of A? Explain.

Q37.3. A rocket is moving to the right at $\frac{1}{2}$ the speed of light relative to the earth. A light bulb in the center of a room inside the rocket suddenly turns on. Call the light hitting the front end of the room event A and the light hitting the back of the room event B (Fig. 37.27). Which event occurs first, A or B or are they simultaneous, as viewed by (a) an astronaut riding in the rocket and (b) a person at rest on the earth?

Figure **37.27** Question Q37.3.

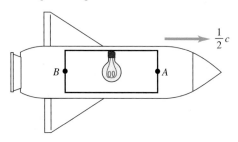

Q37.4. What do you think would be different in everyday life if the speed of light were 10 m/s instead of 3.00×10^8 m/s?

Q37.5. The average life span in the United States is about 70 years. Does this mean that it is impossible for an average person to travel a distance greater than 70 light-years away from the earth? (A light-year is the distance light travels in a year.) Explain.

Q37.6. You are holding an elliptical serving platter. How would you need to travel for the serving platter to appear round to another observer?

Q37.7. Two events occur at the same space point in a particular inertial frame of reference and are simultaneous in that frame. Is it possible that they may not be simultaneous in a different inertial frame? Explain.

Q37.8. A high-speed train passes a train platform. Larry is a passenger on the train, Adam is standing on the train platform, and David is riding a bicycle toward the platform in the same direction as the train is traveling. Compare the length of a train car as measured by Larry, Adam, and David.

Q37.9. The theory of relativity sets an upper limit on the speed that a particle can have. Are there also limits on the energy and momentum of a particle? Explain.

Q37.10. A student asserts that a material particle must always have a speed slower than that of light, and a massless particle must always move at exactly the speed of light. Is she correct? If so, how do massless particles such as photons and neutrinos acquire this speed? Can't they start from rest and accelerate? Explain.

Q37.11. The speed of light relative to still water is 2.25×10^8 m/s. If the water is moving past us, the speed of light we measure depends on the speed of the water. Do these facts violate Einstein's second postulate? Explain.

Q37.12. When a monochromatic light source moves toward an observer, its wavelength appears to be shorter than the value measured when the source is at rest. Does this contradict the hypothesis that the speed of light is the same for all observers? Explain.

Q37.13. In principle, does a hot gas have more mass than the same gas when it is cold? Explain. In practice, would this be a measurable effect? Explain.

Q37.14. Why do you think the development of Newtonian mechanics preceded the more refined relativistic mechanics by so many years?

Exercises

Section 37.2 Relativity of Simultaneity

37.1. Suppose the two lightning bolts shown in Fig. 37.5a are simultaneous to an observer on the train. Show that they are *not* simultaneous to an observer on the ground. Which lightning strike does the ground observer measure to come first?

Section 37.3 Relativity of Time Intervals

37.2. The positive muon (μ^+), an unstable particle, lives on average 2.20×10^{-6} s (measured in its own frame of reference) before decaying. (a) If such a particle is moving, with respect to the laboratory, with a speed of $0.900c$, what average lifetime is measured in the laboratory? (b) What average distance, measured in the laboratory, does the particle move before decaying?

37.3. How fast must a rocket travel relative to the earth so that time in the rocket "slows down" to half its rate as measured by earth-based observers? Do present-day jet planes approach such speeds?

37.4. A spaceship flies past Mars with a speed of $0.985c$ relative to the surface of the planet. When the spaceship is directly overhead, a signal light on the Martian surface blinks on and then off. An observer on Mars measures that the signal light was on for 75.0 μs. (a) Does the observer on Mars or the pilot on the spaceship measure the proper time? (b) What is the duration of the light pulse measured by the pilot of the spaceship?

37.5. The negative pion (π^-) is an unstable particle with an average lifetime of 2.60×10^{-8} s (measured in the rest frame of the pion). (a) If the pion is made to travel at very high speed relative to a laboratory, its average lifetime is measured in the laboratory to be 4.20×10^{-7} s. Calculate the speed of the pion expressed as a fraction of c. (b) What distance, measured in the laboratory, does the pion travel during its average lifetime?

37.6. As you pilot your space utility vehicle at a constant speed toward the moon, a race pilot flies past you in her spaceracer at a constant speed of $0.800c$ relative to you. At the instant the spaceracer passes you, both of you start timers at zero. (a) At the instant when you measure that the spaceracer has traveled 1.20×10^8 m past you, what does the race pilot read on her timer? (b) When the race pilot reads the value calculated in part (a) on her timer, what does she measure to be your distance from her? (c) At the instant when the race pilot reads the value calculated in part (a) on her timer, what do you read on yours?

37.7. A spacecraft flies away from the earth with a speed of 4.80×10^6 m/s relative to the earth and then returns at the same speed. The spacecraft carries an atomic clock that has been carefully synchronized with an identical clock that remains at rest on earth. The spacecraft returns to its starting point 365 days (1 year) later, as measured by the clock that remained on earth. What is the difference in the elapsed times on the two clocks, measured in hours? Which clock, the one in the spacecraft or the one on earth, shows the shortest elapsed time?

37.8. An alien spacecraft is flying overhead at a great distance as you stand in your backyard. You see its searchlight blink on for 0.190 s. The first officer on the spacecraft measures that the searchlight is on for 12.0 ms. (a) Which of these two measured times is the proper time? (b) What is the speed of the spacecraft relative to the earth expressed as a fraction of the speed of light c?

Section 37.4 Relativity of Length

37.9. A spacecraft of the Trade Federation flies past the planet Coruscant at a speed of $0.600c$. A scientist on Coruscant measures the length of the moving spacecraft to be 74.0 m. The spacecraft later lands on Coruscant, and the same scientist measures the length of the now stationary spacecraft. What value does she get?

37.10. A meter stick moves past you at great speed. Its motion relative to you is parallel to its long axis. If you measure the length of the moving meter stick to be 1.00 ft (1 ft $= 0.3048$ m)—for example, by comparing it to a 1-foot ruler that is at rest relative to you—at what speed is the meter stick moving relative to you?

37.11. Why Are We Bombarded by Muons? Muons are unstable subatomic particles that decay to electrons with a mean lifetime of 2.2 μs. They are produced when cosmic rays bombard the upper atmosphere about 10 km above the earth's surface, and they travel very close to the speed of light. The problem we want to address is why we see any of them at the earth's surface. (a) What is the greatest distance a muon could travel during its 2.2-μs lifetime? (b) According to your answer in part (a), it would seem that muons could never make it to the ground. But the 2.2-μs lifetime is measured in the frame of the muon, and muons are moving very fast. At a speed of $0.999c$. what is the mean lifetime of a muon as measured by an observer at rest on the earth? How far would the muon travel in this time? Does this result explain why we find muons in cosmic rays? (c) From the point of view of the muon, it still lives for only 2.2 μs, so how does it make it to the ground? What is the thickness of the 10 km of atmosphere through which the muon must travel, as measured by the muon? It is now clear how the muon is able to reach the ground?

37.12. An unstable particle is created in the upper atmosphere from a cosmic ray and travels straight down toward the surface of the earth with a speed of $0.99540c$ relative to the earth. A scientist at rest on the earth's surface measures that the particle is created at an altitude of 45.0 km. (a) As measured by the scientist, how much time does it take the particle to travel the 45.0 km to the surface of the earth? (b) Use the length-contraction formula to calculate the distance from where the particle is created to the surface of the earth as measured in the particle's frame. (c) In the particle's frame, how much time does it take the particle to travel from where it is created to the surface of the earth? Calculate this time both by the time dilation formula and from the distance calculated in part (b). Do the two results agree?

37.13. As measured by an observer on the earth, a spacecraft runway on earth has a length of 3600 m. (a) What is the length of the runway as measured by a pilot of a spacecraft flying past at a speed of 4.00×10^7 m/s relative to the earth? (b) An observer on earth measures the time interval from when the spacecraft is directly over one end of the runway until it is directly over the other end. What result does she get? (c) The pilot of the spacecraft measures the time it takes him to travel from one end of the runway to the other end. What value does he get?

Section 37.5 The Lorentz Transformations

37.14. Solve Eqs. (37.21) to obtain x and t in terms of x' and t', and show that the resulting transformation has the same form as the original one except for a change of sign for u.

37.15. An observer in frame S' is moving to the right ($+x$-direction) at speed $u = 0.600c$ away from a stationary observer in frame S. The observer in S' measures the speed v' of a particle moving to the right away from her. What speed v does the observer in S measure for the particle if (a) $v' = 0.400c$; (b) $v' = 0.900c$; (c) $v' = 0.990c$?

37.16. Space pilot Mavis zips past Stanley at a constant speed relative to him of $0.800c$. Mavis and Stanley start timers at zero when the front of Mavis's ship is directly above Stanley. When Mavis reads 5.00 s on her timer, she turns on a bright light under the front of her spaceship. (a) Use the Lorentz coordinate transformation derived in Exercise 37.14 and Example 37.7 to calculate x and t as measured by Stanley for the event of turning on the light. (b) Use the time dilation formula, Eq. (37.6), to calculate the time interval between the two events (the front of the spaceship passing overhead and turning on the light) as measured by Stanley. Compare to the value of t you calculated in part (a). (c) Multiply the time interval by Mavis's speed, both as measured by Stanley, to calculate the distance she has traveled as measured by him when the light turns on. Compare to the value of x you calculated in part (a).

37.17. A pursuit spacecraft from the planet Tatooine is attempting to catch up with a Trade Federation cruiser. As measured by an observer on Tatooine, the cruiser is traveling away from the planet with a speed of $0.600c$. The pursuit ship is traveling at a speed of $0.800c$ relative to Tatooine, in the same direction as the cruiser. (a) For the pursuit ship to catch the cruiser, should the speed of the cruiser relative to the pursuit ship be positive or negative? (b) What is the speed of the cruiser relative to the pursuit ship?

37.18. Equation 37.23 gives the transformation for only the x-component of an object's velocity. Suppose the object considered in the derivation also moved in the y/y'-direction. Find an expression for u_y in terms of the components of u', v, and c, which represents the transformation for the y-component of the velocity. (*Hint:* Apply the Lorentz transformations and relationships like $u_x = dx/dt$, $u'_x = dx'/dt'$, and so on, to the y-components.)

37.19. Two particles are created in a high-energy accelerator and move off in opposite directions. The speed of one particle, as measured in the laboratory, is $0.650c$, and the speed of each particle relative to the other is $0.950c$. What is the speed of the second particle, as measured in the laboratory?

37.20. Two particles in a high-energy accelerator experiment are approaching each other head-on, each with a speed of $0.9520c$ as measured in the laboratory. What is the magnitude of the velocity of one particle relative to the other?

37.21. Two particles in a high-energy accelerator experiment approach each other head-on with a relative speed of $0.890c$. Both particles travel at the same speed as measured in the laboratory. What is the speed of each particle, as measured in the laboratory?

37.22. An enemy spaceship is moving toward your starfighter with a speed, as measured in your frame, of $0.400c$. The enemy ship fires a missile toward you at a speed of $0.700c$ relative to the enemy ship (Fig. 37.28). (a) What is the speed of the missile relative to you? Express your answer in terms of the speed of light. (b) If you measure that the enemy ship is 8.00×10^6 km away from you when the missile is fired, how much time, measured in your frame, will it take the missile to reach you?

Figure 37.28 Exercise 37.22.

Enemy   Starfighter

37.23. An imperial spaceship, moving at high speed relative to the planet Arrakis, fires a rocket toward the planet with a speed of $0.920c$ relative to the spaceship. An observer on Arrakis measures that the rocket is approaching with a speed of $0.360c$. What is the speed of the spaceship relative to Arrakis? Is the spaceship moving toward or away from Arrakis?

*Section 37.6 The Doppler Effect for Electromagnetic Waves

***37.24.** Rewrite Eq. 37.25 to find the relative velocity u between the electromagnetic source and an observer in terms of the ratio of the observed frequency and the source frequency of light. What relative velocity u will produce (a) a 5.0% decrease in frequency and (b) an increase by a factor of 5 of the observed light?

***37.25. Tell It to the Judge.** (a) How fast must you be approaching a red traffic light ($\lambda = 675$ nm) for it to appear yellow ($\lambda = 575$ nm)? Express your answer in terms of the speed of light. (b) If you used this as a reason not to get a ticket for running a red light, how much of a fine would you get for speeding? Assume that the fine is $1.00 for each kilometer per hour that your speed exceeds the posted limit of 90 km/h.

***37.26.** Show that when the source of electromagnetic waves moves away from us at $0.600c$, the frequency we measure is half the value measured in the rest frame of the source.

Section 37.7 Relativistic Momentum

37.27. (a) A particle with mass m moves along a straight line under the action of a force F directed along the same line. Evaluate the derivative in Eq. (37.29) to show that the acceleration $a = dv/dt$ of the particle is given by $a = (F/m)(1 - v^2/c^2)^{3/2}$. (b) Evaluate the derivative in Eq. (37.29) to find the expression for the magnitude of the acceleration in terms of F, m, and v/c if the force is perpendicular to the velocity.

37.28. When Should you Use Relativity? As you have seen, relativistic calculations usually involve the quantity γ. When γ is appreciably greater than 1, we must use relativistic formulas instead of Newtonian ones. For what speed v (in terms of c) is the value of γ (a) 1.0% greater than 1; (b) 10% greater than 1; (c) 100% greater than 1?

37.29. (a) At what speed is the momentum of a particle twice as great as the result obtained from the nonrelativistic expression mv? Express your answer in terms of the speed of light. (b) A force is applied to a particle along its direction of motion. At what speed is the magnitude of force required to produce a given acceleration twice as great as the force required to produce the same acceleration when the particle is at rest? Express your answer in terms of the speed of light.

37.30. Relativistic Baseball. Calculate the magnitude of the force required to give a 0.145-kg baseball an acceleration $a = 1.00$ m/s^2 in the direction of the baseball's initial velocity when this velocity has a magnitude of (a) 10.0 m/s; (b) $0.900c$; (c) $0.990c$. (d) Repeat parts (a), (b), and (c) if the force and acceleration are perpendicular to the velocity.

Section 37.8 Relativistic Work and Energy

37.31. What is the speed of a particle whose kinetic energy is equal to (a) its rest energy and (b) five times its rest energy?

37.32. Annihilation. In proton–antiproton annihilation a proton and an antiproton (a negatively charged proton) collide and disappear, producing electromagnetic radiation. If each particle has a mass of 1.67×10^{-27} kg and they are at rest just before the annihilation, find the total energy of the radiation. Give your answers in joules and in electron volts.

37.33. A proton (rest mass $1.67 \times 10^{\times 27}$ kg) has total energy that is 4.00 times its rest energy. What are (a) the kinetic energy of the proton; (b) the magnitude of the momentum of the proton; (c) the speed of the proton?

37.34. (a) How much work must be done on a particle with mass m to accelerate it (a) from rest to a speed of $0.090c$ and (b) from a speed of $0.900c$ to a speed of $0.990c$? (Express the answers in terms of mc^2.) (c) How do your answers in parts (a) and (b) compare?

37.35. (a) By what percentage does your rest mass increase when you climb 30 m to the top of a ten-story building? Are you aware of this increase? Explain. (b) By how many grams does the mass of a 12.0-g spring with force constant 200 N/cm change when you compress it by 6.0 cm? Does the mass increase or decrease? Would you notice the change in mass if you were holding the spring? Explain.

37.36. A 60.0-kg person is standing at rest on level ground. How fast would she have to run to (a) double her total energy and (b) increase her total energy by a factor of 10?

37.37. An Antimatter Reactor. When a particle meets its antiparticle, they annihilate each other and their mass is converted to light energy. The United States uses approximately 1.0×10^{19} J of energy per year. (a) If all this energy came from a futuristic antimatter reactor, how much mass of matter and antimatter fuel would be consumed yearly? (b) If this fuel had the density of iron (7.86 g/cm^3) and were stacked in bricks to form a cubical pile, how high would it be? (Before you get your hopes up, antimatter reactors are a *long* way in the future—if they ever will be feasible.)

37.38. A ψ ("psi") particle has mass 5.52×10^{-27} kg. Compute the rest energy of the ψ particle in MeV.

37.39. A particle has rest mass 6.64×10^{-27} kg and momentum 2.10×10^{-18} kg · m/s. (a) What is the total energy (kinetic plus rest energy) of the particle? (b) What is the kinetic energy of the particle? (c) What is the ratio of the kinetic energy to the rest energy of the particle?

37.40. Starting from Eq. (37.39), show that in the classical limit ($pc \ll mc^2$) the energy approaches the classical kinetic energy $\frac{1}{2}mv^2$ plus the rest mass energy mc^2.

37.41. Compute the kinetic energy of a proton (mass 1.67×10^{-27} kg using both the nonrelativistic and relativistic expressions, and compute the ratio of the two results (relativistic divided by nonrelativistic) for speeds of (a) 8.00×10^7 m/s and (b) 2.85×10^8 m/s.

37.42. What is the kinetic energy of a proton moving at (a) $0.100c$; (b) $0.500c$; (c) $0.900c$? How much work must be done to (d) increase the proton's speed from $0.100c$ to $0.500c$ and (e) increase the proton's speed from $0.500c$ to $0.900c$? (f) How do the last two results compare to results obtained in the nonrelativistic limit?

37.43. (a) Through what potential difference does an electron have to be accelerated, starting from rest, to achieve a speed of $0.980c$? (b) What is the kinetic energy of the electron at this speed? Express your answer in joules and in electron volts.

37.44. Creating a Particle. Two protons (each with rest mass $M = 1.67 \times 10^{-27}$ kg) are initially moving with equal speeds in opposite directions. The protons continue to exist after a collision that also produces an η^0 particle (see Chapter 44). The rest mass of the η^0 is $m = 9.75 \times 10^{-28}$ kg. (a) If the two protons and the η^0 are all at rest after the collision, find the initial speed of the protons, expressed as a fraction of the speed of light. (b) What is the kinetic energy of each proton? Express your answer in MeV. (c) What is the rest energy of the η^0, expressed in MeV? (d) Discuss the relationship between the answers to parts (b) and (c).

37.45. Find the speed of a particle whose relativistic kinetic energy is 50% greater than the Newtonian value for the same speed.

37.46. Energy of Fusion. In a hypothetical nuclear fusion reactor, two deuterium nuclei combine or "fuse" to form one helium nucleus. The mass of a deuterium nucleus, expressed in atomic mass units (u), is 2.0136 u; the mass of a helium nucleus is 4.0015 u (1 u $= 1.6605402 \times 10^{-27}$ kg). (a) How much energy is released when 1.0 kg of deuterium undergoes fusion? (b) The annual consumption of electrical energy in the United States is of the order of 1.0×10^{19} J. How much deuterium must react to produce this much energy?

37.47. The sun produces energy by nuclear fusion reactions, in which matter is converted into energy. By measuring the amount of energy we receive from the sun, we know that it is producing energy at a rate of 3.8×10^{26} W. (a) How many kilograms of matter does the sun lose each second? Approximately how many tons of matter is this? (b) At this rate, how long would it take the sun to use up all its mass?

37.48. A 0.100-μg speck of dust is accelerated from rest to a speed of $0.900c$ by a constant 1.00×10^6 N force. (a) If the nonrelativistic form of Newton's second law ($\sum F = ma$) is used, how far does the object travel to reach its final speed? (b) Using the correct relativistic treatment of Section 37.8, how far does the object travel to reach its final speed? (c) Which distance is greater? Why?

Problems

37.49. After being produced in a collision between elementary particles, a positive pion (π^+) must travel down a 1.20-km-long tube to reach an experimental area. A π^+ particle has an average lifetime (measured in its rest frame) of 2.60×10^{-8} s; the π^+ we are considering has this lifetime. (a) How fast must the π^+ travel if it is not to decay before it reaches the end of the tube? (Since u will be very close to c, write $u = (1 - \Delta)c$ and give your answer in terms of Δ rather than u.) (b) The π^+ has a rest energy of 139.6 MeV. What is the total energy of the π^+ at the speed calculated in part (a)?

37.50. A cube of metal with sides of length a sits at rest in a frame S with one edge parallel to the x-axis. Therefore, in S the cube has volume a^3. Frame S' moves along the x-axis with a speed u. As measured by an observer in frame S', what is the volume of the metal cube?

37.51. The starships of the Solar Federation are marked with the symbol of the federation, a circle, while starships of the Denebian Empire are marked with the empire's symbol, an ellipse whose major axis is 1.40 times longer than its minor axis ($a = 1.40b$ in Fig. 37.29). How fast, relative to an observer, does an empire ship have to travel for its marking to be confused with the marking of a federation ship?

Figure **37.29** Problem 37.51.

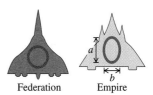

Federation   Empire

37.52. A space probe is sent to the vicinity of the star Capella, which is 42.2 light-years from the earth. (A light-year is the distance light travels in a year.) The probe travels with a speed of $0.9910c$. An astronaut recruit on board is 19 years old when the probe leaves the earth. What is her biological age when the probe reaches Capella?

37.53. A particle is said to be *extremely relativistic* when its kinetic energy is much greater than its rest energy. (a) What is the speed of a particle (expressed as a fraction of c) such that the total energy is ten times the rest energy? (b) What is the percentage difference between the left and right sides of Eq. (37.39) if $(mc^2)^2$ is neglected for a particle with the speed calculated in part (a)?

37.54. Everyday Time Dilation. Two atomic clocks are carefully synchronized. One remains in New York, and the other is loaded on an airliner that travels at an average speed of 250 m/s and then returns to New York. When the plane returns, the elapsed time on the clock that stayed behind is 4.00 h. By how much will the readings of the two clocks differ, and which clock will show the shorter elapsed time? (*Hint:* Since $u \ll c$, you can simplify $\sqrt{1 - u^2/c^2}$ by a binomial expansion.)

37.55. The Large Hadron Collider (LHC). Physicists and engineers from around the world have come together to build the largest accelerator in the world, the Large Hadron Collider (LHC) at the CERN Laboratory in Geneva, Switzerland. The machine will accelerate protons to kinetic energies of 7 TeV in an underground ring 27 km in circumference. (For the latest news and more information on the LHC, visit www.cern.ch.) (a) What speed v will protons reach in the LHC? (Since v is very close to c, write $v = (1 - \Delta)c$ and give your answer in terms of Δ.) (b) Find the relativistic mass, m_{rel}, of the accelerated protons in terms of their rest mass.

37.56. A nuclear bomb containing 8.00 kg of plutonium explodes. The sum of the rest masses of the products of the explosion is less than the original rest mass by one part in 10^4. (a) How much energy is released in the explosion? (b) If the explosion takes place in 4.00 μs, what is the average power developed by the bomb? (c) What mass of water could the released energy lift to a height of 1.00 km?

37.57. Čerenkov Radiation. The Russian physicist P. A. Čerenkov discovered that a charged particle traveling in a solid with a speed exceeding the speed of light in that material radiates electromagnetic radiation. (This is analogous to the sonic boom produced by an aircraft moving faster than the speed of sound in air; see Section 16.9. Čerenkov shared the 1958 Nobel Prize for this discovery.) What is the minimum kinetic energy (in electron volts) that an electron must have while traveling inside a slab of crown glass ($n = 1.52$) in order to create this Čerenkov radiation?

37.58. A photon with energy E is emitted by an atom with mass m, which recoils in the opposite direction. (a) Assuming that the motion of the atom can be treated nonrelativistically, compute the recoil speed of the atom. (b) From the result of part (a), show that the recoil speed is much less than c whenever E is much less than the rest energy mc^2 of the atom.

37.59. In an experiment, two protons are shot directly toward each other, each moving at half the speed of light relative to the laboratory. (a) What speed does one proton measure for the other proton? (b) What would be the answer to part (a) if we used only nonrelativistic Newtonian mechanics? (c) What is the kinetic energy of each proton as measured by (i) an observer at rest in the laboratory and (ii) an observer riding along with one of the protons? (d) What would be the answers to part (c) if we used only nonrelativistic Newtonian mechanics?

37.60. For the protons in Problem 37.59, suppose that their speed is such that each proton measures a speed of half the speed of light for the other proton. (a) What does an observer in the laboratory measure for the speeds of these protons? (b) What is the kinetic energy of each proton as measured by (i) an observer in the lab and (ii) the other proton?

37.61. Frame S' has an x-component of velocity u relative to frame S, and at $t = t' = 0$ the two frames coincide (see Fig. 37.3). A light pulse with a spherical wave front is emitted at the origin of S' at time $t' = 0$. Its distance x' from the origin after a time t' is given by $x'^2 = c^2 t'^2$. Use the Lorentz coordinate transformation to transform this equation to an equation in x and t, and show that the result is $x^2 = c^2 t^2$; that is, the motion appears exactly the same in frame of reference S as it does in S'; the wave front is observed to be spherical in both frames.

37.62. In certain radioactive beta decay processes, the beta particle (an electron) leaves the atomic nucleus with a speed of 99.95% the speed of light relative to the decaying nucleus. If this nucleus is moving at 75.00% the speed of light, find the speed of the emitted electron relative to the laboratory reference frame if the electron is emitted (a) in the same direction that the nucleus is moving and (b) in the opposite direction from the nucleus's velocity. (c) In each case in parts (a) and (b), find the kinetic energy of the electron as measured in (i) the laboratory frame and (ii) the reference frame of the decaying nucleus.

37.63. A particle with mass m accelerated from rest by a constant force F will, according to Newtonian mechanics, continue to accelerate without bound; that is, as $t \to \infty$, $v \to \infty$. Show that according to relativistic mechanics, the particle's speed approaches c as $t \to \infty$. [*Note:* A useful integral is $\int (1 - x^2)^{-3/2} \, dx = x/\sqrt{1 - x^2}$.]

37.64. Two events are observed in a frame of reference S to occur at the same space point, the second occurring 1.80 s after the first. In a second frame S' moving relative to S, the second event is observed to occur 2.35 s after the first. What is the difference between the positions of the two events as measured in S'?

37.65. Two events observed in a frame of reference S have positions and times given by (x_1, t_1) and (x_2, t_2), respectively. (a) Frame S' moves along the x-axis just fast enough that the two events occur at the same position in S'. Show that in S', the time interval $\Delta t'$ between the two events is given by

$$\Delta t' = \sqrt{(\Delta t)^2 - \left(\frac{\Delta x}{c}\right)^2}$$

where $\Delta x = x_2 - x_1$ and $\Delta t = t_2 - t_1$. Hence show that if $\Delta x > c \, \Delta t$, there is *no* frame S' in which the two events occur at

the same point. The interval $\Delta t'$ is sometimes called the *proper time interval* for the events. Is this term appropriate? (b) Show that if $\Delta x > c \, \Delta t$, there is a different frame of reference S' in which the two events occur *simultaneously*. Find the distance between the two events in S'; express your answer in terms of Δx, Δt, and c. This distance is sometimes called a *proper length*. Is this term appropriate? (c) Two events are observed in a frame of reference S' to occur simultaneously at points separated by a distance of 2.50 m. In a second frame S moving relative to S' along the line joining the two points in S', the two events appear to be separated by 5.00 m. What is the time interval between the events as measured in S? [*Hint:* Apply the result obtained in part (b).]

37.66. Albert in Wonderland. Einstein and Lorentz, being avid tennis players, play a fast-paced game on a court where they stand 20.0 m from each other. Being very skilled players, they play without a net. The tennis ball has mass 0.0580 kg. You can ignore gravity and assume that the ball travels parallel to the ground as it travels between the two players. Unless otherwise specified, all measurements are made by the two men. (a) Lorentz serves the ball at 80.0 m/s. What is the ball's kinetic energy? (b) Einstein slams a return at 1.80×10^8 m/s. What is the ball's kinetic energy? (c) During Einstein's return of the ball in part (a), a white rabbit runs beside the court in the direction from Einstein to Lorentz. The rabbit has a speed of 2.20×10^8 m/s relative to the two men. What is the speed of the rabbit relative to the ball? (d) What does the rabbit measure as the distance from Einstein to Lorentz? (e) How much time does it take for the rabbit to run 20.0 m, according to the players? (f) The white rabbit carries a pocket watch. He uses this watch to measure the time (as he sees it) for the distance from Einstein to Lorentz to pass by under him. What time does he measure?

*37.67. One of the wavelengths of light emitted by hydrogen atoms under normal laboratory conditions is $\lambda = 656.3$ nm, in the red portion of the electromagnetic spectrum. In the light emitted from a distant galaxy this same spectral line is observed to be Doppler-shifted to $\lambda = 953.4$ nm, in the infrared portion of the spectrum. How fast are the emitting atoms moving relative to the earth? Are they approaching the earth or receding from it?

*37.68. Measuring Speed by Radar. A baseball coach uses a radar device to measure the speed of an approaching pitched baseball. This device sends out electromagnetic waves with frequency f_0 and then measures the shift in frequency Δf of the waves reflected from the moving baseball. If the fractional frequency shift produced by a baseball is $\Delta f/f_0 = 2.86 \times 10^{-7}$, what is the baseball's speed in km/h? (*Hint:* Are the waves Doppler-shifted a second time when reflected off the ball?)

37.69. Space Travel? Travel to the stars requires hundreds or thousands of years, even at the speed of light. Some people have suggested that we can get around this difficulty by accelerating the rocket (and its astronauts) to very high speeds so that they will age less due to time dilation. The fly in this ointment is that it takes a great deal of energy to do this. Suppose you want to go to the immense red giant Betelgeuse, which is about 500 light-years away. (A light-year is the distance that light travels in a year.) You plan to travel at constant speed in a 1000-kg rocket ship (a little over a ton), which, in reality, is far too small for this purpose. In each case that follows, calculate the time for the trip, as measured by people on earth and by astronauts in the rocket ship, the energy needed in joules, and the energy needed as a percentage of U.S. yearly use (which is 1.0×10^{19} J). For comparison, arrange your results in a table showing v_{rocket}, t_{earth}, t_{rocket}, E (in J), and E

(as % of U.S. use). The rocket ship's speed is (a) 0.50c; (b) 0.99c; (c) 0.9999c. On the basis of your results, does it seem likely that any government will invest in such high-speed space travel any time soon?

*37.70. A spaceship moving at constant speed u relative to us broadcasts a radio signal at constant frequency f_0. As the spaceship approaches us, we receive a higher frequency f; after it has passed, we receive a lower frequency. (a) As the spaceship passes by, so it is instantaneously moving neither toward nor away from us, show that the frequency we receive is not f_0, and derive an expression for the frequency we do receive. Is the frequency we receive higher or lower than f_0? (*Hint:* In this case, successive wave crests move the same distance to the observer and so they have the same transit time. Thus f equals $1/T$. Use the time dilation formula to relate the periods in the stationary and moving frames.) (b) A spaceship emits electromagnetic waves of frequency $f_0 = 345$ MHz as measured in a frame moving with the ship. The spaceship is moving at a constant speed $0.758c$ relative to us. What frequency f do we receive when the spaceship is approaching us? When it is moving away? In each case what is the shift in frequency, $f - f_0$? (c) Use the result of part (a) to calculate the frequency f and the frequency shift $(f - f_0)$ we receive at the instant that the ship passes by us. How does the shift in frequency calculated here compare to the shifts calculated in part (b)?

*37.71. The Pole and Barn Paradox. Suppose a *very* fast runner $(v = 0.600c)$ holding a long, horizontal pole runs through a barn open at both ends. The length of the pole (in its rest frame) is 6.00 m, and the length of the barn (in *its* rest frame) is 5.00 m. In the barn's reference frame, the pole will undergo length contraction and can all fit inside the barn at the same time. But in the runner's reference frame, the *barn* will undergo length contraction and the entire pole can *never* be entirely within the barn at any time! Explain the resolution of this paradox.

37.72. The French physicist Armand Fizeau was the first to measure the speed of light accurately. He also found experimentally that the speed, relative to the lab frame, of light traveling in a tank of water that is itself moving at a speed V relative to the lab frame is

$$v = \frac{c}{n} + kV$$

where $n = 1.333$ is the index of refraction of water. Fizeau called k the dragging coefficient and obtained an experimental value of $k = 0.44$. What value of k do you calculate from relativistic transformations?

Challenge Problems

37.73. Lorentz Transformation for Acceleration. Using a method analogous to the one in the text to find the Lorentz transformation formula for velocity, we can find the Lorentz transformation for *acceleration*. Let frame S' have a constant x-component of velocity u relative to frame S. An object moves relative to frame S along the x-axis with instantaneous velocity v_x and instantaneous acceleration a_x. (a) Show that its instantaneous acceleration in frame S' is

$$a_x' = a_x \left(1 - \frac{u^2}{c^2}\right)^{3/2} \left(1 - \frac{uv_x}{c^2}\right)^{-3}$$

[*Hint:* Express the acceleration in S' as $a_x' = dv_x'/dt'$. Then use Eq. (37.21) to express dt' in terms of dt and dx, and use

Eq. (37.22) to express dv_x' in terms of u and dv_x. The velocity of the object in S is $v_x = dx/dt$.] (b) Show that the acceleration in frame S can be expressed as

$$a_x = a_x' \left(1 - \frac{u^2}{c^2}\right)^{3/2} \left(1 + \frac{uv_x'}{c^2}\right)^{-3}$$

where $v_x' = dx'/dt'$ is the velocity of the object in frame S'.

37.74. A Realistic Version of the Twin Paradox. A rocket ship leaves the earth on January 1, 2100. Stella, one of a pair of twins born in the year 2075, pilots the rocket (reference frame S'); the other twin, Terra, stays on the earth (reference frame S). The rocket ship has an acceleration of constant magnitude g in its own reference frame (this makes the pilot feel at home, since it simulates the earth's gravity). The path of the rocket ship is a straight line in the $+x$-direction in frame S. (a) Using the results of Challenge Problem 37.73, show that in Terra's earth frame S, the rocket's acceleration is

$$\frac{du}{dt} = g\left(1 - \frac{u^2}{c^2}\right)^{3/2}$$

where u is the rocket's instantaneous velocity in frame S. (b) Write the result of part (a) in the form $dt = f(u)\, du$, where $f(u)$ is a function of u, and integrate both sides. (*Hint:* Use the integral given in Problem 37.63.) Show that in Terra's frame, the time when Stella attains a velocity v_{1x} is

$$t_1 = \frac{v_{1x}}{g\sqrt{1 - v_{1x}^2/c^2}}$$

(c) Use the time dilation formula to relate dt and dt' (infinitesimal time intervals measured in frames S and S', respectively). Combine this result with the result of part (a) and integrate as in part (b) to show the following: When Stella attains a velocity v_{1x} relative to Terra, the time t_1' that has elapsed in frame S' is

$$t_1' = \frac{c}{g} \operatorname{arctanh}\left(\frac{v_{1x}}{c}\right)$$

Here arctanh is the inverse hyperbolic tangent. (*Hint:* Use the integral given in Challenge Problem 5.124.) (d) Combine the results of parts (b) and (c) to find t_1 in terms of t_1', g, and c alone. (e) Stella accelerates in a straight-line path for five years (by her clock), slows down at the same rate for five years, turns around, accelerates for five years, slows down for five years, and lands back on the earth. According to Stella's clock, the date is January 1, 2120. What is the date according to Terra's clock?

*37.75. Determining the Masses of Stars. Many of the stars in the sky are actually *binary stars,* in which two stars orbit about their common center of mass. If the orbital speeds of the stars are high enough, the motion of the stars can be detected by the Doppler shifts of the light they emit. Stars for which this is the case are called *spectroscopic binary stars.* Figure 37.30 (next page) shows the simplest case of a spectroscopic binary star: two identical stars, each with mass m, orbiting their center of mass in a circle of radius R. The plane of the stars' orbits is edge-on to the line of sight of an observer on the earth. (a) The light produced by heated hydrogen gas in a laboratory on the earth has a frequency of 4.568110×10^{14} Hz. In the light received from the stars by a telescope on the earth, hydrogen light is observed to vary in frequency between 4.567710×10^{14} Hz and 4.568910×10^{14} Hz. Determine whether the binary star system as a whole is moving toward or

Figure **37.30** Challenge Problem 37.75.

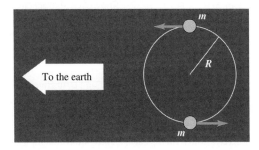

away from the earth, the speed of this motion, and the orbital speeds of the stars. (*Hint:* The speeds involved are much less than c, so you may use the approximate result $\Delta f/f = u/c$ given in Section 37.6.) (b) The light from each star in the binary system varies from its maximum frequency to its minimum frequency and back again in 11.0 days. Determine the orbital radius R and the mass m of each star. Give your answer for m in kilograms and as a multiple of the mass of the sun, 1.99×10^{30} kg. Compare the value of R to the distance from the earth to the sun, 1.50×10^{11} m. (This technique is actually used in astronomy to determine the masses of stars. In practice, the problem is more complicated because the two stars in a binary system are usually not identical, the orbits are usually not circular, and the plane of the orbits is usually tilted with respect to the line of sight from the earth.)

37.76. Relativity and the Wave Equation. (a) Consider the Galilean transformation along the x-direction: $x' = x - vt$ and $t' = t$. In frame S the wave equation for electromagnetic waves in a vacuum is

$$\frac{\partial^2 E(x, t)}{\partial x^2} - \frac{1}{c^2}\frac{\partial^2 E(x, t)}{\partial t^2} = 0$$

where E represents the electric field in the wave. Show that by using the Galilean transformation the wave equation in frame S' is found to be

$$\left(1 - \frac{v^2}{c^2}\right)\frac{\partial^2 E(x', t')}{\partial x'^2} + \frac{2v}{c^2}\frac{\partial^2 E(x', t')}{\partial x'\partial t'} - \frac{1}{c^2}\frac{\partial^2 E(x', t')}{\partial t'^2} = 0$$

This has a different form than the wave equation in S. Hence the Galilean transformation *violates* the first relativity postulate that all physical laws have the same form in all inertial reference frames. (*Hint:* Express the derivatives $\partial/\partial x$ and $\partial/\partial t$ in terms of $\partial/\partial x'$ and $\partial/\partial t'$ by use of the chain rule.) (b) Repeat the analysis of part (a), but use the Lorentz coordinate transformations, Eqs. (37.21), and show that in frame S' the wave equation has the same form as in frame S:

$$\frac{\partial^2 E(x', t')}{\partial x^2} - \frac{1}{c^2}\frac{\partial^2 E(x', t')}{\partial t'^2} = 0$$

Explain why this shows that the speed of light in vacuum is c in both frames S and S'.

37.77. Kaon Production. In high-energy physics, new particles can be created by collisions of fast-moving projectile particles with stationary particles. Some of the kinetic energy of the incident particle is used to create the mass of the new particle. A proton–proton collision can result in the creation of a negative kaon (K^-) and a positive kaon (K^+):

$$p + p \rightarrow p + p + K^- + K^+$$

(a) Calculate the minimum kinetic energy of the incident proton that will allow this reaction to occur if the second (target) proton is initially at rest. The rest energy of each kaon is 493.7 MeV, and the rest energy of each proton is 938.3 MeV. (*Hint:* It is useful here to work in the frame in which the total momentum is zero. See Problem 8.100, but note that here the Lorentz transformation must be used to relate the velocities in the laboratory frame to those in the zero-total-momentum frame.) (b) How does this calculated minimum kinetic energy compare with the total rest mass energy of the created kaons? (c) Suppose that instead the two protons are both in motion with velocities of equal magnitude and opposite direction. Find the minimum combined kinetic energy of the two protons that will allow the reaction to occur. How does this calculated minimum kinetic energy compare with the total rest mass energy of the created kaons? (This example shows that when colliding beams of particles are used instead of a stationary target, the energy requirements for producing new particles are reduced substantially.)

APPENDIX A

THE INTERNATIONAL SYSTEM OF UNITS

The Système International d'Unités, abbreviated SI, is the system developed by the General Conference on Weights and Measures and adopted by nearly all the industrial nations of the world. The following material is adapted from B. N. Taylor, ed., National Institute of Standards and Technology Spec. Pub. 811 (U.S. Govt. Printing Office, Washington, DC, 1995). See also **http://physics.nist.gov/cuu**

Quantity	Name of unit	Symbol	Equivalent units
SI base units			
length	meter	m	
mass	kilogram	kg	
time	second	s	
electric current	ampere	A	
thermodynamic temperature	kelvin	K	
amount of substance	mole	mol	
luminous intensity	candela	cd	
SI derived units			
area	square meter	m^2	
volume	cubic meter	m^3	
frequency	hertz	Hz	s^{-1}
mass density (density)	kilogram per cubic meter	kg/m^3	
speed, velocity	meter per second	m/s	
angular velocity	radian per second	rad/s	
acceleration	meter per second squared	m/s^2	
angular acceleration	radian per second squared	rad/s^2	
force	newton	N	$kg \cdot m/s^2$
pressure (mechanical stress)	pascal	Pa	N/m^2
kinematic viscosity	square meter per second	m^2/s	
dynamic viscosity	newton-second per square meter	$N \cdot s/m^2$	
work, energy, quantity of heat	joule	J	$N \cdot m$
power	watt	W	J/s
quantity of electricity	coulomb	C	$A \cdot s$
potential difference, electromotive force	volt	V	J/C, W/A
electric field strength	volt per meter	V/m	N/C
electric resistance	ohm	Ω	V/A
capacitance	farad	F	$A \cdot s/V$
magnetic flux	weber	Wb	$V \cdot s$
inductance	henry	H	$V \cdot s/A$
magnetic flux density	tesla	T	Wb/m^2
magnetic field strength	ampere per meter	A/m	
magnetomotive force	ampere	A	
luminous flux	lumen	lm	$cd \cdot sr$
luminance	candela per square meter	cd/m^2	
illuminance	lux	lx	lm/m^2
wave number	1 per meter	m^{-1}	
entropy	joule per kelvin	J/K	
specific heat capacity	joule per kilogram-kelvin	$J/kg \cdot K$	
thermal conductivity	watt per meter-kelvin	$W/m \cdot K$	

Quantity	Name of unit	Symbol	Equivalent units
radiant intensity	watt per steradian	W/sr	
activity (of a radioactive source)	becquerel	Bq	s^{-1}
radiation dose	gray	Gy	J/kg
radiation dose equivalent	sievert	Sv	J/kg
SI supplementary units			
plane angle	radian	rad	
solid angle	steradian	sr	

Definitions of SI Units

meter (m)   The *meter* is the length equal to the distance traveled by light, in vacuum, in a time of 1/299,792,458 second.

kilogram (kg)   The *kilogram* is the unit of mass; it is equal to the mass of the international prototype of the kilogram. (The international prototype of the kilogram is a particular cylinder of platinum-iridium alloy that is preserved in a vault at Sévres, France, by the International Bureau of Weights and Measures.)

second (s)   The *second* is the duration of 9,192,631,770 periods of the radiation corresponding to the transition between the two hyperfine levels of the ground state of the cesium-133 atom.

ampere (A)   The *ampere* is that constant current that, if maintained in two straight parallel conductors of infinite length, of negligible circular cross section, and placed 1 meter apart in vacuum, would produce between these conductors a force equal to 2×10^{-7} newton per meter of length.

kelvin (K)   The *kelvin,* unit of thermodynamic temperature, is the fraction 1/273.16 of the thermodynamic temper-ature of the triple point of water.

ohm (Ω)   The *ohm* is the electric resistance between two points of a conductor when a constant difference of potential of 1 volt, applied between these two points, produces in this conductor a current of 1 ampere, this conductor not being the source of any electromotive force.

coulomb (C)   The *coulomb* is the quantity of electricity transported in 1 second by a current of 1 ampere.

candela (cd)   The *candela* is the luminous intensity, in a given direction, of a source that emits monochromatic radiation of frequency 540×10^{12} hertz and that has a radiant intensity in that direction of 1/683 watt per steradian.

mole (mol)   The *mole* is the amount of substance of a system that contains as many elementary entities as there are carbon atoms in 0.012 kg of carbon 12. The elementary entities must be specified and may be atoms, molecules, ions, electrons, other particles, or specified groups of such particles.

newton (N)   The *newton* is that force that gives to a mass of 1 kilogram an acceleration of 1 meter per second per second.

joule (J)   The *joule* is the work done when the point of application of a constant force of 1 newton is displaced a distance of 1 meter in the direction of the force.

watt (W)   The *watt* is the power that gives rise to the production of energy at the rate of 1 joule per second.

volt (V)   The *volt* is the difference of electric potential between two points of a conducting wire carrying a constant current of 1 ampere, when the power dissipated between these points is equal to 1 watt.

weber (Wb)   The *weber* is the magnetic flux that, linking a circuit of one turn, produces in it an electromotive force of 1 volt as it is reduced to zero at a uniform rate in 1 second.

lumen (lm)   The *lumen* is the luminous flux emitted in a solid angle of 1 steradian by a uniform point source having an intensity of 1 candela.

farad (F)   The *farad* is the capacitance of a capacitor between the plates of which there appears a difference of potential of 1 volt when it is charged by a quantity of electricity equal to 1 coulomb.

henry (H)   The *henry* is the inductance of a closed circuit in which an electromotive force of 1 volt is produced when the electric current in the circuit varies uniformly at a rate of 1 ampere per second.

radian (rad)   The *radian* is the plane angle between two radii of a circle that cut off on the circumference an arc equal in length to the radius.

steradian (sr)   The *steradian* is the solid angle that, having its vertex in the center of a sphere, cuts off an area of the surface of the sphere equal to that of a square with sides of length equal to the radius of the sphere.

SI Prefixes   The names of multiples and submultiples of SI units may be formed by application of the prefixes listed in Appendix F.

APPENDIX B

USEFUL MATHEMATICAL RELATIONS

Algebra

$$a^{-x} = \frac{1}{a^x} \qquad a^{(x+y)} = a^x a^y \qquad a^{(x-y)} = \frac{a^x}{a^y}$$

Logarithms: If $\log a = x$, then $a = 10^x$. $\log a + \log b = \log(ab)$ $\log a - \log b = \log(a/b)$ $\log(a^n) = n\log a$

If $\ln a = x$, then $a = e^x$. $\ln a + \ln b = \ln(ab)$ $\ln a - \ln b = \ln(a/b)$ $\ln(a^n) = n\ln a$

Quadratic formula: If $ax^2 + bx + c = 0$, $x = \dfrac{-b \pm \sqrt{b^2 - 4ac}}{2a}$.

Binomial Theorem

$$(a + b)^n = a^n + na^{n-1}b + \frac{n(n-1)a^{n-2}b^2}{2!} + \frac{n(n-1)(n-2)a^{n-3}b^3}{3!} + \cdots$$

Trigonometry

In the right triangle ABC, $x^2 + y^2 = r^2$.

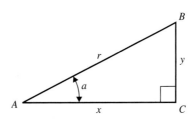

Definitions of the trigonometric functions: $\sin a = y/r$ $\cos a = x/r$ $\tan a = y/x$

Identities: $\sin^2 a + \cos^2 a = 1$ $\tan a = \dfrac{\sin a}{\cos a}$

$\sin 2a = 2\sin a \cos a$ $\cos 2a = \cos^2 a - \sin^2 a = 2\cos^2 a - 1$
$$= 1 - 2\sin^2 a$$

$\sin\frac{1}{2}a = \sqrt{\dfrac{1 - \cos a}{2}}$ $\cos\frac{1}{2}a = \sqrt{\dfrac{1 + \cos a}{2}}$

$\sin(-a) = -\sin a$ $\sin(a \pm b) = \sin a \cos b \pm \cos a \sin b$

$\cos(-a) = \cos a$ $\cos(a \pm b) = \cos a \cos b \mp \sin a \sin b$

$\sin(a \pm \pi/2) = \pm\cos a$ $\sin a + \sin b = 2\sin\frac{1}{2}(a + b)\cos\frac{1}{2}(a - b)$

$\cos(a \pm \pi/2) = \mp\sin a$ $\cos a + \cos b = 2\cos\frac{1}{2}(a + b)\cos\frac{1}{2}(a - b)$

Geometry

Circumference of circle of radius r: $C = 2\pi r$

Area of circle of radius r: $A = \pi r^2$

Volume of sphere of radius r: $V = 4\pi r^3/3$

Surface area of sphere of radius r: $A = 4\pi r^2$

Volume of cylinder of radius r and height h: $V = \pi r^2 h$

Calculus

Derivatives:

$$\frac{d}{dx}x^n = nx^{n-1}$$

$$\frac{d}{dx}\sin ax = a\cos ax$$

$$\frac{d}{dx}\cos ax = -a\sin ax$$

$$\frac{d}{dx}e^{ax} = ae^{ax}$$

$$\frac{d}{dx}\ln ax = \frac{1}{x}$$

$$\int \frac{dx}{\sqrt{a^2 - x^2}} = \arcsin\frac{x}{a}$$

$$\int \frac{dx}{\sqrt{x^2 + a^2}} = \ln\left(x + \sqrt{x^2 + a^2}\right)$$

$$\int \frac{dx}{x^2 + a^2} = \frac{1}{a}\arctan\frac{x}{a}$$

$$\int \frac{dx}{(x^2 + a^2)^{3/2}} = \frac{1}{a^2}\frac{x}{\sqrt{x^2 + a^2}}$$

$$\int \frac{x\,dx}{(x^2 + a^2)^{3/2}} = -\frac{1}{\sqrt{x^2 + a^2}}$$

Integrals:

$$\int x^n\,dx = \frac{x^{n+1}}{n+1} \quad (n \neq -1)$$

$$\int \frac{dx}{x} = \ln x$$

$$\int \sin ax\,dx = -\frac{1}{a}\cos ax$$

$$\int \cos ax\,dx = \frac{1}{a}$$

$$\int e^{ax}\,dx = \frac{1}{a}e^{ax}$$

Power series (convergent for range of x shown):

$$(1 + x)^n = 1 + nx + \frac{n(n-1)x^2}{2!} + \frac{n(n-1)(n-2)}{3!}x^3 + \cdots \quad (|x| < 1)$$

$$\sin x = x - \frac{x^3}{3!} + \frac{x^5}{5!} - \frac{x^7}{7!} + \cdots \quad (\text{all } x)$$

$$\cos x = 1 - \frac{x^2}{2!} + \frac{x^4}{4!} - \frac{x^6}{6!} + \cdots \quad (\text{all } x)$$

$$\tan x = x + \frac{x^3}{3} + \frac{2x^2}{15} + \frac{17x^7}{315} + \cdots \quad (|x| < \pi/2)$$

$$e^x = 1 + x + \frac{x^2}{2!} + \frac{x^3}{3!} + \cdots \quad (\text{all } x)$$

$$\ln(1 + x) = x - \frac{x^2}{2} + \frac{x^3}{3} - \frac{x^4}{4} + \cdots \quad (|x| < 1)$$

APPENDIX C

THE GREEK ALPHABET

Name	Capital	Lowercase	Name	Capital	Lowercase
Alpha	A	α	Nu	N	ν
Beta	B	β	Xi	Ξ	ξ
Gamma	Γ	γ	Omicron	O	o
Delta	Δ	δ	Pi	Π	π
Epsilon	E	ϵ	Rho	P	ρ
Zeta	Z	ζ	Sigma	Σ	σ
Eta	H	η	Tau	T	τ
Theta	Θ	θ	Upsilon	Y	υ
Iota	I	ι	Phi	Φ	ϕ
Kappa	K	κ	Chi	X	χ
Lambda	Λ	λ	Psi	Ψ	ψ
Mu	M	μ	Omega	Ω	ω

APPENDIX D

PERIODIC TABLE OF THE ELEMENTS

Group	1	2	3	4	5	6	7	8	9	10	11	12	13	14	15	16	17	18
Period																		
1	1 **H** 1.008																	2 **He** 4.003
2	3 **Li** 6.941	4 **Be** 9.012											5 **B** 10.811	6 **C** 12.011	7 **N** 14.007	8 **O** 15.999	9 **F** 18.998	10 **Ne** 20.180
3	11 **Na** 22.990	12 **Mg** 24.305											13 **Al** 26.982	14 **Si** 28.086	15 **P** 30.974	16 **S** 32.065	17 **Cl** 35.453	18 **Ar** 39.948
4	19 **K** 39.098	20 **Ca** 40.078	21 **Sc** 44.956	22 **Ti** 47.867	23 **V** 50.942	24 **Cr** 51.996	25 **Mn** 54.938	26 **Fe** 55.845	27 **Co** 58.933	28 **Ni** 58.693	29 **Cu** 63.546	30 **Zn** 65.409	31 **Ga** 69.723	32 **Ge** 72.64	33 **As** 74.922	34 **Se** 78.96	35 **Br** 79.904	36 **Kr** 83.798
5	37 **Rb** 85.468	38 **Sr** 87.62	39 **Y** 88.906	40 **Zr** 91.224	41 **Nb** 92.906	42 **Mo** 95.94	43 **Tc** (98)	44 **Ru** 101.07	45 **Rh** 102.906	46 **Pd** 106.42	47 **Ag** 107.868	48 **Cd** 112.411	49 **In** 114.818	50 **Sn** 118.710	51 **Sb** 121.760	52 **Te** 127.60	53 **I** 126.904	54 **Xe** 131.293
6	55 **Cs** 132.905	56 **Ba** 137.327	71 **Lu** 174.967	72 **Hf** 178.49	73 **Ta** 180.948	74 **W** 183.84	75 **Re** 186.207	76 **Os** 190.23	77 **Ir** 192.217	78 **Pt** 195.078	79 **Au** 196.967	80 **Hg** 200.59	81 **Tl** 204.383	82 **Pb** 207.2	83 **Bi** 208.980	84 **Po** (209)	85 **At** (210)	86 **Rn** (222)
7	87 **Fr** (223)	88 **Ra** (226)	103 **Lr** (262)	104 **Rf** (261)	105 **Db** (262)	106 **Sg** (266)	107 **Bh** (264)	108 **Hs** (269)	109 **Mt** (268)	110 **Ds** (271)	111 **Rg** (272)	112 **Uub** (285)	113 **Uut** (284)	114 **Uuq** (289)	115 **Uup** (288)	116 **Uuh** (292)	117 **Uus**	118 **Uuo**

Lanthanoids

57 **La** 138.905	58 **Ce** 140.116	59 **Pr** 140.908	60 **Nd** 144.24	61 **Pm** (145)	62 **Sm** 150.36	63 **Eu** 151.964	64 **Gd** 157.25	65 **Tb** 158.925	66 **Dy** 162.500	67 **Ho** 164.930	68 **Er** 167.259	69 **Tm** 168.934	70 **Yb** 173.04

Actinoids

89 **Ac** (227)	90 **Th** (232)	91 **Pa** (231)	92 **U** (238)	93 **Np** (237)	94 **Pu** (244)	95 **Am** (243)	96 **Cm** (247)	97 **Bk** (247)	98 **Cf** (251)	99 **Es** (252)	100 **Fm** (257)	101 **Md** (258)	102 **No** (259)

For each element the average atomic mass of the mixture of isotopes occurring in nature is shown. For elements having no stable isotope, the approximate atomic mass of the longest-lived isotope is shown in parentheses. For elements that have been predicted but not yet detected, no atomic mass is given. All atomic masses are expressed in atomic mass units (1 u = 1.66053886(28) $\times$ 10^{-27} kg), equivalent to grams per mole (g/mol).

APPENDIX E

UNIT CONVERSION FACTORS

Length
1 m = 100 cm = 1000 mm = 10^6 μm = 10^9 nm
1 km = 1000 m = 0.6214 mi
1 m = 3.281 ft = 39.37 in.
1 cm = 0.3937 in.
1 in. = 2.540 cm
1 ft = 30.48 cm
1 yd = 91.44 cm
1 mi = 5280 ft = 1.609 km
1 Å = 10^{-10} m = 10^{-8} cm = 10^{-1} nm
1 nautical mile = 6080 ft
1 light year = 9.461 × 10^{15} m

Area
1 cm^2 = 0.155 $in.^2$
1 m^2 = 10^4 cm^2 = 10.76 ft^2
1 $in.^2$ = 6.452 cm^2
1 ft = 144 $in.^2$ = 0.0929 m^2

Volume
1 liter = 1000 cm^3 = 10^{-3} m^3 = 0.03531 ft^3 = 61.02 $in.^3$
1 ft^3 = 0.02832 m^3 = 28.32 liters = 7.477 gallons
1 gallon = 3.788 liters

Time
1 min = 60 s
1 h = 3600 s
1 d = 86,400 s
1 y = 365.24 d = 3.156 × 10^7 s

Angle
1 rad = 57.30° = 180°/π
1° = 0.01745 rad = π/180 rad
1 revolution = 360° = 2π rad
1 rev/min (rpm) = 0.1047 rad/s

Speed
1 m/s = 3.281 ft/s
1 ft/s = 0.3048 m/s
1 mi/min = 60 mi/h = 88 ft/s
1 km/h = 0.2778 m/s = 0.6214 mi/h
1 mi/h = 1.466 ft/s = 0.4470 m/s = 1.609 km/h
1 furlong/fortnight = 1.662 × 10^{-4} m/s

Acceleration
1 m/s^2 = 100 cm/s^2 = 3.281 ft/s^2
1 cm/s^2 = 0.01 m/s^2 = 0.03281 ft/s^2
1 ft/s^2 = 0.3048 m/s^2 = 30.48 cm/s^2
1 mi/h · s = 1.467 ft/s^2

Mass
1 kg = 10^3 g = 0.0685 slug
1 g = 6.85 × 10^{-5} slug
1 slug = 14.59 kg
1 u − 1.661 × 10^{-27} kg
1 kg has a weight of 2.205 lb when g = 9.80 m/s^2

Force
1 N = 10^5 dyn = 0.2248 lb
1 lb = 4.448 N = 4.448 × 10^5 dyn

Pressure
1 Pa = 1 N/m^2 = 1.450 × 10^{-4} $lb/in.^2$ = 0.209 lb/ft^2
1 bar = 10^5 Pa
1 $lb/in.^2$ = 6895 Pa
1 lb/ft^2 = 47.88 Pa
1 atm = 1.013 × 10^5 Pa = 1.013 bar
$\qquad$ = 14.7 $lb/in.^2$ = 2117 lb/ft^2
1 mm Hg = 1 torr = 133.3 Pa

Energy
1 J = 10^7 ergs = 0.239 cal
1 cal = 4.186 J (based on 15° calorie)
1 ft · lb = 1.356 J
1 Btu = 1055 J = 252 cal = 778 ft · lb
1 eV = 1.602 × 10^{-19} J
1 kWh = 3.600 × 10^6 J

Mass–Energy Equivalence
1 kg ↔ 8.988 × 10^{16} J
1 u ↔ 931.5 MeV
1 eV ↔ 1.074 × 10^{-9} u

Power
1 W = 1 J/s
1 hp = 746 W = 550 ft · lb/s
1 Btu/h = 0.293 W

APPENDIX F

NUMERICAL CONSTANTS

Fundamental Physical Constants*

Name	Symbol	Value
Speed of light	c	2.99792458×10^8 m/s
Magnitude of charge of electron	e	$1.60217653(14) \times 10^{-19}$ C
Gravitational constant	G	$6.6742(10) \times 10^{-11}$ N · m^2/kg^2
Planck's constant	h	$6.6260693(11) \times 10^{-34}$ J · s
Boltzmann constant	k	$1.3806505(24) \times 10^{-23}$ J/K
Avogadro's number	N_A	$6.0221415(10) \times 10^{23}$ molecules/mol
Gas constant	R	$8.314472(15)$ J/mol · K
Mass of electron	m_e	$9.1093826(16) \times 10^{-31}$ kg
Mass of proton	m_p	$1.67262171(29) \times 10^{-27}$ kg
Mass of neutron	m_n	$1.67492728(29) \times 10^{-27}$ kg
Permeability of free space	μ_0	$4\pi \times 10^{-7}$ Wb/A · m
Permittivity of free space	$\epsilon_0 = 1/\mu_0 c^2$	$8.854187817 \ldots \times 10^{-12}$ C^2/N · m^2
	$1/4\pi\epsilon_0$	$8.987551787 \ldots \times 10^9$ N · m^2/C^2

Other Useful Constants*

Name	Symbol	Value
Mechanical equivalent of heat		4.186 J/cal (15° calorie)
Standard atmospheric pressure	1 atm	1.01325×10^5 Pa
Absolute zero	0 K	-273.15°C
Electron volt	1 eV	$1.60217653(14) \times 10^{-19}$ J
Atomic mass unit	1 u	$1.66053886(28) \times 10^{-27}$ kg
Electron rest energy	$m_e c^2$	$0.510998918(44)$ MeV
Volume of ideal gas (0°C and 1 atm)		$22.413996(39)$ liter/mol
Acceleration due to gravity (standard)	g	9.80665 m/s^2

*Source: National Institute of Standards and Technology (**http://physics.nist.gov/cuu**). Numbers in parentheses show the uncertainty in the final digits of the main number; for example, the number 1.6454(21) means 1.6454 ± 0.0021. Values shown without uncertainties are exact.

Astronomical Data[†]

Body	Mass (kg)	Radius (m)	Orbit radius (m)	Orbit period
Sun	1.99×10^{30}	6.96×10^8	—	—
Moon	7.35×10^{22}	1.74×10^6	3.84×10^8	27.3 d
Mercury	3.30×10^{23}	2.44×10^6	5.79×10^{10}	88.0 d
Venus	4.87×10^{24}	6.05×10^6	1.08×10^{11}	224.7 d
Earth	5.97×10^{24}	6.38×10^6	1.50×10^{11}	365.3 d
Mars	6.42×10^{23}	3.40×10^6	2.28×10^{11}	687.0 d
Jupiter	1.90×10^{27}	6.91×10^7	7.78×10^{11}	11.86 y
Saturn	5.68×10^{26}	6.03×10^7	1.43×10^{12}	29.45 y
Uranus	8.68×10^{25}	2.56×10^7	2.87×10^{12}	84.02 y
Neptune	1.02×10^{26}	2.48×10^7	4.50×10^{12}	164.8 y
Pluto[‡]	1.31×10^{22}	1.15×10^6	5.91×10^{12}	247.9 y

[†]Source: NASA Jet Propulsion Laboratory Solar System Dynamics Group (**http://ssd.jpl.nasa.gov**), and P. Kenneth Seidelmann, ed., ***Explanatory Supplement to the Astronomical Almanac*** (University Science Books, Mill Valley, CA, 1992), pp. 704–706. For each body, "radius" is its radius at its equator and "orbit radius" is its average distance from the sun (for the planets) or from the earth (for the moon).

[‡]In August 2006, the International Astronomical Union reclassified Pluto and other small objects that orbit the sun as "dwarf planets."

Prefixes for Powers of 10

Power of ten	Prefix	Abbreviation	Pronunciation
10^{-24}	yocto-	y	*yoc*-toe
10^{-21}	zepto-	z	*zep*-toe
10^{-18}	atto-	a	*at*-toe
10^{-15}	femto-	f	*fem*-toe
10^{-12}	pico-	p	*pee*-koe
10^{-9}	nano-	n	*nan*-oe
10^{-6}	micro-	μ	*my*-crow
10^{-3}	milli-	m	*mil*-i
10^{-2}	centi-	c	*cen*-ti
10^3	kilo-	k	*kil*-oe
10^6	mega-	M	*meg*-a
10^9	giga-	G	*jig*-a or *gig*-a
10^{12}	tera-	T	*ter*-a
10^{15}	peta-	P	*pet*-a
10^{18}	exa-	E	*ex*-a
10^{21}	zetta-	Z	*zet*-a
10^{24}	yotta-	Y	*yot*-a

Examples:

1 femtometer = 1 fm = 10^{-15} m

1 picosecond = 1 ps = 10^{-12} s

1 nanocoulomb = 1 nC = 10^{-9} C

1 microkelvin = 1 μK = 10^{-6} K

1 millivolt = 1 mV = 10^{-3} V

1 kilopascal = 1 kPa = 10^3 Pa

1 megawatt = 1 MW = 10^6 W

1 gigahertz = 1 GHz = 10^9 Hz

ANSWERS TO ODD-NUMBERED PROBLEMS

Chapter 21

21.1 a) 2.0×10^{10} b) 8.58×10^{-13}
21.3 2.10×10^{28} electrons, 3.35×10^9 C
21.5 3.71×10^3 m
21.7 a) 7.42×10^{-7} C on each sphere
  b) 3.71×10^{-7} C on one and 1.48×10^{-6} C on the other
21.9 1.43×10^{13}, away from each other
21.11 a) 2.20×10^4 m/s
21.13 $+0.750$ nC
21.15 1.8×10^{-4} N, $+x$-direction
21.17 $x = -0.144$ m
21.19 2.58×10^{-6} N, $-y$-direction
21.21 a) $F_x = 0, F_y = +2kqQa/(a^2 + x^2)^{3/2}$
  c) $2kqQ/a^2$, $+y$-direction
21.23 b) $kq^2(1 + 2\sqrt{2})/2L^2$
21.25 a) 4.40×10^{-16} N b) 2.63×10^{11} m/s^2
  c) 2.63×10^5 m/s
21.27 a) 3.31×10^6 N/C, to the left
  b) 1.42×10^{-8} s c) 1.80×10^3 N/C, to the right
21.29 a) -21.9μC b) 1.02×10^{-7} N/C
21.31 a) 8.75×10^3 N/C, to the right
  b) 6.54×10^3 N/C, to the right
  c) 1.40×10^{-15} N, to the right
21.33 a) 364 N/C b) no, 2.73 μm downward
21.35 1.79×10^6 m/s
21.37 a) $mg = 8.93 \times 10^{-30}$ N; $F_e = 1.60 \times 10^{-15}$ N; yes
  b) 1.63×10^{-16} kg $= 1.79 \times 10^{14} m_e$ c) no
21.39 a) $-\hat{\jmath}$ b) $(\hat{\imath} + \hat{\jmath})/\sqrt{2}$ c) $-0.390\hat{\imath} + 0.921\hat{\jmath}$
21.41 a) 6.33×10^5 m/s b) 1.59×10^4 m/s
21.43 a) 0 b) $E_x = -2kq(x^2 + a^2)/(x^2 - a^2)^2$, for $x < -a$; $E_x = +2kq(x^2 + a^2)/(x^2 - a^2)^2$, for $x > +a$
21.45 a) (i) 574 N/C, $+x$-direction
  (ii) 268 N/C, $-x$-direction
  (iii) 404 N/C, $-x$-direction
  b) (i) 9.20×10^{-17} N, $-x$-direction
  (ii) 4.30×10^{-17} N, $-x$-direction
  (iii) 6.48×10^{-17} N, $+x$-direction
21.47 1.04×10^7 N/C, to the left
21.49 a) $E_x = E_y = E = 0$
  b) $E_x = +2.66 \times 10^3$ N/C, $E_y = 0$;
  $E = 2.66 \times 10^3$ N/C, $+x$-direction
  c) $E_x = +129$ N/C, $E_y = -510$ N/C;
  $E = 526$ N/C, $284°$ clockwise from $+x$-axis
  d) $E_x = 0, E_y = E = +1.38 \times 10^3$ N/C, $+y$-direction
21.51 a) $E_x = -4.79 \times 10^3$ N/C, $E_y = 0$;
  $E = 4.79 \times 10^3$ N/C, $-x$-direction
  b) $E_x = +2.13 \times 10^3$ N/C, $E_y = 0$;
  $E = 2.13 \times 10^3$ N/C, $+x$-direction
21.53 a) $\vec{E} = \dfrac{2k\lambda}{x\sqrt{x^2/a^2 + 1}}\hat{\imath}$ b) $\vec{E} = \dfrac{2k\lambda}{x}\hat{\imath}$
21.55 a) $(7.0\,\text{N/C})\hat{\imath}$ b) $(1.75 \times 10^{-5}\,\text{N})\hat{\imath}$
21.57 a) 0 b) 0 c) σ/ϵ_0 directed downward
21.59 a) yes b) no
21.61 An infinite line of charge has a radial field in the plane through the wire, and constant in the plane of the wire, mirror-imaged about the wire
21.63 a) 1.4×10^{-11} C $\cdot$ m from q_1 toward q_2
  b) 860 N/C
21.65 b) This also gives the correct expression for E_y since y appears in the full expression's denominator squared, so the signs carry through correctly.
21.67 b) Opposite charges are closest so the dipoles attract.
21.69 a) The torque is zero when $\vec{p}$ is aligned either in the *same* direction as $\vec{E}$ or in the *opposite* directions
  b) The stable orientation is when $\vec{p}$ is aligned in

the *same* direction as $\vec{E}$
21.71 1680 N, from $+5.00\,\mu$C charge toward $-5.00\,\mu$C charge
  b) 22.3 N $\cdot$ m, clockwise
21.73 a) $\sqrt{\dfrac{kqQ}{m\pi^2 a^3}}$ b) accelerating along the y-axis away from origin
21.75 b) 2.80×10^{-6} C c) $39.5°$
21.77 a) 2.09×10^{21} N b) 5.90×10^{23} m/s^2 c) no
21.79 a) $6kq^2/L^2$, away from vacant corner
  b) $(3kq^2/2L^2)(1 + 2\sqrt{2})$, toward center of square
21.81 a) 6.0×10^{23}
  b) $F_g = 4.1 \times 10^{-31}$ N, $F_e = 5.1 \times 10^5$ N
  c) yes for F_e and no for F_g
21.83 a) $(2kq/x^2)[1 - (1 + a^2/x^2)^{-3/2}], -x$-direction
  b) $3kqa^2/x^4$
21.85 a) 3.5×10^{20} b) 1.6 C; 2.4×10^{10} N
21.87 a) $(mv_0^2\sin^2\alpha)/2eE$ b) $(mv_0^2\sin 2\alpha)/eE$
  c) $h_{max} = 0.418$ m, $d = 2.89$ m
21.89 a) $E_x = \dfrac{kQ}{a}\left(\dfrac{1}{r} - \dfrac{1}{a + r}\right), E_y = 0$
  b) $\dfrac{kqQ}{a}\left(\dfrac{1}{x - a} - \dfrac{1}{x}\right)\hat{\imath}$
21.91 a) $-(7850\,\text{N/C})\hat{\imath}$ b) smaller c) 18 cm
21.93 a) $+(0.89\,\text{N/C})\hat{\imath}$ b) smaller c) (i) 1.2%
  (ii) 4.5%
21.95 a) $F = \dfrac{2kqQ}{a}\left(\dfrac{1}{y} - \dfrac{1}{\sqrt{a^2 + y^2}}\right), -x$-direction
  b) $F = \dfrac{kqQ}{a}\left(\dfrac{1}{x - a} - \dfrac{1}{x + a} - \dfrac{2}{x}\right)$, $+x$-direction
21.97 $E_x = E_y = 2kQ/a^2$
21.99 a) 6.25×10^4 N/C, $225°$ measured counterclockwise from $+x$-axis
  b) 1.00×10^{-14} N, $45°$ measured counterclockwise from $+x$-axis
21.101 a) 1.19×10^6 N/C, to the left
  b) 1.19×10^5 N/C, to the left
  c) 1.19×10^5 N/C, to the right
21.103 $\vec{E} = \dfrac{\sigma}{2\epsilon_0}\left[-\dfrac{x}{|x|}\hat{\imath} + \dfrac{z}{|z|}\hat{k}\right]$
21.105 b) $q_1 < 0, q_2 > 0$ c) $0.844\,\mu$C d) 56.2 N
21.107 a) $\dfrac{kQ}{L}\left[\dfrac{1}{x + a/2} - \dfrac{1}{x + L + a/2}\right]$

Chapter 22

22.1 a) 1.75 N$\cdot$m^2/C b) no c) i) 0 ii) $90°$
22.3 a) 3.53×10^5 N $\cdot$ m^2/C b) 3.13×10^{-6} C
22.5 $\Phi = E\pi r^2$
22.7 a) 2.71×10^5 N $\cdot$ m^2/C
  b) 2.71×10^5 N $\cdot$ m^2/C
  c) 5.42×10^5 N $\cdot$ m^2/C
22.9 a) zero b) 3.75×10^7 N/C radially inward
  c) 1.11×10^7 N/C radially inward
22.11 b) no
22.13 a) 1.81×10^5 N $\cdot$ m^2/C b) no change
22.15 a) 4.50×10^4 N/C b) 9.18×10^2 N/C
22.17 a) 3.00×10^{-7} C b) 1.20×10^5 N/C
22.19 a) $q = 3.27 \times 10^{-9}$ C b) $n_e = 2.04 \times 10^{10}$
22.21 8.06×10^5 N/C, toward negatively charged sphere
22.23 a) 5.73×10^{-6} C/m^2 b) 6.48×10^5 N/C
  c) -5.65×10^4 N $\cdot$ m^2/C
22.25 a) 2.59×10^{-7} C/m^3 b) 1.96×10^3 N/C
22.27 a) $E = \sigma/\epsilon_0$ b) 0
22.29 a) $\lambda = 2\pi r\sigma$ b) $\sigma R/r\epsilon_0$
22.31 a) yes; $+Q$ b) no c) yes d) no; no
  e) no; yes; no
22.33 a) 750 N $\cdot$ m^2/C b) 0 c) 577 N/C
22.35 a) -5.98×10^{-10} C
22.37 a) $\lambda/2\pi\epsilon_0 r$, radially outward

b) $\lambda/2\pi\epsilon_0 r$, radially outward
  d) inner: $-\lambda$; outer: $+\lambda$
22.39 a) i) $\alpha/2\pi\epsilon_0 r$, radially outward ii) 0 iii) 0
  b) i) $-\alpha$ ii) 0
22.41 $\theta = 19.8°$
22.43 a) $0 < r < R$, $E = 0$
  $R < r < 2R$, $E = Q/4\pi\epsilon_0 r^2$, radially outward;
  $r > 2R$, $E = 2Q/4\pi\epsilon_0 r^2$, radially outward
22.45 a) i) 0 ii) 0 iii) $q/2\pi\epsilon_0 r^2$, radially outward
  iv) 0 v) $3q/2\pi\epsilon_0 r^2$, radially outward b) i) 0
  ii) $+2q$ iii) $-2q$ iv) $+6q$
22.47 a) i) 0 ii) 0 iii) $q/2\pi\epsilon_0 r^2$, radially outward
  iv) 0 v) $q/2\pi\epsilon_0 r^2$, radially inward b) i) 0
  ii) $+2q$ iii) $-2q$ iv) $-2q$
22.49 a) $Qq/4\pi\epsilon_0 r^2$, toward the center of the shell
  b) 0
22.51 a) The given σ is on both sides, so E is twice as great b) $\Phi = (\sigma A)/\epsilon_0$, but $E_{out} = \sigma/\epsilon_0$, so $E_{in} = 0$
22.53 $d = R/2$
22.55 b) for $|x| \le d$: $\vec{E} = (\rho_0 x^3/3\epsilon_0 d^2)\hat{\imath}$;
  for $|x| \ge d$: $\vec{E} = (\rho_0 d/3\epsilon_0)(x/|x|)\hat{\imath}$
22.57 c) $E(r) = \dfrac{Q}{\pi\epsilon_0 R}\left(\dfrac{r}{R} - \dfrac{3r^2}{4R^2}\right)$
  e) $E_{max} = Q/3\pi\epsilon_0 R^2$ at $r = 2R/3$
22.59 a) $\Phi = 4\pi Gm$ b) $\Phi = -4\pi GM_{encl}$
22.61 $\rho\vec{b}/3\epsilon_0$
22.63 a) $-(Q/16\pi\epsilon_0 R^2)\hat{\imath}$ b) $(Q/72\pi\epsilon_0 R^2)\hat{\imath}$
22.65 a) $Q(r) = Qe^{-2r/a_0}[2(r/a_0)^2 + 2(r/a_0) + 1]$
  b) $E = \dfrac{kQe^{-2r/a_0}}{r^2}[2(r/a_0)^2 + 2(r/a_0) + 1]$
22.67 c) 0.807

Chapter 23

23.3 3.46×10^{-13} J
23.5 a) 12.5 m/s b) 0.323 m
23.7 a) 0.198 J b) i) 26.6 m/s ii) 36.7 m/s
  iii) 37.6 m/s
23.9 a) -3.60×10^{-7} J b) $x = 0.0743$ m
23.11 $-q/2$
23.13 B: larger C: smaller D: same
23.15 7.42 m/s; faster
23.17 a) 0 b) $+7.50 \times 10^{-4}$ J
  c) -2.06×10^{-3} J
23.19 a) 2.50 mm b) 7.49 mm
23.21 a) -737 V b) -704 V c) $+8.2 \times 10^{-8}$ J
23.23 b) 0 d) 0
23.25 b) $V = \dfrac{q}{4\pi\epsilon_0}\left(\dfrac{1}{|x|} - \dfrac{2}{|x - a|}\right)$
23.27 1.02×10^7 m/s
23.29 a) b b) 800 V/m c) -4.8×10^{-5} J
23.31 a) increase of 156 V b) decrease of 182 V
23.33 a) oscillatory b) 1.67×10^7 m/s
23.35 a) $\lambda = 9.51$ C/m b) no. less.
  V decreases in direction of $\vec{E}$.
  $\lambda > 0$: V inversely proportional to r c) 0
23.37 a) 7.81×10^4 V b) 0
23.41 a) 8.00 kV/m b) 1.92×10^{-7} N
  c) 8.64×10^{-7} J d) -8.64×10^{-7} J
23.43 b) -20 nC c) no
23.47 a) $E_x = -Ay + 2Bx, E_y = -Ax - C, E_z = 0$
  b) $x = -C/A, y = -2BC/A^2$, any value of z
23.49 a) i) for $r < r_a$, $V = \dfrac{q}{4\pi\epsilon_0}\left(\dfrac{1}{r_a} - \dfrac{1}{r_b}\right)$
  ii) for $r_a < r < r_b$, $V = \dfrac{q}{4\pi\epsilon_0}\left(\dfrac{1}{r} - \dfrac{1}{r_b}\right)$
  iii) for $r > r_b$, $V = 0$
  b) $V_{ab} = \dfrac{q}{4\pi\epsilon_0}\left(\dfrac{1}{r_a} - \dfrac{1}{r_b}\right)$
  c) for $r_a < r < r_b$, $E = \dfrac{V_{ab}}{\left(\frac{1}{r_a} - \frac{1}{r_b}\right)}\dfrac{1}{r^2}$
  d) $E = 0$

23.51 a) concentric cylinders
b) 10 V: 2.90×10^{-2} m; 20 V: 4.20×10^{-2} m
23.53 a) -2.15×10^{-5} J   b) $W_E = +2829$ V
c) $E = 3.54 \times 10^4$ V/m
23.55 a) 7.85×10^4 V/m$^{4/3}$
b) $\vec{E} = (-1.0 \times 10^5 \text{ V/m}^{4/3})x^{1/3}\hat{\imath}$
c) $\vec{F} = (3.13 \times 10^{-15} \text{ N})\hat{\imath}$
23.57 a) $-1.46q^2/\pi\epsilon_0 d$
23.59 a) -8.62×10^{-18} J   b) 2.87×10^{-11} m
23.61 a) i) $V = (\lambda/2\pi\epsilon_0)\ln(b/a)$
ii) $V = (\lambda/2\pi\epsilon_0)\ln(b/r)$ iii) $V = 0$
d) $(\lambda/2\pi\epsilon_0)\ln(b/a)$
23.63 a) 1.76×10^{-16} N, downward
b) 1.93×10^{14} m/s, downward   c) 8.24 mm
d) $15.4°$ e) 4.12 cm
23.65 a) 9.71×10^4 V/m   b) 3.03×10^{-11} C
23.67 a) $r \le R$: $V = \left(\dfrac{\lambda}{4\pi\epsilon_0}\right)[1 - (r/R)^2]$;
$r \ge R$: $V = -\left(\dfrac{\lambda}{2\pi\epsilon_0}\right)\ln(r/R)$
23.69 $Q/4\pi\epsilon_0\sqrt{x^2 + a^2}$
23.71 $Q^2/8\pi\epsilon_0 R$
23.73 a) $Q/8\pi\epsilon_0 R$ b) i) center   c) ii) surface
23.75 b) yes   c) no
23.77 $Q/8\pi\epsilon_0 R$
23.79 a) $(Q/4\pi\epsilon_0 a)\ln[1 + (a/x)]$
b) $(Q/4\pi\epsilon_0 a)\ln\left[(a/y) + \sqrt{1 + (a/y)^2}\right]$
c) in (a), $(Q/4\pi\epsilon_0 x)$ in (b), $(Q/4\pi\epsilon_0 y)$
23.81 a) 1/3   b) 3
23.83 a) $E = Q_1/4\pi\epsilon_0 R_1^2$; $V = Q_1/4\pi\epsilon_0 R_1$
b) sphere 1: $Q_1 R_1/(R_1 + R_2)$;
sphere 2: $Q_1 R_2/(R_1 + R_2)$
c) $V = Q_1/4\pi\epsilon_0(R_1 + R_2)$ for either sphere
d) sphere 1: $E = Q_1/4\pi\epsilon_0 R_1(R_1 + R_2)$;
sphere 2: $E = Q_1/4\pi\epsilon_0 R_2(R_1 + R_2)$
23.85 a) 7.6×10^6 m/s   b) 7.3×10^6 m/s
c) 2.3×10^9 K; 6.9×10^9 K
23.87 a) 5.9×10^{-15} m   b) 4.14×10^{-11} J
c) 2.55×10^{25} nuclei
23.89 a) 1.01×10^{-12} m, 1.11×10^{-13} m,
2.54×10^{-14} m
23.91 a) 3 electrons, 0.507 μm

Chapter 24

24.1 1.82×10^{-4} C
24.3   a) 604 V   b) 9.1×10^{-3} m^2
c) 1.84×10^6 V/m   d) 1.63×10^{-5} C/m^2
24.5   a) 120 μC   b) $C = \epsilon_0 A/d$ c) 480 μC
24.7   2.8 mm
24.9   a) 4.35×10^{-12} F   b) 2.30 V
24.11 a) 6.56×10^{-11} F/m   b) 6.43×10^{-11} C
24.13 a) 1.50×10^{-11} F   b) 3.08 cm
c) 3.13×10^4 N/C
24.15 a) $C_{eq} = 2.40\ \mu$F; $Q_{total} = 6.72 \times 10^{-5}$ C;
$Q_{12} = 2.24 \times 10^{-5}$ C; $Q_3 = 4.48 \times 10^{-5}$ C;
$Q_1 = Q_2 = Q_{12} = 2.24 \times 10^{-5}$ C
24.17 a) $Q_1 = 1.56 \times 10^{-5}$ C; $Q_1 = 2.6 \times 10^{-4}$ C
b) 52.0 V
24.19 $V_2 = 50$ V; $V_3 = 70$ V
24.21 $C_{eq} = \dfrac{\epsilon_0 A}{d_1 + d_2}$
24.23 57 μF
24.25 0.0283 J/m^3
24.27 19.6 J
24.29 a) $Q^2 x/2\epsilon_0 A$ b) $(Q^2/2\epsilon_0 A)dx$ c) $Q^2/2\epsilon_0 A$
24.31 b) yes   c) flat sheets parallel to the plates
24.33 a) 24.2 μC
b) $V = 220$ V: $Q_{35} = 7.7\ \mu$C, $Q_{75} = 16.5\ \mu$C
c) 2.66 mJ   d) 35 nF: 0.85 mJ; 75 nF: 1.81 mJ
e) 220V for each capacitor
24.35 a) 1.60 nC   b) 8.0
24.37 a) $U_{parallel} = 4U_{series}$ b) $Q_{parallel} = 2Q_{series}$
c) $E_{parallel} = 2E_{series}$
24.39 a) 6.20×10^{-7} C/m^2 b) 1.28
24.41 0.0135 m^2
24.43 a) 2.3×10^{-11} C^2/N·m^2 b) 40 kV
c) $\sigma = 4.6 \times 10^{-4}$ C/m^2, $\sigma_i = 2.8 \times 10^{-4}$ C/m^2

24.45 a) 10.1 V   b) 2.25
24.47 a) 3.6 mJ; 13.5 mJ   b) increased by 9.9 mJ
24.49 a) $Q/k\epsilon_0 A$ b) $Qd/k\epsilon_0 A$ c) $k\epsilon_0 A/d$
24.51 a) 2.4×10^{-11} F   b) 2.9×10^{-10} C
c) 1.3×10^3 d) 1.7×10^{-9} J
24.53 a) 421 J   b) 5.39×10^{-9} F
24.55 for $d \ll r_a$: $C \approx \dfrac{\epsilon_0 A}{d}$
24.57 a) $U_{tot} = 158\ \mu$J   b) $U_{4.5} = 72.1\ \mu$J
24.59 a) 2.5 μF   b) $Q_1 = 5.5 \times 10^{-4}$ C, $V_1 = 66$ V ;
$Q_2 = 3.7 \times 10^{-4}$ C, $V_2 = 88$ V ;
$Q_3 = 1.8 \times 10^{-4}$ C, $V_3 = 44$ V ;
$Q_4 = 1.8 \times 10^{-4}$ C, $V_4 = 44$ V ;
$Q_5 = 5.5 \times 10^{-4}$ C, $V_5 = 66$ V
24.61 a) 76 μC   b) 1.4×10^{-3} J   c) 11 V
d) 1.2×10^{-3} J
24.63 a) 2.3 μF   b) $C_1 = 9.7 \times 10^{-4}$ C;
$C_2 = 6.4 \times 10^{-4}$ C   c) 47 V
24.65 a) 3.91   b) 22.8 V
24.67 c) 710 μF
24.69 a) 6.5×10^{-2} F   b) $Q = 2.3 \times 10^4$ C
c) 4.0×10^9 J
24.71 $C_{eq} = \dfrac{2\epsilon_0 A}{d}\left(\dfrac{K_1 K_2}{K_1 + K_2}\right)$
24.73 b) 14 μF   c) 72.0 μF: 505 μC, 7.02 V;
28.0 μF: 259 μC, 9.24 V;
18.0 μF: 229 μC, 12.7 V;
27.0 μF: 276 μC, 10.2 V;
6.0 μF: 14.9 μC, 2.49 V
24.75 a) $(\epsilon_0 L/D)[L + (K - 1)x]$
24.77 b) 2.38×10^{-9} F

Chapter 25

25.1 3.89×10^4 C
25.3   a) 3.13×10^{19} b) $J = 1.51 \times 10^6$ A/m^2
c) $v_d = 1.11 \times 10^{-4}$ m/s
d) J would decrease; v_d would decrease
25.5   a) 110 min   b) 442 min   c) $v_d \propto 1/d$
25.7   a) 329 C   b) 41.1 A   c) 1333 min
25.9 5.86×10^{28} e$^-$/m^3
25.11 a) $1.216\Omega\cdot$m @ 20 °C
25.13 a) tungsten $E = 5.16 \times 10^{-3}$ V/m
b) aluminum $E = 2.70 \times 10^{-3}$ V/m
25.15 a) $E_{max} = 1.21$ V/m   b) $R = 1.45 \times 10^{-2}\ \Omega$
c) $V_{max} = 1.82 \times 10^{-1}$ V = 0.182 V
25.17 0.125 Ω
25.19 15 g
25.21 $1.53 \times 10^{-8}\ \Omega$
25.23 a) $1.53 \times 10^{-8}\ \Omega$ b) $R = 2.4\ \Omega$
25.25 a) 11.1 A   b) 3.13 V   c) 0.28 Ω
25.27 a) 99.54 Ω b) 0.0158 Ω
25.29 a) $4.67 \times 10^{-8}\ \Omega$ b) $6.74 \times 10^{-4}\ \Omega$
25.31 a) 0.219 Ω b) $P = 3422$ J/s, $E = 1.23 \times 10^7$ J
25.33 a) $\mathcal{E} = 9.0$ V   b) $r = 4.5\ \Omega$
25.35 a) $I = 0$ b) $\mathcal{E} = 5.0$ V   c) 5.0 V
25.37 a) $\mathcal{E} = 3.08$ V   b) $r = 0.067\ \Omega$ c) 1.8 Ω
25.39 a) 1.41 A   b) -13.7 V   c) -1.0 V
25.41 b) yes; linear
25.43 a) 144 Ω b) $2.40 \times 10^2\ \Omega$
c) 100 W bulb, $I = 0.833$ A
d) 120 W bulb, $I = 0.500$ A
25.45 a) 29.8 W   b) 0.248 A
25.47 a) $P = JE$ b) $p = J^2\rho$ c) $p = E^2/\rho$
25.49 a) 2.59×10^6 J   b) 0.062 L   c) 1.6 h
25.51 12.3%
25.53 a) 24 W   b) 4.0 W   c) 20 W
25.55 a) 26.7 Ω b) 4.5 A   c) 454 W
25.57 a) $3.65 \times 10^{-8}\ \Omega\cdot$m   b) 172 A
c) 2.58×10^{-3} m/s
25.59 0.060 Ω
25.61 a) 2.5 mA   b) 2.14×10^{-5} V/m
c) 8.55×10^{-5} V/m   d) 1.80×10^{-4} V
25.63 a) $R = \dfrac{\rho h}{\pi r_1 r_2}$ b) $R = \dfrac{\rho L}{A}$
25.65 $I = \dfrac{Q}{\kappa\epsilon_0\rho}$
25.67 a) 0.057 Ω b) $3.34 \times 10^{-8}\Omega\cdot$m   c) 0.86 mm
d) $2.40 \times 10^{-3}\ \Omega$
e) 1.1×10^{-3} (°C)$^{-1}$
25.69 a) 0.2 Ω b) 8.7 V

25.71 a) 1000 Ω b) 100 V   c) 10 W
25.73 1.42 A
25.75 a) $I_A\left(1 + \dfrac{R_A}{r + R}\right)$ b) 0.0425 Ω
25.77 b) 8-gauge   c) 106 W
d) 66 W, 175 kWh, $19.25
25.79 a) 0.40 A   b) 1.6 W   c) 4.8 W   d) 3.2 W
25.81 a) $\dfrac{a}{E}$ b) 2.59×10^6 J   c) 4.32×10^5 J
d) 0.96 Ω e) 1.73×10^6 J
25.83 a) $I = \dfrac{v_0 A}{\rho_0 L(1 - e^{-1})}$
b) $E(x) = \dfrac{v_0 e^{-x/L}}{L(1 - e^{-1})}$
c) $V(x) = V_0\dfrac{(e^{-x/L} - e^{-1})}{(1 - e^{-1})}$

Chapter 26

26.1 $\dfrac{3R}{4}$
26.3   a) $R_q < R_1$ b) $R_{eq} < R_1$
26.5   a) $I = 3.50$ A   b) $I = 4.50$ A   c) $I = 3.15$ A
d) $I = 3.25$ A
26.7   0.769 A
26.9   a) 8.8 Ω b) 3.18 A   c) 3.18 A
d) $V_{2.4} = 7.64$ V; $V_{1.6} = 5.09$ V; $V_{4.8} = 15.3$ V
26.11 $R_{eq} = 5.00\ \Omega$; $I_{total} = 12.0$ A; $I_{12} = 3.00$ A;
$I_4 = 9.00$ A; $I_3 = 8.00$ A; $I_6 = 4.00$ A
26.13 a) $I_1 = 1.50$ A, $I_2 = I_3 = I_4 = 0.50$ A
b) $P_1 = 10.1$ W, $P_2 = P_3 = P_4 = 1.12$ W;
c) $I_1 = 1.33$ A, $I_2 = I_3 = 0.667$ A
d) $P_1 = 8.00$ W, $P_2 = P_3 = 2.00$ W
e) $R_2 + R_3$ is brighter; R_1 is dimmer
26.15 a) 18.0 V; 3.00 A
26.17 a) 0.100 A for each
b) 400-Ω bulb: 4.00 W; 800-Ω bulb: 8.00 W
c) 400-Ω bulb: 0.300 A; 800-Ω bulb: 0.150 A
d) 400-Ω bulb: 36.0 W; 800-Ω bulb: 18.0 W;
total: 54.0 W
e) in series, 800-Ω bulb is brighter; in parallel,
400-Ω bulb is brighter and total light output is
greater
26.19 1010 s
26.21 a) 2.00 A   b) 5.00 Ω c) 42.0 V   d) 3.50 A
26.23 a) 8.00 A   b) $\mathcal{E}_1 = 36.0$ V, $\mathcal{E}_2 = 54.0$ V
c) 9.00 Ω
26.25 a) 1.60 A, 1.40 A, 0.20 A b) 10.4 V
26.27 a) $\mathcal{E} = 36.40$ V   b) 0.500 A
26.29 a) -2.14 V, a is at a higher potential
b) $I_{100} = 0.250$ A; $I_{75} = 0.200$ A;
$I_A = 0.500$ A downward; V = 0
26.31 a) 0.641 Ω b) 975 Ω
26.33 a) 17.8 V   b) 22.7 V   c) 27.5%
26.35 c) 3.34 V
26.37 a) 543 Ω b) 1.88 mA   c) 203 Ω
26.39 a) $C = 8.49 \times 10^{-7}$ F   b) $\tau = 2.89$ s
26.41 a) $t = 4.21 \times 10^{-3}$ s   b) $I = 0.125$ A
26.43 190 μC
26.45 $I = 13.6$ A
26.47 a) 0.938 A   b) 0.606 A
26.49 a) 1.33×10^{-4} C
b) $v_R = 9.12$ V, $v_C = 8.88$ V
c) $v_R = v_C = 8.88$ V   d) 6.75×10^{-5} C
26.51 900 W
26.53 a) 6.0 A, 720 W   b) 3.5 A, 420 W
26.55 a) 13.6 $\mu\Omega = 1.36 \times 10^{-5}\ \Omega$
b) $2.14 \times 10^{-8}\ \Omega$
26.57 a) 9.9 W   b) 16.3 W, brighter
26.59 a) 18.7 Ω b) 7.5 Ω
26.61 $I_1 = 0.848$ A, $I_2 = 2.14$ A, $I_3 = 0.171$ A
26.63 2.00-Ω resistor: 5.21 A; 4-Ω resistor: 1.11 A;
5-Ω resistor: 6.32 A
26.65 a) 0.222 V   b) 0.464 A
26.67 12.7 V
26.69 a) 186 V, upper terminal +
b) 3.00 A from $-$ to + terminal
c) 20.0 Ω
26.71 a) $P_1 + P_2$ b) $\dfrac{P_1 P_2}{(P_1 + P_2)}$
26.73 a) -12.0 V   b) 1.71 V   c) 4.20 V

26.75 $R_3 = 10.8\ \Omega,\ R_2 = 1.08\ \Omega,\ R_1 = 0.12\ \Omega$
26.77 a) 114.4 V   b) 263 V   c) 266 V
26.79 b) 1897 Ω
26.81 a) 224-Ω resistor: 24.8 V; 589-Ω: 65.2 V
    b) 3.87 kΩ c) 62.6 V   d) no

Chapter 27

27.1 a) $(-6.68 \times 10^{-4}\ \text{N})\hat{k}$
    b) $(+6.68 \times 10^{-4}\ \text{N})\hat{i} + (7.27 \times 10^{-4}\ \text{N})\hat{j}$
27.3 a) positive   b) 5.05×10^{-2}N
27.5 9.47×10^6 m/s
27.7 a) $\vec{B}_x = -0.175$ T, $\vec{B}_z = -0.256$ T
    b) yes, $\vec{B}_y$ d) zero, 90°
27.9 a) $\vec{B} = 1.46$ T at 40.0° from the +x-axis,
    toward the z-axis in the xz plane
    b) $\vec{F} = 7.48 \times 10^{-16}$ N, at 50° from the
    +x-axis toward the +z-axis
27.11 a) 3.05×10^{-3} Wb   b) 1.83×10^{-3} Wb   c) 0
27.13 -7.79×10^{-4} Wb
27.15 a) 1.60×10^{-4} T, into the page
    b) 1.11×10^{-7}s
27.17 7.93×10^{-10} N, south
27.19 a) 1.2×10^7 m/s   b) 0.10 T
27.21 a) 8.35×10^5 m/s   b) 2.62×10^{-8} s
    c) 7.26 kV
27.23 a) 107 T   b) no
27.25 a) 8.38×10^{-4}T
27.27 a) no   b) 1.40 cm
27.29 $B = 4.45 \times 10^{-2}$T
27.31 1.29×10^{-25} kg, 78
27.33 a) 1.34×10^4A   b) horizontal
27.35 $F = 0.724$ N, at 63.4° below the +x-axis
27.37 9.7 A
27.39 a) 817 V   b) 113 m/s²
27.41 a) $-(ILB)\hat{j}$ b) yes
27.43 a) 1.5×10^{-16}s   b) 1.1 mA
    c) 9.3×10^{-24}A·m²
27.45 a) rotates about axis A_z b) $\alpha = 294$ rad/s²
27.47 -2.42 J
27.49 a) 1.13 A   b) 3.69 A   c) 98.2 V   d) 362 W
27.51 a) 4.7 mm/s
    b) 4.5×10^{-3}V/m in the +z-direction
    c) 53 μV
27.53 a) F_2/qv_1 in the $-y$-direction   b) $F_2/\sqrt{2}$
27.55 $\vec{B} = 3.68$ T at a right angle to v_i
27.57 a) 8.9×10^{-17}J $= 5.5 \times 10^5$ eV
    b) 7.7×10^{-8}s   c) 1.2 T   d) same as in (a)
27.59 4.46 A
27.61 a) -1.98×10^{-6}C
    b) $(9.69 \times 10^{14}$ m/s$)(4\hat{i} + 3\hat{j})$
    c) $R = 5.69$ cm
    d) 1.47×10^7 Hz   e) $(R, 0, 1.72$ m$)$
27.63 9τ
27.65 1.6 mm
27.67 $(Mg\tan\theta/LB)$, right to left
27.71 a) 8.46×10^{-3} T   b) 0.271 m
    c) 2.14×10^{-2}m
27.73 1.80 N to the left
27.75 0.0242 T, in the +y-direction
27.77 a) 0.0442 N·m clockwise   b) stretched
    c) 7.98×10^{-3} J
27.79 0.444 N, in the $-y$-direction
27.81 b) side $(0,0)$ to $(0,\text{L})$: $(B_0IL/2)\hat{i}$;
    side $(0,\text{L})$ to (L,L): $(-B_0IL)\hat{j}$;
    side (L,L) to $(\text{L},0)$: $(-B_0IL/2)\hat{i}$;
    side $(\text{L},0)$ to $(0,0)$: 0   c) $(-B_0IL)\hat{j}$
27.83 2.52 m/s   b) 7.60 A   c) 0.197 Ω
27.85 a) $\vec{\mu} = -IA\hat{k}$ b) $B_x = 3D/IA$, $B_y = 4D/IA$,
    $B_z = -12D/IA$
27.87 $-\beta r/2$
27.89 a) 5.14 m   b) 1.72×10^{-6} s   c) 6.09 mm
    d) 3.04 cm

Chapter 28

28.1 a) $(-1.92 \times 10^{-5}\ \text{T})\hat{k}$ b) 0
28.3 a) $\vec{B} = 6.00 \times 10^{-10}$ T out of the paper
    b) $\vec{B} = 1.20 \times 10^{-9}$ T out of the paper   c) 0

28.5 a) 0   b) $(-1.31 \times 10^{-6}\ \text{T})\hat{k}$ out of the paper
    c) $(-4.62 \times 10^{-7}\ \text{T})\hat{k}$
    d) $(1.31 \times 10^{-6}\ \text{T})\hat{j}$
28.7 a) attractive   b) 1.00×10^{-6}
28.9 a) 4.00×10^{-7} T out of the paper
    b) 1.52×10^{-8} T out of the paper   c) 0
28.11 a) $(5.00 \times 10^{-11}\ \text{T})\hat{j}$ b) $(-5.00 \times 10^{-11}\ \text{T})\hat{i}$
    c) $(-1.77 \times 10^{-11}\ \text{T})\hat{k}$ d) 0
28.13 1.76×10^{-5} T into the paper
28.15 a) 8.0×10^{-4} T
    b) 4.00×10^{-5} T, 20 times larger
28.17 a) 10.0 A   b) above the wire
    c) directly east of the wire.
28.19 a) $(-1.0 \times 10^{-7}\text{T})\hat{i}$
    b) $(2.19 \times 10^{-6}\text{T})$, $\theta = 46.8°$ from x toward z
    c) $(7.9 \times 10^{-6}\text{T})\hat{i}$
28.21 a) 0   b) 6.67×10^{-6} T
    c) 7.53×10^{-6} T to the left
28.23 a) 0   b) 0   c) 4.0×10^{-4} T to the left
28.25 a) 6.00×10^{-6} N, repulsive
    b) 2.40×10^{-5} N
28.27 4.6×10^{-5} N/m, repulsive but negligible
28.29 $\mu_0 I^2/2\pi\lambda g$
28.31 $m_0|I_1 - I_2|/4R, 0$
28.33 a) 9.42×10^{-3} T   b) 1.34×10^{-4} T
28.35 a) 305 A   b) -3.83×10^{-4} T·m
28.37 a) $\dfrac{\mu_0 I}{2\pi r}$ b) 0
28.39 $B = \dfrac{\mu_0 I}{2\pi r}$; $r = R/2$; $r = 2R$
28.41 a) 1790 turns/m   b) 63.0 m
28.43 a) 3.72×10^6 A   b) 2.49×10^5 A   c) 237 A
28.45 1.11×10^{-3} T
28.47 a) 0.0725 A   b) 0.0195 A
28.49 a) i) 1.1×10^{-3} T   ii) 4.7×10^{-6} A/m
    iii) 5.9 T
28.51 a) 1.00×10^{-6} T into the paper
    b) $(7.49 \times 10^{-8}\ \text{T})\hat{j}$
28.53 a) 1.1×10^{13} m/s², away from the wire
    b) 62.5 N/C, away from the wire
    c) $mg \approx 10^{-29}$ N, negligible
28.55 5.75×10^{-6} T; 2.21×10^{-21} N perpendicular
    to line ab and to velocity
28.57 a) ±607 m/s   b) 9.2×10^{-6} T
28.59 a) 2.00 A out of the paper
    b) 2.13×10^{-6} T, to the right
    c) 2.06×10^{-6} T
28.61 a) 1.11×10^{-5}N/m
    b) out of page: 1.11×10^{-5} N/m upward
28.63 23.2 A
28.65 a) $\mu_0 \pi NN'II'a^2 a'^2 (\sin\theta)/2x^3$
    b) $-\mu_0 \pi NN'II'a^2 a'^2 (\cos\theta)/2x^3$
28.67 a) $(\mu_0 NIa^2/2)[((x + a/2)^2$
    $+ a^2)^{-3/2} + ((x - a/2)^2 + a^2)^{-3/2}]$
    c) $(\mu_0 NI/a)(4/5)^{3/2}$
    d) 0.0202 T   e) 0, 0
28.69 $\mu_0 I/8R$, out of the page
28.71 a) $3I/2\pi R^3$ b) i) $\mu_0 Ir^2/2\pi R^3$ ii) $\mu_0 I/2\pi r$
28.73 zero
28.75 $16a/3$
28.77 b) $\mu_0 I_0/2\pi r$
    c) $(I_0 r^2/a^2)(2 - r^2/a^2)$
    d) $(\mu_0 I_0 r/2\pi a^2)(2 - r^2/a^2)$
28.79 $\mu_0 I$
28.81 a) $\mu_0 nI/2$, in the +x-direction
    b) $\mu_0 nI/2$, in the $-x$-direction
28.83 7.73×10^{-23} J/T $= 0.0833\ \mu_B$
28.85 c) 6.15 mm
28.87 $\mu_0 Qn/a$

Chapter 29

29.1 a) 4.50 Wb   b) 20.3 V
29.3 a) $Q = NBA/R$ b) no
29.5 a) +34 V   b) counterclockwise
29.7 a) $I = i$:$B = \dfrac{\mu_0 i}{2\pi r}$ into the page
    b) $d\Phi_B = \dfrac{\mu_0 i}{2\pi r}L\,dr$ c) $\Phi_B = \dfrac{\mu_0 iL}{2\pi}\ln(b/a)$

    d) $\mathcal{E} = \dfrac{\mu_0 L}{2\pi}\ln(b/a)\dfrac{di}{dt}$
29.9 a) 5.44 mV   b) clockwise
29.11 a) $\mathcal{E} = +Abv$ b) clockwise   c) $\mathcal{E} = -Abv$
    d) counterclockwise
29.13 10.4 rad/s
29.15 a) counterclockwise   b) clockwise   c) $I = 0$
29.17 a) a to b b) b to a c) b to a
29.19 a) clockwise   b) 0   c) counterclockwise
29.21 a) $V_{ab} = 0.675$ V
    b) b at higher potential than a
    c) $E = 2.25$ V/m from b to a
    d) b has excess of positive charge   e) i) 0
    ii) 0
29.23 46.2 m/s; no
29.25 a) 3.00 V   b) clockwise
    c) 0.800 N to the right
    d) 6.00 W $= P_{\text{mech}} = P_{\text{elec}}$
29.27 a) 4.23 V   b) 4.23 V   c) 0
    d) for width $w \ll L$, it does not matter.
    $\mathcal{E} = 4.23$ V as long as the longitudinal axis of
    the rod is in the x-y plane.
29.29 a) $\pi r_i^2 \dfrac{dB}{dt}$ b) $\dfrac{r_1}{2}\dfrac{dB}{dt}$ c) $\dfrac{R^2}{2r_2}\dfrac{dB}{dt}$ e) $\dfrac{\pi R^2}{4}\dfrac{dB}{dt}$
    f) $\pi R^2 \dfrac{dB}{dt}$ g) $\pi R^2 \dfrac{dB}{dt}$
29.31 9.21 A/s
29.33 9.50×10^{-4} V
29.35 $K = 2.34$
29.37 a) 5.99×10^{-10} C
    b) 6.00×10^{-3} A
    c) 6.00×10^{-3} A
29.39 a) 0.15 V/m   b) 38 V/m·s
    c) 3.4×10^{-10}A/m²
    d) $B_D = 2.38 \times 10^{-21}$ T, negligible;
    $B_C = 5.33 \times 10^{-5}$ T
29.41 For any continuous superconducting path,
    $R_{\text{total}} = 0$
29.43 a) $-(4.38 \times 10^4$ A/m$)\hat{i}$ b) $(15.0$ T$)\hat{i}$
29.45 a) 3.7 A   b) 54 μA   c) counterclockwise
29.47 a) $\dfrac{\mu_0 i\pi a}{2C}$ c) $i = i_0\exp(-2Rt/\mu_0 \pi a)$
    d) 45 μs
29.49 a) $\mu_0 Iabv/2\pi r(a + r)$ b) clockwise
29.51 191 rpm
29.53 a) 0.126 V   b) a to b
29.55 b) $FR/B^2 L^2$
29.57 1.2 V
29.59 $\dfrac{\mu_0 IW}{4\pi}$
29.61 a) $(\mu_0 IV/2\pi)\ln((L + d)/d)$ b) a c) 0
29.63 a) 0.165 V   b) 0.165 V   c) 0; 0.0142 V
29.65 $B^2 a^2 V/R$
29.67 a) $(qr/2)\dfrac{dB}{dt}$, to the left
    b) $(qr/2)\dfrac{dB}{dt}$, upward   c) 0
29.73 a) 1.96×10^{-4}A/m²
    b) 3.00×10^{-9}A/m²
    c) 7.82×10^6 Hz
29.75 b) $\dfrac{a}{2}\dfrac{dB}{dt}$ c) 7.37×10^{-4} A
    d) 1.75×10^{-4} V
29.77 a) a to b b) $v_t = \dfrac{Rmg\tan\theta}{L^2 B^2\cos\theta}$ c) $\dfrac{mg\tan\theta}{LB}$
    d) $\dfrac{Rm^2 g^2(\tan\theta)^2}{L^2 B^2}$ e) same as (d)

Chapter 30

30.1 a) 0.270 V, yes   b) 0.270 V
30.5 a) 1.96 H   b) 7.12×10^{-3} Wb
30.7 a) 0.250 H   b) 4.5×10^{-4} Wb
30.9 a) 4.68 mV   b) a
30.11 $\dfrac{\mu_0 N^2 A}{l}$
30.13 2850
30.15 a) 1.61×10^{-1} T   b) 1.03×10^4 J/m³

c) 0.129 J   d) 4.03×10^{-5} H

30.19 a) 2.40 A/s   b) 0.800 A/s   c) 0.413 A
d) 0.750 A

30.21 a) $17.3\mu s$ b) $30.7\mu s$

30.25 a) 0.250 A   b) 0.137 A   c) 32.9 V, c
d) 4.62×10^{-4} s

30.27 a) $(4.50 \text{ W})[1 - \exp(-(3.20 \text{ s}^{-1})t)]$
b) $(4.50 \text{ W})[1 - \exp(-(3.20 \text{ s}^{-1})t)]^2$
c) $(4.50 \text{ W})[\exp(-(3.20 \text{ s}^{-1})t)$
$- \exp(-(6.40 \text{ s}^{-1})t)]$

30.29 a) 25.0 mH   b) 9.00×10^{-8} C
c) 5.40×10^{-7} J   d) 6.57 mA

30.31 a) 105 rad/s, 59.6 ms   b) 7.20×10^{-4} C
c) 4.32×10^{-3} J   d) $-543 \,\mu$C
e) -49.9 mA   f) 2.45×10^{-3} J, capacitor;
1.87×10^{-3} J, inductor

30.33 a) $f = 2.13 \times 10^3$ Hz   b) $V_E = 0.225$ J
c) $V_B = 0.223$ J

30.35 a) $U_C = (Q^2/2C)\cos^2(\omega t + \phi)$;
$U_L = (Q^2/2C)\sin^2(\omega t + \phi)$

30.37 $\sqrt{LC} = \sqrt{(V \cdot s/A)(A \cdot s/V)} = \sqrt{s^2} = s$

30.41 a) 298 rad/s   b) 83.8 Ω

30.43 a) $m = 4.80 \times 10^{-6}$ H
b) $\mathcal{E} = \pm 1.80 \times 10^{-4}$ V

30.49 a) $\dfrac{\mu_0 i}{2\pi r}$ b) $\left(\dfrac{\mu_0 i^2 l}{4\pi r}\right) dr$ c) $\left(\dfrac{\mu_0 i^2 l}{4\pi}\right)\ln(b/a)$

30.51 a) $L = 8.89$ H   b) $l = 56.3$ m; no

30.53 a) 0.281 J   b) 0.517 J   c) 0.236 J

30.57 222 μF; 9.31 μH

30.59 2×10^4 m/s

30.61 a) solenoid   c) 50 V   d) 3.5 A
e) 4.3 Ω;43 mH

30.63 a) $V_1 = 40.0$ V; $A_1 = A_4 = 0.80$ A, all others
are zero
b) $V_1 = 24.0$ V, $V_2 = 0$, $V_3 = V_4 = V_5 = 16.0$;
$A_1 = 0.48$ A, $A_2 = 0.16$ A, $A_3 = 0.32$ A,
$A_4 = 0$ c) 192 μC

30.65 a) $A_1 = A_4 = 0.45$ A, $A_2 = A_3 = 0$
b) $A_1 = 0.58$ A, $A_2 = 0.32$ A, $A_3 = 0.16$ A,
$A_4 = 0.11$ A

30.67 a) 60.0 V   b) a c) 60.0 V   d) c
e) -96.0 V   f) b g) -156 V   h) d

30.69 a) $i_0 = 0$, $V_{ac} = 0$, $V_{cb} = 36.0$ V
b) $i_0 = 0.180$ A, $V_{ac} = 9.0$ V, $V_{cb} = 27.0$ V
c) $i_0 = (0.180 \text{ A})[1 - \exp(-(50.0\text{s}^{-1})t)]$,
$V_{ac} = (9.00 \text{ V})[1 - \exp(-(50.0\text{s}^{-1})t)]$,
$V_{cb} = 27.0 \text{ V} + (9.00 \text{ V})\exp(-(50.0 \text{ s}^{-1})t)$

30.71 a) 0; 20 V   b) 0.267 A; 0   c) 0.147 A; 9.0 V

30.75 a) $i_1 = \mathcal{E}/R_1$, $i_2 = (\mathcal{E}/R_2)[1 - \exp(-R_2t/L)]$
b) $i_1 = \mathcal{E}/R_1$, $i_2 = \mathcal{E}/R_2$
c) $i = (\mathcal{E}/R_2)\exp(-(R_1 + R_2)t/L)$

30.77 a) $d = [(L - L_0)/(L_F - L_0)]D$
b) 0.63024 H, 0.63048 H, 0.63072 H, 0.63096 H
c) 0.63000 H, 0.62999 H, 0.62999 H, 0.62998 H

30.79 a) $i_1 = (\mathcal{E}/R_1)[1 - \exp(R_1t/L)]$,
$i_2 = (\mathcal{E}/R_2)\exp(-t/R_2C)$,
$q_2 = C\mathcal{E}[1 - \exp(-t/R_2C)]$
b) 0, 9.6 mA   c) 1.9 A, 0   d) 1.6 ms
e) 9.4 mA   f) 0.22 s

Chapter 31

31.1 a) $I_{rms} = 0.34$ A   b) $I = 0.48$ A   c) 0
d) $(i^2)_{av} = 0.12$ A^2

31.3 a) 31.8 V   b) 0

31.5 a) 0.0132 A   b) 0.132 A   c) 1.32 A

31.9 a) 1.51 kΩ b) 0.239 H   c) 497 Ω d)16.6 μF

31.11 13.3 μF

31.13 a) $i = (0.0253 \text{ A})\cos[(720 \text{ rad/s})t]$
b) 180 Ω
c) $v_L = (-4.56 \text{ V})\sin[(720 \text{ rad/s})t]$

31.15 b) $v = 20.5$ V, $v_r = 7.6$ V, $v_L = 12.9$ V
c) $v = -15.2$ V, $v_R = -22.5$ V, $v_L = 7.3$ V

31.17 a) 696 Ω b) 0.0431 A
c) $v_R = 8.62$ V, $v_c = 28.7$ V   d) $-73.3°$

31.19 a) 601 Ω b) 49.9 mA   c) $-70.6°$, lags
d) $v_R = 9.98$ V, $v_L = 4.99$ V, $v_c = 33.3$ V

31.21 a) 113 Hz; 15 mA   b) 7.61 mA; lag

31.23 50.0 V

31.25 a) $P_{max} = 40.0$ W   b) $I_{rms} = 0.167$ A
c) $R = 7.20 \times 10^2$ Ω

31.29 a) $+45.8°$,0.697   b) 344 Ω c) 155 V

d) 48.6 W   e) 48.6 W   f) 0   g) 0

31.31 a) 150 V   b) 150 V, 1290 V, 1290 V
c) 37.5 W

31.33 a) 1.00   b) 75.0 W   c) 75.0 W

31.35 a) $Z = 115$ Ω b) $Z = 146$ Ω c) $Z = 146$ Ω

31.37 a) 10   b) 2.40 A   c) 28.8 A   d) 500 Ω

31.39 a) $N_2 = \frac{1}{2}N_1$ b) 13 A   c) 9.0 Ω

31.41 0.124 H

31.43 a) $t_1 = \pi/2\omega$, $t_2 = 3\pi/2\omega$ b) $2I/\omega$
c) $I_{rav} = 2I/\omega$

31.45 a) inductor   b) 0.133 H

31.47 a) $I = 1.15$ A, $V_L = 31.6$ V, $V_R = 57.5$ V,
$V_C = 14.7$ V
b) $I = 0.860$ A, $V_L = 47.3$ V, $V_R = 43.0$ V,
$V_C = 5.47$ V

31.49 $\sqrt{(R^2 + \omega^2L^2)}/[R^2 + (\omega L - 1/\omega C)^2]$

31.53 b) $V_B = LV^2/4[R^2 + (\omega L - 1/\omega C)^2]$,
$V_E = V^2/4\omega C[R^2 + (\omega L - 1/\omega C)^2]$
d) $\omega = 0$; $U_B = 0$; $U_E = CV^2/4$; $\omega \to \infty$;
both U_B and $U_E \to 0$;
$U_B = U_E$ at $\omega = \omega_0 = 1/\sqrt{LC}$

31.57 a) $I_R = V/R$, $I_L = V/\omega L$, $I_C = \omega CV$
c) $\omega = 0$: $I_L \to \infty$, $I_C \to 0$; $\omega \to \infty$: $I_L = 0$,
$I_C \to \infty$ d) 159 Hz   e) 0.50 A
f) $I_R = 0.50$ A, $I_L = I_C = 0.050$ A

31.59 a) 102 V   b) 0.882 A   c) 270 V

31.61 a) 0.750 A   b) 160 Ω c) 619 Ω, 341 Ω
d) 341 Ω

31.63 $i_{av} = 0$, $i_{rms} = I_0/\sqrt{3}$

31.65 a) ω_0 decreases by $\dfrac{1}{2}$ b) X_C doubles
c) X_C decreases by $\dfrac{1}{2}$ d) no

31.67 a) L and C b) factor of $\dfrac{1}{2}$

31.69 a) $V/\sqrt{R^2 + 9L/4C}$
b) $[2V/\sqrt{R^2 + 9L/4C}]\sqrt{L/C}$
c) $[V/2\sqrt{R^2 + 9L/4C}]\sqrt{L/C}$
d) $2LV^2/(R^2 + 9L/4C)$
e) $LV^2/2(R^2 + 9L/4C)$

31.73 a) $V_RI/2$ b) 0   c) 0

31.75 a) 0.400 A   b) 36.9°
c) $Z_{cpx} = (400 \,\Omega) - i(300 \,\Omega)$, $Z = 500$ Ω
d) $I_{cpx} = (0.320 \text{ A}) - i(240 \text{ A})$

Chapter 32

32.1 a) 1.28 s   b) 8.15×10^{15} km

32.3 a) 6.0×10^4 Hz   b) 6.0×10^7 Hz
c) 6.0×10^{13} Hz   d) 6.0×10^{16} Hz

32.5 a) $f = 6.94 \times 10^{14}$ Hz   b) $E_{max} = 375$ V/m

32.7 $\vec{E}(z,t) = (1.74 \times 10^5 \text{ V/m})\hat{\imath} \times$
$\cos[(1.28 \times 10^7 \text{ rad/m})z -$
$(3.83 \times 10^{15} \text{ rad/s})t]$
$\vec{B}(z,t) = (5.80 \times 10^{-4} \text{ T})\hat{\jmath} \times$
$\cos[(1.28 \times 10^7 \text{ rad/m})z -$
$(3.83 \times 10^{15} \text{ rad/s})t]$

32.9 a) $+y$-direction   b) 7.11×10^{-4} m
c) $\vec{B}(y,t) = (-1.03 \times 10^{-2} \text{ T})\hat{\imath} \times$
$\sin[(8.84 \times 10^3 \text{ rad/m})y -$
$(2.65 \times 10^{12} \text{ rad/s})t]$

32.11 a) 361 m   b) 0.0174 rad/m
c) 5.22×10^6 rad/s   d) 0.0144 V/m

32.13 a) 381 nm   b) 526 nm   c) 1.38   d) 1.91

32.15 a) 330 W/m^2 b) 500 V/m; 1.7 μT

32.17 1.33×10^{-8} T, $+ y$-direction

32.19 a) 1.1×10 W/m^2 b) 3.0×10^{-10} T
c) 840 W; assuming isotropic transmission

32.21 2.5×10^{25} J

32.23 $E_{max} = 12.0$ V/m, $B_{max} = 4.00 \times 10^{-8}$ T

32.25 8.5×10^5 W

32.27 a) 8.68×10^{-15} kg/m$^2 \cdot$ s
b) 2.60×10^{-6} kg/m $\cdot$ s^2

32.29 $S = \epsilon_0 cE^2$

32.31 a) 7.10 mm   b) 3.55 mm   c) 1.56×10^8 m/s

32.33 a) 4.38 mm   b) 1.38 mm   c) 4.38 mm

32.35 a) $L = 30.5$ cm   b) $f = 2.46 \times 10^9$ Hz
c) $L = 35.5$ cm: $f = 2.11 \times 10^9$ Hz

32.39 a) $I = 0.00602$ W/m^2
b) 2.13 N/C, 7.10×10^{-9} T
c) 1.20×10^{-12} N

32.41 a) $E_{max} = 701$ V/m, $B_{max} = 2.34 \times 10^{-6}$ T
b) $\mu_E = \mu_B = 1.09 \times 10^{-6}$ J/m^3
c) 1.07×10^{-11} J

32.43 a) $r = R$: $I = 6.4 \times 10^7$ W/m^2, $p_{rod} = 0.21$ Pa;
$r = R/2$: $I = 2.6 \times 10^8$ W/m^2, $p_{rod} = 0.85$ Pa

32.45 7.78×10^{-13} rad/s

32.47 a) $I\rho/\pi a^2$ in direction of current
b) current out of page: $\mu_0 I/2\pi a$, clockwise
c) $I^2\rho/2\pi^2 a^3$, radially inward
d) $I^2\rho l/\pi a^2 = I^2R$

32.49 0.0368 V

32.51 a) 23.6 h   b) throw it

32.53 a) 2.66×10^7 m   b) 0.0673 s
c) 6.50×10^{-23} Pa   d) 0.190 m

32.55 a) $4\pi R^3\rho Gm^3/3r^2$ b) $LR^2/4r^2c$
c) 1.90^{-7} m, independent of r

32.57 b) 1.4×10^{-11} s^{-1} c) 2.6×10^{-8} s^{-1}

Chapter 33

33.1 39.4°

33.3 a) 1.55   b) 549 nm

33.5 a) 5.17×10^{-7} m   b) 3.40×10^{-7} m

33.7 a) 47.5°   b) 66.0°

33.9 2.51×10^8 m/s

33.13 a) frequency $= f$; wavelength $= n\lambda$;
speed $= nf\lambda = nv$ b) frequency $= f$;
wavelength $= \left(\dfrac{n}{n'}\right)\lambda$; speed $= \left(\dfrac{n}{n'}\right)f\lambda = \left(\dfrac{n}{n'}\right)v$

33.15 71.8°

33.17 a) 51.3°   b) 33.8°

33.19 a) 58.1°   b) 22.8°

33.21 1.77

33.23 24.4°

33.25 a) A: $I_0/2$ B: $I_0/8$ C: $3I_0/32$ b) 0

33.27 a) 1.40   b) 35.5°

33.29 $\alpha = \arccos\left(\dfrac{\cos\theta}{\sqrt{2}}\right) = \cos^{-1}\left(\dfrac{\cos\theta}{\sqrt{2}}\right)$

33.31 6.38 W/m^2

33.33 a) first: $I = I_0/2$, second: $I = 0.25I_0$,
third: $I = 0.125I_0$ all linearly polarized along
the axis of their respective filters.

33.35 a) $I_R = 0.374I$ b) $I_V = 2.35I$

33.39 a) $\sin\theta_3 = (n_1\sin\theta_1)/n_3$ c) yes

33.41 72.0°

33.45 1.53

33.47 1.8

33.49 a) 48.6°   b) 48.6°

33.51 39.1°

33.53 a) $n = 1.11$ b) i) 9.75 ns
ii) 4.07 ns; total $= 8.95$ ns

33.55 b) 0.22°

33.61 b) 38.9°   c) 5.0°

33.63 a) 35°   b) 10.1 W/m^2, 19.9 W/m^2

33.67 a) $\Delta = 2\theta_a^A - 6\sin^{-1}\left(\dfrac{1}{n}\sin\theta_a^A\right) + 2\pi$
b) $\cos^2\theta_2 = (n^2 - 1)/8$
c) red: $\theta_2 = 71.9°$; $\Delta = 230.1°$;
violet: $\theta_2 = 71.6°$, $\Delta = 233.2°$; violet

Chapter 34

34.1 39.2 cm to right of mirror; 4.85 cm

34.3 image at (x_0, y_0)

34.5 b) 33.0 cm to left of vertex, 1.20 cm tall,
inverted, real

34.7 0.213 mm

34.9 18.0 m from convex side of glass shell, 0.50 cm
tall, erect, virtual

34.11 a) $m = \dfrac{f}{(f - s)}$ c) $s > f$ d) $s < f$ e) $-\infty$
f) $s = f$ g) $s' = 0$ i) $s < f$ j) $s > f$
k) $s > 2f$ l) it becomes infinite

34.13 a) concave   b) $f = 2.50$ cm, $R = 5.00$ cm

34.15 2.67 cm

34.17 a) at the center of the ball, $m = +1.33$ b) no

34.19 $s = 0.395$ m

34.21 8.35 cm to left of vertex, 0.326 mm, erect

34.23 a) 1.06 m to right of lens, 17.7 mm tall, real, inverted   b) all same as (a)
34.25 71.2 cm to right of lens, $m = -2.97$
34.27 $f = 3.69$ cm, object is 2.82 cm to left of lens
34.29 $n = 1.67$
34.33 Object is 26.3 cm from lens with height 1.24 cm; image is erect; same side
34.35 10.2 m
34.37 a) 1.4×10^{-4} b) 5.25×10^{-4} c) 1.50×10^{-3}
34.39 a) 85 mm   b) 135 mm
34.41 a) 11   b) 2.160×10^{-3} s
34.43 a) convex   b) 50 mm to 56 mm
34.45 a) 80.0 cm   b) 76.9 cm
34.47 a) $+2.33$ diopters   b) -1.67 diopters
34.49 a) 6.06 cm   b) 4.12 mm
34.51 4.17 cm from lens; image is located on same side as ant
34.53 a) 8.37 mm   b) 21.4   c) 297
34.55 19.4 m
34.57 a) -6.33 b) 1.90 cm   c) 0.126 rad = 7.22°
34.59 a) 66.1 cm   b) -59.1
34.61 4.80 m/s
34.63 $n/2$
34.65 a) 13.3 cm   b) 26.2 cm
34.67 a) 46.2 cm from mirror, on opposite side of mirror; virtual   b) 2.88 cm, erect   c) no
34.69 a) -12.0 cm $< s < 0$ b) erect
34.71 $f = \pm 4.4$ cm, ± 13.3 cm
34.73 $v = 31$ m/s
34.75 b) i) 120.00 cm from mirror, 119.96 cm from mirror   ii) $m = -0.600$, $m' = -0.360$ c) faces perpendicular to axis: squares with side 0.600 mm; faces parallel to axis: rectangles with sides of length 0.360 mm (parallel to axis) and 0.600 mm (perpendicular to axis)
34.77 b) image = 2.4 cm high; $m = -0.13$
34.79 a) -3.3 cm   b) virtual   c) 1.9 cm to right of vertex at right end of rod   d) real, inverted   e) 105 mm
34.81 a) $f = 58.7$ cm, converging   b) $h = 4.47$ mm, virtual
34.83 a) 2.53 mm
34.85 a) $R = 8.8$ mm   b) no. behind the retina   c) $s' = 14$ mm from the cornea. In front of the retina. Yes. The lens needs to complete the focusing.
34.87 2.00
34.89 a) 3.75 cm to left of first lens   b) 332 cm   c) real   d) $h = 60.0$ mm. inverted.
34.91 10.6 cm
34.93 a) 0.24 m   b) 0.24 m
34.95 Inside the glass, 72.1 cm from the spherical surface
34.97 0.80 cm
34.99 -26.7 cm
34.101 1.24 cm above page
34.103 a) 46.7 m   b) 35.0 m
34.105 134 cm to left of object

Chapter 35

35.1 a) 2.50 m   b) 1.00 m, 4.00 m
35.3 0.75 m, 2.00 m, 3.25 m, 4.50 m, 5.75 m, 7.00 m, 8.25 m
35.5 a) 2.0 m   b) constructively   c) 1.0 m; destructively
35.9 0.83 mm
35.11 590 nm
35.13 12.6 cm
35.15 1200 nm
35.17 a) $m = 19$, 39 bright fringes   b) $m = \pm 19$, $\theta = \pm 73.3°$

35.19 a) $0.750I_0$ b) 80 nm
35.21 1670 rad
35.23 a) 0.888 mm   b) 0.444 mm
35.25 71.4 m
35.27 114 nm
35.29 0.0235°
35.31 a) $\Delta T = 56$ nm   b) i) 2180 nm   ii) 198.5 nm; 11.0 wavelengths
35.33 a) 514 nm; green   b) 603 nm; orange
35.35 0.11 μm
35.37 0.570 mm
35.39 1.82 mm
35.41 $n = 1.730$
35.43 27.3°, 66.5°
35.45 $n = 1.57$
35.47 b) constructive: $r_2 - r_1 = (m + \phi/2\pi)\lambda$, $m = 0, \pm 1, \pm 2, \pm 3, \ldots$; destructive: $r_2 - r_1 = \left(m + \dfrac{1}{2} + \phi/2\pi\right)\lambda$, $m = 0, \pm 1, \pm 2, \pm 3, \ldots$
35.49 a) $\sqrt{x^2 + (y+d)^2} - \sqrt{x^2 + (y-d)^2} = m\lambda$ c) $\sqrt{x^2 + (y+d)^2} - \sqrt{x^2 + (y-d)^2} = \left(m + \dfrac{1}{2}\right)\lambda$
35.51 6.8×10^{-5} (C°)$^{-1}$
35.53 $\lambda/2d$, independent of m
35.55 b) 72 cm
35.57 $n = 1.42$
35.59 a) pattern moves down the screen   b) $I = I_0 \cos^2[(\pi/\lambda)(d\sin\theta + (n-1)L)]$ c) $d\sin\theta = m\lambda - (n-1)L$
35.61 14.0

Chapter 36

36.1 506 nm
36.3 $m_{max} = 113$; 226 dark fringes
36.5 ± 45.4 cm
36.9 $\pm 16.0°$, $\pm 33.4°$, $\pm 55.6°$
36.11 0.920 μm
36.13 a) 10.8 mm   b) 5.4 mW
36.15 a) 6.75 mm   b) 2.43×10^{-6} W/m^2
36.17 a) 668 nm   b) $9.36 \times 10^{-5}I_0$
36.19 a) $\pm 13.0°$, $\pm 26.7°$, $\pm 42.4°$, $\pm 64.1°$ b) $I = 2.08$ W/m^2
36.21 a) 3   b) 2
36.23 a) $\pm 0.0627°$ b) $0.249I_0$ c) $0.0256I_0$
36.25 cases (i), (iii): slits 1 and 3 and slits 2 and 4; case (ii): slits 1 and 2 and slits 3 and 4
36.27 $a = 1.50 \times 10^4$ nm in width; $d = 4.50 \times 10^4$ nm in separation
36.29 a) 4790   b) 19.0°, 40.7°   c) no
36.31 a) yes   b) 13.3 nm
36.33 23.3°, 52.3°
36.35 10.5°, 21.3°, 33.1°
36.37 a) $R = 17{,}500$ b) yes   c) i) 587.8170 nm   ii) 587.7834 nm   iii) 587.7834 nm $< \lambda < 587.8170$ nm
36.39 0.232 nm
36.41 a) 0.461 m
36.43 1.9 m
36.45 92 cm
36.47 1.45 m
36.49 a) Hubble: 77 m; Arecibo: 1.1×10^6 m   b) 1500 km
36.51 no
36.53 a) i) 25.6°   ii) 10.2°   iii) 5.1°   b) i) 60.0°   ii) 23.1°   iii) 11.5°
36.55 2.07
36.57 a) 1.80 mm   b) 0.798 mm

36.59 $\Delta\theta_{\pm} = \dfrac{2\lambda}{dN}$
36.61 b) for $3\pi/2$: any two slits separated by one other slit; for the other cases: any two slits separated by three other slits
36.65 513 nm
36.67 second order
36.69 c) ± 2.6 rad
36.71 492 km

Chapter 37

37.1 Flash at AA'
37.3 2.60×10^8 m/s
37.5 a) 0.998c   b) 126 m
37.7 1.12 h, clock on spacecraft
37.9 92.5 m
37.11 a) 6.6×10^2 m   b) 4.92×10^{-5} s, 1.48×10^4 m; yes   c) 447 m
37.13 a) 3.57 km   b) 9.00×10^{-5} s   c) 8.92×10^{-5} s
37.15 a) 0.806c   b) 0.974c   c) 0.997c
37.17 0.385c
37.19 0.784c
37.21 $v = 0.611c$
37.23 0.837c, away
37.25 a) 0.159c   b) 1.72×10^8
37.27 b) $a = (F/m)(1 - v^2/c^2)^{1/2}$
37.29 a) $a = (\sqrt{3}/2)c = 0.866c$ b) $c\sqrt{1 - \left(\dfrac{1}{2}\right)^{2/3}} = 0.608c$
37.31 a) $(\sqrt{3}/2)c = 0.866c$ b) $\sqrt{35/36}c = 0.986c$
37.33 a) 4.50×10^{-10} J   b) 1.94×10^{-18} kg·m/s   c) 0.968c
37.35 a) 3.3×10^{-14} %; no   b) 4.0×10^{-16} kg; increases; no
37.37 a) 1.1×10^2 kg   b) 0.24 m
37.39 a) 8.68×10^{-10} J   b) 2.71×10^{-10} J   c) 0.453
37.41 a) nonrelativistic: 5.34×10^{-12} J; relativistic: 5.65×10^{-12} J; 1.06   b) nonrelativistic: 6.78×10^{-11} J; relativistic: 3.31×10^{-10} J; 4.88
37.43 a) 2.06×10^6 V   b) 3.30×10^{-13} J   c) 2.06 MeV
37.45 $v = 0.652c$
37.47 a) 4.2×10^9 kg/s; 4.6×10^6 tons   b) 1.5×10^{13} y
37.49 a) $\Delta = 2.11 \times 10^{-5}$ b) 2.15×10^4 MeV
37.51 0.700c
37.53 a) 0.995c   b) 1.0%
37.55 a) $v = (1 - 9 \times 10^{-9})c$ b) $m_{rel} = 7 \times 10^3 m$
37.57 1.68×10^5 eV
37.59 a) 0.800c   b) 1.00c   c) i) 2.33×10^{-11} J   ii) 1.00×10^{-10} J   d) i) 1.88×10^{-11} J   ii) 4.81×10^{-11} J
37.65 b) $\Delta x' = \sqrt{(\Delta x)^2 - (c\Delta t)^2}$ c) 1.44×10^{-8} s
37.67 0.357c, receding
37.69 a) 140%   b) 5500%   c) 63000%
37.75 a) 13.1 km/s, toward   b) 5.96×10^9 m = 0.040 Earth-sun distance (AU); 5.55×10^{29} kg = $0.279m_{sun}$
37.77 a) 0.7554c   b) 2.526   c) center of momentum: less energy

PHOTO CREDITS

About the Author Hugh D. Young; John P. Surey

Chapter 21 Opener: Ilja C. Hendel/The Image Works; 21.5: Journal-Courier/The Image Works; 21.8a: Richard Megna/Fundamental Photographs; 21.30a: Reproduced from *PSSC Physics*, 2nd ed. (1965), D.C. Heath & Company with Education Development Center, Inc., Newton, Massachusetts; 21.31b: Tony Craddock/Photo Researchers

Chapter 22 Opener: Department of Energy/Photo Researchers; 22.10: AKG London Ltd.; 22.28b: Russ Kinne/Comstock

Chapter 23 Opener: Ted Kurihara/Getty Images; 23.9: NASA/JPL/Caltech; 23.11: © Lester V. Berman/Corbis: 23/13: Fermilab Visual Media Services; 23.18: Hulton Archive/Keystone/Getty Images; 23.23: U.S. Geological Survey, Denver

Chapter 24 Opener: Digital Vision/Agefotostock; 24.3: Design Pics/Indexstock; 24.4: Andrew Lambert/Photo Researchers; 24.7: Paul Silverman/Fundamental Photographs; 24.11: Sandia National Laboratories; 24.17: Stanford Linear Accelerator/Science Photo Library/Photo Researchers

Chapter 25 Opener: David Sacks/Getty Images; 25.4: Fundamental Photographs; 25.5: PhotoDisc/Getty Images; 25.8: Mitch Wojnarowicz/The Image Works; 25.13: Doug Scott/Agefotostock

Chapter 26 Opener: Maximilian Stock/Photo Researchers; 26.2: Corbis; 26.5: John P. Surey; 26.13: John P. Surey; 26.18: Richard Megna/Fundamental Photographs; 26.20: Mehau Kulyk/Photo Researchers; 26.26a: Banana Stock/Alamy; 26.26b: Wikipedia

Chapter 27 Opener: Simon Fraser/Photo Researchers; 27.2b: Bill Aron/PhotoEdit Inc.; 27.20: Cenco; 27.20b: Paul McCormick/Getty Images; 27.21: Lawrence Berkeley National Laboratory; 27.40: Jeremy Burgess/Photo Researchers

Chapter 28 Opener: David Parker/Photo Researchers; 28.8: Definitive Stock; 28.11: Jeremy Walker/Photo Researchers; Test Your Understanding, page 976: Mark Antman/The Image Works

Chapter 29 Opener: James Leynse/Corbis; 29.9: Maximilian Stock Ltd./Photo Researchers; 29.18a: Photodisc Red/Getty Images; 29.18b: Toyota/AP Wide World; 29.18c: CIRRUS Design Corporation; 29.20b: NASA/JPL/Caltech; 29.26: Ken Gatherum, Boeing Computer Services

Chapter 30 Opener: Martin Barraud/Getty Images; 30.7: Photodisc/Getty Images; 30.10: John Walsh/Photo Researchers

Chapter 31 Opener: John P. Surey & Caroline J. Robillard; 31.5: Rubberball/Getty Images; 31.14: Lawrence Migdale/Photo Researchers; 31.22: John P. Surey; 31.23: Roger A. Freedman

Chapter 32 Opener: David Davis Photoproductions; 32.1: Bettmann/Corbis; 32.2a: Peter Barrett/Masterfile; 32.2b: Malcolm Fife/Getty Images; 32.16: The Image Bank/Getty Images; 32.18: Volker Steger/Photo Researchers; 32.20: NASA/JPL-Caltech/E.Churchwell (University of Wisconsin-Madison); 32.23: Michael Porsche/Corbis

Chapter 33 Opener: Peter Aprahamian/Photo Researchers; 33.1: Michael Newman/PhotoEdit; 33.2: National Institutes of Health/Photo Researchers; 33.9: Roger A. Freedman; 33.10a: NASA/John F. Kennedy Space Center; 33.10b: Spencer Grant/PhotoEdit; 33.13b: Susan Schwartzenberg, The Exploratorium; 33.16: Barry S. Blanchard; 33.17: Matthias Kulka/Masterfile; 33.20a: Randy O' Rourke/Corbis; 33.22a: Dougal Walters/Getty Images; 33.22b: Pixtal/AGE Fotostock; 33.26: Diane Hirsch/Fundamental Photographs; 33.31: Sepp Seitz/Woodfin Camp & Associates; 33.33: Dennis Frates/Alamy; 33.37a: K. Nomachi/Photo Researchers

Chapter 34 Opener: Tek Image/Photo Researchers; 34.8: Marshall Henrichs; 34.12a: NASA; 34.12b-c: NASA Headquarters; 34.23: PhotoLink/Getty Images; 34.27: Richard Megna/Fundamental Photographs; 34.34: PhotoDisc/Getty Images; 34.41a-c: Marshall Henrichs; 34.43c: THK Photo Products, Inc.; 34.44b: Omikron/Photo Researchers; 34.52c: Jan Hinsch/Photo Researchers; 34.54d: National Optical Astronomy Observatories

Chapter 35 Opener: Paul A. Souders/Corbis; 35.11: Peter Aprahamian/Photo Researchers; 35.17b: Bausch & Lomb Incorporated; 35.18: Bausch & Lomb Incorporated

Chapter 36 Opener: Digital Vision/Getty Images; 36.2a-b: From Sears, Zemansky, and Young, *College Physics*, 7th Ed., ©1991 Pearson Addison Wesley; 36.6: Pearson Addison Welsey; 36.9b: Richard Megna/Fundamental Photographs; 36.11: Dane Hornsleth; 36.12b: Pearson Addision Wesley; 36.17: Tom Boyden Photography; 36.18: Photodisc Green/Getty Images; 36.19a: NSO/AURA/NSF; 36.19b: Physics Dept., Imperial College/Photo Researchers; 36.21b: Estate of Bertram Eugene Warren; 36.25: Science Photo Library/Photo Researchers; 36.27: From Sears, Zemansky, and Young, *College Physics*, 7th Ed., ©1991 by Pearson Addison Wesley; 36.28a-c: From Sears, Zemansky, and Young, *College Physics*, 7th Ed., ©1991 by Pearson Addison Wesley; 36.29a: National Radio Astronomy Observatory/Associated Universities, Inc./National Science Foundation; 36.29b: European Southern Observatory; 36.32: Paul Silverman/Fundamental Photographs

Chapter 37 Opener: Brookhaven National Laboratory/Corbis; 37.4: Güven Güner/Alamy; 37.7: NASA/John F. Kennedy Space Center; 37.11: Jack Fields/Photo Researchers; 37.18: Adam Hart-Davis/Photo Researchers; 37.19: NASA and The Hubble Heritage Team (STScI/AURA); 37.22: Digital Vision/Getty Images; 37.26: Mauro Fermariello/Photo Researchers

INDEX

NUMERICAL CONSTANTS

Fundamental Physical Constants*

Name	Symbol	Value
Speed of light	c	2.99792458×10^8 m/s
Magnitude of charge of electron	e	$1.60217653(14) \times 10^{-19}$ C
Gravitational constant	G	$6.6742(10) \times 10^{-11}$ N $\cdot$ m^2/kg^2
Planck's constant	h	$6.6260693(11) \times 10^{-34}$ J $\cdot$ s
Boltzmann constant	k	$1.3806505(24) \times 10^{-23}$ J/K
Avogadro's number	N_A	$6.0221415(10) \times 10^{23}$ molecules/mol
Gas constant	R	$8.314472(15)$ J/mol $\cdot$ K
Mass of electron	m_e	$9.1093826(16) \times 10^{-31}$ kg
Mass of proton	m_p	$1.67262171(29) \times 10^{-27}$ kg
Mass of neutron	m_n	$1.67492728(29) \times 10^{-27}$ kg
Permeability of free space	μ_0	$4\pi \times 10^{-7}$ Wb/A $\cdot$ m
Permittivity of free space	$\epsilon_0 = 1/\mu_0 c^2$	$8.854187817 \ldots \times 10^{-12}$ C^2/N $\cdot$ m^2
	$1/4\pi\epsilon_0$	$8.987551787 \ldots \times 10^9$ N $\cdot$ m^2/C^2

Other Useful Constants*

Mechanical equivalent of heat		4.186 J/cal ($15°$ calorie)
Standard atmospheric pressure	1 atm	1.01325×10^5 Pa
Absolute zero	0 K	$-273.15°$C
Electron volt	1 eV	$1.60217653(14) \times 10^{-19}$ J
Atomic mass unit	1 u	$1.66053886(28) \times 10^{-27}$ kg
Electron rest energy	$m_e c^2$	$0.510998918(44)$ MeV
Volume of ideal gas ($0°$C and 1 atm)		$22.413996(39)$ liter/mol
Acceleration due to gravity (standard)	g	9.80665 m/s^2

*Source: National Institute of Standards and Technology (**http://physics.nist.gov/cuu**). Numbers in parentheses show the uncertainty in the final digits of the main number; for example, the number 1.6454(21) means 1.6454 ± 0.0021. Values shown without uncertainties are exact.

Astronomical Data[†]

Body	Mass (kg)	Radius (m)	Orbit radius (m)	Orbit period
Sun	1.99×10^{30}	6.96×10^8	—	—
Moon	7.35×10^{22}	1.74×10^6	3.84×10^8	27.3 d
Mercury	3.30×10^{23}	2.44×10^6	5.79×10^{10}	88.0 d
Venus	4.87×10^{24}	6.05×10^6	1.08×10^{11}	224.7 d
Earth	5.97×10^{24}	6.38×10^6	1.50×10^{11}	365.3 d
Mars	6.42×10^{23}	3.40×10^6	2.28×10^{11}	687.0 d
Jupiter	1.90×10^{27}	6.91×10^7	7.78×10^{11}	11.86 y
Saturn	5.68×10^{26}	6.03×10^7	1.43×10^{12}	29.45 y
Uranus	8.68×10^{25}	2.56×10^7	2.87×10^{12}	84.02 y
Neptune	1.02×10^{26}	2.48×10^7	4.50×10^{12}	164.8 y
Pluto[‡]	1.31×10^{22}	1.15×10^6	5.91×10^{12}	247.9 y

[†]Source: NASA Jet Propulsion Laboratory Solar System Dynamics Group (**http://ssd.jpl.nasa.gov**), and P. Kenneth Seidelmann, ed., ***Explanatory Supplement to the Astronomical Almanac*** (University Science Books, Mill Valley, CA, 1992), pp. 704–706. For each body, "radius" is its radius at its equator and "orbit radius" is its average distance from the sun (for the planets) or from the earth (for the moon).

[‡]In August 2006, the International Astronomical Union reclassified Pluto and other small objects that orbit the sun as "dwarf planets."